Mexico
a travel survival kit

Tom Brosnahan
John Noble
Nancy Keller
Mark Balla
Scott Wayne

Mexico – a travel survival kit

4th edition

Published by
    Lonely Planet Publications
    Head Office: PO Box 617, Hawthorn, Vic 3122, Australia
    Branches: PO Box 2001A, Berkeley, CA 94702, USA, and London, UK

Printed by
    Singapore National Printers Ltd, Singapore

Photographs by
    Greg Alford (GA)
    Ross Barnet (RB)
    Gregory Elms (GE)
    James Lyon (JL)
    Rowan McKinnon (RMcK)
    John Noble (JN)
    Dan Spitzer (DS)
    Scott Wayne (SW)
    Paul Wentford (PW)
    Tony Wheeler (TW)
    Department of Tourism

    Front cover: Indian woman's handicrafts stall, San Christóbal de las Casas (Dallas & John Heaton), Scoopix
    Back cover: Quetzalcóatl, Teotihuacán (JN)

First Published
    1982

This Edition
    December 1992

Although the authors and publisher have tried to make the information as accurate as possible, they accept no responsibility for any loss, injury or inconvenience sustained by any person using this book.

National Library of Australia Cataloguing-in-Publication Data

    Mexico – a travel survival kit.

    4th ed.
    Includes index.
    ISBN 0 86442 166 4.

    1. Mexico – Guidebooks. I. Brosnahan, Tom. II. Noble, John, 1951
    Oct. 11 – . Mexico, a travel survival kit.

917.204835

Tom Brosnahan

Tom Brosnahan was born and raised in Pennsylvania, went to college in Boston, then set out on the road. After travelling in Europe he joined the Peace Corps training program. Following graduate school he travelled throughout Mexico and Central America writing travel articles and guidebooks for various publishers, and in the past two decades his 25 books covering numerous destinations have sold over two million copies in twelve languages. Tom is the author of *Turkey – a travel survival kit*, *La Ruta Maya – a travel survival kit*, and co-author of *Central America on a shoestring* and *Mediterranean Europe on a shoestring*.

John Noble

John Noble was born and grew up in the valley of the River Ribble, England. After a Cambridge University degree in English and Philosophy and a decade of journalism that led him from the Ribble valley's *Clitheroe Advertiser* via London's *Observer*, *Guardian* and *Times* to Latin America and South-East Asia, he updated Lonely Planet's *Sri Lanka – a travel survival kit*. Since then he has co-authored *Mexico – a travel survival kit* and, with his wife Susan Forsyth, helped update *Australia* and *Indonesia*. He then co-authored and coordinated LP's *USSR – a travel survival kit* before returning to Mexico to help produce this edition. John, Susan and their two children have home base in the Ribble valley.

Nancy Keller

Nancy was born and raised in northern California, and worked in the alternative press during the '70s, doing every aspect of newspaper work from editorial and reporting to delivering the papers. She returned to university to earn a master's degree in journalism, finally graduating in 1986 after many breaks for extended stays on the west coast of Mexico. Since then she's been travelling and writing in Mexico, Israel, Egypt, Europe, various South Pacific islands, New Zealand and Central America.

Mark Balla

Mark Balla started travelling at the tender age of three months. He started writing at age five in his first year at school. In the 2½-odd decades that have since passed he hasn't found the time to stop doing either. Somewhere along the way Mark managed to pick up around half a dozen languages and a degree before coming to LP in 1987 as our inaugural Phrasebook editor. After 18 months, the call of Europe became too strong to ignore and Mark departed for Spain, leaving behind the manuscript to LP's *Brazilian Phrasebook*. Having written the Spain chapter for the LP's Europe series, Mark travelled to northern Mexico to research his part of this book, before returning to Australia.

Scott Wayne

Scott was born in Philadelphia, Pennsylvania, but grew up in Newport Beach, California. He has travelled extensively and written about Mexico, Europe, the Middle East and Africa. His recent work for Lonely Planet includes *Egypt – a travel survival kit* and *Baja California – a travel survival kit*.

From the Authors
From John Thanks to Conrad Richter (Canada) for interesting correspondence, the ·Velasco family of Oaxaca and Jim Richardson of Los Angeles for genuine hospitality, and Susan Forsyth (Australia) and Isabella Noble (UK/Australia) for great company and (Susan) help with research.

From Nancy Nancy extends a big *muchísimas gracias por su ayuda* to the staff of the tourist offices in all the places she visited, who collectively answered thousands of questions. Thanks also to those people met along the way who were helpful and made the journey brighter, especially Clarence, Xochitl and Diego in San Miguel de Allende; Mike 'The Kid', Mark and the other folks in San Miguel de Allende; Michiel in Michoacán; Rhona, Maggie, Jesús Pérez, his mother and the family in Guanajuato; Don Teo in Taxco, and Philomena in Melaque. Greatest thanks, as always, to Rudy and to Tom.

From Mark I would like to dedicate my Mexican experience to Professor Emeritus Robert 'Wally' Thompson who taught me to love the Spanish language and its people.

I would also like to thank many people who helped me in Mexico. Thanks to Javier (Matamoros), Javier and Estella (Saltillo), Maria Ardeño (Monterrey), David Simpson (Ciudad Juárez), Eichi Neimura (Chihuahua and Creel), Nick Williams and Nicola Undritz and friends (Creel, Zacatecas and San Blas), Roberto for helping me bail a bunch of drunken Aussie surfers out of jail in Creel, Paul Ryan (Guaymas), a nameless English couple (Los Mochis), half the aging expats in Alamos, and José (Alamos).

Thanks to all the tourist office staff who made my life as easy as possible. Special thanks to the staff at Zacatecas, Chihuahua, Matamoros, Monterrey (for opening the office on a Sunday), Los Mochis and Alamos.

Thanks also to Hanna, Rainer and Gerard who didn't desert me in the Hamburg winter. Also to Greg, James and Margaret at LP for their patience, and Tom Brosnahan and Robert Strauss for their expert guidance.

Finally I wish to thank my new-found friends, Cuauhtémoc and Mónica, for their company, hospitality, ideas and enthusiasm in La Pesca, Ciudad Victoria, and of course Cuauhtémoc (Chihuahua state).

From the Publisher
This edition of LP's Mexico guide was edited and coordinated by Greg Alford. For editing/proofing help, thanks to: Stephanie Bunbury, Michelle Coxall, Simone Calderwood, Miriam Cannell, James Lyon and Kristin Odijk. Map updating, design, illustration and layout was done by Margaret Jung. Thanks to Sharon Wertheim for indexing.

This Book
This is the fourth edition of Lonely Planet's Mexico guide. For this edition, Tom covered the Maya areas of the Yucatán, Tabasco and Chiapas chapters, and did a complete rewrite of Mexico City. John wrote the rest of the Chiapas chapter, as well as Oaxaca, the Gulf Coast region and the area around Mexico City. Nancy researched the central highlands and central Pacific coast areas, while Mark Balla covered the north of the country. Baja California was contributed by Scott Wayne.

Thanks to many travellers who wrote in; a list of your names is on pages 923-4.

Warning & Request
Things change – prices go up, schedules change, good places go bad and bad places go bankrupt – nothing stays the same. So if you find things better or worse, recently opened or long since closed, please write and tell us and help make the next edition better.

Your letters will be used to help update future editions and important changes will be included in a Stop Press section in reprints.

We greatly appreciate all information that is sent to us by travellers. Back at Lonely Planet we employ a hard-working readers' letters team to sort through the many letters we receive. The best ones will be rewarded with a free copy of the next edition or another Lonely Planet guide if you prefer. We give away lots of books, but, unfortunately, not every letter/postcard receives one. .

Contents

Map Legend

BOUNDARIES

—·—·—·—	International Boundary
—··—··—	Internal Boundary
+++++++++	National Park or Reserve
---------	The Equator
··············	The Tropics

SYMBOLS

◉	NEW DELHI	National Capital
●	BOMBAY	Provincial or State Capital
●	Pune	Major Town
•	Barsi	Minor Town
■		Places to Stay
▼		Places to Eat
⬒		Post Office
✈		Airport
i		Tourist Information
◉		Bus Station or Terminal
66		Highway Route Number
⚲ ✝ ⚱		Mosque, Church, Cathedral
∴		Temple or Ruin
✚		Hospital
✳		Lookout
⚑		Camping Area
⌅		Picnic Area
⌂		Hut or Chalet
▲		Mountain or Hill
		Railway Station
		Road Bridge
		Railway Bridge
		Road Tunnel
		Railway Tunnel
		Escarpment or Cliff
		Pass
		Ancient or Historic Wall

ROUTES

	Major Road or Highway
-----------	Unsealed Major Road
	Sealed Road
----------	Unsealed Road or Track
	City Street
++++++++++	Railway
—●—	Subway
··············	Walking Track
----------	Ferry Route
++++++++	Cable Car or Chair Lift

HYDROGRAPHIC FEATURES

	River or Creek
	Intermittent Stream
	Lake, Intermittent Lake
	Coast Line
	Spring
	Waterfall
	Swamp
	Salt Lake or Reef
	Glacier

OTHER FEATURES

	Park, Garden or National Park
	Built Up Area
	Market or Pedestrian Mall
	Plaza or Town Square
	Cemetery

Note: not all symbols displayed above appear in this book

Introduction

Mexico is a land of extraordinary diversity. Great cultures and empires flourished here over a thousand years ago, and their descendants – over 50 distinct Indian peoples, each with its own language – maintain vestiges of traditional lifestyles even in the midst of rampant modernisation. Traditional sources of wealth such as mining, fishing and agriculture coexist with modern manufacturing industries and services. Tourism is very important.

The country's diversity stems partly from topography: mountains and more mountains allowed indigenous peoples to pursue their destiny in some degree of isolation. Only in this century have modern roads, airlanes, radio and television knitted the various regions together into a national consciousness. Even so, being Mexican still means very different things to people in the nation's many distinct regions.

For the traveller, Mexico holds inexhaustible fascination in its cultures, cuisines, handcrafts, art and history. To explore Mexico is to travel through vast deserts, past snow-capped volcanoes, along tropical jungle-clad beaches, amidst ancient ruins, in teeming modern cities, timeless villages and posh resorts. The adventure is endless. Mexico has it all. What you make of it is up to you.

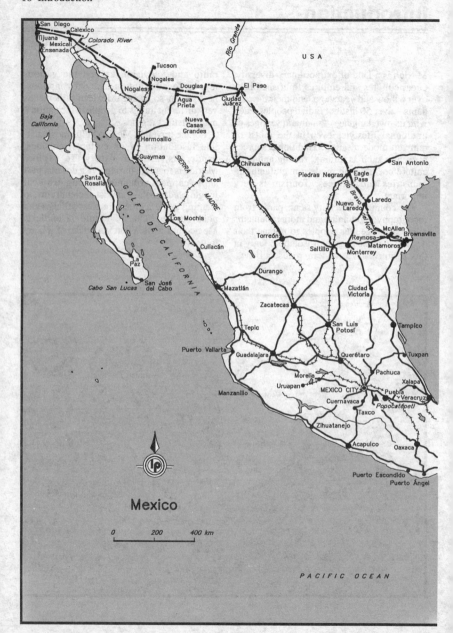

Mexico

0   200   400 km

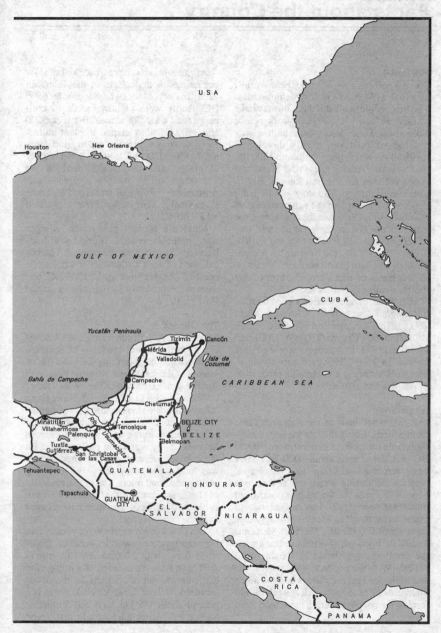

Facts about the Country

HISTORY

There is nothing new about the 'New World', as a look at Mexico's history demonstrates. The first people to inhabit this land may have arrived as many as 20,000 years before Columbus. Their descendants built a succession of brilliant, highly developed civilisations which flourished from 1500 BC to 1500 AD. Among these, the Maya and Aztec cultures are the best known. But in your travels through Mexico you'll have the opportunity to explore the achievements of the mysterious Olmecs of the Gulf Coast, the Zapotecs of Oaxaca, the great imperial city of Teotihuacán near Mexico City, the warlike Toltecs from Tula, the artistically accomplished Totonacs from northern Veracruz, the Huastecs of north-central Mexico, and the Tarascans of Michoacán.

Historians divide Mexico's pre-Hispanic history into four periods – Archaic (up to 1500 BC), Preclassic (or Formative, 1500 BC to 250 AD), Classic (250 to 900 AD), and Postclassic (900 to the conquest of the Aztec Empire in 1521). However you divide it, Mexico's history is a fascinating procession of peoples and cultures.

Beginnings

The first inhabitants of the Americas came from Siberia during the last ice age in migrations that may have begun before 30,000 BC and lasted until about 8000 BC. They came across a land bridge now submerged beneath the Bering Strait, but at that time exposed because the freezing of oceans had made sea levels fall. The earliest human traces so far found in Mexico probably date from about 20,000 BC. The first Mexicans hunted the big herds of mammals that grazed the cool wet grasslands of the highland valleys. With the rise in temperatures at the end of the ice age, the valleys became much drier, ceasing to support such animal life and forcing the people to derive more food from plants.

Archaeologists have traced the slow beginnings of agriculture in the Tehuacán valley in Puebla state, where soon after 6500 BC people were planting seeds of chili pepper and a kind of squash. Between 5000 and 3500 BC they started to plant mutant forms of a tiny wild maize and to grind it into meal. After 3500 BC a much better variety of maize, and also beans, enabled the Tehuacán valley people to live semi-permanently in villages and spend less time in seasonal hunting camps. Pottery appeared by 2300 BC.

Mexico's earliest year-round villages were probably coastal, living by a combination of agriculture and seafood. There is evidence of such settlements on the Pacific coast of Chiapas from about 1500 BC, and there were probably similar places on the Gulf coast.

The Olmecs

Mexico's first civilisation arose near the Gulf Coast, in the humid lowlands of southern Veracruz and neighbouring Tabasco. These were the Olmecs, People from the Region of Rubber, a name coined in the 1920s. Olmec civilisation is famed for the awesome 'Olmec heads', stone sculptures of human heads up to three metres high with grim, pug-nosed features and wearing curious helmets. If the snarls and pitiless gazes on these heads are any guide, Olmec society was held together by fear – of terrifying gods, priests and rulers. The heads, typically of Olmec art, combine the features of human babies and jaguars – a mixture now referred to as the 'were-jaguar'.

The first known great Olmec centre, San Lorenzo near Acayucan in Veracruz, flourished from about 1200 to 900 BC. It may well have been the creation of a ruling elite that emerged out of conflicts for the flood-fertilised lands of the area. San Lorenzo is a plateau about 1¼ km long and 50 metres high, at least partly human-made, that served chiefly as a politico-religious centre. Eight Olmec heads and many other carved stone monuments have been identified as originating here. Their basalt material was probably dragged, rolled or rafted from 60 to 80 km away. Finds at San Lorenzo of objects from far away, such as artefacts of the glasslike volcanic stone obsidian from Guatemala and the Mexican highlands, suggest that it may have controlled trade over a very large area.

The second great Olmec centre was La Venta in Tabasco, which flourished from about 800 to 400 BC. Several tombs have been found here. In one of them, jade, a favourite pre-Hispanic ornamental material, makes its appearance. La Venta produced many more fine stone carvings, including at least five Olmec heads. Like San Lorenzo, it was violently destroyed long ago.

Olmec sites found far from the Gulf coast heartland may well have been trading postscum-garrisons placed to ensure the supply of jade, iron ore for mirrors, and other luxuries for the Olmec elite. The most impressive is Chalcatzingo, Morelos.

The Olmecs were Mexico's ancestral civilisation. Their art, their religious beliefs and quite possibly their social organisation strongly influenced the civilisations that followed. Apart from the were-jaguar which seems to have been linked with rain, Olmec gods included fire and maize deities and the feathered serpent, all of which persisted throughout the pre-Hispanic era.

The Ball Game

Probably all pre-Hispanic Mexican cultures, including the Olmec, played the ball game, which may have varied from place to place and era to era but had certain lasting features. Special I-shaped ball courts appear at ceremonial centres all over the country. The game seems to have been played between two teams and its essence was apparently to keep a rubber ball off the ground by flicking it with hips, thighs and possibly knees or elbows. The vertical or sloping walls around the courts were probably part of the playing area, not stands for spectators. The game had – at least sometimes – deep religious signif-

icance. It perhaps served as an oracle, with the result indicating which of two courses of action should be taken. Games could be followed by the sacrifice of one or more of the players – whether winners or losers, no one is sure!

Monte Albán

By 300 BC settled village life, based on agriculture but supported by hunting, had developed throughout the southern half of Mexico. At this time Monte Albán, the hilltop centre of the Zapotec people of Oaxaca, was growing into a town of perhaps 10,000, probably the biggest settlement in Mexico or Central America. Some of the stone carvings known as Danzantes (Dancers) from this era at Monte Albán show figures with Olmec-like downturned mouths and are considered 'Olmecoid' in style. Many of them have undeciphered hieroglyphs or dates in a dot-and-bar system, which quite possibly mean that the elite of Monte Albán were the inventors of writing and the written calendar in Mexico and Central America. The Zapotec seem never to have tried extending their control beyond the rugged, mountainous Oaxaca region.

Izapa & the Early Maya

The large temple centre of Izapa near the Pacific coast of Chiapas, almost on the border of Guatemala, flourished from about 200 BC to 200 AD. Among its pyramids stood many tall stone slabs, called stelae, fronted by round altars and carved with mythological scenes showing Olmec-derived gods. Izapan culture was distributed from the former Olmec heartland to the Guatemalan highlands and is considered the link between the Olmec and the next great civilisation in southern Mexico, the Maya. Izapa and the early Maya shared several characteristics like the stele-altar pairing, 'Long Count' dates (see Maya Writing & the Calendar), and a cluttered style of pictorial, narrative carving.

It may have been that Izapan civilisation was carried to the lowland Maya, in the Petén forest of northern Guatemala and the

Yucatán Peninsula, via Kaminaljuyú, an ancient centre on the outskirts of modern Guatemala City. By the close of the Pre-classic period in 250 AD, these Maya were already building stepped temple pyramids and a type of roof – the corbel vault – which would be characteristic of the great Maya florescence during the Classic period.

Teotihuacán

The first great civilisation of central Mexico emerged in a side-valley off the Valley of Mexico, about 50 km north-east of the centre of modern Mexico City. Teotihuacán grew into Mexico's biggest pre-Hispanic city, with an estimated 200,000 people at its height in the 6th century AD, and the capital of probably its biggest pre-Hispanic empire.

A collection of small villages began to develop into a town here in the 2nd century BC, and the building of a magnificent planned city began about the time of Christ. Teotihuacán was built on a grid plan and divided into quarters by two great avenues meeting in its centre. The greatest of its buildings, the 70-metre-high, 220-metre-square Pyramid of the Sun, the second biggest pyramid in Mexico and third biggest in the world, was constructed within the first 150 years AD. Most of the rest of the city, including the almost-as-big Pyramid of the Moon, was built between about 250 and 600 AD.

Culture & Economy Teotihuacán was a true city in that many classes of people lived and worked in it. It had writing and books, the bar-and-dot number system and the 260-day sacred year (see Maya Writing & the Calendar). Literacy probably spread throughout its empire except perhaps the west. But what economic base its achievements were built on, in a not especially fertile valley, has long been debated. Some suggest irrigation, others *chinampa* agriculture – the draining and cultivating of the swampy margins of the lakes which then filled the Valley of Mexico. Exports of locally mined obsidian may also have been crucial.

Empire Teotihuacán almost certainly became an imperialistic state, probably after about 400 AD. At its peak it may have controlled, one way or another, all of civilised Mexico and Central America – roughly the southern two-thirds of Mexico, plus Guatemala, Belize and bits of Honduras and El Salvador. But it was an empire probably geared to tribute-gathering, to feed the mouths and tastes of Teotihuacán's big population, rather than to full-scale occupation.

Cholula, near Puebla, with a pyramid bigger even than the Pyramid of the Sun, was part of Teotihuacán's cultural sphere. Teotihuacán may have had hegemony over the Zapotec of Oaxaca during the zenith of their capital Monte Albán, which grew into a city of perhaps 25,000 between about 300 and 600 AD. In about 400 AD Teotihuacán invaders built almost a miniature replica of their home city in Kaminaljuyú, Guatemala. From there they probably extended their sway over some of the Maya in the Petén, where even at Tikal, perhaps the mightiest of all Maya cities, a 445 AD stele shows a Maya king standing between two Teotihuacán soldiers.

Fall of Teotihuacán In the 7th century the heart of Teotihuacán was put to the torch and the city was plundered and largely abandoned. Whether the destroyers were invaders from outside or revolutionaries from within, it is likely that the state was already economically weakened – perhaps by the rise of rival powers in central Mexico, a drying-up of the climate, or by erosion and dessication caused by the denuding of the surrounding hillsides for wood.

Teotihuacán's influence on all of Mexico's other pre-Hispanic cultures was huge. Many of its gods, such as the feathered serpent Quetzalcóatl, an all-important symbol of fertility and life itself, and Tláloc, the rain god, were still being worshipped by the Aztecs a millennium later.

The Classic Maya

The Maya area falls into three regions – southern, the highlands and Pacific coast of

Guatemala; central, the Petén forest of northern Guatemala and adjacent lowlands in Mexico (to the west) and Belize (east); and northern, the Yucatán Peninsula. It was the central and northern regions – the lowlands – that produced pre-Hispanic America's most brilliant civilisation, the Classic Maya, between about 250 and 900 AD.

Maya Cities A typical Maya city centred on plazas surrounded by tall temple pyramids (usually the tombs of probably deified rulers), and lower buildings, the so-called 'palaces', with warrens of small rooms. The corbel vault became universal, stelae and altars were carved with dates and elaborate, typically Maya, human and divine figures. Stone causeways, probably for ceremonial use, led out from the plazas.

The rulers and artisans are thought to have lived close to these centres, which were probably a focus for ceremonial, political and market activity for groups of farming hamlets. In late Classic times, estimates of the population of Tikal, the biggest Maya site, range from 10,000 to 40,000. The impossibility of intensive agriculture amid forests made large settlements unlikely, but the ceremonial centres and their associated lesser settlements constituted city states.

Early Classic Period Most of the major Classic Maya sites, especially from the first half of the era, are in Guatemala's Petén, with Tikal, which may have been the capital of much of the Maya lowlands, supreme among them. Since the early Classic Maya were probably partly controlled by Teotihuacán, it is not surprising that the era of Teotihuacán's decline was also one of disturbances among the Maya. No stelae at all were erected by the lowland Maya in the second half of the 6th century. However in the 7th century life seems to have resumed much as before.

Chiapas Classic Maya centres in Mexico fall into four zones: one in Chiapas, in the central Maya region, and three in the Yucatán peninsula, in the northern Maya region. The chief Chiapas sites are Yaxchilán, its tribu-

tary Bonampak (where famous, vivid battle murals were found in 1948), and Palenque, which to many people is the most beautiful of all Maya sites. Palenque rose to prominence under the 7th-century ruler Pakal, whose treasure-loaded tomb deep within the fine Temple of the Inscriptions was discovered in 1952. Perhaps the most exquisite buildings at Palenque however are the three delicate Temples of the Cross, built around a single plaza by Pakal's son Chan-Balum.

Río Bec & Chenes North of the Petén in Mexico's Campeche state are the wild, little-investigated Río Bec and Chenes zones, noted for their lavishly carved building facades. Río Bec pyramids and palaces tend to be fronted by unclimbable false stairways leading to dummy rooms, and flanked by false towers.

Puuc Further north, in Yucatán state, is the Puuc zone, the focus of northern Classic Maya culture. The most important of the many Puuc ceremonial centres was Uxmal, an architectural treasure trove south of modern Mérida. Puuc ornamentation, which reaches its peak on the Governor's Palace at Uxmal, featured intricate stone mosaics on the upper parts of buildings' facades, part-geometric but also incorporating faces of the hook-nosed, sky-serpent-cum-rain-god Chac. The facade of the amazing Palace of Masks at Kabah, 18½ km south of Uxmal, is covered with over 300 Chac faces.

Maya Art The art of the Maya was typically cluttered and narrative in content. Many paintings or carvings on wood, gourds and other perishables have disappeared. Fine carved stelae showing historical and mythological events crop up almost everywhere, but those in the central region are generally superior. Maya potters achieved marvellous multicoloured effects on grave vessels to accompany the dead to the next world. Jade, the most precious substance, was turned into beads or thin plaques carved in relief.

Maya Writing & the Calendar Classic Maya

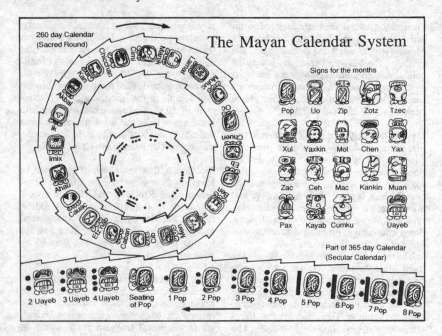

The Mayan Calendar System

260 day Calendar (Sacred Round)

Signs for the months

Pop · Uo · Zip · Zotz · Tzec

Xul · Yaxkin · Mol · Chen · Yax

Zac · Ceh · Mac · Kankin · Muan

Pax · Kayab · Cumku · Uayeb

Part of 365 day Calendar (Secular Calendar)

2 Uayeb · 3 Uayeb · 4 Uayeb · Seating of Pop · 1 Pop · 2 Pop · 3 Pop · 4 Pop · 5 Pop · 6 Pop · 7 Pop · 8 Pop

intellectual achievements were among their greatest of all. They had a very complex writing system with 300 to 500 symbols, primarily pictorial but also often with a sound component, which only a minority then, and no one today, could fully understand.

The Maya also refined a calendar possessed by other pre-Hispanic peoples into a tool for exact recording of earthly and heavenly events. They could predict eclipses of the sun and the movements of the moon and Venus. Time was counted in three ways: in sacred or almanac years *(tzolkins)* composed of thirteen 20-day periods; in 'vague' solar years *(haabs)* of 18 cycles of 20 days followed by a special five-day 'portentous' period; and in units of one, 20, 360, 7200 and 144,000 days.

All Mexico's pre-Hispanic civilisations used the first two counts, whose interlocking enabled a date to be located precisely within any period of 52 years called a Calendar Round. But the Maya were the pre-eminent users (though not the inventors) of the third count, known as the Long Count, which was infinitely extendable. Their inscriptions enumerate the Long Count units elapsed from a starting (Creation) point of 13 August 3114 BC. Numbers were written in a system of dots (counted as one) and bars (counted as five), but actually reading inscriptions is complicated.

Maya Religion Religion permeated every facet of Maya life, though it is debated whether the priests were also rulers. The Maya believed in predestination, and had a complex astrology. However they also carried out complex rituals, involving incense offerings, the alcoholic drink *balche*, bloodletting from ears, tongues or penises, dances, feasts and sacrifices, to win the gods' favours. The Classic Maya seem to have practised human sacrifice on a small scale, the Postclassic on a bigger scale. Beheading was probably the most common method. At Chichén Itzá, victims were thrown into a deep *cenote* (well) to bring rain. Maya wars seem mostly to have been aimed at winning captives for sacrifice and slavery than at empire building.

The Maya inhabited a universe with a centre and four directions – each associated with a tree, a bird and a colour (east, red; north, white; west, black; south, yellow; the centre, green) – plus 13 layers of heavens and nine layers of underworld to which the dead descended. The earth was thought of as the back of a giant reptile floating on a pond (it's not *too* hard to imagine yourself as a flea on this creature's back as you look across a Maya landscape!).

The Maya believed themselves descended from people made from maize gruel. The current world was just one of a succession of worlds created and then destroyed. It too would end in cataclysm and be succeeded by another, and this cyclical nature of things enabled the future to be predicted by looking at the past.

Important Maya gods included Itzamná (who was the fire deity and either the supreme creator or the son of the supreme creator), and gods for each layer of the heavens and the underworld and for each time period, Chac the rain god, Yum Kaax the maize and vegetation god, and Ah Puch the death god. The feathered serpent, known here as Kukulcán, was introduced from central Mexico in the Postclassic period. Another important aspect of religion was the worship of dead ancestors, particularly rulers, who were thought to be a race apart, descended from the gods.

The Maya Collapse In the second half of the 8th century, trade between Maya states started to shrink and conflict began to grow. By 830 building had stopped almost throughout the central region, which by the early 10th century had been virtually abandoned, most of its people probably migrating to the northern region or the highlands of Chiapas. Population pressure and consequent ecological damage are considered possible causes of the collapse; invasion or revolt are regarded as secondary causes at most.

In the north the Puuc sites didn't reach their final form till the late 9th century and were occupied till the second half of the 10th century.

Classic Veracruz Civilisation

Along the Gulf Coast, in what are now central and northern Veracruz, the Classic period saw the rise of a number of independent power centres with shared culture – together known as the Classic Veracruz civilisation. Its hallmark is a style of abstract carving, featuring pairs of curved and interwoven parallel lines. Classic Veracruz appears to have been particularly obsessed with the ball game and its most important centre, El Tajín near Papantla, at its height from about 600 to 900 AD, contains at least 11 ball courts.

The Toltecs

One chief power centre in central Mexico after the decline of Teotihuacán was Xochicalco, a hilltop site in Morelos with both Maya influence and impressive evidence of a feathered-serpent cult. Another may have been Cholula. A third was Tula in Hidalgo, 65 km north of Mexico City. Tula is a common Mexican place name, but it is widely accepted that this was the Tula described in later Aztec 'histories' as the capital of a great empire ruled by the Toltecs (Artificers).

It is particularly hard to disentangle myth and history in the Toltec story because dubious written accounts as well as archaeology form part of the evidence. A widely accepted version is that the Toltecs were one of a number of semicivilised tribes from dry northern Mexico which moved into the Valley of Mexico after the fall of Teotihuacán. Tula became their capital, probably in the 10th century, growing into a city of 30,000 or 40,000. The Tula ceremonial centre is dedicated primarily to the feathered serpent god Quetzalcóatl. and its tall, fearsome warrior statues (Atlantes) apparently represent Quetzalcóatl in his guise as the morning star.

The annals relate however that Quetzalcóatl was displaced by Tezcatlipoca (Smoking Mirror), a newcomer god of warriors and sorcery, one of whose aspects was Huitzilopochtli the sun god, who demanded a regular diet of the hearts of sacrificed warriors. A Quetzalcóatl king fled to the Gulf Coast and set sail eastward on a raft of snakes, promising one day to return.

Tula seems to have become capital of a militaristic kingdom that dominated central Mexico. Warriors were organised in orders dedicated to different animal-gods – the coyote, jaguar and eagle knights. Mass human sacrifice may have started at Tula. Fortification and sombre stone carvings concerned with death and war became widespread.

The influence of the Toltecs – if that's who they were – was enormous. They probably founded the La Quemada fortress in Zacatecas to guard the route of turquoise commerce from present-day New Mexico in the USA. Their hand is seen at Gulf Coast sites like Castillo de Teayo and in western Mexico. They had some hold over the early Mixtecs of northern Oaxaca. Pottery from as far south as Costa Rica has been found at Tula. There's even probable Toltec influence in old temple mounds and artefacts found in Tennessee and Illinois in the USA.

Tula was abandoned about the start of the 13th century, seemingly destroyed by Chichimecs, as the periodic hordes of barbaric raiders from the north came to be known. Its people apparently dispersed to the southern part of the Valley of Mexico and further afield. Many later Mexican peoples revered the Toltec era as a golden age. Some rulers, including Maya leaders and Aztec emperors – whose capital, Tenochtitlán, contained many artistic and architectural similarities to Tula – claimed to be descended from the Toltecs.

Chichén Itzá Maya scripts relate that towards the end of the 10th century much of northern Yucatán was conquered by one Kukulcán (Feathered Serpent). The partly Puuc Maya site of Chichén Itzá in northern Yucatán also contains very many Tula-like features, from flat beam-and-masonry roofs (contrasting with the Maya corbel roof) to gruesome chac-mools – reclining human figures with their heads turned to one side, holding on their stomachs dishes which are popularly thought to have been receptacles for human hearts torn out during sacrifices. There's a resemblance that can hardly be coincidental between Tula's Pyramid B and Chichén Itza's Temple of the Warriors, plus many other parallels between the two sites. Many writers therefore believe Toltec exiles invaded Yucatán and created a new, even grander version of Tula at Chichén Itzá.

To confuse matters however, there's a respectable body of opinion that the Tula-style features at Chichén Itza *predated* Tula, implying that Chichén Itza, not Tula, was the epicentre of whatever culture this was, and even perhaps that the great Toltecs referred to in the annals were the people, not of Tula, Hidalgo, but of Teotihuacán.

The Aztecs

Rise of the Aztecs The Aztecs' own legends relate that they were the chosen people of the sun god Huitzilopochtli. They were originally northern nomads who were led to the Valley of Mexico by their priests. They settled on islands in the series of interconnected lakes that then filled much of the valley, because they saw there an eagle which was standing on a cactus and eating a snake – the sign, as their prophecies had told them, to show where to stop their wandering.

The Aztec capital Tenochtitlán was, according to this story, founded in the first half of the 14th century. Aztecs also founded Tlatelolco on a neighbouring island which, as the intervening swamps were drained, became joined to Tenochtitlán and was eventually subdued politically. For half a century or more the Aztecs served the rulers of Azcapotzalco on the lake shore, which was gaining control over some of the dozens of rival statelets in the valley. Then, around

1426, the Aztecs successfully rebelled against Azcapotzalco and themselves became the most powerful people in the valley.

The Aztec Empire In the mid-1400s, with their sense of being a chosen people growing, the Aztecs formed the Triple Alliance with two other valley states, Texcoco and Tlacopan, to wage war against Tlaxcala and Huejotzingo, outside the valley to the east. The prisoners they took would form the diet of sacrificed warriors that the Aztecs' sun god demanded, enabling them to fulfil their mission to keep the sun rising. For the dedication of Tenochtitlán's Great Temple in 1487, Ahuizotl had 20,000 captives sacrificed.

In the second half of the 15th century the Triple Alliance, led by the Aztec kings Moctezuma I Ilhuicamina, Axayácatl and Ahuizotl, brought most of central Mexico, in a broad band from the Gulf Coast to the Pacific (though not Tlaxcala), under its control. One province, Xoconochco, was even established on the far-off coast of Chiapas. The total population of the empire's 38 provinces may have been about five million. The empire's purpose was to exact tribute of resources absent from the heartland – such as jade, turquoise, cotton, paper, tobacco, rubber, lowland fruits and vegetables, cacao, and precious feathers – which were needed for the glorification of its elite or to support the many nonproductive servants of its war-oriented state.

Ahuizotl's successor was Moctezuma II Xocoyotzin, a reflective character who believed – perhaps fatally – that the Spaniard Hernán Cortés, who arrived on the Gulf Coast in 1519, might be Quetzalcóatl, returned from the east to reclaim his throne.

Economy & Society By 1519 Tenochtitlán-Tlatelolco probably had over 200,000 inhabitants – many of them non-food-producing specialists – and the Valley of Mexico as a whole probably over a million. These were supported by a variety of intensive farming methods using only stone and wooden tools, but including irrigation, terracing and lake and swamp reclamation.

The basic unit of Aztec society was the *calpulli*, a few dozen to a few hundred extended families, owning land communally and forming a taxation, labour and military unit. The Aztec king held immense wealth and absolute power but delegated important roles like priest or tax collector to members of the *pilli* (nobles). Military leaders were usually *tecuhtli*, elite professional soldiers. Another special group was the *pochteca*, militarised merchants who helped extend the empire, brought goods to the capital and organised the large important markets, held daily in big towns. Many commoners were specialist artisans. At the bottom of society were pawns (paupers who could sell themselves for a specified period), serfs and slaves.

Culture & Religion Tenochtitlán-Tlatelolco had hundreds of temple complexes, the greatest of which, located just off modern Mexico City's Zócalo, included three big and six small pyramid temples, several plazas, a ball court, a wooden rack for the skulls of sacrificed victims, and a sacred pool. The main temple pyramid, dedicated to Huitzilopochtli and the rain god Tláloc, was over 30 metres high and 100 metres long on each side.

Much Aztec culture was drawn from earlier Mexican civilisations. They had writing, bark-paper books, and the Calendar Round. They observed the movements of heavenly bodies in great detail for astrological purposes. A routine of great ceremonies, many of them public, was performed by celibate professional priests. Typically these would include offerings, sacrifices and masked dances or processions enacting myths.

Like the Maya, the Aztecs believed they lived in a world whose predecessors had been destroyed – in this case the fifth world. The other four had each been ended by the death of the sun, wiping out humanity each time. Aztec human sacrifices were designed to keep the sun alive. Like the Maya, the

Aztecs saw the world as having four directions, 13 heavens and nine hells. Those who died by drowning, leprosy, lightning, gout, dropsy or lung disease went to the paradisal gardens of Tláloc, who had killed them; warriors who were sacrificed or died in battle, merchants killed travelling far away, and women who died giving birth to their first child all went to heaven as companions of the sun; everyone else travelled for four years under the northern deserts, the abode of the death god Mictlantecuhtli, before reaching the ninth hell where they vanished altogether.

Other Postclassic Civilisations

On the eve of the Spanish conquest the basic modes of existence of many of Mexico's peoples, including the Aztecs, held deep similarities. Each was politically centralised, with government, taxation, trade and markets highly organised. Societies were divided into classes and many people were occupied in specialist tasks, including professional priests.

Agriculture was very productive despite the lack of draft animals, metal tools and the wheel. Maize tortillas and *pozol* (maize gruel) were staple foods. Beans provided important protein, and a great variety of other crops was grown in different regions, from squashes, tomatoes and chiles to avocados, peanuts, papayas and pineapples. Luxury foods for the elite included turkey, domesticated hairless dog, game, and chocolate drinks. The exchange of foods between different regions was an important reason for trade. All peoples worshipped a multiplicity of powerful gods (very often shared with other cultures), some of which demanded human sacrifices. Warfare was widespread, often in connection with the need to take prisoners for sacrifice.

Maya The 'Toltec' phase at Chichén Itzá lasted until about 1200 when the place was abandoned. It's conventionally thought that it was reoccupied by a probably-Maya people called the Itzá, who went on to found the town of Mayapán, south of modern Mérida. Mayapán, under the Cocom line of Itzá, came to dominate most of the Yucatán city states until the 15th century when the Cocom were overthrown in a rebellion and Mayapán was destroyed. Yucatán became a quarrelling-ground of numerous city states with a culture much decayed from Classic Maya glories.

Oaxaca Zapotec civilisation had declined in the 8th century, with Monte Albán and many other sites abandoned. From about 1200, those that remained, such as Mitla and Yagul, came under growing dominance of the Mixtecs, famed metalsmiths and potters from the uplands around the Oaxaca-Puebla border. Mixtec and Zapotec cultures became entangled before much of their territory fell to the Aztecs in the 15th and 16th centuries.

Gulf Coast The Totonacs, a people who may have occupied El Tajín in its later years, established themselves in much of what is now Veracruz state. To their north, the Huastec civilisation, another web of probably independent statelets, flourished from 800 to 1200. In the 15th century the Aztecs subdued most of the Totonac and Huastec areas.

The West One civilised people who avoided conquest by the Aztecs were the Tarascans who ruled the area of modern Michoacán from their capital Tzintzuntzan, beside Lago Pátzcuaro, about 200 km west of Mexico City. Like the Mixtecs they were skilled artisans and jewellers; fire and the moon were among their chief deities.

The Spanish Conquest

Ancient Mexican civilisation, nearly 3000 years old, was shattered in two short years from 1519 to 1521. A tiny group of invaders destroyed the Aztec Empire, brought a new religion and reduced the native people, including their all-powerful overlords, to second-class citizens and slaves. So alien to each other were the newcomers and the Indians that each doubted the other was human.

From this traumatic meeting arose modern Mexico. Most Mexicans, being *mestizo* (of mixed Indian and European blood), are descendants of both cultures. While Cuauhtémoc, the last Aztec emperor, is now an official hero, Cortés, the leader of the Spanish conquerors, is a villain, and the Indians who helped him are seen as traitors. Nevertheless, Spanish is the national language, Catholicism is the national religion and European and American influence is obvious and pervasive.

Early Expeditions The Spaniards had been in the Caribbean since Christopher Columbus arrived in 1492, with their main bases on the island of Santo Domingo (now occupied by the nations of Haiti and the Dominican Republic) and Cuba. Realising that they had not reached the East Indies, they began looking for a passage through the land mass to their west but were distracted by tales of gold, silver and a rich empire. Trading, slaving and exploring expeditions from Cuba were led by Francisco Hernández de Córdoba in 1517 and Juan de Grijalva in 1518, but didn't penetrate inland from Mexico's Gulf Coast where they were driven back by hostile natives.

In 1518 the governor of Cuba, Diego Velázquez, asked Hernán Cortés to lead a new expedition westward. As Cortés gathered ships and men, Velázquez became uneasy about the costs and Cortés' loyalty, and cancelled the expedition. Cortés ignored him and set sail on 15 February 1519 with 11 ships, 550 men and 16 horses.

Cortés' cunning and Machiavellian tactics are legendary, but it is less widely known that the Aztecs played military politics too. A first-hand, detailed account may be found in the *True History of the Conquest of New Spain* by one of Cortés' soldiers, Bernal Díaz del Castillo.

Cortés & the Aztecs Landing first at Cozumel off Yucatán, the Spaniards were joined by Jerónimo de Aguilar, a Spaniard who had been shipwrecked there several years earlier, and who now spoke the Indians' language. Moving west along the coast to Tabasco, they defeated some hostile Indians and Cortés delivered the first of many lectures to Indians on the importance of Christianity and the greatness of King Carlos V of Spain. The Indians gave him 20 maidens, among them La Malinche who became his interpreter, aide and lover.

The expedition next put in near the present city of Veracruz, where the local Totonac Indians were friendly. Meanwhile, in the Aztec capital of Tenochtitlán tales of 'towers floating on water' (the Spanish ships) bearing fair-skinned beings had been carried to Moctezuma II, the Aztec god-emperor. Lightning struck a temple, a comet sailed through the night skies, a bird 'with a mirror in its head' was brought to Moctezuma, who saw warriors in it, and according to the Aztec calendar, 1519 would see legendary god-king Quetzalcóatl's return from the east. Moctezuma discouraged Cortés from travelling to Tenochtitlán.

The Spaniards were well received at the nearby Totonac towns of Zempoala and Quiahuiztlán, which resented Aztec domination. Cortés thus gained his first Indian allies. Cortés then set up a settlement called Villa Rica de la Vera Cruz, and appointed town officials who duly elected him their leader. Still facing doubts and hostility among his own men, Cortés apparently scuttled his remaining ships to remove any ideas of retreat. Then, leaving about 150 men at Villa Rica, the Spaniards and Zempoalan carriers set off inland for Tenochtitlán. On the way Cortés convinced the Tlaxcalan Indians that he was their friend, and they became his most valuable allies.

Moctezuma finally invited Cortés to meet him, denying responsibility for an ambush at Cholula. The Spaniards and 6000 Indian allies thus approached the Aztecs' lake-island capital – a city bigger than any in Spain. Entering Tenochtitlán on 8 November 1519 along one of the causeways which joined it to the lakeshore, Cortés was met by Moctezuma, who was carried by nobles in a litter with a canopy of feathers and gold. They exchanged courtesies and the

Spaniards were lodged – as befitted gods – in the former palace of Axayácatl, Moctezuma's father.

Though attended to with considerable luxury, the Spaniards were trapped; one wrong move and the Aztecs could easily have retaliated. Some of the Aztec leaders advised Moctezuma to attack the Spaniards, even though they might be gods. The emperor's hesitation eventually made the decision for him.

To guarantee their own safety, the Spaniards took Moctezuma hostage. Moctezuma, believing Cortés a god, kept his people from rebelling by telling them that he went willingly. But hostile voices rose in the city, aggravated by the Spaniards' destruction of Aztec idols.

The Fall of Tenochtitlán After the Spaniards had been in Tenochtitlán about six months, Moctezuma told Cortés that another fleet had arrived on the Veracruz coast. This was led by Pánfilo de Narváez, sent by Diego Velázquez to arrest Cortés. Cortés left 140 Spaniards under Alvarado in Tenochtitlán and sped to the coast with his remaining forces. They routed Narváez' much bigger force one night in May 1520 and most of the defeated men joined Cortés.

In their absence the long-feared confrontation took place in Tenochtitlán. Apparently fearing an attack, the Spaniards under Alvarado had struck first and killed about 200 Aztec nobles trapped in a square during a festival. Cortés and his enlarged force returned to the Aztec capital and were allowed to rejoin their comrades – only then to come under the fiercest attack they had yet encountered. Trapped in Axayácatl's palace, Cortés persuaded Moctezuma to try to pacify his people. According to one version, the emperor went onto the roof to address the crowds but was unable to calm them and, wounded by missiles, died soon afterwards; other versions have it that the Spaniards killed him.

The Spaniards, hopelessly outnumbered, had no choice but to flee, which they tried to do in secret on the night of 30 June 1520.

Their Aztec enemies discovered their plan, however, and several hundred Spaniards and thousands of their Indian allies were killed on this Noche Triste (Sad Night).

To their relief the Spanish survivors were welcomed at Tlaxcala, whose leaders had been impressed by the Spaniards' valour. They prepared for another campaign by building boats in sections which could be carried across the mountains for a water-borne assault on Tenochtitlán. When the 900 Spaniards re-entered the Valley of Mexico, they were accompanied by 100,000 native allies. For the first time, the odds were in their favour.

Moctezuma had been replaced by his nephew, Cuitláhuac, who then died of small-pox, a new disease brought to Mexico by one of Narváez's soldiers. He was succeeded by another nephew, the 18-year-old Cuauhtémoc. The attack started in May 1521 and the Spaniards' boats soon bested the Aztecs' canoes. But the besieged Aztecs refused surrender, and Cortés resorted to razing Tenochtitlán to the ground building by building in order to give his horses and cannon the advantage of open ground. By 13 August 1521 the last resistance ended. Cuauhtémoc was captured. He asked Cortés to kill him, but was denied his request.

The Colonial Era
The Encomienda System Establishing their headquarters at Coyoacán on the southern shore of the lake, the Spaniards organised the rebuilding of Tenochtitlán as the capital of New Spain. In an unsuccessful bid to discover the whereabouts of the fabled treasure hoards, they reputedly tortured Cuauhtémoc and other Aztec nobles by burning the soles of their feet.

To satisfy his soldiers, who were disgruntled at the lack of material reward for their efforts, Cortés began giving them Indian towns as *encomiendas*. Under this system the Spaniards were entitled to Indian tribute and labour and in return were supposed to look after 'their' Indians' welfare and convert them to Christianity. In reality, encomiendas were often little more than slave encampments. The rest of the 16th century saw a long and largely successful struggle by the Spanish crown to bring the conquistadors under royal control since the crown was uneasy about letting them and their descendants have such power.

By 1524 virtually all of the Aztec Empire, plus some outlying regions such as Colima, the Huasteca and the Tehuantepec area, were under at least loose Spanish control.

In 1528 Cortés was granted 22 towns as encomiendas and given the title Marqués del Valle de Oaxaca, but was denied the role of governor. He returned to Spain in 1540 and died near Seville in 1547.

Audiencias & Viceroys In 1527 the Spanish king set up Mexico's first *audiencia*, nominally a high court but with government functions. Its leader, Nuño de Guzmán, was among the worst of Mexican history's long list of corrupt, violent leaders. Guzmán made an enemy of Mexico City's first bishop, Juan de Zumárraga, who was shocked by the maltreatment of the Indians. Guzmán then set off on a bloody conquest of western Mexico, from Michoacán up to Sonora. Eventually he was recalled to Spain.

The second audiencia (1530-35) brought some order to the colony. The king then appointed Antonio de Mendoza as Mexico's first viceroy – his personal representative to govern Mexico. Mendoza, who ruled for 15 years, gave the colony the stability it badly needed, limited the worst exploitation of the Indians, encouraged the spread of Christianity and ensured steady revenue to the Spanish crown.

Yucatán was subdued in the 1540s by two men both called Francisco de Montejo (relatives of a conquistador of the same name who had failed in the same task in 1527). This meant that all of 'civilised' Mexico was in Spanish hands. That left the huge 'Chichimec frontier' – roughly, the area north of a line between modern Tampico and Guadalajara – inhabited by the fierce seminomads known to the Aztecs as Chichimecs (Barbarians or Descendants of Dogs).

The discovery of big silver deposits in Zacatecas in the mid-1540s, followed soon after by major finds at Guanajuato, San Luis Potosí and Pachuca, spurred Spanish attempts to pacify the Chichimec area, but these were not successful until the 1590s.

Racial Politics Despite the efforts of Bishop Zumárraga and Viceroy Mendoza, the position of the natives deteriorated fast, not only because of harsh treatment at the hands of the colonists but also because of a series of plagues, many of them new diseases brought by the Spaniards. The Indian population of New Spain, as the colony was called, was decimated from 20 million at the time of conquest to two million in 1580. It reached its low point of one million in the mid-17th century. At one point the Indians had been thought by some to be incapable of reason and thus less than human. (In 1537 the Pope ruled that they were human.)

The Indians' only real allies were some of the Christian monks who started arriving in New Spain in 1523 to convert them. Many were compassionate and brave men; the Franciscans and Dominicans distinguished themselves by protecting the Indians from the colonists' worst excesses. One Dominican monk, Bartolomé de Las Casas, persuaded the King to enact new laws in 1542 and 1543 to protect the Indians. When this nearly caused a rebellion among the encomienda holders the laws were not put into practice.

But the monks' missionary work also helped extend Spanish control over Mexico. By 1560 they had built over 100 monasteries, some fortified, and had carried out millions of conversions. These monastic orders were distinct from the 'secular' clergy under bishops, a division which later gave rise to serious rivalry.

Under the second viceroy, Luis de Velasco, Indian slavery was abolished in the 1550s, to be partly replaced by black slavery. Forced labour on encomiendas was also stopped, but since the population of workers was plummeting, a new system of about 45 days' forced labour a year for all Indians was introduced – the *cautequil*. This too was widely abused by the Spaniards until abolished about half a century later.

From the 16th to the 18th centuries, a sort of political-economic 'apartheid' system was in effect in Mexico. One's place in society was determined by skin colour and birthplace. Although they were a minuscule part of Mexico's population, *peninsular* Spaniards or *gachupines* were at the top of the socio-economic ladder and were automatically considered nobility in Mexico, however humble their status in Spain.

Next on the ladder were *criollos*, people born of Spanish parents in Mexico. By the 18th century some criollos had managed to acquire fortunes in ranching, mining, agriculture and commerce; not surprisingly, they also sought political power commensurate with their wealth.

In the first half of the 18th century, the Spanish Kings Philip V and Ferdinand VI assented to appointing eight criollos to the 12-member audiencia of Mexico. They hoped that the appointments would bring greater cooperation and increased tax revenues from a growing Mexican population of criollos and non-Whites. Spain desperately needed the additional revenue.

King Charles III (1759-88) sought not only policy reforms, but also a complete revamping of the political-economic structures of both Spain and Mexico. He believed this was necessary because Mexico was increasingly threatened by British and French encroachments on its northern flank. Several important changes were made. Most notably, the Jesuits (two-thirds of whom were criollos) were expelled from Mexico because they were regarded as too influential in Mexican society.

Expulsion of the Jesuits was only the beginning of an attack on church organisations. From bequests of money, property and personal belongings, the Catholic Church in Mexico had amassed a fortune large enough to allow it to lend money to local entrepreneurs. To the Spaniards this represented a loss of control. In 1804 the Amortisation & Consolidation Law was passed, which called for the immediate transfer of all church funds to the royal coffers. Most of the church property holdings had to be sold to meet royal demands. The result was economic chaos and the creation of conditions ripe for rebellion. The catalyst came in 1808 when Napoleon Bonaparte invaded Spain and crown control over Mexico suddenly rested solely with loyalists in Mexico.

Independence, Empire & Republic

War of Independence In 1810 Miguel Hidalgo y Costilla, a parish priest in the town of Dolores, began actively planning a rebellion. News of his plans leaked to the government, so Hidalgo acted immediately. On 15 September 1810 he summoned his supporters to the church and issued the *Grito de Dolores*, a call to rebel against the Spaniards:

My children, a new dispensation comes to us this day. Are you ready to receive it? Will you be free? Will you make the effort to recover from the hated Spaniards the lands stolen from your forefathers 300 years ago? We must act at once.

An angry mob formed, marched on Guanajuato and, over the next month and a half, also captured Zacatecas, San Luis Potosí and Valladolid. They scored a few minor victories as they tried to take Mexico City, but were forced northward where Spanish troops captured them and executed the rebel leaders, including Hidalgo.

José María Morelos y Pavón, also a parish priest, assumed the leadership of the rebel forces. He led them back to Mexico City where they besieged the city for several months. Meanwhile he convened a congress of representatives at Chilpancingo (in modern Guerrero state). The congress adopted guiding principles including the abolition of slavery, elimination of royal monopolies, universal male suffrage and, most importantly, popular sovereignty. Morelos, however, was captured in 1815 and his forces were dispersed into several bands of guerrillas, the most successful of which was led by Vicente Guerrero.

Emperor Agustín I Sporadic fighting continued until 1821 when Viceroy Agustín de Iturbide defected and conspired with the rebels to declare independence from Spain. By September 1821 a compromise called the Plan de Iguala had been worked out between various factions in Mexico. The plan established 'three guarantees' – religious dominance of the Catholic Church, a constitutional monarchy, and equality of rights for criollos and peninsular Spaniards. The plan was accepted by both loyalists and rebels. Under the terms of the Plan de Iguala, Iturbide ascended to the throne as Emperor Agustín I.

Antonio López de Santa Anna Iturbide's reign lasted less than two years, after which a junta consisting of Nicolás Bravo, Guadalupe Victoria and Pedro Celestino Negrete drew up a constitution (1824). This established a federal republic of 19 states and four territories. Victoria became Mexico's first president. During the next seven years, Victoria was overthrown by Bravo who, in turn, later lost an election to a centrist candidate. Guerrero staged a coup d'état and in 1829 had General Antonio López de Santa Anna lead the final expulsion of Spanish troops from Mexico. Santa Anna turned around in 1831 and had Guerrero executed.

Santa Anna became president in 1833. His tenure marked the beginning of a 22-year period of severe political instability in which the presidency changed hands 36 times; 11 of these terms went to Santa Anna. His main contributions to Mexico were manifestations of his megalomaniac personality. Most memorably, he had his amputated, mummified leg (which he lost in an 1838 battle with the French) disinterred in 1842 and paraded through the streets of Mexico City with a full military guard in attendance.

Santa Anna is also remembered for his attempts to keep Texas a part of Mexico. After a war with the USA, the Mexican government signed the Treaty of Guadalupe Hidalgo on 2 February 1848 which ceded Texas, California and New Mexico to the USA. Crippled by the war and a weakened economy, Santa Anna's government decided to raise much-needed capital by ceding – for a price – more land to the USA. In 1853 the US government negotiated what is known as the Gadsden Purchase and bought the Mesilla Valley (today Arizona and southern New Mexico) from Mexico for US$10 million. This loss precipitated the Revolution of Ayutla, which ousted Santa Anna from power in 1855.

Juárez & French Intervention A provisional government was formed to implement the Plan of Ayala, drawn up the year before by Benito Juárez, a Zapotec Indian turned liberal politician and lawyer. Several reform laws were passed, which along with a new constitution, precipitated the War of the Reform (1858-61) between liberals, with their 'capital' in Veracruz, and conservatives based in Mexico City.

The liberals under Juárez won the war and came to power in 1861, with Juárez as president. But the country was in shambles – roads, bridges, public buildings and fields of crops were all in ruins – and heavily in debt to England, France and Spain. These three countries agreed among themselves to temporarily occupy Mexico to collect their debts, but France decided to go even further and colonise Mexico, leading to yet another Mexican civil war.

Though the French army was defeated at Puebla by General Ignacio Zaragoza on 5 May 1862, the French took Puebla a year later, and went on to capture Mexico City. In 1864 Emperor Napoleon III of France invited Austrian Archduke Maximilian of Hapsburg to become emperor of Mexico. Juárez and his government were forced by the French army to withdraw to the interior as a government of opposition.

Emperor Maximilian and Empress Carlota entered Mexico City on 12 June 1864 and moved into Chapultepec castle. Their reign lasted only a year and a half. Under pressure from the USA, Napoleon III withdrew many of the troops which enforced Maximilian's rule. In May 1867, Maximilian was defeated at Querétaro by forces loyal to

Juárez, and was executed there by firing squad on 19 June.

The war over, Juárez immediately set an agenda emphasising economic and educational reform. The education system was completely revamped and, for the first time, schooling was made mandatory. A railway line was built between Mexico City and Veracruz. A rural police force was organised to secure the transportation of cargo through Mexico. Juárez, Mexico's great indigenous statesman, had only a few years to enjoy his triumphs, however.

The Porfiriato José de la Cruz Porfirio Díaz, who opposed Juárez in the election of 1871, rebelled in November 1871, and propelled Sebastián Lerdo de Tejada into the presidency after Juárez's death in 1872. Four years later, Díaz sent Lerdo into exile, grabbed control of Mexico, and began the long era of dictatorship known as the Porfiriato.

Díaz spent his first four-year presidential term implementing various economic reforms and clamping down on smuggling and banditry. He left office in 1880 and was followed by Manuel González, who continued Díaz's modernisation programme for four more years. Díaz then returned to power in 1884 with a modernisation philosophy based on the Positivistic writings of Auguste Comte and the slogan 'order and progress'.

Buildings and public-works projects were constructed throughout Mexico, particularly in Mexico City. Telephone and telegraph lines were strung and underwater cables laid. In 1876, Mexico had 640 km of railway track; by the 1890s, 3200 km, and by 1911, more than 20,000 km.

Mexico's stability and prosperity attracted foreign investors. Mining and oil exploration were opened up to greater foreign investment.

Díaz believed that order and progress could not be maintained in the presence of political opposition, free elections and a free press. He made Mexico's rich richer, but kept the country under control with a repressive army and rural police force.

In the early 1900s a liberal opposition formed, but was forced into exile in the USA. The most important group of exiles included Antonio Villareal, Librado Rivera, Juan Sarábia and the Flores Magón brothers. In 1906, in St Louis, Missouri, they issued an independence proclamation and began an opposition publication, *La Redención*. Their actions precipitated strikes throughout Mexico which led, in late 1910, to the Mexican Revolution.

The Mexican Revolution

Madero & Villa In 1910, Francisco Madero, a liberal from a wealthy family in the state of Coahuila, campaigned for the presidency and probably would have won if Díaz hadn't imprisoned him. Madero was released and immediately began organising an anti-Díaz opposition. After he drafted the revolutionary Plan of San Luis Potosí in November 1910 the revolution spread quickly across the country and prompted Díaz to suspend all civil liberties and to allow the use of force against the opposition. By May, however, revolutionaries under the leadership of Francisco 'Pancho' Villa (born Doroteo Arango) took Ciudad Juárez and caused Díaz to resign later that month. Madero was elected president in November 1911.

Madero was unable to create a stable government and contain the various factions fighting for power throughout the country. Emiliano Zapata, a peasant leader from Morelos, withdrew support from Madero because of Madero's reluctance to immediately restore hacienda land to the peasants. Madero sent federal troops to Morelos to disband Zapata's rebel forces, and the Zapatista movement was born.

In November 1911, Zapata promulgated the Plan of Ayala calling for the restoration of all land to the peasants. Zapatista forces won battles against federal troops in the present-day states of Morelos, Guerrero, México, Tlaxcala, Puebla and in Mexico City. Other rebellious forces took up local causes in other parts of the country. Soon all of Mexico was plunged into military chaos.

Chaos in the Capital In October 1912, Félix Díaz, nephew of Porfirio, organised a conservative, counter-revolutionary army in Veracruz – the Felicistas – and unsuccessfully tried to march out of the city. Félix was imprisoned in the Mexico City penitentiary where he met Bernardo Reyes. Together, they plotted yet another revolt.

Reyes and Díaz were sprung from prison in February 1913 by General Manuel Mondragón and several artillery regiments. The fighting quickly spread to the streets of Mexico City as Díaz (Reyes died in the first street battle) and the soldiers took control of the Ciudadela, a major army arsenal in the city. From 9 February to 18 February – a period now called the *decena trágica* or 10 tragic days – the city was besieged by artillery fire. Thousands of civilians and soldiers were killed and many buildings were destroyed. The fighting ended only after the US ambassador to Mexico, Henry Wilson, negotiated for Madero's General Huerta to support the rebels in deposing Madero's government. As Madero and his vice president, José María Pino Suárez, were executed by the rebels, Huerta stepped into the ensuing power vacuum to take control of the government.

Huerta & Carranza Huerta did nothing for Mexico except foment greater opposition and strife. In March 1913, three revolutionary factions united against Huerta under the Plan of Guadalupe: Francisco 'Pancho' Villa in Chihuahua, Venustiano Carranza in Coahuila and Álvaro Obregón in Sonora. Zapata and his forces were also fighting against the government. Terror reigned in the countryside as Huerta's troops fought unsuccessfully on three fronts, and in reprisal pillaged and plundered many villages. Huerta was forced to resign on 8 July 1914.

Carranza called all the revolutionary leaders to a conference in the hope that a new government could be formed. Instead, another civil war erupted and each faction formed its own government. Carranza eventually emerged as the victor and formed a government that was recognised by the USA. A constitutional convention was held in 1916 and the Constitution of 1917 resulted. Carranza was sworn into office on 1 May 1917.

Unfortunately for Carranza, the revolution continued, especially in Morelos where the Zapatistas demanded more social reforms. However, he was able to eliminate the Zapatista threat by having Jesús M Guajardo, a colonel in the federal army, feign defection to the Zapatistas. Guajardo called a meeting with Zapata on 10 April 1919 at a hacienda in Chinameca. As Zapata entered the building, Guajardo's men shot him point-blank. Carranza's problems, however, were not over yet. The following year, opposition leaders Adolfo de la Huerta and Álvaro Obregón raised an army, chased Carranza out of office and had him assassinated.

From Revolution to World War II
The 1920s brought political stability, peace and prosperity as the economy was rebuilt. Mexican art and culture flourished. President Álvaro Obregón (1920-24) and his Minister of Education, José Vasconcelos, regarded art an important part of their new educational structure. Vasconcelos commissioned Mexico's top muralists – Diego Rivera, David Alfaro Siqueiros and José Clemente Orozco – to decorate important public buildings.

Plutarco Elías Calles, who succeeded Obregón in 1924, continued the political stability and economic prosperity. Calles expanded the education system by 2000 schools, implemented many agricultural reforms, and distributed more than three million hectares of land to small farmers. With the appointment of Dwight Morrow as US ambassador to Mexico, relations with the USA improved.

However, Calles' administration was not without problems. Like some of his predecessors, he took measures against the power of the Catholic Church in Mexico. These included the closure of all monasteries and convents, deportation of all foreign priests and nuns, and the prohibition of religious processions. These drastic measures precipitated the bloody Cristero Rebellion, which lasted until 1929.

At the end of his term in 1928, Calles called for the return of Obregón to office, this time for the newly expanded presidential term of six years. Obregón won re-election, but was assassinated not long after. On Calles' recommendation, Emilio Portes Gil was then elected for a two-year interim term while Calles reorganised his political supporters to found the National Revolutionary Party (El Partido Nacional Revolucionario or PNR), Mexico's first well-organised political party and initiator of a long list of official acronyms.

Although important reforms had been implemented since the Revolution, there was still much to do. In 1934 Lázaro Cárdenas, formerly governor of Michoacán, won the presidency with the support of the PNR and actively continued the reform programme.

During his six-year term, Cárdenas instituted an extensive land reform system by redistributing almost 20 million hectares, mostly through the establishment of *ejidos* (lands owned collectively). He encouraged better church-state relations and reorganised the labour movement into the Confederation of Mexican Workers (Confederación de Trabajadores Mexicanos, CTM).

The act for which Cárdenas is generally remembered was his bold expropriation of foreign oil company operations in Mexico (1938); formation of the Mexican Petroleum Company (Petróleos Mexicanos, or Pemex); and reorganisation of the PNR into the Party of the Mexican Revolution (Partido de la Revolución Mexicana or PRM), a coalition party of representatives from four sectors of Mexican society – agrarian, military, labour and the people-at-large.

After the oil expropriation, foreign investors avoided Mexico. Combined with the tremendous cost of implementing various social programmes, this slowed the Mexican economy, but only temporarily. Cárdenas had laid the foundation for Mexico's future development.

In 1940 Cárdenas established a political tradition: during his last year in office the Mexican president recommends a successor, who receives the ruling party's candidacy and is invariably elected president. Cárdenas recommended a conservative candidate, Manuel Ávila Camacho, who easily won.

WW II was the key event during Camacho's presidency (1940-46). As a supporter of the Allied war effort, he sent Mexican troops to help the Allies in the Pacific, and supplied raw materials and labour to the USA. At home, the war proved a boost to Mexico's economy: because many manufactured goods could no longer be imported from the industrialised countries, they had to be produced in Mexico. This fostered local industry as well as increasing exports.

After WW II

As the Mexican economy expanded, new economic and political groups demanded power, which meant influence in the ruling party (the PRM). To recognise their inclusion, the party was renamed the Institutional Revolutionary Party (El Partido Revolucionario Institucional, or PRI). In 1946 the postwar boom ushered in Miguel Alemán Valdés as president (1946-52).

Alemán continued the industrialisation and development of Mexico by building the National Autonomous University of Mexico (Universidad Nacional Autónoma de México or UNAM), hydroelectric stations and irrigation projects, and by expanding Mexico's road system fourfold. In addition, Pemex drilling operations and refineries grew dramatically and, with the rapid rise of other industries, spawned some of Mexico's worst corruption.

Alemán's successor, Adolfo Ruiz Cortines (1952-58), tried to eliminate much of the graft and corruption that had plagued his predecessor's administration. Cortínes also began to tackle a new problem – explosive population growth. In the previous two decades Mexico's population had doubled and many people began migrating to urban areas to search for work.

Confronting the problems of the poor became one of the priorities of Cortínes' successor, Adolfo López Mateos (1958-64).

His social reforms included redistribution of 12 million more hectares of land to small farmers, nationalisation of foreign utility concessions, implementation of social-welfare programmes for the poor, and public-health campaigns to combat tuberculosis, malaria and polio. Almost every village was given assistance in the construction of schools and provided with teachers and textbooks. His programmes were helped by strong economic growth, particularly in tourism and exports.

Recent Decades

President Gustavo Díaz Ordaz (1964-70) came to power on a platform that emphasised business more than social programmes. One of his first actions was to fire the new liberal-minded president of the PRI, Carlos Madrazo. His reputation, already soured by his pre-presidency nullification of Baja California's elections, was worsened by this action against liberals. Groups of university students in Mexico City were the first to express their outrage with the Díaz Ordaz administration.

Protests began at the National University in the spring of 1966, but were quelled by federal troops. Student discontent came to a head in 1968 at the summer Olympic Games, the first ever held in a Third World country. More than half a million people rallied in Mexico City's Zócalo on 27 August; on 2 October, with the Olympics in progress, a rally was organised at the Plaza de las Tres Culturas in Tlatelolco. The government, fearing the rally would disrupt the games, sent in riot police with tear gas, clubs and firearms. In the ensuing confrontation, several hundred people died.

When President Luis Echeverría Álvarez (1970-76) took office, Mexico was a political and economic mess. He sought a strategy by which Mexico could continue to expand economically and wealth could be redistributed more equitably. His first target of reform was the agricultural sector where technical assistance and government investment were desperately needed to forestall a complete collapse. He instituted new government credit projects and expanded rural health clinics, the social security system and family planning.

Despite Echeverría's progressive actions, though, civil unrest in Mexico was increasing, including political kidnappings, bank robberies, and an insurrection in Guerrero, all of which were partially fuelled by the corruption rife among government officials.

Echeverría's successor, José López Portillo (1976-82), presided during the jump in world oil prices following the Arab boycott. For Mexico this meant rapidly rising oil revenues, which could be applied to both industrial and agricultural investments. Suddenly, Mexico was seen as a safe investment; international banks and lending institutions lent Mexico billions of dollars until, just as suddenly, a glut of oil on the world market sent oil prices plunging. The peso collapsed and Mexico's worst economic recession since the Depression began.

The administration of López Portillo was considered the most corrupt in living memory. The most infamous case of corruption was that of Mexico City's chief of police, Arturo Durazo. Officially he earned a salary of US$65 per week; unofficially, he bought race horses, built palatial residences in Mexico City, Zihuatanejo and various foreign cities, and funnelled more than US$600 million into Swiss bank accounts.

Disaster & Political Reform

Miguel de la Madrid (1982-88) was largely unsuccessful in coping with the problems left to him by his predecessors. The population continued to grow at Malthusian rates; the economy made only weak progress, crushed by the huge debt burden assumed during the oil boom years; and the social pot continued to simmer.

De la Madrid's economic policies were not helped by the earthquake of 19 September 1985, which registered eight on the Richter scale, and caused more than US$4 billion in damage. Hundreds of buildings in Mexico City were destroyed, thousands of people were dislocated, and at least 8000 were killed.

AN HISTORICAL WHO'S WHO

Jerónimo de Aguilar
Spanish priest shipwrecked on the Yucatán Peninsula seven years before Cortés arrived. He had learned the Maya language and proved an invaluable ally to Cortés.

Ahuizotl
Aztec emperor from 1486 to 1502, who expanded the empire.

Captain Ignacio Allende (1779-1811)
One of the instigators of the independence struggle in 1810.

Pedro de Alvarado (1486-1541)
One of the leading conquistadors who accompanied Cortés; later he conquered Guatemala and El Salvador.

Axayácatl
Aztec emperor from 1469 to 1481, father of Moctezuma II Xocoyotzin.

Luis Echeverría Álvarez
President of Mexico from 1970 to 1976, he increased government technical assistance for agriculture and expanded rural social services. His administration, however, was blighted by violent civil unrest and the beginnings of severe corruption.

Empress Carlota Marie Charlotte Amélie (1840-1927)
Daughter of King Leopold I of Belgium, she married Archduke Maximilian of Hapsburg (1857), and accompanied him to Mexico in 1864 to become empress. After her husband's execution in 1867, she lived on for 60 years, mentally unstable, a ward of the Vatican.

Plutarco Elías Calles (1877-1945)
Mexican Revolution leader and then president of Mexico from 1924 to 1928. He started to unite regional political elites into a national party while president, creating a modicum of stability in the country. In 1929 Calles' national party became the National Revolutionary Party, the precursor to the PRI, Mexico's dominant party today.

Lázaro Cárdenas (1895-1970)
A general and a statesman, he was considered a true president of the people; he served from 1934 to 1940. Cárdenas carried out major land reforms, established the system of ejidos, expropriated foreign oil company operations, and reorganised the PNR into the PRM (Party of the Mexican Revolution), consolidating one-party domination.

Venustiano Carranza (1859-1920)
Succeeded the intensely disliked Huerta as president (1914-1920), but he wasn't able to end Mexico's revolutionary anarchy. One of his most memorable actions was the ambush and execution of rebel leader Zapata. He was overthrown by the alliance formed by Álvaro Obregón and Huerta and assassinated while fleeing the country with five million pesos in gold.

Bernal Díaz del Castillo (1492-1581)
Captain in the army of Cortés. He was the author of the *True History of the Conquest of New Spain*, an eyewitness account of the Spanish conquest of Mexico and Guatemala.

Hernán Cortés (1485-1547)
Spanish conquistador, sometimes known as Hernando or Fernando, who invaded Mexico and conquered the Aztecs. Much maligned today in Mexico, Cortés was the person chiefly responsible for introducing Hispanic civilisation into Mexico.

Miguel Hidalgo y Costilla (1753-1811)
Parish priest of Dolores who sparked the independence struggle in 1810 with his famous *Grito* or call for independence. He led an unsuccessful attempt to take Mexico City.

Cuauhtémoc
Last Aztec emperor, successor to Moctezuma II Xocoyotzin and Cuitláhuac. Cuauhtémoc was defeated and later executed (1525) by Cortés.

Cuitláhuac
Aztec emperor who succeeded Moctezuma II Xocoyotzin in 1520, but died in the same year.

Porfirio Díaz (1830-1915)
Elected president in 1876 and re-elected on numerous occasions on a slogan of 'order and progress', he began as a reformer but later became a dictator. He pursued many public works projects and encouraged foreign investment, though at the expense of certain freedoms. His policies precipitated the Mexican Revolution in 1910 and forced his resignation in 1911.

Ricardo Flores Magón
One of two brothers who were leading opponents of Porfirio Díaz.

Juan de Grijalva
Leader of a Spanish expedition to the Mexican Gulf Coast in 1518; he died in 1527.

Guadalupe Victoria (1786-1843)
Born Manuel Félix Fernández, he fought alongside Hidalgo and Morelos, and contested (along with Santa Anna) Iturbide's accession as emperor of Mexico. After Iturbide's removal in 1823, he was a member of the provisional government, and then president, serving under his nom de guerre.

Vicente Guerrero (1782-1831)
A leader in the later stages of the struggle for independence from Spain. Subsequently a liberal president but deposed and executed by the conservative Anastasio Bustamante in 1829.

General Victoriano Huerta (1854-1916)
Huerta quashed rebel leader Orozco's attack on Mexico City in March 1912. The following year he stepped into a power vacuum and became one of Mexico's most disliked and ineffective leaders. He was forced to resign in 1914.

Agustín de Iturbide (1783-1824)
An officer in the royalist army, he worked to suppress the rebellion of Hidalgo and Morelos. When sent to defeat Guerrero, he instead negotiated with the rebels to declare independence from Spain (1821). Instead of the liberal revolution envisaged by Hidalgo, Iturbide established a conservative state and was proclaimed Emperor Agustín I of Mexico, but his reign lasted less than two years (1822-1823).

Benito Juárez (1806-72)
A Zapotec Indian from Oaxaca, a politician and lawyer who led a group of liberals in deposing Santa Anna, then passed laws against the church that precipitated the three-year War of the Reform. Elected president in 1861, he ran the country until forced to flee because of the French takeover by Napoleon III and Emperor Maximilian. After Napoleon III recalled his soldiers from Mexico, Juárez resumed the presidency, which he held until his death.

Frida Kahlo (1907-54)
An artist, crippled by a bus accident at 18, she went on to achieve mastery of the surrealist idiom, projecting her physical suffering vividly – and with a wry humour – onto painted canvas. Wife of Diego Rivera, also a celebrated Mexican artist.

Bartolomé de Las Casas (1474-1566)
Spanish missionary and historian, he was a leading campaigner for Indian rights, and Bishop of Chiapas from 1544 to 1547.

José López Portillo
President from 1976 to 1982, López Portillo's administration borrowed enormous sums from foreign banks on the strength of Mexico's oil wealth. When the price of oil fell precipitously, Mexico's debt

burden all but crushed the economy. His administration is thought by many to have marked a high point in government corruption.

Francisco I Madero (1873-1913)
A liberal politician, Madero led the first major opposition to Díaz and succeeded in forcing him to resign. He proved unable to quell the factional fighting throughout Mexico and only made matters worse. His term ended in 1913 in front of a firing squad.

La Malinche
Cortés' Indian mistress and interpreter, she is considered to have had a major influence on Cortés' strategy in subduing the Aztecs.

Ferdinand Maximilian
Hapsburg archduke sent by Napoleon III of France to rule as emperor of Mexico. His rule was short-lived (1864-1867) and he was forced to surrender to Benito Juárez's forces, who executed him by firing squad in 1867.

Moctezuma I Ilhuicamina
Aztec emperor from 1440 to 1468.

Moctezuma II Xocoyotzin
Aztec emperor at the time of the Spanish invasion in 1519.

Francisco de Montejo (El Adelantado) (1479-1548)
Conquistador who failed to conquer Yucatán in 1527 and later became governor of Honduras. His son (El Mozo) and his nephew, both also named Francisco de Montejo, brought Yucatán under Spanish colonial control in the 1540s.

José María Morelos y Pavón (1765-1815)
A liberal priest like Hidalgo, he proved to be a brilliant leader and military strategist. Assuming leadership of the revolution after Hidalgo's capture and execution, he was elected generalissimo by the Congress of Chilpancingo (1813). Captured and executed in 1815 by Iturbide's forces, he was succeeded in his struggle by Vicente Guerrero and Guadalupe Victoria.

Álvaro Obregón (1880-1928)
An enlightened farmer, general and revolutionary leader, he led a force from Sonora in support of Madero, and later supported Carranza against Huerta and Villa. After serving as Carranza's minister of war, he rebelled when Carranza tried to keep power illegally. Obregón's term as president (1920-1928) saw the implementation of revolutionary reforms, especially in education. He was assassinated in 1928.

José Clemente Orozco (1883-1949)
One of the three great 20th century Mexican muralists, with Rivera and Siqueiros.

Diego Rivera (1886-1957)
Founder of a Mexican tradition of mural painting linking art and politics, he sought to bring political art into public spaces. Though his life was spent working for socialist causes, he embraced the Roman Catholic church just before his death. He was the husband of Frida Kahlo, also a celebrated Mexican artist.

Carlos Salinas de Gortari
Elected president in 1988 with 50.36% of the official vote count – the lowest of any PRI candidate in history – he has undertaken important economic and political reforms. His term lasts until 1994.

General Antonio López de Santa Anna (1794-1876)
A thorn in the side of newly independent Mexico for 30-odd years, Santa Anna unseated Iturbide, the head of Mexico's first independent government, in 1823. During the first 30 years of Mexico's independence there were 50 governments, 11 of them headed by Santa Anna. He was a lead player in Mexico's conflicts with the USA, and when Texans cry 'Remember the Alamo' they are recalling Santa Anna's massacre of the US defenders of the Alamo mission in what is today San Antonio, Texas.

David Alfaro Siqueiros (1898-1974)
One of the three great 20th century Mexican muralists, with Rivera and Orozco. His works were enormous and highly dramatic, as in the Poliforum Cultural Siqueiros in Mexico City.

Leon Trotsky
A Bolshevik organiser, founder of the Red Army and a leader of the Russian Revolution, Trotsky was outmanoeuvred by Stalin after Lenin's death. Forced to flee the Soviet Union, he sought refuge in Mexico City in 1937 with Diego Rivera's help, but was murdered by a Stalinist agent in 1940.

Francisco 'Pancho' Villa (1877-1923)
Born Doroteo Arango, he rebelled from his *peon* (peasant) roots and became a bandit in Chihuahua and Durango on the model of Robin Hood. His support was an important element in the victories of Madero over Díaz. Though he later supported Carranza against Huerta, Carranza turned on him when Huerta was out of the way. After a string of military defeats, Villa's forces invaded the USA, and General Pershing invaded Mexico in pursuit of him – but never caught him. Villa was assassinated in 1923.

Emiliano Zapata (1879-1919)
A peasant rebel leader from what is now the state of Morelos, he organised one of Mexico's first land-reform fights with the Plan of Ayala in 1911. After winning numerous battles throughout Mexico during the revolution (some in association with Pancho Villa), he was ambushed and executed in 1919 on President Carranza's orders. ∎

Not surprisingly, in this climate of economic helplessness people began to question the country's political system. The 1980s saw an increase in organised political dissent, even within the PRI.

Northern Mexico, where comparisons with the affluent USA are all too easy to make, saw growing support for the right-wing opposition party PAN (Partido de Acción Nacional). Frustrated by PRI electoral fraud, protesters marched in Monterrey. At Piedras Negras in December 1984, when the PAN claimed 16 victories in 38 seats at local elections but was awarded only a few, the city hall was set on fire.

Discontent on all sides finally mounted to the point where it at last made an impact on even the *official* results of the 1988 presidential election. Cuauhtémoc Cárdenas, son of the charismatic 1930s president Lázaro Cárdenas, walked out of the PRI to lead the new centre-left National Democratic Front (FDN) into the election. One of his close aides was murdered on the election eve, but despite discouragement many people believe Cárdenas received more votes than anyone else. Officially he was awarded 31% of the vote, while the PRI candidate, Carlos Salinas de Gortari (a former member of De la

Madrid's cabinet), received 50.36% – the lowest of any PRI presidential candidate in history. The PAN candidate Manual Clouthier won 17%.

Today & Tomorrow
At the root of Mexico's problems is population growth. Since 1970 Mexico's population has increased from about 47 million to more than 80 million. This increase has dramatically outpaced economic growth, particularly in the agricultural sector, and boosted migration to big cities.

President Salinas de Gortari, who serves until 1994, seems to have heard the call for electoral and social change. Though the population bomb keeps ticking, he has taken important actions against corruption, drug smuggling and election fraud, often at the urging of huge crowds gathered in the Zócalo. In the autumn of 1991, opposition protests brought the resignation of the PRI governors-elect of Guanajuato and San Luis Potosí, both of whom, it was alleged, won their posts through fraud. In January 1992, the Zócalo again filled, this time with protestors from Tabasco, and the result was the resignation of the state's newly-seated PRI governor.

Salinas, a fervent advocate of the North American Free Trade Agreement (a common-market plan for Canada, the USA and Mexico), sees reform as essential to implementation of the plan. His economic measures have revitalized the Mexican economy, kept inflation low and kept the peso strong (some would say overvalued). The real test of his achievement, however, will come in 1994. Will Mexico then be part of one huge North American economic community, will the peso still be strong, will the national elections be relatively free of fraud, and will Mexico have a clue how to control its population growth? All of Mexico is waiting to see.

GEOGRAPHY
Size & Borders

Covering almost two million square km, Mexico is shaped like a wide-handled scythe that narrows towards the south/south-east at the Isthmus of Tehuantepec and then curves north-eastward into the Yucatán Peninsula. It's bordered by the Sea of Cortés (also known as the Gulf of California) on the north-west, and by the Pacific Ocean along the Baja California coast and the western and south-western mainland coasts. Mexico's east coast is bordered by the Gulf of Mexico and curves south-east and then east from Veracruz and north-eastward to Campeche and the Yucatán Peninsula. This curved part of the Gulf is called the Bahía de Campeche (Bay of Campeche). Heading east along Yucatán and then south, the peninsula is bordered by the Caribbean Sea.

Mexico is big: it's nearly 3500 km as the crow flies from Tijuana in the north-west to Cancún in the south-east, or about 4600 km by road. To travel from the US border at Ciudad Juárez to Mexico City, one must ride almost 1700 km (about 24 hours). From Mexico City to the Guatemalan border at Ciudad Cuauhtémoc is almost 1200 km by road.

Mexico has a 3326-km northern border with the USA and, along the south and south-

NORTH

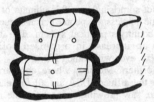

SOUTH

EAST

WEST

Glyphes for the world directions

east, an 871-km border with Guatemala and a 251-km border with Belize.

Topography

Northern and central Mexico – as far south

as Mexico City – have coastal plains on east and west, and two north-south mountain ranges framing broad central plateaux.

On the west coast, a relatively dry coastal plain stretches south from Mexicali almost to Tepic. Several rivers cut through the plain and empty into the Sea of Cortés and the Pacific Ocean, including the Río Colorado, Río Sonora, Río Yaqui, Río Fuerte and, just north of Tepic, the Río Grande de Santiago. The rivers flow out of the Sierra Madre Occidental mountain range, which joins the Sierra Nevada range in the USA. The mountains are rugged and have made this area almost completely impassable. There are only two surface transportation routes from the coast through the mountains to the great plateaux – the Copper Canyon train from Los Mochis to Chihuahua and the harrowing highway from Mazatlán to Durango.

The plateaux are divided into northern and central parts and range in altitude from about 1000 metres in the north to around 2000 metres near San Luis Potosí, 1500 metres around Guadalajara and 2300 metres in Mexico City. The Sonoran Desert occupies much of the northern plateau and extends northward into the southern fringes of Arizona and California. The central plateau is mostly a series of rolling hills and broad valleys, and includes some of the best farming and ranching land and the two largest cities (Mexico City and Guadalajara) in the country. Not surprisingly, more than half the population lives on this plateau.

Both plateaux are bounded to the east by the Sierra Madre Oriental mountain range, which runs as far south as the northern part of the state of Puebla and includes peaks as high as 3700 metres (over 12,000 feet).

On the east side of the Sierra Madre Oriental is the Gulf Coast plain, an extension of a similar coastal plain in Texas. In the north-eastern corner of Mexico the plain begins as a wide area, semi-marshy near the coast, and gradually narrows as it nears Veracruz, a major port.

The central plateau, Sierra Madre Oriental range and Gulf Coast plain reach as far as the Cordillera Neo-Volcánica mountain range,

just south of Mexico City. This range runs east-west and includes Mexico's highest peaks – Pico de Orizaba (5639 metres), Popocatépetl (5452 metres) and Iztaccíhuatl (5286 metres) – as well as the smaller extinct volcanoes of Paricutín (2700 metres) and Nevado de Colima (4330 metres).

To the west, the Pacific coastal lowlands become a narrow coastal plain as the Sierra Madre Occidental mountains become the Sierra Madre del Sur just south of Cabo Corrientes (west of Guadalajara). The Sierra Madre del Sur extends south all the way to the 250-km-wide Isthmus of Tehuantepec, the narrowest part of Mexico. As the range approaches the Isthmus, a lower range called the Oaxacan highlands branches northward from Oaxaca.

From the isthmus a narrow stretch of lowlands runs along the Pacific coast south to Guatemala. The lowlands are demarcated to the north-east by the Sierra Madre de Chiapas (also called the Sierra de Soconusco), beyond which is the Río Grijalva basin and then the Chiapas highlands. Travelling farther north-east past the highlands is a lush tropical rainforest area called El Petén. The jungle melts into a region of tropical savanna on the Yucatán Peninsula and, at the tip of the Peninsula, a very arid desert-like region. North of El Petén the jungle and isthmus open onto the marshy Tabasco plain.

The other major geographic feature of Mexico is Baja California, a 1300-km-long peninsula of mountains, deserts, plains and beaches – the world's longest peninsula.

CLIMATE

The Tropic of Cancer cuts across Mexico just north of Mazatlán and Fresnillo. It's hot and humid along the coastal plains of both coasts south of the Tropic of Cancer; however, inland at higher elevations such as in Guadalajara or Mexico City, the climate is much more dry and temperate with mountain peaks that are often capped with snow.

The hot, wet season is May to October, with June to September the hottest and wettest months of all. Low-lying coastal areas get more rain and higher temperatures than elevated inland ones. In the east, rainfall is particularly high on the eastern slopes of the Sierra Madre Oriental and on the northern side of the Isthmus of Tehuantepec. The Altiplano Central (high central plateau) is one of the driest parts of the country. December to February are generally the coolest months and north winds can make inland northern Mexico chilly, with temperatures (in °C) often in single figures, approaching freezing.

Weather by Phone
You can obtain an up-to-the-minute weather report for a Mexican city from the USA with a tone telephone by using The Weather Channel Connection. Call (900) 932-8437 (that's (900) W-E-A-T-H-E-R), and for US$0.95 per minute (plus tax) you can check the current time and date, current weather, three-day extended forecast, and normal weather patterns for trip planning in 600 US cities and 225 other cities throughout the world. You can also hear travel information such as visa requirements and current US Department of State travel advisories.

To hear the full weather report for one city (local time, temperature, dewpoint, general conditions, relative humidity, wind speed and direction, barometer reading and status), you will normally spend between two and three minutes on the line, which means that the average call costs US$2.85, plus tax (you can expect to pay slightly over US$3 total). To hear the extended forecast as well, expect to pay a bit more. Remember that some businesses, most hotels and all pay telephones disallow 900-number calls.

Press the buttons for the first four letters in a Mexican city's name to hear the forecast. Here are the Mexican cities for which weather information is available:

Acapulco	2227
Cancún	2262
Ensenada	3673
Guadalajara	4823
Ixtapa-Zihuatanejo	4982
Mazatlán	6394, then follow instructions
Mexico City	6394
Puerto Vallarta	7837
Tijuana	8458
Veracruz	8372

FAUNA & FLORA
Mexico has an impressive list of wild animals, from the fabled jaguar to the volcano rabbit *(Romerolaqus diazi)*, which only exists around Popocatépetl and Iztaccíhuatl volcanoes. There is also much splendid bird life, from the abundant coastal species and the hawks, eagles and buzzards which roam the mountain areas to magnificent tropical creatures such as the multicoloured red macaw and a few quetzal birds said to inhabit the Mexico-Guatemala border area. Unfortunately much of this wildlife is disappearing because of hunters and the destruction of the forests. Conservation laws, where they exist at all, are widely disregarded.

Nor is Mexico geared up for visitors who merely want to observe animals in the wild, rather than shoot them. The best places to see wildlife are zoos, and probably the best zoo

in the country is at Tuxtla Gutiérrez in Chiapas, where animals are kept in fairly spacious enclosures in an extensive forest area. All the species in the zoo are native to the state of Chiapas. Here you'll see jaguar, tapir, ocelot, puma and lynx, as well as vicious-looking snakes (including boa constrictors) and spiders that will put paid to any dreams you might have of unaccompanied jungle safaris.

If you're interested in the wildlife – particularly the birds – of the Gulf and Yucatán coasts, get hold of Donald Schueler's *Adventuring Along the Gulf of Mexico* (Sierra Club Books, San Francisco, 1986).

GOVERNMENT

Mexico is a republic with some similarities to both the American and European systems of democracy. A bicameral legislature makes the laws, a president carries them out, and an independent judiciary decides disputes according to Napoleonic law. Women gained the right to vote in 1955, and achieved passage of an Equal Rights Amendment to the constitution in 1974. The governors and legislatures of Mexico's various states, which need not be of the same party as that which dominates the federal government, are elected by their citizens.

So much for theory. In practice, Mexican political life has been dominated for more than half a century by the Institutional Revolutionary Party (PRI), and the president of Mexico – head of the PRI – has ruled in the tradition of strong leadership going back to Moctezuma and Cortés. Though the Chamber of Deputies and the Senate may debate the president's proposals, his will is rarely denied.

Each president serves one six-year term of office *(sexenio)*; he is not eligible for re-election. At the end of his term, the president selects a candidate to succeed him from within PRI party ranks, and since 1929 that candidate has invariably won.

The presidential elections of 1988 signalled the possibility of change, however. Following a split in the PRI, Carlos Salinas de Gortari, the official PRI candidate, won

the presidency with the smallest PRI majority ever (50.36%). Taking this signal to heart, President Salinas announced that 'the era of one-party rule is over'. Since then, the PRI has refrained on some occasions from using its powerful mechanisms for fraud, and opposition party candidates have won election as mayors and governors.

President Salinas de Gortari, a Harvard-trained economist who serves until 1994, has carried out important political and economic reforms which have met with wide local and international acclaim. If the PRI wins the presidential elections of 1994, it will be due largely to his leadership. If the PRI loses to an opposition candidate, it will signal a revolution in Mexican political life.

Human Rights

In 1984 and 1985 the international human rights body Amnesty International sent teams to investigate reports of killings, disappearances and torture of peasants in land disputes in Oaxaca and Chiapas. The quarrels arose mainly from local elections, peasant occupations of disputed lands, and arguments over boundaries between Indian communities. Amnesty International stated, 'In some cases such disputes have apparently led to deliberate killings of members of peasant organisations in circumstances suggesting that municipal authorities or members of the security forces were involved...'.

Peasant organisations reported the killing of 37 Triqui Indians between 1976 and 1981, 22 protest-organisation members or supporters between 1974 and 1984, more than 20 Tzotzil Indian leaders in Chiapas since the mid-1960s, and 12 peasants in Huizitlán de Serdán, Puebla, in 1984. Amnesty also documented the killing of 12 other protest-organisation supporters in Hidalgo since 1983. The victims tended to be supporters of groups opposed to landowners, commercial interests, or municipal or state authorities.

Amnesty added: 'The available evidence suggests that when members of opposition peasant organisations are killed by armed civilians, those responsible have rarely been

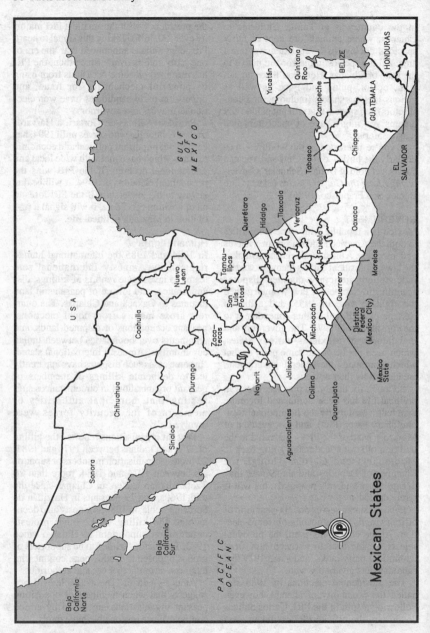

Mexican States

brought to justice...(it was) frequently alleged that internal divisions within communities were fostered and exploited by landowners closely associated with the municipal authorities...(there were) clear differences in the success rate of police investigations according to the political affiliation of the victim...'.

Another tactic open to the peasants is to make highly public protests. Amnesty International named Jorge Enrique Hernández, a Chiapas peasant, one of its 'Prisoners of the Month' in January 1987, after he had taken part in a demonstration on the Pan-American Highway demanding a maize subsidy. The protest dispersed peacefully when police and soldiers arrived, and the Chiapas state government apparently agreed to receive a delegation from the protesters, but the delegation members were then arrested. Hernández, one its members, was charged with terrorism.

Other protests included hunger strikes in April 1987 by Chiapas peasants in Mexico City's Zócalo (demanding release of political prisoners and punishment for murderers of peasants) and by three women in San Luis Potosí's main plaza (demanding to be shown 24 prisoners who had disappeared).

In a few places the Church gives the peasants some support, but clergy who speak out are usually branded leftists. Samuel Ruíz García, the bishop of San Cristóbal in Chiapas, is called the Obispo Rojo (Red Bishop) for this reason.

ECONOMY

After WW II, Mexico entered an era of statism, with the federal government taking control of many aspects of the national economy. By the 1970s, the government ran the telephone company, the oil monopoly, railways, banks, airlines, hotels and other enterprises. As with many government-controlled enterprises, they were very inefficient, with jobs given out as political favours and subsidies granted to make up for losses. Despite the heavy hand of government, Mexican business and commerce has grown substantially. In 1910, Mexico was an agricultural country. Though agriculture remains important, Mexico today produces motor vehicles, processed food, chemicals, paper, glass and apparel as well as the traditional exports of sugar, coffee, oil, lead, copper and zinc.

With the oil boom of the 1970s, Mexico undertook ambitious development projects; with the oil bust that followed, the country found itself with a crushing burden of debt which could not be paid from shrinking oil revenues. Debt was rescheduled, austerity measures introduced, and government enterprises were privatised. By the early 1990s the Mixican economy had largely regained health – just in time for the worldwide recession.

The economic reforms instituted by President Carlos Salinas de Gortari since 1988 have strengthened the economy and stabilised (some would say overvalued) the peso.

With the establishment of the North American Free Trade Agreement (NAFTA) in 1992, Mexico is on its way to membership in the world's largest and richest trading bloc (Canada, Mexico and the USA). It is hoped that NAFTA will help Mexico to develop more rapidly, raise the income of the poorest members of society, and cut rampant population growth and resulting societal pressures.

PEOPLE

Mexico's population according to the 1990 census was 81.14 million, but there are credible claims that this figure was several million too low, because of doctoring of the tallies for electoral purposes. The official increase since 1980 was 14.29 million, 4 million less than in the previous decade.

About two-thirds of the people live in towns or cities. The major cities were given in the census as; Mexico City (with officially 13.63 million in its metropolitan area but really perhaps 20 million if you include fringe settlements), Guadalajara (metropolitan area 2.85 million), Monterrey (metropolitan area 2.52 million), Puebla

(1.05 million), León (872,000), Ciudad Juárez (798,000) and Tijuana (743,000).

Ethnic Groups

The major ethnic division is between *mestizos* and *indígenas* (Indians). Mestizos are people of mixed ancestry – usually Spanish and Indian, although African slaves and other Europeans were also significant elements. Indians are those descendants of Mexico's pre-Hispanic inhabitants who have retained their distinct culture, language and identity. Mestizos are the overwhelming majority, and together with the few people who consider themselves of pure Spanish descent, hold most positions of power in Mexican society.

Researchers have listed at least 139 vanished Indian languages. The 50 or so Indian cultures that have survived, some now with only a few hundred people, have done so largely because of rural isolation. Indians in general remain second-class citizens, often occupying the worst land and exploited by mestizos. Their main wealth is traditional and spiritual, their way of life imbued with communal custom and rituals bound up with nature. Indian traditions, beliefs, arts, crafts and their colourful costumes are fascinating subjects of study. There is more information on them in the various regional chapters, and in this chapter under Culture, Religion and Festivals & Holidays.

Official figures count as Indians only those who list themselves in censuses as speakers of Indian languages. The real number is probably between 5 and 10 million. The biggest Indian people is the Nahua, 1.5 million or more of whom are spread over at least 12 states, with the greatest numbers in Puebla, Veracruz, Hidalgo, Guerrero and San Luis Potosí. The ancient Aztecs were Nahua. The 700,000-plus Maya of the Yucatán Peninsula, the 350,000 or more Zapotec of Oaxaca, the 300,000-plus Mixtec of Oaxaca, Guerrero and Puebla, the 200,000 or more Totonac of Veracruz and Puebla, and over 100,000 Tarasco or Purépecha in Michoacán are all also descendants of well-known pre-Hispanic peoples.

Descendents of less-known pre-Hispanic peoples include over 300,000 Otomí (mainly in Hidalgo and México states), 200,000 or more Mazahua in México state, and over 100,000 Huastec in San Luis Potosí and northern Veracruz. The 300,000-plus Tzotzil and Tzeltal of the Chiapas highlands are probably descendants of lowland Maya who migrated at the time of the Classic Maya downfall. The Huichol Indians of Jalisco and Nayarit are renowned for the importance of peyote in their religious life, and the Mazatec of northern Oaxaca for their use of hallucinogenic mushrooms.

National Character

The Mexican character is complex to say the least – try reading Octavio Paz's *The Labyrinth of Solitude* for an assessment of it. Two general features of Mexican society which quickly become apparent are strong nationalism, and a greater stereotyping of gender than in many other countries.

Machismo is an exaggerated masculinity aimed at impressing other males rather than women. Its manifestations range from aggressive driving and the carrying of weapons to heavy drinking. Women, in turn, exaggerate their femininity and don't question male authority.

The macho image probably has its roots in Mexico's violent past, and seems to hinge on a curious network of family relationships: as several writers have pointed out, it's not uncommon for Mexican husbands to have

mistresses. In response, wives lavish affection on their sons, who end up idolising their mothers and, unable to find similar perfection in a wife, take a mistress...The strong mother-son bond also means that it's crucial for a Mexican wife to get along with her mother-in-law. And while the virtue of daughters and sisters has to be protected at all costs, other women are often seen as 'fair game' by Mexican men. This applies particularly to foreign women without male companions.

Despite tensions – or perhaps to hide them – family loyalty is very strong. One gringo who has lived in Mexico for several years commented that Mexicans never really reveal their true selves outside the family: 'However well you think you know someone, you eventually realise that everything they say or do is an act of one kind or another – but that doesn't stop them being friendly, loyal or charming'. If you have any friends or contacts who live in the country, don't waste the opportunity. An invitation to a Mexican home is an honour for an outsider; as a guest you will be treated royally and will enter a part of real Mexico to which surprisingly few outsiders are admitted.

Nationalism stems from Mexico's 11-year war for independence from Spain in the early 19th century and subsequent struggles against Spanish, US and French invaders on Mexican soil. Foreign economic domination – by the British and Americans around the turn of this century and more recently by the Americans again – has also been impossible to throw off. But while Mexicans present a fiercely patriotic front to foreigners, they are well aware that their country, like any other, has its shortcomings. Politicians, police and public officials are universally despised for their corruption, and inefficiency in public organisations is accepted as the rule, not the exception. As one Mexican passenger at the Dallas airport confided when our Continental flight to Mexico City was delayed four hours: 'We're not in Mexico, we're not travelling on a Mexican airline, but we are going to Mexico, so we are late'.

More often than being macho, Mexicans are friendly, humorous and willing to help. Language difficulties can obscure this fact; some people are shy or will ignore you because they haven't encountered foreigners before and don't imagine a conversation is possible – just a few words of Spanish will often bring you smiles and warmth, not to mention lots of questions. Then someone who speaks a few words of English will pluck up the courage to try them out.

Some Indian peoples adopt a cool attitude to visitors; they have learned to mistrust outsiders after 4½ centuries of exploitation by whites and mestizos. They don't like being gaped at by crowds of tourists and are sensitive about cameras, particularly in churches and at religious festivals.

If you have a white skin in Mexico, you will be assumed to be a citizen of the USA and may provoke any reaction from curiosity or wonder to fear or, occasionally, hostility. The classic Mexican attitude to the USA is a combination of the envy and resentment that a poor neighbour feels for a rich one. While the USA is still seen by some as the land where everything you touch turns to dollars (or at least cars, cassette players and Disneyland T-shirts), enough Mexicans have worked as labourers for it to be known that the USA doesn't share its wealth too willingly. The *norteamericanos* have also committed the sin of sending their soldiers into Mexican territory three times.

Any hostility towards individual Americans usually evaporates as soon as you show that you are human too. And while the word 'gringo' isn't exactly a compliment – you may hear it in an annoying undertone after you have walked past someone – it can also be used with a brusque friendliness.

If you are not an American, and say so, you may well be seen (in rural areas particularly) as a freak of nature who will get the benefit of the doubt.

Reactions to the revelation that I was *Inglés* have included 'How many days in the bus to England?' (from a trainee teacher in Chiapas); 'England...that is Germany? Or France?' (a Oaxaca restaurant-owner); 'What part of England is Britain in?' (a Mexico City telephone operator); and, from a fisherman on the Chiapas coast, 'Is England that way (pointing out to sea) or that way (inland)?' to which I pointed inland (the more accurate of the two choices) and he replied, 'Ah, in the sierra'. A New Zealander with whom I travelled for a few days usually evoked blank incomprehension with the words *Nueva Zelandia*, nor did the addition of *cerca de Australia* help much.

John Noble

As for the Mexican attitude toward time – the fabled *mañana* syndrome – it's no more casual than in any other developing country and has probably become legendary simply from comparison with the USA. While it's certainly true, especially outside the big cities, that the urgency or promptness Europeans and North Americans are used to is lacking, it must be realized that most Mexicans value *simpatía* (congeniality) over promptness. If something is really worth doing, it gets done. If not, it can wait. Life should not be a succession of pressures and deadlines. In the 'business-like' cultures, life (according to many Mexicans) has been desympathised. Perhaps the Mexicans are right!

ARTS & CULTURE
Traditional Dress

One of the most intriguing aspects of Mexican Indian life is the colourful, usually handmade traditional clothing. This comes in infinite and exotic variety, often differing dramatically from village to village. Under the onslaught of modernity, such clothing is less common in everyday use than a few decades ago, but in some areas – notably around San Cristóbal de las Casas in Chiapas – it is actually becoming more popular as Indian pride reasserts itself and the commercial potential of handicrafts is developed. In general, Indian women have kept to traditional dress longer than men.

Some styles still in common use go back to pre-Hispanic times. Among these (all worn by women) are the *huipil*, a long, sleeveless tunic; the *quechquémitl*, a shoulder cape; and the *enredo*, a wrap-around skirt. Blouses are post-conquest introductions. Indian men's garments owe more to

Spanish influence; modesty was encouraged by the church, so shirts, hats and *calzones* (long baggy shorts) were introduced.

What's most eye-catching about these costumes is their colourful embroidery – often entire garments are covered in a multicoloured web of stylised animal, human, plant and mythical shapes which can take months to complete. Each garment identifies the group and village from which its wearer comes. *Fajas* (waist sashes) are also important in this respect.

The designs often have multiple religious or magical meanings. In some cases the exact significance has been forgotten, but among the Huicholes of Jalisco, for instance, fajas are identified with snakes (fertility symbols) and serve as appeals for rain; the embroidered design of the white *totó* flower which grows in the rainy season is a request for maize. To the Indian weavers of Chiapas, descendants of the Maya, diamond shapes represent the universe (the ancient Maya believed the earth was a cube), while wearing a garment with saint figures on it is a form of prayer.

Materials and techniques are changing but the pre-Hispanic back-strap loom is still widely used. The warp (long) threads are stretched between two horizontal bars, one of which is fixed to a post or tree, while the other is attached to a strap which goes round the weaver's lower back. The weft (cross) threads are then woven in.

Yarn is hand-spun in many villages. Some Otomí women in Hidalgo make cloaks from maguey cactus fibres. Palm hats are common. Vegetable dyes are still in use, and natural indigo is employed in several areas. Red dye from cochineal insects and purple dye from sea snails are used by some Mixtecs in Oaxaca. Modern luminescent dyes go down very well not only with Indians but with other Mexicans, who are happily addicted to bright colours.

The variety of techniques, materials, styles and designs is bewildering. Read Chloë Sayer's *Mexican Costume* (British Museum Publications, London), one of the most fascinating books written in recent years on any aspect of Mexico. (For more on clothing and other handicrafts, see Things to Buy in the Facts for the Visitor chapter.)

Music & Dance

In Mexico you're likely to hear live music at any time on streets, plazas or even buses. The musicians are playing for a living and range from marimba teams (with big wooden 'xylophones') and mariachi bands (violinists, trumpeters, guitarists and a singer, all dressed in 'cowboy' costume) to ragged lone buskers with out-of-tune guitars and hoarse voices. Marimbas are particularly popular in the south-east and on the Gulf coast.

Mexico has a thriving popular music business – old folk songs are in demand alongside rock and even punk music, while styles imported from elsewhere in the Americas include tango, bossanova, salsa and Andean pan-pipe music. The name of one band going the rounds in Oaxaca was 'Mike y Su Tropical Salvaje Show' (Mike & His Wild Tropical Show). Classical music is not neglected; there are several venues in Mexico City and other cities where you can hear recitals.

Music is an important part of the many colourful festivals on the Mexican calendar. The festivals also feature traditional dances. They are mainly performed to honour Christian saints, but in many cases they have pre-Hispanic roots and retain traces of ancient ritual. There are hundreds of traditional dances: some are popular in many parts of the country, others can be seen only in a single town or village. Nearly all of them feature special costumes, often including masks. One of the most spectacular is the *voladores*, performed by Totonac and Nahua Indians in the states of Veracruz and Puebla. Four men 'fly' (with ropes attached to one leg) from the top of a 20-metre-high pole in re-enactment of an old fertility rite. Among the most superb of all dance costumes are those of the Zapotec feather dance in Oaxaca and the Nahua quetzal dance in Puebla, which feature enormous feathered headdresses or shields.

Some dances tell stories that are clearly Spanish or colonial in origin. Moros y Cristianos is a fairly widespread example which re-enacts the victory of Christians over Moors in medieval Spain, while the spring carnival at Huejotzingo, Puebla, sees a mock battle between Mexicans and French. At carnival time in Zaachila, Oaxaca, whip-wielding 'devils' are defeated by 'priests' with crosses and buckets of water. Near San Miguel de Allende in May, the festival of Las Yuntas sees 'Indians' confront 'Federales'.

Other dances – like the voladores – have even older roots. In a tradition which goes back to before the Spanish conquest, groups of dancers from several states meet at a spot outside San Miguel de Allende in late September, then wend their way to the town wearing bells, feather headdresses, scarlet cloaks and masks, carrying flower offerings and in some cases playing lutes made of armadillo-shell. The Huastec dance, Zacamson, from San Luis Potosí state, mimics animal movements to the music of harp and fiddles. It has more than 75 parts, danced at different times of day and night.

Sometimes the meaning of the dances has become confused over time; in one Holy Week dance in Pinotepa Nacional, Oaxaca, white-painted youths called *Judíos* (Jews) recite old Mixtec incantations while firing arrows into the air. The Mardi Gras dance of Los Tejorones in the nearby villages of Pinotepa de Don Luis and San Juan Colorado has four episodes – a tiger or snake hunt, a wedding, a baptism and a cockfight.

Some dances are these days performed outside the religious context as simple spectacles. The voladores, for instance, can regularly be seen at El Tajín, Zempoala and Papantla. The Ballet Folklórico in Mexico City brings together traditional dances from all over the country. Veracruz state also has its own Ballet Folklórico, and folklore festivals like the Guelaguetza in Oaxaca and the Atlixcáyotl in Atlixco, Puebla, also gather performers from wide areas.

Sport
The Bullfight To gringo eyes, the bullfight hardly seems to be sport or, for that matter, entertainment. Mexicans, however, see it as both and more. It's a traditional spectacle, more a ritualistic dance than a fight, that originated in Spain and readily lends itself to a variety of symbolic interpretations, mostly related to machismo. Symbolism aside, the importance of the bullfight to Mexican society is underscored by the oft-heard saying that Mexicans arrive on time for only two events – funerals and bullfights.

The *corrida de toros* (bullfight) begins with the presentation of the matador and his assistants. Everyone leaves the ring except for the matador and his 'cape men', then the first of six bulls is released from its pen. The cape men try to tire the bull by working him around the ring.

After a few minutes, a trumpet sounds to mark the beginning of the first of three parts *(tercios)* of each 'fight'. Two men called *picadores* enter the ring on thickly padded horses with long lances and get close enough to the bull to stick their lances into its shoulder muscles. They weaken the bull just enough to make it manageable.

After the picadores leave the ring, the second tercio begins. Men with *banderillas*, one-metre-long darts, enter the ring on foot.

Their objective is to jam three pairs of banderillas into the bull's shoulders without being gored.

With that done, the third *tercio* – the part everyone has been waiting for – begins. The matador has exactly 16 minutes to kill the bull. First he tires it with fancy cape-work. When he feels the time is right, the matador trades his large cape for a smaller one (the *muleta*) and takes up a sword. He baits the bull towards him and gives it what he hopes will be the death blow, the final *estocada* or lunge from the sword. If the matador succeeds, and he usually does, the bull collapses and an assistant dashes into the ring to slice its jugular. If the applause from the crowd warrants, he will also cut off an ear or two and sometimes the tail for the matador.

Football (Soccer) *Futbol* is probably the country's second favourite sport; Mexico hosted the World Cup finals in 1970 and 1986. On neither occasion did the home team get beyond the quarter-finals – a fair reflection on local standards. If Mexico produces a really good player, chances are he will go to Spain or Italy to improve his game and earn more. There is a decent national professional league and several impressive stadiums, but crowds at games are small – perhaps because games are shown on TV. América (of Mexico City) and Guadalajara are among the top clubs.

Other Sports *Beisbol* (baseball) is popular, and there is a national professional league. Mexican stars often move to the United States, and ageing Americans sometimes stretch out their careers south of the border.

Charreada is the rodeo, held particularly in the northern half of the country, both during fiestas and in regular venues often called *charros*.

Horse racing is held at several *hipódromos* (racecourses) around the country. It's popular in towns on the US border and at the Hipódromo de las Américas in Mexico City.

Jai Alai ('HIGH-lie') is the Basque game *pelota*, brought to Mexico by the Spanish. It is a bit like squash with a hard ball on a very long court, played with curved baskets attached to the arm – and it can be fast and exciting. You can see it played by semi-professionals in Mexico City and Tijuana, among other places.

Tennis and golf are popular among those who can afford them. Many resort and luxury hotels have tennis courts.

ARCHITECTURE

The pre-Conquest Indian civilisations of Mexico produced some of the most spectacular and eye-pleasing architecture ever built. In some places, such as Tenochtitlán, the site of present-day Mexico City, the indigenous architecture has been almost obliterated. But at other sites, such as Teotihuacán near Mexico City, Monte Alban in Oaxaca state, and Chichén Itzá and Uxmal in the Yucatán you can still see largely intact pre-Colombian cities.

One of the Spaniards' first preoccupations upon their arrival in Mexico was to replace 'pagan' temples with Christian churches, often in the same location. A classic case is the Great Pyramid of Cholula, the biggest in the Americas, which is now surmounted by a small colonial church. Religious buildings remained among the most important of all the fine buildings erected in Mexico during the 300 years of Spanish rule. Many of the mansions and plazas which today contribute so much to the beauty of Mexico were also built then. Most of them are in basically Spanish styles but often with unique local variations.

Gothic & Renaissance

These styles and influences dominated the 16th and early 17th-century architecture of Mexico. The Gothic style of the European Middle Ages is typified by soaring buttresses, pointed arches, clusters of round columns and ribbed vaults (ceilings). The Renaissance style saw a return to disciplined ancient Greek and Roman ideals of harmony and proportion; classical shapes like the square and the circle predominated, along with classical motifs; also featured were columns in styles or 'orders', which, from the simplest to the most elaborate, were called Tuscan, Doric, Ionic, Corinthian and composite.

The usual Renaissance style in Mexico was called Plateresque – from the Spanish for silversmith, *platero* – because it often resembled the elaborate ornamentation that went into silverwork. Plateresque is commonly a style of decoration for the façades of buildings, particularly church doorways, which have round arches bordered by classical columns and often a variety of stone sculpture. A later version of the Renaissance style was called 'pure', or Herreresque after the Spanish architect Juan de Herrera. This was more austere and less decorative than Plateresque.

Gothic and Renaissance influences are combined in numerous 16th-century Mexican buildings – including many of the fortified monasteries that were built as Spanish monks carried their missionary work to all corners of the country. Monasteries usually had a large church, a cloister where the monks lived and worked, a big atrium (churchyard) sometimes with small *posa* chapels in the corners where processions would pause, and often a *capilla abierta* (open chapel) from which, in the early days, the priests could address large crowds of Indians gathered in the atrium.

Capillas abiertas – many of which have a simple beauty – are rare outside Mexico. Besides their practical functions before the monastery church was completed, they were probably a subtle attempt to simulate the feeling of pre-Hispanic religious ceremonies, at which the people would gather in plazas while priests carried out their tasks on pyramids or platforms.

Notable monasteries include Actopan, Acolmán and Huejotzingo (all in central Mexico); and Yanhuitlán, Coixtlahuaca and Teposcolula in Oaxaca state. The Casa de Montejo on the main plaza in Mérida, Yucatán, has a fine Plateresque façade. Mérida cathedral shows a mixture of Plateresque and pure Renaissance, while Mexico City and Puebla cathedrals mingle pure Renaissance and the later baroque style. The interior of Guadalajara cathedral is a bit of an anomaly, built later but in more Gothic style.

The influence of the Arabs who had occupied much of Spain until fairly recently was also carried across the Atlantic to Mexico. Examples of this style, which is known as *Mudéjar*, can be seen in some beautifully carved wooden ceilings and in the *alfíz*, a rectangle framing a round arch (such as on the Plateresque side door of San Francisco church in Puebla). The Capilla Real in Cholula is one of the strangest Arabic-influenced buildings in Mexico: its 49 domes almost resemble a mosque.

Baroque

Baroque style first came to Mexico in the early 17th century and was in turn a reaction against the strictness of Renaissance styles. It used classical influences but combined them with other elements and aimed at creating dramatic effect rather than classical proportion. Curving shapes and lines, use of colour, contrasts of light and dark, and a decorativeness that became increasingly elaborate were among its hallmarks. Painting and sculpture were integrated with architecture for further elaborate effect – most notably in ornate, often enormous altarpieces. The classical 'orders' were used, but often the 'wrong' way round, with the lighter or more elaborate columns placed below the heavier, simpler ones.

Mexican baroque went through several phases and, between 1730 and 1780, followed what some people consider a distinct style in itself – Churrigueresque. Named after a Barcelona carver and architect, José Benito de Churriguera, the style was characterised by riotous surface ornamentation of which the hallmark is the *estípite* – a pilaster (vertical pillar projecting only partially from the wall) in the form of a very narrow upside-down pyramid. The estípite helped give Churrigueresque its frequent, dramatic 'top-heavy' effect.

Early, more restrained baroque buildings include the churches of Santiago Tlatelolco in Mexico City, San Felipe Neri in Oaxaca and San Francisco in San Luis Potosí. Later baroque structures are the churches of San Cristóbal in Puebla and La Soledad in Oaxaca, and the Zacatecas cathedral façade. Outstanding Churrigueresque works include the façade of the Sagrario Metropolitano and the La Merced monastery patio in Mexico City; the churches of San Martín in Tepotzotlán, of San Francisco, La Compañía and La Valenciana in Guanajuato and of Santa Prisca and San Sebastián in Taxco; the Ocotlán sanctuary at Tlaxcala; and the interiors of Santa Rosa and Santa Clara churches in Querétaro.

Mexican Indian artisanry came into its own in the baroque era, with a profusion of detailed sculpture in stone and polychrome stucco. Among its most exuberant examples are the Capilla del Rosario in Santo Domingo church, Puebla, and the village church of Tonantzintla, near Puebla. Arabic influence continued with the popularity of coloured tiles (*azulejos*) on the outside of buildings, particularly in and around the city of Puebla. The House of Tiles in Mexico City (now a Sanborns restaurant) and Acatepec church near Puebla are notable tiled buildings, although in these cases the designs are not particularly Arabic.

Neoclassic

This was another return to Greek and Roman ideals. In Mexico it lasted from about 1780 to 1830. Outstanding examples are the Palacio de Minería in Mexico City, El Carmen church in Celaya, the Alhóndiga de Granaditas in Guanajuato and the second tier of the Mexico City cathedral towers.

19th & 20th Centuries

Early independent Mexico mainly saw revivals of earlier styles and imitation of contemporary European fashions. There were Gothic and colonial revivals and towards the end of the century many buildings copied French or Italian styles – none of them very original. The Palacio de Bellas Artes in Mexico City is one of the best.

After the Revolution of 1910 to 1921 there was an attempt to return to pre-Hispanic roots in the search for a national identity – a trend generally known as Toltecism – and many public buildings exhibit the 'heaviness' of, say, Aztec or Toltec monuments. This movement culminated in the famous Mexico City university campus, built in the early 1950s, where many buildings are covered with colourful murals. Since then major buildings in Mexico have been more responsive to international trends and there have been a few dramatic innovations. Perhaps the most spectacular is the Faro del Comercio in Monterrey – a tall, thin block of orange concrete which emits green laser beams across the city at night.

RELIGION
Indian Religion
The Spanish missionaries of the 16th and 17th centuries succeeded less in converting the indigenous people than in grafting Catholicism onto the pre-Hispanic religions. Often old gods were simply given saints' names and old festivals and rituals continued to be celebrated, little changed, on whichever saint's day was nearest to the traditional date. Acceptance of the new religion was greatly helped by the dark-skinned Virgin Mary who appeared in a vision in 1531 to an Indian called Juan Diego, on a hill near Mexico City where Tonantzin, the mother of the Aztec gods, had long been worshipped. Today the 'Virgin of Guadalupe' is the patron saint of Mexico.

The picture has changed little since those early Spanish days, despite some decline in traditional practices as the modern world makes inroads into Indian life. While nearly all Indians are Christian, their Christianity is fused with more ancient beliefs. Indeed, among some of those in more remote regions it is only a sideshow. Triqui witch doctors in Oaxaca, for instance, reputedly carry out magical cures in churches after services, and for the Day of the Dead, Triquis pour a broth made from sacrificed oxen over the church floor to feed the dead.

The Huicholes of Jalisco, who never really accepted Christianity, have two Christs but neither is a major deity. Much more important is Nakawé, the fertility goddess. The hallucinogenic plant peyote is a crucial source of wisdom in the Huichol world. Elsewhere, especially among the Tarahumara in the Copper Canyon, drunkenness is an almost sacred element at festival times. Even among the more orthodox Indians it is not uncommon for saints' festivals in spring, or the pre-Lent carnival, to be accompanied by remnants of fertility rites. The famous Totonac voladores dance of Veracruz is one such ritual, though it is losing much of its sacredness today through being performed as a spectacle for tourists. The Guelaguetza dance festival, which draws thousands of visitors to Oaxaca every summer, has its roots in pre-Hispanic maize god rituals which Christian priests replaced with masquerades.

In the traditional Indian world almost everything has a spiritual (some would say superstitious) dimension – trees, rivers, plants, wind, rain, sun, animals and hills have their own gods or spirits, and travellers have seen offerings of Coca-Cola bottles at festivals in Chamula, Chiapas. Whole hierarchies of 'pagan' gods sometimes co-exist side by side with the Christian Trinity and saints.

Witchcraft and magic survive. As with the deities, beliefs are complicated and differ from one group to the next, but illness is widely seen as a 'loss of soul' caused by the sufferer's wrongdoing or by the influence of someone with magical powers. A soul can be 'regained' if the appropriate ritual is performed by a witch doctor (brujo) and sometimes these ceremonies involve the use of hallucinogenic mushrooms. Another common belief is in the tono or tona – a person's animal 'double' in the spirit world whose welfare closely parallels that of the person's.

Catholicism
More than 90% of the population professes Catholicism. This is remarkably high considering the rocky history that the Roman Catholic Church has had in Mexico, particularly in the last two centuries.

The Catholic Church was present in Mexico from the very first days of the Spanish conquest. It remained the second most important institution after the crown and its royal colonial representatives (the viceroy etc), and was really the only unifying force in Mexican society until independence. Almost everyone – Indians, mestizos and whites – belonged to the Church because, spirituality aside, it was the principal provider of social services and education in Mexico.

The Jesuits were the foremost providers and administrators, having established several missions and settlements throughout Mexico by the late 18th century. In the eyes of the French-influenced Bourbon administration in Spain, they were mistakenly seen as one of the causes of Mexico's economic demise over the previous century and a half, so they were expelled in 1767. This marked the beginning of stormy Church-state relations.

In the 19th and 20th centuries (up to 1940), colonial Mexico and then independent Mexico passed numerous measures restricting the power and influence of the Catholic Church. The bottom line was money and property, both of which the church was amassing faster than the generals and political bosses. The 1917 constitution includes several anti-clerical provisions: marriage is a civil, not a religious, contract; clergy can't speak out about government policies and decisions; religious groups can't own property; and all Church buildings must first be authorised and approved by the government. Most of these provisions are still in the constitution, but they are almost never enforced.

Today, the Church remains the unifying force that it was when Mexico was a Spanish colony. Since 1531, its most binding symbol has been the dark-skinned Virgin of Guadalupe. The appearance of a dark-skinned Virgin has been regarded as a link between the Catholic and non-Catholic Indian worlds. More importantly, since Mexico is now a predominantly mestizo society, the Virgin has come to symbolise a coming-of-age for the country. Evidence of this abounds in Mexico: the name of the Virgin of Guadalupe in invoked in religious ceremonies, political speeches and literature.

Protestantism

With only 4% of the population professing Protestantism, it has not been significant in Mexico. Several denominations, however, are represented: the Methodist Church, Jehovah's Witnesses, Seventh-Day Adventist Church, Seventh-Day Baptist Church, Church of Jesus Christ of Latter-Day Saints (Mormons) and National Presbyterian Church.

Judaism

Jews make up 0.1% of Mexico's population. Most of them live in the state of México and in Mexico City, where there are several synagogues.

LANGUAGE

Spanish is the predominant language of Mexico. Mexican Spanish is unlike Castilian Spanish, the literary and official language of Spain, in two respects: in Mexico, the Castilian lisp has more or less disappeared and numerous Indian words have been adopted.

Travellers in the towns, cities and larger villages can almost always find someone who speaks at least some English. All the same it is still useful and courteous to know at least a few words and phrases of Spanish. Mexicans will generally respond more positively if you attempt to speak to them in their own language.

More than 50 Indian languages are spoken by over four million people in Mexico, of whom about 20% to 25% don't speak Spanish.

Pronunciation

Vowels & Consonants Spanish has five vowels: **a**, **e**, **i**, **o** and **u**. They are pronounced something like the highlighted sections of the following English words: f**a**ther, **e**nd, mar**i**ne, **o**r and p**u**ll.

Most of the consonants in Spanish are pronounced in much the same way as their

English counterparts, but there are a few exceptions:

c is pronounced like 's' in 'sit' when before e or i; elsewhere it is like 'k'.

g is pronounced like English 'h' (with more friction) before e or i; before a or o it is like the 'g' in 'go'.

gu is pronounced like the 'g' in 'go', but the u is not pronounced.

h is not pronounced at all.

j is pronounced like English 'h', only with a lot more friction.

ll is similar to English 'y'.

ñ is like the 'ny' in 'canyon'.

qu is the same as English 'k' (the u is not pronounced).

r is a very short rolled r.

rr is a longer rolled 'r'.

x is like 'j' when it comes after e or i, otherwise it is like English 'x' as in 'taxi'; in many Indian words (particularly Maya ones), 'x' is pronounced like English 'sh'.

z is the same as English 's'; under no circumstances should s or z be pronounced like English 'z' – this sound does not exist in Spanish.

There are a few other minor pronunciation problems, but the longer you spend in Mexico, the easier they will become. The letters **ch**, **ll** and **ñ** are deemed separate letters of the Spanish alphabet and come after c, l and n respectively in alphabetical lists like indexes, dictionaries or phone books.

Accents & Stress Knowing which part of a word to stress in Spanish is a big aid to being understood. The rule is: if the word has an accent, put the stress on the syllable containing the accent; if not, stress the last syllable unless the word ends in a vowel or n or s, in which cases stress the second-last syllable. Examples:

zócalo	SO-ca-lo
kilómetro	ki-LOH-meh-tro
mazatlán	mah-sat-LAN
méxico	MEH-hee-ko
cortés	cor-TESS

favor	fa-VOR
catedral	cat-eh-DRAL
monterrey	mon-te-RREY
comer	coh-MEHR
estoy	es-TOY
acapulco	ah-cah-POOL-co
naranja	na-RAN-ha
estados unidos	es-TA-dos oo-NEE-dos
casa	CA-sa
joven	HO-ven

Gender

Nouns in Spanish are either masculine or feminine. Nouns ending in 'o', 'e', or 'ma' are usually masculine. Nouns ending in 'a', 'ión' or 'dad' are usually feminine. Some nouns take either a masculine or feminine form, depending on the ending, eg *viajero* is a male traveller; *viajera* is a female traveller. An adjective usually comes after the noun it describes, and must take the same gender form.

Greetings & Civilities

hello/hi
  hola
good morning/good day
  buenos días
good afternoon
  buenas tardes
good evening/good night
  buenas noches
goodbye
  adiós
Pleased to meet you.
  Mucho gusto.
How are you? (to one person)
  ¿Como está?
How are you? (to a group)
  ¿Como están?
I am fine.
  Estoy bien.

Grammar

I	*yo*
you (familiar)	*tu*
you (formal)	*usted*
you (pl)	*ustedes*
he/him/it	*el*
she/her	*ella*

we/us	nosotros
they/them (m)	ellos
they/them (f)	ellas
my wife	mi esposa
my husband	mi esposo
my sister	mi hermana
my brother	mi hermano
sir/Mr	señor
madam/Mrs	señora
miss	señorita
I am...	
(condition or place)	Estoy...
tired	cansado
sick/ill	enfermo
I am...	
(state)	Soy...
a student	estudiante
a worker	trabajador

Useful Words & Phrases

For words pertaining to food and restaurants, see the Food and Drinks sections of the Facts for the Visitor chapter.

yes	sí
no	no
please	por favor
thank you	gracias
you're welcome	de nada
excuse me	perdóneme
what did you say?	¿mande? (colloq)
good/okay	bueno
bad	malo
better	mejor
best	lo mejor
more	más
less	menos
very little	poco or poquito

How much?
 ¿Cuánto?
How much does it cost?
 ¿Cuánto cuesta? or ¿Cuánto se cobra?
I want...
 Quiero...
I do not want ...
 No quiero...
Give me ...
 Déme...

What do you want?
 ¿Que quiere?
Do you have ...?
 ¿Tiene usted ...?
Is/are there ...?
 ¿Hay ...?

Nationalities

American (m/f)	(norte-) americano/a
Australian (m/f)	australiano/a
British (m/f)	británico/a
Canadian (m & f)	canadiense
English (m & f)	inglés
French (m/f)	francés/francesa
German (m/f)	alemán/alemana

Languages

I speak...	Yo Hablo...
I do not speak...	No hablo...
Do you speak...?	¿Usted habla...?
Spanish	español
English	inglés
German	alemán
French	francés

I understand.
 Entiendo.
I do not understand.
 No entiendo.
Do you understand?
 ¿Entiende usted?
Please speak slowly.
 Por favor hable despacio.

Crossing the Border

border (frontier)	la frontera
car owner's title	título de propiedad
car registration	registración
customs	aduana
driver's licence	licencia de manejar
identification	identificación
immigration	inmigración
passport	pasaporte
tourist card	tarjeta de turista
visa	visado
birth certificate	certificado de nacimiento

Getting Around

street	calle

boulevard	*bulevar*
avenue	*avenida*
road	*camino*
highway	*carretera*
corner (of)	*esquina (de)*
corner (or) bend	*vuelta*
block	*cuadra*
to the left	*a la izquierda*
to the right	*a la derecha*
on the left side	*al lado izquierdo*
on the right side	*al lado derecho*
left (hand side)	*(mano) izquierda*
right (hand side)	*(mano) derecha*
straight ahead	*adelante*
straight on	*todo recto* or *derecho*
this way	*por aquí*
that way	*por allí*
north	*norte*
south	*sur*
east	*este*
east (in an address)	*oriente* (abbrev. *ote*)
west	*oeste*
west (in an address)	*poniente* (abbrev. *pte*)

Where is ...?
   ¿Dónde está...?
   the bus station
      el terminal de autobúses/central camionera
   the train station
      la estación del ferrocarril
   the post office
      el correo
   a long-distance telephone
      un teléfono de larga distancia
   the airport
      el aeropuerto

Ticket Sales Counter	*Taquilla*
Waiting Room	*Sala (de) Espera*
Baggage check-in	*(Recibo de) Equipaje*
Toilets	*Sanitario*
Arrivals	*Llegada*
Left luggage room/checkroom
Guardería (or Guarda) de Equipaje	

How far is ...?
   ¿Á que distancia está ...?
How long? (how much time?)
   ¿Cuanto tiempo?

(by) short route (usually a toll highway)
   (via) corta

Driving in Mexico

gasoline/petrol	*gasolina*
fuel station	*gasolinera*
unleaded	*sin plomo*
regular/leaded	*regular/con plomo*
fill the tank	*llene el tanque; llenarlo*
full	*lleno; 'ful'*
oil	*aceite*
tyre	*llanta*
spare tyre	*llanta de repuesto*
puncture	*agujero*
flat tyre	*llanta desinflada*

How much is a litre of gasoline (petrol)
   ¿Cuánto cuesta el litro de gasolina?
My car has broken down.
   Se me ha descompuesto el carro.
I need a tow truck.
   Necesito un remolque.
Is there a garage near here?
   ¿Hay un garage cerca de aqui?

Highway Signs

Though Mexico mostly uses the familiar international road signs, you should be prepared to encounter these other signs as well.

road repairs	*camino en reparación*
keep to the right	*conserva su derecha*
dangerous curve	*curva peligrosa*
earthquake zone	*derrumbes*
slow	*despacio*
detour	*desviación*
slow down	*disminuya su velocidad*
school (zone)	*escuela, zona escolar*
men working	*hombres trabajando*
road closed	*no hay paso*
danger	*peligro*
have toll ready	*prepare su cuota*
continuous white line	*raya continua*
speed bumps	*topes*
road being repaired	*tramo en reparación*
narrow bridge	*puente angosto*
via toll highway	*via cuota*
via bypass route
(often a toll road)	*via corta*

free, older road be-
  side a toll highway   *libramiento*
one-lane road 100
  metres ahead   *un solo carril a 100 m*

Accommodation

hotel	*hotel*
guest house	*casa de huéspedes*
inn	*posada*
room	*cuarto, habitación*
single room	*cuarto solo, cuarto sencillo*
double room	*cuarto para dos, cuarto doble*
double bed	*cama matrimonial*
twin beds	*camas gemelas*
with bath	*con baño*
shower	*ducha*
hot water	*agua caliente*
air-conditioning	*aire acondicionado*
blanket	*manta*
towel	*toalla*
soap	*jabón*
toilet paper	*papel higiénico*
the bill	*la cuenta*

What is the price?
  ¿Cuál es el precio?
How much does it cost?
  ¿Cuánto cuesta?
Does that include taxes?
  ¿Están incluidos los impuestos?
Does that include service?
  ¿Está incluido el servicio?

Money

money	*dinero*
travellers' cheques	*cheques de viajero*
bank	*banco*
exchange bureau	*casa de cambio*
credit card	*tarjeta de crédito*
exchange rate	*tipo de cambio*

I want to change some money.
  Quiero cambiar dinero.
What is the exchange rate?
  ¿Cuál es el tipo de cambio?
Is there a commission?
  ¿Hay comisión?

Telecommunications

telephone call	*llamada*
telephone office	*caseta de teléfono*
telephone booth	*cabina de teléfono*
telephone token	*ficha de teléfono*
telephone debit card	*tarjeta de teléfono*
tone	*tono*
area or city code	*clave*
telephone number	*numero telefónico*
credit card phone	*teléfono de tarjetas de crédito*
long-distance telephone	*teléfono de larga distancia, Ladatel*
local call	*llamada local*
long-distance call	*llamada de larga distancia*
operator	*operador(a)*
person to person	*persona a persona*
collect call	*por cobrar*
insert credit card	*inserta tarjeta de crédito*
remove credit card	*remueva tarjeta de crédito*
dial the number	*marque el numero*
please wait	*favor de esperar*
busy	*ocupado*
toll/cost (of call)	*cuota/costo*
time & charges	*tiempo y costo*

Times & Dates

Monday	*lunes*
Tuesday	*martes*
Wednesday	*miércoles*
Thursday	*jueves*
Friday	*viernes*
Saturday	*sábado*
Sunday	*domingo*

yesterday	*ayer*
today	*hoy*
now/in a few minutes	*horita, ahorita*
tomorrow (also maybe, sometime)	*mañana*
morning	*mañana*
tomorrow morning	*mañana por la mañana*
afternoon	*tarde*
night	*noche*
What time is it?	*¿Que hora es?*

Numbers

0	*cero*	18	*diez y ocho*
1	*un, uno* (m), *una* (f)	19	*diez y nueve*
2	*dos*	20	*veinte*
3	*tres*	21	*veinte y uno*
4	*cuatro*	22	*veinte y dos*
5	*cinco*	30	*treinta*
6	*seis*	40	*cuarenta*
7	*siete*	50	*cincuenta*
8	*ocho*	60	*sesenta*
9	*nueve*	70	*setenta*
10	*diez*	80	*ochenta*
11	*once*	90	*noventa*
12	*doce*	100	*cien*
13	*trece*	101	*ciento (y) uno*
14	*catorce*	200	*doscientos*
15	*quince*	1000	*mil*
16	*diez y seis*	2000	*dos mil*
17	*diez y siete*	3000	*tres mil*

Facts for the Visitor

VISAS & EMBASSIES

All visitors to Mexico should have a valid passport and, in most areas, must carry a Mexican government tourist card for visits over 72 hours. Some nationalities also require visas.

Passports

Though it is not recommended, US citizens can enter Mexico without a passport if they have some other proof of American citizenship (birth certificate, notarised affidavit of citizenship, or a certificate of naturalisation from the US Immigration & Naturalisation Service) and a photo identification such as a driver's licence or state-issued identification card. It is much better to have a passport however, because officials are used to passports and may delay those with other forms of citizenship proof. Banks, too, will require your passport when you change money. If you bring a birth certificate it must clearly show official certification from a government agency in the USA.

Citizens of Canada and UK need to show a current passport. Citizens of Australia, New Zealand and European Community countries must obtain visas in their passports as well as tourist cards. No photographs are required. Both visas and tourist cards are issued free.

It would be wise to confirm these requirements at any of the places that distribute tourist cards. US citizens with non-American spouses should be particularly careful. The spouse will be subject to the visa rules governing his or her country of origin (*not* country of residence), and Mexican consulates in the USA may not know those rules (even if they think they do). Check with the embassy or consulate of the country of origin.

Proof of citizenship may be needed for US citizens when returning to the USA. A driver's licence or identity card issued by a state Department of Motor Vehicles is usually sufficient to prove US citizenship; a passport certainly is. Citizens of other countries must have passports and appropriate US visas. Be certain of the entry and re-entry status of your US visa before departing for Mexico.

Tourist Card

The Mexican government tourist card is your 'visa' for entry into and exit from Mexico, and, by Mexican law, must be carried with you at all times. (When in large cities, it may be a good idea to put your tourist card in the hotel safe and carry a photocopy of it instead, in case of theft.) Tourist cards are available at no charge from Mexican government tourist offices, Mexican consulates and embassies, Mexican immigration authorities at border crossings, airlines flying between North America and Mexico, some travel agencies outside Mexico and from several automobile clubs in the USA and Canada. The card must be validated by Mexican immigration authorities at the port of entry.

Two types of tourist card are issued: a single-entry card valid for 90 days, and a card that in theory (but not always in practice) allows unlimited entries over a period of 180 days. Two photographs – sometimes three – are required for the 180-day card. The photograph requirement seems to be more stringent if you apply for a tourist card outside North America.

You do not need a tourist card for visits of less than 72 hours to the Mexican border towns or to places between Tijuana and Maneadero (just south of Ensenada) in Baja California, but you must still have some form of identification with photograph (such as a US driver's licence).

Do not overstay the time limit on your card or you may be subject to a fine. If you need to extend your visit, apply for an extension several weeks before your card is due to expire. You will certainly run into red tape if you attempt to fly out of Mexico without a tourist card. Chances are slim, however, that you will be asked to show your tourist card if you drive, walk or take a bus across the Mexico-US border. Near the border, the most likely places you will be asked for your card are the airports in Tijuana, Mexicali, Ciudad Juárez, Nuevo Laredo and Matamoros, when you arrive from some other point in Mexico.

If you lose your card, prepare yourself for a frustrating and time-consuming bureaucratic tour of the Delegación de Servicios Migratorios.

Mexican Embassies & Consulates

Unless otherwise noted, all details are for embassies.

Australia
>
> 14 Perth Ave, Yarralumla, Canberra, ACT 2600 (☎ (06) 273 -905/47/63)
> Consulate: 49 Bay St, Double Bay, Sydney, NSW 2028 (☎ (02) 326-1292/1311)

Austria
>
> Renngasse 4, 1010 Wien (Vienna) (☎ (222) 535-1776 to 79)

Belgium
>
> Rue Paul-Emile Jansson 6, 1050 Brussels (☎ (2) 648-2671/2703)
> Consulate: Quellinstraat 42, Bus 2, 2018 Antwerpen (☎ 234-1861, 231-7316/7)

Belize
>
> 20 North Park St, Belize City (☎ 45367, 44301, 78742)

Canada
>
> 206-130 Albert St, Ottawa, Ontario KIP 5G4 (☎ (613) 233-8988/9272)
> Consulate: 1000 Sherbrooke West, Suite 2215, Montréal, Quebec H3A 3G4 (☎ (514) 288-2502/4816)
> Consulate: 60 Bloor St West, Suite 203, Toronto, Ontario M4W 3B8 (☎ (416) 922-2718/3196)
> Consulate: 310-625 Howe St, Vancouver, BC V6C 2T6 (☎ (604) 684-3547/5725)

Costa Rica
>
> 7a Avenida No 1371, San José (☎ 22-55-28, 22-54-85)

El Salvador
>
> Paseo General Escalon No 3832, San Salvador (☎ 98-10-84, 98-11-76)

France
>
> 9 rue de Longchamps, 75116 Paris (☎ 45-53-99-34, 45-53-76-43)
> Consulate: 4 rue Notre-Dame des Victoires, 75002 Paris (☎ 40-20-07-32/33, 42-61-51-80)

Germany
>
> Oxfordstrasse 12-16, 5300 Bonn 1 (☎ (228) 63-12-26 to 28)
> Consulate: Neue Mainzer Strasse 57, 6000 Frankfurt 1 (☎ (069) 23-6134, 23-5709)
> Consulate: Hallerstrasse 70-1, 2000 Hamburg 13 (☎ (040) 45-8950, 44-8774)

Guatemala
>
> 16 Calle 1-45, Zona 10, Guatemala City (☎ (02) 68-02-02, 68-28-27)
> Consulate: 13 Calle 7-30, Zona 9, Guatemala City (☎ (02) 36-65-04, 36-35-73, 31-81-65)

Honduras
>
> Calle República del Brasil Suroeste 2028, Colonia Palmira, Tegucigalpa (☎ 32-64-71, 32-40-39)

Israel
>
> 14 Hey I'yar, Kikar Ha-Medina, Tel Aviv (☎ (03) 210-266 to 268)

Italy
>
> Via Lazzaro Spallanzani No 16, 00161 Roma (☎ (6) 440-2319/2323)
> Consulate: Via Cappuccini 4, Milano (☎ (2) 349-8782)

Japan
>
> 2-15-1, Nagata-cho, Chiyoda-Ku, Tokyo 100 (☎ (3) 581-2150, 581-1131 to 35)

Netherlands
>
> Nassauplein 17, 2585 EB The Hague (☎ (70) 60-29-00, 60-68-57)
> Consulate: Groothandelsgebow, Stationsplein 45, Rotterdam (☎ (010) 126-084)

Nicaragua
>
> Km 45, Carretera a Masaya, Colonia 25 Varas Arriba (Altamira), Managua (☎ (2) 75380, 75275 to 79)

Panama
>
> Calle 50 at Calle San José, Bank of America Building, 5th floor, Panama City 7 (☎ 63-50-21)

Spain
>
> Avenida Paseo de la Castellana No 93, 7th floor, Madrid 28046 (☎ (1) 456-1349/1496)
> Consulate: Avenida Diagonal No 626, 4th floor, Barcelona 08021 (☎ (343) 200-6265, 201-1822)

Sweden
>
> Grevgatan 3, 114 53 Stockholm (☎ (8) 661-6175, 660-3970)

Switzerland
>
> Bernestrasse 57, 3005 Berne (☎ (31) 43-18-14, 43-18-75)

UK
>
> 8 Halkin St, London SW1 (☎ (071) 235-6393, 235-6351, 245-9030)

USA
>
> 2829 16th St NW, Washington, DC 20009 (☎ (202) 234-6000 to 6003)

Mexican Consulates in the USA Besides the Mexican embassy in Washington DC, there are consular offices in many other US cities, particularly in the border states:

Arizona
Douglas: 515 10th St, 85607 (☎ (602) 364-2275)
Nogales: 135 Terrace Ave, 85621 (☎ (602) 287-2521)
Phoenix: 700 East Jefferson, Suite 150, 85034 (☎ (602) 242-7398/9)
California
Calexico: 331 West Second St, 92231 (☎ (619) 357-3863/3880)
Fresno: 2839 Mariposa St, 93721 (☎ (209) 233-3065/9770)
Los Angeles: 125 East Paseo de la Plaza, Suite 300, 90012 (☎ (213) 624-9387/8)
Sacramento: 1506 South St, 95814 (☎ (916) 446-4696/9024)
San Bernardino: 588 West 6th St, 92401 (☎ (714) 888-2500/4700)
San Diego: 1333 Front St, Suite 200, 92101 (☎ (619) 231-8414/8427)
San Francisco: 870 Market St, Suite 528, 94102 (☎ (415) 392-5554)
San Jose: 380 North First St, Suite 102, 95112 (☎ (408) 294-3414/5)
Colorado
Denver: 707 Washington St, 80203 (☎ (303) 830-0523/0704)
Florida
Miami: 780 NW LeJeune Road, Suite 525, 33126 (☎ (305) 441-8780 to 441-8783)
Georgia
Atlanta: 410 South Tower, One CNN Center, 30303-2705 (☎ (404) 688-3258/3261)
Illinois
Chicago: 300 North Michigan Ave, 2nd floor, 60601 (☎ (312) 855-1380 to 855-1384)
Louisiana
New Orleans: 1140 World Trade Center Building, 2 Canal St, 70130 (☎ (504) 522-3596/7)
Massachusetts
Boston: 20 Park Plaza, Suite 321, Statler Building, 02116 (☎ (617) 426-4942/8782)
Michigan
Detroit: 1515 Book Building, Washington Blvd at West Grand River, 48226 (☎ (313) 965-1868/9)
Missouri
Kansas City: 823 Walnut St, 64106 (☎ (816) 421-5956)
St Louis: 1015 Locust St, Suite 922, 63101 (☎ (314) 436-3233/3426)
New Mexico
Albuquerque: Western Bank Building, 401 Fifth St, NW, 87102 (☎ (505) 247-2139/2147)
New York
New York: 8 East 41st St, 10017 (☎ (212) 689-0456 to 60)
Pennsylvania
Philadelphia: Independence Mall East, 575 Philadelphia Bourse Building, 19106 (☎ (215) 922-4262/3834)
Texas
Austin: 200 East Sixth St, Suite 200, Hannig Row Building, 78701 (☎ (512) 478-2300/2866/9031)
Brownsville: Elizabeth & East Seventh Sts, 78520 (☎ (512) 542-4431/2051)
Corpus Christi: 800 North Shoreline, One Shoreline Plaza, 410 North Tower, 78401 (☎ (512) 882-3375/5964)
Dallas: 1349 Empire Central, No 100, 75247 (☎ (214) 630-7341/2024)
Del Rio: 1010 South Main St, 78840 (☎ (512) 775-2352/9451)
Eagle Pass: 140 Adams St, 78852 (☎ (512) 773-9255/6)
El Paso: 910 East San Antonio St, PO Box 812, 79901 (☎ (915) 533-3644/5)
Houston: 4200 Montrose Blvd, Suite 120, 77006 (☎ (713) 524-4861/2300)
Laredo: 1612 Farragut St, 78040 (☎ (512) 723-6360/1741)
Lubbock: 1220 Broadway Ave, 79401 (☎ (806) 765-8816)
McAllen: 1418 Beech St, No 102-104, 78501 (☎ (512) 686-0243/4)
Presidio: 730 O'Riety St, 79845 (☎ (915) 229-3745)
San Antonio: 127 Navarro St, 78205 (☎ (512) 227-9145/6)
Utah
Salt Lake City: 182 South 600 East, Suite 202, 84102 (☎ (801) 521-8502/3)
Washington State
Seattle: 1411 Fourth Ave, Fourth Avenue Building, Suite 410, 98101 (☎ (206) 343-3047, 682-8996)

DOCUMENTS

Every visitors should bring a valid passport and carry a Mexican government tourist card, or a copy thereof, at all times. See the Visas & Embassies section above for details of paperwork requirements and issuing authorities. Tourists driving into Mexico must also have a valid driver's licence, car registration papers and a temporary import permit for each vehicle (including motorcycles and boats), obtainable at the border. Local car insurance is also essential. For more details, see the Getting There & Away chapter.

Minors

Every year numerous parents run away to Mexico with their children in order to escape the legal machinations of the children's other parent in North America. In order to prevent this escape from the law, the Mexican authorities may – and often do – require a notarised affidavit *signed by both parents* permitting the minor to enter Mexico, whether alone or with one parent. Don't risk hassles. Write out an affidavit (a statement) of permission to travel, have it notarised, and take it with you when you head for Mexico. If both parents are going, no affidavit is needed.

Other Permits

Hunting & Fishing For information on hunting licences and importing hunting guns into Mexico, contact a Mexican Consulate (see the list above). Anglers 16 years or older need fishing licences, and those importing boats will need boat licences as well. Applications can be obtained from the Mexico Department of Fisheries (☎ (619) 233-6956), 1010 2nd Ave, Suite 1605, San Diego, California 92101. If you plan to take any of your catch out of Mexico, you will have to meet local import requirements, which may be difficult. Contact the authorities of the country to which you wish to take your catch. For importation into the USA or Canada, remember that you will have to meet both federal and state requirements.

Pets You may bring your dog or cat with you from the USA into Mexico, but you must have proof of vaccination (issued within three days of your crossing the border) for rabies and/or any other contagious diseases borne by your species of pet. The proof of vaccination must also be approved by the US Department of Agriculture and the Mexican Consulate. There is a pet visa fee of US$16.

It is also a good idea to carry the International Health Certificate. This can be obtained from any veterinarian.

If you are returning to the USA or Canada, you will have to meet US or Canadian requirements for animal importation. Inquire about these requirements before you take your pet into Mexico.

CUSTOMS

Motor vehicles entering Mexico (except within the limits of the US border towns) must have car permits and should have Mexican insurance (see the Getting There & Away chapter for more details). Firearms are prohibited except when brought in during hunting season with the proper hunting and firearms permits. Officially, adults are allowed to bring in 50 cigars, 200 cigarettes (one carton) and 250 grams of tobacco, one still camera and one 8-mm movie camera or camcorder with 12 rolls of film for each, but these limits are rarely applied strictly.

Returning to the USA

Each US resident returning from Mexico to the USA may bring in duty-free items that do not exceed a total retail value of US$400; the next US$1000 of goods are usually taxed at a flat 10%. These items must be for personal use only. The exemption applies to each 30-day period you are out of the country. This limit is rarely invoked because, according to US Customs, 'Mexico is a developing country'. More than 2700 items produced in Mexico, including most handicrafts, are exempt from this US$400 limit. If the limit is applied at all, it is used to restrict imports of cheap clothes.

Limits on tobacco products, alcohol and perfumes are stricter, and governed by state as well as federal laws. If you plan a heavy liquor run, know state laws. You may find that you will have to pay state tax on *all* imported liquor whether subject to federal duty or not (Texas), or that all alcoholic beverages above the federally allowed one litre duty free must be destroyed at the border (Arizona).

Questions? Contact the US Customs Service, 1301 Constitution Ave, Washington, DC 20229 (☎ (202) 566-8195) and ask for their brochure, *Know Before You Go*.

Returning to Canada

Canadian citizens may bring back CN$100 of souvenirs duty free; once a year you may bring back CN$300 worth of goods if you've been out of Canada for at least a week. For more information, contact Canada Customs & Excise Department, Communications Branch, Mackenzie Ave, Ottawa, ON K1A 0L5 (☎ (613) 957-0275).

Returning to the UK

The limit for duty-free goods on return is £32. For information, contact HM Customs & Excise Office, New King's Beam House, 22 Upper Ground, London SE1 9PJ (☎ (071) 382 54 68).

Returning to Australia

The limit for duty-free goods is A$400 for adults, A$200 for those under 18 years of age. On the next A$160 of goods, the duty is a flat 20% of value. For more information, ask at an office of the Australian Customs Service for the booklet *Customs Information for All Travellers*.

Returning to New Zealand

Duty-free limits are NZ$500 for all goods. Full details are included in the booklets *New Zealand Customs Guide for Travellers* and *If You're not Sure About It, Declare It*.

Luggage Inspection

Normally the Mexican customs officers will not look seriously in your luggage, and they may not look at all. At some border points the amount of search is inversely proportional to the amount of 'tip' you have provided: big tip, no search; no tip, big search. As for expensive items, if you have an expensive camera, electronic gizmo, or jewellery, there is a risk that they may be seen as leverage, or be deemed as liable for duty at customs' discretion. Be prepared, and be firm but flexible. Whatever you do, keep it all formal and polite. Anger, surliness or rudeness can get you thrown out of the country, or into jail, or worse.

La Mordida

In Mexico, as in other Latin American countries, border officials sometimes request small 'tips' or unofficial 'fees' from travellers. Usually the *mordida*, the 'bite', is put on you in an official tone of voice: the officer will scribble something on your tourist card, or in a ledger, or stamp your passport, or do some other little action, then say 'Too dallah'. There are several things you can do to avoid paying.

The first is to look very important by dressing in a suit and tie or other such intimidating clothing. If you are male, wearing dark sunglasses (a favourite expression of machismo) can help.

The second is to scowl quietly and act worldly-wise. Scowl all you want, but whatever you do, keep everything formal. Appear quietly superior and unruffled at all times.

The third thing is to ask for a receipt: *'un recibo'*. Some fees, such as charging for the disinfection of your car, are official and legitimate. If the fee is legitimate, you'll be given an official-looking receipt; often the official will show you the receipt booklet when he makes the request, to prove to you that the fee is legitimate. If you don't get a receipt, you've succumbed to the mordida.

The fourth thing is to offer some weird currency such as Thai baht or Australian dollars. Border officials are usually used to seeing only US dollars (and some Canadian ones), Mexican pesos, and perhaps Belizean dollars and Guatemalan quetzals. At the sight of strange money the officer will probably drop the request. If he doesn't, or if the fee turns out to be legitimate, 'search' for several minutes in your belongings and come up with the dollars you need.

MONEY

When travelling in Mexico, it's useful to carry your money in US dollars or US dollar travellers' cheques. Though you should be able to change other sorts of currency (especially Canadian dollars) in major banks in large cities, it can require some time-consuming hassles, and may be supremely difficult in smaller cities and towns. In many parts of Mexico it can take a lot of time to change US dollars, let alone some European or other foreign currency that is, to a local bank teller, highly exotic. With the privatisation of Mexican banking now under way, this situation may improve. It is often difficult or impossible to exchange travellers' cheques on weekends except in the largest cities.

Try to spend all of your local currency before you cross a border because the exchange rates between countries are often terrible. For example, if you exchange pesos for quetzals in Guatemala the rate will be very low; the same thing happens if you exchange quetzals for pesos in Mexico, and ditto for pesos to Belizean dollars.

For some useful Spanish words dealing with money, see the Language section in the Facts about the Country chapter.

Currency

The Mexican unit of currency is the peso (MX$). The peso is further divided into 100 centavos, although centavos are now worth so little that they are not used. Mexican coins come in denominations of 50, 100, 500, 1000 and 5000 pesos, and perhaps even larger denominations in the future. Bills (notes) are in denominations of 1000, 2000, 5000, 10,000, 20,000, 50,000 and 100,000 pesos, and as well-worn, rarely encountered notes of 500 pesos.

The dollar sign ($) is used to indicate pesos in Mexico, so if you sit down to a plate of tacos and get a bill for $5000, don't panic – it's only pesos, and cheap at that. Since there is often confusion in tourist areas about whether a price is in pesos or dollars, with both currencies using the same sign, prices are often written as '$5000 mn', that is, '5000 pesos, *moneda nacional* (Mexican national currency)'; or as '$5 Dlls' ie US$5.

In such heavily touristed areas as Acapulco, Cancún and Cozumel you can often spend US currency as easily as pesos at hotels, restaurants and shops. Most of the time you won't get as good an exchange rate as if you changed your dollars for pesos at a bank, and it can be downright outrageous. In some establishments, however, dollars are accepted at an exchange rate as good as or better than that of the banks, to get you to spend your money there.

Exchange Rates

The peso floats against the US dollar so the exchange rate changes daily. But as of this writing, the Mexican government is maintaining economic policy support mechanisms for the peso which keep its value artificially high, and make Mexico relatively expensive for what you get (though still a bargain compared with many other countries). Devaluation is quite likely, however, if the government or the policies change. Devaluation of the peso means you get more for your dollar and after any deval-

Stop Press

As this book went to press, it was reported that the Mexican government was going to change the denomination of the peso. At the beginning of 1993, three zeros are to be dropped so that 1000 'old' pesos will be worth one 'new' peso; something priced at 25,500 'old' pesos would be priced at 25 'new' pesos and 50 centavos (MX$25.50). As many experts contend that the peso is presently overvalued, the change in denomination may be accompanied by a devaluation. Thus you may receive something like 4.50 new pesos for each US dollar instead of the present rate of about 3000 old pesos per US dollar. The change in denomination will be phased in gradually, and for at least six months prices will be quoted in both old and new pesos.

These reforms will see the return of the single peso, as well as the centavo coins, which have been virtually out of circulation for several years. ∎

uation the prices given in this book will seem too high compared to actual prices paid.

US$1	=	MX$3123
C$1	=	MX$2700
UK£1	=	MX$6195
FFr1	=	MX$654
A$1	=	MX$2224
NZ$1	=	MX$1688
DM1	=	MX$2118
SpPta100	=	MX$3427

Credit Cards

Major credit cards such as Visa and MasterCard (Eurocard, Access) are accepted at all airline and car rental companies, and at the larger hotels and restaurants in Mexico; American Express cards are often accepted at the larger and fancier places, and at some smaller ones.

In Mexico, many smaller establishments will readily accept your card, even for charges as little as US$5 or US$10; the big cities and resorts live on credit cards, and even have telephones that accept these cards for long-distance calls.

Costs

Bottom End For the very budget-conscious traveller, Mexico has low prices in the smaller towns but surprisingly high prices in resorts such as Acapulco, Cancún and Cozumel. A single budget traveller staying in bottom-end or lower middle-range accommodation and eating two meals a day in restaurants may pay US$8 to US$15 per day, on average, for those basics. Add in the other costs of travel (snacks, purified water and soft drinks, admission to archaeological sites, roughly US$1 per hour on long-distance buses, etc), and you may spend more like US$12 to US$20 per day. If there are two or more of you sharing accommodation, costs per person come down considerably. Double rooms are often only a few dollars more than singles, and triples or quadruples only a little more expensive than doubles.

Camping is the cheapest and sometimes the easiest way to go. You can camp for nothing on almost any beach in Mexico (all beaches are public property). Most official campgrounds are designed for mobile homes. Electrical hook-ups, running water and sewerage are normally provided. Clean bathrooms with hot showers are sometimes available. Prices for two people and a vehicle average US$5 to US$8 per night. To pitch a tent is less expensive; the price is usually subject to negotiation.

In the middle range, you can live quite well for US$25 to US$40 per person per day, even in the large cities and expensive resorts. A couple can easily find a clean, modern room with private bath and TV in Mexico City for US$30 to US$40, and have the other US$30 or US$40 to pay for food, admission fees, transport and incidentals.

At the top end, there are hotels and resorts in Mexico that charge upwards of US$200 per night for a room, and restaurants where you can pay US$50 per person, but you can also stay at very comfortable smaller hotels for only US$60 to US$75 per couple per night and eat extremely well for US$30 to US$40 per person per day. A daily budget of US$50 to US$75 per person is fully sufficient for comfort, unless you plan to fly a lot or to rent a car.

Tipping

In general, staff in the smaller, cheaper places don't expect much in the way of tips, while those in the expensive resort establishments expect you to be lavish in your largesse. Tipping in the resorts frequented by foreigners (Acapulco, Cancún, Cozumel, Ixtapa, Huatulco, etc) is up to American standards of 15% to 20%; elsewhere, 10% is usually sufficient. In small, cheap eateries you needn't tip.

Bargaining

Though you can attempt to haggle down the price of a hotel room, the rates are usually set and fairly firm, especially during the busy winter season. Off-season price reductions are sometimes negotiable.

For handcrafts and other souvenirs, and for anything in an open-air market, haggling is the rule, and you may pay several times the going price if you pay the first price quoted.

Student Discounts

There are few discounts for students who are not members of the Mexican national educational system. A few places offer small discounts on admission fees to students under 26 who hold a card from either the Servicio Educativo de Turismo de los Estudiantes y la Juventud de México (SETEJ) or Consejo Nacional de Recursos para la Atención de la Juventud (CREA). These cards also entitle you to youth hostel membership. CREA cards can be obtained at most youth hostels in Mexico. For more information, write to the Asociación Mexicana de Albergues de la Juventud, AC, Avenida Francisco I Madero No 6, Despachos 314 y 315, Mexico 1, DF.

Consumer Taxes

IVA Mexico's *Impuesto de Valor Agregado* (Value-Added Tax), abbreviated *IVA* (pronounced 'EE-bah'), is levied at 8% to 10%. By law the tax must be *included* in virtually any price quoted to you; it should not be added afterwards. Signs in shops and notices on restaurant menus usually reiterate this fact as *'incluye el IVA'* or *'IVA incluido'*. Thus you won't see IVA on your bill except for a few high-priced items such as luxury hotel rooms, car rentals and air tickets. When in doubt, ask *'¿Está incluido el IVA?'* ('Is IVA included?').

Airport Usage Taxes Mexico levies airport taxes on all passengers: domestic (US$5.75) and international (US$12). If you buy your ticket abroad, the tax will be levied in Mexico when you check in for a flight. If you buy your ticket in Mexico the tax is already included in your fare.

WHAT TO BRING

The clothing you bring should depend upon how, when and where you want to travel, and how you would like to be perceived by Mexicans. You might want to conform to Mexican norms.

Mexicans tend to dress informally but conservatively. In the hot regions, men of all classes, from taxi drivers to business executives, wear long trousers and sports shirts or *guayaberas*, the fancy shirts decorated with tucks and worn outside the belt, which substitute for jacket and tie. Many women still dress traditionally in Indian costume, or stylishly in dresses, or blouses and skirts. In the largest cities (Mexico City, Guadalajara, Monterrey), stylish, fashionable clothing is the rule for those who can afford it.

The local people do not expect you to dress as they do. They allow for foreign ways, but know that shorts and T-shirts are the marks of the tourist.

In lowland areas such as the Pacific and Gulf coasts, Yucatán and Tabasco, both men and women should always have a hat, sunglasses and sunblock cream. If your complexion is particularly fair or if you burn easily, consider wearing light cotton shirts with long sleeves and light cotton slacks. Otherwise, men can wear light cotton trousers or shorts, tennis shoes or sandals and T-shirts, although more conservative wear is in order when visiting churches.

Women can dress similarly, except off the beaten track in villages unaccustomed to tourists. In general, it is better for women to dress somewhat more conservatively when in town – no shorts, tank tops, etc. Seaside resorts are the exception; in resorts such as Acapulco, Cancún, Cozumel, Huatulco and Zihuatanejo, wear whatever you like. Bring a light sweater or jacket for evening boat rides. Blue jeans are often uncomfortably heavy in these warm, humid areas.

In the mountainous interior you will need warmer clothing – a pair of slacks or jeans for sure – plus a sweater or jacket, perhaps both if you plan to be out for long periods in the evening or early morning. A light rainjacket, preferably a loose-fitting poncho, is good to have from October to May, and is a necessity from May to October.

Toiletries such as shampoo, shaving cream, razors, soap and toothpaste are readily available throughout Mexico in all but the smallest villages. You should bring your own contact lens solution, tampons, contraceptives, insect repellent containing DEET, and deodorant.

Other recommended items are sunglasses, flashlight, hat, disposable lighter, pocket knife, two to three metres of cord, sunblock, small sewing kit, money belt or pouch, small Spanish-English dictionary and lip balm.

TOURIST OFFICES

Mexican government tourist offices are a fair source of information; they also issue tourist cards. Address inquiries to the Mexican Government Tourist Office at these locations:

USA & Canada
Chicago
　　Two Illinois Center, 233 North Michigan Ave, Suite 1413, 60601 (☎ (312) 565-2785)
Houston
　　2707 North Loop West, Suite 450, 77008 (☎ (713) 880-5153)
Los Angeles
　　10100 Santa Monica Blvd, Suite 2204, 90067 (☎ (213) 203-8151)
Montréal
　　1 Place Ville Marie, Suite 2409, H3B 3M9 (☎ (514) 871-1052)
New York
　　405 Park Ave, Suite 1002, 10022 (☎ (212) 755-7261)
Toronto
　　181 University Ave, Suite 1112, M5H 3M7 (☎ (416) 364-2455)

Europe
France
　　34 Ave George V, Paris 75008 (☎ (1) 47-20-69-07)
Germany
　　Wiesenhuettenplatz 26, D600, Frankfurt-am-Main 1 (☎ (69) 25-34-13)
Italy
　　Via Barberini No 3, 00187 Rome (☎ (6) 474-2986)
Spain
　　Calle de Velázquez No 126, Madrid 28006 (☎ (1) 261-1827)
UK
　　7 Cork St, London W1X 1PB (☎ (071) 734-1058)

There are also federal, state and local tourist information offices in Mexico.

BUSINESS HOURS

Banks are generally open from 9 am to 1.30 pm, Monday to Friday. Businesses generally open from 9 am to 2 pm, close for siesta, then reopen from 4 to 7 pm, Monday to Friday. Outside Mexico City, some shops and offices in hot regions close roughly from 1 to 4 pm, then stay open until 7 or 8 pm.

Most Mexican churches are in frequent use, so be careful not to disturb services when you visit them. Many – particularly those that contain valuable works of art – are locked when not in use.

Archaeological sites are usually open from 8 am to 5 pm seven days a week. This is unfortunate, because in many hot regions the hours before 8 am and after 5 pm, especially in summer, are cooler and much more pleasant for touring, and there's plenty of golden light.

FESTIVALS & PUBLIC HOLIDAYS

The abundance of fiestas in the Mexican calendar has been explained by some writers, notably Octavio Paz, as an attempt to escape from the horrors of everyday existence – not only poverty, but also a kind of blackness in the soul which perhaps stems from the country's violent past and its roots in the joining of two antagonistic groups, the Indians and the Spaniards. Be that as it may, Mexican fiestas are full-blooded, highly colourful affairs which often go on for several days.

Festivals may be held for harvests of local products such as grapes, apples, lemons, even radishes. There are festivals of the arts, local dance and music. Even trade and business fairs add a bit of a festival atmosphere to a town. Most Mexican festivals are religious at heart and often serve as an excuse for general merrymaking. Parades, special costumes, dancing, lots of music and plenty of drinking are all part of the scene.

Some are celebrated nationwide – for example Carnival, Easter, Independence Day, the Day of the Dead, the Day of the Virgin of Guadalupe and Christmas. Others are very local, such as celebrations for a village's patron saint. But even near-universal events such as the pre-Lenten Carnival have their unique local variations, often comprehensible only to those raised in local traditions.

Here are the main holidays, celebrations and events. Banks, post offices and government offices are closed most of these days. Note especially the effects on travel of *Semana Santa* (Holy Week).

1 January
New Year's Day
5 February
Constitution Day
24 February
Flag Day
Late February-early March
Carnaval (Carnival) – Held the week or so before Ash Wednesday, usually in February. Celebrated all over the country but most grandly in Veracruz and Mazatlán, with huge parades, music, food, fireworks and other events.
21 March
Birthday of President Benito Juárez
April
Semana Santa (Holy Week) – Easter Week is one of the biggest holiday periods in Mexico. It starts with Palm Sunday, one week before Easter, and progresses through Good Friday to Easter Sunday; closures are usually from Good Friday through Easter Sunday. Easter is the first Sunday following the first full moon after the vernal (March) equinox. Almost as awe-inspiring as the movement of the planets is the movement of people in Mexico at this time. Around 60,000 people a day pass through Mexico City's Terminal Norte, and the two national airlines carry the same number of travellers. Virtually the entire population of the Distrito Federal makes at least one trip out of the city. Some parts of the country become so overrun that gasoline has to be rationed. You've been warned!
1 May
Labour Day
5 May
Cinco de Mayo – Anniversary of Mexico's victory over the French Army at Puebla in 1862. Celebrated grandly in Puebla.
10 May
Día de la Madre (Mother's Day)
1 June
Navy Day
Last two Mondays in July
Guelaguetza Festival – Regional dance performances in Oaxaca city.

August
La Pamplonada – A 'running of the bulls' celebrated in Tecate and meant to resemble the running of the bulls in Pamplona, Spain.
15-16 September
Día de la Independencia – Commemoration of Mexico's independence from Spain in 1821. The biggest celebrations take place in Mexico City beginning with a recitation of Hidalgo's *Grito* or cry for independence by the president in Mexico City's Zócalo, followed by fireworks, horse races, folk dances from all over Mexico and mariachi bands.
September
Día de San Miguel – This saint's day, held on one of the last Fridays in September, brings big celebrations in San Miguel de Allende, Guanajuato.
Atlixcáyotl – Dance and music festival held the last weekend in September at Atlixco, Puebla. Performers come from a wide area.
12 October
Día de la Raza – Columbus Day, commemorating Columbus' discovery of the New World, and the Mexican (mestizo) race.
1 November
All Saints Day
2 November
All Souls Day
Día de los Muertos (Day of the Dead) – Festivities take place throughout Mexico with especially colourful celebrations on the island of Janitzio in Lago Pátzcuaro. In many places the celebrations recall ancestor-worship, as families build altars in their homes in honour of their dead and spend the day in the graveyards – which often have quite a festive atmosphere. It is widely believed that the spirits of the dead return on this day. Breads and sweets made to resemble human skeletons are sold in almost every market and bakery; papier-mâché skeletons and skulls appear everywhere.
20 November
Anniversary of the Mexican Revolution of 1910
12 December
Día de Nuestra Señora de Guadalupe (Festival of Our Lady of Guadalupe) – Festival of the patron saint of Mexico. The biggest celebrations take place at the Basílica de Guadalupe in Mexico City.
25 December
Día de Navidad (Christmas Day) – This marks the end of a week of *posadas*, parades of costumed children re-enacting the journey of Mary and Joseph to Bethlehem. The children also break *piñatas* (papier-mâché animals) full of candy. Posadas are held throughout Mexico. Christmas is celebrated with a service in almost every church in the country.

Saints' Days

Our Lady of Guadalupe may be Mexico's patron saint, but every village, town and city has its own patron saint as well. On that saint's official day (according to the Catholic Church calendar), the saint's image – often a particular painting or statue – is venerated and celebrated first in the church and then in the streets. Some claim that the tradition is a throwback to pre-Hispanic days when local gods and goddesses were fêted with the same vigour.

POST & TELECOMMUNICATIONS

Almost every city and town in Mexico has an *oficina de correos* (post office) where you can buy postage stamps and send or receive mail.

Sending Mail

Postal rates change often, so check current rates at the post office. Service is relatively dependable, but not predictable. If you are sending something by air mail, be sure to clearly mark it with the words 'Por Avión'. An air mail letter sent from Mexico to the USA or Canada may take anything from four to 14 days. Mail to Europe can take between one and three weeks. If you need assured speedy delivery, use one of the international courier services such as United Parcel Service, Federal Express, or DHL, all of which have agents or offices in Mexico.

Receiving Mail

This can be tricky. You can send or receive letters and packages care of a post office if they're addressed as follows:

Jane SMITH (last name in capitals)
a/c Lista de Correos
Acapulco, Guerrero
00000 (postal code) MEXICO

When the letter arrives at the post office, the name of the addressee is placed on an alphabetical list which is updated daily. If you can, check the list yourself because the letter may be listed under your first name instead of your last.

To claim your mail, present your passport or other identification; there's no charge. The snag is that many post offices only hold 'Lista' mail for 10 days before returning it to the sender. If you think you're going to pick mail up more than 10 days after it has arrived, have it sent to you at Poste Restante, Correo Central, Town/City, State, Mexico. Poste Restante usually holds mail for up to a month but no list of what has been received is posted. Again, there's no charge for collection.

If you can arrange a private address to send mail to, do so. There's less chance of your mail getting put aside, lost or returned to the sender if you're late in picking it up.

American Express If you have an American Express card or American Express travellers' cheques, you can have mail sent to you c/o the American Express offices in Mexico, which will hold it for your arrival. You must show your card or a travellers' cheque when you collect the mail.

Telephone

Local calls are cheap; international calls are generally very expensive. Don't go to the post office looking for telephones, as the telephone company, Teléfonos de México (TELMEX), is a private corporation (it was formerly a quasi-governmental corporation).

TELMEX is in the midst of a modernisation campaign, installing several new varieties of automatic public telephone and retiring older sets. But more of that in a moment.

Local calls are laughably inexpensive (often free) and easy to place from public telephone boxes and *casetas de teléfonos* (telephone call stations in shops). If you aren't placing the call from a caseta or one of the newer phones, be sure you have the often rare small-denomination coins (10, 20, 50, 100 pesos, etc) accepted by public callboxes.

Telephone numbers in Mexico have different numbers of digits for different cities and· towns. You must dial seven digits in Mexico City, but only six in Mérida, and only five in Palenque, etc. City codes are of differing length as well.

For some words useful when making telephone calls, see Language in the Facts About the Country chapter.

Long-Distance Calls from Mexico You may see the abbreviation Lada in connection with long distance calls; it's short for *larga distancia* (long distance). International and domestic long-distance (trunk) calls are exorbitantly taxed, laden with surcharges, and sometimes difficult to place. Be warned! If you make anything but the shortest possible call, you may be facing a bill of terrifying size. A 20-minute operator-assisted call just to the USA can easily cost close to US$60.

If you are calling the USA or Canada, it is much cheaper to use a short call to ask the person you're ringing to call you back.

Ladatel Phones Special Ladatel call stations are located on the streets of major cities, in the larger hotels, at airports, railway stations and bus terminals in Mexico; keep an eye out for them as you travel, because they can make calling abroad much easier, quicker and cheaper. You can dial direct to any place in the world from a Ladatel phone for much less than an operator-connected call would cost. Calling instructions are posted on most Ladatel phones in Spanish, English, and French. In time, these will replace all the older phones (described below).

Ladatel phones are of three types, depending upon method of payment. Those with blue handsets take coins (100, 500 or 1000-pesos) or telephone tokens (*fichas*). Those with brown handsets take cards; the boxy slot is for major credit cards (Visa, MasterCard, Access, Eurocard etc.); the dimpled slot is for special telephone company debit cards (*tarjetas de teléfono*) obtainable at TELMEX offices in denominations of 20,000, 30,000 and 50,000 pesos.

Cost The cost of a Ladatel call depends upon where you call and when. The cheapest times to call are Saturday and Sunday; the most expensive are business hours on weekdays. Long-distance calls within Mexico are discounted 20% from 5 to 9.59 pm, 63% from 10 pm to 7.59 am Monday to Saturday; Sunday is cheap all day. Calls to the USA and Canada are discounted 33% from 7 pm to 6.59 am Monday to Friday, all day Saturday, and on Sunday till 4.59 pm (except calls to Alaska and Hawaii). Calls to other countries are discounted 33% all day Saturday and Sunday, and at the following times Monday to Friday:

South America and Caribbean: 5 pm to 4.59 am
Europe, Africa, Middle East: 6 pm to 5.59 am
Central America: 7 pm to 6.59 am
Asia & Pacific: 5 am to 4.59 pm

The minimum Ladatel charge for most calls from Mexico to the USA and Canada is about US$1.70 per minute during off-peak hours, US$2.40 during peak hours. There is a three-minute minimum for operator-assisted calls.

Placing a Call Calling from a Ladatel phone, insert your coins or card and begin with the code for the service you want:

- Mexico long-distance station-to-station: 91
- Mexico long-distance person-to-person, collect (reverse-charge), etc: 92
- USA & Canada station-to-station: 95
- USA & Canada person-to-person, collect, etc: 96
- Other countries, station-to-station: 98
- Other countries, person-to-person, collect, etc: 99

Follow the service code with the country code, city code and local number. (Note that you should *not* press '1' as country code for the USA or Canada.)

Casetas If you don't use a Ladatel or a hotel phone you must find a *caseta de larga distancia*, or long-distance call station. These are being phased out, but still exist, especially in many small non-touristy towns and often in shops. An operator will connect your number and you speak from a booth. Ask the agent in the caseta what the charge will be before you call!

A collect (reverse charge) call *(llamada por cobrar)* is usually much cheaper than a normal operator-assisted call, but a hotel or caseta may refuse to place a collect call or levy a fee for doing so, whether the call goes through or not. If you call from a hotel, be sure to ask in advance if a service charge (often a percentage) will be added, and find out the approximate cost per minute of the call.

Fax

Mexico is fairly well provided with fax machines. The post and telegraph offices in some major public places (bus terminals, railway stations, airports, etc) have public fax machines. There are also private fax offices or you may be able to send one from one of the larger hotels. They cost somewhat more than a regular Ladatel telephone call – John paid US$4 per minute plus US$2.75 per page for a fax sent from Oaxaca to Australia.

Telegram

Most towns have a *telégrafos* office where you can send domestic and international telegrams – a simple but not always very quick means of communication (one from Mexico City to Melbourne, Australia, took five days). The usual cost within Mexico is less than US$1 for up to ten words if sent *ordinario*, or US$2 if sent *urgente*. To the USA and Canada, cost is US$4.50 for up to 15 words (US$0.66 for each additional word); to Europe, US$3.50 for up to seven words (US$0.50 for each additional word).

TIME

Most of Mexico is on Central Standard Time (six hours behind Greenwich Mean Time) the same time as Chicago, Dallas and Winnipeg in wintertime, and Guatemala, Honduras, Nicaragua and Costa Rica. Several states in north-western Mexico (Baja California Sur, Sinaloa, Sonora and parts of Nayarit) are on Mountain Standard Time, the same as Calgary, Salt Lake City and Tucson. Baja California Norte is on Pacific Standard Time, the same as California and British Columbia.

Mexico does not observe Daylight Saving (summer) Time, except for Baja California Norte, which always keeps the same time as the US state of California.

ELECTRICITY

Electrical current, plugs and sockets in Mexico are the same as in the USA and Canada: 110 volts, 60 cycles and flat, two-pronged plugs.

WEIGHTS & MEASURES

Mexico uses the metric system. For conversion between metric and US or Imperial measures, see the back of this book. Here are some rules of thumb:

- There are about 2½ centimetres to an inch.
- A metre is slightly longer than a yard.

- A kilometre is about 6/10 of a mile; 10 km equals roughly six miles; 100 km is about 60 miles.
- A litre is a little more than a quart; one gallon is about 3¾ litres; ten gallons is about 38 litres.
- A kilogram is a little over two pounds; a half-kilo (500 grams) is a little over a pound; 250 grams is about half a pound.

BOOKS

Although you can find books in English in most major centres, the choice is not extensive outside Mexico City. The Mexican-produced titles mentioned – such as the guides to pre-Hispanic sites below – are widely available in Mexico, but with other books it is wise to find what you want before arriving in the country.

The Mexican Book Service, 204 Worthington Drive, Exton, Pennsylvania 19341, USA, maintains a comprehensive list of 215 books covering all aspects of Mexico including travel, pre-Hispanic history, mythology and economics. Most of the books mentioned can be obtained from this service.

Travel Guides

La Ruta Maya: Yucatán, Guatemala & Belize – a travel survival kit by Tom Brosnahan (Lonely Planet Publications, Melbourne, 1991) covers south-eastern Mexico and its neighbours in detail, with emphasis on the Maya and their culture.

Baja California – a travel survival kit by Scott Wayne (Lonely Planet Publications, Melbourne, 1991) is one of the best guides available on Baja California. In typical Lonely Planet fashion, it is packed with useful tips and information about Mexico's last frontier.

A handy companion for this book and the two mentioned above is Lonely Planet's *Latin American Spanish Phrasebook*, which contains practical and up-to-date words and expressions in Latin-American Spanish.

Adventuring Along the Gulf of Mexico by Donald G Schueler (Sierra Club Books, San Francisco, 1986) is an interesting guide to the whole Gulf coast from Florida to the Yucatán, concentrating on wildlife, the environment and opportunities to get away from other people.

Mexico's Volcanoes by R J Secor (The Mountaineers, Seattle, 1981) is a thorough guide to routes up the seven main peaks of Mexico's central volcanic belt. It contains much practical information on how to reach the mountains, what to take and safety precautions.

Backpacking in Mexico & Central America by Hilary Bradt & Rob Rachowiecki (Bradt Enterprises, Cambridge, Massachusetts, and Chalfont St Peter, Bucks, England, 1982) covers only a few hikes in Mexico but has some useful general information plus details of hikes in all the other Central American countries.

Camping in Mexico and *The People's Guide to Mexico* by Carl Franz (John Muir Publications, Santa Fe, New Mexico) have long been essential for anyone planning an extended trip. They do not attempt to give hotel-restaurant-transport-sightseeing specifics but instead provide an all-round general introduction to Mexico.

Those who love old guidebooks should try to find a copy of *Terry's Guide to Mexico*, which was produced from 1922 to 1947. It's highly detailed, though hopelessly out of date of course – but look at those wonderful old multicoloured fold-out maps! A copy of the 1935 edition at the Lonely Planet office reveals that the 1934 Mexican Customs regulations didn't have much to say about how many cigarettes or bottles of wine you could bring in with you, but did list exhaustively what clothes a female visitor was permitted to import duty-free:

Eighteen pieces of each kind of underwear, 12 nightdresses or six pyjamas, 24 pairs of stockings, 24 handkerchiefs, six collars, two aprons, one pair of bath slippers, one bathing cap, one bathrobe, one bathing suit, one pair of slippers, 12 pairs of shoes, one pair of riding boots, one pair of rubber shoes, six house robes, one automobile robe, three overcoats or wraps, one mackintosh, three sweaters, four mufflers, six pairs of gloves, six belts, 12 street dresses, two evening dresses, three sports gowns, one parasol, one umbrella and 10 hats.

Those with a passionate interest in pre-Hispanic sights should look for *A Guide to Ancient Mexican Ruins* and *A Guide to Ancient Maya Ruins*, both by C Bruce Hunter (University of Oklahoma Press, 1974 & 1977 and later editions).

Travel & Description

Barbarous Mexico by John Kenneth Turner (University of Texas Press, 1969) is a superb account by a US journalist of travels in Mexico early this century, written to tell North Americans the truth about the barbarity of the Porfirio Díaz regime – a job in which it succeeds admirably and very readably. When translated into Spanish in 1955, the book was entitled *Problemas Agrícolas e Industriales de México* (Agricultural & Industrial Problems of Mexico) – no doubt a less offensive title for a Mexican audience.

Other interesting books by foreigners who have lived or travelled in Mexico are *Life in Mexico* by Frances Calderón de La Barca, the Scottish wife of Spain's ambassador to Mexico in the turbulent 1840s (reissued by Dent, London in 1970); *Viva Mexico!* by Charles Macomb Flandrau (Eland paperback) which tells of life on a coffee plantation at the turn of this century; *Thomas Gage's Travels in the New World* (University of Oklahoma Press, 1969), by a 17th-century English Puritan; and *A Visit to Don Octavio* by Sybil Bedford (Eland paperback).

Incidents of Travel in Central America, Chiapas & Yucatán and *Incidents of Travel in Yucatán* by John L Stephens are fascinating accounts of adventure, discovery and archaeology by the enthusiastic 19th-century amateur archaeologist. Both are available in Dover paperback editions.

Graham Greene's *The Lawless Roads* was originally published in 1939 and entertainingly traces his wanderings through Mexico at a particularly troubled time when violent clashes were taking place between state and Church.

Aldous Huxley travelled through Mexico too; *Beyond the Mexique Bay*, first published in 1934, has interesting observations on the

Maya. It's also worth reading if you're going to be staying long in Oaxaca.

Writers haven't stopped finding Mexico a worthwhile place to travel in and write about. *So Far from God (A Journey to Central America)* by Patrick Marnham (Viking, New York, 1985 and now in Penguin paperback) is an insightful, amusing account of a journey from Texas through Mexico into Central America. Paul Theroux rides the rails through Mexico on *The Old Patagonian Express*.

The Children of Sánchez by Oscar Lewis (Random House) is a brilliant look at the Mexican family. It's essential reading if you want to understand the pivotal importance of the family in Mexican society. *Five Families* (Basic Books) is by the same author.

Literature

Mexico's best known novelist is Carlos Fuentes, who has achieved major international recognition. His most highly regarded novel is *Where the Air is Clear* (Farrar Straus & Giroux, New York, 1971), written in the 1950s. Like *The Death of Artemio Cruz* (Panther), another of his best-known works, it's an attack on the failure of the Mexican Revolution. Fuentes' *Aura* is a magical book with one of the most stunning endings of any novel. His other novels include *Terra Nostra, Distant Relations, A Change of Skin* and *The Old Gringo*, which poses a solution to the mysterious disappearance in Mexico of US writer Ambrose Bierce during the Revolution.

Another Mexican novelist widely known outside the country is Jorge Ibargüengoitia, who was killed in the Madrid air disaster of 1983. *The Dead Girls* and *Two Crimes* (both published in paperback by Chatto & Windus, London), are black comic thrillers; the first based on the real murders of six prostitutes in a provincial Mexican brothel, the second the story of a radical on the run from the security forces.

The Labyrinth of Solitude by Octavio Paz is perhaps the most probing examination of Mexico's myths and the Mexican character. Among Paz's other books, *The Other*

Mexico: Critique of the Pyramid (Grove Press, New York, 1972) is a passionate, insightful book. It was written after the 1968 Tlatelolco massacre and assesses the lingering influence of the savage Aztec world view in modern Mexico. Paz's *Alternating Currents* is a less known but still brilliant collection of essays combining literary criticism, philosophy and political and social insights.

D H Lawrence's *The Plumed Serpent* asks the big questions about life, death and relationships in a Mexican setting. Heavy going even for Lawrence fans, it was first published in 1926 and is available in Penguin paperbacks. *Mornings in Mexico* (also in Penguin paperback) is a collection of short stories by Lawrence set in both New Mexico and Mexico. Lawrence's frail health didn't stand up to the country very well: he got malaria, dysentery and tuberculosis.

Made into a widely acclaimed film with the same name, *Under the Volcano* by Malcolm Lowry (Lippincott 1965; also in Penguin paperback) follows a British diplomat who drinks himself to death. Sounds simple, but it delves deeply into the Mexican psyche at a time (1938) of deep conflict.

Carlos Castaneda's *Don Juan* series of novels (Penguin), which reached serious cult status in the 1970s, tells of a North American's experiences with a peyote guru somewhere in northern Mexico.

History

General *Sons of the Shaking Earth* by Eric Wolf (University of Chicago Press, 1959) is a wonderfully readable introduction to Mexican history. Other good general introductions to the country's history include *A Short History of Mexico* by J Patrick McHenry (Doubleday) and *The Course of Mexican History* by Michael C Meyer & William L Sherman (Oxford University Press, 1986).

There are various worthwhile books to look for on the pre-Hispanic period, on the Spanish conquest and its aftermath, and on recent events in Mexico. Starting at the beginning of the Mexican story there's Nigel

Davies' *The Ancient Kingdoms of Mexico* (Allen Lane, London, 1982; also available in Pelican paperback). This is a succinct but scholarly study of four of Mexico's ancient civilisations: the Olmecs, the builders of Teotihuacán, the Toltecs and the Aztecs. Diagrams, illustrations, plans and maps complement the text.

Atlas of Ancient America by Michael Coe, Dean Snow & Elizabeth Benson (Facts on File, New York and Oxford, 1986) covers North, South and Central America as well as Mexico. It's too big to take along on your trip but is a fascinating, superbly illustrated, up-to-date book.

Of Gods & Men by Anna Benson Gyles & Chloë Sayer (BBC, London, 1980) traces the path of several Indian peoples from pre-Hispanic to modern times.

The Daily Life of the Aztecs by Jacques Soustelle (New York, 1962) is something of a classic on its subject. *Burning Water* by Laurette Séjourné (Shambhala, Berkeley, 1976) is an interesting book on Aztec myths, religion and thought.

The multi-volume *Handbook of Middle American Indians* (University of Texas Press, Austin, 1964-1976) edited by Robert Wauchope is an encyclopaedic work that covers both the pre-Hispanic and more recent Indian history and culture in great detail.

Spanish Conquest *The Conquest of New Spain* by Bernal Díaz del Castillo (Penguin paperback, abridged version) is an eyewitness account of the Spanish arrival. Díaz was one of Cortés' lieutenants. *Cortés & Moctezuma* (Avon Books, 1954 & 1978) is a fast-moving story of the Spanish conquest.

Soldiers, Indians & Silver by Philip W Powell is an interesting history of the bloody and little-known Chichimec War fought by the Spanish for control of northern Mexico in the 16th century.

Mexico Today *Distant Neighbors: A Portrait of the Mexicans* by Alan Riding (originally published by Knopf, New York in 1984 but now available in Viking paperback)

is an insightful look at the country and its people by a *New York Times* reporter once based there. This is probably the best guide to understanding modern Mexico and its love-hate relationship with the United States.

Mexico in Crisis by Judith Adler Hellman (Holmes & Meier, New York and London, 1983) is a well-researched leftist attack on the failure of Mexico's recent governments to provide any real remedies for the country's poverty.

For disturbing documentation of recent political violence against Mexico's poor, dig out *Mexico – Human Rights in Rural Areas*, a short report published by Amnesty International in London in 1986.

Culture, Art & Architecture

A Treasury of Mexican Folkways by Frances Toor (Bonanza Books/Crown Publishers, New York, 1985) was written in the 1940s but its detail on mainly Indian customs, ceremonies, beliefs and ways of life is still interesting.

Mexico South by artist Miguel Covarrubias (Alfred A Knopf, New York, 1946), an account of the life and customs of the Zapotecs on the Isthmus of Tehuantepec, is also fascinating but much of what it describes has sadly disappeared.

Books on Mexico's great 20th-century artists include Diego Rivera's autobiography *My Art, My Life* (Citadel Press, New York), *The Fabulous Life of Diego Rivera* by B D Wolfe (Stein & Day, New York), and *The Mexican Muralists* by Alma M Reed (Crown, New York).

Mexico's colonial architectural heritage isn't nearly so well documented as the pre-Hispanic but *Art & Time in Mexico* by Elizabeth Wilder Weismann & Judith Hancock Sandoval (Harper & Row) is a good, fairly handy, recent book on colonial architecture, with many photos. *A Guide to Mexican Art* by Justino Fernández (University of Chicago Press, 1969) covers architecture as well as art fairly thoroughly.

One of the most fascinating of all recent books on Mexico – but unfortunately too big

to carry along – is Chloë Sayer's *Mexican Costume* (British Museum Publications, 1985). It traces the designs, materials and techniques of the country's highly colourful and varied costumes from pre-Hispanic times to the present, and includes many photos and a great wealth of other intriguing detail about Mexican life past and present. Sayer has also written *Crafts of Mexico* (Aldus Books) and *Arts & Crafts of Mexico* (Thames & Hudson), the latter very good and well illustrated. Another good book in English is *Mexican Folk Crafts* by Carlos Espejel (Editorial Blume, Barcelona, 1978).

Michael D Coe has two interesting books available as Thames & Hudson paperbacks. *The Maya* (fourth edition, 1987) traces the history, art and culture of the Maya while *Mexico* (1984) concentrates on the other pre-Hispanic civilisations of Mexico. These two books give a handy and well-illustrated overall view of the great cultures of Mexico. Charles Gallenkamp's *Maya* is also widely acclaimed.

The Blood of Kings (Dynasty & Ritual in Maya Art) by Linda Schele & Mary Ellen Miller (George Braziller, New York 1986) is a heavily illustrated guide to the art and culture of the Maya period with particular emphasis on sacrifices, bloodletting, torture of captives, the ball game and other macabre aspects of Maya culture.

Books Sold in Mexico

Mexican publisher Minutiae Mexicana produces a range of pocket-size guides to various aspects of Mexico including *A Bird Watcher's Guide to Mexico, A Guide to Mexican Mammals & Reptiles, A Guide to Mexican Archaeology, A Guide to Mexican Ceramics, A Guide to Architecture in Ancient Mexico* and even *A Guide to Tequila, Mezcal & Pulque*. They're useful, compact introductions to specific topics and are widely available in Mexico.

The *Official Guide* series published in Mexico has some good books on important museums and archaeological sites.

Another interesting Mexican-produced paperback series with many titles in English is Panorama. These include *History of Mexico, The Conquest of Mexico, The Mexican Revolution, Truth & Legend on Pancho Villa, Pre-Hispanic Gods of Mexico, Codices of Mexico, Mural Painting of Mexico* and *Indian Costumes of Mexico*.

MAPS

One of the best overall maps of Mexico is published by Bartholomew in its World Travel Map series at a scale of 1:3 million – which means that it folds out to about 1.2 by 0.8 metres. It shows altitudes, rivers, cities and towns, roads, railways and state boundaries clearly and accurately. You can also get a good 1:3.5 million 'Tourist Road Map' of the country, which includes good street plans of some cities, free from many tourist offices. For motorists, the best road atlas is generally reckoned to be the *Pemex Atlas de Carreteras*, available from some Pemex petrol stations.

MEDIA
Newspapers & Magazines
English-language *The Mexico City News* is distributed throughout Mexico, with the price rising the further you get from the capital. Almost every other city or region that attracts English-speaking tourists and retirees – Lake Chapala, Guadalajara, Baja California and Puerto Vallarta, for example – has a small English-language newspaper or newsletter. *Atención San Miguel* is a weekly paper in English published in San Miguel de Allende.

Spanish-language Mexico has a thriving local press as well as national newspapers such as *Excelsior* and *El Tiempo*. Even small cities often have two or three newspapers of their own.

For those interested in a non-establishment view of events, *La Jornada* is a good national daily with a mainly left-wing viewpoint that covers a lot of stories other papers don't. *Proceso* is a weekly news magazine with a similar approach. Both cover international and cultural events as well as domestic news. Another interesting opposition magazine is the weekly *Quehacer Político*. *Fem* is a national feminist magazine.

Ovaciones is a national paper with a whole section devoted entirely to Mexican and international sport. North American baseball and football scores and European soccer results can often be found in *Excelsior* and *El Universal*.

México Desconocido (Unknown Mexico) is a colourful monthly magazine with intelligent coverage of many interesting places. Buy it at newsstands for US$2, or order an annual subscription (which comes with an English supplement) for US$50 to USA or US$75 to Europe, from Editorial Jilguero SA de CV (☎ (5) 202-65-85), Monte Pelvoux 110, Primer piso, Lomas de Chapultepec, México, DF 11000.

Radio & TV
Broadcasting is run by private enterprise. Mexican radio announcers are much given to the use of the dramatic echo chamber. Apart from that, they offer a variety of music, often that of the region where you're listening. In tourist areas such as Mexico City, Acapulco and Cancún, some radio stations give news reports several times daily in English. In the evening you may be able to pick up US stations on the AM (medium wave) band.

Many, if not most hotel rooms above the low end have television sets. The news reports can help you to improve your Spanish. Many hotels have satellite dish antennae and receive some US stations. Most popular are ESPN (the sports channel) and UNO, the Spanish-language US network. Local Spanish-language programming includes hours and hours of talk shows and soap operas, some sports, and reruns of old American movies dubbed in Spanish.

FILM & PHOTOGRAPHY
According to Mexican customs laws you are allowed to bring in no more than one still camera and one eight-mm movie camera or camcorder with 12 rolls of film for each, but these limits are rarely applied strictly. Camera stores, pharmacies and hotels sell

film. Be suspicious of film that is being sold at prices lower than what you might pay in North America – it is often outdated. You may not know this by glancing at the date on the back of the film carton because sometimes it's obscured by a sticker bearing the new lower price. Look under the sticker before you buy the film.

Most types of film are available in the larger cities and resorts. Film prices in Mexico are usually about US$1 or US$2 higher than prices in North America.

Mexico is a photographer's paradise, especially for shots of magnificent landscapes and coastline; a wide-angle lens is useful. It helps to have a polarising filter to cut down glare from reflections of sunlight on the ocean.

For in-depth information and tips on all aspects of travel photography, including hints for Mexico, get a copy of *Travel Photography Pocket Mate* by Jason Rubinsteen (Travel/Photography Press, P O Box 4486, Inglewood, California 90309, USA). It costs US$11 including postage (California residents must add US$0.65 for sales tax).

HEALTH
Predeparture Preparations

Specific immunisations are not normally required for travel in Mexico. All the same, it's a good idea to be up to date on your tetanus, typhoid-paratyphoid and polio immunisations. US citizens born after 1957, who have probably been inoculated against measles in childhood, should check with their doctors to make sure they are still immune; catching measles is not a pleasant prospect for an adult. Those who had a bout of measles as children are definitely immune. If you plan to stay for more than a few weeks, and you're adventurous in your eating, an immune globulin shot is also recommended for protection against infectious hepatitis. You only need a yellow fever certificate to enter the country if, within the last six months, you have been to a country where yellow fever is present.

Mexico is partly in the tropics where food spoils easily, mosquitoes roam freely, and sanitation is not always the best, so you must take special care to protect yourself from illness. The most important steps you can take are to be careful about what you eat and drink, and to stay away from mosquitoes (or at least make them stay away from you). These measures are particularly important for adventurous travellers who enjoy getting off the beaten track, mingling with the locals, and trekking into remote areas.

Before presenting this somewhat disturbing catalogue of potential illnesses, let us say that after dozens of journeys in every region of the country in every season of the year, climbing pyramids in remote jungle, camping out, staying in cheap hotels and eating in all sorts of markets and restaurants, we have never got anything more serious than traveller's diarrhoea (but we've got that frequently!). We have rarely taken medicines to help get rid of diarrhoea, instead preferring to let the body heal itself. We have not taken malarial prevention medicine or gamma globulin, and have not come down with malaria or hepatitis. But we have known people who have got dengue fever and typhoid fever, so we know that it can happen.

If you come down with a serious illness, be very careful to find a competent doctor, and don't be afraid to get second opinions. You may want to telephone your doctor at home for consultation as well. In some cases it may be best to end your trip and fly home for treatment, difficult as this may be. A friend who contracted typhoid fever in Mexico went to the local hospital where a sympathetic doctor strongly recommended that she and her husband fly home to the USA and go to the hospital there, which she did. Medical practice in Mexico is not always what it should be.

Medical Kit It is always a good idea to travel with a small first-aid kit. Some of the items that should be included are: adhesive bandages, a sterilised gauze bandage, elastic bandage, cotton wool, thermometer, tweezers, scissors, antiseptic (Dettol or Betadine), burn cream (Caladryl is good for sunburn, minor burns and itchy bites), insect repellent containing DEET, and multivitamins.

Don't forget a full supply of any medication you're already taking; the prescription may be difficult to match abroad.

Basic Rules
Food & Water Food can be contaminated by bacteria, viruses and/or parasites when it is harvested, shipped, handled, washed (if the water is contaminated) or prepared. Cooking, peeling and/or washing food in pure water is the way to get rid of the germs. To avoid gastrointestinal diseases, avoid salads, uncooked vegetables, and un-pasteurised milk or milk products (including cheese). Make sure the food you eat has been freshly cooked and is still hot. Do not eat raw or rare meat, fish or shellfish. Peel fruit yourself with clean hands and a clean knife.

As for beverages, don't trust any water unless it has been boiled for 20 minutes or treated with purifiers, or it comes in an unopened bottle labelled *agua purificada*. Most hotels have large bottles of purified water from which you can fill your carafe or canteen; some will put smaller capped bottles of purified water in your room. Local people may drink the water from the tap or from the well and their systems may be used to it – or they may have chronic gastric diseases! Some Mexican cities supposedly have purified tap water safe to drink. All the same, we drink bottled water. Purified water and ice are available from supermarkets, small grocery shops *(tiendas)* and liquor stores *(licorerías* or *vinos y licores)*.

Use only pure water for drinking, washing food, brushing your teeth, and ice. Tea, coffee, and other hot beverages should be made with boiled water. If the waiter swears that the ice in your drink is made from agua purificada, you may feel you can take a chance with it.

Canned or bottled carbonated beverages, including carbonated water, are usually safe, as are beer, wine and liquor.

If you plan to travel off the main roads and into the middle of nowhere, bottled water may not be readily available and you will

have to purify water yourself. Your water purification method might be one of these:

- Water purification drops or tablets containing tetraglycine hydroperiodide or hydroclonazone, sold under brand names such as Globaline, Potable-Agua or Coughlan's in pharmacies and sporting goods stores in the USA. In Mexico, ask for *gotas* (drops) or *pastillas* (tablets) *para purificar agua*, sold in pharmacies and supermarkets.
- Boiled water; bringing it to a rolling boil will kill most germs, but you must boil it for at least 20 minutes to kill parasites.
- A portable water filter that eliminates bacteria. Compact units are available from major camping supply stores in the USA such as Recreational Equipment, Inc (REI) (☎ (206) 431-5804), P O Box C-88126, Seattle, Washington 98188; and Mountain Equipment Inc (MEI) (☎ (800) 344-7422), 1636 South Second St, Fresno, California 93702, and through outfitters such as Eddie Bauer and L L Bean.

Protection against Mosquitoes Many serious tropical diseases are spread by infected mosquitoes.

Some mosquitoes feed during the day, others at night. In general, they're most bothersome when the sun is not too hot, in the evening and early morning, and on overcast days, and most prevalent in lowland and coastal regions and during the rainy season (May to October).

Mosquitoes seem to be attracted more to dark colours than to light, so in mosquito-infested areas wear light-coloured long trousers, socks, a long-sleeved shirt and a hat. Clothing should be loose-fitting, as mosquitoes can drill right through the weave of a tight T-shirt. Mosquitoes also seem to be attracted by scents such as those in perfume, cologne, lotions, hair spray, etc. Sleep in screened rooms or beneath mosquito netting after you have disposed of the little suckers who have somehow got in there with you. Check to make sure screens are intact, and that all openings to the outside are either screened or blocked.

Use insect repellent which has at least a 20% concentration of N,N diethylmeta-toluamide (DEET) on any exposed skin. It's best to buy repellent before leaving home as repellents bought in Mexico may or may not have this most effective ingredient. To avoid reactions to the repellent, apply it sparingly only to exposed skin or to clothing, don't inhale the stuff or get it in your eyes or mouth or on broken or irritated skin, and wash it off after you enter a mosquito-free area.

It's probably best not to use a repellent with an especially high – or low – concentration of DEET (concentrations reach 95%!) Be particularly careful with children: don't put it on hands which may be put in the mouth or eyes, use as little as possible, and wash it off afterwards.

In addition, you may want to use a pyrethrum-based insect spray in your sleeping room.

Medical Problems and Treatment

Mexico is partly in the tropics, and has tropical diseases, some of which you may not know about. However, although you should be informed about them, you're unlikely to contract anything more than an unpleasant bout of traveller's diarrhoea.

Traveller's Diarrhoea The food and water in different countries has different bacteria from those your digestive system is used to – germs that your immune system may not be prepared to combat. If you plunge right into the local culture and eat lots of food with high concentrations of these different bacteria, your body's natural defences may be overwhelmed.

Travellers to many less developed countries suffer from what is known medically as traveller's diarrhoea (TD) and informally as Montezuma's revenge, *turista*, or the trots. The condition is defined as having twice as many (or more) unformed bowel movements as normal; typically one has four or five watery stools per day. Other possible symptoms include abdominal cramps, nausea, fever, malaise, a bloated feeling, and urgency of bowel movements. It usually hits within the first week of travel, but may hit at any time and more than once. A bout of TD typically lasts three or four days. It seems to affect younger travellers more than older ones, which may be due to lack of caution among the young, or acquired immunity among the old.

Note that heatstroke (see below) can mimic the symptoms of TD. If you are in a hot region ask yourself: have I been drinking *lots* of fluids, even when not thirsty?

Doctors recommend that you *not* take medicines in the hope they will prevent TD. Taking medicines such as antibiotics, bismuth subsalicylate (Pepto-Bismol), or difenoxine (Lomotil) as prophylactics can actually make it *easier* for you to get the disease later on by killing off the benign digestive bacteria that help to protect you from the 'foreign' bacteria. These strong drugs can also cause side effects, some of them serious. One such side effect is photosensitivity, a condition in which your skin is temporarily oversensitive to sunlight (in the sunny tropics!).

Instead of taking drugs as a precaution, observe the rules of safe eating and drinking, and don't overdo it early in your trip. For the first week after arrival, be careful and conservative in your eating habits, avoid overeating or eating heavy or spicy food, don't get overtired, and don't drink lots of alcoholic beverages or coffee.

If you do come down with a case of TD, take it easy; stay in bed if you can. Be especially careful to replace fluids and electrolytes (potassium, sodium, etc) by drinking caffeine-free soft drinks or glasses of fruit juice (high in potassium) with honey and a pinch of salt added, plus a glass of pure water with a quarter teaspoon of sodium bicarbonate (baking soda) added; weak tea, preferably unsweetened and without milk, is all right.

Avoid dairy products. Eat only salted crackers or dry toast for a day or so. After that, eat easily digested foods that are not fatty or overly acid. Yoghurt with live cultures is particularly good as it helps to repopulate the bowel with benign digestive organisms. When you feel better, be particularly careful about what you eat and drink from then on.

As for medications, it's best if you cure

yourself without them. If you must have some chemical help, go to a doctor, who may recommend one of the following treatments as described in the US Public Health Service's book, *Health Information for International Travel*. Treatments and dosages should be determined by a competent doctor who can tell you about side effects and contraindications; those noted here are the normal ones for otherwise healthy adults *(not* children), and are for information only:

- Bismuth subsalicylate (Pepto-Bismol), one ounce of liquid or the equivalent in tablets every half-hour for four hours. This treatment is not recommended if symptoms last more than more than 48 hours, or if you have high fever, blood in the stool, kidney problems or are allergic to salicylates. Children under the age of two should not be given this medicine.
- Diphenoxylate and loperamide (Lomotil, Imodium) are antimotility agents made from synthetic opiate derivatives. They temporarily slow down the diarrhoea but do not cure it, they increase the risk of getting TD again, and they can make you sluggish or sleepy. They should not be used if you have a high fever, or blood in the stool, or are driving a motor vehicle or operating machinery (your alertness is impaired). In any case, don't use them for longer than two full days.
- Doxycycline (100 mg twice daily); or trimethoprim (200 mg twice daily); or trimethoprim (160 mg)/sulfamethoxazole (800 mg, once daily), known as TMP/SMX and sold in Mexico as Bactrim F (Roche), are antibiotics that may be indicated if there are three or more loose stools in an eight-hour period, especially with nausea, vomiting, abdominal cramps and fever.

It bears repeating: traveller's diarrhoea is self-limiting, and you're usually better off if you can get through it without taking strong drugs. If you feel that you need medicine, go to a doctor. Make sure that you have TD and not some other gastrointestinal ailment for which the treatment may be very different.

Medicines Not to Take You can walk into a chemist's/pharmacy in Mexico and buy medicines – often without a prescription – which might be banned for good reason in your home country. Well-meaning but incompetent doctors or chemists/pharma-cists might recommend such medicines for gastrointestinal ailments, but such medicines may be worse than no medicine at all. Though they may bring some relief from the symptoms of TD, they may cause other sorts of harm such as neurological damage.

Medicines called halogenated hydroxy-quinoline derivatives are among these, and may bear the chemical names clioquinol or iodoquinol, or brand names Entero-Vioform, Mexaform or Intèstopan, or something similar. It's best not to take these medicines without consulting a trusted physician, preferably your regular doctor at home.

Cholera After a recent outbreak in Peru, this serious disease is now spreading throughout South and Central America. There have been some cases reported in Mexico, but the government has sent out special rapid-reaction teams to stifle outbreaks; none has been in a touristy area.

Like dysentery, cholera is a disease of insanitation, and spreads quickly in areas, urban and rural, where sewerage and water supplies are rudimentary. It can also be spread in foods that are parcooked or uncooked, such as the popular *ceviche*, which is made from marinaded raw fish, as well as salads and raw vegetables.

The disease is characterised by a sudden onset of acute diarrhoea with 'rice water' stools, vomiting, muscular cramps and extreme weakness. You need medical help – but first treat for dehydration, which can be extreme. If there is an appreciable delay in getting to the hospital, then begin taking tetracycline (adults, one 250 mg capsule four times a day; children under eight, one-third of this dose; other children, half this dose). Cholera vaccination is not all that effective, but the disease does respond to treatment if caught early.

Dysentery There are two types of dysentery, both of which are characterised by diarrhoea containing blood and/or mucus. You require a stool test to determine which type you have.

Bacillary dysentery, the most common

variety, is short, sharp and nasty but rarely persistent. It hits suddenly and lays you out with fever, nausea, cramps and diarrhoea, but it is self-limiting. Treatment is the same as for traveller's diarrhoea; as it's caused by bacteria, the disease responds well to antibiotics if needed.

Amoebic dysentery is caused by amoebic parasites and is more dangerous. It builds up slowly, cannot be starved out and if untreated will get worse and can permanently damage your intestines. Do not have anyone other than a doctor diagnose your symptoms and administer treatment.

Giardia (Giardiasis) This is caused by a parasite named *Giardia lamblia*, contracted by eating faecally contaminated food or beverages or by contact with a surface that has been similarly contaminated. Symptoms usually last for more than five days (perhaps months!), may be mild or serious, and may include diarrhoea, abdominal cramps, fatigue, weight loss, flatulence, anorexia and/or nausea. If you have gastrointestinal gripes for a length of time, talk to a doctor and have a stool sample analysed for giardia. Medicine is available to rid you of this unpleasant little bug easily and safely.

Hepatitis This is a viral disease of the liver for which there are no medicines, and it can be very serious – even fatal – if not treated with bed rest. There are several types of hepatitis.

Symptoms appear 15 to 50 days after infection (generally around 25 days) and consist of fever, loss of appetite, nausea, depression, lack of energy and pains around the base of the rib cage. Skin turns yellow, the whites of the eyes yellow to orange, and urine deep orange or brown. Do *not* take antibiotics. There is no cure for hepatitis except complete rest and careful diet. The worst is over in about 10 days, but rest is still important.

The hepatitis A virus can be spread by contaminated food, beverages, cutlery or crockery, or by intimate contact with an infected person. You can protect yourself against hepatitis A by getting an immune globulin (IG) injection before you begin your travels, and by being careful of what you eat and how you have sex.

Hepatitis B is spread by direct contact with blood, secretions, or intimate sexual contact with an infected person. Risk is very low if you avoid these situations.

The mysterious hepatitis virus known as Non-A, Non-B is spread in the same way as Hepatitis A, by contaminated food and beverages. Yet another variant, Hepatitis C, is similar to the B virus, but is fairly rare and should not be of too much concern to travellers.

Hepatitis may also be spread by use of contaminated, unsterilised needles for tattooing, acupuncture, drug abuse or medicinal injections. It can be avoided by making sure that needles are sterile.

If you get hepatitis, see a doctor immediately. The treatment is simple: go to bed and stay there for several weeks, eat only easily digestible low-fat foods and drink no alcohol for at least six months. There is no medicine which helps cure hepatitis except B vitamins; on the contrary, many medicines such as antibiotics, which must be detoxified by the already-weakened liver, can cause hepatic (liver) failure which can be fatal. If a doctor prescribes anything but bed rest and B vitamins for hepatitis, consult another doctor.

Typhoid Fever This serious disease is spread by contaminated food and beverages, and has symptoms similar to those of traveller's diarrhoea. If you get it, you should be under close supervision by a competent doctor for a while, and perhaps spend a short time in the hospital. Inoculation can give you some protection, but is not 100% effective. If diagnosed and treated early, typhoid can be treated effectively.

Heatstroke Only slightly less common than traveller's diarrhoea are the illnesses caused by excessive heat and dehydration. These are more dangerous because they display fewer symptoms.

If you exercise excessively in hot regions such as Yucatán, the Gulf and Pacific coasts, or if you fail to replace lost fluids and electrolytes (salt, potassium, etc), you can suffer from dizziness, weakness, headaches, nausea, and greater susceptibility to other illnesses such as traveller's diarrhoea. This is heat exhaustion, heat prostration or, in severe cases, heatstroke. In this last case, exposure to intense heat can cause convulsions and coma.

Protect yourself by drinking lots of fluids. If you urinate infrequently and in small amounts, you're not drinking enough. If you feel tired and have a headache, you're not drinking enough. In hot regions, don't just drink when you're thirsty; make it a habit to drink frequently, whether you're thirsty or not. It's so easy to prevent dehydration that you should feel foolish if you succumb to it.

Alcohol, coffee and tea are diuretics – they make you urinate and lose fluids. They are not a cure for dehydration: they're part of the problem. Drink pure water, fruit juices and soft drinks instead; go easy on the beer. In hot regions, salty food is good to eat as the salt helps your body to retain fluids.

Other measures to take against the heat: don't overdo it. Take it easy climbing pyramids and trekking through the jungle. Wear light cotton clothing that breathes and cools you; wear a hat and sunglasses. Allow yourself frequent rest breaks in the shade, and give your body a chance to balance itself. Use sunblock to prevent bad sunburn. Be doubly cautious if you spend time near or on the water, as the sun's glare from sand and water can double your exposure to the sun. You may want to wear a T-shirt and hat while swimming or boating .

Altitude Sickness Acute Mountain Sickness is the result of the lower levels of oxygen and barometric pressure at higher altitudes – 1500 metres (5000 feet) or higher. Many interesting places in Mexico are above these altitudes: Mexico City is over 2000 metres (7000 feet), Pachuca at close to 2700 metres (9000 feet).

Symptoms are shortness of breath, fatigue, headache, and sometimes nausea.

Your body will adjust to higher altitude in time (it makes more red blood cells to carry more oxygen), but it may take a week or more. When you arrive at an altitude over 1500 metres (5000 feet), refrain from strenuous physical activity for a few days – no jogging, fast walking or climbing. Drink extra fluids, but avoid alcoholic beverages, which are more potent in a low-oxygen environment. If you have respiratory or heart disease, talk to your doctor about pollution in Mexico City, and about what to do at altitudes above 2500 metres (8000 feet).

Dengue Fever Dengue is spread by mosquitoes, so risk of contraction, though low for the average traveller, is greatest where mosquitoes are most common. Symptoms include the fast onset of high fever, severe frontal headache, and pain in muscles and joints; there may be nausea and vomiting, and a skin rash may develop about three to five days after the first symptoms, spreading from the torso to arms, legs and face. It is possible to have subclinical dengue (that is, a 'mild' case of it), and also to contract dengue haemorraghic fever (DHF), a very serious and potentially fatal disease.

There are four different dengue viruses, but no medicines to combat them. The disease is usually self-limiting, which means that the body cures itself. If you are generally healthy and have a healthy immune system, the disease may be unpleasant but it is rarely serious. To protect against dengue, see the earlier section on Protection against Mosquitoes.

Malaria Symptoms of this serious disease may include jaundice (a yellow cast to the skin and/or eyes), general malaise, headaches, fever and chills, bed sweats and anaemia. Symptoms of the disease may appear as early as eight days after infection, or as late as several months after you return from your trip. You can contract malaria even if you've taken medicines to protect yourself.

Malaria is spread by mosquitoes, which bite mostly between dusk and dawn. It is fair to say that somewhere in Mexico you will encounter mosquitoes, which may or may not carry infectious diseases. The best way to protect yourself against malaria is to protect yourself against mosquito bites (see that section). You can also take medicines to protect against malarial infection, usually chloroquine phosphate (Aralen) or hydroxychloroquine sulphate (Plaquenil), though other medicines may be indicated for specific individuals. You must consult a doctor on the use of these medicines, and get a prescription to buy them.

Begin taking the medicine *one or two weeks before you arrive* in a malarial area, continue taking it while you're there, and also for a month after you leave the area, according to your doctor's instructions. Unlike some other countries, Mexico does not have chloroquine-resistant strains of *Anopheles* mosquitoes. Taking medicine does not guarantee that you will not contract malaria, though.

The choice you must make is whether or not to take preventive medicine. As an adventurous traveller, you are more at risk than a person who buys a package tour to Cancún or Acapulco. Although most visitors to Mexico do not take antimalarial medicine, and most do not get malaria, you must decide for yourself.

Talk to your doctor. Call a hospital or clinic which specialises in tropical diseases or an appropriate information service. In the UK, call the Malarial Reference Laboratory on (071) 636 7921, a taped information service that tells you all you need to know. Unfortunately it's very busy. In the USA, call the Center for Disease Control's telephone information system toll-free on (800) 526-6367, or the CDC Malaria Hotline on (404) 332-4555. In Australia, call the Commonwealth Department of Health, Housing & Community Services, or consult a clinic like the Travellers Medical & Vaccination Centre (☎ (03) 650 7600), at Level 2, 393 Little Bourke St, Melbourne. Whether or not you take medicine, do be careful to protect yourself against mosquito bites.

Rabies The rabies virus is spread through bites by infected animals, or (rarely) through broken skin (scratches, licks) or the mucous membranes (as from breathing rabid-bat-contaminated air in a cave, for instance). Typical signs of a rabid animal are mad or uncontrolled behaviour, inability to eat, biting at anything and everything, and frothing at the mouth.

If any animal (but especially a dog) bites you, assume you have been exposed to rabies until you are certain this is not the case – there are no second chances. First, immediately wash the wound with lots of soap and water – this is very important! If it is possible, and safe to do so, try to capture the animal alive, and give it to local health officials who can determine whether or not it's rabid. Begin rabies immunisation shots as soon as possible; if you are taking antimalarial medicine, be sure to mention this to the doctor because antimalarial medicines can interfere with the effectiveness of rabies vaccine. Rabies is a potentially fatal disease, but it can be cured by prompt and proper treatment. Immunisation is also possible, but is expensive and unnecessary for most travellers in Mexico.

Schistosomiasis A parasitic worm makes its way into the bodies of certain tiny freshwater snails and then into humans swimming, wading or otherwise touching the infected water in pools, ponds or cenotes. Two or three weeks after your dip you may experience fever, weakness, headache, loss of appetite, loss of weight, pain in the gut and/or pain in the joints and muscles. You may have nausea and/or coughing. Six to eight weeks after infection, evidence of the worm can be found in the stools.

After this very unpleasant month or two, diagnosis can correctly identify schistosomiasis as the culprit, and you can get rid of it quickly and effectively by taking an inexpensive medicine. To guard against the illness, don't swim in fresh water that may be infected by sewage or other pollution. If you accidentally expose your skin to schistosomiasis-infected water, rub the skin vigorously with a towel, and/or rub alcohol on it.

Typhus If you go to a mountain town and get head lice, they can give you typhus; otherwise, the risk is extremely low. Typhus is treated by taking antibiotics.

Sexually Transmitted Diseases Sexual contact with an infected sexual partner spreads these diseases. While abstinence is the only 100% preventative, using condoms is also effective. Gonorrhoea and syphilis are the most common of these diseases; sores, blisters or rashes around the genitals, discharges or pain when urinating are common symptoms. Symptoms may be less marked or not observed at all in women. Syphilis symptoms eventually disappear completely but the disease continues and can cause severe problems in later years. Gonorrhoea and syphilis are treated with antibiotics.

There are numerous other sexually transmitted diseases, for most of which effective treatment is available. However, there is no cure for herpes and there is also currently no cure for AIDS. Abstinence is the only fully effective preventative; using condoms is usually effective but, as one doctor put it, if your partner is infected with HIV (the AIDS virus) and the condom breaks, you may die.

AIDS can be spread through infected blood transfusions; most developing countries cannot afford to screen blood for transfusions. It can also be spread by dirty needles – vaccinations, acupuncture and tattooing can potentially be as dangerous as intravenous drug use if the equipment is not clean. If you do need an injection it may be a good idea to buy a new syringe from a pharmacy and ask the doctor to use it.

Hospitals & Clinics
Almost every Mexican town and city now has either a hospital or medical clinic, and Cruz Roja (Red Cross) emergency facilities, all of which are indicated by road signs showing a red cross. Hospitals are generally inexpensive for common ailments (diarrhoea, dysentery) and minor surgery (stitches, sprains). Clinics are often too understaffed and overburdened with local problems to be of much help, but they are linked by a government radio network to emergency services.

If you must use these services, try to ascertain the competence of the staff treating you. Compare their diagnoses and prescriptions to the information in this section. If you have questions, call your embassy and get a referral for a doctor, or call home and have your doctor advise you.

Women's Health
Gynaecological problems, poor diet, lowered resistance due to the use of antibiotics for stomach upsets and even contraceptive pills can lead to vaginal infections when travelling in hot climates. Keeping the genital area clean, and wearing skirts or loose-fitting trousers and cotton underwear will help to prevent infections.

Yeast infections, characterised by a rash, itch and discharge, can be treated with a vinegar or even lemon-juice douche or with yoghurt. Nystatin suppositories are the usual medical prescription. Trichomonas is a more serious infection; symptoms are a discharge and a burning sensation when urinating. Male sexual partners must also be treated, and if a vinegar-water douche is not effective medical attention should be sought. Flagyl is the prescribed drug. Those prone to cystitis must be especially careful to drink plenty of fluids; attacks should be treated as soon as the first twinges are felt by drinking as much water as possible and taking a teaspoon of bicarbonate of soda in water every couple of hours. If this doesn't work, an antibiotic should be prescribed.

Pregnancy Most miscarriages occur during the first three months of pregnancy, so this is the most risky time to travel. The last three months should also be spent within reasonable distance of good medical care, as quite serious problems can develop at this time. Pregnant women should avoid all unnecessary medication, but vaccinations and malarial prophylactics should still be taken where possible. Additional care should be taken to prevent illness and particular attention should be paid to diet and nutrition.

WOMEN TRAVELLERS

In this land of machismo, women must make some concessions to local customs. In general, Mexicans are great believers in the *difference* (rather than the equality) between the sexes, and lone women have to expect numerous attempts to chat them up. It's commonly believed that foreign women in Mexico without male companions are easy game for Mexican men. Before AIDS, few middle-class Mexico City males got through their teens without a trip to Acapulco to see whom they could pick up. This can get tiresome at times; the best discouragement is a cool but polite initial response and a consistent, firm 'No'.

Don't put yourself in peril by doing things Mexican women would not do, such as challenge a man's masculinity, drink in a cantina, or hitchhike without a male companion.

DANGERS & ANNOYANCES

Mexico has some reputation as a violent country, thanks mainly to Pancho Villa, foreign movies and machismo. However, there's really little to fear for your physical safety unless you get deeply involved in a quarrel. More at risk are your possessions, particularly those you carry around with you.

Theft & Robbery

Theft, particularly pocket-picking and purse-snatching, is common in all large Mexican cities, and epidemic in Mexico City. Foreign tourists are particularly singled out for theft as they are presumed to be wealthy (by Mexican standards) and to be carrying valuables. Buses, the Metro in Mexico City, markets, pedestrian underpasses, thronged streets and plazas are all prime locations for theft.

You must protect yourself, or you can expect to lose a considerable amount. In Mexican cities, follow the precautions listed below *without fail*.

- Unless you have immediate need of them, leave most of your cash, travellers' cheques, passport, jewellery (earrings, necklaces, bracelets), air tickets, credit cards, expensive watch etc (and perhaps your camera) in a sealed, signed envelope in your hotel's safe. Obtain a receipt for the envelope. Virtually all hotels except the very cheapest provide safe-keeping for guests' valuables. You may have to provide the envelope (buy some at a *papelería*, or stationery shop). Your signature on the envelope and a receipt from the hotel clerk help to ensure that hotel staff won't pilfer your things.
- Leaving valuable items in a locked suitcase in your hotel room is often safer than carrying them with you on the streets of a Mexican city.
- Have a moneybelt or a pouch on a string around your neck, place your remaining valuables in it, and wear it *underneath your clothing*. You can carry a small amount of ready money in a pocket or bag.
- Be aware that any purse or bag in plain sight may be slashed or grabbed. At ticket counters in airports and bus stations, keep your bag between your feet, particularly when you're busy talking to a ticket agent.
- On long-distance buses or trains, particularly the 2nd and 3rd-class ones, keep your baggage with you if you can. If you let it disappear into a bus baggage compartment the chances of not seeing it again increase – or it may emerge considerably the worse for wear. (One reader reported, however, that when highwaymen stopped his bus they took the luggage inside the bus but didn't bother to open the luggage compartments underneath the seating area.)
- Do not leave any valuables visible in your vehicle when you park it in a city, unless it is in a guarded car park.

Pickpockets Crowded buses, bus stops, Metro trains and Metro stations are among the thieves' favourite haunts. They often work in teams: one or two of them may grab your bag or camera (or your arm and leg), and while you're holding on to it for dear life another will pick your pocket. Or one may 'drop' a coin or other object in a crowded bus and as he 'looks for it', a pocket will be picked in the jostling. Pickpockets also often carry razor blades with which they slit pockets, bags or straps. The operative principle is to outnumber you, confuse you, and to get you off balance. Here's what happened to John:

I was sitting in a bus on Insurgentes with my wallet in a front pocket of my jeans and a small bag on my lap. The other seats were all full but there was plenty of standing room. A youth, apparently with a crippled leg, started looking for something behind my seat. I looked too and found a card with his picture on it, which he then showed me, insistently. I didn't understand what he was trying to say until a couple of men beside him started motioning me to stand up – one of them even grabbed my arm and tried to lift me out of my seat. I guessed the card was an authorisation for a disabled person to take a seat on a bus, and stood up.

Suddenly I was off balance, somehow trapped by the three men's arms and legs. One tried to pull my bag from my hand but I clung to it. I tried to get my other hand down to cover my wallet but my arm was being held and I felt another hand lift the wallet out. Then in a flash the three were off the bus. I ran to the door but they had already disappeared.

Robbery Robberies and muggings are much less common than pocket-picking and purse-snatching, but they are on the increase. Tom Brosnahan was robbed at gun and knife-point in Mexico City on a quiet Sunday afternoon – he was not harmed, and lost little, as his valuables were in the hotel safe. Robbery is much easier to prevent than theft, but much more serious when it happens as the robbers may force you to remove your moneybelt or neckstrap pouch, watch, rings etc. Usually robbers will not harm you. What they want is your money, fast.

To avoid being robbed in cities, do not go where there are few other people. This includes empty streets at night, empty Metro carriages at night, little-used pedestrian underpasses, and similar lonely places. Tom was robbed in the pedestrian underpass beneath Reforma near the Cine Diana and Chapultepec park. Robbers work these underpasses regularly.

On beaches and in the countryside, do not camp overnight in lonely places unless you can be sure it's safe.

Reporting a Theft or Robbery There's little point in going to the police after a robbery unless your loss is insured, in which case you'll need a statement from the police to present to your insurance company. You'll probably have to communicate with them in Spanish, so if your Spanish is poor take a more fluent speaker. Also take your passport and tourist card, if you still have them. Say you want to *'poner una acta de un robo'* (make a record of a robbery). This should make it clear that you merely want a piece of paper and aren't going to ask the police to do anything inconvenient like look for the thieves or recover your goods. With luck and polite urging you should get the required piece of paper without too much trouble.

Legal Assistance in Mexico

If you should encounter legal troubles with public officials or local businesspeople anywhere in Mexico, you can contact La Procuraduría de Protección al Turista (Attorney-General for the Protection of the Tourist). English-speaking aides are on the staff at each attorney general's office. There's an office in every state capital and in some other cities as well. The 24-hour national hotline is in Mexico City (☎ (5) 250-01-51, 250-04-93, 250-05-89, 250-01-23); ask the operator for emergency assistance.

WORK

Mexico City is the best place to pick up English-teaching work; Guadalajara is also good. It should also be possible in Monterrey, Puebla and other sizeable cities as well as in places where there are 'gringo' communities, for example San Miguel de Allende and Oaxaca.

English-speaking travellers can find positions teaching in language schools, high schools or universities, or can offer personal tutoring. Positions in institutions are more likely to become available with the beginning of the new school term.

By law, a foreigner working in Mexico must have a permit, but a school will often pay a foreign teacher in the form of a scholarship or *beca*, and thus circumvent the law, or the school's administration will procure the appropriate papers.

The Mexico City News and the yellow pages phone book in large towns are good sources of job opportunities. Contact the various institutions and schools that offer bilingual programmes or classes in English. For universities, arrange an appointment with the director of the language department.

Pay is low but you can live on it. Language schools tend to offer short courses, so that opportunities come up more often, and any commitment is for a shorter time, but they pay less than *preparatorias* (high schools) and universities. The major chain schools pay higher rates, but often require a two-year commitment.

It's helpful to know at least a little Spanish, even though some institutes insist that only English be spoken in class.

ACTIVITIES
Outdoor Sports

Mexicans are not, in general, great lovers of nature or the wilderness experience. There are a few popular day trails; the one up Popocatépetl volcano outside Mexico City can get pretty busy. There is also a small rock-climbing fraternity. For many middle-class Mexicans, the countryside is either a place where peasants work or, if it's picturesque, somewhere to go in your car, have a family picnic, and look at the view.

Fishing and shooting may be bigger news than hiking and camping, but that doesn't keep intrepid gringos from trekking off into what Mexicans consider absurdly rough country. The trails in Copper Canyon (see the North-Central Mexico chapter) are a breeze for the Tarahumara Indians, but a challenge that is increasingly popular among gringo backpackers. *Mexico's Volcanoes* and *Backpacking in Mexico & Central America* are two useful guides (see Books, earlier in this chapter). Nor is cycling a common pastime. Campsites are usually also trailer parks. In some places it is possible to hire horses for the day (see San Cristóbal de las Casas in the Chiapas chapter).

Sport fishing is especially popular off the Pacific coast and in the Sea of Cortés. Check the *Angler's Guide to Baja California* by Tom Miller (Baja Trail Publications).

Water sports are popular in the coastal resorts. Most of the resorts and surrounding towns have shops that will rent equipment such as snorkels, masks and fins, and arrange boat excursions.

Surfing is popular on the Pacific coast of Mexico. A few of the best surf spots include Punta Mesquite and Santa Rosalillita in Baja, and Bahía de Metanche near San Blas where they boast the world's longest wave. Ixtapa and Puerto Escondido are also considered good.

Study Programmes

There are Spanish-language schools in many cities – some private, some attached to the universities. Course lengths range from a week to a year. Often you can enrol in a course on the spot, though some places prefer you to make the arrangements before you come to Mexico.

You may be offered accommodation with a local family as part of the deal – and living with Spanish speakers will help your Spanish as much as any formal tuition. UNAM in Mexico City is one university that offers such courses. The Universidad Vera-cruzana in Xalapa does summer courses, as does the university in Saltillo. Guadalajara also has a Spanish-language school.

Cuernavaca has several private Spanish-language schools, most of which offer courses ranging from a few days to a few months. See the Cuernavaca section of the Mexico City to Acapulco chapter for further information.

There are also a few colleges where foreigners can study Mexico and Latin America in depth – often with credit for college courses at home. Apart from Mexico's regular universities, these include the Universidad de las Américas at Cholula near Puebla, and the Academía Hispano Americana in San Miguel de Allende. Also in San Miguel, the Instituto Allende is popular with foreigners for art, craft and language courses. In Oaxaca, the Instituto Cultural

Oaxaca runs courses in the Spanish, Zapotec and Mixtec languages and in weaving, ceramics and regional dance.

Many Mexican towns have Casas de la Cultura, which are adult education centres offering part-time, usually cheap courses, both practical and theoretical, in a wide variety of arts and crafts. Foreigners are often welcome to join these. In San Miguel de Allende the Bellas Artes offers classes of this kind.

Information is available in the USA about other Spanish-language programmes in Mexico from the National Registration Center for Study Abroad, 823 North Second St, Milwaukee, Wisconsin 53203 (☎ toll-free (800) 558-9988). In Canada contact Ms Doreen Desmarais, 341 Main St, Ottawa, Ontario K1V 8Y6.

The Council on International Educational Exchange, 205 East 42nd St, New York, New York 10017 (☎ (212) 661-1414) lists a wide variety of programmes in various countries. Contact them for more information.

ACCOMMODATION

Accommodation in Mexico ranges from guest houses *(casas de huéspedes)* and youth hostels *(albergues para jóvenes)* through budget hotels and motels to world-class luxury high-rise hotels and lavish holiday resorts.

Advance Reservations

You may want to reserve your room in advance if you plan to travel to touristy areas during the Christmas-New Year holidays, during Semana Santa (Holy Week, the week leading up to Easter), and the summer holiday period during July and August. Hotel reservations may not be necessary in 'business' destinations such as Guadalajara, Mexico City, Monterrey, etc, but will certainly be needed – even in cheap hotels – in Acapulco, Cancún and Veracruz, to name but a few. You should have advance transport reservations as well.

Camping

All beaches in Mexico are public property.

You can camp for nothing on most of them, but you must be very conscious of safety, particularly in tourist areas.

Most equipped campgrounds are set up for travel trailers, RVs and caravans, but accept tent campers at lower rates. You may pay anywhere from US$1 to US$3 to pitch your tent, or up to US$15 for a lavish campground with lots of facilities.

If you plan to camp much, we highly recommend *Camping in Mexico* by Carl Franz (John Muir Publications, Santa Fe, New Mexico) as a resource for what to bring, how and where to camp, outdoor cooking and other camping topics.

Cabañas & Hammocks

These are two of the cheapest forms of accommodation, usually found in low-key beach spots along the coasts. Cabañas are palm-thatched huts – some have dirt floors and nothing inside but a bed; others are more solidly built, with electric light, mosquito nets, fans and even cookers. Prices range from US$2 up to US$15 per person.

You can rent a hammock and a place to hang it for a dollar or two in some beach places – usually under a palm roof outside a small casa de huéspedes or a fishing family's hut. If you bring your own hammock the cost may be even less. It's easy enough to buy hammocks in Mexico; Mérida in Yucatán and Mitla in Oaxaca are two places special-ising in them.

Hostels

Albergues para jovenes (youth hostels) exist in the major university towns and in some resort towns. Sometimes they are of use to travellers; other times cheap hotels are pref-erable. Most hostels are run by the Consejo Nacional de Recursos para la Atención de la Juventud (CREA), which is associated with the International Youth Hostel Association (IYHA). IYHA cards can be used or you can obtain a CREA card at the hostel. The charge is US$3 to US$5 per night for members and slightly more for nonmembers.

Casas de Huéspedes

The cheapest and most congenial lodging is often the casa de huéspedes, a home converted into simple guest lodgings. A double can cost anywhere from US$5 to US$10 with or without meals.

Cheap Hotels

These exist in virtually every Mexican city and town, including the posh resorts. Facilities and prices vary according to location, but you can get a double room with private shower and hot water in the centre of Mexico City for as little as US$10 to US$15. In Cancún you may have to pay US$20 to US$25 for a comparable room; in many smaller, less touristed towns you can get one for US$5 to US$10.

Middle & Top-End Hotels

Mexico specialises in good middle-range hotels where a double room with private shower, TV, and perhaps even air-conditioning, lift and maybe a restaurant and bar costs between US$15 and US$40. These places are usually pleasant, comfortable without being luxurious, respectable and safe.

Among the most charming of the middle-range hotels are the old mansions and inns turned into hotels. Some date from colonial times, others from the 19th century. Most are wonderfully atmospheric. Some are 'authentic' and a bit spartan (but lower in price), others have been 'updated' with modern facilities, and can be quite posh. These are the lodgings you will remember most fondly after your trip.

Mexico has a full selection of large, modern hotels, particularly in the largest cities and resorts. These offer expected levels of luxury at expectedly lofty prices. If you like to stay in luxury but also enjoy saving some money, choose a luxury hotel in a Mexican chain (Krystal, Calinda, Hostales de México, etc) rather than an international chain, or choose a Mexican luxury hotel that is not part of a chain.

If you're on a short holiday from the USA and want as much as possible for your money, sign up for one of the many package deals offered in US Sunday newspaper travel sections. Most travel agents should also be able to help you. The packages often include 25% to 45% discounts on room rates, a rented car and airport transfers.

FOOD

Mexicans eat three meals a day: breakfast (desayuno), lunch (almuerzo) or dinner (comida), and supper (cena). Each includes one or more of three national staples:

Tortillas are thin round patties of pressed corn (maíz) or wheat flour (harina) dough cooked on griddles. Both can be wrapped around or served under any type of food.

Frijoles are beans, eaten boiled, fried, or refried, in soups, on tortillas or with eggs.

Chiles are spicy-hot peppers which come in dozens of varieties and are consumed in hundreds of ways. Some types such as the *habanero* and *serrano* are always very hot, while others such as the *poblano* vary in spiciness according to when they were picked. If you are unsure about your tolerance for hot chiles, ask if the chile is *dulce* (sweet), *picante* (spicy-hot), or *muy picante* (very spicy-hot).

Breakfast

The simplest breakfast is coffee or tea and *pan dulce* (sweet rolls), a basket of which is set on the table; you pay for the number consumed. You can often have dry cereal or cooked cereal such as oatmeal (avena). More elaborate breakfasts include fruit juice (jugo de fruta), toast (pan tostado) with butter *(mantequilla)* and jam *(mermelada)*, and eggs *(huevos)*, which are served in a variety of ways:

huevos cocidos – hard-boiled eggs
huevos estrellados – fried eggs
huevos fritos (con jamón/tocino) – fried eggs (with ham/bacon)
huevos mexicanos – eggs scrambled with tomatoes, onions, chiles and garlic
huevos Motuleños – tortilla topped with slices of ham, then fried eggs, topped with cheese, peas and tomato sauce
huevos poches – poached eggs

Lunch

Almuerzo is perhaps a North American borrowing, as the Hispanic tradition is to eat a large midday meal, the comida (see below). Almuerzo is like the comida, but perhaps lighter.

Dinner

La comida, the biggest meal of the day, is usually served between 1 and 3 or 4 pm. Most restaurants offer special fixed-price menus called *comida corrida, cubierto, menú del día, platillo del día*, or even *lonch comercial*. These constitute the best food bargains, because you get several courses (often with some choice) for much less than such a meal would cost à la carte. Prices range from a mere US$1.50 for a very simple three-course meal of soup, meat dish, rice and coffee, to US$10 or more for elaborate repasts beginning with oyster stew and finishing with profiteroles.

Supper

La cena, the evening meal, is a junior version of la comida, but usually lighter. Fixed-price multi-course value-for-money meals are rarely offered in the evening, so plan to eat your main meal at lunchtime.

Snacks

Antojitos, or 'little whims', are Mexican traditional snacks or light dishes – some are not really all that light. Here are some of the standard ones:

burrito – any combination of beans, cheese, meat, chicken or seafood seasoned with salsa or chile and wrapped in a wheat flour tortilla
chilaquiles – scrambled eggs with chiles and bits of tortillas
chiles rellenos poblano – chiles stuffed with cheese, meat or other foods, dipped in egg whites, fried and baked in sauce
enchilada – ingredients similar to those used in tacos and burritos wrapped in a flour tortilla, dipped in sauce and then baked or fried. Enchiladas Suizas (Swiss enchiladas) come in a blanket of thick cream
machaca – cured, dried and shredded beef or pork mixed with eggs, onions, cilantro and chiles
quesadilla – flour tortilla topped or filled with cheese and occasionally other ingredients and then heated

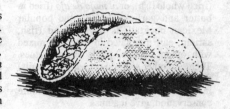

taco – a soft or crisp corn tortilla wrapped or folded around the same fillings as in a burrito
tamale – corn dough stuffed with meat, beans, chiles or nothing at all, wrapped in corn husks and steamed
tostada – flat, crisp tortilla topped with meat or cheese, tomatoes, beans and lettuce

Soup

Besides these soups *(sopas)* there are others made from various vegetables and seafoods.

caldo – broth
gazpacho – chilled vegetable soup spiced with hot chiles

menudo – popular tripe soup made with the spiced entrails of various four-legged beasts

pozole – rich, spicy stew of hominy (large maize kernels) with meat and vegetables.

sopa de ajo – garlic soup with egg yolk

sopa de cebolla – onion soup

sopa de chícharos – pea soup

sopa de fideos – vermicelli soup

sopa de lentejas – lentil soup

sopa de Médula – bone-marrow soup

sopa de pollo – chicken's feet in a thin chicken broth

sopa de verduras – vegetable soup

Note that *sopa de arroz* is not soup at all but rice pilaf.

Seafood

Seafood is good along the coasts, and in the major cities where customers abound. Be suspicious of seafood in out-of-the-way mountain towns.

Fish is often eaten as a *filete* (filet), *frito* (fried whole fish), or *al mojo de ajo* (fried in butter and garlic). *Ceviche*, the popular Mexican cocktail, is raw seafood (fish, shrimp, etc) marinated in lime and mixed with onions, chiles, garlic and tomatoes. There are other seafood *cocteles* (cocktails) as well. *Tortuga* (turtle) is sometimes served in restaurants. In the interests of wildlife conservation, give it a miss.

Fish

anchoas – anchovies

arenques – herring

atún – tuna

robalo – sea bass

corvina – bass

filete de pescado – fish filet

huachinango – red snapper

lenguado – flounder or sole

merluza – hake (type of cod)

mojarra – perch

pescado – fish after it has been caught

pez espada – swordfish

pez – fish which is alive in the water

salmon (ahumada) – (smoked) salmon

sardinas – sardines

sierra – mackerel

tiburón – shark

trucha del mar – sea trout

trucha – trout

Shellfish

abulón – abalone

almejas – clams

calamares – squid

camarones gigantes – prawns

camarones – shrimp

cangrejo – large crab

caracol – snail

jaiba – small crab

langosta – lobster

mariscos – shellfish

ostiones – oysters

Meat

bistec, bistec de res – beefsteak

borrego – sheep

cabrito – kid (small goat)

cabro, cabra – goat

carne – meat, usually beef if not otherwise specified

carne asada – tough but tasty grilled beef

carnero – mutton

carnitas – deep-fried pork

cerdo – pork

chicharrón – deep-fried pork rind; pigskin cracklings

chorizo – spicy pork sausage

conejo – rabbit

cordero – lamb

hígado – liver

jamón – ham

puerco – pork

res – beef

ternera – veal

tocino – bacon
venado – deer (venison)

Fowl

aves – fowl, birds
codorniz – quail
faisan – pheasant; turkey
ganso – goose
guajalote – turkey
pato – duck
pavo – turkey
pechuga – chicken breast
perdiz – partridge
pollo – chicken

Cuts & Preparation

a la parrilla – grilled, perhaps over charcoal
a la plancha – 'planked', split and roasted
a la tampiqueña – sauteed thin slice of meat
a la veracruzana – topped with tomato and green olive sauce
ahumado – smoked
al carbón – charcoal-grilled
al horno – baked
al mojo de ajo – in garlic sauce
alambre – shish kebab, 'en brochette'
asado, asada – roasted
barbacoa – literally 'barbecued', but meat is covered and placed under hot coals.
bien cocido – well done
birria – barbecued on a spit
cabeza – head
chuleta – chop
cocido – boiled
coctel – appetiser (seafood, fruit, etc) in sauce
costillas – ribs
empanizada – breaded
filete – filet of fish or meat
frito – fried
lengua – tongue
lomo – loin
milanesa – breaded (Italian-style)
patas – trotters (feet)
pechuga – chicken breast
pibil – roasted (Yucatán)
pierna – leg
poco cocido – rare
riñones – kidneys

Fruit

chabacanos – apricots
ciruelas – yellow plums
coco – coconut
dátil – date
duraznos – peaches
ensalada de frutas – plain mixed seasonal fruits
frambuesas – raspberries
fresas – strawberries, but also used to refer to any berries
fruta – fruit
granada – pomegranate
guanabana – green pear-like fruit
guayaba – guava
higo – fig
limón – lime or lemon
macedonia de frutas – mixed fruit salad
mamey – sweet orange tropical fruit
mango – mango
manzana – apple
melón – melon
naranja – orange
papaya – papaya
pera – pear
piña – pineapple
plátano – banana
toronja – grapefruit
tuña – prickly pear cactus fruit
uvas – grapes
zapote – sweet fruit of chicle tree

Vegetables

Verduras (vegetables) are rarely served as separate dishes, but are often mixed into salads, soups and sauces or used as garnishes.

aceitunas – olives
aguacate – avocado pear
apio – celery
arroz – rice
calabaza – squash or pumpkin
cebolla – onion
champiñones – mushrooms (see *hongos*)
chícharos – peas
col – cabbage
coliflor – cauliflower
ejotes – green beans

elote – corn on the cob; commonly served from steaming bins on street carts.
ensalada verde – green salad
espárragos – asparagus
espinaca – spinach
frijoles – beans, usually black
hongos – mushrooms
jícama – sweet yellow turnip
lechuga – lettuce
lentejas – lentils
legumbres – vegetables
papas – potatoes
papas fritas – fried potatoes, chips
pepino – cucumber
rabano – radish
tomate – tomato
verduras – vegetables
zanahoria – carrot

Dessert/Sweets *(Postre)*
arroz con leche – rice pudding
flan – custard; crème caramel
galletas – cookies/biscuits
helado – ice cream
nieve – ice cream, sherbet
pastel – pastry or cake
pay – fruit pie
queso – cheese

Street Food
elote – corn on the cob, boiled or roasted
exquisitas – hot dogs
nieve – American 'snow cone': powdered ice flavoured with syrup
paleta – flavoured ice on a stick

Other Foods
bocole – thick tortilla wrapped around beans, etc
crepa – crepe, thin pancake
entremeses – hors d'oeuvres
guacamole – mashed avocados mixed with onions, chile sauce, lemons, tomatoes and other ingredients
hamburguesa – hamburger
lavín – yoghurt
leche – milk
mole – sauce made from chiles and other ingredients, often served over chicken or turkey

mole poblano – Puebla-style mole, with over 30 ingredients including many hot chiles and bitter chocolate
queso – cheese
queso fundido – melted cheese
salchichas – sausages, often knockwurst
salsa – sauce made with chiles, onions, tomato, lemon or lime juice and spices
salsa verde – *salsa* with hot green chiles
sandwich – US-style sandwich on square-loaf bread
torta – Mexican-style sandwich in a roll

At the Table
Note that *el menú* can mean either the menu, or the special set-price meal of the day. If you want the menu, ask for *la lista* or *la carta* or you may inadvertently order the set-price meal.

aceite – oil
azúcar – sugar
bolillo – French-style bread rolls
catsup – ketchup; US-style spiced tomato sauce
cilantro – fresh coriander leaf
copa – glass
crema – cream
cuchara – spoon
cuchillo – knife
cuenta – bill
mantequilla – butter
margarina – margarine
mostaza – mustard
pan (integral) – (whole-grain) bread
pimienta – pepper
plato – plate
propina – the tip; 10% to 15% of the bill
sel – salt
servilleta – napkin
taza – cup
tenedor – fork
vaso – glass
vinagre – vinegar

DRINKS
A variety of drinks *(bebidas)*, both alcoholic and non-alcoholic, are available – as befits a country with such a warm climate.

Tea & Coffee

Mexican *café*, grown mostly near Córdoba and Orizaba and in Chiapas, can be somewhat coarse like the African varieties, but is always flavourful. In a few areas such as Córdoba and Orizaba, sugar is mixed with the coffee after it is ground, and unsweetened coffee is difficult to obtain. Mexican tea, invariably from bags, is usually a profound disappointment to any real tea drinker.

Nescafé – instant coffee
café instantaneo – instant coffee
café sin azúcar – coffee without sugar
espresso – espresso, brewed by steam pressure.
café negro – black coffee
café americano – black coffee
café con leche – coffee with hot milk, half and half
café con crema – coffee with cream, served separately
té de manzanillo – camomile tea
té negro – black tea

Fruit Drinks

Fresh fruit and vegetable juices (*jugos*) are popular in Mexico, and readily available from streetside stalls. All of the fruits and a few of the squeezable vegetables are used.

Licuados are blends of fruit or juice with water and sugar, and perhaps raw egg, milk, ice, and flavourings such as vanilla or nutmeg. The delicious combinations are practically limitless.

Aguas frescas are made by mixing fruit juice or a syrup made from mashed grains or seeds with sugar and water. You will usually see them in big glass jars on the counters of juice stands. Try the *agua fresca de arroz* (literally 'rice water'); it has a sweet nutty taste.

Soft Drinks

Mexico offers a variety of *refrescos* (soft drinks), including some interesting and tasty variations on the overly-familiar colas and lemon-flavoured drinks. *Sidral* and *Manzanita* are two apple-flavoured brands. *Toronja* (grapefruit) is tart and refreshing. Other types such as *fresa* (strawberry), *limón* (lime) and *cereza* (cherry) tend to be too sweet.

Alcohol

Mexico produces a fascinating variety of intoxicating drinks from grapes, grains and cacti.

Drinking Places Everyone knows about Mexican cantinas, those pits of wild drinking and even wilder displays of machismo. Tom has been in a cantina in Mexico City where it was hardly noticed when a man drew his pistol and fired several rounds into the ceiling. Cantinas are usually loud, but not that loud.

Cantinas are not usually marked as such, but can be identified by signs prohibiting minors from entering, from wild-west type swinging half-doors, and from the generally raucous atmosphere.

Cantinas are usually for men only – no women or children allowed. If you enter one, you must be prepared to drink hard. You may be challenged by a local to go one-for-one at a bottle of tequila, mezcal or brandy, and you had better have a cast-iron liver. If you're not up to this, excuse yourself and beat a retreat.

Some of the nicer cantinas don't get upset about the presence of a woman if accompanied by a regular patron. Leave judgement of the situation up to a local, though, and tread lightly or there could be trouble.

Besides cantinas, Mexico has lots of bars, lounges, 'pubs' and cafés to which all are welcome and where the excesses of machismo are toned down. No sign differentiates a cantina from a bar or lounge, though.

Mezcal, Tequila & Pulque Mezcal can be made from the sap of several species of the *maguey* plant, which resembles a porcupine with long, wide, slightly curved spikes. Tequila is made only from the maguey called *agave tequilana* that grows in and around the town of Tequila. The spikes of the maguey are stripped away to expose the plant's core or *piña*. The *piña* is chopped, roasted, shredded and then pressed to remove the juice. Sugar is added to the juice and, after the resulting mixture has fermented for four days, it is put through two distillation processes. During bottling, a repugnant worm (*gusano*) is added to each bottle.

After distillation the mezcal and tequila are aged in wooden casks for periods ranging from four months to seven years. The final product is a clear liquid (sometimes artificially tinted to gold) which is at its most potent as tequila. The longer the ageing, the smoother the drink and the higher the price.

The traditional steps in drinking mezcal or tequila are:

1) lick the back of your hand and sprinkle salt on it
2) lick the salt
3) suck on a lime
4) down a shot of mezcal or tequila in one gulp
5) lick more salt

When the bottle is empty, you are supposed to eat the worm.

For foreigners not used to the potency of straight tequila, Mexican bartenders invented the Margarita, a concoction of tequila, lime juice and orange liqueur served in a salt-rimmed glass. Fresh fruit such as strawberries and peaches can be added.

Pulque is a mildly alcoholic drink derived directly from the sap of the maguey. The foamy, milky drink spoils quickly and thus cannot easily be bottled and shipped throughout Mexico. Most pulque is produced in the region around Mexico City and served in *pulquerías*. There are several excellent pulquerías in Mexico City around the Plaza Garibaldi.

Beer Breweries were first established in Mexico by German immigrants in the late 19th century. Mexico's several large brewing companies now produce more than 25 brands of beer (cerveza). Each major company has a premium beer such as Bohemia and Corona de Barril (usually served in bottles), several standard beers such as Carta Blanca, Superior and Dos Equis, and 'popular' brands such as Corona, Tecate and Modelo. All are blond lagers meant to be served chilled. Some places serve beer barely cooled, so it's a good idea to ask for *una cerveza fría* (a cold beer).

Each of the large companies also produces a dark beer such as Modelo Negro and Tres Equis, but these are sometimes difficult to find in the smaller towns.

There are some regional beers as well, brewed to similar tastes.

Wine & Brandy Wine is not as popular in Mexico as beer and tequila, even though the country's three large vintners produce some quite drinkable vintages.

Pedro Domecq is best known for its Los Reyes table wines and its various brandies. Formex-Ybarra has more than 800 acres of vineyards in the Valle de Guadalupe and is known for its Terrasola table wine. Bodegas de Santo Tomás hopes to eventually produce wines which can compete with California's. It is run by the Tchelistcheffs, a California-based vintner family. They have planted several varieties of grapes from California and have recently begun producing Pinot Noir, Chardonnay and Cabernet wines which are worth a try.

ENTERTAINMENT

Nothing beats a Mexican fiesta for entertainment, but if none is being celebrated at the moment, you have alternatives. The larger cities all have cheap cinemas screening local and foreign films, with most of the foreign films being dubbed in Spanish. Also in the larger cities, the range of nightspots is extensive, with opera, symphony, recitals, theatre (in Spanish), music clubs (jazz, salsa, mariachi, rock, etc), coffee houses, supper clubs, dance halls, bars and lounges abounding.

In smaller towns the best you can expect is a primitive cinema and a bar, perhaps with entertainment, in the best local hotel. Performances of folk dance range from the simple, local and authentic, done at a village fiesta, to the dazzlingly elaborate such as Mexico City's Ballet Folklórico.

THINGS TO BUY

When most visitors to Mexico think of souvenirs, they think of handicrafts. Most *artesanías* (handicrafts) originated in objects made for everyday use or for specific occasions such as festivals. Today many objects are made simply to sell as 'folk art' – some purely decorative, others with a useful function – but that doesn't necessarily reduce their quality. Although traditional materials, particularly textiles, are rarer than they used to be, some artisans have used the opportunity of tourism to develop their artistic talents to high levels.

The places where crafts are made aren't necessarily the best places to buy them. There's wide trade in artesanías, and you'll often find a better selection in towns and cities than in the original villages. Nor are prices necessarily much higher in the bigger centres. Oaxaca city, for instance, is the major clearing-house for handicrafts from all over the state of Oaxaca, and the number of stores selling them helps keep prices competitive. On the other hand, goods from Oaxaca become more expensive when they're transported to Mexico City or elsewhere.

You can get a good overview of the best that's available, and an idea of prices, by looking round some of the city stores devoted to these products. Buying in these places also saves the time and effort of seeking out the sometimes remote towns and villages where items are made. The government-run Fonart shops in several cities usually have a good range of high-quality stock at decent prices. In Mexico City and San Miguel de Allende the shops have a wide range of crafts from all over Mexico. The Bazar Sábado (Saturday Bazaar) at San Ángel in Mexico City always has some of the best of Mexican folk art.

The local markets in San Cristóbal de las Casas, Oaxaca, Toluca, Cuetzalán (Puebla), Ocotlán and Tlacolula (near Oaxaca) are among those with good ranges of crafts.

Pottery

Pots come in a wide variety of shapes, in both unglazed earthenware and sturdier, Spanish-influenced, glazed ware, often highly decorated. Most are fairly cheap.

One of Mexico's most intriguing and distinctive pottery forms is the tree of life. The lavishly worked candelabra-like forms are often colourfully painted, usually with a religious, mythological or contemporary themes. The works of Heron Martínez of Acatlán in Puebla are reckoned to be the best. There are also several artisans in Izucar de Matamoros, Puebla, who use this form. Metepec in the state of Mexico is another tree of life centre, also known for its clay suns. Packing these fragile items to take home is a challenge.

Other styles include Talavera, a glazed, colourfully painted pottery (plates, cups, tiles) from Puebla.

The villages of San Bartolo Coyotepec and Atzompa, both close to Oaxaca city, are the two main pottery centres in that state. San Bartolo produces attractive and reasonably priced unglazed black pottery in multiple forms. Atzompa turns out 'embroidered' clay pieces – including interesting pagan-looking 'earth mother' figures and Last Supper scenes – as well as distinctive green-glazed ware.

The Chiapan village of Amatenango del Valle turns out earthenware jugs, vases and animals, fired not in kilns but in open fires, and painted in pleasing 'natural' colours.

Tonalá, a suburb of Guadalajara, produces animals glazed in red, blue and brown on cream backgrounds. The town of Patamba, Michoacán makes green-glazed pineapple-shaped pots and jars.

Tarascan pottery, decorated with simple swan, fish and fishing designs, is produced in Tzintzuntzan in Michoacán.

Textiles

The colourful hand-woven and embroidered Indian costumes come in a number of basic shapes and as many designs as there are weavers. The states of Oaxaca, Chiapas and Puebla boast a truly bewildering variety of patterns, and Yucatán has good textiles as well.

Some of the finest huipiles (traditional smock-like embroidered blouses) are made in Mérida, Yucatán. Cheaper are the colourful waist fajas (sashes) available in several of the good textile states.

A *sarape* is a type of blanket which can also be worn poncho-style: among the best are those of Jocotepec near Guadalajara and Pátzcuaro in Michoacán. Teotitlán del Valle in Oaxaca turns out an enormous number and variety of blankets and rugs in excellent designs.

Santa María del Río near San Luis Potosí and Tenancingo in the state of Mexico produce some of the best wool or cotton shawls known as *rebozos*.

The Huichol Indians of Jalisco make colourful and interesting 'yarn paintings' with designs clearly influenced by peyote, which is central to Huichol culture.

Attractive table cloths and wall hangings, embroidered with multitudes of colourful animals and plants, are produced in several places in central and southern Mexico. Tenango de Doria (Hidalgo), San Pablito (Puebla) and San Mateo del Mar (Oaxaca) are three villages where they are made, but they can be found in many towns and cities.

Other Woven Goods

Many goods are woven all over the country from palm, straw, reeds or sisal (rope made from the henequén cactus). Mérida is a centre for sisal mats, hammocks, bags and hats. The state of Oaxaca also turns out many palm mats and baskets, as well as useful string bags *(bolsas)*. Ocotlán and Oaxaca markets are good places to find them. The Tarascan Indians of Tzintzuntzan in Michoacán produce mats and figurines from reeds.

Leather Goods

Shoes, boots and leather accessories are often of good quality in Mexico, and much cheaper than at home. The city of León is a shoe-making centre, but in fact every city has dozens of good shoestores. Check quality and fit carefully before you buy. Mexicans use metric footwear sizes.

Silver, Gold & Copper

Taxco, between Cuernavaca and Mexico City, is Mexico's main silversmithing centre; San Miguel de Allende and Oaxaca also have good jewellery. Guanajuato is a centre for gold jewellery, sometimes decorated with turquoise. Santa Clara del Cobre in Michoacán, a copper-mining centre since 1553, has over 50 workshops producing well-worked bowls, candlesticks, lamps and hand-hammered plates. A cheap and quite attractive product found widely is tinplate, beaten and painted into a multitude of designs – the sort of thing that would hang well on a Christmas tree.

Woodwork

Ceremonial masks are widely used and you can buy them in cities like Oaxaca, San Cristóbal de las Casas and Mexico City. San Miguel de Allende and Cuernavaca are centres for wooden furniture. Probably the finest guitars are made in Paracho, Michoacán. Some villages around Oaxaca city are now producing attractive, colourfully painted wooden animals and birds. *Amate* paintings (done on tree bark) are widely available and make pleasing, affordable souvenirs.

Lacquerware This attractive craft involves the decoration of wood – boxes, trays, etc – or gourds with layers of colourful and protective lacquer paint. Several towns specialise in it, and the best work is from Olinalá in Guerrero and Uruapan in Michoacán.

Getting There & Away

Most visitors to Mexico arrive by air, but there are also approaches by road and rail from the USA and Guatemala, and by road from Belize. There's also a little-known jungle route via back-country bus and riverboat from Flores in Guatemala's El Petén to Tenosique in Tabasco and and Palenque in Chiapas.

AIR

To/From the USA & Canada
American, Canadian Airlines International, Continental, Delta, Northwest and United are the US and Canadian airlines with the most services to Mexico. Aeroméxico and Mexicana are the large Mexican airlines connecting Mexican and foreign cities. Aeroquetzal, Aeronica, Aviateca, COPA, LACSA and TACA are regional Central American airlines with flights between Mexico and the USA.

You can fly nonstop to Mexico from any of these North American cities: Atlanta, Chicago, Dallas/Fort Worth, Denver, Detroit, Houston, Los Angeles, McAllen (Texas), Miami, New Orleans, New York, Orlando, Phoenix, San Antonio, San Diego, San Francisco, San Jose, Tampa/St Petersburg, Toronto, Vancouver and Washington, DC. There are one-stop connecting flights from many others.

If you want to travel overland through northern Mexico, you can fly to a US city on the Mexican border. Continental, for instance, serves Laredo, McAllen (Texas) and San Diego. Transtar links Brownsville (Texas) with several cities in the southeastern USA.

Fares There are dozens of airfares for any given route. Travel agents are the first people to consult about fares and routes. Once you've discovered the basics of the airlines flying, the routes taken and the various discounted tickets available, you can consult your favourite bucket shop, consolidator or charter airline to see if their fares are better. Consolidators in North America are similar to bucket shops in Europe: they buy bulk seats from airlines at considerable discounts and resell them to the public, usually through travel agents. Though there are some shady dealers, most consolidators are quite legitimate. Ask your travel agent about buying a consolidator ticket, or look for the consolidator advertisements in the travel section of the newspaper (they're the ones with tables of destinations and fares and toll-free '800' numbers to call).

Here are some sample full economy round-trip fares and also some round-trip excursion fares (called fixed-date return fares in the UK) from various cities to Mexico City:

City	Full fare	Excursion
Chicago	US$802	US$464-US$543
Dallas/		
Fort Worth	US$556	US$300-US$380
Los Angeles	US$806	US$480-US$625
Miami	US$600-US$800	US$350-US$400
New York	US$1000	US$450-US$613
Toronto	US$780	US$662-US$707

To/From Europe
Few European airlines fly nonstop to Mexico. Most take you to one of the US hub cities (Atlanta, Dallas/Fort Worth, New York, Miami), where you may change to a US or Mexican airline.

If you want to stop over in the USA on the way to Mexico, there are many options: several airlines including Aeroméxico, American, Continental, Delta and United serve Europe, the USA and Mexico, or you can simply get a ticket to the USA and buy another ticket to Mexico or the border from there. You may have to show 'sufficient funds' to enter the USA if you haven't already got an onward ticket.

The most common types of ticket from

Europe to Mexico are one-ways, fixed-date returns, open returns, circle trips and open-jaws ('ticketed surface sectors'). Most of them are available at discount rates from cheap ticket agencies in Europe's bargain flight centres like London, Amsterdam, Paris and Frankfurt.

Open tickets are usually valid for 180 days or a year and are a bit more expensive than fixed-date returns. Circle trips and open-jaws are useful if you want to travel from one part of Mexico to another, or between Mexico and elsewhere on the American continents without backtracking. You usually depart from, and return to, the same city in Europe: circle trips give you flights between your different destinations in Mexico or Latin America en route, while with open jaw tickets you make your own way between your entry and exit points in Latin America.

Some bargain fares are only open to students, teachers or people under 26. Fares can also vary considerably between high and low seasons.

London For cheap tickets, pick up a copy of *Time Out, TNT* or any of the other magazines that advertise discount (bucket shop) flights, and check out a few of the advertisers. The magazine *Business Traveller* also has a great deal of good advice on air fare bargains. Most bucket shops are trustworthy and reliable but the occasional sharp operator appears – *Time Out* and *Business Traveller* give some useful advice on precautions to take.

Agents offering good-value fares to Mexico include Journey Latin America (☎ (081) 747-3108) at 16 Devonshire Rd, Chiswick, London W4 2HD (this company also has an information service for its customers and runs some small-group tours to Mexico); STA (☎ (071) 581-1022) at 74 Old Brompton Rd, London W1 and 117 Euston Rd, London NW1; and London Student Travel (☎ (071) 730-3402) at 52 Grosvenor Gardens, London SW1. Standard fares to Mexico City from London start at about £250 one way and £400 return.

An unusual and potentially interesting route to Mexico is via Paris and Havana with the Cuban airline Cubana. Journey Latin America quotes around US$350 one-way and US$550 return for this.

Elsewhere in Europe Discount tickets are available at prices similar to London's in several European cities. Amsterdam, Paris and Frankfurt are among the main cheap flight centres. Tickets on Air France, KLM, Iberia and the Colombian airline Avianca are sold through discount agents. KLM, Air France and Iberia all offer open jaw fares between Europe and numerous places in Latin America (Iberia's are particularly good value), and Avianca has some interesting round-trip options.

To/From Australasia

There are no direct flights from Australia or New Zealand to Mexico. The cheapest way to get there is via the USA, often through Los Angeles. From Sydney/Melbourne to Mexico City via Los Angeles costs from A$1050 one way and A$1750 return. A fixed date return (excursion) fare from Auckland, New Zealand, to South America stopping in Los Angeles, Mexico, Buenos Aires, Lima and Santiago, is around NZ$2700.

Discount returns from Sydney to Los Angeles start around A$1300. Cheap flights from the USA to Mexico are hard to find in Australia. Regular Los Angeles-Mexico City fares are US$400 one way, US$806 return – but you should be able to pick up a cheaper ticket (say, US$500 or so return) if you stop a day or two in Los Angeles. There are also numerous flights between North American cities and several other destinations in Mexico (see To/From the USA & Canada).

Round-the-World Tickets RTW tickets have become very popular in the last few years and many of these pass through Australia; some have a Mexico option. The official airline RTW tickets are usually put together by a combination of two airlines, and permit you to fly anywhere you want on their route systems so long as you do not backtrack.

An alternative type of RTW ticket is one put together by a travel agent using a combination of discounted tickets. Round-the-world tickets with a Mexico option are sometimes available in Australia. STA Travel, with 40 offices around the country, is one of the most popular discount travel agents in Australia. It also has sales offices or agents all over the world.

RTW fares including Latin American connections cost about A$3200. You may also be able to get a Circle Pacific ticket which includes Mexico City for around A$2800.

To/From Guatemala & Belize

Inter (formerly Aerocaribe) flies from Flores (near Tikal), Guatemala, to Cancún several times weekly for US$150 to US$175 one way (single). They also connect Cancún and Belize City for US$100 with daily flights. Aeroquetzal, a small but growing Guatemalan airline, flies from Guatemala City to Cancún twice a week for US$175 one way.

To/From Latin America & the Caribbean

Aeroméxico flies between Mexico City and Panama City, Caracas and Bogotá. Mexicana links Mexico City with Guatemala City, San Juan (Puerto Rico), Havana and San José (Costa Rica); it also has flights between San Juan and Cancún, and Havana and Mérida. Avianca, the Colombian airline, also links Mexico with South America. Cubana flies between Havana and Mexico City.

Departure Tax

A departure tax equivalent to approximately US$12 is levied in Mexico. If you buy your air ticket in Mexico, the tax will be included in your ticket cost; if you bought your ticket abroad, you will have to pay the tax in cash (preferably pesos, or US dollars) at airport check-in.

LAND

You can enter by road from the USA or Belize, or by road or boat from Guatemala.

To/From the USA

There are over 20 official crossing points in these US states on the USA-Mexico border:

Arizona: Douglas/Agua Prieta and Nogales/Nogales (both open 24 hours); Naco/Naco, San Luis/San Luis Río Colorado, Sasabe/Sasabe and Lukeville/Sonoita.

California: San Diego/Tijuana and Calexico/Mexicali (both open 24 hours); Otay/Mesa (open 6 am to 10 pm); and Algodones/Tecate (open 7 am to 8 pm).

New Mexico: Columbus/Palomas.

Texas: El Paso/Ciudad Juárez, Brownsville/Matamoros and Laredo/Nuevo Laredo (all open 24 hours); Rio Grande City/Camargo, Del Rio/Ciudad Acuña, Los Saenz/Ciudad Alemán, Fabens/Guadalupe Bravos, Progreso/Nuevo Progreso, Presidio/Ojinaga, Eagle Pass/Piedras Negras, Fort Hancock/Praxedis Guerrero and McAllen/Reynosa, all with more limited hours.

Bus Greyhound buses serve Brownsville, Calexico, El Paso, Laredo and San Diego. To reach other border crossings, transfer from Greyhound to a smaller line. At the border, transfer to a Mexican bus.

From bus stations in US border towns, a few Mexican buses depart for destinations deep inside Mexico, but these buses usually cost significantly more than buses from the towns on the Mexican side. For a better selection of companies, routes and fares, walk or take a local bus or taxi across the border to the Mexican bus terminal. See the sections on the Mexican border towns for details.

If you plan to travel extensively by bus in the USA, you might consider purchasing a bus pass. Greyhound's Ameripass, sold at most Greyhound terminals, allows you unlimited travel for seven, 15 or 30 days at set prices. The International Ameripass, available to foreign students, research scholars and lecturers (with their families) who have been in the USA for less than a year, costs even less. The International Ameripass can be bought only at Greyhound terminals in New York City, Miami, Los Angeles and San Francisco after completing an affidavit and presenting your passport to Greyhound officials.

Train Travelling by train through the USA to the Mexican border can be quite enjoyable, but it certainly takes more time than flying and it may not be much cheaper when you add in the cost of meals and incidental expenses. Compare prices and times before you decide.

Amtrak (☎ (800) 872-7245) serves three US cities from which access to Mexico is easy. From El Paso (Texas) you cross to Ciudad Juárez to continue your trip by bus, air or on the Ferrocarriles Nacionales de México (Mexican National Railways). From San Antonio (Texas) you can take a bus to the border at Eagle Pass, Del Rio or Laredo and continue your trip by bus or air. From the Santa Fe Amtrak terminal in San Diego (California) you can take a 'San Ysidro' trolley directly to the border, cross to Tijuana, and continue your journey by bus or air.

Car You can easily drive through the USA to Mexico, but when you get to the border, there are some things to consider.

You can leave your car on the US side of the border and continue into Mexico by public transport. Negotiate with a car park or garage owner in one of the US border towns for a safe place to leave your car.

If you take your car into Mexico, you must deal with the problem of unleaded fuel – or, rather, the lack of it. Most US and Canadian cars require unleaded fuel, as fuel with lead will damage their anti-pollution catalytic converters. Several years ago when Pemex, the Mexican government oil company, introduced its unleaded *Magna Sin* petrol, it vowed to make it readily available on all major highways. Availability is still uneven, however, and you cannot expect to find it whenever you need it. You have two choices, then:

• Plan to drive only on routes where you may reasonably expect to find unleaded fuel, such as along major highways to major cities. Obviously, this limits the scope of your travel, even if you carry extra cans of fuel with you.

• Across the border in Mexico, have a Mexican mechanic cut out the catalytic converter from your car's exhaust system and weld a straight piece of exhaust pipe in its place. Take your converter with you, and have a mechanic replace it before you re-enter the USA (but after you've used up any leaded fuel in your tank). Note that it is against US federal law to remove pollution control equipment from a vehicle in the USA.

If you plan to travel extensively and independently, the second choice is the one for you.

Car Insurance Mexican law only recognises Mexican car insurance *(seguro)*, so your insurance from any other country will not help you in Mexico.

Though not actually required by law, it is foolish to travel without Mexican liability insurance because if there is an accident and you cannot show a valid insurance policy, you will be arrested and forbidden to leave the immediate area until all claims are settled, which could take weeks or months. Mexico's legal system is modelled on the Napoleonic Code, under which all persons involved in an incident are assumed to be guilty until proven innocent; trial is by a court of three judges, not by jury. Your embassy can do little to help you in such a situation, except to tell you how stupid you were to drive without local insurance.

Mexican insurance is sold in US, Guatemalan and Belizean towns near the Mexican border. Approaching the border from the USA you will see billboards advertising offices selling Mexican policies. At the busiest border-crossing points (Tijuana, Mexicali, Nogales, Agua Prieta, Ciudad Juárez, Nuevo Laredo and Matamoros), there are insurance offices open 24 hours a day.

Prices for Mexican policies are set by law in Mexico, so you can do little in the way of bargain-hunting. Instead of discounts (which cannot be offered), insurance offices offer incentives such as free travel information and/or maps, connections to motoring clubs (American Automobile Association etc) and other treats.

Those seeking short-term policies are pen-

Top: Mexican-made VWs cruise past the Palacio de Bellas Artes, Mexico City (GE)
Bottom: Mexico City (Dept of Tourism)

Top: Xochimilco, Mexico City (PW)
Left: Car park food stall, Mexico City (GE)
Right: Christmas day clean up, the Zócalo, Mexico City (GE)

alised with extremely high rates. Up to 30 days full coverage of a US$5000 car will cost about US$6 per day (US$180 total); after 30 days the daily premium drops. A year's coverage costs only about US$220 to US$300.

Car Permit To drive a motor vehicle (car, motorcycle, boat, etc) into Mexico, you will need a valid driver's licence. Mexican police will recognise US and Canadian licences; international driver's licences and those from other countries may be unfamiliar, but should pass.

You will also need the car's current valid registration. If the registration is in a different name, you will also need some other proof that you own it, such as a notarised bill of sale. If you don't own it, bring a notarised affidavit of authorisation from the car's owner stating that you are allowed to take the car out of the country where it is registered, together with your current valid driving licence. All vehicles must also carry a temporary import permit from the Mexican authorities.

Temporary import permits good for 90 days (and sometimes up to 180 days) are issued for free at the border when you enter, to be surrendered as you leave. You may drive without a permit into the towns on the Mexican side of the US-Mexican border, and all through Baja California, but if you venture further into Mexico you must have one. Customs officials will require it at posts a few km south of each border town, and at the mainland ports for ferries crossing from Baja (get your permit stamped and approved at the Registro Federal de Vehículos in either Tijuana or La Paz).

You must have a permit for each vehicle you bring in. For example, if you have a motorcycle attached to your car, you must also have a permit for the motorcycle, but there is a catch: the Tourist Card and Temporary Import Permit are one and the same document, so one person cannot have more than one permit even if that person owns both vehicles. Consequently, another person travelling with you must obtain the second permit/tourist card.

As with all rules of this sort, however, they are not written in stone. Changes, exceptions and neglect of the rule are not unheard of, especially if the official who might enforce the rule has somehow been induced to do otherwise in the past. (But if you are not requested to provide a 'tip' or 'special fee', don't initiate one.)

Another rule for drivers intending to travel in Mexico: you cannot leave the country without your vehicle. If it breaks down or is wrecked, you must obtain permission from either the Registro Federal de Vehículos (Federal Registry of Vehicles) in Mexico City or a Hacienda (Treasury Department) office in another city or town to leave the car in the country.

This rule means that you should not drive someone else's car across the border unless you're bringing it back yourself. The car will be registered on your tourist card, and you will not be permitted to leave the country without taking the car or paying a huge customs import duty.

To/From Central America
For detailed information on travel in and through Central America, see *La Ruta Maya: Yucatán, Guatemala & Belize – a travel survival kit* and *Central America on a Shoestring*, both published by Lonely Planet.

There is one official crossing point between Mexico and Belize, at Santa Elena/Subteniente López (near Corozal and Chetumal respectively).

There are three official border crossings between Mexico and Guatemala: Tecún Umán/Ciudad Hidalgo, El Carmen/Talisman, and La Mesilla/Ciudad Cuauhtémoc. It is also possible, but not as easy, to cross at El Naranjo/La Palma in the jungles between Flores (Guatemala) and Palenque (Mexico).

Bus A direct bus service connects Guatemala City with the border crossings at La Mesilla/Ciudad Cuauhtémoc in the highlands (on the way to San Cristóbal de las

Casas), and the Pacific slope crossings at Ciudad Tecún Umán/Ciudad Hidalgo and El Carmen/Talismán (both near Tapachula).

The borders are open 24 hours a day but you may have to pay a few 'extra charges' on the Guatemalan side if you want to go through the border before 9 am, after 6 pm or between noon and 2 pm. At night you'll probably also have to wait longer for onward transport into Mexico. There's more information on these border points in the Chiapas chapter.

From Guatemala City to La Mesilla is 342 km (seven hours). Transportes El Condor (☎ (2) 2-85-04), 19 Calle 2-01, Zona 1, Guatemala City, goes to La Mesilla, on the Pan-American Highway at the border with Mexico, at 4, 8 and 10 am, and 1 and 5 pm daily for US$3.

From Guatemala City to Ciudad Tecún Umán is 253 km (five hours). Fortaleza (☎ (2) 51-79-94), 19 Calle 8-70, Zona 1, Guatemala City, has buses at 5.30 and 9.30 am, stopping at Escuintla, Mazatenango, Retalhuleu and Coatepeque.

There is also a direct daily bus service from Flores (near Tikal), in Petén province in Guatemala, right through Belize to Chetumal, in Quintana Roo state (Mexico); it's 350 km and takes nine hours. A special direct 1st-class bus (US$30) departs from the Hotel San Juan in Flores each morning, bypasses Belize City and goes straight to Chetumal. At Chetumal it connects with an ADO bus heading north along the coast to Cancún at 2 pm.

To go 2nd class you must take the Transportes Pinita and Novelo buses to Belize City, then a Batty bus (US$4) to Chetumal. It's slower, less convenient and less comfortable, but less than half the price of the special 1st-class bus.

From Belize City there are frequent services north, via Orange Walk and Corozal, right into Chetumal's bus terminal, a journey of 160 km (four hours; express 3¼ hours). Venus has buses departing from Belize City every hour on the hour from noon to 7 pm for US$3.50. Batty's has buses every two hours on the hour for the same price.

Train There is a passenger service between Guatemala City and Ciudad Tecún Umán/Ciudad Hidalgo (near Tapachula), but it is exceedingly slow, uncomfortable, unreliable and unsafe. Take the bus instead.

There are no railways in Belize.

Car Driving into Mexico from Guatemala or Belize is similar to approaching from the USA. You must obtain a Mexican car permit at the border; you can buy Mexican car insurance at the border or in the first Mexican city along your way. See the section To/From the USA above for more details.

RIVER
Adventurous travellers may want to consider the route from Flores (near Tikal), Guatemala, to Palenque, Mexico. Buses depart from the Hotel San Juan in Flores daily at 5 am and 12.30 pm for El Naranjo on the Río San Pedro (seven hours, US$3). From El Naranjo you must catch a boat on the river and cruise for about four hours to the border town of La Palma. From La Palma you go by bus to Tenosique (1½ hours), then to Emiliano Zapata (40 km, one hour), and from there to Palenque.

It's best to have camping gear. Once an exhausting and perhaps even dangerous trip, this route is now showing up on the itineraries of trekking and adventure tour companies, so it may soon be fast, safe, and even relatively comfortable. Even so, you may want to consult your embassy or consulate before venturing into the jungle.

TOURS
Package holidays to Mexico are available from many countries. Many of them are of the 'nine nights in Acapulco, two in Taxco' variety but others are more varied and worth considering if you want to pack a lot of Mexico into a little time.

Mexican government tourist offices around the world can give you armfuls of brochures about these trips. Most US travel agents can book the packages for you.

Green Tortoise Alternative Travel (☎ (415) 821-0803, or toll-free for all other areas (800) 227-4766), PO Box 24459, San Francisco, California 94124, is a national organisation that offers bus trips through Mexico and Belize.

Mayan Adventure Tours (☎ (206) 523-5309), PO Box 15204, Wedgwood Station, Seattle, Washington 98115-15204, offers small-group tours of obscure Mayan sites that are not easily accessible.

Toucan Adventure Tours (☎ (213) 438-6293), 3135 E. Fourth St, Long Beach, CA 90814, also offers trips for small groups. Their European office (☎ (41-61) 281 08 18; fax 281 08 20) is at Bachlettenstrasse 47, 4054 Basel, Switzerland.

Journey Latin America (☎ (081) 747-8315; fax (081) 747-8315), 14-16 Devonshire Rd, Chiswick, London W4 2HD, runs small-group tours and packages aimed at individual travellers.

Explore Worldwide has offices in Aldershot, England (☎ (025) 231-9448); Sydney, Australia (☎ (02) 290-3222); Remuera, Auckland, New Zealand (☎ 545-118); Edmonton, Canada (☎ (403) 439-9118); Oakland, California (☎ (415) 654-1879); and Hong Kong (☎ 5-225181).

The Travel Business of Dulwich (☎ (081) 299-0214) at 94 Dulwich Village, London SE 21 offers a tour covering Mexico City, the Copper Canyon railway trip and a week at a coastal resort.

Swan Hellenic offers a 20-day Maya art treasures tour from London with 1st-class hotels and guest lecturers.

Mancunia Travel of Manchester, England (☎ (061) 228-2842) and Mississauga, Ontario (☎ (416) 823-3640), specialises in religious destinations. Once a year this company runs a two-week trip which takes you to the Basilica of Guadalupe in Mexico City plus other sites in Mexico.

Getting Around

Certain times are especially busy for travellers in Mexico, and you will want to have advance transport reservations. The peak travel periods of Semana Santa (the week before Easter) and Christmas/New Year are hectic and heavily booked everywhere.

AIR

Aeroméxico and Mexicana, traditionally the country's two largest airlines, have many international routes that also serve numerous domestic cities. In recent years, however, these large airlines have left many of the domestic routes to new, smaller airlines. These new companies have established useful route systems, some of which bypass Mexico City, something unheard-of for Mexicana or Aeroméxico, but efficient for many passengers.

Information about these 'start-up' airlines changes often; new ones are founded, older ones founder. The larger among them, such as Aero California and Inter (formerly Aerocaribe), will be included in travel agents' computerised reservations systems both in Mexico and abroad; the smaller ones such as Litoral and Aviacsa may not be. You may find it difficult or impossible to get information on the smaller airlines until you get to a city served by them.

Fares vary somewhat between the airlines, with the newer, smaller airlines generally offering cheaper fares. Though some excursion (fixed-date return) tickets are offered, the fare structure is quite simple, with few discounts. Most flights have only one fare. You pay it and go; you pay the same amount to return.

Details for the smaller regional airlines are given in the sections on the places they serve.

Flights in Mexico are no longer particularly cheap, although flying often still represents good value for money, especially considering the long, hot bus trip that may be the alternative. Here are some sample one-way fares from Mexico City:

Acapulco	US$53-US$70
Cancún	US$190
Ciudad Juárez	US$243
Guadalajara	US$80
Monterrey	US$73
Tijuana	US$234
Villahermosa	US$75

BUS

Intercity buses are frequent and go almost everywhere, usually for about US$1 or so per hour (50 to 80 km) of travel. For short (one hour) to medium-length (up to three or four hours) trips on heavily travelled routes, you can usually just go to the bus terminal, buy a ticket and head out without too much delay. For longer trips, or trips on routes not heavily travelled, reserve a seat and buy a ticket at least a day in advance and preferably two or three.

Refunds of 80% to 100% of your ticket price are often available if you cancel your reservation up to three hours before the listed

departure time. This policy allows you to book ahead at busy times and on busy routes, but to change your mind as well.

On long journeys it helps to work out which side the sun will be on, and sit on the other side. If the bus is not air-conditioned, it's a good idea to get a seat where you can control the opening and shutting of the window – Mexicans often have odd ideas about what's too warm or too cool! If the bus is air-conditioned, carry a sweater or jacket with you. Air-conditioned buses are often frigid, even in torrid climates.

Conventional wisdom on luggage is of two minds. One says you should keep your luggage with you in the passenger compartment, where, under your watchful eye, it will be safer. The other says you should have it safely locked in the luggage compartment underneath. (One reader wrote that when his bus was stopped by bandits, they only took things from the passenger compartment, not bothering to open the luggage compartments.) We suggest that you carry your valuables on your person in a money belt or pouch, and store most of your stuff in the luggage compartment on the better buses. However, don't allow it to be hoisted on to the open luggage rack atop a 2nd or 3rd-class bus unless you feel you can keep an eye on it (which is nearly impossible).

Pure water and other drinks, snacks and travel provisions are on sale in the larger bus terminals, but at prices higher than those in the city centre. You'd do well to stock up while at your hotel. Carry some toilet paper.

Local buses in towns are described under Local Transport in this chapter.

Terminals & Schedules

Most cities and towns now have a single bus station where all long-distance buses arrive and depart. This is called the Terminal Central, Central Camionera, Central de Autobuses, Central de Camiones or simply El Central, and is usually on the outskirts, a long way from the centre of town. This reduces heavy traffic downtown but is a lot less convenient for bus users, though frequent city buses often link bus stations with town centres. Note the crucial difference between the *Central* (bus station) and the *Centro* (town centre). Sometimes there are separate Centrales for 1st and 2nd-class buses.

If there is no central terminal, the different bus companies will have their own terminals scattered around town; this is potentially confusing but at least they are usually close to the town centre.

Most bus lines have schedules posted at ticket offices, but these are by no means comprehensive, so always ask. There may well be more services than are listed – and even if your destination isn't listed, it may be en route to one that is.

Classes

Long-distance buses range enormously in quality from comfortable, nonstop, air-conditioned 1st-class services to ancient, decaying, suspensionless ex-city buses grinding out their dying years on dirt tracks to remote settlements. Here are the classes of service, from best to worst:

De Lujo – Deluxe services are run by some of the major companies on their most heavily travelled routes, such as Mexico City to Acapulco, Guadalajara and Monterrey. These services bear names like Plus, Uno, Gran Turismo and the like. De lujo buses are big, new and very comfortable, and are fitted with comfortable reclining seats, toilets and video monitors. They have stewards serving snacks and beverages. The cost may be two to three times the normal 1st-class fare, but cheaper than the plane, which is often the competition. You should reserve your seat in advance.

Primera (1a) clase – 1st class, usually with air-conditioning, a comfortable numbered *(numerado)* seat for each passenger, and sometimes a locked toilet to which the driver may or may not have a key. They make infrequent stops and serve all sizable towns. You can usually book 1st-class tickets several days even weeks in advance, which is useful at busy times like Semana Santa, Christmas/New Year and the July-August holiday period. Some offices even have computer terminals showing seating plans that enable you to choose your seat.

Segunda (2a) clase – 2nd class, but service level varies, and some 2nd-class buses can be almost as quick and comfortable as 1st-class buses. Other 2nd-class buses are older, tattier, less comfortable, more prone to break down, and considerably slower than 1st-class ones because they'll stop anywhere for someone to get on or off. There's no apparent limit on capacity, which means that if you board mid-route you might not be seated (*sentado*) but standing (*parado*). Don't confuse *parado* with *parada* (bus-stop). Often there are no tickets: you just pay the conductor, so beware of rip-offs. Fares are about 10% less than 1st class.

Tercera (3a) clase – 3rd class consists of old city buses with low seat-backs and poor suspension. In some areas these serve outlying villages.

Types of Service

It is also important to know the type of service offered. How many times will the bus stop, if any? Will you have a reserved seat? Here are the types of service:

Directo – 'nonstop' (1st class) between departure point and destination; which sometimes means a few stops anyway.

Semi-directo – a few more stops than directo.

Ordinario – stops wherever passengers want to get on or off. First-class and de lujo buses are never ordinario.

Express – ultra-directo, nonstop on short to medium trips, very few stops on longer trips.

Local – bus that starts its journey from the town in which you start yours. You can usually reserve your seat in advance on *local* buses, and they usually leave on time.

De paso – what a *local* bus becomes after it departs its point of origin: a bus which started its journey somewhere else, but which is stopping where you are to let down and take on passengers. Often late, a de paso bus may or may not have empty seats, and you may have to wait until it arrives before any tickets are sold. You won't know whether you're leaving on this bus until you actually leave on this bus.

Viaje Redondo – round trip (return). Round-trip tickets are only available on some journeys, most starting in Mexico City.

TRAIN

The Ferrocarriles Nacionales de México (Mexican National Railways), have a chequered reputation, perhaps because they offer chequered service. Some trains are fairly comfortable and, if not as rapid as the bus, are sometimes cheaper and more atmospheric. Other trains are mediocre to unpleasant; yet others are ridiculous and downright unsafe.

As a rule, major trains north and west of the Isthmus of Tehuantepec (Mexico's narrow 'waist') are worth considering, and some should not be missed. East of the isthmus, take the bus or the plane, or prepare for unpleasantness.

Classes

Most travellers will probably prefer to take 1st-class seats or sleepers; 2nd class is strictly for the more adventurous.

Primera (1a) Especial – Special 1st-class carriages are air-conditioned, with reclining seats better than those in 1st class. Reservations are obligatory. Fares are usually more than twice as much as regular 1st-class fares, but still offer excellent value, and often include boxed meals of a decent standard. Some top trains are all Primera Especial. Middle-class Mexicans consider Primera Especial the 'basic' class of train service.

Primera (1a) clase – 1st-class carriages are better than 2nd, but are not air-conditioned. Fares are 60% higher than 2nd, but are very cheap. You must beware of pickpockets and luggage thieves. On a few trains, 1st-class seats can be reserved in advance, but usually they cannot.

Segunda (2a) clase – 2nd-class carriages are very basic, usually dirty, hot, overcrowded and uncomfortable, and sometimes rife with pickpockets and livestock. The poorest Mexicans walk; the next poorest ride segunda. If you're an adventurous sort who wants to see the 'real Mexico' at the lowest possible cost, you might consider segunda. Note that most of the best trains don't have 2nd-class carriages.

Coche Dormitorio – Sleeping car. In addition to your sleeping car ticket (which must be reserved in advance) you must have a 1st-class or special 1st-class rail ticket (depending upon the train), also reservable. This fare includes fairly presentable meals in the dining car. There are currently two classes of accommodation in service, both of acceptable but not exceptional cleanliness:

• *Camarín* – Private 'roomette' with washbasin and toilet (under the seat/bed, which must be moved for use). During the day, a seat in a private compartment; at night, a single lower berth folds out to occupy the entire compartment.

• *Alcoba* – Private 'bedroom' with separate upper and lower berths which are converted to seats during the day. They're comfortable for one adult each and minimum occupancy is two adults, but up to four adults and one child are permitted. Washbasin and toilet are always accessible.

Types of Service

Some trains are slower and stop more frequently than others:

Rápido – Trains, sometimes all one class, that make a limited number of stops. They are usually more modern, cleaner and more pleasant than other trains.

Local – Local trains make all stops, take forever, and are usually tatty and forlorn. (Note that *local* trains are completely different from *local* buses.)

Schedules & Reservations

Each place in this book ` has information about rail services, if they are available, under its Getting There & Away heading.

Mexico's top trains are listed in the *Thomas Cook Overseas Timetable*, perhaps the most convenient way to check current schedules outside Mexico. The timetable, published 12 times a year, is available in the UK from bookshops or from Thomas Cook Timetable Publishing Office (☎ (0733) 26-8937 or 26-8943), PO Box 36, Peterborough PE3 6SB, England. In the USA it is on sale in good travel bookshops or by mail from Forsyth Travel Library, Inc (☎ (800) 367-7984), PO Box 2975, Shawnee Mission, KS 66201.

Reservations are required for special 1st-class seats and all sleeping accommodation. Note that some intermediate stations have no sleeping-car space assigned for sale. If you plan to board at San Miguel de Allende, for example, you must reserve and pay for your sleeping car at a larger station.

Cancellations should be made at least 24 hours before trains depart. After this time, no refund will be granted.

In theory, you can make reservations through Mexican National Railways agents at stations in Mexico. In practice this can take months, and is successful only if everything goes just right (the space you request is avail-able, you have paid in advance in pesos, by bank cheque or certified cheque etc).

A far easier, faster and more reliable way, if a bit more expensive (20%), is to reserve through Mexico by Rail (☎ (800) 228-3225, (512) 727-3814; fax (512) 727-8520), PO Box 3508, Laredo, TX 78044, USA. They will confirm your reservations (usually within 48 hours) and post your tickets to you, so the whole process can be completed in a week or two rather than months. They accept Visa, MasterCard or a personal cheque.

For information about reserving through Mexican National Railways offices, write months in advance to Sr Javier Olivares Larraguivel, Jefe, Departamento de Pasajeros Comerciales, Ferrocarriles Nacionales de México, Estación Buenavista, 06358 México, DF (☎ (52-5) 547-86-55).

Fares

For a good selection of sample fares, see Getting There & Away in the Mexico City chapter.

When accompanied by a ticketed adult, children from five to 11 years old pay half-fare, plus a small fee for insurance. One child under five years of age, not occupying a separate seat, may travel free with each ticketed adult.

Stopovers are allowed if requested when the ticket is bought; there's a 15% surcharge.

CAR

Driving a car in Mexico is not as easy as it is in North America, but it is often easier and more convenient than the bus and sometimes the only way to get to some of the most beautiful places and isolated towns and villages. Wherever you drive in Mexico you must have a driver's licence, Mexican car insurance, a forgiving attitude about road conditions, and lots of patience.

As for traffic laws, speed limits etc, they rarely seem to be enforced on the highways. In the cities, you'll want to obey the laws strictly so as not to give the police an excuse to hit you with a 'fine' payable on the spot.

Fuel & Service

All motor vehicle fuel in Mexico is sold by the government-controlled Pemex (Petróleos Mexicanos) company for cash (no credit cards). Motor oil and other automotive fluids are sold by Pemex and by foreign companies. Almost every town, village and major road junction has a Pemex station.

Nova (leaded, blue pump) is 81 octane, Magna Sin (unleaded, silver pump) is 89 octane. Magna Sin is often, but not always, available in the larger cities and at major highway stations, but may be scarce elsewhere. As Mexico is now requiring newly manufactured cars to use unleaded fuel, this situation should improve with time.

Petrol prices in Mexico are US$0.27 per litre for Nova, US$0.36 per litre for Magna Sin (US$1.02 and US$1.36 per US gallon). These are lower than in the USA and Canada, but the fuel is of a lower octane rating as well, so you may end up getting about the same distance per dollar. If you live in Europe, you'll find Mexican fuel quite cheap.

There are no self-service stations. Attendants, particularly in touristy places, are not always trustworthy. When buying fuel, get out of your car, unlock your fuel cap, and tell the attendant the amount you want. It's better to ask for a peso amount than to say *lleno* (full) as lleno usually finishes with fuel gushing down the side of your car. Before the attendant pumps, check that the pump registers zero pesos. Afterwards, check that you have been given the amount you requested: in some stations the attendants will reset the pump immediately and start to serve another customer.

If you need oil, water, air, or any other service, get it only after fuelling is complete. Do each thing in order, and watch; don't have the attendants do two or three things at once or you may not get what you paid for.

Road Conditions

Mexican highways, even the new toll highways, are not up to the standards of European or North American ones. Still, the major highways are serviceable and fairly fast when traffic is not heavy.

In towns and cities you must be especially wary of stop *(alto)* signs, speed bumps *(topes)* and potholes. These are often not where you'd expect, and missing one can cost you in traffic fines or car damage.

Breakdown Assistance

Ángeles Verdes (Green Angels) are bilingual mechanics in bright green trucks. They patrol each major stretch of highway in Mexico at least twice daily searching for motorists in trouble. They make minor repairs, replace small parts, provide fuel and oil, and arrange towing and other assistance by radio if necessary. Service is free; parts, gasoline and oil are provided at cost. If you are near a telephone when your car has problems, you can contact them through the national 24-hour tourist information number in Mexico City, ☎ (5) 250-01-23.

Most serious mechanical car problems can be fixed efficiently and inexpensively by mechanics in towns and cities as long as the parts are available. Don't expect miracles if your car's problems are linked to its state-of-the-art computerised systems. Volkswagens (without fuel-injection engines) are the easiest cars to have repaired in Mexico; American models are next, followed by some Japanese makes.

For information on parts suppliers, consult the Yellow Pages telephone directory in any major city under *Refacciones y Acesorios para Automóviles y Camiones*. For information on authorised dealer service, look under *Automóviles – Agencias*.

Rental

If you can find a reasonable deal, and two or three people to share the costs with, car hire can be economical. It's certainly useful if you want to visit several different places in a short time, or to go off the beaten track where public transport is slow or scarce.

Cars can be hired in most of Mexico's cities, at their airports and sometimes even at their bus and railway stations. In some towns the supply of rental cars isn't equal to demand and it is necessary to book a week or more ahead.

Renters are usually required to be at least 25 years of age; all must have valid driver's licences and passports. A major credit card is usually required as well; if not, a huge cash deposit. You should ensure that the price you're quoted includes all taxes etc. You should also get a signed rental agreement and read its small print.

You usually pay a daily rental rate, plus insurance, plus a fee for each km you drive; you pay for fuel as well. For one day and 200 km in a Volkswagen Beetle – often the cheapest car available – this can amount to between US$45 and US$60. Some agencies offer rates for unlimited distance, which are often preferable if you intend to do some hard driving (and if you don't, why are you renting a car?).

You can reserve from abroad, which sometimes gets you lower rates, by calling one of the large firms. In the USA call: Hertz (☎ (800) 654-3131), National (☎ (800) 328-4567), Budget (☎ (800) 527-0700); and Avis, (☎ (800) 331-2112).

Small private car-rental agencies operate in many cities. Their rates tend to be slightly lower, but prices vary widely from town to town. Where car hire is particularly useful, and where good deals exist, we've put details in the text.

BICYCLE

Cycling is an interesting way to tour Mexico, but it has its drawbacks. Roads are generally rough, people drive fast and are often unobservant, and some of the climatic challenges (altitude, tropical heat) make this method of transport suitable only for the very experienced long-distance rider. There is also the problem of safety in some rural areas. Be careful, choose your itinerary carefully, and – if possible – don't travel alone.

HITCHING

Hitchhiking is relatively easy in Mexico as long as you stick to the highways and main roads, have a sign, and don't look scruffy. If the driver is another tourist or a private motorist, you may get the ride for free. If it is a work or commercial vehicle, you should expect (and offer) to pay.

BOAT

Ferries are used in several parts of Mexico. Car and passenger ferries connect Baja California with the Mexican mainland at Guaymas/Santa Rosalía, La Paz/Mazatlán, La Paz/Topolobampo and Cabo San Lucas/Puerto Vallarta. For details, see the sections on the relevant towns in the North-West Mexico chapter. Ferries also run between the mainland and the Caribbean islands of Isla Mujeres and Cozumel. See those sections in the Yucatán chapter for details.

LOCAL TRANSPORT
Bus

Generally known as *camiones*, local buses are the cheapest way of getting around cities and to nearby villages. They run everywhere, are dirt cheap (in most cities the fare is rarely more than US$0.40), and as often as not are noisy, dirty and crowded. In cities they halt only at specific points *(paradas)*, which may or may not be marked. Mexico City buses are notorious haunts for thieves and pickpockets, so be careful.

Combi, Colectivo & Pesero

These minibuses, minivans or large sedans are halfway between taxis and buses. They're cheaper than taxis, quicker and less crowded than buses. They run along set routes – sometimes displayed on the windscreen – and will pick you up or drop you on any corner along that route.

Go to the curb and wave your hand when you see one. As the driver approaches, he may indicate how many places are free by holding up the appropriate number of fingers. Tell the driver where you want to go and pay at the end of the trip. The fare, established by the government, depends on how far you go. By the way, a *combi* is a VW minibus (microbus), a *colectivo* is any vehicle of this kind and a *pesero* is Mexico City's word for colectivo.

Taxi

Taxis are common in towns and cities and are often surprisingly economical – useful if you have a lot of baggage, or need to get from A to B quickly, or are worried about theft on public transport. In Mexico City they're usually yellow Volkswagen Beetles. Some taxis, especially in Mexico City, have meters – but the metered fare sometimes has to be converted in line with a chart which should be displayed in the vehicle. If a taxi has a meter, ask the driver if it's working (*'¿Funciona el taxímetro?'*) and if it's not, establish the price of the ride before getting in.

Finding Your Way in Cities

Mexican street naming and numbering can be quite confusing. When asking directions, it's better to ask for a specific place, such as the Hotel Central, the Museo Regional or the Correos, than for the street it's on. To achieve any degree of certainty, ask three people and take the average.

Some cities laid out to a grid plan have streets numbered to the points of the compass, as 1 Norte, 2 Norte, 1 Oriente, 2 Oriente (1 North, 2 North, 1 East, 2 East) and so on. Simple though this sounds, in practice it can be confusing. Hints on how to negotiate it are included in the sections on the cities with this street system.

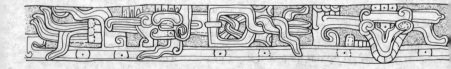

Mexico City

Population of Mexico City: 10,00,000
Population of Greater Metropolitan Area: 20,000,000
Altitude: 2240 metres

Mexico City is a place to love and loathe. It has everything you might expect in the world's largest metropolitan area (2018 square km or 779 square miles) and second-largest city (after Shanghai). Like mysterious ingredients added to a bubbling cauldron, the best and worst of the country have been combined in the high valley where Mexico City sprawls. The result is a bustling cosmopolitan megalopolis of music and noise, brown air and green parks, colonial palaces, world-renowned museums, sprawling slums and infinite variety.

HISTORY

As early as 10,000 BC, humans and animals were attracted to the shores of the lake, later named Texcoco, in the Valley of Mexico. Sometime after 7500 BC the lake began to shrink and hunting became more difficult, so the early inhabitants turned their energies to agriculture. Food production increased and settlements grew as they developed sophisticated farming techniques such as the *chinampas* or 'floating gardens', versions of which are still seen in Xochimilco on the southern outskirts of Mexico City.

Teotihuacán & Tula

Although a loose federation of farming villages evolved around Lago de Texcoco by approximately 200 BC, its influence in the region palled compared to that of Teotihuacán or Place of the Gods, a rapidly developing ceremonial centre of pyramids and temples to the north-east. After centuries of greatness, its influence spreading as far as Guatemala and beyond, Teotihuacán fell in 650 AD. The resulting power vacuum was filled by the Toltecs, a nomadic Chichimec tribe from north of the Valley of Mexico,

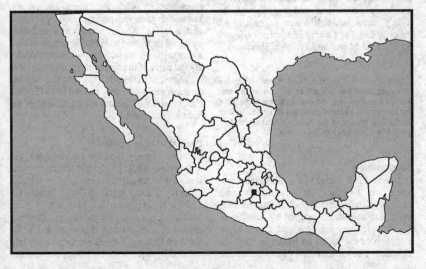

who founded Tula 81 km (50 miles) north-west of present-day Mexico City.

By the 12th century the Tula Empire had also collapsed, leaving yet another vacuum. The villages around the lake had by this time evolved into small city-states, all of which were vying for control of the Valley of Mexico or, as the Indians called it then, Anáhuac, meaning Near the Water. It was another Chichimec tribe invading from the north, though, that eventually won the power struggle.

These latest arrivals were called Mexica ('meh-SHEE-kah') or Aztecs. At first they settled on the hill of Chapultepec, but other valley inhabitants strongly objected to certain Aztec practices such as wife-stealing, human sacrifice and interference in the volatile relations between the various city-states. By the early 14th century Coxcox, the leader of Culhuacán, had pushed the Aztecs on to poor land, but he offered to resettle them on better land if they helped him in a battle against Xochimilco. The Aztecs won the battle and sent Coxcox 8000 human ears as gruesome proof of their victory.

He granted the Aztecs land and even complied with their request to make his daughter an Aztec queen and goddess, though he didn't know what this was to entail. As described in *The Course of Mexican History* by Michael Meyer and William Sherman:

...the princess was sacrificed and flayed. When her father attended the banquet in his honour, he was horrified to find that the entertainment included a dancer dressed in the skin of his daughter. Having finally had enough of the Aztecs, Coxcox raised an army which scattered the barbarians...

Tenochtitlán

Between 1325 and 1345 – historians disagree over the exact year – the Aztecs came to believe that Huitzilopochtli, one of their gods, had sent them a signal by causing an eagle, which was eating a snake, to land on a *tenuch* or cactus on an island in Lago de Texcoco. They interpreted this to mean that the island should become Tenochtitlán or the Place for the High Priest of Tenuch.

Tenochtitlán became a sophisticated city-state, which over the next century and a half was the centre of an empire that extended throughout central and southern Mexico. From 1450 to 1455, though, the empire was beset with terrible floods and famines caused by what the Aztec priests thought were angry gods. To appease the gods, daily rituals of human sacrifice were institutionalised to assure a steady supply of human hearts.

In 1487 these sacrificial rituals were performed at a frenzied pace to dedicate a new temple to the bloodthirsty god Huitzilopochtli. Meyer and Sherman write in *The Course of Mexican History*:

In a ceremony lasting four days sacrificial victims taken during campaigns were formed in four columns, each stretching three miles. At least twenty thousand human hearts were torn out to please the god...In the frenzy of this ghastly pageant, the priests were finally overcome by exhaustion...

Aside from appeasing the gods, these rituals also probably served to intimidate the Aztecs' potential rivals. The resulting peace and prosperity allowed them to build an immense city of canals, streets, causeways, botanical gardens, ponds, zoos, pyramids and temples. At the centre was a double pyramid dedicated to Huitzilopochtli, which today is the great plaza known as the Zócalo. By the early 16th century the population was estimated at 100,000. This was the city the Spanish saw when they arrived in 1519. (See Facts about the Country for the history of the Spanish conquest.)

Capital of New Spain

The first viceroy, Antonio de Mendoza, did not arrive until 1535, but once he was installed in power, Mexico City developed quickly as the capital of New Spain. By 1550, the last year of Mendoza's rule, Mexico City was the beautiful, thriving capital of a viceroyalty that extended as far south as Panama. Streets were carefully laid out and baroque-style buildings constructed according to Spanish designs using local materials such as *tezontle*, a light red, porous volcanic rock that the Aztecs had used to build their temples. Hospitals, schools, churches, palaces, cathedrals, parks, a university and even an insane asylum were built.

From 1550 until struggles for independence from Spain began in 1821, 60 viceroys ruled over New Spain from Mexico City. During the 16th and 17th centuries the economy flourished under the centralised political control of the viceroys, but not without periods of civil unrest. Throughout this period and even up to the late 19th century, Mexico City was also threatened by severe floods caused by the partial destruction in the 1520s of the Aztecs' drainage canals. Lago de Texcoco often overflowed into the city, damaging streets and buildings, and necessitating the relocation of thousands of people.

Independence
On 30 October 1811, parish priest Miguel Hidalgo y Costilla, whose *Grito* or cry for

independence is considered one of the main catalysts of the independence struggle, led an unsuccessful march on Mexico City with 80,000 peasant-soldiers. Two years later, parish priest José María Morelos y Pavón attempted to encircle Mexico City with rebels, but the Spaniards broke through his defences.

Sporadic fighting continued until 1821, when former Viceroy Agustín de Iturbide entered Mexico City to assume control as Emperor Agustín I. Two years later he was booted from power and the United Mexican States was formed by a three-man junta.

During the violent three-year civil war which started in 1858, Mexico had two capital cities: Mexico City for the conservatives and Veracruz for the liberals. By 1860 liberals led by Benito Juárez had taken control of Mexico City and in early 1861 Juárez was installed in power.

The French intervention brought Maximilian of Hapsburg to Mexico City in 1864 to rule as emperor of Mexico. By early 1867, however, the city was again under the control of Juárez.

By this time Mexico City was a booming city of 200,000 that was quickly being transformed into an urban monster of both great beauty and extreme ugliness. Porfirio Díaz came to power in 1876 and ushered in an unprecedented building boom in the capital. He solved the city's drainage problem, and parts of Baron Haussmann's magnificent plans for Paris were adapted to Mexico City's needs. Díaz' most famous project was one of his last, the column topped with a gilded angel in honour of Mexico's independence.

The 20th Century
After Díaz fell from power late in 1910, the chaos of the Mexican Revolution stopped most new building projects, and brought warfare to the city's streets.

The 1920s ushered in a modicum of peace and prosperity as political stability was regained and the economy rebuilt. Álvaro Obregón served as president from 1920 to 1924 and, through his Minister of Education

José Vasconcelos, stimulated a significant trend in Mexican art. Vasconcelos commissioned Mexico's top artists – Diego Rivera, David Alfaro Siqueiros and José Clemente Orozco – to paint murals on the walls of several public buildings. The murals were intentionally painted with dramatic colours and scenes to convey a clear sense of Mexico's past and present, especially during the world Depression. Today, these and other murals painted in subsequent years are on display throughout Mexico City.

The growth and reconstruction of Mexico City were temporarily stymied by the Depression, but by 1940 a drive to industrialise was attracting more people – 1,726,858 by 1940 – and money to the city. In the 1940s and '50s factories and skyscrapers rose almost as quickly as Mexico City's population, which was growing at an average annual rate of 7%.

Recent Times

Despite the continuation of this rapid economic growth into the 1960s, political and social reform lagged far behind. Protest demonstrations began at the university in the spring of 1966, but were quelled by federal troops. The discontent came to a head as Mexico City prepared for the 1968 summer Olympics. More than half a million students rallied in Mexico City's Zócalo on 27 August. A few weeks later on 2 October the Olympics had already begun, and at the Plaza de las Tres Culturas protesters were encircled by riot police. To this day, no one is certain how many people died in the ensuing massacre, but estimates have been put at 300 to 400.

Mexico City in the 1970s continued to expand and spread into the surrounding Federal District. In the mid-1970s rises in world oil prices spawned an economic boom in the city. Petroleum was regarded as the panacea of Mexico's economic ills, but when the price dropped there was an economic recession and in the early 1980s people migrated in droves from the countryside hoping to find work in Mexico City. The population of metropolitan Mexico City

began increasing at an annual rate of 700,000, or 2000 people daily.

People have continued to flow into Mexico City at the same rate despite the earthquake on 19 September 1985 which registered eight on the Richter Scale, caused more than US$4 billion in damage to hundreds of buildings, killed at least 8000 people and displaced thousands more.

In 1986 the population of Mexico City and surrounding areas was estimated at 18 million, with a daily increase of 3000, making it one of the world's most densely populated metropolitan areas. The United Nations estimates that by the year 2000 the population will be at least 37 million.

Mexico City Today

Mexico City is the centre of Mexico's industry, retail businesses, banking, transportation and communications. There are more than 450 industrial plants – about half the country's industries – in the metropolitan area. Tourism is also a big industry: more than one million tourists visit annually. As much as 70% of the country's banking transactions occur here. The city has five television stations, 20 daily newspapers (whose circulation in Mexico City accounts for more than half of the country's total), and 30 radio stations.

The effects of overcrowding have been predictable. Crime has risen to the point where a robbery is committed every five minutes and a murder every 90 minutes. The one million-plus vehicles on the streets daily create grid-locked traffic that, with the presence of heavy industry in metropolitan Mexico City, produces some of the worst smog in the world.

ORIENTATION
Geography

The broad Valley of Mexico, at an altitude of 2309 metres (7525 feet), is surrounded by mountains. Mexico City's 350 *colonias* or neighbourhoods and suburbs sprawl across the ancient bed of Lago de Texcoco and beyond. Groups of colonias are organized as mini-cities called *delegaciones*. Though this vast expanse of urban landscape is daunting at first, the main areas of interest to visitors are fairly well defined and easily traversable.

El Zócalo

The historic heart of the city is the spacious Plaza de la Constitución, universally known as El Zócalo (Metro: Zócalo), surrounded by the National Palace, Metropolitan Cathedral, and Federal District headquarters. The neighbourhoods to the north, west and south of the Zócalo have many good low-end and middle-range hotels and restaurants. To the west of the Zócalo are many shops, to the south (Metro: Pino Suárez) the big department stores and several good museums, and to the east the gigantic food markets of La Merced.

Alameda Central & Bellas Artes

Two important transport streets, Avenida Madero (eastbound) and Avenida Cinco de Mayo (or 5 de Mayo, westbound) link the Zócalo with the verdant park named the Alameda Central, seven blocks to the west (Metro: Hidalgo or Bellas Artes). On the eastern side of the Alameda stands the magnificent Palacio de Bellas Artes (Metro: Bellas Artes). The major northbound thoroughfare running along the east side of the Bellas Artes is Avenida Lázaro Cárdenas (or Eje Central – see Getting Around, below, for an explanation of 'ejes'). Across this major street from the Bellas Artes is the Correo Mayor, Mexico City's main post office. The central telegraph and fax office is nearby at Calle de Tacuba 8. The area of the Alameda is bound on its west side by the grand boulevard known as the Paseo de la Reforma.

Plaza de la República

Due west of the Alameda across Paseo de la Reforma is the Plaza de la República (Metro: Revolución), marked by the sombre, domed Art Deco-style Monumento a la Revolución. This is a fairly quiet, mostly residential area with many decent low-end and a few middle-range hotels.

Paseo de la Reforma

Mexico City's 'main street', this grand boulevard runs for many km through the city's heart, connecting the downtown districts of the Alameda to the Zona Rosa (Pink Zone) and Bosque de Chapultepec (Chapultepec Park). Many major hotels, embassies, banks and businesses rise on either side. Landmark *glorietas* (traffic roundabouts) along its route are marked with statues, including those commemorating Christopher Columbus, Cuauhtémoc (the last Aztec emperor), and, most notably, Mexican independence (the gilded angel).

Zona Rosa

The Pink Zone is the high-life and nightlife district anchored on the independence (angel) monument and bound by these streets: Paseo de la Reforma, Avenida Insurgentes Sur and Avenida Florencia. Many of the city's top hotels, restaurants, clubs, galleries and boutiques are located here. Whether or not your budget allows you to sleep, eat and buy here, it's a fascinating place for a stroll. If you know where to look, the Zona Rosa (Metro: Insurgentes) can yield some good budget surprises as well.

Bosque de Chapultepec

Chapultepec park, to the west of the aforementioned districts (Metro: Chapultepec, Auditorio or Constituyentes), is Mexico City's 'lungs', a vast expanse of trees, lawns, gardens and artificial lakes. It holds the city's major museums, including the renowned Museo Nacional de Antropología, the Museo Tamayo, the Museo de Arte Moderno, and Chapultepec castle, now officially the Museo Nacional de Historia. There are also amusement parks, a large National Auditorium, and the official residence of the president of Mexico.

North of the Centre

Besides these central areas of interest, you may find yourself in several neighbourhoods to the north. The Buenavista railway station (Metro: Guerrero), the rail terminus for the city, is six blocks due north of the Plaza de

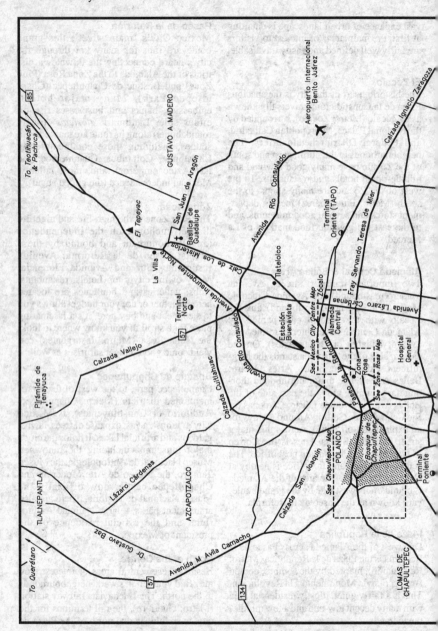

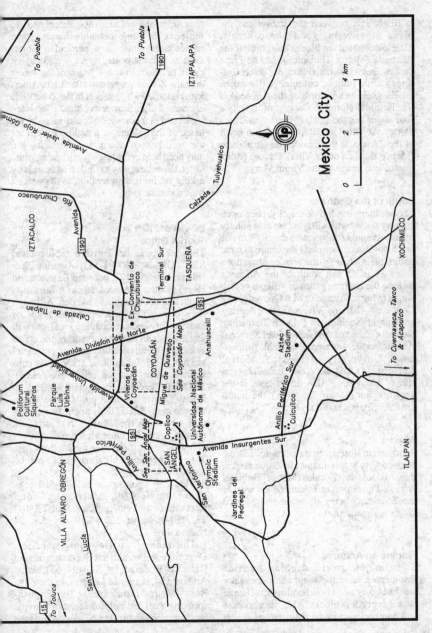

la República; between the station and the plaza are several good cheap hotels. Tlatelolco, about ten blocks due north of the Alameda (Metro: Tlatelolco), has its Plaza de las Tres Culturas (Plaza of Three Cultures) with Indian, colonial and modern buildings. Five km north of the Alameda is the Terminal Norte, the largest of the city's four major bus terminals (Metro: Autobuses Norte). At Villa Guadalupe, seven km north of the Zócalo, is the Basílica de Guadalupe (Metro: Basílica or La Villa), famous for its miraculous image of the Virgin Mary.

South of the Centre

The southern reaches of the city, once open country dotted with villages, are now solidly urban. Avenida Insurgentes, the city's major north-south axis, connects the centre to most points of interest in the south. Attractions about 11 to 15 km south of the Alameda include the charming former villages of San Ángel (Metro: Viveros or M A Quevedo) and Coyoacán (Metro: Viveros), the floating gardens of Xochimilco (Metro: Tasqueña), the vast campus of the Universidad Nacional Autónoma de México (National Autonomous University of Mexico; Metro: Universidad), and the Aztec archaeological site of Cuicuilco. Also down here is the Terminal Sur (Metro: Tasqueña), the southern intercity bus station.

Airport

Aeropuerto Internacional Benito Juárez, Mexico City's only major airport, is six km due east of the Zócalo (Metro: Terminal Aerea). The airport at Toluca, 66 km west of the Zócalo, is being developed as Mexico City's second airport.

Finding an Address

Some major streets, such as Avenida Insurgentes, have the same name for many km, but many neighbourhood streets change names every few blocks. Also, street names and numbering systems may change as you pass from one colonia (neighbourhood) to the next. In some neighbourhoods, street names concentrate on a particular subject such as famous poets, rivers, world capital cities, or Mexican states. Many of the streets near the Zócalo are named after Latin American countries while streets in the Zona Rosa are named after European cities.

All street addresses should include the name of the colonia, if possible. Except for the well-known downtown districts, you may need help in finding a particular colonia. Often the easiest way to find an address is by asking where it is in relation to the nearest Metro station.

INFORMATION
Tourist Office

The Secretaría de Turismo (abbreviated SECTUR; ☎ 250-01-51), Avenida Presidente Masaryk 172, between Emerson and Hegel (Metro: Polanco), stocks information about tourism throughout Mexico. Although they have some brochures and maps of Mexico City and surrounding areas and will assist you with hotel reservations, the office is inconveniently located and the personnel are not as helpful as those at the more convenient district tourism office (see below). SECTUR headquarters is open Monday to Friday from 8 am to 8 pm. On the Chapultepec map, SECTUR is about five blocks due north of the Museo Nacional de Antropología (National Museum of Anthropology). To get there, take the Metro (Linea 7) to Polanco and walk three blocks east on Avenida Masaryk.

SECTUR sponsors a multilingual telephone service for information, hotel reservations and emergencies. Call 250-01-23, 250-01-51 or 250-84-19 any day, 24 hours a day.

The federal district tourism office, Dirección de Turismo del Departamento del Distrito Federal (☎ 528-94-69), is at Amberes 54, corner of Londres, in the Zona Rosa (Metro: Insurgentes). The English-speaking staff are helpful and can provide brochures and maps, but be sure to visit the adjacent lobby/waiting room where several shelves of detailed brochures are available. Hours are 9 am to 9 pm daily.

The district office also maintains the Infotur telephone line (☎ 525-93-80) with English-speaking operators who can answer any tourist or travel-related queries you may have about Mexico City. This free service is available daily from 9 am to 9 pm.

There are small tourist offices at Mexico City's four intercity bus terminals, the Buenavista railway station and Benito Juárez International Airport. Hours are 8 am to 4 pm, daily.

The Mexico City Chamber of Commerce (La Cámara de Comercio de la Ciudad de México, ☎ (5) 592-26-77, ext 226), Paseo de la Reforma 42 between Avenida Juárez and Morelos, is helpful and has useful booklets and maps. Hours are Monday to Friday 9 am to 2 pm and 4 to 7 pm, Saturday 9 am to 2 pm.

Tourist Card Extensions Tourist card extensions should be requested at least two weeks in advance of expiration by visiting the Secretaría de Turismo (☎ 250-01-51, 250-05-89; 24 hours); ask for the Dirección General de Protección al Turista and for specific instructions about the extension process. If your card is lost or expired, contact your consulate and they will advise you about the necessary paperwork.

Money

Banks Mexico City is full of banks, most open Monday to Friday 9 am to 1.30 pm. However, some bank branches do not exchange currrency, and others may do it only at certain hours. Many banks have *cajas permanentes*, which are automatic cash-dispensing machines (ATMs or 'holes in the wall'). If you have a major bank credit card (Visa, MasterCard/Access/Eurocard, etc) or an ATM cash card, look for the bank system logo (VISA, Cirrus, Plus Systems, etc) on the machine. If you see the logo, you can probably withdraw money from your home account. (While you do, take precautions against robbery.) The machine will pay out in pesos at a favorable exchange rate, and save you lots of time and money.

Banamex has over 35 cajas permanentes in Mexico City, including these:

Calle Isabel la Católica 55, corner of Uruguay a few blocks west of the Zócalo.

Avenida Juárez 91, near the Palacio de Bellas Artes.

Avenida Insurgentes Norte 105, beside the VIPs restaurant near Buenavista railway station.

Calle Florencia 7, near the Independence (Angel) Monument in the Zona Rosa.

Calle Plateros 7, corner of Insurgentes Sur in the neighbourhood of San José Insurgentes.

Calle Allende 15, at Plaza Coyoacán in Coyoacán.

Casas de Cambio Casas de cambio (exchange houses) have longer hours and shorter procedures than banks, but the rate of exchange may not be as good, and they may charge fees. There are several casas de cambio near the Independence (Angel) Monument at the intersection of Paseo de la Reforma and Avenida Florencia in the Zona Rosa. Here are some of the casas de cambio we've found useful:

Near the Zócalo

Casa de Cambio Forex, corner of 16 de Septiembre and Bolívar, four blocks west of the Zócalo, open Monday to Friday 9 am to 1.30 pm and 3 to 5 pm.

Casa de Cambio Intercenter, on the east side of Palma just south of 16 de Septiembre; open Monday to Friday 9 am to 5 pm, Saturday 10 am to 1 pm.

Near the Alameda

Casa de Cambio Plus, on the south side of Avenida Juárez facing the Alameda, open Monday to Friday 9 am to 4 pm, Saturday 9 am to 2 pm; exchange rates are not the best, though.

Near the Independence (Angel) Monument

Asesorería Cambiaria Casa de Cambio, on Avenida Florencia at Paseo de la Reforma, open Monday to Friday 9 am to 5.30 pm, Saturday 9 am to 2 pm.

Casa de Cambio Atlantico, next to the VIPS restaurant facing the Angel Monument, open Monday to Friday 9 am to 2 pm.

Casa de Cambio Mexicana de Devisas, Avenida Florencia at Reforma, on the north-east corner of the intersection, open Monday to Friday 9 am to 4.30 pm, Saturday 10 am to 2 pm.

Casa de Cambio Indice, Paseo de la Reforma 422, at Sevilla; very bad rate for exchanging travellers' cheques.

Airport
> The airport casas de cambio claim to be open 24 hours daily, though it seems they are open only when a big international flight arrives. In the main terminal at Aeropuerto Internacional Benito Juárez, the Casa de Cambio Aeropuerto SA, Local (shop) 47 opposite Sala B (Aeroméxico and Mexicana), is open seven days a week, and offers exchange rates similar to, or better than, those offered by casas de cambio in the city centre. They also change all sorts of European currencies.

American Express The main American Express Company office (☎ 533-03-80), Paseo de la Reforma 234, gives the best rate of exchange for its own travellers' cheques. The office also has other financial services, a travel bureau and a mail pick-up desk. The staff speak English and are helpful with mail enquiries and American Express card and cheque questions. A 24-hour 'lost cheque' hotline staffed by English-speaking operators can be called collect from anywhere in Mexico at (5) 598-79-66, extension 2367 or 2368.

The travel bureau and mail pick-up desk are open Monday to Friday from 9 am to 6 pm. The cashier (for money exchange and other financial matters) is open from 9 am to 5 pm. Both are open on Saturday from 9 am to 1 pm; closed Sunday.

If you need to have money wired to you from outside Mexico, do not go through a Mexican bank. Instead, have it wired through the American Express office, the Barclays Bank representative's office (☎ (5) 525-18-70), at Paseo de la Reforma 390, Suite 1203, México, DF 06695, or the main Mexico City telegram and telex offices, Telegramas Internacionales (☎ (5) 519-59-20), Central de Telégrafos, in the Museo Nacional del Arte building, Calle de Tacuba 8, (east of Avenida Lázaro Cárdenas). The telegraph office is open for *giros internacionales* (international wire transfers) from Monday to Friday 9 am to 1 pm and 2.30 to 6.30 pm, Saturday 9 am to 1 pm, Sunday 9 to 11 am.

Post
The Correo Mayor, the central post office of Mexico City, is on Avenida Lázaro Cárdenas at Tacuba across from the north-east corner of the Palacio de Bellas Artes. The stamp windows are marked with signs reading '*estampillas*' and the poste restante or general delivery window is marked 'Lista de Correos'. Hours for all services are 8 am to 12 midnight Monday to Saturday, and 8 am to 4 pm on Sunday.

Other post office branches are at these locations; look for the 'Correos' sign:

Zócalo – in the arcade on the west side of the plaza (in the passage marked 'Almacenes Nacionales de Depósito').
Plaza de la República – corner of Mariscal and Arriaga.
Zona Rosa – corner of Varsovia and Londres.

If you are a customer of the American Express Company (that is, if you carry their charge card or travellers' cheques), you can use their office as your mailing address in Mexico City. See the information under Money in this section.

Telecommunications
Telephones See the Facts for the Visitor chapter for details on the various sorts of telephones, how to place calls, and rates. Beware making telephone calls from your hotel room phone unless you understand the rate structure! Hotels may add enormous service charges; you can end up spending US$60 for a short call to the USA. Ask the hotel operator or receptionist about rates before you call.

The easiest and cheapest sorts of phones to use for international calls are the ones which accept a major credit card. These are found in the important transportation termini and in the lobbies of posh hotels. Almost as easy are the phones which take telephone company debit cards. As yet, these are still difficult to find. Ladatel phones, which accept coins and tokens, are in evidence throughout the city.

With the advent of Ladatel and card phones, the old system of casetas de larga distancia (long-distance telephone offices) is obsolescent and may soon disappear.

Telegram & Fax You can send domestic and international telegrams from the Central de Telégrafos on the east side of the Museo Nacional del Arte at Tacuba 8, just east of Avenida Lázaro Cárdenas (Metro: Bellas Artes). It's open until 11 pm. See Facts for the Visitor for more on sending telegrams.

Many Mexican telegraph offices now offer fax service as well. Rates are similar to those for telephone calls. Here is a list of the most convenient offices, and their fax numbers:

Administracion Central, Tacuba 8 (the main telegraph office; fax 510-16-21); Metro: Bellas Artes

Aeropuerto, Aeropuerto Internacional Benito Juárez, Sala A, Local 4 (fax 571-32-52); Metro: Terminal Aerea

Central de Autobuses Norte, the Terminal Norte bus station (fax 587-58-97); Metro: Autobuses Norte

Central de Autobuses Oriente, or TAPO, the eastern bus station (fax 522-15-71); Metro: San Lázaro

Central de Autobuses Poniente, the western bus station, (fax 271-08-56); Metro: Obervatorio

Central de Autobuses Sur, the southern bus station (fax 549-80-15); Metro: Tasqueña

Estacion Buenavista, Buenavista railway station (fax 547-11-39); Metro: Guerrero

Hotel María Isabel Sheraton, facing the Independence (Angel) Monument at Paseo de la Reforma 325, at Río Tiber (fax 207-45-74); Metro: Insurgentes

You may also be able to send and receive faxes at your hotel for a fee. For more on sending faxes, see Facts for the Visitor.

Foreign Embassies & Consulates
Officially, a country's embassy is the residence of its ambassador. Often the larger embassies do business in a separate office building well away from the ambassador's house. When going to find an embassy, be sure that the building you're searching for (which is usually the consular office) is the one for business.

Embassies and consulates often keep strange, limited business hours, and close on both Mexican and their own national holidays. It's best to telephone ahead before you make the trek to find one.

'CP' in the addresses below refers to the *codigo postal* (postal code) for each embassy; the postal code can help you to locate the embassy's street in an atlas such as the *Guía Pronto Ciudad de México* (see Maps in this section), or on another map which gives postal codes.

Australia
    Paseo de la Reforma 195, 5th floor, CP 06500, near the Independence (Angel) Monument (☎ 566-30-55)
Belize (Belice)
    Thiers 152-B, CP 11590 (☎ 203-56-42, 203-59-60)
Canada
    Schiller 529, Polanco, CP 11580, a few blocks due north of the Anthropology Museum (☎ 254-32-88, or 254-38-07 for emergencies); open 9 am to 1pm and 3 to 5 pm Monday to Friday
Costa Rica
    Río Po 113, CP 06500, near the Independence (Angel) Monument (☎ 525-77-64)
Cuba
    Avenida Presidente Masaryk 554, Polanco, CP 11560 (☎ 259-00-45); Metro: Polanco
Denmark (Dinamarca)
    Tres Picos 43, Polanco, CP 11560 (☎ 250-85-77, 545-53-76); Metro: Auditorio
El Salvador
    Paseo de las Palmas 1930, Lomas de Chapultepec, CP 11000 (☎ 596-73-66)
France (Francia)
    Havre 15 between Hamburgo and Paseo de la Reforma, Zona Rosa, CP 06600 (☎ 533-13-60; Consulate 207-63-74)
Germany (Alemania)
    Lord Byron 737, Polanco, CP 11580 (☎ 545-66-55); Metro: Auditorio
Guatemala
    Explanada 1025, Lomas de Chapultepec, CP 11000 (☎ 540-75-20; Consulate 520-92-49)
Honduras
    Alfonso Reyes 220, CP 06140 (☎ 515-66-89); Metro: Juanacatlán
India
    Musset 325, Polanco, CP 11560 (☎ 531-08-50)
Israel
    Luis G Urbina 58, Polanco, CP 11560 (☎ 520-75-53)

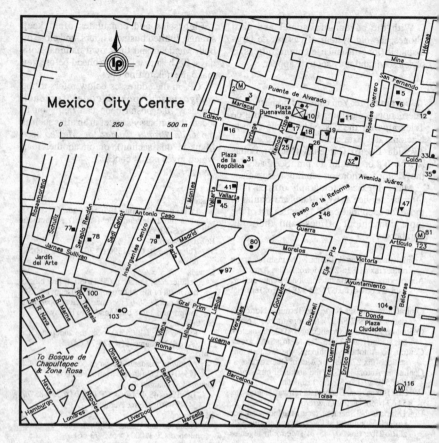

Mexico City Centre

0   250   500 m

Italy (Italia)
Paseo de las Palmas 1994, Lomas de Chapultepec, CP 11000 (☎ 596-36-55)

Japan (Japon)
Paseo de la Reforma 395, 2nd floor, CP 06500, near the Independence (Angel) Monument (☎ 211-00-28)

Nicaragua
Consulate: Avenida Nuevo León 144, Hipódromo, CP 06170 (☎ 553-97-91)

Netherlands (Paises Bajos)
Sierra Gorda 555, Lomas de Chapultepec, CP 11000 (☎ 202-71-26), or Montes Urales 635, Suite 201, Lomas de Chapultepec, CP 11000 (☎ 540-77-88)

New Zealand (Nueva Zelandia)
Homero 229, 8th floor, Chapultepec Morales, CP 11570 (☎ 250-59-99); Metro: Polanco

Panama
Campos Elíseos 111-1, Polanco, CP 11560 (Consulate: ☎ 250-40-45); Metro: Auditorio

Spain (España)
Blvd M Ávila Camacho 191, 5th floor, Lomas de Chapultepec, CP 11000 (☎ 395-66-11; Consulate 540-49-58)

Sweden (Suecia)
Blvd M Ávila Camacho 1, 6th floor, Lomas de Chapultepec, CP 11000 (☎ 540-73-93)

Switzerland (Suiza)
Hamburgo 66, Zona Rosa CP 06600 (☎ 533-07-35); Metro: Insurgentes

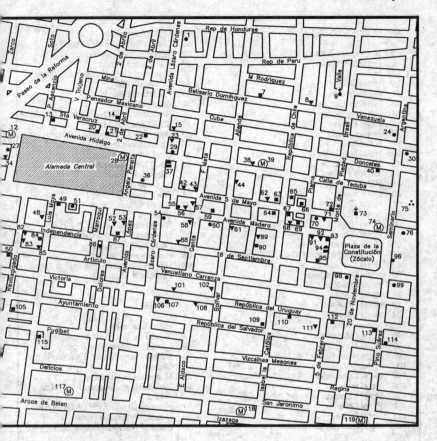

UK (Reino Unido, Gran Bretaña)
Río Lerma 71 at Río Sena, Cuauhtémoc, CP 06500, not far from the Independence (Angel) Monument (☎ 207-24-49, 207-25-69, 207-25-93; emergencies 207-20-89); hours are 8.30 am to 3.30 pm Monday to Friday

USA (Estados Unidos de Norteamérica)
Paseo de la Reforma 305, Cuauhtémoc, CP 06500, not far from the Independence (Angel) Monument (☎ 211-00-42, or 553-33-33 Saturday for emergencies); open 9 am to 5.30 pm Monday to Friday, closed on Mexican and American holidays

Laundry & Dry Cleaning

Lavandería Automática, Edison 91, on the north side of the street between Iglesias and Arriaga near the Plaza de la República (Metro: Revolución), charges US$1.75 for two kilos to wash, the same to dry. Hours are Monday to Friday 10 am to 7 pm, Saturday 10 am to 6 pm.

Two reliable dry cleaners, both named Jiffy (that's 'HEE-fee'), are on Río Tiber a block or two north-west off Reforma from the Independence (Angel) Monument. One is at the corner of Río Tiber and Río Lerma, the other at the corner of Río Tiber and Río Panuco.

■ PLACES TO STAY

3	Gran Hotel Texas
5	Hotel Managua
7	Hotel Antillas
10	Hotel Oxford
11	Hotel Jena
13	Hotel de Cortés
14	Hotel Hidalgo
16	Hotel Edison
17	Hotel Carlton
18	Hotel New York
22	Hotel Mariscala
40	Hotel Catedral
41	Palace Hotel
45	Hotel Corinto
49	Hotel Bamer
50	Hotel Fleming
59	Hotel Ritz
63	Hotel Rioja
64	Hotel Gillow
65	Hotel Juárez
66	Hotel Washington & Café El Popular
67	Hotel Canada
69	Hotel San Antonio
77	Hotel Mallorca
78	Hotel Sevilla
79	Hotel Regente
84	Hotel Metropol
87	Hotel Marlowe
90	Hotel Lafayette
93	Hotel Majestic
95	Gran Hotel Ciudad de México
105	Hotel Conde
107	Hotel Concordia
109	Hotel Isabel
110	Hotel Montecarlo
112	Hotel Ontario
113	Hotel Roble
115	Hotel San Diego

▼ PLACES TO EAT

6	No Name Restaurant
8	Hostería de Santo Domingo
15	Taquería Los Pericos
19	Restaurante Samy
23	Frutería Frutivida & El Correo
25	Restaurante Bracen's
26	Restaurant La Esquina
34	Café Trevi & Café Colón
38	Café de Tacuba
42	Restaurante Café Paris
43	La Opera Bar
44	Restaurante Jampel
47	Fonda Santa Anita

48	El Regiomontano
52	Centro Naturista de México
53	Taquería El Sembrador
56	Restaurant Vasco
57	Restaurante El Vegetariano (Mata)
58	La Baguetelle
61	Restaurant Borda
62	Café La Blanca
68	Restaurante El Vegetariano (Madero)
71	Café Cinco de Mayo
82	Restaurante Presente y Futuro
83	Restaurant Lincoln
85	Los Faroles
86	Hong King (Chinatown)
88	Pastelería Ideal
89	La Casa del Pavo
91	Restaurant El Gallo
92	Cafetería Los Popos
97	Shirley's (Reforma)
100	Restaurante Daruma
101	Restaurant Centro Castellano
102	Hong King (Bolívar)
106	Restaurant Danubio
108	Rincón Mexicano & Antojitos Tere
111	Pastelería Madrid

OTHER

1	Plaza Garibaldi
4	Museo de San Carlos
9	Iglesia de Santo Domingo
20	Museo Franz Mayer & Cafetería del Claustro
21	Museo de la Estampa
24	Secretaría de Educación Pública (murals)
27	Pinacoteca Virreynal de San Diego
29	Museo Nacional de Arte
30	Escuela Nacional Preparatoria (murals)
31	Monumento a la Revolución & Museo Nacional de la Revolución
32	Lotería Nacional
33	Museo Mural Diego Rivera
35	Jardín de la Solidaridad
36	Palacio de Bellas Artes
37	Correo Mayor (Main Post Office)
46	Cámara de Comercio (Info Office)
51	Museo Nacional de Artes e Industrias Populares
54	Torre Latinoamericana
55	Casa de Azulejos (Sanborns)
60	Palacio de Iturbide
72	Nacional Monte de Piedad (Pawn Shop)
73	Catedral Metropolitana & El Sagrario

75	Templo Mayor & Museo	Ⓜ	METRO
76	Museo Nacional de las Culturas		
	(Casa de la Moneda)	2	Revolución
80	Glorieta Cristóbal Colón	12	Hidalgo
94	Correos (Branch Post Office)	28	Bellas Artes
96	Palacio Nacional	39	Allende
98	Departamento del Distrito Federal	74	Zócalo
99	Suprema Corte de Justicia (murals)	81	Juárez
103	Glorieta Cuauhtémoc	116	Balderas
104	La Ciudadela y Centro Artesanal	117	Salto del Agua
114	Museo de la Ciudad de México	118	Isabel la Católica
		119	Pino Suárez

Bookshops

City Centre These are all near the Bellas Artes metro station.

American Bookstore (☎ 512-03-06 or 512-72-84; fax 518-69-31), Avenida Madero 25, Centro, has many English-language books and current magazines and newspapers (usually only two or three days old). Hours are 9.30 am to 6 pm, daily except Sunday. There's another branch in San Ángel suburb.

Librería Británica, Madero 30A in the Hotel Ritz building, specialises in, as its name suggests, English-language books and magazines.

Sanborns, in the Casa de Azulejos (House of Tiles), at Madero and Condesa a block east of Avenida Lázaro Cárdenas, has a good English book and newsstand section, as do most Sanborns stores throughout the city.

Librería Misrachi, Avenida Juárez 4, a few steps west of Avenida Lázaro Cárdenas, facing the Palacio de Bellas Artes, is a good source of English-language books about Mexico and Mexico City and maps for all parts of Mexico.

Zona Rosa Librería Británica (☎ 705-05-85), Serapio Rendon 125, Colonia San Rafael, facing the Hotel Sevilla, is just off the Jardín del Arte, three blocks north-west of the intersection of Insurgentes and Reforma. This branch carries mostly more technical, scientific and academic books for university students.

San Ángel American Bookstore (☎ 550-01-62 or 548-89-01), Avenida Revolución 1570, San Ángel.

Coyoacán Librería Británica, Avenidas Universidad and México, next to the Coyoacán Metro stop in Coyoacán, has a good general collection.

Libraries

Benjamin Franklin Library (☎ 211-00-42), Paseo de la Reforma 295, between Río Danubio and Río Sena just north-east of the Independence (Angel) Monument, is the library of the United States Information Agency, which is part of the US State Department. A wide range of books about the USA, Mexico and other parts of Latin America is available, as well as current English-language periodicals. It is open to the public, but only residents of Mexico City can check out books. Hours are 9 am to 6 pm, Monday to Friday.

The Canadian Embassy Library (☎ 254-32-88), Schiller 529, Polanco (Metro: Polanco), four blocks due north of the Anthropology Museum in Chapultepec park, has a wide selection of Canadian books and periodicals in English and French. Hours are Monday to Friday, 9 am to 5 pm.

Newspapers & Magazines

The most popular and oldest English-language newspaper is the *The Mexico City News*, the best source of information in English about concerts, art exhibitions, plays, movies and English-as-a-second-language teaching positions. Price is US$0.50 to US$0.75, depending upon the current rate of exchange. Ask for it at newsstands (kiosks) in the city centre (some of which carry it), or at the bookshops mentioned elsewhere in this section.

The *Mexico City Daily Bulletin* is a 20-page tabloid distributed free every day except Monday in some shops and in the lobbies of many hotels (usually the ones which advertise in it). There are snippets of daily wire-service news as well as bits of tourist-oriented information, some of it useful, not all of it accurate.

The essential weekly directory for information about cultural and sporting events, restaurants, TV programmes and movies in and around Mexico City is the weekly Spanish-language magazine *Tiempo Libre* (Free Time), published every Thursday. Even if you don't know Spanish, you should be able to recognise some cognates and the names of performers and performances. It can be bought at most newsstands and bookstores for US$0.65 to US$0.85.

Some English-language newspapers and magazines from North America and Europe are sold at major hotel newsstands and at the bookstores listed in this section. The Casa de la Prensa Internacional, Florencia 59, to the right of the Hotel Plaza Florencia in the Zona Rosa, carries the major British and American newspapers and magazines, as well as a few French and German ones; it's closed Sunday.

Maps

The various tourist offices, hotels, shops, travel agencies and crafts stores provide handy street plans of the city. For a thorough and attractive street atlas, get the *Guía Pronto Ciudad de México* for US$10 at the American Bookstore, Avenida Madero 25, and at some other bookstores.

Emergency

Tourist Police The Procuraduría General de Justicia del Distrito Federal (Solicitor-General of Justice of the Federal District) maintains two offices to aid tourists, both Mexican and foreign, with legal questions and problems, including theft and robbery. Offices are in the Zona Rosa, at Avenida Florencia 20 (☎ 625-87-61), and on Calle de Argentina, at the corner of San Ildefonso (☎ 789-08-33), three blocks north of the Zócalo (from the east side of the cathedral, walk north on Seminario, which soon changes names to become Calle de Argentina). There is also a telephone hot line available at any hour on any day: call 625-86-68.

Car Problems If you need information about or assistance with car-related problems within Mexico City, call the Ángeles de Plata or Silver Angels (☎ 250-82-21), the city version of the Ángeles Verdes (Green Angels) who patrol the highways.

Lost & Found City authorities maintain a special telephone number, (5) 658-11-11, to help you find lost things. It probably won't work for your wallet, but it may work for your car.

If you've lost something on the Metro, you can call or visit the Oficina de Objectos Extraviados (☎ (5) 709-11-33, ext 1019), in the Fray Servando station. If it's something that 10 million people wouldn't want, you may find it there.

Dangers & Annoyances

Crime Mexico City is among the most likely places to be robbed. Please read the sections on Theft & Robbery under Dangers & Annoyances in Facts for the Visitor, and follow carefully the precautions outlined there.

Mexico City's buses and Metro are notorious for pickpockets and thieves, particularly when they're crowded. The most dangerous places are those where lots of foreigners go: in the buses along Paseo de la Reforma, near the Anthropology Museum, to the markets and Chapultepec park. You may want to walk or take taxis instead of the buses (in the long run, it's cheaper than having your pocket picked).

If you take taxis, make sure they are licensed and properly authorised (look for the windscreen stickers, rooftop light, driver's permit, meter, etc). When in doubt, ask your hotel to assist you in finding a taxi.

Do not use the services of any guide except a properly licensed and officially authorised guide.

Do not walk into any pedestrian underpass which is empty or nearly so; robbers post spotters at each end, and after you enter they intercept you.

If you participate in any Mexican festivities (rallies or celebrations in the Zócalo, etc.) be aware that every pickpocket in the city will be there as well. At the airport or bus station, keep your bag or pack between your feet, particularly when you are checking in at a counter (thieves tend to snatch them while you're talking with the ticket agent).

On the Metro, the first and last carriages are usually less crowded, but during rush hours (6.30 to 9 am and 4 to 7 pm) all trains and buses in the central area are sardine cans. You may want to walk or take a taxi rather than taking a chance at having your pocket picked.

If you are the victim of a crime, you can report it through the offices of the Procuradoría General de Justicia (see Tourist Police in this section under Emergency).

Air Pollution The severity of air pollution in Mexico City is due to the altitude and consequent lack of oxygen, the abundant sunshine which causes chemical reactions among the pollutants, and to thermal inversion, whereby the layer of smog traps the air below it and further reduces the amount of oxygen. This happens several times a year in Mexico City. When it does, people suffering from severe asthma, bronchitis or other breathing problems are at great risk. On an average day, breathing the air in Mexico City is, for a non-smoker, equivalent to smoking two packets of cigarettes.

AROUND THE ZÓCALO

Start your explorations of the city where the city began. The historic centre of Mexico City is the Plaza de la Constitución, more commonly known as the Zócalo (Metro: Zócalo). Until the early 19th century, the plaza was known variously as the Plaza de Armas and the Plaza Real, but it was more a maze of market stalls and narrow passageways than an open plaza. The market, called the Mercado del Parián, existed for most of the 16th and 17th centuries until it had to be torn down because the many stalls had overcrowded the plaza.

In 1812 the plaza was renamed Plaza de la Constitución to commemorate a liberal constitution drawn up by the local assembly in protest at Napoleon's invasion of Spain. The Aztec word *zócalo*, which means plinth or stone base, was adopted in 1843 when a tall monument to Independence commissioned by President Santa Anna was constructed only as far as the base. The plinth is long gone, but the name remains, and has been adopted informally by many (but by no means all) other Mexican cities and towns for their main plazas.

The plaza was first paved in the 1520s by Cortés with stones from the ruins of what had been the grandest and most important set of temples and palaces of the Aztec Empire. With each side measuring 240 metres (792 feet), it has remained one of the world's largest city plazas. To get a true sense of its immensity, visit the open-air terrace restaurant on the 7th floor of the Hotel Majestic, on the plaza's west side at the corner of Avenida Madero and Monte de Piedad.

The Zócalo is the home of the powers-that-be in Mexico City. To the east is the National Palace, to the north the Metropolitan Cathedral. The buildings on the south side house the government of the Departamento del Distrito Federal (Federal District Government). Just off the south-west corner of the plaza at Avenida 16 de Septiembre 82 is the Gran Hotel Ciudad de México, with a spectacular stained-glass canopy floating above its lobby and ornate birdcage elevators on the left-hand side.

Palacio Nacional

Home to the offices of the president of Mexico, the Federal Treasury, the National Archives, a museum in honour of President Benito Juárez (1855-72) and the dramatic murals of Diego Rivera, the National Palace fills the entire east side of the Zócalo. The present structure was built in the late 17th and early 18th centuries over the ruins of two previous palaces.

The first palace on this spot was built of tezontle (volcanic stone) by Moctezuma II Xocoyotzin in the early 16th century before Cortés and his conquistadors arrived. Cortés destroyed the palace in 1521 and rebuilt it with a large enclosed courtyard so that he could entertain visitors with New Spain's first recorded bullfights. The palace remained in Cortés' family until the king of Spain bought it in 1562 to house the viceroys of New Spain. It was destroyed during riots in 1692, rebuilt again using tezontle and continued in use as the viceregal residence until Mexican independence in the 1820s.

As you face the palace you see three portals: on your right – to the south – is the guarded entrance for the president of Mexico and other officials; the centre door is the entrance to a courtyard surrounded by Diego Rivera's colourful depictions of Mexico's history and people; and the third (north) leads to a courtyard where the seldom-visited El Recinto de Homenaje a Benito Juárez (the place of homage to Benito Juárez) is located. Enter through the centre door.

Diego Rivera's bright, colourful **murals** are the prime attraction of the palace. They summarise the history of Mexican civilisation from the arrival of Quetzalcóatl – the plumed serpent god believed to be personified first in Cortés – to Mexico's 1910 Revolution. Detailed guides to the murals are available at the foot of the stairs just inside the entrance gate. The murals are open for public viewing from 9 am to 3 pm and 6 to 9 pm daily. Admission is free.

If you have time, enter the left (north) door and visit **El Recinto de Homenaje a Benito Juárez** (☎ 522-56-46) on the 2nd floor.

Juárez led Mexico's reform movement in the 1850s and the fight against the French invaders in the 1860s. He served as president until his death in this wing of the National Palace in 1872. His library, the room in which he died, and various personal effects have been preserved. Hours are 10 am to 6 pm Tuesday to Friday, 10 am to 3 pm Saturday and Sunday. Admission is free.

Catedral Metropólitana

The Metropolitan Cathedral on the north side of the Zócalo was one of the first buildings begun by the Spaniards in the 1520s. They placed it right where the Aztecs had had their Tzompantli, or Wall of Skulls, a sort of altar on which the skulls of sacrifice victims were displayed (Cortés found over 136,000 such skulls here and nearby). With a three-naved basilica design of vaults on semicircular arches, the cathedral was constructed to resemble cathedrals in the Spanish cities of Toledo and Granada. Construction was finished in 1548, but the early church was later replaced by a larger cathedral, parts of which were expanded, redesigned or torn down over the years.

The cathedral's grand portals on the south side were constructed in the 17th century with baroque designs that include three levels of exterior columns and marble panels with bas-reliefs.

The tall twin doors on the north side were added in the early 17th century and are a good example of Neoclassical Renaissance-style portals with pilasters that resemble columns.

The cathedral's exterior was not completed until 1813 when architect and sculptor Manuel Tolsá added statues of Faith, Hope and Charity atop the clock tower and a great central dome to create a sense of unity and balance.

Inside, the cathedral includes 14 heavily decorated chapels, a central nave, two processional or side naves and two chapel naves. The eye-catching Chapel of the Holy Angels is an exquisite example of baroque sculpture and painting with its huge main altarpiece that is all one sculpture and three smaller altarpieces decorated by the 17th-century painter Juan Correa. Paintings by Correa also grace the walls of the sacristy with depictions of Jesus' arrival in Jerusalem, the coronation of the Virgin and St Michael's slaying of the dragon.

Most of the rest of the artwork in the cathedral was, unfortunately, damaged or completely destroyed in a 1967 fire. The intricately carved wooden choir stalls of late 17th-century artist Juan de Rojas and the huge gilded Altar of Pardon have been restored, and work continues. Restoration is endless, as the building's immense weight causes it to sink slowly into the spongy soil which was once the bed of Lago de Texcoco.

El Sagrario

Adjoining the cathedral on its east side (nearest the Templo Mayor) is the 18th-century parish church of El Sagrario (The Sacred). Originally built to house the archives and vestments of the archbishop, it is a prime example of the ultra-decorative Churrigueresque style.

Inside, the church was laid out in a square so that it resembles a Greek cross and fits neatly next to the rectangular cathedral.

Templo Mayor & Museo

The Teocalli, or sacred city, of Tenochtitlán lies beneath the cathedral and its precincts. For centuries the precise location of the Aztecs' principal temple (Templo Mayor) was unknown because the Aztec city had been destroyed by the Spaniards in the 1520s. However, in February 1978, municipal workers unearthed an intriguing eight-tonne votive stone as they were digging just north of the National Palace and east of the cathedral. The stone, a replica of which is displayed in the Museo del Templo Mayor (the original is in the Anthropology Museum), was decorated with the figures and symbols of a violent Aztec legend. More excavation showed that this was the site of the Aztecs' principal temple, a twin temple dedicated to the rain god Tláloc and the Aztec tribal god Huitzilopochtli, during the flourishing of Tenochtitlán in the 1400s.

Huitzilopochtli was a symbol to the Aztecs of those warriors who had been sacrificed to the sun to insure its continued rising.

The temple is thought to be on the exact spot where the Aztecs saw the symbol of an eagle with a snake in its beak perching on a cactus – still the symbol of Mexico today. Reconstructed between 1483 and 1487, the temple was rededicated with the sacrifice of 20,000 prisoners in four days.

On your way from the Zócalo to the site, stop at the Fountain of Tenochtitlán, on the east side of the cathedral. A brass model of the ancient city is displayed in the pool, with the water filling its canal-like streets, and surrounding its chinampas (floating gardens) on the outskirts. There's another model of the ancient city in the Museo de la Ciudad de México, described below.

The temple site, on the east side of the cathedral at the corner of Seminario and Moneda, is open Tuesday to Sunday from 9 am to 5 pm. Admission costs US$3.50 and includes entrance to the Museo del Templo Mayor (see below); on Sunday, both are free. Guided tours are given in Spanish (free) Tuesday to Friday at 9.30 am and 4 pm (Saturday at 9.30 am and 1 pm); and in English (US$1) Tuesday to Saturday at 10 am and noon. Refreshments are on sale in the courtyard of the building at No 8, near the Fountain of Tenochtitlán.

A raised walkway around the site gives you some idea of the temple's layout and multiple layers of construction. The temple pyramid that once stood here was rebuilt to a larger scale at least five times, in accordance with the cycles of the Aztec calendar. (Note that the map of the Teocalli of Tenochtitlán shows how it used to be; today much of it has either been destroyed or is buried beneath city streets.)

The beautiful, modern Museo del Templo Mayor (☎ 542-17-17), on the east side of the site, was opened in 1987 to house artefacts discovered here. Prime of place is given to the great wheel-like votive stone of Coyolxauhqui, the moon goddess, who, according to her unpronounceable name, had 'bells painted on her face'. It was

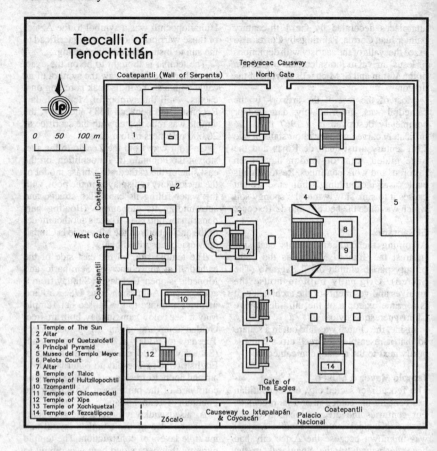

Teocalli of Tenochtitlán

Tepeyacac Causeway
North Gate

Coatepantli (Wall of Serpents)

0   50   100 m

Coatepantli

West Gate

Coatepantli

1 Temple of The Sun
2 Altar
3 Temple of Quetzalcóatl
4 Principal Pyramid
5 Museo del Templo Mayor
6 Pelota Court
7 Altar
8 Temple of Tlaloc
9 Temple of Huitzilopochtli
10 Tzompantli
11 Temple of Chicomecóatl
12 Temple of Xipe
13 Temple of Xochiquetzal
14 Temple of Tezcatlipoca

Gate of
The Eagles

Zócalo   Causeway to Ixtapalapán   Palacio   Coatepantli
& Coyoacán   Nacional

Coyolxauhqui, ruler of the night, who gave virgin-birth to Huitzilopochtli, the triumphant warrior god who demanded so much blood sacrifice from the Aztecs.

Other outstanding exhibits include a mask made of jade and obsidian, and full-size terracotta *guerreros aguilas*, or eagle warriors.

Here is an outline of the exhibit rooms:

Sala 1, Antecedentes – the early days of Tenochtitlán.
Sala 2, Guerra y Sacrificio – Aztec beliefs and practices of war and human sacrifice.
Sala 3, Tributo y Comercio – Aztec government, trade and commerce.

Sala 4, Huitzilopochtli – lord of the Templo Mayor and demander of sacrifices
Sala 5, Tláloc – the rain god and his role in Aztec daily life.
Sala 6, Faunas – animals of the Aztecs and their empire.
Sala 7, Religion – the gods, goddesses and other spirits of Aztec religion.
Sala 8, Caida de Tenochtitlán – the fall of the city, its last two emperors (Moctezuma and Cuauhtémoc) and the conqueror (Cortés).

Leave the Templo Mayor, walk back toward the Zócalo, and turn left onto Calle Moneda. As with many buildings in this historic section of the city, those along Moneda are constructed of tezontle, the local volcanic stone.

Museo Nacional de las Culturas

The National Museum of Cultures (☎ 512-74- 52 or 512-45-99), Calle Moneda 13, has a collection of exhibits showing the art, dress and handicrafts of several cultures. The 2nd-floor rooms each highlight a different set of cultures: for example, there's an Asian room with displays from India and China. The ground-floor rooms include a small temporary exhibit hall, a library with magazines from several countries and a paleontological exhibit. If time is short, you can pass it by.

The museum is in a building constructed in 1567 to house the Casa de la Moneda, the colonial mint. Hours are Tuesday to Saturday 9.30 am to 5.30 pm, and Sunday 9 am to 4 pm. Admission is US$0.50.

Templo de la Santísima

The Church of the Holy Sacrament, a magnificent example of Churrigueresque style, is two blocks east of the National Museum of Cultures on Calle Moneda at Calle de la Santísima. The profusion of ornamental sculptures on the façade is the main reason to visit this church, most of which was designed and carved by sculptor and architect Lorenzo Rodríguez between 1755 and 1783. The most important features of the façade include the ghostly busts of the 12 apostles and the sculpted depiction of Christ with his head in God's lap.

Nacional Monte de Piedad

To the left (west) of the cathedral across the busy Calle Monte de Piedad is Mexico's national pawn shop. Founded in 1775 by the Count of Regla, it's worth a visit to see what must be one of the world's largest 'department stores' for second-hand goods. It is housed in a large, dark building facing the west side of the cathedral and is open daily except Sunday, for free. The site was once occupied by the Palace of Axayácatl, where Cortés and his intrepid companions were first received by Moctezuma II in 1519.

Iglesia de Santo Domingo

Built in 1527, the original Church of Santo Domingo was one of Mexico's first Dominican churches and convents. However, the present building, still on the original site at the intersection of Calles República del Brasil, República de Venezuela and República de Colombia, only dates from 1736.

It is a beautiful example of baroque architecture decorated on its eastern side with the statues of Saint Domingo and Saint Francis. Below the statues, the arms of both saints are symbolically entwined as if to convey a unity of purpose in their lives. The front or southern façade is equally beautiful with its statues and 12 columns around the main entrance. Between the columns are statues of Saint Francis and Saint Augustine and in the centre at the top is a bas-relief of the Assumption of the Virgin Mary.

Murals

Several buildings around the Zócalo hold important works by the great Mexican muralists: Diego Rivera, José Clemente Orozco and David Alfaro Siqueiros. All these buildings are government offices, and thus are open only Monday to Friday from 9 am to 3 pm. Admission is free.

The first is the **Secretaría de Educación Pública** (☎ 510-23-80), on Calle República de Argentina between San Ildefonso/González Obregón and Calle República de Venezuela, 3½ blocks north of the Zócalo. Coming from the Iglesia de Santo Domingo, walk east along Calle República de Venezuela one block and turn right; from the Zócalo, walk north between the cathedral and the Templo Mayor on Calle Seminario, which becomes Calle República de Argentina. Look for the Secretaría on the left-hand side just after you cross Calle San Ildefonso/González Obregón.

Walk into the courtyard to see some of the 235 mural panels done by Diego Rivera in 1921 to 1922 when the building was constructed. Themes in the first courtyard are agriculture, handicrafts and industry; in the second court, festivals and markets. Try to see the murals on the upper floor as well. In addition to Rivera, there are panels by Amado de la Cueva, Jean Charlot, Juan O'Gorman, Carlos Mérida and others.

From the Secretaría de Educación Pública, walk south back toward the Zócalo a half-block. On the left-hand (east) side of the street is the **Escuela Nacional Preparatoria**, at the corner of Argentina and Donceles. Once the Jesuit college of San Ildefonso (1749), it became a teacher training college under President Benito Juárez. From 1923 to 1933, Rivera, Orozco, Siqueiros and other artists were brought in to decorate the walls. Most of the work in the main court and on the grand staircase is by Orozco, inspired by the Mexican Revolution (just ended at the time he painted). In a small patio are Siqueiros' works. The amphitheatre holds a gigantic mural by Rivera with Creation as the subject.

Walk south three blocks (through the Zócalo) to reach the Suprema Corte de Justicia.

Mexico's Supreme Court, just off the south-east corner of the Zócalo at the corner of Pino Suárez and Corregidora, would not be a visitor attraction were it not for the five immense murals painted by José Clemente Orozco on the walls of the 2nd-floor foyer and near the entrance to the library. Enter and go directly up the steps. The mural on the east wall is a bright tribute to workers' rights, while on the opposite wall the pride and national conscience of Mexico are depicted in the form of a great tiger atop the country's mineral wealth. The other two murals are called *La Justicia* and show 'Justice' sleeping while a man is transformed into a destructive fire-bolt. The fifth mural is by American artist G Biddle.

Museo de la Ciudad de México

The Museum of Mexico City (☎ 542-04-87), Pino Suárez 30 at Calle República del Salvador (Metro: Pino Suárez), three blocks south of the south-east corner of the Zócalo, is often skipped by travellers, but it provides an overview of the geological, demographic and political history of Mexico City.

The museum is housed in a mansion built in 1528 as a residence for one of Cortés' cousins and then rebuilt in 1779 to 1780 for the counts of Santiago de Calimaya. A stone sculpture of a feathered serpent embedded in the building's cornerstone at Pino Suárez and República del Salvador shows that the mansion was partly constructed from Aztec ruins.

On the ground floor, models chronicle the volcanic eruptions that created the valley now occupied by Mexico City. Displays (all in Spanish) show that humans began settling the valley in 8000 BC and gradually built the magnificent temples and pyramids of Teotihuacán. By the 14th century AD, the Aztecs had settled in the area of present-day Mexico City to build Tenochtitlán.

An impressive small-scale model of the city is in Room 6. In the next room, a huge mural by Mexican painter Francisco Moreno Capdevila depicts the fiery conquest of Tenochtitlán by Cortés in 1521. An audiovisual show depicting the history of Tenochtitlán is shown (in Spanish) daily at 11 am in the museum's ground-floor conference room.

A 2nd-floor room once served as the studio of Joaquin Clausell, a Mexican Impressionist painter, who used the studio's walls as a floor-to-ceiling canvas.

Museum hours are Tuesday to Sunday, 9.30 am to 7.30 pm; closed Monday. Admission is free.

AROUND THE ALAMEDA

West of Avenida Lázaro Cárdenas and north of Avenida Juárez is the Alameda Central, Mexico City's prettiest park. In the blocks around the Alameda are more than a dozen interesting sights, from colonial mansions to skyscrapers. If you approach the Alameda walking westward from the Zócalo, you'll pass streets filled with hotels, restaurants, shops, stores and street markets, a fascinating area for exploration. Two traffic arteries connect the Zócalo with the Alameda to the west: Avenida Cinco (5) de Mayo carries traffic westbound, Avenida Madero carries it eastbound. Leave the Zócalo walking westward along Avenida Madero (by the Hotel

Majestic). Before reaching the Alameda, stop and have a look at the Palacio de Iturbide and the Casa de Azulejos (described below).

Alameda Central

During the days of Tenochtitlán, what is now a pleasant, verdant park was an Aztec marketplace. In early colonial times, it became the site of the church's auto-da-fé, where heretics were burned or hanged. Then in 1593, Viceroy Luis de Velasco decided the growing city needed a pleasant area of pathways, fountains and trees. By the late 19th century the park was dotted with European-style statuary, a bandstand was the venue for free concerts, and gas lamps gave illumination at night. Today, the park is a popular and easily accessible refuge from the maddening crowds and traffic of the city.

On the south side of the Alameda facing Avenida Juárez is the Juárez Hemiciclo, a gleaming white semicircle of marble columns surrounding a regally seated statue of Benito Juárez (1806-72). Born a poor Zapotec Indian boy in Oaxaca, Juárez rose to become a famous lawyer, president of Mexico, and victor of the battles against the armies of Napoleon III and Maximilian of Hapsburg.

West of the Alameda across Calle Dr Mora is the Jardín de la Solidaridad (Solidarity Garden). Built in 1986 on the site of the old Hotel Regis, it commemorates the struggle of Mexico City's residents to rebuild their city after the disastrous earthquake of 1985.

The Alameda is surrounded by museums. Here they are, starting on the east side, moving to the north, then west and south.

Palacio de Bellas Artes

Dominating the east end of the Alameda is the Palace of Fine Arts (☎ 704-21-11), an impressive concert hall and arts centre commissioned by President Porfirio Díaz. Construction began in 1904 under Italian architect Adam Boari who favoured Neo-classical and Art Nouveau styles. It was supposed to be completed by 1910 in time for the grandiose centennial celebration of

Mexican independence. However, before the interior was finished, the heavy marble shell of the building began to sink into the spongy subsoil, and construction was halted. Then came the Mexican Revolution, which delayed completion until 1934. Architect Federico Mariscal changed and completed the interior so that it would reflect the popular Art Deco style of the 1920s and '30s.

The Palace houses some of Mexico's finest murals, by Siqueiros, Orozco, Rivera, Rufino Tamayo and Jorge González Camarena. They dominate immense wall space on the 3rd level of the Palace. Displayed here are Siqueiros' *Cain en los Estados Unidos*, expressing the artist's indignation at racism against blacks in the USA; and *Nacimiento del Fascismo*, his graphic interpretation of the birth of fascism and dictatorships in the world.

Rivera also used murals as a form of dramatic political expression. On the western wall is one of his most famous murals, *Man at the Crossing of the Ways*, which was first painted at Rockefeller Center in New York as *Man in Control of his Universe*. The Rockefeller family commissioned the piece in the 1930s but had it destroyed because of its rebellious, anti-capitalist themes. Rivera reproduced it here even more dramatically with the same themes of struggle against class systems and dehumanising industrialisation.

Another highlight of the Palace is the beautiful stained-glass curtain hanging in the main theatre that colourfully depicts the Valley of Mexico. Based on the work of Mexican painter Gerardo Murillo ('Dr Atl'), Tiffany Studios of New York assembled the curtain from almost a million pieces of coloured glass. On Sunday mornings and just before performances, the curtain is illuminated for public viewing.

You can view the murals and look around the Palacio Tuesday to Sunday from 10 am to 6 pm. There's a bookshop and an artsy little café also (see Places to Eat).

The Palacio is also home to Mexico City's Ballet Folklorico, a dazzling spectacle of Mexican music and dance that should not be missed. See the Entertainment section for more details.

Palacio de Iturbide

At Avenida Madero 17, between Bolívar and Gante, rises the beautiful baroque façade of the Iturbide Palace (☎ 521-57-97). Built between 1779 and 1785 by Francisco Guerrero y Torres for the marquises of Jarral de Berrio and the counts of San Mateo de Valparaiso, it was claimed in 1821 by General Agustín Iturbide. The general, author of the Plan of Iguala and a hero of the Mexican struggle for independence from Spain, responded favourably to a crowd which gathered in the street in front of his palace in 1822, beseeching him to be their emperor (Iturbide is thought to have instigated the gathering). Proclaiming himself Emperor Agustín I, Iturbide reigned over the first Empire of Mexico for less than a year. Later in 1822, General Santa Anna proclaimed the birth of the Mexican republic, and in 1823 Iturbide abdicated.

The palace was restored in 1972 and now houses the offices of Fomento Cultural Banamex, the bank's cultural promotion section. Art exhibits are hung in several of its rooms; there's a bookshop as well. The courtyard is hung with 17th and 18th-century paintings; on the upper floor is a beautifully restored chapel.

Casa de Azulejos

A block west of the Iturbide Palace at Avenida Madero 4, on the north side of the street on the corner of Condesa, stands one of the city's gems. The House of Tiles dates from 1596, when it was built for the counts of the valley of Orizaba. Although Moorish in style with a combination of Spanish and North African geometric designs, the tiles (added in the 1700s) were actually produced in China and shipped to Mexico on the Manila *naos* (typical Spanish sailing vessels used from the late 16th to the early 19th centuries). Some of the tiles were also produced in Puebla.

The building now houses a Sanborns store (☎ 510-96-13) and restaurant (open 7.30 am to 10 pm), and is a good place to buy a newspaper or have refreshments. The spacious interior courtyard with its Moorish fountain is now enclosed and set with dining tables. On the grand staircase on the north side is a mural painted in 1925 by Orozco.

Torre Latinoamericana

The Latin American Tower, at the corner of Avenidas Madero and Lázaro Cárdenas, has an observation deck on its 42nd floor. It's open every day between 10 am and 11 pm. Admission costs US$3.50 for adults, US$2.75 for children. Buy your tickets at the little booth by the entrance before you reach the elevators. If you want to use the pay telescopes, buy some tokens for them as well. If you'd like to get in without paying admission, go to the Muralto restaurant and bar on the 41st floor, open from 1 pm to 1 am. To enjoy the view you will be required to buy a drink (US$4 and up) or a meal.

The tower also boasts the 'highest aquarium in the world' on the 38th floor at 2358 metres (7736 feet) above sea level. Hours are the same as for the observation deck; admission costs just a bit less.

Museo Nacional de Arte

The National Museum of Art (☎ 512-32-24), Calle de Tacuba 8, just east of Avenida Lázaro Cárdenas and the Bellas Artes, is in the former headquarters of the Secretaría de Comunicaciones y Obras Públicas. You'll recognise it by the distinctive bronze equestrian statue of Spanish King Carlos IV de Borbón (1788-1808) done by the Mexican sculptor Manuel Tolsá. Called *El Caballito* or Little Horse, it once stood in the Zócalo, then in a glorieta on Paseo de la Reforma, and is now here. Note that Mexicans refer to the horse, but not to the rider, who reigned just before Mexico gained its independence.

A grand Italian marble staircase with baroque lampposts, the work of Italian architect Silvio Contri, greets you as you enter. The museum's collections represent every style and school of Mexican art. First-floor collections include works by José Velasco depicting late 19th and early 20th-century life in Mexico City and the countryside. One of his landscapes shows that Mexico City was still surrounded by lakes even in the late 19th century.

Second-floor collections include 17th-century religious paintings by Antonio Rodríguez, Juan Correa and José de Ibarra; 18th and 19th-century sculptures; portraits by Antonio Poblano; sketches and prints of skeletal figures sweeping streets; and anonymous paintings with social and political themes. Hours are 10 am to 5 pm, Tuesday to Sunday. Admission is US$2.75.

Palacio de Minería

Directly across the street from the museum is the Palace of Mines (☎ 510-18-68), Calle de Tacuba 5, a beautiful Neoclassical building designed by architect Manuel Tolsá and built between 1797 and 1813. Four meteorites found in Mexico are on display, echoing the time when this was the nerve centre of Mexican mining activity. But the building is now used for university cultural functions, including art exhibits. Hours are Monday to Friday from 8.30 am to 9 pm. Admission is free.

Museo Franz Mayer

On the north side of Avenida Hidalgo, facing the Alameda, stands the Franz Mayer Museum (☎ 518-22-65), Avenida Hidalgo

45 at Plaza de Santa Veracruz (Metro: Hidalgo or Bellas Artes). It's the repository of a sumptuous once-private collection of Mexican art.

Franz Mayer, born in Mannheim, Germany, in 1882, moved to Mexico, became a citizen, and began to collect masterpieces of Mexican silver, textiles and furniture. You can now admire 'Don Pancho's' collections in what was once the Hospital de San Juan de Dios.

As you enter, rooms to the right hold changing exhibits and displays of antique furnishings. To the left is a gorgeous colonial garden courtyard. The suite of rooms on the courtyard's south side are done in antique furnishings, and are very fine, especially the lovely chapel. To the north is the Cafetería del Claustro, a delightful café serving light meals (see Places to Eat for details). The best gold and silver items are in one room on the upper floor of the courtyard (follow signs to 'Obras maestras de la colección de plata del Museo Franz Mayer').

The museum is open Tuesday to Sunday from 10 am to 5 pm. Admission costs US$1.75 (US$0.35 for students); it's free on Sunday. If you just want to go to the Cafetería del Claustro, tell that to the guard and you needn't buy a ticket.

Museo de la Estampa

To the right (east) of the Museo Franz Mayer is the Museum of Printing (☎ 521-22-44), Avenida Hidalgo 39, with a permanent collection of engravings, lithographs, etc from Mexico's greatest artists, as well as changing exhibits of the graphic arts. Hours are Tuesday to Sunday from 10 am to 5.45 pm. Admission costs US$0.70.

Museo Mural Diego Rivera

Among Diego Rivera's most famous murals is *Sueño de una Tarde Dominical en la Alameda* (Dream of a Sunday Afternoon in Alameda Park), a large work (15 metres long by four metres high) painted in 1947. The artist imagines all the great historical figures who walked in the city, from Cortés and Sor Juana Inez de la Cruz through Juárez,

General Santa Anna, Emperor Maximilian and Empress Carlota, Cuban revolutionary José Martí, Porfirio Díaz, and Madero and his nemesis, General Victoriano Huerta.

The mural was painted in the Hotel del Prado which stood across the street on the south side of Avenida Juárez until it was badly damaged in the earthquake of 1985. The museum, sometimes called the Museo de la Alameda (☎ 510-23-29), was constructed in 1986 to house just this mural. It's on the west side of the Alameda, facing the Jardín de la Solidaridad (Metro: Hidalgo). Hours are Tuesday to Sunday 10 am to 2 pm and 3 to 6 pm. Admission costs US$1.75.

Pinacoteca Virreynal de San Diego
Around the corner to the north of the Museo Mural Diego Rivera is this Viceregal Picture Gallery (☎ 510-27-93), at Calle Dr Mora 7 across from the north-west corner of the Alameda. This is a former church and Dominican monastery that is now home to a collection of 17th and 18th-century baroque and religious paintings. A mural by contemporary painter Federico Cantú is also displayed. Hours are 9 am to 5 pm, Tuesday to Sunday. Admission costs US$0.70, but is free to those under 13 and over 60 years, and to everyone on Sunday.

Museo Nacional de Artes e Industrias Populares
The Museum of Popular Arts and Industries of the National Indigenous Peoples' Institute (☎ 521-66-79 or 518-30-58), Avenida Juárez 44, south of the Alameda across from the Juárez Hemiciclo (Metro: Hidalgo), displays and sells (at fixed prices) high-quality handicrafts from all over Mexico. Items include hide-covered drums, hand-blown glassware, intricately woven baskets and shawls. Store hours are 9 am to 6 pm every day; a small crafts museum is open Monday to Friday 9 am to 3 pm.

AROUND PLAZA DE LA REPÚBLICA
There are a few sights of interest around the plaza, starting with the immense monument right in its centre. Metro station for most of the sights in this district is Revolución.

Monumento a la Revolución
Four short blocks west of the intersection of Avenida Juárez and Paseo de la Reforma is the spacious Plaza de la República and its huge Monument to the Revolution. Built in the early 1900s by Porfirio Díaz, this was supposed to be a meeting-chamber for senators and deputies, but construction (not to mention Díaz's term as president) was interrupted by the Revolution. Instead, the structure was modified in the 1930s and dedicated as a monument to the revolution. The remains of two revolutionary heroes, Venustiano Carranza and Francisco Madero, are buried in its wide pillars.

Museo Nacional de la Revolución
Directly beneath the Monument to the Revolution is the National Museum of the Revolution, with exhibits about life during the 1910 Revolution. A life-size model of a typical bank, the front pages of several newspapers, tools and equipment from various industries, old photographs and a silent movie about the 1910 Centenary celebration are among the exhibits. The place is heavy on text (in Spanish), but also has lots of pictures. Hours are Tuesday to Sunday 9 am to 5 pm. Admission is free, and the experience of seeing this museum is worth the price.

Frontón México
On the north side of the Plaza de la República is Mexico City's yellow Art Deco jai alai arena, recently restored. Jai alai, a fast-moving game that originated in the Basque region of Spain, is played with two teams of two players each in a long, walled-in court. Each player wears a small wicker baskets on one arm and uses it to catch and throw a hard, goatskin-covered rubber ball. Spectators bet on each match. Games are played all year starting at 7 pm Tuesday to Friday, at 6.30 pm on Saturday, and 5 pm on Sunday. A notice at the door translates: 'No entry with guns, cellular phones, radios or cameras'.

There's an elegant branch of the Prendes Restaurant here as well.

Museo de San Carlos

The Museum of San Carlos (☎ 566-85-22), Puente de Alvarado 50, at the corner of Calle Ramos Arizpe 1½ blocks east of the Revolución Metro station, is housed in the former mansion of the Marques de Buenavista, designed by Manuel Tolsá in the early 1800s. Later converted to a fine arts academy, it boasts Diego Rivera and José Clemente Orozco among its graduates.

Ground-floor rooms hold temporary exhibits. The museum's permanent collection of paintings from the 1500s to the 1800s. is upstairs. There are works by Berruguete, Brueghel, Cranach the Elder, Daumier, Goya, Ingres, Rembrandt, José Ribera, Titian, Tintoretto, Zurbarán and others. Hours are Wednesday to Monday 10 am to 6 pm (closed Tuesday). Admission costs US$1.75, free to students and children, and to everyone on Sunday. There's a small bookstore. After you visit, stroll into the pretty little park on the museum's south side.

Lotería Nacional

Mexico's national lottery is a national passion. The tall Art Deco skyscraper on the west side of the intersection of Avenida Juárez and Paseo de la Reforma (Metro: Hidalgo) is the game's headquarters; a tall black glass shaft nearby provides more office space. Walk into the Art Deco building and up the stairs any Monday, Wednesday or Friday after 7.30 pm, take a seat in the cosy auditorium, and at exactly 8 pm the ceremony of picking the winning numbers begins. Cylindrical cages spew out numbered wooden balls which are plucked up by uniformed pages who call out the numbers and amounts as they match winner to prize. Admission is free. Winning is possible, but you've got to have a ticket and an improbable amount of luck.

PASEO DE LA REFORMA & ZONA ROSA

Paseo de la Reforma, the city's main street and status address, proceeds south-west from the intersection with Avenida Juárez all the way to and through Chapultepec park. It is said that Emperor Maximilian of Hapsburg laid out the boulevard to connect his palace on Chapultepec hill with the older section of the city. He could look eastward straight down the street from his bedroom, and he rode to work along the paseo on his way to the National Palace on the Zócalo.

The paseo is lined with banks, embassies, stores, hotels, luxury shops, and – surprisingly – art. A few blocks due south of the Plaza de la República on Reforma is the **Glorieta Cristóbal Colón**, with a statue to Christopher Columbus done by French sculptor Charles Cordier in 1877. Just northeast of the glorieta on the north-west side of the street is a branch of the Sanborns store chain with two **frescoes** by Rufino Tamayo. The one called *Día y Noche* (Day and Night) is among the artist's best. In the lobby of the Banco Internacional building at Reforma 156 there are frescoes painted in 1965 by Juan O'Gorman.

Just west of the busy intersection of Reforma and Avenida Insurgentes is the **Jardín del Arte**, a sliver of shady park which becomes an open-air artists' bazaar on Sundays. Come for a stroll and a browse, if not a buy.

South-west of the Reforma-Insurgentes intersection is the **Zona Rosa** (Pink Zone), the high-life and nightlife district. All of the street names in this section are taken from European cities, accentuating the area's cosmopolitan pretensions. The Zona Rosa (Metro: Insurgentes) is an interesting place for a stroll, whether or not you plan to patronise its hotels, restaurants, shops and nightclubs. For details on how to spend money here, see Places to Stay, Places to Eat, Things to Buy and Entertainment.

Reforma passes along the north-west flank of the Zona Rosa. At the intersection with Avenida Río Tiber/Avenida Florencia stands the symbol of Mexico City, the **Monumento a la Independencia**, a gilded statue of Liberty on a pedestal, called by locals simply El Ángel. The statue was done

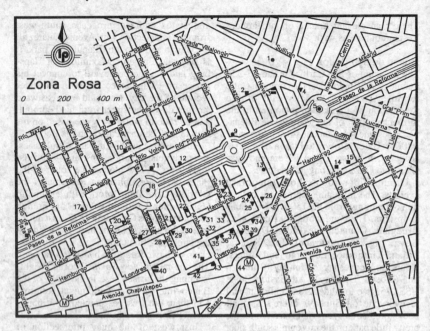

Zona Rosa

0   200   400 m

■ PLACES TO STAY	6	Restaurante Vegetariano Las Fuentes	OTHER
2 Hotel María Cristina	19	Piccadilly Pub	1 Jardín del Arte
7 Casa González	20	Restaurante	3 Correos (Post
10 San Marino Hotel-Suites		Vegetariano Yug	Office)
11 María-Isabel Sheraton Hotel	21	Auseba	5 Glorieta Cuauhtémoc
14 Hotel Parador Washington	23	Pizza Real	8 UK Embassy
15 Hotel Vasco de Quiroga	24	Carrousel Internacional	9 Australian Embassy
16 Hotel Marquis Reforma	25	Chalet Suizo	12 USA Embassy
22 Hotel Marco Polo	26	Luaú	13 French Embassy
27 Hotel Galería Plaza	28	La Crepa Suiza	17 Japanese Embassy
37 Hotel Geneve	29	Salon de Thé Duca d'Este	18 Monumento a la Independencia (El Ángel)
41 Hotel Krystal Zona Rosa	30	Parri	32 City Tourist Office
43 Hotel Century	31	Restaurant Tokyo	36 Fonart Handicrafts Shop
	33	Café Konditori	40 Correos (Post
▼ PLACES TO EAT	34	Shirley's Pink Zone	Office)
	35	Fonda 99.99	
4 Restaurante Daruma	38	Salon Luz	
	39	Restaurante El Gallito	Ⓜ METRO
	42	Fonda El Refugio	44 Insurgentes
			45 Sevilla

by sculptor Antonio Rivas Mercado and erected in 1910, just as the Mexican Revolution got under way. In the north quarter of the angel glorieta is the Hotel María Isabel-Sheraton, which has a **mural** by José Clemente Orozco in its aptly named Orozco Room. Also aptly, the mural revels in the delights of the dinner table. South-west from the Angel the boulevard is lined mostly with large, impersonal modern office buildings.

At the intersection with Calzada General Escobedo and Calzada Melchor Ocampo is a fountain with a **statue of Diana**, and across the paseo from it the six slender columns of the **Monumento a los Niños Héroes** (Monument to the Boy Heroes). Marking the entrance to Chapultepec park and its palace, the monument commemorates six brave cadets at the national military academy. On 13 September 1847, when American troops invaded Mexico and made their way to Mexico City, the military academy was housed in Chapultepec castle. Having defended their school against the invaders as long as they could, the six cadets wrapped themselves in Mexican flags and leapt to their deaths rather than surrender. An annual ceremony on the date remembers their heroism.

From this point the paseo veers from south-westerly to due west and continues through the vast park. But the monumental part of the boulevard, with side roads, trees, glorietas and monuments, ends as it touches the park at the Niños Héroes.

BOSQUE DE CHAPULTEPEC

According to popular legend, Chapultepec first gained prominence when one of the last kings of the Toltecs and Chichimecs escaped from Tula to the woods of Chapultepec, establishing the area as a convenient place of refuge. Later, the hill for which the park was named (Chapultepec means Hill of the Grasshoppers in Nahuatl) served as a refuge for the Mexica tribe and then as a fortress for Moctezuma I (1440-69) before becoming a summer residence for Aztec nobles. In the 1500s, Nezahualcóyotl, the ruler of nearby

Texcoco, gave his official sanction to a plan to make the area a forest reserve.

It has remained Mexico City's largest park for almost 500 years, and attracts hundreds of thousands of visitors daily. The park covers more than four square km (1000 acres) and has lakes, a zoo, botanical gardens, a sculpture garden and several important world-class museums.

There are several ways of getting to and from the park. Buses 55 and 76 ('Zócalo – Km 13') run from the Zócalo along Avenida Cinco de Mayo and Avenida Juárez, and down Paseo de la Reforma straight into the park. The Metro station is Chapultepec. Note that most of the museums in the park offer free admission on Sunday.

Castillo de Chapultepec

Although Cortés built a fortress atop Chapultepec hill, it was abandoned after his death and fell into ruin. Part of the present castle was built in 1785 as a residence for the viceroys of New Spain until it was again briefly abandoned after independence. Some changes were made in 1843 when it was converted into a military academy.

When Emperor Maximilian and Empress Carlota arrived in 1864, they refurbished the castle with the help of painter Santiago Rebull and architect Vicente Manero. After their fall from power the castle remained a residence for Mexico's presidents until 1940, when President Lázaro Cárdenas converted it into the National Museum of History.

Today the **Museo Nacional de Historia** (☎ 553-62-24) has two floors of exhibits chronicling the rise and fall of New Spain, the establishment of an independent Mexico, the dictatorship of Porfirio Díaz and the Mexican Revolution. It's open Tuesday to Sunday from 9 am to 5 pm. Admission costs US$3.50, free on Sunday.

In La Lucha de Independencia (The Struggle for Independence) Hall, a magnificent mural by Diego Rivera covers the walls from floor to ceiling and stretches completely around the room. Don't miss the rooms entered from a garden walkway around the

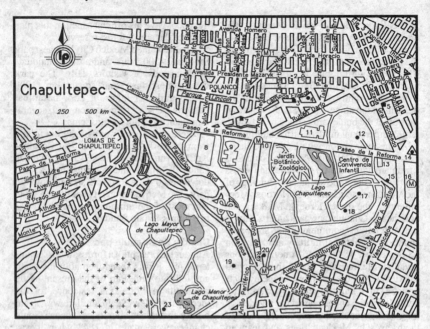

Chapultepec

0 250 500 km

castle, which hold memories of the Hapsburg intervention of Maximilian and Carlota.

To get to the castle from Paseo de la Reforma or Chapultepec Metro station, walk into the park towards the six columns of the Monumento a los Niños Héroes. To the right of the monument, follow the road that curves up towards the castle. You can either take a

10-minute hike up to the hilltop, wait for the free shuttle bus, or take the elevator at the foot of the road.

Museo del Caracol

From Chapultepec castle, stroll down the road to the Museo del Caracol. Shaped somewhat like a snail shell *(caracol)* as it curls down the hillside, this is officially the Museo Galería de la Lucha del Pueblo Mexicano por su Libertad (Museum Gallery of the Struggle of the Mexican People for Liberty). Displays and dioramas cover social and political life in Mexico from Spanish colonial days, the divisions of New Spain in the 18th century, Miguel Hidalgo y Costilla's leadership in the struggle for independence, and Francisco Madero's rule in the early 1900s.

The self-guided tour ends in a circular hall that contains only one item – the 1917 Constitution of Mexico. It is in Chapultepec park near the top of Chapultepec hill, on the south side of Chapultepec castle. Hours are 9 am to 5 pm, Tuesday to Sunday. Hours are Tuesday to Saturday from 9 am to 5 pm, Sunday from 10 am to 4 pm. Admission is free.

Museo de Arte Moderno

At the base of the hill just north-west of the Monumento a los Niños Héroes stands the Museum of Modern Art (☎ 553-93-94; Metro: Chapultepec). Two modern circular structures contain the museum's permanent collection, including works by Mexico's most famous artists – Siqueiros, Cuevas, Rivera, Velasco and O'Gorman – as well as changing exhibits by prominent artists from Mexico and abroad. Refer to *The Mexico City News* or *Tiempo Libre* for information on current exhibits.

Hours are Tuesday to Sunday 10 am to 6 pm. Admission is US$2.75. To the north of the museum, along the way to the Museo Tamayo, is a sculpture garden.

Museo Nacional de Antropología

Along with the Zócalo and the Alameda, the National Museum of Anthropology (☎ 553-62-66) is a sight not to be missed, one of the finest museums of its kind in the world. Hours are 9 am to 7 pm Tuesday to Sunday. Admission is US$3.50, free on Sunday. The museum has a restaurant and a bookshop.

To get there, take bus No 55 or 76 ('Auditorio' or 'Km 13'), or any colectivo ('Auditorio') or bus running south-west along Reforma to the bus stop right at the museum (but watch out for pickpockets as this is a prime route). Alternatively, walk to the museum from Chapultepec castle (500 metres), from the Auditorio Metro station (400 metres), or from the Chapultepec Metro station (600 metres). To return to the Alameda, take a bus or colectivo marked 'La Villa' or 'M(etro) Hidalgo'.

The spacious modern structure is the work of Mexican architect Pedro Ramírez Vásquez, designed and built in the early 1960s at a cost of more than US$20 million. Through the high glass windows of the entrance hall, you can see a long, rectangular courtyard flanked on three sides by the museum's two-storey exhibit halls – a total of four km of hallways. An immense stone 'umbrella' rises from the centre of the courtyard.

In the entrance hall is an orientation theatre featuring a 20-minute film (in Spanish) entitled 'Man in Mesoamerica'.

The museum's ground-floor exhibit halls are dedicated to prehistory and archaeology – the way Mexicans lived in the past. Rooms on the upper level specialise in ethnology – the way Mexicans live today. In general, the ethnological exhibits upstairs cover the same territories as the anthropological exhibits downstairs, so you can see the great Maya city of Palenque as it was in the 700s, then go upstairs and see how the people around Palenque live today.

The museum is fascinating and very large, with more than one can reasonably see (without brain-strain) in a day. Your best plan, unless you have lots of time, is to tour the rooms with exhibits representing regions of Mexico that you plan to visit or have visited. Here's a brief guide to the regions and archaeological sites covered; the tour is in anti-clockwise order around the courtyard:

Introducción a la Antropología – You enter past a mural by González Camarena showing the women of many nations. The exhibits introduce the study of anthropology and ethnology, especially in Mesoamerica and Mexico.

Sala Origenes – The Origins Room shows evidence of the first men and women in this hemisphere with findings from Santa Isabel Ixtapan and the Valley of Mexico.

Sala Preclasica – Preclassic Civilisations date from 2000 BC to 300 AD, and include artefacts from Michoacán, Cuicuilco and Tlaltilco, highlighting the transition from a nomadic life of hunting to a more settled life of farming in Mexico about 1000 BC.

Sala Teotihuacana – The Teotihuacán Room has models of the awesome Teotihuacán ceremonial centre on the outskirts of Mexico City, the Western Hemisphere's first great and powerful state. The room's highlight is a full-sized model of the Temple of Quetzalcóatl.

Sala Tolteca – The Toltecs, the predominant people in Mexico from 900 to 1200 AD, based their first empire at Tula, near Mexico City, and carved great 'Atlantean Men' from stone. This room has one from Tula's Temple of Tlahuizcalpantecutli. Toltec influence later spread to Xochicalco, Campeche, Chichén Itzá and Tenayuca.

Sala Mexica – Look to the far end of the courtyard for the words 'CEM ANAHUAC TENOCHCA TLALPAN' – that's the suite devoted to the Mexica, or, as we know them, the Aztecs. Come here to see the famous Aztec calendar stone, a model of Moctezuma's brilliant feathered headdress, a Tzompantli (Wall of Skulls) and other graphic reminders of ancient Tenochtitlán.

Sala Oaxaca – The cultures of Oaxaca, such as the Zapotec at Monte Albán and the Mixtec at Mitla, are among the earliest and finest. Here, several tombs from Monte Albán have been reconstructed. Note also the finely carved jade objects.

Sala Golfo de México – There are models of the great ceremonial centres along the coast of the Gulf of Mexico, including El Tajín and Zempoala in Veracruz. Exhibits show the Huastec, Totonac and Olmec cultures; there's even one of those enormous Olmec heads.

Sala Maya – The Maya Room includes wonderful exhibits not only from south-eastern Mexico (including Palenque, Yaxchilán, and Bonampak), but from Guatemala, Belize and Honduras as well. The full-scale model of the tomb of King Pakal, discovered deep in the Temple of the Inscriptions at Palenque, is breathtaking. A replica of the famous wall paintings of Bonampak looks much better than the damaged original.

Restaurant – Just past the Maya Room is a flight of stairs down to the museum's restaurant. Prices, though not cheap, are reasonable.

Salas Norte y Occidente – The Northern and Western Mexico rooms cover the cultures of the Mexican deserts, which naturally have many things in common with Indian cultures of the American south-west.

Museo Rufino Tamayo

The Tamayo Museum of Contemporary International Art (☎ 286-58-89 or 286-65-19), a boldly modern, multi-level concrete and glass structure, opened in 1981 to house the modern art collection donated by the renowned Mexican painter Rufino Tamayo and his wife Olga to the people of Mexico. (The Tamayos' pre-Hispanic collection is in the Museo Rufino Tamayo in Oaxaca.)

Part of the collection is devoted to 20th-century art, including paintings by Andy Warhol and Picasso. Other modern works include a mammoth rope wall-hanging that resembles a squirming mass of red, black and brown serpents, and a model of a Rolls-Royce made from twigs and branches. Besides the permanent collection, the museum hosts important world-class travelling shows featuring works by the world's most important contemporary artists; refer to *The News* or *Tiempo Libre* for current exhibits.

The museum is just east of the National Museum of Anthropology and is open Tuesday to Sunday from 10 am to 6 pm. Admission is US$2.75, free on Sunday. To reach the museum, follow the directions for the National Museum of Anthropology, but get off to the east.

Parque Zoológico de Chapultepec

King Nezahualcóyotl established Chapultepec as a forested reserve in the early 1500s, and is said to have set aside part of it as the first zoo in the Americas. After Cortés conquered Tenochtitlán in the 1520s he added a bird sanctuary. In 1975 a gift from the people of China brought pandas. The zoo is fun, particularly for children, and the price is right: admission is free. There's a tram tour for the foot-weary.

Hours are Wednesday to Sunday from 9 am to 5 pm (entrance closes at 4.30 pm).

Look for the zoo south of the Museo Nacional de Antropología (see that heading for directions) and west of the lake (Lago de Chapultepec).

Jardín Botánico
Near the zoo are the Botanical Gardens, a collection of plants and trees from all over Mexico and several other countries. It's open from 9 am to 5 pm and admission is free.

Museo Sala de Arte Público David Alfaro Siqueiros
Less than a month before his death in January 1974, David Alfaro Siqueiros, one of Mexico's greatest painters and muralists, donated his house and studio at Calle Tres Picos 29, corner of Hegel, in Polanco, to the government for use as a museum. Siqueiros' private papers and photographs, along with many of his lithographs, murals and drawings, are on display.

Call 531-33-94 to arrange a free guided tour (which is the only way to visit) Monday to Friday 10 am to 2 pm and 5 to 7 pm, and Saturday 10 am to 2 pm. The house is just outside the park, 150 metres north of the Museo Nacional de Antropología.

TLATELOLCO & GUADALUPE
Tlatelolco – Plaza de las Tres Culturas
About two km north of the Palacio de Bellas Artes and the Alameda up Avenida Lázaro Cárdenas is the Plaza de las Tres Culturas. It was given this name because three cultures and periods of Mexican history are represented on the plaza by the ruins of the Aztec pyramid of Tlatelolco, the 17th-century Spanish colonial church of Santiago and the modern Foreign Affairs building.

Until 1473 when it was annexed to the Aztec capital of Tenochtitlán, Tlatelolco was the seat of an independent dynasty and home to the largest market in the Valley of Mexico. Spaniard Bernal Díaz del Castillo saw the market when he arrived in 1520 and later described it in great detail in his book *The True History of the Conquest of New Spain*.

The Pyramid (Temple) of Tlatelolco was the most prominent feature of the area until the Spanish conquest. Today, you can see the ruins of this and other temples from a causeway erected over them.

The Spanish recognised the religious significance of the temples, so after reducing much of this area to rubble, they built first a church, then a Franciscan monastery and finally, in 1609, the Church of Santiago that stands today. Santiago was the patron saint of Spain, who supposedly enabled the Spanish to conquer the Aztecs. Inside, the principal item of interest on display is the baptismal font of Juan Diego (see under Basílica de Guadalupe).

The easiest way to get to Plaza de las Tres Culturas is to take the Metro to the Tlatelolco station, go out the Manuel González exit and turn right. Walk up to Avenida Lázaro Cárdenas and turn right and you will see the plaza just ahead of you.

Basílica de Guadalupe
On 9 December 1531 a poor Indian peasant named Juan Diego, standing on the Cerro (hill) El Tepeyac about eight km north of the Zócalo, saw a vision of a beautiful lady in a rich blue mantle trimmed in gold. He reported to the local priest that he had seen the Virgin Mary, but the priest didn't believe him. Juan returned to the hill, saw the vision again, and an image of the lady was miraculously emblazoned on the poor man's ragged cloak. The priest believed, and ordered a church built on the spot where Diego had seen the vision. Our Lady of Guadalupe became the patron saint of Mexico.

This first Basílica de Nuestra Señora de Guadalupe (Church of Our Lady of Guadalupe), dating from 1533, is on Tepeyac hill just east of Avenida Insurgentes Norte (Metro: La Villa). For centuries pilgrims came to pay their respects to the image of the Virgin and to pray for her intercession on their behalf. In the twentieth century the crowds swamped the old colonial church, so in 1976 a huge modern structure was built, and Diego's cloak was moved to the place of honour in it. The old basilica is now the Museo de la Basílica de Guadalupe (☎ 577-60-22), with a collection of ecclesiastical furniture, religious images in precious materials, and colonial-era paintings. It's open Tuesday to Sunday from 10 am to 6 pm.

There's no missing the dramatic, huge new basilica, the work of architect Pedro Ramírez Vásquez, already famous for his National Museum of Anthropology.

When you visit, you'll stand in awe of the cavernous building, and of the pilgrims, many of them approaching for hundreds of metres on their knees, who revere the image. To see the image you must wait in line, then step on a moving walkway which takes you past it.

One of the most colourful times to visit the basilica is the week preceding 12 December, the Day of the Virgin of Guadalupe, a national festival day when crowds of pilgrims fill the plaza and celebrate with brightly costumed groups of dancers, artists and musicians from throughout Mexico. A special Virgin-shaped corn cake called *la gordita de la Virgen*, which is eaten only during this week, is available from vendors in the plaza.

The easiest way to get to the basilica is to take the Metro to La Villa station then walk north two blocks along Calzada de Guadalupe (follow the crowds); from the Basilica Metro station, it's a farther walk. By surface transport, take a 'Basilica' or 'La Villa' bus, minibus or combi minivan going north on Avenida Insurgentes Norte and get off at Avenida Montevideo. Walk ¾ km east on Montevideo.

INSURGENTES SUR

The longest thoroughfare in Mexico City goes past several points of interest as it heads south from the intersection with Paseo de la Reforma through the attractive suburb of San Ángel to University City and the Aztec ruins at Cuicuilco.

Siqueiros Poliforum

The bizarre Poliforum Cultural Siqueiros (☎ 536-45-20), Insurgentes at Filadelfia (4½ km south of Reforma), was designed by muralist David Alfaro Siqueiros and opened in 1971. It's an art centre and the site of his last huge mural. The poliforum is open daily from 10 am to 7 pm, but closes from 3 to 4 pm Monday to Friday.

The 12-sided exterior of the building is covered with murals: the atom as the triumph of peace over destruction, the drama unleashed by love during the Spanish conquest, and Moses breaking the Tablets of the Law, among other subjects. The wall backing Insurgentes shows five leaders of the Mexican artistic resurgence of the late 19th and 20th centuries: Diego Rivera, José Clemente Orozco, the cartoonist and printmaker José Guadalupe Posada, the engraver Leopoldo Méndez, and Dr Atl (Gerardo Murillo). Some of them bear a curious resemblance to Stalin, Trotsky and Marx, with whom Siqueiros' life was deeply entangled.

Inside, the ground floor houses contemporary art exhibitions while downstairs are some crafts stores. Entry to these parts is free.

The most important part of the building is upstairs (admission US$0.50). Here the walls and ceiling of an auditorium are covered with an enormous Siqueiros mural with the modest title *The March of Humanity on Earth and Towards the Cosmos*. Grand in scale and concept – it took six years and a team of 50 to finish it – the work combines Mexican and universal themes. The mural is designed to be seen from the rotating, tilting central platform in a daily *luz y sonido* (sound & light) show, but funding or popularity must be waning since you now have to get a group of at least 15 together and book ahead if you want to see it (cost is US$3 per person).

The 50-storey Hotel de México towering behind the poliforum is part of the same complex, which is also supposed to contain a heliport, sports halls, exhibition and conference centres, etc. But money ran out long ago, and the hotel has stood unfinished for years.

Bullfights

About 1½ km south of the poliforum, Calle Holbein leads west off Insurgentes from

Plaza de Baja California to the Ciudad de los Deportes (Sport City), with reputedly the largest bullring in the world (it holds 64,000) and the 65,000-capacity Estadio Nacional soccer stadium.

Bullfights are usually held from December to April every Sunday at 4 pm. The cheapest seats are in the Sol General section in the sun, which is okay if there's a cool breeze. Most other seats should be reserved in advance, especially those in the *sombra* or shady section. Tickets for the better seats can be bought at most major hotels and travel agencies in central Mexico City.

Sunken Garden & Theatre

Parque Luis Urbina, also known as the Parque Hundido (Sunken Garden), is a further half a km south along Insurgentes from Sport City, between the junctions with Porfirio Díaz and Millet. It contains 51 exact copies of the most famous artworks of Mexico's pre-Hispanic civilisations.

Another 1½ km south along Insurgentes, at the corner of Juan Tinoco, the Teatro de los Insurgentes has a mosaic façade by Diego Rivera.

Getting There

Getting to the Poliforum, Hotel de México or the bullfights from the city centre is easy by Metro, bus or colectivo (*pesero*). Take Metro Linea 7 to San Antonio station, exit to Avenida San Antonio and Calle Balderas and walk east/south-east along Eje 6 Sur-Balderas straight to the Plaza de México. Buses '17 Indios Verdes – Tlalpan' and 'Plaza México' (only on Sunday afternoon) run south along Avenida Insurgentes Sur from Paseo de la Reforma. If you're taking bus No 17, get off at Plaza de Baja California. Otherwise, stop any minibus headed south along Insurgentes and ask if they're going to Plaza de México.

Returning north, buses '17 Indios Verdes' and '17 Central Camionera Norte' go straight up Insurgentes to Reforma and far beyond; bus '17 M Insurgentes' goes only to Insurgentes Metro station.

SAN ÁNGEL

This former village ('san ANN-hell') 8½ km south of Reforma, which 50 years ago was still divided from the city by open fields, is filled with quiet cobbled streets lined by old colonial houses. San Ángel is best known for its arts & crafts market the Bazar Sábado (Saturday Bazaar), held at the Plaza San Jacinto, but there's plenty more to see. Besides crafts you can visit several museums and art galleries, a beautiful colonial hacienda, and Diego Rivera's studio. Don't come on Monday as the museums will be closed.

Start your visit at the Plaza San Jacinto, just west of Avenida Revolución along Calle Madero.

Plaza San Jacinto & Bazar Sábado

Walk uphill, south-west on Calle Madero from the intersection of Avenida Revolución with Amargura and La Paz to find this pretty little colonial plaza. Every Saturday it's festive with artists and artisans displaying their work. At lunchtime there's often a brass-band concert.

The Bazar Sábado itself, in one of the houses on the north side of the square, is a market for some of Mexico's best folk art and crafts like jewellery, pottery and textiles. Prices aren't low but quality is high; even if you don't buy anything this is a good place to see what's available. It's open Saturday only, from 10 am to 7 pm. The building which houses the bazaar served as quarters for invading Americans in 1847 and French in 1863. A less expensive crafts market is also held outside, at the north-west corner of the plaza.

The 16th-century church of San Jacinto, off the west side of the plaza, was originally part of a Dominican monastery and has a peaceful garden where you can take refuge from the crowded market areas. You enter it by walking up Juárez, beside the open-air crafts market. Continuing up this street brings you into an area of old colonial villas, side by side with a few expensive modern houses.

Casa del Risco

This 18th-century house, on the north side of Plaza San Jacinto at No 15, contains two courtyards with beautiful tiled fountains and two museums. The Museo Colonial Casa del Risco (☎ 548-58-03), dedicated to European and colonial art, furniture and domestic objects, is open from 10 am to 6 pm daily, closed Monday. The Centro Cultural y Biblioteca Isidro Fábela, housed in the same building, has a library and a display of colonial art open during the same hours. Entry to both parts is free.

San Ángel Inn

Located one km (a ten-minute walk) northwest of Plaza San Jacinto, at the corner of Santa Catarina, Palmas and Altavista, the baroque 18th-century ex-Hacienda de Goicoechea has a beautiful, verdant courtyard, fountain, chapel and colonial gardens. Once the home of the marquises of Selva Nevada and the counts of Pinillos, it is now the San Ángel Inn, a luxurious restaurant serving delicious traditional Mexican and continental cuisine. Order carefully and you can lunch for US$12 per person; order what-

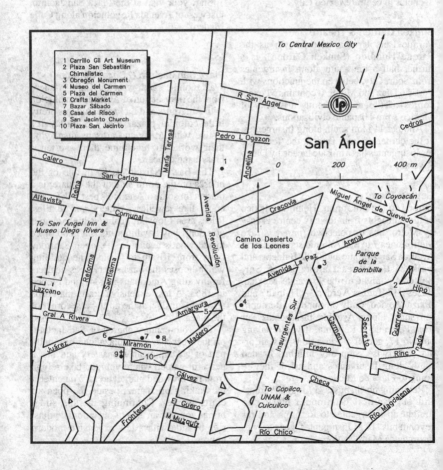

To Central Mexico City

1 Carrillo Gil Art Museum
2 Plaza San Sebastián Chimalistac
3 Obregón Monument
4 Museo del Carmen
5 Plaza del Carmen
6 Crafts Market
7 Bazar Sábado
8 Casa del Risco
9 San Jacinto Church
10 Plaza San Jacinto

San Ángel

To Coyoacán

To San Ángel Inn & Museo Diego Rivera

Camino Desierto de los Leones

Parque de la Bombilla

To Copilco, UNAM & Cuicuilco

ever you like and a three-course meal costs about US$18 to US$25.

To walk from Plaza de San Jacinto, walk due north from the north-west corner of the plaza to reach Calle General Rivera. Turn left and walk along Rivera to the third street (Reina) and turn right, then left onto Lazcano, which leads directly to the San Ángel Inn. The Casa de los Delfines, at Lazcano 18, is an 18th-century ranch house decorated with stone carvings, including dolphins.

You can also go to and from the San Ángel Inn and Museo Estudio Diego Rivera by minibus and pesero. Look for a No 43, which travels between the Viveros Metro station and San Angel Inn and Robles, Camino Desierto de los Leones and Altavista, passing the Museo de Arte Carrillo Gil (see below) along the way.

Museo Estudio Diego Rivera

Just to the right (north-east) of the San Ángel Inn is the Diego Rivera Studio Museum, Calle Diego Rivera at Avenida Altavista, open daily from 10 am to 6 pm, closed Monday; admission costs US$2. Here Rivera lived for several years with artist Frida Kahlo. The ground floor is a gallery for changing exhibits. Upstairs is Rivera's studio, which still contains 6000 artefacts: Aztec statuettes, dozens of fanciful skeleton shapes in various media, self portraits and portraits of women, and much other Riveriana.

Carrillo Gil Art Museum

The Museo de Arte Alvar y Carmen T de Carillo Gil (☎ 548-74-67), Avenida Revolución 1608, is one of Mexico City's best art galleries. It has a permanent collection of Mexican and foreign artists of the first rank, with many works by Rivera, Siqueiros, Orozco (including some of his grotesque, satirical early drawings and watercolours), Picasso, Villon, Nishisawa and Paalen. Temporary exhibits are also excellent. Hours are Tuesday to Sunday from 9.30 am to 6 pm (closed Monday); admission is free.

From the Plaza San Jacinto, walk north-

east down Madero to Avenida Revolución, then two blocks north along Avenida Revolución past a picturesque streetside flower market to the corner with Camino Desierto de los Leones, and the museum. From the San Ángel Inn, take any bus or pesero heading down (east) along Altavista (the No 43 is good), and get out at Avenida Revolución; the museum is on the east side of the boulevard.

Museo del Carmen

The tile-domed church and museum (☎ 548-53-12) of El Carmen are a few metres south-east of the Madero/La Paz intersection on Avenida Revolución at Monasterio. Designed by Andrés de San Miguel, a Carmelite monk, and built between 1615 and 1617, the cool, peaceful church (still in use) has a monumental altarpiece with a number of highly regarded paintings. The museum occupies the former monastic quarters to one side of the church and is mainly devoted to colonial religious art.

Perhaps more interesting to some are the mummified bodies in the crypt, which are probably 18th-century monks, nuns and gentry. Upstairs, the former monastery chapel has been preserved. You can also walk out into the pretty garden, formerly much bigger, which was a source for cuttings and seeds sent all over colonial Mexico, including to California. The museum is open daily from 10 am to 5 pm, closed Monday. Admission costs US$2.

Parque de la Bombilla

Just inside this park, along Avenida La Paz east of Insurgentes, is a monument to Álvaro Obregón, the Mexican revolutionary and ex-president who was assassinated on this spot during a banquet in 1928, just after he had won a new presidential term.

The killer was a young Christian fanatic, José de León Toral, who was connected with the Cristero rebellion against the government's anti-Church policies. Just beyond the far (east) end of this pleasant park is the Plaza San Sebastián Chimalistac, surrounded by old colonial houses and a little church with a 16th-century open chapel.

Places to Eat

Plaza San Jacinto has several popular eateries, including the *Mesón San Jacinto*, Plaza San Jacinto 20, a cool, quiet place with tables both inside and on the sidewalk. Salads of fruit, tuna or chicken sell for US$3.50, cuts of meat for about US$6; a hamburguesa con papas (burger and fries) costs US$4. It's closed Sunday.

The *Fonda San Ángel*, Plaza San Jacinto 9, on the north side of the square, has similar prices; the little place on the east side of the square offers a fine comida corrida for only US$4. Even cheaper eateries can be found in the little streets leading off the square.

There's also the unlikely *Restaurante Hasti Bhawan*, at No 7. Hindustani dishes are delicious and different; full meals range from US$6 to US$10. It's open daily from noon to 11 pm (till midnight Friday and Saturday), noon to 6 pm Sunday.

For very fancy meals, head for the *San Ángel Inn*.

Getting There

To reach San Ángel from the city centre, take the Metro to the Viveros station, then board a minibus marked for San Ángel, asking for the Plaza San Jacinto. The No 42 'Viveros-San Ángel-Monumento Obregón' is good; the No 43 'Viveros-San Ángel-Altavista' goes by the San Ángel Inn and the Museo Estudio Diego Rivera.

The M A Quevedo Metro station, one stop south of Viveros, is 1½ km east of Plaza San Jacinto, a bit closer than Viveros if you want to walk (20 minutes) to the plaza.

If you're heading south along Insurgentes, buses '17 Rectoría' and '17 Ciudad Universitaria (CU)' go south to University City. Buses '17 Fovisste', '17 Villa Olimpica' and '17 Tlalpan' go even further and will take you to Cuicuilco. Ruta 2 colectivos go all the way from Insurgentes to San Ángel. The 'Huipulco' from Insurgentes and La Paz goes on down Insurgentes to the University City and Cuicuilco. In general, there's lots of bus,

minibus and pesero transport in both directions along Insurgentes, which is 250 metres east of Avenida Revolución along Avenida La Paz.

To reach Coyoacán, two km east of San Ángel, one way is to take a 'Río Guadalupe – Ruta 116A – General Anaya' bus from the corner of Camino Desierto de los Leones and Avenida Revolución or Insurgentes. Another is to take a No 43 colectivo to Viveros Metro station and then walk to Coyoacán centre. From Coyoacán to San Ángel, pick up a 'Gen Anaya/San Ángel' bus at the corner of Allende and Malitzin; or hop on a San Ángel minibus from the Viveros Metro station. Taxis between San Ángel and Coyoacán cost about US$3.

COPILCO

One km south of Avenida La Paz along Insurgentes, then 500 metres east along Avenida Copilco and Calle Victoria, is the site of one of the earliest villages in the Valley of Mexico. Copilco probably already existed in 1200 BC when the Olmec civilisation of the Gulf Coast was emerging, and remained inhabited until 400 BC. It was at least partly contemporary with the bigger, Olmec-influenced village of Tlatilco further north, and both were near the shore of the great lake that filled much of the valley at that time. It's thought that Copilco was a trade and religious centre for a large agricultural area and may have been ruled by priests.

The village was buried by an eruption of the volcano Xitle around 100 BC to 100 AD, but archaeologists have found several tombs containing skeletons, pottery, stone implements and clay figurines beneath three metres of lava. Some of these are displayed in a museum which is open from 10 am to 5 pm, except Monday. The nearest Metro station is M A Quevedo, one km north-east of the site.

UNIVERSITY CITY

Breeding-ground of Mexico's most vocal political dissent and the nation's modern architectural showpiece, the main campus

(Ciudad Universitaria) of the Universidad Nacional Autónoma de México (UNAM) is east of Insurgentes, 11 km south of Reforma. It stands on the vast dried-up lava field of El Pedregal.

The university was founded in the 1550s but was suppressed from 1833 to 1910. Most of the present Ciudad Universitaria was built between 1950 and 1953 by a team of 150 young architects and technicians headed by José García Villagrán, Mario Pani and Enrique del Moral. It's a grandiose monument both to national pride, with its buildings covered in optimistic murals linking Mexican and global themes, and to an idealistic education system in which almost anyone, often regardless of qualifications, is entitled to free or cheap university tuition.

UNAM is the biggest university in Latin America, with 340,000 students and 25,000 teachers, but even so has to turn away tens of thousands of applicants a year. The university's problems are as big as it is: the drop-out rate approaches 70%, the budget was cut during the economic crisis of the 1980s, and academic standards are declining (partly because teachers have to take other jobs to make ends meet). In 1987, proposals by university authorities to raise academic entry standards and fees during the economic crisis brought the whole place to a standstill in an 18-day strike while demonstrations of 100,000 or more filed through downtown Mexico City. The reforms were suspended.

Left-wing politics are the norm on this and most other Mexican campuses but they have had little influence on wider national events since the 1968 Tlatelolco massacre, when 300 to 400 people at an open-air meeting were shot dead by soldiers as a student-initiated protest movement gathered momentum on the eve of the Mexico Olympics.

Olympic Stadium

The Estadio Olímpico México 68, on the west side of Insurgentes from the campus, is designed to resemble a volcano cone and holds 80,000 people. The Diego Rivera mosaic over its main entrance was originally intended to be the first of a series. You can peep inside the stadium when it's closed by going to Gate 38 at the south end.

Biblioteca Central

As you enter the campus from Insurgentes, it's easy to spot the Central Library, Mexico's most photographed modern building. Ten floors high, the almost windowless structure is covered on every side with mosaics by Juan O'Gorman.

The south wall, with two prominent circles towards the top, covers colonial times. The theme of the north wall is Aztec culture. The east wall shows the creation of modern Mexico. The mosaic on the west wall is harder to interpret but may be dedicated to Latin American culture as a whole.

La Rectoría

According to one architecture critic, the Rectorate administration building south-west of the library achieves 'a harmonic equilibrium of horizontal and vertical masses'. Whether or not that's so, there's a spectacular 3D mosaic by Siqueiros on its south wall, which shows students urged on by the people.

Museum

With your back to the Siqueiros mural, the building in front and a bit to the left contains the university science & arts museum, open Monday to Friday 10 am to 3.30 pm and 4.30 to 7 pm (free). The archaeological section includes some pieces from Veracruz.

More Murals

Two more interesting mosaics lie just past the far (east) end of the wide grassy Jardín Central, which is reached by steps down from the Rectoría. The science auditorium, fronting the east side of the garden, has on its north end a mural by José Chávez Morado showing the conquest of energy. Humanity progresses from the shadow of the primitive jaguar-god to the use of fire and then the atom, before emerging into an ethereal, apparently female, future. The east side of the same building shows the progression from primitive agriculture to modern science.

A little further east, on the west wall of the medical school, a mosaic in Italian stone by Francisco Eppens interprets the theme of life and death in Mexican terms. The central mask has a Spanish profile on the left, an Indian one on the right, together making up a mestizo face in the middle. A maize cob and symbols of Aztec and Maya gods represent the forces of life and death.

Espacio Escultórico
Still within the Ciudad Universitaria, but a km south of the main buildings, past the Sala Nezahualcóyotl concert hall and close to Insurgentes, is a work by Mathias Goeritz which no one can explain but most people agree is striking. It consists of concrete shapes about a round platform, set on the bare lava bed.

Getting There
Many buses pass along Insurgentes going to and from the centre, passing San Ángel along the way. 'Insurgentes' buses pass between the university stadium on its west side and the campus on the east; the bus stop is only a few metres from both. The nearest Metro station, Copilco, is a km east of the most interesting university buildings; the next station to the south, Universidad, is farther away.

CUICUILCO PYRAMID
Four km south of Ciudad Universitaria is the early archaeological site of Cuicuilco, set in the Parque Ecológico Cuicuilco just east of Insurgentes immediately south of the big intersection with the Anillo Periférico Sur. You can recognise the spot by what's best described as a big round green thing with a hole in the middle.

History
Cuicuilco was near the lake that filled much of the Valley of Mexico and was probably the biggest settlement in the valley from approximately 600 to 200 BC. It was still occupied when it was buried by the eruption of Xitle

volcano, to the south, some time between 100 BC and 100 AD.

The valley at that time was something of a backwater, far from the centres of Mexican civilisation on the Gulf Coast, but Cuicuilco is estimated to have had a population of 20,000 and traces of a street layout have been found. The whole site covered an area 4½ km from north to south and one km from east to west. Its pyramid shows that Cuicuilco must have been, as well as a residential settlement, a ceremonial centre of a priest-dominated society, organised enough to build large monumental structures. Earlier temples in the Valley of Mexico were thatch-roof affairs on low earth mounds. The next important centre to arise in central Mexico was the splendid Teotihuacán (see the Near Mexico City chapter).

Information
The site is open Tuesday to Saturday 10 am to 5 pm, Sundays and holidays 10 am to 4 pm. Entry to the museum (☎ 533-22-63) costs US$2, except on Sundays and holidays when it's free.

Pyramid
The most important excavated structure is the round, tiered pyramid 118 metres across and now 23 metres high which you can see as you approach from Insurgentes. The 10-metre lava layer which buried the lower levels has been removed to show the stone facing of the mound, whose interior is of sand and rubble. The stone facing itself was probably originally plastered with stucco. Ramps on the west and east sides lead to the top of the pyramid, where the remains of an altar are protected by a modern roof. Beneath this altar are the remains of two earlier ones, built over when the whole pyramid was enlarged, which happened at least twice.

Museum
Just south of the pyramid, the museum contains information on Cuicuilco's inhabitants and the development of the valley in ancient times, objects found at the site and a painting of the eruption which destroyed it. There's

an image of the fire-and-volcano god, Xuihtecuhtli, with a brazier on his back, who was – not surprisingly – Cuicuilco's most important deity.

Getting There
From Ciudad Universitaria or San Ángel, take a minibus or pesero marked 'Cuicuilco' heading south along Insurgentes.

COYOACÁN
About eight km south of downtown Mexico City, Coyoacán (Place of Coyotes in Nahuatl) was Cortés' base after the fall of Tenochtitlán and for four centuries remained a small town outside Mexico City until the urban sprawl surrounded it 40 years ago. It still has its own identity, with its own café-ringed plazas and a student-intellectual-artist atmosphere which stems from its closeness to the university and from having been home to people such as Leon Trotsky, Diego Rivera and Frida Kahlo. Their interesting former homes are preserved for the public to visit. Other places to visit in the area are Churubusco monastery – site of a heroic Mexican stand against US invaders – and the Anahuacalli, a building designed by Rivera, which contains his pre-Hispanic art collection and some of his own work.

Coyoacán was on the shore of the lake which covered much of the Valley of Mexico in pre-Hispanic times, and was first settled by the Tepanecs based in Azcapotzalco 18 km to the north. When the Aztecs, who had been subject to the Tepanecs, tu~~~~ tables on their rulers in the~~~~ century, Coyoacán became a~~~~ tary. ~~~~ ea~~~~ ~~~~ ~~~~ an Az

Orientation & Informati~~~~
Coyoacán's wide Plaza C~~~~on y two adjoining plazas, the ea~~~~entr~za Hidalgo, with a statue of Miguel Hidalg~ and the parish church on its south side, and the western Jardín del Centenario, with its coyote fountain. Calle Aguayo/Carrillo Puerto divides the two parts. Most points of interest are within walking distance, or a short ride, from the plaza.

A detailed map of Coyoacán, and leaflets in Spanish, are given out at the Casa de la Cultura, Avenida Francisco Sosa 202, opposite the pretty Jardín de Santa Catarina, one km west of the plaza. Ask for the Delegación de Turismo, which is upstairs. The walk to the Casa de la Cultura along Avenida Sosa takes you past many fine 16th and 17th-century houses, including one owned by Miguel de la Madrid, president of Mexico from 1982 to 1988, but most of the houses are hidden by high walls.

Plaza Central
The former town hall (Casa Municipal, or Ayuntamiento) of Coyoacán, on the north side of Plaza Hidalgo, is also called the **Casa de Cortés**. On this spot, it is said, the Spanish tortured the defeated Aztec emperor Cuauhtémoc to try to make him reveal the whereabouts of treasure. The existing 18th-century building was also the HQ of the Marquesado del Valle de Oaxaca, the Cortés family's private lands in Mexico which included Coyoacán. Above the entrance is the coat of arms bestowed on Coyoacán by Charles IV of Spain.

The parroquía (parish church) of **San Juan Bautista** and adjacent ex-monastery, on the south side of Plaza Hidalgo, were built for Dominican monks in the 16th century. The two lower sections of the main façade are in plain Renaissance style. The doorway beside the tower is Plateresque. The Santísima chapel, to one side of the presbytery (the area in front of the main altar), has an 18th-century altarpiece.

Half a block east of Plaza Hidalgo, at Hidalgo 289, is the **Museo Nacional de Culturas Populares** (☎ 658-12-65), which has good temporary exhibitions on Mexican popular culture such as circuses, *lucha libre* (freestyle wrestling) and *nacimientos* (nativity models). It's free, and open Tuesday and Thursday 10 am to 4 pm, Wednesday, Friday and Saturday 10 am to 8 pm, and Sunday 10 am to 5 pm.

Plaza de la Conchita
Formally called Plaza de la Concepción, this

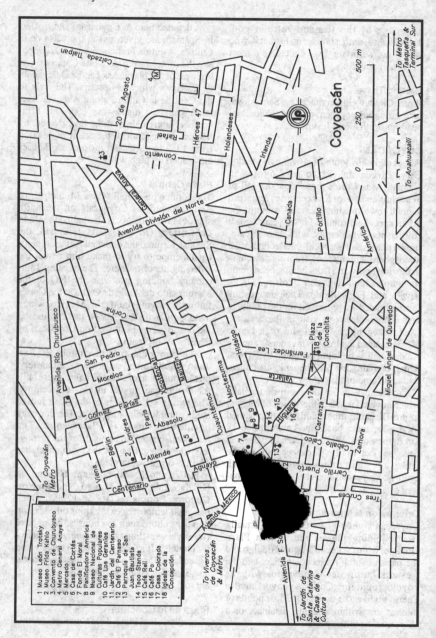

Coyoacán

To Metro
Tasqueña &
Terminal Sur

To Anahuacalli

500 m

250

0

Calzada Tlalpan

20 de Agosto

Héroes 47

Rafael

Holandeses

Convento

General Anaya

Irlanda

Canada

P. Portillo

América

Avenida División del Norte

Avenida Río Churubusco

Corina

San Pedro

Morelos

Xicoténcatl

Matízin

Hidalgo

Fernández Leal

Plaza
de la
Conchita

Miguel Ángel de Quevedo

Gómez Farías

Moctezuma

Vallarta

Cuauhtémoc

Higuera

Carranza

Caballo Calco

Zamora

Viena

Berlín

Londres

Paris

Abasolo

Allende

Aguayo

Centenario

Carrillo Puerto

Tres Cruces

To Coyoacán
Metro

Avenida México

To Viveros
de Coyoacán
& Metro

Avenida F So

To Jardín de
Santa Catarina
& Casa de la
Cultura

1 Museo León Trotsky
2 Museo Frida Kahlo
3 Convento de Churubusco
4 Metro General Anaya
5 Mercado
6 Casa de Cortés
7 Fonda El Moral
8 Panificadora América
9 Museo Nacional de
   Culturas Populares
10 Café La Guadalupana
11 Jardín del Centenario
12 Café El Parnaso
13 Parroquia de San
   Juan Bautista
14 Taco Stands
15 Café Reli
16 Café Po
17 Casa Colorada
18 Iglesia de la
   Concepción

is a peaceful square two blocks east of Plaza Hidalgo. Follow Calle Higuera from the east side of Plaza Hidalgo.

The church of La Concepción is a pretty little 18th-century baroque building on the east side of Plaza de la Conchita. The interior – often closed – has some finely carved wooden altarpieces covered in gold paint. Beyond (east of) the Plaza de la Conchita is the Jardín Frida Kahlo, a park named in honour of Coyoacán's most famous female painter.

The red house (not open to the public), at the corner of Vallarta where Higuera meets the plaza, is the 'Casa Colorada', which Cortés is said to have built for La Malinche, his interpreter and mistress. Cortés' Spanish wife, Catalina Juárez de Marcaida, who disappeared soon after arriving in Mexico, is reputed to have been murdered in this house.

Viveros

Viveros de Coyoacán, the garden nurseries, is actually quite a lush swath of greenery just east of the Viveros Metro station. If you need some oxygenation bio-time among the plants and flowers, you can walk here between 6 am and 7 pm any day for free. There's an entrance on Avenida Progreso near Callejón Retama, around the corner from the Viveros Metro station, and another entrance on Avenida México near Calle Madrid.

Mercado

Three blocks north of Plaza Hidalgo along Allende, between Malitzin and Xicoténcatl, on the east side of the street, is Coyoacán's market. Bustling and picturesque, it's worth a stroll for a look and perhaps a buy before heading further north to the houses of Frida Kahlo and Leon Trotsky.

Museo Frida Kahlo

The blue building (☎ 677-29-84), at the corner of Allende and Londres, six blocks north of Plaza Hidalgo, was the home from 1929 to 1954 of Frida Kahlo, who was born here in 1910, and her husband Diego Rivera.

Kahlo spent most of her life in a wheelchair after a spinal injury in her youth and became an artist with a high reputation in her own right after marrying Rivera, who apparently was not a faithful husband. Given to the nation by Rivera in 1955 in memory of his wife after her death, the house and garden are a very interesting three-in-one gallery/museum. Their fine collection of pre-Hispanic objects and Mexican folk art, as well as works by Kahlo, Rivera, Marcel Duchamp, Orozco, Paul Klee and others, give glimpses of the artist-revolutionary couple's lifestyle.

The paintings, carvings and sculptures by Kahlo express the anguish and hopes of her existence: one called *Marxism Will Give Health to the Sick* shows her casting away her own crutches. Trotsky lived only a few streets away, and Rivera and Kahlo were part of a high-powered but far from harmonious leftist artistic-intellectual circle. Stalin appears as the hero of some of Kahlo's paintings, done after Rivera and Trotsky had fallen out.

Regional costumes (worn by Kahlo), *ex-voto* paintings done to give thanks for miracles, colourful and grotesque papiermâché Easter week procession figures, lacquerware and ceramics are included in the folk art collection.

The house is open daily, except Monday, from 10 am to 6 pm; admission is free. Guided tours (free) are given at 11 am on Saturday and Sunday.

Museo León Trotsky

Having come in second to Stalin in the power struggle in the Soviet Union in 1927, Trotsky fled Russia and eventually found refuge in Mexico under President Lázaro Cárdenas in 1937, thanks to the support of Diego Rivera. Trotsky and Natalia, his wife, lived in Coyoacán at Viena 45, on the corner of Morelos.

To enter, go to Avenida Río Churubusco 410, corner of Morelos, on the north side of the building facing the big boulevard, where there's a modern entrance. Hours are Tuesday to Sunday 10 am to 5 pm. Admission costs US$3.50, half-price for students, civil servants and workers, US$0.75 for children under 12.

The house has been left pretty much as it was on the day in 1940 when Trotsky was killed here. It's a fascinating monument to a revolutionary's life, with secrecy and danger ever-present. High walls and crude watchtowers – once manned by bodyguards with high-powered weapons – surround the house and small garden.

The garden contains a tomb holding the Trotskys' ashes. The watchtowers were put up, the outside walls heightened and the windows made smaller after the first attempt on their lives on 24 May 1940. A group of attackers, which probably included the artist David Alfaro Siqueiros, pumped bullets into the house but the couple survived by hiding under their bedroom furniture. The bullet holes remain. Several interesting old photos in the house include one of Trotsky, Natalia, Rivera, Frida Kahlo and the surrealist painter André Breton in Chapultepec park in 1938.

The most interesting room is Trotsky's study, where he died. The assassin was Ramón Mercader, a Spanish Stalinist agent who managed to become the lover of Trotsky's secretary and gradually gained the confidence of the household, making frequent visits over two or three months. On 20 August 1940 he went to Trotsky, who was sitting at his desk in his study, and asked him to look at a document. Standing beside him, he then pulled an ice-axe from under his coat and smashed it into the back of Trotsky's skull. Trotsky died next day; Mercader was arrested and spent 20 years in prison. Trotsky's desk has been left exactly as it was at the time of his death: books and magazines lying on it include *Should Socialists Support the War? Wall Street's War – Not Ours, If Germany Attacks* and *British Trade Unionism Today*.

Convento de Churubusco

Less than 1½ km east of the Trotsky Museum stands the 17th-century ex-Monastery of Churubusco, scene of one of Mexico's heroic military defeats and now partly given over to an interesting museum

on foreign imperialism in Mexico. The occasion of the heroism was the US invasion in 1847. The Americans had taken Veracruz with high loss of Mexican life and were advancing on Mexico City. On 20 August, Mexicans who had fortified the old monastery resisted a bigger and better armed American force until they ran out of ammunition and were only finally beaten in hand-to-hand fighting. General Pedro Anaya, asked by US General Twiggs to surrender his ammunition, is said to have answered: 'If there was any, you wouldn't be here'. During the Reform War the monastery served again as military quarters and later as a hospital for contagious diseases.

The former monastery is now the Museo Nacional de las Intervenciones (National Interventions Museum, (☎ 604-06-99), open from 9 am to 6 pm Tuesday to Sunday; admission costs US$3.

It's a big museum, and the interesting displays include references to present-day US 'interventions' (eg Libya 1986) and the US military presence in the Caribbean, an American map of the Mexico City area showing operations in 1847 (note how far outside the city Churubusco was at the time), material on the Texas war, the French occupation in the 1860s (with a death mask of Emperor Maximilian), foreign economic dominance in the late 19th and early 20th centuries, and the plot by US Ambassador Lane Wilson to bring down the Madero government in 1913. Numerous interesting old photos include one of US troops in Veracruz in 1914.

Parts of the peaceful old monastery gardens are open to visit. Cannons and memorials outside the monastery recall the events of 1847.

The monastery is on Calle 20 de Agosto at General Anaya, two blocks south of Avenida Río Churubusco and two blocks east of Avenida División del Norte along Catita; it's less than two km from Plaza Hidalgo. General Anaya Metro station is 500 metres south-east along 20 de Agosto, and most peseros between the Metro station and central Coyoacán pass by. Bus and pesero No

59 'Metro División del Norte – Metro Tasqueña', south along Avenida División del Norte from División del Norte Metro station, also pass within a couple of blocks of Churubusco. Get out at the junction with Xicoténcatl and Catita.

Places to Eat

There are several places on or near Coyoacán's Plaza Central. For the cheapest food, walk 50 metres out of the Plaza Hidalgo along Higuera to the municipal building on the left. The building is filled with privately run taco/tostada stands charging less than US$2 for a plateful. A bit farther along is the *Café Reli*, Higuera 22, which offers a daily comida corrida for US$3. A similar cheap café named *Po* is just a bit farther along on the right.

Panificadora América, at the corner of Allende and Hidalgo, on the east side of Plaza Hidalgo, has everything you'll need for a park bench picnic: bread, pastries, sausage, roast chicken, etc.

Café El Parnaso, Carrillo Puerto 2 on the east side of Jardín del Centenario, is an arty sidewalk café with a good bookshop in the back. Sandwiches and burritas cost US$2.50, coffee and pastry about the same or a bit more. Hours are 9 am to 9.30 pm daily. There are three other cafés on this south side of the Jardín del Centenario as well.

Fonda El Moral, Allende at Moctezuma, just a half-block north of Plaza Hidalgo, is a big, busy restaurant with two sections. The left-hand side is open 9 am to 5.30 pm, the right-hand from 7.30 am to 6 pm. Both are decorated in colourful tiles, and both serve bountiful breakfasts for US$3.50 to US$6, and a good four-course comida corrida for only US$5. Plates of enchiladas, tacos and pozole cost US$3.25 to US$5.

Café Los Geranios, Avenida Francisco Sosa 19, a half-block west of Jardín del Centenario, is cool, popular and a touch elegant with a good but not huge portions at moderate prices. Most daily luncheon platters (served after 1.30 pm) go for US$5 to US$10. They open for late breakfasts at 10 am, and stay open for supper till midnight daily.

Getting There

Take the Metro to the Coyoacán station, then a minibus south along Avenida México to the Plaza Central. Or, if you want to walk (two km, 20 to 25 minutes), stay on the Metro to the next station, Viveros, and walk south to Avenida Progreso, then turn left (east) and walk past the Viveros de Coyoacán along Progreso and Valenzuela. Turn north on Ocampo, then east on Domínguez to reach the Plaza Central.

Another way is to take the Metro to General Anaya two km east of Coyoacán, then a 'Santo Domingo/Coyoacán' pesero to Allende in Coyoacán, or a 'Gen Anaya/San Ángel' bus to the corner of Allende and Malitzín. The latter goes on to San Ángel after Coyoacán.

From San Ángel, bus 'Río Guadalupe – Ruta 116A – General Anaya' runs along Camino Desierto de los Leones, Robles, Progreso and Valenzuela, thus close to central Coyoacán. A taxi between Coyoacán and San Ángel costs US$3.

Leaving Coyoacán, take any bus, minibus or pesero marked for a Metro station ('Viveros', 'Coyoacán', or 'General Anaya').

ANAHUACALLI

This dramatic museum (☎ 677-29-84 or 677-28-73), Calle del Museo 150, Coyoacán, was designed by Diego Rivera to house his own excellent collection of pre-Hispanic objects – mostly pottery and stone figures of humans, animals or gods. The name means House of Anáhuac (Anáhuac is the Aztec name for the Valley of Mexico).

The building is a fortress-like edifice of dark volcanic stone incorporating many pre-Hispanic stylistic features of Preclassic, western Mexico, Aztec, Veracruz, Zapotec, Mixtec, Toltec and Teotihuacán cultures. An inscription over the door reads: 'To return to the people the artistic inheritance I was able to redeem from their ancestors'.

Besides the archaeological treasures, the

museum also houses Rivera's studio and some of his own works. The most interesting are studies for major murals like *La Paz* (Peace) and *El Hombre en el Cruce de los Caminos* (Mankind at the Crossroads) done for the Rockefeller Center, New York, in 1933 but now in the Bellas Artes in Mexico City. Another huge sketch shows Mao Zedong offering the dove of peace to Uncle Sam, John Bull and France. If the atmosphere's clear, there's a great view over the city from the roof.

The Anahuacalli is open daily, except Monday, from 10 am to 2 pm and 3 to 6 pm. Entry is free.

Getting There

To get to the Anahuacalli from Coyoacán, go to Avenida División del Norte, just over one km east of Coyoacán's Plaza Hidalgo along Avenida Hidalgo, then catch a No 59 bus, pesero or minibus south less than four km to Calle del Museo. From the Convento de Churubusco, go west two blocks along General Anaya to Avenida División del Norte and get a No 59 south.

To get to the Anahuacalli directly from central Mexico City, take the Metro to Tasqueña, then the Tren Ligero (streetcar) from Tasqueña Metro station to Xotepingo, the fourth stop. Xotepingo station is beside an intersection where a sign points to 'Museo'. Take the direction indicated, continuing three blocks to traffic lights at Avenida División del Norte, then continue ahead for five blocks as the road (Calle Museo) curves left and uphill. The grey, fortress-like Anahuacalli is unmistakable on the right.

Alternatively, take the Metro to División del Norte station, then a bus/pesero No 59 south along Avenida División del Norte for six km to the corner of Calle Museo (check that it's going far enough – some No 59s turn off before reaching Calle Museo).

AZTEC STADIUM

This 100,000-seat soccer stadium, scene of World Cup triumphs by Brazil in 1970 and Argentina in 1986, is five km south of Coyoacán. Games are played here frequently in the Mexican season. The Metro to Tasqueña, then the Tren Ligero to Estadio Azteca is probably the quickest way of getting there from downtown Mexico City.

XOCHIMILCO

Pronounced 'so-chee-MEEL-ko', this Nahuatl word means 'place where flowers grow'. The place is a suburb of 'floating gardens' 24 km south-east of the Zócalo. In the 13th century, the Chinampaneca Indians who settled here built rafts on the lake to grow food and flowers. The rafts eventually became rooted to the lake bottom and were named chinampas. Because of their proliferation the lake was transformed into more than 80 km of canals.

Today, more than 3000 boats, including *trajineras* or colourfully decorated flat-bottom boats, cruise the canals with loads of tourists, mariachi bands, 'official' photographers, taco bars and big steaming pots of corn-on-the-cob. On the weekends the town and waterways are jammed with people trying to arrange a boat, cruising the canals or fast-talking you into buying something. The hawkers are bothersome because they hound you even when you're on the canals. Many of them disappear during the week, so that's a much quieter time to visit, but then you have to pretend that you don't see the mounds of weekend rubbish floating on the water.

You won't have trouble finding a boat: they'll find you, approaching you as you approach the boat landing. Going rate for an hour's ride is about US$10, but you must negotiate, and the price may have something to do with the condition of the boat. Inspect your craft before you embark. When you've had enough, tell the boatman to return. Remember, he's getting paid by the hour.

Getting There

Take Metro Linea 2 to Tasqueña, then any 'Xochimilco' bus. Get off at the end of the line in central Xochimilco and look for 'Embarcaderos' signs.

FESTIVALS

Every major festival described in Facts about the Country is celebrated in Mexico City.

Cinco de Mayo

On Cerro del Peñon hill near the airport (Metro: Oceania), a mock battle between 'French' and Mexican 'soldiers' is conducted in the afternoon to commemorate the Battle of Puebla on 5 May 1862. On that day, Brigadier General Porfirio Díaz led the Second Brigade of the Mexican Army to victory against an invading French army led by General Charles Latrille. It was a temporary victory, though, because about a year later the French army besieged Puebla with two months of mortar and artillery attacks before marching on Mexico City and taking control of the country.

Independence Day

On 15 September thousands of people gather in front of the National Palace in the Zócalo to hear the president of Mexico recite the *Grito de Dolores* (Cry of Dolores), Mexico's most famous speech, from the central balcony. The *Grito*, a call to rebel against the Spaniards, was first proclaimed in 1810 by Miguel Hidalgo y Costilla in the town of Dolores (now named Dolores Hidalgo in his honour). Translated, the gist of the *Grito* is:

My children, a new dispensation comes to us this day. Are you ready to receive it? Will you be free? Will you make the effort to recover from the hated Spaniards the lands stolen from your forefathers 300 years ago? We must act at once...Long live our Lady of Guadalupe! Death to bad government!...Mexicans! Long live Mexico!...

The president then rings the ceremonial bell, and there's lots of cheering and throwing of confetti, usually aimed directly in the faces of other merry-makers. If you go, be sure to leave your valuables in the hotel safe.

Day of the Virgin of Guadalupe

At the Basilica de Guadalupe, north of central Mexico City (Metro: Basilica or La Villa), 12 December caps a week of colourful festivities venerating and celebrating the dark-skinned Virgin who mysteriously appeared before an Indian convert to Christianity in 1531.

PLACES TO STAY

Mexico City has a full range of hotels, from cheap and basic but centrally located hotels (for US$10 to US$20 a double) through the comfortable middle-range hostelries (for US$20 to US$45 a double) to luxurious world-class high rises (for US$50 and up). With the peso strong, these prices seem high. If the peso drops significantly before you arrive in this city, you'll get some fine bargains, no matter what class of hotel you patronise.

In general, the best cheap and moderately priced rooms are in the areas west of the Zócalo, south of the Alameda and north of the Plaza de la República; luxury hotels are in the Zona Rosa, along Paseo de la Reforma, and in the section called Polanco, north of Chapultepec park. Hotels below are described in order of preference. The numbers in brackets, '(06000)', are postal codes, useful if you want to write for reservations.

Places to Stay – bottom end

There are some very cheap hotels on the fringes of the city centre, but I cannot recommend them for safety reasons. Rooms in the hotels recommended here have private baths unless otherwise mentioned, and many also have TVs and carafes or bottles of purified water in each room. If two prices are noted for double rooms, the lower is for two persons in one bed (a double), the higher for twin beds .

West & South of the Zócalo There are many suitable hotels within the area bounded by Avenida Cinco de Mayo on the north, República del Salvador on the south and Avenida Lázaro Cárdenas on the west. Virtually all offer rooms with private bathrooms, and purified drinking water at no extra charge. All are in the 06000 postal code zone.

Hotel Juárez (☎ (5) 512-69-29 or 518-47-18), Primer Callejón de Cinco de Mayo

17, has 39 rooms on a quiet sidestreet only 1½ blocks west of the Zócalo (Metro: Zócalo or Allende). Simple but presentable, it has an excellent location and low prices of US$12 a single, US$13.50 to US$15 a double; triple and quad rooms cost only a few dollars more. The sidestreet *(callejón)* is off Cinco de Mayo between Palma and Isabel la Católica (more precisely, between Nos 48 and 50 on Cinco de Mayo).

Hotel San Antonio (☎ (5) 512-99-06), Segunda Callejón de Cinco de Mayo 29, is just south of the Hotel Juárez across Cinco de Mayo, on the corresponding sidestreet (Metro: Zócalo or Allende). They're not quite as used to gringos and gringas here, but the 40 very simple rooms all have baths, many have TVs, and it's quiet and convenient. Rates are US$12/13.50 a single/double.

Hotel Montecarlo (☎ (5) 518-14-18 or 521-25-59), Uruguay 69 between Isabel la Católica and Cinco de Febrero (Metro: Zócalo), was built in 1772 as a monastery (note the former church, now a library, to its right), and later served as home to D H Lawrence. It's now a 60-room hotel with a good variety of rooms and prices: US$12 a single; US$13.50 to US$20 a double, all with private shower. There's parking space for a few small cars.

Hotel Lafayette (☎ (5) 521-96-40), Motolinía 40, near the corner of 16 de Septiembre (Metro: Zócalo), looks like a plastic sofa showroom as you enter, but in fact is a hotel popular with Mexican families. During the day, radios squawk from the street market out front, but it's quiet at night. Cost is US$13.50 to US$15 a double, with bath. There's a lift.

Hotel Washington (☎ (5) 512-35-02 or 521-11-43), Cinco de Mayo 54 at Palma (near the aforementioned Hotel Juárez; Metro: Allende or Zócalo), has noisy front rooms and slightly higher prices, but is good nonetheless, and very well located. Rooms are US$13.50 a single, US$15 to US$17 a double, up to US$20 for four in two beds; all rooms have baths. The Virgin of Guadalupe presides in the lobby.

Hotel Isabel (☎ (5) 518-12-13), Isabel la Católica 63 at República del Salvador (Metro: Isabel la Católica), is popular with backpackers because of its convenient location, agreeable management, comfy rooms, good little restaurant, bar with Happy Hour (7 to 8 pm, two drinks for the price of one), and free parking nearby. Rates are US$13.50/16 a single/double.

Hotel Rioja (☎ (5) 521-83-33 or 521-82-73), Cinco de Mayo 45 at Isabel la Católica (Metro: Allende), is well-used, worn and fairly noisy, but still popular with travellers on slim budgets because its prices are the lowest: US$8/10 a single/double for rooms sharing communal bathrooms.

Hotel Concordia (☎ (5) 510-41-00), Uruguay 13 just east of Avenida Lázaro Cárdenas (Metro: Bellas Artes), is dark but maintained well enough, with mostly quiet rooms. Prices are good at US$13.50 a double, US$17 a twin. Here you're four short blocks south of the Palacio de Bellas Artes.

Hotel Ontario (☎ (5) 521-09-52), Uruguay 87 between Cinco de Febrero and 20 de Noviembre (Metro: Zócalo), is aging ungracefully but is still serviceable and cheap at US$10 a double. It never seems to be crowded.

Hotel Roble (☎ (5) 522-78-30 or 518-04-72), Uruguay 109 at Pino Suárez (Metro: Zócalo), is a mere two blocks south of the Zócalo on a noisy corner. Used mostly by Mexican businessmen with dealings in the surrounding markets, it has more services – private baths, colour TVs, room service, a lift, restaurant and bar – but also higher prices: US$18 to US$21 a double. The rooms are better than the exterior would lead you to believe.

South of the Alameda The few hotels north of the Alameda are good and quiet, but are a bit higher than a bottom-end budget can afford. South of the Alameda used to be more affordable, but after the 1985 earthquake many hotels upgraded as they rebuilt, raising prices.

Hotel Conde (☎ (5) 521-10-84), Pescaditos 15 at Revillagigedo (06050), five short blocks south of Avenida Juárez (Metro: Juárez or Salto del Agua), advertises itself as *cómodo, limpio y honorable* ('comfortable, clean and honourable'), and also boasts rooms with private baths, phones and TVs, as well as a lift and a car park. It's modern, sterile-looking and clean, and located across the street from a small park. The 80 rooms cost US$17 a single or double.

North of Plaza de la República This quiet residential area (postal code 06030) is drab and slightly less convenient, being about one km west of the Alameda, but prices are good for what you get. The Metro station for all these hotels is Revolución; walk east from the station along Puente de Alvarado, then turn right (south) on Arriaga or Ramos Arizpe.

Hotel Oxford (☎ 566-05-00), Mariscal 67 at Ramon Alcazar (one block east of Ramos Arizpe), beside the quiet Plaza Buenavista and right behind the Museo San Carlos, always seems redolent of fly-spray, but it has clean, carpeted, well-furnished rooms with private bath, plenty of hot water, TV and phone for US$13 to US$15 a double. Ask for a room higher up, overlooking the park.

Hotel Carlton (☎ (5) 566-29-11), Mariscal 32-B, across Plaza Buenavista from the Oxford, is a favourite among budget travellers. Get here early if you want a room; it fills up early. Rooms are clean, carpeted, equipped with TVs, and priced at US$12/ 13.50/17 a single/double/triple. The hotel restaurant serves a comida corrida for US$2.

Hotel Edison (☎ (5) 566-09-33), Edison 106 at Iglesias, has clean rooms set around a pleasant, tiny, plant-filled courtyard. Rates are US$15 a single, US$17 to US$22 a double. There's a bakery just north across the street, and several small restaurants nearby.

Gran Hotel Texas (☎ (5) 705-57-82 or 705-64-96), Mariscal 129 near Arriaga, is popular because of its friendly help. Rooms are stark but clean and serviceable with TVs and potable water, but prices are high for what you get: US$20 to US$22 a double. There's a car park.

Hotel Managua (☎ (5) 521-55-81 or 521-

30-62), Plaza de San Francisco, faces the little park on the north side of Puente de Alvarado just east of Guerrero (Metro: Hidalgo or Revolución). With its parkside location it's fairly quiet. Rooms, though modern, are well used but still livable for US$13.50 a double, US$16 a twin. They have a car park.

Near Buenavista Railway Station Surprisingly, the railway station area (postal code 06300) is not chock-a-block with cheap hotels. Though the many hotels near the Plaza de la Revolución are about 1½ km due south of Buenavista, there are only a few cheap lodgings closer. Walk out the front door of the station to the main street (Martínez de la Torre/Mosqueta) and turn left (east). The nearest Metro station to these hotels is Guerrero, 900 metres east of the station.

Hotel Central (☎ (5) 535-57-24), Mosqueta 248, 1½ blocks east of the station, is all right for one night if you're exhausted, but get a room at the back or the noise will prevent sleep. Price is US$10/12 a single/ double with private bath.

For a look at more hotels, continue walking east two blocks along Mosqueta, then turn right (south) onto Zaragoza.

Hotel Nueva Estación (☎ (5) 546-02-26), Zaragoza 114 between Moctezuma and Meneses, two blocks south of Mosqueta, has clean if bare rooms (with shared baths) around a bare courtyard for US$10 a double. There are several other cheap hotels in the vicinity as well.

Near the Zona Rosa The pricey Zona Rosa is no place to stay on a low budget. But just on the far (north-west) side of Reforma is a low-priced gem.

Casa González (☎ (5) 514-33-02), Río Sena 69 at Río Lerma (06500), is a 500-metre walk from the heart of the Zona Rosa, but more or less behind the US Embassy and just around the corner from the British Embassy. Two beautiful houses set in small plots of lawn have been converted to a charming pensión. All rooms have private bath (some have tubs), and home-cooked meals are available in the pretty dining room. It's perfect for women travellers and those staying more than one or two nights, and it's cheap at US$20 to US$22 per room, single or double. They may have parking. Reserve in advance if you can; no sign marks the houses, and the gate is locked. Ring the bell for admittance.

Places to Stay – middle

Hotels in this range provide comfortable and attractive if small rooms in well-located, modern or colonial buildings. All rooms have private bath (usually with shower, sometimes with tub), colour TVs (sometimes with satellite hook-ups), and lifts.

North of the Zócalo Very convenient to the Zócalo, this neighbourhood, though hardly posh, has lots of small shops and interesting street life.

Hotel Catedral (☎ (5) 518-52-32; fax 512-43-44), Donceles 95 (06020; Metro: Zócalo), just around the corner from the Templo Mayor site and a block north of the cathedral, is shiny, bright and efficient, with a decent restaurant off the lobby. The 140 rooms have TVs and baths (some with tubs); all are well-kept, pleasant and comfortable at US$25/30 a single/double. Some have views of the cathedral. There's parking nearby.

Hotel Antillas (☎ (5) 526-56-74), Belisario Domínguez 34 at Allende (06010; Metro: Allende), six blocks north-west of the Zócalo, has 100 decent rooms with carpeting, bright coloured bedspreads, carafes of purified water, TVs and hot showers for US$22/25 a single/double; triples and suites sleeping four are somewhat more. The restaurant serves a comida corrida for US$3. Parking is available.

West of the Zócalo This area, bounded by Avenida Cinco de Mayo on the north, República del Salvador on the south and Avenida Lázaro Cárdenas on the west, has several excellent moderately priced lodging choices. Metro station for these places is Allende.

Hotel Canada (☎ (5) 518-21-06 to -13), Cinco de Mayo 47 east of Isabel la Católica (06000), is one of my favourite places. Bright, modern and tidy, the staff is welcoming, the location excellent. Machines on each floor dispense hot and cold purified water for your carafe; pure ice can be had as well. The 100 rooms cost US$20/25 a single/double; parking is available.

Hotel Gillow (☎ (5) 518-14-40), Isabel la Católica 17 at Cinco de Mayo (06000), looks old-fashioned as you enter, but the rooms were completely modernised a few years ago, and are now cheerful and up-to-date. Rates are US$22/27 a single/double. The popular restaurant serves a set-price lunch that's good value at US$4.

Hotel Ritz (☎ (5) 518-13-40), Avenida Madero 30 west of Bolívar, right next to the Librería Británica, caters to business travellers and North American tour groups, offering 140 quite comfortable rooms with TVs and mini-bars and an upscale atmosphere at moderate prices of US$50/55 a single/double. There's live music in the lobby daily, a restaurant and a good little bar, parking, and a travel agency. For reservations in the USA call Best Western at (800) 528-1234.

North of the Alameda The neighbourhood north of the Alameda Central, west of Avenida Lázaro Cárdenas, east of Trujano, is quiet yet convenient, and has a few good hotels. The first two are on Calle de Santa Veracruz, one block north of Hidalgo between Avenida Lázaro Cárdenas and Trujano, near the Bellas Artes Metro station.

Hotel Hidalgo (☎ (5) 521-87-71), Calle Santa Veracruz 37 at Dos de Abril (06030), is modern, grey, monolithic, and relatively new. The 100 rooms are carpeted and quite clean; all have telephones, TVs and carafes of purified water. There's a restaurant and garage. Rates are very good at US$22/27/30 a single/double/triple.

Hotel Mariscala (☎ (5) 585-42-88), Santa Veracruz 12 (06010), one block north of the Bellas Artes and just west of Avenida Lázaro Cárdenas, is well-used but serviceable. The rooms are big, and most have telephones, TVs and small desks. A restaurant downstairs serves a comida corrida for US$3.50, and there's a garage as well. Rates are US$17/22 a single/double. The location is very convenient.

Hotel de Cortés (☎ (5) 518-21-81; fax 518-34-66), Hidalgo 85 at Reforma (06300; Metro: Hidalgo), just north of the north-west corner of the Alameda, has a somewhat forbidding façade of dark stone, but inside is a charming colonial courtyard furnished as a relaxing café and restaurant. Built in 1780 as a hospice for Augustinian friars, its 29 rooms are now modern and comfortable with TVs, mini-bars, and small windows that look out on the courtyard. Noise can be a problem, though. Rates are US$66/70 a single/double. The set-price lunch is good at less than US$10.

South of the Alameda Except for one hotel right on Avenida Juárez, these hotels are in a neighbourhood of artisans and shops south of the Alameda, bound by Dolores on the east and Balderas on the west. The closest Metro station is Juárez unless otherwise noted.

Hotel Bamer (☎ (5) 521-90-60; fax 510-17-93), Avenida Juárez 52 at Luis Moya (06050; Metro: Juárez, Hidalgo or Bellas Artes), almost facing the Juárez Hemiciclo, has a prime location looking north over the Alameda. The polished lobby floor, white statues, huge globe and 1960s decor were once expensive to enjoy, but now the 111 large, comfortable rooms, many with fantastic views of the Alameda, are reasonably priced at US$38/40/44/50 a single/double/triple/quad. Most have mini-bars, bathtubs and air-con. The panorama restaurant on the 15th floor serves a comida corrida of salad, two typical Mexican dishes and dessert for US$2.75.

Hotel Fleming (☎ (5) 510-45-30), Revillagigedo 35 south of Artículo 123 (06050), 2½ blocks south of the Alameda, has 100 good, fairly modern rooms with large tiled bathrooms; on the higher floors some have great views. The coffee shop offers a filling comida corrida of four dishes for US$2.75.

Hotel San Diego (☎ (5) 510-3523 or 512-26-53), Luis Moya 98 south of Pugibet (06070; Metro: Salto del Agua), 5½ blocks south of the Alameda, is a bit far from the action, but offers excellent value. The 87 spacious modern rooms boast satellite TVs, lots of coloured marble, and prices of US$20 to US$27 a double. There's a good restaurant, a bar and a garage. The slightly pricier four-star *Hotel Estoril* is just across the street.

Hotel Marlowe (☎ (5) 21-95-40), Independencia 17 between Dolores and López (06050; Metro: Bellas Artes) is an older place that offers good value mostly because of its location just one short block south of Avenida Juárez, and near many cheap restaurants. Rooms are oldish but livable; the brightest are the corner 'junior suites' with numbers ending in 2, and the very best are the highest: 702, 802, etc. Rates are US$20/24 a single/double.

The *Hotel Metropol* (☎ (5) 510-86-60 or 521-49-10; fax 512-12-73), Luis Moya 39 south of Independencia (06050), was totally renovated and modernised in 1991 and now rates four stars. Prices as of this writing are not bad – US$40 per room – but will no doubt rise soon to US$55 or US$60. The hotel's location, only two blocks from the Juárez Metro station and the Alameda, makes it worth the money, though.

Near Plaza de la República Within a few blocks of the Plaza de la República are several comfortable hotels offering very good value. The location, one km west of the Alameda, is only a bit inconvenient.

Hotel Corinto (☎ (5) 566-65-55 or 566-97-11), Vallarta 24 north of Antonio Caso (06030), 1½ blocks south of the plaza, is a great place: sleek, modern and polished, with a good restaurant, bar and travel agent desk. There's even a small swimming pool on the 9th-floor roof. The 155 rooms, though small, are comfortable and quiet. Doubles cost US$30 to US$32. There is no nearby Metro station.

Palace Hotel (☎ (5) 566-24-00), Ignacio Ramírez 7 (06030), a half-block south of the plaza, always has lots of bustle in its lobby as guests (mostly gringos and gringas) arrive and depart. All signs are in English as well as Spanish. The 200 rooms, though aging and characterless, are well kept and suitable, with faint pretensions to luxury, for US$35 to US$40 a single, US$40 to US$46 a double. There's a restaurant, bar, garage and travel agency.

Hotel New York (☎ (5) 566-97-00), Edison 45 at Pedro Bananda (06030), three short blocks north-east of the plaza, used to be a low-budget hotel but has upgraded to the middle class. It has a tidy, busy little restaurant serving a good comida for US$3.50. The 45 rooms are very well kept, and good value at US$24 to US$27 a double. It has a garage.

The *Hotel Jena* (☎ (5) 566-02-77), Jesús Terán 12 at Puente de Alvarado (06030; Metro: Hidalgo), is a modern, gleaming building with some of the most luxurious rooms in the middle range. The 161 rooms are ultra-clean, and the place has a posh feel to it, yet prices are only US$40 a single, US$43 to US$46 a double, US$62 a triple; suites cost US$77.

Near Buenavista Railway Station There are surprisingly few hotels near the railway station, but this one is very close and comfortable.

Hotel Pontevedra (☎ (5) 541-31-60 to - 64), Insurgentes Norte 226, north of Martínez de la Torre/Mosqueta (06400), stands right across Insurgentes from the western side of Buenavista station. Modern, clean and decently priced, it rents good double rooms for US$20 to US$27. Nearest Metro is Guerrero, six blocks east; it's better to use buses on Insurgentes for transport.

Near Terminal Norte *Hotel Brasilia* (☎ (5) 587-85-77), Avenida de los Cien Metros 4823 (07370; Metro: Autobuses Norte), is a five to eight-minute walk (2½ blocks) east of the northern bus terminal; walk out the terminal's front door and turn left. It has 200 comfortable, modern, air-conditioned, TV-equipped rooms ranging from US$20 for the cheapest single to US$34 for a large double. Even larger rooms sleep up to six. There's a restaurant and bar.

Near Jardín del Arte Numerous hotels are within a block of the Jardín del Arte, but there is no convenient Metro station.

Hotel Sevilla (☎ (5) 566-18-66), at Serapio Rendón 126 (06470) north of Sullivan, is popular with Mexican couples and families. It has 150 quiet rooms just a half- block from the park. All the services are here – air-con, purified water taps in all bathrooms, a shop, travel agency, restaurant-bar, and garage. At this writing, many rooms have views of the park, but if they build something next door, the views will disappear. The restaurant serves a very filling comida for US$7. Rates are the best part: US$17 to US$25 a single, US$19 to US$29 a double (one bed), US$28 to US$32 for a double with two large beds.

Hotel Mallorca (☎ (5) 566-48-33), Serapio Rendón 119, across from the Mallorca and under the same management, has similar services but even lower prices. The Librería Británica is just to the left.

Hotel Regente (☎ (5) 566-89-33; fax 592-57-94), at Paris 9 north-west of Madrid (06030), is two blocks north-east of the park. The 138 clean, small, comfortable rooms are favoured by European (often Dutch) tour groups. The location is right near bus routes along Insurgentes and Reforma. Rates are US$44/50 a single/double, and service is quiet and polished. The hotel's Restaurant Korinto serves a decent comida corrida. Parking is available.

Near the Zona Rosa Hotels right in the posh Zona Rosa are expensive, but there are some good, reasonably priced places on the fringes. There is really no convenient Metro station for these hotels.

Hotel María Cristina (☎ (5) 703-17-87; fax 566-91-94), Río Lerma 31 (06500), between Amazonas and Neva, on the north-west side of Reforma 350 metres from the centre of the Zona Rosa, is a colonial-style gem. It has 150 comfy rooms, and staying there is like having your own mansion in the city, complete with manicured lawns, baronial public rooms, and a patio with fountain. There's a fine restaurant (comida: US$9), a bar, and parking; the British Embassy is only a block away. Rates are US$44 to US$50 a single, US$50 to US$64 a double. It's popular with Mexican business executives, families, and foreign tourists, and is often fully booked. Reserve in advance if you can.

Hotel Parador Washington (☎ (5) 592-32-31 or 703-08-93; fax 705-53-51), Dinamarca 42 at Londres (06600), is 300 metres north-east of the centre of the Zona Rosa on a quiet little plaza in a residential neighbourhood. Though built in this century, the building is of colonial inspiration. Families and groups are the preferred guests in the rooms, which cost US$20 to US$24 a double.

Hotel Vasco de Quiroga (☎ (5) 546-26-14 to -16), Londres 15 (06600), north-east of Dinamarca, has 50 elegant, well-furnished rooms. The lobby is up a flight of steps; the public rooms are large and formal, and the place has a quality feel but moderate prices of US$35/39 a single/double.

Places to Stay – top end
Zócalo *Hotel Majestic* (☎ (5) 521-86-00; fax 518-34-66), Avenida Madero 73 (06000) on the west side of the Zócalo, has lots of colourful tiles in the lobby, and a few rooms (the more expensive ones) overlooking the vast plaza. Avoid the rooms facing Avenida Madero (too noisy) and the rooms facing the inner glass-floored courtyard (unless you don't mind people looking in at you). Rates are US$60 to US$80 per room. Be sure to visit the rooftop café/restaurant for a great view of the Zócalo and, rarely, when the smog clears, the snow-capped peaks of Popocatépetl and Iztacchíhuatl.

Gran Hotel Ciudad de México (☎ (5) 512-92-75 or 510-40-40 to -49; fax 512-20-85), Avenida 16 de Septiembre 82 just off the Zócalo (06000), lives up to its name. Enter the spacious lobby and a brilliantly coloured canopy of stained glass soars above you. Sit on one of the plush settees and watch the

open ironwork elevator glide up and down, or listen to the songbirds in the large cages. This is a worthy place, a feast of Mexican Rococo-Victoriana operated, oddly enough, by the Howard Johnson chain. Rates for the 125 large, comfortable rooms are US$70, single or double. There's parking available, and a branch of the Delmonico's restaurant chain. For reservations in the USA call (800) 654-2000.

Zona Rosa Hotels in the Zona Rosa are mostly at the low end of the luxury market in terms of price, and offer excellent, convenient locations as well as good value for money. The Metro station is Insurgentes; postal code is 06600.

Hotel Geneve (☎ (5) 211-00-71), Londres 130 at Genova, is the dowager of Zona Rosa hotels, being older but well-kept, with a formal colonial lobby and a grand glass-canopied restaurant. Rooms have two double beds, mini-bars, and the other luxuries, and cost US$85 a single or double. The restaurant is good, as is the bar and the bookshop.

Hotel Century (☎ (5) 584-71-11; fax 525-74-75), Liverpool 152 at Amberes, is a dramatic high-rise with 143 small rooms furnished in outspoken modern style, including sunken bathtubs, curved balconies, strong coloured textiles, satellite TVs and mini-bars. The hotel has all the services – bars, restaurant and coffee shop, rooftop swimming pool, garage – yet charges less than many others: US$110 a single or double.

Hotel Galería Plaza (☎ (5) 211-00-14 or toll-free in Mexico (91-800) 90-123), Hamburgo 195 at Varsovia, two blocks south of the Angel monument, is classy, comfortable and well-located, with smooth service and a reputation for good and varied cuisine. The 434 rooms cost US$120 a single or double. For reservations in the USA call Westin Hotels at (800) 228-3000.

Hotel Marco Polo (☎ (5) 207-18-93, 511-18-39, or toll-free (800) 90-060; fax 533-37-27), at Amberes 27 between Reforma and Hamburgo, is Mexico City's trendy lodging. Arts and entertainment types (and wannabes) gravitate to its 60 very comfortable, stylishly mod rooms priced at US$124 a single or double. The excellent sidewalk restaurant is called La Boutique after the clientele, not the menu. If you're part of the black turtleneck crowd, this is for you. For reservations in USA call (800) 888-1199, 448-8355, or 223-0888.

Hotel Krystal Zona Rosa (☎ (5) 511-87-79 or 525-26-50; fax 511-34-90), Liverpool 155 at Amberes, is best described as glitzy: it has a mirrored lobby ceiling and walls above a white marble floor, quiet jazz from a combo, plush rooms with satellite TVs, mini-bars, good city views and other luxuries, a heated swimming pool, rooftop Japanese restaurant, and so on. Rooms go for $140 a single or double. For reservations in the USA call (800) 231-9860; fax (619) 792-1872.

Along Paseo de la Reforma The hotels described below are within an easy walk of the Zona Rosa.

Hotel Marquis Reforma (☎ (5) 211-36-00 or 211-49-98, or toll-free (91-800) 90-176; fax 211-55-61), Paseo de la Reforma 465 at Río de la Plata (06500), is among the city's newest hotels, with 125 deluxe guest rooms and 85 lavish executive suites. Design and decor draw from the city's rich Art Deco heritage, and update it for the 21st century. It has lots of coloured marble, well-trained multilingual staff, and facilities such as an outdoor spa with whirlpool baths. The hotel is within walking distance of the Zona Rosa, US Embassy, and Chapultepec park. Rates are US$176 for rooms, US$264 to US$300 for suites, single or double. For reservations in the USA, call (800) 235-2387 or (800) 223-6510.

María Isabel-Sheraton Hotel (☎ (5) 211-00-01), Paseo de la Reforma 325 at Río Tiber (06500), at the Independence (Angel) monument, is Mexico City's standard for solid comfort. Though older (built 1962), it is as plush and attractive as ever with spacious public rooms, excellent food and drink, and all the services of a top-class hotel, including

pool, health club, sauna, two lighted tennis courts, and nightly mariachi entertainment. The 811 deluxe guest rooms offer all the comforts. Rates are US$171 to US$281 a single, US$193 to US$303 a double. For reservations in USA call (800) 325-3535.

San Marino Hotel-Suites (☎ (5) 525-48-86), Río Tiber 107 at Río Lerma (06500), one block north-west of the Independence (Angel) monument, is well located, well kept, and offers a suite with fully equipped kitchenette for less than the price of a regular room in many other luxury hotels. Here you pay US$105. They have a restaurant and a car park.

Chapultepec *Hotel Nikko México* (☎ (5) 203-40-20; fax 255-46-81), Campos Elíseos 204 (11560; Metro: Auditorio), is the best hotel in Chapultepec. Opened in 1987, it successfully blends modern luxury with Asian traditional hospitality in a dramatically designed building within walking distance of the National Museum of Anthropology and Chapultepec castle.

The hotel features a formal French restaurant, a Japanese steakhouse, and a Mexican café, as well as a heated swimming pool, three tennis courts and a health club. Rates are US$187 to US$220 a single, US$198 to US$242 a double. For reservations in the USA call (800) 645-5687.

PLACES TO EAT

This cosmopolitan capital has eateries for all tastes and budgets. The following categories are not strictly defined, so you'd do well to read through the whole section, no matter what your budget. Some of the best places are the cheapest, and some of the more expensive places are well worth the extra money.

Places to Eat – bottom end
Near the Zócalo Cheapest eats near the Zócalo are on Motolinía, a little street three blocks west of the plaza, between Tacuba and Avenida Cinco de Mayo. The street is

lined with shops selling medical apparatus, corsets and bras, and also with a half-dozen big, bright, bare eateries selling tacos, enchiladas and other Mexican traditional dishes at low prices (five tacos for US$1.75). The northern half of the block, right near the Allende Metro station, has the most eateries.

Café El Popular (☎ 518-60-81), Cinco de Mayo 52, between Isabel la Católica and Palma, to the left of the Hotel Washington, is a good neighbourhood place open 24 hours a day. Pastries tempt you as you enter, but they also serve good breakfasts (fruit, eggs, ham, rolls, beans and coffee for US$3), and light meals.

Cafetería Los Popos, Avenida Madero 71 east of Palma, just west of the Hotel Majestic, is a modern lonchería serving tacos, sandwiches, enchiladas, sincronizadas (ham and cheese in tortillas) and pozole (hominy and meat stew) for US$1 to US$2.50. A dozen set-price breakfasts go for US$2 to US$4. Hours are 8 am to 9 pm, closed Sunday.

Restaurant El Gallo (☎ 521-64-75), Palma Norte 28 on the corner of Avenida Madero, is marked by a sign which reads 'Zenón'. Since 1939 this big, bright restaurant with Mexican background music has been satisfying singles, couples and families with platters of meat, potatoes, beans and guacamole for under US$5. Breakfasts are a bit expensive at US$2.50 to US$5. Open every day.

Café Cinco de Mayo (☎ 510-19-95), Avenida Cinco de Mayo 57 east of Palma, open every day, serves good breakfasts, but is best for its set-price lunches, which offer lots of choice (four courses for US$3.50, six courses for US$6). The set-price meals aren't offered at night, making it more expensive. They make their own yoghurt here daily.

At *La Casa del Pavo* (☎ 518-29-16), Motolinía 40-A north of 16 de Septiembre, chefs in white aprons slice roasted turkeys all day long and serve them up at low prices. The comida corrida offers excellent value at US$3. There are several other cheap eateries nearby.

Café La Blanca (☎ 510-03-99), Avenida Cinco de Mayo 40 west of Isabel la Católica, is big, airy, always busy, and good for people-watching. Prices are not the lowest, but you can have their set-price lunch for less than US$5. It's open every day.

Rincón Mexicano (☎ 573-41-80), Uruguay 27 west of Bolívar, and *Antojitos Tere*, Uruguay 29, are tiny hole-in-the-wall eateries with home cooking and very low prices. The *cubierto* (set-price meal) at the Mexicano costs US$3; the comida of three courses at Tere is less than US$2. They're open daily, but close at 5 pm.

Restaurante Café Paris (☎ 521-17-92), Cinco de Mayo 10-F west of Filomeno Mata, is a good place for breakfast. You can get french toast topped with fruit for US$2, other breakfasts for US$2.75 or US$3.50. Set-price lunches range from US$3.75 to US$4.75. It's clean, modern, pleasant, and open daily from 8 am to midnight. Check your bill and count your change, though.

Restaurant Borda (☎ 512-27-97), Avenida Madero 27 or Bolívar 24, is more authentic than fancy, with gilded lettering on the door, strolling guitarists at lunchtime, and excellent prices. The five-course comida corrida is priced at US$4.50, the *menú especial* at US$7. They do good, cheap breakfasts, too. Hours are 8 am to 8 pm; closed Sunday.

Vegetarian Restaurants *Restaurante El Vegetariano* (☎ 521-68-80), Avenida Madero 56 west of Palma, is marked by a plaque on the doorway; the restaurant is up a flight of stairs. Go through to the light, airy, high-ceilinged front rooms where a piano player plunks out old favourites as you dine. The five-course *especialidad del día* goes for US$4; the meatless food is excellent, portions are huge, and the value-for-money is unbeatable. The clientele is mostly young and female.

Restaurante El Vegetariano has a more modern, street-level branch at Filomeno Mata 13 north of Avenida Madero, but I prefer the original place, which opened in 1942.

Bakeries & Pastry Shops The cheapest breakfast is coffee or tea you make yourself (or buy to take away), plus some sweet rolls from a nearby *pastelería*. You enter the pastelería, take an aluminium tray and tongs, fill the tray with what you like, then an attendant will price and bag it. Here are several places:

Pastelería Madrid (☎ 521-33-78), Cinco de Febrero 25 at República del Salvador, two blocks south of the south-west corner of the Zócalo, is huge, with fresh breads and pastries issuing forth from the ovens all the time.

Pastelería Ideal (☎ 585-80-99), 16 de Septiembre 14 west of Gante, has huge wedding cakes in the windows, and looks quite fancy. But prices are still low; all the breads and rolls are at the back.

Panificadora Novedades, Bolívar 78, opens early in the morning so you can pick up fresh pastries for breakfast.

Near the Alameda One block north of the Palacio de Bellas Artes along Avenida Lázaro Cárdenas, at the intersection with Donceles on the north-east corner, is the *Taquería Los Pericos*, serving plates of tacos and tortas (little sandwiches) for US$1.25 to US$1.75. Several similar places are right next door, all open from 8 am to 3 am every day.

On the south-east corner of that same intersection is the *Frutería Frutivida*, with lots of fresh fruit juices and licuados. Look for the fruit colours (orange and yellow) on the awnings, tables and stools.

Next to the Frutería is the *Taquería y Pollería El Correo*, serving tacos for US$0.20 to US$0.50 each, depending upon ingredients.

Café Trevi and *Café Colón*, Calle Colón at Dr Mora, on the west side of the Alameda facing the Jardín de la Solidaridad, are pleasant, cheap, popular and good. The Trevi serves breakfasts from 8 am to noon for US$1.75 to US$3.75, and its set-price meal from noon to 11 pm for US$4. The Colón is even cheaper, with a hearty breakfast of carne asada, chilaquiles, juice and coffee for only US$3.

Head south from the Bellas Artes to find *Taquería El Sembrador*, López 7, a half-block south of Avenida Juárez. New, clean and shiny with bright coloured tiles and white stucco, they serve soups, quesadillas, fajitas, tacos and burritas. A filling bowl of pozole costs US$2.25, a plate of three tacos US$3 to US$6; full meals can be had for US$4. Hours are 7 am to 11 pm every day.

Walk south from the Alameda along Calle Luis Moya, and within a half-block south of Avenida Juárez you'll come to several small, good taquerías on the right-hand (west) side. *El Regiomontano* specialises in cabrito al horno (roasted kid), which you'll see being prepared in the window. This northern Mexican speciality is not cheap, however, at US$12 the portion. But neighbouring shops sell tortas for US$1 or less, plus juices and sweets.

A bit farther along Luis Moya, south of Independencia, is *Los Faroles*, at Luis Moya 41. Beneath the brick arches white-aproned señoras ladle steaming caldo (stew) from huge earthenware *cazuelas* (cooking pots), and prepare authentic and tasty tacos and enchiladas. The dining room can be dark and hot some days, but prices are low. Hours are 8 am to 7 pm every day.

Restaurante Presente y Futuro (☎ 521-19-13), Independencia 72 C at Revillagigedo, is nothing fancy, but it's open long hours (7.30 am to 1 am), and is convenient to the hotels south of the Alameda. Pasta plates cost US$3.50 to US$4, a quarter fried chicken with potatoes is the same; other dishes are more expensive. From 6 to 10 pm, on the mezzanine, a fortune-teller will read your future in the coffee grounds.

Hong King, on Bolívar between Uruguay and Carranza, is a branch of a Chinatown eatery (see below under Places to Eat – middle) which has much cheaper set-price meals than the original place. You can eat here for US$2.50 to US$3.25.

Vegetarian Restaurants *Centro Naturista de México*, Dolores 10, a half-block south of Avenida Juárez, is a shop selling natural foods including pan integral (whole-grain bread). It has a Restaurante Vegetariano serving full meals for US$2.75, and healthy drinks for US$0.50. A photo mural of a forest stream and quiet flute music in the background soothe the soul. Hours are 11 am to 5 pm every day.

Near Plaza de la República A half-dozen small, low-priced restaurants provide for the needs of this neighbourhood.

Among the very cheapest restaurants in this area is one which I call the *No Name Restaurant*, Plaza San Fernando 1, just east of the intersection of Puente de Alvarado and Guerrero. The Café Paris (more expensive) is on the corner, the Restaurante El Pedregal (a noisy cantina) is to the north, and between them is one fairly drab high-ceilinged room, where every day of the week señoras cook up a four-course comida corrida and sell it for US$2. Clerks and secretaries come to fill the tables and themselves at lunchtime. Breakfast and supper are offered as well, for the restaurant is open from 8.30 am to 10 or 11 pm.

Restaurante Samy, Mariscal 12, just south-west of the Hotel Jena, offers fixed-price breakfasts for US$1.25 to US$3.50, and a very popular five-course comida corrida for US$3.50.

Restaurant La Esquina, at the corner of Edison and Emparan, is modern and snazzier, but a bit more expensive. Tacos cost US$0.50 to US$1.25 apiece, but fruit salads sell for under US$1. The set-price lunch costs US$4.

Restaurante Bracen's, at the corner of Edison and Alcazar, is tidy, unpretentious and cheap, with comidas corridas priced from US$2.75 to US$4.75.

The restaurant adjoining the *Hotel New York*, Edison 45 between Emparan and Alcazar, is always popular and usually full because of good food and low prices. You'd do well to come early (1 pm) or late (3.30 pm) for lunch.

Zona Rosa Believe it or not, there are cheap places to eat on the fringes of the Zona Rosa. The first place to look is Plaza Insurgentes,

the great circular construction above the Insurgentes Metro station at the intersection of Genova, Insurgentes and Avenida Chapultepec. Among the many small eateries here is *Taquería Beatriz*, at No 3-B, serving a bewildering assortment of tacos for US$0.50 to US$1 each.

Fonda 99.99, Londres 136-A between Genova and Amberes, serves Yucatecan food at good prices. The menu (in English) offers sopa de lima (lime soup), tacos cochinita, pavo en escabeche, and other Maya favourites. Soup and main course can be had for under US$4.

Places to Eat – middle
Near the Zócalo *La Baguetelle*, Gante 1 just south of Avenida Madero, serves baguette sandwiches for US$2.50 to US$4.50, pizzas for US$4 to US$16, and desserts. Their doughnuts are excellent, as is their whole wheat bread. It has a European café atmosphere, with a few outdoor tables. Hours are 8 am to 8 pm; closed Sunday.

Café de Tacuba (☎ 512-84-82), Tacuba 28 east of Bolívar, just west of the Allende Metro station, is a gem of old-time Mexico City, opened in 1912. Coloured tiles, brass lamps and oil paintings set the mood. The cuisine is traditional Mexican, and delicious. Cakes and tarts are made right here. Daily special platters are priced from US$7 to US$10. Hours are 8 am to midnight every day.

Hostería de Santo Domingo (☎ 510-14-34), Domínguez 72 east of República de Chile, six blocks north-west of the Zócalo, is small but intense. Handicrafts crowd the walls and ceiling, good and unusual regional cooking fills the menu and also the crowds who come at lunchtime. Full three-course, à la carte meals cost about US$15 per person, though you can easily eat for US$10. If you want someplace atmospheric, this is it. Come any day between 9 am and 11 pm; lunch (with live music) is best, at dinnertime the restaurant is fairly empty.

Restaurante Jampel (☎ 521-75-71), Bolívar 8 north of Cinco de Mayo, is three establishments in one. To the left is the fancy

Restaurant-Bar Ejecutivo, open from 2 to 11 pm, with live music and a moderately priced international menu. To the right is the shiny Cafeteria Jampel, and on the mezzanine is the Restaurant-Bar El Golpe, with live music in the evenings. The pleasant cafeteria (open 7.30 am to 11 pm daily, noon to 6 pm Sunday) has good five-course comidas corridas priced from US$4 to US$7.50. Daily except Saturday there's a buffet in the fountain room from 1 to 4.30 pm; weekends there's paella.

Near the Alameda Right inside the Palacio de Bellas Artes, to the left, is the museum's librería y cafetería (bookshop and café). Sandwiches and salads sell for US$3.50 to US$4; coffee and pastry costs US$3 to US$5. Patrons of the café get to use the toilets for free; others must pay US$0.70.

Perhaps the prettiest restaurant in the area is the *Cafetería del Claustro*, the 'Cloister Café', in the Museo Franz Mayer, on the north side of Avenida Hidalgo, facing the Alameda at Hidalgo 45. The museum is open Tuesday to Sunday from 10 am to 5 pm, as is the café (tell the guard you're going to the cafetería and you needn't pay admission). Marble-topped tables are set in the lovely courtyard, where you munch to the restful strains of quiet classical music. The self-service food includes sandwiches, salads and quiche for US$1 to US$3.50; there's also coffee, juices, yoghurt and pastries.

Restaurant Vasco (☎ 518-29-18), Avenida Madero 6 east of Avenida Lázaro Cárdenas, next to the Casa de Azulejos, is entered from the Pasaje América; the restaurant is on the 1st and 3rd floors (ie, 2nd and 4th US-style). There's a lift. Vasco is a Mexico City institution. Its vast old-fashioned dining rooms have a classical stateliness; service is professional. Breakfast, served from 8 am on the 3rd floor, is an experience, but most people come for the abundant six-course cubierto, served in the afternoon on the 1st floor, for US$8.

Restaurant Lincoln (☎ 510-14-68), Revillagigedo 24 at Independencia, 1½ blocks south of Avenida Juárez, is formal and dignified, with dark wood, white tablecloths and black-coated waiters. The food is delicious and prices are moderate, with most meat and fish plates costing US$6 to US$14; however, they offer no set-price lunch. Hours are 8 am to 9 pm every day.

Fonda Santa Anita (☎ 518-46-09), Humboldt 48, a half-block south of Avenida Juárez, is the place to go when you're tired of the same old tacos and enchiladas. The Fonda is a Mexican food fiesta squeezed into a tiny glass-fronted space. The menu is in English, but the food is unusual and authentic, drawing on the country's many regional cuisines. Set-price meals go for US$7, à la carte costs more. Hours are noon to 10 pm; closed Sunday.

Restaurant Danubio (☎ 512-09-12), Uruguay 3 at Avenida Lázaro Cárdenas, is a city tradition. It's been here, specialising in seafood, for half a century, and still does it well. It serves an excellent six-course set-price menú for under US$10. Lobster (langosta) and crayfish (langostinos) are the specialities, but prices for them are stratospheric. Hours are 1 pm to midnight every day.

Sanborns Casa de Azulejos (☎ 512-98-20), Avenida Madero 4 east of Avenida Lázaro Cárdenas, is worth a visit just to see this superb 16th-century Puebla-tile-bedecked building (see Around the Alameda for details). The restaurant is in the covered courtyard around a Moorish fountain. Odd murals of mythical landscapes and creatures cover the walls: two owls (Sanborns' symbol) are in one corner. The food is Mexican and good, but not exceptional, at US$4 to US$9 per meal. Their interesting vegetarian plate features exotica such as ejotes, calabacitas, chícharos and chayote, which are string beans, squash/marrow, peas and chayote-fruit. The lunch counter section in the north-west corner of the building has lower prices, but less atmosphere. Both eating areas are open from 7.30 am to 10 pm. While you're here you could check the Orozco mural on the stairs and the crafts store upstairs.

Restaurant Centro Castellano (☎ 510-14-

61), Uruguay 16 east of Avenida Lázaro Cárdenas, is huge, occupying three floors of its building. The decor is colonial, the menu is long, and heavy on seafood such as red snapper (huachinango) and octopus in its own ink. There's also veal, roast kid – just about everything. The six-course comida corrida costs US$9, as do most à la carte dishes. Hours are 1 pm to 10 pm (till 7 pm on Sunday).

Mexico City has a small Chinatown district on Calle Dolores south of Independencia. *Hong King* (☎ 512-67-03), Dolores 25A, is small and pleasant, with set-price meals from US$6 to US$11 per person and menus in Chinese, Spanish and English. Hours are noon to 11.30 pm every day. (The branch of Hong King on Bolívar between Uruguay and Carranza has much cheaper set-price meals for US$2.50 to US$3.25.) Other restaurants on Dolores include the *Restaurante Daniel*, *4 Mares*, *Oriental*, *Chung King*, and *Shanghai Ming's*.

Along Reforma *Shirley's* (☎ 536-00-86), Reforma 108 north-east of Insurgentes, is a big, comfortable American-style place featuring gringo and Mexican food in clean, pleasant, modern surroundings with super-efficient service. Though all meals are served (they're open 7.30 am to 11.30 pm every day), it's the luncheon eat-all-you-want buffet (US$8) which packs 'em in. There's another Shirley's in the Zona Rosa.

Restaurante Daruma (☎ 546-34-67), Río Tamesis 6, at the intersection with Finlay and Villalongin, is on a tiny side-street just west of the Reforma-Insurgentes intersection. This modern little Japanese place has a sushi bar, teppanyaki griddles and a dozen good-value set-price meals ranging from US$6 to US$10. Hours are 1 to 11 pm Sunday to Friday; closed Saturday.

Around the Zona Rosa The Zona Rosa (Metro: Insurgentes) is packed with restaurants, most moderate in price. Many streets are closed to traffic, making the sidewalk cafés very pleasant.

Restaurante El Gallito, on Liverpool between Insurgentes and Genova, has open-air tables, and standard fare of tacos (US$1), pozole (US$5), quesadillas (cheese in tortillas) and hot tortas (sandwiches). It's open from 10 am to midnight every day.

Parri, Hamburgo 154 between Florencia and Amberes, is a huge barn-like grill house ('parri' is short for *parrilla*, grill) where you can get grilled chicken, beef or pork served up in various ways, from tacos to whole beasts. It's lively and fun, with chefs tending the busy grill and waiters scurrying about. You can eat for US$4, but you're more likely to spend US$8 or US$10.

Salon Luz, Genova 70-A between Liverpool and Londres, is a popular fast food sidewalk café good for people-watching. Have a sandwich or snack and a drink, for US$3 to US$3.75. In the evenings there's live jazz inside.

Shirley's Pink Zone (☎ 514-77-60), Londres 102 at Niza, is efficient and friendly, like the Shirley's on Reforma. The breakfast buffet is bounteous at US$7; luncheon buffets are US$7 on weekdays, US$10 on Saturday and Sunday. Hours for this tried-and-true place are 7.30 am to 11.30 pm.

Chalet Suizo (☎ 511-75-29), Niza 37 between Hamburgo and Londres, has dependably good food well served in pseudo-Swiss rusticity. They have raclette (US$5.50), various fondues (US$10 for two), and pig's knuckles with sauerkraut. Full meals usually cost US$10 to US$20. It's open from 12.30 pm to midnight every day. The menu is in English.

La Crepa Suiza (☎ 511-37-34), Avenida Florencia 33 between Hamburgo and Londres, serves both savoury dinner crepes and sweet dessert crepes, as well as fondues. The luncheon buffet is priced at US$8; dinners cost US$7 to US$11. It's open every day from 7 am to midnight, later on Friday and Saturday, and until 10 pm on Sunday.

Restaurant Tokyo (☎ 525-37-75), Hamburgo 134 at Amberes, is a simple but attractive place up a flight of stairs. Order your sukiyaki, shabu-shabu, sashimi or tempura, and expect to pay US$12 to US$18;

the set-price meals are cheaper. Hours are 12.30 pm to midnight, 2 to 10 pm Sunday.

Luaú (☎ 525-74-74), Niza 38 between Hamburgo and Londres, is an elaborate Chinese-Polynesian fantasy with fountains and miniature gardens. Best bargains are the set-price Cantonese meals priced from US$7.50 to US$15 per person. It opens daily at noon and closes at 11 pm, an hour later on Friday and Saturday, an hour earlier on Sunday.

Café Konditori (☎ 511-15-89), Genova 61 between Londres and Hamburgo, used to be Danish but now serves mostly Italian and other continental fare in its elegant small dining rooms and spacious sidewalk café. Spaghetti costs only US$5, fondue twice as much, but come for the succulent pastries and coffee (US$4 and up) when you're feeling rich. It's open from 7 am to midnight daily.

Pizza Real (☎ 511-88-34), Genova 28 at Estrasburgo, serves pizza 50 different ways (US$2.50 to US$10), as well as lots of pasta and other Italian specialities; tables are indoors and along the sidewalk. Hours are 8 am to 11.30 pm daily.

Carrousel Internacional (☎ 533-64-17), Niza 33 at Hamburgo, is a lively bar/pub and restaurant with mariachis singing energetically most of the time. Come for a sandwich, spaghetti, fruit salad or tuna steak (US$3.50 to US$7), or a drink at the bar (US$1.50 to US$3) and enjoy the music. It's open from 11.30 am to midnight every day.

Vegetarian Restaurants *Restaurante Vegetariano Las Fuentes* (☎ 525-70-95), at Río Panuco 127 on the corner of Río Tiber, two blocks north-west of the Independence (Angel) Monument, is among my favourites. Big, boldly modern and attractive, it serves delicious meatless food in huge portions for moderate prices. Abundant full-course meals cost US$8 to US$10; big breakfasts (8 am to 1 pm) are about US$5. Wine and beer are served. It's open from 8 am to 8 pm daily.

Restaurante Vegetariano Yug (☎ 533-32-96), Varsovia 3 at Reforma, one long block south-west along Reforma from the Angel

Monument, is a small, glass-enclosed place with decent vegetarian food at prices lower than Las Fuentes. The clientele are mostly office-workers from the neighbourhood.

Tearooms The Zona Rosa has numerous sidewalk cafés, and also two wonderful tearooms serving good coffees, teas, other drinks, pastries, breakfasts and light meals.

Auseba (☎ 511-37-69), Hamburgo 159-B north-east of Avenida Florencia, has glass cases filled with delicious sweets, and large windows from which to watch the pedestrian parade on Hamburgo.

Salon de Thé Duca d'Este (☎ 525-63-74), at Hamburgo 164-B, on the corner of Avenida Florencia almost facing Auseba, has very formal French decor and polite service. Tea or coffee and pastry costs US$2.50 and up. Breakfast here is not much more expensive than in cheap restaurants, and a lot cheaper than in most hotels. Hours are 6 am to 10.30 pm every day.

Chain Restaurants Numerous modern chain restaurants have branches in the Zona Rosa, including *Sanborns*, *Denny's*, *McDonald's* and *VIP's*. All are very popular with local citizens, all offer predictable, pleasant if nondescript modern decor and predictable, pleasant if nondescript food at prices slightly higher than you'd like to pay. But then, somebody's got to pay for all that cheery plastic upholstery and the equally cheery plastic smiles of the staff.

Places to Eat – top end
Mexico City has many posh restaurants. Here are a few which offer exceptional Mexican experiences. It's best to reserve a table in advance, and to dress semiformally (a dress for women, a jacket for men).

Fonda El Refugio (☎ 528-58-23), Liverpool 166 between Florencia and Amberes, is a charming old house decorated with antiques and crafts. The chef prepares many of the less well-known Mexican regional dishes with great care. In season, they even have tacos de cuitlacoche, made with that curious corn mould beloved of the Aztecs.

Dinners cost US$20 to US$25 per person. Make reservations for dinner; it's closed Sunday.

Piccadilly Pub (☎ 514-15-15), Copenhague 23 between Reforma and Hamburgo, is a *chilango's* conception of an Olde English pub; that is, far from the real thing. It's a posh restaurant, heavy on English fantasy decor, with quiet live music and both indoor and sidewalk seating. Most dishes are Mexican and international, but they do serve steak and oyster pie, pork in beer, and Cambridge sausages, as well as lots of beefsteak. Full meals cost US$20 to US$25. Hours are noon to 1 am (noon to 6 pm on Sunday).

Restaurant del Lago (☎ 515-95-85/86), Lago Mayor, Segunda Sección del Bosque de Chapultepec, stands at lakeside in the 'Second Section' of Chapultepec park, west of Blvd López Mateos. The lofty, dramatic modern building has a fine view of the lake and the park, an excellent international menu (in English), smooth service, and a dance band for post-prandial exercise. Expect to spend US$25 to US$35 per person. It's open from 1 pm to 2 am, closed Sunday.

Hacienda de los Morales (☎ 540-32-25 or 202-19-73), Calle Vázquez de Mella 525, Colonia Los Morales del Bosque, south of Avenida del Ejercito Nacional, is five km north-west of the Independence (Angel) Monument. It's easiest to go by taxi. Once a grand Spanish colonial country house, it is now surrounded by the city, which makes the spacious rooms and pretty gardens all the more appealing. Popular Mexican, American and continental dishes are served in the numerous dining rooms by experienced waiters. Full dinners cost about US$25 to US$30 per person. It's open daily from 1.30 to 11.30 pm (till 10.30 on Sunday).

ENTERTAINMENT

For information on theatre, concerts, cinema and the like, pick up a copy of *Tiempo Libre* (see Newspapers & Magazines, above), or check out *The Mexico City News*.

Concerts, Ballet & Opera

The performing arts are lively here, with concerts all over town. Ballet and opera are often held in the Palacio de Bellas Artes (Metro: Bellas Artes). Ticket prices range from US$3.50 to US$15 for concerts, US$10 to US$30 for opera. Ticket windows *(taquillas)* at the Bellas Artes are open daily from 11 am to 3 pm and 5 pm to 7 pm (Sunday from 10.30 am to 1 pm and 4 to 7 pm).

The most famous show at the Bellas Artes is the Ballet Folklorico, a festive blur of coloured lights, costumes and music from all over Mexico. The world-famous company has been doing shows like this for decades, so it's a sure hit. Tickets cost US$10, US$20 and US$25. Buy them at the ticket windows in the main lobby at the Bellas Artes rather than from travel agencies and hotels, which mark up the prices. Call 529-05-09, 529-93-20 or 529-78-05 for information.

Cinemas

Most non-Mexican movies are dubbed in Spanish, but now and then you may be able to catch one in the original language with subtitles. Check *Tiempo Libre* or *The News*, then have your hotel clerk locate a cinema in the centre (some are many km from the Zócalo).

Mariachis

Plaza Garibaldi, six blocks north of the Palacio de Bellas Artes along Avenida Lázaro Cárdenas (Metro: Bellas Artes), is where the city's out-of-work mariachi bands gather in the evenings. Fitted out in their fancy costumes, they tune their guitars and drink until someone approaches them, ready to pay for a song (about US$10 to US$20). You can wander and listen for free, and perhaps have a cup of pulque (maguey juice) or a shot of tequila in one of the bars around the plaza. The Tenampa is an old standard, and they're used to foreigners. But don't bring any valuables (except a bit of pocket change) and look out for pickpockets; they'll certainly be looking out for you. Come earlier (8 to 10 pm) rather than later, and don't wander in the neighbouring streets.

Bars & Clubs

Most good bars and nightspots are closed on Sunday.

My favourite is La Opera Bar (☎ 512-89-59), Avenida Cinco de Mayo 14, corner of Filomeno Mata, a block east of the Bellas Artes. Though long a bastion of masculinity, this ornate, turn-of-the-century watering hole opened its doors to the ladies in the 1970s. Gilded ceilings, dark wood booths and a massive bar are all original. Drinks cost US$2 and up; lots of food is served at moderate prices. If you're not up for the machismo, come at lunch; it's open Monday to Saturday from noon to midnight.

For the best view of the sprawling urban maelstrom that is Mexico City, whisk up to the top of the Torre Latinoamericana, Avenida Lázaro Cárdenas at Madero, for a drink at El Muralto. The drinks are expensive (US$4 and up) for what you get, but the view is marvelous.

South of the Alameda, try Catacumbas (☎ 518-41-27), Dolores 16 at Independencia, half a block south of the south-east corner of the Alameda, for salsa, reggae and Cuban-style *tropicale* music. It's for couples only, and there's a US$4 cover charge. It's open from 8.30 pm to 4 am; closed Sunday.

Nearby, the crowd is younger and the cover charge is lower but the music is similar at Zotano's (☎ 518-40-37), Revillagigedo 20 at Independencia.

In the Zona Rosa, the Carrousel Internacional, described in Places to Eat – middle, has live music most of the time, but can get crowded in the evening. Papa's Bar, on Amberes between Londres and Liverpool, is fairly upscale and atmospheric, with live entertainment and a US$5 cover charge. *Harry's Bar*, a few doors away, is funkier and often crowded. Both are closed on Sunday.

Spectator Sports

Football (Soccer) *Futbol* is popular on TV but crowds at most games are small. Mexico isn't a first-rank soccer nation despite hosting the World Cup finals twice. The city has several major league clubs and games in a number of stadiums most weekends. The biggest match of the year is usually América (a Mexico City club) against Guadalajara.

Bullfights The main bull ring is in the Ciudad de los Deportes, off Insurgentes. Sunday is the main bullfight day with fights starting at precisely 4 pm. See the Insurgentes Sur section above for more information.

Horseracing Horse races are held Tuesday (winter only), Thursday, Saturday and Sunday all year (except for a few weeks in September and October) at the Hipódromo de las Américas, north-west of central Mexico City. Most days the races start at 2.15 pm. To get there, take a minibus or colectivo marked 'Hipódromo' going west on Paseo de la Reforma. Admission is free except for the small tax that's paid when you purchase a programme. Obviously, the expectation is that you will bet on the races, which can be done at the windows.

Jai Alai This old Basque game (pronounced 'HIGH-lie'), introduced to Mexico by the Spanish, is a fast, skilful and elegant sporting spectacle when played by experts, and some of the best can be seen every night except Monday or Friday at the Frontón México on the north side of the Plaza de la República.

Jai alai is rather like squash played on a very long court, and even more like the English game of racquets. Instead of a racquet the players – two or four – attach a long curved basket to one arm and use it to catch the hard ball and thump it straight back against the end wall of the court. The ball must not bounce twice before being played, must land between an upper and a lower line on the end wall, and must not go off the open side of the court. Only the server or serving pair can score a point. If they lose a rally, the opposition takes the next serve. Most games end when one side reaches 30 points.

The attraction for the spectators is not just the game but the chance to bet on it. The betting system is complicated but is partly explained in the nightly programme. Bookmakers call out changing odds as each game goes on: if a player or pair is way behind and the game is approaching its end, the odds on them will be very long.

Admission to the Frontón México is US$2. Games are played all year starting at 7 pm Tuesday to Friday, at 6.30 pm on Saturday, and 5 pm on Sunday. There's a restaurant and bar, and you can take drinks in to watch the play.

THINGS TO BUY

There are lots of things to buy in this city. For boutiques, art and antiques, stroll the streets of the Zona Rosa. For information on the Bazar Sábado in the southern suburb of San Ángel, refer to the sightseeing section covering San Ángel.

Mexican Sweets

For delicate Mexican sweets such as candied fruits, sugared almonds, crystallised strawberries, honey and fruit jams, go directly to the Dulcería de Celaya, Cinco de Mayo 39 west of Isabel la Católica. These treats are not cheap, costing from US$0.50 to US$1 apiece, but anyone can afford at least one or two. The dulcería is open every day from 10.30 am to 7 pm.

Across the street on the north side of Cinco de Mayo, east of Isabel la Católica, the Dulcería La Gardenia, Cinco de Mayo 46-C, is not nearly so fancy, and prices are lower, but the sweets are still delicious.

Markets

La Ciudadela y Centro Artesanal A little more than one km south of the south-western corner of the Alameda, is La Ciudadela (The Citadel), which has an important place in the history of the Mexican Revolution. It was from here in February 1913 that supporters of the ousted dictatorial President Porfirio Díaz waged bloody street battles that resulted in the ouster and eventual execution of President Francisco Madero. La Ciudadela is not open to visits.

Most people come here to shop at the nearby Centro Artesanal y Mercado de Curiosidades (Metro: Balderas), and at the nearby open-air market at the Plaza del Buen Tono, at the corner of Ayuntamiento and Dolores (Metro: Salto del Agua). These places have handicrafts from all over Mexico at prices that are fair even before you begin bargaining. You'll find life-size brass storks, brightly dyed sarapes, multicoloured ceramic parrots, paintings on leather or felt, silver jewellery, guitars, plaster-of-paris statuettes, ceramic slices of watermelon and baskets of every shape and size – some large enough to hide in.

Fonart Fondo Nacional para el Fomento de Artesanías (National Fund for the Promotion of Crafts) is a government-supported organisation with shops throughout Mexico that sell quality handicrafts such as glassware, hand-woven wall-hangings, baskets, ceramic animals and many other items from all over the country. No bargaining is allowed because the government sets the prices, which are reasonable. The National Museum of Popular Industrial Arts, at

Avenida Juárez 44 facing the south side of the Alameda (Metro: Hidalgo), is operated by Fonart. There's another Fonart shop in the Zona Rosa at Londres 136-A, between Genova and Amberes.

La Lagunilla On Sundays this is a sprawling flea-market of over 1500 stalls selling antiques, old books (some in English), stamps, pottery, watches, guitars, leather, clothes, blankets, hats and much more. It spreads out from the corner of Comonfort and Rayón, just east of the intersection of Reforma and Avenida Lázaro Cárdenas, about one km north-east of the Alameda.

Guerrero is the nearest Metro station and buses marked 'La Villa' running north-east along Reforma take you within a few blocks.

La Merced Once this gigantic city's gigantic produce and general goods market, La Merced, about one km south-east of the Zócalo (Metro: Merced) has now been purposely diminished and many of its functions moved to modern facilities on the city's ever-expanding outskirts. The streets of this area are still very devoted to buying and selling, however, and it makes for an interesting stroll.

Buenavista Crafts Market Just east of the Buenavista railway station at Aldama 187, this vast handicrafts 'market' (☎ (5) 526-37-00) is actually a huge warehouse store. Much advertised and crassly commercial, it does have a huge assortment of stuff ('90,000 items – no less!'), but you should compare prices with other shops and markets before you buy. Bargains can be scarce. Hours are daily 9 am to 6 pm, Sunday 9 am to 2 pm.

GETTING THERE & AWAY
Air
For international flight information, see the Getting There chapter. For general information on air travel in Mexico, see the Getting Around chapter. For information on transport to and from the airport, railway station and bus terminals, see the Getting Around section which follows this section.

For information on airport usage taxes, see Costs in the Facts for the Visitor chapter.

Airports Aeropuerto Internacional Benito Juárez (☎ (5) 571-36-00), Mexico City's only major airport, is five km due east of the Zócalo (Metro: Terminal Aerea). The airport at Toluca, 66 km west of the Zócalo, is being developed as Mexico City's second airport, but you will probably land at Benito Juárez.

The attractive, modern terminal (there is only one) is divided into five *salas* or halls, lettered from A through E: Sala A – domestic arrivals, Sala B – domestic departures and ticket counters for national airlines, Sala C – European airlines ticket counters, Sala D – North American airlines ticket counters, and Sala E – all international arrivals.

It has restaurants, coffee shops, souvenir shops and newsstands, a post and telegraph office, telephones for domestic and international calls, and currency exchange booths (open when major international flights arrive). Casa de Cambio Aeropuerto SA, shop No 47 opposite Sala B (after you've cleared Customs and Immigration), usually offers quite good rates, and changes many European currencies.

Guarded left-luggage lockers are in Sala A (US$2 for 24 hours).

Car-rental kiosks can be found at the international arrivals section (Sala E). If no one is present, check the kiosk for a telephone number to call.

A tourist information booth in Sala A offers a map and leaflets about Mexico City from 8 am to 9 pm.

Airlines Mexico City has good air connections with all parts of the country. The newer, smaller airlines often charge somewhat less for a ticket than the more established lines, yet comfort, service and safety on the newer lines can be quite similar – and sometimes even superior. If you already have your air ticket onward from Mexico City, you're all set. If not, I'd suggest visiting a Mexican travel agency *(agencia de viajes)*. Ask at your hotel for the nearest full-service agency.

Here's where to find the offices of the major international airlines:

Aerolíneas Argentinas
Estocolmo 8, Zona Rosa (☎ 208-10-50); offices at Paseo de la Reforma 450, 4th floor (☎ 207-73-46)

Aeromar
Sevilla 4, Colonia Juárez (☎ 207-66-66 for reservations)

Aeroméxico
Paseo de la Reforma 445 (☎ 207-60-93), and over 20 other offices throughout the city

Aeronica Aerolíneas Nicaraguenses
Paseo de la Reforma 322 (☎ 511-32-90 or 511-36-17)

Aerovias de México
Campos Elíseos 218 (☎ 203-75-43; at the airport 762-40-22)

Aerovias Oaxaqueñas
Balderas 32-513 (☎ (510-01-62)

Aero California
Paseo de la Reforma 332 (☎ 207-13-92, 207-13-78, 207-55-71, 207-00-68)

Air France
Paseo de la Reforma 404, 15th floor for administrative offices; Paseo de la Reforma 287 for ticket offices (☎ 566-00-66 reservations; 511-38-83 ticket information)

Air Panama
Paseo de la Reforma 116, Torre Empresarial Reforma (☎ 566-68-60, 566-75-57, 566-75-68 or toll free 91-800-70075)

Alitalia
Paseo de la Reforma 390, 10th floor (☎ 533-12-40 to -43)

American Airlines
Paseo de la Reforma 300 (☎ 399-92-22 for reservations and information; 208-63-96 for general offices)

Aviación de Chiapas
Aerpuerto Internacional Benito Juárez , Sala B, Counter 23 (☎ 762-01-99)

Avianca
Paseo de la Reforma 195, 3rd floor (☎ 535-02-27)

Aviateca, Línea Aerea de Guatemala
Paseo de la Reforma 56 (☎ 592-52-89, 566-59-66)

British Airways
M Escobedo 752, 3rd floor (☎ 511-73-79)

Continental Airlines
Paseo de la Reforma 325, corner of Río Danubio (☎ 203-11-48 reservations; 571-36-61 arrivals and departures; 525-37-10 ticket information)

Delta Airlines
Paseo de la Reforma 381 (☎ 202-16-08)

Iberia
Paseo de la Reforma 24 (☎ 592-29-88)

Icelandair
Calle Durango 193-302 (☎ 511-84-61 for information)

Japan Air Lines
Paseo de la Reforma 295 (☎ 533-55-15 to -19)

KLM Royal Dutch Airlines
Paseo de las Palmas 735, 7th floor (☎ 202-44-44, 202-39-36)

LACSA Lineas Aereas Costarricenses SA
Río Nazas 135 (☎ 207-21-27)

Litoral
Felix Cuevas 329 (☎ 524-33-11, 524-34-30)

Lloyd Aéreo Boliviano
Paseo de la Reforma 133 (☎ 592-74-08, 546-46-38)

Lufthansa
Paseo de las Palmas 239, Lomas de Chapultepec (☎ 202-88-66, or toll free 91-800-90600)

Mexicana
Paseo de la Reforma at Amberes, Zona Rosa (☎ 660-44-44 reservations, open 24 hours; 571-88-88 arrivals and departures), and more than a dozen other offices throughout the city

SAS Scandinavian Airlines
Hamburgo 61 at Havre, Zona Rosa (☎ 202-85-33)

Swissair
Hamburgo 66-3, Zona Rosa (☎ 533-63-63)

TACA International Airlines
Morelos 108 (☎ 566-18-50, 546-88-09)

TAESA
Aeropuerto Internacional Benito Juárez (☎ 758-14-87, 758-07-14)

TAN-SAHSA Lineas Aereas Internacionales de Honduras
Paseo de la Reforma 87, 2nd floor (☎ 566-52-11)

United Airlines
Calle Leibnitz 100 (☎ 531-83-44, 531-45-28, 545- 90-25 and 545-51-47 for reservations and ticket information)

Varig
Paseo de la Reforma 80, suite 12 (☎ 546-98-87)

Bus

Mexico City has four main terminals serving the four points of the compass: north *(norte)*, east *(oriente)*, south *(sur)*, and west *(poniente)*. All terminals have left-luggage offices (baggage checkrooms), toilets, newsstands, banks, post, telegraph and telephone offices, restaurants and snack stands. All may be reached by Metro.

Here are some intercity bus travel tips:

For shorter trips (one to five hours), just go to the bus station, buy your ticket and go.

For longer trips (seven or eight hours or more), most buses leave in the evening or at night, and service (except to Monterrey and Guadalajara) may be limited, so buy your ticket in advance.

Some companies have more than one ticket counter in the same bus terminal.

Large companies have ticket counters in several bus stations, so you may be able to buy a ticket at the Terminal Norte for a bus departing later from the Terminal Sur, etc.

Ticket prices vary from company to company, and for different classes of service within each company. You pay more for buses of greater comfort (eg, on fancier buses, with toilets, hot and cold drink service, air-conditioning and perhaps even video) and for faster schedules such as *directo* or *express* service, and *via corta* or *via autopista* (via toll highway).

Check your luggage in at the bus line's baggage counter at least 30 minutes before departure (most companies require this).

Terminal Norte The Terminal Central Autobuses del Norte (☎ (5) 587-59-67), Avenida de los Cien Metros 4907 (Metro: Autobuses del Norte), a half km north off Insurgentes Norte and five km north of the Zócalo, is the largest of the four terminals. It is called many names, including Autobuses del Norte, Central del Norte, Central Camionera del Norte, Camiones Norte (or just 'CN'). The Terminal Norte is for buses to and from northern Mexico, as well as to Pachuca, Papantla and Tuxpan to the north-east of Mexico City; Guadalajara and Morelia in the west and a few other points, not exactly to the north, are served as well.

There's a left-luggage office at the far right (south) end (US$0.20 per piece per hour; don't leave valuables in your bags).

There's a casa de cambio at the centre of the main hall by the entrance, open Monday to Friday 8 am to 10 pm, Saturday 9.30 am to 4.30 pm. There are also Banamex ATM cash machines (cajas permanentes) which accept VISA, Mastercard and Cirrus cards and spew forth cash pesos.

Here is a guide to the locations of the bus company ticket counters, from nearest to farthest, as you enter from the Metro and the street:

To the left (north)
Autobuses Estrella Blanca I
Transportes Frontera
Transportes Monterrey-Saltillo
Transportes del Sur
Mexico-Tuxpan-Tampico
Transportes Norte de Sonora
Flecha Amarilla
Mexico-Pachuca
Herradura de Plata
Autobuses de Occidente Flecha Roja
Autobuses San Juan Teotihuacán
Oriente
Autotransportes Valle del Mezquital
Autotransportes Aculco-Tepozan

To the right (south)
Tres Estrellas de Oro
ADO (Autobuses de Oriente)
Transportes del Pacifico
Transportes del Norte
Transportes Chihuahuenses
Omnibus de México
Estrella de Oro
Autobuses Blancos
Autobuses El Aguila
Autobuses Estrella Blanca II
Transportes Frontera
Autobuses Blancos
ETN
Servicios Coordinados
Primera Plus
Camiones de los Altos Estrella Blanca
Guardería de Equipajes (left luggage room)

Terminal Oriente (TAPO) The Terminal de Autobuses de Pasajeros de Oriente (☎ (5) 702-59-77), Zaragoza 200 (Metro: San Lázaro), usually known by its acronym TAPO, is on Calzada Ignacio Zaragoza between Avenida Eduardo Molina and Avenida Oceánia, about two km east of the Zócalo. This is the terminal for buses serving east and south-east Mexico, including Puebla, central and southern Veracruz, Oaxaca, Chiapas, the Guatemalan border and Yucatán.

As you approach the terminal from the Metro, you pass the taxi ticket stand, then walk down a long tunnel-like passageway and climb some stairs into the terminal's circular main hall. Turn left and go around the circle clockwise, and these are the companies you'll find: Autobuses Unidos, UNO, ATAH, Autotransportes Mexico-Texcoco, Estrella Roja, Omnibus Cristóbal Colón, and ADO (Autobuses de Oriente).

Terminal Sur The Terminal Central de Autobuses del Sur (☎ (5) 544-21-01), Tasqueña 1320 (Metro: Tasqueña), is busy with services to Cuernavaca, Cuautla, Taxco and Acapulco, as well as to a few other destinations.

Here are the ticket counters, from left to right, as you enter the terminal's front door: Estrella Roja, Omnibus Cristóbal Colón, Cuauhtémoc, Flecha Roja (no letters, just a big red arrow); central corridor with taxi ticket kiosk and left-luggage room (Guarda Equipaje); Estrella de Oro, Autos Pullman de Morelos & Autobuses México-Zacatepec, Cristóbal Colón Cuautla-Oaxtepec.

A hotel kiosk at the station entrance is open from 10 am to 5 pm Monday to Friday for making reservations in Acapulco. When you get to your Acapulco hotel, ask the price *before* you tell them that you have a reservation. Sometimes 'reserved' prices are higher than walk-in prices.

Terminal Poniente The Terminal Poniente de Autobuses (☎ (5) 516-48-57), Avenida Sur 122 (Metro: Observatorio), is the smallest and least confusing of the bus terminals. Its main reason for being is the very frequent shuttle services (every two minutes or so) to neighbouring Toluca, but it serves some other western destinations such as Guadalajara and Morelia as well. Most services for much of Mexico's north-western coast (Mazatlán, Guaymas, etc.) is from the Terminal Norte.

Destinations Here are some major destinations served by direct buses from Mexico City, with distances, travel times, bus companies, class and ticket prices. (This is not a complete list of all destinations served.) The name of the terminal from which each destination is served is in brackets. All is subject to change, of course.

Acapulco – 400 km, seven hours (Sur), Estrella de Oro Autobuses de Acapulco runs 14 buses daily (1st, US$9.50), plus three luxury services (luxe, US$28); Flecha Roja charges US$9, with a luxury service costing US$13.50; Cuauhtémoc runs several buses as well (2nd, US$8.50).

Aguascalientes – 468 km, seven hours (Norte), frequent buses by Estrella Blanca (1st, US$11) via corta; also by Estrella de Oro, Servicios Coordinados, and many other companies. Flecha Amarilla (2nd, US$10).

Bahías de Huatulco – 819 km, 18 hours (Oriente), Cristóbal Colón has one bus daily (1st, US$22) at 8.45 pm.

Campeche – 1360 km, 21 hours (Oriente), ADO runs eight per day (1st, US$27).

Cancún – 1772 km, 27 hours (Oriente), ADO runs six per day (1st, US$36.50).

Catemaco – 553 km, eight hours (Oriente), Autobuses Unidos (1st, US$12) runs three buses daily, as does ADO (1st, US$13).

Cempoala – see Zempoala.

Chetumal – 1450 km, 24 hours (Oriente), ADO runs four daily (1st, US$30).

Chihuahua – 1455 km, 20 hours (Norte), several dozen buses a day by Estrella Blanca and Transportes Chihuahuenses (1st, US$30), as well as by many other companies.

Ciudad Juárez – 1830 km, 24 to 26 hours (Norte), several dozen buses daily by Estrella Blanca and Transportes Chihuahuenses (1st, US$37), and many other companies.

Colima – 742 km, 11 hours, (Norte) ten buses daily; Estrella de Oro runs three (1st, US$16), as does Tres Estrellas de Oro (1st, US$15); and Flecha Amarilla (2nd, US$14).

Comitán – 1168 km, 22½ hour, (Oriente), Cristóbal Colón has three buses daily to San Cristóbal de las Casas, two of which (1.30 and 7.30 pm) continue to Comitán (1st, US$26); they also run one luxury bus daily (luxe, US$40).

Córdoba – 303 km, 4½ hours (Oriente), Autobuses Unidos (1st, US$7) has very frequent buses to Córdoba and Orizaba; ADO runs them at least every hour (1st, US$7.50). UNO has deluxe service.

Cuautla – 109 km, two hours (Sur, Oriente), from the Terminal Sur, Cristóbal Colón runs buses every 15 minutes between 6 am and 9.15 pm (1st, US$2.50); from the Terminal Oriente (TAPO), Cristóbal Colón has buses (1st, US$2) every 40 minutes from 6 am to 10 pm.

Cuernavaca – 84 km, 1½ hours (Sur), Pullman de Morelos has buses every 15 minutes (1st, US$2) and deluxe service (luxe, US$4) at least every 30 to 60 minutes from 6.30 am to 6.30 pm; Cuauhtémoc runs buses (1st, US$2; 2nd, US$1.75) at least every 45 minutes; Estrella de Oro has 10 buses daily (1st, US$2).

Durango – 903 km, 12 hours (Norte), a dozen buses daily by Estrella Blanca (1st, US$17), Estrella de Oro (1st, US$18), and several other companies.

Fortín de las Flores – 306 km, 4½ hours (Oriente), ADO has four buses daily (1st, US$7.50).

Guadalajara – 535 km, seven to eight hours (Norte), very many buses daily; Camiones de los Altos Estrella Blanca runs a bus every 30 minutes from 7.30 pm to 12.30 am (1st, US$13); Estrella de Oro, Tres Estrellas de Oro and Oriente have a dozen each (1st, US$13); Flecha Amarilla runs many also (2nd, US$12).

Guanajuato – 355 km, five hours (Norte), many companies run frequent buses, including Estrella Blanca and Tres Estrellas de Oro (1st, US$8); Flecha Amarilla (2nd, US$7.50).

Guatemala City – 1500 km, 26 hours plus border-crossing time (Oriente), Omnibus Cristóbal Colón runs two buses daily (noon and 7.45 pm) via Tapachula to the border at Talismán, with a bus connection for Guatemala City (1st, US$30).

Huatulco – see Bahías de Huatulco.

Ixtapa – 400 km, nine hours (Sur), Estrella de Oro has one bus (1st, US$15) daily at 11.15 pm.

Jalapa – see Xalapa.

Los Mochis – 1478 km, 23½ hours (Norte), several daily buses by Norte de Sonora, Tres Estrellas de Oro, and Transportes del Pacífico (1st, US$32).

Manzanillo – 843 km, 13 hours (Norte), Tres Estrellas de Oro (1st, US$16.50); Flecha Amarilla (2nd, US$15).

Matamoros – 960 km, 15½ hours (Norte), a dozen buses daily by Transportes Frontera, Tres Estrellas de Oro, and Transportes del Norte (1st, US$21).

Mazatlán – 1085 km, 18½ hours (Norte), over a dozen buses daily by Estrella Blanca and Transportes del Pacífico (1st, US$23), Norte de Sonora (1st, US$21), and Tres Estrellas de Oro (1st, US$24).

Mérida – 1505 km, 24 hours (Oriente), ADO has eight buses daily (1st, US$31).

Monterrey – 961 km, 11 hours (Norte), departures at least every hour by Transportes del Norte (1st, US$18.50 to US$19); also by Transportes Frontera and Tres Estrellas de Oro (1st, US$18.50); deluxe service by Estrella Blanca (luxe, US$29).

Morelia – 309 km, four hours (Norte), Herradura de Plata runs hourly (2nd, US$5); Flecha Amarilla (2nd, US$6).

Nogales – 2280 km, 33½ hours (Norte), several buses daily by Norte de Sonora (1st, US$42), Tres Estrellas de Oro and Transportes del Pacífico (1st, US$47).

Nuevo Laredo – 1191 km, 15 hours (Norte), Transportes del Norte (1st, US$24 to US$25) has buses at least every hour; Tres Estrella de Oro (1st, US$24) also runs; Estrella Blanca has deluxe service (luxe, US$37).

Oaxaca – 510 km, nine hours (Oriente), ADO has hourly buses from 7 am to midnight (1st; US$11); Autobuses Unidos (1st, US$10) runs numerous buses, most departing after 7 pm; Cristóbal Colón (1st, US$11) runs eight per day (seven of which depart between 9 and 11.30 pm), as well as two luxury buses (luxe, US$18).

Oaxtepec – 100 km, 1½ hours (Sur), Cristóbal Colón has buses every 15 minutes (1st, US$2.25).

Pachuca – 88 km, 1½ hours (Norte), the Mexico-Pachuca line runs buses every five minutes (2nd, US$1.75); Mexico-Tuxpan-Tampico line every 15 minutes between 6 am and 9 pm (2nd, US$1.75); ADO every 15 minutes (1st, US$2).

Palenque – 1020 km, 14 to 16 hours (Oriente), ADO has two daily (1st, US$21.50) at 4 and 6.10 pm.

Papantla – 310 km, five hours, (Oriente), ADO runs four daily (1st, US$6.50).

Pátzcuaro – 415 km, 6½ hours (Poniente), frequent service by Tres Estrellas de Oro and Autobuses de Occidente(1st, US$8); Flecha Amarilla runs six buses daily (2nd, US$7).

Puebla – 126 km, two hours (Oriente), Estrella Roja runs buses (1st, US$2.75) every five minutes from 6 am to 9 pm, and slightly faster service via autopista (by expressway) every 10 minutes. Autobuses Unidos runs every five to 12 minutes, with highest frequency on weekends (1st, US$2.75). ADO has buses every 10 minutes from 7 am to 10 pm at the same price.

Puerto Vallarta – 931 km, 14 to 15 hours (Norte), Estrella Blanca (1st, US$21); Tres Estrellas de Oro (1st, US$22).

Querétaro – 222 km, 2½ to three hours (Norte), very frequent buses; Estrella Blanca runs hourly buses (1st, US$4.50; 2nd, US$4); Flecha Amarilla runs every 15 minutes (2nd, US$4); Oriente, Tres Estrellas de Oro and Transportes del Norte (1st, US$4.75) also run frequently.

Reynosa – 970 km, 15 hours (Norte), a half-dozen buses daily by Transportes Frontera, Tres Estrellas de Oro and Transportes del Norte (1st, US$21); also Oriente (2nd, US$19).

Saltillo – 876 km, 11 hours (Norte), Transportes del Norte (1st, US$17) runs eight buses daily; or go to Monterrey and transfer immediately to one of the very frequent Saltillo-bound buses.

San Cristóbal de las Casas – 1139 km, 20 hours (Oriente), Cristóbal Colón has three buses daily (1st, US$24) at 1.30, 5.30 and 7.30 pm, as well as one luxury bus (luxe, US$37) daily.

San Juan Teotihuacán – 50 km, one hour (Norte), Autobuses San Juan Teotihuacán runs buses every 15 minutes between 5 am and 10 pm. Buses marked 'San Juan' (2nd, US$1) go to the town only; those marked 'Piramides' (2nd, US$1.10) go to the archaeological zone. Make sure you buy a ticket to 'Piramides'.

San Luis Potosí – 424 km, six hours (Norte), very frequent buses; Estrella Blanca runs every hour from 6 am to 1 am (1st, US$8.50), Oriente, Tres Estrellas de Oro and Transportes del Norte almost as frequently; Flecha Amarilla (2nd, US$7.50).

San Miguel de Allende – 280 km, 4½ hours (Norte), Herradura de Plata (2nd, US$5.50) runs hourly buses; Flecha Amarilla runs some also (2nd, US$5.50).

Tapachula – 1185 km, 21 hours (Oriente), Cristóbal Colón runs seven buses (1st, US$25); two continue to the Guatemalan border at Talismán (see Guatemala City, above). They also have three luxury buses daily (luxe, US$37).

Taxco – 185 km, three hours (Sur), Estrella de Oro has six buses daily (1st, US$3.75); Cuauhtémoc has 12 daily (2nd, US$3.50).

Tehuacán – 241 km, four hours (Oriente), ADO has nine buses daily (1st, US$5.75).

Teotihuacán – see San Juan Teotihuacán.

Tijuana – 2841 km, 42 hours (Norte), several buses daily by Transportes del Pacifico (1st, US$58), and a few by other companies.

Tlaxcala – 113 km, two hours (Oriente), ATAH has buses every 15 minutes (2nd, US$2.50).

Toluca – 66 km, one hour (Poniente), Flecha Roja has buses to Toluca (2nd, US$1.75) every two minutes from 5 am to 11 pm. Turismos Mexico-Toluca runs buses (1st, US$2) every 10 minutes.

Torreón – 1000 km, 15 hours (Norte), Estrella Blanca (1st, US$20; 2nd, US$18), and a few by Transportes del Norte as well.

Tula – 65 km, one hour (Norte), Autotransportes Valle de Mezquital runs every 15 minutes (2nd, US$2).

Tuxpan – 330 km, six hours (Oriente), ADO runs a dozen buses daily (1st, US$7).

Tuxtla Gutiérrez – 1056 km, 16 to 18 hours (Oriente), Cristóbal Colón has 11 buses daily in the afternoon and evening (1st, US$23), as well as three luxury services (luxe, US$34).

Veracruz – 424 km, seven hours (Oriente), Autobuses Unidos (1st, US$8.50) runs very frequent buses; ADO has buses at least hourly from 7 am to midnight (1st, US$9). UNO has deluxe service.

Villahermosa – 863 km, 12 hours (Oriente), ADO has buses almost every hour from 7 am to 11.30 pm (1st, US$19); Autobuses Unidos (1st, US$17) runs three daily; Cristóbal Colón has one bus daily (1st, US$19) at 6.45 pm, as well as one luxury bus (luxe, US$30). UNO has deluxe service as well.

Xalapa (Jalapa) – 313 km, five hours (Oriente), Autobuses Unidos (1st, US$6.50) runs frequent buses daily; ADO has at least hourly buses from 6.45 am to midnight (1st, US$7). UNO has deluxe service.

Zempoala – 435 km, seven hours (Oriente), ADO has three buses daily (1st, US$8.75) at 6.45 am, 10.30 and 11.30 pm.

Zihuatanejo – 410 km, nine hours (Sur), Estrella de Oro has five buses daily (1st, US$14), the first one at 6 am, the rest after 6 pm.

Train

Buenavista Station The city's central station is the Terminal de Ferrocarriles Nacionales de México (FNM), known more commonly as Estación Buenavista (☎ (5) 547-90-60), open daily from 6 am to 10 pm. It's a cavernous building at Insurgentes Norte and Martínez de la Torre/Mosqueta about 1½ km (a 20-minute walk) due north of the Plaza de la República. For local transport to and from the station, see Getting Around, below.

The main hall has an information kiosk (☎ (5) 547-65-93), a long-distance telephone office (but you can use the special Ladatel phones instead), a post and telegraph office (with fax), and ticket windows. Upstairs is a left-luggage office (Guardería de Equipaje or *Paquetería)* and the International Passengers Office (☎ (5) 547-89-71), open daily from 7.30 am to 3 pm (sometimes longer if necessary). Ticket and reservation information in English can be obtained by calling 547-65-93.

Ticket offices (taquillas) are open 6 am to 9.30 pm daily. (For information on classes of seating and sleeping accommodation, see the Getting Around chapter.) Tickets for sleeping accommodation and 1st-class reserved seats must first be reserved at the *módulo de asignaciones* on the main concourse and then purchased at a taquilla. Useful words are *Llegada* (arrival), *Salida* (departure), and *Andenes* (tracks, train platforms).

The station has a slow, overpriced restaurant upstairs. If you have the time, you'd do better to leave the station, go out the front to the corner of Insurgentes and Mosqueta

(Eje 1 Norte), to the chain restaurant named *El Portón*, which sells tacos and other Mexican dishes at moderate prices. Across Insurgentes is *Shakey's Pizza*. The moderately priced *Hotel Pontevedra* is just west of the station across Insurgentes (see Places to Stay).

Reservations You should make reservations for special 1st-class seats and for sleeping accommodation well in advance if possible. According to the Gerencia de Tráfico de Pasajeros (Passenger Traffic Office, ☎ (5) 547-20-32), reservations for train trips originating or ending in Mexico City should be made at least 30 days in advance if you plan to travel during holiday periods and you want a space in a sleeper car. Outside holiday periods, it's easier to find space.

The Buenavista office is open Monday to Friday 9 am to 3 pm and 6 to 8 pm, or you can write to the Gerencia de Tráfico de Pasajeros, Ferrocarriles Nacionales de México, Estación Buenavista, México, DF 06358. Your reservation request should include all itinerary details and the type of seat or space you want. Cancellations or changes are accepted up to 24 hours before departure. For a full explanation of what's available and how to reserve it, see the Getting Around chapter.

Top Trains Here are the daily schedules of the most important trains. The named trains (*El División del Norte, El Regiomontano*, etc) are faster, more comfortable, and more expensive, but worth it. Note that fees for sleeping berths (roomettes and bedrooms) include meals and are *in addition to* the 1st-class fares; so the full fare for a single roomette from Mexico City to Ciudad Juárez is US$117, not US$99. Unless otherwise noted, only the base fare is listed below.

The following schedules will probably change at least slightly by the time you travel, so please use them only as general

guidelines, and confirm times, fares and other details in advance of travel:

To/From Ciudad Juárez El División del Norte, Train 7, has 1st class and special 1st-class seats, roomettes (one or two persons) and bedrooms (two to four persons); all seats and berths reserved (34¾ hours). Fares for 1st/special 1st/one-person roomette are: US$5.50/16/29 to Aguascalientes, US$6.50/19/35 to Zacatecas, US$15/–/80 to Chihuahua, and US$18/–/99 to Ciudad Juárez.

departs	Train 7
Mexico City	8.00 pm
Querétaro	11.30 pm
Aguascalientes	6.50 am
Zacatecas	9.30 am
Torreón	5.10 pm
Chihuahua	1.20 am
arrives	
Ciudad Juárez	6.45 am

departs	Train 8
Ciudad Juárez	10.00 pm
Chihuahua	11.25 pm
Torreón	noon
Zacatecas	8.05 pm
Aguascalientes	10.30 pm
Querétaro	5.40 am
arrives	
Mexico City	9.30 am

To/From Monterrey & Nuevo Laredo *El Regiomontano*, Trains 71 and 72, haul roomettes, bedrooms and dining cars (18¼ hours). Fares (special 1st-class) are US$10 to San Luis Potosí, US$19 to Saltillo, US$21 to Monterrey, US$27 to Nuevo Laredo. For a sleeper, the extra charge is US$41 per person to Monterrey, US$52 to Nuevo Laredo.

Trains 1 and 2 haul 2nd-class coach, 1st-class coach and 1st-class reserved seats (22¾ to 24 hours). Some 1st-class fares (2nd class is 40% lower, 1st-class reserved is 23% higher): US$2 to Querétaro, US$2.50 to San Miguel de Allende, US$4 to San Luis Potosí, US$7 to Saltillo, US$7.75 to Monterrey, US$10 to Nuevo Laredo.

departs	Train 71	Train 1
Mexico City	6.00 pm	9.00 am
Querétaro	–	1.06 pm
San Miguel de Allende	–	2.35 pm
San Luis Potosí	12.01 am	5.35 pm
Saltillo*	5.44 am	12.15 am
Monterrey**	8.10 am	2.50 am
arrives		
Nuevo Laredo	12.15 pm	7.20 am

departs	Train 72	Train 2
Nuevo Laredo	3.15 pm	6.55 pm
Monterrey**	7.00 pm	12.01 am
Saltillo*	10.00 pm	3.00 am
San Luis Potosí	3.45 am	10.35 am
San Miguel de Allende	–	1.09 pm
Querétaro	–	2.47 pm
arrives		
Mexico City	10.00 am	7.00pm

* Trains 181 and 182 run between Saltillo and Piedras Negras, taking 7½ hours and connecting with *El Regiomontano* (Trains 71 and 72).
** *El Tamaulipeco*, Trains 141 and 142, runs between Monterrey, Reynosa and Matamoros, taking 3½ hours (Monterrey-Reynosa) and 1½ hours (Reynosa-Matamoros), and connecting – if you're lucky – with *El Regiomontano* at Monterrey.

To/From Guadalajara *El Tapatío*, Trains 5 and 6, hauls special 1st-class seats, roomettes and bedrooms, and a dining car (11½ hours), and connects at Guadalajara with *El Pacífico* running along the Pacific Coast to and from Nogales and Mexicali. The fare (special 1st class) between Mexico City and Guadalajara is US$21; a camarín (roomette for one) costs an additional US$41, and an alcoba (for two) an extra US$82.

See the Getting There & Away section of Guadalajara, in the Guadalajara, Jalisco & Colima chapter, for information about onward connections.

departs	Train 5
Mexico City	8.30 pm
arrives	
Guadalajara	8.00 am

departs	Train 6
Guadalajara	9.00 pm
arrives	
Mexico City	8.30 am

To/From Querétaro & Guanajuato *El Constitucionalista*, Trains 9 and 10, hauls reserved 1st-class seats only. The fare from Mexico City is US$6.50 to Querétaro, US$9.25 to Irapuato, US$11.25 to Guanajuato.

departs	Train 9
Mexico City	7.00 am
Querétaro	10.20 am
Irapuato	12.05 pm
arrives	
Guanajuato	1.25 pm

departs	Train 10
Guanajuato	2.30 pm
Irapuato	3.40 pm
Querétaro	5.35 pm
arrives	
Mexico City	9.15 pm

To/From Fortín & Veracruz *El Jarocho*, Trains 53 and 54, hauls 1st and 2nd-class coach seats, 1st-class reserved seats, roomettes and bedrooms; Trains 51 and 52 haul coach seats only (11 hours, 26 minutes). Fares (1st/reserved 1st) are US$3/7 to Orizaba, US$3.50/8 to Fortín de las Flores, US$3.50/8 to Córdoba, and US$4.50/10 to Veracruz; a sleeper to Veracruz costs an additional US$17 per person.

Trains 101 and 102 between Veracruz and Tapachula (near the Guatemalan border) connect with Trains 53 and 54 at Veracruz.

departs	Train 51	Train 53
Mexico City	7.34 am	10.02 pm
Fortín de las Flores	4.00 pm	4.54 am
Córdoba	4.27 pm	5.05 am
arrives		
Veracruz	7.00 pm	7.30 am

departs	Train 52	Train 54
Veracruz	8.00 am	10.00 pm
Córdoba	10.35 am	12.14 am
Fortín de las Flores	10.50 am	12.33 am
arrives		
Mexico City	7.12 pm	8.08 am

To/From Morelia, Pátzcuaro & Uruapan *El Purépecha*, Trains 31 and 32, hauls 1st-class reserved seats, roomettes and bedrooms (12

hours). Fares (1st/roomette for one person) are US$3.75/16.50 to Morelia, US$4.50/19 to Pátzcuaro, and US$5.25/22.50 to Uruapan.

departs	Train 31
Mexico City	10.00 am
Morelia	5.35 am
Pátzcuaro	6.45 am
arrives	
Uruapan	10.10 am

departs	Train 32
Uruapan	7.15 pm
Pátzcuaro	9.00 pm
Morelia	10.55 pm
arrives	
Mexico City	7.17 am

To/From Puebla & Oaxaca *El Oaxaqueño*, Trains 111-112 and 112-111, haul special 1st-class reserved seats, roomettes and bedrooms (14½ hours). Fares (special 1st class/roomette for one person) are US$4.75/12 to Puebla, US$7.50/18.50 to Tehuacán, and US$13/31.50 to Oaxaca.

Trains 113-114 and 114-113 haul 1st and 2nd-class coach seats only (14½ hours). Fares (2nd/1st) are US$1/1.75 to Puebla, US$2.50/4.50 to Oaxaca.

departs	Train 111-112	Train 113-114
Mexico City	7.00 pm	5.32 pm
Puebla	11.30 pm	10.35 pm
Tehuacán	2.19 am	-
arrives		
Oaxaca	9.30 am	8.05 am

departs	Train 112-111	Train 114-113
Oaxaca	7.00 pm	6.20 pm
Tehuacán	1.35 am	-
Puebla	4.05 pm	3.50 am
arrives		
Mexico City	9.20 am	8.52 am

To/From Mérida Train 49 has 1st and 2nd-class coach seats only (35½ hours). Fares (2nd/1st) are US$4.75/8 to Palenque, US$6.50/11.25 to Campeche, and US$7.25/12.50 to Mérida. This train is not recommended as it is chronically late and

subject to bandit raids east of the Isthmus of Tehuantepec. Take the bus instead.

departs	Train 49
Mexico City	6.30 pm
Córdoba	1.36 am
Tierra Blanca	3.50 am
Medias Aguas	8.15 am
Coatzacoalcos	1.10 pm
Teapa	5.19 pm
Palenque	7.45 pm
Campeche	3.00 am
arrives	
Mérida	6.00 am

departs	Train 50
Mérida	10.00 pm
Campeche	1.27 am
Palenque	8.37 am
Teapa	11.17 am
Coatzacoalcos	4.30 pm
Medias Aguas	6.45 pm
Tierra Blanca	11.17 pm
Córdoba	1.55 am
arrives	
Mexico City	9.15 am

Car

Touring Mexico City by car is strongly discouraged, unless you are familiar with the streets and have a healthy reserve of stamina and patience. You may, however, want to rent a car here for a tour outside the city.

Any hotel above the lowest class can put you in touch with a car rental agency, often the hotel owner's brother-in-law. Most of the international car rental companies have offices in or near the Zona Rosa; ask at any of the large hotels there. For more information on car rentals, see the Getting Around chapter.

If you're still keen to drive in town, be warned that a sticker system banning each car for one day a week operates in Mexico City. Cars registered in Mexico City must bear a coloured sticker in the windscreen; the colour indicates on which day the car may not be driven in the city. In the absence of a sticker, the last digit of the registration number indicates the day. Any car may operate on Saturday and Sunday. The system works as follows:

Last Digit	Sticker Colour	Prohibited Day
1, 2	green	Thursday
3, 4	red	Wednesday
5, 6	yellow	Monday
7, 8	pink	Tuesday
9, 0	blue	Friday

GETTING AROUND

Besides their historic names, many major north-south and east-west avenues in Mexico City bear the designation *Eje* (axis). Eje Central is Avenida Lázaro Cárdenas. Thus major avenues to the west of it bear the designations Eje 1 Poniente, Eje 2 Poniente, etc; to the east of it, Eje 1 Oriente, Eje 2 Oriente and so on. The same goes for major avenues to the north and south of the Alameda Central and Zócalo: Avenida Rayón is Eje 1 Norte, and Avenida Fray Servando Teresa de Mier is Eje 1 Sur. The Eje system superimposes a large-scale and more easily comprehensible grid of priority roads on top of this sprawling city's maze of smaller streets, making transport easier and quicker.

To/From the Airport

Unless you are renting a car (not recommended for travel in this city), use the Metro or taxi to go the six km between the Zócalo and the airport. Buses and minibuses run near the airport, but they're inconvenient if you have baggage.

Bus Route No 22 buses go near the airport; see the relevant section under Bus & Minibus below. There are no direct buses or hotel courtesy buses to the airport.

Metro Officially, you're not supposed to travel on the Metro with anything larger than a shoulder bag. However, this rule isn't always enforced, especially before 7 am and after 9 pm, and on Sunday.

The airport Metro station is 200 metres from the terminal. As you enter the main hall from your plane, turn left and walk past Sala A and out of the terminal. Continue in the same direction (there'll be a big parking garage on your right) until you see the Metro

logo and stairway down. This is the Terminal Aerea station (*not* Aeropuerto) on Linea 5. To get to the hotel areas in the city centre, follow signs for 'Dirección Pantitlán'; at Pantitlán, follow signs for 'Dirección Observatorio' (Linea 9), and get out at Chabacano; then follow signs for 'Dirección Cuatro Caminos' (Linea 2), which takes you to the Zócalo, Allende, Bellas Artes, Hidalgo and Revolución stations. The fare is a few pennies.

Taxi Taxis carrying passengers away from the terminal are usually large, comfortable cars marked 'Transporte Terrestre'. They give good service, and they're controlled by a ticket system. You look at the zone map on display near Sala E to determine your destination's zone, and buy a fixed-price ticket (US$5 to US$9) from the ticket window just outside Sala E. (If you mention your hotel name, or a nearby landmark such as 'Plaza de la República' to the ticket agent, he'll know the zone.) Hold onto your ticket and your luggage, and walk outside to the taxi rank. Put your luggage in the car's trunk/boot, and hand the ticket to the driver only after getting into the car. (Various 'assistants' will want to take your ticket and your luggage the five steps to the taxi, and will then importune you for a tip.) At the end of a trip the driver is not supposed to expect a tip, but (surprise!) it'll be readily accepted.

However, you can get into the centre for half the fare and hassle by using a normal street taxi. Do not go with the drivers of non-regulated taxis who hang out in the terminal calling 'Taxi? Taxi?'. Rather, walk to the Metro station (see above). Just beyond it is the busy Blvd Puerto Aereo, with lots of small Volkswagen, Nissan and other normal taxis. They're not as comfortable as the Transporte Terrestre cars, but they do the job for half the price.

Going to the airport from the city centre, use a normal VW taxi or the Metro.

To/From the Bus Terminals

The Metro is the fastest and cheapest way to get to any bus terminal, but the prohibition against luggage may keep you from using it. Each terminal is reachable by bus, minibus and/or trolleybus, and also by taxi. Unlike the ticket-controlled taxis from the airport and railway station, the ticket taxis at the bus terminals offer good value.

Terminal Norte The Metro station (on Linea 5) just outside the front door is named Autobuses (del) Norte, but on some Metro maps it's marked 'T A N' for Terminal de Autobuses del Norte. If you're travelling from the Terminal Norte into the centre, enter the Metro station and follow signs for 'Dirección Pantitlán' (Linea 1), then change at La Raza, or at Consulado and Candelaria. If you change lines at La Raza, be aware that you must walk for seven or eight minutes and negotiate one long flight of steps in La Raza station.

Another way to get to the centre is by trolleybus or minibus. Trolleybuses waiting in front of the terminal are marked 'Eje Central', going south along Avenida Lázaro Cárdenas, and 'Terminal Sur' to the southern bus station at Tasqueña some 18 km due south; bus No 17-B, 'Central Camionera del Norte-Villa Olimpica' goes down Avenida Insurgentes to the centre and to points farther south.

For other city buses to downtown, cross under the road through the Metro subway. Bus No 27 goes to Tlatelolco Metro station and Bellas Artes Metro station near the Alameda Central. Bus No 17 goes down Insurgentes, passing near Estación Buenavista and the Plaza de la República, crossing Reforma at the edge of the Zona Rosa, and continuing to Insurgentes Metro station. Bus No 17 'Rectoría' follows the same route and continues to San Ángel and the university in the south of the city.

To reach the Terminal Norte by trolleybus or minibus, take a northbound vehicle on Avenida Lázaro Cárdenas near the Bellas Artes, or take bus No 17 'Central Camionera Norte' going north on Insurgentes. Those stopping at the Terminal Norte will be marked (in the front window) with some variation of the terminal's name.

A taxi ticket from Terminal Norte to Buenavista railway station (Zone 2) costs US$2.25, to the Plaza de la República, Alameda, Terminal Oriente (TAPO), or Zócalo (Zone 3) the cost is US$3, to Chapultepec park and the airport (Zone 4) it's US$3.75, to the university and Tasqueña (Zone 7) it's US$6.50.

Terminal Oriente (TAPO) TAPO is next door to San Lázaro Metro station. For city buses from TAPO, follow the signs to Calle Eduardo Molina and when you hit the street the bus stop is 50 metres to the right. Bus No 16 'Alameda' goes to the Alameda Central; bus No 24 links TAPO with the Alameda Central and the Plaza de la República, passing Hidalgo and Revolución Metro stations on the street named Puente de Alvarado.

To get to TAPO from the centre, bus No 20 ('Hipódromo-Pantitlán') runs along Puente de Alvarado and Hidalgo, then along Donceles (two blocks north of the Zócalo) to the terminal.

Taxi ticket fare to the Zócalo (Zone 1) is US$1.75; to the Alameda, Plaza de la República or airport (Zone 2) it's US$2.25; to the Zona Rosa or Terminal Norte (Zone 3) it's US$3; to Chapultepec park or Coyoacán it's US$3.75.

Terminal Sur Metro station Tasqueña is just across the street from the Terminal Sur. Trolleybus 'Eje Central' runs from the Terminal Sur to Avenida Lázaro Cárdenas downtown and then all the way to the Terminal Norte.

A taxi ticket to Plaza Hidalgo in Coyoacán (Zone 1) is US$1.75; to the university (Zone 2) is US$2.25; to San Ángel (Zone 3) is US$3; to the Zona Rosa, Alameda or Zócalo (Zone 4) it's US$3.75; to the Plaza de la República, Buenavista station and the airport (Zone 5) it's US$4; and to the Terminal Norte (Zone 6) it's US$5.

Terminal Poniente Metro station is Observatorio. Bus No 76 ('Zócalo-Km 13') runs from the Terminal Poniente to Paseo de la Reforma, Avenida Juárez, Avenida Madero and the Zócalo.

The taxi ticket cost to most points downtown (Zone 3) is US$3.

To/From the Train Station

The nearest Metro station to Estación Buenavista is Guerrero, 900 metres east of the station along Martínez de la Torre/Mosqueta.

Bus Buses and minibuses (No 17 'Indios Verdes' and others) along Insurgentes go right past the station, as do many peseros. Catch these near the intersection with Reforma. Look for any vehicle with 'Buenavista' or 'FFCC' on the windscreen.

Going to the station from the city centre heading north along Avenida Insurgentes, the station is just north of a big 'Suburbia' shopping centre; the street sign says 'Eje 1 Norte'. Look for the letters 'Ferrocarriles Nacionales de México' atop the station, and the small antique locomotive in front.

Taxi Taxis from the railway station operate under a zone ticket system. As at the airport (but unlike at the bus terminals), the ticket-taxis running from the railway station are about twice as expensive as normal street cabs. You'll pay less if you just go out the door of the station and catch a regular Volkswagen or Nissan taxi running along Insurgentes or Martínez de la Torre/Mosqueta. The fare to any of the major hotel areas should be US$2 or less.

Bus & Minibus

Over 15 million people use Mexico City's thousands of buses and minibuses daily; they run from 5 am to midnight. Even-numbered buses run east-west, odd ones go north-south. Routes are most crowded during the morning and late afternoon/early evening rush hours. During other hours, those routes of interest to the traveller are not too crowded. Pickpockets and thieves are worst on the lines frequented by tourists, especially along Paseo de la Reforma – you'd do well to avoid this route altogether, despite the inconvenience. See Crime at the beginning of this chapter, and also Theft & Robbery under Dangers & Annoyances in Facts for the Visitor, for ways to protect yourself.

Full-sized buses and the smaller minibuses (as distinct from combi microbuses) are operated by the city government. They often have useful route information painted chaotically in the windscreens. Fares are only a few pennies per ride.

Here are a few major routes:

Route 17 – Various No 17 buses and minibuses cover different lengths of Insurgentes. Southbound, 'Rectoría', 'Villa Olimpica' and 'Fovisste' all go past Buenavista railway station and close to the Plaza de la República, cross Reforma at the edge of the Zona Rosa, then continue to Insurgentes Metro station, San Ángel and the university. Northbound, 'Indios Verdes' buses follow the same route in reverse, and pass close to the Basílica de Guadalupe before terminating at Indios Verdes in the north of the city. 'Central Camionera Norte' buses turn off before the Basílica de Guadalupe to go to the Terminal Norte. 'M Insurgentes', in either direction, only go as far as Insurgentes Metro station.

Route 20 – 'Pantitlán-Metro Colegio Militar' buses run from Pantitlán near the Terminal Oriente (TAPO) and the Alameda along Avenida Hidalgo, and continue along Puente de Alvarado near the Plaza de la República.

Route 22 – 'Metro Pantitlán-Metro Cuatro Caminos' pass the Buenavista railway station on Mosqueta and continue east to pass the intersection of Norte 17 and Blvd Puerto Aereo (on the south-east corner of the airport runways, a bit less than a km from the terminal). You can change to any northbound bus on Blvd Puerto Aereo if you don't feel like walking.

Route 24 – 'Santa Martha-Metro Cuatro Caminos' pass along Puente de Alvarado near the Plaza de la República, Avenida Hidalgo near the Alameda and near the Terminal Oriente (TAPO).

Route 26 – 'Sta Cruz Meyehualco-Hipódromo' run from beyond Pino Suárez Metro station along 20 de Noviembre, República de Uruguay and Victoria to the Hipódromo.

Route 55 – 'La Villa-Auditorio Nacional' run from La Villa Metro station (Linea 6, near the Basílica de Guadalupe), Plaza de Tlatelolco, along Paseo de la Reforma to the National Museum of Anthropology and the Auditorio.

Route 76 – 'Zócalo-Km 15.5' buses run from the Zócalo to the Alameda, Paseo de la Reforma, the National Museum of Anthropology and the Auditorio Nacional. From the Auditorio, 'Por Palmas' buses proceed along Paseo de las Palmas and join Paseo de la Reforma later. The 'Por Reforma' buses stay on Reforma to the end of the route.

Combi, Pesero & Colectivo

Volkswagen microbuses and other makes of minivans (usually coloured white or light green), plus the occasional large American sedan, are called combi (Mexican for VW microbus), pesero (they used to cost one peso many years ago), or colectivo (jitneys). They're privately owned and operated, but run along routes approved by the city government. Routes often begin and/or end at a Metro station. You can often get a combi to stop for you anywhere along the route. Present plans call for these vehicles to be phased out of service as the new minibuses come into service.

Route 2 (Ruta Dos) is the most useful downtown route because it goes between the Zócalo and Chapultepec park along Juárez and Paseo de la Reforma. Peseros 'Indios Verdes' (northbound) and 'San Ángel' (southbound) run up and down most of the length of Insurgentes. Fares vary with the distance travelled and the vagaries of inflation, but are currently thus: up to five km, 500 pesos (US$0.17); five to 12 km 700 pesos (US$0.24), 12 to 17 km 800 pesos (US$0.26), over 17 km 1000 pesos (US$0.33).

Metro

Mexico City's Metro system offers the cheapest, quickest and most crowded way to get around Mexico City. The fare is only a few pennies per ride, including transfers.

Over five million people ride the Metro on an average day. The stations are generally clean and well organised, but always crowded, sometimes fearfully so. The station platforms become dangerously packed with passengers, especially during the morning and evening rush hours, and it's not unusual to see police officers with clubs shoving people into each car. When it gets crowded enough to require the police, separate cars are made available to women and children. Boarding for these cars is done through special 'Solo Mujeres y Niños' lanes. Best times to ride the Metro are midday, evening and Sunday.

With such crowded conditions, it is not surprising that major baggage is not allowed and pickpocketing is rife. Be careful with your belongings; read Crime, in the introduction to this chapter, and also Dangers & Annoyances in the Facts for the Visitor chapter.

The Metro is easy to use. Upon entering the station, consult the map for the Dirección you want. Signs reading 'Dirección Pantitlán', 'Dirección Universidad' and so on name the station at the end of the Metro line. Buy a ticket (boleto) or a more convenient strip of tickets at the booth, feed a ticket into the turnstyle, and you're on your way.

'Andenes', by the way, means boarding platforms; 'Salida' means exit. Information desks give out maps of the system at La Raza, Hidalgo, Insurgentes, Pino Suárez and other stations. The Metro operates from 6 am to midnight.

On display at the Pino Suárez station is a small Aztec pyramid unearthed during construction.

Taxi

Mexico City has several classes of taxi. Cheapest are the yellow Volkswagen Beetles and small Nissans and other Japanese models. Slightly more expensive are the coral-coloured Sitio (taxi rank) cars. Most expensive are the large, comfortable Transporte Terrestre and the full-size American sedans with black bags over the meters and no taxi markings. These last operate more like hired limousines than taxis, charging set prices rather than metered fares.

In the yellow and coral cars, fares are according to the digital meters. Some of the meters have kept pace with inflation, and the fare shown is the fare you pay. Others have

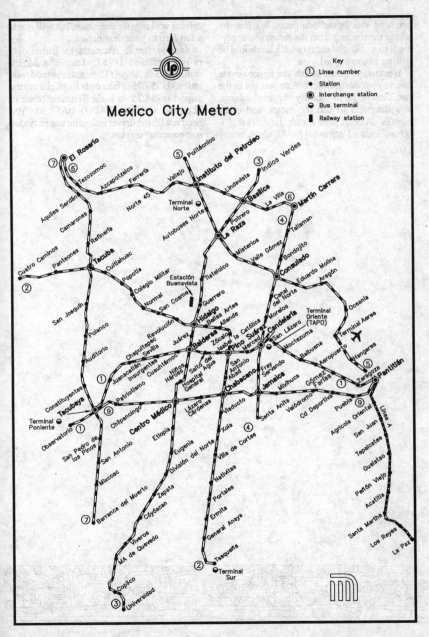

Mexico City Metro

Key
1 Linea number
• Station
◉ Interchange station
⊟ Bus terminal
▮ Railway station

not, and the driver computes the fare by taking the reading from the meter and applying it to an official chart (which he should be willing to show you).

It's always good to ask the approximate fare to your destination before you get in the car. This helps to identify 'broken' meters, unwillingness to use the meter, and other ripoffs. Ask if the meter is working – '¿Funciona el contador?'. At night, many drivers will not use the meter, but will quote a flat fare to your destination.

Sample fares: Alameda to Buenavista railway station US$2; Tasqueña Metro station to San Ángel (15 minutes in moderate traffic) US$3.75; Plaza de la República to the airport US$3.75, or to the Terminal Norte or Terminal Oriente (TAPO) US$2.50. You need not tip the driver unless he has provided some special service.

Near Mexico City

Staying in Mexico City doesn't mean you have to spend all of every day in the capital. Indeed you will be missing out on some of the country's splendours if you do. The ancient city of Teotihuacán, with its giant pyramids of the Sun and the Moon, and the volcanoes Popocatépetl and Iztaccíhuatl, can easily be visited in day trips.

Other highlights outside the city are Tula, probable capital of the pre-Hispanic Toltecs, with its fearsome warrior statues; the great baroque church of Tepotzotlán; and probably Mexico's biggest market, held on Fridays at Toluca.

This chapter covers most of the sights in the states of México and Hidalgo. The Cuernavaca area to the south of Mexico City, and the Puebla area to the east, which can be visited in day trips from Mexico City but are also worth longer stays, are covered in the Mexico City to Acapulco and Mexico City to Veracruz chapters.

West of Mexico City

DESIERTO DE LOS LEONES

The name of this 2000-hectare national park, 25 km west of the city and 800 metres higher, means Desert of the Lions but it is actually a pine forest. The name comes from a 17th century Carmelite monastery called the Desierto de Santa Fe, with pleasant gardens and nowadays the setting for exhibitions and free concerts on Sundays – when the forest may be packed with picnickers. Also in the park are walking trails and a campsite. You can reach the park from Highway 15 to Toluca or by Camino del Desierto from San Ángel. The latter is closed from 6 pm to 7 am.

TOLUCA

Population: 490,000
Altitude: 2680 metres
Toluca, 60 km west of Mexico City, is 400 metres higher and the extra altitude is notice-

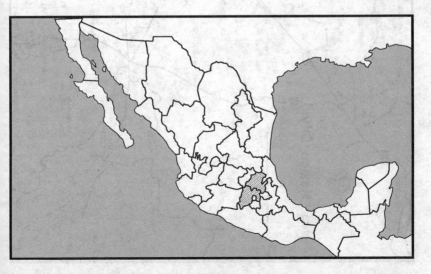

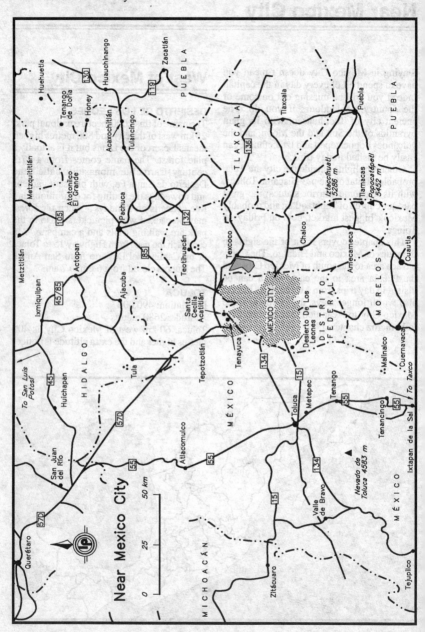

Near Mexico City

able. Industry lines the approach from the capital but Toluca city centre is surprisingly attractive. Toluca was an Indian settlement from at least the 13th century and the Spanish founded the city in the 16th century after defeating the Aztecs and Matlazincas who lived in the valley. It became part of the Marquesado del Valle de Oaxaca, Hernán Cortés' personal estates in Mexico. Since 1830 it has been capital of the state of México, which surrounds the Distrito Federal on three sides like an upturned U.

Orientation
The road from Mexico City becomes Paseo Tollocan, a dual carriageway, as it approaches Toluca. On reaching the east side of the city proper, Paseo Tollocan veers south-west as a southern bypass, passing the Casart crafts centre on the left after about 1¼ km and, about 500 metres later, also on the left, Calle Isidro Fabela, down which lie the bus station and the Juárez Market. Buses take a slightly circuitous route to the bus station but pass both Casart – where they may let you get off – and the market.

The city centre is two km north-west of the bus station and market.

Information
Tourist Office The Dirección General de Turismo of the State of México, in office E307 of the Edificio Oriente (East Building) of the Plaza Toluca, on Lerdo de Tejada facing Plaza Garibay, can answer some questions and has a good *State of Mexico Tourist Atlas* to give away. The entrance to the building is the same as for Cinemas Plaza Toluca.

Money You can change money or travellers' cheques at Banamex at Hidalgo Pte 223 on the corner of Galeana, opposite Portal Madero, and Bancomer at Hidalgo Pte 100 under Portal Madero.

Post & Telecommunications The main post office is at the corner of Hidalgo and De la Cruz, 500 metres east of Portal Madero. There is a LADATEL caseta, for long-distance phone calls, at Allende 200.

Juárez Market & Casart
The Mercado Juárez, on Isidro Fabela behind the bus station, is open daily but on Fridays it becomes a *tianguis*, an Indian market, and villagers from all around swarm in to sell hens, pigs, pots, odd socks, etc. Then the market turns into a heaving madhouse and gringos attract extra-hard hustle from the multitudes of hawkers. You need to bargain hard if anything grabs your fancy. Crafts from nearby Indian villages include Tenancingo rebozos, Temoaya hand-knotted carpets, Metepec pottery and Tianguistengo sarapes.

More peaceful shopping can be enjoyed at Casart, the excellent State of México crafts store 700 metres north-east of the market on Paseo Tollocan. The range is big, the quality higher than in the market – often even higher than you will find in the villages where the crafts are made – and the prices are fixed. You can gauge prices here before diving into the market.

To our taste, Toluca wares aren't generally as appealing as, say, those of Oaxaca or Chiapas, but *something* will catch your eye, and if you aren't going to any other major Indian market or craft town in Mexico, Toluca is worth the experience.

City Centre
Toluca's centre, remodelled in recent decades, is surprisingly calm and stately. You may well reach it by way of the quarter-km-long, 19th-century **Portal Madero** (Madero Arcade) along Hidalgo. A block north is the broad **Plaza de los Martires**, lined on all sides by fine old-style government buildings. On the south side are the 19th-century **cathedral** and the 18th century **Santa Veracruz church**.

Immediately north-east of the Plaza de los Martires is the fountained **Plaza Garibay**, at the east end of which stands the unique **Cosmo Vitral Jardín Botanico** (Cosmic Glass Botanic Garden). Built in the early 20th century as a market, and until 1972 the site of the weekly tianguis, this now houses 3500 sq metres of tranquil and lovely botanic garden, lit since 1980 through 48 colourful

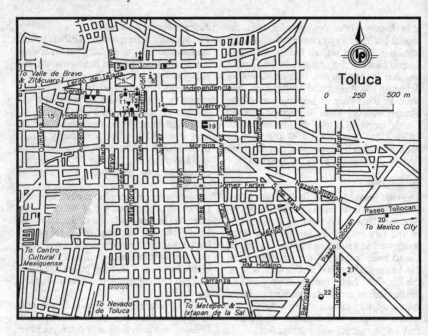

1   El Carmen Church & Fine Arts
     Museum
2   Palacio de Gobierno
3   Plaza Garibay
4   Cosmo Vitral Jardín Botanico
5   Plaza de los Martires
6   Tourist Office
7   Hotel Plaza Morelos
8   Restaurant Concorde
9   Cathedral
10 Santa Veracruz Church
11 Fonda Rosita
12 Hostería Las Ramblas
13 Hotel San Carlos
14 Hotel Colonial
15 Alameda
16 Comedor Familial y Café L'Ambient
17 Banamex
18 Hotel Rex
19 Post Office
20 Casart
21 Mercado Juáez
22 Bus Station

stained glass panels on the theme of duality
– life and death, day and night, creation and
destruction – by the Tolucan artist Leopoldo
Flores. Opening hours are 9 am to 5 pm,
Tuesday to Sunday.

On the north side of Plaza Garibay is the
18th-century **El Carmen Church**. The adjacent ex-convent buildings house Toluca's
Fine Arts Museum. The pleasant **Alameda**
park is three blocks west of the Portal
Madero along Hidalgo.

Centro Cultural Mexiquense

The impressive State of México Cultural
Centre, in a former hacienda eight km west
of the city centre, groups three good
museums and a library. The **Museo de Arte
Moderno** includes paintings by Tamayo,
Orozco and many more. The **Museo de Arte
Popular** gives a comprehensive introduction
to the crafts of México state, including some
astounding Metepec trees of life. The **Museo
de la Antropología e Historia** also has a

fine collection from México state, including a superb carved wooden Aztec *huehuetl* (war drum) from Malinalco.

The museums are open daily, except Monday, from 10 am to 6 pm. Bus 'Línea 2 de Marzo' from the bus station or the Plaza de los Martires goes there about every 20 minutes.

Places to Stay

The *Hotel San Carlos* (☎ (721) 4-94-22) on Hidalgo at Portal Madero 210 and the *Hotel Rex* (☎ (721) 5-93-00), a few metres away at Matamoros Sur 101, are both dingy but acceptable. The San Carlos is the better, with reasonably sized, clean singles/doubles for US$11.75/16.75. The Rex's more faded rooms are US$10/13.50. In both you get a private bathroom and a TV on which it's nigh impossible to get a decent picture.

A lot better – though it doesn't look much from outside – is the *Hotel Plaza Morelos* (☎ (721) 5-92-00) at Serdán 115 on the corner of Ascensio. An agreeable lobby leads to clean and comfortable, if not huge, rooms with working TV and phone, which cost US$20/23.50. There's a pleasant stairwell-lounge and a reasonable restaurant too. For colonial ambience at a similar price, the *Hotel Colonial* (☎ (721) 5-97-00) at Hidalgo Ote 103, just east of Juárez, has smallish, old-fashioned but comfortable enough rooms around an interior courtyard.

Places to Eat

Downtown, one of the best and most atmospheric places is the *Hostería Las Ramblas* at Portal 20 de Noviembre 105 on Constitución. A starter of champiñones al ajillo (mushrooms in garlic) for two at US$5.50 could be followed by a fonda or a variety of special antojitos, served only from 6 pm, for around US$2 to US$3. Meat courses are mainly US$4 or US$5.

The *Fonda Rosita* in the passage between Portal Madero and the cathedral has a slightly more cosmopolitan menu – eg avocado salad for US$2, antojitos around US$3.50, meat dishes from US$5 up to a sirloin steak· at US$8.50. The Franco-Mexican *Restaurant Concorde* on Serdán next door to the Hotel Plaza Morelos offers salmon-trout dishes for US$9.50, a host of steaks from US$10 up to Chateaubriand for two at US$19.50, or a plate of French cheeses for two at US$12.75.

There is more basic but still acceptable fare at the *Comedor Familial y Café L'Ambiant*, at Hidalgo Pte 229 opposite Portal Madero. In the reasonable US$3.50 comida corrida you get a choice of three soups and five meat dishes as well as rice, frijoles and dessert. There is an à la carte menu too with enchiladas, egg dishes and ensalada de verduras all around US$1.75, meats US$3.50 to US$5.

Getting There & Away

Bus Toluca's bus station is at Berriozábal 101, two km south-east of the centre. Buses enter from Isidro Fabela to the rear, opposite the Juárez market.

In Mexico City, Toluca buses use the western bus terminal. The all-round best service between the two cities is by the 1st-class TMT line, which runs directo buses every five minutes in both directions from 6 am to 10 pm. The trip takes one hour for US$1.75. The luxury buses of ETN make the trip hourly for US$5. Other departures from Toluca include:

Cuernavaca – 110 km, three hours; 2nd-class buses by Lineas Unidas del Sur half-hourly, 5.30 am to 7 pm.
Guadalajara – 500 km, nine hours; three luxury buses daily by ETN for US$26.75, a few 1st-class buses daily for US$11.75.
Morelia – 250 km, 4½ hours; a few 1st-class buses daily for around US$4.50.
Pátzcuaro – 305 km, 5½ hours; a few 1st-class buses daily.
Uruapan – 360 km, 6½ hours; a few 1st-class buses daily.

Car Drivers from Mexico City can take either Highway 15 or the Toluca toll road. On the toll road you must pay the US$2.75 fee in coins of 100, 500 or 1000 pesos.

Getting Around

A taxi between the bus station or market and city centre costs US$1. City buses are poor and the streets they travel often congested. 'Centro' buses outside the bus station go to the centre; 'Terminal' buses from Juárez just south of Lerdo de Tejada in the centre go to the bus station.

AROUND TOLUCA
Nevado de Toluca

The extinct volcano Nevado de Toluca or Xinantécatl, 4583 metres high, lies across the horizon south of Toluca. Though a road runs up the 48 km to the two lakes in its crater, El Sol and La Luna, buses go no nearer than Highway 134, the Toluca-Tejupilco road, 27 km from the crater.

TOLUCA TO IXTAPAN DE LA SAL

Highway 55 from Toluca to the spa Ixtapan de la Sal, 80 km south, goes through or near several places of interest. They are also all reachable from Mexico City, or Taxco, 67 km beyond Ixtapan de la Sal, or even Cuernavaca, to the east. (See the Mexico City to Acapulco chapter for Taxco and Cuernavaca coverage.) Handicraft seekers may do just as well in Toluca, which seems to cream off much of the best ware.

The 2nd-class Tres Estrellas del Centro line runs buses from Toluca bus station to Tenango (US$0.50) and Tenancingo every 10 minutes, to Ixtapan de la Sal (US$1.75) every half-hour, and from Mexico City's western terminal to all three places (Ixtapan US$3.25) every 30 minutes. For drivers, a toll highway parallels part of Highway 55, bypassing Tenango and Tenancingo.

Metepec

The potters of Metepec, seven km south of Toluca by Highway 55 and barely separated from it now, produce elaborate trees of life and 'Metepec suns', large earthenware sun discs with brightly painted faces. Frequent 2nd-class buses go from Toluca bus station to Metepec for US$0.25. Beside the stop in Metepec is a triangular building with a moderately accurate village map showing potters' workshops (alfarerías). On Mondays a sprawling market takes over the village centre but the pottery there is everyday ware.

Tenango & Teotenango

Tenango, 25 km south of Toluca on Highway 55, is overlooked from the west by the large, well-restored hilltop ruins of Teotenango, a Matlazinca ceremonial centre dating from the 9th century. The site, with several pyramids and plazas and a ball court, is open daily except Monday. It is reached by a road to the west just before Tenango. There is a museum at the final turning up to the hilltop. The town has a Sunday market.

Malinalco

One of the few reasonably well-preserved Aztec temples stands on a hillside above Malinalco, 25 km south-east of Highway 55 via Joquicingo, from a turning 12 km south of Tenango. The site is about one km uphill west of the town centre by a good dirt road.

The Aztecs conquered this area in 1476 and were still building a ritual centre here when they were themselves conquered by the Spanish. The Temple of Eagle and Jaguar Warriors, where sons of Aztec nobles were initiated into the Jaguar and Eagle orders of warriors, survived because it is hewn from the mountainside itself. It is recognisable by its reconstructed thatched roof. Its entrance is carved in the form of a fanged serpent or earth god, who devours each person entering the temple by virtue of the fact that you must walk over its tongue. Pedestals beside this entrance supported warrior statues, and there are more carvings – jaguars and eagles – inside. The site is open daily except Monday from 10 am to 4.30 pm. Entry is US$3.50.

Second-class buses of Lineas Unidas del Sur go from Toluca bus station to Malinalco, a two-hour trip, every 1½ or two hours from 6.30 am till late afternoon.

Chalma

One of Mexico's most important shrines is at the small village of Chalma, 12 km east of Malinalco on the road from Mexico City or

Cuernavaca. In 1533 an image of Christ, El Señor de Chalma, 'miraculously' appeared in a cave to replace one of the local god Oxtéotl, and proceeded to stamp out dangerous beasts locally and do other wondrous things. The Señor now resides in Chalma's 17th century church. The biggest of many annual pilgrimages here is for Pentecost (3 May) when thousands of people from Mexico City and elsewhere camp, hold a market and perform traditional dances.

Buses to Chalma are only 2nd-class: Lineas Unidas del Sur goes from Toluca bus station; Autotransportes Aguila and the México, Tenango del Valle, Chalma lines go from Mexico City's western bus terminal. From Cuernavaca's Flecha Roja bus station there are four buses a day (morning and early afternoon).

Tenancingo
This town of 50,000, 50 km from Toluca on Highway 55, is famous for its brightly coloured rebozos and fruit liqueurs. Market days are Thursday and Sunday.

Ixtapan de la Sal
Ixtapan is a spa town of 25,000 people, 1900 metres high. The Balneario Nuevo Ixtapan (New Ixtapan Spa), a kind of giant curative water fun park, combines thermal water pools with waterfalls, lakes, waterslides and a miniature railway. Most of the middle-range hotels, as well as the luxury *Hotel Ixtapan* (☎ 3-00-21) with 250 big, comfortable rooms at over US$100 a day including meals, line up along Blvd San Román where the balneario is.

North of Mexico City

TENAYUCA & SANTA CECILIA ACATITLÁN
Two Aztec sites that enthusiasts might visit lie just beyond the Distrito Federal's northern border, swallowed up by Mexico City's urban sprawl.

Tenayuca was settled at least as far back

as the 11th century but its last ruler was a son of Moctezuma and the double-temple pyramid he left is a dead ringer for the Templo Mayor in the Mexico City Zócalo, though smaller. Striking serpent sculptures surround three sides of its base – imagine what they looked like when they were painted bright red, yellow and green.

At Santa Cecilia Acatitlán, two km north of Tenayuca in a more pleasant neighbourhood, is the only surviving complete Aztec temple – dedicated to the war god Huitzilopochtli – atop a small but fine pyramid behind a 16th-century church. The museum at Acatitlán has Aztec sculptures and a replica sacrificial skull rack.

Both sites are open 10 am to 5 pm daily, except Monday, for US$2.75.

Getting There & Away
Tenayuca pyramid is next to Tenayuca zócalo, two blocks north of Avenida Aqueducto Tenayuca. Take a 'Pirámide' pesero from La Raza metro. You can reach Santa Cecilia Acatitlán by taking a pesero or bus that's going north up Avenida Santa Cecilia, on the east side of Tenayuca pyramid, to Avenida de los Alfanjes. Ask for Santa Cecilia, which is on the left of Avenida de los Alfanjes soon after a petrol station. There are also peseros between Basilica metro and Santa Cecilia.

TEPOTZOTLÁN
About 35 km north of central Mexico City, but only just past the edge of its urban sprawl, in the pleasant little town of Tepotzotlán stand probably Mexico's most riotous example of Churrigueresque architecture and the Museo Nacional del Virreinato, the National Museum of the Viceregal (Colonial) Period.

The Jesuit church of San Francisco Javier beside the zócalo was originally built from 1670 to 1682, but it was the elaborations carried out in the 18th century that made it one of Mexico's most lavish churches. The façade, with its single tower, is a phantasmagoric array of carved saints, angels, people, plants and more, while the interior walls, and the Camarín del Virgen adjacent to the altar, are covered with a riot of gilded and multicoloured ornamentation. One sparkling altarpiece gives way artfully to another, each adorned with mirrors accentuating the dazzle.

In the 1960s the church and adjacent monastery – including its peaceful gardens – were restored and transformed into the Museo del Virreinato. Among the fine art and folk art gathered here are silver chalices, pictures created from inlaid wood, porcelain, furniture, and some of the finest religious paintings and statues from the epoch. Don't miss the Capilla Doméstica (Domestic Chapel) whose Churrigueresque main altarpiece is thick with mirrors.

Opening hours are 11 am to 5.30 pm daily except Monday, and admission is US$3.50 (free on Sundays and holidays). Classical concerts are sometimes given on the premises. There are eateries around Tepotzotlán zócalo – the comida corrida at the *Virreyes Restaurant* is good value – and in the monastery itself.

Getting There & Away

Tepotzotlán zócalo is 1½ km west of the Caseta Tepotzotlán, the first toll booth on Highway 57-D from Mexico City to Querétaro. Avenida Insurgentes leads from the highway, 200 metres south of the toll booth, to the zócalo.

There are two routes by public transport from Mexico City. Both take about 1½ hours from downtown. The one we have tried and trusted is a 2nd-class Autotransportes Valle del Mezquital 'Tula Ordinario vía Refinería' bus from the capital's northern bus terminal to the Caseta Tepotzotlán. These go every 15 or 30 minutes and cost US$1. You could also use them to combine Tepotzotlán and Tula visits in one day. The ticket office is at the northern end of the terminal. From the Caseta Tepotzotlán take a local bus or walk along Avenida Insurgentes. Alternatively, colectivos or buses to Tepotzotlán reportedly leave Tacuba metro about every 10 minutes.

TULA

Population: 40,000
Altitude: 2060 metres

The probable capital of the ancient Toltec civilisation stood 65 km north of what is now Mexico City. Though less spectacular than Teotihuacán, Tula is still an absorbing site, best known for its fearsome 4½-metre-high stone warrior figures. There's little exciting about dusty, industrial, modern Tula.

History

There's still debate about whether Tula was the capital of the people referred to by later Aztec annals as the Toltecs – mighty empire-builders to whom the Aztecs themselves looked back with awe, claiming them as royal ancestors – but there is little doubt that it was an important city from about 900 to 1150 AD, reaching a peak population of 30,000 or 40,000.

Assuming Tula was the Toltec capital, the events described by the annals as happening here are worth relating. The story goes that it was a king called Topiltzin, fair skinned, long haired and black bearded, who founded the city in the 10th century as the capital of his Toltec people – who until recently had been Chichimecs wandering in the north.

Topiltzin was supposedly a priest-king dedicated to the peaceful, non-human-sacrificing worship of the feathered serpent god Quetzalcóatl. But Tula also housed followers of the less likeable Tezcatlipoca (Smoking Mirror), god of warriors, witchcraft, life and death. The story goes that Tezcatlipoca appeared in various guises to provoke Topiltzin: as a naked chili-seller he aroused the lust of Topiltzin's daughter and ended up marrying her, as an old man he persuaded the sober Topiltzin to get drunk.

Eventually the humiliated leader left for the Gulf coast, where he set sail eastward on a raft of snakes, promising one day to return and reclaim his throne (which caused the Aztec emperor Moctezuma much consternation when Hernán Cortés arrived on the Gulf Coast in 1519...). The conventional wisdom is that Topiltzin set up a new Toltec state at Chichén Itzá in Yucatán, while the Tula

Top: Agave cactus, Mexico state (GE)
Left: Temple of Quetzalcóatl, Teotihuacán, near Mexico (GA)
Right: Pyramid of the Sun, Teotihuacán (JN)

Top: On the beach, Veracruz (GE)
Left: San Gabriel monastery, Cholula, Puebla state (GE)
Right: Mariachi, Veracruz (GE)

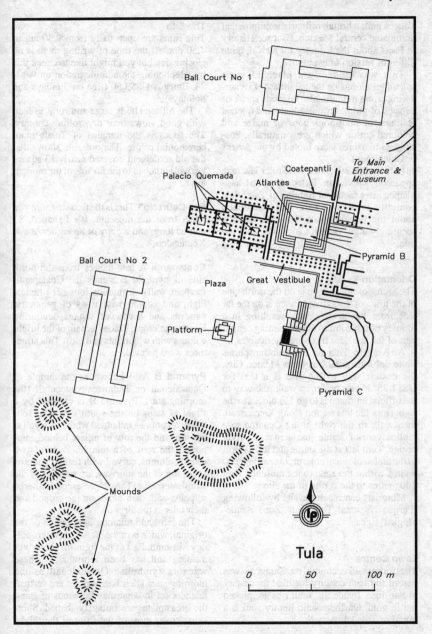

Ball Court No 1

To Main
Entrance &
Museum

Coatepantli

Palacio Quemada

Atlantes

Pyramid B

Ball Court No 2

Plaza

Great Vestibule

Platform

Pyramid C

Mounds

Tula

0   50   100 m

Toltecs built a brutal, militaristic empire that dominated central Mexico. (But see History in Facts about the Country for a rival, quite different version of events.)

Tula was evidently a place of some splendour alongside the harshness of its surviving stone monuments. Legends speak of palaces of gold, turquoise, jade and quetzal feathers, of enormous cobs of maize and coloured cotton which grew naturally. Possibly its treasures were looted by the Aztecs or Chichimecs.

In the mid-12th century the ruler Huémac apparently moved the Toltec capital to Chapultepec after factional fighting at Tula, then committed suicide. Tula was abandoned about the beginning of the 13th century, seemingly after violent Chichimec destruction.

Orientation

The archaeological zone is on the north side of the town of Tula. Its entrance is on the far side from the town centre, resulting in a journey of three km to the interesting central part of the site. But there are alternatives...

Arriving in Tula on an Autotransportes Valle del Mezquital bus from Mexico City, the easiest way to the site is a taxi for US$1.25. If you prefer to walk, the way to the official entrance is to go 1½ blocks to the right from the bus station along Xicoténcatl, then walk to the right along Ocampo to a replica warrior statue just across the river bridge. Turn left at the statue and it's 1¾ km to the archaeological zone entrance, then 500 metres within the zone to the museum, then 700 metres to the centre of the site.

Motorists can reach the site by following 'Parque Nacional Tula' and 'Zona Arqueológica' signs.

Town Centre

The fortress-like church on Zaragoza was part of the 16th century fortified monastery of San José. Inside, its vault ribs are picked out in gold. On the zócalo library wall is a mural of Tula's history.

The Site

Tula ruins are open daily from 9.30 am to 4.30 pm. At the time of writing there is no closing day but you might like to check this by telephoning the administration on 9-17-73. Entry is US$3.50 (free on Sundays and holidays).

The hilltop site is large and rural in feel, with good views over dry, rolling country. The focus is the remains of Tula's main ceremonial centre. The museum shows that the old settlement covered nearly 13 square km and stretched to the far side of the modern town.

Ball Court No 1 This is the first structure you reach from the museum. It's I-shaped, 37 metres long, and a copy of an earlier one at Xochicalco.

Coatepantli A few metres from the north side of pyramid B stands the Coatepantli (serpent wall), 40 metres long, 2¼ metres high, and carved with rows of geometric patterns and a row of snakes devouring human skeletons. Traces remain of the bright colours with which this and most Tula structures were painted.

Pyramid B Also known as the temple of Quetzalcóatl or Tlahuizcalpantecuhtli (the morning star), Pyramid B is climbed by a flight of steps on the south side. The four basalt telamones (atlantes) which face you at the top, and the row of pillars behind, supported the roof of a temple. Parts of two round columns, carved with feather patterns at the top of the stairway, are remains of the temple entrance. They represented feathered serpents with their heads on the ground and their tails in the air.

The left-hand telamon is a replica of the original, which is in the National Anthropology Museum. Part of the right-hand one was missing and has been reproduced. These warriors symbolise Quetzalcóatl as the morning star. Their headdresses are vertical feathers set in what may be bands of stars; the breastplates are butterfly-shaped. Short skirts cover most of the front of the thighs but leave the buttocks bare and are held in place behind by discs representing the sun. Their right hands hold spear-throwers called *atlatls*; in their left hands are spears or arrows and incense bags. The columns behind the atlantes depict crocodile heads (symbolising the earth), warriors, symbols of warrior orders, weapons and the head of Quetzalcóatl.

Tula telamon

On the east wall of the pyramid, protected by scaffolding, are some of the carvings which once surrounded all four sides. These show the symbols of the warrior orders: jaguars, coyotes, eagles eating hearts and what may be a human head in the mouth of Quetzalcóatl.

The Great Vestibule, a now roofless colonnaded hall, extends along the front of the pyramid, facing the open plaza. The stone bench carved with warriors originally ran the length of the hall, possibly for priests and nobles observing ceremonies in the plaza.

Palacio Quemada The 'Burnt Palace' immediately west of Pyramid B is a series of halls and courtyards with more low benches and relief carvings, one showing a procession of nobles. It was probably used for meetings or ceremonies, and the walls were painted with frescoes.

Plaza The plaza in front of Pyramid B would have been the scene of religious and military displays. At its centre is a small altar or ceremonial platform. Pyramid C on the east side of the plaza is Tula's biggest structure but is unexcavated. To the west is Ball Court No 2, the largest in central Mexico at over 100 metres long, with alarming chac-mools at each end.

Places to Stay
Casa de Huéspedes Rodríguez at Zaragoza 20 has basic but tolerably clean singles/doubles with communal bathrooms for US$5.50/7.50. It's at the far end of Zaragoza from the church, on the right.

Auto Hotel Cuéllar at Cinco de Mayo 23 has bare, smallish rooms with private baths for US$10/13.50 (extra for TV). Turn left along Cinco de Mayo at the end of Zaragoza. *Motel Lisbeth* (☎ 2-00-45) at Ocampo 42 is the best place in town, charging US$14/17.50 for comfortable rooms with private bath and colour TV.

Places to Eat
The large, clean *Restaurant Casa Blanca*, at the corner of Zaragoza and Hidalgo, does

antojitos for around US$2.50 and meat courses at US$4 or US$5. *Cafetería El Cisne*, 100 metres from the zócalo at the end of the pedestrian street Juárez, does moderate Western-type snacks and light meals. Hamburguesas are US$1.50, fried chicken and salad US$2.75.

Getting There & Away
Autotransportes Valle del Mezquital runs 2nd-class buses to Tula from Mexico City's northern terminal every 15 to 30 minutes from 5 am to 10 pm. Fare is US$2.25. The ticket office is at the northern end of the terminal – to the left as you enter. 'Directo vía Refinería' is the best service, leaving half-hourly or hourly and taking 1¼ hours. 'Ordinario vía Refinería' buses are more frequent but slower; 'Vía Cruz Azul' services take a more roundabout route.

In Tula, Autotransportes Valle del Mezquital has its own amazingly gleaming terminal on Xicoténcatl (see Orientation). The last 'Directo vía Refinería' bus to Mexico City leaves at 7 pm, though there are ordinarios up to 11 pm. Buses to Pachuca (US$2) leave every 15 minutes or so, and there are five daily services to Querétaro and one (in the morning) to Guanajuato.

PACHUCA
Population: 180,000
Altitude: 2426 metres
Pachuca, capital of the state of Hidalgo, lies 90 km north-east of Mexico City. Whitewashed or brightly painted houses climb the dry hillsides around the centre of this pleasant, calm town.

Silver was found in the area by the Spanish as early as 1534 and the mines of Pachuca and Real del Monte, nine km northeast, still produce 6% of world silver output – over a million ounces a year. Pachuca was also the gateway by which football (soccer) entered Mexico, brought by miners from Cornwall, England, in the 19th century.

Orientation
Pachuca's centre is the rectangular Plaza de la Independencia, with its central clock tower – the *reloj monumental*. The main market is on Plaza Constitución, a couple of blocks north-east of the Plaza de la Independencia.

Important streets include Matamoros, along the east side of Plaza de la Independencia, and Allende, running south from the plaza's south-west corner. Guerrero runs roughly parallel to the plaza, about 100 metres west. To the south, both Guerrero and Matamoros reach the modern Plaza Juárez after about 700 metres.

Information
The Hidalgo state tourist office (☎ (771) 3-25-31) at Allende 406, near the corner of Matamoros, is helpful, with good give-away maps, and open 8.30 am to 9 pm, Monday to Friday.

There are banks on the Plaza de la Independencia. The post office is at the corner of Juárez and Iglesias.

City Centre
A couple of streets east of the Plaza de la Independencia have been pedestrianised and several small modern plazas have been added to the older ones. The Plaza de la Independencia **clock tower** was built in 1904 in the French style then popular. Four marble sculptures, one on each side, represent Independence, Liberty, the Constitution and Reform.

The old **Cajas Reales** (Royal Treasuries) are behind the north side of the Plaza Constitución.

Centro Cultural de Hidalgo
The former monastery of San Francisco, about 750 metres south-east of the Plaza de la Independencia, has become the Centro Cultural de Hidalgo which contains Mexico's national photography museum, a regional museum, theatres and an exhibition gallery. Admission is free (except for performances) and the centre is open from 10 am to 6 pm, Tuesday to Saturday.

Go three blocks south down Matamoros from the Plaza de la Independencia to a crossroads with a fountain. One of the best of Pachuca's **murals**, inspired by Hidalgo's Otomí Indian heritage, covers a wall just south of this fountain, depicting animals and plants. From the fountain go east along Arista to the monastery, which is beside the Jardín Colón at the junction of Hidalgo, after about two blocks.

The **Museo Nacional de la Fotografía** combines early film technology – such as a recreated daguerrotype studio – with selections from the 1.5 million photos in the archive of INAH, the national anthropology and history institute. These provide fascinating glimpses into Mexico's past (since 1873) and present, capturing both the big names and the ordinary people. The collection is particularly strong on the revolutionary period: you will see folk heroes Emiliano Zapata and Pancho Villa, as well as the pomp and circumstance of dictator Porfirio Díaz.

The **Museo Regional de Hidalgo** exhibits Indian dress, lifestyles and crafts as well as the state's archaeology and history. There is a fine stone jaguar from Tula. The 17th-century **La Asunción church** next door contains the mummified body of Santa Columba (who died in Europe in 273 AD) on one of the side altars.

Places to Stay

The *Hotel Grenfell* (☎ (771) 2-02-77) occupies an imposing building on the west side of Plaza de la Independencia but is much less impressive inside. Sizeable but bare rooms with private bath around a large but wasted courtyard give it an institutional feel. Rooms are US$6.75 with one single or double bed, US$8.50 with two beds.

The *Hotel Noriega* (☎ (771) 2-50-00) at Matamoros 305, two blocks south of Plaza de la Independencia, is an excellent-value colonial-style place with a good restaurant. There's a covered courtyard, a fine staircase, wide rambling corridors, and lots of plants. Pleasant rooms with TV and private bath cost US$13 single or double.

Hotel Plaza Eldorado (☎ (771) 2-52-85) at Guerrero 721 has 92 pleasant and sizeable rooms at US$11.75/14.50. Take the short street off the middle of the west side of the Plaza de la Independencia and turn left along Guerrero at the first corner.

Places to Eat

The Cornish miners who brought soccer to Pachuca also brought Cornish pasties – meat, potato, carrot and onion in a pastry shell – and you can still find *pastes* in Pachuca shops, though the filling nowadays is likely to contain its share of chile or mole.

The *Restaurant Noriega* in the Hotel Noriega has a touch of elegance (including prints of old London on the walls), but prices are reasonable. It is especially popular for Sunday lunch, for which you pay US$5. *Chip's Restaurant*, attached to the Hotel Emily on the south side of the Plaza de la Independencia, is more of a cappuccino, antojito and ice cream bar, though it does do comida corrida for US$2.50.

The large *Restaurant La Blanca* (☎ 2-18-96), also on the plaza at the corner of Matamoros and Valle a few metres from the clock tower, serves fairly ordinary Mexican food. The five-course comida corrida is US$2.75.

Restaurant Ciro's is a few steps down from street level on the north side of the plaza. The usual aves and carnes are in the US$2.75 to US$5 range. There are also antojitos (enchiladas Suizas are tasty at US$2.50) and eggs.

Things to Buy

The Casa de las Artesanías (☎ 3-04-12), by the Glorieta Independencia roundabout on Avenida Juárez (the Mexico City road) two km south-west of Plaza de la Independencia, displays and sells Hidalgo crafts.

Getting There & Away

Bus First-class ADO buses leave Mexico City's northern terminal for Pachuca every 10 or 15 minutes, taking 1½ hours for the US$2 trip. Apart from one or two daily ADO buses to/from Poza Rica (US$4, four hours) and Tampico (US$9.75, nine hours), other buses serving Pachuca are 2nd class.

There are frequent buses to/from Tula (1½ hours), Tulancingo (one hour),

Tamazunchale (six hours) and Ciudad Valles (eight hours), several daily to/from Huejutla (six hours) and Querétaro (five hours via the surfaced but rough Highway 45 between Ixmiquilpan and San Juan del Río), and a few a day to/from Matamoros, Tampico, Tuxpan and Poza Rica.

Getting Around

The bus station is some way south-west of the centre, not far off the road to Mexico City. Green-and-white colectivo taxis (US$0.20) or regular taxis (US$1) wait outside it to take you to the Plaza de la Independencia.

ACTOPAN & IXMIQUILPAN

The finest of Hidalgo's many 16th-century fortress-monasteries is at **Actopan** (population 26,000), 37 km north-west of Pachuca on Highway 85 (the Pan-American). Frequent 2nd-class buses take 45 minutes.

Founded in 1548, the monastery is in excellent state of preservation. Its church has a lovely Plateresque façade and a single tower showing Mudéjar (Moorish) influence. The nave has Gothic vaulting. Mexico's best 16th-century frescoes are in the cloister: hermits are depicted in the Sala De Profundis, while on the stairs are shown saints, leading Augustinian monks and a meeting between Father Martín de Acevedo, an important early monk at Actopan, and two Indian nobles, Juan Inica Actopa and Pedro Ixcuincuitlapilco. To the left of the church a large, vaulted capilla abierta is also decorated with frescoes.

Actopan's Wednesday market goes back at least 400 years.

Ixmiquilpan (population 35,000), 75 km from Pachuca on Highway 85 (1½ hours by frequent buses), is a former capital of the Otomí Indians, very anciently established inhabitants of Hidalgo. The arid Mezquital valley in which the town stands remains an Otomí enclave. About 125,000 of Mexico's 300,000 Otomí live in Hidalgo, more than in any other state. Traditional Otomí women's dress is a quechquémitl over an embroidered cloth blouse. The Mezquital valley Otomí make Mexico's finest *ayates*, cloths woven from *ixtle*, the fibre of the maguey cactus. The Otomí also use maguey to make food, drink, soap and needles.

There's a Casa de Artesanías displaying and selling Otomí crafts on Felipe Ángeles, but Ixmiquilpan's busy Monday market is the best place to find products like miniature musical instruments made of juniper wood with pearl or shell inlay, colourful drawstring bags, or embroidered textiles.

The church of Ixmiquilpan's monastery has a huge Gothic vault. In the cloister are old frescoes by Indian artists showing combats between Indians and mythical pre-Hispanic figures, as well as religious scenes.

Places to stay include the *Hotel Saisa* (☎ 3-01-12) at Insurgentes 99, the *Hotel Jardín* (☎ 3-03-08) and *Hotel Palacio* (☎ 3-01-08) both on Plaza Juárez, and the more expensive *Hotel Club Alcantara* (☎ 3-04-90), which has a swimming pool, at Peña Juárez 8.

There are also frequent buses to Actopan and Ixmiquilpan from Mexico City's northern bus terminal.

NORTH & EAST OF PACHUCA

North of Ixmiquilpan, Highway 85 crosses the forested, sometimes foggy Sierra Madre to Tamazunchale and Ciudad Valles in San Luis Potosí state (see the San Luis Potosí section in the Bajío chapter).

Pachuca is the starting point for two other scenic roads through the Sierra Madre: Highway 105 to Huejutla and Tampico, and Highway 130 to Tulancingo and Poza Rica. Information on these is given in the Tampico to Pachuca and Northern Veracruz to Pachuca sections of the Gulf Coast chapter. See under Pachuca, Ciudad Valles and Tampico for buses on these routes.

TEOTIHUACÁN

If there is any 'must see' attraction in the vicinity of Mexico City, it is Teotihuacán ('teh-oh-tih-wah-KAN'), some 50 km north-east of the city centre in a mountain-ringed offshoot of the Valley of Mexico. Site of the huge Pyramids of the Sun and Moon,

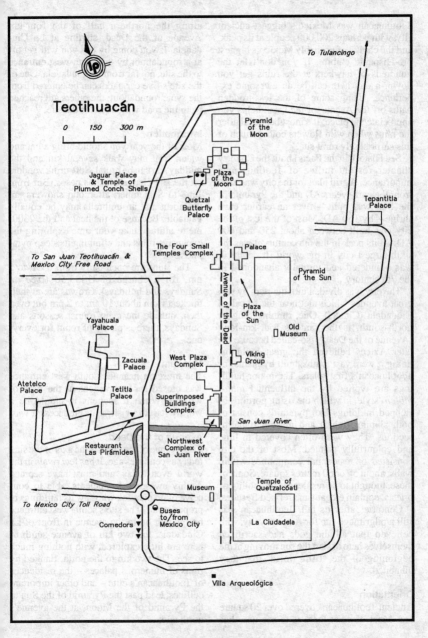

Teotihuacán

0   150   300 m

To Tulancingo

Pyramid of the Moon

Jaguar Palace & Temple of Plumed Conch Shells

Plaza of the Moon

Quetzal Butterfly Palace

Tepantitla Palace

To San Juan Teotihuacán & Mexico City Free Road

The Four Small Temples Complex

Palace

Pyramid of the Sun

Plaza of the Sun

Avenue of the Dead

Old Museum

Yayahuala Palace

Zacuala Palace

Viking Group

Ateteico Palace

Tetitla Palace

West Plaza Complex

Superimposed Buildings Complex

San Juan River

Restaurant Las Pirámides

Northwest Complex of San Juan River

To Mexico City Toll Road

Museum

Temple of Quetzalcóatl

Buses to/from Mexico City

Comedors

La Ciudadela

Villa Arqueológica

Teotihuacán was Mexico's biggest ancient city, with perhaps 200,000 people at its peak, and the capital of probably Mexico's biggest pre-Hispanic empire. If you don't let the hundreds of hawkers at the ruins get you down, a day here can be an awesome experience. Using some of the less-trodden paths off the Avenue of the Dead helps you appreciate the place. It's most beautiful after the rains when wild flowers colour much of this surprisingly rural site.

See History in the Facts about the Country chapter for an outline of Teotihuacán's importance. A grid plan for the city was used from the early years AD and the Pyramid of the Sun was built – over an earlier cave shrine – by 150 AD. Most of the rest of the city was built between about 250 and 600 AD. At its peak in the 6th century it was the sixth-largest city in the world. It declined, was plundered and virtually abandoned in the 7th century.

The city was divided into quarters by two great avenues which met near the so-called Ciudadela (Citadel). One, running roughly north-south, is the famous four-km-long 'Avenue of the Dead' – so-called because the later Aztecs believed the great buildings lining it were vast tombs, built by giants for Teotihuacán's first rulers. The major buildings are typifed by the influential *talud-tablero* style, in which the rising portions of stepped buildings like pyramids consist of both sloping (talud) and upright (tablero) sections. They were often covered in lime and colourfully painted. Most of the city consisted of residential compounds within walls, about 50 or 60 metres square. Some of these, thought to be residences of nobility or priests, contain elegant and refined frescoes.

Centuries after its fall, Teotihuacán was still a pilgrimage site for Aztec royalty, who believed that all the gods had sacrificed themselves here to start the sun moving at the beginning of the 'fifth world' that they inhabited.

Orientation

Ancient Teotihuacán covered over 20 square km. Most of what there is to see now lies along the northern half of the four-km Avenue of the Dead, starting at La Ciudadela. If you come by bus you will get off at a roundabout by the south-west entrance to the site, not far from La Ciudadela. One of the site's five car parks can be entered from the same roundabout; the others are reached from the road which circles the site.

Information

Most of the year you should bring a hat and water. You may walk several km and the midday sun can be brutal. Soft-drink vendors on the site charge muchos pesos. But from June to September, afternoon showers are the norm and an umbrella may be equally valuable. Because of the heat and the 2300-metre altitude take your time exploring the expansive ruins and climbing its steep pyramids.

The ruins are open daily from 8 am to 5 pm, for a charge of US$3.50 (free on Sundays and holidays). Crowds are at their thickest from about 10 am to 2 pm but even then, outside the main tourist seasons and Sundays, there is plenty of room for everyone.

Museum

The museum near the south-west entrance was closed for renovations at the time of writing. When it reopens it should be a worthy start to a visit, as its predecessor was.

Avenue of the Dead

The Avenue of the Dead is the axis of the site, today as centuries ago. It has few rivals in the world even today, and must have seemed doubly awesome to ancients, able to conceive of no parallel, who saw its buildings in proper repair. The site's south-west entrance brings you on to the avenue in front of La Ciudadela; the two km of avenue south of here are little explored, with nothing much to see. The two km to the north, flanked by ruins of numerous palaces – the residences of Teotihuacán's elite – and other important edifices, lead past the Pyramid of the Sun to the Pyramid of the Moon, at the avenue's north end.

Teotihuacán stone mask

La Ciudadela

The large square complex called La Ciudadela (The Citadel) is believed to have been the residence of the city's supreme ruler. Four wide walls 390 metres long, topped by a total of 15 pyramids, enclose a huge open space of which the main feature, towards the east side, is a larger pyramid, the Temple of Quetzalcóatl. The temple is flanked by two large ruined complexes of rooms and patios, which may have been the city's administrative centre.

Temple of Quetzalcóatl The fascinating feature of this temple is the facade of an early version from around 250 to 300 AD, revealed by excavation from beneath a later version. The four surviving 'steps' of this facade – there were originally seven – are encrusted with striking carvings. In the upright tablero panels the sharp-fanged feathered serpent deity, its head emerging from a 'necklace' of 11 petals, alternates with a four-eyed, two-fanged creature often named as the rain god Tláloc but perhaps more authoritatively reckoned to be the fire serpent, bearer of the sun on its daily journey across the sky. On the sloping talud panels are side-views of the plumed serpent, its

body snaking along behind its head. Sea shells, an important Teotihaucán motif, form part of the background in both sets of panels.

Pyramid of the Sun

The world's third-largest pyramid stands on the east side of the Avenue of the Dead, towards its north end. The Pyramid of the Sun is surpassed in size only by the pyramid of Cholula and Egypt's Cheops. Built originally around 100 AD and reconstructed in 1908, it has a base about 222 metres square, roughly equal to that of Cheops. It's just over 70 metres high and had a wood and thatch temple on top. Remind yourself that this pyramid was fashioned from some 3 million tons of stone, brick and rubble without metal tools, pack animals or the wheel!

The Aztec belief that the structure was dedicated to the sun god was unsubstantiated until 1971, when archaeologists uncovered a 100-metre-long underground tunnel leading from near the pyramid's west side to a cave directly beneath its centre. Here they found religious artefacts. It is thought the sun was worshipped here before the pyramid was built and that the city's ancient inhabitants traced the very origins of life to this grotto.

At Teotihuacán's height, the pyramid's plaster was painted bright red, which must have been a radiant sight at sunset. Climb its 248 steps for an overview of the entire city.

Pyramid of the Moon

The Pyramid of the Moon, at the north end of the Avenue of the Dead, is not as expansive or tall as the Pyramid of the Sun, but seems more gracefully proportioned. Its summit is virtually at the same height, because it was built on higher ground. It was finished about 300 AD.

The artfully laid-out Plaza of the Moon before it includes the remains of 12 temple platforms. Some archaeologists attribute astronomical symbolism to the total 13. The altar in the plaza's centre is thought to have been the site of religious dancing.

Palace of the Quetzal Butterfly

Off the south-west corner of the Plaza of the

Moon is the Palace of the Quetzalpapálotl, or Quetzal Butterfly, where it is thought a high priest or ruler lived. A flight of steps leads up to a roofed portico with an abstract mural, off which is a well-restored patio with thick columns carved with designs representing the quetzal bird or a hybrid quetzal-butterfly.

Jaguar Palace & Temple of the Plumed Conch Shells

These structures lie behind and below the Palace of the Quetzal Butterfly. On the lower walls of several of the chambers off the patio of the Jaguar Palace are parts of murals showing the jaguar god in feathered headdresses, blowing conch shells and apparently praying to the rain god Tláloc.

The Temple of the Plumed Conch Shells, entered from the Jaguar Temple patio, is a now-subterranean structure of the 2nd or 3rd century AD. Carvings on what was its facade show large shells – possibly used as musical instruments – decorated with feathers, and four-petalled flowers. The base on which the facade stands has a green, blue, red and yellow mural of birds with water streaming from their beaks.

Tepantitla Palace

Teotihuacán's most famous fresco, the *Paradise of Tláloc*, is in the Tepantitla Palace, a priest's residence about 500 metres east of the Pyramid of the Sun. A full-size copy of the mural in the National Anthropology Museum is easier to make out than the original, so don't hike out to Tepantitla unless you are keen. The mural flanks a doorway in a covered patio in the north-east corner of the building. The rain god Tláloc, attended by priests, is shown on both sides. Below, on the right of the door, appears his paradise, a garden-like place with tiny people, animals and fish swimming in a river flowing from a mountain. Left of the door, tiny human figures are engaged in a unique ball game. Frescoes in other rooms show feather-head-dressed priests.

Tetitla & Atetelco Palaces

Another group of palaces lies west of the main part of the site, about one km from the south-west entrance. Their many murals, discovered in the 1940s, are often well-preserved or restored and perfectly intelligible. The Tetitla Palace is a large complex of perhaps several adjoining houses. No less than 120 walls have murals, with Tláloc, jaguars, serpents and eagles among the easiest to make out. Some 400 metres west is the Atetelco Palace, whose vivid jaguar or coyote murals – a mixture of originals and restoration – are in the so-called Patio Blanco in the north-west corner. Processions of these creatures in shades of red perhaps symbolise warrior orders. There are also criss-cross designs of priests with Tláloc and coyote costumes.

Places to Stay & Eat

The Club Med-run *Villa Arqueológica* (☎ (595) 6-02-44) at the south end of the site ring road has very comfortable air-conditioned rooms for around US$60 single or double. There is a pool, library, tennis court and French-Mexican restaurant.

Other restaurants are dotted around the ring road, the cheapest being the *comedors* lined up south of the roundabout outside the site's south-west entrance.

Getting There & Away

The 2nd-class buses of Autobuses San Juan Teotihuacán run from Mexico City's northern terminal to the ruins every 20 or 30 minutes during the day, costing US$1.25 for the journey of about an hour. The ticket office is at the north end of the terminal. Make sure your bus is going to 'Los Pirámides', because some only go to the village of San Juan Teotihuacán, two km west of the ruins.

You get off at a roundabout outside the site's south-west entrance, which is also where you catch the bus to go back to Mexico City. Fewer return buses may come by before about 1 pm: if you have waited too long, get a taxi to San Juan Teotihuacán, from where buses leave every 20 minutes. The last bus back to the capital from the roundabout leaves about 6 pm. Some terminate at Indios Verdes metro station on Insurgentes Norte in the north of Mexico City. If you don't fancy the metro you can get a pesero or taxi down Insurgentes to the city centre.

Numerous tours from Mexico City go to Teotihuacán.

East of Mexico City

POPOCATÉPETL & IZTACCÍHUATL

The snow-capped peaks of Mexico's two most famous mountains ('po-po-ka-TEH-pettle' and 'iss-ta-SEE-wattle') form the eastern rim of the Valley of Mexico, 60 km south-east of Mexico City and 45 km west of Puebla. They used to be visible almost daily from Mexico City, but nowadays, because of the smog, are hardly ever seen.

There are better views from the Puebla side, or from the Mexico City-Puebla road – from which Iztaccíhuatl (5286 metres) is the nearer, Popocatépetl (5452 metres) the more cone-shaped peak. Best of all is to go up on the mountains themselves, easily done in a day from Mexico City without hiking a metre. This is a popular weekend jaunt for people from the capital. When the weather's clear the mountains are magnificent – but be ready for winds which can produce a distinct chill even in sunshine.

A road goes up to Tlamacas, 3950 metres high on the saddle between the two mountains. Here, on the edge of a pine forest, is a lodge with dormitory beds, from which there are plenty of strolls and walks. It is possible to walk from Tlamacas to the top of Popo and back in a strenuous day if you have the right equipment. The heights of Izta, however, are mainly for climbers.

The peaks are Mexico's second and third highest and their names are Aztec. Popocatépetl means Smoking Mountain, Iztaccíhuatl White Woman. The legend is that Popo was a warrior, in love with Izta, the emperor's daughter. She died of grief while he was away at war. On his return, he built

the two mountains, laid her body on one and stood holding her funeral torch on the other. Steam still sometimes rises from Popo's crater and, with a touch of imagination, Izta – popularly known as La Mujer Dormida (The Sleeping Woman) – does look a bit like a woman lying on her back.

Different sections are named after parts of her body. As you approach from Mexico City you can, if the weather's clear, make out four peaks from left to right known as La Cabeza (head), El Pecho (breast), Las Rodillas (knees) and Los Pies (feet). Between head and breast is El Cuello (neck).

History

The mountains' present shape dates from 2.5 million years ago. Both are classified as dormant volcanoes, but while Iztaccíhuatl is now craterless, Popocatépetl sometimes belches steam. As recently as 1921, a small new cone formed on the floor of its crater.

High on the rugged lower peak of Popocatépetl called the Ventorrillo is a small enclosure dating from 900 AD, reckoned to be the work of Toltecs. The conquistadors who reached Cholula in October 1519, curious about a mountain that emitted smoke, sent 10 Spaniards and some Indians up Popo, which was erupting at the time. Cortés wrote to the King of Spain that the party hadn't quite reached the top because of snow, flying ashes, wind and cold.

After the fall of Tenochtitlán in 1521, five conquistadors were sent back to collect sulphur from Popo's crater for making gunpowder. Again it was erupting. The expedition managed to dodge the flying hot rocks and four reached the top, one having retired exhausted. Two men were lowered by rope towards the molten lava in the crater, 13 times between them, each time coming up with a bag of sulphur. They were received as heroes by Indians waiting at the foot of the mountain. Their exploits were equalled on a daily basis nearly four centuries later by workers of a sulphur-mining company.

Information
Altitude Anyone can be affected by altitude

problems – which if acute can kill. There is no hard and fast rule about how high is too high – Acute Mountain Sickness has been fatal at 3000 metres, although 3500 to 4500 metres is the usual range. Fitness helps avoid these problems, and acclimatisation is another key. Most people going to Tlamacas (3950 metres) have already spent a few days around Mexico City (2240 metres) which makes a lot of difference. A day at Tlamacas before an ascent is also a good idea. It is wise to sleep at a lower altitude than the highest you have reached during the day.

The lack of oxygen at high altitudes affects most people to some extent. Take it easy at first, increase your liquid intake and eat well. Even with acclimatisation you may still have trouble adjusting.

Mild altitude problems generally abate after a day or so but if the symptoms persist or become worse the only treatment is to descend – even 500 metres can help – and seek medical help. Breathlessness, a dry, irritative cough – which may progress to the production of pink, frothy sputum – severe headache, loss of appetite, nausea, sometimes vomiting, are all danger signs. Increasing tiredness, confusion and lack of coordination and balance are real danger signs. Any of these symptoms individually, even just a persistent headache, can be a warning.

Books R J Secor's guide *Mexico's Volcanoes* (The Mountaineers, Seattle) covers hikes and many rock-climbing routes on Popo and Izta. *Backpacking in Mexico & Central America* by Hilary Bradt and Rob Rachowiecki (Bradt Enterprises, Cambridge, Massachusetts, and Chalfont St Peter, England) includes hiking routes on Popo and Izta.

Groups & Guides At Tlamacas you may be invited to join a group of Mexican climbers or hikers. In Mexico City you can try contacting the Club de Exploraciones de México (☎ 578-57-30) for information on climbing the mountains. The club apparently runs some trips which are open to nonmembers.

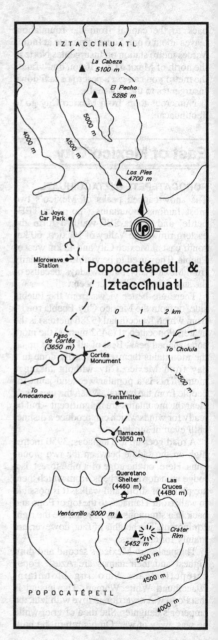

Another possibility is the Mountain Rescue Club at Lázaro Cárdenas 80, No 305, in central Mexico City, which reportedly rents equipment.

Coordinadores de Guías de Montaña (☎ 584-46-95), at Tlaxcala 47 in Colonia Roma, Mexico City, provides qualified guides for Popo, Izta and other Mexican peaks. For a 28-hour trip from Mexico City to the top of Popo and back they charge US$180 per person including transport, accommodation and two meals. You can usually also find guides at Tlamacas – but for the Las Cruces route on Popo it's not really necessary because the trail is well-worn and sometimes busy.

Accommodation & Food See the Amecameca, Paso de Cortés & Tlamacas, and Climbs sections for info on accommodation and food. On a day trip to Tlamacas, it is advisable to take some food and drink unless you know that the restaurant there will be open.

Amecameca

From the Mexico City side, the town of Amecameca (population 22,000, altitude 2470 metres), 60 km by road from the city, is the key staging post for a visit to the volcanoes. There are a few restaurants and a dingy hotel, the *San Carlos*, here. A lively little crafts and food market is held on Saturdays and Sundays in the zócalo.

Paso de Cortés & Tlamacas

The road to Paso de Cortés – the pass between the two volcanoes and Tlamacas branches east from the Amecameca-Cuautla road one km south of Amecameca, then winds its way up through pine woods. It is 25 km from Amecameca to Paso de Cortés (3650 metres), 29 km to Tlamacas (3950 metres).

The Cortés monument at Paso de Cortés is one of only two in the country – old Hernán isn't too popular among Mexicans! It was here that the conquistadors saw in the distance for the first time the lake cities at the heart of the great empire they were to conquer. At Paso de Cortés two dirt roads branch off – one goes eight km to La Joya car park on the south-west side of Iztaccíhuatl, passing a TV transmitter on the way; the other heads east down to Cholula 45 km away, emerging on the Cholula-Tonantzintla road, and is reportedly passable in dry weather.

The paved road ends at the Tlamacas lodge, the *Albergue Vicente Guerrero*, at the base of the black, towering cone of Popo. The lodge is a modern 98-bed establishment which charges US$3.50 per person for a dormitory bed and locker (bring your own padlock). There is hot water at certain hours. It is highly advisable to make a reservation in advance through the lodge's Mexico City office (☎ 553-58-96) at Río Elba 20, Noveno Piso (9th floor), Colonia Cuauhtémoc. The lodge has a bar and a restaurant but these were closed at the time of writing, awaiting a new concessionary. Normally they are open to non-residents. You can rent ice axes and crampons at the lodge and get advice about the mountains.

Walks

For some, a ramble through the woods around Tlamacas or a stroll in the general direction of Popo is enough at this altitude. Another possibility is to walk the four km between Paso de Cortés and Tlamacas, which are 300 metres apart in altitude; there are several short cuts between the bends in the road. Longer but flatter is the eight km from Paso de Cortés to La Joya car park on the flank of Izta – take drinks (at least) with you. From La Joya there are trails across the west flank of Izta to the Chalchoapan hut beneath El Cuello, and back down to Amecameca (six hours).

To experience Popo itself without going all the way to the top, you can walk to Las Cruces at 4480 metres, three hours from Tlamacas (see Climbs).

It is ill-advised to leave anything in a vehicle anywhere – the lockers at Tlamacas hut are probably the only safe refuge for belongings you don't want to carry.

Climbs

Register at the Tlamacas lodge or with the Mountain Rescue people (Socorro Alpino) at Tlamacas before embarking on any ascent more demanding than the walk to Las Cruces. It is advisable to have experience in at least mountain-snow hiking before embarking on Popo, and it is not at all wise to go alone. Izta is even more formidable. People have died on these mountains.

Conditions & Seasons It can be windy and well below freezing on the upper slopes of either mountain any time of year and is nearly always below freezing near the summits at night. Ice and snow are permanent; the average snow line is 4200 metres but it is higher in October and November. The best months for ascents are December and January, when there is a reasonable amount of snow for cramponing. February and March are sometimes prone to storms and poor visibility. The rainy season, April to September, is least suitable: there is lots of snow but it is often soft, and there can be thunderstorms, clouds, white-outs and even avalanches. Crevasses (*grietas*) exist on parts of Popo at any time of year.

Equipment Unless you are just walking to Las Cruces, take ice axes and crampons, since you will be going up steep, icy or snowy slopes. You can rent them at Tlamacas lodge (about US$6 each). You should also have, at least, good boots; clothing for temperatures below freezing and, at some times of year, for rain; head protection against sun and cold; first-aid gear; food and water (though you can melt snow once you reach the snow line); sunglasses and sunblock for glare; and a very warm sleeping bag if you are thinking of sleeping in a hut or tent.

Shelters on Popo Above Tlamacas, there are three shelters (*refugios*) without equipment or facilities – one on the summit and two on rock-climbers' routes. They hold eight people each and at weekends and holidays can be full.

Las Cruces Route This is the hiker's route up Popocatépetl, an ascent of 1500 metres from Tlamacas. It takes an average of eight hours to reach the summit, a bit less just to the crater rim, and two to four hours to come down, so a 3 am start is normal. You can walk the beginning of the route – to Las Cruces and back – as a few hours' stroll. From Tlamacas, take the clear trail going east across the base of the volcano. Las Cruces, where there used to be a hut, is 2.7 km along this path and 550 metres above Tlamacas, at 4480 metres.

From Las Cruces to the lower edge of the crater at 5100 metres you head straight up the 30° slope – by far the hardest part, but if you make it you will be rewarded by spectacular views into the crater. Its sides are sheer with a depth of 380 metres. On the floor is a small lake and a few minor cones. The crater is 2.7 km round. If you turn right on reaching the crater and follow the rim round, you reach the shelter on the 5452-metre summit after an hour or so.

Other Popo Route The trip to the Queretano shelter on the Ventorrillo – the craggy formation visible between Tlamacas and the crater – is a possibility for adventurous hikers. You fork right off the Las Cruces trail at 4100 metres, following the path to the north-east ridge of the Ventorrillo, from which it reaches the Queretano shelter hut at 4460 metres, overlooking the canyon between the Ventorrillo and Popocatépetl's glaciers.

Iztaccíhuatl Nearly all the routes to Izta's peaks – the highest is El Pecho at 5286 metres – involve some rock-climbing and a night on the mountain. Three shelter-huts (one ruined) between 4500 and 4900 metres on the way from La Joya car park to Las Rodillas could be used during an ascent of El Pecho. On average, it takes six hours from La Joya to the huts, another four to six hours from the huts to El Pecho, and four to six hours to descend. There are a few other huts and many other routes on Izta, which is in many ways a more beautiful mountain than

Popo. Before tackling any of them, make full information, equipment and physical condition preparations.

Getting There & Away

Cristóbal Colón 1st-class buses to Cuautla from Mexico City's eastern bus station, TAPO, stop at Amecameca. They leave TAPO every 40 minutes from 6 am to 10 pm and take 1¼ hours to Amecameca, for US$1.25. The last bus back to Mexico City leaves Amecameca at 9 pm and the last to Cuautla at 10.15 pm. Frequent 'Candelaria-Amecameca-San Lázaro' microbuses, which run back and forth between San Lázaro metro (beside TAPO) and Amecameca zócalo up to about 8 pm, are an alternative for US$1.

From the bus station in Amecameca walk a couple of blocks to the zócalo, where taxis wait to take people up to Paso de Cortés or Tlamacas. The standard one-way fare for the 45-minute drive to Tlamacas is US$10. Drivers ask US$3.50 an hour waiting time if you want them to take you back down to Amecameca later, but if you agree to an all-in price you should be able to make a saving somewhere.

At weekends, it is not too hard to hitch lifts between Amecameca and the volcanoes, even along the road to Izta from Paso de Cortés.

Mexico City to Veracruz

Ever since Cortés landed near what's now the steamy Gulf port of Veracruz and made his way up to Tenochtitlán, the Veracruz-Mexico City corridor has been vital in the Mexican story. Veracruz remained Mexico's chief gateway to the outside world until well into the 20th century, and through here have flowed invaders, settlers, saints, slaves, trade, diseases, laws and ideas.

It's about 430 km by road between capital and coast – only some seven hours by bus, but there are good reasons to break the trip. Some places on the way are worth visiting even if you aren't travelling all the way through the corridor. One is Puebla, one of Mexico's best preserved colonial cities and a pivot of its history, but also a lively modern metropolis, the fourth-biggest in the country. From Puebla the conventional route to Veracruz is by Orizaba and Córdoba, but going instead via Xalapa, the surprising Veracruz state capital and a stimulating cultural and university centre, is rewarding.

The Mexico City-Puebla-Veracruz corridor is also the start of the two main routes from the capital to south-east Mexico. One, via Oaxaca, diverges not far east of Puebla, through Tehuacán. The other, towards Tabasco and the Yucatán Peninsula, heads off from the Córdoba-Veracruz road, shortly before Veracruz.

The small colonial town of Tlaxcala, a little north of Puebla, is capital of a tiny state (population 700,000) of its own. Tlaxcala and the nearby pre-Hispanic site of Cacaxtla, with its well preserved frescoes, can both be visited in a day trip from Puebla. The state of Puebla extends nearly 200 km north and over 100 km south from Puebla city, wrapping around Tlaxcala. Its northern mountains, the Sierra Norte de Puebla, are beautiful and remote, with a high Indian population.

Geography
From Mexico City the first part of your trip

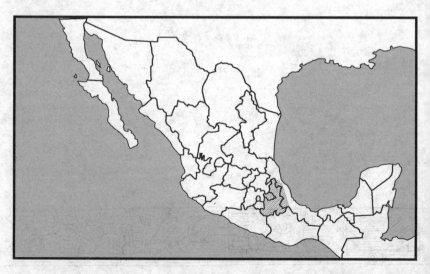

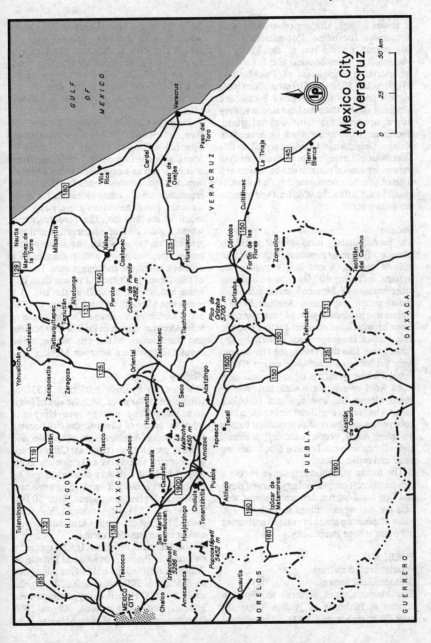

is across a high, dry region studded with volcanoes including Popocatépetl and Iztaccíhuatl on the rim of the Valley of Mexico (see Near Mexico City), La Malinche rising north-east of Puebla, and 5700-metre Pico de Orizaba, Mexico's highest peak, on the border of Puebla and Veracruz states. Then the land slopes steeply down towards the Gulf coastal plain, immediately becoming much more verdant. Xalapa, Orizaba and Córdoba are all on this slope which is more moderate in climate than the sweaty coastal plain. It can be subject any time of year to a persistent drizzle known as *chipichipi*. Coffee, flowers, fruit and tobacco are grown here.

People

The predominantly rural state of Puebla is Mexico's fifth most populous, with over four million people. About half a million are Indians, including 400,000 – more than any other state – of Mexico's most numerous Indian people, the Nahua. Another 200,000 Nahua live in western parts of Veracruz state, some of which are covered by this chapter. The Nahua language was spoken by the Aztecs and, like the Aztecs, the Nahua here were probably of Chichimec origin. Traditional Nahua women's dress consists of a black wool *enredo*, waist sash, and embroidered blouse and *quechquémitl* (shoulder cape). The Nahua are Christian but often also believe in a pantheon of supernatural beings including *tonos*, people's animal 'doubles', and witches who can become blood-sucking birds and cause illness.

The Indian presence helps give Puebla a rich handicraft output; pottery, carved onyx and fine hand-woven and embroidered textiles are among the things to look out for. Most of these are made in villages and towns but often sold in Puebla city.

PUEBLA

Population: 1.5 million
Altitude: 2162 metres
Few Mexican cities preserve the Spanish imprint as faithfully as Puebla. There are over 70 churches and 1000 other colonial buildings in the central area alone – many adorned with the hand-painted tiles for which the city is famous. Strategically located on the Veracruz-Mexico City road, and set in a broad valley with Popocatépetl and Iztaccíhuatl rising to the west, Puebla has always played a major role in national affairs.

Strongly Catholic, criollo and conservative, its people (Poblanos) maintained Spanish affinities longer than most in Mexico. In the 19th century their patriotism was regarded as suspect and today Puebla's wealthy, Spanish-descended families have a reputation among other Mexicans for snobbishness. Nevertheless it's a lively city with much to see and do. The historic centre, where a great deal of conservation and restoration has taken place, has a prosperous modern dimension too, with its share of slick dressers, boutiques and burger bars. The Hill of Guadalupe is a peaceful retreat from city noise and smells, as well as the site of a renowned Mexican military victory in 1862 and a clutch of museums. On the negative side, accommodation in Puebla is expensive and some areas of the city are as noisy, squalid and polluted as any in Mexico.

History

Founded by Spanish settlers in 1531 as Ciudad de los Ángeles, with the aim of overshadowing the nearby pre-Hispanic religious centre of Cholula, the city became Puebla de los Ángeles eight years later and quickly grew into an important Catholic religious centre. Good clay and colonists' skills helped make it a pottery centre too and by the late 18th century it was also an important textile and glass producer. With 50,000 people by 1811, it remained Mexico's second biggest city until Guadalajara overtook it in the late 19th century.

The French invaders of 1862 expected a welcome in Puebla, but General Ignacio de Zaragoza fortified the hill of Guadalupe and on 5 May his 2000 men defeated a frontal attack by 6000 French, many of whom were handicapped by diarrhoea. About 1000 French were killed. This rare Mexican mili-

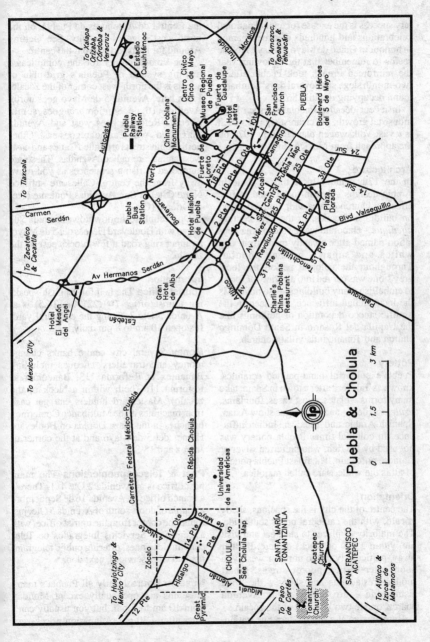

Puebla & Cholula

tary success is the excuse for annual national celebrations and hundreds of streets named in honour of Cinco de Mayo (5 May). No one seems to remember that the following year the reinforced French took Puebla after a two-month siege and several days' bombardment, occupying it until 1867.

In recent decades Puebla has seen huge industrial growth, the clearest sign of which is a vast Volkswagen plant built in 1970 on the approach from Mexico City.

Architecture

In the 17th century local tiles – some in Arabic designs – began to be used to fine effect on church domes and, with red brick, on buildings' façades. In the 18th century *alfeñique* – elaborate white stucco ornamentation named after a candy made from egg whites and sugar – became popular. Throughout the colonial period the local grey stone was carved into a variety of forms to embellish many buildings. Also notable is the local Indian influence, best seen in the prolific stucco decoration of buildings like the Capilla del Rosario in Santo Domingo church and Tonantzintla village church.

Pottery

Puebla's colourful hand-painted ceramics, known as Talavera after a town in Spain, take many forms – plates, cups, vases, fountains, *azulejos* (tiles) – and its designs show Asian, Spanish-Arabic and Mexican Indian influence. In colonial times Puebla pottery was not used by the rich, who preferred silver or Chinese porcelain. The finest Puebla pottery of all is the white ware called majolica.

Orientation

The centre of the city is the spacious, shady zócalo, with the cathedral on its south side. The majority of places to stay, eat and visit are within a few of blocks of here. Further away, particularly to the north or west, you soon enter dirtier, poorer streets. Smart modern restaurants and shops – the Zona Esmeralda – are dotted along Avenida Juárez, one to two km west of the zócalo.

Buses arrive at a big modern bus station,

the Central de Autobuses de Puebla, on the north-west edge of the city. See Getting Around for transport to/from the centre.

The crucial corner for the complicated naming system of Puebla's grid-plan of streets is the north-west corner of the zócalo. From here, Avenida 5 de Mayo goes north, Avenida 16 de Septiembre goes south, Avenida Reforma goes west and Avenida Maximino Avila Camacho goes east. Other north-south streets are called Calles and east-west streets are called Avenidas. These are numbered in rising sequences as you move away from the centre. Calles are suffixed Norte (Nte) or Sur, Avenidas Poniente (Pte) or Oriente (Ote).

Don't confuse the downtown Avenida 5 de Mayo with Boulevard Héroes del 5 de Mayo, an inner ring road a few blocks east of the zócalo.

Information

Tourist Office The helpful, English-speaking tourist office (☎ (22) 46-12-85) is at Avenida 5 Ote 3, facing the cathedral yard. It's open 10 am to 8 pm daily.

Money Several city centre banks change money and travellers' cheques including Banamex at Reforma 113, Bancomer at Reforma 116 (both within a block of the zócalo). Mastercard holders can get cash from machines in the Multibanco Comermex branches in the Plaza Dorada on Boulevard Héroes del 5 de Mayo and at the corner of Juárez and 13 Sur.

Post & Telecommunications The main post office is at Avenida 2 Ote 411. There's a branch office on Avenida 16 de Septiembre a couple of doors south of Avenida 5 Ote, just round the corner from the tourist office, with a Centro de Servicios Integrados de Telecommunicaciones, offering public telegram, fax and telex services, next door.

Museum Hours Nearly all Puebla's many museums are open daily except Monday from 10 am to 5 pm, but you usually can't enter after 4.30 pm. Admission prices vary but most are free on Sunday. The main exception to these rules is the Museo Amparo.

City Centre – Zócalo & South

Puebla's central plaza was a marketplace where hangings, bullfights and theatre took place before it acquired its current garden-like appearance in 1854. The *portales* (arcades) are 16th century.

Cathedral The massive cathedral occupying the block south of the zócalo is considered one of Mexico's best proportioned. It blends severe Herreresque Renaissance style and early baroque. Building began in 1550 but most took place under the dynamic Puebla Bishop Juan de Palafox in the 1640s. The towers are the highest in the country at 69 metres; some of their bells date from the 17th century and are celebrated in the traditional rhyme *'Para mujeres y campanas, las Poblanas'* – 'For women and bells, Puebla's (are best)'. The dome is covered with local glazed tiles.

Casa del que Mató al Animal The House of He who Killed the Animal, now a newspaper office, at the corner of Avenida 3 Ote and 2 Sur, has a 16th-century carved doorway showing hunters and dogs in a style similar to 15th-century French tapestries. It recalls the Puebla legend of a monstrous snake from La Malinche that terrorised the city. A wealthy citizen, whose child it had killed, offered a reward to whoever would get rid of the monster. A young soldier who arrived in town heard of this and managed to cut off the creature's head.

Bishop's Palace On Avenida 5 Ote, facing the south side of the cathedral, the old Bishop's Palace is a classic brick-and-tile Puebla building now housing government offices (at the Avenida 16 de Septiembre end), the tourist office, and (at No 5) the Casa de la Cultura, devoted to local cultural activities, with a cafeteria. Upstairs in the Casa de la Cultura is the Biblioteca Palafoxiana (Palafox Library), with thousands of valu-

able books, including the 1493 Nuremberg Chronicle with more than 2000 engravings. It's open normal museum hours.

Museo Amparo The theme of this excellent modern museum, opened in 1991 on 2 Sur at the corner of Avenida 9 Ote, is 'Meeting with our Roots' – an encounter which takes place by means of displays of pre-Hispanic, colonial and republican Mexican art. The eight pre-Hispanic rooms display their artefacts well and interpret them and their societies in English and Spanish, tracing the course of pre-Hispanic art from its Olmec roots.

The museum is attractively housed in two linked colonial buildings, one of which was the family home of its founder Manuel Espinosa Yglesias, to whose late wife it's a homage. It's open 10 am to 6 pm daily except Tuesday. Entry is US$1.75 but free on Monday. For a further US$1.75 plus US$1.75 deposit you can rent headphones for interactive video sets which give further explanation in a choice of languages including English. The museum also has a library, cafeteria and good bookshop.

Museo Bello This house at Avenida 3 Pte 302 is filled with the very diverse art and craft collection of 19th-century industrialist José Luis Bello and his son Mariano. Among the more curious or outstanding items are beautiful French, English, Japanese and Chinese porcelain; a 17th-century wooden Mexican organ; nuns' spiked flagellation chains; and a door of glass columns, each with a different musical pitch. Admission is US$1 (free on Saturdays). Tours are given in Spanish and English and guides ask for a tip.

City Centre – East & North-East

Casa de los Muñecos The big tiles on the House of the Puppets on 2 Nte, just off the north-east corner of the zócalo, caricature the city fathers who took the house's owner, Agustín de Ovando y Villavicencio, to court because his building was taller than theirs. Inside is the Museo Universitario (free) telling the story of education in Puebla.

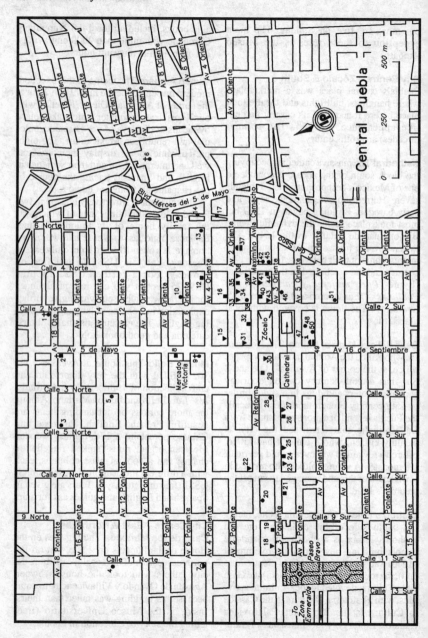

■ PLACES TO STAY

8 Hotel Embajadoras
12 Hotel Imperial
16 Hotel Posada San Pedro
19 Hotel Virrey de Mendoza
21 Hotel San Miguel
24 Hotel San Agustín
26 Hotel Teresita
29 Hostal de Halconeros
32 Hotel & Restaurant/Bar Royalty
35 Hotel Palacio San Leonardo
40 Hotel Del Portal
44 Hotel Colonial

▼ PLACES TO EAT

15 Sanborns
18 Fonda Santa Clara, 3 Pte 920 Branch
22 Teorema bookshop/café
23 Mesón de los Frailes
25 El Vegetariano
27 Fonda Santa Clara, 3 Pte 307 Branch
30 Restaurant-Café El Vasco
31 Café Foto Aguirre
33 VIPs
34 Restaurants La Concordia, La Grecia
   & Venecia
36 Restaurant Nevados Hermilo
39 Fonda Carolina
41 Café El Carolo
43 Vittorio's

OTHER

1 San José Church
2 Santa Monica Convent
3 Mercado Cinco de Mayo
4 Museo del Ferrocarril
5 Santa Rosa Convent & Museo de
   Artesanías del Estado de Puebla
6 San Francisco Church
7 Colectivos to Cholula
9 Santo Domingo Church
10 Museo de la Revolución
11 Teatro Principal
13 Casa del Alfeñique
14 Barrio del Artista
17 El Parián
20 Palacio de Gobierno
28 Museo Bello
37 Post Office
38 Casa de los Muñecos
42 La Compañía Church
45 University
46 Casa del que Mató al Animal
47 Tourist Office
48 Casa de la Cultura
49 Post Office & Centro de
   Servicios Integrados de
   Telecommunicaciones
50 Creart
51 Museo Amparo

La Compañía Church This Jesuit church with a 1767 Churrigueresque façade, at the corner of Avenida Maximino Avila Camacho and 4 Sur, is also called Espíritu Santo. Beneath the altar is a tomb said to be that of a 17th-century Asian princess who was sold into slavery in Mexico and later freed. She is supposed to have originated the colourful China Poblana costume of shawl, frilled blouse, embroidered skirt and gold and silver adornments a kind of peasant chic fashionable in the 19th century. But *china* also meant maid-servant and the style may have developed from Spanish peasant costumes.

University The 16th-century Edificio Carolino, next door to La Compañía on 4 Sur, formerly a Jesuit college, is now the main building of Puebla University. It has pretty courtyards and the upstairs Salón Melchor de Covarrubias has a typical Puebla 'sugar candy' ceiling of Churrigueresque stucco.

Casa del Alfeñique This house, at the corner of 6 Nte and Avenida 4 Ote, is the outstanding example of the 18th-century decorative style alfeñique. Inside is the Museo del Estado (entry US$0.50) with 18th and 19th-century Puebla paraphernalia such as China Poblana gear, carriages and furniture.

Teatro Principal & Barrio del Artista The theatre on 6 Nte between Avenidas 6 and 8 Ote dates from 1756 – one of the oldest in the Americas. You can look inside between 10 am and 5 pm when it's not in use. It went up in flames in 1902 but was rebuilt in the

1930s. Nearby, 8 Nte, between Avenidas 4 and 6 Ote, is occupied by artists' and sculptors' workshops and showrooms – the so-called 'Artists' Quarter'.

San Francisco Church The north doorway of San Francisco, just east of Boulevard Héroes del 5 de Mayo on Avenida 14 Ote, is a good example of 16th-century Plateresque; the tower and fine brick-and-tile façade were added in the 18th century. In a glass case in the church's north chapel is the body of San Sebastián de Aparicio, a Spaniard who came to Mexico in 1533 and planned many of the country's roads before becoming a monk. His body is in a remarkable state of preservation and attracts a stream of worshippers. The chapel contains many paintings of his life, and his statue stands outside the church.

Museo de la Revolución This house at Avenida 6 Ote 206 was the scene of the first battle of the 1910 Revolution. Betrayed on 18 November 1910, two days before the planned uprising against Porfirio Díaz's dictatorship, the Serdán family (Aquiles, Máximo, Carmen and Natalia) and 17 others fought 500 soldiers and police until only Aquiles, their leader, and Carmen were left alive. Aquiles, hidden under the floorboards, might have survived if the damp hadn't provoked a cough which gave him away. The house contains a bullet-shattered mirror and other Revolution memorabilia. Entry is US$0.50.

City Centre – North
Santo Domingo Church The chief glory of Santo Domingo, 2½ blocks north of the zócalo on Avenida 5 de Mayo, is the Capilla del Rosario (Rosary Chapel) south of the main altar. Built between 1680 and 1720, the chapel is a sumptuous baroque proliferation of gilded plaster and carved stone with angels and cherubim popping out from behind every leaf. Some locals call it the Eighth Wonder of the World. See if you can spot the heavenly orchestra.

Mercado Victoria A few paces up Avenida

5 de Mayo from Santo Domingo, then to the left, Puebla's former main market is an elegant 1912 roofed construction where everything from vegetables and clothes to herbal medicines was sold. It's being revamped as part of the city centre's clean-up and had been closed for at least four years at the time of writing.

Santa Rosa Convent This 17th-century nunnery, on 3 Nte between Avenidas 12 and 14 Pte, houses the excellent Museo de Artesanías del Estado de Puebla – an extensive collection of Puebla state handicrafts. Guided tours in Spanish are compulsory. You'll see Indian costumes, fine pottery (including superb trees of life), onyx, glass, even *amate* (bark paper). Finally you reach the kitchen where mole Poblano (spicy chocolate sauce – see Places to Eat) is said to have been invented. The kitchen is full of old pottery and beautified with 20th-century tiles. Entry is US$0.50.

Santa Monica Convent Another nunnery-museum, with an exquisite tiled courtyard, is at Avenida 18 Pte 101 near the corner of Avenida 5 de Mayo. The story that Santa Monica functioned secretly during the anti-clerical movements of the 19th century is now disputed – but it's a nice tale. Today it houses mainly religious art, but you can look into some of the old nuns' cells where, among other items, their self-flagellation weapons are laid out. Entry is US$1.75.

Museo del Ferrocarril A dozen vintage locomotives ranging from the majestic to the quaint repose with fresh coats of paint outside the city's old station, facing the junction of 11 Nte and Avenida 12 Pte. You can reminisce about the age of steam and wonder whether trains ever were a really serious transport option in Mexico. Entry is free.

Hill of Guadalupe
The hilltop park stretching a km east of 2 Nte, two km north-east of the zócalo, contains two of Puebla's most historic sites – the Forts of Loreto and Guadalupe – as well as

the Centro Civico Cinco de Mayo, a group of museums and exhibitions. Good views, relatively fresh air and eucalyptus woods add to the appeal. Take bus 'Fuertes' (US$0.20) from the corner of Avenidas 5 de Mayo and 10 Pte to get there.

The **Fuerte de Loreto** at the west end of the hilltop was one of the Mexican defence points on 5 May 1862, when a French invasion army was defeated in one of the few successful episodes of Mexican military history. Today it houses the Museo de la Intervención, chronicling the French invasion and occupation of Mexico (entry US$1.75).

A short walk east of the fort, beyond the domed auditorium, are the **Museo Regional de Puebla** (US$2.75), tracing human history in the state, the **Museo de Historia Natural** (US$1), a pyramid-shaped Planetarium, and the Puebla headquarters of INAH. At the east end of the hilltop is the **Fuerte de Guadalupe** (US$1.75), which also played its part on 5 May 1862, when the chapel inside was ruined.

Places to Stay

Anything above the most basic bottom-of-bottom-end places is at least US$15 double. For colonial ambience you need to move into the middle range and pay at least US$33 double. Even then, the better value places are often full. Why on earth doesn't someone revamp one of the many still decrepit colonial buildings near the city centre into a properly cared-for budget hostelry?

Places to Stay – bottom end

Some of Puebla's cheapest budget hotels bear a strong resemblance to prisons, with gloomy concrete walkways, clanging doors and Spartan rooms. The most appealing lower bottom-end place is the rambling *Hostal de Halconeros* (☎ (22) 42-74-56) at Avenida Reforma 141, half a block west of the zócalo, which nearly always has a few rooms vacant. Only the rooms on the noisy street side have windows to the outside world, and many don't even have windows to a corridor, but despite this and lumpy pillows and flaky plaster most manage to be somehow cosy. Ceilings are high and the place is splashed with colourful tiles and paintwork. Staff are friendly and keep it pretty clean. Singles/doubles/triples with private bath are US$13.75/17.50/21.

The little *Hotel Teresita* (☎ (22) 41-70-72) at Avenida 3 Pte 309, 1½ blocks west of the zócalo, has small, windowless rooms with little escape from other guests' noise, but it's clean, friendly and often full. Singles or doubles are US$6.75 with shared bath, US$13.50 with private bath. Hot water is limited. The *Hotel Victoria* (☎ (22) 41-89-92) across the street at 3 Pte 306 is typically gloomy and faded, though friendly enough and kept just about clean. Singles/doubles with private bath are US$10.50/13.50.

Rooms at the *Hotel Embajadoras* (☎ (22) 41-26-37), on 5 de Mayo between 6 and 8 Ote, are only US$5 single or double with shared bath, US$9.50 with private shower. They're on three floors around a big covered courtyard, and are quite big and reasonably clean, but dark, bare and, apart from a few newly concreted shower areas, very, very tired.

A trio of 'top of the bottom end' hotels are a distinct step up from everything else. The *Hotel Imperial* (☎ (22) 42-49-82) at Avenida 4 Ote 212 is the most central. Its top floor rooms – clean, with TV are bigger and airier than those below, with tiles to brighten the bare walls. Singles/doubles are US$18.50/22.75, and the staff are friendly.

The *Hotel Virrey de Mendoza* (☎ (22) 43-39-03) at Avenida 3 Pte 912 has large, clean, wood-beamed rooms along two wide balconies above a courtyard where locals garage their cars (their movements create little disturbance). Some beds are a little lumpy, hot water is mornings only, and paint in some bathrooms a bit flaky, but the place has a friendly owner and isn't at all bad for this price range. Rooms are US$16.75/21.75. Prices are identical at the *Hotel San Miguel* (☎ (22) 42-48-60), nearby at Avenida 3 Pte 721, but the rooms, though clean, respectably sized and perfectly tolerable, are bare and characterless.

Places to Stay – middle

Best value in this range – and therefore often full – is the *Hotel Colonial* (☎ (22) 46-47-09) at 4 Sur 105 on the corner of 3 Ote, a block east of the zócalo. Singles/doubles are US$28.50/33.50. Once part of a 400-year-old Jesuit monastery, it maintains a colonial atmosphere despite being comfortably modernised. Most of the 70 rooms are spacious and prettily tiled. All have TVs. Upstairs exterior rooms are among the brightest and best. The hotel has an old glass-domed dining room with a carved stone fountain and several attractive sitting areas. Ring between 9 am and 1 pm for a room reservation.

The 54-room *Hotel Royalty* (☎ (22) 42-47-40) is another well-kept colonial-style place, with friendly staff. You couldn't find a more central location: it's in the middle of the north side of the zócalo at Portal Hidalgo 8. Rooms are comfortable, with carpets and TVs, though mostly only moderately sized, and cost US$31.50/39. Prices are the same at the *Hotel Palacio San Leonardo* (☎ (22) 46-05-55) at Avenida 2 Ote 211, where the rooms are quite spacious and modern but unremarkable. The elegant lobby has a fountain and coloured glass ceiling.

The colonial *Hotel Del Portal* (☎ (22) 46-02-11) at Maximino Avila Camacho 205 on the north-east corner of the zócalo, has been modernised and raised its prices, which means it's now poorer value for money. Still, the rooms are comfortable, if small for US$38.50/45.

The 52-room *Hotel Lastra* (☎ (22) 35-97-55) at Calzada de los Fuertes 2633, two km north-east of the zócalo on the Hill of Guadalupe, is well worth considering for its peaceful location, good views and pleasant garden. Rooms (US$42/54) are comfortable, sizeable and come in assorted shapes. The walk to and from the city centre is agreeable enough but you'd probably want your own car or taxis if you plan a long stay.

Places to Stay – top end

The *Hotel Posada San Pedro* (☎ (22) 46-50-77) in a colonial building at 2 Ote 202, has a small pool and two restaurants but the rooms,

while pleasant, are none too big and some could be noisy. They cost US$66/70.75.

The three topmost hotels, all out of the centre, charge US$77/100. The best is generally reckoned to be the 190-room *Hotel El Mesón del Ángel* (☎ (22) 48-21-00, toll-free 800-22333) at Avenida Hermanos Serdán 807, six km north-west of the centre, ½ km off the Mexico City autopista. There are two pools, tennis courts, several restaurants and bars, etc. The others are the 400-room *Gran Hotel de Alba* (☎ (22) 48-60-55), three km nearer the centre at Avenida Hermanos Serdán 141, and the *Hotel Misión de Puebla* (☎ (22) 48-96-00) at 5 Pte 2522, which occupies three six-storey towers between 25 and 27 Sur in the Zona Esmeralda.

Places to Eat

Specialities Mole Poblano, found on almost every menu in Puebla and imitated Mexico-wide, is a spicy chocolate sauce usually served over turkey (pavo or guajolote) or chicken – a real taste sensation if well prepared. Supposedly invented by Sister Andrea de la Asunción of Santa Rosa Convent for a visit by the viceroy, it traditionally contains fresh chile, chipotle (smoked chile), pepper, peanuts, almonds, cinnamon, aniseed, tomato, onion, garlic and of course chocolate.

A seasonal Puebla dish, available in August and September, is chiles en nogada, said to have been created in 1821 to honour Agustín de Iturbide, the first ruler of independent Mexico. Its colours are those of the national flag: large green chiles stuffed with meat and fruit are covered with a creamy white walnut sauce and sprinkled with red pomegranate seeds.

An excellent place to sample Poblano food is the *Fonda Santa Clara* which has two branches on Avenida 3 Pte, at least one of them open every day and night of the week. Both have the same menu. The one at No 307 (☎ 42-26-59), which closes on Monday, is nearer to the city centre and usually busier, but the cooking at No 920 (☎ 46-19-19), which closes on Tuesday, is equally good. The Santa Clara's delicious mole Poblano comes with chicken for US$6 or on enchiladas for US$5.50. Other dishes we have enjoyed are mixiotes (seasoned lamb steamed in cactus leaves, with guacamole) for US$7.50 and succulent champiñones al ajillo (large mushrooms lightly fried with lots of garlic) for US$6. In April and May you can try gusanos de maguey and in March escamoles – respectively maguey worms and their eggs, prepared with avocados or hen eggs.

The little *Mesón de los Frailes* at Avenida 3 Pte 531 serves up cheaper but still tasty Poblano fare, and you'll be made welcome. Mole Poblano with chicken here is US$4, mixiotes US$5, and there's a four-course comida corrida for only US$2. There are non-Poblano dishes too – enchiladas US$2.75, meats US$4 to US$7, seafood and Pernod (!) soup US$6.75 – and it's open till 10 pm.

The *Restaurant Nevados Hermilo* (☎ 41-79-63), at the corner of Avenida 2 Ote and 4 Nte, is a Poblano favourite for its tortas (US$1.50), enchiladas in mole Poblano (US$5), consomé Atlixqueño (a chicken soup with floating chile, US$2.75), and tasty little cocktails called nevados – try Marijuana (mint and vodka) or Popocatépetl (tequila and mint), both US$1.50. Breakfast is good too – huevos a la Mexicana US$2, a good fruit cocktail US$1.50 – and so are steaks (US$7 to US$10).

Zócalo & Nearby The zócalo culinary highlight is *Vittorio's* (☎ 32-79-00) on the east side at Portal Morelos 106. This Italian-run restaurant bills itself 'La Casa de la Pizza Increible' in memory of a 20-square-metre monster pizza it baked as a stunt back in 1981, and the pizza it serves up today is still 'increible', with tasty, generous toppings on a light, crisp base. Prices are US$5 to US$7 for chico (one-person) size, US$8 to US$11 for mediana (two-person), US$13 to US$16 for grande (three or four-person). You can eat in or take away. Also on the menu are spaghettis (Bolognese US$3.50), and salads (verde US$1.75, Roquefort US$2.50).

The *Restaurant-Café El Vasco* in Portal Juárez on the opposite (west) side of the zócalo is the kind of place where couples and old friends meet for a chat – and worth a visit for a look at its bilingual menu alone. Sadly, the 'ostopussy into its own ink' which used to adorn this document has become plain old octopus but you can still feast on 'veal chicken friend steak', 'friend chicken 1/2', 'filet sol overflow', 'shrimps at curry' and 'pathé de foie grass'. The fare is good and the portions sizeable. Steaks and seafood are US$7 to US$10, enchiladas Suizas US$3.50, avocado with tuna and sardines US$6.

At the smart *Restaurant-Bar Royalty* (☎ 42-47-40), at Portal Hidalgo 10 on the north side of the zócalo, the octopus is simply 'into its tint'. Its outdoor tables are a good place to watch the world go by but the view doesn't come cheap – café con leche is US$1.50, breakfasts US$4 to US$7.

Just off the zócalo on Avenida 5 de Mayo, the *Café Foto Aguirre* is a busy but clean and orderly place popular with locals. A breakfast of a small orange juice, café con leche, scrambled eggs and bolillo costing US$3.75. The rest of the menu is of the typical antojitos, carnes, aves variety.

There's a *Sanborns* at Avenida 2 Ote No 6 and a *VIPs* in a beautifully restored 19th-century cast-iron building at the corner of Avenida 2 Ote and 2 Nte – and just east of VIPs on Avenida 2 Ote, three cheaper but good local places. The popular *La Concordia* does a range of four-course comidas corridas for US$2.75 to US$4; *La Grecia* has some interesting breakfast offers such as jelly, eggs, sweet bread and coffee for US$2; and the *Restaurant Venecia's* four-course comida corrida is also only US$2.

The *Café El Carolo* on Avenida Maximino Avila Camacho, less than a block east of the zócalo, serves up deluxe fruit salad with a tub of tasty plain yoghurt for US$3, and a good if small cappuccino for US$1. In the atmospheric old restaurant of the *Hotel Colonial* at the corner of Avenida 3 Ote and 4 Sur, US$3 buys you a breakfast of huevos, fruit, toast, butter, jam and coffee.

Elsewhere *El Vegetariano* at Avenida 3 Pte

525, open 8 am to 8 pm, has a long menu of meatless dishes like chiles rellenos, nopales rellenos (stuffed cactus ears), crepas or enchiladas Suizas, any of which comes with salad, soup and a drink for around US$4 or on its own for about US$ 2.50.

For a splash-out meal in semi-Westernised surroundings – enjoyed by many Mexicans – go to *Charlie's China Poblana* (☎ 46-31-59) at Juárez 1918 in the Zona Esmeralda. A good meal with wine from a Mexican and international menu will be US$20 to US$30. The Zona Esmeralda has lots more swish restaurants – including German, Italian and Chinese.

Until the Mercado Victoria reopens, the most central food market is the Mercado Cinco de Mayo at the corner of 18 Pte and 5 Nte.

Entertainment

Teorema at the corner of Avenida Reforma and 7 Nte is a bookshop-cum-café which fills up in the evenings with an arty/studenty crowd attracted by nightly live music from about 8.30 pm to 1 am. A pair of able guitar balladeers were in residence on our last visit. Snacks (cakes US$2) and drinks are sold.

The serious nightlife is at Cholula, a few km west (see separate section), and as a consequence the Puebla-Cholula road is an accident blackspot! The bar at Charlie's China Poblana restaurant at Juárez 1918 in the Zona Esmeralda has a reputation as a pick-up spot. At night mariachis lurk around the Callejón del Sapo, a pedestrian street between Avenidas 5 and 7 Ote, just east of 4 Sur.

For cultural events check the notice boards in the tourist office and Casa de la Cultura on Avenida 5 Ote and the university building on 4 Sur.

Things to Buy

Probably the prettiest Puebla ceramics are made, displayed and sold at a small work-

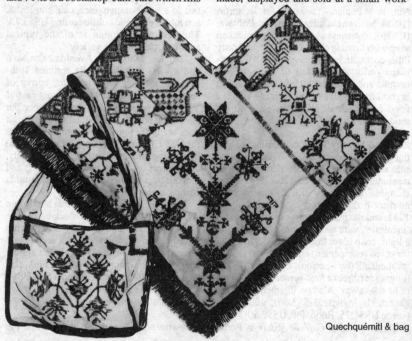

Quechquémitl & bag

shop at Avenida 18 Pte 111, a few doors from Santa Monica convent. Small square tiles cost from US$1.50 to US$3.50. The Uriarte Talavera workshop and showroom at Avenida 4 Pte 911, with similar prices, is also well worth a visit. It's open daily.

The city is also a good place to look for crafts from elsewhere in the state like Indian textiles, Tecali onyx, and pottery from Acatlán de Osorio, Amozoc, or Izucar de Matamoros. The trees of life made by Héron Martínez in Acatlán are probably the finest in the country. There's a good selling exhibition of the state's crafts in the tourist office at Avenida 5 Ote 3. The Creart shop on Avenida 7 Ote just east of Avenida 16 de Septiembre (its address is 16 de Septiembre 506-5) has a superb range of beautiful ceramics and glass from all over Mexico.

El Parián craft market between 6 and 8 Nte and Avenidas 2 and 4 Ote has, beside the sorts of leather, jewellery and textiles that you find in other cities, local Talavera, onyx and trees of life. Quality isn't the highest but prices are generally good. Callejón del Sapo, between Avenidas 5 and 7 Ote, just east of 4 Sur, is lined with shops selling antiques, old books and bric-a-brac.

The three smart shopping areas are the streets just north of the zócalo, the Zona Esmeralda, and the Plaza Dorada beside Boulevard Héroes del 5 de Mayo.

Getting There & Away

Air The only scheduled flights into Aeropuerto Hermanos Serdán, 22 km west of Puebla on the Cholula-Huejotzingo road, are daily to/from Guadalajara and Tijuana by AeroCalifornia. Mexicana (☎ 48-56-00) has an office at 23 Sur 506 on the corner of Avenida Juárez; Aeroméxico (☎ 32-00-13/14) is at Avenida Juárez 1514A.

Bus Puebla's big modern bus station, the Central de Autobuses de Puebla (CAPU), is four km north of the zócalo and 1½ km off the autopista, by the corner of Blvds Norte and Carmen Serdán.

To/From Mexico City Mexico City to Puebla buses use the capital's eastern terminal, TAPO. The 130-km trip takes around two hours. Three bus lines have very frequent services. The most straightforward are ADO's 1st-class directo service for US$3, every 10 or 20 minutes from 6 am to 10 pm, and AU's 2nd-class directo 'Premier' service, every five to 15 minutes from 6 am to 10 pm for US$2.75. Estrella Roja has four services of which one, the 'autopista' 2nd-class ordinario service (US$2.75), goes continuously 24 hours.

Buses from Puebla to Mexico City are pretty much the same in reverse. After 7 pm, there can be long queues for the Estrella Roja continuous autopista service. Estrella Roja runs buses to Mexico City airport every one or two hours from 4 am to 8 pm.

Other There are bus services from Puebla to just about everywhere in the south and east of Mexico, including:

Acapulco – 510 km, nine hours; one luxury (Gran Turismo) bus (US$30) and one 1st-class bus (US$11.75) daily by Autobuses Oro; five 2nd-class buses daily by ABC for US$10

Córdoba – 170 km, three hours; 11 1st-class buses daily by ADO for US$4.50, 30 2nd-class by AU for US$4

Cuernavaca – 180 km, three hours; four luxury (Gran Turismo) buses (US$11) and six 1st-class buses (US$4.75) daily by Autobuses Oro; hourly directo 2nd-class buses from 5 am to 8 pm by ABC for US$3.50

Mérida – 1390 km, 22 hours; one daily 1st-class bus by ADO for US$27.75

Oaxaca – 450 km, nine hours; five 1st-class locales daily by ADO and two by Cristóbal Colón, for US$8; three 2nd-class directos each by AU and ABC for US$7.25

Tampico – 730 km, 14 hours; one 1st-class bus daily by ADO for US$11.50

Tuxtla Gutiérrez – 1070 km, 17 hours; one 1st-class bus daily each by ADO (US$18.75) and Cristóbal Colón (US$19.50)

Veracruz – 300 km, five hours; one luxury afternoon departure by Uno for US$18; 10 1st-class buses daily by ADO for US$6.25; 15 2nd-class buses by AU for US$6

Villahermosa – 690 km, 12 hours; one luxury evening departure by Uno for US$45; five 1st-class ADO buses daily for US$15.75

Xalapa – 185 km, 3½ hours; one luxury morning
departure by Uno for US$12; eight 1st-class
buses daily by ADO for US$4; 13 2nd-class
buses daily by AU for US$3.75

Train The daily *El Oaxaqueño* Mexico City-
Oaxaca train is scheduled to leave Puebla at
11.30 pm and reach Oaxaca at 9.30 am, but
is usually an hour or so late out of Puebla and
two or three hours late reaching Oaxaca. It
therefore passes through the dramatic Sierra
Madre de Oaxaca in daylight. The reverse
trip from Oaxaca to Puebla is nearly all in
darkness, and the train's too slow to be useful
between Puebla and Mexico City.

Puebla-Oaxaca fares are primera especial
for US$8 (including breakfast but take your
own drinks), primera regular US$3.25.
Primera especial seats are sold at the station
from noon to 2 pm Monday to Friday and 11
am to noon on Saturday. Primera regular are
sold during the hour before the scheduled
departure. Camarines and alcobas are not
available. Don't confuse *El Oaxaqueño* with
the 10.30 pm train to Oaxaca which has only
primera regular and segunda (US$1.75)
classes, seats being sold in the hour before
scheduled departure.

Puebla station is in the north of the city,
about 200 metres north of the corner of 9 Nte
and Avenida 80 Pte. Ruta 1 'Estación Nueva'
colectivos take 20 minutes from 9 Sur at the
corner of Avenida 5 Pte in the city centre.
They run until about 9 pm. In the reverse
direction, board the colectivo about 200
metres straight ahead from the station
entrance and get off at Paseo Bravo. A taxi
between the station and zócalo is US$2.50.

Car Puebla is 130 km from Mexico City by
a fast toll autopista, Highway 190-D. There
are views of Iztaccíhuatl and Popocatépetl to
the south as you climb out of the Valley of
Mexico. East of Puebla, the toll highway
continues as 150-D to just east of Córdoba
(about 175 km), negotiating a cloudy,
winding 22-km descent from the 2385-metre
Cumbres de Maltrata en route, then joining
Highway 150 for the last 130 km to Veracruz.
The route to Veracruz via Xalapa is about 10

km shorter, but takes a bit longer because of
some potholed stretches between Puebla and
Xalapa.

Getting Around
Most hotels and places of interest are within
walking distance of the zócalo but you need
transport to/from the bus station. Simplest on
arrival at the bus station is to buy a taxi ticket
– US$2 to the zócalo – from the 'Boletos de
Taxi' kiosk in the main hall. You then join
the quick-moving taxi queue at the entrance.
For public transport, exit the bus station and
walk left along Boulevard Norte to its hectic
junction with Boulevard Carmen Serdán.
Here you have two options: either go straight
over to the far side of the junction and get a
'Blvd 5 de Mayo/Plaza Dorada' bus or colectivo, east along Boulevard Norte to
Boulevard Héroes del 5 de Mayo, where you
can get off at the corner of Avenida Maximino Avila Camacho, three blocks east of
the zócalo. Or turn right and get a 'Paseo
Bravo' colectivo south down Carmen Serdán
to Paseo Bravo, a park beside 11 Sur, five
blocks west of the zócalo. Either way the ride
is 15 to 20 minutes.

From the city centre to the bus station, get
any 'CAPU' colectivo from 9 Sur or 9 Nte,
four blocks west of the zócalo. All city buses
and colectivos cost 20c.

CHOLULA
Population: 40,000
Altitude: 2146 metres
Ten km west of Puebla stands the biggest
ancient pyramid in the Americas, the Great
Pyramid of Cholula. At 425 metres square
and 60 metres high it's even larger in volume
than Egypt's Pyramid of Cheops – though
because much of it is overgrown, and reconstruction has been limited, it's less
impressive than the pyramids of Teotihuacán. Cholula was one of the largest
cities and religious centres in pre-Hispanic
Mexico. Cortés vowed to build a church here
for each day of the year, or one on top of
every pagan temple, depending which
legend you prefer. At any rate there are 38 or
39 now. The village churches of Tonantzintla

and Acatepec, a few km south, are more splendid than any in Cholula itself.

Modern Cholula is scruffy but has more cosmopolitan services than most other small Mexican towns because the University of the Americas, with many North American students, is sited on its eastern fringe.

History

Between 1 and 600 AD Cholula grew into one of central Mexico's most important cities while powerful Teotihuacán flourished 100 km north-west. The Great Pyramid was built over several times. Around 600 AD Cholula fell under the sway of the Olmeca-Xicallanca who built nearby Cacaxtla but, some time between 900 and 1300, it was taken over by Toltecs and/or Chichimecs. Later it fell under Aztec dominance. There was also artistic influence from the Mixtecs to the south. The colourful glazed Mixteca-Puebla pottery was the finest in the land when the Spanish arrived: Moctezuma, it was said, would eat off no other.

In 1519 Cholula had a population of 100,000, although the Great Pyramid was

1 Colectivos to Puebla
2 Estrella Roja Bus Stop
  & Bus 'Chipilo' Stop
3 San Pedro Church
4 Café y Artes Los Portales
5 Hotel Calli Quetzalcóatl
6 Restaurant El Virrey
7 La Casona
8 San Gabriel Monastery
9 Museum
10 Hotel Las Américas
11 Villa Arqueológica
12 San Andrés Church

Cholula

0   250   500 m

already overgrown. Cortés, having made friends with the nearby Tlaxcalans, had travelled here at Moctezuma's request. But the Spanish had walked into an ambush, as Aztec warriors were waiting outside the city. Deciding to strike first, the Spanish launched the Cholula massacre, killing up to 6000 Cholulans before the city was looted by the Tlaxcalans.

After a severe plague in the 1540s, Cholula, overshadowed by the new city of Puebla, never regained its old importance.

Orientation & Information
Approaching Cholula from Puebla you can see the Great Pyramid, topped by a church, to your left. Buses and colectivos will drop you a short distance north of Cholula zócalo, 400 metres north-west of the pyramid.

For changing money you have a choice between Bancomer and Banamex on the zócalo, and the Casa de Cambio Azteca half a block south of it on 2 Sur. The post office is at Miguel Alemán 314, two blocks from the zócalo.

Great Pyramid
The pyramid, probably originally dedicated to Quetzalcóatl, is topped by one of the chapels built by the Spanish – a classic symbol of their conquest. You can ascend by a path from the pyramid's north-west corner, by the railway. The path and chapel are not part of the Zona Arqueológica, which includes tunnels under the pyramid, excavated and restored areas around it, and a small museum down some steps on its north side. Entry to the zona, from 10 am to 5 pm daily, is US$3.50 (free on Sunday and holidays).

Tunnels Archaeologists have burrowed eight km of tunnels beneath the pyramid. You can walk through some of them to see early layers of the building. Guides who approach you at the entrance, on the north side, can be useful in explaining the unlabelled structures in the bowels of the pyramid. They don't have an official fee but

expect a tip – US$2.50 or US$3 is reasonable.

Great Plaza The Great Plaza, or Patio de los Altares, on the south side, was the main approach to the pyramid. It is surrounded by platforms and unique diagonal stairways. Three large stone slabs on its east, north and west sides are carved in the Veracruz interlocking-scroll design. At its south end is an Aztec-style altar in a pit dating from shortly before the Spanish conquest. Human bones indicate this was possibly a sacrificial site.

One of the buildings just west of the plaza, not open to the general public, contains a 50-metre-long mural, probably from the 3rd century AD, depicting a drinking ceremony whose life-size participants are mostly naked and in an advanced state of inebriation. If you want to see it, try applying to INAH at 18 Pte 103 in Puebla (☎ 32-01-78).

Zócalo
San Gabriel Monastery, along the east side of Cholula's wide zócalo, includes three fine churches. On the left is the Arabic-style Capilla Real, dating from 1540, unique in Mexico with 49 domes. In the middle is the 17th-century Tercer Orden church, and on the right the San Gabriel church, founded in 1530 on the site of a pyramid. On the north side of the zócalo stands the parroquia (parish church) of San Pedro (1640).

Festivals
Cholula's firework-makers are renowned for their spectacular shows. There are said to be at least 10 festivals a year in each of its many churches. Among the most important is the Festival de la Virgen de los Remedios and regional feria in the first week of September, with daily traditional dances on the Great Pyramid.

Places to Stay
Cholula is a very easy day trip from Puebla but there are options if you fancy staying. *Hotel Calli Quetzalcóatl* (☎ 47-15-55) on the zócalo at Portal Guerrero 11 has good modern rooms, a dining room and a bar, all

Top: Puebla cathedral (PW)
Bottom: Boy outside barber's shop, Puebla (PW)

Top: Acapulco fort (TW)
Left: La Quebrada divers, Acapulco (TW)
Right: Acapulco (TW)

around a courtyard with a fountain. Doubles cost US$39. The best bottom end choice is the clean *Hotel Las Américas* (☎ 47-09-91) at 14 Pte 6, 2½ blocks east of the Great Pyramid. Singles/doubles are US$13/17. Rooms are a good size and comfortable, with TVs, and there's a pleasant courtyard and restaurant.

The 50-room air-conditioned *Villa Arqueológica* (☎ 47-19-66) at 2 Pte 601, a couple of fields south of the Great Pyramid, is one of the best hotels in the Puebla area, with tennis, swimming pool, and rooms at around US$80.

The well kept *Trailer Park Las Américas* (☎ 47-01-34), at 30 Ote 602 just off the Carretera Federal on the north edge of Cholula, charges US$10 for two people with all hook-ups.

Places to Eat

At the north end of Portal Guerrero on the zócalo, *Café y Artes Los Portales* is a friendly place whose English-speaking manager Roberto Malagón also gives out tourist info and puts on art exhibitions and sometimes live music. Good tortas are US$1.50 to US$2.75, and there are 10 breakfast menus, 18 types of coffee, yoghurt and some vegetarian dishes. Comida corrida is US$4 for four courses. Several other eateries along the portales offer pizza, tacos and almost anything else.

La Casona, a block south of the zócalo along Miguel Alemán, then half a block left at 3 Ote 9, is one of the best places in town, with tables in rooms around a pleasant courtyard. On offer are a variety of local specialities, or more straightforward main courses like steaks, for US$5 to US$8, plus soups and starters mostly for US$2 to US$4.

Entertainment

Cholula's student population makes it a nightlife centre for the Puebla area. The disco 'ghetto' comes to life about 10 pm from Thursday to Saturday, a couple of blocks east of the Great Pyramid in the streets around the corner of 14 Pte and 5 de Mayo. But probably the glitteriest place of all is Disco Porthos,

halfway back to Puebla. Cover price in the better establishments is about US$7.

Getting There & Away

Frequent colectivos to Cholula leave from the corner of Avenida 4 Pte and 11 Nte in Puebla. They cost US$0.25 and the ride is about 20 minutes. They drop you at the corner of 5 de Mayo and 10 Pte, three blocks from Cholula's zócalo. To return to Puebla, board one on 3 Nte at the corner of 8 or 10 Pte. They enter Puebla along 8 Pte: get off at the corner of 11 Nte. 'Puebla' buses passing the Great Pyramid go to Puebla bus station, not the city centre. In your own vehicle, the Vía Rápida Cholula is the quicker route from Puebla to Cholula.

Estrella Roja runs buses both ways between Mexico City (TAPO) and Puebla bus station via Huejotzingo and Cholula, every 15 or 20 minutes until 9 pm. In Cholula they stop at the corner of 3 Nte and 6 Pte. Mexico City to Cholula costs US$2.50.

AROUND CHOLULA
Tonantzintla & Acatepec

The small churches in these quiet villages, four and five km south of Cholula respectively, are among the loveliest examples of Puebla architecture. Both are open to visitors from 10 am to 1 pm and 3 to 5 pm.

The interior of the baroque church of Santa María Tonantzintla is among the most exuberant in Mexico. Under the dome, every available inch is covered with colourful stucco saints, devils, flowers, fruit, birds and more – a great example of Indian craftsmanship applied to Christian themes. Blue, white and gold are prominent colours. Tonantzintla holds a procession and traditional dances for the Festival of the Assumption on 15 August.

The church of San Francisco Acatepec, 1½ km south-east of Tonantzintla, dates from about 1730. Here, the exterior is the main attraction, with inspired use of blue, green and yellow Puebla tiles set in red brick on an ornate Churrigueresque façade. Some of the tiles are painted with animals and birds.

Getting There & Away Autobuses Puebla-Cholula runs 'Chipilo' buses from Puebla bus station to Tonantzintla and Acatepec. In Cholula you can pick them up at the corner of 6 Pte and 3 Nte. Between the two villages you can wait for the next bus or walk; it's only 1½ km.

Huejotzingo

Huejotzingo ('w eh-hot-ZIN-goh'), 14 km north-west of Cholula on Highway 150, was capital of a small pre-Hispanic state friendly with the Tlaxcalans at the time of the conquest. Huejotzingo is now a town of 25,000 known for its cider and sarapes.

The churchyard of its fine 16th-century Plateresque-style monastery has four posa chapels with Moorish-style alfizes, and the fortified church has Gothic ribbing on its roof. In the cloisters are some old frescoes and, upstairs, a small museum. On Shrove Tuesday, a masked Carnival dance in Huejotzingo re-enacts a battle between French and Mexicans. There's a cider festival there at the end of September. Market days are Tuesday and Saturday. See Cholula Getting There & Away for bus info.

CACAXTLA

Pieces of a highly coloured mural dug by looters in 1974 from unexplored hilltop ruins at Cacaxtla, 35 km north-west of Puebla and 20 km south-west of Tlaxcala, led archaeologists to one of the most exciting discoveries of recent decades in Mexico – a fortified ceremonial and palace complex of the 8th and 9th centuries AD, embellished with some of the most vivid, best-preserved pre-Hispanic paintings in the country.

History

Cacaxtla was the capital of a group of Olmeca-Xicallanca or Putún Maya, a Campeche-based, Maya-speaking, trading and seafaring people, probably no relation to the earlier Olmec. Some of them first came to central Mexico possibly as early as 400 AD and after the decline of Cholula about 600 AD (which they may have helped bring about), they became the chief power in

southern Tlaxcala and the Puebla valley. Cacaxtla peaked from 650 to 900 AD before being abandoned about 1000 or 1100 AD in face of possibly Chichimec newcomers.

Orientation & Information

From the car park it's about a 200-metre walk to the ticket office, small museum and cafeteria, then 500 metres to the main part of the site, a natural platform 200 metres long and 25 metres high called the Gran Basamento (Great Base). The site is open daily from 10 am to 5 pm, the museum has the same hours but is closed Monday. Entry to both is US$3.50 (free on Sunday and holidays). There are good explanatory signs in English as well as Spanish.

Gran Basamento

As you approach the Gran Basamento you pass an outlying pyramid on the right, then you cross one of the Gran Basamento's defence ditches.

On the Gran Basamento stood Cacaxtla's main religious and civil buildings and the residences of its ruling priestly classes. In front at the top of the entry stairs is an open space called the Plaza Norte. From here you follow a clockwise path round the Gran Basamento, passing first through El Palacio, which was living quarters of some kind. Bones of sacrificed children, associated with a cult of the rain god Tláloc, were found here. Murals showing plants with human heads, similar to the art of the Usumacinta basin in the Maya region, have been uncovered on a lower level immediately west of El Palacio. The path also passes a room with a clay lattice-window *(celosía)* unique in Mexico.

Building B Facing the north side of the Plaza Norte is this building with remains of a six-pillared portico and, flanking a stairway facing the plaza, the Mural of the Battle, dating from just before 750 AD. It shows people dressed as jaguars and birds engaged in a battle – probably a real one in which the Olmeca-Xicallanca were involved – which the jaguar-warriors, with round shields, are

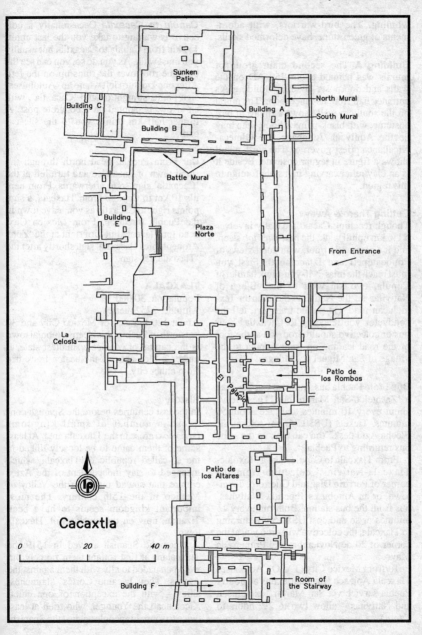

Sunken Patio

Building C

Building A

North Mural

South Mural

Building B

Battle Mural

Building E

Plaza Norte

From Entrance

La Celosía

El Palacio

Patio de los Rombos

Patio de los Altares

Cacaxtla

0   20   40 m

Building F

Room of the Stairway

winning. The bird-warriors, with adornments of green stone, have deformed skulls.

Building A The second main group of murals was painted about 750 AD on the walls and doorposts dividing Building A's entrance hall from its inner room. The mural on the southern wall shows a figure in bird costume, with black-painted body, who may be the Aquiyach Amapane, the Olmeca-Xicallanca priest-governor. The north mural shows a figure in jaguar costume. Beside it is an clay relief carving in a style foreign to this region.

Getting There & Away
Though reaching Cacaxtla usually involves a 1½ km uphill walk, the hike isn't *too* steep, and it's pleasantly rural, with good views of Popocatépetl and Iztaccíhuatl. First you must reach the miss-it-if-you-blink hamlet of Capula, two km west of the village of Nativitas on the Nativitas-San Martín Texmelucan road. On public transport, tell the conductor you're going to Cacaxtla. Your bus or colectivo should drop you at the foot of the road leading up from Capula to the village of San Miguel del Milagro.

Bus From Puebla bus station to Capula, take a 'Zacatelco-San Martín' bus. These leave about every 10 minutes and take about 50 minutes. Tickets (US$0.75) are sold at the Flecha Azul desk. You can pick up the same bus returning to Puebla.

From Tlaxcala to Capula, take a 'Texoloc-Tlaxcala-Nativitas' colectivo from the corner of Porfirio Díaz and Guerrero, downtown, or an Autobuses Tepetitla 'Nativitas' bus from the bus station. Both run every 15 minutes or so and cost US$0.50. Returning to Tlaxcala, the colectivo will drop you at the corner of 20 de Noviembre and Primero de Mayo.

To/from Mexico City (TAPO), Autobuses Tlaxcala Apizaco Huamantla runs an hourly Puebla service via San Martín Texmelucan and Nativitas – allow two to 2¼ hours to Capula.

Capula to Cacaxtla Occasionally a colectivo is waiting to take you the last uphill 1½ km from Capula to Cacaxtla, but usually you must walk. As you do so, you can see the big blue roof over the ruins up on the left. After one km, turn left where an 'Autobuses' sign points straight on and 'Cacaxtla', with an arrow, is painted on a concrete post. A further half km brings you to the site car park.

Car From Puebla, head north through the small town of Zacatelco and turn left at the 'Cacaxtla' sign soon afterwards. From here it's 10 km to Capula. From Tlaxcala, a sign points right to Cacaxtla as you leave town in the Puebla direction. From Mexico City, head for Tlaxcala but turn right at the 'Zona Arqueológica Cacaxtla' sign shortly after the 'Tlaxcala 25' sign.

TLAXCALA
Population: 30,000
Altitude: 2252 metres
About 120 km east of Mexico City and 30 km north of Puebla, this sleepy colonial town is the capital of Mexico's smallest state. It makes a pleasant, off-the-beaten-track trip from either city.

History
In the last centuries before the Spanish conquest, a number of small kingdoms *(señoríos)* arose in the Tlaxcala area. At least some of them came to be loosely linked in the so-called republic of Tlaxcala, which managed to stay independent of the Aztec empire that spread out from the Valley of Mexico in the 15th century. The most important kingdom seems to have been Tizatlán, now on the outskirts of Tlaxcala town.

When the Spanish arrived in 1519 the Tlaxcalans at first fought them fiercely but were persuaded to ally with them against the Aztecs. They became Cortés' staunchest allies – with the exception of one chief, Xicoténcatl the Younger, who tried at least twice to rouse his people against the Spanish, who hanged him in 1521. Xicoténcatl is now a Mexican hero.

The Spanish rewarded the Tlaxcalans with privileges and used them to help pacify Chichimec areas to the north. Tlaxcalans were among the early settlers in San Miguel de Allende, San Luis Potosí and Saltillo. In 1527 Tlaxcala became the seat of the first bishopric in New Spain, but a plague in the 1540s decimated the population and the town never played an important role again.

Orientation

Most things of use or interest are near two central plazas, which meet at the corner of Independencia and Diego Muñoz. The squarer of the plazas, surrounded by colonial buildings, is the zócalo, called the Plaza de la Constitución. The other more rectangular plaza is the Plaza Xicohténcatl. Tlaxcala's bus station (Central Camionera) is a km south-west of the town centre.

Information

The Tlaxcala state tourist office (☎ 2-00-27) is at the corner of Juárez and Lardizabal, just off the zócalo. It's open 9 am to 3 pm and 5 to 7 pm Monday to Friday and is helpful with leaflets and information, but the staff speak little English.

The post office is on the west side of the zócalo and Bancomer is at the zócalo's south-eastern corner. Banamex is on the south side of Plaza Xicohténcatl.

Zócalo

The zócalo is one of the best-looking in Mexico. Most of its north side is taken up by the 16th-century Palacio de Gobierno, inside which are vivid murals of Tlaxcala's history by local artist Desiderio Hernández Xochitiotzin. On the same side of the square, the Palacio Municipal, a former grain storehouse, has some fine 16th-century Moorish-style arches. Just off the zócalo's north-west corner is the pretty brick, tile and stucco parish church of San José, with one tower.

San Francisco Monastery

The Ex-Convento de San Francisco, as it's properly known, is up a short pathway, Calzada San Francisco, from the south-east corner of Plaza Xicohténcatl. This was one of Mexico's earliest monasteries, built between 1537 and 1540, and its church has a beautiful Moorish-style wooden ceiling. One side chapel, the Capilla del Tercer Orden, contains a font in which it is said the four chiefs of the republic of Tlaxcala were baptised. Next to the church is the Tlaxcala Regional Museum (open daily except Monday, 9 am to 5 pm, entry US$1.75).

Museum & Handicrafts Exhibition

The Museo de Artes y Tradiciones Populares on Boulevard Mariano Sánchez, opposite the end of Lardizabal, covers Tlaxcalan village life in some detail. Next door, the Casa de Artesanías sells modern handicrafts like pottery and textiles. Both are open 10 am to 5.30 pm daily except Monday. Museum entry is US$0.75.

Ocotlán Sanctuary

The Santuario de Nuestra Señora de Ocotlán is one of Mexico's most spectacular churches and an important pilgrimage goal. It stands on a hill a km from the zócalo where the Virgin is believed to have appeared in 1541. Take an Ocotlán bus or colectivo from the bus station, or walk north from the zócalo along Juárez for three blocks, then turn right up Zitlalpopocatl. The church's 18th-century façade is a classic example of Churrigueresque, with white stucco 'wedding-cake' decoration contrasting with plain red tiles, and towers that look so top-heavy you wonder how they stay up.

Inside, the area before the main altar and the Camarín de la Virgen behind it (the 'dressing room' for the image of the Virgin which stands on the main altar in memory of the 1541 apparition) are riots of gilded and coloured decoration. The 18th-century Indian Francisco Miguel spent 25 years decorating the *camarín* and altarpieces. On the third Monday in May the Virgin's image is

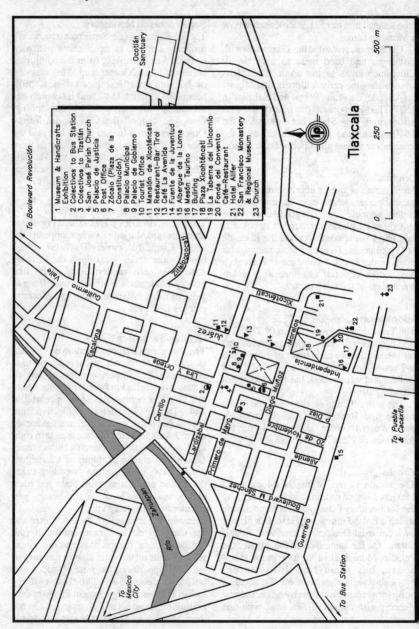

1 Museum & Handicrafts Exhibition
2 Colectivos to Bus Station
3 Colectivos to Tizatlán
4 San José Parish Church
5 Palacio de Justicia
6 Post Office
7 Zócalo (Plaza de la Constitución)
8 Palacio Municipal
9 Palacio de Gobierno
10 Tourist Office
11 Mansión de Xicoténcatl
12 Restaurant–Bar Tirol
13 Café La Avenida
14 Fuente de la Juventud
15 Albergue de la Loma
16 Mesón Taurino
17 Bullring
18 Plaza Xicohténcatl
19 La Taberna del Unicornio
20 Fonda del Convento
21 Café–Restaurant
21 Hotel Alifer
22 San Francisco Monastery & Regional Museum
23 Church

To Boulevard Revolución

Tlaxcala

500 m

250

0

Valle

Guillermo

Escalona

Carrillo

Lira y Ortega

Lardizábal

Primero de Mayo

20 de Noviembre

Diego Muñoz

Allende

Boulevard M Sánchez

Guerrero

Río Zahuapan

Zitlalpopocatl

Juárez

Morelos

Independencia

Xicoténcatl

To Boulevard Revolución

To Puebla & Cacaxtla

To Mexico City

To Bus Station

Ocotlán Sanctuary

carried round other churches in a procession that attracts many pilgrims and onlookers.

Tizatlán

The scanty remains of Xicoténcatl's HQ stand on a small hill four km north of the town centre, with views of three volcanoes if the weather's clear. Take a 'Tizatlán' colectivo (US$0.10) from Tlaxcala bus station or from the corner of Primero de Mayo and 20 de Noviembre behind the parish church. Get off at the bottom of a lane on the left leading up to a church with a yellow dome.

In the remains of a palace are two altars with some faded frescoes in Mixteca-Puebla style showing gods like Tezcatlipoca (Smoking Mirror), Tlahuizcalpantecutli (Morning Star) and Mictlantecuhtli (Underworld).

San Estéban Church next to the ruins has a 16th-century Franciscan *capilla abierta* with frescoes showing angels playing medieval instruments. There's also a small religious art museum and a statue of Xicoténcatl the Younger looking out towards La Malinche. Everything's closed on Mondays.

La Malinche

The dormant 4450-metre volcano named after Cortés' Indian interpreter and lover is 30 km south-east of Tlaxcala and 30 km north-east of Puebla. Its long, sweeping slopes dominate the skyline north of Puebla.

The approach to the summit is from the Tlaxcala-Huamantla road. Only three or four hours' relatively easy walking are needed if you have a vehicle. Turn south from Highway 136, halfway along its 26-km stretch between Apizaco and Huamantla. From this turn-off there's 15 km of road (mostly paved) past a microwave radio station and a government resort, IMSS La Malintzin. The road becomes impassable at 3000 metres. Then it's 1000 metres by footpath, through trees at first, on to the ridge leading to the summit. La Malinche has snow only for a few months of the year.

Places to Stay

Tlaxcala's cheapest option is the *Mansión Xicoténcatl* (☎ 2-19-00) at Juárez 15. Biggish but slightly grubby rooms are US$10.75/13.50. The modern *Hotel Alifer* (☎ 2-56-78) at Morelos 11 has very clean rooms, friendly management and its own restaurant. Rooms are US$13.50/18.50. The *Albergue de la Loma* (☎ 2-04-24), on a small height overlooking the town at Guerrero 58 on the corner of 20 de Noviembre, charges US$10.75/17.25. Rooms are big with clean, tiled bathrooms, and the exterior ones are bright.

The more expensive places are on Blvd Revolución, the northward continuation of Juárez and Valle. *Jeroc's Hotel* (☎ 2-16-77) at No 4B and *Challet's Hotel* (☎ 2-03-00) at No 3 both charge around US$30 a double.

Places to Eat

The *Restaurant-Bar Tirol* on Juárez, next to the Mansión Xicoténcatl hotel, has good food at reasonable prices. There's a three-course comida corrida for US$2.50; à la carte choices range from spaghetti dishes at US$2 to US$4 to shrimps stuffed with cheese (US$5.50) or steaks at US$6 to US$7.75. It's open till 10 pm. The US$2 comida corrida at the *Café La Avenida*, just along the street, is also popular.

On the zócalo the *Fuente de la Juventud* (no sign) has loud rock music, and chess in the back room, but the fare is dull. Better for snacks is the *Fonda del Convento Café-Restaurant* on Calzada San Francisco. Probably the classiest place in town is the *Mesón Taurino* at Independencia 15, just off Plaza Xicohténcatl, with elegant décor and helpful waiters. Pasta or queso fundido costs US$2 to US$3, fish or meat US$4 to US$6, a few other dishes up to US$8.

Getting There & Away

Only 2nd-class buses serve Tlaxcala. Flecha Azul and Autobuses Puebla-Tlaxcala-Calpulalpan run a joint directo service to/from Puebla every few minutes for US$0.75. Autobuses Tlaxcala-Apizaco-Huamantla (ATAH) runs an hourly 'directo numerado' service to/from Mexico City (TAPO) from 6.30 am to 7.30 pm, costing US$2.50 for the two-hour trip, and an ordinario service every 15 minutes.

Getting Around
Colectivos and buses within Tlaxcala cost US$0.10. Most colectivos at the bus station go to the town centre. You can get off at the corner of Independencia and Diego Muñoz, where the two central plazas meet. Returning to the bus station from the centre, catch a colectivo on the corner of Lira y Ortega and Lardizabal.

SIERRA NORTE DE PUEBLA
The Sierra Norte de Puebla covers much of the remote northern arm of Puebla state. The mountains often rise over 2500 metres before falling away to the Gulf coastal plain. Even though some of the land is deforested, it's fertile and beautiful with pine forests at higher altitudes and luxuriant semi-tropical vegetation lower down.

The area has a high Indian population, mostly Nahua and Totonac. The ancestors of these Nahua are thought to have reached the Sierra Norte in the 14th century, probably from the Valley of Mexico and southern and central Puebla. For more on the Nahua see the introduction to this chapter; for the Totonacs see the Gulf Coast chapter.

Sierra Norte handicrafts – among them *rebozos*, quechquémitls, wood-carving and baskets – are sold in markets at Cuetzalan, Zacapoaxtla, Teziutlán, Tlatlauquitepec and elsewhere, as well as in Puebla and Mexico City.

A trip to the Sierra Norte could be combined with visiting Xalapa or El Tajín. The main town is Teziutlán, but Cuetzalan is the most attractive initial destination. Some places in the lower-lying far north of Puebla state are covered under 'Northern Veracruz to Pachuca' in the Gulf Coast chapter.

Cuetzalan
The colonial town of Cuetzalan, 1200 metres high in a lush coffee-growing area and dominated by its large church, is famed for its Sunday market which draws Nahua and Totonac Indians from many miles around. Flowers, embroidered blouses and quechquémitls are just a few of the items bargained over.

Yohualichán Eight km from Cuetzalan by a poor dirt road, this is the only known pre-Hispanic site with a pyramid of niches similar to El Tajín, 50 km north-east. It's in seven tiers, less impressive than its famous cousin, beside a plaza with more pyramids on the other sides. Traces of the original red paint remain and some restoration has been done. The site is open Wednesday to Sunday. The modern town plaza of Yohualichán is adjacent.

Festivals For several days around 4 October Cuetzalan holds lively celebrations of the festival of San Francisco de Assisi, combined with the Feria del Café y del Huipil. A traditional dance festival in mid-July attracts groups from all over the area. Among the dances is the Quetzales, whose performers wear huge circular headdresses of feathers, ribbons and reeds. On special occasions like these, Nahua women of Cuetzalan wind strips of fabric known as *maxtahual* into their hair to raise it up to a hat-like appearance.

Places to Stay Singles/doubles are around US$15/20 in the *Posada Las Garzas* on the zócalo at the corner of Guadalupe Victoria and 2 Abril, the *Posada Jackelin* next door and the *Posada Cuetzalan* (☎ 1-01-54) at Zaragoza 8. The Posada Cuetzalan is the only one where all the rooms have private baths: ring ahead if you're keen to stay on a weekend. There are also the *Hotel Rivello* at Guadalupe Victoria 3 and the *Hotel Marquéz* at Alvarado 11.

Getting There & Away Cuetzalan is where the paved roads end, some 50 km north of Highway 129 from a turning 50 km north of Oriental and 45 km west of Teziutlán. Three 2nd-class buses of the Teziutecos line make the 4½-hour trip from Puebla each day for

US$4. Autotransportes México-Texcoco has a daily evening departure from Mexico City (TAPO) to Cuetzalan for US$6.

SOUTHERN PUEBLA
Tepeaca & Tecali

Tepeaca (population 16,000, altitude 2256 metres), 40 km east of Puebla on Highway 150, has a big Friday market noted, among other things, for its *metates* (grinding stones) and *petates* (mats). There's also a Franciscan monastery. Lineas Unidas del Sureste buses go from Puebla. The village of Tecali, 11 km south-west of Tepeaca, is a centre for the carving of onyx from the nearby quarries. Stalls and shops in the plaza and on the roadside sell the stuff.

Tehuacán

In the high, dry Tehuacán Valley in southeast Puebla, archaeologists have traced the beginnings of agriculture in Mexico in detail. Caves, rock shelters and other sites show that probably by 7000 BC a few small groups were moving around the valley with the seasons, eating plant foods and hunting animals such as horses, jack rabbits and antelope. By 7000 to 5000 BC they were planting avocados, chiles, cotton and squashes, and around 5000 BC cultivating the first tiny forms of maize. Later, stone metates were made for grinding these crops. Pottery, the sign of a truly settled existence, appeared about 2000 BC.

Modern Tehuacán, 115 km from Puebla on the way to Oaxaca, is a sizeable spa of 80,000 people, 1677 metres high and famed for its mineral waters sold in bottles all over Mexico. It has a fine zócalo, Parque Juárez, a block east of the main intersection where Independencia (running east-west) meets Reforma (north-south). The Museo del Valle de Tehuacán, explaining the finds of the archaeologists led by Richard MácNeish in the 1960s, is in the Ex-Convento del Carmen, two blocks north and one west of the zócalo. Among the exhibits are tiny cobs of maize which were among the first to be cultivated.

Places to Stay At the bottom end, the *Hotel Madrid* (☎ 2-00-72) at 3 Sur 105 has singles/doubles for US$7/9. A little dearer is the *Hotel Posada de Tehuacán* (☎ 2-04-91) at Reforma Nte 213, a block west of the zócalo then 1½ blocks north. The *Hotel Iberia* (☎ 3-15-00) at Independencia 211, just east of the zócalo, is old but cared-for, with rooms for US$11/13.50, some round a courtyard.

At the top end it's hard to beat the *Hotel México* (☎ 2-00-19), at Independencia Pte 101, on the corner of Reforma a block west of the zócalo, where rooms are US$35/40. There's a good restaurant, and the comfortable rooms mostly face a central patio. The roof garden has a lion fountain modelled on the famous one in the Alhambra Palace in Granada, Spain.

Getting There & Away Thirty 1st-class ADO buses come from Puebla daily for US$2.50, as well as frequent 2nd-class services by AU. ADO runs four buses daily from to/Veracruz (US$4.25, 3½ hours). Its station is at Independencia 119. All Puebla-Oaxaca buses go through Tehuacán. From Tehuacán they take either a longer but smoother route via Huajuapan de León, or a slightly quicker but rougher one through Teotitlán del Camino. The Tehuacán-Orizaba road crosses the dramatic Cumbres de Acultzingo where it zig-zags 800 metres down an often cloudy mountainside in just four km.

Atlixco

The Atlixcáyotl festival on the last weekend in September on the Cerro de San Miguel at Atlixco, 31 km from Puebla on Highway 190 to Huajuapan de León, is a chance to see many traditional costumes, dances and music from Puebla state and further afield. Atlixco has 50,000 people and is known for its avocados and near-perfect climate.

XALAPA (JALAPA)
Population: 250,000
Altitude: 1427 metres

Cool, clean and civilised, Xalapa (sometimes spelt Jalapa, always pronounced

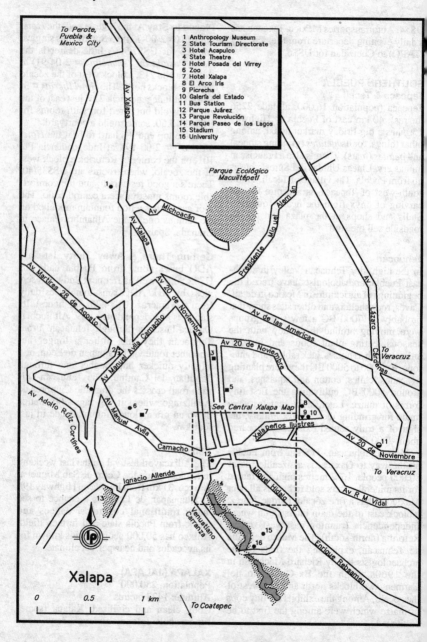

To Perote,
Puebla &
Mexico City

Av Xalapa

Parque Ecológico
Macuiltépetl

Av Michoacán

Av Xalapa

Presidente Miguel Alemán

Av Lázaro

Av Martires 28 de Agosto

Av 20 de Noviembre

Av de las Americas

Av Manuel Ávila Camacho

Av 20 de Noviembre

To Cárdenas

Av Adolfo Rúiz Cortines

Av Manuel Ávila
Camacho

See Central Xalapa Map

Xalapeños Ilustres

Av 20 de
Noviembre

Ignacio Allende

Miguel Hidalgo

To Veracruz

Av R M Vidal

Venustiano Carranza

Enrique Rebsamen

1 Anthropology Museum
2 State Tourism Directorate
3 Hotel Acapulco
4 State Theatre
5 Hotel Posada del Virrey
6 Zoo
7 Hotel Xalapa
8 El Arco Iris
9 Picrecha
10 Galería del Estado
11 Bus Station
12 Parque Juárez
13 Parque Revolución
14 Parque Paseo de los Lagos
15 Stadium
16 University

Xalapa

0   0.5   1 km

To Coatepec

'ha-LAP-a') is one of Mexico's least-known gems. A hill-country colonial city and the capital of Veracruz state, it has been home to the Universidad Veracruzana (University of Veracruz) since 1944 and enjoys a lively artistic and entertainment scene, a convivial café life and some good restaurants. Its setting on the semi-tropical slope between the coast and the central highlands makes for a pleasant environment, allowing fine parks and panoramas – though peak hour traffic can be as vile as anywhere!

Many people come to Xalapa just to see its superb anthropology museum, but leave wishing they had allowed more time to get to know the town.

A pre-Hispanic town became part of the Aztec Empire around 1460. Cortés and his men passed through in 1519. The Spanish town didn't take off until the annual trade fair of Spanish goods was held here from 1720 to 1777. Today Xalapa is a commercial hub for the coffee and tobacco grown on the slopes, and well known for its flowers.

Orientation

The bus station is on 20 de Noviembre two km east of the centre. The city centre is on a hillside with Parque Juárez more or less in the middle of things. The main streets include Enríquez, which crosses the north side of Parque Juárez, and Zaragoza which heads east from it. Two other important streets are Revolución and Dr Lucio, heading uphill (north) from Enríquez either side of Xalapa's cathedral. Most hotels, restaurants and places of interest are within a few minutes' walk of Parque Juárez, the big exception being the anthropology museum.

Information

Tourist Office There's a helpful, English-speaking tourist information kiosk in the bus station. The State Tourism Directorate (☎ (281) 8-72-24) at Manuel Avila Camacho 191, equally far from the centre in the opposite direction, should also be able to answer questions.

Money Rates at the Casa de Cambio Jalapa at Gutiérrez Zamora 36, are better than at most casas de cambio in other cities. It's open Monday to Friday 9 am to 1 pm and 4.30 to 6.30 pm.

Post & Telecommunications The main post office, open 8 am to 7 pm Monday to Friday and 9 am to 1 pm Saturday, is in the Palacio Federal on the corner of Gutiérrez Zamora and Diego Leño. Next door on Gutiérrez Zamora is the Centro de Servicios Integrados de Telecommunicaciones, with public fax, telex and telegram services, open 9 am to 8 pm Monday to Friday and 9 am to noon Saturday. There's a clutch of Ladatel phones on the wall of the Palacio de Gobierno, on Enríquez facing Dr Lucio.

City Centre

Parque Juárez, a formal garden on a terrace overlooking the town below, is the best place to imbibe the Xalapeño atmosphere and get your bearings. The pillared Palacio Municipal (City Hall) faces its north side; the Palacio de Gobierno on its east side is the seat of the Veracruz state government. Facing the Palacio de Gobierno across Enríquez is the 1772 cathedral, from where Revolución and Dr Lucio both lead up to the bustling area around and above the market. Coming down from there you can descend steps from Dr Lucio to Madero and return to Enríquez by older little streets like Callejón Diamante.

Galería del Estado

The Veracruz state art gallery was opened in 1991 in a fine renovated colonial building on Xalapeños Ilustres a km east of the centre, just past Arteaga. If its exhibitions continue to be as good as the early display we saw of Rufino Tamayo's graphic work, the gallery will be a major attraction. Hours are 10 am to 7 pm daily except Monday.

Anthropology Museum

The Museo de Antropología de la Uni-

versidad Veracruzana (☎ 5-49-52), devoted
to the archaeology of Veracruz state, is one
of the best museums in Mexico. Its large
collection includes no fewer than seven huge
Olmec heads, and its spacious layout is a
textbook example of museum design.

The museum is a long, low grey building
with a fountain outside, on the west side of
Avenida Xalapa four km north-west of the
city centre. Take a 'Tesorería-Centro-SEP'
bus (cream with a red stripe, US$0.25) from
the Restaurant Terraza Jardín on Enríquez.
The same or a blue-striped 'Centro' colectivo
will return you to the centre. The museum is
open 10 am to 5 pm daily except Monday;
admission is US$1.75 (free on Sunday). It
has an excellent bookshop.

The exhibits, in a series of galleries
descending a gentle slope, are arranged in a
general south-to-north order. You reach the
Olmec material, from southern Veracruz,
first, and the El Tajín display near the
bottom. The largest Olmec head here, from
San Lorenzo, is 2.7 metres high. Another San
Lorenzo head is pocked with hundreds of
small holes, thought to be a deliberate muti-
lation at the time of San Lorenzo's fall. Apart
from many more fine Olmec carvings, other
museum highlights include an array of beautiful *yugos* and *hachas* from central
Veracruz, murals from the Classic Veracruz
centre Las Higueras, and a collection of huge
Classic-period pottery figures from El
Zapotal.

Parks

Just a block south of Parque Juárez is **Parque
Paseo de los Lagos**, winding a km along
either side of a lake, with the Universidad
Veracruzana campus above it. At its northern
end is the Casa de Artesanías, where local
handicrafts are shown and sold. **Parque
Ecológico Macuiltépetl**, in the north of the
city, occupies the highest ground in Xalapa
– the thickly-treed cap of an old volcano. The
park is 800 metres east of Avenida Xalapa
along Michoacán: the turning is about 200
metres back towards town from the anthropology museum. Paths spiral to the top
where there are good views.

Places to Stay – bottom end

Xalapa has a good range of budget lodgings.
The central *Hotel Limón* (☎ (281) 7-22-07)
at Revolución 8 has small tiled rooms and a
tiled courtyard with a fountain and trees. It's
clean, rooms have private bath and hot water
and the management is friendly. Singles are
US$6, doubles US$7.50 with one bed,
US$9.50 with two. A km up the hill from the
centre, the *Hotel Acapulco* (☎ (281) 5-16-
41) on Julian Carrillo between Revolución
and Dr Lucio has absolutely basic and bare
but very clean, well-kept rooms, all with
private bath. Singles are US$6.75, doubles
US$8.75 with one bed, US$11 with two.

The central *Hotel Continental* (☎ (281)
7-35-30) at Gutiérrez Zamora 4 is a friendly,
shabby place with a roofed courtyard and big
rooms. Some are much better than others and
traffic noise at the front is hideous. Most are
bare and mildly decayed but kept clean
enough. All have private baths but hot water
is very erratic. Singles/doubles/triples are
US$7.75/11/14.50. What a beautiful place
this *could* be.

The best rooms in the bottom end – good,
clean and spacious, with hot water – are at
the *Hotel Principal* (☎ (281) 7-64-00), also
central at Zaragoza 28. Singles or doubles
with one bed cost US$13.50, with two beds
US$15. Beware noise in street-side rooms.

Places to Stay – middle

The large *Hotel Salmones* (☎ (281) 7-54-31)
at Zaragoza 24 has a small garden, big lobby,
restaurant and rooms with carpets, phones
and sometimes TV. Singles/doubles are
US$16.75/20. The *Hotel Posada del Virrey*
(☎ (281) 8-61-00) at Dr Lucio 142, about
700 metres uphill from the city centre, is a
comfortable modern hotel with TV in rooms,
a bar and restaurant. Rooms are only moderately sized but not bad value at US$23.50/30.

The number-one downtown hotel is the
114-room *Hotel María Victoria* (☎ (281) 8-
60-11) at Zaragoza 6. Very clean though not
huge rooms with phone, TV and air-conditioning or heating cost US$27.75 to US$31
single, US$33.50 to US$36.75 double.
There's a restaurant and bar, too.

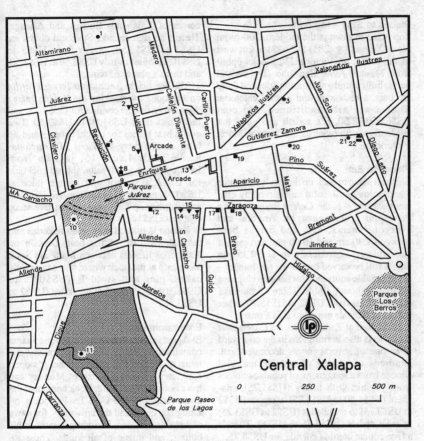

Central Xalapa

0   250   500 m

1	Market
2	Taquería El Coral
3	Dauzón
4	Hotel Limón
5	Mariscos El Estacionamiento
6	Palacio Municipal
7	Restaurant Terraza Jardín
8	Cathedral
9	Palacio de Gobierno
10	El Agora
11	Casa de Artesanías
12	Hotel María Victoria
13	Café Nuevo
14	Restaurant Monroy
15	Café y Restaurant La Parroquia
16	La Casona del Beaterio
17	Hotel Salmones
18	Hotel Principal
19	Hotel Continental
20	Casa de Cambio Jalapa
21	Centro de Servicios Integrados de Telecommunicaciones
22	Post Office

Places to Stay – top end

Top place in town is the modern, 200-room *Hotel Xalapa* (☎ (281) 8-22-22), a km west of the centre on Victoria 1½ blocks uphill from Manuel Avila Camacho. The central part is built round a swimming pool and there are bars, a restaurant and a good cafeteria. Rooms are air-conditioned and cost US$65.50/72.50. It's stylish and good but not really worth twice as much as the María Victoria.

Places to Eat

The best place to soak up the city's ambience – and enjoy good, solid fare served by efficient waiters – is the *Café y Restaurant La Parroquia* at Zaragoza 18. Anyone and everyone meets, eats and drinks here between 7.30 am and 10.30 pm, and even if you squeeze breathlessly in at 10.25 pm you'll still be served one of the set dinners – say vegetable soup and chicken and chips for US$6 – without quibble. There's a range of set breakfasts from US$2 to US$5.75; other snacks and meals are up to US$8 or so.

Next door at Zaragoza 20, *La Casona del Beaterio* is also inviting. Sit in the courtyard or in one of several rooms decorated with hundreds of photos of old Xalapa, and choose from a long menu of reliable choices from yoghurt with honey (US$1.25), spaghetti (US$1.50 to US$2.25) or crepes (US$2 to US$3.75) to enchiladas (US$2 to US$3.25) or meat dishes (US$3.75 to US$8). There's a five-course comida corrida for US$4.75.

Also on Zaragoza, the clean *Restaurant Monroy* concentrates on antojitos; there's also a four-course comida corrida for US$4. The Monroy and the *Aries Restaurant* in the Hotel María Victoria along the street are both open 24 hours. Good for late night coffee or snacks is the *Café Nuevo* on Enríquez, open till 12.30, with antojitos from US$1.50 to US$2. A plate of sweet breads comes with Nescafé con leche – you pay for what you eat.

A km east of the city centre but well worth the walk for its candlelit, mildly Bohemian atmosphere and good Italian and Mexican food at reasonable prices is *Picrecha*, on the corner of Xalapeños Ilustres and Arteaga. There's no sign outside. Spaghetti dishes are US$3 to US$3.50, pizzas from US$5 to US$10, antojitos mostly US$2.50 to US$3.50, and there's plenty of wine.

The big, bright *Restaurant Terraza Jardín* on Enríquez overlooking the Parque Juárez does a five-course comida for US$4.25, and breakfasts from US$1.50 to US$3.50. Two of the best places for quick, cheap stand-up bites are the busy *Mariscos El Estacionamiento* at Dr Lucio 15, just up from Enríquez, with good-value shrimp cocktails for US$2.50, carrot and orange juice at US$0.75, and tortas, and *Taquería El Coral* a bit further up Dr Lucio, where five tacos cost just US$1.50 to US$2.

Xalapa is littered with good bakeries and cake shops. One of the best, *Dauzón* on Xalapeños Ilustres between Mata and Soto, has a café at the back where you can sample cakes, pies and strudels (US$0.75 to US$1.50) or down a full breakfast (US$2 to US$3.50).

Entertainment

El Agora, an arts centre in the Parque Juárez containing a cinema, theatre and gallery, is a focus of Xalapa's busy arts scene. It's open 8.30 am to 9 pm daily except Monday and has a bookshop and café. Look here, or at the notice board in the Café La Parroquia on Zaragoza, or around the university, for news of what's on in town including theatre, exhibitions, and music of all kinds. The state theatre (Teatro del Estado Ignacio de la Llave), at the corner of Manuel Avila Camacho and De la Llave, stages performances by the Xalapa Symphony Orchestra and the Ballet Folklórico de la Universidad Veracruzana.

Getting There & Away

Air The nearest airport is Veracruz.

Bus Xalapa's gleaming, modern, well-organised bus station, known as CAXA (Central de Autobuses de Xalapa) for short, is two km east of the city centre on 20 de Noviembre. Departures include:

Mexico City – 315 km, five hours; three luxury buses daily by Uno for US$21; 24 1st-class buses daily by ADO for US$7

Papantla – 260 km, 5¼ hours; nine 1st-class buses daily by ADO for US$5.25

Puebla – 185 km, 3¼ hours; 11 1st-class buses daily by ADO for US$4; 12 2nd-class directo buses by AU for US$3.75

Tampico – 540 km, 11 hours; two 1st-class buses daily by ADO for US$11.50

Veracruz – 100 km, two hours; 1st-class buses by ADO every 20 or 30 minutes from 5.30 am to 10 pm for US$2.25

Villahermosa – 575 km, nine hours; six 1st-class buses daily by ADO for US$11.50

Other places served by ADO include Acayucan, Campeche, Catemaco, Córdoba, Fortín de las Flores, Mérida, Orizaba, Poza Rica, San Andrés Tuxtla and Santiago Tuxtla. AU goes to Salina Cruz.

Car Xalapa is 185 km from Puebla by Highways 140 and 150-D. There are some potholed stretches between Puebla and Perote. The Veracruz-Xalapa roads are better: the quickest route is Highway 140 via Paso de Ovejas. Coming to Xalapa from the northern Gulf coast, it's easiest to follow Highway 180 to Cardel, then turn inland, but the inland Highway 127 via Martínez de la Torre is likely to be more scenic.

Car rental firms in Xalapa include Renta Car Xalapa (☎ 4-11-61) at Lázaro Cárdenas 696 and Acmosa (☎ 5-11-55), which rents Nissans, at Avenida Xalapa 564.

Getting Around

For buses from the bus station to the city centre, walk to the foot of the bus station's approach road: the stop is a few metres to the right on 20 de Noviembre. Any microbus, bus or colectivo combi saying 'Centro' will take you within a short walk of Parque Juárez. All microbus rides are US$0.25.

A taxi from the bus station to the centre is US$1.25. If the queue immediately outside the bus station is too slow, walk down to 20 de Noviembre, where you won't have to wait long.

To return to the bus station from the city centre or the anthropology museum, take a 'Tesorería-SEP-Centro' microbus (cream with a red stripe). The most central stop is on Zaragoza, a few metres west of the Hotel María Victoria. Any 'CAXA' bus east along Zaragoza will get you to the bus station too.

AROUND XALAPA
Cofre de Perote

Cofre de Perote is a 4282-metre-high volcano south-west of Xalapa. The name means 'coffer', which is what its summit looks like. A rough dirt road (initially Calle Allende) from the town of Perote, 50 km west of Xalapa on Highway 140 to Puebla, climbs 1900 metres in 24 km to just below the summit.

Coatepec & Xico

Coatepec, 15 km south of Xalapa, is known for its locally-grown coffee and orchids. The María Cristina orchid garden, on the main square, is open daily. The 40-metre Texolo waterfall is a pleasant two-km walk through coffee plantations from Xico, a small town in verdant surroundings eight km south of Coatepec.

Buses of the Excelsior line go about every 15 minutes to Coatepec or Xico from Parque Revolución, about a km west of the centre along Allende.

ORIZABA

Population: 175,000
Altitude: 1219 metres

Orizaba is an industrial and transport centre 16 km west of Córdoba, with a few colonial buildings and lots of church domes rising above its streets – a lively, pleasant town, without any compelling attractions.

There was an Aztec garrison here from the mid-15th century. Later the Spanish founded a town to guard the Veracruz-Mexico City road. Orizaba developed as an industrial centre in the late 19th century and some of the area's factories were early centres of the unrest that led to the unseating of dictator Porfirio Díaz. Today it has big brewery, cement, textile and chemical industries.

Orientation

The central square, Parque del Castillo, has the parish church of San Miguel on its north side. Madero, running down the west side of the parque, and Avenidas Pte 7 and Ote 6, crossing Madero three blocks south of the parque, are the busiest streets. The market is just north of the parque, in the block east of Madero and north of Ote 5.

Information

There's a tourist office in the Casa Consistorial, on Norte 1 between Pte 2 and 4, behind the Palacio Municipal (Town Hall). It's open 10 am to 1.30 pm and 5 to 7 pm Monday to Friday, and 10 am to 1 pm Saturday. The post office is at the corner of Sur 7 and Ote 2.

Things to See

The iron and steel **Palacio Municipal** (Town Hall), off the north-west corner of Parque del Castillo, was the Belgian pavilion at the Paris International Exhibition in the late 19th century. Orizaba bought it for 105,000 pesos and had it dismantled, shipped across the Atlantic and rebuilt.

San Miguel, the big parish church on the north side of Parque del Castillo, is mainly 17th century in style with several towers and some Puebla-style tiles. The 18th-century **La Concordia, El Carmen** and **Santa Gertrudis** churches all have Churrigueresque façades.

You can arrange to tour the big **Cervecería Moctezuma** brewery at Pte 7 and Sur 10 by calling 5-11-50 or 5-10-38. The formal **Alameda** park is four blocks west of the centre along Colón.

The **Centro Educativo Obrero** (Workers' Education Centre) on Colón between the Parque del Castillo and the Alameda, has a 1926 mural by Orozco.

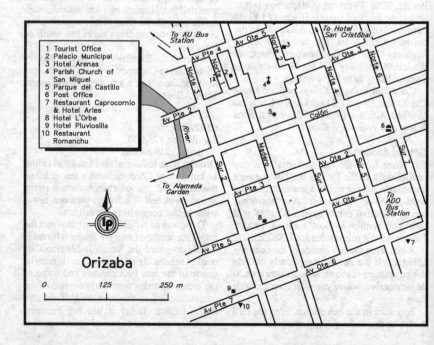

1 Tourist Office
2 Palacio Municipal
3 Hotel Arenas
4 Parish Church of San Miguel
5 Parque del Castillo
6 Post Office
7 Restaurant Caprocornio & Hotel Aries
8 Hotel L'Orbe
9 Hotel Pluviosilla
10 Restaurant Romanchu

Orizaba

0   125   250 m

Pico de Orizaba

Mexico's highest mountain, 5700-metre Pico de Orizaba, is often visible to the north-west from Orizaba. It's a dormant volcano with a small crater, a permanent snow-cap and a seasonal pattern similar to Popocatépetl. The only higher peaks in North America are Mt McKinley in Alaska and Mt Logan in Canada.

The mountain is popular with climbers but is not for hikers. The most common route to the top is a steep, crevasse-ridden glacier. The main approach is from the village of Tlachichuca (2700 metres), 23 km east of the Xalapa-Puebla road. From Tlachichuca a rough dirt road, requiring 4WD, leads 23 km east to two huts at Piedra Grande (4230 metres) on the north flank of the mountain, from where the ascent is six to nine hours. Señor José Amador Reyes (☎ Tlachichuca 26) can arrange lodging in Tlachichuca and transport to Piedra Grande. He has two representatives in Mexico City, Señor Francisco Reyes Rodríguez (☎ 595-12-03) and Señora Ofelia Carlín de Mulliert (☎ 595-13-97). Coordinadores de Guías de Montaña (☎ 584-46-95) at Tlaxcala 47 in Colonia Roma, Mexico City, can provide guides for the mountain.

Places to Stay

Orizaba's best bottom-end value is the *Hotel Arenas* (☎ 5-23-61) at 169 Norte 2, half a block south of Ote 5. It's family-run and friendly, with a tropical courtyard garden. Clean rooms with bath are US$8.25 single, US$11 to US$14 double. The *Hotel San Cristóbal* (☎ 5-11-40) at 243 Norte 4, half a block north of Ote 5, has clean rooms with bath for US$8.25 single or double.

Middle-range places include the *Hotel L'Orbe* (☎ 5-50-33) at 33 Pte 5, with air-conditioned rooms with TV from US$25 single, US$30 double. The *Hotel Pluviosilla* (☎ 5-52-65) at 163 Pte 7 has rooms for US$20.50/22.50 round a central courtyard where you can park a car.

Places to Eat

Most restaurants are along Madero, Sur 3

and Pte 7/Ote 6; they usually close by 8.30 pm. One of the best is the *Restaurant Romanchu* opposite the Hotel Pluviosilla on Pte 7. The Hotel Pluviosilla has its own restaurant, *La Borda*, where quite substantial breakfasts cost from US$4.50, dinners from US$6.50 to about US$10. *Restaurant Capricornio*, attached to the Hotel Aries at 265 Ote 6, does moderately tasty pizza ranging from US$3.50 for a small cheese pizza to US$10.50 for a large Napolitana.

Getting There & Away

Bus Most buses out of Orizaba are de paso. The 1st-class ADO bus station is at 577 Ote 6 between Sur 11 and 13. AU (2nd-class) is at 425 Zaragoza Pte. To reach the town centre from AU, turn left outside the station, take the first fork right and head for the church domes two or three blocks ahead. Outbound services include:

Córdoba – 16 km, 30 minutes; 20 1st-class buses daily by ADO for US$0.50; 50 2nd-class buses daily by AU for US$0.50

Mexico City – 285 km, four hours; about 30 1st-class buses daily by ADO for US$7.25; about 40 2nd-class buses daily by AU for US$6.50

Puebla – 155 km, 2½ hours; eight 1st-class buses daily by ADO for US$4; about 30 2nd-class buses daily by AU for US$3.75

Veracruz – 150 km, 2¼ hours; 18 1st-class buses daily by ADO for US$3; 20 2nd-class buses daily by AU for US$2.75

Xalapa – 242 km, four hours; seven 1st-class buses daily by ADO for US$4.25

There are also 1st-class services to Tehuacán, Oaxaca, Tuxpan, Catemaco, Villahermosa, even Mérida.

Train Orizaba is on the route of the El Jarocho night sleeper between Mexico and Veracruz. Add or subtract 50 minutes from Córdoba schedules. The station is south of the city centre at the corner of Pte 19 and Sur 10.

Car Autopista 150-D by-passes central Orizaba, heading east to Córdoba and west to Puebla (145 km). Highway 150 runs east to Córdoba and Veracruz (140 km), and south-west to Tehuacán, 65 km away over the hair-raising Cumbres de Acultzingo (see Tehuacán).

FORTÍN DE LAS FLORES

Population: 16,000
Altitude: 970 metres

From April to June the gardens, *viveros* (nurseries) and plazas of Fortín ('forr-TEEN') de las Flores blossom with a riot of gardenias, orchids, camellias, azaleas and more. In these months Fortín is a good place to stop between the highlands and the coast. There's a week-long flower festival at the end of April and start of May. Year-round, Fortín is a weekend retreat for the Mexico City middle class.

Information & Orientation

Fortín is seven km from Córdoba (the two places nearly run into each other) and 11 km from Orizaba. It has a big open plaza, the Parque Central, with the Palacio Municipal (town hall) in the middle and a church at the south end. The Córdoba-Orizaba Highway 150 runs across the north end of the parque as Avenida 1; Avenida 3 goes across the middle; Avenida 5 forms the south end. Calle 1 runs down the west side of the parque, Calle 3 down its east side. There's a market area a block south of the parque and a couple of blocks east.

Places to Stay & Eat

The *Hotel Bugambilia* (☎ (272) 3-05-22), two blocks east of the Parque Central at the corner of Avenida 1 and Calle 7, has ordinary singles/doubles with private bath but no fan for US$9.50/11.50.

Hotel Fortín de las Flores (☎ (272) 3-00-55, 3-01-08), on Avenida 2 between Calles 5 and 7, one block north and 1½ east of the north-east corner of the Parque Central, is a good middle range hotel with gardens, table tennis and a gardenia-strewn pool with bar and tables. All 66 rooms have fans, some have a balcony and/or air-conditioning. A fan room is US$26.75/33.50. You can get a full meal in the hotel restaurant for as little as US$5.

The *Hotel Posada Loma* (☎ (272) 3-06-58) is one km out of town, set back above Highway 150 towards Córdoba. The rooms are in bungalows in big gardens; singles cost US$35, doubles US$35 to US$48. Facilities include swimming pool and a squash court.

There are a few restaurants along Calle 1, both on the Parque Central and north of it, and a Chinese restaurant at the corner of Avenida 1 and Calle 5.

Getting There & Away

You can reach Fortín de las Flores by bus or train.

Bus Frequent blue 'Fortín' buses (U$$0.20) leave the corner of Calle 3 and Avenida 5 in Córdoba for the 15-minute trip to Fortín. Going back, buses leave from the upper half of the west side of Fortín's Parque Central. There are also frequent buses to/from Orizaba.

The ADO (1st-class) bus station is at the corner of Avenida 2 and Calle 4, two blocks west of the Parque Central along Avenida 1, then one block north. There are seven de paso buses daily to Mexico City (US$7.75), three each to Veracruz (US$2.50) and Puebla (US$4.50), and nine to Xalapa (US$3.25).

Train Like Córdoba, Fortín is on the El Jarocho route. Add or subtract 30 minutes from Córdoba schedules. The station is two blocks north of the north-west corner of the Parque Central on Calle 1 Norte.

CÓRDOBA

Population: 150,000
Altitude: 924 metres

Córdoba ('CORR-do-ba'), 126 km from Veracruz in the foothills of Mexico's central mountains, has a long colonial history and a pleasant enough centre but Xalapa and Puebla are more interesting stopovers – though the verdant, dramatic hill country around the town is enticing.

History

Córdoba was founded in 1618 by 30 Spanish families to stop attacks by escaped black slaves on travellers between Mexico City and the coast. It's known as La Ciudad de los Treinta Caballeros (City of the 30 Knights). Today it's a prosperous commercial and processing centre for sugar cane, coffee and tobacco from the surrounding hillsides and fruit from the lowlands.

Orientation

Everything of importance is within a few blocks of the central Plaza de Armas. The parroquia (parish church) occupies the plaza's south-east end. Streets running north-west to south-east are called Avenidas; Calles are at right angles to Avenidas.

Information

The Cámara Nacional de Comercio, Servicios y Turismo (☎ (271) 2-11-47) at 308 Calle 5, between Avenidas 3 and 5, can give some tourist information. It's open 9 am to 1 pm and 4 to 7 pm Monday to Friday, 9 am to 1 pm Saturday.

The post office is at 3 Avenida 3 just north-west of the Plaza de Armas, open 8 am to 8 pm Monday to Friday and 9 am to 1 pm Saturday and Sunday.

The market is bounded by Calles 7 and 9 and Avenidas 8 and 10. Shops are in the blocks south-east of the Plaza de Armas.

Hotel Zevallos

This is not a hotel but the former home of the Condes (Counts) of Zevallos, built in 1687. It's on the north-east side of the Plaza de Armas, now partly occupied by the Café Parroquía.

Plaques in the courtyard record that Juan O'Donojú and Agustín de Iturbide met here after mass on 24 August 1821 and agreed on terms for Mexico's independence from Spain. O'Donojú, the new viceroy, had concluded it was useless for Spain to try to cling to its colony; Iturbide was the leader of the anti-imperial forces, a former royalist general who had changed sides. Contrary to the Plan de Iguala, in which Iturbide and Vicente Guerrero had proposed a European monarch as Mexican head of state, O'Dono-

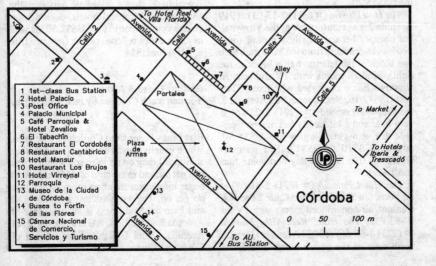

1 1st-class Bus Station
2 Hotel Palacio
3 Post Office
4 Palacio Municipal
5 Café Parroquia & Hotel Zevallos
6 El Tabachín
7 Restaurant El Cordobés
8 Restaurant Cantabrico
9 Hotel Mansur
10 Restaurant Los Brujos
11 Hotel Virreynal
12 Parroquia
13 Museo de la Ciudad de Córdoba
14 Buses to Fortín de las Flores
15 Cámara Nacional de Comercio, Servicios y Turismo

Córdoba

jú and Iturbide agreed that a Mexican could hold that office. Iturbide went on to a brief reign as Emperor Agustín I.

Other Sights

The 18th-century **Portales** stretching down from the Hotel Zevallos are lively with a string of busy cafés. Draughts is the favourite game here. The big late-18th-century **Parish Church** in the Plaza de Armas, La Parroquía de la Inmaculada Concepción, has famously loud bells. The **Museo de la Ciudad de Córdoba**, in a 17th-century house at 303 Calle 3, has a small, well displayed collection including Classic Veracruz palmas.

Places to Stay

Rooms in the *Hotel Mansur* (☎ (271) 2-60-00), on the Plaza de Armas at 301 Avenida 1, aren't enormous but are well kept and the lobby is elegant. Singles or doubles with a TV, phone and air-conditioning are US$17/20.75. The *Hotel Virreynal* (☎ (271) 2-23-77), also on the plaza, facing the parroquia at the corner of Avenida 1 and Calle 5, has spacious and clean but bare rooms with tiled floors, private bath and fan for US$15/20.

The *Hotel Iberia* (☎ (271) 2-13-01) at 919 Avenida 2 is as comfortable as the Virreynal, but cheaper because it's less central (only two blocks downhill from the Virreynal, then one block to the left and half a block to the right). Modern rooms with TV and pointed windows line a courtyard with trees. They cost US$12/16. Next door at 909 Avenida 2, the *Hotel Tresscadó* (☎ (271) 2-23-66) is very bare and a bit smelly but maybe tolerable for a night. Singles are US$8.50, doubles US$10 to US$12. Hot water is limited to five hours a day and some fans don't work.

The *Hotel Palacio* (☎ (271) 2-31-68) at the corner of Avenida 3 and Calle 2 has big, pleasant, air-conditioned rooms with TV for US$30/35. The *Hotel Real Villa Florida* (☎ (271) 4-66-66) at 3002 Avenida 1, 1.5 km north-west of the centre where Avenida 1 meets Highway 150, has tasteful, modern, air-conditioned rooms for about US$45/55, attractive gardens, a cafeteria and a restaurant.

Places to Eat

The *Restaurant Virreynal* in the Hotel Virreynal is popular at breakfast and also for its excellent comida corrida (US$4.50), of which an example is vegetable soup, two enchiladas, rice, beef with bananas, and jelly or flan.

The Plaza de Armas portales are lined with cafés and restaurants where you can dine and drink the local coffee in a variety of ways. The long menu at the *Restaurant El Cordobés* for instance includes meat filetes (US$10), spaghetti (US$3 to US$6) and seafood cocktails (US$5 to US$7). Its five-course comida corrida is good value at US$5. At the top of the portales, *El Tabachín* makes a speciality of freshwater prawns (langostinos).

Just off the Plaza de Armas the *Restaurant Cantabrico* at 11 Calle 3 is a tasteful place with piped music and plenty of choice of fish and meat in the US$5 to US$10 range as well as antojitos. *Restaurant Los Brujos* at 306 Avenida 2, down an alley between the Mansur and Virreynal hotels, does a four-course comida corrida for US$2.50, as well as meat, chiles rellenos or fish (mojarra frito is tasty) for US$4.

Getting There & Away

You can reach Córdoba by bus, train or car.

Bus Many buses from Córdoba are de paso, which usually means waiting around the bus station till they come in to see whether you can get on, and in the case of AU (2nd-class) buses may mean standing-room only if you *do* get on. The 1st-class bus station (ADO and Estrella Azul lines) is at the corner of Avenida 3 and Calle 4. AU is at the corner of Avenida 7 and Calle 9. Services out of Córdoba include:

Mexico City – 305 km, 4½ hours; two luxury morning departures by Uno for US$21; hourly 1st-class buses by ADO for US$7.50; 29 directo 2nd-class buses (16 locales, 13 de paso) daily by AU for US$7

Oaxaca – 317 km, seven hours; two 1st-class buses daily by ADO for US$7.75; one 2nd-class evening departure by AU for US$6.50

Orizaba – 16 km, 30 minutes; 19 1st-class buses daily by ADO for US$0.50; 50 2nd-class buses daily by AU for US$0.50

Puebla – 175 km, three hours; 18 1st-class buses daily, including five locales, by ADO for US$4.50; 42 2nd-class buses daily including seven locales by AU for US$4.25

Veracruz – 125 km, two hours; 13 1st-class buses daily, including five locales, by ADO for US$2.50; 20 2nd-class buses daily by AU for US$2.25

Xalapa – 200 km, 3½ hours; five 1st-class buses daily by ADO and nine by Estrella Azul for US$3.50

Train The El Jarocho night sleeper between Mexico City and Veracruz (see Veracruz in the Gulf Coast chapter) stops at Córdoba. Eastward, it is scheduled to leave Córdoba at 4.30 am; westward, at 11.30 pm. A camarín from Mexico City costs US$12.50 for one person. The station is at the corner of Avenida 11 and Calle 33 in the south of the town.

Car The toll autopista 150-D from Puebla bypasses Fortín de las Flores and Orizaba. Highway 150 from Veracruz continues west from Córdoba through those towns to Tehuacán.

Mexico City to Acapulco

The route from Mexico City to Acapulco passes through the states of Morelos and Guerrero. Coming from Mexico City, Highways 95 and 95D climb more than 3000 metres from the Valley of Mexico and into refreshing pine forests; as you leave the valley, look back at the capital for a breathtaking view before the descent into the Valley of Morelos and the city of Cuernavaca, capital of Morelos.

Either Highway 95 or Highway 95D can be used to reach Cuernavaca, 1½ hours' drive from Mexico City. After Cuernavaca, Highway 95 heads south through Taxco, joining Highway 95D again at Iguala, from where both continue as Highway 95 through Chilpancingo and on to Acapulco, 400 km south of Mexico City.

The trip straight through from Mexico City to Acapulco takes seven hours on the bus, somewhat less if you're driving. The toll road, Highway 95D, is the faster route, missing out on the mountainous twists and turns that take you to Taxco. A new toll highway, the *autopista*, under construction in 1992, is planned to reduce the driving time between Mexico City and Acapulco by several hours.

There are several interesting places to see along the way, which could break up the journey into an interesting few days. Most places in the state of Morelos are close enough to Mexico City to be visited in a day trip, though they're also popular places to stay a few days, providing a pleasant relief from the smog, traffic and crowds of the national capital. Cuernavaca, the capital of Morelos, has lively plazas, beautiful colonial-style architecture, sidewalk cafés and the imposing palace of Hernán Cortés, now a museum.

Morelos' surrounding towns and countryside are also interesting. They include the pre-Columbian ruins of Teopanzolco, Xochicalco and Tepozteco; Tepoztlán, a mystical town steeped in Aztec, Tlahuica and

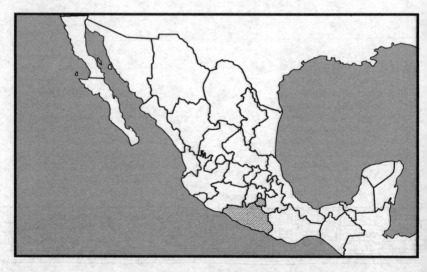

colonial history, with the Dominican ex-Convento cathedral; Cuautla, a bustling market town known for its sulphurous *balnearios* (swimming areas); and Oaxtepec, a tiny town with a huge holiday resort complex featuring 25 swimming pools, some sulphurous.

Crossing into the state of Guerrero, the old Spanish mining town of Taxco is famed for its fine silverwork, the extravagant Churrigueresque Catedral de Santa Prisca, and for its winding, cobblestoned streets, reminiscent of Old Spain; the government of Mexico has declared the entire city a national historical monument. Further on towards the coast are Iguala and Chilpancingo, two other cities important in Mexico's history.

Acapulco, of course, is a world-famous holiday destination, and the granddaddy of Mexico's Pacific coast resorts. Growing rapidly, the city now boasts over a million inhabitants, beaches, nightlife and a thriving tourism industry.

Also in the state of Guerrero is the smaller town of Zihuatanejo, 239 km north-west up the coast from Acapulco, on a beautiful bay of the same name. It's one of the Pacific's most pleasant towns, with nearby Ixtapa an expensive resort designed especially to bring big-spending tourists to Mexico. You can stay economically in Zihuatanejo, though, spend a few cents to reach Ixtapa on the local bus, and enjoy Ixtapa's beaches just as easily as if you were staying there.

Morelos

Morelos is named after José Maria Morelos y Pavón, a mestizo priest who was a follower of Miguel Hidalgo's 1810 rebellion and, after Hidalgo was executed in 1811, the leader of the independence movement. Although Chilpancingo, in the neighbouring state of Guerrero, became the site of the constitutional congress (the Congress of Chilpancingo, 1813), much of his support came from peasants in the area of the present state of Morelos. He was able to use this area as both a base and refuge until Spanish royalist forces caught and executed him in 1815.

Morelos followed a long line of Aztecs and Spaniards who considered this area, especially Cuernavaca, either a refuge from political problems or a holiday retreat or.

Before Cortés built a palace in Cuernavaca in 1531, the Tlahuica and Aztec Indians established religious centres in Morelos, with the construction of pyramids and temples in Xochicalco, Tepoztlán and Cuauhnáhuac (now Cuernavaca). In the 18th century the Taxco silver magnate José de la Borda, king of Mexico's silver mines, was attracted to Morelos by the pleasant climate and established a palatial residence and beautiful garden in Cuernavaca, later used by Emperor Maximilian and Empress Carlota. During the revolutionary years, Morelos was a favourite stomping grounds for Emiliano Zapata and his rebellious Zapatistas.

Today, Morelos is still a popular refuge for international celebrities and *chilangos* (residents of Mexico City). Covering 4941 square km, the state is one of Mexico's smallest and most densely populated; despite its small size it is a prominent agricultural centre, particularly for fruits, vegetables, maize (corn), rice, sugar cane and wheat. Much of the state lies on the steep southern slopes of the central Mexican plateau. Small valleys at different elevations throughout Morelos have give it a variety of micro-climates, which make the area suitable for a variety of fruits, vegetables and grains.

Guerrero

The state of Guerrero, named after the Independence War hero General Vicente Guerrero, is a mountainous area of 64,281 square km. Four mountain ranges dominate the state, the most important being the Sierra Madre del Sur, which parallels the Pacific Ocean from the Río Balsas border with Michoacán to the border with Oaxaca.

If you're travelling from the interior to the coast, on the western side of the Sierra Madre be prepared for the descent from the relatively cool, dry air of the mountains to the hot, humid, tropical climate of the coast.

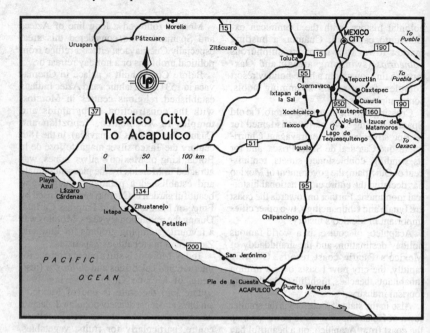

CUERNAVACA

Population: 280,000
Altitude: 1542 metres

Before the Spanish conquistadores arrived in the early 1520s Cuernavaca was inhabited mostly by Tlahuica Indians, who called their city Cuauhnáhuac or 'Place at the Edge of the Forest'. The surrounding valley was filled with trees which, according to legend, whispered when the wind rustled the leaves. The symbol for speech in the Indians' pictographic language was a three-branched tree; today this is the city's shield.

In 1521, shortly after conquering the Aztecs, Cortés torched the city and renamed it Cuernavaca, a more pronounceable (to the Spanish) version of its original name. Destroying the city pyramid, Cortés used the stones to build a fortress-palace on the pyramid's base, a strong message to the natives that there had been a shift of power. He also constructed from the rubble a large cathedral, the Catedral de la Asunción, also

quite a fortress; in the 1520s there was not much reason to trust in the benign favour of the new Catholic converts. Cortés also introduced sugar cane and more efficient agricultural methods, which eventually transformed Cuernavaca into a major colonial agricultural centre.

Early in its history, Cuernavaca became a refuge for the rich and powerful from Mexico City. The German Baron Alejandro von Humboldt called Cuernavaca 'the City of Eternal Spring' for its flowers and benign climate. The Taxco silver magnate José de la Borda, said to have been the richest man in Mexico at one time in the 18th century, built a lavish home and garden here, the Jardín Borda, which was later lived in by Emperor Maximilian and Empress Carlota.

In this century, Cuernavaca achieved literary fame as the setting for Malcolm Lowry's novel *Under the Volcano*, published in 1965 and later made into a widely acclaimed film of the same name.

Cuernavaca is still a haven for people from the capital, especially the rich, who have built magnificent estates in Cuernavaca over the centuries. With modern transport, the number of visitors has increased, especially on weekends, when hotel rooms can be hard to come by, elbow-to-elbow crowds flow through the zócalo, and patrons at sidewalk cafés can't take a sip without an aggressive pedlar waving blankets, cheap paintings or doilies in their faces.

During the week the situation is not much better; the construction of an industrial complex just outside the city, and the massive influx of former Mexico City residents since the 1985 Mexico City earthquake, have brought to Cuernavaca many of the capital's problems, including crowding, traffic, smog and crime.

Cuernavaca is still worth visiting though, if only to see the famed Palacio de Cortés and some other historic sights. You can also enjoy some good restaurants and sidewalk cafés, and stroll through the zócalo. Cuernavaca is also famed for its many language schools – this is one of the principal places in Mexico where foreigners come to learn Spanish, and the city has 17 different language institutes to choose from.

Orientation

Cuernavaca is 85 km south of Mexico City, a 1½-hour drive on Highway 95 or Highway 95D. If you're on Highway 95D, the autopista or toll road which circles Cuernavaca on its way to Acapulco, take the Cuernavaca or Highway 95 exit. Highway 95 runs right through the centre of town. Entering from the north, Highway 95 becomes Boulevard Emiliano Zapata and then one-way (northbound) Avenida Morelos. Turn off onto Avenida Matamoros, or onto Rayón or Hidalgo, to reach the zócalo.

If you come in by bus, getting to the zócalo will depend on which bus line you came with; all four bus companies have different terminals, but all are within easy walking distance of the zócalo.

The zócalo, also called the Plaza de Armas

or Plaza de la Constitución, is the heart of the city and the best place to begin a tour of Cuernavaca.

Information

Tourist Office The Dirección General de Turismo (☎ (73) 14-38-60, 14-39-20, 14-38-72) at Avenida Morelos Sur 802 is a few blocks south of the cathedral and one block north of the Estrella de Oro bus station. It's open Monday to Friday from 9 am to 3 pm and 6 to 8 pm; weekends from 9 am to 6 pm with fewer staff. The staff are helpful and can provide heaps of information on hotels, language schools, archaeological sites, balnearios (swimming areas) and cultural activities in Morelos.

The same office operates a small information kiosk in the Plaza de Armas, opposite the Palacio de Cortés; it's open every day from 9 am to noon and from 3 to 6 pm.

Post & Telecommunications The post office is on the south side of the Plaza de Armas. It's open Monday to Friday from 8 am to 7 pm, Saturday 9 am to 1 pm.

Telegraph, telegram and fax services are offered in the telecomunications building, next door to the post office. Hours for sending or receiving telegrams are Monday to Friday from 9 am to 2 pm and 3 to 5 pm, Saturday from 9 am to noon. Fax services are offered Monday to Friday from 9 am to 2 pm and 3 to 8 pm, Saturday from 9 am to 1 pm.

There are several public telephones in front of the post office. Local or long distance (national or international) telephone calls can be made from the caseta de larga distancia at the Farmacia Central, on Galeana facing Jardín Juárez; it's open every day from 7 am to 10 pm.

Laundry The Euro Klin laundry (☎ 14-06-22) is at Avenida Morelos Sur 801, on the corner of Morelos and Calle del Zapote, a couple of blocks north of the tourist office. It's open Monday to Saturday from 7 am to 9 pm, Sunday from 10 am to 6 pm; cost for wash, dry and fold is US$4 for 3.5 kg or US$6.35 for seven kg.

To
Mexico
City

Ricardo Linares

1

2

Avenida

Morelos

I. Valle

Madero

G. Farias

Victoria

Guerrero

Cuailla

Arco

del Parque

Jardín de la
Estación F F C C

López Mateos

Arista

3

Matamoros

López Mateos

4

Boulevard Ayala

Degollado

Salinas

5
Aragón y León

6

Morrow

No. Reelección

Arteaga

Zarco

8

Tejada

9

11
12

Juan Gutemberg

Atlacomulco

Cuauhtémoc

Rayón

13
14

15

16

18
17

19

Salazar

20

Hidalgo
21

22

Netzahualcóyotl

23

24

Las Casas

Juárez

20 de
Nov

25

26

Abasolo

27

Alvaro Obregon

Motolinia

28

Galeana

Leyva

Humboldt Palmira

Cuauhtémotzin
29

Cuernavaca

0   250   500 m

Approximate Scale

González Bocanegra

30

Avenida

Morelos

Sur

31

Nimno

Nacional

32

San Juan

To Acapulco

■ **PLACES TO STAY**

1 Motel Los Canarios & Restaurant
   Julius
2 Hotel & Restaurant Las Mañanitas
5 Motel Royal
6 Hotel Colonial
14 Hotel Iberia
23 Hotel Juárez
27 Posada de Xochiquetzal
28 Hotel Papagayo

▼ **PLACES TO EAT**

7 Restaurant La India Bonita
8 Restaurant Vienés, Los Pasteles del
   Vienés
11 Restaurant La Parroquia
12 Harry's Grill
15 Restaurants El Portal, La Cueva,
   Pollo y Más
24 Restaurant Vegetariana & Restaurant
   Taxco
25 Restaurant Casa de Campo

OTHER

3 Flecha Roja Bus Station
4 Mercado
9 Farmacia Central (long distance
   telephones)
10 Jardín Juárez
13 Cinema Morelos
16 Palacio del Gobierno
17 Post Office & Telecomm Building
18 Plaza de Armas (Zócalo)
19 Palacio de Cortés/Museo de
   Cuauhnáhuac
20 Jardín Borda
21 Catedral de la Asunción
22 Palacio Municipal (City Hall)
26 Autos Pullman de Morelos Bus
   Station
29 Estrella Roja Bus Station
30 Euro Klin laundry
31 Dirección General de Turismo
   (Tourist Office)
32 Estrella de Oro Bus Station

Plaza de Armas (Zócalo)

The Plaza de Armas, also called the Plaza de la Constitución or simply the zócalo, is Cuernavaca's main plaza. It is flanked on the east by the Palacio de Cortés, on the west by the Palacio del Gobierno (the seat of the state government), and on the north by a smaller plaza, the Jardín Juárez.

Jardín Juárez

The small Jardín Juárez, on the north-west corner of the zócalo opposite the Palacio del Gobierno, is a smaller plaza sporting a gazebo designed by Gustave Eiffel, of Eiffel Tower fame. You can get a simple snack from one of the booths on the gazebo's ground floor, or sit at one of the sidewalk cafés facing the plaza and watch the people flow by. At sunset there's a cacophony of birds in the trees.

Palacio de Cortés – Museo de Cuauhnáhuac

Cortés' imposing medieval-style fortress stands at the south-eastern end of the Plaza de Armas. Construction of this two-storey

stone palace was accomplished between 1522 and 1532, on the base of a large pyramid which Cortés destroyed. During the 1530s when Charles V finally bestowed a title of nobility upon him, Cortés resided here as Marquis del Valle de Oaxaca; he departed for Spain in 1540. The palace remained with Cortés' family for most of the next century, but by the 18th century it was being used as a prison and, during the days of Porfirio Díaz in the late 19th century, it served as a government palace.

Today the palace houses the Museo de Cuauhnáhuac, with two floors of exhibits highlighting the history and cultures of Mexico. On the ground floor, exhibits focus on several prominent pre-Hispanic cultures including the Aztec, Maya, Olmec, Xochilimilca, Chalcha and Tlahuica. The base of the original pyramid can still be seen at various places around the museum's ground floor.

Upstairs, exhibits cover events from the Spanish conquest to today. On the balcony is a fascinating mural by Diego Rivera, which is one of the museum's most outstanding

Olmec jadeite mask

features and is said to be one of Rivera's best murals. Commissioned in the mid-1920s as a gift to the people of Cuernavaca by Dwight Morrow, the US ambassador to Mexico, the right-to-left chronological mural is yet another stunning Rivera monument to Mexico's history. With scenes from the conquest to the 1910 revolution, the giant mural emphasises the cruelty, oppression, the violent taking of power and subjugation by force which have characterised Mexican history.

The museum is open Tuesday to Sunday from 10 am to 5 pm. Admission is US$3.35 (children under 12 free), except on Sunday when it's free for everyone.

Palacio Municipal

For more wall paintings showing Mexico's history, visit the Palacio Municipal (City Hall), also known as the Honorable Ayuntamiento de Cuernavaca (Honourable Town Council of Cuernavaca), at the corner of Avenida Morelos and Callejón Borda, on the south side of the Jardín Borda. The large paintings, displayed around the inner court-

yard of the 1883 building on both the ground and upstairs floors, show life in pre-Hispanic Cuernavaca and Morelos.

The Palacio Municipal is open Monday to Friday from around 8 am until 6 pm; you can come in for nothing to see the paintings.

Jardín Borda

The Jardín Borda (Borda Garden) was laid out with pools and fountains by Manuel de la Borda in 1783 as an addition to the stately residence built by his father José de la Borda, the Taxco silver magnate. From 1866, the house was the summer residence of Emperor Maximilian and Empress Carlota, who entertained their courtiers in the gardens.

Now restored, the Jardín Borda is one of Cuernavaca's main tourist attractions. From the entrance on Avenida Morelos at Calle Hidalgo, opposite the cathedral, you can tour the house and gardens to get an idea of how Mexico's aristocracy lived. Several large paintings show scenes of the garden in Maximilian's time, with ladies and gentlemen rowing on the pond; one of the most famous paintings depicts Maximilian and La India Bonita, the Beautiful Indian Girl who was to become his lover.

The house and garden is open Tuesday to Sunday from 10 am to 6 pm; admission is US$0.70. The gardens are great for a picnic; you might bring something extra for the ducks on the pond. You can hire a little rowboat to row on the pond like the emperor's court used to do; cost is US$1.70 for half an hour or US$3 for an hour, payable at the entrance.

Beside the house is the Parroquia de Guadalupe church, also built by José de la Borda, and dedicated on 12 December 1784. The schedule of masses is posted behind the iron gate; the church may not be open at other times.

La Catedral de la Asunción

Cuernavaca's large 16th-century cathedral stands in a large high-walled compound at the corner of Morelos and Hidalgo, opposite the Jardín Borda and the Palacio Municipal. Built by Cortés from the rubble of Cuauhnáhuac, it was started in 1526 and is one of the earliest cathedrals in Mexico. The cathedral compound also holds two smaller churches, one on either side of the Calle Hidalgo entrance. Like the Palacio de Cortés, this cathedral was built on a grand scale and in a fortress-like style, as a defence against the natives and to impress and intimidate them.

Over the main entrance is a skull and crossbones topped by a cross, symbol of the Franciscan order that once maintained a monastery here. Inside is a hodge-podge of architectural and artistic styles. Though most of the building was constructed as a plain, sturdy fortress with high walls and towers, the wall reliefs are good examples of churrigueresque style.

Early 17th-century Japanese frescoes on the interior walls were accidentally discovered in this century, when the nave was renovated. The frescoes show the persecution of Christian missionaries in Sokori, Japan and are believed to have been painted by a Japanese convert to Christianity who settled in Cuernavaca. This church was renowned as a centre for Franciscan missionary activities that extended throughout the Orient.

La Casa del Olvido

The 'House of Forgetfulness' was one of Maximilian's favourite hideouts, where he and La India Bonita would meet. Legends abound concerning this simple house, which was a country house in 1866 when Maximilian bought it, though Cuernavaca has now grown to surround it. One story goes that the house, actually named La Casa de Olindo, got its nickname 'Olvido' because Maximilian 'forgot' to include a room for his wife there – though he did remember to include a small house for La India Bonita. Another story goes that he named the house 'La Casa del Olvido' because he wanted it as a haven where he could forget the pressures of being the emperor of Mexico, and the pressures of his reportedly unhappy marriage.

Today, the house is the Museo de la Herbolaria, a museum of traditional herbal medicine, and the gardens have been planted as a botanical garden of medicinal plants. The museum was closed for remodelling in 1992, but is expected to reopen soon. Meanwhile you can still visit the house and the botanical garden; they're open every day from 10 am to 5 pm; admission is free.

The house is at Calle Matamoros 200 in the Colonia Acapantzingo, about 1½ km south-east of the zócalo. It is also called the 'Casa Maximiliano'.

Pyramid of Teopanzolco

This small archaeological site is on Calle Río Mayo in the colonia Vista Hermosa. The pyramid is actually two pyramids, one inside the other – this was a typical Tlahuica Indian method of expanding pyramids by using an original pyramid as a base and building a second one all around it.

The older (inside) pyramid was built over 800 years ago; the outside one, under construction at the time Cortés arrived in Cuauhnáhuac, was never completed. The site is probably much older than the pyramid itself, however; the name Teopanzolco translates as 'Place of the Ancient Temple' (*teopantli* = temple, *zol-tic* = ancient or old, and *co* = place). The term may relate to an ancient construction to the west of the current pyramid, where artefacts dating from around 7000 BC have been found, plus a number of artefacts with a marked Olmec influence.

Several other smaller platform structures surround the pyramid. The rectangular platform west of the double pyramid is notable because human remains, mixed with ceramic pieces, were found there; they are believed to be products of human sacrifice in which decapitation and dismemberment were practised.

The archaeological site, with 14 structures in total, is open every day from 10 am to 5 pm. Admission is US$2.70, except on Sunday and holidays, when it's free; children under 13 are always admitted for free.

Other Sights

If you're going to be in Cuernavaca for a

while, there are a few other interesting sights you might want to check out.

The great Mexican muralist Alfaro Siqueiros had his workshop here in Cuernavaca; he lived and worked in it from 1964 until his death in 1974. On 12 December 1973 he donated the shop to the people of Mexico. Known as the **Taller Alfaro Siqueiros**, at Calle Venus 7 in the Fraccionamiento Jardines de Cuernavaca, the shop is open Tuesday to Sunday from 10 am to 2 pm and 4 to 6 pm (free admission). On display are four murals left unfinished at the artist's death, a photographic display of his principal works, various writings, and other mementos of his life.

Another notable residence is the **house of Baroness Barbara Hutton**, a replica of a Japanese mansion including a Japanese theatre. The mansion, in the Colonia José G Parres, now houses the Restaurant Sumiya, and it's open to the public.

Martín Cortés, who took over from Hernán Cortés to become the second Marquis of the Valle de Oaxaca, constructed the **Hacienda de San Antonio Atlacomulco** in the 17th century. In the late 19th century, after various changes, it was used as an aguardiente factory; during the revolution, Emiliano Zapata took it over and used it as a base for his troops. After the revolution the estate deteriorated until, in 1973, it was restored and served as the Instituto de Investigaciones para el Hombre. In 1980 it was renovated once more, and is now open to the public as the Hotel Hacienda de Cortés, with a restaurant and bar. It's about four km outside the city, in Atlacomulco.

In the district of San Antón, the Salto de San Antón is a 40-metre waterfall cascading over a walkway built into the cliff where it falls. It's a picturesque place, with many trees.

If you like water and swimming, ask the tourist office about balnearios – they have brochures with info on many swimming areas in the state of Morelos, most within an hour's drive of Cuernavaca. Some of the notable places are the lake of Tequesquitengo, the river at Las Estacas, and the

balnearios at Oaxtepec, Cuautla, Atotonilco and El Rollo. All of these are some distance from the city, maybe an hour's drive or so; the balneario at the ex-Hacienda de Temixco is closer, being in an outlying area just to the south of the city and accessible by a local city bus route. Several of the balnearios provide camping areas.

Courses

Cuernavaca is one of the most prominent places in Mexico for foreigners coming to study Spanish, with a number of well-known language schools. The tourist office can provide you with a list of 17 language institutes in the city; any of the schools will send you a free brochure explaining their programmes and fees.

The best schools offer small-group (four or five students) or private instruction, at all levels from beginning to advanced, with the option of special programmes adapted to special needs (for medical or legal workers, diplomats, etc), with several hours per day of intensive instruction. Accompanying cultural programmes include weekend tours to archaeological and cultural sites; extracurricular classes in related subjects like Mexican folk-dancing, handcrafts, guitar, etc are also offered. Classes begin each Monday; you can study for as many weeks as you want, or take off to travel for a while and come back to resume studies. Tuition is paid by the week.

Most of the schools offer students the option of staying in regular accommodation (hotels, apartments, etc), or living with a Mexican family. The families, screened for suitability by the schools, offer the advantage of 'total immersion' in the culture as well as the language. Cost for staying with families is normally around US$14 per day with shared room and bath, or around US$20 per day with private room and bath, including three daily meals.

One of the most renowned schools for learning Spanish in Cuernavaca is Cuauhnáhuac – Instituto Colectivo de Lengua y Cultura (☎ (73) 18-92-75, fax 18-26-93), on Avenida Morelos Sur 1414, Colonia Chipitlán. Their registration fee is US$75; tuition is US$155 per week, or US$575 for four weeks. In March, April, September, October and November the rates are reduced to US$130 per week or US$485 for four weeks. Their mailing address is Apdo Postal C-26, Cuernavaca 62050, Morelos, México. Their representative in the USA is Ms Karin Wigren, 4000 Cherryvale, Soquel, CA 95073 (☎ (408) 462-9399).

Experiencia – Centro de Intercambio Bilingüe y Cultural (☎ (73) 18-52-09) at Calle Leyva 1130, Colonia Las Palmas, is another popular, reputable school. Tuition cost is US$110 per week, or US$400 for four weeks; their accommodation plans, at the school or with a family, include options priced anywhere from US$5 (without meals) to US$18 per day (with three meals). Their mailing address is Apdo Postal C-96, Cuernavaca, Morelos, México. In the USA one of their representatives is Patricia Damron (☎ (915) 886-4802), PO Box 1812, Anthony, NM 88021; in Canada you could contact Clubtour-Sat (☎ (514) 844-2851, fax 844-2621), 666 Rue Sherbrooke Quest, Suite 507, Montreal, Quebec H34 1E7; they also have representatives in Europe.

The Center for Bilingual Multicultural Studies (☎ (73) 17-10-87, fax 17-05-33) at Calle San Jerónimo 304, Colonia San Jerónimo, has a similar programme, with a US$100 registration fee and US$150 per week tuition. You can write to them at Apdo Postal 1520, Cuernavaca 62000, Morelos, México.

Instituto IDEAL (Instituto de Estudios de América Latina) (☎ (73) 17-04-55), at Privada Narciso Mendoza 107, Colonia Pradera, has a registration fee of US$100 and a US$130 per week tuition fee. Their mailing address is Apdo Postal 22-B, Cuernavaca 62910, Morelos, México.

Then there's the Instituto Teopanzolco (☎ (73) 13-64-21) at Avenida Universidad 5, Casa 110 (mailing address Apdo Postal 1195, Cuernavaca, Morelos, México). In addition to their regular courses they also offer from time to time a unique programme specially designed for deaf or hearing-impaired stu-dents. Their normal courses cost US$100 per week, with a US$60 registration fee.

Festivals
Carnaval Late February or early March, in the five days before Ash Wednesday, is the time for this colourful week-long celebration of Mardi Gras that includes street perfor-mances by the Chinelo dancers of Tepoztlán, among others, with parades, art exhibits, dances and more.

Feria de la Primavera Cuernavaca's Spring Fair, held from 21 March to 10 April, includes cultural and artistic events, con-certs, and a beautiful exhibit of the city's spring flowers.

San Isidro Labrador On 15 May, the Day of Saint Isidro the Farmer, local farmers adorn their mules and oxen with flowers and bring them to town for an annual blessing.

Día de la Virgen de Guadalupe The day of the Virgen de Guadalupe, Mexico's patron saint, is celebrated in Cuernavaca on 12 December, as it is everywhere in Mexico.

Places to Stay
Cuernavaca offers a good selection of places to stay, but if you're planning to arrive on a weekend or holiday, when the town fills up with visitors from the capital, you might want to phone ahead to reserve a hotel room, as they can be difficult to come by at these times. If you do come without a reservation at these times, try to arrive early in the day and secure yourself a room. At other times, the hotels are not so full.

Places to Stay – bottom end
The *Hotel Colonial* (☎ (73) 18-64-14) at Aragón y León 104, three blocks north of the zócalo, is clean, quiet and small, with 14 rooms arranged around a peaceful interior courtyard. Some of the rooms have big windows with plenty of light and ventilation; other's don't. Ask for one of the rooms with windows. Singles/doubles here cost US$11.70/14.35.

Down the block from the Colonial, near Matamoros, are several basic casas de huéspedes which are cheaper, but they are known for being of 'questionable' character. The Colonial, on the other hand, is a 'decent' place and quite pleasant at that.

If you have a car with you, you might consider the *Motel Royal* (☎ (73) 18-64-80) at Matamoros 19. Its rooms, with doors and windows opening onto walkways around a central court with parking spaces for cars, don't have much personality but they're clean and economical at US$11.70/13.35 for singles/doubles. If you're bringing a car and can afford it, you'd probably find it more enjoyable to stay at one of the middle-range motels, which cost not that much more.

Places to Stay – middle

The *Hotel Juárez* (☎ (73) 14-02-19), at Netzahualcóyotl 117 about a block south-west of the zócalo, is a good place to stay, centrally located but quiet, with a large garden and swimming pool behind the hotel. The 13 rooms are simple but large, light and airy, some with windows to the street and others to the garden; singles/doubles are US$15/20.

The *Hotel Iberia* (☎ (73) 12-60-40) at Rayón 9, just west of the Jardín Juárez, is an old dependable hostelry long patronised by travellers and foreign students. Rooms in the big old hotel, costing US$17/22.50 for singles/doubles, are set around a courtyard with lots of plants and a couple of parking spaces for cars.

A few blocks north of the zócalo, the *Motel Los Canarios* (☎ (73) 13-00-00, 13-44-44) at Avenida Morelos 713 is a good place if you have a car or children with you. The rooms, at US$14.70/29.35, are rather spartan and functional, but each has its own outdoor terrace with tables and chairs. There's plenty more garden space too, including a large area behind the hotel with two large swimming pools (one for adults, one for children) and playground equipment for the kids. Two economical restaurants serving all meals are another convenience.

The *Hotel Papagayo* (☎ (73) 14-17-11,

14-19-24) at Motolinia 13, between Avenida Morelos and Calle Netzahualcóyotl, is another old favourite, a large, pleasant hotel whose 77 rooms are arranged around a large garden courtyard with two swimming pools (the adults' pool has high dives), again with childrens' play equipment and plenty of parking spaces. During the week, the single/double rate of US$23.35/40 includes two meals, which can be breakfast and lunch or breakfast and dinner. On Friday and Saturday, the rate of US$31.70/56.70 includes all three meals.

Places to Stay – top end

If price is no object, by all means stay at Cuernavaca's best, the *Hotel Las Mañanitas* (☎ (73) 14-14-66, 12-46-46, fax 18-36-72), at Ricardo Linares 107. Prices start at US$60/82 for standard rooms and go up in steps to US$200/234 for garden suites (these are incredibly beautiful) and even to US$300 a night for a two-bedroom suite; it is very impressive, with every luxury including a large private garden (for guests only) where peacocks stroll around while you enjoy the elegant pool. This hotel has been included in several listings of the world's finest hotels and its restaurant is also justly famous.

If Las Mañanitas is full (which it often is), try the *Hostería Las Quintas* (☎ (73) 12-88-00) at Avenida Las Quintas 107, a couple of km from the centre. It's in the same general vein as Las Mañanitas, with gardens, pool, restaurant, bar, etc; standard rooms are US$61/70, terrace suites US$88/100.

Or there's the more centrally located *Posada de Xochiquetzal* (☎ (73) 18-57-67, 18-69-84) at Leyva 200, on the corner of Abasolo, with rooms ranging from US$69 (standard) to US$106 (suites). This is not as luxurious but it's one of Cuernavaca's well-known, long-time favourites.

Places to Eat – bottom end

For a simple snack of yoghurt with fruit, escamochas (a kind of fruit salad), corn on the cob, ice cream, or fresh fruit or vegetable juice, you could patronise one of the booths on the ground floor of the *Jardín Juárez gazebo*, then eat it on one of the park benches and watch the people strolling by. This is an especially popular activity on Sundays and Thursdays at around 6 pm, when concerts are held in the plaza.

On the east side of Jardín Juárez, *La Parroquia*, open every day from 7.30 am to 11.30 pm, is one of Cuernavaca's favourite restaurants: it serves all meals, is open long hours, and has a good view of the plaza. Its extensive reasonably-priced menu of meals, coffees and desserts includes an unusual feature, a section of Arabic specialties-of-the-house, which is unusual and exotic for Mexico.

The *Restaurant Los Arcos*, with umbrella-covered tables right out on the Plaza de Armas, on the south side next to the post office, is a pleasant place for a meal or just to hang out, sip coffee or a soda, and watch the action on the plaza. Their varied bilingual menu has something for everyone and is not expensive; they're open every day from 8 am to 11 pm.

In the block just south (down the hill) from Jardín Juárez on Galeana, *El Portal* and *La Cueva*, open every day from around 7 am to 11.30 pm, do a brisk business, competing with one another to offer good food at an inexpensive price. In the early afternoon they post their comida corrida menus out front. Prices will be around US$4, more or less, for a three or four-course meal; though they're not much on atmosphere, they serve pretty good food. You could also get a roast chicken to go, which for around US$4 comes with tortillas, chiles, etc, and take it to the nearby Jardín Borda for a picnic.

Vegetarians will like the small, simple *Restaurant Vegetariana*, also on Galeana, in the next block down the hill at Galeana 110. It's open every day from 9 am to 9 pm; starting at 1 pm they serve a delicious four-course comida corrida which, at US$2.35, is the cheapest in town. It changes daily but usually consists of a choice of salads (fruit and yoghurt or vegetable), good vegetable soup, choice of hot main dish, served with

brown rice, and tea and dessert. They sometimes have live music at lunch time.

Next door, the non-vegetarian *Restaurant Taxco*, with savoury aromas wafting out into the street, is also popular.

If you're travelling with children (or even if you're not), a good place for a quiet, enjoyable meal is the *Restaurant Julius*, in the rear of the Motel Los Canarios which is at Avenida Morelos 713. It's a pleasant covered-garden restaurant, open from 8 am to 8 pm; for US$3.35 you can get the comida corrida in the afternoon; they also serve seven different breakfast combos, and other selections. There are swings, a carousel, etc in the garden, where children can play while adults linger over coffee. There are also two swimming pools, one for adults and one for kids, which could make for a pleasant afternoon's outing.

Places to Eat – middle

La India Bonita, a block north-west of Jardín Juárez at Calle Morrow 6, is a pleasant restaurant with good traditional Mexican food. The house specialities are mole poblano (chicken mole), with that great mole sauce which is a combination of chocolate, chiles, and about 20 other ingredients (US$10.50); charcoal-grilled filet mignon (also US$10.50); or a special Mexican plate with seven different selections (US$6.50). La India Bonita is open Tuesday to Saturday from 8.30 am to 7.30 pm, Sunday 8.30 am to 6.30 pm (closed Monday).

Restaurant Vienés, at Tejada 201 also a block from Jardín Juárez, is a charming European-style restaurant founded some years ago by a Swiss/German couple. It offers a delicious variety of traditional European dishes from Switzerland, Germany, Hungary, Italy, Denmark – and, of course, Vienna. The 'farmer's plate' of smoked pork ribs, roast veal, frankfurter potatoes and sauerkraut costs around US$9.50, as does a big knackwurst served with sauerkraut and German fried potatoes, or stuffed roast meatloaf served with potatoes, vegetables and salad. They're open every day except Tuesday, 1 pm to 10 pm.

Next door, *Los Pasteles del Vienés* serves the best coffee, cakes, cookies, cream puffs and chocolate/rum truffles you've seen since the last time you were in Vienna. Their coffee, probably the best in the city, comes with free refills. Connected to the Restaurant Vienés, it's more like a café and it also serves breakfast; hours are from 8 am to 10 pm every day. Both Vienés restaurants have comfortable European-style decor, with cloths on the tables and plenty of windows.

Harry's Grill, at Juan Gutenberg 3 just off the Plaza de Armas, is one of the Carlos Anderson chain of bar/restaurants where rock & roll music shakes the photos and posters lining every inch of wall space. All the Anderson restaurants provide a good time for the gringos, and this one is no exception; prices aren't bad either, with beef, chicken, seafood, etc from around US$6.50 to US$10. Harry's is open from 2 to 10.30 pm every day.

Places to Eat – top end

If you can afford a splurge, try the *Restaurant Las Mañanitas*, at the hotel of the same name at Ricardo Linares 107. One of Mexico's best and most famous restaurants, its decor will make your eyes pop, with peacocks and flamingos strolling through an emerald green garden and swans gliding around on a pool. Tables are on the garden terrace or inside the mansion; the menu features meals from around the world, which might cost around US$15 (wine extra). It's a good idea to phone ahead for reservations (☎ 14-14-66, 12-46-46); they're open every day from 1 to 5 pm and from 7 to 10.30 pm, but they may close earlier if they're full.

Cuernavaca has long been a haven for the rich and it boasts a number of other sumptuous restaurants. You could try the restaurant/bar at the *Hostería Las Quintas* (mentioned under Places to Stay), or the *Casa de Campo* restaurant on Abasolo 101, in a similar style to Las Mañanitas but not quite as grand. Or there's the *Restaurant Sumiya*, in the lavish Japanese-style mansion built by Baroness Barbara Sutton, in the colonia José G Parres (phone 15-30-55 for reservations).

Entertainment

The good discos in Cuernavaca are usually open only on Friday and Saturday nights; Barba Azul and Kaova are two of the best. For live salsa dance music, try Sammaná, open Thursday, Friday and Saturday nights.

Some of Cuernavaca's better hotels have live music in their bars every night; you could try the bars at the Villa Bejar or the Villa del Conquistador.

For quieter drinks in elegant surroundings, the garden bar at the Hotel Las Mañanitas is hard to beat; it's open every day from noon to midnight.

The Cinema Morelos (☎ 18-82-50), on the corner of Morelos and Rayón, is the state theatre of Morelos, hosting a variety of cultural offerings including quality film series, plays, dance performances, etc.

Getting There & Away

Bus Four bus companies serve Cuernavaca. Each has its own separate terminal, but all are within walking distance of the zócalo. They are:

Estrella de Oro –Avenida Morelos Sur 900 (☎ 12-30-55, 12-82-96)
Estrella Roja – corner of Galeana & Cuauhtémotzin (☎ 18-59-34)
Flecha Roja – Avenida Morelos 503, between Arista & Victoria (☎ 12-81-90)
Autos Pullman de Morelos – corner of Abasolo & Netzahualcóyotl (☎ 14-36-50)

Buses from Cuernavaca include:

Acapulco – 315 km, five hours; four daily with Estrella de Oro (US$9.20); five daily with Flecha Roja (ordinario US$7.35, directo US$9.35, servicio de lujo US$12.70).
Chilpancingo – 180 km, three hours; same buses as to Acapulco (US$5).
Cuautla – 42 km, one hour; every 20 minutes, 5 am to 10 pm, with Estrella Roja (US$1.15).
Grutas de Cacahuamilpa – 80 km, 2½ hours; hourly, 6 am to 6 pm, with Flecha Roja (US$1.50).
Iguala – 90 km, 1½ hours; same buses as to Acapulco (US$2.60).
Izucar de Matamoros – 100 km, two hours; hourly, 5 am to 8 pm (US$2.35).

Mexico City – 85 km, 1½ hours; every 15 minutes, 5 am to 9.30 pm, with Pullman de Morelos (ordinario US$2, servicio de lujo US$2.10, ejecutivo dorado US$4.35); every 30 minutes, 6.30 am to 10 pm, with Flecha Roja (US$1.85); seven daily with Estrella de Oro (US$2.10).

Oaxtepec – 31 km, 50 minutes; every 30 minutes, 6 am to 10 pm, with Estrella Roja (US$1.15).

Puebla – 175 km, 3½ hours; hourly, 5 am to 8 pm, with Estrella Roja (US$4.10).

Taxco – 80 km, 1½ hours; every 30 minutes, 6 am to 10.15 pm, with Flecha Roja (US$1.85); five daily with Estrella de Oro (US$1.75).

Tepoztlán – 23 km, one hour; every 15 minutes, 5.30 am to 10 pm, depart from local bus terminal at mercado (US$0.55).

Xochicalco – 38 km, one hour; same bus as to Grutas de Cacahuamilpa (US$0.70).

Zihuatanejo – 550 km, nine hours; two daily with Estrella de Oro (US$13.90).

Train It's possible to reach Cuernavaca by train, but this is so inconvenient it's not worth describing, with all the trains being either slow 2nd-class or goods trains. The train station is in the north-east part of the city on the road to Cuautla, about a km north of the zócalo.

Getting Around

Although most of central Cuernavaca is within walking distance, numerous local buses and taxis are available for outlying destinations. Avenida Morelos is the principal thoroughfare for the buses before they veer towards the colonia (neighbourhood) marked on their signs. The average bus fare is US$0.25. The tourist office can help you work out which route to take if you want to go to a particular destination.

Taxis are plentiful but expensive; a taxi ride in town, even if only going a few blocks, costs around US$1.70 at the least, often US$2 or more.

XOCHICALCO

Atop a desolate plateau 15 km south-west of Cuernavaca as the crow flies, but about 38 km by road, is the ancient ceremonial centre of Xochicalco ('so-chee-CAL-co'), one of the most important archaeological sites in central Mexico. In Nahuatl, the language of the Aztecs, Xochicalco means Place of the

House of Flowers, which it probably was for Toltecs in the 7th century.

Today it is a collection of white stone ruins covering approximately 10 sq km, some of them yet to be excavated. They represent the various cultures – Toltec, Olmec, Maya, Zapotec, Mixtec and Aztec – that once ruled empires or parts of empires from here. Xochicalco was a commercial, cultural and religious centre. When Teotihuacán began to weaken around 650 to 700 AD, Xochicalco began to rise in importance, achieving its maximum splendour between 650 and 850 AD with far-reaching commercial and cultural relations. Around the year 650 a congress of spiritual leaders met in Xochicalco, representing the Zapotec, Mayan and Gulf Coast peoples, to correlate their respective calendars.

The most famous monument here is the Pyramid of the Plumed Serpent; from its well-preserved bas-reliefs archaeologists have surmised that astronomer-priests met here at the beginning and end of each 52-year cycle of the Aztec calendar. Xochicalco remained an important centre until around 1200, when its excessive growth caused a fall similar to that which happened in Teotihuacán.

Unless you have your own transport, getting to Xochicalco can be difficult. Autos Pullman de Morelos buses heading from Cuernavaca to Miacatlán will drop you off at the crossroads, about an hour's ride from Cuernavaca; from there, it's a four-km hike uphill to the principal site. The site is open every day from 10 am to 5 pm; admission US$3.35 (children under 13 free).

TEPOZTLÁN

Population: 12,300
Altitude: 1701 metres
Situated in a beautiful valley surrounded by high jagged cliffs 23 km north-east of Cuernavaca, the town of Tepoztlán justifiably claims to be a magical place. A variety of soothsayers, astrologists, writers, artists and just ordinary folk frequent Tepoztlán in hopes of experiencing the legendary force that spawned the birth of Quetzalcóatl, the

omnipotent serpent god of the Aztecs, more than 1200 years ago.

The name Tepoztlán means Place of Copper. The old people in the village still speak Nahuatl among themselves; though the young people have abandoned the Nahuatl language for everyday use, it is now being taught in the town's secondary school.

If you come to Tepoztlán from Cuernavaca, you'll see the craggy mountains rising behind the village of Santa Catarina. With the snowcapped peak of the Popocatépetl volcano towering in the distance behind them, they look like something out of a mystical fantasy painting. Tepoztlán is around the other side of these mountains, tucked into a valley with cliffs on every side.

Orientation
The town is small enough for everything except the Pyramid of Tepozteco to be easily accessible by walking.

As in many other Mexican cities and towns, streets in Tepoztlán change names. All the east-west streets have different names on either side of Avenida Cinco de Mayo, which changes names itself, becoming Avenida Tepozteco north of the main plaza. The north-south streets also all have two names, one on the north side of the main plaza and another on the south side.

Information
The post office and telegraph office are in the large building on the north side of the main plaza.

Long-distance and local telephone calls can be made from the caseta de larga distancia at the Farmacia Villamar, on Avenida Cinco de Mayo on the west side of the main plaza. It's open every day from 9 am to 9 pm.

Pyramid of Tepozteco
The 10-metre-high Pyramid of Tepozteco was built on a cliff three km above Tepoztlán to honour Tepoztécatl, the Aztec god of fertility, the harvest and pulque (fermented maguey juice). Gazing up from town, the pyramid is visible way up at the top of the cliffs to the north, looking like a tiny toy so

high up in the distance. Each year on the night of 7 September a pilgrimage up to the pyramid takes place to honour the god (see Festivals).

The pyramid is accessible by a steep, narrow path beginning at the end of Avenida Tepozteco. It takes about one to 1½ hours to climb up to the pyramid, depending how athletic you are; at the top you're rewarded with a spectacular view of Tepoztlán and the valley. The pyramid site is open every day from 10 am to 5 pm; admission is US$1.60.

Ex-Convento de Tepoztlán
Properly called the 'Ex-Convento Dominico de la Natividad', the huge convento (monastery) built by Dominican priests between 1580 and 1588 is by far the dominant feature of the town. It is still in use as a church; school children play in the grounds in front of the church after school. On the arch of the church façade are Dominican seals interspersed with floral designs and various figures including the sun, moon and stars, animals, angels and the Virgin Mary. The church is open every day from around 7 am to 8 pm.

The monastery section to one side of the church is no longer in everyday use. It is quiet and impressive, with remnants of murals of centuries past on the walls. The rear terrace on the upper floor offers a magnificent view of the valley of Tepoztlán. The convent can be visited Wednesday to Sunday from 9.30 am to 5 pm (closed Monday and Tuesday). Admission is free, but you could make a donation to help the restoration project.

Museo Arqueológico
The Archaeological Museum at Calle Pablo González 2 (behind the church) is small but interesting, with a good collection of pieces from many parts of Mexico donated to the people of Tepoztlán by the Tabascan poet Carlos Pellicer Cámara. Pellicer had a great love for Mexico's pre-Hispanic art; the objects on display here are lively and vibrant, with an emphasis on human figures but also some animals thrown in. There's quite a

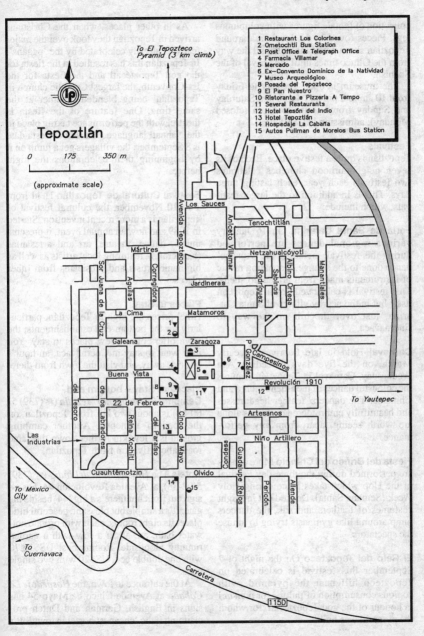

Tepoztlán

0   175   350 m

(approximate scale)

To El Tepozteco
Pyramid (3 km climb)

1 Restaurant Los Colorines
2 Ometochtli Bus Station
3 Post Office & Telegraph Office
4 Farmacia Villamar
5 Mercado
6 Ex–Convento Dominico de la Natividad
7 Museo Arqueológico
8 Posada del Tepozteco
9 El Pan Nuestro
10 Ristorante e Pizzeria A Tempo
11 Several Restaurants
12 Hotel Mesón del Indio
13 Hotel Tepoztlán
14 Hospedaje La Cabaña
15 Autos Pullman de Morelos Bus Station

Los Sauces

Avenida Tepozteco

Aniceto Villamar

Tenochtitlán

Mártires

Netzahualcóyotl

P Rodríguez

Sabinos

Albino Ortega

Manantiales

Corregidora

Sor Juana de la Cruz

Aguilas

Jardineras

La Cima

Matamoros

Galeana

Zaragoza

P González

Campesinos

Buena Vista

Revolución 1910

22 de Febrero

Reina Xochitl

del Paraíso

Cinco de Mayo

del Tesoro

de los Labradores

To Yautepec

Artesanos

Niño Artillero

Las
Industrias

Cuauhtémotzin

Olvido

Campesino

Guadalupe Rejos

Pericón

Allende

To Mexico
City

To Cuernavaca

Carretera

115D

collection of female figures with voluptuous legs. Pieces found in the local area around Tepoztlán show it was inhabited all the way from the Olmec times until the arrival of the Spanish.

The museum is open Tuesday to Friday from 10 am to 2 pm and 4 to 6 pm, Saturday and Sunday from 10 am to 6 pm (closed Monday); admission is US$0.70.

Festivals

Tepoztlán is quite a festive place. Each of its seven neighbourhood churches celebrates two festivals each year, each lasting three days. This is in addition to the larger festivals, which include:

Feria de Santa Catarina On 16 January various regional dances are performed during this festival, including the 'Apache' dance done to the strange, resonating music of instruments made from armadillo shells. This festival is celebrated not in Tepoztlán itself but in the nearby village of Santa Catarina, just over the hill on the way to Cuernavaca.

Carnaval Held in late February or early March, on the five days preceding Ash Wednesday, Carnaval in Tepoztlán features the colourful dances of the Huehuenches and Chinelos. The dancers' feather headdresses and beautifully embroidered costumes alone are worth seeing, apart from any performance.

Fiesta del Brinco del Chinelo More dances are performed during the three-day Festival of the Hop which takes place during Holy Week (Semana Santa). Decked out in bright costumes of feathers and silk, the dancers jump around like gymnasts trying to amuse the spectators.

El Reto del Tepozteco On the night of 7 September this festival is celebrated on Tepozteco hill near the pyramid, with copious consumption of pulque (or *ponche*) in honour of the god Tepoztécatl, for whom the pyramid was built.

As in other places, when the Christians arrived in Tepoztlán they took over the major festivals already celebrated by the 'pagans'. In Tepoztlán this has resulted in the fiesta for the god Tepoztécatl and the fiesta for the Ex-Convento, the largest Catholic church in Tepoztlán, being blended together at the same time. One feature of the fiesta is theatre, with the performance taking place in the Nahuatl language. The actual fiesta date is 8 September; the villagers get a jump on it by beginning their celebrations the night before.

Festival Cultural de Tepoztlán Held from 1 to 10 November, the cultural festival of Tepoztlán is a more recent invention. Started in 1989 and now an annual event, it presents music, dance, theatre, art and artesanías (handcrafts), featuring local artists as well as big-name artists and musicians from other places.

Places to Stay

Hotel prices are high in Tepoztlán, particularly for the bottom-end establishments; the town offers only a few places to stay. You may want to stay in Cuernavaca, an hour's bus ride away, and visit the town from there.

Places to Stay – bottom end

Camping *Campamento Meztitla* (☎ (739) 5-00-68) is about two km from Tepoztlán, on the road to Yautepec. Another camping ground is a few km further down the same road, about five km from Tepoztlán.

Hotels The *Hotel Mesón del Indio* (☎ (739) 5-02-38), at Avenida Revolución 44, has no sign out front but there's a big '44' beside the gate. It's a simple but pleasant, peaceful little place; its eight rooms, each with private hot-water bath, are all in a row with a garden running alongside. Rooms cost US$16.70 with one double bed, US$20 with two single beds.

At the entrance to town, the *Hospedaje La Cabaña* at Avenida Cinco de Mayo 54 has signs in English, German and Dutch proclaiming it the 'cheapest hostel in town'. It's a step down in comfort, with 10 very basic rooms sharing two toilets and two showers – the beds were much better at the Mesón del Indio. Nonetheless it's clean, there's hot water in the showers, a garden where you can sunbathe and meet other guests, and the friendly management provides purified water, coffee and tea. At US$20 per room, though, it's overpriced and not even really the cheapest.

Places to Stay – top end

The *Posada del Tepozteco* (☎ (739) 5-00-10, 5-03-23) at Calle Paraíso 3 was built as a hillside hacienda in the 1920s and added to as time went by. This is the more attractive of the top-end places, with two swimming pools, a restaurant/bar, and terraces with panoramic views of the town and valley. The seven rooms cost US$47 or US$59; the six suites, all with private spa baths, cost US$70. The same management is planning to build another top-end hotel seven km from Tepoztlán at Amatlán de Quetzalcóatl, with horse riding and many luxuries.

The *Hotel Tepoztlán* (☎ (739) 5-05-03, 5-05-22/23) at Calle Las Industrias 6 is a resort-style hotel with 36 rooms and two suites (some with good views), a heated swimming pool, and a restaurant and bar. Singles/doubles cost US$37/47 for during the week, US$45/63 on Saturday night. The suites, each with private jacuzzi, cost US$94 during the week, US$110 on Saturday. A buffet breakfast on Sunday is included in the Saturday rates.

Places to Eat

For a simple meal, there are many small restaurants and outdoor eating places set up in the mercado, in front of the church.

All in the same block, on Avenida Revolución opposite the mercado, are a number of restaurants including *El Quinto Sol* at No 6 for natural fruit juices, licuados and health-food drinks; the *Restaurante Veg-etariano* at No 12 which may serve food only on weekends; and *Naty's* at No 7 on the market side of the street. *Coquis* at No 10 and

La Luna Mextli at No 16 are combination restaurants, bars, and art galleries.

For good traditional Mexican food you could try the *Restaurant Los Colorines* at Avenida Tepozteco 13, 1½ blocks north of the main plaza. A small restaurant with an attractive decor, it offers a variety of meals from US$3.35 to US$6.

Just south of the main plaza at Avenida Cinco de Mayo 26, *El Pan Nuestro* is a pleasant cafeteria and cake shop with good desserts and coffee, open daily from 10.30 am to 8.30 pm. In the same block, on Avenida Cinco de Mayo at the corner of 22 de Febrero, *A Tempo* is an Italian ristorante and pizzeria.

Getting There & Away

Buses to Cuernavaca depart from in front of the Ometochtli bus terminal on Avenida Tepozteco, one block north of the main plaza. They go every 15 minutes from 5 am to 9 pm; cost is US$0.55 for the one-hour trip.

Buses to Mexico City and Yautepec depart from the terminal of Autos Pullman de Morelos and Autobuses México-Zacatepec (☎ (739) 5-05-20), at Avenida Cinco de Mayo 35 at the southern entrance to town. Buses to Mexico City depart nine times daily from 5.15 am to 5.30 pm and cost US$2 for the 1¼-hour, 70-km trip. Buses to Yautepec, on the way to Cuautla, depart eight times daily, roughly every two hours between 9 am and 8 pm; the 18-km trip takes 30 minutes and costs US$0.50.

CUAUTLA

Population: 110,250
Altitude: 1291 metres

First impressions of Cuautla ('KWOUT-la') are deceiving because it doesn't appear to live up to its reputation as a favourite resort for Mexico City's rich and powerful. Mexico's pre-Hispanic and Spanish past is visible only in a few old churches.

However, mineral springs (balnearios) and a pleasant year-round climate have been attractions at least as far back as Moctezuma; he was reputedly an avid fan of soaking in the sun and sulphur springs. Cuautla has also catered to Mexico's beleaguered political bosses and earned itself a place in the history books.

In 1811 it was more than just hot springs that attracted José Maria Morelos y Pavón, one of Mexico's first leaders in the independence struggle. Morelos' military strategy was to use Cuautla as a base from which his forces would encircle the royalist forces in Mexico City. However, before he could launch an attack, the royalist army under General Calleja besieged the city from 19 February to 2 May 1812 (both dates are now street names in Cuautla). Morelos and his army were forced to evacuate when their food gave out and many people died of starvation. The town remains proud of Morelos: the house on the main plaza where he lived is marked with a plaque, there's a small Morelos museum, and a huge statue of an angry Morelos wielding a machete towers over the Plaza Galeana.

A century later Cuautla was again significant in Mexico's history, this time as a key centre of support for the revolutionary army of Emiliano Zapata. In June 1916 the federal army of then-President Carranza attempted to wrest control of the state of Morelos from the Zapatistas, but their success was limited to the execution or deportation of thousands of peasants. Zapata remained in control and was able to rout the federalist forces from Cuautla.

An epidemic of Spanish influenza in 1918, however, killed thousands of his soldiers and opened the door to another federalist offensive which had the Zapatistas on the run. When a federalist colonel named Jesús Guajardo pretended to defect to Zapata's side, Zapata welcomed the additional support and agreed to have lunch with the colonel at a hacienda in Chinameca. He was shot dead as he rode through the gate. Today, every year on 10 April the Agrarian Reform Minister lays a wreath at Zapata's statue in Cuautla and makes a speech quoting his ideas about land reform.

Orientation

Cuautla lies 42 km east of Cuernavaca and is the second largest city in the state of Morelos. The city extends from north to south approximately parallel to the Río Cuautla, and may have the distinction of being the only city in the world where many of its streets have a different name in *every single block*. Why this is, no one knows – maybe to honour more heroes than there were streets to give names to, or maybe just to make things interesting and keep you on your toes. For example, one of the main avenues coming into town, Avenida Insurgentes, becomes Batalla 19 de Febrero as it nears town, changing names again to Galeana where it passes the Plaza Galeana; it remains Galeana for three blocks until it reaches the main plaza but changes names again, to Zemano, south of the main plaza. Note that there is also a Calle Insurgentes, which runs east-west.

The main plaza (zócalo) is the city centre and a good point from which to get your bearings. The church is on the east side of the plaza, the Palacio Municipal (City Hall) on the west; the Hotel Colón, with a popular open-air corner restaurant, is on the south side, and the Restaurant El Cid is on the north side, beside Calle Galeana, which departs the plaza as a pedestrian mall before turning into a regular traffic street one block north. Three blocks further north on Galeana are the tourist office, the Morelos museum, and Plaza Galeana.

Information

Tourist Office The Oficina de Turismo (☎ (735) 2-52-21) is at the former terminal of the Scenic Train *(Ferrocarril Escénica)*, which unfortunately is no longer running. The building is on Galeana at the corner of Defensa del Agua, facing Plaza Galeana. The tourist office is in the first door as you enter the old train platform entrance; hours are Monday to Saturday from 9 am to 7 pm, Sunday 9 am to 5 pm. A free city map is available which will help you to clarify the changes of the street names, find the balnearios, etc.

It's a large and historic building, constructed by the Franciscans as the Templo y Convento de San Diego in the 16th and 17th centuries. It contains a large church, and was also used as a fort – the Fort of San Diego. Much later, it became the terminus of the scenic train line and, even more recently, the site of the José María Morelos museum.

Post & Telecommunications The post office is on Calle Insurgentes, half a block west of Galeana. It's open from 8 am to 7 pm Monday to Friday, 9 am to 1 pm on Saturday. The telegraph office is opposite the post office, a couple of doors further west.

Several businesses around the main plaza have 'larga distancia' signs posted; local or long-distance telephone calls can be made from any of them.

Museo José María Morelos

The has been moved from his house on the main plaza beside the Hotel Colón (the house is still marked by a plaque) to the building also housing the former Scenic Train station and the tourist office, facing Plaza Galeana at the corner of Galeana and Defensa del Agua. There's not much in the museum, but the price is right (free); it's open Tuesday to Sunday from 10 am to 5 pm.

The museum is upstairs over the Casa de la Cultura de Cuautla, which offers an intriguing mixture of classes: Jazz-Rap, Nahuatl and Literature were being offered on our most recent visit.

Balnearios

The most resplendent and largest of the local balnearios is the 25-pool centre at Oaxtepec, 10 km north-west of Cuautla (see Around Cuautla). It takes only about 15 minutes to reach Oaxtepec from Cuautla and minibuses (combis) make the trip every few minutes.

In Cuautla itself there are a number of balnearios. Probably the best known is Agua Hedionda (☎ (735) 2-00-44), known for its health-giving mineral waters, which smell faintly of sulphur, have all kinds of other minerals, and spring from the earth medium-warm (27°C) to fill two giant swimming pools. The complex also includes a number of private pools which can be hired for families or groups of 10 people or less. General

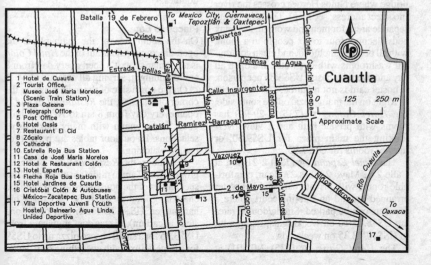

Key to map:
1 Hotel de Cuautla
2 Tourist Office,
   Museo José María Morelos
   (Scenic Train Station)
3 Plaza Galeana
4 Telegraph Office
5 Post Office
6 Hotel Oasis
7 Restaurant El Cid
8 Zócalo
9 Cathedral
10 Estrella Roja Bus Station
11 Casa de José María Morelos
12 Hotel & Restaurant Colón
13 Hotel España
14 Flecha Roja Bus Station
15 Hotel Jardines de Cuautla
16 Cristóbal Colón & Autobuses
   México–Zacatepec Bus Station
17 Villa Deportiva Juvenil (Youth
   Hostel), Balneario Agua Linda,
   Unidad Deportiva

Cuautla

0   125   250 m
Approximate Scale

To Mexico City, Cuernavaca, Tepoztlán & Oaxtepec

To Oaxaca

admission to the large pools is US$1.65 Monday to Friday, US$2 on weekends; the private pools cost US$6.70 per hour. The complex is open every day from 7 am to 7 pm.

To get to Agua Hedionda from the centre, take the 'Agua Hedionda' combi from the corner south of the tourist office, or from behind the Palacio Municipal on the main plaza, or from either side of the bridge where Avenida Niños Héroes crosses the river (the balneario is in the Agua Hedionda district, on the east side of the river). Cost is US$0.25.

Other balnearios in Cuautla include El Almeal; walk four blocks east from the tourist office on Calle Defensa del Agua, then turn left (north), walk two more blocks on Centinela Gabriel Tepepa and you're there. Or there's the Balneario Agua Linda, just across the Niños Héroes bridge from the centre, or the Balneario Las Tazas, in the colonia of the same name.

Places to Stay – bottom end

Cuautla has a youth hostel, the *Villa Deportiva Juvenil* (☎ (735) 2-02-18), commonly known as the albergue. It's around behind the swimming pool and bleachers of the Balneario Agua Linda, in the Unidad Deportiva sports centre on the east side of the bridge where Niños Héroes crosses the river (no street address; see map). The hostel, with separate areas for men and women, has bunk beds sleeping four to six people in a room, with all bedding included, and clean communal washrooms with hot water. It's open all day and evening; cost is US$3.35 per person. A hostel card is not required.

Right on the main plaza, on the south side, the *Hotel Colón* (☎ (735) 2-29-90) has rooms with private bath and a view overlooking the main plaza for US$9.50, or interior rooms for US$7.95.

The *Hotel España* (☎ (735) 2-21-86), at Calle 2 de Mayo 22, has 27 clean, comfortable rooms with private bath and hot water arranged around an interior court where a few cars can be parked. Single/double rates are US$8.35/10 on weeknights, rising a bit to US$10/13.35 on weekends.

The *Hotel Oasis* (☎ (735) 2-01-01) at

Galeana 21 has 23 rather dark rooms whose windows, opening onto an interior walkway, are high enough that not everyone can look into your room. Singles/doubles here are US$10/13.35.

Places to Stay – middle

The *Hotel Jardines de Cuautla* (☎ (735) 2-00-88, 2-51-35), opposite the Cristóbal Colón bus terminal at Calle 2 de Mayo 94, has cool, stark rooms with private bath and windows opening onto lawn areas, some onto the garden in the rear of the hotel where there are two tiny swimming pools (one for adults, one for children) and a parking area for cars. Some rooms have small balconies. Singles/doubles are US$13.35/23.35.

Places to Stay – top end

The *Hotel de Cuautla* (☎ (735) 2-72-33/55/77) at Batalla 19 de Febrero 114, half a block north of Plaza Galeana, is a spotless, modern hotel with squash and tennis courts, table tennis, a physical fitness gym, a large swimming pool in the garden behind the hotel, a restaurant/bar, and enclosed parking. The rooms, all with air-conditioning, colour TV and phone, cost US$41.35/51 for singles/doubles.

Places to Eat

On the south side of the main plaza, the open-air corner restaurant of the *Hotel Colón* is a popular spot; it's open every day from 8 am to midnight, serving all meals.

On the north side of the main plaza on the corner of Galeana, the *Restaurant El Cid* is open every day from 8 am to 10 pm, with a good, varied menu with many inexpensive selections. Its outdoor tables are perfect for people-watching.

Next door, the *Restaurant/Bar El Portal* is open from 7 am to midnight every day. The specialities of the house are the pizza and the charcoal-grilled meats (US$1.85 for a big hamburger, US$4.70 for sirloin or T-bone steak al carbón). Pizzas cost anywhere from US$3.35 for a small cheese pizza up to US$9 for a large deluxe with everything on it. Here, too, the tables out on the main plaza are great for watching the world go by.

In the blocks around the main plaza, especially on Calle 2 de Mayo between the main plaza and the bus stations, and on Galeana heading north from the main plaza, there are many other inexpensive little restaurants, cafés, fruit juice stalls and ice cream shops.

Getting There & Away
The Cristóbal Colón and Autobuses México-Zacatepec companies share a large bus station at Calle 2 de Mayo 97, at the corner of Calle Segundo Viernes (☎ (735) 2-62-77). The Flecha Roja bus station (☎ (735) 2-20-65) is a block away, at Calle 2 de Mayo 74, on the corner of Mongoy. A block north of this, at the corner of Vazquez and Mongoy, is the Estrella Roja bus station (☎ 2-09-59).

Flecha Roja has only one bus route from Cuautla; starting at Cuautla it goes to Jojutla, Zacatepec, Iguala, Chilpancingo, and Acapulco.

Other buses from Cuautla include:

Cuernavaca – 42 km, one hour; every 20 minutes, 5 am to 8 pm, with Estrella Roja (US$1.15).
Mexico City – 70 km, two to 2½ hours; every 30 minutes, 5 am to 7.30 pm, with Estrella Roja (US$2.55); every 20 minutes, 4.30 am to 8.45 pm, with Cristóbal Colón (US$2.60). There are two routes to Mexico City, one via Pera (two hours) and another via Ameca (2½ hours).
Oaxaca – 410 km, seven hours; three buses daily with Cristóbal Colón (US$9.35).
Puebla – 125 km, 2½ hours; hourly, 5.45 am to 6.45 pm, with Cristóbal Colón (US$2.95).

OAXTEPEC
Ten km north-west of Cuautla, Oaxtepec is a small town but it is the home of the largest balneario and holiday centre in the state of Morelos. Sponsored by the Mexican Social Security Institute (IMSS), the 20-hectare Centro Vacacional Oaxtepec has 25 pools, with some large ones for swimming, some deep ones for diving, and some with medicinal sulphur springs. It also has restaurants, picnic areas, a supermarket, sports areas, a theatre, movies, an aerial cable car (funicular) taking you to the top of a hill for a bird's

eye view of the centre, and plenty of places to stay. The giant park can accommodate 42,000 bathers at once, and often does on weekends and holidays.

For day use, the balneario is open every day from 8 am to 6 pm. Entrance costs US$3.35 for adults, half price for children (age four to 11) and seniors (over 60).

Places to Stay
If you want to stay over, you can make arrangements to stay in the centre's cabañas (with or without private pool), hotels, or camping grounds. Cost is US$4 per person (half price for children) for camping (tent or trailer); US$16 for up to four people in the Hotel Económico; US$37.35 for up to six people in the Hotel Familiar; US$64 for four people in a cabin with private pool; or US$80 per night for a house sleeping seven. Phone (5) 543-0059 or 669-0521 in Mexico City; or the centre itself (☎ (735) 6-01-01, 6-02-02) for reservations and information.

Getting There & Away
The bus station in Oaxtepec is beside the entrance to the centre. The Cristóbal Colón, Autobuses México-Zacatepec, and Estrella Roja bus companies all make the 1½-hour trip between Oaxtepec and Mexico City approximately every 20 minutes from 5.30 am to 11 pm (US$2.40). They also offer bus services from Oaxtepec to Cuautla (US$0.35) and Tepoztlán (US$0.45).

From Cuernavaca, Estrella Roja buses to Oaxtepec depart every 30 minutes from 6 am to 10 pm for the 50-minute trip (US$1.15). Or you can take one of their buses heading for Cuautla, which will let you off on the highway opposite the centre.

Local combis run between Oaxtepec and Cuautla every five or 10 minutes, stopping at the entrance to the centre; cost is US$0.50 for the 15-minute trip.

TAXCO
Population: 42,000
Altitude: 1755 metres
Taxco was called Tlachco ('place where ball is played') by the Aztecs, who had domi-

nated the region since 1440. The Spanish arrived in 1529, and the city was founded by Captain Rodrigo de Castañeda, acting under a mandate from Hernán Cortés. The town's first residents were three Spanish miners – Juan de Cabra, Juan Salcedo and Diego de Nava – and the carpenter Pedro Muriel. Here, in 1531, they established the first Spanish mine on the North American continent.

The Spaniards came searching for tin, which they found in small quantities, but by 1534 they had also discovered tremendous lodes of silver, beginning a courtship with silver still going strong today.

In 1534 the Hacienda del Chorrillo was built, complete with water wheel, smelter and aqueduct. The old arches standing over the highway to Mexico City at the northern end of Taxco are all that remains of the aqueduct. The water wheel and smelter have long since vanished, but the hacienda has gone through several metamorphoses and is now part of an art school.

The prospectors quickly emptied the first veins of silver from the hacienda and left Taxco. Further significant quantities of silver were not discovered until two centuries later, in 1743. Don José de la Borda, who had arrived in 1716 from France at the age of 16 to work with his miner brother, accidentally uncovered one of the area's richest veins. According to a frequently related Taxco legend, Borda was walking near where the church of Santa Prisca now stands when his horse stumbled, dislodged a stone and exposed the silver.

Borda went on to make a fortune and build mansions, gardens (such as the Jardín Borda in Cuernavaca) and the church of Santa Prisca. His new-found wealth attracted many prospectors and the newly found veins were also emptied.

With most of the silver gone, Taxco once more became a quiet town with a dwindling population and economy. In 1932 an American professor named William Spratling arrived and, at the suggestion of then-US Ambassador Dwight Morrow, set up a small silver workshop as a way to rejuvenate the town. The workshop became a factory and Spratling's apprentices began establishing their own shops. Today there are more than 300 silver shops in Taxco selling some of the finest silverwork in the world.

Taxco is also an attraction in itself. With its labyrinth of winding cobblestone streets and passageways and a jumble of red-tiled buildings, the town conjures up romantic images of old Spain. Local laws preserve Taxco's colonial-style architecture and heritage; the federal government has gone a step further and declared the entire city a national monument.

Orientation

Taxco is 85 km south-west of Mexico City along Highway 95 to Acapulco. It's a hilly town of steep, narrow cobblestoned streets and hidden plazas, and you may feel like a mouse in a maze when you try to find your way to the town's main square, the Plaza Borda, sometimes called the zócalo.

As Highway 95 enters the city and winds through the hills around the perimeter of central Taxco, it becomes Avenida John F Kennedy. If you follow Avenida Kennedy from the north, Calle La Garita will be the first major street on your right, opposite the Pemex station and the entrance to the Hotel de la Borda. La Garita winds through the city to the Plazuela de Bernal and the Plaza Borda. From the Plazuela de Bernal, the first major street on your left, Calle Juan Ruiz de Alarcón, leads back down the hill to Avenida Kennedy.

The next major street off Kennedy is Calle de Santa Ana, which changes names to Calle San Nicolás (also called Calle Hidalgo) as it climbs back towards central Taxco to end west of the Plaza Borda at the Plazuela de San Juan. Farther along Kennedy, Calle de San Miguel also climbs towards central Taxco to intersect with Calle Santa Ana/San Nicolás at the church of La Santísima. The last major street going off Kennedy towards Plazuela de San Juan is Calle de Pilita, heading up the hill from opposite the Estrella de Oro bus station.

Information

Tourist Office The Secretaría de Fomento Turístico (☎ (732) 2-22-74/79) has an office in the Centro de Convenciones de Taxco, on Avenida John F Kennedy beside Los Arcos at the north end of town, where the old aqueduct arches over the highway. It's open Monday to Friday from 9 am to 3 pm and 6 to 8 pm; on Saturday and Sunday from 9 am to 8 pm with fewer staff. Both the state and federal government tourist offices are here; a couple of other tourist information offices are also on the highway near town.

Post The post office is at Benito Juárez 6, upstairs in the Palacio Municipal, where a large historical mural graces the outside wall. It's open Monday to Friday from 8 am to 7 pm, Saturday 9 am to 1 pm, closed Sunday. There are rumours that the post office is going to move, but no one knows to where.

Telecommunications Long-distance telephone calls can be made from the caseta at the Farmacia de Cristo at Calle San Nicolás 12 (also called Calle Hidalgo), a block or so down the hill from the Plazuela de San Juan. It's open every day from 8 am to 10 pm.

Another caseta is in the Farmacia Oscarín, on the highway at John F Kennedy 47, opposite the Flecha Roja bus terminal. Hours are Monday to Saturday from 9 am to 8 pm, Sunday 9 am to 3 pm.

The most convenient way to make long-distance calls from Taxco is to use a Ladatel telephone debit card. The post office is the central place for buying these cards but they're also sold at several hotels, banks, etc, and by the fellow who sells lottery tickets in the Plaza Borda opposite the church of Santa Prisca. There are many card phones near the Plaza Borda and in hotel lobbies.

The telecommunications office (telegram, telegraph and fax) is beside the post office; hours are 9 am to 3 pm, Monday to Friday.

Iglesia de Santa Prisca

Located on Plaza Borda, this is Taxco's second most popular attraction after the silver shops. Constructed by Spanish architects Diego Durán and Juan Caballero from 1748 to 1758 for Don José de la Borda and his son Manuel, a priest, the rosy-stoned church is a masterpiece of baroque architecture. The façade is a Churrigueresque riot of elaborately sculpted figures and decorations. Over the doorway, the bas-relief depicts Christ's baptism.

Inside, the intricately sculpted altarpieces covered with gold leaf are equally fine examples of Churrigueresque art. On both sides of the main altar and in the sacristy are paintings by Miguel Cabrera, including one showing Mary pregnant. Another painting depicts San Sebastián, Taxco's other patron saint along with Santa Prisca, being martyred by arrows. It's said that Santa Prisca was chosen for the town's patron saint because she is the saint of lightning.

Other Churches

Other colonial churches in Taxco include La Santísima, San Nicolás, San Miguel, Santa Veracruz, Chavarrieta, and the Ex-Convento de San Bernardino. Up on the hill above the Plaza Borda are the churches of Ojeda and Guadalupe. The little square in front of the church of Guadalupe affords a fine view over the town.

Museo de Taxco Guillermo Spratling

This three-storey museum of archaeology and history is at Calle Profesor Porfirio A Delgado 1, directly behind the church of Santa Prisca. Pre-Hispanic art exhibits on the two upper floors include jade statuettes, Olmec crafts and ceramics and other interesting pieces, mostly from the private collection of William Spratling. The ground floor is devoted to temporary exhibits.

The museum is open Tuesday to Saturday from 10 am to 5 pm, Sunday 9 am to 3 pm, closed Monday. Guided tours are offered Tuesday to Saturday at 10.30 am and 1.30 pm. Admission is US$3.35 (children under 13 free).

Casa Humboldt

On Calle Juan Ruíz de Alarcón a couple of

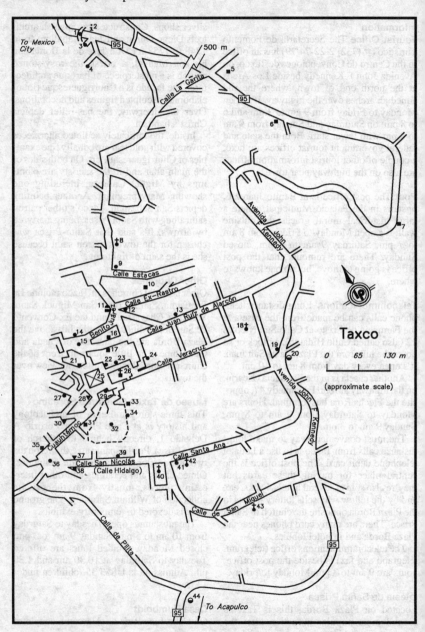

To Mexico City

Calle La Garita

95

500 m

95

Avenida John F. Kennedy

Calle Estacas

Calle Ex-Rastro

Benito Juárez

Calle Juan Ruiz de Alarcón

Calle Veracruz

Avenida John F. Kennedy

Taxco

0   65   130 m

(approximate scale)

Museo de Taxco

Cuauhtémoc

Calle San Nicolás
(Calle Hidalgo)

Calle Santa Ana

Calle de San Miguel

Calle de Pilita

To Acapulco

95

blocks down the hill from the Plazuela de Bernal stands one of the oldest colonial homes in Taxco. In 1803 this was the house of German explorer and naturalist Baron von Friedrich Heinrich Alexander von Humboldt. In 1992 it was closed for restoration, expecting to reopen as a museum of colonial religious art.

Casa de Figueroa

On the Plazuela de los Gallos just a few steps from the Plaza Borda opposite the church of Santa Prisca, the Casa de Figueroa is another of Taxcós famous old houses, built in 1767 by the Count de la Cardena. It acquired the name 'House of Tears' because it was built by workers who had neglected to pay their taxes. After the death of the count, the house served as a monastery and reformatory before it was bought by the Figueroa family in 1848. Over time, the Figueroas made

changes to the house and dug a labyrinth of tunnels underneath, supposedly leading all the way to the church of Santa Prisca and up into the hills of Taxco, to escape revolutionaries who harrassed them in the early 1900s.

In the 1950s and '60s Richard Nixon, Bette Davis and General MacArthur stayed at the house at different times. The last time we checked, the house was closed for repairs.

Museo de la Platería

Taxco's small Museum of Silver has exhibits and explanations (all in Spanish) relating to the history of silver in Taxco and in Mexico. The museum is at Plaza Borda 1, downstairs from the Patio de Artesanías (enter from the sidewalk as if you were going to Señor Costilla's restaurant, turn left instead of right on the patio, and go down the stairs). The museum is open every day from 10 am to 5 pm; admission US$1 (children free).

Silver Shops

Silver is the main attraction of Taxco and among the hundreds of silver shops are several that are particularly noteworthy, with some of the finest silverwork in Mexico. Several are in the Patio de las Artesanías building at Plaza Borda 1, in the corner of the plaza to your left as you face Santa Prisca. Pineda's, also on the Plaza Borda, on the corner of Calle Celso Muñoz between the Patio de las Artesanías building and Santa Prisca, is one famous shop; a couple of doors down Muñoz, at No 4, the Joyería Elena Ballesteros is another.

On the Plazuela de Bernal, just a short block north of the Plaza Borda, Los Castillo Plateros at Bernal 10 is worth visiting. The Castillo family has been working in silver for over 60 years and they present a remarkable display, not only of jewellery but also of statues, large vases, silverware, ceramic/silver creations, and many other unusual items. You're welcome to walk through the workshop behind the display rooms and see how everything is made. The shop is open daily from 9 am to 1 pm and from 3 to 7 pm, Sunday from 9 am to 3 pm.

Cable Car (Teleférico)

At the northern end of Taxco near Los Arcos is an unexpected sight – a million-dollar Swiss cable-car system that ascends 173 metres to the luxurious Monte Taxco resort. The panoramic view of Taxco from the cable car and resort is fantastic, and on the far side, away from Taxco looking over the tennis courts, on a clear day you can see all the way to the Popocatépetl and Iztaccíhuatl volcanoes.

The cable car runs daily from 7.30 am to 7 pm; fare is US$1.70 one-way or US$3.35 return (children half-price). From Los Arcos, over the highway, enter at the gate of the Instituto de Artes Plásticas de Taxco, a silversmith school; you can see the cable-car terminal from the gate.

Up at the resort you can use their facilities for a price: it's US$6.70 for an hour of tennis or horseback riding or for all-day use of the swimming pool, US$5 an hour to use the gym and steam baths, or US$23.50 for a round of nine holes of golf. The bar overlooking the pool has a superb view of Taxco, and there's also a restaurant and a discothèque.

Festivals

Try to time your visit to Taxco during one of its several annual festivals, but be sure to make hotel reservations in advance because finding a room can be difficult.

Santa Prisca & San Sebastián The festivals of Taxco's two patron saints are celebrated on 18 January (Santa Prisca) and 20 January (San Sebastián). Mass is celebrated in the cathedral while people parade by the entrance with their pets and farm animals in tow for an annual blessing. Game booths are set up outside the cathedral's gates and groups of dancers entertain the many pilgrims who come for the mass.

En El Atrio de la Parroquia de Ojeda The celebration In the Front Court of the Parish Church of Ojeda on 24 February includes colourful performances by various music and dance groups.

Palm Sunday Jesus Christ's triumphant entrance into Jerusalem on a donkey is re-enacted in the streets of Taxco on the Sunday before Easter.

Maundy Thursday On the Thursday before Easter, the institution of the Eucharist is commemorated with beautiful presentations and street processions of hooded penitents. Some of the penitents, bearing crosses, flagellate themselves with thorns as the procession winds through the streets. All during Semana Santa (Holy Week), visitors from around the world pour into the city to see the processions and events.

Día de San Miguel Regional dance groups perform in the front court of the beautiful 18th-century chapel of Archangel San Miguel on 29 September.

El Día del Jumíl *Jumiles* are small beetles, about one cm long, which migrate annually to the Cerro de Huixteco (the hill behind Taxco) to reproduce. They begin to arrive around September; the last ones are gone by about January or February. During this time, the jumiles are a great delicacy for the people of Taxco, who eat them alone, or mixed in salsa with tomatoes, garlic, onion, chiles etc, or even *alive*, rolled into tortillas. (You can buy live jumiles in the mercado during this time; the Restaurant Santa Fe serves *salsa de jumíl* prepared in the traditional way.)

El Día del Jumíl is celebrated on the first Monday after the Day of the Dead (which is on 2 November). Traditionally, the entire population of the town climbs the Cerro de Huixteco on this day, collecting jumiles, bringing picnics and sharing food and fellowship. Many families come early and camp on the hill over the weekend preceding the Monday, but the Monday is the actual day. In old tradition, this celebration represented the giving of energy and life by the jumiles to the townspeople of Taxco for another year.

Feria de la Plata The week-long national silver fair is held during the last week in November or the first week in December (check with the tourist office for exact dates). National silverwork competitions are held in various categories (statuary, jewellery, etc) and some of Mexico's best silverwork is on display. Other festivities include organ recitals in Santa Prisca, rodeos, burro races, concerts and dances.

Las Posadas From 16 to 24 December, nightly candle-lit processions pass through the streets of Taxco singing from door-to-door, going from one church to another each night, finally arriving at the church of Santa Prisca on Christmas Eve. The children are usually dressed up to resemble various Biblical characters. At the end of the processions, decorated *piñatas* (clay pots in the shape of an animal, pineapple etc) stuffed with candy are hung from ropes in the streets and blindfolded children take turns trying to break them open while adults control the ropes.

Places to Stay – bottom end

The *Casa de Huéspedes Arrellano* (☎ (732) 2-02-15) at Calle los Pajaritos 23 offers 10 simple but clean rooms in a central location tucked away in a backstreet across from the Mercado de Artesanías Plata. It's a family-run place with sitting terraces and a place on the roof for washing clothes. Single rooms cost US$6.70 with shared bath (hot water) or US$10 with private bath; doubles are US$11.70. To find it, walk about 15 metres down the alley going down the right side of Santa Prisca (as you face the church) until you reach a staircase going off to your right. Follow it, winding down, until you come to the next place you can take stairs down, to your left; walk down these and the casa de huéspedes is 30 steps down, on your left as you enter the tiny plaza with the Mercado de Artesanías Plata.

Much easier to find is the *Hotel Casa Grande* (☎ (732) 2-01-23), right on the Plazuela de San Juan, upstairs in the same building with the Cine Ana Maria. It has 12 clean, basic rooms arranged around an inner courtyard; the rooftop rooms are the most pleasant, with plenty of windows and cross-ventilation, opening onto a large rooftop terrace. On one side is a *lavadero* where you can wash clothes. Singles/doubles are US$9.50/14.35, all with private hot-water bath.

Places to Stay – middle

One of the most attractive places to stay in Taxco at any price is the *Hotel Posada de las Palmas* (☎ (732) 2-31-77, 2-02-31), at Ex-Rastro 4 and Estacas 1, half a block down the hill from the Palacio Municipal. Though it's centrally located, it's quiet and peaceful, with a private parking area, and a lovely, large enclosed garden with a big swimming pool. The high-ceilinged rooms are clean, spacious and pleasant, with firm beds, and many have private terraces. Singles/doubles cost US$15.65/20.70; there are also several apartments which rent for around US$250 to US$350 per month.

The *Hotel Los Arcos* (☎ (732) 2-18-36), Juan Ruíz de Alarcón 2, is near the Plaza Borda and has 26 beam-ceilinged rooms around a cool courtyard. In 1620 the building was a monastery; it retains a splendid architecture, with a pleasant courtyard, sitting areas and rooftop terrace. The rooms are tastefully decorated and cost US$16/24 for singles/doubles, all with private bath.

Opposite the Los Arcos, the *Hotel Posada de los Castillo* (☎ (732) 2-13-96, fax 2-29-35) at Juan Ruíz de Alarcón 3 is another place with colonial charm. Singles/doubles here cost US$16/20.70.

The *Hotel Meléndez* (☎ (732) 2-00-06), Cuauhtémoc 6, is an older place, but it has many pleasant terrace sitting areas, a pleasant off-street restaurant, and it's in a good location between the Plazuela de San Juan and the Plaza Borda. Singles/doubles are US$16.70/25.

Right on the zócalo, the *Hotel Agua Escondida* (☎ (732) 2-07-26/36), Calle Guillermo Spratling 4, has several attractive terraces, a large terrace swimming pool, and a basement car park. The comfortable, airy rooms cost US$28.35/33.35.

On the south side of the Plazuela de San Juan, the colonial-style *Hotel Santa Prisca* (☎ (732) 2-00-80, 2-09-80), Cena Obscuras 1, is an elegant place with a quiet interior patio, a bright, comfortable sitting room with a library of books in English, and a pleasant restaurant where breakfast is served from 7.30 to 9.30 am. Rooms, most with private terraces, are US$30/36.

On the highway near town, the motel-style *Hotel Loma Linda* (☎ (732) 2-02-06, 2-07-53) at Avenida John F Kennedy 52 is perched on the ledge of a vast and beautiful chasm; each of the spotlessly clean rooms has a private terrace with a sweeping vista, and they're far enough back from the highway to be quiet and peaceful. There's a swimming pool with a slide for the kids, a restaurant, and a pleasant lawn area; singles/doubles are US$23.35/28.35. It's worth considering whether or not you've come by car; combis

pass by on the highway every few minutes to take you up the hill to town.

Places to Stay – top end

The four-star *Hotel de la Borda* (☎ (732) 2-00-25), Cerro del Pedregal 2 opposite the junction of Avenida Kennedy and Calle La Garita, is a 120- room, modern mission-style hotel with large, clean standard rooms for US$50, junior suites for US$60 and master suites for US$130, some overlooking the swimming pool. A few rooms offer panoramic views of the city. Rooms on the ground floor are still comfortable, but views of the city are blocked by trees.

The five-star *Posada de la Misión* (☎ (732) 2-00-63, 2-05-33, fax 2-21-98), also on the highway at Avenida John F Kennedy 32, is a luxurious place whose 120 large rooms have private terraces with a view of Taxco; there are also several spacious suites and a large swimming pool with jacuzzi. The single/double rates of US$90/100 include breakfast.

Way up on top of the mountain overlooking Taxco, the five-star *Hotel Monte Taxco* (☎ (732) 2-13-00/1/2, fax 2-14-28) is probably the most luxurious place to stay in Taxco. It can be reached by car, taxi or cable car; the rates of US$95 for standard rooms, or US$117 for suites, include use of the hotel's facilities: golf, tennis, horseback riding, gym, steam baths, and a large swimming pool with a marvellous view. There are also restaurants, bars and a disco.

Places to Eat

The *Restaurant Santa Fe* at Hidalgo 2, a few doors downhill from the Plazuela de San Juan, is the one that locals most often recommend for good food at a good price, and it does indeed serve delicious food. The comida corrida for US$5.50, with a choice of soups, then spaghetti or Mexican rice, a choice of main courses with beans and rolls, and finally dessert or coffee, is tasty and filling; they also serve good breakfasts. It's open from 8 am to 11 pm, every day of the year.

Overlooking the Plaza Borda, the open-air

Restaurant/Bar Paco is great for people-watching, and is open every day from noon to 11 pm. Two of the house specialities are the ensalada Popeye (a spinach salad with mushrooms, bacon and nuts), and the queso cilantro (cheese fondue with potato skins, salsa verde, cilantro and sesame, served with tortillas). They also serve garlic, onion, mushroom, and cream of corn soups.

Señor Costilla's, upstairs in the Patio de las Artesenías overlooking the Plaza Borda, is one of the Carlos Anderson chain and resembles the gringo-style Carlos 'n Charlie's restaurants that have sprouted up all over Mexico, with loud rock & roll music shaking the many old photographs and pictures on the walls. A lot of gringos and Mexicans alike come here to party and the prices on the menu, though a bit high by Mexican standards, are not unreasonable. It's open every day from 1 pm to midnight.

If you enter the same building at the Plaza Borda entrance, as if you were going to Señor Costilla's, but turn to your left instead of your right, you come to a stairway leading up to the *Pizzería Mario*. This small open-air restaurant, with only a few tiny tables out on a terrace, has one of the best views in all Taxco; it's worth eating here or having a coffee just to enjoy the airy view over the canyon. It's open every day from 10 am to midnight. The pizza, and the spaghetti served with garlic bread, are pretty good too.

Bora Bora Pizza at Delicias 4, just off Calle Cuauhtémoc not far from the Plaza Borda, is an attractive restaurant with a pleasant decor and the locals swear it serves the best pizza in Taxco. Prices range from US$3.35 to US$5.70 for a small, up to US$8 to US$13.35 for a maxi; they also serve spaghetti, cheese fondue and good desserts, dishing it up every day from 1 pm to midnight.

Restaurant La Hacienda, just off the Plaza Borda, can be reached through the lobby of the Hotel Agua Escondido or through the separate entrance around the corner. Their specialty, cecina hacienda, is a large, delicious special Mexican meal of tender beefsteak served with sausage, rice, beans, guacamole, cheese, chicharrones (crisp pork rinds) and a chalupita (a tiny tostada), all for US$8.70. Of course they also have many other things on the menu; they're open every day from 7 am to 10 pm.

Opposite the Palacio Municipal, the *Restaurant Los Reyes* at Benito Juárez 9 is a quieter place for a meal, away from the Plaza Borda. It's another upstairs restaurant, with colourful woven tablecloths and some tables out on the terrace, and is open every day from 8 am to 10 pm.

If you want to spend more at one of Taxcós fancier restaurants, try *La Taberna* at Benito Juárez 8, beside the Palacio Municipal, or the restaurant at the luxurious *Hotel Monte Taxco*, on the mountaintop overlooking the city, with a splendid view. In addition to the à la carte menu, the Monte Taxco's restaurant serves all-you-can-eat buffet meals which are actually quite reasonably priced for what you get: US$10 for breakfast, US$11.70 for lunch, and US$13 for dinner. Take the time to enjoy a drink at the bar overlooking the swimming pool and that great view; after dinner, you could dance the night away at the hotel's disco.

Entertainment

For drinks and people-watching over the Plaza Borda, try the terraces of the Restaurant/Bar Paco, Señor Costilla's, or the Bar Berta beside Santa Prisca. The Berta, opened by a lady of the same name in the early 1930s, is known for its house drink, also called Berta; another claim to fame is that William Spratling supposedly invented the Margarita here.

Taxco has several discothéques, including the *Escapar Artes*, a downstairs disco on the north-eastern corner of the Plaza Borda; Bugambilias near the Palacio Municipal; Corsario on Calle La Garita; Güiri Güiri on Calle Cuauhtémoc; Salsa Romántica on Avenida John F Kennedy; and Windows, at the mountaintop Hotel Monte Taxco.

On the Plazuela de San Juan, in the same building as the Hotel Casa Grande, is a movie house, the Cine Ana Maria. Also in the same building, the Café/Bar La Concha

Nostra has table tennis, a billiards table, chess, and other games, and a few tables on tiny terraces overlooking the plazuela. It's open every day from 9 am until 10 pm or later.

Things to Buy

Silver is why many people come to Taxco. There are more than 300 shops specialising in silverwork; the selection of jewellery is mind-boggling. If you are careful and willing to bargain a bit, good deals can be obtained. Don't buy anything that doesn't have the Mexican government '.925' stamp and spread-eagle hallmark (sometimes only one symbol appears), which certify that the piece is 92.5% pure sterling silver. Anything else might be silver-plated tin or copper or *alpaca*, a cheap silver-like metal. Anyone who is discovered selling forged .925 pieces is sent to prison. The shops in and around the Plaza Borda tend to have higher prices than shops farther from the centre.

Getting There & Away

Bus Taxco has two long-distance bus terminals, both on Avenida John F Kennedy, the local name for Highway 95. The Flecha Roja terminal (☎ (732) 2-01-31), at Avenida John F Kennedy 104, also serves as the terminal for the Cuauhtémoc bus line. The Estrella de Oro terminal (☎ (732) 2-06-48) is at Avenida John F Kennedy 126, where Calle Pilita meets the highway.

Combis pass the Flecha Roja terminal every few minutes and will take you up the hill to the Plaza Borda for US$0.20 (get one marked 'zócalo'). From the Estrella de Oro terminal you must walk or take a taxi (US$1).

Long-distance buses from Taxco include:

Acapulco – 260 km, five hours; seven daily with Cuauhtémoc (US$6.35); four daily with Estrella de Oro (US$7.40). These buses stop at Iguala (one hour, US$1) and Chilpancingo (three hours, US$3.35) on the way to Acapulco.
Cuernavaca – 80 km, 1½ to 2½ hours; hourly from 6.30 am to 6.30 pm with Flecha Roja; three daily with Estrella de Oro (both US$1.70).

Grutas de Cacahuamilpa – 30 km, 45 minutes; take bus heading to Toluca and get off at the 'Grutas' crossroads (US$1). Or, take an hourly combi from in front of the Flecha Roja terminal (US$1).
Iguala – 35 km, one hour; every 15 minutes from 5 am to 9 pm with Cuauhtémoc (US$1).
Ixtapan de la Sal – 68 km, two hours; every half hour, 6.20 to 5.30 pm, with Flecha Roja (US$2.35).
Mexico City (Central Sur terminal) – 140 km, three hours; hourly from 5 am to 8 pm with Flecha Roja (US$3.45); five daily with Estrella de Oro (US$3.75).
Toluca – 145 km, three hours; six daily with Cuauhtémoc (US$4.75).
Zihuatanejo – 520 km, 10 hours; one daily with Estrella de Oro (US$12.30).

Car & Motorbike Cars can be hired from Renta de Autos Satturno (☎ (732) 2-11-30, 2-14-91, 2-12-10), located at Avenida John F Kennedy 32.

Moto Renta (☎ (732) 2-25-67), on the highway at Avenida John F Kennedy 24, hires Honda 50 motorcycles; cost is US$8.35 per hour, or US$50 for eight hours.

Getting Around

Combi Aside from walking, combis and taxis are the most popular ways of getting around the steep winding streets of Taxco. Combis, white Volkswagen microbuses, are an excellent way to get around Taxco; departing every five minutes or so, they operate every day from 7 am to 8 pm and cost US$0.20.

The 'Zócalo' combi departs from Plaza Borda, goes down Calle Cuauhtémoc to the Plazuela de San Juan, then heads down the hill on Calle de San Nicolás/Hidalgo, makes a right at Calle San Miguel, turns left at the highway, and follows it until turning upwards towards town on Calle La Garita.

The 'Arcos/Zócalo' combi follows basically the same route except that it continues past Calle La Garita to Los Arcos.

The 'Guadalupe' combi, also departing from the Plaza Borda, heads up the hill above Taxco to the church of Guadalupe, from where there's a marvellous view over town.

The 'Panorámica' combi, departing from the Plazuela de San Miguel, is another good one for views, going to the top of the mountain overlooking town.

Several other combis serve various small farming communities near Taxco.

Taxi Taxis are plentiful in Taxco; the average taxi ride costs US$1. You can phone for a taxi (☎ 2-03-01).

AROUND TAXCO
Las Grutas de Cacahuamilpa

The caverns of Cacahuamilpa are a beautiful, natural wonder of stalactites, stalagmites and twisted rock formations 30 km north-east of Taxco. The huge caves, protected as a national park, are truly impressive and worth visiting.

You are required to enter the caves with a guide, who leads groups two km into the cave along an illuminated walkway, pointing out interesting formations and features of the 25-metre-high caverns. When you reach the end, you're free to walk the two km back out at your own pace, contemplating the wonders of the cave. The entire tour takes about two hours.

Cave tours depart from the visitors' centre at the entrance every hour on the hour from 10 am to 5 pm; cost is US$5 (US$3.35 for children aged five to 12).

There are restaurants, snacks, souvenir shops, etc at the visitors' centre; if you want to stay near the caves, the *Hotel Las Bugambilias* is about a 10-minute drive away, at Km 2 on the highway from Michapa to Puente de Ixtla. A map at the visitors' centre shows you how to get there.

To get to the caves from Taxco, hourly combis depart from in front of the Flecha Roja bus terminal; the trip takes about 45 minutes and costs US$1. This combi goes right to the visitor's centre at the caves. Alternatively, you can take any bus heading for Toluca or Ixtapan de la Sal; after 30 km (about 45 minutes), get off at the 'Grutas' crossroads and walk one km down the road to the visitors' centre.

The caves are further from Cuernavaca than from Taxco but some people do visit them from there. Flecha Roja buses make the 80 km, 2½-hour trip from Cuernavaca hourly from 6 am to 6 pm. If you're coming from Mexico City, Autos Pullman de Morelos buses depart from the city's Central Sur terminal every two hours from 6.50 am to 2.50 pm.

Tehuilotepec

In the village of Tehuilotepec (often called simply 'Tehui' by locals), five km north of Taxco on the road to Cuernavaca, is a mining museum, the Museo de la Minería, in a historic house built by José de la Borda. The museum is right on the town plaza, where there is also an old colonial church. Take a 'Tehui' combi from Avenida John F Kennedy in Taxco.

Ixcateopan

The village of Ixcateopan, 26 km south-west of Taxco, was the birthplace of Cuauhtémoc, the final Aztec emperor, who was defeated and later executed by Cortés. After the emperor's death his remains were returned to his native village; they are entombed in the church on the town plaza. A historical museum, the Museo de la Mexicanidad, is also on the plaza.

Ixcateopan is also interesting due to the marble quarries nearby. Marble being the most common stone in the area, it was used to construct buildings, houses and even the streets, making Ixcateopan one of the few towns in the world with streets made of marble.

A combi marked 'Ixcateopan' departs Taxco from in front of the Seguro Social, where Calle de San Miguel meets the highway, approximately every hour from around 7 am to 5 pm; the trip takes about one to two hours and costs around US$1.70.

IGUALA
Population: 83,400

Iguala is an industrial city on Highway 95 about 35 km south of Taxco and 170 km south of Mexico City. The city is of interest for its past rather than its present.

On 24 February 1821, at the height of Mexico's struggle for independence from

Spain, Viceroy Agustín Iturbide and rebel leader Vicente Guerrero met here and issued the historic Plan de Iguala, an unusual declaration of independence. The declaration was the result of Iturbide's defection from the Spanish crown and offer to make peace with Guerrero.

Iturbide and Guerrero recognised the need for conservative support in Mexico for a new government to succeed. They also wanted to appease liberal factions clamouring for an independent republic. Consequently, rather than berate Spain in the declaration, they stated that Spain was the most magnanimous of nations but, after 300 years as a colony, it was time for Mexico to become a nation in its own right. After some badgering, Spain agreed to the plan, Mexico's first flag was sewn and raised in Iguala and a provisional junta was installed in Mexico City as a prelude to an independent Congress.

When the Congress was formed, it immediately began chopping away at Iturbide's military support. Iturbide sensed that his hope of being ruler of Mexico was slipping away, so he engineered a demonstration of soldiers who demanded that he declare himself emperor. The ruse succeeded and, on 19 May 1822, Congress was intimidated into proclaiming him constitutional emperor of Mexico. So much for Mexico's break with Spain's imperial style of government.

Iguala's only interesting sight is the block-like Monument to the Flag & the Young Heroes of the Revolution on the main plaza. Built in 1942, it features the sculpted figures of Mexico's independence heroes: Morelos, Guerrero and Hidalgo.

Tamarind trees planted around the plaza in 1832 in honour of the Plan de Iguala established tamarind as the city's fruit. Try an *agua de tamarindo* at any of the juice stands near the plaza.

Every year, from 17 to 28 February, Iguala hosts the Flag Fair, a colourful celebration with rodeos, horse-racing, a parade, and exhibits from local farms and businesses.

The *Iguana Loca* (Crazy Iguana) restaurant is a km or two south-east of the town centre, next to the Club de Leones (Lion's Club) on Highway 95. It has been recommended by travellers as the place to go if you have always wondered about the taste of iguana.

CHILPANCINGO

Population: 97,200
Altitude: 1360 metres
Chilpancingo, capital of Guerrero, is a university city and agricultural centre on Highway 95, about 130 km north of Acapulco and 270 km south of Mexico City.

Murals in the former Palacio Municipal showing the 1813 Congress of Chilpancingo are the only remaining signs of the city's important place in Mexico's history. In the spring of 1813, rebel leader José Maria Morelos y Pavón encircled Mexico City with his guerrilla army and then called for a congress to meet in Chilpancingo. The Congress issued a Declaration of Independence and began to lay down the principles of a new constitution. Their achievements, however, were short-lived because Spanish troops broke the circle around Mexico City and recaptured most of Guerrero, including Chilpancingo. Morelos was tried for treason and executed by a firing squad.

ACAPULCO

Population: 1,200,000
Acapulco was the first of the ports and resort cities on Mexico's Pacific coast. Its name is derived from the ancient Nahuatl Indian words meaning Where the Reeds Stood or Place of Giant Reeds. Archaeological finds in the area show that when the Spaniards arrived, Indians had been living around Acapulco Bay and the nearby bay of Puerto Marqués for about 2000 years, and had progressed from a hunting and gathering to an agricultural society.

Spanish sailors discovered the Bay of Acapulco in 1512. Port and ship-building facilities were later established here because of the bay's substantial natural harbour.

In 1523 Hernán Cortés, Juan Rodríguez Villafuerte and merchant Juan de Sala joined to finance an overland trade route between

Acapulco and Mexico City. This route, known as the 'Camino de Asia', was the principal trade route between Mexico City and the Pacific; the 'Camino de Europa', continuing on from Mexico City to Veracruz on the Caribbean coast, formed a link between the Orient and Spain.

Acapulco became the only port in the New World authorised to receive the naos (Spanish trading galleons) from the Philippines and China. During the annual 'Acapulco Fair', lasting from three to eight weeks after the galleons arrived from Manila each year in the spring, traders converged on Acapulco from Manila, Mexico City and Peru.

By the 17th century, trade with the Orient was flourishing and Dutch and English pirate ships abounded in the Pacific Ocean and along the coastlines of Mexico and Baja California. To ward off the pirates, Fort San Diego was built atop a low hill overlooking the bay. It was not until the end of the 18th century that Spain permitted its colonies in the Americas to engage in free trade, ending the monopoly of the naos and the Manila-Acapulco route for trade with the Orient. The naos continued trading until the early 19th century when they were replaced by bigger and better sailing ships.

With independence, Mexico severed most of its trade links with Spain and its colonies, and Acapulco declined as a port city. It became relatively isolated from the rest of the world until a paved road was built in 1927 linking it with Mexico City. As Mexico City grew larger its citizens began flocking to the Pacific coast for vacations. With a new international airport, Acapulco became a booming resort by the 1950s.

Today Acapulco is a fast-growing city of dual personalities. Along the bay and for two blocks inland, it's a place of beaches, hotels, motels, discos, designer shopping plazas and restaurants with trilingual menus (many French Canadians come here). Beyond this is a city of auto parts stores, a polluted river, tacky billboards, crowded apartment buildings and long lines of fuming buses that choke passers-by.

Throughout the year you can expect average daytime temperatures of 27 to 33°C and night-time temperatures of 21 to 27°C. Afternoon showers are common from June to September, but rare the rest of the year.

Orientation

Acapulco is on a narrow coastal plain along the 11-km shore of the Bahía de Acapulco. Reached by Highway 200 from the east and west and by Highway 95 from the north, it is 400 km south of Mexico City and 242 km south-east of Zihuatanejo/Ixtapa.

At the western end of the city, the Peninsula de las Playas (Peninsula of Beaches) juts south from downtown Acapulco. From Playa Caleta on the southern edge of the peninsula, Avenida López Mateos climbs west and then north to Playa La Angosta and La Quebrada before curling east back towards downtown.

Playa Caleta also marks the beginning of Avenida Costera Miguel Alemán (known simply as 'La Costera'), Acapulco's principal avenue. Most of Acapulco's major hotels, restaurants, discos and other points of interest are along or just off La Costera. From Playa Caleta, La Costera cuts north/northwest across the peninsula and then hugs the shore all the way to the Icacos naval base at the east end of the city. After passing the naval base, La Costera becomes La Carretera Escénica (the Scenic Highway) for nine km, at which point it intersects Highway 200 on the left and the road to Puerto Marqués on the right. The airport is 2½ km straight ahead.

As in most Spanish colonial cities, the heart of the old downtown district is the church and its adjacent plaza. In Acapulco this plaza is called the zócalo, with the sea on one end and the church on the other.

From north/north-west of the zócalo, Vicente Guerrero and Escudero/Aquiles Serdán lead to Calzada Pie de la Cuesta, which, in turn, goes to Pie de la Cuesta, a lagoon and beach area 13 km to the west. Avenida Cuauhtémoc, Acapulco's main business street, branches right from Aquiles Serdán and runs approximately parallel to La

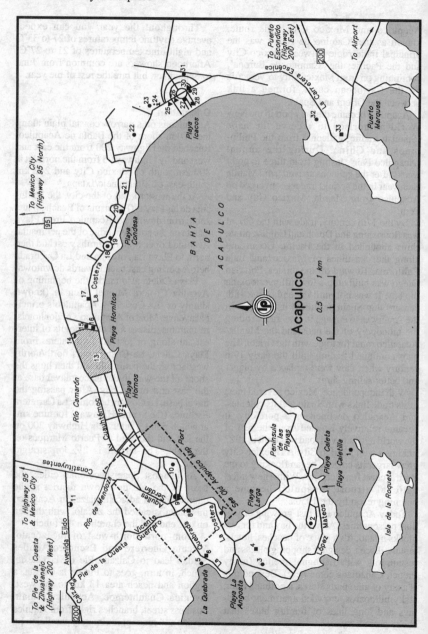

To Puerto
Escondido
(Highway
200 East)

To Airport

200

La Carretera Escénica

Puerto
Marques

32

33

BAHIA
DE
ACAPULCO

Acapulco

N

0   0.5   1 km

31

30
26
27 28 29
25
24
23

22

Playa
Icacos

Playa
Condesa

21

20

19
18

17

16
15

14

13

Playa
Hornitos

Playa
Hornos

Playa
Camarón

12

Port

Av. Cuauhtémoc

Acapulco Map
See

Old

10

9
8
7

6
5

La Costera

La Quebrada

Playa La
Angosta

Aquiles
Serdán

Vicente
Guerrero

Río de Mendoza

11

Constituyentes

To Highway 95
& Mexico City

Avenida Ejido

To Pie de la Cuesta
& Zihuatanejo
(Highway 200 West)

200

Cda. Pie de la Cuesta

1

2

3

4

Playa
Larga

Playa
Caletilla

Playa Caleta

Peninsula
de las
Playas

López Mateos

Isla de la Roqueta

To Mexico City
(Highway 95 North)

95

La Costera

■ PLACES TO STAY

4   Hotel Casablanca
6   Hotel El Faro & Hotel La Torre Eiffel
15 Auto Hotel Ritz
16 Hotel Jacqueline & Hotel del Valle
17 Hotel Club del Sol
20 Romano Palace Hotel
28 Motel Quinta Mica & Suites Selene
33 Hotel Las Brisas

▼ PLACES TO EAT

21 Carlos 'n Charlie's
25 Mariscos Pipo
26 Hard Rock Café
30 Fersato's

OTHER

1   La Capilla Submarina (Underwater Statue)
2   Bull Ring
3   French Consulate
5   Plaza La Quebrada (Divers)
7   Yacht & Boat Docks
8   Cathedral & Zócalo (Plaza)
9   Palacio Federal, Post Office & Telecomm
10 Fort of San Diego
11 Estrella Blanca Bus Station
12 Delegación Federal de Turismo (Federal Tourist Office)
13 Parque Papagayo
14 Estrella de Oro Bus Station
18 Diana Statue ('La Diana')
19 American Express
22 Club de Golf
23 Centro Internacional Acapulco (Convention Centre)
24 Tourist Assistance Bureau (State Tourist Office)
27 CICI Watersports Centre
29 Centro Cultural
31 German Consulate
32 Icacos Naval Base

Costera until it turns inland north of Playa Condesa.

Just south of the Peninsula de las Playas is the popular Isla de la Roqueta and, nearby, the so-called 'underwater shrine', a submerged bronze statue of the Virgin of Guadalupe.

Information

Tourist Office The state-run Tourist Assistance Bureau or Procuraduria del Turista (☎ (74) 84-44-16, 84-45-83) is at La Costera 4455, with an office near the sidewalk in front of the Centro Internacional Acapulco convention centre. Speaking English, Spanish and French, they offer assistance with all manner of needs, questions and complaints. Opening hours are 9 am to 9 pm every day; Friday and Saturday they're open later, until 3 am.

The federal tourism office, the Delegación Federal de Turismo (☎ (74) 85-10-41), is in a white office building on the ocean side at La Costera 187, on Playa Hornos. Opening hours are 8 am to 8 pm Monday to Friday, 10 am to 6 pm on weekends. They offer basically the same services, though the state-run office may be a bit more prepared for dealing with visitors' needs.

Both offices have plenty of printed information about Acapulco, in English, Spanish, and some in French; ask for free copies of the tourist magazines *Acapulco Inside, Info Acapulco* and *Adventure in Acapulco Mágico*.

Money You can change money at many places around Acapulco. The numerous banks give the best rates; they are open Monday to Friday from 9 am to 1 pm. Most of the casas de cambio pay a lower rate; it pays to check around as they vary quite a bit. There are many casas de cambio all along La Costera and they are open longer, more convenient hours than the banks. Hotels will also change money; their rates are usually not good, but their hours are convenient.

The American Express office (☎ (74) 84-15-10/20), at La Costera 709A just east of the Diana statue, is a full-service office, with travellers' cheques services, mail service and a travel agency. It changes travellers' cheques at the same rates as the banks, but is less crowded and is open more convenient hours: 9 am to 6 pm Monday to Friday, 9 am to 1 pm Saturday.

Post The main post office is at La Costera

125, in the Palacio Federal beside the Sanborns department store, a couple of blocks east of the zócalo. Opening hours are 8 am to 8 pm Monday to Friday, 9 am to 8 pm Saturday, and 9 am to noon on Sunday.

Telecommunications Also in the Palacio Federal beside Sanborns is the Telecomm office, with telex, telegram, money order and fax services. Hours are 9 am to 7.30 pm Monday to Friday, 9 am to noon on Saturday.

Long-distance telephone calls can be made from several casetas around town; look for signs saying 'larga distancia'. Near the zócalo, the Tabaquería Alameda on Calle La Paz, just a few steps west of the zócalo, offers long-distance, collect, and fax services. It's open Monday to Friday from 9 am to 2 pm and 3 to 8 pm, Saturday from 9 am to 5 pm, and Sunday from 9 am to 2 pm. On the other (east) side of the zócalo, the Caseta Carranza on Avenida Carranza offers services for local and long-distance calls. It's open every day from 8 am to 10 pm, but is a noisier place.

There are several other casetas along La Costera, though many of them won't let you make a collect call. You can make collect calls from any public coin phone; public phones are plentiful in Acapulco.

Foreign Consulates Consulates in Acapulco include:

Canada
    Hotel Club del Sol, La Costera & Reyes Católicos, Local No 9 (☎ (74) 85-66-00/21).
France
    Costa Grande 235, Fraccionamiento Las Playas (☎ (74) 82-33-94).
Germany
    Avenida Alaminos 26, Fraccionamiento Costa Azul (☎ (74) 84-18-60, 84-74-37).
UK
    Hotel Las Brisas, Carretera Escénica 5255 (☎ (74) 84-16-50, 84-66-05).
USA
    Hotel Club del Sol, La Costera & Reyes Católicas, Local No 8 (☎ (74) 85-66-00, 85-72-07).

Other consulates in Acapulco include those of Austria, Finland, Holland, Italy, Norway,

Panama, Spain and Sweden. The tourist offices have a complete list.

Laundry There's a laundry in the Club del Sol, at La Costera & Reyes Católicos. Another, the Lavandería Automática Acapulco (☎ 82-60-04), is at Tadeo Arredando 6, about one block back from La Costera on the same street as the Comercial Mexicana department store.

Travel Agencies Apart from American Express, Acapulco has about 50 other travel agencies, including Acuario Tours (☎ 85-61-00) at La Costera 186-2, opposite the Acapulco Plaza Hotel. Look for others in the telephone directory under 'Agencias de Viajes'.

Beaches – in town
Doing nothing on Acapulco's beaches tops most visitors' lists of things to do here. The beaches heading east around the bay from the zócalo – Playas Hornos, Hornitos, Condesa and Icacos – are the most popular. (The high-rise hotel district begins on Playa Hornitos, at the eastern side of Parque Papagayo, and heads east from there.) City buses constantly ply La Costera, the beachside avenue, making it easy to get up and down this long arc of beaches.

Playas Caleta and Caletilla are two small, protected beaches beside one another in a cove on the south side of the Peninsula de las Playas. An aquarium on a tiny point of land separates the two beaches. Boats depart from here for Isla de la Roqueta, which has a zoo and another popular beach. Any bus marked 'Caleta' heading down La Costera will take you to these beaches.

Playa La Angosta is another beach in a tiny, protected cove on the south side of the peninsula. From the zócalo it takes about 20 minutes to walk there, or you can take any 'Caleta' bus and get off near the Hotel Avenida, on a corner of La Costera. From the Hotel Avenida the beach is just one short block to the west.

Beaches – out of town

Pie de la Cuesta For less crowded beaches, try Pie de la Cuesta, 8½ km north-west of the zócalo. Pie de la Cuesta is a narrow peninsula stretching for two km between the ocean and the large fresh-water Laguna de Coyuca. It's a popular place and there are many restaurants and places to stay; it's a good alternative to the city glitz of Acapulco, and a great place for watching the sunset.

Coyuca Lagoon is three times as large as Acapulco Bay and contains the islands of Montosa, Presido and Pájaros, a bird sanctuary. Swimming and water-skiing are good in the lagoon; swimming in the ocean can be dangerous due to the shape of the waves, which sometimes get very large and crash straight down with immense force. Be extremely cautious if you swim on the ocean side; people do swim here, but each year a number of people are killed in the surf, or by the rip tide. Sometimes the waves aren't so large and swimming is easier.

To get to Pie de la Cuesta, take the 'Pie de la Cuesta' bus on La Costera opposite the post office (the one next to Sanborns, near the zócalo), on the bay side of the street. This is one of its first stops, so you'll get a seat. The ride takes about 35 minutes and costs US$0.25. Buses depart every 15 minutes from 6 am until around 7 or 8 pm; be sure to find out what time the last bus leaves Pie de la Cuesta for the return trip, unless you intend to stay the night. A taxi ride between Pie de la Cuesta and downtown Acapulco costs US$5 one-way.

Puerto Marqués About 18 km south-east of Acapulco is the beach at Puerto Marqués, which is not so different from the other beaches in town. The main reason for going there is to see the stunning view of the bay as the Carretera Escénica climbs south out of the city. Las Brisas Resort, one of Acapulco's finest hotels, is just off the highway. Buses marked 'Puerto Marqués' depart from along La Costera every 10 minutes from 4 am to 9 pm and cost US$0.30, the same as the other La Costera buses.

Beach & Water Activities

Just about everything that can be done on, under and above the water is offered at most of Acapulco's beaches.

On Acapulco Bay, waterskiing costs US$50 an hour; jet-skiing US$50 for half an hour; a ride on a huge 'banana' dragged behind a speed boat is US$3.50; or a para-sailing ride (hanging from a parachute being towed by a speedboat) is US$10. Or you can hire a small motor boat for two people for about US$27 per hour.

On the smaller Playas Caleta & Caletilla, flatboats hire for US$5 per hour, canoes for US$7 per hour, small sailboats for US$20 per hour (with a free lesson if you need one), and motor boats for US$40 per hour. Here, too, are jet skis, waterskiing, the 'banana', etc.

From Playas Caleta & Caletilla a glass-bottom boat departs for Isla de la Roqueta, giving you a view of the underwater sights and La Capilla Submarina ('The Underwater Chapel'), a submerged bronze statue of the Virgen de Guadalupe. The round trip takes about 45 minutes and costs US$7. You can get off on the island and come back on a later boat if you like – the island has a beach, a zoo, and various snorkelling and diving possibilities. You can hire snorkelling gear on Playa Caleta for US$8.50 per hour.

Scuba-diving trips and/or instruction can be arranged on Playa Caleta, on Acapulco Bay, or by contacting any of several diving operators. These include Aqua Mundo (☎ 82-10-41), La Costera 100, open 9 am to 6.30 pm; Divers de México (☎ 82-13-98), La Costera 100, open 10 am to 9 pm; Hermanos Arnold (☎ 82-18-77), La Costera 205; Long Dog (☎ 82-46-05), La Costera 143; or Mantarraya (☎ 82-60-59, 82-69-70), Gran Via Tropical 2 .

Deep-sea fishing is another possibility; cost is around US$160 for a five-hour trip. Phone Deep Sea Fishing Acapulco (☎ 82-41-91/71, 84-86-71), Barracuda's Fleet (☎ 83-85-43, 82-52-56), ask on the beaches or at travel agencies, or just stroll along the malecón near the zócalo and see which boats look likely.

Waterskiing is popular on the Coyuca

Lagoon at Pie de la Cuesta, where there are several waterski clubs. Boat trips on the lagoon are also popular, taking you across the lagoon to the place where Sylvester Stallone filmed *Rambo*. Prices for the boat trips are subject to negotiation and are set by the boat rather than the person.

The calm water at Puerto Marqués makes it another good place for waterskiing, sailing, etc.

Cruises Various boats and yachts offer cruises, departing from the Malecón (waterfront street) near the zócalo. They range from multi-level boats with blaring salsa music and open bars to yachts offering quiet sunset cruises around the harbour. You can make reservations by calling them directly, through any travel agency or at most hotels.

The large *Aca Tiki* catamaran offers a four-hour cruise to Isla de la Roqueta, beginning at 11 am; a buffet lunch and open bar are included in the US$15 price, or they also offer a dinner cruise (☎ 84-61-40, 84-67-86 for reservations).

The large *Hawaiano*, with three decks, three dance floors, three bars, live music and disco, also costs US$15 (children under 10 free); it leaves the Malecón at 4.30 and 10.30 pm, goes out near Isla de la Roqueta where the later cruise holds a beach party, passes by to see the cliff divers at La Quebrada, crosses over to Puerto Marqués, and comes back around the bay (☎ 82-12-17, 82-07-85 for reservations).

The *Bonanza* offers a morning cruise from 11 am to 2 pm (US$12), a sunset cruise from 4.30 to 7 pm (US$17), a 'pirate's cruise night' from 8 pm to midnight including all you can eat and drink plus an 'international show' and disco (US$47), and a moonlight cruise from 10.30 pm to 1 am (US$40) (☎ 83-18-03, 83-25-31 for reservations).

Divers of La Quebrada

The famous cliff divers *(clavadistas)* at La Quebrada have been amazing visitors to Acapulco ever since 1934. They dive with graceful finesse from heights of 25 to 45 metres into a narrow crevasse, with the ocean

swells rising and falling inside. Not surprisingly, the divers pray at a small shrine before leaping over the edge. So did Elvis Presley in the film *Fun in Acapulco*.

Diving times are every day at 1 pm in the afternoon, and at 7.30, 8.30, 9.30 and 10.30 pm in the evening. Admission is US$1.65 at 1 pm, US$1.35 in the evening (free for children under 12), with three divers leaping each hour.

You can also get a great view from the restaurant and bar of the Plaza Las Glorias/El Mirador Hotel. It costs US$10 to enter the bar while the diving's going on (the price includes two drinks); the view is even better from the restaurant, which offers a buffet for US$27 every evening from 7 pm until midnight.

To get to La Quebrada you can either walk up the hill from the zócalo on Calle La Quebrada, which takes about 15 minutes (it's only a few blocks but it's quite a steep hill), or take a taxi. La Quebrada is also an excellent place to come and watch the sunset.

Bullfights

South-east of La Quebrada and north-west of Playas Caleta and Caletilla is Acapulco's Plaza de Toros or bull ring. Bullfights are held on Sundays at 5 pm; you can buy tickets at the bull ring starting at 4.30 pm. Phone the tourism office for exact details and times. The traditional bullfighting season is from December to April (Christmas to Easter) but sometimes it's been ending earlier. The 'Caleta' bus passes near the bull ring. For a description of a bullfight, see the Facts About the Country chapter.

Parque Papagayo

Papagayo amusement park is opposite Playas Hornos and Hornitos; La Costera goes underground here to allow free access between the park and the beach without having to dodge across the busy avenue. It's a large park full of tropical trees and many attractions for both kids and adults.

Within the park is a hill from which there's an excellent view of all Acapulco. To get up there you can take a cable car *(teleférico)* one way, and a chair lift *(telesilla)* the other; they meet at the top. Cost is US$1 or less for the round trip. A toboggan for hurtling down the hill was out of order in 1992 but may be repaired one day. Other attractions include a roller skating rink, a lake with paddle boats for hire, a children's train, and many rides. The rides operate every afternoon and evening; the park is always open, with no admission charge.

Fuerte de San Diego & Museo Histórico

Built in 1616 atop a hill just east of the zócalo, the five-sided Fuerte de San Diego was supposed to protect the naos or galleons that conducted trade between the Philippines and Mexico from marauding Dutch and English pirates. It must have done some good because this trade route lasted until the early 19th century. Apparently it was also strong enough to forestall independence leader Morelos' takeover of the city for four months. The fort had to be rebuilt after a 1776 earthquake which damaged it along with the rest of Acapulco. It remains basically unchanged today, and has been restored to top condition.

The fort is now the home of the Museo Histórico de Acapulco, a museum with interesting exhibits on the history of the Bahía de Acapulco, including several on the commercial and cultural exchange between Mexico and the Orient during colonial times, and the role of the fort. The exhibit rooms, in the rooms of the old fort, are all air-conditioned; many posted explanations are in both Spanish and English.

The museum is open from 10.30 am until 4.40 pm, Tuesday to Sunday (closed Monday). Admission is US$3.35, but free on Sundays and holidays, and also free to everyone under 13 or over 60 years of age, and to students with proper identification.

Mercado de Artesanías

Acapulco's main crafts market is a few blocks east of the zócalo between Avenida Cuauhtémoc and Vicente de León. The 400-stall market is paved and pleasant, and is a good place to get better deals on everything that you see in the hotel shops and on the beaches – serapes, hammocks, silver jewellery, huaraches, T-shirts, etc. Bargaining is definitely the rule here.

Centro Internacional de Convivencia Infantil (CICI)

The Centro Internacional de Convivencia Infantil (all it's ever called is CICI), on La Costera on the east side of Acapulco, is a family watersports park. Dolphin and seal shows are held at 12.30, 3.30 and 5.30 pm; there's also a 30-metre-high water toboggan, a pool with artificial waves, a small tidepool aquarium, and other kids' games.

CICI is open 365 days a year from 10 am to 6 pm, with the last tickets sold at 5.30 pm. Admission is US$7.35 for adults, US$6 for children ages two to 10. Any bus marked 'CICI', 'Base' or 'Puerto Marqués' will take you there.

Centro Cultural

The Centro Cultural complex, which includes the Centro Cultural de Acapulco, the Museo Arqueológico and the Instituto Guerrerense de la Cultura, is a group of buildings set around a garden at La Costera 4834, just east of CICI. The archaeological museum has a sign on the door saying it's open every day from 9 am to 2 pm and from 5 to 8 pm; it was closed for remodelling last time we checked. The Galería Ixcáteopan in the centre was open daily from 10 am to 3 pm and from 5 to 8 pm, with permanent and changing art exhibits. Four-month and summer courses in English, music, dance and other arts are held at the centre.

Centro Internacional Acapulco

The Centro Internacional Acapulco, also called the Acapulco Convention Centre or Centro de Convenciones, is a large complex on the mountain side of La Costera, not far from CICI. The centre has a permanent crafts gallery (Galería de Artesanías), temporary special exhibitions, a large plaza where celebrations are held on holidays, and several

To Playa Hornos

To Pie de la Cuesta & Zihuatanejo (Highway 200 West)

Av Constituyentes

Humboldt

Aquiles Serdán

Av Cuauhtémoc

Parana

Acapás

J. de León

Zaragoza

Mina

5 de Mayo

Galeana

Mendoza

Escudero

Terraplen

Domingillo

5 de Mayo

Hornitos

Morelos

La Costera (Costera Miguel Alemán)

Malecón

Vicente Guerrero

To Pie de la Cuesta & Zihuatanejo

Progreso

Madero

Carranza

Old Acapulco

0   125   250 m

Approximate Scale

BAHÍA DE ACAPULCO

Hidalgo

José María Iglesias

Calle Felipe Valle

Benito

Argueta

Juárez

Constancio Martínez

Matías

Calle La Quebrada

Avenida López

La Pinzona

La Costera

To La Quebrada (1 block)

To La Quebrada (1 block)

To Playa Caleta & Playa La Angosta

1 ·
2
3
4
5
6
7
8
9
10
11
12
13 14
15
16
17
18
19
20
21
22
23
24
25
26
27
28
29

■ PLACES TO STAY

16 Hotel Misión
17 La Mama Hélène
18 Hotel Sutter
19 Casa de Huéspedes Aries & Casa de
    Huéspedes La Tía Conchita
20 Hotel Maria Antonieta
22 Hotel Fel-Mar
23 Hotel Mariscal
24 Hotel Angelita
25 Hotel Asturias
26 Casa de Huéspedes Guadalajara
27 Hotel Coral
28 Hotel Casa Amparo

▼ PLACES TO EAT

7   Cafetería Astoria
8   Mi Parri Pollo, Maggi's Pizzas
9   La Flor de Acapulco
13 Restaurant Ricardo & Restaurant San
    Carlos
14 Restaurant/Bar Caballero
15 The Fat Farm
21 El Amigo Miguel

OTHER

1   Mercado de Artesanías
2   Fort of San Diego
3   Woolworth's
4   Palacio Federal, Post Office, Telecom
    Building
5   Sanborns Department Store
6   Caseta Carranza
10 Cathedral
11 Zócalo (City Plaza)
12 Tabaquería Alameda
29 Yacht & Boat Docks

theatres where plays, music and dance programmes are performed. You can phone the
centre (☎ 84-70-50) to ask about current
offerings, or stop by their information kiosk
by the sidewalk in front of the centre.

Aquarium & Zoo

There's an aquarium on a small point of land
between Playas Caleta and Caletilla, open
every day from 9 am to 7 pm. Admission is
US$5 (children US$3.35).

Out on the Isla de la Roqueta is a zoo,

which also features telescopes and childrens'
games. It's open every day except Tuesday,
10 am to 5 pm; admission US$1.

Festivals
Nao de China This arts and crafts festival
from 7 to 30 November commemorates the
galleons that conducted trade between
Mexico and the Philippines from the 16th to
the early 19th centuries. Oriental exhibits,
local music groups and various cultural
events are featured.

Nuestro Señora de Guadalupe Celebrated
all night on 11 December and all the following day, with processions accompanied by
small marching bands, fireworks and folk
dances in the streets, all converging on the
cathedral in the zócalo, where children are
brought dressed in costumes. It's a lesser
version of the Mexico City festival.

Expo-Acapulco An industrial and commercial exposition is held from 20 December to
7 January to encourage greater investment in
Acapulco.

Places to Stay
Acapulco has a great number of hotels and
over 25,000 hotel rooms, but its tourism is
seasonal. High season is in winter, from the
middle of December until the day after
Easter; the rest of the year tourism is much
slower. Most hotels raise their rates during
high season, when they can be as much as
double the low-season (summer) price,
though some do this for only part of the
season or even not at all. At other times of
year you can often bargain for a better rate,
especially if you plan to stay a while. If you
come to Acapulco at an especially busy time,
like Christmas/New Year or Easter week, be
sure to have hotel reservations or you may
do a lot of walking looking for a room. We're
giving the high-season prices here.

Places to Stay – bottom end
Most of Acapulco's budget hotels are con-
centrated around the zócalo area, and on
Calle La Quebrada, the street going up the

hill from behind the cathedral to La Quebrada, where the divers do their stuff. There are many more hotels in this area, if all the ones listed are full. All the hotels mentioned in this section come with fan and private bath, unless otherwise noted.

A favourite with many travellers (especially those who speak French) is *La Mama Hélène* (☎ (74) 82-23-96; fax 83-86-97) at Benito Juárez 12, near the corner of Calle Felipe Valle. Hélène, the proprietress, comes from France, speaks English, French and Spanish, and does indeed treat her guests like a 'mama', with special care. Though it's right downtown, the place has a quiet and pleasant atmosphere, with nicely decorated rooms and an interior courtyard with aquariums, table tennis, and tables where breakfast with good French coffee is served. Rates are US$10/15 for singles/doubles, breakfast extra.

Nearby, the *Hotel Misión* (☎ (74) 82-36-43) at Calle Felipe Valle 12 is another special place. Higher priced than most other hotels in this district, it's also the finest; in an old Spanish colonial compound, rooms with private hot-water bath are set around a lovely, shady courtyard decorated with plants, tiles and heavy Spanish furniture. Breakfast is served in the courtyard; singles/doubles are US$15/28.35.

Other recommendable places in the area include the *Hotel Sutter* (☎ (74) 82-02-09) at Azueta 10 on the corner of La Paz, with rooms at US$10/20, and on the opposite corner of the same intersection at Azueta 17, the *Hotel Maria Antonieta* (☎ (74) 82-50-24), with rooms at US$8.35/16.65. The *Hotel Fel-Mar* (☎ (74) 82-29-82) at Constancio Martines 5 is a bit run-down but its rooms have private balconies and plenty of windows; the upper-floor rooms have a view of Acapulco Bay. Singles/doubles here are US$10/20.

Many good budget hotels are found along Calle La Quebrada. *Hotel Angelita* (☎ (74) 83-57-34) at No 37 is clean, popular, and its rooms have good ventilation and hot water in the private baths; singles/doubles are US$8.35/16.65. Next door, the *Hotel Maris-*

cal (☎ (74) 82-00-15) at No 35 also has ho water, and the rooms, with small private balconies, cost US$10/13.35 (less ir summer).

Also on La Quebrada, at No 45 , the *Hotel Asturias* (☎ (74) 83-65-48) is another popular spot; its clean rooms open onto a courtyard with a small swimming pool, and there is hot water. Rates are US$6.65 per person most of the year, rising to US$8.35/16.65 for December and Semana Santa.

Other hotels with swimming pools on La Quebrada include the *Hotel Coral* (☎ (74) 82-07-56) at No 56, with rooms at US$10. 20, and the *Hotel Casa Amparo* (☎ (74) 82-21-72) up the hill at No 69, with private parking and rooms at US$13.35/16.70.

If you're trying to economise, check ou the *Casa de Huéspedes Aries* (☎ (74) 83-24-01) at La Quebrada No 30 and the *Casa de Huéspedes La Tía Conchita* (☎ (74) 82-18-82) right beside it at No 32. They both have tiny rooms, with partitions not fully reaching the ceiling, but they're small, friendly and family-run, making you feel like you're par of the family. Cost is US$5 per person at both places, with a few private baths at the *Aries* and shared but clean baths at the *Tía Conchita*.

Just up the street at La Quebrada 51, the *Casa de Huéspedes Guadalajara* (☎ 82-76-53) is another family-run cheapie with the same rates of US$5 per person; here they have private baths, but look at a room first as they're sometimes a bit grotty. The 'Misc elanea Guadalajara' shop is in the front.

A couple of blocks further up the hill at the top of La Quebrada is the Plaza La Quebrada overlooking the sea where the cliff diver perform. The large parking lot here is a safe place to park a car (there are attendants) bu it gets very busy and loud in the evening when the divers are one of Acapulco's majo attractions. The hotels here have sea-facing balconies and are somewhat cooler than places down the hill in town, since they catcl the sea breezes.

The *Hotel El Faro* (☎ (74) 82-13-65) right on the plaza at Quebrada 83, has large rooms with private balconies, good ventilation and hot water at US$10/16.70. Perched on a hill above the plaza, but easily reached from the plaza by a stairway, *La Torre Eiffel* (☎ (74) 82-16-83) at Inalambrica 110 has a small swimming pool and several large balconies with tables and sitting areas set up for a view of the sea. Its bright rooms have hot water and cost US$10/20 most of the year, but may be double the price in the high season. Bargain for a good rate here.

Places to Stay – middle

On the east side of Parque Papagayo, just a few metres from La Costera and the popular Playa Hornitos, the *Hotel Jacqueline* (☎ (74) 85-93-38) at Gonsalo Gómez 6 has 10 rooms, all with private bath, hot water and air-con, arranged around a pleasant little garden. Prices are reasonable at US$16.70/23.35 for singles/doubles.

Next door to the Jacqueline, the *Hotel del Valle* (☎ (74) 85-83-36/88), whose address is Costera y Gonzálo G Espinosa 150, is another pleasant place, with rooms at US$22 with overhead fan or US$25 with air-con. They have a small swimming pool, terraces with tables, and two kitchens on each floor. Use of a kitchen costs an extra US$5 per day – it's your own private kitchen, not shared with other guests.

Not far from here, also just half a block from the Playa Hornitos beach, the *Auto Hotel Ritz* (☎ (74) 85-80-23, fax 85-56-47) on Avenida Wilfrido Massieu (no number) is an attractive six-storey hotel whose sparkling white air-conditioned rooms all have large private balconies overlooking the swimming pool. Rates during most of the year are around US$24/29, jumping to US$53 in the winter high season. Three children up to age 14 can stay free in the same room with adults; free indoor parking is another feature.

Further east, near the CICI watersports park and Playa Icacos, are a number of other hotels. The *Hotel Quinta Mica* (☎ (74) 84-01-21/22) at Cristobal Colón 115, across the street to the east of CICI, charges US$55 throughout the high season for two or three

persons in rooms that can easily hold four; summer rates will be much less.

Closer to the beach on the same road, *Suites Selene* (☎ (74) 84-29-77) at Cristobal Colón 175 has large one-bedroom and two-bedroom apartments with private balconies, sitting rooms and private bathrooms. It's just one door from the beach. High-season rates here are US$57 for one-bedroom apartments, US$113.35 for two bedrooms. These two places are especially good value because their air-conditioned rooms are actually little apartments, with bedrooms and fully-equipped kitchens; both also have swimming pools. The 'Super Super' supermarket nearby is convenient for groceries.

The high-rise hotels along La Costera tend to be expensive; many are four and five-star hotels. One of the more economical ones, and quite luxurious, is the four-star *Romano Palace Hotel* (☎ (74) 84-77-30) at La Costera 130. All the rooms come with refrigerator, air-con, two double beds, colour TV, and a private balcony with flowers in the planter box. The full-wall windows, with chiffon curtains, offer a great view of Acapulco; try to get one of the upper-storey rooms for the best view (there are 22 floors). Rates are US$55 most of the year, rising to US$74 during high season; the cost is the same for one to four people.

Another place for a great view is the fancy *Hotel Casablanca* (☎ (74) 82-12-12/15, fax 82-15-17) at Cerro de la Pinzona 195, Fraccionamiento Las Playas, way up on a hill on the Peninsula de las Playas. Rooms with private balcony and a sweeping view cost US$29/45 most of the year, rising to US$42/64 in winter.

Places to Stay – top end

If you want to spend up, there's plenty of opportunity for it in Acapulco – there are at least 25 four-star, eight five-star, three 'grand tourism' and four 'special category' hotels to choose from. The super luxury 'special category' hotels include Las Brisas (see below), the *Acapulco Princess* (☎ (74) 84-31-00), the *Pierre Marqués* (☎ (74) 84-20-00) and the *Hyatt Regency Acapulco*

(☎ (74) 84-28-88). Grand Tourism hotels include the *Acapulco Plaza* (☎ (74) 85-80-50), the *Sheraton Acapulco Resort* (☎ (74) 81-22-22) and the *Villa Vera* (☎ (74) 84-03-33).

Many of the four and five-star hotels are found on the beachfront along La Costera; the high-rise hotel zone begins at the east end of Parque Papagayo and runs east around the bay. Travel agents should have literature on most of these hotels.

One of Acapulco's best hotels, *Las Brisas* (☎ (74) 84-16-50) is worth visiting just to see it. In the USA it has topped lists of favourite honeymoon destinations, with 300 private *casitas*, many with their own private swimming pools, set on a hillside of manicured gardens. The views of Acapulco Bay, especially at night, seem too good to be true. Rates are US$180 per night for rooms with shared pool, US$230 with private pool, from April to December, rising in high season to US$250 and US$350.

There are a couple of quirks in the price structure for Acapulco's top-end hotels. You can sometimes get particularly good deals by buying a combination hotel-and-airfare package from Canada or the USA, even in winter. On the other hand, some of these hotels pad their prices for the foreign tourist market; a room rate might be twice as much when quoted by a travel agent in the USA, Canada or Europe as it would be if you walked in off the street and asked, or if you made your arrangements in Mexico.

Places to Stay – Pie de la Cuesta

Pie de la Cuesta is a good alternative to staying in Acapulco – it's quieter, cleaner, closer to nature, much more peaceful, and it has great sunsets. There's no nightlife so if you're looking for excitement you're probably better off staying in the city. Buses to downtown Acapulco run every 15 minutes from 6 am until around 8 pm, take about 35 minutes to get there and cost US$0.25; a taxi from town costs US$5.

Pie de la Cuesta has a number of places to stay – some 14 hotels and two trailer parks spread along the two-km stretch of road between the beach and the lagoon – and

many beachside restaurants, mostly specialising in seafood. There are no telephones yet, though telephone service, potable water and floodlights for the beach are supposed to be installed sometime during 1992.

Since there's only one road, you can easily walk along and check out what Pie de la Cuesta has to offer. There are a few very attractive, higher priced places to stay, and a number of small family-run casas de huéspedes with just a few rooms. Most of these also have beachside restaurants, where a fish dinner costs around US$4, enchiladas half that. All of the places to stay have private parking areas.

The *Villa Nirvana*, owned by a Canadian/Mexican couple, is one of the most attractive places on the beach, with just seven rooms set around a big garden with a beachside swimming pool; you can do your own cooking and use the refrigerators in the outdoor patio kitchens. Rates are US$25 for one or two people, US$40 for four, but 20% less from May to September.

The *Hotel Puesta del Sol*, right by the beach, has not only a swimming pool and attractive grounds, but also a tennis court. Rates are US$20 for one or two people, US$10 each for three or four; the larger rooms have private kitchens, and there's also a bar and restaurant. *Quinta Karla*, also near the beach and with a swimming pool, has single/double rooms at US$13.35/16.65 all year round.

Aside from these places, there are a number of smaller, family-style casas de huéspedes on the beach side of the road, all of them simple, clean little places with fan, private bath, off-street parking and little beachfront restaurants.

The first one you come to when you enter Pie de la Cuesta is the *Hotel & Restaurant Rocío*. Rooms with one double bed cost US$11.70, or US$20 with two beds. Félix López, the resident bartender, chef, guitarist and songster provides music, entertainment and good times. The *Hotel, Restaurant & Bar La Cabañita* is another simple place, with a swimming pool and a terrace with hammocks overlooking the beach; rates are US$10/13.35 for singles/doubles.

Further along the road, *Bungalows María Cristina*, run by a friendly family, is a relaxing place with a barbecue on the beach and many hammocks around. All the rooms have two double beds; cost is US$16.65 in summer, US$20 in winter (15 December to 15 April). Next door, *Estacionamento Juanita* is a similar place with rooms for one to four people at US$16.65.

Still further along, the *Hotel & Restaurant Casa Blanca* has singles/doubles for US$10/16.65; nearby, the *Casa de Huéspedes Playa Leonor* charges US$15 for rooms with two double beds.

Camping There are two trailer and camping parks in Pie de la Cuesta, down at the far end of the road from the highway and near the end of the bus line coming from Acapulco. Both have full hook-ups for trailers and RVs, but are also good for tents. Take a look at both parks and ask the prices before you choose your spot; they're only about a two-minute walk from each other but most campers have a distinct preference for one or the other.

The *Trailer Park Quinta Dora*, run by a friendly and helpful family, has camping grounds on both the beach and lagoon sides; it's clean, pleasant, and their casual beachside restaurant is about the most economical in the area. Cost is US$8.35 for a space for two people, US$1.70 for each extra person. Nearby, the *Acapulco Trailer Park*, with grounds on the ocean side of the road and a small grocery store at the entrance, charges about the same; rates are less for tents than for RVs.

Places to Eat
Near the Zócalo On the east side of the zócalo, *La Flor de Acapulco* is a long-time Acapulco favourite, with an indoor dining room and tables under umbrellas out on the plaza good for people-watching. Further back in the plaza, hidden away in the northeast corner to the right of the church, the *Cafetería Astoria* also has outdoor tables; it's

a pleasant, shady, quieter spot for a coffee, meal or snack. Both places are open every day from 8 am to 11 pm.

Just a few steps from the east side of the plaza on the Carranza walking street, *Mi Parri Pollo* and *Maggi's Pizzas*, with umbrella tables on the sidewalk under a large shady tree, are open 24 hours every day, serving a variety of meals and snacks.

On the west side of the plaza are two upstairs restaurants. The *Restaurant/Bar Caballero* at the corner of La Costera specialises in paella (US$8.70), while the *Terraza Las Flores* features German food. Both are open in the afternoon and evening.

Coming out of the zócalo on the west side, Calle Benito Juárez has about a dozen restaurants. *Restaurant Ricardo* is a popular choice with the locals, often brimming with diners at all hours. Their comida corrida, with a selection of soups, rice, 15 main courses, and dessert or coffee, all for US$2.70, is a good deal. It's open every day from 7.30 am to 1 am. A couple of doors nearer the zócalo, the *Restaurant San Carlos*, with a pleasant open-air patio, is also popular.

In the next block west, *The Fat Farm* at Benito Juárez 10 boasts 'the best cup of coffee in Acapulco' and they're probably right. They have attractive seating in the rear patio hung with a colourful collection of paintings, piñatas and masks, and an extensive English book exchange along one whole wall; US$0.50 brings you a big mug of coffee, with all the free refills you want, while you enjoy yourself and listen to the classical music. They also boast 'the best plate of spaghetti in town', 'real Tex-Mex chili con carne', sandwiches, and an extensive dessert menu. Open daily, 9 am to 10 pm.

There are many other restaurants in this same district west of the zócalo, including many specialising in seafood. At the corner of Juárez and Azueta, the open-air *El Amigo Miguel* is one of the most patronised. With a bilingual English-Spanish menu and meals from around US$3.35 to US$8, the seafood here is indeed delicious. A seafood soup for

US$3.35, brimming with shrimp, fish, shellfish and other goodies from the sea, served with French bread and butter, makes a filling lunch. There are several other seafood restaurants on the same corner and nearby.

La Costera There are dozens of restaurants as you head east down La Costera toward the big high-rise hotels. They tend to get more expensive as you move from the zócalo and into the tourist area. Nonetheless, there are many pleasant restaurants down this way, if you don't mind spending a bit more. Of course all the fancy hotels have restaurants and cafeterias, too.

Juice stands and restaurants in the *100% Natural* chain are found throughout Acapulco; there are many spread all along La Costera. Some of them are simple juice stands, where you can get a big, freshly made fruit or vegetable juice concoction or licuado (fruit blended with milk) for anywhere from US$1 to US$3. Others are small or large restaurants, serving vegetarian and other fresh, natural fare; the one just west of the Centro Cultural, all the way down by the CICI watersports centre, is quite large and pleasant.

Opposite the Centro Cultural, *Fersato's* is a long-standing family establishment, with an attractive open-air decor of brick walls, stone arches and ceiling fans. Meals cost from US$3.70 up to US$13.35 for surf & turf (filet mignon with sea bass); it's open every day from 7 am to midnight.

One block west of CICI, on the same (beach) side of La Costera, the *Hard Rock Café* is a sister to its namesakes in London, New York, Amsterdam, etc; the first one was established in London on 14 June 1971. Beatles and other rock memorabilia decorates the British pub-like interior; live rock music starts at 11 pm every night except Tuesday, but there's always rock playing. A burger with fries here costs US$7.50, and they also sell a collection of T-shirts, jackets, etc emblazoned with their famous logo. It's open every day from noon to 2 am.

Another block west, *Mariscos Pipo* is famous for its seafood. Try a combination seafood plate for US$7.35 (small) or US$9 (large). It's open every day from 1 to 9.30 pm.

Back along the main drag of La Costera, *Carlos 'n Charlie's* at La Costera 999, opposite the Hotel Los Gemelos, is one of the Carlos Anderson chain found throughout Mexico, with a fascinating collection of old photos, etc covering every inch of wall space, rowdy music always going on, and a quirky bilingual menu with 'moo' for beef, 'crunch' for salad, etc. It's not cheap (a 'heartburn steak' is US$11.35) but the Anderson restaurants always put on a good time for the tourists. It's open every day from 6.30 pm to midnight. Another Anderson restaurant, *Sr Frog's*, is also in Acapulco.

About two doors west of Carlos 'n Charlie's is another *La Flor de Acapulco*, a more sedate place, related to its namesake in the zócalo; yet another *Flor*, also on La Costera, is opposite the Hotel Continental Plaza. All are open daily from 8 am to 11 pm and are a dependable place to get a good meal.

La Quebrada For a splurge, you might want to try the *Restaurant La Perla* (☎ 83-11-55), at the Plaza Las Glorias Hotel on the Plaza La Quebrada, some evenings when the divers are performing. This fancy restaurant, with a great view of the divers, offers a nightly buffet every evening from 7 pm to midnight for US$27, with dining on terraces under the stars.

Supermarkets The large Super Super, Comercial Mexicana and Gigante combination supermarkets and discount department stores are along La Costera between the zócalo and Parque Papagayo; Super Super has another branch opposite CICI.

Pie de la Cuesta The restaurants at Pie de la Cuesta, most of which are attached to hotels and casas de huéspedes, are renowned for their seafood. A fish dinner or lunch costs around US$4 at most places, a snack of enchiladas or quesadillas about half that. The *Restaurant El Zanate* beside the road is a small restaurant with good food; opposite this, on the shore of the lagoon with a terrace right over the water, *Steve's Hideaway* is an attractive place also frequently recommended, though it seemed to be up for sale on our last visit.

Most of the other restaurants are open-air places right beside the beach. The *Tres Marias* is known to have some of the best food in the area. The restaurant at the *Trailer Park Quinta Dora*, down at the far end of the road, is also fine and it's only about half the price of most of the other restaurants. Other good restaurants, attached to hotels and guest houses, are those at the *Rocío*, the *Quinta Karla*, *La Cabañita* and the *Puesta del Sol*.

Entertainment

Acapulco's active nightlife rivals its beaches as an attraction of the city.

Much of the nightlife revolves around the many discos and nightclubs, with new ones always opening up to challenge the old. Extravaganza, in the Las Brisas area in the south-east part of the city, is the major current rave. Fantasy, also in the Las Brisas area, has a laser light show, disco dancing and a 2 am fireworks show. Baby O's, at La Costera and Horatio Nelson, also has a laser light show and is supposedly one of the best discos in Acapulco, attracting a younger crowd. Magic, across from Baby O's, is an exclusive place with a bouncer at the door who selects the clientele. The News disco and concert hall at La Costera 12, billing itself as 'one of the largest & most spectacular discos in the world', is another favourite, as are Atrium, a smaller disco at La Costera 30, and Le Dome at La Costera 402.

Disco Beach is another popular disco, right on the beach on Playa Condesa. Nina's, Eve and Delirio are other popular discos right on La Costera. Don't forget the Hard Rock Café; this Acapulco branch of the famous chain, at La Costera 37 just west of CICI, is open every day from noon until 2 am, with live music starting nightly at 11 pm. B and B in the Caleta area is a newer disco with two dance floors, one for fast music and one for slow, with music of the '60s to '80s.

The Rock Hola Café, at the corner of Juan de la Cosa and La Costera near the Diana traffic circle, has live music from the '50s, '60s and '70s. Afroantillanos, half a block behind it, features live tropical and salsa music. Faces, nearby, is an after-hours spot continuing into the wee hours; it opens at midnight and stays open until around 6 or 7 am.

Acapulco has an active gay scene and several predominantly gay bars and clubs. The Gallery, at Avenida de los Deportes 11 near the Calinda Quality Inn, is a disco also known for its 11 pm and 1 am shows of female impersonators. The Peacock is another mostly-gay bar and is said to have some of the best music in Acapulco.

Most of the discos open around 10 pm and have a cover charge of around US$5 to US$8 or more; some charge more to get in but have an open bar.

If you don't feel up to a disco, most of the big hotels along La Costera have bars with entertainment, be it quiet piano bars or live bands.

Apart from the disco scene there are plenty of other things to do around Acapulco at night. El Fuerte, at La Costera 239, features a show of Flamenco dancers, singers, guitarists and Spanish folklore nightly except Sunday at 10 and 11.30 pm; phone ahead for reservations (☎ 82-61-61). The theatres at the Centro Internacional Acapulco (☎ 84-70-50) present plays, music, dance and other cultural performances. Acapulco has several cinemas; there's one on the zócalo, one with several salons on La Costera, and several more around town.

Evening cruises are another possibility. And then there are the cliff divers at La Quebrada. Or it's pleasant to sit at one of the sidewalk restaurants on the zócalo, feel the warm night air, and watch the activity in the plaza.

Getting There & Away

Air Acapulco has a busy international airport, with direct flights connecting it with a great many destinations in Mexico, the USA, Canada and Central America. Flying into Acapulco can be an excellent alternative to flying into Mexico City.

Airlines serving Acapulco include:

Aeroméxico
Offices at the airport, at La Costera 251 near Playa Hornos, and in the Torre Acapulco at La Costera 1252 (☎ (74) 85-16-25, 85-16-00, 85-15-43)
American Airlines
Airport (☎ (74) 84-17-34, 84-18-14, 84-12-44)
Continental Airlines
Airport (☎ (74) 84-70-03, 84-03-16)
Delta Airlines
Airport (☎ (74) 84-04-46, or reservations toll-free 91-800-90-221)
Mexicana
Torre Acapulco, La Costera 1252 (☎ (74) 84-68-90, 84-69-43, 84-68-37)
Taesa
Hotel Imperial, La Costera 251 (☎ (74) 86-45-76)

Bus Acapulco has two major long-distance bus stations: Estrella de Oro and Estrella Blanca.

The Estrella de Oro terminal (☎ (74) 85-96-74) is on the corner of Avenidas Cuauhtémoc and Wilfrido Massieu, roughly on the north-east corner of Parque Papagayo. A tourism information kiosk in the arrivals lobby will help you to make hotel or airline reservations when you get off the bus; though they have 'deals' with various hotels and may encourage you to book into these, they will telephone around to find you a room in any hotel you choose. The Base-Cine Río-Caleta local bus passes by this terminal; you can catch it opposite the Sanborns department store, on La Costera two blocks east of the zócalo.

The Estrella Blanca terminal (☎ (74) 82-11-00, 83-11-15, 83-12-51) is at Avenida Ejido 47; any local bus marked 'Ejido' departing from opposite the Sanborns department store will get you there.

Both companies offer various services to Mexico City, with various levels of luxury for the 400-km, seven-hour trip. Estrella Blanca offers *primera clase* (US$11.20), *plus* (US$15.30) and *turista* (US$17). Estrella de Oro has *primera clase* (US$11.20), *plus* (US$15.40), *crucero* (US$18.30), and *diamante* (US$30). Both companies have

buses to both the Central Sur and Central del Norte terminals in Mexico City. Estrella Blanca buses depart every half-hour from 6 am to 9.30 pm, and every 15 minutes from 10 pm to 2 am. Estrella de Oro has 14 departures daily to the Central Sur terminal, and three to the Central del Norte.

Other buses connections from Acapulco include:

Chilpancingo – 132 km, 2½ hours; every 10 minutes from 5.15 am to 10 pm with Estrella Blanca (US$4.35); 10 daily with Estrella de Oro (US$4).
Cuernavaca – 315 km, five to six hours; every half hour from 3.40 am to 10 pm with Estrella Blanca (US$9.70); two daily with Estrella de Oro (US$8.90).
Iguala – 231 km, four hours; every half-hour from 3.40 am to 10 pm with Estrella Blanca (US$6.70); seven daily with Estrella de Oro (US$5.40),
Puerto Escondido – 370 km, seven hours; two daily with Estrella Blanca (US$9.40).
Taxco – 266 km, five hours; five daily with Estrella Blanca (US$7.70); two daily with Estrella de Oro (US$7.20).
Zihuatanejo – 239 km, five hours; every 20 minutes from 4 am to midnight with Estrella Blanca (US$5.20); also buses with Estrella de Oro.

Car & Motorbike Many car rental companies hire Jeeps as well as cars; several have offices at the airport as well as in town, and/or offer free delivery to wherever you choose. As always, it's a good idea to call around to compare prices.

Companies include: Avis (☎ 84-16-33, 85-64-67); Budget (☎ 84-82-00); Dollar (☎ 84-30-66, 84-31-04); Economovil (☎ 84-28-28, 84-88-89); Fast (☎ 84-48-44, 85-64-04); Hertz (☎ 85-89-47, 85-69-42); Inter Renta (☎ 84-48-16, 84-48-89); National (☎ 85-55-96, 85-55-96); Odin (☎ 85-37-67, 85-85-58); Quick (☎ 85-86-99, 84-75-55); Saad (☎ 84-34-45, 84-53-25); Sands (☎ 84-10-31, 84-28-32).

Rental motorcycles and scooters can be hired from CICI Renta de Motos (☎ 84-19-71), set up under a sidewalk awning on La Costera outside the CICI watersports centre. Honda 50s cost US$6.70 per hour, US$11.70 for two hours, US$23.35 for eight hours or US$33.50 for 24 hours. Honda 80s are

US$20 for four hours, US$30 for eight hours, or US$40 for 24 hours. You must have a driver's licence (a licence for cars will do) and a credit card is extremely helpful; otherwise you'll be asked for a large deposit. Hours are 10 am to 6 pm daily.

Getting Around

To/From the Airport Acapulco's airport is 22½ km south-east of downtown, beyond the junction for Puerto Marqués. If you arrive by air, buy a ticket for transport into town from the Transportaciones de Pasajeros desks before you leave the terminal. The minibus (colectivo) fare is US$5 per person; it will take you directly to your hotel; taxis cost US$20.

Leaving Acapulco, telephone the same company 24 hours in advance to reserve your transport back to the airport (☎ 85-23-32, 85-17-84, 85-29-71). They'll pick you up 90 minutes before your departure for domestic flights, two hours ahead for international flights.

Bus Acapulco has a good city bus system, with buses going every few minutes to most anywhere you'd want to go. They operate every day from 4 am to 11 pm and cost US$0.30.

Along La Costera the bus stop shelters are prominently marked with names and numbers, making it easy to identify the stop you want. Inside are posted large colour-coded maps of the city and the four La Costera bus routes.

From the zócalo area, the bus stop opposite Sanborns department store is a good place to catch buses. It's on La Costera two blocks east of the zócalo, and it's at the beginning of several bus routes so you can usually get a seat.

The most useful city bus routes include:

Base-Caleta
   from the Icacos Naval Base at the south-east end of Acapulco, along La Costera, past the zócalo to Playa Caleta.

Base-Cine Río-Caleta
   from the Icacos Naval Base, cuts inland from La Costera on Avenida Wilfrido Massieu to Avenida Cuauhtémoc, heads down Cuauhtémoc through the business district, turning back to La Costera just before reaching the zócalo and continuing west to Caleta.

Puerto Marqués-Centro
   from opposite Sanborns, along La Costera to Puerto Marqués.

Zócalo-Pie de la Cuesta
   from opposite Sanborns, to Pie de la Cuesta.

Taxi Taxis are plentiful in Acapulco and taxi drivers are happy to take gringos for a ride, especially for fares higher than the government-set rates. Stop at a taxi stand sometime to ask what the fares should be. Always agree on the fare you'll pay before you climb into the cab; it never hurts to bargain with taxi drivers.

ZIHUATANEJO & IXTAPA

Population: 38,000

Not so long ago, Zihuatanejo ('see-wah-tah-NAY-ho') was a small fishing village and nearby Ixtapa ('ees-STOP-pah') was a coconut plantation. Then Fonatur, the Mexican government tourism development organisation that built Cancún, decided that the Pacific coast needed a Cancún-like resort to bring more tourist dollars into Mexico.

Using various market studies of American tourists, Fonatur economists chose Ixtapa, 210 km north of Acapulco, for their new resort complex. Proximity to the USA, an average temperature of 27°C, tropical vegetation and, most importantly, the quality of the beaches were their criteria. They bought the coconut plantation, laid out streets, built reservoirs, strung electrical lines and invited the world's best-known hotel chains to begin construction.

Today, Ixtapa is a string of impressive resort hotels spread out along the Bahía del Palmar; the Club Méditerranée and Playa Linda Ixtapa are farther west beyond Punta Ixtapa. Zihuatanejo, 10 km to the south, is supposed to be a 'typical' Mexican fishing village, but it has been spruced up so that visitors can be impressed by 'old' Mexico.

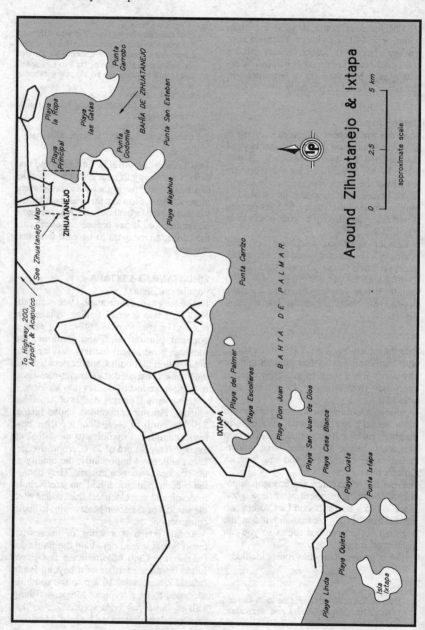

Around Zihuatanejo & Ixtapa

The hotels, restaurants and shops of Ixtapa are expensive, and many travellers cringe at Ixtapa's artificial glitz created for the gringos. Zihuatanejo, on the other hand, though quite touristy, retains an easy-going coastal town ambience, and its setting on a magnificent bay with a number of fine beaches makes it an idyllic place to visit. Small-scale fishing still forms an important part of the town's economy; if you walk down on the beach near the pier in the early morning you can join the pelicans in greeting the returning fishermen and see the morning's catch.

Orientation

Though Zihuatanejo's suburbs are growing considerably, spreading out around the Bahía de Zihuatanejo and starting to climb up the hills behind the town, the city centre is quite compact, with everything within a few square blocks. It's difficult to get lost in Zihuatajeno; there are only a few streets and the street names are clearly marked. Ixtapa, 10 km away, is easily reached by frequent local buses or by taxi.

Information

Tourist Office The government Secretaría de Turismo (☎ (743) 3-19-67) used to be in Zihuatanejo but it's been moved to Ixtapa, near the police station and opposite the Hotel Stouffer Presidente.

In Zihuatanejo there are many kiosks and small offices set up with tourist information. They are actually in business to promote various time-share schemes, tourist activities, etc in Ixtapa, but they will also provide free maps of Ixtapa/Zihuatanejo and answer any questions you may have. Then they'll try to encourage you to go for a free breakfast, cocktail or whatever at some new place in Ixtapa.

Money Zihuatanejo has a number of banks and casas de cambio where you can change US dollars and travellers' cheques. The banks give the best rate of exchange and are they're open Monday to Friday from 9 am to 1.30 pm. The casas de cambio give a less favourable rate but are open longer, more convenient hours. Casa de Cambio Ballesteros, on Galeana near the corner of Nicolás Bravo, is open every day from 8 am to 9 pm.

American Express (☎ (743) 3-08-53, 3-21-21) has an office in Ixtapa at the Hotel Westin Ixtapa, open Monday to Saturday from 8 am to 8 pm, Sunday from 8 am to 1 pm.

Post The post office is on a curving side street a few doors from Vicente Guerrero. Hours are 8 am to 7 pm Monday to Friday, 9 am to 1 pm on Saturday.

Since the post office has been moved to this slightly inconvenient location, several other places in town, all of them near post boxes which are serviced daily, have started selling stamps. Among them is the Terminal Portuario building at the foot of the pier; it's open Monday to Saturday, 8 am to 6 pm.

Telecommunications The telegraph office has also been moved; it's now in the old airport, on the other side of Avenida Morelos from town.

Long-distance telephone and fax services are available at a number of casetas de larga distancia. The Caseta Telefónica at the corner of Galeana and Pedro Ascencio is open Monday to Saturday from 8 am to 9 pm, Sunday from 8 am to noon and from 6 to 9 pm. Casa de Cambio Ballesteros also has telephone and fax services; it's open every day from 8 am to 9 pm. The Terminal Portuario building at the foot of the pier has long-distance telephone, fax and postal services; it's open Monday to Saturday, 8 am to 6 pm.

Laundry Lavandería Super Clean, at Catalina González 11 on the corner of Galeana, offers laundry services for US$1.35 per kilo; it's open Monday to Saturday from 8 am to 8 pm. Lavandería Disney, on the corner of Cuauhtémoc and Antonio Nava, charges the same prices; it's open every day from 9 am to 9 pm.

Travel Agencies Viajes Ixtamar (☎ 4-35-

Zihuatanejo

0   125   250 m

To Ixtapa

Highway 200
to Acapulco

To Playa
La Ropa

Paseo del Palmar

Paseo la Boquilla

Canal

Calle Eva S. de López Mateos

Playa Madera

Footbridge

Bahía
de
Zihuatanejo

Paseo del Cocotal

Paseo Benito Juárez

Avenida Benito Juárez

Catalina González

Ejido

Nicolás Bravo

A Ramírez

Juan

Playa del Pescador

Playa Principal

Vicente Guerrero

Avenida Morelos (Paseo Zihuatanejo)

Ignacio Altamirano

Antonio Nava

Galeana

Cuauhtémoc

Cinco de Mayo

Pedro Ascencio

Álvarez

Muelle

La Noria

To CREA
Youth Hostel

90) is in a convenient location at Paseo del Pescador 20-A, near the foot of the pier. Or there's the Agencia de Viajes Abassa (☎ 4-33-44, 4-28-04, fax 4-43-48) at Ejido 24, between Galeana and Vicente Guerrero.

Beaches
Waves are gentle at all of the beaches on Bahía de Zihuatanejo. If you want big ocean waves you'll have to go over to Ixtapa, which takes only a few minutes on the local bus.

Playa Principal This beach, right in front of Zihuatanejo town, is the least appealing for

swimming. If you're on Playa Principal facing towards the water you can see several other beaches spread around the bay, starting with Playa Madera just past the rocky point on your left, then the long, white stretch of Playa la Ropa past that, and finally, directly across the bay, Playa las Gatas.

Playa Madera. There are several good hotels and bungalows at Playa Madera. To get there, walk a couple of blocks out of town on Paseo de la Boquilla until you come to the footbridge crossing over the canal. Go over the footbridge, continue on the other side and

■ PLACES TO STAY

1 Hotel Playa de la Madera, Hotel
   Palacios
2 Bungalows Allec, Bungalows Ley
3 Bungalows Sotelo
5 Bungalows Pacíficos
11 Hotel Casa Bravo
12 Posada Citlali
14 Casa de Huéspedes Miriam
15 Hotel Imelda
18 Hotel Amueblados Valle
19 Hotel Casa Aurora
22 Hotel Avila
24 Casa de Huéspedes Juve
27 Hotel Maver
35 Hotel Lari's
41 Hotel Raúl Tres Marias

▼ PLACES TO EAT

16 Natural de Splash, Restaurant/Bar
   Splash
17 Los Braceros
20 La Mesa del Capitán
21 Panificadora El Buen Gusto
23 Tata's Restaurant/Bar, Cevichería Los
   Paisanos

31 Cafetería Nueva Zelanda
32 Chez Juan
33 Al Andaluz Expresso
37 Casa Elvira
38 La Sirena Gorda
42 Casa Puntarenas

OTHER

4 Estrella de Oro Bus Station
6 Telegraph Office (Former Airport)
7 Mercado
8 Bus Stop for Local Buses to Ixtapa
9 Cinemas Vicente Guerrero
10 Mercado Municipal de las Artesanías
13 Post Office
25 Casa de Cambio Ballesteros
26 Caseta Telefónica
28 Basketball Court
29 Lavandería Disney
30 Lavandería Super Clean
34 Church
36 Aeroméxico Office
39 Ticket Office for Boats to Playa Las
   Gatas & Isla Ixtapa
40 Terminal Portuario

take the first right turn; the street heads up a steep hill and just on the other side is Playa Madera. It takes only about 10 or 15 minutes to walk there from town.

Playa la Ropa Keep walking along the coast for about another 10 minutes or so from Playa Madera, and you reach the broad, two-km expanse of Playa la Ropa. It's bordered by palm trees and palapa-covered fish restaurants, and is actually about the best beach for swimming. It's a pleasant walk, with the road rising up onto cliffs offering a fine view over the bay.

Playa las Gatas You can take a boat to Playa las Gatas from the pier in town. Buy your ticket at the ticket booth at the foot of the pier; save your ticket because you'll need it for the return trip. Cost is US$2 for the round

trip and the boats depart every 10 minutes from 8 am to 5 pm, with the last boat leaving las Gatas for the return trip at 5 pm.

Las Gatas is a protected beach, good for snorkelling and for swimming for children – Calzontzin, a Tarascan chief, built a stone barrier there in pre-Hispanic times to keep the waves down and prevent sea creatures from entering, making it a sort of private swimming pool. You can hire snorkelling gear from any of several palapa-covered shacks on the beach for around US$3.35 to US$5; they also offer scuba diving for around US$40 per dive.

Ixtapa The big hotels in Ixtapa are lined up along **Playa del Palmar**, a long, broad stretch of white sand. Be very careful if you swim on this beach: the large waves tend to crash straight down, and there's a powerful undertow. The west end of this beach, just before the entrance to the lagoon, is called

Playa Escolleras by the locals and it's a favourite spot for surfing.

Heading further west, past the marshy entrance to the lagoon and the future marina, are three small beaches which are some of the most beautiful but least accessible in the area: **Playa San Juan**, **Playa Casa Blanca** and **Playa Cuata**.

Other Beaches To the west, past Punta Ixtapa, are **Playa Quieta** and **Playa Linda**. Unless you have a private vehicle, you'll have to take a taxi from Ixtapa to reach them.

From Playa Quieta boats run every 10 minutes to **Isla Ixtapa** just offshore, which has several more beaches. Cost is US$2 for the round-trip boat ride; the boats operate every day from 8 am to 5 pm, with the last boat returning at 5 pm. You can also reach Isla Ixtapa by taking a boat from the pier in Zihuatanejo. It departs once a day at 11 am, departing the island at around 4 pm to be back in town at 5 pm. The trip takes about an hour from town and costs US$5.85 for the round trip. Tickets are sold at the ticket office at the foot of the pier.

Activities

Most of the activities around Zihuatanejo are naturally oriented towards the sea. Swimming is said to be best at Playa la Ropa, where you can also hire sailboards, sailboats and arrange waterskiing.

Snorkelling is good at Playa Las Gatas, Playa Quieta and on Ixtapa Island; you can hire snorkelling gear at any of these beaches for around US$3.35 to US$5. The same beaches also have diving operators, who will take you for a dive for around US$40, or give you scuba lessons in the quiet water.

The most professional scuba diving operation in Zihuatanejo is the NAUI-affiliated Zihuatanejo Scuba Center (☎ (743) 4-21-47, fax 4-44-68). They are presently located at Paseo del Pescador 4, near the foot of the pier, but are scheduled to move to a larger shop on Avenida Cuauhtémoc between Álvarez and Ascencio, near the Hotel Maver. They do a morning and an afternoon dive every day, tailoring their dives to the level of expertise of the divers. Cost is US$40 for a morning or afternoon dive; US$65 for both, including lunch; US$50 for night dives; and US$40 for a video of your dive. They also offer certified instruction at US$65 for a resort diving course, or US$350 for a full NAUI diving certification course, which takes a minimum of five days to complete. They have many diving photos on display and can answer any questions you may have about diving in this area. There is an abundance of species here due to a convergence of currents, and there is sometimes great visibility, up to 35 metres.

Sportfishing is another popular sport in Zihuatanejo. The sportfishing office at Paseo del Pescador 20-6, near the foot of the pier (☎ 4-41-62), can arrange a seven-hour deep sea fishing trip at US$100 for two people in a small boat, US$150 for four in a medium boat, or US$200 for six people in a large boat. Or you can just walk around on the pier and talk with the various fishermen, many of whom speak some English and frequently make fishing trips.

The surf shop on Guerrero beside the Hotel Amueblados Valle can recommend good surfing spots in the area, for the time of year you're there.

Golf and tennis are available at the Ixtapa Golf Club (☎ 3-10-62).

Museum

On the north end of Paseo del Pescador in Zihuatanejo, a building is being prepared and materials collected for the future opening of an archaeological museum there. You could stop by and see how it's going.

Places to Stay

The reasonably-priced places to stay are in Zihuatanejo; Ixtapa's big resort hotels are quite pricey, upwards of US$150 a night in winter. If you want to stay in Ixtapa, arrange a package deal through a travel agent, which could include airfare from your home country.

During the high season, from mid-December until Easter, many hotels in Zihuatanejo may be full. Phoning ahead to reserve a hotel room is a good idea at this time; if you don't like what you get, you can always look for another room early the next day, but at least you'll have somewhere to stay on the first night.

The busiest times of all for tourism are Semana Santa and the week between Christmas and New Year's Day. If you plan to come at this time, you must reserve a room and be prepared to pay more.

The rest of the year, from around mid-April to mid-December, is the slow season for tourism. At this time you can bargain for a discount and probably get it, as the hotels are competing for what few tourists there are.

Places to Stay – bottom end

Camping Two good camping grounds offer spaces for both tents and trailers. These are *Camping Playa Ropa*, on Playa la Ropa near the fancy Hotel Sotavento, and *Camping Playa Linda*, at Playa Linda on the west end of Ixtapa.

Hostels The least expensive place to stay is at the *CREA Youth Hostel* (☎ (743) 4-46-62), on Paseo de las Salinas (no number), about a 10-minute walk from town. To find it, head west from town on Avenida Morelos, follow the curve around and it will be on your right. They charge US$5 per night for a bed in a clean, single-sex dormitory with four beds. The hostel is open all day and evening.

Hotels *Casa de Huéspedes Juve* (☎ (743) 4-25-41), at Pedro Ascencio 3, is a block from the beach. It's a very basic place which you'd probably only go to because it's about the cheapest place in town, after the youth hostel. Single/double rooms with private bath cost US$6.70/13.35, with a discount if you stay a few days.

Hotel Lari's (☎ (743) 4-21-14), at Ignacio Altamirano 42, is a simple but clean casa de huéspedes, with off-street parking. Singles/doubles with private baths are US$10/16.70.

A similar place, simple but clean (but without parking spaces) is the *Casa de Huéspedes Miriam* (☎ (743) 4-38-90), at Antonio Nava 8, with singles/doubles at US$8.35/16.70.

The *Hotel Raúl Tres Marias* (☎ (743) 4-21-91, 4-25-91), on Calle La Noria 4, Colonia Lázaro Cárdenas, is just across the water from town. (It used to be connected to town by a small footbridge, but the last time we were there the bridge had been taken down and you got back and forth on little boats pulled by ropes.) This is many budget travellers' all-time favourite place to stay in Zihuatanejo, with many of its 25 rooms opening onto large terraces with flowers and a fine view overlooking town and the bay. The amiable family, which has run the place since 1963, keeps it immaculately clean and functioning smoothly. Single/double rooms with private bath are US$12.35/17.35.

Back in the centre of town the *Hotel Casa Bravo* (☎ (743) 4-25-48), at Nicolás Bravo 11, has six clean pleasant rooms for US$20, which come with private hot-water bath, overhead fan, windows and good ventilation; some rooms also have balconies.

The *Hotel Maver*, at Cuauhtémoc 5, has some rooms with large balconies overlooking the shopping street down below; ask for one of these, as the interior rooms are not as good. All come with private cold bath and cost US$11.65/23.35 for singles/doubles.

At the same prices, the *Hotel Casa Aurora* (☎ (743) 4-30-46), at Nicolás Bravo 27, also has some rooms better than others; the upstairs rooms have windows, good cross-ventilation, and a pleasant common terrace sitting area. Ask for one of these; the downstairs rooms are a bit dark.

Places to Stay – middle

Posada Citlali (☎ (743) 4-20-43), at Vicente Guerrero 3, is very pleasant, with several terrace sitting areas and its rooms arranged around a courtyard filled with trees and plants. The rooms are comfortable and clean, with private bath, hot water, good windows and plenty of light and ventilation. Singles/doubles are US$20/26.70.

With the same prices, the *Hotel Imelda* (☎ (743) 4-31-99), at Catalina González 11, has enclosed parking and was remodelled and upgraded in 1992. Some of the rooms are small but all are clean and comfortable, with windows facing outside and private hot-water bath. Their downstairs restaurant is open every day from 7.30 am to 11 pm.

The *Hotel Avila* (☎ (743) 4-20-10), at Calle Juan N Alvarez 8, is right by the beach, with terraces overlooking the sea, but the rooms don't have a private sea view. At US$47 the rooms seem a bit overpriced.

Apartments The *Hotel Amueblados Valle* (☎ (743) 4-32-20, 4-20-84), at Vicente Guerrero 14, is a good deal, with five one-bedroom and three two-bedroom apartments. All are large and ample, bright and airy, with everything you need including fully-equipped kitchens, sitting rooms, etc. The one-bedroom apartments, sleeping up to three people, cost US$30 per night; the two-bedroom apartments can sleep five people and cost US$50 per night, with discounts available in the off-season or by the month.

If they're full (which they often are in the high season), you could try the *Hotel Amueblados Isabel* (☎ (743) 4-36-61, 4-26-69), on Pedro Ascencio (no number). The apartments aren't quite as bright but they certainly have everything you need, with fully-equipped kitchen, phone, sitting room, etc. Two-bedroom apartments sleeping four people cost US$51.35 per night; three-bedroom apartments sleeping up to six people cost US$62.35.

Playa Madera Playa Madera, only a 10 or 15-minute walk from the centre of town, has several excellent places to stay. They're a bit more peaceful and, being perched on the hillside over the beach, they take advantage of the natural setting with large terraces offering magnificent views of the bay and the sparkling lights of town. All will give discounts off-season.

Closest to town, *Bungalows Pacíficos* (☎ & fax (743) 4-21-12), on Calle Eva S de López Mateos, has six very attractive bungalows, all with large terraces with a splendid

view and fully-equipped kitchens. Cost is US$44 for one or two people, US$10 for each extra person. It opens onto a little sheltered beach that is practically private; this is one of the loveliest places in Playa Madera.

All the rooms at *Bungalows Sotelo* (☎ (743) 4-35-45), at Calle Eva S de López Mateos 3, also have terraces with great views. The three large, two-bedroom bungalows come with fully-equipped kitchen, private terrace, spa bath, air-conditioning and colour TV; they cost US$100 a night. There's also a one-bedroom bungalow with kitchen, renting for US$67 a night, and two one-bed rooms without kitchen, which cost US$50 per night.

Near the Sotelo, *Bungalows Allec* (☎ (743) 4-20-02, 4-36-79) and *Bungalows Ley* (☎ (743) 4-45-63, 4-40-87) are similar places, each with bungalows with kitchens and terraces, sleeping two or three people, renting for around US$40 a night. Bungalows Allec also has some larger two-bedroom units, sleeping four to six people, which cost US$84 per night.

The rooms at the *Hotel Playa de la Madera* (☎ (743) 4-21-42), also on Calle Eva S de López Mateos, don't have kitchens but it's a pleasant hotel with a large swimming pool. Singles/doubles cost US$20/30, and there are larger rooms for up to six people for US$47. The *Hotel Palacios* (☎ (743) 4-20-55), with singles/doubles at US$21.70/33.35, is another reasonably-priced hotel, with two small terrace swimming pools overlooking the beach.

Places to Stay – top end
The *Hotel Sotavento* (☎ (743) 4-20-32) on the hill overlooking Playa la Ropa has one of Zihuatanejo's most beautiful settings; its white terraces are visible from all around the bay. Singles/doubles here cost US$71/96 in the high season, including two daily meals; in the low season the rates drop to around US$47 per room.

Villa del Sol (☎ (743) 4-32-39), also on Playa la Ropa, is a luxury resort where the high-season rates of US$180/210 also include breakfast and the evening meal; off-season rates are US$120 with no meals.

Other top-end hotels are all in Ixtapa. They include the Club Méditerranée (☎ (743) 4-33-40), the Ixtapa Sheraton (☎ (743) 3-18-58), the Holiday Inn (☎ (743) 3-10-66), the Westin Ixtapa (☎ (743) 3-21-21), the Omni Ixtapa (☎ (743) 3-00-03) and the Stouffer Presidente (☎ (743) 3-00-18), among others. Most travel agents can arrange packages at any of Ixtapa's big top-end hotels.

Places to Eat
As with the hotels, the reasonably priced restaurants are clustered in Zihuatanejo, not in Ixtapa.

Seafront *La Sirena Gorda*, on Paseo del Pescador near the foot of the pier, is a popular place for all meals from breakfast to a late-night snack; it's open every day except Wednesday from 7 am to 10 pm. It's a casual open-air hang-out with breakfasts around US$2 and a variety of unusual seafood dishes from around US$2 to US$5 for lunch and dinner. Their logo is a fat mermaid (just as the name says): it's quite charming and customers have donated a variety of fat-mermaid artwork to liven up the walls.

Further up Paseo del Pescador at No 8, *Casa Elvira* is famous for having some of the best food in town. It's a pleasant restaurant with a variety of seafood, poultry and meat dishes from around US$8.50 to US$15; open every day from noon to 10 pm.

Still on Paseo del Pescador, past the basketball court, *Restaurant/Bar Tata's* and *Cevichería Los Paisanos* have tables under palapas right on the sandy beach and offer a great view of the bay. Tata's is open every day from 7 am to 11 pm, with good breakfasts and a popular happy hour from 5 to 7 pm. Los Paisanos is open every day from 9 am to 6 pm; they serve many seafood dishes but their speciality is ceviche, a cold lemon-marinated fish salad, for US$2.70.

Bakeries & Cafés Zihuatanejo has several good bakeries where you can get baked goods to eat there or take away. The *Panadería Francesa*, at Catalina González 15 near the Hotel Imelda, is open every day from 7 am to 9 pm. It has a variety of doughnuts, croissants, cookies, rolls, baguettes, and breads including whole wheat, black and soy bread.

The *Panificadora El Buen Gusto* at Vicente Guerrero 8-A is another good bakery, with a couple of tables out in front where you can enjoy your coffee and baked goodies. It's open Monday to Saturday, 7.30 am to 10 pm.

Cafetería Nueva Zelanda at Cuauhtémoc 23, stretching right through the block to Galeana on the other side, is a clean café with fresh fruit juices, licuados, tortas, sandwiches, omelettes, enchiladas, cappuccino and café con leche. You can get anything they have 'to go' (*'para llevar'*) for a few cents extra. It's open every day from 7.30 am to 9.30 pm.

Also on Cuauhtémoc, at No 12-B, *Al Andaluz Expresso* is a New York-style deli with some tables on the sidewalk and others inside. It serves big torpedo sandwiches, hot dogs with sauerkraut, hamburgers, BBQ ribs, espresso coffee and so on, and is open every day from 8 am to 10.30 pm.

Natural food lovers should try the *Natural de Splash* restaurant beside the *Splash* restaurant/bar, which is on the corner of Ejido and Vicente Guerrero. It's a casual open-air place, open every day from 9 am to 11 pm, serving natural treats like whole-wheat hot cakes with raisins and nuts, whole-wheat French toast with a variety of toppings, a selection of omelettes, veggie-burgers, and a great variety of fresh juices made with carrot, celery, beet, pineapple, apple, banana, guava, papaya and so on.

Meat Restaurants *Pollos Locos*, at Nicolás Bravo 15 near the Hotel Casa Bravo, is not fancy to look at, just an open-air place with simple folding tables and chairs, but it serves some of the best wood-grilled chicken on the coast. A quarter chicken, served with a grilled onion, salad, salsa and hand-made tortillas, costs US$3.20; a soda is another

US$0.65. It's a popular place, open every day from 1 to 11 pm.

Los Braceros at Ejido 21 is another popular meat restaurant, with a sidewalk grill where you can see the meat being cooked. Their menu features a variety of meat and vegetable combinations; 'the whale', for example, at US$4.85, includes beef steak, bacon, BBQ pork, green pepper, tomato, onion, melted cheese and tortillas. They also serve crepes (for meals or desserts), melted cheese, and tacos al pastor. It's open daily from 4 pm to 1 am.

Other Other notable restaurants around Zihuatanejo include *Chez Juan*, on the corner of Galeana and Nicolás Bravo, a Chinese restaurant/bar with mostly Szechuan but also some Cantonese dishes (Szechuan/Chez Juan – get it?). For Italian food there's the *Ristorante-Bar-Pizzeria Da Giuseppe* and the *Video Bar Il Piccolo*, next door to each other on Nicolás Bravo near the Hotel Casa Aurora, both serving pizza, lasagne, spaghetti, etc.

Casa Puntarenas is just across the water from town, about six doors from the Hotel Raúl Tres Marias. It's a simple, family-run patio restaurant, open for breakfast daily from 8.30 to 11 am and for dinner from 6.30 to 9 pm. The atmosphere is relaxed and enjoyable, and its reputation for serving large portions of good, inexpensive food keeps the family busy.

Top End Zihuatanejo has a number of fancier restaurants if you want to spend more for a fancy night out. *La Mesa del Capitán*, on the corner of Vicente Guerrero and Nicolás Bravo, is open every day from 2 to 11 pm and it's one of the town's best restaurants.

Entertainment
Happy hour from 5 to 7 pm at Tata's Restaurant/Bar, right on the beach on Playa Principal, was attracting a jolly sunset crowd every evening.

For more serious nightlife, head for Ixtapa. All of the big hotels have bars and nightclubs, and most also have discos. You could try the Euforia Disco near the Posada Real Hotel, or the Magic Circus Disco, Flash Le Club, Visage Disco or the Tropicana Night Club, all in the Ixtapa shopping centre. Or there's the Christine disco at the Hotel Krystal.

Also in Ixtapa, La Cantina, with live Mexican music, boasts an 'absolutely genuine Mexican cantina atmosphere'; it's open every day from noon to 3 am. Or there's Carlos 'n Charlie's, a lively restaurant/bar which always guarantees a good time for the gringos, with sassy waiters and customers dancing on the tables.

Getting There & Away
Air The Ixtapa/Zihuatanejo international airport is 19 km from Zihuatanejo, about two km off Highway 200 heading towards Acapulco. The airport is served by three airlines – Aeroméxico, Mexicana and Delta – and between them they connect Ixtapa/Zihuatanejo with a great number of cities throughout Mexico, the USA and other countries, with both direct and connecting flights.

The Aeroméxico office (☎ (743) 4-20-18/19/22) is in Zihuatanejo at Calle Juan N Álvarez 34, on the corner of Calle Cinco de Mayo; it also has an office at the airport (☎ (743) 4-22-37, 4-26-34). Mexicana has offices in Ixtapa (☎ (743) 3-22-08) and at the airport (☎ (743) 4-22-27). Delta has only one office, at the airport (☎ (743) 4-33-86).

Bus Flecha Roja and Estrella Blanca share a large bus terminal, the Central de Autobuses (☎ (743) 4-34-77), on Highway 200 about two km out of town, heading towards Acapulco.

Estrella de Oro (☎ (743) 4-21-75) has its own small terminal, closer to town at Paseo del Palmar 54. Estrella de Oro has only one route, going to Mexico City via Acapulco, Chilpancingo and Cuernavaca six times daily.

Buses from Zihuatanejo include:

Acapulco – 239 km, four hours; hourly from 5.30 am to 6.45 pm, with Flecha Roja, ordinary service with many stops (US$5.10); 10 buses daily between 6 am and 6 pm, with Estrella Blanca, nonstop direct (US$5.20); six buses daily with Estrella de Oro (US$4.90).

Lázaro Cárdenas – 72 km, two hours; 12 daily with Flecha Roja (US$2.35); 11 daily with Estrella Blanca (US$2.50).

Mexico City – 640 km, US$16; three daily with Flecha Roja, with stops, 11 hours; two daily with Estrella Blanca, stops only at Chilpancingo, Iguala and Cuernavaca, 10 hours; six daily with Estrella de Oro, via Acapulco, 10 hours.

Estrella Blanca also has one bus daily which goes all the way to Nuevo Laredo at the US border; it takes 28 hours to get there, passing through Querétaro, San Luis Potosí, Saltillo and Monterrey.

Car & Motorbike Several car rental companies serve Ixtapa/Zihuatanejo and, as always, it's best to phone around to compare prices. Several have offices at the airport. Offices in Ixtapa include: Avis (☎ 4-22-48); Budget (☎ 3-21-62, 4-48-37); Dollar (☎ 4-23-14); Econo Rent (☎ 3-10-66); Hertz (☎ 4-22-55); National (3-03-33); Quick (☎ 3-21-21).

The liquor store on Galeana near the corner of Pedro Ascencio has a sign announcing it rents scooters, and several scooters lined up in front to prove it. Honda 50s cost US$11.70 per hour, or US$50 per day (9 am to 6 pm). Honda 80s cost US$20 per hour, or US$60 per day.

Getting Around

To/From the Airport The best way to get to the airport is by taxi; US$8.35 from the centre of Zihuatanejo. Otherwise you could take a bus heading for Petatlán, get off at the crossroads on Highway 200, and walk two km to the airport.

Bus Local buses run frequently between Zihuatanejo and Ixtapa, departing every 15 minutes from around 6.30 am to 10 pm. Cost is US$0.20 for the 10-km, 15-minute ride. In Zihuatanejo the buses depart from a bus stop on the corner of Avenida Benito Juárez and Avenida Morelos. In Ixtapa the bus stops all along the main street, in front of all the large hotels.

Taxi Taxis are plentiful in both Ixtapa and Zihuatanejo. Prices seem to be fixed, with not as much taxi rip-off as in some other places (Acapulco, for example). Cost for a taxi from the centre of Zihuatanejo is US$1.70 to Playa la Ropa, US$3.35 to Ixtapa, and US$8.35 to the airport.

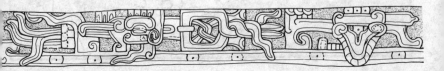

North-East Mexico

This chapter covers the states of Tamaulipas, Nuevo León, and Coahuila – a huge area, stretching nearly 1000 km from north to south and 500 km from east to west. Many travellers enter Mexico at one of the five border crossings from the USA, and take one of the several routes heading south to the Bajío region, central Mexico or the Gulf coast. The major inland cities are of interest – Monterrey, capital of Nuevo León, is now a large, modern-looking industrial city, and Saltillo, capital of Coahuila, which is quieter and older in appearance. The coast offers remote beaches and lagoons, and the Huasteca country west of Tampico is verdant and subtropical with a substantial Indian population.

Although there are large tracts of rugged, sparsely populated country, distant from Mexico City and close to the USA, the north-east is far from being a barren desert to be crossed before you reach the 'real' Mexico. On the contrary, the people from this region are an independently minded lot with a high degree of local pride and a good deal of antagonism towards the politicians and bureaucrats in the capital.

Tamaulipas

MATAMOROS
Population: 350,000

This is the most interesting and least hybrid of the three main US-Mexico border crossing points. It has fewer tourists entering than the other two, a town centre with a real Mexican feel to it, an interesting museum, and a reasonable beach 37 km away.

First settled during the Mexican colonisation of Tamaulipas in the mid-18th century, Matamoros used to be called Congregación de Nuestra Señora del Refugio. It was renamed after Father Mariano Matamoros, a hero of the independence war.

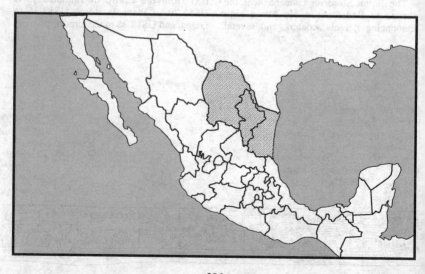

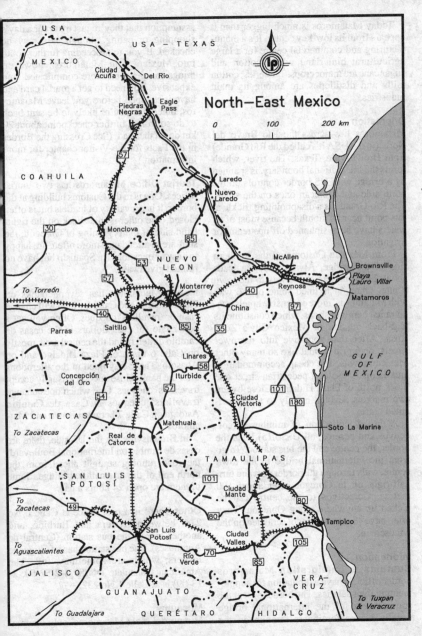

North–East Mexico

Today Matamoros is much bigger than it appears from its low-key centre. It's a manufacturing and commercial centre for a large agricultural hinterland where cotton and sugar cane are major crops. Tanneries, cotton mills and distilleries are among its main industries.

Orientation

Matamoros lies across the Río Bravo del Norte (in the USA it's called the Río Grande) from Brownsville, Texas. The river, which forms the international boundary, is spanned by a bridge with US border controls on the north side and Mexican ones on the south. The Río Grande is a disappointing trickle at this point near its mouth because most of its waters have been siphoned off upstream for irrigation.

From Mexican Customs on the southern side of the bridge, Álvaro Obregón leads about three-quarters of the way to the town centre. Obregón is lined some of the way with Matamoros' more expensive hotels, restaurants, bars and shops, which constitute its laid-back version of Mexico City's Zona Rosa. After that you dive into narrower streets, on a grid format like so many other Mexican towns. The cheap accommodation area is on Abasolo, a pedestrian street one block north of Plaza Hidalgo. Close by are two markets devoted mainly to tourist-oriented crafts.

A motley collection of minibuses (colectivos and peseros, all US$0.15) links the border, the centre and the bus station. To go from the international bridge to the town centre, walk through the border post and turn half-right on to Obregón after about 100 metres. Colectivos to the centre can be picked up anywhere along Obregón. They often have 'Sexta-Mercado' scrawled on the windscreen.

Information

Customs & Immigration Matamoros border officials have a reputation for supplementing their salaries. The border post at the southern end of the international bridge usually waves foreigners through on the assumption that they're just there for a day's shopping or eating, though cars may be checked. If you're proceeding further south into Mexico from Matamoros, however, things can get a bit more complicated, and expensive. You need to get a tourist card and have it stamped before you leave Matamoros, otherwise you're likely to be sent back to do so from a further checkpoint about 20 km down the road. (See Crossing the Border in the Facts for the Visitor chapter for more information.)

Tourist Office Matamoros has two tourist offices. One is in the Customs building at the border. It has a variety of leaflets but is often closed. The other is in a shack on the right-hand side of the beginning of Obregón; the staff are in attendance more often, are happy to answer questions (in Spanish) but have no printed giveaways.

Money Matamoros has several banks on Plaza Hidalgo and Calle 6 which will change cash or travellers' cheques. Often you get a better rate for cash dollars in the casas de cambio dotted round the central area, mostly on Calle 6 north of Plaza Hidalgo and on Abasolo. These stay open in the afternoons after the banks close but don't usually accept travellers' cheques. One which does change travellers' cheques is Casa de Cambio Astorga on Calle 7 between Bravo and Matamoros.

In Brownsville, on the US side, there are casas de cambio on International Boulevard, the road running straight ahead from the north end of the international bridge. Some of them are open 24 hours a day.

Other There is a post office at Calle 6 No 214, between Herrera and Iturbide, and another one in the bus station (Central de Autobuses). The bus station has left-luggage lockers, which are sometimes full. The American Consulate (☎ (891) 2-52-50, 2-13-09) is at Calle 1 No 232.

Museums

Museo del Maíz Matamoros' only one real

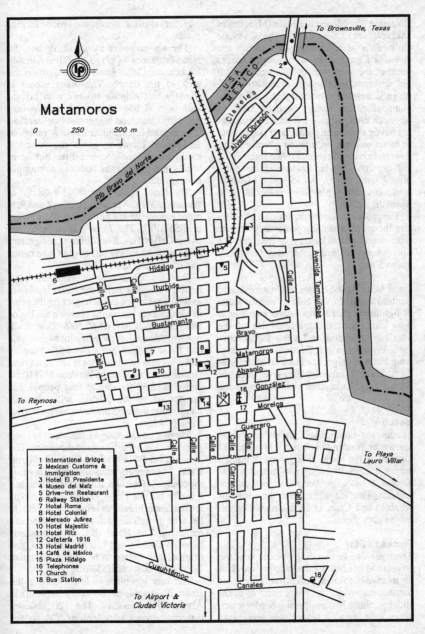

Matamoros

0   250   500 m

To Brownsville, Texas

USA
MEXICO

Río Bravo del Norte

Claveles

Álvaro Obregón

Avenida Tamaulipas

Calle 1

Hidalgo
Iturbide
Herrera
Bustamante

Bravo
Matamoros
Abasolo
González
Morelos
Guerrero

Calle 10
Calle 9

Calle

To Reynosa

Calle 8
Calle 7
Calle 6
Calle 5
Calle 4 (Carranza)
Calle 1

To Playa
Lauro Villar

Cuauhtémoc

Canales

To Airport &
Ciudad Victoria

1 International Bridge
2 Mexican Customs &
   Immigration
3 Hotel El Presidente
4 Museo del Maíz
5 Drive-Inn Restaurant
6 Railway Station
7 Hotel Roma
8 Hotel Colonial
9 Mercado Juárez
10 Hotel Majestic
11 Hotel Ritz
12 Cafetería 1916
13 Hotel Madrid
14 Café de México
15 Plaza Hidalgo
16 Telephones
17 Church
18 Bus Station

attraction, the Museo del Maíz (Museum of Maize/Corn), also called the Casa de Cultura, is at the corner of Calle 5 and Avenida Constitución, about seven blocks north of the main square. This well thought out museum, with lots of imaginative displays, is devoted to one subject – maize, the plant which has always been the basis of Mexican civilisation – but uses that subject to convey a powerful political message about *la lucha que aún no termina* – *latifundistas frente a la posesión comunal* (the fight which still goes on – big landowners against communal ownership). As in most Mexican museums, all explanatory material is in Spanish.

The museum displays culminate in a life-size model of protesting peasants, complete with sound-effects! Entry is free and it's open every day except Monday from 9.30 am to 5 pm.

Casa Mata At the corner of Guatemala and Santos Degollado, this old fort was the scene of fighting in the Mexican-American War. It now contains some memorabilia of the Mexican revolution and a few Indian artefacts. Entrance is free. To reach this museum from Plaza Hidalgo, head east on Morelos as far as Calle 1, turn right, go five blocks to Santos Degollado, then two blocks to the left.

Beach

Matamoros' beach, Playa Lauro Villar (also known as Washington Beach), is in fact 37 km east of the town on Highway 2, but it's empty and clean enough to attract a few Texans. It has a few beachside seafood restaurants. The 'Playa' bus from the corner of Abasolo and Calle 11 in downtown Matamoros goes there.

Places to Stay

There are one or two dingy places near the bus station but better value is to be found on or near Abasolo, a pedestrianised street running east-west, one block north of Plaza Hidalgo. Since Matamoros is a border town, prices here are a bit higher than you might pay for similar accommodation further south.

There's nowhere outstanding but the *Hotel Majestic* (☎ (891) 3-36-80) at Abasolo 89, between Calles 8 and 9, is marginally the pick of the bunch. The management is friendly and helpful. Rooms with private bathroom (US$8/10 a single/double) are basically clean, and bigger and brighter than in comparable establishments. A range of antiquated furniture gives the rooms a modicum of atmosphere and the hot water works, but some of the beds sag alarmingly in the middle.

The *Hotel México* (☎ (891) 2-08-56) at Abasolo 807, also between Calles 8 and 9, is more expensive but not significantly better at US$10/13. The *Hotel Continental*, between Calles 7 and 8 on Abasolo, is a grubby place with a balcony full of old Coke crates and rooms at US$9/11.50.

On González, west of Plaza Hidalgo between Calles 8 and 9, the *Hotel Madrid* is as well-kept as you could expect for the price in Matamoros, but rooms are none too big or airy. Here you pay US$5.50/8. One block north of Abasolo, at the corner of Matamoros and Calle 6, the *Hotel Colonial* is friendly and a bargain of sorts if there are more than two of you. Prices range between US$10.50 and US$12.50 for one to four people, but interior rooms are gloomy with signs of damp while those on the street have a traffic-noise problem.

Moving up the scale a little, there are two places within a few blocks of the centre. The *Hotel Roma* (☎ (891) 3-61-76, 6-05-73), on Calle 9 between Matamoros and Bravo, is the cheaper of the two. It's modern, clean and friendly but for US$25/27.50 its 30 rooms are neither as big nor as bright as they should be, even though they have TV, telephone and carpeting. The *Hotel Ritz*, on Matamoros between Calles 6 and 7, is altogether bigger, brighter and better with a large attractive lobby and rooms at US$27/34.

The very top place in Matamoros is the *Hotel El Presidente* (☎ (891) 3-94-40) at Álvaro Obregón 249. The 120 air-conditioned rooms with colour TV go for

US$48/53. For this you also get gardens and a swimming pool.

Places to Eat

The town has a pleasant range of eating places, from small cafés to the expensive haunts of visiting Texans and wealthier locals. Of the town centre's places, the clean *Café de México* (☎ 2-50-23), on González between Calles 6 and 7, is popular from morning to evening and the food isn't bad, with a tasty comida corrida going for around US$4. Decor is basic – this is really just a friendly, slightly up-market 'eating hall'.

Another good option in the lower budget range is *Café y Restaurant Nuevo León*, on Calle 9 more or less opposite Hotel Roma. It can get awfully hot in here, but the decor is great and a filling comida corrida costs only US$3.

Also popular, the *Cafetería 1916*, on Calle 6 between Matamoros and Abasolo, pays more attention to atmosphere and cuisine than the Café de México and is a bit more expensive. A big three-course lunch goes for US$6.50, a large chicken salad for US$3.50.

Slightly further up the scale there's the *Restaurant y Bar Piedras Negras*, at 175 Calle 6, half a block north of the main square. Favoured by better-off Mexicans and a few gringos, a meal could well set you back US$10. Elsewhere, in a similar price range, there's *El Fandango* (☎ 2-50-14) at the corner of Abasolo and Calle 5, with some outdoor tables. They specialise in charcoal grills.

Things to Buy

Matamoros has two central tourist-oriented craft markets and a few interesting but expensive folk art shops along Obregón. The larger of the two markets, the Mercado Juárez, is on Abasolo between Calles 9 and 10. A lot of the stuff is second-rate – including blankets, hats, pottery and glass – but you may find something appealing. Vendors also set up on the pavement outside and some of them sell attractive-looking leather belts. You'll have to bargain hard to beat prices down to levels that you'd get further south.

The second market, selling similar goods, is on Bravo between Calles 8 and 9. Piñatas,

those colourful decorated containers which are filled with gifts and smashed open at festival times, seem to be on sale almost year-round. They're not the handiest items to carry with you, but if you're on your way to the USA, Matamoros would be one of the least inconvenient points to pick one up. You will notice that piñata manufacturers do their best to keep up with the latest trends – you are bound to see papier-mâché Teenage Mutant Ninja Turtles if you pass through Matamoros.

Getting There & Away

Air Matamoros has an airport (☎ (891) 2-20-56) 17 km out of town on the road to Ciudad Victoria. There is a direct Aeroméxico flight from and to Mexico City every afternoon and an extra one each way on Tuesday and Saturday mornings. Aeroméxico also flies Matamoros/Ciudad Victoria/Mexico City and vice-versa on Wednesday, Friday and Sunday mornings. The Aeroméxico office (☎ (891) 3-07-01) in Matamoros is at Obregón 21.

Aeromonterrey flies to/from Monterrey, Tampico and Veracruz five days a week.

Bus Matamoros is linked by bus to almost everywhere in Mexico. Both 1st and 2nd-class buses run from the bus station (☎ (891) 2-01-81) on Canales near the corner of Aguiles. The bus station has a 24-hour restaurant, a post office and left-luggage lockers (US$1 for 12 hours).

Four of the better 1st-class bus lines serve Matamoros – ADO, Transportes del Norte (T del N), Omnibus de México (O de M), and Tres Estrellas de Oro (TE de O). Both 1st and 2nd-class services are offered by Transportes Monterrey-Cadereyta-Reynosa (TM-C-R), while 2nd-class service only is offered by Autotransportes Mante (AM), Oriente (O) and Transportes Frontera (TF).

Chihuahua – 1061 km, 15½ hours; US$23.50 with O de M

Ciudad Victoria – 312 km, 4½ hours; US$6.50 1st class, US$6.25 2nd class with TE de O, AM, O, TF

Culiacá – 1402 km, 23 hours; US$37.50 with TE de O

Durango – 858 km, 14 hours; US$18.50 with T del N, O de M

Guadalajara – 1009 km, 15½ hours; US$21.50 1st class, US$19.50 2nd class with T del N, O de M, TE de O, O

Guaymas – 1831 km, 32 hours; US$48 with TE de O

Hermosillo – 1967 km, 34 hours; US$51 with TE de O

Los Mochis – 1608 km, 26 hours; US$41 with TE de O

Mazatlán – 1176 km, 20 hours; US$32.50 with TE de O

Mexicali – 2545 km, 34 hours; US$65 with TE de O

Mexico City – 1172 km, 18 hours; US$22 1st class, US$19 2nd class with T del N, O de M, TE de O, TF

Monterrey – 243 km, six hours; T del N, O de M, TE de O, TM-C-R, US$7 1st class, US$6.50 2nd class

Querétaro – 960 km, 15 hours; US$16.50 with TE de O, O, TF

Reynosa – 98 km, two hours; US$2 1st class, US$1.75 2nd class with TE de O, TM-C-R

Saltillo – 328 km, seven hours; US$8 with TE de O

San Luis Potosí – 658 km, 10½ hours US$12.50 1st class, US$11.50 2nd class with T del N, TE de O, O

Tampico – 555 km, eight hours; US$12 1st class, US$11 2nd class with ADO, AM, O, TF

Tijuana – 2734 km, 35½ hours; US$68 with TE de O

Torreón – 605 km, 10 hours; US$14 with O de M

Tuxpan – 748 km, 12 hours; US$16.50 1st class, US$16 2nd class with ADO, TF

Veracruz – 1050 km, 18 hours; US$26 with ADO

Villahermosa – 1549 km, 25 hours; US$35.50 with ADO

Train Matamoros railway station (☎ (891) 2-02-55) is on Hidalgo, eight blocks north of González along Calle 10. There's one service a day in each direction between Matamoros and Monterrey, via Reynosa. Though cheap, it's neither quick nor reliable. The 6.50 am departure from Matamoros is scheduled to arrive in Reynosa at 8.43 am and Monterrey at 1.55 pm. In the other direction, the train leaves Monterrey at 6 am and Reynosa at 10.50 am, reaching Matamoros at 1.05 pm. The fare between Matamoros and Monterrey is about US$2.50 in 1st class, US$1.50 in 2nd.

Car For information on routes heading south into Mexico, see the South from Matamoros section.

To/From Brownsville, Texas If you're going straight through Matamoros deeper into Mexico, or out of interior Mexico into the US, it's worth considering the buses run by the Mexican lines Tres Estrellas de Oro (1st class) and Autotransportes Ciudad Mante (2nd class) between the Trailways station in Brownsville and several cities inside Mexico. They may save you effort – but they certainly lose you money and possibly time. Prices are about 50% higher than to or from Matamoros and these buses can take up to two hours to get over the international bridge, through customs and immigration, and to/from the Matamoros bus station.

Trailways in Brownsville (☎ (512) 546-7171) is at 1165 Saint Charles on the corner of 12th St. Facing into the USA from the north end of the international bridge, walk left (west) on Elizabeth, then two blocks south on 12th. The Tres Estrellas de Oro departures from here are to Ciudad Victoria, San Luis Potosí, Querétaro and Mexico City twice daily; to Monterrey, Saltillo and Guadalajara once; and to Ciudad Victoria, San Luis Potosí, Lagos de Moreno, León, Irapuato, Salamanca and Morelia once. Autotransportes Ciudad Mante runs to Tampico three times a day; to Ciudad Victoria and Ciudad Valles twice.

Most of these buses will also take you between Brownsville Trailways and Matamoros bus station for US$2.50. But it's generally a lot quicker to walk over the international bridge, which is close to downtown Brownsville, and take local transport between the border and downtown Matamoros.

Getting Around

Matamoros is served by buses and colectivos/peseros. The fare on any of these is US$0.25. You can stop them on almost any street corner. They usually have their destinations painted on the front windscreen but check before getting in; the town centre is 'Centro', the bus station 'Central de Autobuses' and the international bridge 'Puente Internacional'.

From the border to the bus station, walk along Obregón until you reach a right-angled crossroads, turn left and wait on the next corner for a pesero.

From the border to downtown, pick up a pesero (usually saying 'Sexta-Mercado') on Obregón. Most transport to the centre runs along Morelos; get off at Calle 6 or 7 for Plaza Hidalgo. From the bus station to the centre, get a bus from directly opposite the main bus station entrance, or a pesero by turning right out of the entrance, left at the nearby crossroads and waiting on the other side of the road.

From the centre to the border, buses and peseros ('Carranza-Claveles') run north along Calle 6, then east along Hidalgo and north on Obregón, before taking a back street called Claveles to reach the border post. From the centre to the bus station, pick up a green 'Canales' bus at the corner of Abasolo and Calle 11.

There are plenty of taxis in Matamoros, as in other Mexican towns. From the border to the centre or the bus station costs US$5.

SOUTH FROM MATAMOROS
Highway 2 – patrolled by Green Angels – goes west to Reynosa, 98 km away. Highway 101 is not as good as the other main arteries leading south from the border, but it is the start of the shortest way from the border to Mexico City (1016 km). From Matamoros to Ciudad Victoria by Highway 101 is 312 km.

For Tampico, Highway 180 (rougher but still adequate) branches off Highway 101 at La Coma, 183 km south of Matamoros. It's another 315 km to Tampico from the intersection, making it 498 km from Matamoros to Tampico. After Tampico, Highway 180 carries on south to Veracruz. A longer but better road from Matamoros to Tampico is Highway 101 to Ciudad Victoria, then Highway 85 south to Ciudad Mante, then Highway 80 east to Tampico.

Matamoros to Tampico
Most of this 498-km road is 30 to 40 km inland from the coast, crossing several rivers but passing mainly through flat drab low-lands – though there are stretches where the outliers of the Sierra Madre Oriental come close to the coast. For the first 183 km the route follows Highway 101 to Ciudad Victoria, then turns off along Highway 180. There are basic hotels in San Fernando (137 km from Matamoros), Soto La Marina (269 km) and Aldama (381 km).

If you're interested in exploring this or any other part of Mexico's Gulf coast in detail, check out Donald Schueler's excellent *Adventuring Along the Gulf of Mexico* (Sierra Club Books, San Francisco), which gives full coverage of the ecology and wildlife.

El Mesquital This is a small fishing village with a lighthouse and beach, on the long, thin spit of land that divides the Laguna Madre (biggest of the lagoons on this stretch of coast) from the Gulf of Mexico. The road to El Mesquital leads about 60 km off the highway from a little south of Matamoros airport.

La Carbonera Another fishing village, this one is on the inland side of the lagoon. You can get a boat out to the lagoon barrier island, where there is quite good surf and porpoises can sometimes be seen. A road leads here from San Fernando.

La Pesca Forty-eight km from Soto La Marina, La Pesca has a long beach that attracts a few American surfers, plus some fishermen for the Laguna de Morales or the Río Soto La Marina.

You can reach La Pesca by bus from Soto la Marina (US$1, 1 hour). The same bus continues on from La Pesca to the beach (US$0.30, 15 minutes), with the last bus leaving the beach for Soto la Marina at 17.30.

There is a restaurant at the beach, but if you want a roof over your head you'll have to go back into La Pesca. The hotel attached to Restaurant Ramón is the best value in town. Rumour has it that there are major development plans for the beach.

Barra del Tordo From Aldama, 117 km from

Tampico, a road goes through the eastern fringes of the Sierra de Tamaulipas to Barra del Tordo, another hamlet with a beach and good fishing.

REYNOSA

Population: 350,000
Altitude: 90 metres

Across the Río Bravo from the small settlement of Hidalgo, Texas, with the bigger US town of McAllen nine km away, Reynosa is one of north-east Mexico's most important industrial towns. It has oil refineries, petrochemical plants, cotton mills and distilleries. Pipelines from here carry natural gas to the USA and Monterrey. It's also the centre of a big cattle-raising, cotton, sugar cane and maize-growing area.

More important as a border crossing than Matamoros, less so than Nuevo Laredo, Reynosa has a pleasant enough town centre on a small hill not far from the international bridge, some distance from the industries which have grown up on the southern side of town. It's as good as any border town for onward transportation into Mexico and is well geared to the Texan tourist trade.

Reynosa was founded in 1749 as Villa de Nuestra Señora de Guadalupe de Reynosa, 20 km from its present location, during the Spanish colonisation of Tamaulipas. Flooding forced the move to the present site in 1802. Reynosa was one of the first towns to rise up in the independence movement of 1810.

Orientation

Reynosa's central streets are laid out on a grid pattern aligned north-south and east-west. The wide and airy central square, with a church, a cinema, a few hotels and restaurants, sits on top of a small hill less than a km south-west of the international bridge. Between the bridge and the centre lies a 'zona rosa' with the town's most expensive restaurants and bars. Cheaper accommodation is a couple of blocks south of the square. The bus station is 1½ km south-east of the bridge and centre.

The walk from bridge or bus station to town centre takes about 15 to 20 minutes. From the bridge and the Mexican border post, walk straight ahead off the exit ramp, crossing one road to reach a desolate-looking three-way junction, where you take the right fork. This street is Zaragoza, and you can see the central square at the top of the hill a few blocks straight ahead. From the bus station, turn left out of the main entrance, and walk to the end of the block to another desolate-looking junction. Turn left here on to Colón and walk about seven blocks until you reach Hidalgo or Díaz, where a right turn and six blocks uphill will bring you to the square.

Ramshackle but frequent local buses and colectivos (US$0.25 or US$0.20) link the bridge, centre and bus station.

Information

Customs & Immigration US immigration is at the north end of the international bridge. Mexican customs and immigration are at the south end, and there's another immigration post in Reynosa bus station. Get a tourist card stamped at either post if you're proceeding beyond Reynosa deeper into Mexico.

Tourist Office There's a friendly and quite knowledgeable tourist office (☎ (892) 2-11-89) inside the customs and immigration building on the Mexican side of the international bridge. Some of the staff speak English.

Money The customs building has a bank. You can also change money in Bánamex, on Guerrero between Hidalgo and Juárez. There are several casas de cambio in the downtown area, particularly on Hidalgo south of the square, plus one in the bus station. Casa de Cambio Principal, at Hidalgo 820 Norte, stays open until 8.30 pm and cashes travellers' cheques. Some shops also change money at competitive rates.

Post The post office is on the corner of Díaz and Colón.

Things to See

Apart from a stroll around the pleasant, open

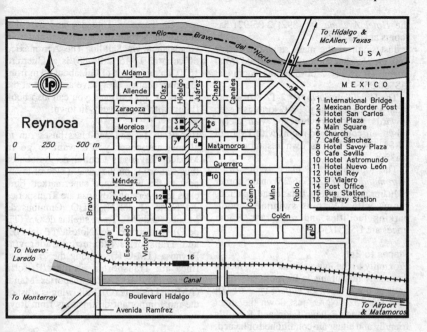

Reynosa

0   250   500 m

1 International Bridge
2 Mexican Border Post
3 Hotel San Carlos
4 Hotel Plaza
5 Main Square
6 Church
7 Café Sánchez
8 Hotel Savoy Plaza
9 Cafe Sevilla
10 Hotel Astromundo
11 Hotel Nuevo León
12 Hotel Rey
13 El Viajero
14 Post Office
15 Bus Station
16 Railway Station

main square, there's little to do in Reynosa. Hidalgo is pedestrianised for a couple of blocks south of the square. There's a basic market a few blocks further south bounded by Hidalgo, Juárez, Colón and the railway tracks. The zona rosa, with a few tourist-oriented craft shops, restaurants, bars and the odd musician, stretches along Allende and Zaragoza between the main square and the international bridge.

Reynosa's major festival is that of Our Lady of Guadalupe, the city's patroness, on 12 December. Pilgrims start processions a week early and there are afternoon dance performances in front of the church.

Places to Stay

Since it's a border town, Reynosa's room prices are a bit high. Best value is to be found in a couple of places on Díaz, a few minutes' walk from the main square. The cheaper of the two, the *Hotel Nuevo León* (☎ (892) 2-

13-10) on Díaz between Méndez and Madero, has quite sizeable, clean rooms with private bathrooms and a bit of newish furniture at US$12 for one person, US$15 for two, US$18.75 for three and US$23 for four.

On the west side of the main square, a few doors from the bigger Hotel San Carlos, the *Hotel Plaza* (☎ (892) 2-00-39) has rooms from US$10 for one, US$13.50 for two. The *Hotel San Miguel* (☎ (892) 2-75-27) on Colón, 2½ blocks from the bus station, is OK if you can't be bothered to go into town, with rooms at US$17/22.50. They rent showers for US$2.75.

The *Hotel Rey* on Díaz between Méndez and Madero, a couple of doors down from the Hotel Nuevo León, has clean, bright rooms with TV at US$20 for one person, US$24 for two and US$27.50 for three. It's very popular and may not have a room if you arrive late.

On the edge of the small zona rosa, at Zaragoza 885 Ote on the corner of Canales, the *Hotel Avenida* (☎ (892) 2-05-92) has rooms at US$21/26.

Just south of the main square at Juárez 860, the pleasant, although overpriced *Hotel Savoy* (☎ (892) 2-00-67) has rooms at US$30/35.

The *Hotel San Carlos* (☎ 2-12-80), on the main square at Hidalgo 970 Norte, is a step towards the luxury bracket with clean, bright, air-conditioned rooms with TV from US$31/34. It has its own restaurant and parking.

The top downtown place is the *Hotel Astromundo* (☎ (892) 2-56-25) on the corner of Juárez and Guerrero. It has clean, spacious rooms with TV, plus swimming pool, parking facilities and restaurant. Room prices are US$31/34.

Places to Eat

Proximity to the international border means that many restaurants in Reynosa stay open until 11 pm or later. *El Viajero* (☎ 2-61-00) is at Díaz 520 Norte, just down the street from the hotels Nuevo León and Rey. It's friendly and either air-conditioned or heated, depending on the season. The food is good and reasonably priced, with a comida corrida for US$4.50.

Half a block from the main square at Morelos 575, the *Café Sánchez* is a restaurant-cafeteria-type place popular with locals, but a little on the expensive side. *Cafe Sevilla* on the corner of Matamoros and Díaz is a much better deal with main courses from US$2 and a comida corrida for US$3.25. In theory it is open 24 hours a day.

Places in the zona rosa have prices appropriate for the day-tripping Texans who make up a lot of their clientele, but in the evenings the *Restaurant Carrusel/Hostelería del Bohemio* on Zaragoza Ote is filled with mostly young local people enjoying live Mexican music in a convivial atmosphere.

Getting There & Away

Air Reynosa airport is eight km out of town, off the Matamoros road. There are two Aeroméxico flights direct to Mexico City daily, except Saturday when there is only one. On Tuesday, Thursday and Saturday afternoons Aeroméxico also flies to and from Guadalajara via Saltillo. The Aeroméxico office (☎ 2-11-15, 2-24-88) is at Guerrero 1510, on the corner of Gil, about a km from the town centre. They have an office at the airport (☎ 3-00-40) and you can also book flights with travel agents in town.

Bus Both 1st and 2nd-class buses run to almost anywhere you'd want to go in Mexico. Reynosa's Central de Autobuses (bus station) is on the eastern side of town, next to the big Blanco supermarket. First class lines serving Reynosa are Transportes del Norte (T del N), ADO, Omnibus de México (O de M), Tres Estrellas de Oro (TE de O), Transportes del Noreste (T del NE) and Transportes Monterrey-Cadereyta-Reynosa (TM-C-R). Among the 2nd-class lines are Transportes Frontera/Estrella Blanca (TF/EB), Autotransportes Mante (AM) and Oriente (O). Following is a list of the most important destinations from Reynosa.

Aguascalientes – 747 km, 10 hours; US$17 with T del N, O de M

Chihuahua – 1043 km, 15 hours; US$24 with O de M

Ciudad Juárez – 1437 km, 20 hours, one a day; US$33 with O de M

Ciudad Victoria – 322 km, 4½ hours; US$7 1st class, US$6.50 2nd class, with TE de O, TF/EB, AM, O

Durango – 840 km, 13½ hours; US$19 with T del N, O de M

Guadalajara – 930 km, 14½ hours; US$23.50 with T del N, O de M, TE de O, O

Matamoros, 98 km, two hours; US$2.25 with T del N, O de M, TM-C-R

Mexico City – 973 km, 16 hours; US$25.50 1st class, US$22.50 2nd class, with T del N, O de M, TE de O, TF/EB

Monterrey – 225 km, four hours; US$5.50 with T del N, O de M, TE de O, T del NE, TM-C-R

Querétaro – 781 km, 12½ hours; US$20 with T del N, TF/EB

Saltillo – 310 km, five hours; US$7 with T del N, O de M, TE de O

San Luis Potosí – 579 km, nine hours; US$15 with T del N, TE de O, T del NE, O, T del N, TF/EB

Tampico – 508 km, 11 hours; US$18.50 1st class, US$17.50 2nd class, with ADO, TF/EB, AM, O

Torreón – 587 km, 8½ hours; US$13.50 with T del N, O de M

Tuxpan – 705 km, 12 hours; US$19.50 1st class, US$18 2nd class, with ADO, TF/EB

Veracruz – 1007 km, 18 hours; US$29 with ADO

Villahermosa – 1506 km, 25 hours, two a day; US$39.50 with ADO

Zacatecas – 673 km, nine hours; US$14.50 with T del N, O de M

Train Reynosa railway station is at the southern end of Hidalgo, six blocks from the main square. You probably wouldn't know it was a station if it weren't next to the railway tracks. There's one slow train daily in each direction (leaving for Matamoros at 12.15 and for Monterrey at 15.25). The fare to Monterrey is about US$6 in 1st class, US$2 in 2nd class.

Car For information on routes heading south from Reynosa, see the following section, South from Reynosa.

To/From McAllen, Texas The nearest Texas transport centre, McAllen, is nine km from the border. Valley Transit Company (VTC) runs buses both ways between McAllen and Reynosa bus station for US$3.50 one way, every 20 minutes between 6 am and 7 pm. There are three later services, with the last leaving Reynosa bus station at 11 pm. Coming from McAllen, if you don't want to go all the way to the Reynosa bus station, you can get off at the Greyhound office on the US side of the border and walk over the international bridge and into Reynosa. Leaving Mexico, you can walk over the bridge and pick up the buses at the same Greyhound office.

The Mexican bus line Transportes Monterrey-Cadereyta-Reynosa also runs between Reynosa's bus station and McAllen. Another option is to take a jitney taxi. In Reynosa they wait on Allende to take passengers to McAllen; they leave when they're full.

Getting Around
To/From the Airport The airport is eight km out of town, off the Matamoros road. Buses don't go all the way to the airport. A taxi from town costs US$12.

Local Transport Hundreds of decrepit buses and microbuses (colectivos) rattle their way round Reynosa's rutted one-way streets, providing an effective if bone-jarring urban transport system. All fares are US$0.20.

From the international bridge to the bus station, take No 14, or catch a free ride on one of the Valley Transit Company or Transportes Monterrey-Cadereyta-Reynosa coaches coming from McAllen. The latter will pick you up as they pull out of the Mexican border building; they're not officially supposed to take you but usually will.

If you don't feel like the short walk from the bridge to the town centre, walk down the bridge exit ramp, straight over the first road, and wait on the next corner (a three-way junction). Most buses going right from here, including '17 Obrera', run close to the central square.

From the town centre to the bridge, most buses or colectivos running along Guerrero, a one-way street, will get you there. The corners of Díaz and Hidalgo are convenient places to pick them up. From the centre to the bus station, catch the '17 Obrera' from Madero, at the corner of Díaz or Hidalgo.

From the bus station to the centre, turn left out of the bus station main entrance, walk to the end of the block, turn left, and catch a '17 Obrera' on the next corner (Colón and Rubio).

SOUTH FROM REYNOSA
You have the choice of going west to Monterrey, or south to Ciudad Victoria or Tampico. Tampico's the place to head for if you're aiming for Veracruz and the south; Ciudad Victoria is en route to San Luis Potosí and Mexico City.

Highway 40, a good road patrolled by Green Angels, goes west to Monterrey (225 km). At China, 109 km from Reynosa, Highway 35 branches south-west off Highway 40 to meet Highway 85, which runs south-east from Monterrey to Ciudad Victoria (402 km from Reynosa by this route). East of Reynosa, Highway 2 goes to Matamoros (98 km), with Highway 97 branching south a few km out of Reynosa to meet Highway 101 coming south from Matamoros to Ciudad Victoria (322 km from Reynosa to Ciudad Victoria this way but the roads are inferior).

CIUDAD VICTORIA
Population: 170,000
Altitude: 333 metres

About 40 km north of the Tropic of Cancer, the capital of Tamaulipas state has no special attractions, but the central Plaza Hidalgo is pleasant, with one middle-range and two expensive hotels if you want to stop overnight.

Ciudad Victoria is quite a big transport centre, a five-way highway junction and the first major town south of Monterrey, Matamoros and Reynosa.

Forty km north-east of Ciudad Victoria, Lago Guerrero is a huge reservoir which attracts Mexicans and North Americans for bass fishing and duck, goose and dove hunting.

Balcón de Montezuma
Although this site has been known by archaeologists for a number of years, it was not until late 1988 that any excavations were done. Very little is known about these ruins but it is generally thought to have been a Huasteca settlement. The site is made up of numerous circles set around two open spaces which were probably public plazas. While the Balcón de Montezuma cannot compete with the better known ruins further south, it is surely one of the dwindling number of sites which can still be seen in their 'raw' state.

1	Market
2	Post Office
3	Hotel Condesa
4	Hotel San Juan
5	Hotel Santorín
6	Laundrette
7	Museum
8	Plaza Hidalgo
9	Hotel Los Monteros
10	Local buses to Main Bus Station
11	Hotel San Bernabe
12	Cafeteria La Ola
13	Hotel Everest
14	Banorte (Bank)

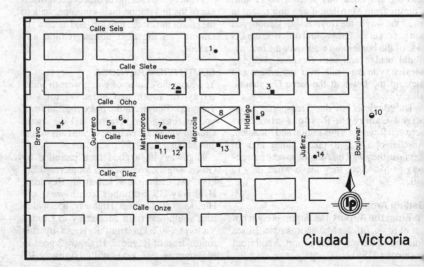

Ciudad Victoria

Getting to the Balcón de Montezuma is no mean feat. First you need to get to Ejido de Alta Cumbre, a tiny hamlet some 25 km south of Ciudad Victoria on Highway 101. If you don't have a car, you can either hitch or take a bus bound for Jaumave, Tula or San Luis Potosí and ask the driver to let you off. Once you get into Ejido de Alta Cumbre, follow the 'main street' to the end of town, then down the hill to the right. It is about an hour's walk down a 4WD track to the ruins, although if you time it right you may get a lift down with some archaeologists.

Places to Stay

Hotel Los Monteros (☎ (131) 2-03-00), on Plaza Hidalgo, is a lovely old colonial building. Considering the quality of the rooms, it is undoubtedly the best deal in town with singles/doubles from US$13/15. If you just can't afford to part with those extra dollars, then try *Hotel San Juan* (☎ (131) 2-79-93), on Calle Nueve (9) between Guerrero and Bravo, with singles/doubles from US$10/13; *Hotel San Bernabe* (no phone), on the corner of Calle Nueve and Matamoros (singles/doubles from US$10); or *Hotel Condesa* (no phone) on Calle Ocho (8) between Hidalgo and Juárez (singles/doubles from US$11.50/15).

Hotel Everest (☎ (131) 2-40-50) and *Hotel Sierra Gorda* (☎ 2-22-80) both cost from US$35/45 with air-con, TV in rooms and restaurant. The top place in town is *Hotel Santorín* on Calle 9 between Guerrero and Matamoros. Singles/doubles start at US$50/65.

Getting There & Away

Ciudad Victoria has an airport, east of town off the Soto La Marina road. There are three Aeroméxico flights a week to and from Matamoros, and daily ones to and from Mexico City, some of which stop at Poza Rica. The Aeroméxico office (☎ (131) 2-87-97, 2-97-40) in town is at Morelos 155B on the corner of Hidalgo.

From Ciudad Victoria, you can continue south-west to San Luis Potosí (346 km away) by Highways 101, 80 and 57. For Mexico City, Highway 85 south via Ciudad Mante and Ciudad Valles, is the most direct.

A 1st-class bus to Mexico City costs US$14 and takes about 13 hours; Tampico US$4.50, about 3½ hours; Matamoros or Reynosa US$5.75, five hours; Monterrey US$6.50, four hours; San Luis Potosí US$7, 5½ hours; Ciudad Valles US$4.50, 3½ hours.

NUEVO LAREDO

Population: 300,000

More foreign tourists enter Mexico through Nuevo Laredo than any other town on the north-east, and the untidy collection of low-rise buildings that greets you on the south side of the international bridge fits the traditional border-town image better than Reynosa or Matamoros. Nuevo Laredo has more restaurants, shops and hotels catering to the US tourist trade than anywhere else in the region, but prices are not well-suited to budget travellers.

Orientation

Drivers can avoid most of Nuevo Laredo and head on south by crossing the border on a new road bridge to the east. The old bridge brings you into Mexico at the north end of Guerrero, Nuevo Laredo's main street, which stretches for two km. The downtown area spreads along either side of Guerrero for the first km from the bridge. Its main plaza, with a kiosk in the middle, the Palacio de Gobierno on the east side, and a few hotels and restaurants around it, is seven blocks along Guerrero from the bridge.

Street numbers on Guerrero tell you how far they are from the bridge: 109 would be in the block nearest the bridge, 509 in the fifth block down, 2009 would be 20 blocks from the bridge, etc. Other north-south streets, parallel to Guerrero, are numbered in the same way. The most important of these are Matamoros, Juárez, Ocampo and Galeana.

Nuevo Laredo's Central Camionera, the arrival and departure point for long-distance buses, is way out on the southern side of town. Local buses run between it and the town bus station, which is on Matamoros,

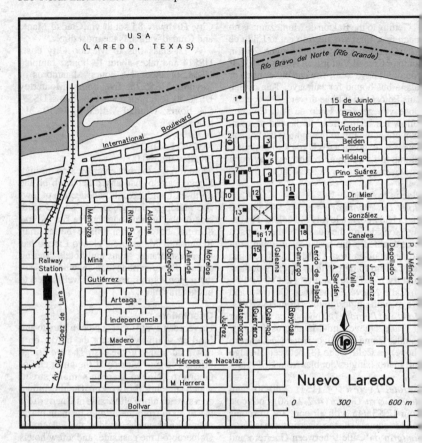

two blocks south and one block west of the international bridge. The railway station, also linked by bus with the town bus station, is 10 blocks south on Guerrero from the bridge, then 10 blocks west on Gutiérrez.

Information

Customs & Immigration Mexican immigration and customs are in the border post at the south end of the international bridge. Get a tourist card stamped here if you're going on south beyond Nuevo Laredo.

Tourist Office There's a small but helpful tourist office (☎ (871) 2-01-04) in the border building, with a copious selection of leaflet on Nuevo Laredo and northern Mexico When it's open (9 am to 3 pm and sometime in the evening) there's usually at least one English-speaker on duty.

Money Banamex/Euromex has a casa de cambio on Guerrero between Canales and Mina, which is the only bank or casa de cambio in town that will change travellers cheques. Its rate for cash is better than the other casas de cambio, a few of which are on

1	Mexican Border Post & Tourist Office
2	Town Bus Station
3	Hotel Reno
4	Cadillac Restaurant
5	Hotel Ramirez
6	Hotel La Llave
7	Hotel Ajova
8	Hotel Sam's
9	Motor Hotel Fiesta
10	Hotel Regis
11	Post Office
12	Café Quinto Patio
13	Hotel Mesón del Rey
14	Main Plaza
15	Casa de Cambio
16	Hotel Texas
17	Café Almanza
18	Motel Don Antonio

Guerrero just south of the international bridge.

Post The post office is on the corner of Reynosa and Dr Mier.

Foreign Consulates There's a US Consulate (☎ (871) 4-05-12) in Nuevo Laredo.

Places to Stay

There's only one worthwhile place in the cheaper bracket but it's one of the better deals to be found in any border town. Nothing special – just cheap, popular with Mexican families, and clean and friendly enough. This is the *Hotel la Llave* (☎ (871) 2-23-80) at Juárez 313, just a few blocks from the international bridge. With singles/doubles from US$11/12, you won't find much better value. Elsewhere, *Hotel Ajova*, on Hidalgo half a block west of Guerrero, is modern but pretty shoddy with singles/doubles from US$11/14.

Hotel Sam's (☎ (871) 2-59-32) at Hidalgo 2903, is not too bad at US$9 for one bed, US$11 for two. For the same price *Hotel Texas* (☎ (871) 2-18-07) at Guerrero 837 comes in a distant second. *Hotel Reno* on the corner of Ocampo and Belden is similar and costs US$12 for one or two people.

A little further up the scale is *Motel Don*

Antonio (☎ (871) 2-11-40) at González 2435. It is reasonable value with big clean rooms, large comfortable beds, and US stations on TV in the room for US$17/19 single/double. Like all motels, it's a bit soulless.

Hotel Mesón Del Rey (☎ (871) 2-63-60) at Guerrero 718 on the main plaza is comfortable enough but not as luxurious as you'd expect for US$27/31. *Hotel Palacio Del Rio* (☎ (871) 2-24-83) at Ocampo 101 is as close as you can get to the Río Bravo (turn left immediately off the international bridge) but the view's nothing special. Singles/doubles are pretty steep at US$40/47.

Places to Eat

Avoid the places on Guerrero for the first few blocks south of the bridge if you want value for money.

For a top value comida corrida you can't go beyond *Restaurant el Farol* on Victoria near the corner of Ocampo. The servings are most generous, and at around US$3.50 they won't break too many budgets.

On the south side of the plaza at the corner of Ocampo and González, the *Café Almanza* is a small, cosy, family-run place, reasonably clean and not too expensive. The menu includes fish, soups and breakfasts (for US$3), and it's open from 7 am to midnight.

Two places very popular with the townsfolk lie a km or so down Guerrero from the international bridge. The *Río Mar* (☎ 2-91-94) at Guerrero 2403 is small and unassuming but packed out at night with people tucking into mouth watering seafood dishes starting at US$5. It's closed on Monday. A few blocks north, at Guerrero 2114 between Venezuela and Lincoln, *El Rancho* (☎ 4-87-53) is a not-so-poor person's taco-and-beer hall, offering a long list of different types of tacos.

Among Nuevo Laredo's classy eateries are *The Winery* (☎ 2-08-95) at Matamoros 308, and *La Fittes* (☎ 2-22-08) at the corner of Matamoros and Victoria, which specialises in seafood.

Entertainment

Nuevo Laredo has horse and greyhound

racing at the *Hipódromo-Galgódromo* on the south side of town. Signposts point to it. Dates and times are irregular but at the last count the horses ran on Sunday afternoon, the dogs on Saturday at 6 pm and on Sunday at 1 pm. You can usually bet with US dollars.

Nuevo Laredo holds an agricultural, livestock, industrial and cultural fair during the second week of September.

Things to Buy

If you've got your travelling ahead of you, the less you buy the better. But if you're on the way home it may be worth browsing round some of the shops and markets for the odd souvenir. There's a craft 'market' on the east side of Guerrero half a block north of the main plaza, another one on the west side of Guerrero half a block south of Hidalgo, and a small mall on the west side of Guerrero between Hidalgo and Belden. Thee are also lots of individual shops all along this northern section of Guerrero.

Getting There & Away

Air Nuevo Laredo airport is off the Monterrey road, 14 km south of town. Mexicana has one or two direct flights to and from Mexico City every day except Tuesday, and one to Guadalajara on Tuesday, Thursday and Sunday, returning on Monday, Wednesday and Friday. The Mexicana office (☎ (871) 2-20-52, 2-22-11) is at Héroes de Nacataz 2335.

Bus Nuevo Laredo's bus station (Central Camionera) is about three km from the international bridge on the southern side of town. It has a left-luggage section and restaurant, and 1st and 2nd-class buses to every city in the northern half of Mexico. The companies servicing the bus station here are Transportes Frontera (TF), Tres Estrellas de Oro (TE de O), Transportes del Norte (T del N), Tamaulipas-Zuazua (T-Z), Autobuses Blanco (AB) and Transportes del Noreste (T del NE).

Aguascalientes – 787 km, 11 hours; US$17.50 with TF, T del N

Ciudad Victoria – 512 km, 7-1/5 hours; US$12 with TF, AB

Durango – 775 km, 12 hours; US$18 with TF

Guadalajara – 976 km, 15 hours; US$24 with TF, TE de O, T del N, AB

Matehuala – 518 km; US$14 with T del N

Mexico City – 1113 km, 16 hours; US$27.50 with TF, TE de O

Monterrey – 230 km, three hours; US$6.50 with TF, TE de O, T del N, T-Z, AB

Querétaro – 921 km, 14 hours; US$22.50 with TF, de O, T del N

Reynosa – 251 km, four hours; US$6 with T del NE

Saltillo – 315 km, 4½ hours; US$8.50 with TF, TE de O, T del N, AB

San Luis Potosí – 719 km, 11½ hours; US$18.50 1st class, US$18 2nd class with TF, TE de O, T del N

Tampico – 755 km, 12 hours; US$17 with TF

Zacatecas – 658 km, nine hours; US$14 with TF, T del N

Train Nuevo Laredo railway station is on Avenida César López de Lara, at the western end of Gutiérrez, 10 blocks from Guerrero. The timetable seems to change every year but, especially if there are sleeping carriages, the trains from here can make a comfortable if slower alternative to a long bus haul south.

There are two daily departures for Mexico City by way of Monterrey, Saltillo and San Luis Potosí. Train 72 (*El Regiomontano*), with sleeping accommodation and dining car, leaves Nuevo Laredo at 3.15 pm. Train 2 (*Aguila Azteca*), with nothing other than 1st-class reserved seats, departs at 6.55 pm. *El Regiomontano* is quicker – about four hours to Monterrey, six to Saltillo, 12 to San Luis Potosí and 18¼ to Mexico City. The *Aguila Azteca* takes 24 hours to Mexico City and also stops at San Miguel de Allende and Querétaro.

For trains from Mexico City to Nuevo Laredo, see Getting There & Away in the Mexico City chapter.

Special 1st-class (primera especial) seats on *El Regiomontano* from Nuevo Laredo cost US$27 to Mexico City and US$6 to Monterrey. Roomettes to Mexico City are around US$52 single, US$87 double; a double bedroom is US$104. Breakfast is included with all accommodation.

Regular 1st and 2nd-class seats on the *Aguila Azteca* are significantly cheaper.

To/From Laredo, Texas Transportes del Norte and Transportes Frontera run buses between Laredo, Texas and cities inside Mexico – including Mexico City, Guadalajara and Mazatlán – but these are dearer than their services from Nuevo Laredo. You can use these buses to go between Laredo and Nuevo Laredo bus station, then use a town bus to get into Nuevo Laredo – though it's cheaper and often quicker just to walk over the international bridge. Transportes del Norte (1st class) has 10 buses a day between Laredo Greyhound station and Nuevo Laredo bus station (fare US$3.50).

Getting Around

Frequent city buses (US$0.20) make getting around Nuevo Laredo easy enough. From the international bridge or downtown to the bus station, take Bus No 48 from the town centre terminal on Matamoros, two blocks south and one west of the bridge. You can also pick it up on the main square at the corner of Galeana and Dr Mier, or Galeana and González. From the bus station, the same Bus No 48 brings you into town to near the international bridge: catch it across the road as you walk out of the bus station's main entrance.

To get to the railway station from downtown, catch a blue-and-white 'Arteaga González' bus from the town centre terminal.

SOUTH FROM NUEVO LAREDO

It's mostly cacti and eagles all the way along Highway 85 to Monterrey, with occasional cattle. The town of Sabinas Hidalgo, half way there, has a few motels and restaurants. Forty km west of Sabinas Hidalgo are the Bustamante Caves, a series of chambers three km long. The caves are being developed for visitors.

You can go past Monterrey and push on to Saltillo, 98 km beyond, by the excellent Highway 40. This Saltillo route is now the main one from Nuevo Laredo to Mexico City (1223 km away). It's possible to cover the 773 km from Nuevo Laredo to San Luis Potosí in one very long day's driving.

From Nuevo Laredo to the Gulf coast,

going via Monterrey is most direct if you're heading for Ciudad Victoria, Tampico and points south. If your destination is north of Ciudad Victoria, Highways 2 and 97 via Reynosa are shorter.

Green Angels patrol Highway 85 from Nuevo Laredo to Monterrey, Ciudad Victoria and Ciudad Valles, and Highway 40 from Monterrey to Saltillo.

Nuevo Léon

It was the search for silver (not found) and slaves, and the desire of missionaries to spread their word, which first brought the Spanish to this sparsely inhabited region. In 1579 Luis de Carvajal was commissioned to found Nuevo León. He set up abortive settlements in Monterrey and Monclova but also fought with the Spanish governors of the Pánuco region. Eventually arrested as a lapsed Jew, he died in prison in Mexico City.

Slowly, ranching became viable around the small new towns, despite raids by hostile Chichimecs which continued into the 18th century. Nuevo León had an estimated 1.5 million sheep by 1710. Huge empty areas could be taken over by a few people, laying the foundations of the enormous landholdings and the power of the land owners who came to dominate the area. As the 19th century progressed and the railways arrived, ranching continued to expand, and industry developed, especially in Monterrey. By 1900 Nuevo León had 328,000 inhabitants.

MONTERREY

Population: 2.18 million
Altitude: 540 metres
Monterrey, capital of Nuevo León, and Saltillo, capital of Coahuila, are less than 100 km apart but a world away from each other in atmosphere. Monterrey is Mexico's third biggest city and second biggest industrial centre – new, hectic, noisy, polluted but exciting – a unique place that makes an impression on everyone who visits it. It is also a good base for some worthwhile side

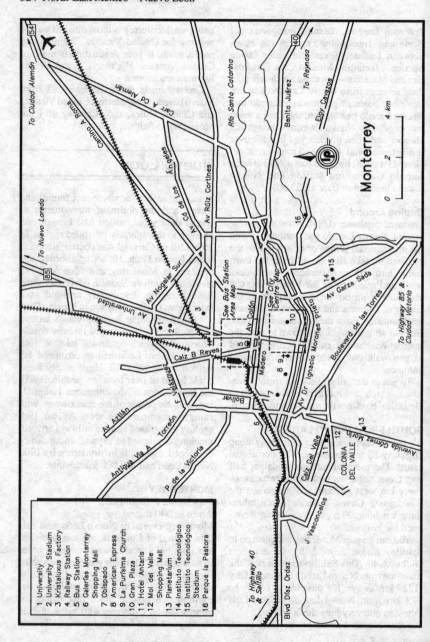

Monterrey

To Ciudad Alemán
To Nuevo Laredo
To Ciudad Alemán
Carr A Cd Alemán
Camino A Roma
Río Santa Catarina
To Reynosa
Benito Juárez
Eloy Cavazos

Av Cd de Los Ángeles
Av Nogalar Sur
Av Universidad
Av Ráiz Cortines
Av Colón
Av Garza Sada
Av Gómez Morín
Boulevard de las Torres
To Highway 85 & Ciudad Victoria

See Bus Station Area Map
See City Centre Map

Calz B Reyes
E Velázquez
Av Aztlán
Torreón
La Purísima Church
Madero
Bolívar
Av Dr Ignacio Morones Prieto
Avenida Gómez Morín

P de la Victoria
Antigua Vía A Victoria

Calz Del Valle
COLONIA DEL VALLE

J Vasconcelos

To Highway 40 & Saltillo
Blvd Díaz Ordaz

1 University
2 University Stadium
3 Kristaluxus Factory
4 Railway Station
5 Bus Station
6 Galerías Monterrey
   Shopping Mall
7 Obispado
8 American Express
9 La Purísima Church
10 Gran Plaza
11 Hotel Antaris
12 Mol del Valle
   Shopping Mall
13 Planetarium
14 Instituto Tecnológico
15 Instituto Tecnológico
   Stadium
16 Parque la Pastora

0   2   4 km

trips into the surrounding mountains and forests.

Everything else comes second to industry in Monterrey. Young, unfettered by the past, the city pursues profit with a single-mindedness unique in the country. Factories belch dirt and noise on the edges of the city; buses do the same just about everywhere. Only the downtown area and the extensive wealthy suburbs are screened from the immediate effects of Monterrey's sources of lucre. But it's also a grand city with one of the world's biggest plazas, a few relics of the early Spanish years and a partly pedestrianised downtown area of towering hotels, chic restaurants and shops – all surrounded by dramatic mountains.

Life is faster and everything is more efficient here than anywhere else in Mexico. Monterrey's people – known as *Regiomontanos* – have a reputation for tight-fistedness (though they seem to have enough time to point the way in a friendly fashion to enquiring visitors). Extremes of poverty and wealth rub shoulders: you can see a man stagger into a café and gobble up leftovers at empty tables; then, a few minutes later, see another man carry his poodle to keep its feet from getting dirty.

Monterrey is an assault on the senses – not a place to relax but a fascinating, extreme example of urban Mexico. Even its civic architecture is exciting: several entire blocks have been demolished to open up the enormous Macro Plaza and vistas of the dramatic mountains which circle the city, including the distinctive saddle-shaped Cerro de la Silla (1740 metres). In the plaza, towering over a delicate colonial cathedral, stands the Faro del Comercio, a tall, thin, orange concrete shaft, from which green laser beams sweep over the entire city at night.

Monterrey and the villages it has swallowed sprawl 30 km from east to west. The surrounding country offers caves, canyons, lakes and waterfalls, but most of the foreign visitors here are business people.

For budget travellers, Monterrey's disadvantage is that cheaper accommodation is mainly in a seedy area near the bus station, a 20-minute ride from the downtown. Also, some of the out-of-town sights are hard to reach by public transport.

History

There were three attempts to found a city here before it got off the ground. The first was in 1577; the second, by the ill-fated Luis de Carvajal, was in 1592; and the third, in 1596, by Diego de Montemayor who christened his 34-person settlement Ciudad Metropolitana de Nuestra Señora de Monterrey, after the Conde de Monterrey who was viceroy of Mexico at the time.

Monterrey struggled as a remote northern outpost, but it slowly became the centre of a sheep-ranching area, often at odds with the Chichimec Indians who lived in the area. Its importance grew with the colonisation of Tamaulipas in the mid-18th century, since it was on the trade route to the new settlements. In 1777, when Monterrey had about 4000 inhabitants, it became the seat of the new bishopric of Linares.

In 1824 it became capital of the state of Nuevo León in newly independent Mexico. In the Mexican-American War, Monterrey was occupied by Zachary Taylor's troops – but only after three days of fierce fighting by the Mexicans led by General Pedro de Ampudia. The city was occupied again in the 1860s by French troops, who were driven out by Benito Juárez's forces in 1866.

Monterrey's location close to the US gave it advantages in trade and smuggling: in the American Civil War it was a staging post for cotton exports by the blockaded Confederates. It began to emerge as an industrial centre in the 1860s and by the early 20th century was one of Mexico's biggest cities; its population grew from 27,000 in 1853 to about 80,000 in 1910. Railway lines ran to Monterrey in 1881, and tax exemptions for industry under state governor Bernardo Reyes during the Porfiriato had attracted Mexican, American, British and French investment.

The city was the site of the first heavy industry in Latin America – the iron and steel works of the Compañía Fundidora de Fierro y Acero de Monterrey. In 1890 José Schneider founded the Cervecería Cuauhtémoc, which became Mexico's biggest brewery, as well manufacturing glass, cartons, and bottle caps. Other industries – producing furniture, clothes, cigarettes, soap, cement and bricks – sprang up, and today they have been joined by innumerable others. Two intermarried families, the Garzas and the Sadas, came to dominate business and built a huge empire – the Monterrey Group – that owned many of the city's biggest companies.

Monterrey has grown steadily during the 20th century, and especially since the 1940s when the spread of electricity enabled hundreds of new industries to set up. Little planning went into the city's growth, and the environment and the poor were mainly left to look after themselves, but education was promoted by the Garza and Sada families, and today Monterrey has four universities and a famous Technological Institute.

Economic success and distance from the national power centre have given Monterrey an independent turn of mind. Relations between its leaders and those in Mexico City are marked by suspicion and sometimes even hostility. Monterrey resents 'meddling' in its affairs by the central government, which in turn sometimes accuses the city of being too capitalistic or, worse, too friendly with the USA.

Relations reached their lowest point under the left-leaning Mexican President Echeverría in the early 1970s. After the ageing head of the Monterrey Group, Eugenio Garza Sada, was murdered in 1973 (apparently by left-wing guerrillas), it was alleged that Echeverría had been trying to pressure the old man into turning his enormous steel company over to the government. The Garza Sadas, perhaps in fear of wholesale nationalisation, broke the Monterrey Group into two parts – the Alfa Group and the VISA Group.

President López Portillo, Echeverría's successor, fostered better relations with the powers of Monterrey. In 1978 the city was responsible for more than one-third of Mexico's exports, the production of its 14 biggest companies was worth US$4 billion. The economic crisis of the 1980s struck Monterrey hard. The Alfa Group went broke, the city government ran short of money, and a government-owned steel mill was closed.

Today there are great hopes that the free-trade agreement with the US and Canada will once again bring prosperity to the city. Time will tell.

Orientation

Downtown Monterrey focuses on the zona rosa, an extensive area of pedestrianised streets with the more expensive hotels, shops and restaurants. On the eastern edge of the zona rosa is the Plaza Zaragoza, with the cathedral on its east side and the Palacio Municipal (city hall) on its south side. South of this area is the nearly dry bed of the Río Santa Catarina, which cuts across the city from west to east. The bus station and most of the cheap accommodation are 2½ km north-west of downtown, the railway station 3½ north-west. Frequent, noisy buses run all over the city (see Getting Around).

Streets in the downtown and bus station areas are on a grid pattern. The corner of Juárez and Aramberri, roughly halfway between downtown and the bus station, is the centre of town as far as addresses are concerned. North of Aramberri, north-south streets have the suffix 'Norte' or 'Nte'; south of Aramberri, they have the suffix 'Sur'. West of Juárez, east-west streets have the suffix 'Poniente' or 'Pte'; east of Juárez, they have the suffix 'Oriente' or 'Ote'. Numbers get higher as they move further away from the intersection.

Information

Tourist Office Monterrey has a friendly, modern tourist office called Infotur (☎ (83) 45-08-70, 45-09-02), at the corner of Matamoros and Zaragoza underneath the Gran Plaza. Staff speak fluent English, are knowledgeable about both Monterrey and the state of Nuevo León, and have lots of leaflets to hand out, including good maps of Mexico and street directory maps of Monterrey. They can also tell you about cultural and entertain-

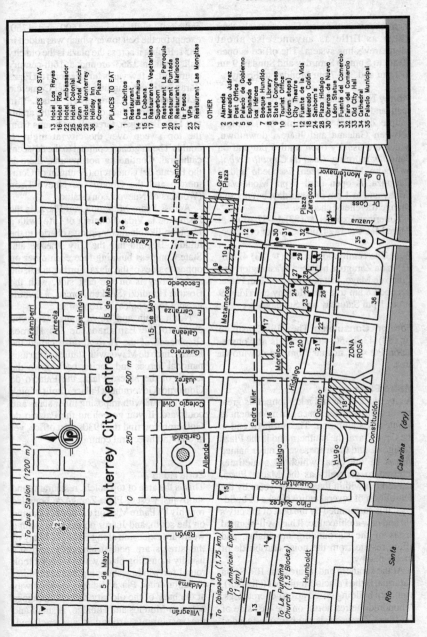

Monterrey City Centre

PLACES TO STAY

- 13 Hotel Los Reyes
- 16 Hotel Río
- 22 Hotel Ambassador
- 25 Hotel Colonial
- 26 Gran Hotel Ancira
- 29 Hotel Monterrey
- 36 Holiday Inn
- 36 Crowne Plaza

PLACES TO EAT

- 1 Los Cabritos
- Restaurant
- 14 Das Bierhaus
- 15 La Cabaña
- 17 Restaurante Vegetariano
- Superbom
- 19 Restaurant La Parroquia
- 20 Restaurant Puntada
- 21 Restaurant Mariscos
- la Pesca
- 23 VIPs
- 27 Restaurant Las Monglitas

OTHER

- 2 Alameda
- 3 Mercado Juárez
- 4 Post Office
- 5 Palacio de Gobierno
- 6 Esplanada de
- los Héroes
- 7 Bosque Hundido
- 8 State Library
- 9 State Congress
- 10 Tourist Office
- (down steps)
- 11 City Theatre
- 12 Fuente de la Vida
- 18 Mercado, Colón
- 24 Sanborns
- 28 Plan Hidalgo
- 30 Obreros de Nuevo
- León Statue
- 31 Fuente del Comercio
- 32 Faro del Comercio
- 33 Old City Hall
- 34 Cathedral
- 35 Palacio Municipal

ment events in the city. Unfortunately they know as little as anyone else about Monterrey's bus system. The office is open 10 am to 5 pm on Saturday and Sunday, 9 am to 1 pm and 3 to 7 pm Monday to Friday.

Money Numerous downtown banks change cash and travellers' cheques. There are a couple of casas de cambio on Ocampo, between Galeana and Juárez, downtown, which are usually open until 6 pm and on Saturday morning. *Casa de Cambio Trebol*, on Padre Mier between Escobedo and E Carranza, is open until 6 pm Monday to Friday and to 1 pm on Saturday, but doesn't change travellers' cheques.

American Express (☎ (83) 44-52-41) is at Padre Mier Pte 1424, on the corner of Bravo.

Post The central post office (☎ (83) 42-40-03) is on Zaragoza between Washington and Cinco de Mayo, just north of the Gran Plaza. It's open 8 am to 8 pm Monday to Friday, 9 am to 1 pm Saturday and Sunday.

Foreign Consulates The US Consulate (☎ (83) 43-06-50, 46-06-50) is at Constitución Pte 411, not far from the downtown area.

Macro Plaza

A city block wide and a km long, this great swath of urban open space is a monument to Monterrey's ambition. The northern end is the Gran Plaza, the southern end is the Plaza Zaragoza, and there are several other named plazas in the area, which is sometimes referred to generally as the Macro Plaza. Carved out within the past few years by the demolition of several entire blocks of buildings, it is surrounded by the best of the city's old and new architecture. It has well-planned vistas of the surrounding mountains, and offers respite from the noise and bustle of streets nearby.

At the southern end, nearest the Río Santa Catarina, is the Palacio Municipal (city hall), a modern building raised up on concrete legs. A hundred metres north, on the east side of the Plaza Zaragoza, is the baroque-façaded cathedral, built between 1600 and 1750, except for the bell tower which was added in 1851. Facing it across the plaza is the old city hall, built in 1853 around a 16th-century courtyard. A few yards further north on Plaza Zaragoza is the stunning Faro del Comercio (Lighthouse of Commerce), a tall, thin orange concrete shaft designed by the architect Luis Barragán. Green laser beams from the top sweep over the city at night. It couldn't be in greater contrast to the adjacent cathedral. Continuing northwards, there is the Fuente del Comercio (Fountain of Commerce) and the Obreros de Nuevo León (Workers of Nuevo León) statue.

Across Padre Mier, on Gran Plaza, is the Fuente de la Vida (Fountain of Life) with a Neptune-like character riding a chariot in the middle. Beyond this the City Theatre and State Congress building face each other on opposite sides of the plaza. Further north, the state library is on the east side, with the Bosque Hundido (Sunken Forest), a favourite spot for couples, in front of it.

North again and down some steps you come to the Esplanada de los Héroes (Esplanade of the Heroes), also called the Plaza Cinco de Mayo, with statues of various national heroes and, facing back down the length of the Macro Plaza, the Palacio de Gobierno (Government Palace), built of pink stone in 1908 with imposing inner stairs and courtyard. If you go behind the Palacio de Gobierno you find the 1930s post office, yet another architectural contrast.

Zona Rosa

This is the area of top hotels, restaurants and shops just west of Plaza Zaragoza, bounded roughly by Padre Mier on the north, Ocampo on the south, and Juárez on the west, with a westward extension along Hidalgo. Many of the streets are pedestrians-only and it's usually a bustling place worth taking a look round for window shopping and something to eat or drink. Plaza Hidalgo, tucked away at the back of the old city hall off Zaragoza between Morelos and Hidalgo, is small and the restaurants around it are enclosed, making it a far cry from the traditional Mexican town square.

The Obispado

The former bishop's palace stands on a hill, 2½ km west of the zona rosa, along Matamoros, and gives fine views over the city and surrounding mountains. Built in 1786-87, it served as a fort during the US attack on Monterrey in 1846, the French intervention of the 1860s, and confrontations between local Constitutionalists and the forces of Pancho Villa in the Revolution years. It was also a yellow-fever hospital before becoming what it is now – the Regional Museum of Nuevo León. You can trace the history of the state through exhibits and displays, which include remains of a mammoth found locally. All explanatory material is in Spanish. The Obispado is closed on Monday.

Cuauhtémoc Brewery & Museums

Brewery and more, this curious complex features an art gallery, a sports museum, a baseball hall of fame, brewery tours and ... free beer! It's in the gardens of the Cervecería Cuauhtémoc, the maker of Bohemia, Carta Blanca and Tecate beer, and is a km north of the bus station at Avenida Universidad 2202.

The art gallery (Museo de Monterrey, (☎ 72-48-94) has a not-very-interesting permanent collection but some excellent visiting exhibitions, which have included Picasso, Siqueiros, Miró, Giacometti and Moore. The baseball hall of fame (salon de la fama) has pictures, memorabilia and facts and figures on Mexican baseball. American fans can spot not only Mexican players who later made names for themselves in the USA but also Americans whose careers made more headway south of the border. The sports museum (Museo Deportivo de Monterrey) features boxing, bullfighting, rodeo and soccer.

Brewery tours are at 11 am, noon and 3 pm, Tuesday to Friday. You don't have to go on one to get the free beer, which is served outdoors to all who visit any of the exhibits, which are also free. The complex is open

from 9.30 am to 5.30 pm Tuesday to Friday, 10.30 am to 6.30 pm on Saturday and Sunday. There's also a café set among old brewing vats, where tasty sweet pastries are served.

Colonia del Valle & Chipinque

Colonia del Valle, six km south-west of the centre, used to be Monterrey's most exclusive suburb. It's still one of them, but the richest people have now moved a km or two south, up the slopes of the Mesa de Chipinque, which rise to 835 metres above the city. The whole area is called Garza García and gives a glimpse of the way Mexico's wealthy live – in big houses behind high walls, with satellite TV dishes sprouting like mushrooms.

Colonia del Valle contains the Mol del Valle shopping mall and other areas of classy shops in the streets off Calzada del Valle. The Planetarium (☎ 78-58-19), at Avenida Gómez Morin 1100, has a science and technology museum too, and is open from 3 to 7 pm, Tuesday to Sunday. Colonia del Valle also has lots of restaurants. There's an automobile museum at the corner of Vasconcelos and Río Suchiate.

Mesa de Chipinque, several km up the hill from Colonia del Valle, offers woodland walks, fine views back over the city and the luxury Hotel Chipinque, where there are horses for hire. Unfortunately you need a taxi or your own vehicle to get there, since buses don't run beyond Colonia del Valle (see 'Getting Around').

A good landmark in Colonia del Valle is the roundabout where six roads meet next to the Mol del Valle, which is serviced by buses. A sculpture containing a lot of pipes stands in the middle of the roundabout. Calzada del Valle runs west, past the north side of Mol del Valle, for three km from here; Avenida Gómez Morin runs south to the Planetarium (about 1½ km away) and on towards the Mesa de Chipinque.

La Purísima Church

About a km west of downtown by a pleasant little park at the corner of Hidalgo and Peña, this church is a fine example of modern architecture, designed by Enrique de la Mora and built in 1946. It is constructed round several parabola-shaped arches. The statues on the façade are of the 12 disciples.

Alameda

Occupying several blocks, a km north-west of downtown, this park is bounded by Pino Suárez, Aramberri, Villagrán and Washington. It has a zoo on the west (Villagrán) side, and sometimes Sunday morning concerts.

Parque La Pastora

There's a bigger zoo here, woodlands and canoe rides, but it's five km east of the centre, off Avenida Eloy Cavazos.

Instituto Tecnológico

The Technological Institute, in the south-east of the city on Avenida Garza Sada between Pernambuco and Avenida del Estado, is one of Mexico's best-regarded higher-education schools. It has fine facilities, including a stadium which hosted World Cup soccer games and a library with a huge collection of different editions of *Don Quixote*.

Art Galleries

Monterrey has several galleries, including the Museo de Monterrey. Another, the Casa de Cultura on the corner of Colón and Escobedo, is more interesting for the curious building that houses it (a gothic-style ex-railway station) than for the temporary shows inside, which are not usually of high quality. Among the commercial galleries, a good one concentrating on modern work is Arte Actual Mexicano at Río Bravo 210 in Colonia del Valle.

Lead Crystal Workshop

You can see artisans turning lead crystal into jugs, glasses, etc at the factory of Kristaluxus (☎ 51-98-69, 51-93-93) in the north of the city at J M Vigil 400, between Zuazua and E Carranza, Colonia del Norte. Tours are available at 10.30 am Monday to Friday (telephone first) and there's a showroom where you can buy the products.

Festivals

Independence Anniversary Monterrey's biggest celebrations are held on 15 and 16 September, with a big parade on the 16th.

Spring Fair There are many festivities during the spring fair, which begins on Palm Sunday (the Sunday before Easter).

Nuestra Señora de Guadalupe Held on 12 December, but attracting thousands of pilgrims and worshippers several days before, this festival is centred on the Santuario de Guadalupe, a big modern church south of the Río Santa Catarina, visible from the Gran Plaza. The festival is also celebrated in a big way in Abasolo, a village about 25 km from Monterrey off the Monclova road, where there are pilgrimages, a fair, a parade of floats and horseback-riders, and folk-dancing.

Organised Tours

A company called Osetur runs sightseeing and shopping tours to places in and out of the city in small coaches. Destinations covered depend on the day of the week but include the Gran Plaza, the Cuauhtémoc Brewery complex, the Planetarium, the Kristaluxus lead crystal factory, Galerías Monterrey shopping mall, craft shops, a rodeo, Mesa de Chipinque, Grutas de García and Horsetail Falls. A morning city tour which is basic and covers two or three destinations costs around US$8. Osetur (☎ (83) 43-66-16, 44-68-11) is based in Colonia Loma Larga south of the Río Santa Catarina, but tours leave from downtown at the corner of Escobedo and Ocampo. Telephone first or ask the tourist office where the tour goes on a particular day.

Places to Stay

Nearly all the cheaper hotels are within a few blocks of the bus station, where a room away from the street and the growling buses is a decisive plus. There's middle-range accommodation in this area and in the zona rosa, while the top-end places are nearly all in the zona rosa.

Places to Stay – bottom end

Some of the best value is on Calle Amado Nervo within two blocks of the enormous bus station. If you leave the bus station and stand facing the dual carriageway (Avenida Colón) immediately outside, Amado Nervo runs south from the far side of Colón.

The first place you come to, at Amado Nervo 1138, the *Hotel Posada* (☎ (83) 72-39-08) has clean rooms with fans, plenty of hot water in the shower, and even spyholes in the doors for the suspicious. Prices are US$17 for a single and US$18.50 for a double. Some rooms on the upper floors have views over the city. For an extra fee you can have TV in the room. In winter the rooms can be cold because there's no heating.

Half a block further down at Amado Nervo 1007, the *Hotel Nuevo León* (☎ (83) 74-19-00) is also clean and fairly modern, with plenty of hot water. The interior rooms are pretty quiet for this part of town but don't have very much light. Singles/doubles are US$15.50/22.

The *Hotel Amado Nervo* (☎ (83) 75-46-32), at Amado Nervo 1110 has smaller, dingier rooms for US$15.50/17, and the *Hotel Virreyes* (☎ (83) 74-66-10), at Amado Nervo 902, has larger but tattier rooms for US$15.50/19.

Three other cheap places in the bus station area are the *Hotel Roosevelt* (☎ (83) 75-76-02), Universidad 1295 at the corner of Gutiérrez, where rooms vary considerably and cost from US$14 single or double (many of them are grubby); the *Hotel América* (☎ (83) 75-17-86), at Cuauhtémoc Nte 1114 on the corner of Reforma, where uninspiring singles/doubles cost US$10.50/12; and *Hotel Reforma* (☎ (83) 75-70-68), at Avenida Universidad Nte 1132 (between Reforma and Colón), with basic singles/doubles also going for US$10.50/12.

If you arrive at the railway station late at night, the nearest hotel is the *Hotel Estación*, at Victoria 1450, the street running straight ahead as you walk out of the southern exit road of the station. It's very basic but probably tolerable for a night, with singles/doubles at US$14/21.

Places to Stay – middle

The middle range in Monterrey starts at around US$25 for a single. Be forewarned that there are very few great bargains in this range.

Bus Station Area The *Hotel Patricia* (☎ (83) 75-07-50) is at Madero Ote 123 between Juárez and Guerrero, and has clean, quite pleasant rooms with air-conditioning costing from US$28. The hotel has a parking lot.

The *Hotel 5a Avenida* (Quinta Avenida) (☎ (83) 75-65-65), at Madero Ote 234 between Guerrero and Galeana, has comfortable air-conditioned rooms with TV for US$32.50. It also has its own clean, modern restaurant.

Hotel Jandal (☎ (83) 72-46-06, 72-36-36), at Cuauhtémoc Nte 825 on the corner of Salazar, has comfortable, spotless, air-conditioned singles/doubles with TV for US$27/32; there's parking and a restaurant. Despite its name it doesn't appear to have any New Zealand connections (actually it's pronounced 'han-DAL').

Nearer the bus station the *Hotel Son Mar* (☎ (83) 75-44-00) at Universidad Nte 1211, close to the corner of Colón, has slightly bigger, equally comfortable, though grossly overpriced, rooms for US$40 single or double. The Son Mar has its own restaurant and parking.

The top place (for price) in this area is the big *Fastos Hotel* (☎ (83) 72-32-50, 74-14-68), over the road from the bus station at Colón Pte 956, on the corner of Villagrán. The hotel's 'económico' rooms may well be worth considering if there are three or four of you travelling together. They go for US46.50/50/53.50/57 for 1/2/3/4 people.

Downtown West of the zona rosa at Hidalgo Pte 543, the slightly ageing *Hotel Los Reyes* is the nearest thing to a downtown bargain, with big, clean, air-con singles and doubles for US$34.

The very central location of the *Hotel Colonial* (☎ (83) 43-67-91), at Hidalgo Ote 475, makes it a tempting splurge. Admittedly

Monterrey Bus Station Area

1 Cuauhtémoc Brewery & Museums	8 Market	15 Market
2 Railway Station	9 Fastos Hotel & Fastory Restaurant	16 Hotel Jandal
3 Hotel Estación	10 Hotel Posada	17 Hotel Patricia
4 Restaurant Posada	11 Hotel Nuevo León	18 Hotel & Restaurant Quinta Avenida
5 Bus Station	12 El Pastor Restaurant	19 Casa de Cultura
6 VIPs	13 Hotels Amado Nervo	20 Gran Hotel Yamallel
7 Hotel Son Mar	14 Hotel Vireyes	

it has air-con, but they have a gall charging US$32 for their pitiful little rooms. Also close to the centre is the modern, 120-room *Hotel Jolet* (☎ (83) 40-55-00 to 09), at Padre Mier Pte 201, where singles/doubles with air-con and TV cost US$46 per night at weekends and US$62 during the week.

Elsewhere Near neither the bus station nor downtown but somewhere between the two is the towering *Gran Hotel Yamallel* (☎ (83) 75-35-98), at Zaragoza Nte 912. Modern in style, it offers parking and TV but in fact it's slightly decrepit. The only real reason to stay here is the view over the city from the upper floors. Singles and doubles cost US$31.50.

Places to Stay – top end
In the downtown area, you have the pick of a clutch of places in the US$50 plus bracket. At all of them you can expect restaurants and bars, and carpeted rooms with air-conditioning, TV and phone. For atmosphere none

rivals the *Gran Hotel Ancira* (☎ (83) 43-20-60), at the corner of Escobedo and Plaza Hidalgo. It's been going since 1912, which gives it several decades over other Monterrey hotels. During its early years, it is said, Pancho Villa once rode into the lobby, which is now a sitting area with piano player and hovering waiters, a restaurant and shops. Big rooms and plenty of old-fashioned elegance go for US$69 at weekends and US$126 during the week.

The *Hotel Royalty* (☎ (83) 40-98-00), at Hidalgo Ote 402, has rooms for US$60 at weekends and US$74 during the week. The 200-room *Hotel Monterrey* (☎ (83) 43-51-20), fronting onto the Plaza Zaragoza at Morelos Ote 574, has an electric band in its lobby bar and is one of the more popular top-end places. It charges US$58 at weekends and US$106 during the week for singles or doubles.

The enormous *Hotel Río* (☎ (83) 44-90-40, 44-95-10) occupies a whole block between Morelos and Padre Mier; its address is Padre Mier Pte 194. It has a swimming pool and its 400 rooms cost from US$55 at weekends and US$90 during the week. The *Hotel Ambassador* (☎ (83) 42-20-40), at the corner of Hidalgo and E Carranza, has 241 rooms at US$71 at weekends and US$108 during the week. The *Holiday Inn Crowne Plaza* (☎ (83) 44-93-00), at Avenida Constitución Ote 300, is a huge 390-room place with blue-lit elevators gliding up and down above a cavernous restaurant/lounge where a rock band plays in the evenings. It is the most expensive place in town with rooms going for US$84 at weekends and a very international US$168 during the week.

Places to Eat

Monterrey abounds in *norteño* ('northern-style') ranch cooking, of which *cabrito al horno* (roast kid) is perhaps the best-known dish: whole young goats are split open, flattened on racks and roasted before charcoal or wood fires. It can be greasy and somewhat tough, but also quite flavourful, tasting a bit like lamb. It is not particularly cheap.

Downtown Every block of the zona rosa seems to have at least one restaurant or café. There's a wide range of prices and types of food, but real value-for-money is hard to come by at either end of the scale. The cheapest places of all are the comedors (basic cookshops) in the markets – benches and tables set up around a couple of gas rings where the cooks turn out local staples.

At Hidalgo 123 Ote, *Restaurant Puntada* has a long menu of Mexican items with nothing above US$2.50 and is always packed.

More expensive but with a pleasant atmosphere is *La Cabana*, on Matamoros between Pino Suárez and Cuauhtémoc. It's a kind of large but comfortable log cabin where you can just drink beer or eat seafood, meat, chicken enchiladas with mole sauce, or soup with the most expensive item on the menu costing US$7.

Vegetarians will find a haven at *Restaurante Vegetariano Superbom* (☎ 45-26-63),

upstairs at the corner of Padre Mier and Galeana. They do an excellent buffet for US$5. The Superbom is open from 8 am to 8 pm Monday to Thursday, 8 am to 4 pm on Friday, and 10 am to 6 pm on Sunday. Other vegetarian restaurants are on Escobedo, half a block north of Padre Mier, and at the corner of Ocampo and Cuauhtémoc.

A few blocks west of the zona rosa proper, *Das Bierhaus*, at the corner of Hidalgo Pte and Rayón, is a quite pleasant German-style beerhouse where you can down mugs while perching on stools at high tables, or sit in a bit more comfort and eat. Beer from the barrel costs US$1.30 (with free peanuts); food is in the US$2 to US$9 range.

Restaurants of the *VIPs* chain are worth considering, although if you're on a tight budget you have to choose carefully. There is one at the corner of Hidalgo and E Carranza. Sandwich plates cost about US$3.50, and shrimp US$5.50.

For good international fare in a bizarre setting try *Las Mongitas*, on Escobedo between Morelos and Plaza Hidalgo. You are served by waitresses dressed as nuns and accompanied by a live marimba duet as you sit in the cloisters and contemplate the wall paintings of smiling nuns preparing and serving food. Very generous main courses go for between US$2.50 and US$5. Breakfast can cost as little as US$2. The same menu, with serving sisters to boot, can be had at *La Parroquia*, nearby on the corner of Morelos and Galeana, but it is nowhere near as atmospheric as Las Mongitas.

Incidentally, if you fancy sampling the atmosphere of the *Gran Hotel Ancira*, you should know that a coffee at a table in the lobby costs US$1.50.

Bus Station Area Ordinary Mexican eateries in this part of town are pretty poor. There are, however, a few reasonably priced places around if you know where to look.

Although a little on the expensive side, *El Pastor*, at Madero Pte 1067 near the corner of Alvárez, is worth serious consideration. They serve nothing but cabrito, the roast kid speciality of this part of Mexico. El Pastor does a variety of different parts of the animal, usually charcoal-grilled (al pastor), at prices between US$5 and US$10. El Pastor is open from 11 am to 11 pm.

Fastory Restaurant, in the Fastos Hotel on Colón opposite the bus station, is a tidy modern place, open 24 hours, with Mexican and Western food. Spaghetti bolognese (no trimmings) costs US$3, enchiladas US$4, breakfasts up to US$5.50, steaks up to US$8. There's a *VIPs* on Pino Suárez, just north of Colón, with the same menu as the downtown VIPs. Two places with a similar style but smaller and slightly cheaper, are the *Restaurant York*, in Hotel Quinta Avenida, and the restaurant in the *Hotel Jandal*. Courses start at around US$3 in both of these restaurants.

Elsewhere Near the alameda, *Los Cabritos*, at the corner of Aramberri and Villagrán, is another place specialising in cabrito. It's slightly dearer than El Pastor. Also popular in this part of town, but not cheap, is the *Café Lisboa*, on Aramberri on the north side of the park.

If you find yourself in Colonia del Valle and don't want to hit one of the many expensive restaurants there, *Bambis Pizza* (☎ 78-64-27), on the west side of the Mol del Valle nearly opposite the Hotel Antaris, is quite good value from US$3.

Entertainment
Monterrey has numerous cinemas and an active cultural life including concerts, theatre and art exhibitions. The tourist office can tell you what's on, and posters are placed in strategic spots around town listing events. You might also come across some street theatre in the zona rosa.

There are bullfights and rodeos every Sunday. The bullfights are held in the afternoons at the big covered Plaza de Toros at Universidad 2401 in the north of the city. Rodeos (charreadas) take place in several different places, usually on Sunday mornings. Two better known venues are in Guadalupe, on the eastern edge of the city, and Cryco, 35 km south by Highway 85.

Monterrey also has professional football (soccer) and baseball teams.

A disco popular with the wealthier young is the Baccaratt (☎ 78-65-48), at Grijalva 50 in Colonia del Valle. Video bars are in fashion too; try Heaven (☎ 78-10-18) at Orinoco 108, Colonia del Valle.

Things to Buy
Monterrey has several markets, at least three plush shopping areas and some interesting craft shops. There are few distinctive local handicrafts but, as elsewhere in northern Mexico, plenty of leather goods around.

The two main downtown markets are the Mercado Colón, bounded by the streets Constitución, Garibaldi, Ocampo and Juárez, and the Mercado Juárez, bounded by Juárez, Aramberri, Guerrero and Arreola. Both are big, bustling places selling everything ordinary Mexicans need and containing numerous cookshops (comedors), the cheapest places to eat in town. Two markets near the bus station are between Universidad and Jiménez, a block north of Colón, and along Reforma east of Cuauhtémoc.

Interesting crafts shops with folk art items from different parts of Mexico – some of them surprisingly cheap – are Carápan, at Hidalgo Ote 305, and Tikal, at Río Guadalquivir 319 in Colonia del Valle. Casa de las Artesanías, near the Gran Plaza at the corner of Coss and Allende, has an interesting range of modern art objects influenced by folk tradition, as well as some clothes.

Getting There & Away
Air Aeroméxico (☎ (83) 40-87-60, 40-87-66 to 69; at the airport 44-77-30, 44-77-40) is at the corner of Padre Mier and Cuauhtémoc 818 Sur. Mexicana has offices at the corner of Zaragoza and Matamoros (☎ (83) 45-30-77), at Hidalgo Pte 922 (☎ (83) 44-11-22), Cuauhtémoc Nte 716 (☎ (83) 74-14-74, 74-14-77), on the corner of Hidalgo and Escobedo (☎ (83) 45-64-82, 45-64-22), and at the airport (☎ (83) 45-08-11, 45-08-71). Continental Airlines (☎ (83) 43-70-01, 44-70-25) is at Padre Mier Pte 188.

Aeroméxico has daily non-stop flights to Chihuahua (two), Guadalajara (three), Houston (one), and Mexico City (five), with connections from these cities to many other cities in Mexico and abroad. Mexicana has a similar roster of flights.

Aeromonterrey, a regional airline founded in 1991, flies F-27s between Monterrey and Harlingen and San Antonio in Texas, and to/from Tampico. It is also developing non-stop routes between Monterrey and south-eastern Mexico. You can make reservations on Aeromonterrey through Mexicana, or through a local travel agent.

Litoral, a small airline based in Ciudad del Carmen, Campeche (☎ (938) 2-43-64; fax 2-43-63) flies daily on the route Ciudad del Carmen-Villahermosa-Veracruz-Tampico-Monterrey and return. Inquire at the airport or at a travel agency for more information.

Bus Monterrey bus station (Central de Autobuses) occupies three blocks along Colón between Pino Suárez and Reyes. It's a small city in itself, with ticket desks strung out along its whole length. The first class lines servicing Monterrey are Omnibus de México (O de M) (☎ (83) 75-71-21), Transportes del Norte (T del N) (☎ (83) 75-42-80), Tres Estrellas de Oro (TE de O) (☎ (83) 74-24-10) and Anáhuac (A) (1st and 2nd class). Among the second class lines are Transportes del Noreste (T del NE), Estrella Blanca (EB), Transportes Tamaulipas (TT) (☎ 75-32-02), Transportes Monterrey-Cadereyta-Reynosa (TM-C-R), Transportes Frontera (TF), Linea Verde (LV) and Autobuses El Aguila (AEA). Following are some of the more important destinations from Monterrey.

Aguascalientes – 577 km, eight hours; US$12.75 with O de M, LV
Chihuahua – 818 km, 11½ hours; US$18.50 with O de M
Ciudad Acuña – 492 km, seven hours; US$11 1st class, US$10 2nd class with A
Ciudad Juárez – 1212 km, 17 hours; US$27.50 with O de M
Ciudad Valles – 512 km, 7½ hours; US$11.50 1st class, US$11 2nd class with T del N, TT

Ciudad Victoria – 282 km, 4½ hours; US$6.75 1st class, US$6.25 2nd class with T del N, TT
Durango – 615 km, 10 hours; US$14 with O de M
Guadalajara – 766 km, 10½ hours; US$17 with O de M, A, LV
Laredo, Texas – 225 km, 3½ hours; US$7 with T del N
Matamoros – 323 km, six hours; US$7.50 with O de M, T del N, TE de O, TM-C-R
Matehuala – 203 km, five hours; US$8 1st class, US$7.25 2nd class with T del N, A, T del NE, TT, TF, TF
Mexico City – 788 km, 12 hours; US$22 1st class, US$20 2nd class with T del N, TE de O, A, EB
McAllen, Texas – 235 km, five hours; US$6.50 with TM-C-R
Nuevo Laredo – 220 km, three hours; US$6.50 1st class, US$6 2nd class with T del N, TE de O, TF
Querétaro – 596 km, 10 hours; US$16.50 with A
Reynosa – 225 km, four hours; US$5.50 with O de M, T del N, TE de O, T del NE, TM-C-R, AEA
Saltillo – 85 km, 1½ hours; US$2.25 with T del N, TF
San Luis Potosí – 394 km, six hours; US$11.75 1st class, US$11 2nd class with T del N, TE de O, A, T del NE, EB, TT, TF
Tampico – 525 km, eight hours; US$14.50 1st class, US$13 2nd class with O de M, T del N, TT, TF
Torreón – 362 km, 5½ hours; US$8.50 with O de M
Zacatecas – 448 km, 6½ hours; US$10 with O de M, A, LV

Train Monterrey railway station (☎ (83) 75-46-53) is about half a km west of the bus station along Colón, then three blocks north on Nieto.

There are two trains daily to Mexico City. *El Regiomontano*, Train 72, also known as the Pullman, has special 1st-class (primera especial) sleeping accommodation and a dining car. It leaves Monterrey at 7 pm, reaching Saltillo at 10 pm, San Luis Potosí at 3.45 am and Mexico City at 10 am.

The *Aguila Azteca*, Train 2, has only 1st and 2nd-class seats. It departs Monterrey at 12.01 am, reaches Saltillo at 3 am, San Luis Potosí at 10.35 am, San Miguel de Allende at 1.09 pm, Querétaro at 2.47 pm and Mexico City at 7 pm.

A special 1st-class ticket to Mexico City costs US$21; sleeping accommodation costs US$41 for one person, twice that for two people. Regular 1st-class fare is US$7.75, 2nd-class fare is US$5.

Heading north, train 71 (*El Regio-*

montano) and Train 1 (*Aguila Azteca*) come from Mexico City and continue past Monterrey to Nuevo Laredo – four or five hours from Monterrey. The fare to Nuevo Laredo is US$6 primera especial (special 1st-class, on *El Regiomontano*), US$2.50 1st-class and US$1.50 2nd class (on the *Aguila Azteca*). For departures from Mexico City, see that chapter.

Trains 181 and 182 run between Saltillo and Piedras Negras, taking 7½ hours and connecting with *El Regiomontano* (Trains 71 and 72) at Monterrey.

El Tamaulipeco, Trains 141 and 142, runs between Monterrey, Reynosa and Matamoros, taking 3½ hours (Monterrey-Reynosa) and 1½ hours (Reynosa-Matamoros), and connecting – if you're lucky – with *El Regiomontano* at Monterrey.

There are also daily slow trains between Monterrey and Tampico (11 hours) via Ciudad Victoria, and between Monterrey and Torreón.

The fare from Monterrey to Reynosa is US$2.25 in 1st class, US$1.25 2nd class; to Matamoros is US$2 in 1st class, US$1.25 in 2nd class.

Car For routes to/from the US border, see under Nuevo Laredo, Reynosa and Matamoros in the Tamaulipas section, earlier in this chapter.

If you're going to the north-west Mexico, Mazatlán, Zacatecas or Guadalajara, head for Saltillo initially – go west along Colón or Constitución until you reach the Saltillo road, Highway 40.

The best route south, to San Luis Potosí (546 km from Monterrey), Querétaro and Mexico City (960 km), is also via Saltillo. The alternative route south, Highway 85, which passes through Montemorelos, Linares, Ciudad Victoria, Ciudad Mante and Ciudad Valles is not only further to Mexico City (984 km), it's also an inferior road, especially in some of the stretches south of Ciudad Valles. Highway 40 to Saltillo and Highway 57 from Saltillo to Mexico City are patrolled by Green Angels all the way, but there are stretches on Highway 85 south of Ciudad Valles which aren't.

If you're heading to Tampico and points south along the Gulf coast, Highway 85 is the one to follow as far as Ciudad Mante, where you turn east on Highway 80.

For rental, Avis (☎ (83) 40-22-20) is at Ocampo 370 and at the airport (☎ (83) 44-47-23). Hertz (☎ (83) 44-70-83) is at Garibaldi 814.

Getting Around

To/From the Airport Monterrey airport is off the road to Ciudad Alemán (Highway 54) north-east of the city, about 15 km from the city centre. There is no shuttle service to the airport. A taxi costs about US$15 to US$20.

Bus Buses (US$0.20) are noisier when you're outside them than inside, and they go frequently to just about everywhere in Monterrey, but often by roundabout routes. Unfortunately there's no centralised source of info on which ones go where. People on the street often know how to get from where you are to where you want to go; if they don't, ask a bus driver.

A few useful numbers follow. Don't worry if they appear to be going in the opposite direction to the one you want; their routes are sometimes extremely convoluted.

Bus Station to Centre – Buses 17 and 18, from the corner of Amado Nervo and Reforma, go to the edge of the zona rosa, then do a dogleg around it. For Gran Plaza, the best place to get off is the corner of Juárez and 15 de Mayo. For the zona rosa, get off at the corner of Juárez and 15 de Mayo, or on Pino Suárez at the corners of Padre Mier, Hidalgo or Ocampo.
Centre to Bus Station – No 39 (orange) can be picked up on Juárez at the corners of Ocampo, Hidalgo, Morelos or Padre Mier. It takes you to Colón. No 17, going north from the corner of Cuauhtémoc and Padre Mier, also goes to Colón.
Bus Station to Obispado, La Purísima & Downtown – No 1 from the corner of Amado Nervo and Reforma goes within a few blocks of the Obispado, passes La Purísima church, then goes along Ocampo to Zaragoza.

Centre to Obispado – No 4 from the corner of Padre Mier and Garibaldi goes west along Padre Mier. For the Obispado, get off when it turns left at Degollado, walk straight up the hill, turn left at the top of the steps, then take the first right (a 10-minute walk).

Centre or Bus Station to Cuauhtémoc Brewery – No 1 'San Nicolás-Tecnológico' goes up Juárez from downtown and passes the corner of Cuauhtémoc and Colón (near the bus station) on its way up Universidad to the brewery. No 17 'Universidad' goes north up Cuauhtémoc from Padre Mier to Colón, then on up Universidad to the brewery.

Cuauhtémoc Brewery to Bus Station & Centre – Nos 17 and 18 go south along Universidad, then right along Colón and left down Amado Nervo before heading downtown.

Centre to Colonia del Valle/Garza García – Bus 'San Pedro' from the corner of Ocampo and Pino Suárez goes to the big roundabout in Colonia del Valle (where Gómez Morin, Vasconcelos and Calzada del Valle meet), then heads west along Vasconcelos.

Centre to Instituto Tecnológico – Take No 1 from the corner of Padre Mier and Pino Suárez.

Metro The first line of Monterrey's Metro opened in mid-1991. It is not yet of much interest to tourists as it only runs east to west in the north of the city, primarily going to outlying residential areas. However, there are stops near the bus station and the Casa de Cultura and a second line running north to south is expected to open in 1994. This line will include at least one stop near the Gran Plaza. Fares range from US$0.20 to US$1.50 depending on how far you travel.

AROUND MONTERREY

Don't go looking for the cable car up Cerro de la Silla – it was closed after an accident a few years ago.

Grutas de García

An illuminated, 2½-km route leads through 16 chambers in this cave system high in the Sierra del Fraile, approached by a 700-metre cable-car ascent. The caves were formed about 50 million years ago and discovered by the parish priest in 1843. There are lots of stalactites and stalagmites, as well as petrified seashells. Each chamber has a different

name such as 'The Eagle's Nest', 'Chamber of Clouds' and 'The Eighth Wonder'.

This is a popular weekend outing among Monterrey people. Sunday is the only day you can get a bus there; it's operated by Transportes Monterrey-Saltillo and leaves Monterrey main bus station at 9, 10 and 11 am and at noon, returning in the afternoon (US$2.50 for the round trip). On other days the same line runs buses every half-hour to Villa de García, nine km from the caves, where you could try hiring a donkey if you're very keen. To get there by car from Monterrey, take Highway 40 towards Saltillo. After about 25 km a sign points the way to the caves, turn right and go another 18 km to the start of the cable car.

The caves and cable car are open from 9 am to 4.30 pm, Tuesday to Sunday. Entrance fee (including cable car) is US$2.25.

Cañón de la Huasteca

On the western edge of Monterrey, 16 km from the centre, this canyon ('wass-TEK-a') is 300 metres deep with some dramatic rock formations. There is a shanty town at one end of it and children's playground in the middle, which reduce its attraction as a wilderness area. Reach the mouth of the canyon by taking a 'Santa Catarina/Huasteca' bus (US$0.20) from the corner of Padre Mier and Juárez, or Cuauhtémoc and Madero, in downtown Monterrey. The same bus brings you back to the city centre. The town of Santa Catarina, at the north end of the canyon, celebrates the festival of the Virgen de San Juan de Los Lagos with dances and fireworks from 10 to 15 August.

Cascadas Cola de Caballo

Horsetail Falls, a 25-metre waterfall, is six km up a rough road from El Cercado, a village 35 km south of downtown Monterrey by Highway 85. The waterfall is on private land and open from 8 am to 6 pm, Tuesday to Sunday. Like many Mexican 'beauty spots', it has its share of hawkers and food stalls. Horses and donkeys can be hired from a car park about one km before the falls. Autobuses Monterrey-Villa de Santiago-El

Cercado go to El Cercado from Monterrey bus station. The village of Santiago, close to El Cercado, is the scene of some of the region's biggest celebrations of the apple harvest – the Fiesta de la Manzana – in the second half of August.

On the way to El Cercado you pass close to the **Rodrigo Gómez Dam**, known as La Boca – an artificial lake where Regiomontanos go swimming, sailing and water-skiing.

If you have your own vehicle, you can drive 33 km up a rough road from El Cercado to the **Laguna de Sánchez**, a mountain lake surrounded by pine forests.

MONTERREY TO CIUDAD VICTORIA

The 287 km of this road pass through Mexico's most important citrus-growing area, centred on the towns of Allende, Montemorelos, Hualahuises and Linares. The Sierra Madre rises to the west. There are hotels in Montemorelos and Linares. Montemorelos is the centre for celebrations of the orange harvest (Fiesta de la Naranja) in November.

Sierra Madre

From Linares a scenic road (Highway 58) heads west up into the Sierra Madre to the towns of Iturbide (44 km from Linares) and, with an eight-km northward detour, Galeana (72 km from Linares), climbing 1000 metres from the valley. Highway 58 continues west down on to the altiplano central, where it meets Highway 57 between Saltillo and Matehuala, 98 km from Linares.

Iturbide This area has several caves, canyons and waterfalls. There's a hotel in town where you can hire horses to reach some of them. Nine km before Iturbide, a giant bas-relief, **Los Altares**, dedicated to road builders, stands beside the road.

Galeana High on a wheat-producing plateau, Galeana is a centre for hand-loomed wool shawls and blankets. The town celebrates the festival of San Pablo with fireworks and processions from 20 to 25 January. Seven km north is a 15-metre-high

natural bridge called the **Puente de Dios**, over which a local road passes. The 3635-metre peak of Cerro Potosí, one of the highest in the Sierra Madre Oriental, is 35 km west of Galeana.

Coahuila

The state of Coahuila is sparsely populated and has little to offer the traveller except for a couple of not-very-convenient border crossings, and the city of Saltillo, which is definitely worth a visit.

As with Nuevo León, the Spanish came to Coahuila in search of silver, slaves and souls, but stayed to establish sheep and cattle ranches which became viable despite raids by Chichimec Indians which continued into the 18th century. Huge empty areas were taken over by a few people, and these big land owners came to dominate the area. One south-east Coahuila holding of 89,000 hectares in 1731 (bought from the crown for 250 pesos) grew to 5.87 million hectares by 1771, becoming the Marquesado de Aguaya which was protected by a private cavalry.

In the early years of Mexican independence after 1821, Coahuila and Texas were one state of the new republic, but Texas was lost in 1848 after the Mexican-American war. As the 19th century progressed, ranching grew in importance, helped by the arrival of railways. By 1900 Coahuila had 297,000 inhabitants.

PIEDRAS NEGRAS & CIUDAD ACUÑA

There are border crossings at Piedras Negras, from the US town of Eagle Pass, and Ciudad Acuña, from the US town of Del Rio. These crossings are less frequently used than those further south-east in Tamaulipas – the road connections into Mexico and the USA are not as convenient for most travellers.

Heading south from Piedras Negras & Ciudad Acuña, it's a seven or eight-hour bus ride through the state of Coahuila to Saltillo or Monterrey. Highway 57 south from Piedras Negras to Saltillo (445 km) is a good road, fairly straight and level, with only isolated towns and villages. Along the way, 25 km south of Monclova, Highway 53 branches south-east to Monterrey (there are no fuel stations on Highway 53).

The Saltillo route is the main one from Piedras Negras to Mexico City, 1340 km away. It's patrolled by Green Angels all the way. The main route to the Gulf coast is via Monterrey.

An unrecommendable alternative to the bus is the train (2nd class only) which leaves Piedras Negras at 9 am, arriving in Saltillo at 7.10 pm (it doesn't go to Monterrey).

SALTILLO

Population: 300,000
Altitude: 1599 metres

Set high in the arid Sierra Madre, Saltillo was founded in 1577 and is the oldest city in the north-east. It's on the main road and rail routes between the north-east border and central and western Mexico, and it is a pleasant place to break a journey. Like Monterrey, it has excellent transport links with the rest of Mexico.

Its quiet central area has a small-town feel and some lovely colonial buildings that make it a pleasant place to stop – if you're coming south from the US, it's here that you'll find both the first gem of colonial architecture and the first reasonably priced colonial-style hotel. Saltillo is a city with the confidence, even stateliness, of old capitals, as well as new shops and housing that give it a prosperous air.

The pace of life is much slower than in Monterrey – the people of Saltillo even seem to speak at a more comprehensible speed! A few mariachi bands hang around the downtown area at night, blowing on their trumpets and hoping for customers. Saltillo has industries too, but it's a much smaller city than Monterrey. It lies 1000 metres higher, and has some fine views over the mountains.

History

During Saltillo's first two centuries, Indians from Tlaxcala were brought to help the Spanish stabilise the area, and they set up a colony beside the Spanish one at Saltillo. The Tlaxcalans' skill on the treadle-loom and the abundance of wool in the area led to the development of a unique type of sarape, for which Saltillo became famous in the 18th and 19th centuries.

Work on Saltillo's cathedral started in 1746, and the city's growth was helped by the colonisation of Tamaulipas over the following decade, since it was on the trade route to that area. Saltillo was made capital of the province of Coahuila later that century, but by 1800 it still had less than 7000 people.

Capital of the state of Coahuila & Texas after Mexican independence in 1821, it was occupied by US troops under Zachary Taylor in 1846 during the Mexican-American War, which was sparked off by the dispute over Texas. At Buenavista, 10 km south of Saltillo, the 20,000-strong army of General Santa Anna was repulsed by Taylor's men in 1847, the decisive battle for control of the north-east during that war.

President Benito Juárez came to Saltillo during his flight from the invading French forces in 1864 and the city was occupied again by foreign troops before being freed in 1866. During the Porfiriato (1876-1910), agriculture and ranching prospered in the area, and the coming of the railway helped trade and the first industries in the city, but Monterrey was by this time fast overtaking Saltillo in size and importance.

Nevertheless the two cities, although only 85 km apart, are separated by the Sierra Madre and are in distinct regions. Today Saltillo in no way lives in the shadow of its more famous neighbour. It has its own industries – flour and textiles among them, as well as big Chrysler and Pemex plants – and is a commercial and communications centre for a large livestock and agricultural area. Saltillo is still the capital of Coahuila, but it has been outgrown by the modern city of Torreón in the south-west of the state.

Orientation

Downtown Saltillo is on a slightly higgledy-piggledy grid format, with two plazas as the main landmarks. The Plaza de Armas, with the cathedral on its east side and fine colonial buildings around the other sides, is the more monumental of the two. Hidalgo, an important street, runs across the east side of the plaza, in front of the cathedral. The dividing point for Saltillo's street addresses is the junction of Hidalgo and Juárez at the south-west corner of the cathedral. With your back to the main façade of the cathedral, up the hill on Hidalgo (to the left) is south (Sur), downhill to the right is north (Nte), behind you is east (Ote), in front of you is west (Pte).

If you leave the west side of the Plaza de Armas and walk one block further, you come out on another main thoroughfare, Allende. A right turn here (northward) and a few blocks down the hill brings you to the Plaza Acuña, with the market building on its north side. Most places to stay and eat, and almost all the city's activity, are within five minutes' walk of these two plazas. The busiest street is Aldama, running across the south side of Plaza Acuña. Victoria, parallel to and south of Aldama, has a number of up-market shops.

The bus station is out on the south-west side of town – a good 15-minute bus ride away. The railway station is a 20-minute walk from the centre; from Plaza Acuña, walk up the hill on Allende three blocks, turn right on Victoria, go down Victoria and straight across the alameda (park) at the bottom. One more block straight on brings you to a crossroads where you turn left on E Carranza (named not after revolutionary hero Venustiano Carranza, but Emilio Carranza, who made the first non-stop flight from Mexico City to New York). After three long blocks you see the station on your right.

Information

Money You can change cash and travellers' cheques at the banks or at the casa de cambio on the north side of the Plaza de Armas, open till 6 pm, Monday to Friday.

Post The post office, open Monday to Saturday plus Sunday morning, is at Victoria Pte 223, a few doors down from the Hotel Urdinola.

Plaza de Armas

In contrast to the bustling Plaza Acuña, the Plaza de Armas is spotlessly clean and rela-

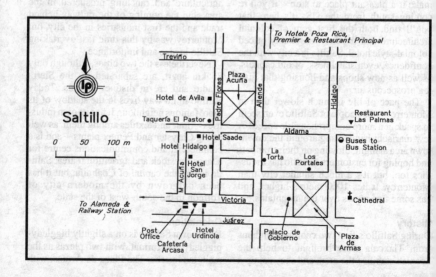

tively tranquil, with street vendors seemingly banished.

Cathedral Built between 1746 and 1801, the cathedral of Santiago dominates the plaza and has one of Mexico's finest Churrigueresque facades, its columns of elaborately carved pale grey stone in pristine condition. It's particularly splendid when lit up at night. Inside, the transepts (side-arms of the cross-shaped ground plan) are full of gilt ornamentation – and no, the human figure perched on a ledge at the top of the dome, seemingly about to fall, isn't real! You can go up the smaller of the two towers if you ask the man in the religious goods shop underneath. At the top of the stairway you come out among the bells, with good views over the city and surrounding mountains.

Palacio de Gobierno On the opposite side of the plaza to the cathedral is the state government headquarters. You are free to wander into the elegant building, which has a fountain in its inner courtyard.

Los Portales This is the covered section behind the arches on the north side of the plaza. It harbours a few café-restaurants and a video-games parlour.

Museo Cavie This art gallery is in a courtyard on the south side of the plaza. They put on temporary exhibitions of work by promising local artists.

The Alameda
The park, full of shady trees and pathways like other alamedas in Mexico, has a children's playground and is a favourite spot for young couples. A pond at the southern end is alleged to be shaped like Mexico, but the resemblance is far from obvious.

Plaza México
Also known as the Fortín de Carlota (Carlota's Fortress), this spot in the south of the city offers the best views over Saltillo and the surrounding country. It's a 10-minute bus ride from downtown (see 'Getting Around').

Festivals
Día del Santo Cristo de la Capilla On 6 August, the Day of the Holy Christ of the Chapel brings dance groups from different parts of Coahuila to Saltillo to honour a holy image. The best-known group is the Matachines.

Feria Anual The city holds its annual fair in mid-August.

Feria de San Nicolás Tolentino Ramos Arizpe, about 10 km north of Saltillo on the Monterrey road, has dances by the Matachines from before dawn on 10 September and a parade at about 5 pm.

Places to Stay – bottom end
Of the cheaper downtown possibilities, *Hotel Metropoli* (☎ (841) 4-81-44), at Allende Nte 436, is reasonable value at US$12/13.50 for a single/double. *Hotel Hidalgo* (☎ (841) 4-98-53), at Padre Flores 217, is basic but fair value for money with singles/doubles going for only US$7.50/9.

Hotel De Avila (☎ (841) 2-59-16), at Padre Flores 211 in the north-west corner of Plaza Acuña, is pretty seedy and the staff does not do much to make you feel welcome. Singles/doubles cost US$11/14.

There are two hotels over the road from the bus station. The *Hotel Central* is much the better of the two, with singles/doubles for US$10/11. The poky *Hotel Siesta* charges US$9/10.50.

Places to Stay – middle
Best value of any hotel in Saltillo is the *Hotel Urdinola* (☎ (841) 4-09-40), at Victoria Pte 207. From Plaza Acuña, walk south up the hill on Allende three blocks and turn right on Victoria. The hotel is about 200 metres along on the left. There's a glamorous lobby with a couple of model knights-in-armour standing at the bottom of a wide white stairway that sweeps upward to a stained-glass window. Rooms at the back are around a long courtyard with a fountain. For big, clean

rooms with TV you pay US$20 for one person, US$25 for two. The hotel also has a pleasant, if not cheap, dining room and very friendly and helpful staff. The only minor drawback is that they sometimes ask for a deposit of more than a night's lodging when you check in (any balance refundable).

The *Hotel Premier* (☎ (841) 2-10-50), at Allende Nte 566, is comfortable enough but without the atmosphere of the Urdinola. Singles/doubles are US$20/22.

Places to Stay – top end

The top downtown establishment is the *Hotel San Jorge* (☎ (841) 2-22-22) at M Acuña Nte 240. From Plaza Acuña, go west down Aldama one block, then turn left onto M Acuña. This hotel has recently been upgraded; it has a restaurant and swimming pool, and clean, quite big rooms with TV go for US$35 single, US$20.75 double.

Motel Huizache (☎ (841) 6-10-00), 1½ km north of the city centre at Boulevard V Carranza 1746 where Highway 40 to Torreón meets Highway 57 going north to Monclova, has doubles at US$30.

Places to Eat

Saltillo is short on inviting restaurants but has several good snack places and fast-food joints.

Among the restaurants, *Cafetería Arcasa*, on Victoria next door to Hotel Urdinola, does reasonable Mexican and Western food. A comida corrida costs around US$4.50. The restaurant has a selection of local and national newspapers to help you pass the time.

Restaurant Principal (☎ 4-33-84), at Allende Nte 710 four blocks down the hill from Plaza Acuña, specialises in cabrito (roast kid). If neither of these places grabs you, try the more expensive restaurants in the hotels Urdinola or San Jorge.

Pastelería y Cafetería Daisy Queen (☎ 3-33-49), at Allende Nte 515A, does cakes as well as yoghurt with fruit (US$0.75 small size, US$1.50 large – but beware un-defrosted strawberries). Its tacos are small and overpriced.

Much better for tacos is *Taquería El Pastor*, on Plaza Acuña at the corner of Aldama and Padre Flores. Delicious *tacos al pastor* (beefsteak) are US$0.40 each, *tacos de lengua* (tongue) are US$0.60 each. There's another place with the same name, menu and prices two blocks down Aldama from the plaza.

For truly delicious sandwiches try *La Torta*, on Allende around 75 metres to the south of Aldama. The Torta Cubana is excellent.

At the bottom (west) end of Victoria near the alameda are a couple of places selling mostly yoghurt. *Hugos La Juerta – La Casa del Yoghurt*, half a block up Victoria from the alameda, does a bewildering variety of forms and flavours of yoghurt and a huge range of things to mix with it. You can try yoghurt licuados, 'nieve' (mixed with ice cream) or cocktails.

Restaurant Las Palmas, at Aldama Nte 198 B, is open 24 hours a day. Breakfast costs US$2.50. A comida corrida goes for US$4.50.

Things to Buy

Saltillo used to be so famous for its sarapes that a certain type was known as a 'Saltillo' even if it was made elsewhere in Mexico. The technique involves leaving out colour fixatives in the dyeing process so that the different bands of colour *se lloran* (merge, or literally weep) into each other. The finest ones would have silk or gold and silver threads woven into them. Nowadays the local workshops have sadly stopped making all-wool sarapes and seem to be obsessed with jarring combinations of bright colours. But you can still get ponchos and blankets in more 'natural' colours, some of which are pure wool.

Shops where you can see these and other handicrafts include El Saltillero (☎ 4-11-36) at the corner of Victoria and M Acuña, and the Sarape Factory on Hidalgo a couple of blocks up the hill from cathedral. In the latter you can watch people at work on treadle looms.

Getting There & Away

Air

Aeroméxico (☎ (841) 4-10-11, 4-10-66; at the airport (841) 8-04-39, 8-06-99) is at Allende Nte 815.

Bus Saltillo's modern bus station is way out on a bypass on the south-west edge of town, but it's clearly a matter of some pride to the city since you can buy postcards of it. It has no left-luggage section. First-class lines have their ticket desks to the right-hand end of the booking hall as you enter, 2nd class to the left.

Lots of buses serve Saltillo but few start their journeys here. This means that on 2nd-class buses in particular, you often can't buy a ticket until the bus has arrived and the ticket clerk knows how much room there is for new passengers. It also means that, on 2nd-class buses, you may have to stand for a while. Whatever, it pays to buy your ticket early and board the bus first – if you can.

The 1st-class lines which service Saltillo are Transportes del Norte (T del N), Omnibus de México (O de M) and Tres Estrellas de Oro (TE de O). Anáhuac (A), Transportes Monterrey-Saltillo (TM-S) and Transportes Coahuila-Zacatecas (TC-Z) all have 1st and 2nd-class buses, while Transportes Frontera (TF), Blancos (B) and Linea Verde (LV) have 2nd-class buses only.

Aguascalientes – 492 km, 6½ hours; US$10 1st class, US$9.50 2nd class, with O de M, A, T del N

Chihuahua – 713 km, 12 hours; US$14.50 with T del N

Ciudad Juárez – 1107 km, 14 hours; US$22 1st class, US$20 2nd class, with T del N, O de M, TM-S, TC-Z

Ciudad Victoria – 355 km, five hours; US$8 with T del N

Durango – 530 km, seven hours; US$11 1st class, US$10 2nd class, with T del N, O de M, A, TM-S, TC-Z

Guadalajara – 681 km, nine hours; US$14.50 1st class, US$13 2nd class, with T del N, O de M, A, TF, B, LV

Matamoros – 408 km, seven hours; US$8 with T del N, O de M

Matehuala – 203 km, four hours; US$5.50 with A, TF, B, LV

Mazatlán – 848 km, 10½ hours; US$17 1st class, US$16 2nd class, with T del N, TM-S, TC-Z

Mexico City – 788 km, 11 hours; US$17.50 1st class, US$15.75 2nd class, with T del N, O de M, A, TF, B, LV

Monterrey – 85 km, 1½ hours; US$2.25 with T del N, TM-S, TC-Z

Nuevo Laredo – 315 km, 4½ hours; US$7.50 with T del N

Querétaro – 596 km, eight hours; US$13 1st class, US$11.75 2nd class, with T del N, TE de O, A, TF, B, LV

Reynosa – 310 km, four hours; US$6.50 with T del N, O de M

San Luis Potosí – 394 km, five hours; US$9 1st class, US$8.25 2nd class, with T del N, TE de O, A, TF, B, LV

Tampico – 598 km, 10 hours; US$13.50 with T del N

Tepic – 808 km, 11 hours; US$18 with O de M

Torreón – 277 km, 3½ hours; US$6 with T del N, O de M, A, TM-S, TC-Z

Zacatecas – 363 km, five hours; US$7.75 1st class, US$7 2nd class, with T del N, O de M, A, TM-S, TC-Z, TF, B, LV

Train Saltillo railway station (☎ (841) 3-55-84) is just off E Carranza, south-west of the city centre. 'El Regiomontano' (Trains 71 and 72) is the best train; it has sleeping accommodation and a dining car and leaves at 10 pm for San Luis Potosí (5¾ hours away) and Mexico City (12 hours); and at 5.44 am for Monterrey (2½ hours) and Nuevo Laredo (6½ hours).

The 'Aguila Azteca' (Trains 1 and 2), with 1st-class reserved, regular 1st-class and 2nd-class seats, leaves Saltillo at 12.20 am for Monterrey (two hours) and Nuevo Laredo (seven hours); and at 3 am for San Luis Potosí (seven hours), San Miguel Allende (10 hours), Querétaro (11½ hours) and Mexico City (16½ hours).

There are also trains to Monterrey at 3.35 pm, San Luis Potosí at 12.40 pm and Piedras Negras at 7 am and 8.05 am.

The station is open for advance ticket sales from 11.30 am to 4 pm. Fares to Mexico City are US$19 (special 1st class), US$36 (sleeping accommodation for one person), US$7.25 (regular 1st class) and US$4.50 (2nd class).

Car Saltillo is the junction of five good major

roads. Highway 40 heads north-east to Monterrey and west to Torreón (277 km), on the way to Mazatlán, Chihuahua and the north-west border. Highway 57 goes north to Monclova and Piedras Negras and south to Mexico City (852 km). To the south-west, Highway 54 crosses high, dry plains towards Zacatecas (363 km) and Guadalajara (680 km). Outside Saltillo it climbs to over 2000 metres, then descends gradually along the altiplano central to Matehuala (260 km) and San Luis Potosí (451 km) through barren but often spectacular country.

Getting Around

Most of Saltillo's activity is within a few minutes' walk of the two central squares, the Plaza de Armas and the Plaza Acuña.

To reach the city centre from the bus station, walk out of the entrance of the bus station and you will see minibuses waiting to your right, past the end of the bus station. No 9 takes you downtown (US$0.20). Convenient points at which to get off are the cathedral (easily recognised as you pass it on the right coming down Hidalgo) or the main downtown bus stop at the corner of Allende and Treviño (from where you walk one block uphill on Allende to reach Plaza Acuña). Returning to the bus station from downtown,

pick up No 9 at the corner of Aldama and Hidalgo.

To reach downtown from the railway station, walk 200 metres straight ahead out of the station, cross a single-track railway line, and go left down the road (E Carranza) for three blocks until you meet Madero, where you turn right. Walk straight across the alameda park which you reach after one block on Madero, then straight on up Victoria, which meets Allende at the top. Three blocks to the left brings you to Plaza Acuña; one to the left then one to the right brings you to Plaza de Armas.

To reach Plaza México take bus 'Zapoliname' (US$0.20) from Aldama and Hidalgo.

AROUND SALTILLO
Parras

A small town 150 km west of Saltillo off the Torreón road in a wine and brandy-producing area, Parras has a week-long grape fair, the Feria de la Uva, in early August. It includes religious celebrations on Assumption Day and traditional dances by descendants of early Tlaxcalan settlers. Parras has some colonial buildings, a house where Francisco Madero lived and several hotels.

North-Central Mexico

This chapter covers the states of Chihuahua, Durango and Zacatecas. The central route from El Paso/Ciudad Juárez to Mexico City is considerably less attractive than Mexico's Pacific coastal highways and takes substantially longer than the road from the Gulf Coast. Nonetheless, if you decide to come this way, the central route has some interesting sights to offer.

South from Ciudad Juárez, the towns along the central route are good places to get away from other tourists. You are certain to sharpen your Spanish, as relatively few locals speak English.

For scenic splendour, the train ride through the Copper Canyon is among the world's more spectacular rail trips. Cutting through majestic mountain scenery, the train runs between Chihuahua and the Pacific coastal port of Los Mochis.

Further south Zacatecas, one of the Silver Cities, will awe you with its fine colonial architecture. It is an inspiring legacy of Mexico's turbulent yet vibrant history.

CIUDAD JUÁREZ

Population: 1,100,000
Altitude: 1145 metres

Although Ciudad Juárez is not as dull as El Paso, its allure for certain visitors lies in its cheap dental work and other dubious services. It's one of those frontier towns where inhabitants do what they can to survive while grafting onto their culture the worst aspects of gringoland across the border. It's not a pretty picture.

Nor is the climate all that hospitable. Ciudad Juárez is insufferably hot in summer; in winter wind may swirl off the desert, sweeping stinging sand in its wake.

Don't let this put you off. Just to the south, the atmosphere is far friendlier, the scenery more *simpático* and the climate relatively mild. You can choose between staying in Ciudad Juárez or El Paso for one night; see the Places to Stay section below.

Orientation

El Paso's Stanton St and El Paso St bridges

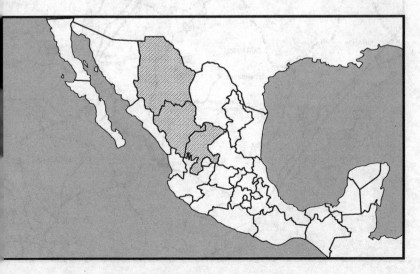

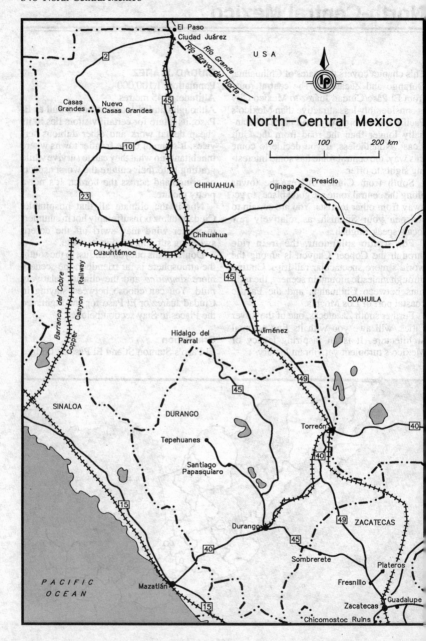

North-Central Mexico

0   100   200 km

continue as Lerdo and Juárez on the Mexican side of the border. Juárez is the most important street in Ciudad Juárez, lined with shops, restaurants and hotels. Follow it if you are heading for the bus station or the centre of town.

Information

Tourist Office You will find the government tourist office near the immigration checkpoint on Malecón between Juárez and Lerdo. Look for it in the basement of the high-rise government building. The staff are particularly friendly and there is usually someone there who speaks English. Unfortunately the city maps which they stock are atrocious; however, they do have a fairly comprehensive list of hotels and restaurants. The office is open Monday to Friday from 9 am to 2 pm, and 4 to 7 pm.

Money There are banks on Avenida 16 de Septiembre and near the bus station, but they are only open Monday to Friday, 9 am to 1 pm. If you arrive in Ciudad Juárez in the afternoon, you shouldn't have trouble finding somewhere to change cash (no travellers' cheques) among all the souvenir shops along Juárez.

Post The post office is at the intersection of Lerdo and Ignacio Peña. Hours are 8.30 am to 7.30 pm Monday to Saturday.

Foreign Consulates If you don't intend to venture more than 32 km south of Juárez, you won't need a tourist card. Travellers may move freely between El Paso and Juárez (although to return to the USA you must be able to show proof of US citizenship or, if you're not a US citizen, a visa).

For those moving deeper into Mexico, a stop at the immigration office, at the foot of the Stanton St bridge on the Mexican side, is required to secure your tourist card.

If you are having tourist card/visa problems and are a US citizen, call (16) 13-40-48. For other emergencies, call this number in El Paso: (915) 525-6060.

Museo Chamizal

Known to many locals by its old name, Museo Arqueológico, the Museo Chamizal is in Parque Chamizal and, given Juárez's impossible-to-decipher bus system, best reached by taxi. Admission is US$0.25. Although there are some ancient statues and pottery on display, the museum has more copies than originals. Hours are 9 am to 6.30 pm daily.

Old Presidencia

The Old Presidencia on 16 de Septiembre is one of the last vestiges of colonial architecture in Ciudad Juárez. It contains an interesting historical museum.

Places to Stay – bottom end

Ciudad Juárez Most of the real cheapies in Juárez prefer to rent their rooms by the hour, and cannot really be recommended. The one notable exception is *Casa de Huéspedes El Refúgio*, on Mina near Corregidora, with singles/doubles for US$6/7. The rooms are pretty simple and do not have bathrooms, but the pleasant courtyard adds a touch of character to the place.

Hotel Viajero, on Mina near the corner of Noche Triste directly in front of Mercado Hidalgo, is uninspiring, but with singles/doubles from US$8/9 you shouldn't expect much better. *Hotel Maya*, on the corner of Ahumada and La Paz, with singles/doubles for US$8/16 is pretty scummy, but the rates may be negotiable. None of these places have telephones.

El Paso The *Gardner Hotel* (☎ (915) 532-3661), 311 East Franklin St near the intersection of Stanton St, is the top budget choice for those who do not want to stay overnight in Juárez. The Gardner's dorms, with shared bath, have earned the hotel the status of an American Youth Hostel. A bed in a dorm costs US$9.95 for IYHF/AYH members and US$12.50 for nonmembers. There is a brand new kitchen with excellent facilities, but it is available only to IYHF/AYH members.

Places to Stay – middle

Far and away your best choice for moderately priced comfort and safety in Juárez is the *Hotel Impala* (☎ (16) 2-04-18), a two-minute walk from immigration and the Stanton St Bridge in the first block of Lerdo at No 828. All 38 rooms have air-conditioning, hot water and TV. Singles/doubles both cost US$26.50.

The *Hotel Parador* (☎ (16) 15-91-24) at Ahumada 615 has rooms with TV, VCR and microwave oven (!) for US$20, but note that the place has absolutely no Mexican feeling to it at all. *Hotel Imperial* (☎ (16) 15-03-23) at Guerrera 206 (near the corner of Juárez) is a slightly less plush version of the Parador with singles/doubles for US$20/21.

Places to Stay – top end

Those seeking luxury accommodation in Juárez should consider the *Plaza Juárez* (☎ (16) 13-13-10), on Lincoln at Coyoacán near the Pronaf Center. Air-conditioned rooms with colour TVs cost US$58 a single, US$63 a double. Another recommended place is *Hotel Calinda* (☎ (16) 6-34-21) a Avenida Hermanos Escobar 3515 with singles/doubles for US$57.

Places to Eat

Ciudad Juárez Exercise discretion if you are just entering Mexico. It's best to build up some immunity to new bacilli for a few day before you become too adventurous with local fare.

There are cheap *taquerías* everywhere in Juárez. A favourite among locals is *Res taurant El Norteño* on Juárez just north of 1 de Setiembre (opposite Hotel Koper). Tacos cost US$0.50 and a quarter chicken with chips costs around US$2. For those willing to spend more money, there are high-gloss eateries on Avenida Juárez Norte like *Martino Restaurant* at 412, *Villa Española*

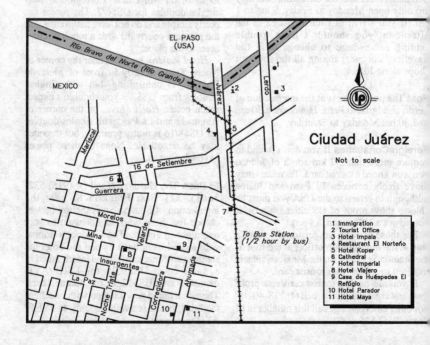

Ciudad Juárez

Not to scale

1 Immigration
2 Tourist Office
3 Hotel Impala
4 Restaurant El Norteño
5 Hotel Koper
6 Cathedral
7 Hotel Imperial
8 Hotel Viajero
9 Casa de Huéspedes El Refúgio
10 Hotel Parador
11 Hotel Maya

nearby where Juárez intersects Colón, *Florida Steak House* at 301 and *Jet Set* at 668. If you are shopping at the Pronaf Center and willing to spend the bucks, *Casa Del Sol* offers Mexican and Continental cuisine accompanied by strolling mariachis.

El Paso In El Paso you can't do better than the luxury *Hotel Westin* on the corner of El Paso and Texas Sts. They have a buffet from 4pm to 8 pm where food is free so long as you buy drinks. Beers cost US$1, and nobody seems to mind if you sit on one beer all evening. There are a couple of places with excellent breakfast deals on Mills between Stanton and Kansas.

Things to Buy

The primary shopping emporium in Juárez, the Pronaf Center, is about three km from the Mexican border post. Reminiscent of a US shopping mall, Pronaf boasts some quality crafts amidst its sea of junk, but at prices significantly higher than elsewhere in Mexico. There are also numerous souvenir and craft shops along Juárez, but unless this is your last stop and you must bring back a knick-knack for Aunt Tilly or a bottle of mezcal for Uncle Bob, don't waste your time shopping in Ciudad Juárez.

Getting There & Away

Air There are connecting or direct flights to Ciudad Juárez via Chihuahua from most major cities in Mexico. El Paso is also an important hub and is easy to reach from most US cities.

Bus For information on getting to the bus station in Ciudad Juárez see the Getting Around section. This is one of the biggest bus stations you are likely to see in Mexico and it has the flow of buses to match. Regular destinations include Chihuahua, Tijuana (including border points along the way), Torreón, San Luis Potosí, Monterrey and Mexico City. Most other places to the south can be reached via Chihuahua.

Train Juárez's train station is an easy walk from the Mexican side of the Stanton St Bridge. Just keep walking straight on Lerdo some 11 blocks, but note that Lerdo's name changes to Corona. You will find the Ferrocarriles Nacionales station at the intersection of Corona and Insurgentes.

Train No 8, *El División del Norte*, departs Ciudad Juárez each evening bound for Mexico City via Chihuahua, Torreón, Zacatecas, Aguascalientes and Querétaro. For more information, see Getting There & Away in the Mexico City chapter.

Getting Around

To get to the Ciudad Juárez bus station (Central de Autobuses), walk down Juárez from the immigration office to Guerrera, then go left and walk to Corona. Buses marked 'Lomas' or 'Granjera' stop on the south-east corner and will drop you directly in front of the bus station. Allow a minumum of one hour from the border to the Central de Autobuses.

From the bus station to the centre any passing local bus marked 'Centro' will drop you close to the cathedral – just get off at the end of the line.

CASAS GRANDES & NUEVO CASAS GRANDES

Although Nuevo Casas Grandes, four hours south-west of Ciudad Juárez, is a more comfortable place to stay your first night in Mexico than Juárez, the city of Chihuahua is on a more direct route to Mexico City and may be a preferable first stop for those in a hurry. The only reason to visit Nuevo Casas Grandes is to see the ruins of Paquimé, adjacent to the small town of Casas Grandes. While Paquimé is the region's major archaeological site, it is hardly in the league of the spectacular sites to the south.

Information

Money Change money at the International, open from 9 am to 1.30 pm, at the intersection of Obregón and 5 de Mayo.

Post The post office is a block from 5 de Mayo at 16 de Septiembre and Madero.

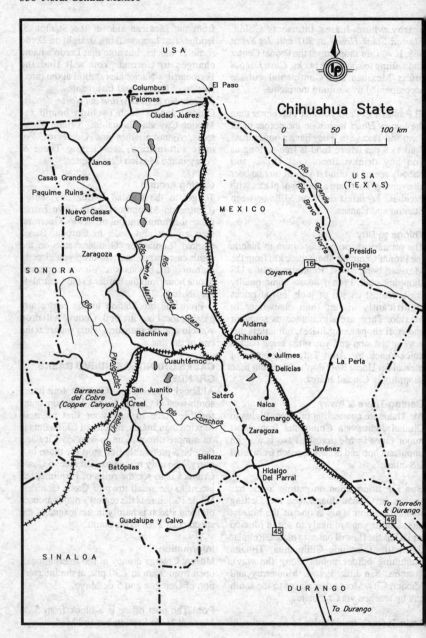

Paquimé Ruins

Buses run to the start of the Casas Grandes trail to the ruins. They leave from a stop on Constitución, a block from where it intersects 5 de Mayo. The buses run every half-hour, daily from 9 am to 5 pm. These buses may be distinguished by a 'Casas Grandes/Col Juárez' sign on their sides. The eight-km journey takes about 15 minutes.

You will be let off at old Casas Grandes' main plaza where a sign will direct you to the 10-minute walk to the ruins. This walk is unshaded, so bring a hat. While you are supposed to pay a small admission fee at the site, you may find that Paquimé's caretaker is either absent or asleep.

Set beneath the attractive backdrop of the Sierra Madre, Paquimé was the major Indian trading settlement in northern Mexico between 1000 and 1200 AD. Agriculture flourished here as well, and poultry (largely turkeys) was raised in adobe cages to protect the fowls from harsh climatic extremes.

Two major cultural influences shaped the architecture of Paquimé. The initial settlement had adobe structures similar to Pueblo structures of the US Southwest. As the city grew in prominence, it was influenced through trade with southern Indian civilisations, particularly the Toltecs. This contact introduced the inhabitants of Paquimé to Toltec architectural designs of religious, sporting and agricultural structures. You can still see this interesting legacy of religious step pyramids, a *pelota* (ball) court, and part of the network of canals that once made the area fertile.

Despite fortified walls and unique interior water systems, including hidden cisterns, Paquimé fell prey to outside invaders (some say Apaches) in 1340. The city was sacked, burned and abandoned, and its once-great structures were left alone for more than 600 years. Unfortunately, after the site was partially excavated in the early 1970s, exposure to the elements led to erosion of the structures; during your visit you may see work crews patching Paquimé with adobe.

Paquimé's inhabitants were great potters and jewellers. While some of their finest works are displayed in Mexico City's National Museum of Anthropology, you can see some of the exceptional animal-shaped Casas Grandes pottery, with striking red, brown or black geometric designs over a cream background, on exhibit at the Museo Arqueológico in Ciudad Juárez.

Places to Stay

All the following places are in Nuevo Casas Grandes.

Places to Stay – bottom end

Hotel Juárez (☎ (169) 4-02-33) has a convenient location at Obregón 110, a few doors from the bus depot, but that's its only favourable attribute. The place is fairly decrepit and overpriced. Singles cost US$13, doubles US$17. Showers may only occasionally be hot and there's no extra charge for the *cucarachas*.

Places to Stay – middle

In Nuevo Casas Grandes moderately priced hotels are your best bet, with the *Motel Piñon* (☎ (169) 4-06-55) at the top of the list. The motel is a 15-minute walk from the bus station at Avenida Juárez 605. It is by far the most comfortable of the town's middle-range lodging, offering well-maintained air-conditioned rooms with TVs and hot showers. Singles cost US$24, doubles US$29.

Second choice and five-minutes' walk closer to the bus station is *Hotel California* (☎ (169) 4-11-10), at Constitución 209. Here you will find air-conditioned singles with bath at US$25 and doubles at US$31.50.

Places to Stay – top end

The *Motel La Hacienda* (☎ (169) 4-10-48) features a swimming pool, tennis court and restaurant. Its air-conditioned rooms with TV cost US$58 a single, US$63 a double. La Hacienda is 1½ km north of town on Highway 10.

Places to Eat

Nuevo Casas Grandes has a number of good, reasonably priced restaurants. You'll find excellent meat dishes right next to Motel Piñon at *México Español*. The owners are from Argentina; their specialities are grilled meats. Good standard Mexican fare is available at the *Constantino*, across the street and two blocks towards 5 de Mayo from Motel Piñon.

If your tastes run slightly to the exotic, try the little Mormon-run *La Boquilla Restaurant* at 5 de Mayo 111b (look closely or you'll miss it – it's not far from Avenida Juárez). La Boquilla serves up shrimp and turtle (!) tacos. Those with more conventional palates will find *Dinno's Pizza* at the intersection of 5 de Mayo and Obregón convenient to the bus depots. For those watching their pesos more than their palates, there are a host of cheap taquerías on Obregón around the bus station.

Getting There & Away

Buses run regularly to and from Ciudad Juárez (about four hours, US$7) and Chihuahua (about 4½ hours, US$9.50). Omnibus de México is generally faster than Transportes Chihuahenses. Note that the direct road to Chihuahua often gets cut off during the rainy season, leaving Chihuahua accessible only via Ciudad Juárez.

CHIHUAHUA

Population: 800,000
Altitude: 1392 metres

Although Chihuahua is a comfortable, prosperous city, most travellers find little purpose in staying here other than to catch the Barranca del Cobre (Copper Canyon) train or to stay overnight during their journey to points south. Nonetheless, there are a few sights of interest that you can easily see within half a day. The modern marketplace is visited early in the morning by colourfully attired Mennonites and Tarahumara Indians. Most of the men of Chihuahua will remind you that this is true *caballero* country through their everyday dress of cowboy hats and boots.

History

Today the capital of Mexico's largest state, Chihuahua was originally settled by miners seeking silver. Although Franciscan and Jesuit missionaries Christianised the agrarian-oriented tribes in the area, brutal treatment by the Spaniards led to rebellions by even the most tranquil tribes. Not only did Spanish settlers have to deal with these uprisings, they also faced constant depredations by Apache raiders. When you take in the rugged nature of the area's desert and mountain terrain, it's easy to understand why the region stayed sparsely populated for some time.

The city of Chihuahua gradually grew in size to administer the territory and serve as a commercial centre for cattle and mining interests. It also played a major role in the War of Independence. Rebel leader Miguel Hidalgo fled here, only to be betrayed. Imprisoned by the Spaniards, he was executed here with his head displayed in Guanajuato as a warning to the rebels. Instead of turning the people from rebellion, Hidalgo's severed head became a symbol of martyrdom, a catalyst for subsequent independence.

President Benito Juárez made Chihuahua his headquarters for a while when forced to flee northward by the French troops of Emperor Maximilian. The city also served as a major garrison for cavalry guarding the vulnerable settlements from the incessant raids of the fierce Apaches. Ultimately, the legendary Mexican Indian fighter, Colonel Joaquín Terrazas, defeated the Apache chief Victoria and brought a short period of relative tranquillity to the region.

The era of peace was brief, as social inequities – particularly the huge cattle fiefdoms – created the conditions conducive to revolution. (One *latifundista* owned a ranch the size of Belgium.) Enter Pancho Villa, patriot to some, *bandido supremo* to others, who enlisted oppressed *campesinos* in revolt. The mansion that served as Villa's headquarters is the primary site of interest for tourists today in Chihuahua.

Currently, the cattle, timber and mining industries have made Chihuahua one of the most prosperous cities in Mexico. But the heritage of dissent remains and many citi-

Top: Girls at a small station, Copper Canyon railway, Chihuahua state (GA)
Bottom: Brown pelicans & seagulls on a harbour breakwater, Cabo San Lucas, Baja
California (RB)

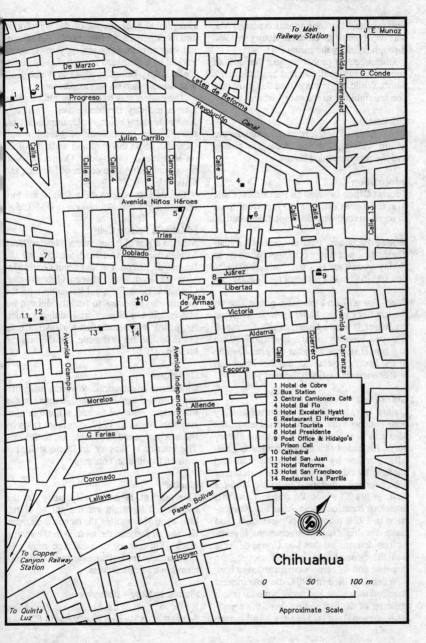

1 Hotel de Cobre
2 Bus Station
3 Central Camionera Café
4 Hotel Bal Flo
5 Hotel Excelaris Hyatt
6 Restaurant El Herradero
7 Hotel Tourista
8 Hotel Presidente
9 Post Office & Hidalgo's
   Prison Cell
10 Cathedral
11 Hotel San Juan
12 Hotel Reforma
13 Hotel San Francisco
14 Restaurant La Parrilla

Chihuahua

0   50   100 m

Approximate Scale

To Copper
Canyon Railway
Station

To Quinta
Luz

To Main
Railway Station

J E Munoz

G Conde

De Marzo
Progreso
Letes de Reforma
Revolución   Canal

Julian Carrillo

Calle 10
Calle 6
Calle 4
Calle 2
Camargo
Calle 3
Calle 9
Calle 13

Avenida Niños Héroes

Trias
Doblado

Juárez
Libertad

Plaza
de Armas

Victoria

Aldama

Escorza

Morelos

Allende

G Farias

Coronado

Lallave

Paseo Bolivar

Irigoyen

Avenida Ocampo
Avenida Independencia
Calle
Guerrero
Avenida V Carranza

Avenida Universidad

zens maintain that the opposition party, PAN, was deprived of an election victory in 1988 through fraud by the ruling PRI.

Chihuahua is probably most famous, of course, for the small dog that bears the city's name. While originating from this province, you are unlikely to see many around today.

Orientation
Most areas of interest in Chihuahua are within walking distance of the bus station and the recommended hotels.

Information
Tourist Office Located on Reforma at Calle 31a, the tourist office is too far out of town to serve anyone who does not have a car.

Money Banamex, next to the Hotel Presidente, is open for exchange Monday to Friday from 9 am to 1 pm. Numerous casas de cambio give decent rates for dollars.

Post You will find the main post office on the top floor of the Padre Hidalgo Museum on Juárez between Guerrero and Carranza. It's open Monday to Saturday from 9.30 am to 6 pm. If stamps are your only need, some of the luxury hotels, like the San Francisco at 409 Victoria, will sell them to you.

Quinta Luz
Quinta Luz, mansion of the revolutionary hero Pancho Villa, is also a museum of the Mexican Revolution and a must for history buffs. Regarded as a tactical genius in guerrilla warfare by some, a charlatan and bandido by others, Villa – once a victim of debt peonage – believed in living *la dulce vida*, as his 22 wives, 24 children and this luxurious mansion attest. After his assassination in 1923, many of his paramours filed claim for his estate. Government investigations determined that Luz Corral de Villa was the generalissimo's legal spouse; the mansion and its name were awarded to her.

When Luz died in 1981, the government acquired the estate and transformed it into a museum of the Revolution. Inside is a veritable arsenal of weaponry, and some exceptional photographs of the Revolution and its principals. Unfortunately, the accompanying explanations are only in Spanish. Parked in a courtyard is the bullet-spattered black luxury Dodge roadster in which Villa was riding when he was assassinated.

The easiest way to get to Quinta Luz is to take a red city bus designated 'Avaloz y Juárez' running south on Ocampo. Get off the bus on the corner of Mendez and Ocampo, cross the road and walk downhill on Mendez for two blocks. Quinta Luz will be on your left on the corner of Mendez and Calle 10a.

Quinta Luz is open daily from 9 am to 1 pm and 3 to 7 pm. Admission is US$0.35.

Hidalgo's Prison Cell
Mexico's War of Independence leader Padre Miguel Hidalgo was held prisoner by the Spaniards, just prior to his execution in 1811, in a jail on Juárez between Guerrero and Carranza. Look for a golden eagle with the inscription 'Libertad' to find the door to his prison cell. On display are Hidalgo's crucifix, pistol, letters and other personal effects, but note that this is the site, not the original building.

Cathedral
Chihuahua's cathedral, towering magnificently over the Plaza de Armas, has a marvellous baroque façade. Although construction began in 1717, continual raids by Indians postponed its completion until 1789. The interior is simpler, in Doric style, but with 16 Corinthian columns.

Market
The market is especially busy in the morning. You might catch sight of blond, blue-eyed Mennonites, the men in their overalls and straw hats, the women in their long, black 19th-century dresses. You may also spy Tarahumara Indian women in their picturesque traditional dress.

Places to Stay – bottom end
By far the best of the cheapies is *Hotel San Juan* (☎ (14) 10-26-83) at Victoria 823. An

older hotel with a courtyard, the San Juan is heated and offers singles with bath for US$8 and doubles for US$11.50. The proprietor, Señor José Talámes, speaks some English and is helpful. The San Juan is less than 15 minutes' walk from the bus station.

If you are absolutely exhausted after arriving by bus, the *Hotel del Cobre* (☎ (14) 15-17-58), across from the bus station on Calle 10a at Progreso, offers clean singles with air-conditioning, TV and bath for US$12.50 a single, US$15 a double.

Another place which is marginally acceptable is *Hotel Reforma* (☎ (14) 12-58-08) at Victoria 814. Here spartan rooms are US$9 a single and US$12.50 a double.

Places to Stay – middle
The *Hotel Bal Flo* (☎ (14) 16-03-00), at the intersection of Avenida Niños Héroes and Calle 5a No 702, offers pleasant air-conditioned rooms with bath, and charges US$20 for singles/doubles and US$24 for triples. The Bal Flo is owned by Balthazar Flores, who speaks English fluently and can tell you a good deal about Chihuahua. The hotel is a 15-minute walk or US$2 taxi ride from the bus station.

Places to Stay – top end
Chihuahua's deluxe hotel is the *Exelaris Hyatt Chihuahua* (☎ (14) 16-60-60) at Avenida Niños Héroes and Independencia. Other three-star hotels are *Hotel Presidente* (☎ (14) 16-00-48) on the zócalo at Libertad 9, and the *San Francisco* (☎ (14) 16-75-50) at Victoria 504. All three have rooms starting at around US$50.

Places to Eat
For good standard breakfasts and Mexican fare, try the cafeterias of the hotels *Bal Flo*, *San Juan* and *Del Cobre*. Surprisingly good, especially for breakfast, is the *Central Camionera* café. This is a real cafeteria where you stand in line – the service is good, the food cheap and filling with breakfast for around US$2 to US$3. Two other spots for decent breakfasts are the *Comedor Familiar* at Victoria 830, and *Mí Café* at Victoria 807.

Or try *Lonchería Jiménez* just outside the train station.

There are two excellent places for meat dishes. Near the Bal Flo is *El Herradero*, on Calle 5a between Trias and Avenida Niños Héroes. A short walk from Hotel San Juan is *La Parrilla*, at Victoria 420, known for its barbecued meats.

Vegetarians and those in the mood for pizza will find *Dinno's Pizza*, on Independencia across from the Hyatt, to their taste. *Restaurant la Diligéncia*, on the corner of Progreso and Diligéncia near the bus station, does a good comida corrida for around US$4 or a serving of tacos or enchiladas with a beer for US$3.

Entertainment
For bullfights, go on Sunday to the Plaza de Toros at the intersection of Canal and Cuauhtémoc. Some Saturdays and Sundays, you will find rodeos scheduled at the Lienza Charro in the western part of the town. In the evening, there are discos at the Hyatt, Presidente and Victoria hotels.

Things to Buy
For Tarahumara Indian crafts, ponchos, sweaters and silver jewellery, visit the Museo de Artes y Industrias Populares at Reforma 5 (closed Monday), and Arte Popular Mexicano at Aldama 710. For jewellery, try Artesanías y Gemas Naturales de México at Calle 10 No 3019.

Getting There & Away
Bus The main companies running from Chihuahua are Estrella Blanca (EB) (2nd class), Omnibus de México (O de M), Transportes del Norte (T del N) and Tres Estrellas de Oro (TE de O). In addition there are a number of smaller companies which do the regional rounds including hourly buses to Cuauhtémoc for US$3.

Acapulco – 1959 km, 27 hours; (US$43) with EB.
Aguascalientes – 961 km, 16½ hours; (US$22) with O de M.
Ciudad Juárez – 394 km, six hours; (US$9.50) with O de M, T del N, EB.

Creel – 240 km, five hours; (US$7.50) with EB.

Cuauhtémoc – 104 km, 1½ hours; (US$3) with O de M.

Durango – 709 km, 11 hours; (US$16) with O de M.

Guaymas – 841 km, 16 hours; (US$24.50) with TE de O.

Hermosillo – 605 km, 14 hours; (US$21.50) with TE de O.

Hidalgo del Parral – 301 km, 4½ hours; (US$5.50) with O de M, EB.

Mazatlán – 1027 km, 16 hours; (US$24) with EB.

Mexicali – 1308 km, 18½ hours; (US$29.50) with TE de O.

Mexico City – 1412 km, 20 hours; (US$33) with O de M, EB.

Monterrey – 818 km, 12½ hours; (US$19.50) with O de M, T del N.

Nogales – 811 km, 12 hours; (US$19) with TE de O.

Nuevo Casas Grandes – 371 km, six hours; (US$9) with four buses a day, EB.

Nuevo Laredo – 1048 km, 15½ hours; (US$21.50) with T del N.

Saltillo – 733 km, 11 hours; (US$17.50) with T del N.

San Luis Potosi – 1028 km, 16 hours; (US$23) with EB.

Tampico – 1470 km, 19 hours; (US$31) with O de M.

Tijuana – 1497 km, 20 hours; (US$33) with TE de O.

Torreón – 456 km, 7½ hours; (US$12) with T del N, EB.

Zacatecas – 832 km, 13½ hours; (US$20) with O de M, EB.

Train Chihuahua is an important stop on the line between Ciudad Juárez and Mexico City travelled by *El División del Norte* (Train No 7 and 8). Chihuahua is also the north-eastern terminus of the Chihuahua al Pacífico line, for *Barranca del Cobre* (Copper Canyon) trains. Different stations serve these two different lines.

The Ferrocarriles Nacionales de México station (for *El División del Norte* and other trains between Ciudad Juárez and Mexico City) is accessible via 'Granjas Colón' or 'Villa Colón' buses running from the centre. Since you can't see the station from the road, ask the driver to let you know when you have reached it. For train schedules, see Getting There & Away in the Mexico City chapter.

Copper Canyon Trains The Chihuahua al Pacífico station for Copper Canyon trains is off Avenida Ocampo, nearly two km southwest of the Plaza de Armas and a block from

the prison. To get to the station, take a 'Col Rosalía' or 'Sta Rosa' bus and get out at the prison – it looks like a medieval castle, you can't miss it. Walk behind the prison to the station.

Air-conditioned special 1st-class *vistatrens* haul dining cars and depart daily on the 13½-hour run down through the canyon to the Pacific coast town of Los Mochis. There is also a regular, far less comfortable *mixto* train which departs on Monday, Wednesday and Friday, taking about five hours longer.

From Chihuahua to Los Mochis, the schedule is as follows:

departures	vistatren	mixto
Chihuahua	7.00 am	7.20 am
Cuauhtémoc	9.13 am	10.41 am
La Junta	10.05 am	12.00 pm
Creel	12.16 pm	2.47 pm
Divisadero	1.58 pm	4.35 pm
San Rafael	2.30 pm	5.15 pm
Temoris	4.24 pm	7.32 pm
El Fuerte	7.08 pm	10.48 pm
Sufragio	7.51 pm	11.42 pm
Los Mochis	8.38 pm	12.49 am

For a description of the train journey and stops along the way, see the chapter on North-West Mexico under Barranca del Cobre – Copper Canyon, following the Los Mochis section.

Getting Around

All of the recommended sites and hotels are only a walk from the train and bus stations. There is good city bus service when you need it, and taxi fares are reasonable if you bargain. The most convenient way to get to the airport is to take a colectivo. You need to make your reservation 24 hours in advance by calling (14) 20-11-24. They will pick you up anywhere in town and drop you at the airport for US$6.

AROUND CHIHUAHUA
Cuauhtémoc Mennonite Colony

The Mennonites' major population centre is the town of Cuauhtémoc, 2½ hours by bus or 3½ hours by train west of Chihuahua. A guided tour is offered by Chihuahua's Viajes Cañon del Cobre agency (☎ (14) 12-88-93) in the Hotel Victoria. The cost is US$26 per person, with a four-person minimum. To do it more cheaply, take a bus there yourself.

Founded by the Dutchman Menno Simonis in the 16th century, the Mennonite sect takes no oaths of loyalty other than to God, and eschews military service. Persecuted for their beliefs, its members moved from Germany to Russia to Canada, and thousands settled in the tolerant, post-Revolutionary Mexico of the 1920s.

In Cuauhtémoc, you will see Mennonites in traditional dress, driving their horse-drawn buggies and speaking their own dialect of German. They lead a spartan existence, speak little Spanish, and marry only among themselves. Their substantial population increase in Mexico has led many to emigrate to Paraguay and Brazil. The Mexicans praise the Mennonites' hard work and cheese and meat products (especially sausage), but find the austere life style and work ethic hard to fathom.

HIDALGO DEL PARRAL

For those en route to Durango, Hidalgo del Parral is a town rich in revolutionary history. Believing that the infamous revolutionary Pancho Villa would sooner or later pass by a house on Calle Gabino Barreda in his 1919 Dodge, nine conspirators staked it out for 103 days. On 20 July 1923 Villa approached the house with his six bodyguards, and the assassins opened fire. While five of his bodyguards lay mortally wounded, Villa, bleeding profusely from 17 bullet wounds, crawled alongside his black automobile. With his last gasp, he took aim and shot one of his assassins.

Seven conspirators escaped into the desert. Their leader, Jesús Salas Barraza, calmly gave himself up to Parral's authorities, saying he had planned the assassination because he cared about Mexico's future and believed Villa was only out for his own gain with dictatorship in mind. Apparently the revolutionary government concurred, for although Salas was sentenced to 20 years, he was released from jail a few months after the trial.

The campesinos of the state of Chihuahua, many of whom Villa had led into battle, saw the generalissimo as a great advocate of the people. A few caballeros can recall that 30,000 mourners attended Villa's funeral in Parral, where Villa remains a folk hero. A few years ago Villa's body was moved to Mexico City, an action which has unfortunately hurt Parral's tourist industry quite badly. Don't let that keep you away as Parral is a very pleasant place to break up a long journey.

Parral was best known for centuries as a mining centre where, in the 16th century, enslaved Indians and later their descendants mined the rich veins of silver, copper and lead.

During the French intervention (1861-67) a fort on Parral's Cerro de la Cruz was occupied by French troops under orders from Emperor Maximilian.

Places to Stay

Few travellers stay the night in Parral, most moving on to Durango. If you do stay, you will not be disappointed with the clean and friendly *Hotel Acosta* (☎ 2-06-57), on Agustín Barbachano just off the main square. Singles/doubles cost US$12/15.50.

Getting There & Away

The bus station on the outskirts of town is most easily reached by taxi (US$1.50 to

US$2). There are buses to Chihuahua (US$5), Ciudad Juárez (US$15), Durango (US$9), Monterrey (US$15) and Mexico City (US$29) among others.

DURANGO
Population: 340,000
Altitude: 1912 metres

Don't be too put off by the modernisation you will see as you come by bus from the outskirts of the city. Proceed immediately to Durango's delightful old Plaza de Armas, where you'll discover fine colonial architecture.

Some 14 km from the city's centre you can visit the sets of many Westerns, some of which starred John Wayne and were directed by the legendary John Ford. Given its superb architecture and relaxed atmosphere, Durango is a good place to break a journey.

History
Founded in 1523 by the conquistador Don Francisco de Ibarra, and named after the Spanish city of his birth, Durango became prominent thanks to the mineral wealth in the region. Just north of the city, the Cerro del Mercado – a mountain of iron – is one of the world's largest iron deposits. Using the Río Tunal for irrigation also encouraged Durango's growth. Farmers reap excellent harvests of wheat, corn, cotton and barley.

More recently, the city's prosperity has increased due to the timber industry's harvest of paper products from the forested slopes of the Sierra Madre. Also, the dusty 'Western' scenery in the vicinity leads Hollywood to construct 'Wild West' towns here for its movies. When films are in production, numerous local craftspeople, carpenters and extras are employed.

Orientation
Virtually all sights are within walking distance of each other.

Information
Tourist Office Durango's tourist office is at Hidalgo 408 between 5 de Febrero and Pino Suárez. The staff are very friendly and quite knowledgeable, though their English is limited.

Money For currency exchange you will find a Bancomer just off the Plaza de Armas, open Monday to Friday from 9 am to 1.30 pm.

Post To reach the post office, go four blocks north of the plaza to Constitución 213. Hours are Monday to Friday from 8 am to 8 pm.

Cathedral
On the Plaza de Armas stands the town's baroque cathedral. Under construction from 1695 to 1750, the cathedral's twin-domed bell towers dominate the plaza. Although the interior decor cannot compare with the exterior architecture, the cathedral is a fine example of northern Mexican colonial construction. On Sunday, musicians perform on the plaza's bandstand while locals promenade.

Teatro Principal
From the cathedral, walk down Avenida 20 de Noviembre and on your right you will see the beautifully constructed 19th-century Teatro Principal, which has succumbed to cultural hard times and now functions as a cinema.

Palacio de Gobierno
From the Teatro Principal, go south on Bruno Martínez; beyond the Teatro Victoria, on the north side of another plaza, you will see the Palacio de Gobierno. Built on the estate of a Spanish mine owner, the Palacio was expropriated by the government following the War of Independence. Inside are colourful murals depicting state history and the economic activities of local residents.

Casa de los Condes de Suchil
From the university, take 5 de Febrero back to the Casa de los Condes de Suchil. This mansion is a striking example of early 17th-century Hispanic colonial architecture. Its detail and carvings have been well cared for and you can easily picture it housing the Spanish governor of Durango, the Conde

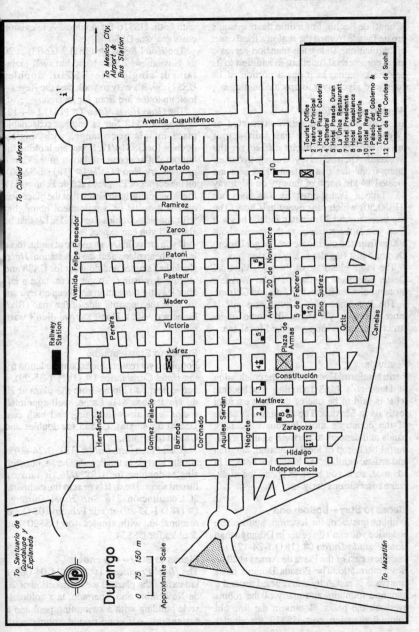

Durango

0   75   150 m

Approximate Scale

To Santuario de
Guadalupe y
Explanada

To Ciudad Juárez

To Mexico City,
Airport &
Bus Station

To Mazatlán

Avenida Cuauhtémoc

Apartado

Ramirez

Zarco

Patoni

Pasteur

Madero

Victoria

Juárez

Constitución

Martínez

Zaragoza

Hidalgo

Independencia

Avenida Felipe Pescador

Hernández

Gomez Palacio

Barreda

Coronado

Aquiles Serdan

Negrete

Pereira

Avenida 20 de Noviembre

5 de Febrero

Pino Suárez

Ortiz

Canelas

Plaza de
Armas

Railway
Station

1 Tourist Office
2 Teatro Principal
3 Hotel Plaza Catedral
4 Cathedral
5 Hotel Posada Duran
6 La Única Restaurant
7 Hotel Presidente
8 Hotel Casablanca
9 Hotel Reyes
10 Teatro Victoria
11 Palacio del Gobierno &
   Tourist Office
12 Casa de los Condes de Suchil

(Count) de Suchil. For a time the mansion's ornate facade fronted the region's local court of Inquisition. Today the mansion serves a more commercial function, in addition to its landmark status, as it has a portion of its courtyard given over to upscale boutiques.

Western Movie Towns

To visit Hollywood sets constructed as 'Western' towns, you can join a tour organised by the tourist office on the weekend. Alternatively, you can get yourself there from the bus station. The sets are located 14 km north of the city on Highway 45. Take a Transportes El Ranchero bus (US$0.50) which runs every half-hour. The trip takes around 30 minutes and the bus will drop you at the entrance to the towns about 500 m from the old movie set. To get back to Durango just flag down any passing bus.

The more elaborate of the two, Villa del Oeste, was used in two of John Wayne's more mediocre efforts, *Big Jake* and *Chisum*.

The less impressive Chupaderos site is more decrepit, yet ironically some of its structures shelter impoverished local families.

Festivals

Feria Nacional Every 8 July, the celebration of Durango's 1563 founding has become what is said to be one of the most exciting festivals in Mexico. The fiesta brings some of the country's most famous musicians, bands and dancers to perform against a colourful backdrop of local industrial, agrarian and artistic exhibits. All hotels are booked in advance, so if you hope to spend the night, make reservations early.

Places to Stay – bottom end

Without question, for location, atmosphere and price you can't do better in Durango than *Hotel Posada Duran* (☎ (181) 1-24-12), situated just east of the Plaza de Armas at 20 de Noviembre 506. The Posada Duran's inner courtyard is tastefully constructed around a romantic fountain, and many of the rooms overlook the plaza. Rooms in the fine old colonial mansion cost US$13 for singles

with bath, US$16 for doubles. A television costs an extra US$0.50.

The *Hotel Reyes* (☎ (181) 3-02-03) at 20 de Noviembre 220 is basic but well maintained; singles are US$10, doubles US$11.50. It's easy to walk past the Reyes – look up to the 3rd floor for its sign.

The *Gran Hotel Matar* (☎ (181) 1-44-12) at Progreso 112 Sur is another reasonable place in this price range, with singles/doubles for US$14/17. If you are looking for bottom-dollar accommodation in the centre of town, try *Hotel Gallo* (☎ (181) 1-52-90), on the corner of Progreso at 5 de Febrero 117 Pte. You get the impression that the place was once a hospital or a retirement home, but with singles/doubles for US$8/12 that is about all you can expect.

If you arrive in Durango late at night, there is one cheap place near the bus station. *Hotel Karla* has singles and doubles for US$8 and is truly disgusting. To get there, take a left after leaving the station and keep an eye out for it on the opposite side of the road (Blvd Francisco Villa). Don't say we didn't warn you.

Places to Stay – middle

For plush yet reasonable accommodation try the *Hotel Casablanca* (☎ (181) 1-35-99), a convenient two blocks from the plaza at 20 de Noviembre 811. Large, well-appointed rooms with air-conditioning and bath cost US$20 for singles, US$25 for doubles and US$30 for triples.

Hotel Plaza Catedral (☎ (181) 3-24-80) is similar in style to the Posada Duran, but with singles/doubles for US$22/26, it ranks a distant second best. It is next to the cathedral at Constitución 216 Sur. *Hotel Durango* (☎ (181) 1-55-80) at 5 de Febrero 103 Ote is reasonable, with singles for US$20 and doubles for US$24.

Places to Stay – top end

The *Hotel Presidente* (☎ (181) 11-04-08), 1 km east of the plaza at the intersection of 20 de Noviembre and Apartado, is a colonial-style building with a swimming pool and a restaurant. Air-conditioned rooms with phones and TV cost US$58 a single, US$63 a double.

Places to Eat

If you arrive late and are hungry, walk three blocks from the plaza down 20 de Noviembre until it intersects with Pasteur. There you will find a cheap, filling taquería, *La Única*, where a fine mariachi band plays until midnight. For excellent, low-cost food, try *Fil-Bet's*, also on 20 de Noviembre at 212 Ote. Their inexpensive comida corrida is substantial and good.

If you are hankering for decent pizza and willing to spend a bit more, try the outdoor patio of *Restaurant La Terraza* on the 2nd floor of a building on 5 de Febrero overlooking the plaza. Pizzas here cost US$4 to US$8.50.

For those willing to spend a bit for continental cuisine, the *Café Nevería La Bohemia*, at 20 de Noviembre 907, serves decent spaghetti and German dishes like sausage with cabbage. A serve of spaghetti costs US$2.50, a Bohemia Burger US$4.50 and German Pork Shanks US$8. Their Mexican food is cheaper and their afternoon comida corrida, although a little steep at US$5, is a good deal.

Getting There & Away

Bus The Central Camionera is far from the centre of town; the centre can be reached in 15 minutes by local buses designated 'Centro'. Going to the bus station, take a bus marked 'Central Camionera' from the market near the plaza. There are also slightly more expensive colectivo vans to the bus station from near the plaza. Most convenient of all, taxis are reasonably priced – bargain one down to about US$3.50.

There are four 1st-class bus companies providing direct or connecting services to virtually every part of Mexico. There are regular services to Mexico City (almost hourly), Guadalajara, and to Mazatlán via a scenic mountain road. There are frequent services to Zacatecas; the trip takes 4½ hours for US$6. There are also 1st-class services to Durango from most urban centres.

To reach Chihuahua from Durango takes 11 hours and costs about US$16.

Train Train services to and from Durango are slower than 1st-class buses. If you are coming from the north and wish to avoid 11 hours of less-than-electrifying scenery, consider an overnight sleeper. It's slow but at least you will sleep through the tedium.

To get from the train station into town, take a bus from the front of the station direct to the main plaza via Constitución; or walk some seven blocks down Martínez to the intersection of 20 de Noviembre, turn left and walk one block to the plaza.

ZACATECAS

Population: 165,000
Altitude: 2445 metres

If you've come from the north, welcome to the first of Mexico's justly fabled Silver Cities. If you've been visiting Silver Cities like Guanajuato in the south, don't hesitate to journey a few hours further, as Zacatecas is particularly fascinating.

In fact, at 2445 metres (over 8000 feet) altitude, Zacatecas literally takes your breath away. The town is carved into the slopes of the Cerro de la Bufa, a mountain whose silhouette resembles a Hispanic wineskin or *bufa*. As you climb stone-stepped streets, you will see some of Mexico's finest colonial buildings, including what may be the most beautiful Churrigueresque cathedral in Mexico. This historic, friendly town is all the more to be appreciated for its lack of tourists.

History

Long before the first conquistadors arrived, the Zacateco Indians were mining silver here. Then an Indian gave a piece of the fabled metal to a conquistador.

After subduing the Indians, the Spaniards moved in, founding a settlement and starting mining operations in 1548. Caravan after caravan of silver was sent off to Mexico City. While some treasure-laden wagons were raided by nomadic Indians, enough silver reached its destination to create fabulously wealthy silver barons. Agriculture and

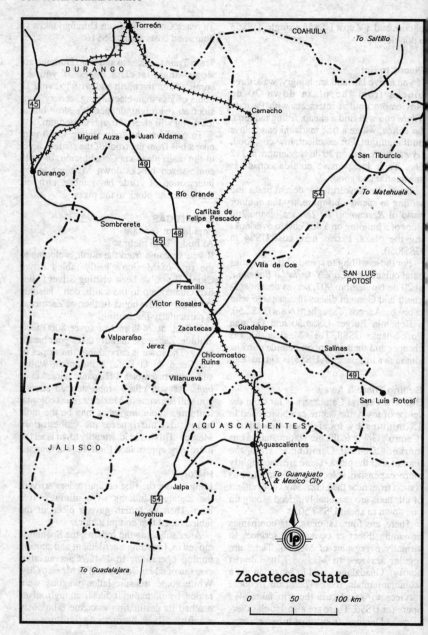

Zacatecas State

0   50   100 km

ranching developed to serve the rapidly increasing populace of the town.

Thanks to Zacatecas' mineral wealth, the city and Crown prospered. In the first quarter of the 18th century, Zacatecas' mines were producing 20% of the colony's silver. However, in the 19th century the volatile course of political events somewhat diminished the flow of silver as various forces fought to control the city. In 1871, Benito Juárez decisively defeated local rebels here.

Although silver production later improved under Díaz, the Revolution disrupted it. Here in 1914 Pancho Villa, through brilliant tactics, defeated a stronghold of 12,000 soldiers loyal to the self-seeking General Huerta. This may have led to Villa's undoing, as he violated the orders of the man who would become Mexico's first post-Revolutionary president, Venustiano Carranza.

After the Revolution, Zacatecas continued to thrive due to silver. To this day it remains a mining centre, with the 200-year-old El Bote mine still productive.

Orientation

The major sites are all within walking distance of the centre. To keep your bearings in this colonial city of twisting, inclined streets, take note of the two major thoroughfares, Avenidas Hidalgo and Juárez. When you get lost, as you invariably will, just have a local point you back to one of the main streets. Avenida Hidalgo becomes González Ortega at a point south-west of its intersection with Juárez.

Information

Tourist Office The tourist office is easy to find; it's next to the cathedral on Plaza Hidalgo. The helpful staff here speak English and offer plenty of brochures describing Zacatecas' attractions (although these are in Spanish). It's open Monday to Friday from 8 am to 3.30 pm, but is closed on the weekend.

Money For currency exchange, you will find two banks at the intersection of Avenida

Hidalgo and Callejón de la Caja, open Monday to Friday from 9 am to 1.30 pm.

Post The post office is conveniently located just off Avenida Hidalgo, one block north-east of Avenida Juárez at Allende 111. Its hours are Monday to Friday from 8 am to 7 pm and Saturday from 9 am to noon.

Cathedral

The cathedral is one of the true masterpieces of colonial Mexican architecture, with its carved pink sandstone façade. Although the ground was broken in 1612, the cathedral was not completed until 1752, and in this city of affluent silver barons no expense was spared. The interior was once festooned with elaborate gold and silver ornaments and adorned with tapestries and paintings. However, in the course of the country's turbulent history, the cathedral's wealth was plundered. The towers and façade laced with Churrigueresque carvings still make it worth a trip to Zacatecas.

Palacio de Gobierno

Looking north from the cathedral, you will see the Palacio de Gobierno on Plaza Hidalgo. It was originally built in 1727 as a mansion for the silver baron Count Santiago de la Laguna, and was acquired by the state. In the city hall portion of the building, you will see a fine mural of the region's history which was painted in 1970 by Antonio Rodríguez.

Mercado González Ortega

Walking south away from the cathedral on Hidalgo, you will come to a colonial structure, the Mercado González Ortega. On the upper level, fronting Hidalgo, an upscale shopping mall complete with restaurants has replaced the old market. The lower level opens onto Calle Tacuba and if you follow Tacuba you will come to Zacatecas' lively daily marketplace.

Teatro Calderón

Across Avenida Hidalgo from the Mercado González Ortega is the beautiful 19th-

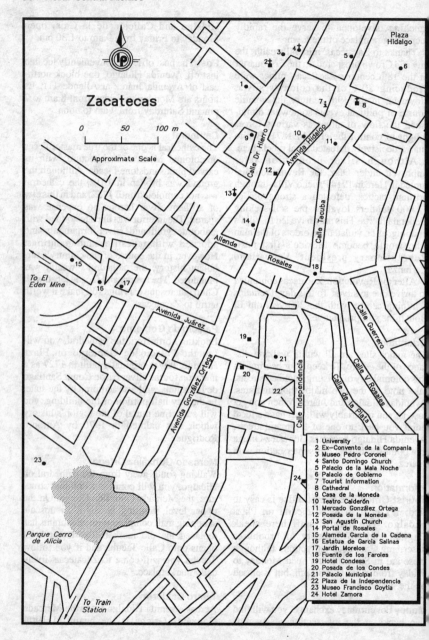

Zacatecas

0   50   100 m

Approximate Scale

To El Eden Mine

To Train Station

Parque Cerro de Alicia

Plaza Hidalgo

1 University
2 Ex-Convento de la Compania
3 Museo Pedro Coronel
4 Santo Domingo Church
5 Palacio de la Mala Noche
6 Palacio de Gobierno
7 Tourist Information
8 Cathedral
9 Casa de la Moneda
10 Teatro Calderón
11 Mercado González Ortega
12 Posada de la Moneda
13 San Agustín Church
14 Portal de Rosales
15 Alameda García de la Cadena
16 Estatua de García Salinas
17 Jardín Morelos
18 Fuente de los Faroles
19 Hotel Condesa
20 Posada de los Condes
21 Palacio Municipal
22 Plaza de la Independencia
23 Museo Francisco Goytia
24 Hotel Zamora

century Teatro Calderón, an ornate example of colonial architecture.

Santo Domingo Church

Perched atop a steep street looking down upon the cathedral, the Santo Domingo church is in a more sober baroque style than the cathedral. Inside, however, are some fine gilded altars and paintings, and a graceful horseshoe staircase with a fountain. The church was designed to form a Latin cross, with two side aisles and a dome above the transept. Beside the church is the former Jesuit college, with an elaborate doorway and pleasant cloister. The church served as the monks' place of worship. The college now serves as the regional museum.

Museo Pedro Coronel

Next to the Santo Domingo Church is the Museo Pedro Coronel. An affluent Zacatecan artist bequeathed to his home town this collection of artefacts from all over the world. Coronel also amassed works by Picasso, Roualt, Chagall, Hogarth, Daumier and Goya as well as artwork from the Orient.

Although this is only a regional museum, it is truly special. Allow extra time to fully enjoy it. Admission is free on Sundays, otherwise US$0.60; hours are Tuesday to Sunday from 10 am to 5 pm.

University & Mint

If you want to talk with Mexican students, you will find the Universidad Autónoma de Zacatecas nearby on the same street as the museum. Just beneath the university, on Calle de Hierro, you will see the building that housed Zacatecas' mint, the Casa de la Moneda. Inside is a display of early coins.

Church of San Agustín

Walk further along and you will come to the partially restored Church of San Agustín, with a Plateresque doorway. Built in the 18th century, this finely constructed church functioned for a time as a casino. The bas-relief depicts the life of St Augustine. The church's visiting hours are Monday to Saturday, 8 am to 2 pm, and 4 to 5 pm; closed on Sunday. Admission is free.

Teleférico

For a view of the city, ride Zacatecas' cable car. The lower station is close to the Motel del Bosque. Taking the teleférico tram to the top of the Cerro de la Bufa (US$2.75 round trip), you will be treated to the spectacle of the city spread out beneath you. The hours of operation are Tuesday to Sunday, 12.30 to 7.30 pm, weather permitting (cars do not run in high wind).

Museo de la Toma de Zacatecas

Atop the Cerro de la Bufa near the cable car station is the Museo de la Toma de Zacatecas, commemorating the victory of Pancho Villa's revolutionaries over the Federales in 1914. Some historians say that Villa's taking of Zacatecas insured his victory in this battle. The museum is open daily from 10 am to 6 pm. Admission is free.

La Capilla

Adjacent to the Museo de la Toma de Zacatecas is La Capilla de la Virgen del Patrocinio. Named for the patron saint of miners and thus also of Zacatecas, the 18th-century chapel has a portrait of the virgin said to be capable of healing the sick. On the cliffside near the church is a meteorological observatory.

Mausoleo de los Hombres Ilustrios de Zacatecas

Behind La Capilla is the Mausoleo de los Hombre Ilustrios de Zacatecas. Here, with a commanding view of the city, are the graves or memorials of Zacatecan revolutionaries.

El Eden Mine

La Mina El Eden, once one of Mexico's richest mines, is a 'must' for visitors to Zacatecas for the dramatic insight it gives into the source of wealth in this region – and the terrible price paid for it. Digging for what proved to be a fabulous yield of silver, gold, iron, copper and zinc, enslaved Indians, many of whom were between eight and 10 years old, worked under horrific conditions. As your guide will tell you, each day at least eight mining slaves met their doom.

As you take a miniature mine train into the middle level of the mine and are guided along lit walkways over treacherous shafts below, it is easy to see why so many lost their lives to accidents and diseases like silicosis and tuberculosis. After you disembark from the train, you are led along creaky wooden boards through dark passageways and over subterranean pools. Visible beneath are water-filled lower shafts which flooded due to a miscalculated explosion and ultimately closed the mine. Today the mine is open only for tourism and, in the evenings, for a disco (see the Entertainment section).

There are two entrances to the mine. The lesser known is near the cable car's lower embarkation station, and you may well have to wait a while before a guide shows up. For more certain success, walk up Avenida Juárez and stay on it after its name changes to Avenida Torreón at Alameda park until you see the huge Seguro Social Hospital. Make a right here and a short left on Calle de la Loma, and you will be at the entrance to La Mina. Or take a bus from Jardín Independencia up Avenida Juárez to the hospital. Tours are offered from 12.30 to 7.30 pm, Tuesday to Sunday; closed Monday. Admission is US$2.75.

The excellent guides here are paid a very low wage. Some are university students working their way through school, and a generous tip may be in order.

Museo Francisco Goytia

The Museo Francisco Goytia, a gallery of painting and sculpture, is worth visiting. Set above the pleasantly pastoral Cerro de Alicia park (great for picnics) where part of the city's ancient aqueduct system remains intact, the museum has ground-floor exhibits of the works of the great early 20th-century painter Goytia (1882-1960). Goytia was a Zacatecan whose paintings of Indians are particularly good. The upper floor of the former governor's mansion is given over to the works of local artists and exhibits on tour.

The museum hours are 9 am to 1.30 pm and 5 to 8 pm Tuesday to Sunday, closed Monday. Admission is free. To reach the Museo Francisco Goytia, follow Avenida Hidalgo south to Avenida Juárez where its name changes to Avenida González Ortega. Follow it up the steep hill until you see Cerro de Alicia park. The museum is behind the park.

Festivals

Zacatecas holds a fiesta from late August into September. On the principal day, 27 August, a battle between Moors and Christians is recreated atop the Cerro de la Bufa. Renowned *toreadores* are imported to fight the famous bulls bred in this region.

Places to Stay – bottom end

The basic but clean *Hotel Colón* (☎ (492) 2-04-64) at López Velarte 508, is a 15 to 20-minute walk from Plaza de la Independencia. A room here with private bath costs US$13.50 a single, US$16 a double.

One of the cheapest places in town worth considering is the *Hotel Río Grande* (☎ (492) 2-53-49), offering singles/doubles for US$7.75/10. From the old bus station, go over the road bridge and then left 150 metres up the hill to the hotel at Calzada de la Paz 313. Another one is the well-located *Hotel Zamora* (☎ (492) 2-12-00) on Zamora near Independencia. Rooms start at US$9.

Places to Stay – middle

For a slight splurge, the top choice in Zacatecas is the *Posada de los Condes* (☎ (492) 2-10-93), conveniently located near the intersection of Avenidas Hidalgo and Juárez at Avenida Juárez 18. The building itself, over three centuries old, is a national landmark. Singles/doubles cost US$21/27.

A good second choice is the *Posada de la Moneda* (☎ (492) 2-08-81), a block south of the cathedral at Avenida Hidalgo 413. Singles with bath, telephone and hot water cost US$15, doubles US$21.

Across the street from the Posada de los Condes is the less attractive but cheaper

Hotel Condesa (☎ (492) 2-11-60) at Avenida Juárez 5. Singles/doubles cost US$17/18.50.

Places to Stay – top end
Hotel Aristos (☎ (492) 2-17-88), located on the periphery of town at the Lomas de la Soledad, has a good view of Zacatecas as well as a fine restaurant and a swimming pool. Rooms start at US$70.

The *Gallery* (☎ (492) 2-33-11), at López Mateos and Callejón del Barro is the best luxury hotel in town. Rooms here also start at US$70.

Places to Eat
There are good, filling, comidas corridas in the restaurant of the *Posada de los Condes* for US$5, inexpensive breakfasts at the café of the *Hotel Condesa* (under US$2 for hotcakes and a cup of tea) and adequate Mexican standard dishes at the restaurant of the *Posada de la Moneda*.

A terrific place to snack and meet students just opposite the tourist office is the *Café y Nevería Acropolis*. The varied fare includes great coffee (rare in Mexico), burgers, fries, and all sorts of sodas and desserts.

For cheap roast chicken dishes, try the little 2nd-floor *Rosticería El Pastor*, across from the library at Plaza Independencia 214 (look up to see it). For less than US$2 you can fill up on chicken and chips. Notice the sign out the front commemorating this residence as the birthplace of the first journalist in America.

For cheap Mexican meat dishes, try the *Mesón La Mina*, conveniently located at Juárez 15 near Avenida Hidalgo. You can also get beer and decent coffee here. Another aptly named cheap café is *El Carnerito* at Avenida Juárez 105.

Restaurant La Troje (☎ 2-05-09) at Avenida Hidalgo 111, with live (non-touristy) music and a dance floor is a fun place for a night out. It is open until 2 am or 3 am and is very popular with locals, so it could be worth reserving a table. Food is expensive, although pizzas start at US$3. Beers are expensive at US$2 or more.

For excellent Chinese food and very friendly service, try *El Dragón de Oro* directly opposite the Museo Pedro Coronel. It is not the cheapest place in town, but you get what you pay for.

Entertainment
The bizarrely situated disco in La Mina El Eden features a rock-and-roll club complete with light show Thursday to Saturday from 9 pm to 2 am. Numbers are limited, so it is a good idea to reserve a table. The only sure way of doing this seems to be to go to the mine during the day and ask to speak with someone who knows about the disco.

For a pretty place to dance, with a romantic view of the city, try El Elefante Blanco Disco next to the cable car station. The luxury hotels Aristos and Calinda have their own nightly discos.

Things to Buy
Zacatecas is famous for its fine leatherwork, colourful sarapes and wood and stone carvings. Bargain at shops in and around the old market on Tacuba and Avenida Hidalgo.

The best sarapes in the region are said to come from Guadalupe (see below). A family by the name of Ruelas has a certain fame, and their workshop, Sarapes Ruelas, is known to almost anyone you ask in Guadalupe.

Getting There & Away
Bus There is frequent 1st-class bus service between Zacatecas and Mexico City (US$15, nine hours), Guadalajara (US$9, four hours), Durango (US$6.75, 4½ hours) and Aguascalientes (US$3, two hours).

Train Zacatecas is on the main rail route to Mexico City and Ciudad Juárez. For timetable information, see Getting There & Away in the Mexico City chapter.

Getting Around
Although the modern bus station is far from the city centre, reaching the centre is neither expensive nor difficult. Buses charging less than US$0.20 run regularly for the 15-minute trip. If you are in a hurry, you can bargain a taxi down to about US$1. The

railway station, too, has buses and taxis running regularly to the centre. Once you are in town, the major sights are all within walking distance, but allow extra time to reach your destination because of the high altitude and steep streets.

AROUND ZACATECAS
Convento de Guadalupe

To visit one of Mexico's most beloved religious sites, the Convento de Guadalupe, you must take a local bus about eight km to the town of Guadalupe. To catch the bus, walk from the Plaza de Independencia past the old bus station and make a left on the Callejón de Tampico. Just past the overhead passenger walk you will see an alley where the Guadalupe bus is parked. The fare is US$0.08 and buses depart every 15 minutes for the 20-minute ride.

Founded in the early 18th century, the convent served as an educational centre for Franciscan monks preparing to proselytise what is now northern Mexico and the US Southwest. You may visit the convent's interior on your own or wait for a tour guide. Inside, the walls are covered with some of the finest religious paintings in colonial Mexico. Walk to the top of the convent and ask to be admitted to the Coro Alto, a choir overlooking the interior of the ornate church.

The convent/museum is open daily from 9 am to 1 pm and 3 to 5 pm. Admission is a hefty US$3.50.

CHICOMOSTOC RUINS

The Chicomostoc ruins, also known as Quemada ruins, lie in a valley some 56 km from Zacatecas. The ruins are quite interesting, but the hefty entry fee (US$3.50) is hard to justify if you're on a strict low budget, unless you are a real ruins buff.

If you've been to Monte Albán near Oaxaca, you'll see some similarity in the design of the pyramids here. Only the largest, known as The Temple, has been fully restored. Some archaeologists say the site, founded during the late 12th century, served as a fortress for the Nahuatlacas Indians during the pre-Aztecan Empire period; others believe it was a religious site for local royalty and the priestly class.

Getting There & Away

Buses no longer run directly to the Chicomostoc ruins. Instead, take a bus bound for Guadalajara and get the driver to drop you off on the road, just by the Restaurant Siete Cuevas, about 30 to 40 minutes' walk from Chicomostoc. Catching transport back can be pretty slow going. It may be easier to hitch to the small town of Villanueva and then catch a bus back to Zacatecas.

North-West Mexico

This chapter includes Baja California and the opposite coastline on the Gulf of California, as far south as the beach resorts of Mazatlán and San Blas. It covers the states of Sonora, Sinaloa, Nayarit, Baja California Norte and Baja California Sud.

Nogales to Tepic

The 1505-km stretch of Highway 15 from Nogales on the US border to Tepic, capital of the state of Nayarit, cuts through the harsh Sonoran desert to the agricultural boomtown of Hermosillo, then down along Mexico's beautiful north-western Pacific coast, passing several very popular seaside resorts such as Guaymas and Mazatlán.

The Pacific littoral is mostly cut off from central and eastern Mexico by the high wall of the Sierra Madre Occidental. Travel from the coast up to the high plateaux of inland Mexico is practicable at only a few points: on the Chihuahua al Pacífico railway from Los Mochis up through the Copper Canyon to Chihuahua, from Mazatlán up to Durango, and from Tepic to Guadalajara.

By the way, the fertile agricultural land in the back country of Sinaloa is used extensively by illegal drug farmers, and the Sinaloan capital of Culiacán is the money centre of this local drug trade. It's best not to wander too far off the main roads in Sinaloa state.

NOGALES
Population: 75,000
Altitude: 1170 metres
Like its border-city cousins Tijuana, Ciudad Juárez, Nuevo Laredo and Matamoros, Nogales in the Mexican state of Sonora is a major transit point for goods and people travelling between the USA and Mexico. On the northern side of the border in Arizona is its US counterpart, also named Nogales

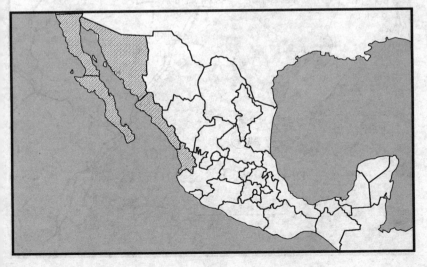

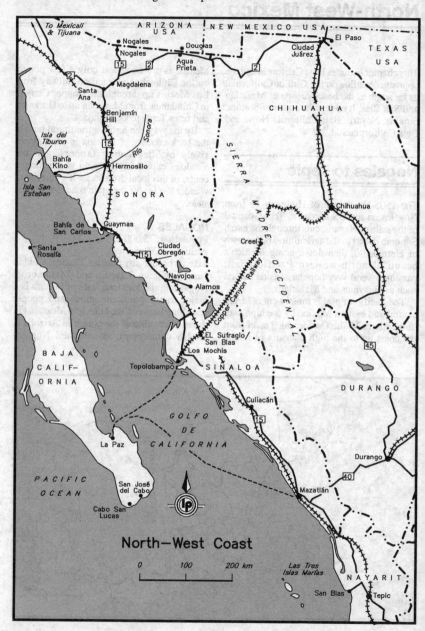

North—West Coast

0   100   200 km

(walnuts) because of the many walnut trees that once flourished here.

The Ferrocarril del Pacífico (Pacific Railway) passes through on its way between Mexicali (Baja California) and points south. Several major bus lines, including the USA-based Greyhound lines, begin and end routes in Nogales, Arizona. As a transit point, you can't beat it.

As a place to visit, Nogales presents an easier introduction to Mexico than Tijuana. Nogales has everything Tijuana has – curio shops overflowing with wrought-iron bird cages, tacky felt paintings, plaster renditions of Mickey Mouse, cheap bars and plenty of liquor stores – but all on a much smaller scale.

For details on crossing borders, see Crossing the Border in the Getting There & Away chapter.

Information & Orientation

The commercial section of Nogales is only a few blocks in width, being hemmed in on either side by hills. The main street is Obregón, which eventually runs into Highway 15. Almost everything is within walking distance of the border; it's virtually impossible to get lost here.

If you plan to head south, don't forget to get your tourist card validated at the Mexican immigration office just after crossing from Nogales, Arizona. And, if you're driving, be sure to get a vehicle permit from the *aduana* (customs office), next to the immigration office. The border offices are open 24 hours daily.

Places to Stay

There are plenty of hotels and motels in Nogales, but if you're travelling on a low budget you might want to continue straight through town to a place where lodgings are cheaper. If you do stay the night, try the *Hotel Martinez* (☎ (631) 2-54-89), at Juarez 33 just a couple of minutes walk from the border crossing, with singles/doubles from US$17/20. If you want to clean up before crossing back into the USA, they will rent you a shower for $2. Another option is *Hotel Olivia*

(☎ (631) 2-22-00) at Avenida Obregón 125 which has air-conditioned rooms with telephones and TVs for US$32.50 per single/double.

Places to Eat

For food, try the *Café Olga*, Juárez 37, open 24 hours a day. *The Apolo*, at Km 6 on Highway 15, reputedly serves some of the best turtle soup (called *cahuama*) in northern Sonora. *El Cid*, Avenida Obregón 124 overlooking the street, has an excellent menu but is expensive by Mexican standards with meals starting at around US$7.

Getting There & Away

Unfortunately the bus station is well out of the centre on the highway south of the town. You don't really have much choice but to take a taxi (at least $5).

There are only three bus companies operating out of the small bus station here. Transportes Norte de Sonora (TN de S), Transportes Norte del Pacifico (TN del P) and Tres Estrellas de Oro (TE de O). Here are the major destinations they serve:

Chihuahua – 839 km, 12 hours; US$18 with TE de O.
Guadalajara – 1600 km, 24 hours; US$38 with TE de O, TN del P.
Hermosillo – 277 km, four hours; US$6 with TN de S, TE de O.
Los Mochis – 763 km, 10 hours; US$17 with TE de O, TN de S.
Mazatlán – 1195 km, 16½ hours; US$27 with TE de O.
Mexicali – 562 km, nine hours; US$14 with TE de O.
Mexico City – 2167 km, 32 hours; US$51 with TN de S, TE de O, TN del P.
Tijuana – 751 km, 11½ hours; US$16 with TN de S, TE de O.

HERMOSILLO

Population: 500,000
Altitude: 238 metres
Founded in 1700 by Juan Bautista Escalante for the resettlement of Pima Indians, Hermosillo is now the capital of the state of Sonora. It's right on Highway 15 approximately 227 km due south of Nogales and La Frontera (the international border). Like many cities in Mexico, Hermosillo is quickly industrialising; in little more than a decade,

the city has gone from being primarily an agricultural and administrative centre of 45,000 to a multi-industry city of more than 500,000.

Most travellers use Hermosillo as a base for trips to beaches on the Gulf of California especially during the oppressively hot summer months. The nearest beaches to Hermosillo are at Old and New Kino on Bahía Kino, 120 km to the west. Unless you want to camp on the beach or in a trailer park, however, there is no budget accommodation in the twin Kinos.

Orientation

Highway 15 enters Hermosillo from the north-east and becomes Blvd Francisco Eusebio Kino, a wide street lined with orange and laurel trees. Kino continues east through the city, curves south-west and initially becomes Blvd Rodríguez, then Blvd Rosales and Blvd Agustín de Vildosola before regaining its designation as Highway 15.

The major business and administrative sections of town lie on either side of this main thoroughfare and along the Blvd Transversal which transects Kino from north/north-west to south-east. The Periférico, a highway originally designed to circumscribe the periphery of Hermosillo, has almost become an inner loop due to the city's rapid expansion.

The central section of Hermosillo, which is also the oldest and most charming, lies to the south just after the adjoining community of Villa de Seris. The Cerro de la Campana (Hill of the Bell) is the most prominent landmark in the area and an easy point of reference night or day. The panoramic view from the top is beautiful and well worth the climb.

Information

Tourist Office The city tourist office (☎ (62) 17-29-64) is on the ground floor of the Palacio de Gobierno and offers some information in English and Spanish about Hermosillo and the rest of the state of Sonora.

Money There are several banks on Blvd Rosales. Casas de cambio are scattered throughout downtown Hermosillo.

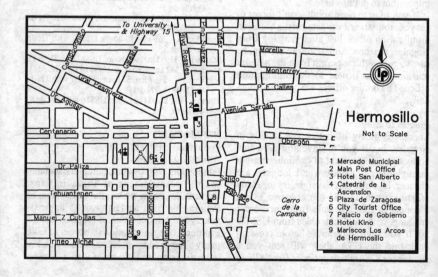

Hermosillo

Not to Scale

1 Mercado Municipal
2 Main Post Office
3 Hotel San Alberto
4 Catedral de la Ascensión
5 Plaza de Zaragosa
6 City Tourist Office
7 Palacio de Gobierno
8 Hotel Kino
9 Mariscos Los Arcos de Hermosillo

Post The main post office is at Blvd Rosales and Avenida Serdán and is open 8 am to 7 pm Monday to Friday, and 9 am to 1 pm Saturday and Sunday.

Laundry Lavarama laundromat is at the corner of Yañez and Sonora. Lavandería Automática de Hermosillo is a self-service laundry at Juárez and Periférico 2 Poniente; it's open Monday to Saturday from 8 am to 8 pm, and Sunday from 8 am to 2 pm.

Plaza de Zaragosa

A visit to the Plaza de Zaragosa is highly recommended, especially at sundown when thousands of yellow-headed blackbirds flock in to roost in the park trees for the night. On the west side is the lovely **Catedral de la Ascensión** (also called Catedral Metropolitana). On the east side is the **Palacio de Gobierno** (Government Palace and municipal offices) with colourful courtyard murals depicting various episodes in the history of Sonora. The cathedral and palace are open daily; admission is free.

Museo de Sonora

The Sonora Museum hugs the eastern side of the Cerro de la Campana. Most of the exhibits cover various aspects of Sonora's history and anthropology. Hours are Wednesday to Saturday 10 am to 5.30 pm, and Sunday 10 am to 3.30 pm. Admission is free.

Centro Ecológico de Sonora

The Ecological Centre of Sonora is a wonderful zoo and botanical garden 2½ km south of downtown Hermosillo near the Periférico Sur and just off Highway 15. Many animals and plants indigenous to Sonora and other desert environments around the world are displayed. It's open Wednesday to Sunday at varying hours.

Universidad Autónoma de Sonora

The Autonomous University of Sonora has a fine arts complex across from the campus at the main traffic circle formed by the intersection of Blvds Rosales (Rodríguez) and Transversal. A variety of theatrical and musical events and art exhibits are presented throughout the year. Check with the university or the tourist office for the latest information.

Places to Stay

If you spend a night here in the summer, you must have a room with air-conditioning that works. Some hotels advertise air-conditioning, but the cool air may blow with barely more force than a whisper. Check the room before you accept it.

Many of Hermosillo's motels and hotels are strung out along Blvd Francisco Eusebio Kino (Highway 15) in the north-east corner of the city. One of these is the *Motel El Encanto* (☎ (62) 14-47-30), Blvd Kino 901 three blocks west of the Holiday Inn. The rooms are clean and air-conditioned with tiled floors, telephones and TVs. There's also a swimming pool. Singles/doubles are US\$25/33.

Closer to downtown is the *Hotel Kino* (☎ (62) 13-31-31), Pino Suárez 151 at the base of the Cerro de la Campana right before Pino Suárez merges with Blvd Rosales. This no-nonsense hotel is a favourite among Mexican businesspeople. Rooms have private baths, air-conditioning, colour TVs and mini-refrigerators. Singles/doubles are US\$30/33.50.

Nearby is the *Hotel Montecarlo* (☎ (62) 12-33-54), at Juárez and Sonora just off Blvd Transversal. This reasonably priced older hotel has clean, air-conditioned rooms. It fills up quickly each day, so make reservations or show up before sundown. Singles/doubles are US\$20/23.50.

The *Hotel San Alberto* (☎ (62) 13-18-40), Avenida Serdán and Blvd Rosales, attempts modern elegance, but it's overpriced. Single/double rooms with air-conditioning, cable TV and continental breakfast are US\$41/47. It also has a swimming pool.

The only cheap places to stay in town are the few dingy casas de huéspedes on Sonora between Garmendia and Matamoros. Even there you will be pushing to find a single for under US\$13. Most of the rooms seem to be rented out long term to students or short term to hookers. At night the hookers tend to be noisy, so make your selection carefully.

Places to Eat

The state of Sonora is known for both beef and seafood dishes. *Jardín Xochimilco*, at Obregón 51 in the adjoining community of Villa de Seris, offers a complete dinner that includes tripe, kidneys, ribs and steak charcoal-broiled in huge ovens for US$4.

The *Restaurant La Huerta*, San Luis Potosí 109, has been recommended for its seafood.

The *Hotel Kino* restaurant has a reputation for good, moderately priced meals, including an excellent comida corrida for under US$6.

Rene's Café, on Blvd Rosales at Moreno and Michel, is a bright, cheery place that also does a good comida corrida.

Some of the cheapest food in town can be bought from any of the numerous street-corner hot-dog carts and cheap foodstalls in the *Mercado Municipal*. Situated only three blocks south of the plaza, the Mercado is a large indoor market at Guerrero and Calles. The tacos here can usually be trusted not to wreak havoc on your innards. The hot dogs are surprisingly good, especially when piled with condiments such as mustard, guacamole, chiles, relish and refried beans. Another street-cart treat is the pico de gallo, a delicious melange of chunks of orange, apple, pineapple, cucumber, jicama, watermelon and coconut – refreshing on a hot day.

Things to Buy

If you always wanted to buy a pair of cowboy boots and a 10-gallon hat, you'll probably find what you want in Hermosillo. The city's shops offer one of the best selections in Mexico of these and other cowboy-related paraphernalia.

Getting There & Away

Bus The Central de Autobuses at Blvd Transversal 400 handles most of Mexico's major bus lines. Tres Estrellas de Oro is the principal line, with 1st-class air-conditioned buses to Agua Prieta six times daily, Mexicali every hour 24 hours daily, Nogales

hourly from 2.30 am to 6.30 pm, and Guaymas every hour 24 hours daily.

Train The Ferrocarril del Pacífico railway station is just off Highway 15 about 2½ km north of central Hermosillo. The train to Los Mochis and other points south departs in the evening while the northbound train departs in the morning.

AROUND HERMOSILLO

Bahía Kino – Old & New Kino

Named for Father Eusebio Kino, a Jesuit missionary who established a small mission here for Seri Indians in the late 17th century, the bayfront town of Kino is divided into old and new parts that are as different as night and day. The old quarter is a dusty, run-down fishing village, while New Kino is a winter gringoland of trailer parks and condominiums. The twin Kinos are 120 km west of Hermosillo on Highway 16.

If you're on a tight budget, you'll have to camp out at one of the trailer parks for US$10 to US$15 per night or sleep for free under a thatched *palapa* on the New Kino beach.

You can eat cheaply though, in the old quarter at any of several open-air restaurants that serve fresh barbecued fish. *La Palapa* restaurant is often recommended.

Buses to Kino run four times daily from Hermosillo (US$2). The last bus from Kino to Hermosillo usually leaves between 4 and 6 pm.

GUAYMAS

Population: 105,000

Founded in 1769 by the Spaniards at the site of Yaqui and Guaymas Indian villages, the city of Guaymas today is the main port of Sonora. With so much commerce and industry in Guaymas, tourism isn't a priority. The main reasons to stop here are to escape from the oppressive heat of Hermosillo and get to the Bahía San Carlos resort beaches 20 km north of Guaymas. Since the ferry from Santa Rosalía in Baja California lands here, the city is also a popular transit point. Except for a small tree-lined plaza, however, the city

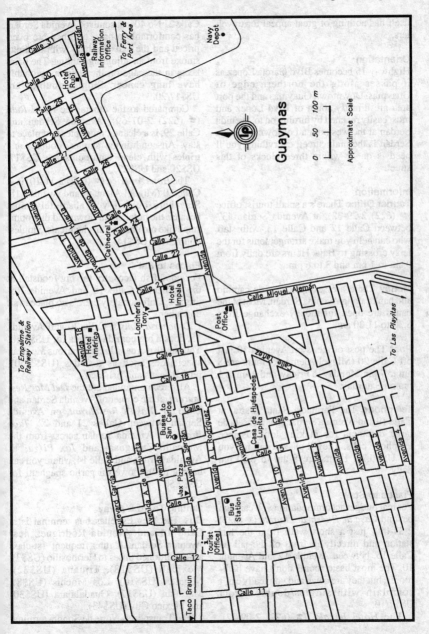

itself has nothing of great appeal for travellers.

Orientation
Highway 15 becomes Blvd García López as it passes along the northern edge of Guaymas. Downtown Guaymas and the port area are directly south of Blvd López and most easily reached by turning on to Avenida Serdán at the western end of town. Avenida Serdán is the main street; everything you'll need is on or within three blocks of this street.

Information
Tourist Office There's a small tourist office (☎ (622) 2-29-32), at Avenida Serdán 437 between Calle 12 and Calle 13, with staff who can help you make arrangements for the ferry crossing to Baja. Hours are daily from 9 am to 1 pm and 3 to 6 pm.

Money There are several casas de cambio and banks along Avenida Serdán. Most of the banks are open for money exchange from 8.30 to 11.30 am.

Post The post office is on Avenida 10 just off Calle 20 (Miguel Alemán). Hours are 8 am to 7 pm Monday to Friday, and 9 am to 1 pm on Saturday.

Telephone The Farmacia Santa Marta, at Calle 19 and Avenida Serdán, has a caseta de larga distancia for making long-distance telephone calls. They'll place a call for you for US$0.75. Hours are 8 am to 8.30 pm daily.

Places to Stay
For real budget accommodation you can't go beyond *Casa de Huéspedes Lupita* (☎ (622) 2-84-09), just a short walk from the bus station and directly in front of the jail on Calle 15, between Avenida 12 and Avenida 10. The most basic rooms don't have bathrooms, but they are clean and you really can't complain with singles/doubles from US$7/10.

The *Hotel Impala* (☎ (622) 2-09-22),

Calle 21 No 40 just south of Avenida Serdán, has comfortable rooms, but they are overpriced and the halls are hazy with cigarette smoke from an adjoining cantina. The parakeets in the cage on the stairway probably have lung cancer. Singles/doubles are US$17/20.

Compared to the others, the *Hotel Rubi* (☎ (622) 2-01-69), Avenida Serdán and Calle 29, is a cleaner, more pleasant place to stay. Air-conditioned singles, doubles and triples with clean bathrooms are US$17, US$20 and US$23.

The *Hotel América* (☎ (622) 2-11-10) is at Calle 20 (Miguel Alemán) and Avenida 18. Stay here only if you absolutely must because the hotel is run-down and the rooms smell like old dark-room chemicals. Singles/doubles are US$14.

Places to Eat
For good fish tacos, try the big foodstall at the corner of Calle 18 and Avenida Rodriguez. Unfortunately there's no place to sit down here.

Lonchería Tony's, Calle 20 and Avenida 15, does a big comida corrida for US$2.50. You can also order à la carte various Mexican specialities such as tostadas (US$1.50), refried beans and fish tacos.

Also recommended are the *Del Mar Restaurant*, at the corner of Avenida Serdán and Calle 17, *Pako's Restaurant*, on Avenida Serdán between Calles 21 and 22, *Taco Braun*, on Avenida Serdán across from the Mercado Zaragosa, and *Jax Pizza*, at Avenida Serdán and Calle 14, where you can have a really powerful garlic spaghetti for US$2.50.

Getting There & Away
Bus The Tres Estrellas bus terminal is at Calle 14 and Avenida Rodríguez near Avenida Serdán. It runs frequent 1st-class air-conditioned buses to Hermosillo (US$3), Mexicali (US$18), Tijuana (US$22), Nogales (US$10), Los Mochis (US$8), Mazatlán (US$17), Guadalajara (US$30) and Mexico City (US$43).

The Transportes Norte de Sonora terminal

is across the street and has almost exactly the same routes, frequency of departures and fares.

Train The railway information office (☎ (622) 2-49-80) is at the south-eastern end of the city on Avenida Serdán near Calle 29. The station is 10 km east of the city at the town of Empalme. The southbound express stops there at 9.30 pm and the northbound express at 5.30 am. The trains stop in Hermosillo (US$5), Nogales (US$13), Mazatlán (US$23), Tepic (US$30) and Guadalajara (US$40).

Boat The Transbordador (ferry) terminal is at the eastern end of town with ferries to Santa Rosalía, Baja California. Departures are at 8 am on Tuesday, Friday and Sunday. You can usually buy tickets the day before at the ticket office (7 am to 2 pm only). The basic single fare (one way) is $10.

Getting Around

Getting around Guaymas is easy. Buses run at least every half-hour along Avenida Serdán from the ferry terminal to Bahía San Carlos.

AROUND GUAYMAS
Bahía San Carlos

Bahía San Carlos is similar to Bahía Kino – a beautiful landscape full of gringos, trailer parks with monstrous motor homes and overpriced accommodation. The cheapest place to stay is the *Motel Creston* (☎ (622) 6-00-20) at Km 15 on the main road into San Carlos. It has a swimming pool and restaurant. Air-conditioned singles/doubles are US$40.

Trailer-park camping is possible, if space is available, at the *Teta Kawi Trailer Park* (☎ (622) 6-02-20) 9½ km west of the Highway 15 San Carlos exit. Near the marina docks is the *Shangri-la & Trailer Park* where campsites with full hook-ups are also sometimes available.

Buses to San Carlos from Guaymas run about every half-hour along Avenida Serdán in Guaymas. The beaches are worth a day

visit from Guaymas. Part of *Catch-22* was filmed on the beach near the Club Mediterranée; only a few rusty pieces of the set remain.

The San Carlos Diving Center (☎ (622) 6-00-49) rents scuba and snorkeling equipment and conducts boat trips for sightseeing, fishing and diving around the bay. You can probably arrange some trips on your own for less if you negotiate with local fishermen.

CIUDAD OBREGÓN & NAVOJOA

The highway south from Guaymas passes through Ciudad Obregón, a modern agricultural town with nothing of touristic interest, and Navojoa, a similarly mundane place. In Navojoa there are several banks along Highway 15.

From Navojoa, however, a side road leaves Highway 15 and heads east 53 km into the foothills of the Sierra Madre Ocidental to the picturesque town of Alamos, once a mining centre, now a desert retreat for those in the know.

The bus station to Alamos is inconveniently located at least 40 minutes' walk from the main bus station. Unless you want to breathe in lots of noxious fumes and experience heat exhaustion, don't even consider walking. A taxi between the two bus stations is worth every last cent of the US$3 fare.

ALAMOS

Population: 5000

In 1540, Francisco Vázquez de Coronado camped here on his way to subjugating the Mayo Indians, attempting to subdue the Yaqui Indians (not fully achieved until 1928) and becoming the governor of New Galicia (presently western Mexico). If he had known about the vast amounts of gold and silver that prospectors would later find, he would have stayed.

By 1781, Alamos was a busy mining centre with a population of more than 30,000. A well-trodden mule trail through the foothills connected Alamos with

Culiacán and El Fuerte to the south. Several opulent haciendas, a cathedral, tanneries, metal works and blacksmith shops were built.

After Mexico won independence from Spain, Alamos became the capital of the newly formed state of Occidente, which comprised the present states of Sonora and Sinaloa. Don José María Aldama, was appointed provisional vice governor. By that time the Aldama family was well established in Alamos. Throughout much of the 19th century and up to the Mexican Revolution, Alamos and the surrounding area festered with political strife and violence, a situation not unlike most of Mexico at that time. By the 1920s, most of the population had left and many of the once-beautiful haciendas were in disrepair. Alamos became a sleepy little town until the late 1940s.

After WW II, Alamos was awakened by the arrival of William Levant Alcorn, a dairy farmer from Pennsylvania. He moved to Alamos and bought the 15-room Aldama hacienda on Plaza de Armas and restored it as the Hotel Los Portales. After making a fortune in selling Alamos' real estate, he attracted the attention of the American media and was written up in the *Saturday Evening Post*, *National Geographic* and other magazines.

Alcorn, and his company and hotel, are still alive and well. You may find Alcorn himself sitting on the front veranda of his hotel recounting intriguing stories about Alamos.

Orientation

The paved road from Navojoa enters Alamos from the west end and leads to Plaza Alameda and the municipal market. Plaza de Armas and cathedral are two blocks south of the market. The Arroyo La Aduana (Custom-house Stream, which is usually dry) runs along the town's northern edge; the Arroyo Agua Escondida (Secret Waters Stream, also usually dry) along the southern edge. Both converge at the east end with the Arroyo La Barranca (Ravine Stream) which runs from the north-west.

Information

Tourist Office The tourist office (☎ (642) 8-00-53) is under the Hotel Los Portales on Plaza de Armas. Hours are 9 am to 3 pm and 5 to 7 pm Monday to Saturday, 9 am to noon Sunday, though sometimes the woman who runs the place has to leave early to go to her English class.

In addition to the tourist office, there are three tourist guides in town. One of them, José Rosario Yocupicio M, is likely to be either in the tourist office or on Plaza de Armas.

Money You can change money at a bank on the Plaza de Armas.

Telephone There's a caseta de larga distancia in Polo's Restaurant at the corner of Calle Zaragoza and Calle Allende. Long-distance collect calls can be made for a small fee.

La Catedral

The cathedral is the tallest building in Alamos and also one of its oldest. It dates back to 1783 when Bishop Antonio de los Reyes, appointed by King Carlos III of Spain to head the newly established Bishopric of Sonora, Sinaloa and the Californias, established himself at Alamos. According to a town legend, everyone in Alamos contributed something to the construction of the cathedral. Some of the most unusual contributions included fine china plates that were placed at the bases of the pilasters in the church tower.

A three-tiered belfry was built in the tower. Inside, the altar rail, lamps, censers and candelabra were fashioned from silver. All of these items were ordered to be melted down in January 1866 by General Ángel Martínez after he booted French imperialist troops out of Alamos.

El Museo Costumbrista de Sonora

The Museum of Sonoran Customs is on the eastern side of Plaza de Armas. The displays and exhibits covering the history of Sonora and Alamos include photographs from the

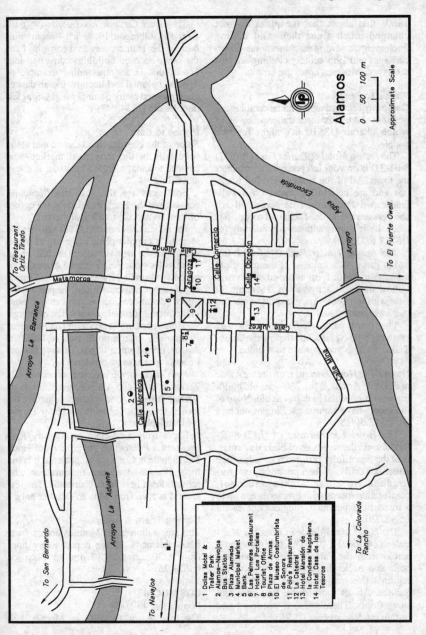

Alamos

0   50   100 m

Approximate Scale

To Restaurant
Ortiz Tirado

To El Fuerte Owell.

Matamoros

Calle Allende

Calle Comercio

Calle Obregón

Zaragoza

Calle Juárez

Calle Morelos

Calle Mina

Arroyo La Barranca

Arroyo La Aduana

Agua Escondida

Arroyo

To San Bernardo

To Navajoa

To La Colorada
Rancho

1 Dolisa Motel &
   Trailer Park
2 Alamos–Navojoa
   Bus Station
3 Plaza Alameda
4 Municipal Market
5 Bank
6 Las Palmeras Restaurant
7 Hotel Los Portales
8 Tourist Office
9 Plaza de Armas
10 El Museo Costumbrista
   de Sonora
11 Polo's Restaurant
12 La Catedral
13 Hotel Mansión de
   la Condesa Magdalena
14 Hotel Casa de los
   Tesoros

1860s that show that the plaza has not changed much since then. Old mining implements, a sewing machine, horse-drawn carriages and 19th-century clothing are also displayed. Museum hours are erratic.

Places to Stay

Camping Tent and motor-home camping are possible at Alamos' three trailer parks, all of which charge US$10 per night for two people.

The *Dolisa Motel & Trailer Park* (☎ (642) 8-01-31) is on your left just before you enter the town. All of the spaces have full hook-ups and are behind the motel on a well-landscaped lot. Clean bathrooms and hot showers are available. The motel section has clean, basic rooms with air-conditioning for US$17 to US$20.

The *Acosta Trailer Park* (☎ (642) 8-02-46) is just over a km east of the municipal market on a fruit farm at the edge of town. Follow the signs across town. There are 30 sites with full hook-ups, a laundry room and two swimming pools.

The third park, *Real de los Alamos* (☎ (642) 8-03-32) is a little before the Dolisa Trailer Park as you come in to Alamos.

Hotels The *Hotel Enríquez*, on the west side of Plaza de Armas, is in a 250-year-old building with rooms that look just as old. None of the rooms have bathrooms. Singles/doubles are US$7.50/15.

The *Hotel Los Portales* (☎ (642) 8-02-01), also on the west side of Plaza de Armas, is in the beautifully restored hacienda of the Aldama family. A central courtyard surrounded by stone arches and cool, comfortable rooms with fireplaces add up to a romantic experience. Singles/doubles are US$27/30.

The *Hotel Mansión de la Condesa Magdalena* (☎ (642) 8-02-21), Calle Obregón 2 across from the Palacio de Gobierno, was built as a hacienda in 1685 for one of the region's first major mining families, the Salidos. All 13 rooms have fireplaces and stone floors. There's also a whirlpool and restaurant. Rooms cost US$30.

The *Hotel Casa de los Tesoros* (☎ (642) 8-00-10), Obregón 10, is a 14-room 'inn' built in the 18th century as a convent. Like the other restored buildings converted into hotels, this is an outstanding example of Spanish colonial architecture. Indian dances are presented every Saturday night. Singles/doubles are US$40/47.

Places to Eat

Some of the cheapest food can be had at the foodstalls in the municipal market. The ceviche tostada, a seafood tostada, is cheap and filling.

For tacos try the *Taquería Blanquita* across from the Plaza Alameda at the corner of Rosales and the municipal market.

For delicious tortas (at US$1 each), try the incredibly popular place at the top of Matamoros (across the river and up the hill) about 15-minutes walk from Plaza de Armas. Supposedly it is called *Restaurant Ortiz Tirado*, but everyone just knows it as 'the place at the top of Matamoros where you can get those great tortas'. It is only open in the evenings.

'Home cooking' is served at *Las Palmeras Restaurant*, on the north side of Plaza de Armas, from 7 am to 10 pm. This is a favourite among expatriate residents.

Polo's Restaurant is on the corner of Calle Zaragosa and Calle Allende, just off Plaza de Armas. It has a good reputation among the locals, though it seems to be better known for its telephones.

For a truly first-class splurge try *Restaurant La Pithaya* on the grounds of Hotel Mansión de la Condesa Magdalena. It is run by a French-Moroccan restaurateur who moved down here from California. The restaurant is open from May to October only.

Getting There & Away

The bus station is on Morelos across from Plaza Alameda. Buses depart every hour from 6.30 am to 6.30 pm for Navojoa (US$1.25).

LOS MOCHIS

Population: 130,000
The only reason to visit Los Mochis is to

catch a train, boat or bus to someplace else. The Chihuahua al Pacífico railroad from Topolobampo through Los Mochis to the Copper Canyon and Chihuahua was completed in 1961 and instantly considered an engineering marvel.

Orientation

It's difficult to get lost in Los Mochis because, unlike the streets in many Mexican cities, the streets here don't have more than one name. Avenida Gabriel Leyva, the main street through the city, runs directly south-west from Highway 15.

Central Los Mochis can be considered the area that is within two or three blocks of the intersection of Avenidas Leyva and Álvaro Obregón.

Information

Post The post office is on Hidalgo between Guerrero and Flores. Hours are 8 am to 6 pm Monday to Friday, and 8 am to noon on Saturday.

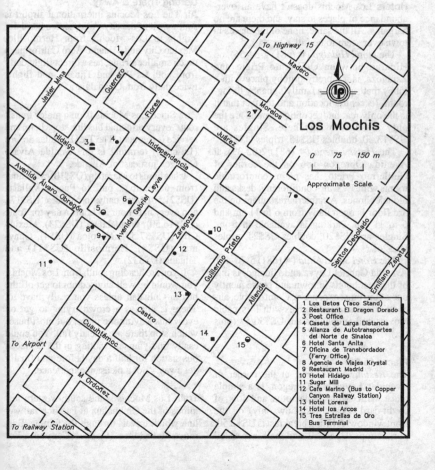

Los Mochis

0   75   150 m

Approximate Scale

1 Los Betos (Taco Stand)
2 Restaurant El Dragon Dorado
3 Post Office
4 Caseta de Larga Distancia
5 Alianza de Autotransportes del Norte de Sinaloa
6 Hotel Santa Anita
7 Oficina de Transbordador (Ferry Office)
8 Agencia de Viajes Krystal
9 Restaurant Madrid
10 Hotel Hidalgo
11 Sugar Mill
12 Cafe Marino (Bus to Copper Canyon Railway Station)
13 Hotel Lorena
14 Hotel los Arcos
15 Tres Estrellas de Oro Bus Terminal

Telephone A caseta de larga distancia can be found on Flores between Independencia and Hidalgo, in a casa de cambio next to the Hotel Monte Carlo.

Places to Stay

Camping The *Los Mochis Trailer Park* (☎ (681) 2-00-21), one km west of Highway 15, has 140 spaces with full hook-ups. There are also hot showers, a laundry room and restaurant. They charge US$10 for two per night.

Hotels Los Mochis doesn't have an overabundance of places to stay, and there are no bargains. All the same, none of the places in town ever seem to be full.

The *Hotel Hidalgo* (☎ (681) 2-34-56), on Hidalgo between Guillermo Prieto and Zaragoza, is a a pretty grubby place with a lobby that's part of a family's shabby livingroom. Its central location and the fact that it is the only real budget option around are the only reasons to stay here. Singles are US$13.50, doubles US$15, triples US$17.

The *Hotel Lorena* (☎ (681) 2-02-39), at Avenida Obregón 186 on the corner of Guillermo Prieto, has plain, comfortable rooms with TVs, air-conditioning, desks and old telephones. A cafeteria/restaurant on the 3rd floor is open daily from 6 to 11 am and 6 to 11 pm. Parking is available in front. Singles are US$20, doubles US$24, triples US$26.

The *Hotel Santa Anita* (☎ (681) 5-70-46), Avenida Gabriel Leyva and Hidalgo, is one of the best hotels in town and consequently one of the most expensive. Comfortable, airconditioned singles/doubles with TVs, cable movies and telephones are US$50/57 (plus tax).

Places to Eat

The *Restaurant Madrid*, at the corner of Avenidas Leyva and Obregón, is a simple place with white tablecloths and lots of credit-card decals (for show only) on the front window. A filling breakfast is US$2.50, pork chops US$3.50 and half a roasted chicken US$2.50. All dishes are served with tortillas and refried beans.

The best tacos in Los Mochis are at *Los Betos*, corner of Juárez and Guerrero. Another decent taco stand is *El Taquito* on Avenida Gabriel Leyva between Independencia and Hidalgo.

The *Restaurant El Dragon Dorado*, at Morelos and Zaragoza, is a Chinese restaurant without chopsticks and with chop suey. You can get a fairly good-sized meal here for under US$5.

Getting There & Away

Air The Los Mochis international airport is south-west of the city. Aeroméxico has daily flights to Los Mochis from Hermosillo, Mexico City and Tijuana. Aero California, a much smaller airline, has a direct flight daily from both La Paz and Tijuana, and flights twice daily from Guadalajara.

Bus Since Los Mochis is on a major transit route, every principal bus line stops here, and service is frequent. The Tres Estrellas de Oro (1st-class) terminal is on Avenida Álvaro Obregón just east of Allende.

It has buses to Mazatlán (US$10) every hour from 6 am to 2 pm, to Puerto Vallarta (US$21.50) twice daily, to Nogales (US$17), and every half-hour 24 hours a day to: Tepic (US$16.50), Guadalajara (US$23), Mexico City (US$37.50), Navojoa (US$4), Guaymas (US$8), Hermosillo (US$11) and Tijuana (US$32).

If you are heading south from Los Mochis, you would be well advised not to get off the bus in Culiacán unless you really have to. There is always a crowd trying to get on every bus leaving the place, but most buses which stop there are already full. You could easily find yourself waiting in the Culiacán bus station for half a day before you finally get away – not a pleasant experience.

Train Los Mochis is the south-western terminus of the Chihuahua al Pacífico railway line which travels through the famous Barranca del Cobre (Copper Canyon). For details on this train, see the Barranca del Cobre – Copper Canyon section.

Ferrocarril del Pacífico trains do not stop in Los Mochis proper, but in El Sufragio/San Blas about 52 km to the north. See the Barranca del Cobre – Copper Canyon section for details.

Boat The ferry to La Paz departs from Topolobampo, 24 km south of Los Mochis, at 10 am on Monday, Thursday and Friday. Tickets can be bought the day before departure from the Oficina de Transbordador (ferry office) (☎ (681) 2-00-35) in Los Mochis at Juárez 125 between Allende and Guillermo Prieto. Office hours are 8 am to 12.30 pm Monday to Friday, and 8 am to 1.30 pm Saturday and Sunday. A salon seat costs US$10.

Getting Around

Everything in Los Mochis except the Chihuahua al Pacífico railway station is within walking distance of the centre (the intersection of Avenidas Leyva and Obregón). The railway station for the Chihuahua al Pacífico railway to Copper Canyon and Chihuahua is at the south-eastern edge of Los Mochis, two km from the centre.

To get to the railway station, you can either take a taxi (US$5, even at 5 am) or a bus (not possible at 5 am when you most need it) from Café Marino, on Zaragoza between Avenidas Obregón and Hidalgo. At 5 am taxis to the train station can also always be found in front of the Hotel Santa Anita, at the corner of Avenida Gabriel Leyva and Hidalgo. For details on trains, see the Getting There & Away and Copper Canyon sections.

The closest railway station for the Ferrocarril del Pacífico to Mexicali and Guadalajara is 52 km north-east of Los Mochis at San Blas/El Sufragio.

Buses north to San Blas (for El Sufragio, the Ferrocarril del Pacífico railway station) and south to Topolobampo (the Baja ferry terminal) leave from two terminals on Avenida Álvaro Obregón, between Avenida

Gabriel Leyva and Flores across from the Agencia de Viajes Krystal. Alianza de Autotransportes del Norte de Sinaloa and Transportistas del Valle del Fuerte buses run from each terminal.

BARRANCA DEL COBRE – COPPER CANYON

The Chihuahua al Pacífico train route between Los Mochis and Chihuahua is among Mexico's most scenic rail journeys. A considerable feat of engineering, the line is used heavily to transport passengers and freight, but it is also becoming one of the country's prime touristic excursions.

You can take the train from either Los Mochis or Chihuahua. If you start from Los Mochis, you have a better chance of seeing the dramatic scenery. The trains are almost always late, so pray that the inevitable delays occur after, not before, you've seen some of the best parts of the landscape. The trains from Chihuahua seem to run late more often and by more hours than the ones from Los Mochis.

Starting from Los Mochis, the journey to Chihuahua takes almost 14 hours, with stops at El Sufragio/San Blas (the junction with Ferrocarril del Pacífico trains) and Creel in the Copper Canyon. There are two trains – the vistatren and the mixto. The first train costs more, but it's faster, cleaner, more comfortable and usually air-conditioned or heated. It affords better views of the canyon too.

To be absolutely sure of a seat, you can buy your ticket well in advance from Mexico by Rail (☎ (512) 727-3814 or toll-free in the USA (800) 228-3225; fax (512) 727-8520), PO Box 3508, Laredo, TX 78044-3508 USA. This costs considerably more (US$80 to Creel, US$100 for the entire run between Los Mochis and Chihuahua), but assures you of a seat, and includes a box lunch. Mexico by Rail also arranges tours with overnight stops in Los Mochis, Creel and Chihuahua.

Otherwise, tickets for the vistatren (US$28.50 to Chihuahua, US$16.50 to Creel) may be available the day before departure in Los Mochis at the Agencia

Viajes Flamingo (☎ (681) 2-19-29), at Hidalgo 419 around the corner from the Hotel Santa Anita. If there are still seats, tickets can be bought on departure day after 5 am (Mountain Time), but be prepared to elbow through a crowd to get to the station's only ticket window. Mixto tickets to Chihuahua and Creel cost US$8.50 and US$5.25, a good deal only if you're ready for what might be either a cold or hot (no heating or air-con), crowded trip that passes the most spectacular scenery after dark.

Warning: the Copper Canyon train runs on Central Time (the time in Chihuahua), even though Los Mochis runs on Mountain Time. Thus, the train schedule in Los Mochis will read 'departure at 7 am', which means that the train leaves Los Mochis at 6 am Mountain Time. The rule is to expect departures *one hour earlier* if you're boarding in Los Mochis, El Sufragio/San Blas or El Fuerte, all of which are in the Mountain Time zone. Here's the schedule :

Copper Canyon Train Timetable (in Central Time)

departures	vistatren	mixto
Los Mochis	7.00 am*	8.00 am*
El Sufragio	7.46 am	9.11 am
El Fuerte	8.28 am	10.04 am
Temoris	11.12 am	1.24 pm
San Rafael	1.17 pm	4.03 pm
Divisadero	1.58 pm	4.46 pm
Creel	3.20 pm	6.18 pm
La Junta	5.41 pm	9.05 pm
Cuauhtémoc	6.29 pm	10.15 pm
Chihuahua	8.43 pm	1.05 am

* Note: this is 6 & 7 am in Los Mochis

Trains tend to run late; cargo trains en route cause delays. For a timetable of departures from Chihuahua, see the Getting There & Away section for that town in the North-West Mexico chapter.

The Ferrocarril del Pacífico trains stop at El Sufragio/San Blas, and you can theoretically transfer there to or from the Copper Canyon train. But train schedules are not usually adhered to closely, so don't plan a close connection; it's better to take a bus to Los Mochis and arrange your ticket there. Remember also that the Copper Canyon train runs on Central Time, but El Sufragio is in the Mountain Time zone. Ferrocarril del Pacífico trains stop at El Sufragio/San Blas at the following times (Mountain Time):

northbound	southbound
arr 12.10 am	arr 8.30 pm
dep 12.20 am	dep 9.00 pm
arr 8.55 am	arr 2.10 am
dep 9.30 am	dep 2.25 am

Along the Way

As the sun rises, the train passes through flat, gray farmland and gradually begins to climb through fog-shrouded hills. The land takes on the bluish-white hue of dawn until the first rays of sunlight creep over the hilltops and colour everything pale yellow. Like fingers popping up from beneath the desert, dark pillars of cacti become visible.

About three hours from Los Mochis the train passes over the harrowing Río Fuerte bridge and through the first of 88 tunnels. The train will pass over 38 more bridges: the Copper Canyon is deeper and grander than the USA's more famous Grand Canyon. The railway line from Chihuahua to Los Mochis cost US$90 million and took almost 90 years to build.

The train cuts through small canyons and hugs the sides of cliffs as it climbs higher and higher through the mountains of the Sierra Tarahumara, a sub-range of the Sierra Madre Occidental. The trip becomes a whirlwind of dramatic geological images – sheer craggy cliffs towering above and vertical canyon walls leading to a riverbed far below. Seven hours out of Los Mochis, the train stops for 15 minutes at Divisadero for the first and only true view of the Copper Canyon. Along the rest of the trip, the train runs through pine forests skirting the edge of the canyon, but not close enough to see down into it. Unless you plan to hike into the 2300-metre-deep

Top: Pacific Ocean-side beach at Cabo San Lucas; Land's End in the distance, Baja California (RB)

Bottom: Rock formations at Land's End, including El Arco (The Arch); Los Cabos, Baja California (RB)

Top: Port of Ensenada, Baja California (GA)
Left: Agua Caliente tower, Tijuana (SW)
Right: Bullfight poster (SW)

canyon, the viewpoint at Divisadero is the only chance you'll get to see it.

This will also probably be the first time you see some of the Tarahumara Indians who inhabit the canyon. The Indians come up from the canyon to display and sell their handicrafts to visitors.

The *Posada Barranca del Cobre* hotel (Chihuahua (☎ (14) 6-59-50) is also at Divisadero near the canyon rim. Double

Tarahumara Indians

More than 50,000 Tarahumara Indians live in the canyons of the Sierra Tarahumara, the Copper Canyon being only one of them. Although the Tarahumara are the second-largest Indian tribe north of Mexico City (the largest is the Navajo), they have also been one of the most isolated groups and have therefore been able to maintain many of their traditions.

One such tradition is the *tesquinada*, the object of which is to consume copious amounts of potent *tesquino* or corn beer. Between tesquinadas the Indians run nonstop through many km of rough, often vertical, terrain along the canyon sides.

Many of them still live in caves, a few of which can be seen near Creel, and subsist on corn tortillas and refried beans.

Catholic missionaries have made some progress improving living conditions for the Tarahumara, but they haven't been entirely successful in converting them to Catholicism. Many of the Tarahumara attend church services, but their ancestral gods are still worshipped, particularly Raiénari, the sun god and protector of men, and Mechá, the moon god and protector of women. Sorcerers are as important as Catholic priests and are the only members of the Tarahumara permitted to consume peyote, a hallucinogen derived from a small cactus. They often take peyote in order to perform a bizarre peyote dance to cure the sick. ■

rooms with fireplaces, which you'll need in winter, are US$68, including all meals.

Although the hotel will arrange a guided tour for you into the canyon, you can arrange a far better deal with one of the Tarahumara Indians yourself. You must have your own food for the trip; there are two restaurants, but no stores in Divisadero. For US$22 your guide will lead you down 1820 metres to the Río Urique. Carry enough water for the descent and be prepared for a change in climate from very cold – Divisadero is over 2460 metres (8070 feet) high – to warm and humid near the river. Fall is the best time to come because flash floods and suffocatingly high temperatures are a problem in the summer.

Books & Maps

One of the best books written about the Copper Canyon trails is Rick Fisher's *National Parks of Northwest Mexico, Volume II*, available from Sunracer Publications, PO Box 40092, Tucson, Arizona 85717, USA.

Topographical maps of the canyon can be obtained from the Dirección General de Geografía del Territorio Nacional, San Antonio Abaz No 124, 5th floor, Mexico City, Mexico DF. The *San Jacinto map no 6 13-1, Chihuahua* map is recommended. A general map of the Copper Canyon region can be ordered from the International Map Company, 5316 Santa Teresa, El Paso, Texas, USA. Decent topographical maps and the general map can be bought at the Tarahumara Mission Store in Creel, which is the next train stop after Divisadero.

CREEL

Altitude: 2338 metres

It's easier to begin a trek into the canyon from Creel because, in addition to maps, you can stock up on staples and catch a bus to Batopilas, a village 140 km away deep in the heart of the canyon and Tarahumara country. Creel is also a convenient jump-off point for an all-day trip to Basaseachic Falls or Cusárare Falls or half-day hikes to nearby lakes.

Information

Money Banca Serfin on the plaza changes money from 10.30 am to noon, Monday to Friday. If possible don't leave your money-changing until Friday, as the bank has been known to run out of cash.

Post The post office is on the other side of the plaza in the Presidencia Municipal.

Telephone There's a caseta de larga distancia in the Hotel Nuevo, across the tracks from the railway station.

Hikes & Tours

Daniel, husband of Margarita (of Casa de Margarita described below), offers several trips to the surrounding countryside, a few of which could probably be done on your own. The following are condensed descriptions of the trips:

Recohuata Hot Springs The day trip begins with a 1½-hour truck ride and then a hike down 607 metres (1991 feet) into the canyon to the hot springs. It's for groups only, and costs US$10 per person.

Lago Arareco Lake Arareco is an easy seven-km hike from town along the graded dirt road to Cusárare. Hitchhiking is also relatively easy. A few caves inhabited by Tarahumara Indians can be seen along the way. At the lake there's an old log cabin that was used as a set for the filming of a Mexican movie, *El Refugio del Lobo* (Refuge of the Wolf).

Cascada Cusárare The 30-metre-high Cusárare waterfall is 22 km south of Creel near the village of Cusárare. As you get near the town, look for a small roadside shrine and km marker on the right side of the road. Just past that is a small sign that marks the road to the 'Cascada – Waterfall Hotel'. Follow that road to the right for three km, crossing the river three or four times. When the road ends, follow the trail to the top of the waterfall. The trail winds around to the bottom of the falls. Hitchhiking to the 'hotel' road is usually easy. A group is needed for this and it also costs US$10 per person.

San Ignacio & Tarahumara Caves Follow Avenida Mateos south, passing the town cemetery on your left, and continue straight ahead. Caves will appear on both sides of the road before you eventually arrive at the small village of San Ignacio, where there's a 400-year-old mission church.

Valley of the Monks The valley is nine km away and is considered a day trip by horse. Ask Daniel about renting one.

Río Urique On the map this excursion looks like a long one because the river flows along the bottom of the Copper Canyon; but it can be done in a day for US$22 per person.

Río Oteros The Río Oteros walk is considered a day hike; ask before you go.

Baseachic Falls These and other tours can also be arranged by the Hotel Nuevo, and the Motel Parador, on Mateos about five blocks from the plaza. The Parador offers full-day tours to Basaseachic Falls, 140 km northwest of town. The waters of Basaseachic fall 245 metres, the second-highest drop in the world (the biggest drop is at Angel Falls in Venezuela), and are worth the bumpy four-hour drive and 1½-hour hike from Creel (each way). The best deal on this works out at around US$25 per person. The Parador also offers a general tour of the Copper Canyon.

Places to Stay
At an elevation of 2338 metres (7670 feet), Creel can be cold, even snowy, especially in the winter. Warm rooms are available in town at a few hotels and guest houses.

One of the homiest places to stay is the *Casa de Margarita*, Mateos 11, in a house on the corner of the plaza. Margarita or her son usually meet the train each evening to snare any backpackers who need a place to stay. There are around 40 beds, and prices start at US$5 for a simple bunk berth in an open

dormitory and move up to around US$22 for a single with a private bathroom.

The price includes a reasonable breakfast and an excellent dinner. Both meals are shared (in two or three sittings due to the crowd) with the family. For reservations write to Margarita Quintero de González, Avenida López Mateos y Parroquia 11, Creel, Chihuahua 33200, México. Otherwise call Margarita no more than 24 hours before you arrive on (145) 6-00-45.

The *Hotel Korachi* has clean, log cabin-style rooms with wood stoves and hot-water showers. It is directly next to the bus station. Singles are US$7 to US$14; doubles are US$9 to US$22; and triples are US$14 to US$27.50.

The *Motel Parador de la Montaña* (Chihuahua ☎ (14) 15-54-08, 12-20-62) is a favourite with tour groups. It has very comfortable singles for US$31, doubles for US$40, and triples at US$48, including TVs and hot showers.

The *Hotel Nuevo*, across from the railway station, has clean, comfortable rooms. Some of them have wood-burning stoves, others have fireplaces. Singles/doubles start at US$17.50/22. The best rooms cost US$53.

Places to Eat
Creel doesn't have many restaurants. *Restaurant Mary* is one of the few that serves passable food. Basically most people have dinner and breakfast in their hotel, and lunch while taking in the surrounding natural wonders.

There are two grocery stores on Mateos where you can buy fruit, vegetables and a few other staples. For some reason, peanuts are in abundance.

Things to Buy
The Tarahumara Mission Store is open from 9.30 am to 1 pm and 3 to 6 pm. The money earned from selling Tarahumara handicrafts, photographs and books about the Indians goes back to them. The Catholic missionaries who run the store are a fount of knowledge about the Indians and the various canyons and rivers of the Copper Canyon and Sierra Tarahumara.

Getting There & Away

Bus There are daily buses from Creel to Chihuahua (US$6.50, five hours) via San Juanito, La Junta and Cuauhtémoc at 7 am, 9 am, 10 am, 11.30 am, 1 pm, 2.30 pm, 4 pm and 5.30 pm; the trip takes four to six hours. The ticket office and departure point is on the other side of the train tracks across from the plaza.

Buses to Batopilas (US$8, seven to 10 hours) leave on Tuesday, Thursday and Saturday at 7 am. The bus departs from a shop one block from the Chihuahua bus office on the second street from the train tracks. There's always a broken-down red-and-white bus in front of the shop. Tickets are sold until 8 pm. The return bus from Batopilas to Creel departs at 4 am on Monday, Wednesday and Friday.

Train See the Barranca del Cobre – Copper Canyon section for rail schedules from Los Mochis. For schedules from Chihuahua, see that section in the North-Central Mexico chapter.

BATOPILAS

The village of Batopilas, 140 km south of Creel deep in the heart of the canyon country, is a great starting point for treks into the canyons. There are a few small hotels and guest houses where you can rent rooms, including the hotels *Batopilas, Samachique, Napuchi* and *Parador*. The bus from Creel costs US$8.

MAZATLÁN

Population: 260,000

Mazatlán ('mah-zaht-LAHN'), a beach resort jammed with package tourists, is also a shrimp-packing and port city. The Spaniards began using the area as a port in 1531 to send off galleons full of Sierra Madre gold. They were the ones who named it Mazatlán, which means Place of the Deer in Nahuatl. Today the only deer in sight are plastered on billboards advertising tobacco. There are few signs of the long-standing Spanish presence here, even in 'old' Maz-

atlán. All the same, Mazatlán can be fun if you need some beach time.

Orientation

Old Mazatlán is concentrated on a wide peninsula at the southern end of the city, bound on the west by the Pacific Ocean and on the east by the Bahía Dársena. Highways 15 and 40 merge before they enter the city from the east and south-east and become Calzada Gabriel Leyva just after passing the railway station.

Just after Calzada Gabriel Leyva passes the marina on the left, Avenida del Puerto forks off to the south and continues along the edge of the peninsula, passing docks for launches to Isla de la Piedra, cruise-ship docks and the Baja ferry terminal. After the ferry terminal, Avenida del Puerto curves around to the Pacific Ocean side of the peninsula and runs along the coast passing two *miradores* (look-out points) and briefly becomes Paseo Centenario. It changes names again to Paseo Olas Altas as it curves around a small cove that was once *the* resort centre of Mazatlán, and finally becomes Paseo Claussen.

Calle Ángel Flores cuts across the peninsula from Olas Altas north-eastward through downtown Mazatlán and almost all the way to the cruise-ship docks on the other side. It passes old Mazatlán's two principal plazas – Plaza Hidalgo and Plaza de la República (also called the zócalo). Almost everything of interest to travellers, including budget hotels, can be found from Ángel Flores north/north-westward towards Paseo Claussen and Avenida del Mar (the continuation of Paseo Claussen).

The Golden Zone (Zona de Oro), part of 'new Mazatlán', is a long stretch of resort hotels and time-share condominiums that begins just after the traffic circle junction for Highway 15 (alternate route) across from the Hotel Los Sábalos. Avenida del Mar splits into two streets and changes names to Avenida Camarón-Sábalo (the inland branch) and R T Loaiza (the coastal branch, more commonly known just as Playa Las Gaviotas). This area is rapidly expanding

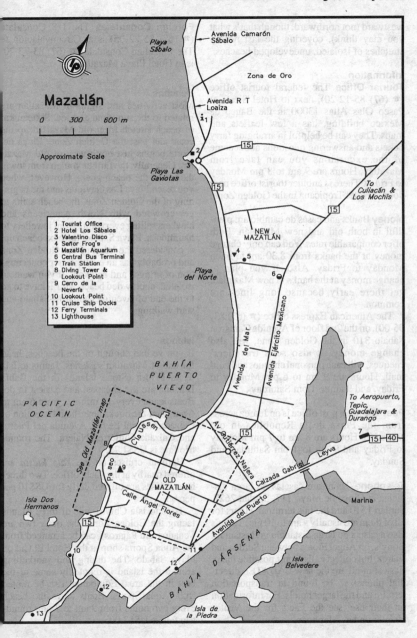

Mazatlán

0   300   600 m

Approximate Scale

1 Tourist Office
2 Hotel Los Sábalos
3 Valentino Disco
4 Señor Frog's
5 Mazatlán Aquarium
6 Central Bus Terminal
7 Train Station
8 Diving Tower & Lookout Point
9 Cerro de la Nevería
10 Lookout Point
11 Cruise Ship Docks
12 Ferry Terminals
13 Lighthouse

Playa Sábalo

Avenida Camarón Sábalo

Zona de Oro

Avenida R T Loaiza

Playa Las Gaviotas

To Culiacán & Los Mochis

NEW MAZATLÁN

Playa del Norte

Avenida del Mar

Avenida Ejército Mexicano

BAHÍA PUERTO VIEJO

PACIFIC OCEAN

Claussen

Paseo

See Old Mazatlán map

Isla Dos Hermanos

OLD MAZATLÁN

Av Gutiérrez Nájera

Calle Ángel Flores

Calzada Gabriel Leyva

To Aeropuerto, Tepic, Guadalajara & Durango

Marina

Avenida del Puerto

BAHÍA DÁRSENA

Isla Belvedere

Isla de la Piedra

westward (not northward, though that's what you may think), covering the last nearby stretches of isolated, undeveloped beaches.

Information

Tourist Office The federal tourist office (☎ (67) 85-12-20), next to Hotel Siesta at Paseo Olas Altas 13000 in the Banco de México building, has a few leaflets and maps. They can be helpful in arranging ferry tickets and answering questions about some of the excursions you can take from Mazatlán. Hours are 9 am to 8 pm Monday to Friday. There is another tourist office next door to Hotel Tropicana in the Golden Zone.

Money Banks and casas de cambio are plentiful in both old and new Mazatlán. Both offer comparable rates. You can only change money at the banks from 8.30 am to noon Monday to Friday. Also, if you plan to change money at the banks in new Mazatlán, get there early because long lines are common.

The American Express office (☎ (67) 83-06-00), on the 2nd floor of Avenida Camarón Sábalo 310 in the Golden Zone, will also change money. It also sells travellers' cheques, will cash personal cheques and hold mail. Hours are 9 am to 6 pm Monday to Friday, and 9 am to 1 pm Saturday .

Post The main post office is on Juárez across from the Plaza de la República in old Mazatlán. Hours are 8 am to 7 pm Monday to Friday and 9 am to 1 pm Saturday and Sunday.

Telephone There are casetas de larga distancia at Cinco de Mayo 117, Serdán 2627, Serdán 1510 and the bus terminal. Hours for all of them are usually 9 am to 10 pm. There's also a caseta de larga distancia in Restaurant Bony's, on Ángel Flores between Serdán and Juárez, but collect calls aren't possible there. Easiest of all are the new LADATEL direct-dial phones to be found in transportation termini and the larger hotels. For information on their use, see the Facts for the Visitor chapter under Telephone.

Foreign Consulates The US Consulate (☎ (67) 85-22-05) is at Circunvalación 6. The Canadian Consulate (☎ (67) 83-73-20) is in Hotel Playa Mazatlán.

Beaches

Most activities and sights in Mazatlán are related to the sun, sand and sea. Sixteen km of beach stretch from old Mazatlán up the coast and past the Golden Zone. Playa del Norte begins just north-west of old Mazatlán. Generally, the farther you go from town, the fewer the beach-goers. However, when you reach Playa Las Gaviotas and the beginning of the Golden Zone, the beach starts to get crowded with North Americans and hawkers selling everything from jewellery to hammocks. Playa Sábalo, the next beach up, is considered the heart of the Golden Zone and probably has an even greater concentration of gringos and hawkers. If you want an isolated, uncrowded beach, you'll have to go to the end of Avenida Camarón-Sábalo and start walking.

Islands

If you've had enough of the beaches, head for one of Mazatlán's islands. Jaunts to Isla de la Piedra (Stone Island) in the Bahía Dársena are the cheapest and easiest to do. Boats leave every 15 minutes from 6 am to 6 pm from the docks near the intersection of Calzada Gabriel Leyva, Avenida del Puerto and Calzada Gutiérrez Najera. The round-trip fare is US$1.75.

Harbour cruises on the *Yate Fiesta* are offered nearby at the yacht office. Two three-hour cruises are offered daily for US$10 per person.

Trips to Isla Chivas, one of three islands facing the Golden Zone (the other two are Venados and Pájaros), can be arranged from the Aqua Sports shop at the Hotel El Cid on Playa Sábalo. The diving and snorkelling around the island is reputedly some of the best in the area. Equipment can be rented from Aqua Sports. Boats leave the beach every two hours from 9 am to 7 pm; round-trip fare is US$3.00.

Acuario Mazatlán

The Mazatlán Aquarium is on Avenida de los Deportes, just north of the Sands Hotel and about a block from Playa del Norte. They claim to have over 200 kinds of fish, including piranhas and marlins, in 51 tanks. Hours are 9.30 am to 6 pm daily. Admission is US$3.50. There are sea lion shows at 1 pm, 3 pm and 4 pm.

High Divers

When the weather permits, there are high divers in Mazatlán similar to Acapulco's famous La Quebrada high divers. The divers' towers are near the lookout point at the base of the Cerro de la Nevería. The divers perform in high season and at weekends at around 10 am and again at 4 pm.

Places to Stay – bottom end

Most of Mazatlán's bottom-end accommodation is concentrated near the Plaza de la República and the intersection of Serdán and Avenida del Mar.

Camping Tent space is available at any of the trailer parks in the Golden Zone, but expect to pay resort rates – US$16 to US$20 per night. The parks are often packed with motor homes and portable satellite dishes. Since most of the motor homes have their own bathrooms and showers, the park owners rarely, if ever, clean or repair the park's facilities. You can camp for free on the beach at the end of Avenida Camarón-Sábalo, but safety may be a concern.

Hotels – Old Mazatlán The *Hotel del Centro* (☎ (67) 81-26-73), J M Canizales 18, has several clean, basic singles, doubles and triples with fans for US$10, US$13.50 and US$14. It's near the cathedral and the corner of Juárez and Canizales.

The *Hotel Milan* (☎ (67) 81-35-88), J M Canizales 10, has clean, air-conditioned rooms with telephones and shower/bath combinations. Potted plants and rocking chairs grace the hallways. Singles/doubles are US$12/14.

The *Hotel Beltran* (☎ (67) 82-27-76), Serdán 819, has simple, dormitory-like rooms with fans and hot showers. Singles cost US$8.50, doubles US$10, triples US$12.

The *Hotel México* (☎ (67) 81-38-06), Serdán and México across from the Beltran, is the place to stay only as a last resort. The walls are cracking and full of holes that probably date from the Mexican Revolution. In fact, you could easily imagine Pancho Villa's men staying here. Rooms go for US$8.50, single or double.

The *Hotel San Jorge* (☎ (67) 81-36-95), Serdán 2710 across from the beach, has a sign painted on the front window advertising 'absolutely clean' rooms. The 2nd-floor rooms are pink, clean and cheery, but the walls are smudged with a mysterious substance. Singles/doubles are US$12.50/15.

Hotels – New Mazatlán The *Hotel Emperador* (☎ (67) 82-62-88), Río Panuco s/n across from the bus terminal, is not the best place to stay – hard beds, clean basic rooms, drab halls and dirty stairs. Singles and doubles both cost US$10.

Places to Stay – middle

Marco's Suites (☎ (67) 83-59-98), Avenida del Mar 1234 about halfway between new and old Mazatlán, is a great deal for this price range. Its Icelandic owners, the Arnasons, keep the place super-clean; they live in one of the suites. The suites can accommodate two to four persons and most of them have ocean views and fully equipped kitchens. They charge US$18 per night for each suite.

The *Hotel Siesta* (☎ (67) 81-26-40), Paseo Olas Altas 11 in old Mazatlán, is above El Shrimp Bucket restaurant with most of the rooms overlooking a courtyard full of tropical plants and the Bucket's tables. Everything is painted a different shade of green, which amplifies the tropical atmosphere. Singles cost US$15.45, doubles US$19, triples US$23.

Places to Stay – top end

Mazatlán is full of top-end places to stay. Rates range from US$28/35 for singles/

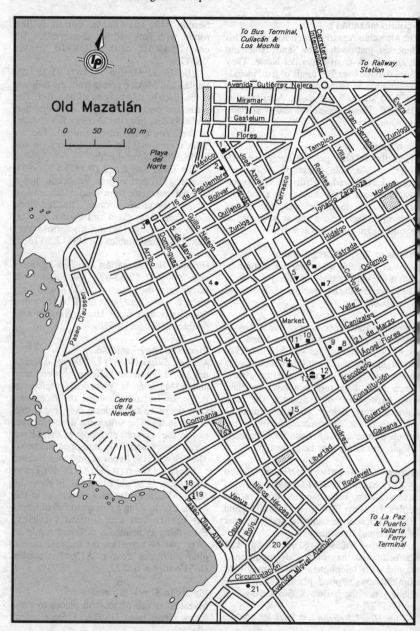

Old Mazatlán

0   50   100 m

Playa
del
Norte

To Bus Terminal,
Culiacán &
Los Mochis

To Railway
Station

Carretera Internacional

Avenida Gutiérrez Nájera

Miramar

Gastelum

Flores

México

16 de Septiembre

Guillo Nelson

Arrillo

Domínguez

5 de Mayo

Bolívar

Quijano

Zúñiga

Merida

José Azueta

Carrasco

Tampico

Fran Serrano

Villa

Rosales

Ignacio Zaragoza

Hidalgo

Estrada

Corlola

Ocampo

Valle

Canizales

21 de Marzo

Ángel Flores

Escobedo

Constitución

Guerrero

Galeana

Market

Paseo Claussen

Cerro
de la
Nevería

Companía

Libertad

Juárez

Roosevelt

To La Paz
& Puerto
Vallarta
Ferry
Terminal

Paseo Olas Altas

Venus

Niños Héroes

Osuna

Rojo

Circunvalación

Avenida Miguel Alemán

Evers

Zúñiga

Morelos

1	Hotel México
2	Hotel Beltran
3	Mexicana Office
4	Parque Zaragoza
5	Lonchería Mary Sol de los Arcos
6	Hotels Vialta & Victoria
7	Casa Familiar Aurora
8	Hotel San Lorenzo
9	Caseta de Larga Distancia
10	Hotel Milan
11	Hotel del Centro
12	Restaurant Bony's
13	Main Post Office
14	Cathedral & Plaza de la República
15	Restaurant Dony
16	Plaza Hidalgo
17	High Divers of Mazatlán
18	El Shrimp Bucket
19	Federal Tourist Office
20	Immigration
21	US Consulate

doubles at the *Sands Hotel* (☎ (67) 82-00-00), on Avenida del Mar, to US$115 for singles and doubles at the *Camino Real* (☎ (67) 83-11-11) at Playa Sábalo.

Places to Eat

The restaurant attached to the *Hotel del Centro*, J M Canizales 18, serves a decent meal that includes a fillet of fish, beans and rice for US$3.

Fresh fish, shrimp and squid can be bought from the street market at the corner of Serdán and Quijano.

The *Restaurant Gypsy*, Avenida del Mar and Río Tamazula facing the ocean, is a good place to have a cheap drink and people-watch. Their food, on the other hand, is not so cheap. They serve a number of different shrimp dishes (from US$13.50) and various fish fillets (from US$8.50).

Avenida Cafetería & Nevería, Avenida del Mar 880, is a big sidewalk café renowned for its coffees and freshly squeezed juices.

Señor Frog's, Avenida del Mar next to the Avenida Cafetería & Nevería, is a Mazatlán landmark that's almost always packed with Americans. Part of the Carlos Anderson chain, Señor Frog's advertises 'lousy food

and warm beer', but actually the food is good (just overpriced) and the beer only warm when they can't cool the bottles fast enough to keep up with demand.

El Shrimp Bucket, Paseo Olas Altas 11, is another eatery that's popular with gringos. Founded in 1962, it was the first of 50 Carlos Anderson bars and grills established in the USA, Mexico, Spain and South America. The shrimp bucket is their speciality at US$13. Other dishes include shrimp cocktail (US$5.50), lobster thermidor (US$15) and a Mexican combo platter (US$7).

Entertainment

Mazatlán is full of discos, most of which are in the Golden Zone. Often recommended are El Caracol at the Hotel El Cid, the Tango Palace, Frankie Oh! and Oh Baby!. Valentino disco is in the very out-of-place, white-washed fairytale castle which dominates new Mazatlán's beachfront. For slightly more mellow entertainment, try Joe's Oyster Bar right on the beach behind Los Sábalos resort hotel (five minutes walk north along the coast from the castle).

Getting There & Away

Air Aeroméxico, Mexicana and Delta all have offices in Mazatlán. Aeroméxico has offices at Serdán 2511 (☎ (67) 84-11-11), the international airport (☎ (67) 82-34-44) and in the Golden Zone at Avenida Camarón Sábalo 310 (☎ (67) 84-16-21), which is their main passenger office.

Mexicana offices may be found at 16 de Septiembre 443 (☎ (67) 81-30-95), Paseo Claussen and Belisario Domínguez (☎ (67) 82-79-69), and the international airport (☎ (67) 82-57-67).

Delta is at the Hotel El Cid (☎ (67) 83-54-55), Avenida Camarón-Sábalo; hours are 9 am to 6 pm Monday through Friday.

Delta Airlines operates direct flights between Mazatlán and Los Angeles daily. Aeroméxico and Mexicana have direct daily flights to Mazatlán from Los Angeles and several Mexican cities including Tijuana, La Paz, Guadalajara and Mexico City.

Bus The central bus terminal is just off Avenida Ejército Mexicano (also known as Avenida Juan Carrasco) and the corner of Avenida de los Deportes, about three blocks inland from Playa Norte.

Tres Estrellas de Oro (1st class) has frequent departures to many major cities, including Mexico City (US$24.50, 18 hours) five times daily, Guadalajara (US$12, nine hours) twice daily, Tijuana (US$42, 26 hours) twice daily, Nogales (US$27.50, 18 hours) and most major points in between twice daily, Tepic (US$7.50, four hours) every hour and Puerto Vallarta (US$11.50, eight hours) twice daily.

Transportes del Pacífico (2nd class) has departures to the same cities at slightly lower prices.

Train The railway station is at the eastern end where Highways 15 and 40 enter the city. The Ferrocarril del Pacífico trains make daily stops in Mazatlán, northbound at 1 am and southbound at 5.40 am.

Average 1st-class fares for the following destinations are: Guadalajara US$4.50, Hermosillo US$7, Nogales US$9 and Mexicali US$12. Tickets can be bought at the train office in the Hotel Hacienda (☎ (67) 82-70-00), Avenida del Mar and Calle Flamingos.

Boat There are daily ferries between Mazatlán and La Paz, Baja California. The ferry departs at 6 pm from a dock at the southern end of town; the trip averages 18 hours. Hard plastic seats are the rule; there are supposedly cabins for rent as well, but reservations are difficult to obtain in normal times, and practically impossible during holidays, especially Semana Santa (Easter Week) and Carnaval (Mardi Gras).

Call the ferry office to make reservations as soon as you arrive in town (☎ (67) 82-21-59). The office is open from 8 am to 3 pm Monday to Friday. Cancellations are sometimes available on the day of departure. Get to the office very early, some say 5 am, if you plan to buy your ticket on the day of departure.

Salon seats cost US$12; per-person rates

for cabins are US$24 (four-person cabin) US$36 (four-person, bathroom and shower in room), and US$48 (two-person deluxe suite).

Ferries from La Paz arrive at about 10 am

Getting Around
To/From the Airport The Mazatlán international airport is 30 km south of the city. There are no buses; you have to take a taxi for US$16 from Old Mazatlán or US$14 from the Golden Zone.

Bus The 'Sábalo' bus runs from the municipal market to the beach via Juárez and then continues along Avenida del Mar all the way to the Golden Zone.

The 'Playa Sur' bus runs along Avenida Ejército Mexicano (Avenida Juan Carrasco) near the central bus terminal and through the city to the municipal market and the ferry terminal.

The 'Villa Galaxia' bus follows the same route as the 'Playa Sur' bus, but doesn't continue past the market.

The 'Insurgentes' bus also runs near the bus terminal and through the city to the market, but goes on to the railway station.

To get into downtown Mazatlán from the bus terminal, go to Avenida Ejército Mexicano and catch a 'Playa Azul' bus going to your right if the bus terminal is behind you. It runs to the ferry terminal through old Mazatlán, near the market, almost every 10 minutes from 6 am to 8 pm.

The 'Cerritos-Juárez' and the 'Insurgentes' buses shuttle between the train station and old Mazatlán.

Taxi Taxis are the most expensive way to get around, but they're also the easiest. Set the price before getting in. If you bargain hard, taxis are only slightly more expensive than *pulmonías*. You should be able to get the fare from old Mazatlán to the Golden Zone down to around US$5. A taxi to Old Mazatlán from the bus station costs around US$3.50.

Pulmonía After buses, pulmonías are the cheapest way to get around the city, particu-

arly along the coast from the Golden Zone
o Playa Olas Altas. Although 'pulmonía'
iterally means 'pneumonia', here it means
golf cart', a small open-air motorised
vehicle. You can flag one down almost anywhere along the Mazatlán coast. From the
Golden Zone to Serdán costs US$4.

TEPIC

Tepic, capital of the state of Nayarit, has
nothing of interest for travellers except a bus
terminal and a railway station. If you have to
stop here, catch the next bus or train as soon
as possible to Mazatlán, which is 278 km
away and five hours by bus, for US$6; Puerto
Vallarta, 169 km, three hours, US$5; Guada-
lajara, 127 km, five hours (because the bus
stops at every village en route); or San Blas,
70 km, approximately one hour, US$1.75.

Norte de Sonora buses to San Blas depart
at 6 am, 9 am, 2.15 pm, 4.30 pm, 5.30 pm
and 6.30 pm.

Southbound Ferrocarril del Pacífico trains
stop here at 11.15 am and 1.45 pm and arrive
in Guadalajara at 5.10 and 7 pm. Northbound
trains stop in Tepic at 2.05 and 6.30 pm and
arrive in Mazatlán at 6.45 pm and 1 am.

SAN BLAS

Population: 6000
The small fishing village of San Blas, 70 km
north-west of Tepic, was an important
Spanish port from the late 16th to the 19th
centuries. The Spanish built a fortress here
to protect their naos (trading galleons) from
marauding British and French pirates.
Today's visitors come to enjoy a paradise
that may seem too good to be true, with
isolated beaches, exotic colourful birds, a
thick tropical jungle where mangos and
papayas are plentiful, navigable rivers and an
estuary.

The village has been discovered by travellers and has the amenities of a small beach
resort town – a few hotels, restaurants,
grocery stores, etc. Fortunately, however, it
is far enough off the beaten track to have the
broken cobblestone streets, muddy potholes
and small shops of a wild frontier town.

One suspects, though, that the real reason

the village hasn't been developed as a major
resort is due to the proliferation of *jejenes*
(nicknamed 'no-see-ums' because they're
difficult to see) at dusk and dawn. No-see-
ums are tiny fly-like creatures with huge
appetites for human flesh that aren't deterred
from attack by normal window screens or
weak insect repellents. These guys slip
through all but the finest mesh screening,
have their fill and leave you with an indom-
itable itch.

Orientation

San Blas sits on a tongue of land bound on
the west/south-west by El Pozo estuary, on
the east by the San Cristóbal estuary, and on
the south by Playa El Borrego and the Pacific
Ocean. The only road into and out of the
village is the 36-km paved road to Highway
15 and onward to Tepic.

Just west of the bridge over the San
Cristóbal estuary, the road passes the Cerro
de la Contaduría and the ruins of the old
Spanish fortress. At the Pemex station, the
road splits into three branches with the centre
one, Juárez, becoming the main street and
leading to the village's small zócalo. Calle
Batallón de San Blas runs along the western
side of the zócalo and leads south to the
beach; this could be considered the village's
other main street. From the zócalo, everything in the village is within walking
distance.

Information

Tourist Office There's a small tourist office
in the Palacio Municipal on the west side of
the zócalo, but they aren't very helpful. You
would be better off trying to get your travel
questions answered at one of the hotels, such
as the Hotel Las Brisas.

Money The only place in town to change
money is the Banco Nacional de México
(Banamex) on Juárez about a block east of
the zócalo. You can change money only from
8.30 to 10.30 am. It is best to turn up early,
as the bank has been known to run out of
money.

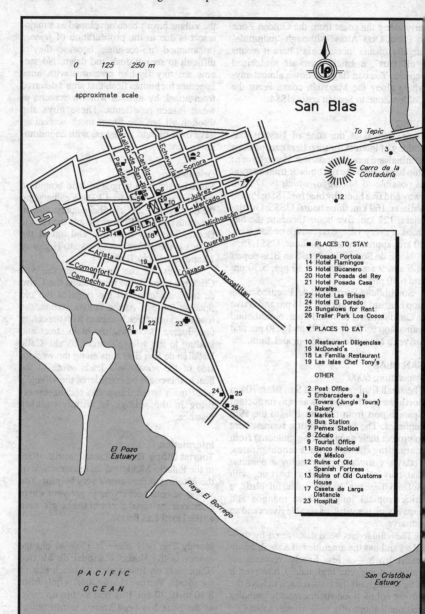

Post The post office is on Michoacán near the south-west corner of the zócalo. Hours are 9 am to 1 pm and 3 to 7 pm Monday to Friday, and 9 am to 1 pm Saturday.

Telephone The small shop and newsstand on the south side of the zócalo doubles as a caseta de larga distancia with two lines for making long-distance telephone calls. Be patient because it could take more than an hour to reach an operator. There are also telephones and a fax and modem service (!) in the bus station.

Beaches
San Blas's best attractions are its natural wonders – the beaches and jungles. The nearest beach is Playa El Borrego at the end of Calle Batallón de San Blas.

The best beaches are south-east of the village around the Bahía de Metanchén, starting with Playa Las Islitas seven km away. A paved road that veers south from the road to Highway 15 passes the dirt road to Playa Las Islitas and continues past an Oceanography School and through the village of Aticama eight km from Playa Las Islitas. Between Playa Las Islitas and Aticama the beach is wonderfully isolated and popular with surfers who claim that the world's longest wave sweeps ashore here.

After Aticama, Playa Los Cocos and Playa Miramar have palapas under which you can lounge and drink from a coconut. You can either walk or take a taxi from San Blas to Playa Las Islitas for US$4 one way. There's also a bus three times daily from San Blas to the village of Santa Cruz, just past Playa Miramar. Occassionally the bus does a detour down to Playa Las Islitas.

Jungle Boat Ride
A maximum of ten passengers hop in a boat at the Embarcadero a la Tovara, to your left as you cross the bridge into town. The guide steers the boat into the San Cristóbal estuary and up a river to the freshwater spring of La Tovara, and beyond to visit a crocodile farm. A jungle full of exotic birds and lush, tropical plants and trees surrounds you. Bring your bathing suit because you can swim at La Tovara. The price is fixed at US$50 for the first four passengers (US$12.50 each) plus US$3.50 per extra person.

Festivals
Father José María Mercado Every year on 31 January the anniversary of the death of Father José María Mercado is commemorated with a parade, a demonstration march by Mexican marines and fireworks in the zócalo. Mercado lived in San Blas in the early 19th century and helped Miguel Hidalgo with the independence movement by sending him a set of old Spanish cannons from the village.

San Blas Day Festivities on 3 February are mainly an extension of those begun on 31 January. Dance and musical presentations are also featured.

Places to Stay
Considering its small size, San Blas has a fair selection of places to stay. Look at the room before you accept it and be sure that the window screens are without holes or tears.

Camping The *Trailer Park Los Cocos* (☎ (321) 5-00-55) is near Playa El Borrego, almost at the end of Calle Batallón de San Blas, in a grassy area with lots of trees. Electricity and showers are available. Beware of the hungry mosquitoes that swarm into the bathrooms at sunset.

At Playa Los Cocos there's a trailer park on the beach next to a few palapa restaurants.

Hotels *Posada Portola* (☎ (321) 5-03-81), at Paredes 118, is one of the best deals you are likely to come across if you are not a solo traveller. Very spacious bungalows with private cooking facilities, a fridge and laundry service go for US$20 for one or two people, US$27 for three and US$33 for four. The place has good security, and the owner, Federico Rodríguez, is always there when you need him.

The *Hotel Las Brisas* (☎ (321) 5-01-12), Cuauhtémoc 106, has 32 large rooms with fans and a suite with a full kitchen. There's a great restaurant, swimming pool and yard full of exotic birds. You can buy ice, soft drinks, snacks and postcards in the reception area. The staff speak English and are extremely helpful. Singles/doubles are US$43/50.

The *Hotel Posada del Rey* (☎ (321) 5-01-23), on the corner of Campeche and a short nameless alley, is a simple, relatively modern place with a small swimming pool. Clean rooms have fans and hot-water showers. Singles cost US$17, doubles US$23, triples US$27.

The *Hotel Bucanero* (☎ (321) 5-01-01), at Juárez 75 one block from the end of the street, is full of character. Stuffed crocodiles greet you at the door. Wagon wheels and chunks of an old stone column are scattered around the inner courtyard. The rooms are OK, but a bit humid and musty even though there are fans. Singles cost US$13, doubles US$17, and triples US$20.

The *Hotel Flamingos*, at the end of Juárez just past the Bucanero, has rooms around a courtyard full of plants with a well in the middle. Singles cost US$13.50, doubles US$15, and triples US$18.50.

Places to Eat

The restaurant at the *Hotel Las Brisas* serves breakfast from 8 to 10 am for US$3 and dinner from 4 to 8.30 pm under a big thatched palapa enclosed with screening. They serve a different Mexican seafood speciality every night.

Sí Simon restaurant at Playa El Borrego serves a variety of seafood dishes, including an octopus salad and shrimp and oyster cocktails. A full meal costs US$5 to US$7.

Las Islas Chef Tony's, Paredes and Arista, has a chef whom locals claim is the best in town. They serve various seafood specialities from US$4.

McDonald's, on Juárez a little way to the east of the zócalo, is a favourite place for a good breakfast. It's clean, usually cool and popular with travellers. Their specialities include breaded oysters, fish fillet, oysters

'casino', shrimp omelettes and shrimp kebabs. A filling meal shouldn't set you back more than US$5 to US$7.

La Familia Restaurant, near the corner of Calle Batallón de San Blas and Mercado, serves fresh lobster every day.

There are also a couple of good eating places on the square. For a sensational (very spicy) prawn dish, try camarones a la diabla at *La Terraza* on the east side of the square.

There is a good selection of places to eat on the beaches. Seafood dishes run from US$4 to US$7.

Getting There & Away

The bus station is at Sinaloa and Canalizo, at the north-east corner of the zócalo. Buses to Santa Cruz, the village at the far end of Bahía de Matanchén, leave at 9 am, 11 am and 1 pm to return shortly after arriving in Santa Cruz.

Buses depart for Tepic (US$1.75) at 6.30, 7.30, 8.30 and 9.30 am and at 1, 4 and 5 pm. Buses depart for Guadalajara (US$6.50, six hours) at 7.30 am and 4 pm.

Baja California

Baja California (Lower California) – the world's longest peninsula – stretches 1300 km south from Tijuana to Cabo San Lucas. It is divided along the 28th parallel into the states of Baja California Norte and Baja California Sur.

Spanish explorers first landed on the Baja peninsula in 1533. For them, Baja was both enticing and forbidding. A beautiful coastline of fine, white beaches, peaceful bays and lagoons and imposing cliffs disguised a harsh interior. Settlement attempts repeatedly failed until the late 17th century, when Jesuit priests arrived and began establishing self-sufficient missions. They converted local Indians to Catholicism, taught them to work the fields and build the churches, all with the hope of 'civilising' them. In less than a century, though, this 'civilising' mission began to collapse as the Indians fell

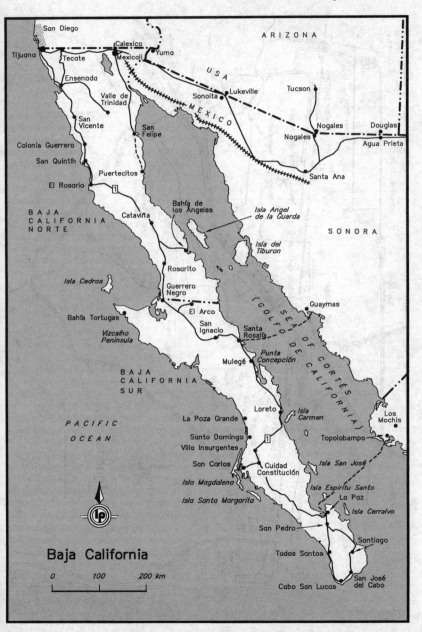

Baja California

0   100   200 km

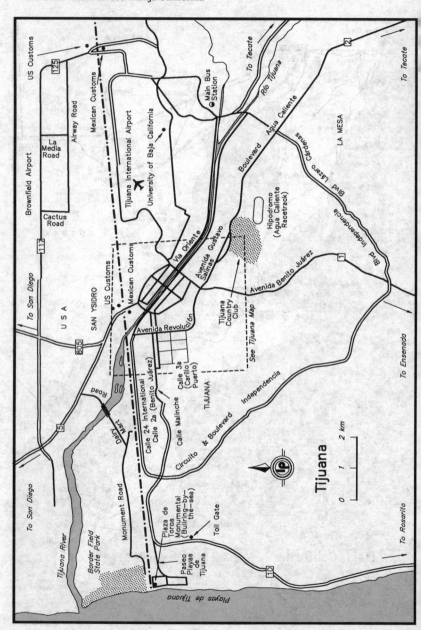

Tijuana

prey to European diseases and the Jesuits, suspected of hoarding royal treasures, were booted out.

In the 19th century, parts of Baja were tamed and settled by ranchers and fishers. Mines were dug, ports were set up and huge tracts of land were sold to foreign companies. Foreigners, encouraged by great mining discoveries, poured into the peninsula. Although small fortunes were made, Baja remained largely undeveloped and unaffected. When most of the mines closed in the early 20th century, many foreigners took whatever money they had and left the area.

The 20th century ushered in a new era for Baja; it became a land of escape. Some of the first escapees were Magonistas, a splinter group of revolutionaries and mercenaries who briefly 'conquered' Northern Baja while fleeing from Mexican federal troops. Criminals fleeing the law found Baja a convenient place to hide. Then, with Prohibition in the USA, Baja also became a convenient place for gambling, drinking and other vices unobtainable north of the border. Hotels, restaurants, racetracks, bullrings and casinos were built. A new type of escapee was lured to Baja – the American tourist.

Today, many of Baja's cities and towns are thriving with a prosperity brought by millions of annual visitors. The border cities are the most visited because they offer short, inexpensive escapes: shopping sprees, sumptuous meals, exotic drinks, bullfights and jai alai matches. Baja's duty-free status has spawned American-style shopping malls where designer jeans and shirts and French perfumes sell at discount prices.

South of the border cities, the attraction is outdoor activities: horseback riding in the mountains or on the beach, roaring over sand dunes in an all-terrain vehicle, scuba diving or snorkelling in the Sea of Cortés, windsurfing, clam-digging, whale-watching, fishing, sailing, kayaking, bicycling, surfing or hiking.

Though Baja has its attractions, it is certainly not cheap by Mexican standards. Remoteness from the mainland, long distances, and hordes of well-heeled visitors keep the price structure high.

For more detailed information on all parts of Baja, see Lonely Planet's *Baja California – a travel survival kit* by Scott Wayne.

TIJUANA

Population: 1,900,000

Tijuana ('tee-WAH-na'), sometimes called 'TJ', is a fast-growing city with multiple personalities. For most of its existence Tijuana was a tawdry border town famous among gringos for booze and sex. It was also a gaudy place where curio shops overflowed with cheap, wrought-iron bird cages, theatrical sombreros (never worn by Mexicans) and bright multicoloured sarape blankets. All this still exists, but Tijuana is quickly becoming a big modern city as well – a place of business deals, glass skyscrapers and housing developments.

US dollars and Mexican pesos can be spent – and are accepted – with equal ease in TJ.

For details on border crossings, see the Land section of the Getting There & Away chapter.

Orientation

Tijuana parallels the USA border for about 12 miles (20 km). The border – La Frontera or La Linea – at Tijuana is open 24 hours a day. The border post is 1½ km (one mile) from Avenida Revolución, Tijuana's main commercial street. 'Central Camionera' buses depart from a street just beyond the taxi lot, charging US$0.25 for the trip to the centre or the bus station.

Information

Tourist Office The Tijuana Chamber of Commerce Tourism Office (☎ (66) 88-16-85 or 85-95-20), at the corner of Avenida Revolución and Comercio, has lots of information and English-speaking staff to provide it for you. The Tourism & Convention Bureau can be called on (66) 83-14-05. The Procuraduría de Protección al Turista (Attorney-General for the Protection of the Tourist,

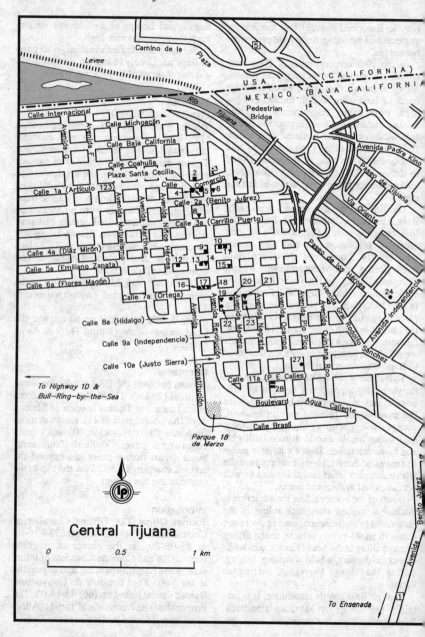

Camino de la
Plaza

Levee

USA (CALIFORNIA)
MEXICO (BAJA CALIFORNIA)

Río Tijuana

Pedestrian
Bridge

Calle Internacional

Avenida G
Avenida F

Calle Michoacán

Calle Baja California

Calle Coahuila

Plaza Santa Cecilia

Calle 1a (Artículo 123)

Avenida Mutualismo
Avenida Martínez
Avenida Niños Héroes

Calle

Calle Comercio

Calle 2a (Benito Juárez)

Calle 3a (Carrillo Puerto)

Calle 4a (Díaz Mirón)

Calle 5a (Emiliano Zapata)

Calle 6a (Flores Magón)

Calle 7a (Ortega)

Avenida Padre Kino

Paseo de Tijuana

Vía Oriente

Paseo de los Héroes

Avenida Gral. Rodolfo Sánchez

Avenida Independencia

Calle 8a (Hidalgo)

Calle 9a (Independencia)

Calle 10a (Justo Sierra)

Avenida Revolución
Avenida Madero
Avenida Negrete
Avenida Ocampo
Avenida Pío Pico
Quintana Roo

To Highway 1D &
Bull–Ring–by–the–Sea

Avenida Constitución

Calle 11a (P E Calles)

Boulevard Agua Caliente

Calle Brasil

Parque 18
de Marzo

Benito Juárez

Avenida Benito Juárez

Central Tijuana

0   0.5   1 km

To Ensenada

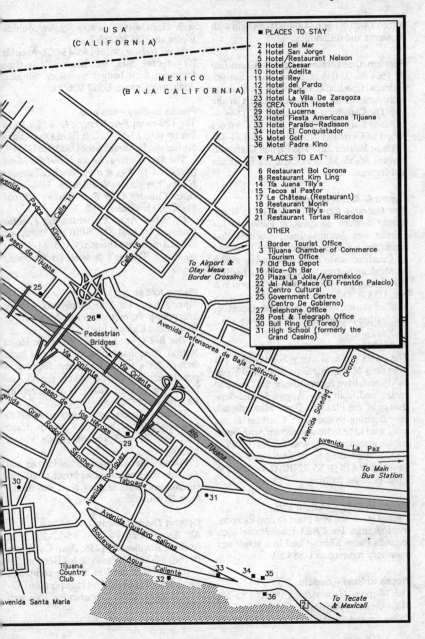

■ PLACES TO STAY
2 Hotel Del Mar
4 Hotel San Jorge
5 Hotel/Restaurant Nelson
9 Hotel Caesar
10 Hotel Adelita
11 Hotel Rey
12 Hotel del Pardo
13 Hotel Paris
23 Hotel La Villa De Zaragoza
26 CREA Youth Hostel
29 Hotel Lucerna
32 Hotel Fiesta Americana Tijuana
33 Hotel Paraíso–Radisson
34 Hotel El Conquistador
35 Motel Golf
36 Motel Padre Kino

▼ PLACES TO EAT
6 Restaurant Bol Corona
8 Restaurant Kim Ling
14 Tía Juana Tilly's
15 Tacos al Pastor
17 Le Château (Restaurant)
18 Restaurant Monin
19 Tía Juana Tilly's
21 Restaurant Tortas Ricardos

OTHER
1 Border Tourist Office
3 Tijuana Chamber of Commerce Tourism Office
7 Old Bus Depot
16 Nica–Oh Bar
20 Plaza La Jolla/Aeroméxico
22 Jai Alai Palace (El Frontón Palacio)
24 Centro Cultural
25 Government Centre (Centro De Gobierno)
27 Telephone Office
28 Post & Telegraph Office
30 Bull Ring (El Toreo)
31 High School (formerly the Grand Casino)

☎ (66) 84-21-81 or 684-94-92) can help with problems and difficulties.

Foreign Consulates The US Consulate (☎ (66) 86-00-01) is at Tapachula Sur 96, Colonia Hipódromo, near the Agua Caliente racecourse in the south-eastern part of the city. The Canadian Consulate (☎ (66) 84-04-61) is at Calle Gedovius 5-202 in Zona del Río. The German Consulate (☎ (66) 81-82-74) is at Mérida 221. The French Consulate (☎ (66) 86-55-54) is at Carretera Ensenada and Balarezo 2900.

Centro Cultural Tijuana

The Cultural Centre (☎ 84-11-11) is the boldly modern complex at Paseo de los Héroes and Avenida Independencia that resembles a nuclear power plant. It houses an Omnimax-style cinema featuring a film on Mexican history and culture (the English version at 2 pm, US$5; Spanish version at 6 pm, US$1). Other sections of the complex hold art shows, exhibitions on Mexican life, and feature performances of the lively arts.

Bullfights

The fights are held every Sunday at 4 pm from early May to late September at El Toreo de Tijuana, Blvd Agua Caliente 100, near the centre; and from early August to mid-September at the Plaza de Toros Monumental, the 'Bullring-by-the-Sea'. Corridas at the latter tend to be more spectacular, with better known matadors. Buy your tickets (US$5 to US$25, depending upon where you sit) at Revolución 815 (☎ 85-22-10) from 10 am to 7 pm, or at the bullring.

Places to Stay – bottom end

Tijuana is not the best place to find inexpensive lodgings. The *CREA Youth Hostel* is on Avenida Padre Kino. A bed in a single-sex dormitory room costs US$4.50.

Places to Stay – middle

The 74-room *Motel Alaska* (☎ (66) 85-36-81), Avenida Revolución 1950 between Calles 1a and Coahuila, is an aging motel

with clean, basic rooms. Singles/doubles/triples are US$24/27/32.

Hotel Nelson (☎ (66) 85-43-02), Avenida Revolución 503, has been a long-time favourite with budget travellers. Singles/doubles/triples are US$24/26/34.

Places to Stay – top end

The 120-room *Best Western Hotel La Mesa Inn* (☎ (66) 81-65-22), at Blvd Díaz Ordaz 50, has singles/doubles for US$50 to US$69.

The *Best Western Hacienda Del Río Hotel* (☎ (66) 84-86-44), at Blvd Sánchez Taboada 10606, has singles/doubles for US$60/65. *Hotel Country Club Best Western* (☎ (66) 81-77-33) is similar.

On Blvd Agua Caliente, the *Paraíso Radisson* (☎ (66) 81-72-00) and the *Hotel Fiesta Americana Tijuana* (☎ (66) 81-71-16) are two of Tijuana's classiest (and priciest) hotels.

Places to Eat

Tijuana has over 200 restaurants serving everything from traditional Mexican to Balkan and Chinese food.

The *Bol Corona*, across from the Hotel Nelson, specialises in burritos; one is large enough for a meal. *Tía Juana Tilly's* is a popular gringo hang-out next to the Jai Alai Palace; a second *Tilly's* is on Avenida Revolución at Calle 5a.

There's a great taco stand at Avenida Revolución 925-7, between Calles 5a (Calle Emiliano Zapata) and 6a (Calle Flores Magón).

Plaza Fiesta, at Paseo de los Héroes and Avenida Independencia, is home to 20 restaurants and cafés serving food and drinks from 10 countries.

Getting There & Away

Air Aeroméxico (☎ (66) 85-22-30) is at Avenida Revolución 1236; Aero California (☎ (66) 84-20-06), Paseo de los Héroes 619-C (in the Plaza del Río Tijuana complex). Mexicana (☎ (66) 81-72-11; airport (66) 82-41-83) is at Calle Gobernador Balarezo 2800.

Aeroméxico has flights between Tijuana

and cities throughout Mexico. Mexicana flies from Tijuana to La Paz, Mexico City and Zacatecas. Aero California has flights from Tijuana to Los Mochis (the Copper Canyon train departure point).

Bus The Central Camionera (main bus station) is a cavernous modern building on the outskirts about five km (three miles) south-east of the centre, where Blvd Lázaro Cárdenas becomes the airport highway. To get there take any 'Buena Vista', 'Central Camionera' or 'Centro' bus from Calle 2a.

It seems as though half the towns in Baja are named Rosarito, Rosario or Rosalía, perhaps because of the immense number of rosary beads which can be counted on any Baja bus journey. Both Baja California Norte (BCN) and Baja California Sur (BCS) have their own separate towns bearing these names. You must work to keep your roses straight here.

Ensenada – 114 km, 1½ hours, US$4; hourly buses run by Autotransportes de Baja California.
Guadalajara – 2306 km, 37 hours, US$45; a dozen buses daily by Transportes Norte de Sonora, with an express bus departing at 9 am.
Guerrero Negro – 686 km, 10 hours, US$15; three buses daily by Autotransportes de Baja California.
La Paz – 1457 km, 23 hours, US$30; several daily by Autotransportes de Baja California.
Los Mochis – 1383 km, 24 hours, US$30; several buses daily by Transportes Norte de Sonora.
Mazatlán – 1819 km, 30 hours, US$36; several buses daily by Transportes Norte de Sonora.
Mexicali – 185 km, three hours, US$4; very frequent departures by most of the bus lines.
Mexico City – 2841 km, 42 hours, US$58; four buses daily by Transportes Norte de Sonora (express at 11.30 am), also several by Transportes del Pacífico.
Mulegé – 986 km, 17 hours, US$23; one bus daily by Autotransportes de Baja California.
Rosarito – BCN, 30 km, one hour, US$1; Autotransportes de Baja California runs buses every hour from Tijuana's old bus station in the centre at Madero and Calle 1a, a block from the tourist office on Revolución.
San Diego (California, USA) – 20 km, 45 minutes; Greyhound Lines operates a daily bus service between San Diego and Tijuana, with connections to other destinations in the USA.

Trolley The San Diego Trolley (☎ (619) 233-3004) is one of the cheapest ways (US$1.50) to travel between downtown San Diego and the international border at San Ysidro.

ENSENADA
Population: 200,000
Though Ensenada, 109 km (68 miles) south of Tijuana, is a major fishing and shipping port, at first it seems quiet and unassuming, almost boring. From Monday to Thursday everything appears to move in slow motion – people on the sidewalks, boats and trawlers in the harbour, cars and, occasionally, donkey carts. On Friday evening Ensenada sheds its serene veneer and becomes the city of Bacchus, full of revelling gringos.

Orientation & Information
Most hotels and restaurants are on Blvd Lázaro Cárdenas/Blvd Costero. The state tourism office (☎ (667) 6-22-22), Avenida López Mateos 1350 at Avenida Espinosa, is open Monday to Saturday from 9 am to 7 pm. The Chamber of Commerce's office (☎ (667) 8-37-70), Avenida López Mateos 693 at Macheros, is another good source, open Monday to Friday from 9 am to 6 pm.

El Mirador
Atop Chapultepec hill is El Mirador, a scenic viewpoint with a spectacular panoramic view of the area. To get there go right up Avenida Alemán from Calle 2a.

Winery Tour
Bodegas de Santo Tomás (☎ (667) 8-25-09), Avenida Miramar 666, is one of Baja California's premier wineries, profiting from northern Baja's excellent wine-growing climate. Daily public tours, which include wine tastings, are offered at 11 am, 1 and 3 pm. Admission is US$1.50.

Places to Stay
Although Ensenada has many hotels, on weekends even the cheap and sleazy ones are full. Weekend reservations are strongly recommended.

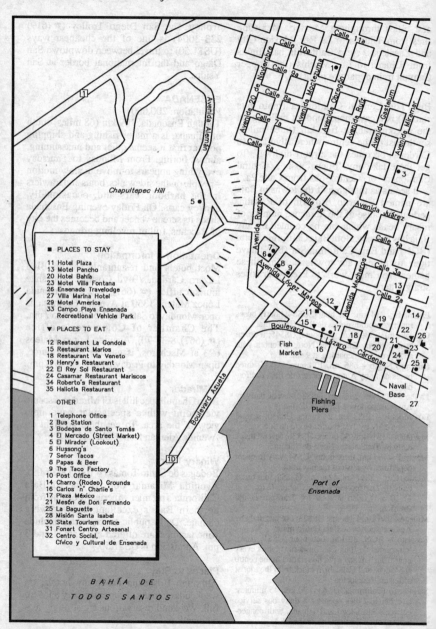

PLACES TO STAY

11 Hotel Plaza
13 Motel Pancho
20 Hotel Bahía
23 Motel Villa Fontana
26 Ensenada Travelodge
27 Villa Marina Hotel
29 Motel America
33 Campo Playa Ensenada
   Recreational Vehicle Park

▼ **PLACES TO EAT**

12 Restaurant La Gondola
15 Restaurant Marios
18 Restaurant Via Veneto
19 Henry's Restaurant
22 El Rey Sol Restaurant
24 Casamar Restaurant Mariscos
34 Roberto's Restaurant
35 Haliotis Restaurant

OTHER

1 Telephone Office
2 Bus Station
3 Bodegas de Santo Tomás
4 El Mercado (Street Market)
5 El Mirador (Lookout)
6 Hussong's
7 Señor Tacos
8 Papas & Beer
9 The Taco Factory
10 Post Office
14 Charro (Rodeo) Grounds
16 Carlos 'n' Charlie's
17 Plaza México
21 Mesón de Don Fernando
25 La Baguette
28 Misión Santa Isabel
30 State Tourism Office
31 Fonart Centro Artesanal
32 Centro Social,
   Cívico y Cultural de Ensenada

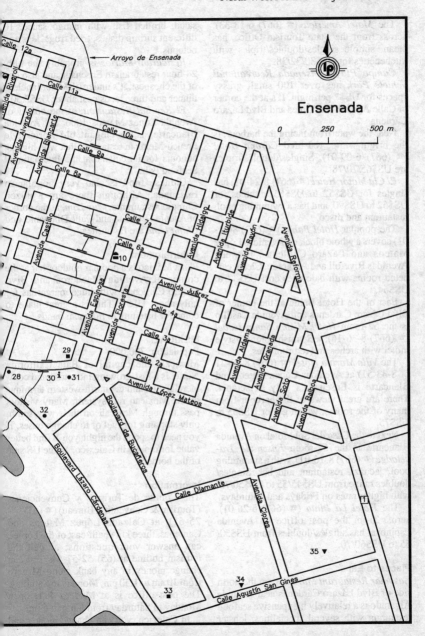

Ensenada

0   250   500 m

The *Motel America* (☎ (667) 6-13-33), across from the State Tourism Office, has clean, simple singles/doubles/triples with kitchenettes for US$30/32/38.

Campo Playa Ensenada Recreational Vehicle Park has over 100 small grassy spaces for US$7 per night. It's at the corner of Calle Agustín San Gines and Blvd Lázaro Cárdenas.

Near the waterfront facing the harbour, is the bright-white, red-tiled *Corona Hotel* (☎ (667) 6-09-01). Singles/doubles/triples are US$65/70/78.

El Cid Motor Hotel (☎ (667) 8-24-01) has singles for US$52 to US$65, doubles for US$52 to US$90, and has a swimming pool, restaurant and disco.

The popular *Hotel Bahía* (☎ (667) 8-21-01) covers a whole block on Avenidas López Mateos and Lázaro Cárdenas, between Avenidas Riveroll and Alvarado. Clean, carpeted rooms with balconies cost US$32 to US$64.

East of the Hotel Bahía at the corner of Blvd Lázaro Cárdenas and Avenida Castillo is the 52-room *Hotel Misión Santa Isabel* (☎ (667) 8-36-16), a Spanish colonial-style motel with arches and red roof tiles.

The *Villa Marina Hotel* (☎ (667) 8-33-21 or 8-33-51) at Avenidas López Mateos and Blancarte is Ensenada's only skyscraper. There are great views of the harbour from many of the rooms, which go for US$55 to US$75.

Next to the Casa del Sol Motel on Avenida Blancarte is the 52-room *Ensenada Travelodge* (☎ (667) 8-16-01), with a swimming pool, jacuzzi, restaurant and bar. Singles/doubles range from US$45/55 to US$50/75, with higher rates on Fridays and Saturdays.

The *Hotel La Pinta* (☎ (667) 6-26-01), across from the post office on Avenida Espinosa, has singles/doubles from US$50/55 to US$60/70.

Places to Eat

Casamar Restaurant Mariscos, on the north side of Blvd Lázaro Cárdenas near Avenida Alvarado is a relatively inexpensive seafood restaurant with several specialities: lobster salad, broiled fish with mango sauce, 10 different shrimp dishes, fried frogs' legs and octopus.

Restaurant Marios is probably the only 24-hour restaurant in Ensenada and also one of the cheapest; it's under US$4 for lunch or dinner and three tacos cost about US$2.50.

El Rey Sol Restaurant, at the corner of Avenida López Mateos 1000 and Avenida Blancarte, is an elegant old-world-style French-Mexican restaurant that won highest honours for its cuisine at the International Seafood Fair.

Chinese food is also very popular in Ensenada. Although there are a dozen Chinese restaurants, *Muy Lam*, at the corner of Avenida Ejército and Calle Diamante, and *China Land* are favourites.

Entertainment

Plaza México is a popular outdoor bar at the corner of Avenida Macheros and Blvd Lázaro Cárdenas, with huge margaritas for only about US$3. This is a great place to come for listening to mariachi bands.

MEXICALI

Population: 700,000

Mexicali, the capital of Baja California Norte, is a fast-growing industrial and commercial city, and the north-western terminus of the Mexican rail system. Many visitors pass through Mexicali on their way south, only stopping for fuel or to change buses. If you need to spend the night, you'll find better value for money in Calexico, on the US side of the border.

Information

The Comite de Turismo y Convenciones (Tourism & Convention Bureau) (☎ (65) 57-25-61), at Calzada López Mateos and Camelias, three km south-east of the border, can answer your questions; or call the tourism hotline at (65) 52-57-44. You can change money in any bank along Madero from 10 am to 1.30 pm, Monday to Saturday. The post office is at Madero 491, open Monday to Saturday from 8 am to 6 pm.

In Calexico, you can change money and

buy automobile insurance along Imperial Avenue, which leads straight to the border crossing. The Calexico casas de cambio usually offer slightly better rates than their Mexicali competitors. Exchange services at banks are only open from 9 am to 1.30 pm, but try to exchange money before 12.30 pm because the last hour is chaotic. In Calexico there is a First Interstate Bank with a 24-hour teller machine at 250 East 4th St, across from the De Anza Hotel.

Getting There & Away

Bus The Central Camionera (bus station) is on Avenida Independencia near Calzada López Mateos, about five km south of the international border. There is good, frequent service to most points in Baja, and to most other major cities in mainland Mexico.

Train The main railway station is at Calle Ulises Irigoyen (Calle F). Passenger services go from Mexicali to Mexico City via Hermosillo, Guaymas (Empalme), El Sufragio/San Blas (the Copper Canyon train junction for Los Mochis and Chihuahua), Mazatlán and Guadalajara. For information, call (6) 57-23-86, ext 213 or 222/3, between 6.30 am and 1 pm daily.

GUERRERO NEGRO

The first town south of the 28th parallel, Guerrero Negro is renowned for a lagoon that annually becomes the mating and breeding grounds of California grey whales.

The breeding grounds are in Scammon's Lagoon, south of the town's salt works and about 24 km (15 miles) from the junction of Highway 1. Each year the whales migrate 6000 miles from the Bering Sea to Scammon's Lagoon, now designated Parque Natural de Ballena Gris (Grey Whale Natural Park), where they stay from early January to early March.

Places to Stay & Eat

Motel El Morro, on the north side of Blvd Zapata, has clean, basic rooms for US$15 to US$20. *Hotel La Pinta Guerrero Negro* has

an excellent restaurant and bar and very comfortable rooms for US$60.

You can camp free at most beaches in the area. Also, the *Malarrimo Trailer Park*, a small RV park at the edge of town, charges US$10 a night for two people. *Malarrimo*, the best place to eat, offers a variety of seafood from abalone and shrimp to fish and clams, including octopus cocktail, halibut fillet, fish burritos, San Carlos shrimp and lobster.

SAN IGNACIO

The lush town of San Ignacio is a welcome sight after the scrub brush and dense cacti of the Vizcaíno Desert. In the late 18th century, Jesuit priests planted date palms and citrus trees that now fill the area around the town. After the expulsion of the Jesuits, Dominican missionaries built a beautiful lava-block church and mission that continues to dominate the town's cool tree-shaded plaza.

There are 46 caves with primitive paintings that can be visited by mule from ranchos Santa Marta or San Francisco. See Oscar Fischer in town to arrange a tour.

Places to Stay & Eat

La Posada Motel is the town's only budget accommodation; spartan doubles with hot showers cost US$30. More upscale in price and quality is the *Hotel La Pinta San Ignacio*, which has singles/doubles for US$60/70.

Camping is possible behind the PEMEX station (and within earshot of the highway traffic) and in the palm groves closer to town.

The small, family-run *Loncheria Chalita* is about the only place to eat in San Ignacio. You eat whatever the family feels like serving that day.

SANTA ROSALÍA

Population: 15,000

Santa Rosalía was founded in the 1880s by the French-owned El Boleo Copper Company. The mine closed in 1953, but a few vestiges of French influence remain – colonial-style homes, an iron church built by

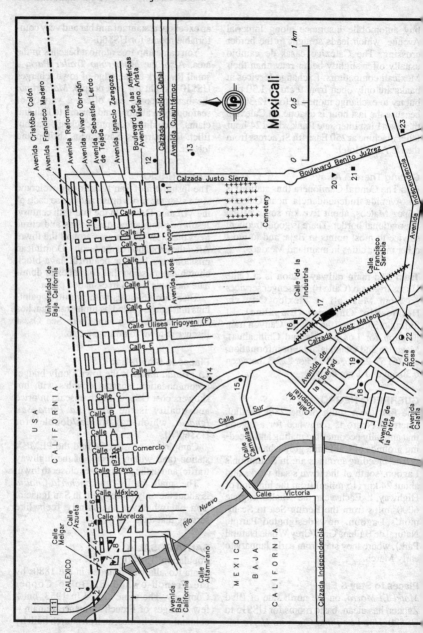

Mexicali

1 km
0.5
0

Boulevard Benito Ju2rez

Avenida Cristóbal Colón
Avenida Francisco Madero
Avenida Reforma
Avenida Alvaro Obregón
Avenida Sebastían Lerdo de Tejada
Avenida Ignacio Zaragoza
Boulevard de las Américas
Avenida Mariano Arista
Calzada Aviación Canal
Avenida Cuauhtémoc

Calzada Justo Sierra

Cemetery

Calle I
Calle K
Calle J
Calle I
Calle H
Calle G
Calle Ulises Irigoyen (F)
Calle E
Calle D
Calle C
Calle B
Calle A
Calle del Comercio
Calle Bravo
Calle México
Calle Morelos

Avenida José Larroque

Universidad de Baja California

Calle de la Industria

Calzada López Mateos

Calle Francisco Sarabia

Avenida de la Libertad
Avenida de Patria
Avenida Calafia

Hospital Civil
Calle del
Zona Rosa

Calle Sur
Calle Camelias
Calle Victoria

Río Nuevo

Calle Altamirano
Avenida Baja California

Calzada Independencia

Avenida Independencia

U S A
CALIFORNIA

Calle Melgar
Calle Azueta
CALEXICO

111

M E X I C O   B A J A   C A L I F O R N I A

1 US Customs
2 Mexican Customs
3 Hotel del Norte/Restaurant del Norte
4 Parque Chapultepec
5 Post Office
6 Fortín de las Flores Hotel
7 Marisco Olympo
8 Plaza Hotel
9 State Tourism Office
10 Museum
11 Coca-Cola Bottler
12 La Casa del Patrón
13 Baseball Stadium
14 El Teatro del Estado
15 Tourism & Convention Bureau
16 Motel Azteca de Oro
17 Railway Station
18 Centro Cívico-Comercial
19 Plaza de Toros Calafía
20 El Dragon Restaurant
21 Holiday Inn
22 Bus Station (Central Camionera)
23 Hotel Lucema
24 La Misión Dragon Restaurant

Alexandre Gustave Eiffel (of Tower fame) and a quasi-French-style bakery.

There are several small hotels, motels and restaurants in and just south of town, but most travellers just pass through to see the church and catch the ferry to the mainland.

Santa Rosalía is the northernmost ferry depot on the Baja peninsula. Ferries (transbordadores) customarily depart Santa Rosalía for Guaymas, seven-hours cruise away, at 11 pm on Sunday, Tuesday and Thursday; tickets (which are in fierce demand) go on sale at 4.30 pm on sailing days. For information, go to the Transbordadores dock, or call (685) 2-00-13.

In the USA, the Mexico West Travel Club (☎ (619) 585-3033), in Chula Vista, California (near San Diego), can often provide the latest ferry information as well.

MULEGÉ

Mulegé is a small tropical town with a calm river, thatched huts, lots of palm trees, a plaza, and an 18th-century mission. It is a good place to stock up for camping on the beaches around Bahía Concepción to the south.

Information

Ask your questions at the Hotel Las Casitas, Madero 50. You can change money at Banamex, a block north of the plaza, from 8.30 am to 1 pm Monday to Friday. Long-distance calls can be made from Abarrotes Padilla on San Martín at Zaragoza, a block north of the plaza.

Places to Stay & Eat

Because of its beach-oasis reputation, Mulegé is not cheap. Try the *Casa de Huéspedes Nachita* (☎ (685) 3-01-40), on the outskirts of town; it's a very simple place, but cheap at US$8/10 a single/double. *Hotel Rosita* (☎ (685) 3-02-70), on Madero just east of the main plaza, has air-conditioned suites available for US$30 a double, and US$36 for up to four persons; reserve in advance if possible.

The hotel *Las Casitas* (☎ (685) 3-00-19), on Calle Madero, has hot showers and air-conditioning, and rooms from around US$20 to US$35. *Hotel Terrazas* (☎ (685) 3-00-09), two blocks north of the plaza, has some of the comfiest rooms in town, with air-con and hot water, for US$20/25/30 a single/double/triple.

As for food, scavenging from food shops and 'dining' (to use the term loosely) in the few little restaurants is all there is. Perhaps the best food is that served in the hotels.

Getting There & Away

Mulegé has no bus station; you have to wait near the highway for de paso buses, which are usually late and usually jam-packed. Hitching is sometimes possible.

LORETO

Population: 5000

Loreto, 210 miles north of La Paz and 84 miles south of Mulegé, was the first permanent European settlement in the Californias. Founded on 25 October 1697 with the establishment of Misión Nuestra Señora de Loreto, the town became the first capital of the Californias.

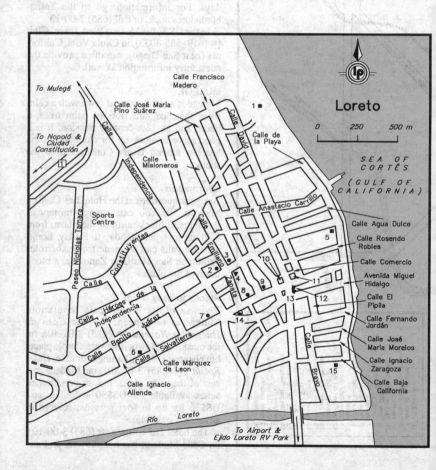

Camping is possible at the *Ejido Loreto RV & Trailer Park*. Most of the hotels are in the middle to upper range. These include the *Hotel Misión de Loreto* (☎ (683) 3-00-48), the *Hotel La Pinta Loreto* (☎ (683) 3-00-25), and the lavish resort complex of the *Stouffer Presidente Loreto*, which was struggling to survive when last visited.

For places to eat, try *Caesar's Restaurant* for a filling seafood platter, *Rancho Viejo* for steak and lobster, and *Asadero Las Brasas* for tacos.

LA PAZ
Population: 170,000
La Paz, capital of Baja California Sur, means Peace, a suitable description today. Spectacular sunsets over the bay, a palm-lined corniche, colonial-style buildings and beautiful beaches on the Pichilingue peninsula are La Paz's main attractions. It is also a principal terminus for the ferries to Topolobampo/Los Mochis and to Mazatlán on the mainland.

Information
For tourist information, the latest ferry and bus schedules, hotel bookings, and advice on which beaches to visit, stop by the State Tourism & Tourist Protection Office (☎ (682) 2-59-39) on the waterfront at the corner of Paseo Álvaro Obregón and Calle 16 de Septiembre. The staff speak English and can be extremely helpful. Hours are 8 am to 8 pm daily except weekends and holidays.

Places to Stay & Eat
At the bottom end, the *Pensión California* (☎ (682) 2-28-96), Calle Degollado 209, and *Hotel Posada San Miguel* (☎ (682) 2-18-02), Calle Belisarío Dominguez 1510, are two of the most popular among budget travellers. *Hotel Lorimar* (☎ (682) 5-38-22), Calle Bravo 110, has a variety of well-kept, air-conditioned rooms for prices starting at US$12 per night. Check out the *Hotel Yeneka* at Calle Madero 1520 for a good laugh and a fair place to stay.

For more comfortable places, try the *Hotel Gran Baja La Paz* (☎ (682) 2-39-00), at the end of Calle Nayarit, the *Hotel Los Arcos* (☎ (682) 2-27-44), at Paseo Álvaro Obregón 498, or the *Hotel Palmira* (☎ (682) 2-40-00), which is on the road to Pichilingue about 2km from central La Paz.

The *Restaurant Camarón Feliz* (Restaurant Happy Shrimp), corner of Calles Bravo and Madero, usually stays true to its name with a variety of spicy shrimp dishes. *El Quinto Sol* is a popular vegetarian restaurant and health-food market that is worth trying.

Getting There & Away
Air There are daily Aeroméxico and Mexicana flights between La Paz and several Mexican cities. Aero California also operates several flights to and from La Paz, including flights to and from Los Angeles, California. Aeroméxico is on Paseo Álvaro Obregón between Calles Hidalgo and Morelos; Mexicana at Paseo Álvaro Obregón 340; and Aero California at Paseo Álvaro Obregón near the corner of Calle Bravo.

Bus At least three intercity bus companies operate from La Paz's Central Camionera to almost every town in Baja. Local buses to Pichilingue and the ferry terminal depart

1	Hotel La Pinta Loreto
2	Pemex Gasoline Station
3	Focandi Department Store
4	Caesar's Restaurant
5	Hotel Misión de Loreto
6	Motel Salvatierra
7	Public Telephones
8	Dive Shop
9	Misión de Nuestra Señora de Loreto/Museum
10	Post Office/Telegraph Office
11	Plaza Civica (Zócalo)
12	La Casita Restaurant
13	Café Olé
14	Bus Station
15	Hotel Oasis

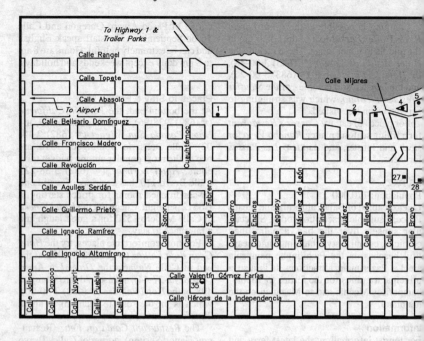

■ PLACES TO STAY

3	Hotel Los Arcos
9	Hotel La Perla/Hertz/Las Brisas Restaurant
19	Hostería del Convento
20	Hotel Palencia
21	Hotel Posada San Miguel
23	Pensión California
27	Clark Hotel
28	Hospedaje Mareli

▼ PLACES TO EAT

2	Restaurant/Bar El Cheff
14	Restaurant Kiwi
22	El Quinto Sol
31	La Flor de Michoacán
32	Bismark II Restaurant

OTHER

1	Registro Federal de Vehículos
4	Las Casas de las Artesanías de Baja California Sur
5	Aero California
6	Wharf
7	Post Office/Telegrams
8	Immigration Office
10	Banks
11	Dive Shop
12	Tourist Office
13	Medrita Travel (Bus to Pichilingue)
15	Aeroméxico
16	Dorian's Department Store
17	Chinatown
18	Palacio de Gobierno
24	Plaza Constitución
25	Bookstore
26	Post Office/Telegrams
29	Public Market (Local Buses)
30	Misión de Nuestra Señora de La Paz
33	Anthropology Museum
34	Ferry Office
35	Central Bus Station (Central Camionera)

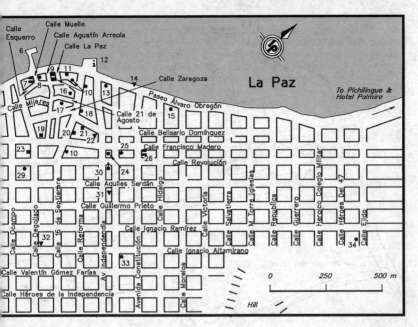

Calle Esquerro
Calle Muelle
Calle Agustín Arreola
Calle La Paz
Calle Zaragoza
La Paz
To Pichilingue & Hotel Palmira
Paseo Álvaro Obregón
Calle Mijares
Calle 21 de Agosto
Calle Belisario Domínguez
Calle Francisco Madero
Calle Revolución
Calle Aquiles Serdán
Calle Guillermo Prieto
Calle Ignacio Ramírez
Calle Ignacio Altamirano
Calle Valentín Gómez Farías
Calle Héroes de la Independencia
Calle Hidalgo
Calle Victoria
Calle Salvatierra
Calle M. Torre Iglesias
Calle República
Calle Guerrero
Calle Heroico Colegio Militar
Calle Héroes Del 47
Calle Ejido
Calle Ocampo
Calle Degollado
Calle 16 de Septiembre
Calle Reforma
Av Independencia
Avenida Constitución
Calle Morelos
Hill
0   250   500 m

from the Medrita Travel agency, Paseo Álvaro Obregón and Calle 5 de Mayo.

Boat The terminal is on the Pichilingue peninsula about 22 km (14 miles) from the centre. Tickets should be bought by 2 pm a day in advance from the ferry terminal, or in town at the Contreras travel agency, Calle 16 de Septiembre about a block from the tourist office. Hours are 8.30 am to 8 pm daily except Sunday 8 am to 1 pm.

Marítima Turística del Mar de Cortés operates hydrofoils from La Paz (Pichilingue ferry terminal) to Mazatlán and Topolobampo (with ground transportation provided to Los Mochis).

SAN JOSÉ DEL CABO
Population: 12,000

A quaint town of small streets, Spanish-style buildings and a tree-shaded plaza, San José del Cabo is quickly being transformed into a major tourist resort. It is one of the two large

resort towns of Los Cabos, the name given to the southern tip of the Baja peninsula.

Beaches
Pueblo La Playa and Playa de Nuevo Sol/Playa de California are near town. The former is a small fishing community about 2½ km from the junction of Calle Benito

Land's End

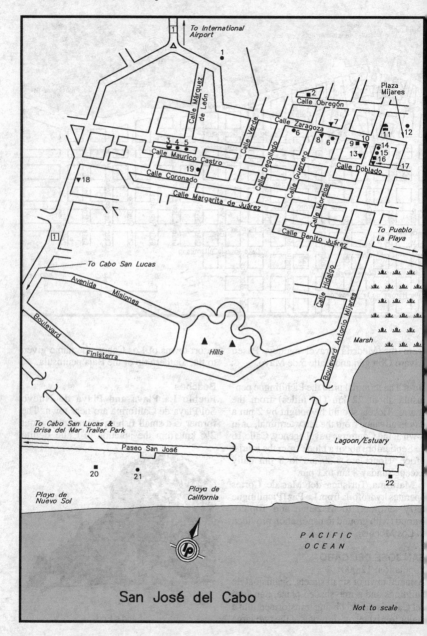

To International
Airport

Plaza
Mijares

1

2
Calle Obregón

Calle Zaragoza

7
6

Calle Verde

3 4 5
Calle Maurico Castro

9
10
14
15
16

11
12

8 6

13
17

Calle Doblado

19
Calle Coronado

Calle Degollado

Calle Guerrero

18

Calle Margarita de Juárez

Calle Morelos

Calle Benito Juárez

To Pueblo
La Playa

To Cabo San Lucas

Avenida   Misiones

Boulevard

Finisterra

Calle Hidalgo

Boulevard Antonio Mijares

Marsh

Hills

To Cabo San Lucas &
Brisa del Mar Trailer Park

Lagoon/Estuary

Paseo San José

20

21

22

Playa de
Nuevo Sol

Playa de
California

PACIFIC
OCEAN

San José del Cabo

Not to scale

Hotel Calinda Aquamarina-Comfort Inn (☎ (684) 2-01-55) is also moderately priced (for Baja) and located right on the beach.

Places to Eat

If you crave seafood or 'hickory burgers' eaten to the beat of a Mexican rock and roll band that sings in English, then head for *Pancho & Lefty's Restaurant/Bar.* The *Damiana Restaurant* is a romantic seafood restaurant in a restored 18th-century house facing the plaza. Other recommended restaurants include *Le Bistrot*, *La Fogata*, and the *Restaurant Diana*.

Getting There & Away

Alaska Airlines, Aeroméxico, Mexicana and Aero California all have daily flights between Los Cabos and the USA. The Los Cabos international airport is 11 km (seven miles) north of San José del Cabo. Official taxis and minibuses operate between the airport and Cabo San Lucas and San José del Cabo. The bus station is on Calle Doblado.

CABO SAN LUCAS

In the last five years, Cabo San Lucas has become a booming tourist resort with many hotels and restaurants springing up. Cruise ship lines include Cabo in their itineraries.

Beaches

Most people come to Cabo San Lucas for the beaches, diving and fishing. Some of the better known beaches include Medano beach, the Hotel Solmar beach, Lover's Beach, and several others between Cabo San Lucas and San José del Cabo.

Places to Stay

At US$18 per night, the *Hotel Casablanca* is the cheapest place. Also cheap is the *Hotel Dos Mares* (☎ (684) 3-03-30), on Calle Zapata between Calles Hidalgo and Matamoros.

Hotel Mar de Cortez is a colonial-style building in the centre of town. Rooms range from about US$35 to US$75. The *Hotel Marina* has overpriced motel-style rooms at similar rates. The *Giggling Marlin Inn*

Juárez and Blvd Antonio Mijares. The other beaches are south of this junction in front of a row of resort hotels.

Places to Stay

Hotel Ceci at Calle Zaragoza 22 has singles/doubles/triples for US$11/15.50/20. The *Hotel Colli* on Calle Hidalgo has singles/doubles for about US$30. The *Hotel San Jose Inn* (☎ 2-09-24; formerly the Hotel Pagamar) on Calle Obregón has singles/doubles for US$20/30.

The fancier hotels start at US$65 per room. *Stouffer Presidente Los Cabos Hotel* (☎ (684) 2-02-11) is in a beautiful location with the beach on one side and the lagoon on the other. The four-star Best Western *Hotel Posada Real* is also on the beach, but its rooms are more moderately priced. The

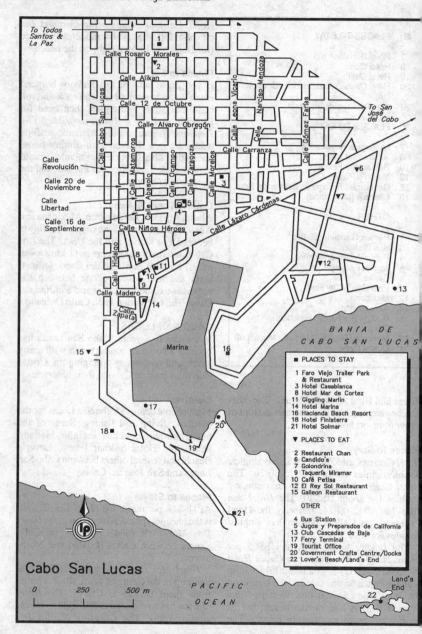

To Todos
Santos &
La Paz

Calle Rosario Morales
Calle Alikan
Calle 12 de Octubre
Calle Alvaro Obregón
Calle Cabo San Lucas
Calle Leona Vicario
Calle Narciso Mendoza
Calle Gómez Farías
Calle Carranza
Calle Revolución
Calle 20 de Noviembre
Calle Libertad
Calle 16 de Septiembre
Calle Matamoros
Calle Ocampo
Calle Zaragoza
Calle Morelos
Calle Abasolo
Calle Niños Héroes
Calle Lázaro Cárdenas
Calle Hidalgo
Calle Madero
Calle Zapata

To San
José
del Cabo

Marina

BAHÍA DE
CABO SAN LUCAS

PACIFIC
OCEAN

Cabo San Lucas

0   250   500 m

Land's
End

■ PLACES TO STAY

1 Faro Viejo Trailer Park
  & Restaurant
3 Hotel Casablanca
8 Hotel Mar de Cortez
11 Giggling Marlin
14 Hotel Marina
16 Hacienda Beach Resort
18 Hotel Finisterra
21 Hotel Solmar

▼ PLACES TO EAT

2 Restaurant Chan
6 Candido's
9 Golondrina
10 Taquería Miramar
10 Café Petisa
12 El Rey Sol Restaurant
15 Galleon Restaurant

OTHER

4 Bus Station
5 Jugos y Preparados de California
13 Club Cascadas de Baja
17 Ferry Terminal
19 Tourist Office
20 Government Crafts Centre/Docks
22 Lover's Beach/Land's End

(☎ (684) 3-06-06) is an outgrowth of the usually rambunctious Giggling Marlin restaurant and bar next door.

There are numerous very comfortable top-end hotels, including the *Hotel Meliá San Lucas* (☎ (684) 3-10-00), the *Hacienda Beach Resort* (☎ (684) 3-01-22), *Hotel Solmar* (☎ (684) 3-00-22), *Hotel Finisterra* (☎ (684) 3-00-00), and the massively gaudy *Plaza Las Glorias* (☎ (684) 3-00-29).

Places to Eat
The restaurants here cater to affluent tourists, not locals, thus prices are higher than in other more isolated towns in Baja. A lunch of three fish tacos, for example, costs about US$4 to US$5 in a restaurant, whereas the same is about US$1.50 from a corner taco stand.

Good restaurants include *Candido's*, *Golondrina*, *El Rey Sol Restaurant*, and

Romeo y Julieta restaurant. Calle Hidalgo offers several restaurants, but they tend to be very touristic with names such as *Papi's Deli*, the *Broken Surfboard*, and the *Restaurant Coral*.

Getting There & Away
Aero California has an office in the Centro Comercial plaza at the corner of Calles Lázaro Cárdenas and Hidalgo; Mexicana Airlines is at the corner of Calles Niños Héroes and Zaragoza.

The bus station is at the corner of Calle Zaragoza and Calle 16 de Septiembre. There are frequent departures for La Paz and San José del Cabo.

There used to be a daily ferry service to Puerto Vallarta, but services appear to be indefinitely suspended. Check with the tourist office in town.

The Bajío

The Bajío ('ba-HEE-oh') is the name given to the rich lands immediately north of Mexico's central volcanic belt, where the southern end of the Altiplano Central is broken by a number of low ranges. This fertile area stretches almost from coast to coast and is between 1500 and 1800 metres high. Broadly speaking it encompasses the states of Guanajuato and Querétaro, apart from their mountainous north-eastern fringes. This chapter covers both those states as well as the neighbouring states of Aguascalientes and San Luis Potosí.

Some highlights of the region include the spectacular colonial silver city of Guanajuato; the town of San Miguel de Allende, noted for its artists and schools where foreigners come to study Spanish; the colonial city of Querétaro; and Dolores Hidalgo, the 'cradle of independence' where the cry for Mexico's independence from Spain was sounded in the parish church in 1810.

San Luis Potosí State

The state of San Luis Potosí ('poh-toh-SEE') has two of the most interesting destinations on the way south from Mexico's north-east border: the mountain ghost town of Real de Catorce and the city of San Luis Potosí itself, steeped in history and the first major colonial town reached on this route into Mexico.

The state is mostly in Mexico's Altiplano (high plain) region, with the exception of a small part of its south-eastern side, which drops into a tropical valley. It is bordered on the north by Coahuila, on the north-east by Nuevo León and Tamaulipas, on the east by Veracruz, on the south by Querétaro, Guanajuato and Hidalgo, on the south-west by Jalisco, and on the west by Zacatecas; there is little rainfall and the average altitude is around 2000 metres, giving it a temperate climate.

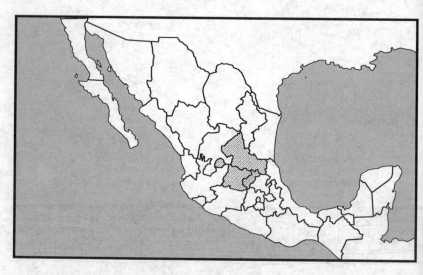

Bajío

0   25   50 km

The eastern part of the state is home to about 50,000 Huastec Indians, descendants of an advanced pre-Hispanic civilisation.

Before the Spanish conquest of Mexico in 1521, western San Luis Potosí was inhabited by hunters and collectors known as Guachichiles (the Aztec word for sparrows), from their custom of wearing little but loincloths and sometimes pointed bonnets resembling sparrows. The Guachichiles, like other Chichimec tribes, were warlike; they often sacrificed their prisoners. One of their settlements, Tangamanga, is believed to have been on the site of the present city of San Luis Potosí.

A couple of religious missions entered the south-west of the state in the 1570s and 1580s, but it was the discovery of silver in the Cerro de San Pedro mountains that really awakened Spanish interest. The city of San Luis Potosí was founded near the silver deposits in 1592. Cattle ranchers moved into the area in the 1590s too. Indians from further south – Tlaxcalans, Tarascans and Otomíes – were brought to work the mines and haciendas.

In the 18th century the area was noted for maltreatment of Indians, partly because a number of parishes were transferred from the hands of the Franciscans, who did their best to protect the Indians, into the control of the secular (non-monk) clergy. In 1767 there was an uprising sparked by the appalling conditions in the mines and discontent over the expulsion from all Spanish territory of the Jesuits, who ran the best schools in Mexico and managed their estates relatively well.

An administrative reform in 1786 divided New Spain into 12 local government *intendencias*, one of which was based at San Luis Potosí and included what are now the states of San Luis Potosí, Tamaulipas, Nuevo León, Coahuila and Texas. But such power lasted only until Mexican independence: in 1824 the state of San Luis Potosí was formed with its present area.

San Luis Potosí is a fairly rich state; its silver mines, mostly in the northern area, are some of the richest in the country, and gold, copper, zinc and other minerals are also produced. Other sources of wealth are agriculture (maize, beans, wheat and cotton), livestock and industry, which is mainly concentrated in the capital city.

SAN LUIS POTOSÍ

Population: 490,000
Altitude: 1860 metres

The capital of the state named after it, this town has played a succession of important roles in Mexican history, first as a major silver-producing centre, later as host to a line of governments-in-exile and revolutionaries. Today its main importance is as a regional capital and centre of industry, including brewing, textiles and metal foundries. But the colonial heart of the city, which is an architectural feast of nearly every different Mexican style, has been preserved from the onslaught of industry, and its plazas, markets, cafés, restaurants, churches, museums and other buildings make it a very attractive halt between Mexico City and the north-east.

San Luis is far enough from Mexico City to maintain an independent, self-assured air and its citizens take as much pride in being

Potosinos as in being Mexicans. It has a university and a fairly active cultural life.

History

Diego de la Magdalena, a Franciscan friar, started a small settlement of local Guachichil Indians about 1585 on the approximate site of the university building in what is now the city's Plaza de los Fundadores.

Another early leading light was Miguel Caldera, a mestizo who had spearheaded the Spanish side in the later part of the Chichimec War and carried out the ultimately successful policy of giving the Chichimecs food and clothing in return for peace. Caldera came to Mexquitic, 23 km north-west of San Luis, for this purpose in 1587 and a Franciscan monastery was set up there in 1590. As in other northern settlements, the Spanish used trusted Tlaxcalan Indians in San Luis and Mexquitic to help them 'civilise' the local Chichimecs.

A Guachichil told the head of the monastery about the existence of silver in the area, and Caldera sent out prospecting parties. They found silver in the Cerro de San Pedro, 20 km east of the present city, in March 1592; the city was officially founded near Magdalena's village and its springs in November of the same year. It was named Real de Minas de San Luis Potosí – the 'Potosí' coming from the immensely rich Bolivian silver town of the same name, which the Spanish hoped San Luis would rival.

It didn't; yields from the mines started to decline in the 1620s, but the city was by then well enough established as a ranching centre to ensure its continued importance. It became a communications, trade and government centre too and was the major city of north-east Mexico for three centuries – which makes it an interesting contrast to Monterrey, the upstart that overtook San Luis by sheer economic power at the turn of this century.

San Luis was one of the first cities to fall to the forces of Hidalgo and Allende in 1810 at the beginning of the independence war. In 1846 Santa Anna trained his army here before heading north in an unsuccessful

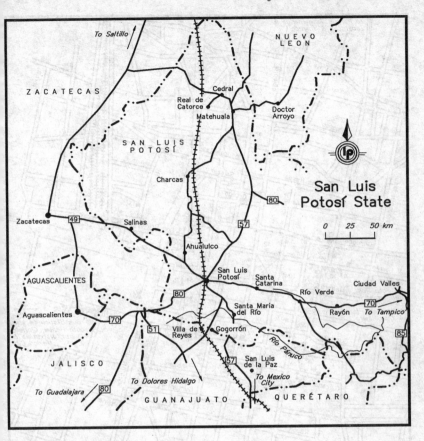

San Luis Potosí State

effort to throw the invading Americans out of Mexico. During the French intervention of the 1860s, Mexican President Benito Juárez set up his government in San Luis twice – once when he was fleeing before French forces, once when he was on the way back to oust Emperor Maximilian.

Later in the century San Luis was renowned as one of Mexico's most ostentatiously rich cities, known for its lavish houses and luxury goods imported from the USA and Europe. It also played an important part in national politics. It became, too, a breeding ground for the liberals who started the campaign to remove dictator Porfirio Díaz.

A national liberal convention here in 1901 was the first gathering of anti-Díaz elements. In 1910 Francisco Madero, the liberal candidate running against Díaz in that year's election, spent polling day, 21 June, in jail in the city. Bailed out by his family, Madero hatched a strategy in San Luis with other colleagues who had avoided jail. Then he went to San Antonio, Texas, where in October 1910 he announced the Plan de San Luis Potosí; this declared the recent election illegal, named Madero as provisional presi-

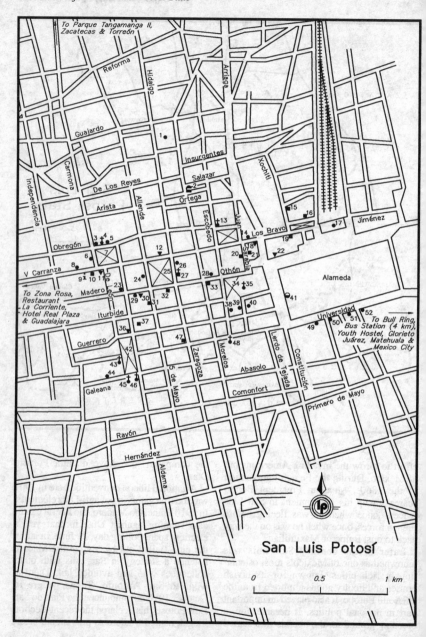

San Luis Potosí

0   0.5   1 km

■ PLACES TO STAY

10	Hotel Panorama
15	Hotel Anáhuac
16	Hotel Guadalajara
19	Hotel Jardín Potosí
20	Hotel Principal
21	Hotel Maria Cristina & Hotel Nápoles
31	Hotel de Gante
32	Hotel Plaza
33	Hotel Concordia
37	Hotel Progreso
47	Hotel Filher

▼ PLACES TO EAT

11	Restaurant La Parroquia
12	Restaurant La Posada del Virrey
18	Café Pacífico
22	Café Tokio
30	Restaurant/Bar Castillo
36	Restaurant El Bocolito

OTHER

1	Mercado Hidalgo
2	Post Office
3	Capilla de Loreto
4	Church of La Compañía
5	University (Rectory)

6	Ipiña Building
7	Plaza de los Fundadores
8	Computel
9	Tourist Office
13	Iglesia de San Juan de Dios
14	Caseta de Larga Distancia
17	Train Station
23	Caja Real
24.	Palacio del Gobierno
25	Plaza de Armas
26	Palacio Municipal
27	Cathedral
28	Casa Museo de Manuel José Othón
29	Palacio Monumental
34	Plaza del Carmen
35	Iglesia del Carmen
38	Telecomm
39	Museo Nacional de la Máscara
40	Teatro de la Paz
41	Bus Stop
42	Plaza San Francisco
43	Iglesia de San Francisco
44	Museo Regional Potosino
45	Iglesia del Tercer Orden
46	Iglesia del Sagrado Corazón
48	Iglesia de San Agustín
49	Caseta de Larga Distancia
50	Computel
51	Centro de Difusión Cultural IPBA
52	Santuario de San José

dent, and designated 20 November as the day for Mexico to rise in revolution.

Since the revolution years San Luis has made steady progress as an industrial centre, helped initially by the arrival of widespread electricity supplies in the 1940s. It's a fairly prosperous city, with a laid-back kind of zona rosa, some luxury suburbs and plenty of fine architecture.

Orientation

Central San Luis Potosí is a compact area, easy to walk around and centred on four plazas, stretching about a km from the Alameda park in the east to the Plaza de los Fundadores and the Plaza San Francisco in the west. Within this triangle lie the Plaza del Carmen, surrounded by a clutch of fine buildings a block west of the Alameda, and the Plaza de Armas or zócalo, a block east of the Plaza de los Fundadores. Hotels and res-

taurants are mainly in this central area, with cheaper lodgings concentrated close to the Alameda, near the train station. There is also a youth hostel and a couple of more expensive hotels near the bus station, which is out on the eastern edge of the city. Most shops and markets are in the streets north of the Plaza de Armas.

A small zona rosa, with some scattered up-market restaurants and shops, stretches a couple of km along Carranza, heading west from the Plaza de los Fundadores.

Information

Tourist Office The state Dirección General de Turismo (☎ (481) 12-99-06, 12-30-68, fax 12-62-03) is at Carranza 325, next door to the Hotel Panorama half a block west of the Plaza de los Fundadores. It's open Monday to Friday from 9 am to 8 pm, Saturday 9 am to 1 pm and 4 to 8 pm. They give out free city maps and a series of interesting brochures on the city and state of San Luis Potosí.

Money Numerous banks around the Plaza de Armas and Plaza de los Fundadores change cash and travellers' cheques; they're open Monday to Friday from 9 am to 1.30 pm.

The American Express office (☎ 17-60-04) at Carranza 1077, several blocks west of the Plaza de los Fundadores, is open Monday to Friday from 9 am to 2 pm and 4 to 6 pm, Saturday 10 am to 1 pm. They sell travellers' cheques and will replace lost or stolen ones, but will not change cheques to pesos; for that you must go to a bank or casa de cambio. The American Express travel agency, Grandes Viajes, shares the same office.

Post The main post office is at Morelos 235 between Ortega and Salazar, three blocks north and two blocks west of the Alameda. It's open Monday to Friday from 8 am to 7 pm, Saturday 9 am to 1 pm. Another branch of the post office, open Monday to Friday from 8 am to 7 pm, is in the 1st-class hall of the bus station.

Telecommunications The Telecomm office, with telegram, telex and fax services, is at Escobedo 200 on the south side of the Plaza del Carmen, at the rear entrance of the building housing the National Mask Museum. It's open Monday to Friday from 9 am to 8 pm, Saturday 9 am to 1 pm. Another Telecomm branch with the same services is in the 1st-class hall of the bus station; it's open Monday to Friday, 9 am to 3 pm.

Computel, with long-distance telephone and fax services, is at Universidad 700 on the south side of the Alameda; it's open every day from 7 am to 10 pm. Another branch of Computel, with the same services and hours, is at Carranza 360-B half a block west of the Plaza de los Fundadores.

Other casetas de larga distancia include one at the Cafetería El Carmen at Universidad 686 on the south side of the Alameda, open Monday to Saturday from 5 am to 11 pm and Sunday from 8 am to 3.30 pm, and another at Los Bravo 423 between Constitución and Juan Sarabia, one block north of the Alameda; it's open Monday to Saturday, 9.30 am to 8 pm. Two more casetas, open every day from 8 am to 10 pm, are in the central bus station.

Foreign Consulates There's a US consular office (☎ 17-25-01) at Carranza 1430, several blocks west of the Plaza de los Fundadores; it's open Monday to Friday from 9 am to noon.

Laundry The Super Wash laundromat at Carranza 1093, several blocks west of the Plaza de los Fundadores, is open Monday to Saturday from 8 am to 8 pm, Sunday 9 am to 2 pm. You can drop off your laundry or stay to do it yourself.

Alameda

The large Alameda park marks the eastern boundary of the downtown area. It is behind the Del Carmen church and used to be the vegetable garden of the monastery attached to the church. Today it's an attractive park with shady paths and a small pond with an island.

Santuario de San José The Sanctuary of San José faces the south side of the Alameda. Inside is the image of El Señor de los Trabajos, a Christ figure attracting pilgrims from near and far. Numerous *retablos* around the statue testify to miracles received in finding jobs, regaining health and having other petitions answered.

Centro de Difusión Cultural IPBA Sponsored by the Instituto Potosino de Bellas Artes (Potosino Institute of Fine Arts), this cultural centre in a large modernistic building facing the south side of the Alameda contains art galleries with changing exhibitions and a theatre hosting performances of theatre, dance, music and other arts. The galleries are open Tuesday to Saturday, 10 am to 2 pm and 5 to 8 pm, Sunday 10 am to 2 pm and 6 to 8 pm; admission is free.

Plaza del Carmen

The Plaza del Carmen, dominated by the Iglesia del Carmen church, is one short block west of the Alameda.

Iglesia del Carmen This is the most spectacular building in San Luis, a Churrigueresque church built between 1749 and 1764. The vividly carved stone façade has the upside-down pyramid-shaped pillars known as estípites which are a hallmark of the Churrigueresque style. Perching and hovering angels show the influence of Indian artisans. The Camarín of the Virgin, with a splendid golden altar, is to the left of the main altar inside. The entrance and roof of this chapel are a riot of small plaster figures. The main altar is by Neoclassical architect Eduardo Tresguerras.

Teatro de la Paz The Peace Theatre stands next to the Iglesia del Carmen. The Neoclassical building, constructed between 1889 and 1894, contains a concert hall and exhibition gallery as well as a theatre. Posters announce upcoming events; they usually have something on. The art gallery, called the Sala German Gedovius, is open Tuesday to Sunday from 10 am to 2 pm and 4 to 7 pm; admission is free. Its entrance is to the right of the main theatre entrance.

Casa Museo Nacional de la Máscara Opposite the Teatro de la Paz on the south side of the plaza, the National Mask Museum in an attractive late-19th-century building featuring exhibits of masks from many regions of Mexico, with explanations of the dances and rituals in which they are used, and comments on the use and role of masks in the human experience. The museum is open Tuesday to Friday from 10 am to 2 pm and 4 to 6 pm, Saturday and Sunday 10 am to 2 pm; admission is free.

Casa Museo de Manuel José Othón Also called the Museo Othoniano, this museum at Othón 225, half a block west of the Plaza del Carmen, is in the birthplace of the poet and playwright Manuel José Othón, born here on 14 June 1858. The house features period furniture and memorabilia relating to the poet, his family and his work. The museum is open Tuesday to Friday from 10 am to 2 pm and 4 to 6 pm, Saturday and Sunday 10 am to 2 pm; admission is free.

Iglesia de San Agustín This church, a block south of Plaza del Carmen down Escobedo, is an amalgam of architectural styles constructed over the centuries, with a 17th-century baroque façade, an 18th-century Churrigueresque tower and a Neoclassic interior.

Plaza de Armas

Also known as the Jardín Hidalgo, this is the city's main square, popular with Potosinos for chatting and watching the world go by from the seats dotted around it. There are several cafés and restaurants around the plaza. The kiosk in the middle is inscribed with names of Mexican musicians.

Cathedral The cathedral faces the east side of the Plaza de Armas. When originally completed in 1710, this three-nave baroque building had only one tower. The northern (left-hand) one was added this century and is an exact copy of the other. The Carrara marble statues of the apostles on the façade are smaller copies of the statues in the interior of the San Juan de Letran Basilica in Rome. Inside, the church has a Gothic feel, with towering, sweeping arches carved in pink stone; the leaf motif carved on the arches is repeated in blue and gold on the ceiling. On the altar is a large pipe organ. In 1935 the church was declared a national monument.

Palacio Municipal Beside the cathedral, on its north side, the 19th-century city hall is a stocky building with powerful stone arches. Finished in 1838, it was the home of Bishop Ignacio Montes de Oca from 1892 to 1915, when it was turned over to the city. In the rear of the patio is a stone fountain carved with the heads of three lions; the coat of arms of San Luis Potosí in stained glass overlooks the double staircase. Upstairs, over the entrance to the building, the Cabildo Hall has a ceiling painted by the Italian artist Erulo Eroli.

Palacio del Gobierno This Neoclassical building constructed between 1798 and 1816 occupies the entire west side of the square. Numerous Mexican VIPs have lodged here, including presidents Iturbide and Santa Anna, but its most illustrious occupant was Benito Juárez – first in 1863 when he was fleeing from invading French forces, then in 1867 when he confirmed here the death sentence of Emperor Maximilian, who had been installed by the French. You can visit the rooms he occupied, upstairs inside, which contain life-size models of Juárez and, kneeling before him, Princess Ines de Salm Salm, an American who had married into Maximilian's family and came to San Luis in June 1867 to make one last plea for the emperor's life. The Sala Juárez is open Monday to Friday from 9 am to 2 pm; admission is free.

Palacio Monumental In the block west of the plaza at Madero 175 is the Neoclassical Monumental Palace, designed by the French architect Henri Guindon and finished in 1909. It was here that Francisco Madero and others worked out their revolutionary manifesto, the Plan de San Luis Potosí.

Caja Real The old Royal Treasury on the corner of Madero and Aldama, a block west of the Plaza de Armas, is a pretty baroque building completed in the latter part of the 18th century. Above the typical Potosino balcony on the corner façade stands La Purísima, a stone statue of the Virgin given to the city by King Carlos III of Spain. In 1935 the building was declared a national monument.

Plaza San Francisco
Dominated by the red bulk of the San Francisco church, this quiet square is one of the most beautiful in the city.

Iglesia de San Francisco The 18th-century San Francisco church has a baroque façade. The interior was remodelled this century but the sacristy (priest's dressing room), reached by a door to the right of the altar, is original 18th century with a fine dome, carved pink stone and a number of historic religious paintings. The room through the arch at the south end of the sacristy is called the Sala De Profundis and has more paintings and a stone fountain carved by Indians. A beautiful crystal ship hangs from the main dome into the church's sanctuary.

Iglesias del Tercer Orden & Sagrado Corazón These two small churches, both formerly part of the monastery, stand together at the south end of the plaza. The Tercer Orden church, on the right, was finished in 1694 and restored in 1959-60. Sagrado Corazón dates from 1728-31.

Museo Regional Potosino The regional museum at Galeana 450, along the street to the left of the San Francisco church, is in a large building built in 1592 that was originally part of the Franciscan convent founded in 1590. The ground floor has exhibits on pre-Hispanic Mexico, especially covering the Huasteca Indians but also the peoples of other parts of Mexico.

Upstairs is the lavishly decorated Capilla de Aranzazú, an elaborate mixture of Churrigueresque and baroque styles constructed in the mid-18th century by a Franciscan monk who lived in the convent. A private chapel for the Franciscan order, it is dedicated to the cult of the Virgin of Aranzazú; according to legend, a shepherd found a statue of the Virgin in a thorn bush *(zarzas)* and named it Aranzazú, a Basque word meaning *entre espinas, tu* (among thorns, you).

The museum is open Tuesday to Saturday from 10 am to 6 pm, Sunday 10 am to 2 pm; admission is free.

Plaza de los Fundadores
The Founders' Plaza is where the city started. On the north side is a large building con-

structed in 1653 as a Jesuit college. It was abandoned when the Jesuits were expelled by Spain's King Carlos III. It was later used for a variety of purposes until 1923, when the first autonomous university in Mexico was founded there. It now serves as the rectory.

To the left (west) of this is the church of La Compañía, also called del Sagrario, built by the Jesuits in 1675 with a baroque façade. Further to the left is the Capilla de Loreto, a 1700 Jesuit chapel with picturesque twisted 'Solomonic' pillars. The west side of the plaza is occupied by the Ipiña building, a large Neoclassical edifice. Construction began in 1906 but was interrupted by the Revolution in 1910; originally designed to occupy the entire block, the building was never completed.

Casa de la Cultura

Several blocks west of the Plaza de los Fundadores at Carranza 1815, the Casa de la Cultura occupies a fine turn-of-the-century Neoclassical building surrounded by landscaped grounds. Among its offerings are art exhibits, concerts, theatre and other cultural events; the monthly schedule is posted at the entrance. Free French films are presented by the Alianza Francesa on Saturday at 6 pm; Sunday at noon they show free music videos.

The cultural centre is open Tuesday to Friday from 10 am to 2 pm and 4 to 6 pm, Saturday 10 am to 2 pm and 6 to 8 pm, and on Sunday from 10 am to 2 pm.

Centro Taurino Potosino

A few blocks east of the Alameda on Avenida Universidad at the corner of Triana, past the Plaza de Toros, is a bullfighting museum with a collection of items relating to bullfighting, including intricately decorated matador suits and capes, historical posters and photos, stuffed bulls' heads and more. It's open Tuesday to Saturday from 11 am to 1.30 pm and 5.30 to 7.30 pm; admission is free.

Parks

Two or three km south-west of the centre, the giant 411-hectare **Parque Tangamanga I**

has museums, a planetarium, an outdoor theatre, mechanical games, two large lakes, sports fields and hectares of green open spaces. To get there, take the 'Perimetral' bus from the west side of the Alameda.

Two or three km north of the centre is the newer **Parque Tangamanga II**, also a large park with sports fields and green open spaces. The 'Perimetral' or 'Saucito' buses heading north from the stop on the west side of the Alameda will take you there.

The **Parque Juan H Sánchez**, another lovely green park, is on Carranza, about four km west of the centre.

Festivals

Día de San Sebastián San Sebastián, patron saint of the *barrio* (neighbourhood) of the same name, is fêted in the barrio on 20 January with games, rides, fireworks, etc.

Semana Santa Holy Week, the week before Easter, is celebrated with a number of events including concerts, exhibitions, conferences, an international open tennis tournament and other activities organised for people visiting the city at this time. On Good Friday morning Christ's passion is re-enacted in the barrio of San Juan de Guadalupe, followed by a silent procession through the city with various neighbourhoods and religious brotherhoods carrying images through the streets.

Festival de Arte Primavera Potosina The Spring Arts Festival, normally celebrated during the last two weeks of May, features national and international artists presenting music concerts, symphonies, art exhibits, theatre, classical and contemporary dance, art films, conferences and more. Exact dates are changeable; check with the tourist office for details.

Festival Nacional de Danza During the last two weeks of July the National Dance Festival presents Mexico's most advanced contemporary dance groups at various venues around the city, culminating in the presentation of the National Award for Choreography.

Santiago Apóstol Celebrations similar to those for San Sebastián take place in the Santiago barrio for the barrio's patron saint on 25 July.

Maraton Internacional Tangamanga The International Tangamanga Marathon attracts national and international runners to compete in the 42-km marathon race. Beginning at Tangamanga Park, the runners race through the city, ending back at the park with a giant party of food, music and awards to the winners. The race is held in August, with the date changing each year; check with the tourist office for dates and details.

Feria Nacional Potosina The San Luis Potosí National Fair features cultural, artistic and popular events including concerts, bullfights, rodeos, cockfights and sports events; there's an industrial and commercial pavilion, and exhibits of livestock and agriculture. On 25 August, day of San Luis Rey de Francia (Saint Louis King of France), patron saint of San Luis, various events are organised including a large parade with floats. The national fair goes on for two weeks, normally the last two weeks of August, though the tourist office says the dates may be changing; ask them for details.

Virgen de los Remedios This fiesta is held the first week of September in the Tequisquiapan barrio, with fireworks, games, etc.

San Miguel Arcángel This festival on 29 September features processions and dances in front of the church of San Miguelito, in the barrio of the same name.

Festival Internacional Cervantino The International Cervantes Festival, an extension of the famous festival of the same name in Guanajuato, is held for two weeks around the end of October and beginning of November. National and international arts groups present theatre, dance, music and other cultural events.

Virgen de Guadalupe Dances and fireworks take place on 12 December in the barrio of San Juan de Guadalupe.

Places to Stay – bottom end
Camping The *Motel Mezquite* (☎ (481) 12-03-65) is 13½ km north of the city centre on Highway 57, the highway to Matehuala. It has a trailer park with a swimming pool and 50 trailer spaces with full hook-ups; cost is US$8.35 per space.

Hostels San Luis' youth hostel is the Villa Deportiva Juvenil (☎ (481) 18-16-17), operated by CONADE (the Comisión Nacional del Deporte). It's 1½ blocks from the bus station on Avenida Diagonal Sur, between the bus station and the Glorieta Juárez; from the 2nd-class hall in the bus station turn right out of the entrance, walk to the main road, then go 1½ blocks left to reach the hostel. From the 1st-class hall, go left out of the entrance and walk 1½ blocks

Separate-sex dorms sleep four to a room; cost is US$3.70 a night, with no hostel card required. On the grounds are a swimming pool, a running track and various sports courts. The office is open daily from 6 am to 11 pm.

Hotels Many hotels in every price range are conveniently situated in the city centre. The *Hotel Principal* (☎ (481) 12-07-84) at Juan Sarabia 145, a short block west of the Alameda, is a bit run-down but the beds are OK and it's clean enough. The 18 rooms each have a private bath with 24-hour hot water and cost US$10/13.35 for singles/doubles.

Nearby, the *Hotel Jardín Potosí* (☎ (481) 12-31-52) at Los Bravo 530 is another basic but clean hotel, with 56 rooms with bath at US$12/14.

The *Hotel Anáhuac* (☎ (481) 12-65-04/05, fax 14-49-04) at Xochitl 140, a block north of the Alameda, is a more cheerful place, with its own restaurant and parking facilities. The 43 rooms, all with ample

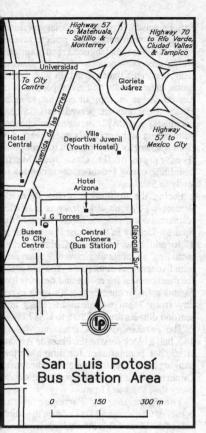

Highway 57
to Matehuala,
Saltillo &
Monterrey

Highway 70
to Río Verde,
Ciudad Valles
& Tampico

Universidad

To City
Centre

Glorieta
Juárez

Highway
57 to
Mexico City

Villa
Deportiva Juvenil
(Youth Hostel)

Hotel
Central

Hotel
Arizona

J G Torres

Buses
to City
Centre

Central
Carnionera
(Bus Station)

Diagonal Sur

San Luis Potosí Bus Station Area

0   150   300 m

bath (some with bathtub as well as shower) open onto a comfortable 2nd-floor TV sitting area in a covered courtyard; others have French doors opening onto wrought-iron balconies. Singles/doubles are US$13.35/18.35. For a couple of dollars more you can get colour TV in your room.

Just off the Plaza de Armas, the *Hotel de Gante* (☎ (481) 12-14-92/93) at 5 de Mayo 140 is another older but comfortable hotel, with singles/doubles at US$17.20/19.75.

Half a block north of the Plaza San Francisco, the *Hotel Progreso* (☎ (481) 12-03-66) at Aldama 415 is also an older hotel, with statues of classical-looking ladies overlooking the staircase and lobby. In its day it was probably a very classy place. The 51 high-ceilinged rooms come in various prices depending on the newness of the furniture, colour TV, etc; singles/doubles start at US$15/16.70 and go up to US$21.35/23.35.

Places to Stay – middle

The *Hotel Maria Cristina* and the *Hotel Nápoles* stand side by side on Juan Sarabia, a short block north-west of the Alameda. The large nine-storey *Maria Cristina* (☎ (481) 12-94-08, fax 12-88-23) at Juan Sarabia 110 has comfortable rooms with satellite colour TV, carpet, phone, fan and plenty of windows; cost is US$26.70/30 for singles/doubles. Next door, the *Nápoles* (☎ (481) 12-84-18, ☎ /fax 14-21-04) at Juan Sarabia 120 has comfortable, modern rooms with the same facilities at the same price. Parking is available at both hotels; each also has its own restaurant.

Also at the same price, the *Hotel Concordia* (☎ (481) 12-06-66, fax 12-69-79), on the corner of Morelos and Othón, is an older hotel but in a modern style; its 94 rooms all have colour TV, carpeting and other amenities, and there's parking and a lobby restaurant/bar.

Near the bus station are a couple of other middle-range hotels. Opposite the station doors, at J Guadalupe Torres 158, is the *Hotel Arizona* (☎ (481) 18-18-48, fax 22-21-82).

windows, cost US$14.65/17 for singles/doubles; add an extra US$4.70 if you want colour TV.

The *Hotel Guadalajara* (☎ (481) 12-46-12), half a block north of the Alameda at Jiménez 253, has enclosed parking and 33 clean, comfortable rooms with ample windows, carpeting, colour TV, phone and fan; cost is US$16.70/18.35 for singles/doubles.

Facing the south side of the Plaza de Armas, the *Hotel Plaza* (☎ (481) 12-46-31) at Jardín Hidalgo 22 is in a refurbished 18th-century building. Some of its 32 rooms with

It's clean and modern, with 92 rooms at US$26.70/30, but it seems a bit overpriced. Around the corner at Avenida de las Torres 290, the *Hotel Central* (☎ (481) 12-14-44) is cheaper but more pleasant, with 70 clean rooms with colour TV, phone, carpet and ample windows; singles/doubles are US$18.35/21.70. It has its own restaurant and parking.

Places to Stay – top end
Near the south-west corner of the Plaza de los Fundadores, the *Hotel Panorama* (☎ (481) 12-17-77, fax 12-45-91) at Carranza 315 is a luxury 10-storey, four-star hotel with 126 rooms. Those on the south side have full-wall windows and private balconies overlooking the swimming pool; singles/doubles are US$50/58.35. Up on the 10th floor is an elegant restaurant/bar with dancing every night except Sunday, when there's a pianist; there's also a piano bar and one of the city's best discos.

Further west on Carranza, the *Hotel Real Plaza* (☎ 14-60-55, 14-69-69, fax 14-66-39) at Carranza 890 is another elegant, modern four-star hotel with every amenity; its 270 rooms cost US$49.70/58.70.

Places to Eat
There are many good, popular places to eat around the centre, especially near the various plazas. The *Café Tokio* at Othón 415, facing the north-west corner of the Alameda, is a large, clean, shiny air-conditioned restaurant good for all meals; the comida corrida is US$3.85, antojitos (enchiladas, tacos, etc) US$2.95 to US$3.50, meat and seafood meals US$3.35 to US$7.85. It's open every day from 7 am to midnight.

Café Pacífico is a pleasant corner café/restaurant on the corner of Los Bravo and Constitución, half a block from the north-west corner of the Alameda. It has a similar menu and prices and is open 24 hours a day.

El Bocolito is a small, unassuming little café/restaurant on the corner of Guerrero and Aldama, on the north-east corner of the Plaza San Francisco. It offers a variety of local specialities with names like gringa, zarape, mula, alambre, pelangocha and capricho, which are combinations of meats (bacon, ham, beef, etc) lightly fried up with herbs, onion, chile, tomato and green pepper, with melted cheese on top; all cost the same at US$5. Breakfasts are served for US$2.35, enchiladas for US$2, or there are cheaper hamburgers and tortas. It's open every day from 8.30 am to 10.30 pm and is a cooperative venture of the Casa José Martí, benefiting young Indian students coming to study in San Luis.

Facing the north side of the Plaza de Armas, *La Posada del Virrey* is a fancier restaurant occupying the former home of the Spanish viceroy in San Luis; it was built in 1736 and now has several dining areas including an attractive covered courtyard with live music at dinnertime. You can come for meals or just for coffee and desserts like banana splits or cheesecake; it's open every day from 7 am to midnight. Meat and seafood dinners are US$5.35 to US$7.85.

The *Restaurant/Bar Castillo* at Madero 145, half a block west of the Plaza de Armas, is another popular spot for dining or just hanging out over coffee, with some beautiful Durán murals of Paris street scenes. It's open every day, 8 am to 11 pm.

The *Restaurant La Parroquia* at the corner of Carranza and De León on the south side of the Plaza de los Fundadores is another large, clean, popular corner restaurant. The comida corrida is US$4.20 every day except Sunday, when they have a special one for US$6.20; it's open every day from 7 am to midnight.

One of the most attractive restaurants in the city is the *Restaurant La Corriente* at Carranza 700, a few blocks west of the Plaza de los Fundadores. This fancy restaurant/bar is in an elegant covered courtyard with a fountain, ferns and plants all around, and specialises in ranch-style food and Mexican antojitos. You can eat well here for less than US$5, including a meal and a soft drink. The hearty comida corrida, with nine selections of main dishes, is served every day except

Sunday; cost is US$4, or if you prefer you can get a selection of all nine main dishes for just US$6.70. It's open every day from 8 am to midnight.

More expensive, but elegant for a special lunch or evening out, is the *Sky Room* penthouse restaurant/bar up on the 10th floor of the Hotel Panorama at Carranza 315, near the south-west corner of the Plaza de los Fundadores. They serve an array of international and European dishes and its full-wall windows offer a great view over the entire city. There's music for dancing every night from 9 pm to 2 am, except Sunday night when there's a pianist; after dining you could also go to the piano bar or disco in the same hotel.

Entertainment

San Luis has several downtown cinemas and a fairly active cultural life. Ask in the tourist office for what's on and keep your eyes on the posters around town for concerts (popular and classical) and exhibitions. The Teatro de la Paz has something on most nights; theatre and other cultural events are also presented at the Centro de Difusión Cultural IPBA on the south side of the Alameda, at the Casa de la Cultura at Carranza 1815, and the Teatro de la Ciudad and Teatro Infantil Carlos Amador, both in the Parque Tangamanga I.

Bullfights take place at the Plaza de Toros on Universidad, east of the Alameda. There's also a bullfighting museum here.

Numerous cultural and popular events take place during San Luis' many annual festivals.

There are a few discos in town and in the motels on the outskirts. Most popular are La Jaula del Jaguar in the Hotel Panorama at Carranza 315 in the centre; Arusha at Prolongación Muñoz 195; Oasis in the Hotel Maria Dolores on Highway 57, the exit to Mexico City, just pass the Glorieta Juárez on the eastern outskirts of the city; and Dulcinea at the Motel Hostal del Quijote, further out on Highway 57 heading towards Mexico City.

Things to Buy

The Mercado Hidalgo is five blocks north of the Plaza de Armas, between Morelos and Zaragoza. The main area of shops lies between Mercado Hidalgo and the Plaza de Armas. There are also a number of more expensive shops and boutiques along Carranza, west of the Plaza de los Fundadores in the zona rosa.

Getting There & Away

Air The airport is 23 km from the centre of town, on Highway 57 heading towards Monterrey. Airlines and flights serving San Luis include Mexicana (flights to Mexico City four times weekly, and to Monterrey and Chicago four times weekly), Aeromar (daily flights to Mexico City), Aerolitoral (daily flights to Monterrey), Aeroponiente (flights to Guadalajara six times weekly), Aeroguadalajara (flights to Guadalajara six times weekly, and to Tampico and Puerto Vallarta four times weekly).

There are a number of travel agencies around the centre where you can make flight arrangements, especially in the zona rosa blocks of Carranza heading west from the Plaza de los Fundadores.

Bus The Central de Autobuses is on the eastern outskirts of the city, just south of the Glorieta Juárez, on J Guadalupe Torres at the corner of Avenida Diagonal Sur. It's a large bus station with separate halls for 1st, 2nd and 3rd-class buses. Also here are a restaurant, a post office open Monday to Friday from 8 am to 7 pm, a Telecomm office beside it open Monday to Friday from 9 am to 3 pm, and a couple of casetas de larga distancia, open daily from 8 am to 10 pm.

Local buses marked 'Centro' go from the bus station into the centre of town; the local bus stop is on the corner to your left as you exit from the 2nd-class hall of the station. In the centre, local buses arrive and depart from the bus stop at the western end of the Alameda. Any 'Central' bus will take you from there back to the bus station.

San Luis Potosí is a major hub of bus transport, with buses heading out to everywhere in northern Mexico. Bus routes departing from San Luis Potosí include:

Aguascalientes – 168 km, 2½ hours; 17 daily with Estrella Blanca (US$4.30).

Ciudad Victoria – 346 km, four to five hours; hourly buses, 8 pm to 4 am, with Estrella Blanca (US$8.35); six daily with Transportes Chihuahuenses (US$10); six daily with Servicios Huastecos (US$7.50); five daily with Transportes Frontera (US$9); four daily with Tres Estrellas de Oro (US$9).

Guadalajara – 354 km, five to six hours; hourly, 24 hours, with Transportes Oriente (US$8.20); nine daily with ETN (US$13.35); four daily with Estrella Blanca (US$9); one or two daily with several other lines.

Matehuala – 191 km, 2½ hours; same buses as to Monterrey (US$4.35 to US$5.20).

Mexico City – 425 km, five to six hours; hourly buses, 24 hours, with Estrella Blanca (US$11.35); hourly, 24 hours, with Transportes Frontera (US$11.35); 20 daily with ETN (US$20); 15 daily with Omnibus de México (US$11.35); 13 daily with Transportes Chihuahuenses (US$12.35); six daily with Autobuses Blancos (US$11.35); six daily with Autobuses El Águila (US$10.35); four daily with Servicios Coordinados (US$11.35); two daily with Primera Plus (US$13.35); two daily with Tres Estrellas de Oro (US$11.35).

Monterrey – 537 km, six to seven hours; hourly buses, 5.30 am to 2 pm, then every half hour, 2 pm to 1.30 am, with Estrella Blanca (US$12.70); hourly, 2 pm to 4 am, with Transportes Frontera (US$13.70); six daily with Transportes Chihuahuenses (US$15); four daily with Tamaulipas Altiplano (US$13.95); three daily with Tres Estrellas de Oro (US$13.95); three daily with Autobuses Blancos (US$12); three daily with Autobuses El Águila (US$12); two daily with Omnibus de México (US$13.70).

Querétaro – 200 km, 2½ hours; same buses as to Mexico City (US$4.60 to US$7.70).

Río Verde – 131 km, 2½ hours; same buses as to Tampico (US$3.25).

Saltillo – 260 km, five to six hours; same buses as to Monterrey (US$10.35 to US$12.70).

Santa María del Río – 47 km, 45 minutes; buses every half hour, 6.20 am to 11.15 pm, with Autobuses Rojos de Potosí (US$1.15); every half hour, 6.30 am to 11 pm, with Autobuses Potosinos (US$1.15).

Tampico – 392 km, six to seven hours; hourly, 24 hours, with Transportes Oriente (US$12.50); four daily with Servicios Huastecos (US$9); two daily with Omnibus de México (US$10); one daily with Tres Estrellas de Oro (US$10); one daily with Transportes Chihuahuenses.

Zacatecas – 189 km, three hours; nine daily with Omnibus de México (US$4.70); two daily with Estrella Blanca (US$4.35).

Train The Estación del Ferrocarril (☎ 12-21-23) is on the north side of the Alameda. Tickets for night trains can be bought at the station from 2 to 7 pm; tickets for other trains are sold an hour before departure time.

Trains departing from San Luis include:

El Regiomontano – 1st-class train; 3.55 am – southbound to Mexico City, 8½ hours (US$13.70); 12.11 am – northbound to Monterrey, 6½ hours (US$15.35).

Train 1 – 2nd-class train; 5.35 pm – northbound to Nuevo Laredo, 11 hours (US$6.70).

Train 2 – 1st & 2nd-class train; 10.35 am – southbound to Mexico City, nine hours (1st-class cars US$13.70, 2nd-class cars US$4.40).

Train 352 – 2nd-class train; 10.35 am – westbound to Aguascalientes, six hours (US$2).

El Huasteco – 2nd-class train; 8.00 am – eastbound to Tampico, 11 hours (US$4).

Though these are the scheduled times, in practice the trains are often late, and schedules are subject to change. Check the current schedules at the station.

Car & Motorbike The excellent Highway 57 runs 425 km south to Mexico City; northward it goes to Matehuala (191 km) and Saltillo (260 km). Highway 45 goes northwest to Zacatecas (189 km). To the east, Highway 70 goes to Ciudad Valles (268 km) and Tampico (392 km). Highway 70 also continues west of San Luis Potosí to Aguascalientes (168 km). For Guadalajara (354 km from San Luis), take Highway 70 west until just after the small town of Ojuelos de Jalisco, where you branch left on Highway 80 through Lagos de Moreno.

Car rental agencies include Budget (☎ 14-50-59), National (☎ 18-24-89, 18-26-16, ext 103), Kar (☎ 12-95-00, 12-32-29) and others; they are listed in the yellow pages of the telephone directory under 'Automóviles, Renta de'.

Getting Around
To/From the Airport Taxi Aereo (☎ 12-21-

22) runs a colectivo taxi to and from the airport for US$13.35 per person, but for two or more people a taxi (US$13.35 to US$16.70) is cheaper for the half-hour trip.

Bus Local buses operate every day from 5.30 am to around 10 pm; cost is US$0.20. The main bus stop in the city centre is on the west side of the Alameda; from here buses depart to most places in the city.

Taxi Taxis cost around US$2 from the bus station to the centre.

MATEHUALA
Population: 50,000
Altitude: 1600 metres

The only town of any size on Highway 57 between Saltillo and San Luis Potosí, Matehuala ('ma-te-WAL-a') is an unremarkable but pleasant and quite prosperous place high on the Altiplano Central. Matehuala was founded in the 17th century, and its winding central streets give it a colonial air, but the main reason for going there is because it's the major jumping-off point for Real de Catorce.

Orientation
Central Matehuala lies between two plazas about 400 metres apart: the formal Plaza de Armas with a kiosk in the middle, and the bustling Placita del Rey to the north, in front of the large concrete church. Cheaper hotels and the town's restaurants are in this area; motels are on Highway 57 as it bypasses the town to the east.

The bus station is about two km south of the centre. To walk to the centre from the bus station, turn left out of the entrance, then go straight along the road (5 de Mayo) for about 1½ km until you reach the corner of Guerrero, where you turn left. Guerrero ends after a few blocks when it meets Morelos. The Plaza de Armas is a few metres to the left along Morelos.

Festivals
Fiesta del Cristo de Matehuala Held the first two weeks of January, the festival includes religious ceremonies and processions, fireworks, folk dances, rodeos and cockfights. The main day is 6 January.

Founding of Matehuala From 8 to 16 July a feria celebrates the founding of the town.

Places to Stay
In Town The place with the most atmosphere is the *Hotel Matehuala* (☎ (488) 2-06-80) at the corner of Bustamante and Hidalgo. The departure point for buses to Real de Catorce is only a few doors away. The hotel has a

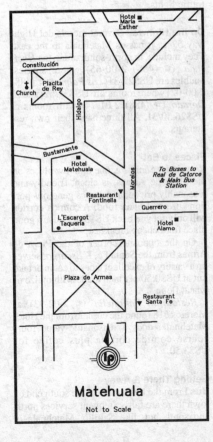

Matehuala

Not to Scale

large central courtyard with rooms on two levels around it. Rooms are basic, but the place has a pleasant atmosphere and friendly staff. Singles/doubles are US$10.50/12. Rooms away from the street are much quieter.

Elsewhere, the *Hotel Alamo* (☎ (488) 2-00-17) on Guerrero near the Morelos end is dingy and grubby with singles/doubles at US$7/8. The *Hotel María Esther* is a family-run place where singles/doubles with private bath cost only US$5.50/7. It is on the northern section of Morelos which you reach by walking along Hidalgo from the Hotel Matehuala, past the church and turning right at the traffic lights.

On the Highway Several motels dot Highway 57 as it passes Matehuala to the east. They include, in north-south order, the *Hacienda* (☎ (488) 2-00-65) where singles/doubles are US$22/31; *Las Palmas* (☎ (488) 2-00-02) where rooms are US$37/52; and *El Dorado* (☎ (488) 2-01-74) with rooms at US$26.50/31. All three have their own restaurants.

Places to Eat

Restaurant Santa Fe, one of a few places on the Plaza de Armas, is clean, friendly and reasonably priced, and serves generous portions of good plain food. A comida corrida will only set you back US$3. It is also a good place for a cheap breakfast.

On the opposite corner of the Plaza de Armas from the Santa Fe, *L'Escargot* serves up a variety of excellent tacos to eat in or take out at US$0.50 per taco made with maize or wheat flour.

Restaurant Fontinella (☎ 2-02-93), at Morelos 618 round the corner from the Hotel Matehuala, does a reasonable-value four-course comida corrida plus coffee for US$3.50.

Getting There & Away

Bus From the bus station at the south end of town there are fairly frequent services north and south but, like Saltillo, Matehuala is mid-route for most buses so you can usually buy tickets only when the bus arrives.

The companies which pass through Matehuala are Transportes del Norte (1st class) (T del N), Autobuses Anáhuac (1st and 2nd class) (AA), Transportes Frontera (2nd class) (TF), Transportes Tamaulipas (2nd class) (TT). The main destinations are:

Guanajuato – 401 km, five hours; (US$7.50) with TF.
Guadalajara – 542 km, seven hours; (US$10.50) with TF.
Mexico City – 585 km, eight hours; (US$12.50) with T del N, AA, TF.
Monterrey – 288 km, 5 hours; (US$7 1st class, US$6.50 2nd class) with T del N, AA, TF, TT.
Nuevo Laredo – 518 km, eight hours; (US$11) with T del N, TF.
Querétaro – 393 km, five hours; (US$8) with T del N, AA, TF.
Reynosa – 388 km, 7½ hours; (US$9.50) with AA, TT.
Saltillo – 203 km, four hours; (US$5) with T del N, AA, TF.
San Luis Potosí – 191 km, 1½ hours; (US$3.75 1st class, US$3.50 2nd class) with T del N, AA, TF, TT.

Getting Around

Orange buses marked 'Centro' run from the bus station to the town centre but aren't very frequent. It's often quicker to make the 25-minute walk.

Buses for Real de Catorce leave at 8, 10 am, noon, 2 and 6 pm from Guerrero, a little way to the east of the Hotel Alamo and on the other side of the road. One-way fare is US$1.30. Get to the office an hour ahead to buy your ticket.

REAL DE CATORCE

Population: 800
Altitude: 2756 metres

This is a place with a touch of magic. High in an offshoot of the Sierra Madre Oriental, Real de Catorce was a wealthy and important silver-mining town of 40,000 people until early this century. Today it's almost deserted, its paved streets lined with decaying or boarded-up stone houses, its mint a ruin. Thirty km north-west of Matehuala and reached by a 2⅓-km road tunnel through former mine shafts, the town lies in a narrow valley at a high elevation, with spectacular views westward to the plain below.

Its remaining 800 or so souls now eke an existence from old mine workings and from pilgrims who come to pay homage to the figure of Saint Francis of Assisi in the town's church. The festival of St Francis (San Francisco) is on 4 October, and between 100,000 and 200,000 people flock to the tiny settlement between 25 September and 12 October.

The rugged mountains surrounding the town are a source of the hallucinogenic cactus peyote. The Huichol Indians, who live 400 km away on the Durango-Nayarit-Jalisco-Zacatecas borders, believe that their peyote and maize gods live here. Every May or June they make a pilgrimage to the hills around Catorce, known to them as Wírikuta, for rituals involving peyote.

You can visit Real de Catorce on a day trip by bus from Matehuala, or stay in one of its few hostelries to soak up the mountain air and strange, peaceful atmosphere – which have attracted a tiny handful of Americans and Europeans to make this place home.

History
The name Real de Catorce literally means 'Royal of 14': the '14' probably comes from 14 soldiers killed by Indians in the area about 1700. The town was founded in the mid-18th century and the church built between 1783 and 1817.

The mines had their ups and downs: during the independence war years (1810-1821) some of the shafts were flooded and in 1821-22 an Englishman called Robert Phillips made a year-long journey from London to Catorce bringing a 'steam machine' for pumping the water from the mines.

Real de Catorce reached its peak in the late 19th century when it was producing an estimated US$3 million in silver a year, and had a theatre, a bull ring and shops selling imported European goods. Numbers of large houses still standing today bear witness to this period of opulence for some of its citizens. The dictator Porfirio Díaz journeyed

here from Mexico City in 1895 to inaugurate two mine pumps bought from San Francisco, California. Díaz had to travel by train, then by mule-carriage, then on horseback to reach Catorce.

Quite why Catorce was transformed into a ghost town within three decades is a slight mystery. Locals in the town will tell you that during the revolution years (1910-20) *bandidos* took refuge here and scared away the other inhabitants. The official state tourist guidebook explains, perhaps more plausibly, that the price of silver slumped after 1900.

Orientation
The bus from Matehuala drops you at the end of the 2⅓-km Ogarrio tunnel, from where the town spreads out before you. A rough street, Lanza Gorta, leads straight ahead (west) to the church, which is roughly the centre of town.

Parroquia
The parish church is quite an impressive Neoclassical building but it's the reputedly miraculous image of St Francis of Assisi on one of the side altars that is the attraction for thousands of Mexican pilgrims. A cult has grown up this century around the statue, whose help is sought in solving problems. Some believe it can cleanse their sins. Also in the church are numerous grateful offerings from people whom St Francis has helped, including paintings of 'miraculous' incidents attributed to him.

Casa de la Moneda
Opposite the main entrance of the church, the old House of Money is now empty and crumbling. Coins were minted here for a few years in the 1860s. A friendly old fellow who usually hangs around on the steps of the mint is full of stories about the town's past and has the key to the cockpit (see below). He doesn't ask for money but you may want to give him some coins.

Plaza Hidalgo
Further west along the street that leads from

the bus halt to the church and mint, you reach this small plaza raised above the right side of the street. The plaza was constructed in 1888 with a fountain in the middle; the kiosk you see now replaced the fountain in 1927.

Palenque de Gallos & Plaza de Toros

A block or so north-west of the plaza lies this monument to the town's heyday, a cockpit built like a Roman amphitheatre. It was restored in the 1970s and now hosts occasional theatre or dance performances. It's normally locked – the man on the steps of the mint has the key and will open the cockpit for you. Further up the hill (Zaragoza) past the cockpit, you soon reach the edge of the town. Here, opposite the graveyard, is the bull ring (Plaza de Toros), also recently restored.

Museum

In the bowels of the church, with its entrance on Lanza Gorta, is a small museum containing photos, documents and whatever else has been rescued from the crumbling town that pertains to its heyday including a rusting, ancient car, said to be the first to reach Catorce. Entry to the museum costs US$0.25.

Places to Stay & Eat

Real de Catorce has a couple of cheap casas de huéspedes and three middle-range hostelries, all catering mainly to pilgrims.

There are a few casas de huéspedes and food stalls along Lanza Gorta and near the bus stop. *Casa de Huéspedes La Providencia* on Lanza Gorta has basic but cleanish singles/doubles for US$6/9. The attached restaurant does an excellent comida corrida for around US$4.

If you are looking for real rock-bottom accommodation, you may be able to rent a room from Doña Celia. To find her house, walk to the church, then up the stairs into the small square at the top. As you face the church from this position, the house is the second one on the left of the church (blue door). Doña Celia's rooms are very basic, but they rent for US$7 (single or double). If this

is too expensive for you, she will rent you floor space for around US$1.50.

El Real, up the hill to the right off Lanza Gorta one block after the church, is an old house restored to provide a few quite comfortable bedrooms at US$17.50 double. The communal bathroom is clean. Its restaurant serves Italian and other food; main dishes are US$1 to US$5. There is an excellent Huichol yarn picture on the dining-room wall.

If you go up Zaragoza, the street running uphill to the north from Plaza Hidalgo, you soon find yourself on the edge of the town. Here, near another church, is the modern *Quinta La Puesta Del Sol* with superb views down the valley to the west, where rooms with TV and private bath cost US$20.

Getting There & Away

Bus Five buses a day make the journey from Matehuala to Real de Catorce and back. One-way fare is US$1.30 and the journey takes at least 1¼ hours. In Matehuala the buses leave at 8, 10 am, noon, 2 and 6 pm from Guerrero, not far from the Hotel Alamos. It's advisable to get there an hour before departure if you want a seat. You can buy return (round-trip) tickets.

Car & Motorbike The road up the hill to Catorce is mostly well paved. The Ogarrio tunnel is only wide enough for one vehicle; men stationed at each end with telephones control traffic. If you're driving south down Highway 57 you can turn off through Cedral to reach Catorce, rather than going to Matehuala and then back northwards again.

RÍO VERDE

Population: 42,000

Río Verde, 131 km east of San Luis Potosí on the Ciudad Valles road, is a small town in an agricultural area surrounded by orange and avocado trees, beans and maize. The town was founded in 1617; the church on the plaza was built by the Franciscans in 1761. Around the town are a number of thermal pools good for swimming, including La Plata, Los Anteojitos, San Diego and Palma

Larga. Food and lodging are available in the town.

A few km from Río Verde is a small lake, Laguna de la Media Luna, from which a mammoth's bones and pre-Hispanic pottery vessels containing small figures have been recovered. The waters are warm and clear except during the rainy summer months, and the lake attracts snorkellers and divers. It's sometimes possible to rent equipment in the town; facilities at the lake are limited. To get there, take the turn-off from Highway 70, four km west of the town, and go nine km down a rough road to reach the lake.

CIUDAD VALLES

Population: 320,000

Ciudad Valles ('VAH-yes'), sometimes just called Valles, lies on Highway 85, the Pan-American, a little over halfway from Matamoros (540 km) or Monterrey (520 km) to Mexico City (475 km), at the junction of Highway 110 from Tampico (140 km) and Highway 70 to San Luis Potosí (270 km). It's a convenient overnight stop for motorists. Commerce in cattle and coffee are among the most important activities. The town's Museo Regional has a Huastec collection.

Orientation

The bus station (Central de Autobuses) is on the eastern edge of town. Local buses waiting outside go along Highway 85 before turning left along Hidalgo to approach the central plaza, which is about seven blocks west of the highway.

Places to Stay

Two adequate places are the *Hotel Rex* (☎ (138) 2-03-45) at Hidalgo 60, 3½ blocks from the plaza, and the *Hotel Piña* (☎ (138) 2-01-83) at Juárez 210, a little closer to the plaza (Juárez is parallel to Hidalgo, one block north). Both are clean and unspectacular, with moderately-sized singles/doubles at US$9/10.50.

A km north of the town along Highway 85, the *Hotel Valles* (☎ (138) 2-00-50) is a luxurious motel with good, large air-con rooms for around US$40/44. It has a big swimming pool and a 25-site campground/trailer park where full hook-ups cost around US$10.

Places to Eat

Pizza Bella Napoli next to the Hotel Piña at Juárez 210 does good spaghetti (US$2.25 to US$3) and pizzas (US$2.50 to US$7.50). For Mexican food, including comida corrida, try the *Restaurant Malibu* at Hidalgo 109, a few doors from the central plaza. Hotel Valles has a steakhouse, the *Restaurant Del Bosque*, in its grounds.

Getting There & Away

Bus There are fairly frequent but mainly 2nd-class buses to most places in north-east Mexico. Few are locales. Departures include:

Matamoros – 545 km, 10 hours; several 2nd-class buses daily for US$9.75

Mexico City – 465 km, 10 hours; four 1st-class buses daily by Omnibus de México for US$9, hourly 2nd-class buses by Flecha Roja

Monterrey – 520 km, nine hours; half a dozen 1st-class and 2nd-class buses daily for about US$10

Pachuca – 380 km, 8½ hours; several 2nd-class buses daily for US$7.50

San Luis Potosí – 270 km, 4½ hours; two 1st-class buses daily for US$5.25 and one or two 2nd-class buses hourly

Tampico – 140 km, 2½ hours; seven 1st-class buses daily, mostly by Omnibus de Oriente, for US$2.75, and two or three 2nd-class buses an hour

Car Highway 70 west to San Luis Potosí is spectacular as it rises across the Sierra Madre to the Altiplano Central. But it's twisting with a sometimes poor surface. East to Tampico the road is in the same condition but straighter.

Southward on Highway 85 there's fine, rugged highland after Tamazunchale (105 km) as the road climbs above 2000 metres in the Sierra Madre (be ready for fog between Tamazunchale and Zimapán). Pachuca is the only sizeable town before Mexico City.

TAMUÍN

The important Huastec ceremonial centre of Tamuín, which flourished from about 700 to

1200 AD, is seven km from the town of the same name, 30 km east of Ciudad Valles on Highway 110, the Tampico road. The ruins are not spectacular but this is one of the few Huastec sites worth visiting at all. Turn south down a road marked 'San Vincente' from Highway 110 about one km east of the town, and continue for 5½ km. From a small sign indicating the 'zona arqueológica', it's about an 800-metre walk to the ruins. Frequent buses between Tampico and Ciudad Valles go through Tamuín. The rest of the way you must walk or take a taxi.

The only cleared part of the 170,000-sq-metre site is a plaza with platforms made of river stones on all four sides. A low bench with two conical altars, extending from the east side of a small platform in the middle of the plaza, bears the remains of frescoes (probably 8th or 9th-century) which may represent priests of Quetzalcóatl.

TANCANHUITZ & AQUISMÓN

The small town of Tancanhuitz, also called Ciudad Santos, in a narrow, tree-covered valley 52 km south of Ciudad Valles, three km east of Highway 85, is in the heart of the area inhabited by modern-day Huastecs. A lively market takes place on Sunday. There are pre-Hispanic Huastec remains near Tampamolón, a few km east.

The Huastec village of Aquismón, 11 km north-west of Tancanhuitz, holds its market on Saturday. In the wild country nearby, not accessible by vehicle, are the 105-metre **Cascada de Tamul**, which are 300 metres wide when in flood, and the **Sótano de las Golondrinas** (Pit of the Swallows), a 300-metre-deep hole which is home to tens of thousands of swallows and parakeets.

Tancanhuitz and Aquismón are centres for the festivals of San Miguel Arcángel and the Virgen de Guadalupe on 28 and 29 September and 12 December respectively. Huastec dances performed then include Las Varitas (The Little Twigs) and Zacamson (Small Music), which imitate the movements of wild creatures. Zacamson, danced especially around Aquismón, has in its full version more than 75 parts, danced at different times

of day and night, and is accompanied by much drinking of sugar-cane alcohol.

TAMAZUNCHALE
Population: 65,000

Quaint Tamazunchale, 95 km south of Ciudad Valles on Highway 85, is in a low-lying area of tropical vegetation with exuberant bird and butterfly life. There are a few hotels and restaurants, mainly on 20 de Noviembre, and a colourful Sunday market. For the Day of the Dead (2 November) the people spread carpets of confetti and marigold petals on the streets, leading to family altars.

SANTA MARIA DEL RÍO
Population: 9600

Forty-seven km south of San Luis Potosí, just off the highway to Mexico City, this small town is famed for its excellent hand-made rebozos. They are usually made of synthetic silk thread called *artisela* in patterns which appear to involve some tie-dyeing, with garish colours less in evidence than in many Mexican textile centres. It takes about two weeks to make one, and prices in Santa Maria are lower than in San Luis.

You can see and buy the rebozos at the Escuela del Rebozo (Rebozo School) on the central Plaza Hidalgo, and in a few private workshops. A Rebozo Fair is held each year in August or December; check with the tourist office in San Luis for exact dates. There's a smart motel and restaurant, *La Puesta del Sol*, at the entrance to Santa Maria from the highway; other lodging is also available. The Autobuses Rojos de Potosí and Autobuses Potosinos bus companies link the town with San Luis Potosí.

Ten km before the town is the **Ojo Caliente** thermal springs, a bathing resort with swimming pools and baths.

Also in the area is **Lourdes**, another thermal-spring resort, whose waters are said to be beneficial for digestion, the skin, nerves and for rheumatism. Lodging and food are available. To get there, go 53 km south from San Luis on the highway to

Mexico city, then turn off and go another 10 km down a gravel road to the springs.

GOGORRÓN

This is another hot-springs resort; its waters reach 42°C and are allegedly beneficial for rheumatism and arthritis. Facilities include four large swimming pools, two smaller children's pools, private Roman baths, large green areas, basketball and volleyball courts and horse riding. The resort is open every day from 9 am to 6 pm; cost for day use is US$4 (children US$2.70).

Gogorrón can easily be visited on a day trip from San Luis. From the central bus station, take a Flecha Amarilla bus heading towards San Felipe – they depart every 20 minutes, 5 am to 9 pm. It takes about an hour to reach Gogorrón and the bus will drop you off right at the gate. Flag down a bus at the entrance for the return trip.

If you want to stay over, accommodation is available in comfortable cabins. With three meals a day included, cost is US$58/69 for singles/doubles in smaller cabins, US$85.35/99.70 in large ones; two children under 10 years old can stay for free with their parents. A stay without meals is available only from Sunday to Thursday nights; cost is US$40.35 for one or two people. All the cabins have private Roman baths.

You can make reservations and get more information at the Gogorrón office (☎ 12-15-50, 12-36-36) in San Luis, up on the 4th floor at Othón 100, opposite the cathedral on the Plaza de Armas. The office is open Monday to Friday from 9 am to 8 pm, Saturday 9 am to 2 pm. Or you can contact the resort directly (☎ /fax 22-08-06).

Aguascalientes State

The state of Aguascalientes, bordered on the south by Jalisco and on the east, north and west by Zacatecas, is one of Mexico's smallest and was originally part of the state of Zacatecas; according to legend, a kiss planted on the lips of dictator Santa Anna by the attractive wife of a prominent local politician brought about the creation of Aguascalientes state, independent of Zacatecas.

Aguascalientes is primarily an agricultural state, with fertile lands where maize (corn), beans, chiles, fruits and grains are grown for use within the state and for export. Livestock is also important and the state's ranches raise famous bullfighting stock for bullfights all over Mexico as well as cattle for meat and hides. Industry is concentrated in and around the capital city, Aguascalientes.

AGUASCALIENTES

Population: 440,500
Altitude: 1800 metres

Aguascalientes (Hot Waters), named for its hot springs, is the capital of Aguascalientes state. It's a booming, prosperous, industrial city with just enough colonial legacies to justify a brief visit.

History

Before the conquistador invasion, indigenous people built a labyrinth of catacombs which made the first Spaniards here dub Aguascalientes La Ciudad Perforada – the perforated city. Archaeologists still have no explanation for the tunnels, which are off limits to visitors.

Cortés dispatched Pedro de Alvarado to subdue the tribes in this region. When Alvarado reached Aguascalientes in 1522, a fierce attack by Indians forced him to retreat. King Philip II decreed Aguascalientes a settlement in 1575, naming it Villa de la Asunción, but continual raids by the Chichimecs limited settlement for years. The initial settlement was a fortress with 16 soldiers, one official and two neighbours, from which the soldiers protected outlying miners, silver convoys from Zacatecas and cattle drovers.

As the Indians were suppressed, the city grew. The springs at Ojo Caliente served as the basis for the growth of the town; in the 16th century, Juan de Montoro built a large tank beside the springs, which served as a public fountain and irrigation for local farms

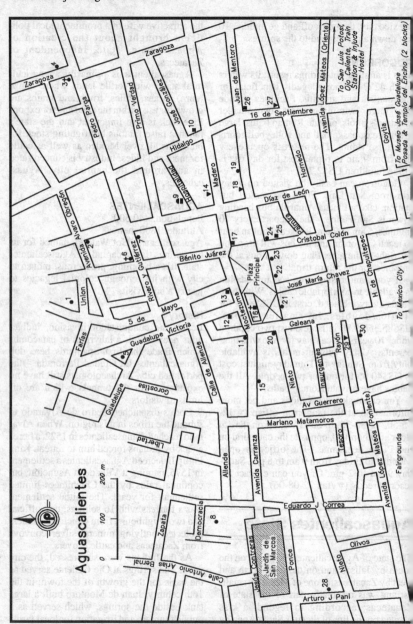

Aguascalientes

where fruits, vegetables and grains were cultivated both for home use and for the regional market. By 1611 the town, with houses and farms, was declared a villa, with the name of Villa de Nuestra Señora de la Asunción de las Aguas Calientes.

Today, more than half of the state's population lives in the city, where industry, textile crafts, and the region's ranches, vineyards and orchards provide employment. While this has benefited the people of Aguascalientes, urban expansion has significantly diminished the former colonial charm of the city. Nonetheless, there are a few interesting things to see and places to visit.

Orientation

Aguascalientes is flat and easy to get around. The centre of town is the Plaza Principal, also sometimes called the Plaza de la Patria or Plaza de Armas. Around this plaza are the cathedral, the Palacio del Gobierno and Palacio Municipal, the elegant Hotel Francia, and the city's commercial centre. Most hotels, restaurants, and sites of interest are within a few blocks of the plaza; others are easily accessible by local bus from the centre. The bus and train stations, both on the outskirts of town, are served by frequent local buses.

Information

Tourist Office The tourist office (☎ (491) 15-11-55), called the Delegación de Turismo del Estado de Aguascalientes, is on the ground floor of the Palacio del Gobierno on the south side of the Plaza Principal. It's open Monday to Friday from 8 am to 3 pm and 5 to 8 pm, Saturday 10 am to 1 pm. They give out free city maps and information on the city and state of Aguascalientes.

Money Several banks on and near the Plaza Principal will change money; they're open Monday to Friday from 9 am to 1.30 pm.

Post The post office is at Hospitalidad 108, a couple of blocks north-east of the Plaza Principal. It's open Monday to Friday from 8 am to 7 pm, Saturday 9 am to 1 pm. Another post office, open the same hours, is in the central bus station.

Telecommunications There's a caseta de larga distancia upstairs over the Tortas Estilo México restaurant on the south-east corner of the Plaza Principal, on the corner of Colón and Juan de Montoro, open every day from 8 am to 10 pm. Another caseta, Sendetel, with telephone and fax services, is in the central bus station; it's open every day from 7 am to 9.30 pm.

The Telecomm office, with services of telegraph, telex and fax, is on the corner of Galeana and Nieto, a block from the Plaza Principal. It's open Monday to Friday from 9 am to 8 pm, Saturday 9 am to noon. Another Telecomm office, open the same hours, is in the central bus station.

Bookshops Publicaciones Excelsior, in the Centro Comercial El Parian on Rivero y Gutierrez near the corner of Morelos, has a selection of magazines in English, plus a few English paperbacks.

Cathedral
The 18th-century baroque cathedral on the Plaza Principal is more magnificent on the inside than the outside; inside is the renowned *Last Supper* by the great colonial Zapotecan Indian artist Miguel Cabrera, as well as other excellent 17th and 18th-century religious paintings.

Teatro Morelos
Alongside the cathedral is the Teatro Morelos, which in 1914 played host to a revolutionary convention in which Pancho Villa suggested to supporters of his rival Carranza that the two leaders resolve their differences and save the Revolution by having the state execute them both! The wily Villa was hardly serious, knowing that Carranza would not even show up at the convention, let alone entertain the idea.

Palacio del Gobierno
The most noteworthy example of colonial architecture in Aguascalientes is the Palacio del Gobierno on the south side of the Plaza Principal. The building, once the mansion of the feudal baron the Marqués de Guadalupe, was constructed in 1665 and has been refurbished on numerous occasions. Built of red sandstone, tezontle (porous rock) and pink cantera quarried stone, the palace opens into a striking courtyard of arches and pillars. The mural on the back wall, painted in the 1960s by the Chilean Oswaldo Barra (no surprise

that his mentor was Diego Rivera), is a compendium of the historic and economic forces that forged Aguascalientes. Other murals were in the process of being painted in 1992.

Palacio Municipal
Next to the Palacio del Gobierno is the similarly styled but more contemporary Palacio Municipal.

Museo Regional de Historia
The regional history museum at Carranza 18. one block west of the cathedral, was designed by Refugio Reyes, the same self-taught architect who designed the Church of San Antonio. It was built in 1914 as a family home; in its history it has been a convent, a school, and now a museum. It's open Tuesday to Sunday from 10 am to 2 pm and 5 to 8.30 pm; admission is US$1.70, but free for children and students (with student cards), and free for everyone on Sundays and holidays.

Museo de Aguascalientes
The Museo de Aguascalientes is located in a beautiful turn-of-the-century building at Zaragoza 505 near the corner of Pedro Parga. opposite the Church of San Antonio. It houses a permanent exhibit of the art of native son Saturnino Herran, born in Aguascalientes in 1887, plus other temporary art exhibits. It's open Tuesday to Sunday from 10 am to 2 pm and 4.30 to 7.30 pm; admission is free.

Church of San Antonio
Opposite the Museo de Aguascalientes is the Church of San Antonio, a crazy-quilt of architectural styles by the local self-taught architect Refugio Reyes. The interior is highly ornate, with huge round paintings and intricate decoration highlighted in gold.

Museo de Arte Contemporaneo
The museum of contemporary art is at Juan de Montoro 222, 1½ blocks east of the plaza. It's open Tuesday to Sunday from 10 am to 2 pm and 5 to 8 pm; admission is free.

Museo José Guadalupe Posada

This museum is in the former convent of the Templo del Encino at the corner of Diaz de León and Pimentel, about five blocks south of the Plaza Principal. Aguascalientes' most famous patriot, José Guadalupe Posada, was a fine artist whose political engravings and cartoons lampooning the dictator Porfirio Díaz spurred on the local impulse to revolt. The museum houses a large collection of his work, including the metal engravings the prints were made from; also included are his political and social commentary, plus his art work in many other areas. Also here are various temporary art exhibits.

The museum is open Tuesday to Sunday from 10 am to 2 pm and 4 to 8 pm; admission is free. Each Sunday at 12.30 pm, free cultural events – music concerts, dance, theatre, etc – are presented in the museum's central courtyard.

Templo del Encino

Beside the museum is the Templo del Encino. Some believe that the temple's black statue of Jesus is growing and that when it eventually reaches an adjacent column, a worldwide calamity will ensue.

Jardín de San Marcos

This pretty enclosed park on Avenida Carranza, a couple of long blocks west of the Plaza Principal, is a popular, shady place to relax.

Thermal Springs

With a name like Aguascalientes, it's no surprise that there are hot springs in this town.

The best known thermal springs is Ojo Caliente (☎ 15-47-21). It's on the northern outskirts of town, beyond the train station, at the intersection of Alameda and Boulevard Tecnológico; any local bus marked 'Ojo Caliente' or 'Tecnológico' heading east on Avenida López Mateos will take you there from the centre. The large pool, and some other smaller pools, have cool water; the hot water is in the private pools, which rent by the hour. Also here are large park-like grounds, with tennis, volleyball and squash courts. Entrance is US$1.35 per day; the private pools, holding up to six people, cost US$11.70 per hour, and there are also individual baths at US$1.70 per hour. It's open every day from 7 am to 7 pm. There's also space for trailers and camping.

Another hot springs is the Balneario Valladolid (☎ 18-18-15/21, ext 234), about 20 km north of Aguascalientes on the road to Jesús Maria. Any bus marked 'Valladolid' or 'Jesús Maria' departing from Avenida López Mateos will take you there; the trip takes about half an hour. The water here is hotter than at Ojo Caliente; they also have saunas, tennis and squash courts, and park-like grounds.

Other Attractions

If you have your own wheels you can go a few km north on the highway to Zacatecas for a tour of the **San Marcos Winery**, at km 543. It's open to the public Monday to Friday from 9 am to 2 pm. The brandy made here is cheap and surprisingly good.

Go a little further north and you may visit the region's most famous **bull-breeding ranch**, Hacienda Las Bóvedas. If you don't have a car, you might get the 'Valladolid' or 'Jesús Maria' bus from Avenida López Mateos to stop here. Tell the driver where you want to get off. Other bull-breeding ranches in the area include the Hacienda Chichimeco, also on the highway to Zacatecas, and the Hacienda Peñuelas, about 25 km south of Aguascalientes on the highway to Mexico City, a km or so before the airport. Tours can be arranged through the tourist office in Aguascalientes.

Festivals

Feria de San Marcos This is the biggest national fair in Mexico, attracting around a million visitors each year for the exhibits, cultural events, bullfights, cockfights, free concerts, and a big national-scale parade taking place on the saint's day itself, 25 April. The fair starts in the second week of April and lasts 22 days, ending in early May.

Fiesta de Santiago Apostol This fiesta, featuring traditional dances of the Chicahuale Indians, is held from 26 July to 4 August in the town of Jesús María, about 20 minutes north of Aguascalientes.

Feria de la Guayaba The guayaba (guava) fair is held from 1 to 15 December in the town of Calvillo, about an hour from Aguascalientes.

Places to Stay – bottom end
Camping The Ojo Caliente thermal springs (☎ (491) 15-47-21), at the intersection of Alameda and Boulevard Tecnológico on the northern outskirts of the city, has a trailer park and space for camping. Local buses operate frequently between here and the centre.

Hostels Cheapest place to stay is the INJUDE hostel (☎ (491) 15-34-63, 16-08-78), on the western outskirts of the city at Avenida López Mateos and Calzada de la Juventud. It has 160 beds, with separate men's and women's dorms sleeping up to eight in a room; cost is US$3.70, with no youth hostel card required. In the park-like grounds are a swimming pool, gym, and various ball courts. To get there, go about 800 metres past the train station on Alameda, turn right onto Avenida Circunvalación, go about 400 metres and you'll see it on your left.

Hotels Right in the centre of town are a number of good budget hotels. One of the best is the *Hotel Maser* (☎ (491) 16-35-62) at Juan de Montoro 303 on the corner of 16 de Septiembre. It has 47 clean, pleasant rooms with private bath set around a covered inner courtyard, and enclosed parking in the rear. Singles/doubles are US$13.35/17.35.

A block away at Hidalgo 207, the *Hotel San José* (☎ (491) 15-51-30), also with parking, has simple but clean singles/ doubles at US$16.70/21.70.

The *Hotel Señorial* (☎ (491) 15-16-30, 15-14-73), at Colón 104 near the corner of Juan de Montoro, is on the south-east corner

of the Plaza Principal. Its 32 rooms include some with balconies overlooking the plaza, some interior rooms, and some with beds for up to six people. Singles/doubles are US$13.35/17.35.

On the opposite side of the Plaza Principal, at 5 de Mayo 106 on the corner of Moctezuma, the *Hotel Imperial* (☎ (491) 15-16-64/50) has economical interior rooms at US$12.85/16.50 for singles/doubles. The exterior rooms, with French doors opening onto balconies facing the cathedral, are US$19.10/23.85.

Half a block north of the cathedral, the *Hotel Rosales* (☎ (491) 15-21-65/79) at Guadalupe Victoria 104 is a basic hotel with 43 simple rooms, all with private bath, at US$10/13.35 for singles/doubles.

If you're just passing through town and want to stay near the bus station on the outskirts, there are a couple of basic but clean hotels to your left as you come out the bus station's front door. Both have ground floor restaurants. At the *Hotel Gómez* (☎ (491) 17-04-09), all the rooms have windows facing outside to the street or onto an airshaft; singles/doubles cost US$12.20/14. Behind it, the *Hotel Continental* (☎ (491) 15-55-48) has singles/doubles at US$10.70/ 13.35.

Places to Stay – top end
The luxury place to stay in the centre is the elegant *Hotel Francia* (☎ 15-60-80) on the north-east corner of the Plaza Principal. It has private parking, a restaurant, cafeteria and bar, and 99 rooms, all with air-con, colour TV and phone. Singles/doubles cost US$47/59.

Places to Eat
There are several good places to eat around the centre. The *Restaurant La Veracruzana* on the corner of Hornedo and 16 de Septiembre is nothing fancy, just a small, simple family restaurant with good food at a good price: the comida corrida is a bargain at US$2.85. It's open Monday to Saturday from 9 am to 5 pm.

The *Restaurant El Greco* at Madero 436,

one block east of Zaragoza, is a popular family restaurant open every day from 8 am to 11.30 pm, serving an ample comida corrida for US$4.

The *Restaurant Mitla* at Madero 220 is large, clean and pleasant, with a wide variety of dishes on the menu. The comida corrida is US$5.20, enchiladas US$4, and meat, chicken or seafood dinners from US$4.35 to US$9.70 for filet mignon. On Sundays there's a buffet breakfast for US$5.70 from 8 am to noon. The Mitla is open every day from 8 am to 11.30 pm.

A good deal for quantity is *Baby Pizza* at Juan de Montoro 204, a block east of the Plaza Principal. Every day from 1 to 6 pm they feature an all-you-can-eat buffet of pizza, spaghetti, hamburgers, hot dogs, and a variety of salads, vegetables and fruits, all for US$4 (children US$2). Pizza and fried chicken 'Kentucky style' are the specialities of the house. It's open every day from 11 am to 1 am.

The *Pizza Palace* at López Mateos Poniente 207 near the corner of Galeana is a family restaurant with the same buffet at the same price, every day from noon to 6 pm. They, too, are open every day from 11 am to 1 pm.

There are several mercados (markets) a few blocks north of the Plaza Principal: Mercado Juárez, Mercado Jesús Terán and Mercado Morelos. The big Comercial Mexicana supermarket is on Avenida López Mateos near the corner of Galeana.

Entertainment

The Casa de la Cultura (☎ 15-00-81/97) on the corner of Carranza and Galeana, opposite the rear end of the cathedral, hosts art exhibits, music concerts, theatre and dance performances, and other cultural events; stop by for their monthly schedule, *Correo de la Casa*.

The Teatro Morelos, facing the south side of the cathedral, presents all kinds of performances, as does the Teatro de Aguascalientes at the corner of Boulevard Aguascalientes and Boulevard José Maria Chávez, on the outskirts of town on the road to Mexico City.

Local buses marked 'Centro Comercial Aurrera' or 'Ciudad Industrial', stopping at the bus stop on the north side of the cathedral and heading south along Galeana, will take you there.

Free cultural events – music, dance, theatre, etc – are presented every Sunday at 12.30 pm in the courtyard of the Museo José Guadalupe Posada, about five blocks south of the Plaza Principal on the corner of Diaz de León and Pimentel.

The Centro Superación Familiar at Díaz de León 412, a block north of the Museo José Guadalupe Posada, is a family amusement park with rides, swimming pool, gym, theatre and more. It's the private amusement park for employees of the JM Romo factory across the street, but foreigners are welcome to visit – you just need to present your ID at the gate. It's open Sunday from 11 am to 5 pm; admission is free.

Aguascalientes has several discos; the two most popular are El Cabus in the fancy Hotel Las Trojes about 20 km (15 minutes) from the centre on the highway to Zacatecas, and Meneos in the Centro Comercial El Dorado on Avenida Las Américas, about seven km from the centre.

Cockfights are held in the Palenque at the Casino de la Feria building on Calle Arturo J Pani, half a block south of the Jardín de San Marcos. Bullfights are also popular in Aguascalientes; there's an old bull ring just north of the Jardín de San Marcos, and a new one in the fairgrounds off Avenida López Mateos, a couple of blocks south of the Jardín de San Marcos. Large concerts are also held in the bull rings, especially during the Feria de San Marcos.

Getting There & Away

Air The Jesús Terán airport (☎ 17-24-04) is about 26 km from Aguascalientes, on the road to Mexico City. Colectivo vans run from the airport into town, but not from town to the airport; a taxi to the airport costs around US$12.

Flights from Aguascalientes include: to Guadalajara, daily (except Sunday) flights with Aerolitoral; to Los Angeles, four flights weekly with Aeroméxico; to Mexico City, daily flights with Aero California and Aeroméxico; to Monterrey, daily flights with Aerolitoral; to Puerto Vallarta, four flights weekly with Aeroméxico; to Tijuana, two flights daily with Aeroméxico and Aero California.

There are several travel agencies around the city centre where you can make flight arrangements; a convenient one is Wagons-lits Viajes (☎ 15-56-25, 15-59-73, fax 15-38-70) in the lobby of the Hotel Francia, right on the Plaza Principal.

Bus The Central Camionera is on the southern outskirts of town on Avenida Circunvalación, also called Avenida de la Convención, at the corner of Quinta Avenida, a km or two from the centre. It has a post office, a long-distance telephone office with fax, a Telecomm office for telegrams, a restaurant, a guarda equipaje for storing luggage, a pharmacy and various shops.

Several local bus routes marked 'Centro' and 'Central' run between the bus station and the centre of town. Going from town to the station, they stop on Moctezuma at the bus stop on the north side of the cathedral and then head south on Galeana.

Buses from Aguascalientes include those to:

Guadalajara – 251 km, 3½ to four hours; hourly buses, 24 hours, with Estrella Blanca (US$6.35); hourly, 24 hours, with Rojo de los Altos (US$6.35); 14 daily with Norte de Jalisco (US$6.35); 14 daily with Omnibus de México (US$6.70); eight daily with ETN (US$10); six daily with Transportes Chihuahuenses (US$6.50); five daily with Transportes del Norte (US$6.50); two daily with Servicios Coordinados (US$5.85).

Guanajuato – 184 km, three hours; three daily with Servicios Coordinados (US$4.30).

Mexico City – 468 km, 6½ to seven hours; 19 buses daily with Estrella Blanca (Primera Plus US$16.35, primera normal US$14.20); 13 daily with Omnibus de México (US$14.20); nine daily with ETN (US$28.35); eight daily with Servicios Coordinados (US$14); three daily with Transportes Chihuahuenses (US$16.70).

Morelia – 319 km, six hours; three daily with Servicios Coordinados (US$10).

San Luis Potosí – 168 km, three hours; 10 daily with Estrella Blanca (US$4.25).

Zacatecas – 135 km, two to 2½ hours; buses every half hour, 6 am to 8.30 pm, with Rojo de los Altos (US$3); hourly buses, 24 hours, with Transportes de Guadalupe (US$2.95); 12 daily with Transportes Chihuahuenses (US$3.40); 10 daily with Omnibus de México (US$3.35); five daily with Transportes del Norte (US$3.40).

Train The Estación del Ferrocarril (☎ 15-21-51) is on Avenida Alameda about a km north of the centre. Local buses marked 'Centro' run frequently from the train station into the centre of town. The ticket office is open every day from 6 to 9 am, noon to 1.30 pm, and from 8 to 10.30 pm.

The 'División del Norte' train from Mexico City to Ciudad Juárez stops at Aguascalientes; the northbound train (Train 7) departs Aguascalientes at 6.50 am, the southbound train (Train 8) at 10.30 pm. See the Mexico City train section for the full schedule of this train.

Heading south, primera regular/primera especial fares from Aguascalientes are US$1/3.60 to Lagos de Moreno, US$1.50/5.50 to León, US$2/7.45 to Irapuato, and US$5.10/18.90 to Mexico City. Heading north, the primera especial service extends only as far as Zacatecas; primera regular/primera especial fares to Zacatecas are US$1.10/3.90. Beyond that, primera regular fares from Aguascalientes are US$4.95 to Torreón, US$9.30 to Chihuahua, and US$12.50 to Ciudad Juárez.

A 2nd-class train, Trains 13 and 14, also operates the Mexico City to Ciudad Juárez route. Fares are about the same as primera regular on the División del Norte train, but the 2nd-class train is slower and the cars not as good. Northbound Train 13 to Ciudad Juárez departs Aguascalientes at 9 pm; southbound Train 14 to Mexico City departs at 8 am.

Getting Around

Most places of interest are within easy walking distance of the centre. Places further

Top: Ghost town of Real de Catorce, San Luis Potosí (JN)
Bottom: Guanajuato (DS)

Top/Bottom: Street scenes, Guadalajara (PW)

out, including the bus and train stations, are served by local bus routes; local buses run every day from 6 am to 10 pm and cost US$0.25.

The centre has plenty of taxis; a taxi to the bus or train stations costs around US$1.35.

Guanajuato State

The state of Guanajuato, bordered by Michoacán, Jalisco, San Luis Potosí and Querétaro states, was historically one of Mexico's richest states. After silver was found in Zacatecas, Spanish prospectors combed the rugged lands north of Mexico City and were rewarded by discoveries of gold, iron, lead, zinc, tin and, in the most spectacular of veins, silver.

The richest mines were worked in Guanajuato, where for two centuries 30% to 40% of the world's silver was mined. Guanajuato city became one of the three greatest silver-mining centres in the Americas, along with Zacatecas and Potosí in Bolivia. Silver barons in the wealthy mining cities lived opulent lives at the expense of Indians who worked the mines, first as slave labour and then as wage slaves.

The growing well-heeled criollo class of Guanajuato and Querétaro states – people of Spanish blood but born here in New Spain – began to resent the dominance and arrogance of the Spanish-born in the colony. After the occupation of much of Spain by Napoleon Bonaparte's troops in 1808 and subsequent political confusion in Mexico, some provincial criollos began to draw up plans for rebellion while meeting as 'literary societies'.

The house of Miguel Dominguez, a member of one such group in Querétaro, was raided on 13 September 1810. Three days later his colleague, parish priest Miguel Hidalgo, declared independence in Dolores, Guanajuato. After Dolores, San Miguel de Allende was the first town to fall to the rebels, Celaya the second, Guanajuato the third. Sometimes called the Cuna de la Independencia (Cradle of Independence), Guanajuato is proud to have given birth to Mexico's most glorious moment and is visited almost as a place of pilgrimage by people from far and wide. The most visited and interesting places in the state of Guanajuato are Guanajuato city, San Miguel de Allende and Dolores Hidalgo.

Guanajuato also has some important industrial centres like León (shoes, saddles, other leather goods, steel, textiles and soap) and Salamanca, which has a big oil refinery. Still Mexico's fourth largest silver producer, it's also an important source of gold and fluorspar, as well as various grains.

GUANAJUATO
Population: 73,000
Altitude: 2017 metres
Welcome to one of the country's outstanding destinations.

Subterranean passageways serve as the town's streets, and houses are crammed onto the steep slopes of a ravine which once contained the Río Guanajuato, until the river flooded the town in 1905, was subsequently diverted, and the riverbed converted to roadways.

This impossible topography was settled in 1559 because the silver and gold mines of Guanajuato were among the richest in the world. The colonial structures built from this wealth remain intact throughout much of the city, making Guanajuato what the government calls a 'colonial monument' to a prosperous, turbulent past.

But it's not only the past that resounds from Guanajuato's narrow cobbled streets and colonial buildings. The University of Guanajuato, known for its arts programmes, attracts 15,000 students to the town each year, giving the city a youthfulness, vibrancy and cultural life equally as attractive as the charm of the colonial architecture and winding streets.

History
One of the hemisphere's richest veins of silver was uncovered in 1558 at La Valenci-

ana Mine, five km north of Guanajuato. For 2½ centuries, the excavation of what is now the periphery above the city produced 20% of the world's silver. Colonial barons benefiting from this mineral treasure were infuriated when King Charles III slashed their share of the wealth in 1765. The King further enraged the city with his 1767 decree banishing Jesuits from Latin America for their anti-monarchical stance. Both the wealthy barons and the poor Indian miners who held allegiance to the Jesuits were alienated from Spanish rule.

This anger found a focus in the War of Independence. In 1810 the priest and rebel leader Father Miguel Hidalgo, whose Grito (Cry for Independence) at his parish church in nearby Dolores set off Mexico's independence movement, led a successful conquest of Spain's Alhóndiga fortress with the assistance of Guanajuato's citizenry – the first military victory of the independence rebellion. When the Spaniards retaliated, furious that locals had lynched royalist prisoners, they retook the city. In the infamous 'lottery of death', names of Guanajuato's citizens

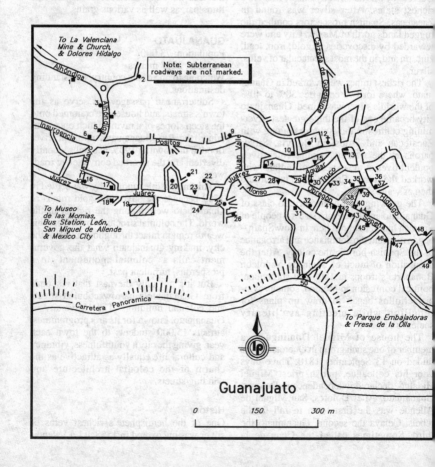

Guanajuato

Note: Subterranean roadways are not marked.

To La Valenciana Mine & Church & Dolores Hidalgo

To Museo de las Momias, Bus Station, León, San Miguel de Allende & Mexico City

To Parque Embajadoras & Presa de la Olla

Carretera Panoramica

0   150   300 m

vere drawn strictly at random and the unlucky 'winners' were tortured and hanged.

The rebels eventually won, freeing the silver barons to acquire mineral wealth with which mansions, churches and theatres were built, making Guanajuato one of Mexico's most handsome colonial cities.

Orientation

Guanajuato's central area is quite compact, with only a few major streets. Juárez, the city's main avenue, heads east from the mercado to the Basilica; the three-way intersection at the Basilica is called Plaza de la Paz. Passing along the south side of this plaza, Juárez changes names first to Obregón and then to Sopeña as it passes the Jardín de la Unión, the city's main plaza, a block further east.

Parallel to Juárez is Positos, with the University of Guanajuato, the Alhóndiga and a couple of museums. Near the University, Positos heads down the hill, intersecting with Hidalgo and then with Sopeña a few blocks further on, on the east side of town. Once you know these streets you'll never get lost in the centre.

Aside from these main streets are a bewildering maze of narrow, crooked callejones, or alleyways, winding up the hills from the centre of the city. One, the Callejón del Beso, is so narrow that you can easily touch the walls of the houses on both sides as you climb up its steps. You can have a great time getting lost among the callejones of Guanajuato.

Another twist on getting around in the city is that several of the major avenues are under the ground.

■ PLACES TO STAY

1 Hotel Socavón
4 Hotel El Minero
5 Hotel Mineral de Rayas
6 Hotel Alhóndiga
17 Hotel Central
18 Hotel Posada San Francisco
27 Hotel Posada de la Condesa
31 Casa Kloster
34 Hotel Museo Posada Santa Fé
41 Hotel San Diego
45 Hostería del Frayle

▼ PLACES TO EAT

15 Centro Nutricional Vegetariano;
    Pastelería La Paz
23 Pizza Piazza
24 Restaurant La Carreta
28 Restaurant El Zaguán
33 Truco 7
35 Restaurant El ágora del Baratillo
36 Pizza Piazza
39 Café/Restaurante Pinguis
40 Restaurant Valadez
44 Café/Restaurant El Retiro

    OTHER

2 Servi Fax

3 Lavandería Automática Internacional
7 Plaza Alhóndiga
8 Alhóndiga de Granaditas
9 Museo y Casa de Diego Rivera
10 Museo del Pueblo de Guanajuato
11 University of Guanajuato
12 Templo de la Compañia de Jesús
13 Post Office
14 Palacio Legislativo de la Paz
16 Tours Kiosk - Transporte Exclusivo de
    Turismo
19 Mercado Hidalgo
20 Jardín de la Reforma
21 Plaza San Roque
22 Plazuela San Fernando & Pizza
    Piazza
25 Plazuela de los Angeles
26 Callejón del Beso
29 Tourist Office & Plaza de la Paz
30 Basílica
32 Rincón del Beso (La Peña Bohemia)
37 Teatro Principal
38 Jardín de la Unión
42 Church of San Diego
43 Teatro Juárez; Telecomm
46 Museo Iconográfico del Quijote
47 Templo de San Francisco
48 Lavandería Automática Internacional
49 Teatro Cervantes; Statues of Don
    Quijote & Sancho Panza
50 Pípila Monument

The bus station, once in the city centre, has now been moved to the south-western outskirts of town.

Information

Tourist Office The state-run tourist office (☎ (473) 2-15-74, 2-00-86), at Plaza de la Paz 14 opposite the Basílica, has a large 'Información Turística' sign over its interior courtyard office. The staff gives out free city maps, and sells larger, more detailed maps for US$1; it also has free brochures about the city and state of Guanajuato printed in Spanish and English. The office is open Monday to Friday from 8.30 am to 7.30 pm, Saturday and Sunday 10 am to 2 pm.

Another branch of the tourist office is in the central bus station. It's open Monday to Friday from 10.30 am to 7 pm, Saturday 10.30 am to 2 pm, closed Sunday.

Money For currency exchange there are a number of banks along the Plaza de la Paz and Juárez, open Monday to Friday from 9 am to 1.30 pm. When the banks are closed, some of the larger hotels will change your money at slightly less favourable rates.

Post The main post office is at the eastern end of Calle Positos, opposite the Templo de la Compañia church. It's open Monday to Friday from 8 am to 8 pm, Saturday 8 am to 1 pm.

Another branch of the post office at the central bus station is open Monday to Friday, 9 am to 1 pm and 3 to 6 pm.

Telecommunications The Telecomm office at Sopeña 1, beside the Teatro Juárez and opposite the Jardín de la Unión, offers telegram, telex, and fax services. It's open Monday to Friday from 9 am to 8 pm, Saturday 9 am to 1 pm. Servi Fax at San Clemente 8 offers slightly cheaper public fax services; it's open Monday to Friday from 8 am to 8 pm, Saturday 8 am to 3 pm.

Guanajuato has several casetas de larga distancia. The one on Calle Positos, opposite the Alhóndiga, is open every day from 10 am to 3 pm and from 5 to 10 pm. Another is in the Miscelanea Unión shop at Calle Hidalgo 18, near the Teatro Principal, just east of the Jardín de la Unión; it's open every day from 10 am to 5 pm and from 6 to 10 pm. The Lonchería Pípila, at Alonso 14 in the same block as the Casa Kloster, also has a caseta; it's open Monday to Saturday from 9.30 am to 9.30 pm, plus at some time on Sunday but with no fixed hours. Another caseta, at the central bus station, is open 24 hours every day.

Laundry The Lavandería Automática Internacional has two laundromats, both with the same hours and prices, where you can drop off your laundry or do it yourself. One is on the eastern end of the centre at Manuel Doblado 28, on the corner of Hidalgo. The other is on the west side of town at Alhóndiga 35-A. Both are open Monday to Saturday from 9 am to 8 pm.

Jardín de la Unión & Other Plazas

At the centre of town is the pretty Jardín de la Unión. This zócalo, the social heart of the city, is surrounded by cafés and shaded by trees. People congregate here in the late afternoons and early evenings, with itinerant guitarists serenading those taking their ease here.

Other notable plazas are the Jardín de la Reforma, on Juárez; just off this, the Plaza San Roque, where *entremeses* theatre is peformed during the annual Festival Cervantino; and, near this, the pleasant Plazuela San Fernando.

The steps of the Plazuela de los Ángeles on Juárez are a popular congregating spot for students, with the Callejón del Beso just a few steps away.

The Plaza de la Paz, in front of the Basilica, is surrounded by buildings which were once the homes of wealthy silver lords. The Plaza Alhóndiga, at the corner of Positos and 5 de Mayo in front of the Alhóndiga, is quite bare.

Teatro Juárez & Other Theatres

Opposite the Jardín Unión sits the magnificent Teatro Juárez, built over a 30-yea period from 1873 to 1903. It was inaugurated by the dictator Porfirio Díaz, whose lavish yet refined tastes are reflected in the interior. The outside is festooned with columns, lampposts and statues; inside the motif is Moorish, with the bar and lobby walls and ceiling gleaming with carved woods, stained glass and precious metals.

The theatre can be visited from 9 am to 1.45 pm and 5 to 7.45 pm, Tuesday to Sunday (closed Monday); admission is US$1, cameras another US$0.50. Performances are held here during the Festival Cervantino and at other times; check for the current schedule.

Other theatres include the Teatro Principal, on Hidalgo near the other end of the Jardín de la Unión, and the Teatro Cervantes, at the eastern end of Calle Hidalgo. These theatres are not as spectacular as Teatro Juárez but they have more frequent performances, plus weekly international film series (see Entertainment). Statues of Don Quijote and Sancho Panza grace the courtyard of the Teatro Cervantes.

Basílica & Other Churches

The Basílica de Nuestra Señora de Guanajuato on the Plaza de la Paz, one block west of the Jardín de la Unión, contains a jewel-covered image of the Virgin, patroness of Guanajuato. The wooden statue was supposedly hidden from the Moors in a cave for 800 years. Philip II, in thanks for the riches which accrued to the Crown, gave the statue to Guanajuato in 1557.

Other fine colonial churches include the Church of San Diego, opposite the Jardín de la Unión, and the Templo de la Compañia de Jesús beside the University. A Jesuit church, La Compañia was the largest of its order when it was completed in 1747. The church was part of a Jesuit seminary which is now the site of the University of Guanajuato.

The Templo de San Francisco, on Sopeña a couple of blocks west of the Jardín de la Unión, is another fine church. As you walk around Guanajuato you'll see many more old churches.

University of Guanajuato

The Universidad de Guanajuato, whose green ramparts are visible above much of the city, is on Calle Positos one block up the hill from the Basílica. The building was originally built to house a large Jesuit seminary. It is considered one of Mexico's finest schools for music and theatre, and it also has a Spanish as a second language programme for foreign students.

Palacio Legislativo de la Paz

Half a block in front of the Basílica, at Plaza de la Paz 77, the Palacio Legislativo de la Paz is the seat of government for the state of Guanajuato. Finished in 1900 under the opulent Porfirio Díaz regime, the building is known for its architecture, an impressive and gaudy medley of styles. It can be visited any day from around 9 am to 10 pm.

Museo de las Mómias

Guanajuato has a number of interesting and special museums, but the Museum of the Mummies, at the cemetery on the outskirts of town, is by far the most famous and most visited. It is the quintessential example of Mexico's obsession with death, to say nothing of commercial possibilities, attracting visitors from far and wide who come to see scores of corpses disinterred from the public cemetery.

The first remains were disinterred from this cemetery in 1865, when it was necessary to remove some bodies to make room for more. To the horror and amazement of the authorities, what they uncovered were not skeletons but flesh mummified in grotesque forms and facial expressions. The mineral content of the soil around the cemetery, along with extremely dry atmospheric conditions, combined to preserve the flesh in this unique way.

Today there are over 100 mummies on display in the museum, including the first mummy to be discovered, the smallest mummy in the world, a pregnant mummy and plenty more. The most recent one died in 1979 and was exhumed in 1984.

Mummies continue to be discovered. It

takes only five or six years for a body to become mummified here, though only 1% or 2% of the bodies exhumed have turned into mummies worthy of display, and these only from the crypts, not from the underground burials. If they're not 'display quality', the remains are cremated.

Why are the bodies disinterred, you might ask? It turns out that Guanajuato's cemetery is a small one, and that when someone is buried they are allowed only five or six years' free residence in the cemetery. At the end of that time, a fee is charged to keep the body in the cemetery 'in perpetuity'; in 1992, when we asked, the fee was about US$50 to US$70. If the fee is not paid, the body is removed and either cremated or put on display.

The museum is open every day from 9 am to 6 pm; admission is US$1 (children five and under free), with an additional charge of US$0.70 for cameras or US$1.70 for video cameras. You can reach the museum by taking any 'Mómias' or 'Panteón' local bus heading west on Juárez.

Alhóndiga de Granaditas

The Alhóndiga de Granaditas on Calle Positos, the site of the first major rebel victory in Mexico's War of Independence, is today a history and art museum.

A massive grain-and-seed storehouse under construction from 1798 to 1808, the Alhóndiga in 1810 became a fortress for Spanish troops and royalist leaders who barricaded themselves in the granary when 20,000 rebel troops led by Padre Hidalgo attempted to conquer the city. The substantial structure allowed the outnumbered Spaniards to hold out and it looked as if they would be able to defend their fortress; but on 28 September a young Indian miner named Juan José de los Reyes Martínez (better known as El Pípila), under orders from Hidalgo, rushed the gates, setting them afire before he succumbed to a hail of bullets. While the Spaniards choked on smoke, the rebels advanced and took the Alhóndiga.

The Spaniards later took their revenge: the heads of four leaders of the rebellion – Aldama, Allende, Jiménez, and Hidalgo himself, who was executed in Chihuahua – were hung from the four outside corners of the Alhóndiga from 1811 to 1821. Instead of intimidating the locals, the display for a decade reminded rebels of their martyrs, spurring them on to eventual independence. The long black hooks holding the metal cages in which the martyrs' heads hung may still be viewed on the top of the four outer corners of the building, with a plaque telling where each head hung.

For a century, beginning in 1864, the massive building was used as a prison. It became a museum in 1967. Historical exhibits range all the way from Guanajuato's pre-Hispanic past, with archaeological artefacts, to the great flood of 1905 which inundated the town, and into modern times. There's also a fine art gallery housing a permanent collection and temporary exhibits. Don't miss the dramatic murals of Guanajuato's history painted in the staircases by Chavez Morado.

The museum is open Tuesday to Saturday from 10 am to 2 pm and 4 to 6 pm, Sunday from 10 am to 3.30 pm (closed Monday). Admission is US$3.35, but it's free to those aged 13 and under or 60 and over, and free to everyone on Sunday.

Museo y Casa de Diego Rivera

The birthplace of Diego Rivera, today a museum honouring the painter, is at Positos 47 between the University and the Alhóndiga. Diego was born in this house on 8 December 1886, together with a twin brother who died at the age of two; the family left the house and moved to Mexico City when Diego was six years old.

In reactionary Guanajuato, where Catholic influence prevails (in the late 1920s the city was a bastion of support for the attempted counter-revolution led by the church), the Marxist revolutionary Diego was *persona non grata* for years. Ultimately, profits prevailed over principle and Guanajuato now honours its once blacklisted native son with a small collection of his work in the house where he was born and raised.

The museum's 1st floor contains the Rivera family's 19th-century antiques and fine furniture. On the 2nd and 3rd-floors are some 70 to 80 paintings and sketches by the master, including Indian and peasant portraits, a nude of Frida Kahlo, and sketches from some of Rivera's memorable murals.

The museum is open Tuesday to Saturday from 9 am to 1.30 pm and 4 to 6.30 pm, Sunday 10 am to 2.30 pm. Admission is US$1.70 (free for those 11 years and under, or 60 years and over).

Museo del Pueblo de Guanajuato

Opposite the university at Positos 7 is the Museo del Pueblo de Guanajuato, occupying the former mansion of the Marqueses de San Juan de Rayas who owned the San Juan de Rayas mine. The mansion, built for them in 1696 with a private church in the interior courtyard, is now an art museum with a collection of art ranging from colonial to modern times, and a powerful mural by José Chavez Morado in the courtyard church.

The museum is open Tuesday to Saturday from 10 am to 2 pm and 4 to 7 pm, Sunday from 10 am to 2.30 pm (closed Monday). Admission is US$1.70 (free for those up to age 11 and over 60).

University Museums

The University of Guanajuato has three art museums, all with changing exhibitions. The Salas de Exposiciones Hermenegildo Bustos and Polivalente are beside one another on the ground floor of the university building; the Sala de Exposiciones El Atrio is under the front courtyard of the Compañia church next door. All three are open Monday to Friday from 9 am to 2 pm and 5 to 8 pm, with free admission.

On the fourth floor of the university building is the Museo de Historia Natural Alfredo Duges, honouring the work of one of the university's foremost naturalists. It contains an extensive collection of preserved and stuffed animals, birds, reptiles and insects, with some strange specimens including a stuffed two-headed goat. It's open Monday to Friday from 10 am to 6 pm, admission free.

At the university's Escuela de Minas campus, overlooking the town a km or two from the centre on the road to La Valenciana, the Museo de Mineralogía is said to be one of the world's foremost mineralogy museums. Its collection of over 20,000 specimens from around the world includes some extremely rare minerals, some of them found only in the Guanajuato area. The museum is open Monday to Friday from 8 am to 3 pm, admission free. To get there, take a 'Presa-San Javier' local bus heading west on Juárez and ask to get off at the Escuela de Minas.

Museo Iconográfico del Quijote

This excellent museum at Manuel Doblado 1, on the tiny plaza in front of the Templo de San Francisco church, presents an impressive collection of art relating to Don Quijote de la Mancha. Items on display range from room-size murals to a tiny painting on an eggshell, with dozens of paintings, statues, figurines, tapestries, and even a collection of postage stamps from several countries honouring the famous hero of Spanish literature.

The museum is open Tuesday to Saturday from 10 am to 6.30 pm, Sunday 10 am to 2.30 pm (closed Monday); admission is free.

Callejón del Beso

Climbing up the hills from Guanajuato's main avenues are a maze of alleyways, called callejones. Most are narrow but one, the Callejón del Beso, is the narrowest of all, with the balconies of the houses on either side of the alley practically touching. In Guanajuatan legend, lovers living on either side of the alleyway used to furtively exchange kisses from these balconies.

The Callejón del Beso is not far off Calle Juárez. From the Plaza de los Ángeles, walk about 40 metres up the Callejón del Patrocinio and you'll see the Callejón del Beso taking off to your left.

Pípila Monument

The Pípila monument, with a torch raised

high over the city, was built to honour the rebel who heroically torched the front doors of the Alhóndiga on 28 September 1810, enabling Hidalgo's forces to win the first victory of the independence movement. At the base of the statue is the inscription 'Aun hay otras Alhóndigas por incendiar' ('There are still other Alhóndigas to burn').

It's worth coming up to the statue for the magnificent view over the city; you can climb up inside the statue for US$0.35 but it's not really worth doing, since the view is just as good from the terraces at the statue's feet.

The walk from the centre of town to the statue is also interesting and worthwhile, passing through some steep, picturesque cobblestone alleyways. One possible route is to walk east on Calle Sopeña from Jardín de la Unión, making a right on Callejón de Calvario (you will see the sign saying 'Al Pípila'). Another ascent, unmarked, goes uphill from the small plaza on Calle Alonso. If the uphill climb is too much for you, take the 'Pípila-ISSSTE' bus heading west on Juárez. It lets you off right at the statue, from where there are footpaths heading down the hill back to the centre of town.

Presa de la Olla

In the hills on the east end of the city are two scenic reservoirs, Presa de la Olla and Presa de San Renovato, with a green park between them and a lighthouse on the hill above. It's a popular family park on Sundays, when you can bring a picnic and hire small rowboats. The rest of the week it is quiet and peaceful. Any eastbound 'Presa' bus will drop you off there.

Ex-Hacienda San Gabriel de Barrera

Built at the end of the 17th century, the Ex-Hacienda San Gabriel de Barrera was the hacienda of Captain Gabriel de Barrera, whose family descended from the first Count of Valencia of the famous La Valenciana mine. One of a number of grand Spanish haciendas built from the wealth gained from silver and gold, this hacienda opened as a museum in 1979. It has been magnificently

restored with period European furniture and art; in the chapel is an ornate gold-covered altar.

Originally the large grounds were devoted to the processing of metals, with ore brought from the La Valenciana mine. Much later, in 1945, the grounds were planted with several terraces of beautiful gardens in various themes. These gardens, with their pavilions, pools, fountains and footpaths, make a lovely and tranquil retreat from the city.

The museum is open every day from 9 am to 6.30 pm. Admission is US$1.35, with an extra charge of US$1 for cameras or US$1.70 for video cameras. The frequent 'Central de Autobuses' local buses heading west on Juárez will drop you off right in front; tell them you want to get off there when you board the bus.

La Valenciana Mine & Church

La Valenciana mine, on a hill overlooking Guanajuato about five km north of the centre, was once one of the richest and most famous in the world; for 250 years it produced 20% of the world's silver, in addition to quantities of gold.

Shut down after the Revolution and at various times throughout its history, it reopened in 1968 and is once again in operation, now cooperatively run. The mine still yields silver, gold, nickel and lead; if you come on a workday you can see the earth being extracted and miners descending an immense main shaft, nine metres in diameter and 500 metres deep.

The mine can be visited any day from around 7 am to 7 pm; admission free. If you want to see the mine in operation, come any day except Sunday.

Near the mine is the magnificent La Valenciana church, also called the Church of San Cayetano. One legend says that the Spaniard who started the La Valenciana mine promised Saint Cayetano that if the mine made him rich, he would build a church to honour the saint; another legend says that the silver baron of La Valenciana, Conde de Rul, tried to atone for exploiting the miners by building the ultimate in Churrigueresque-style churches.

Whatever the motive, ground was broken in 1765, and the church was completed in 1788. La Valenciana's façade is spectacular and its interior dazzling with ornate golden altars, stained glass, filigree carvings and giant paintings. The church is open from around 9 am to 7 pm, every day except Monday.

To get to La Valenciana, take a 'Valenciana' local bus, departing every half hour from Calle 5 de Mayo in front of the Plaza Alhóndiga. Get off at the church; the mine is about 300 metres down the dirt road opposite the church.

Language Courses

Guanajuato is a university town and it has an excellent atmosphere for studying Spanish. The University of Guanajuato offers courses

in Spanish for foreigners. Cost is only US$19 for a two to 2½ month course, with registration four times a year: the last week of January, the second week of April, the first week of August and the second week of October. The university can help you arrange to stay with local Mexican families; cost for students staying under three months is around US$9 to US$13 per day including all meals, or US$200 per month for those staying longer, but arrangements may vary depending on the family you live with.

For information you can write to the university: Universidad de Guanajuato, Departamento de Servicios al Estudiante (☎ (473) 2-27-70, fax 2-02-78), Lascurain de Retana No 5, CP 36000 Guanajuato, Gto, México.

The university also offers a separate summer programme, organised through 11 universities in the USA including the University of Chicago, Northwestern University, Purdue University, and the Universities of Illinois, Indiana, Iowa, Michigan, Minnesota and Wisconsin, among others. Contact any of these for information on the summer Spanish programme.

Another alternative is the Instituto Falcón (☎ (473) 2-36-94), whose mailing address is Callejón de la Mora 158, CP 36000 Guanajuato, Gto, México. Theirs is a more flexible programme, with registration every Monday, smaller classes (maximum six students), and more personal attention, with weekend recreational trips. Cost depends on how many hours of instruction you want per day: one or two hours daily is US$4.25 per hour, five hours daily is US$3 per hour. They, too, help to arrange living with local Mexican families; accommodation cost is US$12.50 per day, including all meals.

Organised Tours

Two companies offer organised tours of several of Guanajuato's major sights. The tours are conducted in Spanish; you can reach all the same places by going on the local bus, which costs only US$0.20 per ride, but if your time is limited it is easier to see several sights in just a few hours if you go with a tour.

Transporte Exclusivo de Turismo (☎ 2-59-68) has a kiosk on the corner of Juárez and 5 de Mayo. Their 3½-hour Guanajuato Colonial tour includes the Mummies, the La Valenciana mine and church, the Pípila monument and the Panoramic Highway with a view over the town; cost is US$4 and it departs three times daily. Another tour goes to Cristo Rey, on the Cerro del Cubilete; it takes 3½ hours, goes three times daily and costs US$4.35. Their other tours go farther away and cost more.

Transportes Turísticos de Guanajuato (☎ 2-21-43, 2-28-38) has an office below the front courtyard of the Basilica, and another in the Hotel El Minero at Alhóndiga 12-A (☎ 2-52-51). Their 3½-hour Patrimonio Cultural de la Humanidad tour departs three times daily, costs US$6.70 and includes the Mummies, the La Valenciana mine and church, the Pípila monument, the Presa de la Olla park, and a city tour to point out other important sights. They also offer a three-hour tour to Cristo Rey (US$6.70) and other, more distant tours.

Festivals
Fiestas de San Juan y Presa de la Olla The Fiestas de San Juan are celebrated at the Presa de la Olla park from 15 to 24 June, with the 24th being the big blowout bash for the saint's day itself; dances, music, fireworks and picnics are all part of the celebrations. On the first Monday in July, everyone comes back to the park for another big party celebrating the opening of the floodgates of the Presa de la Olla dam.

Día de la Cueva This festival, with music and outdoor picnics, is held on 31 July, the day of San Ignacio, at the Cueva de San Ignacio on the Cerro Cantera, a hill overlooking the town. If you're here at this time, ask someone to tell you the legend of the cave.

Fiesta de la Virgen de Guanajuato This festival, celebrated on 8 August, commemo-

rates the date in 1557 when Philip II gave the jewelled wooden Virgin now adorning the Basilica to the people of Guanajuato.

Festival Internacional Cervantino Entremeses, theatre and other cultural events, with internationally renowned music, dance and theatre groups coming in from around the world, are performed during Guanajuato's Cervantes Festival. Exact festival dates vary but it's usually held around the last two weeks of October.

The festival attracts talent and tourists worldwide, so tickets and hotels should be booked in advance. Tickets go on sale around the beginning of October; in Guanajuato they're sold in front of the Basilica, or they can also be bought in Mexico City at the FIC office at Alvaro Obregón 273, Colonia Roma (☎ 514-7365). If you can't find a hotel, plenty of buses run between Guanajuato and not-so-distant destinations like Querétaro, San Miguel de Allende, Dolores Hidalgo, León and Irapuato.

While some events are held in Teatro Juárez and other theatres, the most spectacular of entremeses, with galloping horses and medieval costumes, are performed in the ancient setting of the Plazuela San Roque and in the Plaza Alhóndiga. If your visit to Mexico coincides with the festival dates, don't miss it.

Places to Stay – bottom end
Camping Up a steep hill about a km or two north of the centre of town is the *Trailer Park Móvil*, on Subida de Mellado (no number) just down the hill from the Carretera Panorámica, in Barrio Nuevo. There are two levels of spaces for trailers and tents on the hillside; cost is US$4/6.70 for one/two people if you don't use the electricity, or US$5/8.35 with full hook-ups.

Hotels In Guanajuato, there is no question concerning the top choice for budget lodgings: the *Casa Kloster* (☎ (473) 2-00-88) at Alonso 32, a short block down an alley from the Basilica. Travellers lost a great friend when the fatherly proprietor Don Jesús Pérez died in late 1991, but his wife and family are still there running the place with the same excellence as ever. Birds and flowers still grace the sunny courtyard, the well-cared-for rooms with shared bath are still clean and comfortable, and you still have to light a fire in the old boilers to make hot water for a shower. Cost is US$8.35 per person. Many European travellers congregate here and it's a relaxed, friendly place where it's easy to meet other travellers.

A distant second choice for rock-bottom lodging is the *Hotel Posada de la Condesa* (☎ (473) 2-14-62), at Plaza de la Paz 60, also near the Basilica. It's a large hotel with plenty of rooms, all with private bath and 24-hour hot water; it's a bit tired and run-down, though the rooms are kept clean enough. If you don't like the room you're shown at first, ask to see another – some rooms are large and even have little balconies overlooking the street, others are claustrophobic with no ventilation. All cost US$8.35/11.70 for a single/double.

In the area around the mercado are several other relatively low-priced hotels, including the *Hotel Central*, the *Hotel Granaditas*, the *Hotel Posada San Francisco*, the *Hotel Juárez* and the *Posada Hidalgo*, but none are as cheap or as good as the Casa Kloster or even the Posada de la Condesa.

Places to Stay – middle

Calle Alhóndiga, heading north from the Plaza Alhóndiga, has several good medium-priced hotels. Near the corner of Alhóndiga and visible from the plaza, the *Hotel Alhóndiga* (☎ (473) 2-05-25) at Insurgencia 49 has clean, comfortable rooms with carpeting, colour TV, and some with small private balconies; there's also a restaurant, a sitting area and enclosed parking. Singles/doubles are US$16.70/25.

Around the corner at Alhóndiga 7 is the *Hotel Mineral de Rayas* (☎ (473) 2-19-67, 2-37-49), another clean and comfortable place with a hotel restaurant. Many of the rooms have tiny private balconies overlooking a quiet side street. Singles/doubles are

US$20/23.35, with an extra US$3.35 per day if you want colour TV.

Just a little further down Alhóndiga at No 12-A, the *Hotel El Minero* (☎ (473) 2-52-51) is another good place with small, comfortable rooms, all with carpet and TV, and many with balconies over the street, at US$21.25/23.50.

Further down again at Alhóndiga 41-A, the *Hotel Socavón* (☎ (473) 2-48-85, 2-66-66) is an attractive, well-kept hostelry whose rooms are arranged around a sunny interior courtyard with brick arches, plants and some antique mining implements. All the rooms have copper washbasins, painted tile in the private baths, colour TV, carpeting and plenty of windows; cost is US$26.70/30. There's a restaurant/bar on the 2nd floor.

Near the Jardín de la Unión at Sopeña 3, a few doors east of Teatro Juárez, the *Hostería del Frayle* (☎ (473) 2-11-79) is very attractive. All the rooms have high wood-beamed ceilings, colour TV, telephone and carpet; though it's right in the centre of town, the building's construction with thick adobe walls keeps it quiet. Singles/doubles here are US$31.70/36.70.

If you want to get quite out of the centre of town to a quiet place, but only a five-minute local bus ride from the centre, try the *Motel de las Embajadoras* (☎ (473) 2-00-81) beside the Parque Embajadoras at the corner of Embajadoras and Paseo Madero (no number). It's peaceful and quiet, removed from the hustle and bustle of downtown; there's an elegant but inexpensive hotel restaurant/bar, plenty of parking spaces, and a lovely courtyard full of plants, trees and birds. The rooms are clean, comfortable and well-kept, with carpet, phone and colour TV; singles/doubles are US$31.90/36.70. The 'Embajadoras' buses heading east on Juárez, operating frequently from around 7 am to 10 pm, will let you off right at the door.

Places to Stay – top end

Guanajuato has several good choices in the upper bracket, with two elegant long-time-favourite hotels right on the Jardín de la

Unión. The *Hotel San Diego* (☎ (473) 2-13-00/21, fax 2-56-26) at Jardín de la Unión 1, near Teatro Juárez, has 52 elegant rooms and two suites, a 2nd-floor restaurant overlooking the plaza, and a large rooftop terrace where you can sit in the sun or shade. Singles/doubles are US$55/66.

On the other end of the Jardín de la Unión, the four-star *Hotel Museo Posada Santa Fé* (☎ (473) 2-00-84, fax 2-46-53), whose address is simply Jardín de la Unión, is a sumptuous hotel in an elegant 19th-century mansion. Rooms cost US$65/73 per night; suites are US$147. On the ground floor is an expensive hotel restaurant with some tables out on the plaza.

The four-star *Castillo Santa Cecilia* (☎ (473) 2-04-77/85, fax 2-01-53) on the Carretera Valenciana, Km 1, built of stone and resembling a castle, is known both for its luxurious accommodation and excellent restaurant. Rooms are US$55 for one or two people; there are also suites and junior suites.

Also outside the city, the four-star *Hotel San Gabriel de Barrera* (☎ (473) 2-39-80, fax 2-74-60), beside the Ex-Hacienda San Gabriel de Barrera at Km 2.5 on the Camino Antigua a Marfil has a restaurant, bar, swimming pool, tennis courts, and 139 luxury rooms at US$62/69.

Places to Eat

There are a number of good, inexpensive restaurants around the Jardín de la Unión and the Basilica. Two popular old standbys are the *Restaurant Valadez*, opposite the Teatro Juárez on the corner of the Jardín de la Unión, and the *Café/Restaurant El Retiro*, a few doors down at Sopeña 12. Both are open every day from 8 am to 11 pm, serving a comida corrida for US$4.35 in the early afternoon.

Also on this end of the Jardín de la Unión, the *Hotel San Diego* has an elegant upstairs restaurant with several balcony tables overlooking the plaza. It's rather expensive but you can get a good breakfast special for US$3.35.

On the far corner of the Jardín de la Unión the *Hotel Museo Posada Santa Fé* has a fancy but expensive restaurant inside, and sidewalk tables out on the plaza. Opposite this, the *Café/Restaurante Pinguis* has no sign out front, but it's one of the most popular places in town for its good prices – the comida corrida costs only US$2.70, sandwiches and tortas US$0.85. It's open every day from 8.30 am to 9.30 pm.

Heading out of this far end of the plaza on the pedestrian street curving around to the right, the *Restaurant El Ágora del Baratillo* in the courtyard of the Ágora del Baratillo on the corner of Hidalgo is a pleasant open-air restaurant with inexpensive prices and interesting foods you don't often see in Mexico. The comida corrida is reasonably priced at US$3. It's open Monday to Saturday, 8 am to 9 pm.

Pizza Piazza has a restaurant at Hidalgo 14, on the far end of the Jardín de la Unión; another on the Plazuela de San Fernando; another at Juárez 69-A; and another on the Plaza de los Pastitos heading out of town towards Marfil. All are open every day from 2 to 11 pm; all are known for good pizza, good prices and a casual student atmosphere.

Other good restaurants are near the Basilica. One of our favourites on our last trip was *Truco 7*, at Truco 7 on the side street to the right of the Basilica. A small, intimate, artsy café-restaurant-coffee house-art gallery, it has great atmosphere and delicious food at some of the cheapest prices in town, with a variety of breakfast specials and a comida corrida for US$2.70. Jazz, blues, classical, and other music play during the day and there's a live guitarist in the evening. It's open Monday to Friday from 9 am to midnight, weekends 11 am to midnight.

On the left side of the Basilica at Aguilar 43, the *Centro Nutricional Vegetariano* was the only vegetarian restaurant in town on our last visit. It's a simple little place open every day except Sunday from 10 am to 9 pm. In the same block, the *Pastelería La Paz* at Aguilar 53 is a large bakery and pastry shop, open every day from 7 am to 10 pm.

On the plaza in front of the Basilica, *El Zaguán* at Plaza de la Paz 48 is another small courtyard café with good atmosphere, good coffee, pastries, ice cream, and a comida corrida for US$3.50; it's open from 10 am to 10 pm every day except Monday.

Finally, for delicious chicken, there's the *Restaurant La Carreta* at Juárez 96, heading down towards the mercado. It's a typical Mexican chicken shack with chickens revolving on the spit out front and picnic tables behind. Served with large portions of rice and salad, a quarter chicken costs US$2.35, a half chicken US$4.20, or a whole one US$8, to take away or eat there. It's open every day from 8 am to 10 pm.

Entertainment

Every evening, the Jardín de la Unión comes alive with university students and others congregating there; the sidewalk cafés along one side of the plaza are popular for having a drink, people-watching and listening to the strolling musicians. The state band gives free concerts in the gazebo on Tuesday and Thursday evenings from around 7 to 8 pm and on Sundays from around noon to 1 pm.

On Friday, Saturday and Sunday evenings at around 8 or 8.30 pm, *callejoneadas* depart from in front of the Church of San Diego on one end of the Jardín de la Unión. Also called *estudiantinas*, the callejoneada tradition is said to come from Spain. A group of songsters and musicians start up the music in front of the church, a crowd gathers, and the whole mob takes off winding around through the ancient alleyways of the city, playing and singing heartily, taking along a burro laden with wine. It's good fun and one of Guanajuato's most enjoyable traditions. There's no cost except for the wine you drink.

The Rincón del Beso, at Alonso 21-A not far from the Jardín de la Unión, is also affectionately known as La Peña Bohemia since it's a rather Bohemian club. Every evening at around 10 pm the live music starts off; all kinds of music is presented, sometimes poetry too, and part of the attraction is never knowing what they might come up with next. Often the whole club joins in singing; they stay open as long as there are people there wanting to party, often all night long. There's no cover charge, though the drinks are a bit expensive. The Truco 7 restaurant at Truco 7 also has live music in the evening.

Guanajuato has three fine theatres, the Teatro Juárez, the Teatro Principal and the Teatro Cervantes, all in the area near the Jardín de la Unión. Stop by and check the posters out front to see what's on. Last time we were in town, international films were being shown every Sunday and Monday evening at the Teatro Principal, and the Teatro Cervantes was presenting an international film series every Sunday, Monday and Tuesday evening. Events at Teatro Juárez on the Jardín de la Unión were more sporadic, but it's a magnificent theatre and it would probably be worth going to see anything presented there, just for the experience of the theatre itself.

With its youthful population, Guanajuato has several discos to choose from. Some of the most popular are the Galería in the San Javier district; Sancho's in the Mineral de Cata district; and Jav's on the Las Pastitas park on the west side of the city. All are a short taxi ride from the city centre.

Getting There & Away

Air Guanajuato is served by the Bajío airport, which is about 10 or 12 km from Silao, to the south-west of Guanajuato. It takes about half an hour by car to get from Guanajuato to the airport. Going on the bus, you have to take a bus to Silao and a taxi from there.

Airlines serving this airport include Aerolitorál, Aeroméxico, Continental, Mexicana and SARO. None have offices in Guanajuato; they are represented here by the travel agencies. Viajes Frausto Guanajuato (☎ 2-35-80, 2-01-15, fax 2-66-20) is a convenient one, at Luis González Obregón 10, between the Jardín de la Unión and the Basilica. Another is Viajes Georama (☎ 2-59-09, 2-51-01, fax 2-19-54) at Plaza de la Paz 34, in front of the Basilica.

SETEJ, Mexico's student travel agency, has a representative in the Departamento de Servicios al Estudiante office on the ground floor of the University (☎ 2-27-70, fax 2-02-78). They sell the ISIC card and offer a list of discounts that can be obtained with it, plus various special student package tours. For airline tickets you might as well go to a regular travel agent: ISIC discounts are only 5% on national flights and 3% on international flights.

Bus Guanajuato's central bus station has moved from the city centre to a new Central de Autobuses terminal on the south-western outskirts of town. The bus station has a post office, a long-distance telephone office, a tourist information office, a restaurant and a place where you can store your luggage.

Local 'Central de Autobuses' buses run frequently between the bus station and the city centre, operating every day from around 5 am to midnight and costing US$0.20. If you're in the centre and want to go to the bus station, you can catch these buses heading west on Juárez, or on the north side of the Basilica.

Buses departing from Guanajuato include those to:

Aguascalientes – 184 km, four hours; four daily with Flecha Amarilla (US$4.30).
Celaya – 90 km, 2¼ hours; every 45 minutes, 6 am to 8.30 pm, with Flecha Amarilla (US$2.45).
Dolores Hidalgo – 54 km, one hour; every 20 minutes, 6.20 am to 10.30 pm, with Flecha Amarilla (US$1.70).
Guadalajara – 300 km, five to six hours; five daily with Flecha Amarilla (US$6.90); five daily with Estrella Blanca (US$6.90); four daily with Servicios Coordinados (US$7.55); two daily with Primera Plus (US$9); two daily with ETN (US$14).
Irapuato – 48 km, 45 minutes; every 15 minutes, 6 am to 10.30 pm, with Flecha Amarilla (US$1.10).
León – 56 km, 50 minutes; every 10 minutes, 6 am to 10.30 pm, with Flecha Amarilla (US$1.10); every 15 minutes, 7.45 am to 8 pm, with Azteca de Oro (US$1.10); six daily with Servicios Coordinados (US$1.35); three daily with ETN (US$3.35).
Mexico City – 355 km, 4½ hours; seven daily with Estrella Blanca (US$10); four daily with Servicios Coordinados (US$10); three daily with Primera Plus (US$11.70); two daily with ETN (US$20).
Morelia – 170 km, four hours; hourly, 6.30 am to 7.40 pm, with Flecha Amarilla (US$3.60).
Querétaro – 133 km, three hours; four daily with Flecha Amarilla (US$3.95).

San Luis Potosí – 210 km, four hours; five daily with Flecha Amarilla (US$5.25).
San Miguel de Allende – 82 km, two hours; six daily with Flecha Amarilla (US$2.15).

Train The Estación del Ferrocarril (☎ 2-10-35, 2-03-06) is on Calle Tepetapa on the west side of town. A train leaves daily at 2.25 pm, heading for Mexico City via Silao and Irapuato. It takes seven hours to reach Mexico City and costs US$14.30, making it not only slower and longer but also more expensive than the bus.

Getting Around

Most of Guanajuato's principal sights are in the city centre, within easy walking distance. The local bus system, however, has several useful routes, including the 'Panteón' or 'Mómias' route for visiting the Mummies; the 'Valenciana' route for the La Valenciana mine and church; the 'Presa' route for the Presa de la Olla park; the 'Pípila-ISSSTE' route for getting to the Pípila statue via the Panoramic Highway with a great view over the city; and the 'Central de Autobuses' route for the central bus station and the Ex-Hacienda San Gabriel de Barrera. The local buses operate every day from around 5 am to 10 pm; cost is US$0.20.

The tourist office near the Basilica is very helpful with bus information.

Taxis are plentiful in the centre. Cost for a ride in the centre is around US$1.70; between the centre and the bus station may cost around US$2.35 to US$3.35, or whatever the traffic will bear.

AROUND GUANAJUATO
Cerro de Cubilete & Cristo Rey

Cristo Rey (Christ the King) is a 20-metre bronze statue of Jesus erected in 1950 on the summit of the Cerro de Cubilete near Guanajuato, said to be the exact geographical centre of Mexico. For religious Mexicans, there is a significance in having Jesus at the heart of their country – the statue is a popular tourist attraction for Mexicans visiting Guanajuato.

The tour companies offer 3½-hour trips to

the statue (see Tours). Or you can go more cheaply on your own, for only US$1.35, by taking a bus from the central bus station; they depart every day at 7, 9, and 11 am, 2 and 4 pm, with additional buses at 12.30 pm on weekends. From the central bus station it is possible to see the statue up on the hill in the distance.

LEÓN & IRAPUATO

The industrial towns of León and Irapuato, north-west and south-west of Guanajuato respectively, have little to offer the visitor. Guanajuato city is close enough to stay in instead; buses depart at all hours.

Founded in 1576, León has a few remnants of the colonial past like its Palacio Municipal and cathedral, but industrial and population growth to close to a million inhabitants have robbed the city of its charm. Perhaps the only reason to stop here is to pick up a cheap pair of shoes in Mexico's foremost *zapato*-manufacturing centre; you can get custom-made boots here for a fraction of what they would cost anywhere else. If for some reason you must stay overnight in León, take a local bus from the station to the city centre; Avenida Juárez has inexpensive hotels.

Other than its famed strawberries, industrial Irapuato has no visitor attractions. If you are stuck here for a few hours, make a brief stop at the baroque Iglesia del Hospital built in 1713 and the Templo de San Francisco.

DOLORES HIDALGO

Population: 40,000

The village of Dolores was founded in 1568 on the site of an Otomí Indian settlement, with the Otomí name of Cocomacán (place where turtledoves are hunted). In 1640, when the statue of Nuestra Señora de Dolores was given to the village, the name was changed to Congregación de Nuestra Señora de Dolores. In 1780 the village was decreed a pueblo, and in 1824 a villa, with the new name of Villa de Dolores Hidalgo. In 1948 it was given its nickname of 'Cuna de la Independencia'.

This is where the Mexican independence movement began in earnest. At 5 am on the morning of 16 September 1810, Father Miguel Hidalgo, the parish priest, rang the bells to summon people to church earlier than usual and issued the *Grito de Dolores* (Cry of Dolores), whose precise words have been lost to history but which boiled down to 'Viva Our Lady of Guadalupe! Death to bad government and the gachupines!'

Gachupines was the derisive name for Mexico's Spanish overlords, against whom a powder keg of resentment finally exploded in this small town. Miguel Hidalgo, Ignacio Allende and other conspirators, alerted to the discovery of their plans for an uprising in Querétaro by Doña Josefa Ortiz, wife of Querétaro's mayor, decided to launch their rebellion immediately from Dolores.

After the *Grito* they went to the lavish Spanish house on the plaza, today called the Casa de Visitas, and took prisoner Don Nicolás Fernández del Rincón, local representative of the Spanish viceroy, and Don Ignacio Díaz de Cortina, the Spanish tax collector. They also freed the prisoners in the town jail and, at the head of a growing band of criollos, mestizos and Indians, set off for San Miguel on a campaign that would bring their own deaths within a few months but ultimately led to the independence of Mexico.

Today Hidalgo is Mexico's most revered hero, rivalled only by Benito Juárez in the number of streets, plazas and statues dedicated to him throughout the country. Visiting Dolores has acquired almost pilgrimage status for Mexicans. If you're interested in the country's history, it's well worth a trip. If not, don't bother – there's little else to attract you.

Orientation & Information

Everything of interest in Dolores Hidalgo is within a couple of blocks of the zócalo, called the Plaza Principal. The church on the north side of this plaza is where the *Grito* was cried.

Tourist Office The Delegación de Turismo is on the north side of the Plaza Principal in the Presidencia Municipal building to the left of the church; it's in the last office on the outer right side, facing the church. The staff give out free city maps showing the major points of interest and can answer any questions about the town. The office is open Monday to Friday from 9 am to 3 pm and 5.30 to 8 pm, Saturday and Sunday 9 am to 3 pm.

Money Cash and travellers' cheques can be changed at the Bancomer bank on the northwest corner of the zócalo Monday to Friday from 9 am to 1.30 pm. Outside these hours,

you can change money at the Hotel Posada Las Campanas on Guerrero.

Post & Telecommunications The post and Telecomm offices are in the same building at Puebla 22 on the corner of Veracruz, not far from the zócalo. The post office is open Monday to Friday from 8 am to 7 pm, Saturday 8 am to noon. The Telecomm office, with services of telegraph, telex and fax, is open Monday to Friday from 8 am to 1 pm and 3 to 5 pm, Saturday 8 am to noon.

Coin telephones can be found on the zócalo, in the post office and at other places

---

Miguel Hidalgo

The balding, visionary head of Father Miguel Hidalgo y Costilla is familiar to anyone who's looked at Mexican murals, statues, or books on the country. He was, it seems, a genuine rebel idealist, who had already sacrificed his own career at least once before that fateful day in 1810. And he launched the independence movement clearly aware of the risks to his own life.

Born on 8 May 1753, son of a criollo hacienda manager in Guanajuato, he studied at the College of San Nicolás Obispo in Valladolid (now Morelia), won a bachelor's degree and was ordained a priest in 1778. Returning to teach at his old college, he eventually became rector. But he was no orthodox cleric: Hidalgo questioned the virgin birth and the infallibility of the Pope, read banned books, gambled, danced and had a mistress.

In 1800 he was brought before the Inquisition. Nothing was proved but a few years later, in 1804, he found himself transferred to a new assignment as priest of the remote hick town of Dolores.

Hidalgo's years in Dolores show that he was interested in the economic as well as the religious welfare of the local people. Somewhat in the tradition of Don Vasco de Quiroga of Michoacán, founder of the College of San Nicolás where Hidalgo had studied, he started new industries in the town such as tile, ceramics and pottery-making (still practiced in the town today), plus the production of silk and the growing of vines. He also started a music band upon his arrival in the town and promoted other cultural pursuits, benefiting not only the town's economy but also its cultural life.

When Hidalgo met Ignacio Allende from San Miguel, he became caught up in the criollo discontent with the Spanish stranglehold on Mexico. His standing among the mestizos and Indians of his parish was vital in broadening the base of the rebellion that followed.

When Hidalgo became leader of the independence movement he once again came under the scrutiny of the Inquisition. On 13 October 1810, shortly after his Cry for Independence, he was formally excommunicated for 'heresy, apostasy and sedition'. He answered by proclaiming that he never would have been excommunicated if it had not been for his call for the independence of Mexico, and that, furthermore, the Spanish were not truly Catholic in any religious sense of the word, but only for political purposes, specifically to rape, pillage and exploit Mexico. A few days later, on 19 October, Hidalgo dictated his first edict calling for the abolition of slavery in Mexico.

In the coming months Hidalgo led his growing forces from Dolores to San Miguel, Celaya, Guanajuato, south almost to Mexico City, then west to Guadalajara, north to Zacatecas and further north to Chihuahua. He sent his former student, José Maria Morelos y Pavón, to Acapulco to organise a revolutionary army in the south.

On 30 July 1811, having been captured by the Spanish, Hidalgo was shot by firing squad in Chihuahua. His head was returned to the city of Guanajuato, where his army had scored its first major victory, and hung in a cage for ten years on an outer corner of the Alhóndiga de Granaditas building, along with the heads of Allende, Aldama and Jiménez. Rather than intimidating the people, this lurid display kept the memory, the goal and the example of the heroic martyrs fresh in everyone's mind. ■

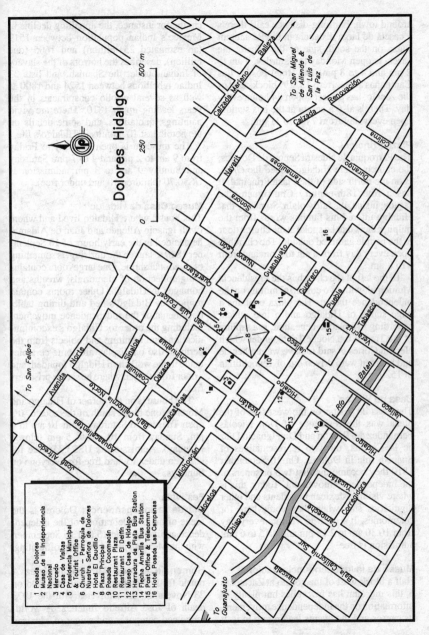

1 Posada Dolores
2 Museo de la Independencia Nacional
3 Mercado
4 Casa de Visitas
5 Presidencia Municipal & Tourist Office
6 Church – Parroquia de Nuestra Señora de Dolores
7 Hotel El Caudillo
8 Plaza Principal
9 Posada Cocomacán
10 Restaurant Plaza
11 Restaurant El Delfín
12 Museo Casa de Hidalgo
13 Herradura de Plata Bus Station
14 Flecha Amarilla Bus Station
15 Post Office & Telecomm
16 Hotel Posada Las Campanes

around town. For long-distance calls there's a caseta de larga distancia in the Restaurant Plaza on the south side of the zócalo; the caseta is open Monday to Saturday, 9 am to 2 pm and 4 to 8 pm. The Hotel Posada Las Campanas at Guerrero 15, 2½ blocks east of the zócalo, has a caseta open 24 hours every day. There's also a caseta at the bus station, open every day from 7 am to 11 pm.

Plaza Principal

The Parroquia de Nuestra Señora de Dolores, the church where Hidalgo issued the *Grito*, is on the north side of the Plaza Principal. It has a fine 18th-century Churrigueresque façade; inside, it's fairly plain. Some say that Hidalgo uttered his famous words from the pulpit, others that he spoke at the church door to the people gathered outside. The church is open every day from 6 am to 2 pm and from 4 to 8 pm.

To the left of the church is the Presidencia Municipal, with two colourful murals on the independence theme. The plaza contains a huge statue of Hidalgo and a tree which, according to a plaque beneath it, is a sapling of the Tree of the Noche Triste, under which Hernán Cortés is said to have wept when he and his men were driven out of Tenochtitlán in 1520.

Casa de Visitas

The Casa de Visitas on the west side of the plaza was the residence of Don Nicolás Fernández del Rincón and Don Ignacio Díaz de la Cortina, the two representatives of Spanish rule in Dolores. On 16 September 1810 they became the first two prisoners of the independence movement. Today, this is where visiting Mexican presidents and other dignitaries stay when they come here for ceremonies. It's open to visitors every day from 10.30 am to 2.15 pm and 4.15 to 6 pm; admission is free.

Museo de la Independencia Nacional

Half a block west of the zócalo at Zacatecas 6, this museum has few relics but plenty of information on the independence movement, its causes and the events leading up to it. It

charts, for instance, the appalling decline in Mexico's Indian population between 1519 (an estimated 25 million) and 1605 (one million), describes the horrors of the slavery of Indians under the Spanish, and lists 23 Indian rebellions between 1524 and 1800 as well as several criollo conspiracies in the years leading up to 1810. There are vivid paintings, quotations, and some details on the heroic last 10 months of Hidalgo's life.

The museum is open Monday to Friday from 9 am to 2 pm and 4 to 7 pm, Saturday and Sunday 9 am to 3 pm; admission is US$0.70 (children 10 and under free).

Museo Casa de Hidalgo

This house, where Hidalgo lived and where (with Ignacio Allende and Juan de Aldama) he decided in the early hours of 16 September 1810 to launch the uprising, is something of a national shrine. One large room contains a big collection of memorials, wreaths and homages to Hidalgo. Other rooms contain replicas of Hidalgo's bed and dining table, documents of the independence movement including the order for Hidalgo's excommunication, and furniture and objects from the period. Also on display are some ceramics made in the workshop Hidalgo founded, and a door from the jail where he set the prisoners free.

The house is on the corner of Hidalgo and Morelos, one block south of the zócalo. It's open Tuesday to Saturday from 10 am to 6 pm, Sunday from 10 am to 5 pm (closed Monday). Admission is US$3.35; free for children under 13, and free for everyone on Sundays.

Festivals

Día de la Independencia Dolores is the scene of major celebrations of the independence anniversary on 15 and 16 September, with the Mexican president often officiating.

Homenaje a José Alfredo Jiménez A music festival and other events are held on 23 November, the anniversary of the 1973 death of José Alfredo Jiménez. A world-renowned composer and singer of Mexican ballads and *rancheras*, he was born in Dolores Hidalgo in 1926 and now lies buried in the town cemetery.

Places to Stay

Most visitors stay in Dolores Hidalgo for only a few hours, just long enough to see the church and museums, eat an ice cream on the plaza, and then they're back on the bus. Only an hour away from either Guanajuato or San Miguel de Allende, Dolores is probably best visited as a day trip from either one; once you've seen the historic sites there's not much else to do in Dolores. If you want to stay over, though, there are a few choices.

Most economical is the *Posada Dolores* (☎ 2-06-42) at Yucatán 8, one block west of the zócalo. It's only a simple casa de huéspedes, but it's friendly and clean. Singles/doubles with shared bath cost US$5/8.35; rooms with private bath are US$10.

On the east side of the zócalo is the fancier *Posada Cocomacán* (☎ 2-00-18); its 50 rooms have private bath, windows for good ventilation, and wooden parquet floors; singles/doubles are US$12.70/16.35. A plaque out front proclaims that Benito Juárez stayed here in 1867.

In the next block, opposite the right side of the church, the *Hotel El Caudillo* (☎ 2-01-98, 2-04-65) at Querétaro 8 has rooms that are carpeted and clean enough, but small and stuffy; singles/doubles are US$15/16.35.

The *Hotel Posada Las Campanas* (☎ 2-04-27, 2-14-24) at Guerrero 15, 2½ blocks east of the zócalo, has 40 well-kept rooms, all with private bath, carpet, TV and phone; singles/doubles are US$22.35/24.70.

Places to Eat

Dolores Hidalgo is famous not only for its historical attractions, but also for its ice cream. On the south-west corner of the zócalo you can get ice cream cones in a variety of unusual flavours including mole, chicharrón, avocado, maize, cheese, honey, and any of about 20 tropical fruit flavours.

You can grab a torta or a snack at many small eateries on and near the zócalo. On the south side of the zócalo, opposite the church, the *Restaurant Plaza* at Plaza Principal 17-B is a good family restaurant offering a view of the plaza. Breakfasts, enchiladas and other antojitos are around US$1.85. The daily comida corrida and other meals are more expensive, at around US$5.50; they also serve pizza. It's open Monday to Saturday from 8 am to 10 pm, Sunday 8 am to 6 pm.

The restaurant/bar at the *Hotel El Caudillo*, facing the right side of the church, is a bit more up-market. The comida corrida here is US$6.70, but you can get breakfast, enchiladas or soup for US$1.50, or sandwiches for US$0.85. They're open from 8 am to 11 pm.

For seafood try the *Restaurant El Delfín* at Veracruz 2, one block east of the zócalo. It's a pleasant family seafood restaurant open every day from 9 am to 7 pm.

Things to Buy

Ceramics, pottery and Talavera tiles have been the special handcrafts of Dolores Hidalgo ever since Father Hidalgo founded the town's first ceramics workshop in the early 19th century. A number of shops sell these and other crafts.

Getting There & Away

Flecha Amarilla and Herradura de Plata are the bus lines serving Dolores Hidalgo. The Flecha Amarilla bus station is on Calle Hidalgo, 2½ blocks south of the zócalo. The Herradura de Plata station is on the corner of Chiapas and Chihuahua, around the corner.

Buses departing from Dolores Hidalgo include those to:

Guanajuato – 54 km, one hour; buses every 30 minutes, 5.20 am to 9 pm, with Flecha Amarilla (US$1.70).

Mexico City – 470 km, five hours; buses every half hour, 4.50 am to 6 pm, plus at 11.10 and 11.50 pm, with Herradura de Plata (US$7.85); nine buses daily with Flecha Amarilla (US$7.85).

San Miguel de Allende – 43 km, one hour; every 20 minutes, 5.20 am to 8.30 pm, with Flecha Amarilla (US$1); same buses as to Mexico City with Herradura de Plata (US$1).

SAN MIGUEL DE ALLENDE

Population: 49,000

Altitude: 1840 metres

A colonial town in a beautiful setting, San Miguel has become known for its large colony of North Americans. Starting around the 1940s, when David Alfaro Siqueiros was an art student here, the town began attracting artists of every persuasion from Mexico and the USA. Over the decades, many painters, sculptors, writers, poets, textile artists and every other kind of creative type came to San Miguel. Neal Cassady, hero of Jack Kerouac's *On the Road*, died here in Febru-

ary 1968, walking on the railroad tracks towards Celaya.

Once San Miguel was entrenched on the gringo circuit, however, it naturally lost some of its bohemian character. Today the town is home to several thousand foreigners, many of them upper-middle-class gringos who have come to retire in Mexico. You can easily visit San Miguel and speak no Spanish at all. With the large population of rich gringos, both the permanent residents and the constant stream of tourists, there are ample tourist facilities but prices are higher than elsewhere in Mexico. There are also

■ PLACES TO STAY

1   San Miguel International Hostel
3   Hotel Quinta Loreto
10 Hotel La Huerta
11 Hotel Sautto
15 Casa de Huéspedes
16 Parador de San Sebastián
17 Posada de las Monjas
21 Hotel Mesón de San Antonio
23 Hotel Central & Restaurant/Bar Casa Mexas
26 Posada San Francisco
44 Pensión Casa Carmen & Caseta de Larga Distancia
46 Posada Carmina, Hotel Vista Hermosa Taboada
47 Posada de Allende
49 Casa de Sierra Nevada
53 Posada de la Aldea
55 Hotel Aristos San Miguel
56 La Mansión del Bosque
59 Hotel Posada La Ermita

▼ PLACES TO EAT

2   Pio Pio Restaurant
13 Pepe Pizzas
14 Andale!! Pizzas & El Ring Disco
22 Plaza Colonial, USA Consulate & Restaurant La Dolce Vita
29 Restaurant Flamingo's
30 Fonda La Mesa del Matador
34 El Tucán
37 Mama Mia
39 La Fragua
43 Rincón Español

45 Café de la Parroquia

OTHER

4   Mercado de Artesanías
5   Mercado El Nigromante
6   Biblioteca Pública
7   Oratorio de San Felipe Neri
8   Church of La Salud
9   Colegio de Sales
12 Pancho & Lefty's, Club de Jazz El Coyote Azul
18 Church of La Concepción
19 Bellas Artes
20 Teatro Angela Peralta
24 Casa de Cambio Mavaq
25 American Express
27 Tercer Orden Chapel
28 Church of San Francisco
31 Casa del Mayorazgo de Canal
32 Casa de los Perros
33 Plaza Principal (Jardín)
35 SCT Telégrafos Nacionales
36 Post Office
38 Museo Histórico de San Miguel de Allende
40 Parroquia
41 Church of San Rafael
42 Tourist Office
48 Inquisition Jail
50 Casa del Inquisidor
51 El Colibrí Bookshop
52 Plaza de Toros
54 Instituto Allende
57 Parque Benito Juárez
58 El Chorro
60 Mirador

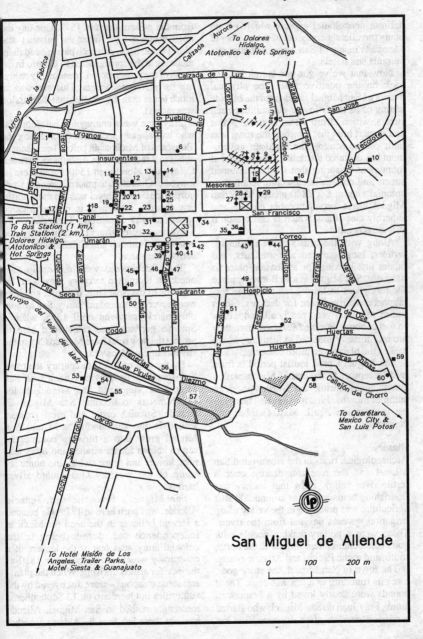

To Dolores
Hidalgo,
Atotonilco & Hot Springs

Calzada Aurora

Calzada de la Luz

San José

To Bus Station (1 km),
Train Station (2 km),
Dolores Hidalgo,
Atotonilco &
Hot Springs

Insurgentes

Mesones

San Francisco

Correo

Umarán

Hospicio

Cuadrante

Terraplén

Huertas

Los Piriles

Diezmo

To Hotel Misión de Los
Angeles, Trailer Parks,
Motel Siesta & Guanajuato

To Querétaro,
Mexico City &
San Luis Potosí

Callejón del Chorro

San Miguel de Allende

0   100   200 m

definite neocolonial aspects which get on many travellers' nerves: count the number of Mexicans in any of San Miguel's better restaurants and hotels.

Now that we've got our *kvetch* in, let's look on the positive side. The physical beauty of San Miguel stems from the hillside setting of its many lovely old buildings and streets, which afford vistas over the plains and distant hills just as when the town was built centuries ago. The Mexican government has declared the entire town a national monument, ensuring that the cobblestoned streets and colonial architecture retain their colonial charm. Set 1840 metres high, San Miguel has a very agreeable climate and superbly clear light, which is one reason it still attracts artists.

Along with the artists come musicians, writers, language and arts students, and others just looking for a pleasant place to hang out. San Miguel is a well-known place for foreigners to learn Spanish. Some foreigners have lived here for decades, others return year after year; nearly all find it easy to feel at home. For the Mexicans' part, they are inordinately addicted to festivals, which makes the place even more colourful.

San Miguel's peak tourist period is from mid-December to the end of March, with a flurry again during the North American summer months, June to August. The quietest months are April, May, October and November.

History

Archaeological ruins in the area around San Miguel and the reservoir nearby, once a fertile river valley, show that society was flourishing here as early as around 200 BC; agriculture was practised in the valley using irrigation systems devised from the rivers. These were a pottery-making people with trade connections extending far to the north, south, and to the Pacific and Atlantic coasts.

The town of San Miguel, the story goes, owes its founding to a few hot dogs. These hounds were dearly loved by a Franciscan monk, Fray Juan de San Miguel, who started a mission near an often-dry river five km

from the present town in 1542. One day the dogs wandered off from the mission and didn't come back. A search party found them reclining at the spring called El Chorro in the south of the present town, presumably enjoying its refreshing waters. This site was so much better than the original that the mission was moved.

Fray Juan was a courageous barefoot friar who had already spent a decade among the Tarascans of Michoacán before being sent as abbot to a monastery in Acámbaro, between Celaya and Morelia, in 1540. From there he moved to Querétaro to push missionary work northwards. San Miguel was the most northerly Spanish settlement in central Mexico when it was founded. Tarascans and Tlaxcalans were brought to help pacify and convert the Otomís and Chichimecas of the surrounding area.

The Chichimecas were not easily subdued; on their own territory they were far superior to the Spaniards in battle, and they were never conquered militarily. San Miguel only barely survived until 1555, when a Spanish garrison was established here to protect the new road from Mexico City to the silver centre of Zacatecas.

By the end of the 16th century the town had forsaken its previous names of San Miguel El Viejo and San Miguel de los Chichimecas to become San Miguel El Grande. Spanish cattle and crop growers settled in the surrounding area and San Miguel grew into a thriving commercial centre known for its sarapes and other textiles, knives and horse tackle, and home for some of the wealthy Guanajuato silver barons.

San Miguel's favourite son, Ignacio Allende, was born here in 1779. He became a fervent believer in the need for Mexican independence and, despite being in the colonial army, was one of the leaders of a conspiracy which set 8 December 1810 as the date for armed uprising. When the plan – and some weapons – were discovered by the authorities in Querétaro on 13 September, a messenger rushed to San Miguel. Allende was not there but Juan de Aldama, another conspirator, was. Aldama sped north to Dolores where, in the early hours of 16 September, he found Allende at the house of the local parish priest Miguel Hidalgo, also one of the coterie.

A few hours later Hidalgo proclaimed rebellion from his church. Within a few days – according to some accounts, the same night – San Miguel was in rebel hands, its local regiment having joined forces with the band of insurgent criollos, mestizos and Indians which had already grown to several hundred. The Spanish population of the town was locked up and some of the rebels set about looting it. Allende was only partly able to restrain them.

The army grew and moved on to many other places, until finally in 1811 Hidalgo, Allende and other leaders were captured in Chihuahua. Allende was executed almost immediately, Hidalgo four months later. It was not until 1821 that Mexico finally achieved independence.

In 1826 San Miguel was rechristened San Miguel de Allende. It began to take on its current character with the founding of the Escuela de Bellas Artes (School of Fine Arts) in 1938 and the Instituto Allende in 1951, both of which attracted many foreign students.

Orientation

The Plaza Principal, called the Jardín, is the focal point of the town. On its south side the Parroquia, with its gothic-like spires, can be seen from far and wide.

As in many other Mexican towns, most streets in San Miguel change names on either side of the plaza. The one-way streets on the north and south sides of the Jardín are the main streets of the central area. The street on the north side of the Jardín is called Canal on the west side, San Francisco on the east. The street on the Jardín's south side is called Umarán on the west side, Correo on the east. The bus station is about one km west of the Jardín on Calle Canal; the train station is at the end of Calle Canal, another km further on.

San Miguel is a compact town and although neighbourhoods are now sprouting up on the surrounding hills, everything of interest in the centre is within easy walking distance. It would require quite an effort to get lost in San Miguel, as the town is so small and the streets so simply laid out.

Information

Tourist Office The tourist office (☎ (465) 2-17-47) is on the south-east corner of the Jardín to the left of the Parroquia, in a glassed-in office behind some tables of the La Terraza restaurant. They give out free maps of the town, printed brochures in English and Spanish, and can answer questions in both languages. The office is open Monday to Friday from 10 am to 2.45 pm and 5 to 7 pm, Saturday 10 am to 1 pm, and Sunday 10 am to noon.

Money There are several banks on Calle San Francisco in the couple of blocks heading east from the Jardín, and another on the Jardín itself, on the west side. They're open Monday to Friday, 9 am to 1.30 pm, and they give the best rates for changing money.

Lloyd's Casa de Cambio in the lobby of the Posada San Francisco, on the north-west corner of the plaza, changes cash and travellers' cheques at only slightly less favourable rates than the banks, and it's not as crowded. It's open Monday to Friday, 9 am to 3 pm. The hotel restaurant will also change money; it's open every day from 7 am to 10.30 pm.

The Casa de Cambio Mavaq on the corner of Hidalgo and Mesones, one block north of the Jardín, also gives only slightly less favourable rates than the banks. It's open Monday to Saturday from 9 am to 7 pm, Sunday from 9 am to 3 pm.

American Express (☎ 2-18-56, 2-16-95) is at Hidalgo 1-A, half a block north of the Jardín. The office has a travel agency, sells travellers' cheques and provides other services, but will not change cheques to pesos. It's open Monday to Friday, 9 am to 2 pm and 4 to 6.30 pm.

Post & Telecommunications The post office is one block east of the Jardín, on the corner of Correo and Calle de la Corregidora. It's open Monday to Friday from 8 am to 7 pm, Saturday 9 am to 1 pm.

The SCT Telégrafos Nacionales office at Correo 16, next door to the post office, has telegram, telex, fax and a coin telephone. Open hours are Monday to Friday from 9 am to 1 pm and 3 to 6 pm, Saturday 9 am to noon.

For long-distance telephone calls there's a caseta de larga distancia upstairs at the corner of Correo and Recreo; it's open every day except Monday, 10 am to 2.30 pm and 5 to 9.30 pm. El Toro, a caseta at Hernández Macías 58-A opposite the Hotel Sautto, is open every day from 9 am to 2 pm and 3 to 8 pm. There's also a caseta in the bus station, open every day from 7 am to 11 pm.

Foreign Consulates The US Consulate (☎ 2-23-57 or in emergencies 2-00-68, 2-09-80) is at Local 6 in the Plaza Colonial, on the corner of Canal and Hernández Macías. Office hours are Monday and Wednesday from 9 am to 1 pm and 4 to 7 pm, Tuesday and Thursday from 4 to 7 pm, and at other times by appointment.

Laundry The ATL Lavandería Automática at Local J in the Pasaje Allende mall at Mesones 5 charges US$4 for a whole basket of laundry if you drop it off, or US$3.35 if you do it yourself. It's open Monday to Saturday from 8 am to 2 pm and 4 to 7 pm.

Bookshops & Libraries The Biblioteca Pública (Public Library) at Insurgentes 25 has a large selection of used books in English on sale at cheap prices; it's open Monday to Saturday from 10 am to 2 pm and 4 to 7 pm (closed Sundays and holidays). The El Colibrí bookshop, at Diez de Sollano 30, 1½ blocks south of the plaza, has an excellent selection of new books and magazines in English, plus a few in Spanish, French and German, but its prices are higher; opening hours are the same. The Lagundi shop in the Plaza Colonial at the corner of Canal and Hernández Macías also has a few books and magazines in English.

Miscellaneous La Conexión (☎ & fax 2-23-12, 2-16-87) at Aldama 1 offers a variety of services including a house-sitting placement agency, answering, mailbox and fax services and more. If you'll be in San Miguel for a while, it might be worth it to check with them about house-sitting.

Newspapers & Notice boards The expatriate community puts out a weekly English-language newspaper called *Atención San Miguel* (US$0.50). It's full of what's on and the comings, goings and doings of long-stayers and their friends, plus lots of small ads offering rooms, apartments, or houses to sell, rent or exchange; furniture sales; house-sitter jobs; classes in yoga, Spanish, art or dance; Alcoholics Anonymous in English; easels for sale; meditation sessions in hot springs and so on. You can buy the paper at the Biblioteca Pública, El Colibrí bookshop and the supermarkets on the zócalo; and at Lagundi and La Dolce Vita in the Plaza Colonial on the corner of Canal and Hernández Macías.

Notice boards in the Biblioteca Pública and the Autotienda supermarket on the west side of the plaza offer the same sort of things. There are also notice boards in Bellas Artes (what's on) and in hotels.

Colonial Buildings
Parroquia The Parroquia, with its pink 'sugar-candy' pointed towers, dominates the Jardín. This strange structure, all soaring pinnacles, is Gothic in impact but really belongs to no architectural school at all. It was designed by an untutored local Indian, Zeferino Gutierrez, in the late 19th century. He reputedly instructed the builders by scratching plans in the sand with a stick. Most of the rest of the church dates from the late 17th century.

The camarín, a chapel beside the main altar which contains ceremonial clothing for saints' images, was designed by Mexico's best-known Neoclassical architect, Eduardo Tresguerras, around 1800. The crypt contains the remains of a 19th-century Mexican president, Anastasio Bustamante. In the chapel to the left of the main altar is a much-revered image of the Cristo de la Conquista (Christ of the Conquest), made by Indians in Pátzcuaro from cornstalks and orchid bulbs, probably in the 16th century.

The church to the left of the Parroquia is San Rafael, founded in 1742, which has also undergone gothic-type alterations.

Museo Histórico de San Miguel de Allende

To the right of the Parroquia at the Cuna de Allende corner of the Jardín stands the house where Ignacio Allende was born, now a museum. Exhibits relate the interesting history of San Miguel and the area around it from prehistoric times up to independence, with special exhibits on Allende and the independence movement he was instrumental in starting. An inscription on the façade says *Hic natus ubique notus* – Latin for 'Here born, everywhere known'. Another plaque points out that the more famous independence hero, Miguel Hidalgo, only joined the movement after being invited by Allende.

The museum is open Tuesday to Sunday from 10 am to 3.30 pm; admission is free.

Casa del Mayorazgo de Canal

This house of the Canal family is one of the most imposing of San Miguel's colonial residences. The entrance is at Canal 4 and it stretches above the arcade on the west side of the plaza. The Neoclassic building has some late baroque touches; the façade has an image of the Virgin of Loreto above the doorway.

The house is now open to the public; art exhibitions are held, movies are presented on Friday, Saturday and Sunday afternoons, and free tours are given for groups. The house is open Monday to Friday from 9 am to 1.30 pm and 4 to 6 pm, Saturday and Sunday 10 am to 5 pm; admission is free.

Casa de los Perros

The House of the Dogs, so-called because of the carved canines supporting its main balcony, is at Umarán 4. Here lived one of San Miguel's many independence heroes, Juan de Umarán. Today it's occupied by the Galería Maxwell shop.

Church of San Francisco

This church on the north side of a small garden at the corner of San Francisco and Juárez has an elaborate late-18th-century Churrigueresque façade. An image of San Francisco de Assisi is at the top, and the Crucifixion appears below it with Our Lady of Sorrows and San Juan on either side. The tower and interior are mainly Neoclassical.

Tercer Orden

This chapel on the west side of the same garden was built in the early 18th century and like the San Francisco church was part of a Franciscan monastery complex. The main façade shows San Francisco and symbols of the Franciscan order. On the side of the building can be seen San Diego and the two-armed cross of Lorraine.

Oratorio de San Felipe Neri

This multi-towered and domed church, built in the early 18th century, stands at the corner of Insurgentes and Llamas. The main façade is baroque with Indian influence. Five niches hold statues of San José, San Juan Bautista, San Felipe, San Pedro and San Pablo. A passage to the right of this façade leads to the east wall, whose Indian-style doorway holds an image of Our Lady of Solitude from an earlier church on the site. The adjacent filled-in doorway is topped by a medallion of San Felipe and a cross of Lorraine. You can also see into the cloister from this side of the church.

Inside the church are 33 oil paintings showing scenes from the life of San Felipe Neri, the 16th-century Florentine who founded the Oratorio Catholic order. In the east transept is a painting of the Virgin of Guadalupe by Miguel Cabrera. The altars are primarily Neoclassical but the main one has some older paintings on mirrors.

In the west transept of the church are two pairs of twisted baroque pillars at the entrance to a lavishly decorated chapel, the Santa Casa de Loreto, built in 1735. It's a replica of a chapel in Loreto, Italy, legendary home of the Virgin Mary. If the chapel doors are open you can see tiles from Puebla, China and Valencia on the floor and walls, gilded cloth hangings and images above the tombs of chapel founder Manuel de la Canal and his wife María de Hervas de Flores. The altar has an image of the Virgin of Loreto in a glass case. Behind the altar, the camarín has six more altars – mostly very elaborate gilded baroque. In one is a reclining wax figure of San Columbano which contains the saint's bones.

Church of La Salud This church, with a big shell carved above its entrance, is just east of San Felipe Neri. The façade is early churrigueresque. Above the door is a figure of La Inmaculada, at the sides are San Joachim and Santa Ana, and below are San Juan Evangelista and El Sagrado Corazón (Sacred Heart). The dome, covered in blue and yellow tiles, has a prickly-pear-shaped lantern. The church's paintings include San Javier by Miguel Cabrera.

Colegio de Sales Next door to La Salud, which used to be part of it, this was once a college run by the order of San Felipe Neri. Founded in the mid-18th century, it counted among its alumni many of the 1810 revolutionaries. The local Spaniards were locked up here when the rebels took San Miguel.

Church of La Concepción A couple of blocks south of the Jardín on Calle Canal is the splendid church of La Concepción, with a fine altar and several large, magnificent old oil paintings. On the interior doorway are painted a number of wise sayings to give pause to those entering the sanctuary. The church was begun in the mid-18th century; its dome, added in the late 19th century by the versatile Zeferino Gutierrez, was possibly inspired by pictures of Les Invalides in Paris.

Bellas Artes This education and cultural centre at Hernández Macías 75 near the corner of Canal, also called the Centro Cultural El Nigromante or the Centro Cultural Ignacio Ramírez, is housed in the beautiful Neoclassical former monastery of the La Concepción church. The building was con-

verted to use as the Escuela de Bellas Artes (School of Fine Arts) in 1938.

One room in the cloister is devoted to an unfinished mural by David Alfaro Siqueiros, done in 1948 as part of a course in mural painting for US war veterans. The subject of the work – though you wouldn't guess it – is the life and work of Ignacio Allende. Other murals were done by Pedro Martínez in the early 1940s. They include *La Cantina, Los Tejedores* (The Weavers) and *El Fanatismo del Pueblo – la caza del vampiro* (The Fanaticism of the People – the vampire hunt).

Inquisition Jail The building at the corner of Cuadrante and Hernández Macías was used as a jail and supposedly also a torture centre during the Spanish Inquisition. The cross carved on the corner of the building is an Inquisition emblem. Today the building has a more cheerful use as a children's centre.

Opposite this at Cuadrante 36 is the Casa del Inquisidor (House of the Inquisitor) where Victorino de las Fuentes, the local delegate of the Inquisition tribunal, lived around 1812. The baroque-style house, built in the second half of the 18th century, is today a house-decorations boutique.

Instituto Allende This large, pleasant building with several patios and an old chapel at Ancha de San Antonio 4 was built in 1736 as the home of the Conde de la Canal, who paid for the Santa Casa de Loreto chapel in the Oratorio de San Felipe Neri. Later it was used as a Carmelite convent, eventually becoming an art and language school in 1951. Above the entrance is a carving of the Virgin of Loreto, patroness of the Canal family. Cardo, the first street heading east from Ancha de San Antonio behind the Instituto, leads to the cool Parque Benito Juárez.

Famous Peoples' Homes Partly thanks to its key role in the independence movement, San Miguel has more than its fair share of homes of the famous. Ones not already mentioned include those of Juan and Ignacio de Aldama (independence) at San Francisco 10;

Luis Malo (independence) at Cuna de Allende 5; Francisco de Lanzagorta (independence) at Correo 4; El Pípila, the man who burned down the door of the Guanajuato Alhóndiga to begin the massacre of the Spaniards inside, at Barranca 90; Mariano Escobedo, leader of the Mexican forces which drove out the French in the 1860s, at Mesones 85; and Ignacio Ramírez, a leading mid-19th century liberal thinker known as El Nigromante (The Sorcerer) at Umarán 28. These are not generally open to the public.

Lookout Point & Park

One of the best views over the town and surrounding country is from the mirador up on Calle Pedro Vargas, also known as the Salida a Querétaro, in the south-east of the town. If you take Calzada del Chorro, the street leading directly downhill from here, and turn left at the bottom you reach El Chorro, the spring where the town was founded. Today it gushes out of a fountain built in 1960. A bit further down the hill is the shady Parque Benito Juárez.

Courses

The reputation of San Miguel's art schools has fallen a little since the heady 1940s when Siqueiros was taking mural-painting courses at Bellas Artes. In part this is due to the many amateurs who come to pursue artistic hobbies rather than careers. It works to the advantage of most people, since there are many easy-to-join courses which demand only enthusiasm. Language courses – group or private – are numerous; some of them are listed here, or just ask around. Most courses run almost year-round with just a three-week break in December.

Instituto Allende (☎ /fax 2-01-90), in an old mansion on Ancha de San Antonio, offers courses in fine arts, crafts and Spanish. Art and craft courses can be joined at any time, usually involve nine hours of attendance a week and cost between US$100 and US$210 a month. They can often count for credits in North American universities. Spanish courses begin about every four weeks and range from conversational (50 minutes a day,

five days a week, US$95 for four weeks) to total impact (individual tuition, three to six hours a day, five days a week, US$490 to US$860 for four weeks). Write to Instituto Allende, San Miguel de Allende, Guanajuato 37700, México for details.

Bellas Artes (☎ 2-02-89), also called the Centro Cultural El Nigromante or Centro Cultural Ignacio Ramírez, is at Hernández Macías 75 on the corner of Calle Canal in a beautiful old former monastery. Courses in art, dance, crafts and music are usually given in Spanish and cost US$70 a month per class; each class is nine hours a week. Registration is at the beginning of each month. Classes are held all year, but some are not held in July, and there are no classes in August.

The Academía Hispano Americana (☎ 2-03-49, (☎ /fax 2-23-33) at Mesones 4 runs Spanish language and culture courses at US$350 for a four-week session, or two weeks for US$200. The school's aim is 'to make available to serious students a complete preparation for a future life among the peoples of Latin America, with special emphasis on Mexico'; the cultural courses are taught in elementary Spanish. The school can arrange for you to live with a Mexican family for about US$450 per month, meals included, or help with other living arrangements.

Inter/Idiomas (☎ 2-21-77) at Mesones 15 is a language school with small classes and an emphasis on conversational skills. Classes are held for two hours daily; tuition is US$45 for one week, US$160 for four weeks.

La Casa de la Luna (☎ 2-23-12, fax 2-16-87) at Recreo 16 begins small-group Spanish-language classes every Monday. Classes can be taken for two hours daily (US$50 per week, US$180 per month) or four hours daily (US$90 per week, US$320 per month).

Activities

Walking Tours A tour of some of the lovely houses and gardens in San Miguel which are otherwise closed to the public departs at 11.30 am every Sunday from the Biblioteca

Pública at Insurgentes 25. Cost is US$8 for the 1½ to two-hour House & Garden tour, with four different houses toured each week.

The Travel Institute of San Miguel (☎ 2-00-78, fax 2-01-21) at Cuna de Allende 11 conducts two-hour historical walking tours of the centre of San Miguel for US$10, plus a variety of other tours; stop by for one of their brochures.

La Conexión (☎ 2-23-12, 2-16-87) at Aldama 1 offers walking tours of San Miguel for US$15.

Riding Club Pegaso (☎ 2-23-12, 2-16-87), run by a North American, offers scenic trail rides for US$15 per hour, jumping or dressage lessons at the same price. La Conexión (☎ 2-23-12, 2-16-87) at Aldama 1 offers riding tours of San Miguel for US$25.

Golf There's a nine-hole golf course about 1½ km out of town on the Guanajuato road.

Festivals

Being so well endowed with churches and patron saints (it has six – San Miguel, San Juan Bautista, the Virgins of Guadalupe and Loreto, La Inmaculada and San José), San Miguel has a multitude of festivals every month of the year. You'll probably learn of some by word of mouth – or the sound of fireworks – while you're there. Some of the more important ones include:

Blessing of the Animals This happens in several churches including the Parroquia on 17 January.

Allende's Birthday On 21 January various official events celebrate this occasion.

Candelaria On 2 February, seeds are blessed in the Parroquia as a plea for good crops, and flowers and plants are sold.

Cristo de la Conquista This image in the Parroquia is fêted on the first Friday in March, with scores of dancers in elaborate pre-Hispanic costumes and plumed headdresses dancing in front of the Parroquia.

Semana Santa Religious ceremonies begin two weekends before Easter with a pilgrimage carrying an image of the Señor de la Columna (Lord of the Column) from Atotonilco, 14 km north, to the church of San Juan de Dios in San Miguel on Saturday night or Sunday morning.

On the Friday before Palm Sunday people visit each others' homes, where images of the Virgin Mary are surrounded by flowers and young wheat plants.

During Semana Santa itself, the week before Easter, the many activities include the lavish Procesión del Santo Intierro on Good Friday and the burning or exploding of images of Judas Iscariot on Easter Day. Families build brightly decorated altars in their homes.

Fiesta de la Santa Cruz This unusual festival traditionally happens on the last weekend in May at Valle del Maíz, one km from the centre of town. Oxen are dressed in lime necklaces and painted tortillas, and their yokes are festooned with flowers and fruit. One beast carries on its back two boxes of 'treasure' (bread and sugar) and is surrounded by characters in bizarre costumes on horses or donkeys. A mock battle between 'Indians' and 'Federales' follows, with a wizard appearing to heal the 'wounded' and raise the 'dead'.

Corpus Christi This moveable feast in June features dances by children in front of the Parroquia. One is called Los Hortelanos (The Gardeners).

Chamber Music Festival Bellas Artes sponsors an annual Chamber Music Festival in the first two weeks of August.

Fiesta de la Independencia The anniversary of the beginning of Mexico's independence movement is celebrated on 15 and 16 September with a parade and other activities.

San Miguel Arcángel Celebrations honouring the town's chief patron saint are held on the saint's day, 29 September (or on the weekend after, if the 29th falls on a weekday). There are cockfights, bullfights and a running of bulls through the streets, but the hub of a general town party is provided by traditional dancers from several states who meet at Cruz del Cuarto, on the road to the train station. Wearing bells and costumes which include feather headdresses, scarlet cloaks and masks, groups carry flower offerings called *xuchiles*, and some play lutes made of armadillo shells. They then walk in procession to the Jardín and the Parroquia. The roots of these performances probably go back to pre-Hispanic times.

Dances continue over a few days and include the Danza Guerrero in front of the Parroquia, which represents the Spanish conquest of the Chichimecas. The dancers also make processions to cemeteries.

Day of the Dead An unusual local touch to this fiesta celebrated on 1 and 2 November is the making of candies from orchid bulbs.

Christmas This starts on 16 December, the first of nine nights of posadas (inns) in which families traditionally get together to make processions through the streets and sing carols, re-enacting Joseph and Mary's search for an inn, with the children dressed in costumes. Afterwards they break piñatas. The nine nights represent the nine-day journey of Joseph and Mary from Nazareth to Bethlehem.

Places to Stay

The price structure for places to stay in San Miguel tends to be higher than in many other parts of Mexico, due to the presence of many foreigners who can pay the price. Some of the best-value places are often full; book ahead if you can, especially during the high season from December to March and during the summer. If you can't book ahead, you'll find a room somewhere but you may have to pay more. The tourist office will ring round for you if you like.

Many hotels give discounts for long-term guests. If you're planning to stay a while in

San Miguel, consider renting your own place or house-sitting for someone. There are plenty of places available; check the newspapers and notice boards, or sign up with the house-sitting service at La Conexión (☎ /fax 2-23-12, 2-16-87) at Aldama 1.

Places to Stay – bottom end

Camping The *Lago Dorado KDA Trailer Park* (☎ (465) 2-23-01), beside the lake five km from town, has a swimming pool, lounge, laundromat and 60 spaces with full hook-ups, plus 40 more spaces without hook-ups. Cost is US$8.35 for one or two people, US$1.70 for each extra person. To get there from town, head south on the Celaya highway, then after three km turn right at the Hotel Misión de los Angeles and continue another two km towards the lake, crossing over the railway tracks. The mailing address is Apartado Postal 523, San Miguel de Allende, Guanajuato, CP 37700.

The *Trailer Park La Siesta* (☎ (465) 2-02-07) is on the grounds of the Motel La Siesta, on the Celaya road two km south of town. It has 62 spaces with full hook-ups; cost is US$9.35 for one or two people. The postal address is Apartado Postal 72.

Hostels The *San Miguel International Hostel* (☎ (465) 2-06-74) at Organos 34 is in a pleasant colonial-style house with a gurgling fountain in the interior courtyard full of flowers and trees. Beds are US$5 in separate-sex dorms, or a few private rooms with bath are US$15/20 (cheaper by the week). Free coffee, tea and continental breakfast are included; kitchen use costs US$1 extra per day, with staples like rice, beans, spaghetti and spices provided. No hostel card is required. (Final negotiations on the hostel were still pending at press time; you might telephone ahead to be sure they're open.)

Hotels Half a block from the plaza, behind the Parroquia, the *Posada de Allende* (☎ (465) 2-06-98) at Cuna de Allende 10 looks a little old and worn; its five rooms, all with private bath and some with balconies over the sidewalk, cost US$8.35/11.70 for singles/doubles.

Heading up Mesones are three good choices in the low-price bracket. The *Casa de Huéspedes* (☎ (465) 2-13-78) at Mesones 27 is a clean, pleasant upstairs hostelry whose rooftop terrace has a good view. All 10 rooms have private bath; regular rooms are US$10/11.70, or US$11.70/15 with private kitchen. There are discounts for stays of three days or more, and a monthly rate of US$200/250. Many European travellers stay here.

Further up the hill at Mesones 7, the *Parador de San Sebastián* (☎ (465) 2-07-07) is quiet and attractive, with a dozen rooms, all with fireplace and private bath, arranged around an arched courtyard full of plants. Singles/doubles are US$14.35/15.70.

Hotel La Huerta (☎ (465) 2-08-81, 2-03-60), off Calle Aparicio, is a bit further up the hill. This is an advantage if you enjoy peace and quiet, as there are many trees, birds, and a running stream which you can hear at night (along with the dogs and roosters). It's a bit more removed from the action of town, though. With singles/doubles at US$6.70/10, this is one of San Miguel's cheapest places.

Places to Stay – middle

San Miguel is brimming with good places to stay in the middle range. Heading out of the Jardín on the right side of the Parroquia, *Posada Carmina* (☎ (465) 2-04-58) at Cuna de Allende 7 is a former colonial mansion with 10 large, attractive rooms at US$21.35/24.70 for singles/doubles, and a pleasant restaurant/bar in the courtyard. In the same block at No 11 is the similar *Hotel Vista Hermosa Taboada* (☎ 2-00-68, 2-04-37), whose 17 rooms with fireplace, carpet and phone are US$24 per night.

Heading out of the Jardín down Calle Canal, the *Hotel Central* (☎ (465) 2-08-51, fax 2-38-65) at Canal 19, half a block from the Jardín, is another colonial place with 22 rooms arranged around two interior courtyards, with a restaurant/bar on the rear patio. Singles/doubles are US$21.35/23.70.

Further down Calle Canal at No 37, the *Posada de las Monjas* (☎ (465) 2-01-71) is a beautiful hotel in a former colonial monastery. The 65 rooms are comfortable and well-decorated, the bathrooms all have slate floors and hand-painted tiles, there are upper terraces for taking sun with a great view over the valley, and there's also a restaurant, bar, laundry and parking. The larger rooms with fireplaces, good sun and views cost US$33.35/38.35. Smaller rooms, at US$20/25, are still good.

The *Hotel Sautto* (☎ (465) 2-00-51/52) at Hernández Macías 59 has 25 rooms, about half with fireplace, set around lovely large garden grounds with plenty of sitting areas and a swimming pool filled in the summer. Singles/doubles are US$22.35/24.70, with discounts for longer stays.

Nearby, the *Hotel Mesón de San Antonio* (☎ (465) 2-05-80, 2-28-97) at Mesones 80 has five regular rooms at US$24.70 and five townhouse-style junior suites at US$30 arranged around an attractive interior courtyard with a lawn and small swimming pool.

Pensión Casa Carmen (☎ (465) 2-08-44) at Correo 31 is a favourite with older folks who return year after year. The 11 rooms in the colonial home, all with high-beamed ceilings and gas heat, are arranged around a pleasant interior courtyard with a fountain, orange trees and flowers. The price of US$30/50 for singles/doubles includes a delicious breakfast and lunch, served in a communal dining room with a friendly European guest house atmosphere. Reserve well in advance if you're coming during the winter or summer high seasons.

The *Hotel Quinta Loreto* (☎ (465) 2-00-42, fax 2-36-16) at Calle Loreto 15 is another long-time favourite. The 38 rooms are simple but pleasant, set around large grounds with gardens, swimming pool, tennis courts and plenty of parking space. The restaurant is one of the best in town and all in all it's an enjoyable and popular place, especially with middle-aged and older foreigners. Single/double rooms are US$21.70/24.70 per night, US$140/160 by the week, or US$563/642 by the month. The management recommends reserving six months in advance for the December to March winter season, one month in advance during summer.

The *Posada San Francisco* (☎ /fax (465) 2-24-25, 2-00-72, 2-14-66), at Plaza Principal 2 on the north-west corner of the Jardín, is another popular place, with singles/doubles at US$31.90/36.70.

Yet another popular place is *La Mansión del Bosque* (☎ (465) 2-02-77), at Aldama 65, opposite Parque Benito Juárez. All 23 rooms are different, all comfortable and attractively decorated with original art on the walls, good furniture and gas heaters; most have both tub and shower, and some also have fireplaces. During the high season from 15 December to 31 March the rates of US$34 to US$44 single, US$59 to US$68 a double include both breakfast and dinner. The rest of the year, singles with two meals are US$28 to US$38, doubles US$48 to US$58, or you can opt for no meals, in which case it's US$23 to US$33 a single, US$40 to US$50 a double.

Places to Stay – top end

The most expensive place in town is the luxury *Casa de Sierra Nevada* (☎ (465) 2-04-15, 2-18-95, fax 2-23-37) at Hospicio 35. Its eight rooms and 14 suites, spaced throughout four colonial mansions, cost US$88 a single, US$110 to US$200 a double.

The *Hotel Posada La Ermita* (☎ (465) 2-07-77) at Pedro Vargas 64 is a steep uphill walk from the centre of town, but it's worth it for the fine view. Its 22 large suites have every luxury, with living rooms, bedrooms, and large private terraces overlooking the town; there's also a large terrace swimming pool, restaurant and bar. Cost is US$66.70 for one or two people; all rooms can hold up to five.

Out on Ancha de San Antonio, near the Instituto Allende, are a couple of other top end hotels. The *Hotel Aristos San Miguel* (☎ (465) 2-03-92, 2-25-94, fax 2-16-31), at Ancha de San Antonio 30, behind the Instituto Allende, has 56 rooms and four suites, all with outdoor terraces, set around a large garden with tennis courts and a swimming pool. Room rates, including breakfast, are US$75 for one or two people in regular rooms, US$134 in suites.

Opposite the Instituto Allende, at Ancha de San Antonio s/n, is another top-end hotel, the *Posada de la Aldea* (☎ (465) 2-10-22, 2-12-96), whose 66 large rooms are US$33.35 per person.

Places to Eat – bottom end

Cheaper places do exist in San Miguel. Just a couple of doors from the north-east corner of the plaza, *El Tucán* at San Francisco 2 makes good hot tortas for US$0.85 up to US$1.20 for the big Cubana with five kinds of meat. Cheeseburgers are US$1.50, or US$2 with salad and French fries. They also serve economical omelettes, quesadillas, enchiladas, juices and licuados. Open every day, 9 am to 10 pm.

The pleasant little *Andale!! Pizzas* at Hidalgo 17 serves a variety of good, economical dishes. Pizzas are US$2.20 (mini) up to US$10 for the big family combo with everything on it. Spaghetti is US$2.70, tortas US$0.85, burgers US$1.50 (Friday is 'two for one' burger day), and they also have various breakfast specials with homemade whole-wheat bread, yoghurt, granola, and orange or carrot juice. It's open every day from 7 am to 11 pm.

Pepe Pizzas at Hidalgo 26, open daily from 1 to 11 pm, is a fancier pizza parlour, but its prices are about double.

The *Pio Pio Restaurant* at Hidalgo 50 is a small family place specialising in fried chicken and fish. On Saturday and Sunday they serve a good buffet for US$6 with Moroccan food as well. The rest of the week, you can get a family pack of chicken (US$5) or fish (US$10) with potatoes, salad, etc. One piece of chicken with potatoes, biscuit and salad is US$1.15, or US$2.70 with fish. They're open every day, 10 am to 7 pm.

Restaurant Flamingo's at Juárez 15 is another small family place. Chickens turn on the spit out front, and behind that is an open steam table where you can choose your food from what you see. The comida corrida, served from 11 am to around 5 or 6 pm, is a good deal (considering this is San Miguel) at US$3.35. It's open daily from 9 am to 10.30 pm.

Places to Eat – middle & top end

San Miguel has a great many restaurants.

Some of the best food in town is found at the little *Fonda La Mesa del Matador* at Hernández Macías 76, between Canal and Umarán. Spaghetti a la Mesa, prepared at your table with shrimp and wine, is US$4.35. A T-bone steak, mixed grill, or pollo suprema Parmesana (sliced chicken breast dipped in Parmesan cheese and fried, served with beetroot, carrots and French fries) is US$6. They're open every day from 8 am to 11 pm.

Mama Mia at Umarán 8, half a block from the Jardín, is in a pleasant, cool courtyard with plants and a fountain. It is a favourite with foreigners, not only for its food but for the live South American music every night from around 8 pm to midnight. Many of their dishes are quite expensive (meats & seafoods US$12, pastas US$6) but their breakfast is a great deal at US$2, with eggs, hash browns, a basket of rolls with butter and jam, fruit or juice, and all the good strong coffee you can drink. They're open every day from 8 am to 12.30 am.

Another popular courtyard restaurant/bar with live music every evening is *La Fragua* at Cuna de Allende 3, beside the museum and just off the Jardín. It's open daily from noon until at least midnight, often later.

The *Rincón Español* at Correo 29 has a comida corrida for US$5.30 served the whole time it's open: noon to 11 pm Monday to Thursday, until 2 am Friday to Sunday. Their other dishes, authentic Spanish specialities, are more expensive. They feature a Flamenco dinner show on weekends (see Entertainment).

Another popular place with the foreign set is the pleasant restaurant of the *Hotel Quinta Loreto* at Calle Loreto 15. Their ample comida corrida for US$5.85, served with soup, salad and spaghetti, features selections like roast beef and orange chicken. The res-

taurant is open every day from 8 to 10.30 am and 1.30 to 5 pm.

The *Café de la Parroquia* at Calle de Jesús 11, between Umarán and Cuadrante, is a pleasant place for breakfast or lunch, or just to have coffee and visit or read. It's in a rear room of a colonial building, with a few tables also out on the courtyard. English, Spanish and French are spoken. It's open Monday to Saturday from 7.30 am to 3 pm, to 1 pm on Sunday.

Casa Mexas at Canal 15, also called Trudy's Lonestar BBQ, is on the expensive side but it's a fun restaurant/bar with Tex-Mex specialities and Texas-size portions. In the back is a bar with a big-screen TV and, further back, a billiards room. It's open daily from noon to 11 pm.

La Dolce Vita in the Plaza Colonial at Hernández Macías 74, opposite Bellas Artes, is also on the expensive side but it's a pleasant European-style place for a good coffee, dessert or Italian gelato, open every day from 10 am to 9.30 or 10 pm. The cafeteria in *Bellas Artes* opposite is another attractive but expensive place for a coffee and dessert.

Entertainment

San Miguel has a thriving cultural and entertainment scene. Keep an eye on the notice boards or buy a copy of *Atención San Miguel* to find out what's on. Some events are held in English.

The movie house near the Jardín plays the usual staples of small-town Mexican cinema, with violence, sex and kung fu films. The Casa del Mayorazgo de Canal often shows a better class of films on Friday, Saturday and Sunday afternoons, with no admission charge. Or try the back room of the Casa Mexas at Calle Canal 15; their parabolic antenna brings in movies in English, played on a large screen TV. If the movies there are no good, you could always go in the back and play billiards.

The Mama Mia restaurant/bar at Umarán 8, half a block from the Jardín, has live South American music every night from around 8 pm to midnight; the pleasant courtyard is a great place to sit under the stars and enjoy

Top: Playa de los Muertos, Puerto Vallarta (SW)
Bottom: Weaver, Puerto Vallarta (SW)

Top: Children at Toluca market, México state (GE)
Left: Fruit market, Veracruz (GE)
Right: Morning parade, zócalo, Veracruz (GE)

the sounds. La Fragua, just off the Jardín at Calle Cuna de Allende 3, is another courtyard restaurant/bar with live music every evening.

The Rincón Español at Correo 29, one block from the Jardín, presents a Flamenco dinner show on Friday at 8.30 pm, Saturday at 8.30 and 10.30 pm, and Sunday at 3 pm.

If you're more in the mood for doing the dancing yourself, Pancho & Lefty's at Mesones 99 has live music of all kinds from around 10 pm to 3 am, Wednesday to Saturday, with a cover charge of US$6.70 and 'two for one' drinks. The Club de Jazz El Coyote Azul, in the same building, upstairs in the back, is open the same hours.

San Miguel has several discos. Most central and therefore most popular is El Ring at Hidalgo 27, open Wednesday to Sunday from 10 pm to 4 am, with a US$10 per person cover charge. Other discos include Laberinto's at Ancha de San Antonio 7 near the Instituto Allende; Los Topos at Hidalgo 96; and Eduardo's on Calle Pedro Vargas, about 100 metres past El Mirador on the highway to Querétaro.

On the more cultural side, Bellas Artes at Hernández Macías 75, near the corner of Canal, hosts a variety of cultural events including art exhibitions, concerts, poetry and literary readings, theatre and the like; check their notice board for the current schedule. They host a chamber music festival the first two weeks of August, and a winter festival from January to March with a schedule of cultural events.

A block from Bellas Artes, the Teatro Angela Peralta at the corner of Mesones and Hernández Macías is another fine venue for performances of all kinds. The theatre was built in 1910.

San Miguel has been attracting artists for over half a century, so art is naturally big around here. Bellas Artes, the Instituto Allende and the Casa del Mayorazgo de Canal all host year-round art exhibitions. Among the many galleries, the Galería San Miguel on the north side of the Jardín at Plaza Principal 14 and the Galería Atenea at Cuna de Allende 15, one block behind the

Parroquia, are two of the best and most established. Casa Armida at Ancha de San Antonio 26, beside the Instituto Allende, is an interesting shop with antiques, decorations, handcrafts, furniture and other assorted oddities. Many other galleries are advertised in Atención San Miguel.

For a great concert of birds in the trees, be on the Jardín at sunset time. The birds make a racket calling to one another from all the trees, while below them the people gather to socialise, doing much the same.

Things to Buy
San Miguel has several markets. The Mercado El Nigromante is on Colegio, behind the Colegio de Sales; market stalls with fruits, vegetables and an assortment of other goods stretch out along Colegio and for a block or two from Colegio down Insurgentes. There's also a Tuesday market; walk west on Canal from the Jardín for about six blocks and you'll run into it. There are two supermarkets facing the Jardín, on the north and west sides.

The Mercado de Artesanías, with a number of small handcrafts shops, is in an alleyway running between Colegio and Calle Loreto, easily reached from the entrance of the Hotel Quinta Loreto. Local crafts include tinware, wrought iron, silver, brass, leather and textiles. Most of these are products of long traditions going back to the 18th century; it is even said the sarape was invented here.

Some of the best handcrafts and folk art from elsewhere in Mexico and even further afield also find their way to San Miguel, where numerous shops sell them at a highly inflated price. You can find almost anything; if the shop you're in hasn't got a Huichol yarn painting or a Guatemalan huipil, ask where to go. Casa Maxwell on Calle Canal, a few doors down from the plaza, has a huge stock of crafts and there are many other shops within a few blocks.

Getting There & Away
Air There is no airport at San Miguel de Allende. The easiest way to fly here is to fly

into the Bajío airport (see the Guanajuato section). From there you can taxi to Silao, then take a bus to Guanajuato, and another bus to San Miguel. Otherwise you can fly into Mexico City and bus from there.

Bus San Miguel has a modern new Central de Autobuses on Calle Canal, about one km west of the centre of town. Any local bus marked 'Central' heading west on Canal will stop there. Coming into town from the bus station, the local bus comes up Insurgentes, winds through the town a bit and terminates at the corner of Mesones and Colegio.

Buses departing from San Miguel include those to:

Aguascalientes – 266 km, four hours; one daily with Omnibus de México (US$6).
Atotonilco – 14 km, 15 minutes; every 20 minutes, 5 am to midnight, with Flecha Amarilla (US$0.50).
Dolores Hidalgo – 43 km, one hour, US$1; buses every 15 minutes, 6 am to 11 pm, with Flecha Amarilla; every 30 minutes, 8.30 am to midnight, with Herradura de Plata.
Guadalajara – 382 km, six hours; two daily with Flecha Amarilla (US$9.80); one daily with Primera Plus (US$11.70).
Guanajuato – 82 km, two hours; 11 buses daily with Flecha Amarilla (US$2.15); two daily with Tres Estrellas de Oro (US$2.70); one daily with Omnibus de México (US$2.70).
León – 138 km, two hours; four daily with Flecha Amarilla (US$3.45).
Mexico City – 273 km, 3½ to four hours; every 30 minutes, 5 am to 6.50 pm, with Herradura de Plata (US$7.35); five daily with Primera Plus (US$8.70); one daily with Omnibus de México (US$7.70).
Morelia – 250 km, three hours; one daily with Flecha Amarilla (US$4.35).
Querétaro – 60 km, one hour; buses every 30 minutes, 5 am to 6.50 pm, with Herradura de Plata (US$1.40); seven daily with Flecha Amarilla (US$1.40); one daily with Omnibus de México (US$1.70).
San Luis Potosí – 153 km, three hours; one daily with Flecha Amarilla (US$4.45).

Train The Estación del Ferrocarril (☎ 2-00-07) is at the end of Calle Canal, about two km west of town. Any local bus marked 'Estación' heading west on Canal will go to the train station, stopping by the bus station on the way.

Trains 1 and 2, going between Mexico City and Nuevo Laredo, stop at San Miguel; see the Mexico City train section for the complete schedule of stops. Heading north, Train 1 departs San Miguel at 2.35 pm; heading south, Train 2 departs at 1.09 pm – though the trains are frequently late. The 1st/2nd-class fares from San Miguel are US$10/2.80 to Mexico City, US$2.75/0.40 to Querétaro, US$5/1.60 to San Luís Potosí, US$4.95 to Saltillo, US$5.85/1.75 to Monterrey and US$8.15 to Nuevo Laredo.

Car Gama (☎ 2-08-15) at Hidalgo 3 is the only car-rental agency in town. Their cheapest cars, VW sedans, rent for US$60 per day with unlimited km, or US$25.50 plus US$0.17 per km. They may be booked up about a week in advance during the winter season (December to March).

Getting Around
To/From the Airport American Express (☎ 2-18-56, 2-16-95) at Hidalgo 1-A offers transport to both the Bajío and Mexico City airports in combis that can hold up to six people, with the cost divided among the number of people making the trip. To the Bajío airport takes 1½ hours and costs US$85 for the whole combi; to the Mexico City airport takes four hours and costs US$145.

Bus Most places you'll want to get to in San Miguel are within walking distance of the centre; the 'Central' and 'Estación' buses heading west on Calle Canal stop at the bus and train stations. The local buses operate every day from 7 am to 9 pm and cost US$0.20.

Taxi San Miguel has many taxis. Between the centre and the bus station costs US$1.35; to the train station it's US$2. A taxi to Taboada costs around US$7.

AROUND SAN MIGUEL
There are several hot springs – or rather

warm springs – near San Miguel, along the highway to Dolores Hidalgo. All have mineral waters, good for the skin.

Hot Springs

Taboada Most popular is Taboada, eight km north of San Miguel and then two km west along a signposted sideroad. It has a large lawn area and three swimming pools, one Olympic-size, filled with thermal waters; the large pool is tepid, but the smaller ones get quite warm. It's open from 10 am to 6 pm every day except Tuesday, when the pools are drained and cleaned; entry is US$3.35.

Buses used to run several times daily between San Miguel and Taboada, but last time we were there, the bus service had been suspended for several months (a bus called 'Taboada' still ran, but it went by another route quite far from the springs). You could check with the Travel Institute (☎ 2-00-78) at Cuna de Allende 11, who sometimes run trips to Taboada; or take any bus heading for Dolores Hidalgo, get off at the turnoff and walk or hitchhike the rest of the way; or take a taxi, which costs around US$7 each way. You can ask the taxi to return for you at an appointed time.

Balneario Santa Veronica This balneario is right beside the highway to Dolores Hidalgo, at the turnoff to Taboada, eight km north of San Miguel. It has a large Olympic-size swimming pool with water a bit cooler than that at Taboada. It's open from 9 am to 6 pm every day except Friday, when the pool is drained and cleaned; admission is US$3.35 (children US$2.70). Any bus heading for Dolores Hidalgo will drop you there.

Centro Naturista Agua Maravillosa (☎ 2-17-00, 1-12-36, 2-07-58). Nine km north of San Miguel on the San Miguel-Dolores Hidalgo highway, this is a natural health centre offering a number of services. If you come just for the day it costs US$5 to swim in their hotel-size thermal pool, or US$45 for a full day health programme with swimming, sauna, jacuzzi, a thermal mud wrap, massage and lunch. They also offer live-in health and

detox programmes (minimum five days) for US$67 per day. They clean the pool on Tuesday or Wednesday; phone to find out which day or to ask about their programmes. The centre is clearly signposted from the road; any bus to Dolores Hidalgo will drop you there.

Atotonilco

Turn off the Dolores Hidalgo highway at the Centro Naturista Agua Maravillosa, continue on past it about one km and you come to the hamlet of Atotonilco, dominated by the Santuario (sanctuary) founded by Father Luis Felipe Neri de Alfaro in 1740 as a spiritual retreat. Here Ignacio Allende was married in 1802; eight years later he returned with Miguel Hidalgo and the band of independence rebels en route from Dolores to San Miguel to take the shrine's banner of the Virgin of Guadalupe as their flag – a clever move which drew the support of Indians who have a special reverence for the Virgin of Guadalupe.

Today Atotonilco is a goal of pilgrims and penitents from all over Mexico. It's also the starting point of an important and solemn procession two weekends before Easter, in which the image of the Señor de la Columna is carried to the church of San Juan de Dios in San Miguel. Inside, the sanctuary has six chapels and is vibrant with statues, folk murals and other paintings. Indian dances are held here on the third Sunday in July.

POZOS

Once a flourishing silver and copper-mining centre, Pozos is now more or less a ghost town. A couple of thousand people live on among abandoned houses and mine workings in what, 90 or so years ago, was a town of about 50,000. Many of them make a living from textile handcrafts. If you've got time to spare, Pozos might make a side trip from San Miguel de Allende or Querétaro.

Unfortunately it's not easy to reach unless you have a vehicle. The most frequent buses are from San Luis de la Paz, 11 km north, which has a few hotels, mostly on Niños Héroes. There are also some buses from San

José Iturbide, 28 km south. Both San Luis and San José are about seven km east of Highway 57, the highway between Querétaro and San Luis Potosí.

To get to Pozos from San Miguel de Allende by bus involves a trip of about two hours on three different buses: first to Dolores Hidalgo, then to San Luis de la Paz, and from there on to Pozos. Coming from San Miguel with your own vehicle, take the Querétaro road, turn left off it after four km towards Dr Mora, follow that road for 35 km crossing Highway 57 on the way, and proceed left at a crossroads from which Pozos is 14 km away.

Querétaro State

The state of Querétaro, bordered by the states of Guanajuato, Michoacán, México, Hidalgo and San Luis Potosí, is primarily an agricultural and livestock-raising state, with industry developing around Querétaro city and in certain other parts of the state, notably San Juan del Río; it also turns out opals, mercury, zinc and lead. Many visitors never get past the capital city, with its fine colonial architecture, active cultural life and its rich history, but the towns of San Juan del Río and Tequisquiapan are also interesting to visit.

QUERÉTARO
Population: 385,500
Altitude: 1762 metres
Two and a half hours from Mexico City yet free of its pollution, crime and chaos, close to San Miguel de Allende yet not inundated with that city's burgeoning gringo population, Querétaro is worth a brief stop. Here you will find some museums, monuments and colonial architecture which, while not spectacular like that of Guanajuato and Zacatecas, still warrants a visit. If you're interested in Mexico's past, don't miss Querétaro, as it has played an important role in Mexican history.

History
First settled by the Otomí Indians, who in the 15th century became absorbed into the Aztec empire, Querétaro was conquered by the Spaniards in 1531. Franciscan monks used the settlement as a base for sending out missionaries to what is now the US Southwest as well as Central America. Later, Querétaro became the site of intrigue, with creole patriots plotting to free Mexico from the yoke of Spanish rule. Conspirators, including Padre Miguel Hidalgo, met secretly at the house of the woman who would become known as La Corregidora, Josefa Ortiz – seen by Mexicans as the catalyst for revolt.

When the conspirators were about to be captured, the mayor locked his wife, Doña Josefa, in a room in the Palacio Municipal. Doña Josefa whispered to a colleague through a keyhole that their co-conspirators were in jeopardy. He galloped off to San Miguel de Allende, warned the rebels, and on 16 September 1810 Padre Hidalgo gave his famous *Grito*, a cry to arms, initiating the War of Independence.

Later in Querétaro on 2 February 1848, a day of tragedy for Mexico, President Pena y Pena acknowledged defeat by the USA and signed a treaty giving the USA over half the country.

In 1867, Emperor Maximilian surrendered to Benito Juárez's General Escobedo at Querétaro. It was here that the ill-fated Maximilian was executed by firing squad.

Querétaro in the early 20th century continued to be the scene of important events. In 1917, the Mexican constitution – still the basis of Mexico's law – was drawn up by triumphant revolutionaries in Querétaro. Mexico's ruling party, PRI, was organised in Querétaro in 1929. To this day, prominent politicians come here in homage to Querétaro's role in the making of Mexican history.

Orientation
The heart of the city is the Plaza Principal, called Jardín Obregón. Running along its west side, by the church of San Francisco, is Corregidora, the main avenue of the down-

town area. Three blocks south on Corregidora is Parque Alameda, a large, green park; the bus station faces the south side of this park. The train station is about one km north of the centre. Getting around in the centre is easy, as the city is laid out in a grid and everything of interest is within walking distance.

In the centre are several other plazas, notably the Plaza de la Corregidora just off the north-east corner of Jardín Obregón, and the Plaza de la Independencia, a block east of Jardín Obregón.

Information

Tourist Office The tourist office (☎ (421) 14-56-23, 13-85-11) is at Pasteur Sur 17, on the south-east corner of the Plaza de la Independencia. Free guided walking tours of the city centre depart from the office every day at 10.30 am, lasting around 1½ to 2½ hours and visiting different places. The office gives out free maps and information on both the city and state of Querétaro. Open hours are Monday to Friday from 9 am to 2 pm and 5 to 8 pm, Saturday and Sunday 9 am to 4 pm.

Money There are several banks on and near the Jardín Obregón, especially on Corregidora Norte, heading north out of the plaza. They are open Monday to Friday from 9 am to 1.30 pm.

Cash and travellers' cheques can also be changed at the Casa de Cambio de Querétaro, in the large building at Madero 6 on the south side of the Jardín Obregón. It's open Monday to Thursday from 9 am to 3 pm, Friday 9 am to 1.30 pm.

Outside these hours some of the larger hotels may change money, but their rates are less favourable.

Post The main post office is at Arteaga Poniente 7, between Juárez and Allende. It's open Monday to Friday from 8 am to 7 pm, Saturday 9 am to noon.

Telecommunications The Telecomm office, with services of telegram, telegraph,

telex and fax is at Allende Norte 4. It's open Monday to Friday from 9 am to 8 pm, Saturday from 9 am to 1 pm. In the patio are some interesting exhibits of old telegraph and communications equipment.

For long-distance telephone calls there's a caseta de larga distancia at 5 de Mayo 33, the pedestrian street taking off to the left of the church of San Francisco on the Jardín Obregón. It's open Monday to Saturday from 9.30 am to 2 pm and 5 to 9 pm. Another caseta, open 24 hours every day, is at the bus station.

Church of San Francisco

Situated on the Jardín Obregón, on the corner of Corregidora and 5 de Mayo, is the magnificent Church of San Francisco. Its dome's pretty coloured tiles were brought from Spain in 1540, around the same time construction on the church began. Inside are some fine religious paintings from the 17th to 19th centuries.

Museo Regional

Beside the Church of San Francisco in its former monastery is the Regional Museum. The ground floor exhibits begin with artefacts and exhibits on pre-Hispanic civilisations in Mexico and archaeological sites around the state of Querétaro, the early Spanish occupation of the area, and ethnography of the state's various Indian groups.

Upstairs is an ornate gilded 17th-century baroque altar with a statue of the Virgen Dolorosa, exhibits on Querétaro's role in the independence movement, the post-independence history of Mexico and Querétaro, and many large religious oil paintings. Included are the table where the Treaty of Guadalupe Hidalgo was signed, the desk of the tribunal that sentenced Maximilian to death, and early military uniforms and weaponry.

The building itself is also an historical place; the building now standing is large, but it's only a small part of the original structure. Begun in 1540, by 1567 the seminary here was the seat of the Provincia Franciscana de San Pedro y San Pablo de Michoacán. Parts of the convent were still being built as late as

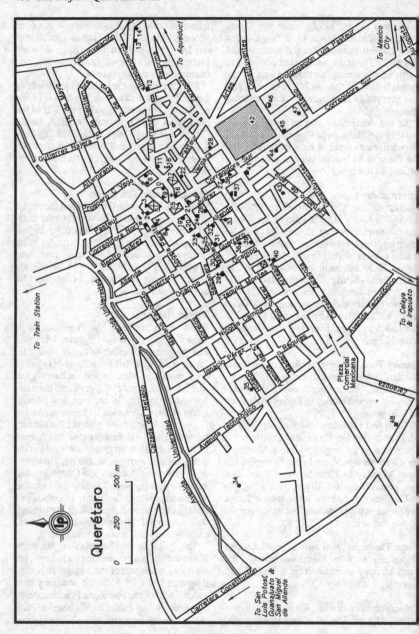

Querétaro

1727, which accounts for the mixture of architectural styles. In 1861, imperialists supporting Maximilian used this building as a fort, as did the North American occupying forces a few years later in 1867 – the building's tower was the highest vantage point in the city. From 1867 on, the building was owned by the federal government, becoming a museum in 1936.

The museum is open Tuesday to Sunday (closed Monday); open hours are 10 am to 6 pm Wednesday to Saturday, 10 am to 3.30 pm Tuesday and Sunday. Admission is US$3.35, but free on Sundays, and always free to those under 13, over 60, and to students with a student card.

Museo de Arte de Querétaro

Querétaro's Museum of Art at Allende Sur 14, beside the Church of San Agustín, is a splendid example of baroque architecture, with angels, gargoyles, statues and other ornamental details all over the building but particularly in the interior courtyard.

The museum occupies the former convent of the church next door. After the Agustinian order had been trying for years for permission to build a church in Querétaro, they finally succeeded, building the Church of San Agustín in 1728. In 1732 they began building the convent beside it, now the museum. The monks occupied the convent in 1743, though it was not finished until

1748. After the monks left, the building went through a period of disrepair; it was restored under the regime of Porfirio Díaz and inaugurated for use as federal offices in 1889, remaining in use as the federal building for around a century until it was converted to its present use.

Today it is a very well-organised museum. Not only are the exhibits well displayed, but if you can read Spanish, the accompanying explanations of each room and each piece make an illustrated course in art history. The top floor contains an introductory room with a photographic display on the history of the convent, pointing out details of its architecture; then there are rooms with art exhibits from 16th-century Mannerism to 18th-century baroque. On the ground floor are exhibits of 16th and 17th-century European painting, tracing interesting influences, for example from Flemish to Spanish to Mexican art; 19th and 20th-century Mexican paintings; a collection of 20th-century Querétaran artists; and a salon for temporary exhibits. The museum bookstore holds many excellent books in Spanish.

The museum is open Tuesday to Sunday from 11 am to 7 pm (closed Monday). Admission is US$0.85, but free for those under 12 and over 60, and free for everyone on Tuesday.

Teatro de la República
One block north of the Jardín Obregón, on the corner of Juárez and Angela Peralta, the Teatro de la República has been the scene of historic events more than once. In 1867 a tribunal met here and decided to execute Emperor Maximilian. Mexico's constitution, still in use today, was signed here on 31 January 1917. The stage backdrop lists the names of its signatories and the states they came from; some states had more delegates, some less, according to their populations. Later on, in 1929, politicians met in this theatre to organise Mexico's ruling party, the PRI.

The theatre is open Monday to Friday from 10 am to 3 pm and 5 to 9 pm, Saturday 10 am to 1 pm (closed Sunday), and admission is free. Cultural events are presented here from time to time; posters at the door announce upcoming events.

Casa de la Corregidora
The Casa de la Corregidora, where Doña Josefa Ortiz informed rebel leaders of the attempt to arrest them, sits on the north side of the Plaza de la Independencia, one block east of the Jardín Obregón. Today the building is used as the Palacio del Gobierno, the state government building.

The room where Doña Josefa was locked up is not marked, but it's the large room upstairs over the entrance to the building. It is now used as the governor's conference room.

The government offices are open Monday to Friday, 10 am to 3 pm, but the building itself can be visited any day from around 7 am to 9 pm; guards on duty will let you in.

Convento de la Santa Cruz
Only about 10 minutes' walk from the centre of Querétaro is one of the city's most interesting sights, the Convento de la Santa Cruz. Construction on the monastery began here in 1654, on the battleground where the alleged miraculous appearance of St James led Otomí Indians to surrender to the conquistadors and Christianity, and continued in stages over 150 years. It is still used today as a religious school.

At various stages in its history the Convento also functioned as a fortress. A Spanish force retreated here toward the end of the War of Independence. Maximilian established his military headquarters here from February to May 1867. After his surrender and subsequent death-sentence, the emperor was jailed here while he awaited the firing squad.

A guide will provide insight into the Convento's history and artefacts. He'll show you sundials, an ingenious water system and unique ways of colonial cooking and refrigeration. The guide will also relate several of the Convento's miracles, including the legendary growth of a tree from a walking stick stuck in the earth by a pious friar in 1697.

The thorns of the tree appear in the pattern of a cross.

The Convento is open Monday to Friday from 9 am to 2 pm and 4 to 6 pm, Saturday and Sunday from 11 am to 6 pm. There's no admission fee, but your guide will request a donation to the convent at the end of your tour. Tours are given in English or Spanish.

Aqueduct & Doña Josefa's Tomb

Walk down the sidewalk to the left of the Convento de la Santa Cruz and you come to a lookout point with a view of Querétaro's aqueduct. Built from 1726 to 1728, the aqueduct with its 76 towering arches, stretching along the Avenida de los Arcos, still brings water about 12 km to the city.

Also here is the tomb of Doña Josefa Ortiz (La Corregidora) and her husband, Miguel Domínguez de Alemán. Behind their tomb is a shrine with photos, lithographs, historical documents and a tribute to Doña Josefa's life.

Other Interesting Buildings

Many other interesting structures are nearby in the centre. One block west of the Jardín Obregón at the corner of Madero and Allende is the pleasant **Neptune Fountain**, designed by the great Mexican architect Tresguerras in 1797. Go inside the **Church of Santa Clara** next to the fountain for an ornate bit of baroque. Around behind the church on Allende, the church's former monastery is now used as offices.

Follow Madero one block further to the **Jardín Guerrero**; on the corner of Madero and Guerrero is the **Presidencia Municipal** or city hall. A block further down Madero at No 70 is the **Archivo Histórico del Estado**. Formerly the state government building, in 1917 it was the provisional National Palace when Benito Juárez established his government seat in Querétaro. On the opposite corner, at Madero and Ocampo, is the rather plain 18th century **Cathedral**.

At the intersection of Arteaga and Ezequiel Montes stands the **Church of Santa Rosa de Viterbos** with its pagoda-like bell tower and impressively gilded,

magnificently marbled interior. The great architect Tresguerras remodelled the church with tiles for the dome and a tower holding what some say is the first four-sided clock built in the New World.

Other notable colonial churches include the **Church of San Antonio** at the corner of Corregidora Norte and Angela Peralta, with two large pipe organs, elaborate crystal chandeliers, gilt red wallpaper and several oil paintings; the **Templo de la Congregación** at the corner of Pasteur Norte and 16 de Septiembre, with some beautiful stained-glass windows and a splendid pipe organ; and the **Church of Santo Domingo** on the corner of Guerrero and Pino Suárez.

The **Casa de los Perros** at Allende 16 near the corner of Pino Suárez has some notable carvings of ferociously ugly, unworldly dogs on the upper reaches of the house's exterior. The house is now used as a children's centre.

Parque Alameda

Opposite the bus station and not far from the city centre, the large Alameda park, shady and green, is a popular place for picnics, jogging, roller skating, strolling around and just taking it easy.

Cerro de las Campanas

At the west end of the city, a good 35-minute walk from the centre, is the Cerro de las Campanas (Hill of Bells), the site of Maximilian's execution by firing squad. The emperor's family constructed a chapel on the site where he was killed. Near it is a statue of Benito Juárez.

Festivals

Querétaro holds its major annual festival, the Exposición Ganadera, Agrícola e Industrial (the state fair), during the entire second week of December.

Places to Stay – bottom end

The CREA youth hostel, called the *Villa Deportiva Juvenil Querétaro* (☎ (421) 14-30-50), is on Ejército Republicano between the Convento de la Santa Cruz and the tomb of Doña Josefa. It has 72 beds, with two bunks (four people) to a room in separate-sex dorms; beds cost US$3.70 per night. No hostel card is required, and people of any age can stay there. The office is open from 7 am to 11 pm.

On the west side of the Jardín Obregón, the *Hotel Plaza* (☎ (421) 12-11-38) at Juárez Norte 23 is a great place to stay in the budget category. All of its 29 rooms are tidy and comfortable, with windows opening onto the interior courtyard, or French doors opening onto small balconies facing the plaza, offering plenty of light and air. Singles/doubles are US$11.70/15, US$16.70 with colour TV, or US$20 with two double beds.

The *Hotel Hidalgo* (☎ (421) 12-00-81), owned and managed by an Englishman, is just a few doors off the Jardín Obregón at Madero 11 Poniente, between Juárez and Allende. Singles/doubles here are US$13.35/15; some large rooms can hold up to seven people, at US$3.35 per extra person. There's parking in the interior courtyard, an economical restaurant open from 8 am to 10 pm, and some of the upper floor rooms have French doors opening onto small balconies overlooking the pedestrian street.

Back-to-back with the Hotel Hidalgo, the *Hotel San Agustín* (☎ (421) 12-11-95, 12-39-19) at Pino Suárez 12 is a modern-style place, not luxurious but OK; all the 35 rooms have colour TV and telephones. Rooms facing the street are the best, with a whole wall of windows and a door opening onto a balcony large enough for sitting out. Singles/doubles are US$16.70/18.35.

Places to Stay – middle

The *Hotel Impala* (☎ (421) 12-25-70, 12-26-76, fax 12-45-15), at the corner of Corregidora Sur and Zaragoza, opposite the Parque Alameda (the official address is Colón 1), is a modern four-storey hotel whose 102 rooms all have colour TV, carpet and phone. Some have a view of the park, but watch the traffic noise as it's a very busy corner; the interior rooms, with ample windows opening onto a large central air

shaft offering plenty of light, are quieter. Singles/doubles are US$20/25.

Also opposite the park, the *Hotel Amberes* (☎ (421) 12-86-04, fax 12-88-32), at Corregidora Sur 188 is similar, with singles/doubles at US$25/31.70.

The *Hotel Mirabel* (☎ (421) 14-39-29, 14-34-99, fax 14-35-85), at Constituyentes Oriente 2, on the corner of Corregidora, to your left as you come out the bus station door, is a step up in luxury. Its six storeys hold 171 modern rooms, all with colour TV and air-conditioning, and some with a view over the park. Singles/doubles are US$38.35/45, or US$60 for doubles with two double beds.

Places to Stay – top end

The *Hotel Jurica Querétaro* (☎ (421) 18-00-22, fax 18-01-36), about 15 km north of the centre of Querétaro, is at Km 229 on Highway 57, in the Fraccionamiento Jurica, Calle Paseo Jurica. It is a magnificent converted 17th-century hacienda with a swimming pool, tennis and squash courts, horses to ride, soccer and volleyball courts, billiards and table tennis, a discothèque, bar and two restaurants, and a golf course five km away. Rooms cost US$115 for one or two people.

The *Holiday Inn* (☎ (421) 16-02-02, fax 16-89-02) is at Avenida 5 de Febrero 110, Colonia Niños Héroes, on Highway 57 a km north of the 45 and 45D interchange. It features a swimming pool, tennis courts, spa baths, miniature golf, a bar, cafeteria and restaurant. Rooms are US$90 for one or two people; two children under 12 can stay for free with their parents.

Places to Eat

La Flor de Querétaro, at Juárez Norte 5 on the west side of the Jardín Obregón, is a good, basic restaurant for all meals; it's open every day from 7.30 am to 10.30 pm. Also on the Jardín Obregón, on the south side in the rear of the large building at Madero 6, *Bisquets Bisquets* is a small, friendly restaurant with good food at good prices, open every day from 7.30 am to 10 pm.

Vegetarians and natural food fans will like the *Restaurante Ibis Natura* at Juárez Norte 47, half a block north of the Jardín Obregón. It's a good vegetarian restaurant, pleasant and popular, open every day except Saturday from 8 am to 9.30 pm. The comida corrida for US$3 is an excellent deal; so are the soyburgers with mushrooms and cheese at US$1.25. They also sell vitamins and other health products. Another branch of the same restaurant, with the same menu and prices, is the *Restaurante Primavera* at Corregidora Sur 130, opposite the Parque Alameda; it's open from 8 am to 9 pm, every day except Sunday.

Plaza de la Corregidora, off the north-east corner of the Jardín Obregón, has a number of attractive, romantic sidewalk café/restaurant/bars: *El Cortijo de Don Juan, El Regio*, the *Fonda del Refugio* and *Pizza La Távola*.

The *Nevería Galy* is a Querétaro institution at 5 de Mayo 8, the pedestrian street to the left of the Church of San Francisco on the Jardín Obregón. It is known for its homemade ice cream; also featured are some unusual specialities like lemon ice cream with mineral water, or cola, or red wine.

A pleasant place for dessert and coffee is the *Cafetería La Mariposa* at Angela Peralta 7, near the corner of Corregidora Norte one block north of the Jardín Obregón. The bright, ice cream parlour-like restaurant is entered through the ice cream and sweets shop to one side; there's an Italian espresso machine in the back, and they also serve basic Mexican meals at good prices. La Mariposa celebrated its 50th anniversary in September 1990 and is still going strong.

Entertainment

Sit in the Jardín Obregón Sunday evenings to watch local families enjoying band concerts; the state band performs every Sunday from around 6 to 8 pm, sometimes accompanied by dancers.

Other outdoor music can be enjoyed at the Jardín de los Platitos, on Juárez at Avenida Universidad. Mariachis, ranchera groups, trios and others start tuning up every evening around dusk and go on until the wee hours, with people requesting their favourite tunes.

Querétaro is a state capital and university town, with many cultural activities. The Teatro de la República, at the corner of Juárez and Angela Peralta a block north of the Jardín Obregón, offers occasional concerts and performances. Posters out front announce upcoming events.

The Casa de la Cultura (☎ 12-56-14) at 5 de Mayo 40 on the corner of Venustiano Carranza sponsors concerts, dance and theatre performances, art exhibits and other cultural events, as does the ISSSTE Centro de Servicios Culturales (☎ 12-73-69) at Arteaga 70. Both publish a monthly schedule of events; stop by during office hours to pick one up.

The Universidad Autónoma de Querétaro has three branches of the Escuela de Bellas Artes (School of Fine Arts) where cultural events are presented regularly. The music campus (☎ 12-05-70), on the corner of Independencia and Juárez Sur, presents the Universitarios en Concierto series of classical music concerts every Friday at 8 pm; admission is US$3.35. On Sundays at 6 pm they have Música Popular, with estudiantinas (lively student sing-alongs), dances, *nueva canción* (new song) and other popular music, usually with no admission charge.

The university's art school, also called Escuela de Bellas Artes (☎ 16-90-22), is on Hidalgo between Avenida Tecnológico and Régules. Art exhibits of one kind or another are usually going on. The Galería Libertad at Libertad 56, on the south side of the Plaza de la Independencia opposite the Casa de la Corregidora, hosts some excellent changing art exhibits; it's open every day from 8 am to 8 pm.

The university's theatre department presents 'theatre, cheese, wine and bread' at El Mesón de los Cómicos de la Legua (☎ 12-49-11), at Guillermo Prieto 7 between 5 de Mayo and 16 de Septiembre, Thursday to Sunday evenings; admission is US$5. Similar is the Corral de Comedias (☎ 12-07-65) at Carranza 39, with dinner and original theatre presented Thursday to Saturday evenings. At both places the action starts around

8.30 pm; it may be a good idea to reserve in advance.

The Conservatorio de Música J Guadalupe Velázquez (☎ 12-59-84) at Vergara 35 presents free music concerts about once a month.

Several of Querétaro's more popular discos feature live music for dancing. The most popular are Qiu at Monte Sinia 102; L'Opera at Circuito Jardín Sur 1; JBJ Disco at Boulevard Zona Dorada 109 in the Fraccionamiento Los Arcos; and Tiffani's at Zaragoza Poniente 67. All except Tiffani's have live music.

There are also several cinemas in the centre.

Getting There & Away

Air Querétaro has a small airport, but it's for small private planes only – no commercial flights go there. The nearest commercial airport is at Mexico City.

Bus Querétaro's Central Camionera is on Constituyentes opposite the Parque Alameda, about six blocks from the Jardín Obregón. Querétaro is a hub for bus transport going in many directions; the bus station is a large, busy terminal with restaurants, shops, a guarda equipaje for storing luggage, and a 24-hour long-distance telephone office.

Buses departing Querétaro include those to:

Aguascalientes – 282 km, five to six hours; eight buses daily with Estrella Blanca (US$7.70); four daily with Flecha Amarilla (US$7.70); hourly, 11.40 am to 3 pm, with Omnibus de México (US$7.50).

Dolores Hidalgo – 103 km, 1½ to two hours; buses every half hour, 6 am to 8.20 pm, with Herradura de Plata (US$2.35); buses every half hour, 6.30 am to 9.30 pm, with Flecha Amarilla (US$2.50); two daily with Omnibus de México (US$2.50).

Guadalajara – 348 km, five to six hours; buses every 20 minutes, 5.20 am to 5 pm, then hourly to 11 pm, with Oriente (US$9.50 to US$12.70); buses every half hour, 5 am to 10 pm, with Flecha Amarilla (US$9.70); seven buses daily with Primera Plus (US$12.70); five daily with ETN (US$18.35); three daily with Omnibus de México (US$10.20), and more.

Guanajuato – 133 km, 2½ hours; six buses daily with Estrella Blanca (US$4.45); two daily with Omnibus de México (US$4.10); two daily with Tres Estrellas de Oro (US$4); or, bus to Irapuato and change buses there, where they leave for Guanajuato every few minutes.

Irapuato – 106 km, 1½ hours; 11 buses daily with Omnibus de México (US$2.70); seven daily with Estrella Blanca (US$3.25).

Mexico City – 213 km, three hours; virtually every bus line in the terminal runs buses between Querétaro and Mexico City. There are buses every 10 minutes, 24 hours a day, with Flecha Roja (US$5.35); buses every 15 minutes, 24 hours a day, with Flecha Blanca (US$5.70); buses every 20 minutes, 24 hours a day, with Estrella Blanca (US$5.70); buses every 15 minutes, 5 am to 10 pm, with Flecha Amarilla (US$5.70); and many more.

Morelia – 195 km, three to four hours; hourly buses, 6 am to 9.40 pm, with Flecha Amarilla (US$4.35); five buses daily with Estrella Blanca (US$5.70); two daily with Primera Plus (US$4.85).

Pachuca – 228 km, five hours; nine buses daily with Estrella Blanca (US$5.20).

San Juan del Río – 52 km, 45 minutes; buses every 10 minutes, 24 hours a day, with Flecha Roja (US$1.20); buses every half hour, 3.30 am to 5.30 pm, with Herradura de Plata (US$1.20).

San Luis Potosí – 204 km, 2½ hours; 15 buses daily with Chihuahuenses (US$5.70); four daily with Primera Plus (US$6.35); four daily with Omnibus de México (US$5); hourly, 5.30 to 11.30 pm, with Tres Estrellas de Oro (US$5.20). Flecha Amarilla runs buses hourly, 7.30 am to 11.30 pm (US$4.85), but they may be slower.

San Miguel de Allende – 60 km, one hour; buses every half hour, 6 am to 8.20 pm, with Herradura de Plata (US$1.35); buses every half hour, 6.30 am to 9.30 pm, with Flecha Amarilla (US$1.50); hourly buses, 6 am to 3.30 pm, with Flecha Verde (US$1.35); two daily with Omnibus de México (US$1.50).

Tequisquiapan – 72 km, 1½ hours; hourly buses, 7 am to 7 pm, with Flecha Azul (US$1.10).

Toluca – 195 km, 3½ hours; buses every 20 minutes, 1 am to 8 pm, with Flecha Roja (US$4.70); buses every half hour, 3.30 am to 5.30 pm, with Herradura de Plata (US$4.50).

Train The Estación del Ferrocarril (☎ 12-17-03) is on Avenida Héroes de Nacozari at the intersection of Calle Cuauhtémoc Norte, about a km north of the centre. The ticket office is open every day from 9 to 10.30 am and from noon to 5 pm. Tickets for Saturday,

Sunday or holiday trips on the *División del Norte* train must be bought in advance.

Querétaro is served by the *Constitucionalista* and *División del Norte* trains, and Train Nos 1 and 2; see the Mexico City train section for the complete schedule of stops of these trains.

First-class fares from Querétaro on the *Constitucionalista* train are US$7.70 to Mexico City, US$5 to Guanajuato. On the *División del Norte* train they are US$7.95 to Mexico City, US$15 to Ciudad Juárez. On Train No 1 they are US$3.20 to San Miguel de Allende, US$6.20 to San Luis Potosí and US$9 to Laredo. On Train No 2 the fare is US$7.95 to Mexico City.

In addition, Train No 6 stops in Querétaro at 4.20 pm on the way to Mexico City; the fare to Mexico City is US$3.20.

Second-class train Nos 13 and 14, going between Mexico City and Ciudad Juárez, also stop in Querétaro, but they are slower than the 1st-class trains. Northbound Train No 13 stops in Querétaro at 2.30 pm; southbound Train No 14 stops in Querétaro at 1 pm. Fares are US$11.90 to Chihuahua (36 hours), US$15 to Ciudad Juárez (48 hours) and US$2.20 to Mexico City (five hours).

Getting Around

Querétaro is a compact city and you will easily reach most major sights on foot.

The local buses, called *urbanos*, operate daily from 6 am until 9 or 10 pm and cost US$0.20. There are buses to the centre from the bus and train stations; going from the centre to the train station, catch 'Ruta 13' going north on Corregidora. To take a local bus to the Cerro de las Campanas, take 'Ruta R', also going north on Corregidora, and get off at the Centro Universitaria. The northbound buses on Corregidora stop outside the church of San Francisco on the Jardín Obregón.

SAN JUAN DEL RÍO

Population: 61,650

Just east of Highway 57, 56 km south of Querétaro and 170 km north of Mexico City, San Juan del Río is something of a craft centre. It is known particularly for its gems and jewellery a business based on local opals but including the polishing and setting of gems and stones from elsewhere. Basket-weaving and furniture are also important industries. The town has a pleasant colonial centre and produces good wine and cheese.

Orientation & Information

The centre of town is about one km east of Highway 57; the bus station is beside the highway. The main road coming into town from the highway and bus station is called Avenida Hidalgo.

The intersection of Avenida Hidalgo and Avenida Juárez, overlooked by the El Santuario church, is the town's principal intersection and commercial area; many businesses, opal and lapidary shops, hotels and restaurants are around this intersection, especially on Avenida Juárez, and within a couple of blocks of it. The town's central plaza, called the Plaza de los Fundadores, is one block further past this intersection on Hidalgo; its two colonial churches are called La Parroquia and El Templo.

The tourist office is near this main intersection of Hidalgo and Juárez, in the Centro Histórico y Cultural at Juárez 30 Oriente. They give out free maps and information about the town.

Museo de la Santa Veracruz

The town museum is in the lovely ex-convent of the colonial church of La Santa Veracruz, up on a hill a short walk from the intersection of Hidalgo and Juárez. To get there from this intersection, walk one block back towards the highway on Hidalgo, turn left onto Calle F de Tapia, walk up the hill a block or two and turn right onto the street marked by a large arrow pointing to 'Museo'. The church and museum are a block or two further on.

The museum itself is a historic building, holding exhibits of archaeology, ethnography, geography and history of the area. It is open Tuesday to Friday from 9.30 am to 2 pm and 4 to 6 pm, Saturday, Sunday and holidays from 10.30 am to 2 pm. The museum entrance is around behind the church.

Places to Stay – bottom end

The *Hotel Layseca* (☎ 2-01-10) at Juárez 9 Oriente, half a block from the intersection of Juárez and Hidalgo, is a pleasant hotel in a well-kept colonial building with enclosed parking. Its 23 clean rooms with high wood-beamed ceilings and private hot-water bath open onto an arched courtyard filled with plants and flowers. Singles/doubles are US$11/12.85.

Opposite this is the *Hotel La Estancia* (☎ 2-00-38, 2-09-30) at Juárez 20 Oriente, with 42 modern, clean rooms and enclosed parking. The rooms facing the street have French doors opening onto tiny balconies; singles/doubles are US$13.35/16.70.

If both these are full, try the *Hotel Jalisco* (☎ 2-04-25) at Hidalgo 15 Sur, a block or two towards the highway from the main intersection of Hidalgo and Juárez. The rooms cost US$13.35 and are basic but clean.

Places to Stay – middle

The *Hotel Colonial* (☎ 2-29-85) is at Juárez 28 & 30 Poniente, 1½ blocks west of the main intersection. It has a swimming pool, parking, and its 55 rooms all have air-conditioning, carpet and colour TV with parabolic antenna; some also have private poolside terraces. Its pleasant restaurant occupies a courtyard covered with stained glass, with a fountain gurgling off to one side. Singles/doubles are US$29.35/40.35; junior and master suites with fridge are more expensive.

Places to Stay – top end

Two resort-hotels in old haciendas to the west of town are used mainly by people from Mexico City for a spot of none-too-cheap relaxation. The *Hotel Estancia de San Juan* (☎ 2-01-55) at Highway 57, Km 172, has tennis, volleyball, a swimming pool and horses; rooms are US$60. The luxurious five-star *Hotel La Mansión Galindo* (☎ 2-00-50, fax 2-01-00) at Carretera Amealco, Km 5, has a swimming pool, horses, golf and

every other amenity; its 163 rooms cost US$147/153.

Places to Eat

There are a number of pleasant restaurants, from cheap ones to high class, on Juárez near the corner of Hidalgo, and around the Plaza de los Fundadores.

Getting There & Away

Bus The bus station is beside Highway 57, about one km from the centre of town. It has a cafeteria, a guarda equipaje for storing your luggage, and a long-distance telephone office open every day from 7 am to 11 pm. Local buses operate frequently between the centre and the bus station, costing US$0.20, or you can make the walk in about 15 minutes.

Buses departing from San Juan del Río include those to:

Mexico City – 170 km, two hours; buses every 15 minutes, 6 am to 8.30 pm, with Herradura de Plata (US$0.50); every 15 minutes, 5 am to 8 pm, with Flecha Roja (US$0.50); hourly, 7.45 am to 5 pm, with Omnibus de México (US$4.85); hourly, 8 am to 8 pm, with Tres Estrellas de Oro (US$4.85); seven daily with ETN (US$8.35).

Morelia – 153 km, 3½ hours; every half hour, 6.30 am to 8.30 pm, with Herradura de Plata (US$4.85).

Querétaro – 56 km, 45 minutes; every 10 to 20 minutes, 5.45 am to 9 pm, with Amealcenses (US$1.20); every half hour, 8 am to 10 pm, with Flecha Roja (US$1.20); hourly, 6 am to 11 pm, with Herradura de Plata (US$1.20); hourly, 7 am to 10 pm, with Estrella Blanca (US$1.20); hourly, 8 am to 5 pm, with Omnibus de México (US$1.35).

San Miguel de Allende – 116 km, two hours; same bus as to Querétaro, with Herradura de Plata (US$2.70).

Tequisquiapan – 26 km, 25 minutes; every 15 minutes, 6 am to 10 pm, with Flecha Blanca (US$0.60); every half hour, 10 am to 7.30 pm, with Flecha Roja (US$0.60).

Tula – 91 km, 1½ hours; seven daily with Flecha Blanca (US$3.80).

Train Some trains running between Querétaro and Mexico City stop at San Juan del Río. The train station is on the northern outskirts of town.

TEQUISQUIAPAN

Population: 19,230

This small town ('teh-kees-kee-AP-an') 26 km north-east of San Juan del Río is a quiet, pleasant retreat from Mexico City or Querétaro. Historically it was known for its hot thermal spring waters – some of Mexico's presidents in earlier times came here to ease their aches and tensions – but the development of a couple of large industries in the area have drained off the hot water. Nonetheless there are still some delightful cool-water pools.

'Tequis' is a quaint, peaceful little town, pleasant for strolling around the brick-paved Spanish streets lined with brilliant purple bougainvilleas. It is also a thriving crafts centre, with interesting goods both in the main market and in a separate Mercado de Artesanías beside it.

Orientation

The central plaza, called Plaza Tequisquiapan, is overlooked by the Church of Santa Maria de la Asunción. Around the plaza are many little restaurants and artesanía shops. The market and the Mercado de Artesanías beside it are one block from the plaza, through a couple of little lanes. Many hotels and restaurants are within a couple of blocks of this area. Parque La Pila, a large verdant park, is a couple of blocks away.

The bus station is on the outskirts of the town; the local bus coming from the station into town will let you off beside the Mercado de Artesanías, between it and the main market. The plaza is one block straight ahead.

Information

Tourist Office The tourist office is at Morelos 23, about a block from the central plaza. It's open Tuesday to Sunday, 10 am to 6 pm, with free maps of the town, brochures and information on Tequisquiapan and the state of Querétaro.

Post Office The post office is in the Presidencia Municipal on Avenida Juárez, about half a km from the plaza.

Balnearios

The large, cool pool at the Hotel Neptuno, at Avenida Juárez Oriente 5 just around the corner from the main market and about 1½ blocks from the central plaza, makes a pleasant place for a swim. It's open Friday to Monday from 8 am to 6 pm; entrance is US$5 per person.

The Hotel El Relox at Morelos 8, just down the block from the Mercado de Artesanías, also has a large pool for day use, but it's more expensive; the entrance fee of US$16.70 per person includes the midday meal. It's open every day from 8 am to 5 pm. They also have private indoor pools, costing US$6.70 per hour.

Organised Tours

Tequisquiapan Tours (☎ 3-13-62/02, fax 31-661) at Callejón 20 de Noviembre 2-A in the centre operates a variety of tours of the local area, as well as regular travel agency services. The Posada Los Arcos (☎ 3-05-66) at Moctezuma 12 also organises tours for guests and non-guests.

Festivals

Festival Turístico Artesanal During Semana Santa (Holy Week) in March or April, this festival features displays of traditional artesanías from townships all over the state of Querétaro.

Feria del Queso y del Vino The Wine and Cheese Fair, held for two weeks in June or July, is the big bash of the year, attracting celebrants from far and wide for the wine and cheese tastings, music and other events. Dates are changeable; check with the tourist office.

Día de la Santa Maria de la Asunción Religious celebrations for Tequisquiapan's patron saint are held from 13 to 17 August; the saint's day itself is on 15 August.

Places to Stay – bottom end

Tequisquiapan has many pleasant hotels in the few blocks around the centre, but not many in the low budget range. One fine budget hostelry, run by a friendly and hospitable family, is the *Posada Mejia* (☎ 3-02-36) at Guillermo Prieto 17, on the corner of 16 de Septiembre. The 16 rooms are simple but clean and pleasant, arranged around a grassy court with trees and roses. Cost is US$11/13.35 for singles/doubles.

Just a bit more expensive is the *Posada Los Arcos* (☎ 3-05-66) at Moctezuma 12, with a small restaurant and nine rooms, each with two double beds, around a fountain courtyard. Singles/doubles are US$15/20.

The *Posada Los Mezquites* (☎ 3-03-65) at Centenario 12 Sur has a small swimming pool in the rear, surrounded by lawn and the 16 rooms, each costing US$22. There's a hotel dining room and parking out behind.

Places to Stay – middle

The *Posada San Francisco* (☎ 3-02-31) at Moctezuma 2, on the corner of Madero, is a pleasant family hotel with a communal sitting room, a dining room, and a large enclosed garden in the rear with a swimming pool overlooked by a statue of a ruminating nymph. The 11 rooms cost US$26.70/53.40 for singles/doubles on weekends, with three meals a day included in the price. Monday to Thursday they offer the same plan, or the option of singles/doubles at US$18.70/37.40 without meals.

Right on the central plaza, the *Hotel La Plaza* (☎ 3-02-89, 3-00-56) has a swimming pool, restaurant, bar and parking, and 17 rooms at US$19.20/28.70.

Places to Stay – top end

Facing onto the central plaza, the *Hotel Maridelfi* (☎ 3-00-52, 3-10-29) is a lovely, luxurious hotel popular with rich Mexican families. Three meals a day are included in the price of US$59/117 for singles/doubles.

Other pleasant hotels with swimming pools include the *Hotel/Balneario Neptuno* at Avenida Juárez Oriente 5, just down the block from the Maridelfi, at US$43.35 per person with three meals or US$25/50 for singles/doubles without meals; the *Hotel/*

Balneario El Relox (☎ 3-00-06/66) near the Mercado de Artesanías with 110 rooms at US$40/80 for singles/doubles including three meals; and the *Posada del Virrey* (☎ 3-02-39, 3-09-02) at Guillermo Prieto Norte 9, on the corner of 16 de Septiembre, with 22 rooms at US$40/80 for singles/doubles, with three meals included.

Places to Eat

There are many restaurants in all price categories around the centre of town. Cheapest place for a good meal or snack is in the rear of the main market, where many clean little *fondas* have tables set out under awnings in the patio. They're open every day from around 8 am to 8 pm.

The restaurant at the *Hotel Maridelfi* on the plaza is good but a little expensive, with the comida corrida at US$9.35. Another good but expensive restaurant for a night out is *El Patio de Tequisquiapan* beside the Hotel El Relox, near the Mercado de Artesanías. Their speciality is Sonora beef, with steak dinners around US$10 to US$13. They have a dance floor with live music on Friday and Saturday night and on Sunday afternoon.

Getting There & Away

Bus Buses arrive and depart from Tequisquiapan at a vacant lot on the outskirts of town. Local buses costing US$0.20 run frequently between the bus station and the centre of town, arriving and departing from beside the Mercado de Artesanías, one block from the central plaza.

Buses departing from Tequisquiapan are all 2nd class. They include:

Mexico City – 196 km, 2¾ hours; buses every half-hour, 6.30 am to 7 pm, with Flecha Amarilla (US$4.85).

Querétaro – 82 km, one hour; hourly, 6 am to 7 pm, with Flecha Azul (US$1.10).

San Juan del Río – 26 km, 25 minutes; every 10 minutes, 5.45 am to 7 pm, with Flecha Amarilla (US$0.60).

Michoacán

South of the Bajío is Michoacán, one of Mexico's most interesting states. It is a beautiful mountainous region of 59,928 sq km extending over part of the Sierra Madre Occidental mountain range in west-central Mexico and down to the Pacific coast. Between the mountains are the river watersheds of the Río Lerma and Río Balsas, with a spiderweb of tributaries and river valleys spread across the state. The volcanic soil, rich and fertile, supports a variety of agriculture.

Home to the Purépeche Indians, also called Tarascans, the mountains are cool and pleasant. Descending to the coast, the vegetation becomes more tropical and the climate more hot and humid, especially in summer.

Many of Michoacán's towns specialise in unique handcrafts passed down through the centuries, making the mountains of Michoacán a patchwork quilt of traditions.

Morelia, the state capital, with its well-preserved colonial architecture is a good starting point for explorations of Michoacán if you're coming from the interior of the country. An hour's ride south-west from Morelia along a well-surfaced two-lane highway is Pátzcuaro, another architectural gem, a lovely, peaceful town at one time the capital of the Tarascan Indian kingdom. Lago Pátzcuaro is known for its Indian fishermen with their traditional butterfly nets, for the island of Janitzio, the largest of five islands, and for several villages on its shores.

Another hour to the south-west again is Uruapan, with a fine national park at the headwaters of the Río Cupatitzio, and the famous Volcano Paricutín nearby. The villages around Pátzcuaro and Uruapan each specialise in particular handcrafts handed down through centuries-old tradition; Michoacán handcrafts are some of the most famous, interesting and colourful in Mexico.

Following Highway 37 from Uruapan to the coast you descend through some spectacular mountain scenery to Highway 200, the

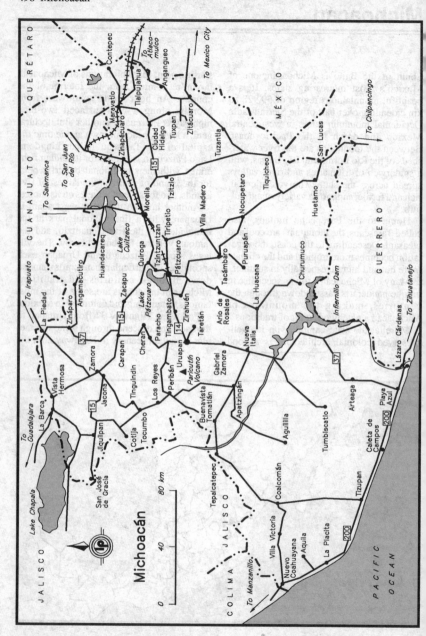

Michoacán

Pacific coastal highway, with the beach resort of Playa Azul and the port of Lázaro Cárdenas nearby.

MORELIA

Population: 428,500
Altitude: 1910 metres

Morelia, the capital of Michoacán, lies in the north-eastern part of the state, 315 km west of Mexico City, 367 km south-east of Guadalajara, and 62 km north-east of Pátzcuaro.

Morelia was officially founded in 1541, although a Franciscan monastery had been in the area since 1537. New Spain's first viceroy, Don Antonio de Mendoza, named it Valladolid in honour of the Spanish city by the same name and encouraged several families of the Spanish nobility to move there. The families remained and maintained Valladolid as a very Spanish city, at least architecturally, until 1828.

By that time, New Spain had become the independent republic of Mexico and hatred of the Spanish was great. The state legislature changed the city's name from Valladolid to Morelia to honour one of its native sons, José María Morelos de Pavón, a key figure in Mexico's independence movement.

Today, with its downtown streets lined with colonial-style buildings, Morelia still looks as Spanish as it probably did before independence. City ordinances now require that all new construction be done colonial-style with arches, baroque façades and carved pink stone walls.

Orientation

Morelia is a fairly compact city, with almost everything of interest within walking distance of the zócalo, also called the Plaza Central, Plaza de los Mártires or Plaza de Armas. Morelia's large cathedral in the middle of the zócalo is one of the city's most famous features; it makes a good orientation point for explorations of the city.

Avenida Madero, running along the north side of the zócalo, is the major avenue of the downtown area. It's called Avenida Madero Oriente to the east of the zócalo, Avenida Madero Poniente to the west. Several hotels, restaurants, historic sites and government offices are on or just off this avenue.

Nine blocks east of the zócalo on Madero Oriente, the Fuente Tarasca (Tarascan Fountain) is another of the city's major landmarks, marking a major intersection; it's here you will enter the city centre of Morelia if you're driving in from Mexico City. Beginning at the fountain, an 18th-century aqueduct runs parallel to Avenida Acueducto for two km, heading south-east and then east out of the city.

Information

Tourist Office The Galería de Turismo (☎ (451) 3-26-54) is on the corner of Avenida Madero Poniente and Nigromante, on an outside corner of the Palacio Clavijero. It has free maps and printed information in Spanish and English on Morelia and the state of Michoacán. Stop by for their free monthly calendar of films and cultural events taking place in the city. Office hours are Monday to Friday from 9 am to 3 pm and 4 to 8 pm, Saturday and Sunday 9 am to 8 pm.

Inside the courtyard of the Palacio Clavijero, the Dirección de Operación y Desarrollo Turístico (☎ 3-26-54) also has tourist information. They offer free walking tours of the historical city centre any time five or more people want to go; all you need do is phone in advance to schedule it. Office hours are Monday to Friday from 9 am to 3 pm and 6 to 8 pm.

Money Banks are plentiful in the zócalo area, particularly on and around Madero. They give the best rates for changing money, but they are only open from 9 am to 1.30 pm, Monday to Friday.

The Casa de Cambio Michoacán, at Calle Valladolid 22 near the south-east corner of the zócalo, changes US dollars and travellers' cheques; it's open Monday to Friday from 9 am to 6 pm, Saturday 9 am to 1 pm.

The Casa de Cambio Majapara at Pino Suárez 166 on the corner of 20 de Noviembre changes US dollars cash and travellers' cheques, plus the currencies of Canada, UK, Germany, Switzerland, France and Spain,

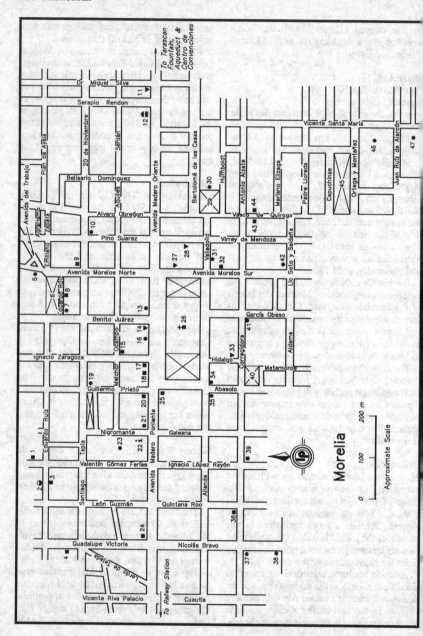

To Tarascan
Fountain,
Aqueduct &
Centro de
Convenciones

Morelia

Approximate Scale

0   100   200 m

and sells Thomas Cook travellers' cheques. It's open Monday to Friday from 9 am to 6.30 pm, Saturday 9 am to 2 pm.

Post & Telecommunications The main post office is in the Palacio Federal at Avenida Madero Oriente 369 on the corner of Serapio Rendon, four blocks east of the zócalo. It's open Monday to Friday from 8 am to 8 pm, Saturday and Sunday 9 am to 1 pm.

Telecomm, with services of telegram, telex, fax and money orders, is in the same building as the post office. Telegram hours are Monday to Saturday from 9 am to 8 pm; telex and fax hours are Monday to Friday from 9 am to 8 pm, Saturday 9 am to noon.

Computel has two casetas de larga dis-

tancia with long-distance telephone and fax services. The one in the central bus station is open 24 hours every day. Another Computel, on Avenida Madero opposite the cathedral at Portal Galeana 157, is open every day from 7 am to 10 pm.

Laundry Lavandería Sandy, at Corregidora 787 on the corner of Nicolás Bravo, is open Monday to Friday from 8 am to 12.30 pm and 4 to 8 pm, Saturday from 8 am to 5 pm.

There's a Lavandería Automática in the Plaza Capuchinas at Ortega y Montañez 318, a few doors to the left of the Templo Capuchinas. You can wash your own clothes there, or drop them off. It's open Monday to Friday from 9 am to 2 pm and 4 to 7 pm, Saturday 9 am to 2 pm.

■ PLACES TO STAY

1 Hotel Concordia
3 Hotel del Matador
4 Hotel Real Victoria
8 Hotel El Carmen
9 Hotel Colonial
15 Hotel Posada de la Soledad
17 Hotel Catedral
18 Hotel Casino, Restaurant Don Quijote, Café Catedral & Sidewalk Cafés
20 Hotel Alameda & Paletería La Michoacana
24 Hotel San Jorge
25 Hotel Virrey de Mendoza
32 Hotel Florida
36 Hotel Mansión del Quijote
39 Hotel D'Atilanos
43 Posada Don Vasco
44 Hotel Mintzicuri

▼ PLACES TO EAT

11 Restaurante Vegetariano La Fuente
14 Restaurant El Paraíso
27 Restaurant Hindu Vegetariano Govinda
28 Restaurant Woolworth
33 Restaurante Vegetariano Acuarius & Restaurant El Tragadero

OTHER

2 Central Bus Station
5 Casa de la Cultura & Museo de la Máscara
6 Plaza del Carmen
7 Museo de Arte Colonial
10 Casa de Cambio Majapara
12 Palacio Federal, Post Office & Telecomm
13 State Government Palace
16 Computel
19 Museo del Estado
21 Colegio de San Nicolás
22 Tourist Office
23 Palacio Clavijero & Mercado de Dulces
26 Cathedral & Zócalo
29 Plaza Valladolid
30 Casa de las Artesanías
31 Casa de Cambio Michoacán
34 Palacio de Justicia
35 Museo Regional Michoacano
37 Lavandería Sandy
38 Mercado Nicolás Bravo
41 Museo Casa Natal de Morelos
40 Plaza San Agustín
42 Museo Casa de Morelos
45 Plaza Capuchinas
46 Lavandería Automática Plaza Capuchinas
47 Mercado Independencia

Cathedral

The cathedral overlooking the zócalo took over a century to build, from 1640 to 1744. Architecturally, it is a combination of baroque, Herreriano (a classical Spanish style) and Neoclassical styles. Its twin 70-metre towers are a prime example of this combination – classical linear bases, baroque mid-sections and multi-columned Neoclassical tops. Inside, much of the baroque relief work was replaced in the 19th century with more balanced and calculated Neoclassical pieces. Fortunately, however, one of the cathedral's interior highlights was preserved: a sculpture of the Señor de la Sacristía made from dried maize and topped with a gold crown from the 16th-century Spanish King Philip II. There's also a large organ with 4600 pipes.

Museo Regional Michoacano

Just off the zócalo at Allende 305 and Abasolo is the Michoacán Regional Museum. Housed in the late 18th-century baroque-style palace of Isidro Huarte, the museum displays a great variety of pre-Hispanic artefacts, 17th and 18th-century paintings and colonial relics, contemporary paintings by local artists, and exhibits on the geology and fauna of the region. One of the museum's highlights is a mural on the stairway, by Mexican painter Alfredo Alce, divided in left and right halves portraying those who have had a positive (right half) and negative (left half) influence on Mexico.

The museum is open Tuesday to Saturday from 9 am to 7 pm, Sunday 9 am to 2 pm (closed Monday). Admission is US$3.35, but free to those under 13 and over 60, and free to everyone on Sunday.

On weekends the Cine Club presents free international films in the museum's auditorium; showings are at noon and 5 pm on Saturday and at noon on Sunday.

Palacio de Justicia

Opposite the zócalo and the Museo Regional Michoacano, the Palacio de Justicia was built between 1682 and 1695 to serve as the town hall. Its façade is an eclectic but well-done mix of French and baroque styles. A dramatic mural by Agustín Cárdenas graces the courtyard.

Museo del Estado

The State Museum of Michoacán at Guillermo Prieto 176, on the corner of Santiago Tapia, is a good place to learn about this very interesting state. Downstairs are exhibits on the history of Michoacán, all the way from prehistoric times and pre-Hispanic societies (principally the Tarascans) up to the time of first contact between the Tarascans and the Spanish. Upstairs are exhibits continuing the story up to the present, with exhibits on many aspects of modern life in Michoacán featuring clothing, handcrafts and agricultural exhibits.

The museum is open Monday to Friday from 9 am to 2 pm and 4 to 8 pm; Saturday, Sunday and holidays it's open the same hours, but only to 7 pm in the evening. Admission is free.

Free cultural events such as regional music, dance, handcraft arts, etc are presented every Wednesday at 7.30 pm.

Museo Casa de Morelos

José Maria Morelos y Pavón, one of the most important figures in Mexico's struggle for independence from Spain, was born and lived in Morelia (then called Valladolid). In 1801 he bought the Spanish-style house at Avenida Morelos Sur 323, on the corner of Soto y Saldaña, adding a second storey in 1806. The house is now a museum with exhibits on Morelos' life and some of the highlights of his role in the independence movement.

The museum is open Monday to Saturday from 9 am to 7 pm, Sunday 9 am to 2 pm. Admission is US$2.70, but free to those under 13 and over 60, and free to everyone on Sunday.

Museo Casa Natal de Morelos

Morelos was born in this house at the corner of Corregidora and García Obeso on 30 September 1765. Two centuries later, the state government declared it a national monument and made it a museum. Morelos memorabilia fills two rooms; a public library, auditorium and projection room occupy the rest of the house. An eternal torch burns next to the projection room, where the Cine Club presents free international films on Wednesday and Thursday at noon, 5 and 7 pm. On Friday evening at 7 pm, the Viernes Culturales series presents free cultural events in the auditorium.

The museum is open Monday to Saturday from 9 am to 2 pm and 4 to 8 pm; admission is free.

Colegio de San Nicolás

Morelos studied at the Colegio de San Nicolás, one block west of the zócalo on the corner of Avenida Madero Poniente and Nigromante. Another of Mexico's illustrious heroes, Miguel Hidalgo y Costilla, was Morelos' teacher there in the days before Hidalgo was transferred to the town of Dolores, there making the famous Cry for Independence in 1810 which started the independence movement. The Colegio later became the foundation for the University of Michoacán; it is still in use as a part of the university.

Upstairs, the Sala de Melchor Ocampo is a memorial room to another Mexican hero, a reformer and governor of Michoacán. Here are preserved Ocampo's library and a copy of the document he signed just before being shot by firing squad on 3 June 1861, donating his library to the college. This room and the rest of the college are open Monday to Friday, 8 am to 2 pm; admission free.

Palacio Clavijero & Mercado de Dulces

In the next block west, between Calles Nigromante and Valentín Gómez Farías, the Clavijero Palace was established in 1660 as a Jesuit school by its chief patron, Fray Javier Clavijero. After the Jesuits were expelled in 1767, the building served alternately as a warehouse and prison until 1970 when it was renovated for use as public offices, including a library and the state tourist office. The public library is attached to the palace.

Be sure to visit the arcade on the western side of the palace to see and taste some of the goodies for sale at the Mercado de Dulces (Market of Sweets). It's open every day from around 8 am to 10 pm. Michoacán handcrafts are also sold in the arcade, but you can find much better handcrafts at the Casa de las Artesanías.

Museo de Arte Colonial

The Museum of Colonial Art is at Benito Juárez 240 on the corner of Eduardo Ruíz, three blocks north of the cathedral. It's open Tuesday to Sunday from 10 am to 2 pm and 5 to 8 pm; admission is free.

Casa de la Cultura & Museo de la Máscara

A block away, across the Plaza del Carmen at Avenida Morelos Norte 485, the Casa de la Cultura hosts performances of dance, music, etc and various temporary art exhibits. Stop by to pick up a free monthly brochure describing cultural events taking place here and around the city.

Also here is a mask museum with masks from many regions of Mexico, all associated with particular dances. The mask museum is open Monday to Friday from 10 am to 2 pm, Saturday, Sunday and holidays from 10 am to 6 pm; admission is free.

Casa de las Artesanías

The House of Artesanías occupies the Ex-Convento de San Francisco, attached to the Templo de San Francisco on the Plaza de Valladolid, three blocks east of the zócalo on Calle Vasco de Quiroga. Arts and handcrafts from all over Michoacán are displayed and sold; they are expensive, but are truly some of the best quality you'll see anywhere in Michoacán. There's also a small selection of cassettes of regional music. It's open every day from 9 am to 8 pm; admission is free.

Upstairs, small shops represent many of Michoacán's towns and villages, with craftspeople demonstrating how the specialities of their areas are made: guitars from Paracho, copperware from Santa Clara del Cobre, lacquerware, weaving, and much more. The shops are open every day from 10 am to 3 pm and 5 to 8 pm.

Fuente Tarasca & El Acueducto

The Tarascan fountain at the end of Avenida Madero Oriente, nine blocks east of the zócalo, consists of a bevy of half-naked Tarascan women in stone, holding aloft a large basket of fruits and vegetables. It is a 1960s replacement of a fountain that mysteriously disappeared sometime in 1940. The effect is strangely beautiful at night.

The aqueduct begins at the Tarascan fountain and extends south-east along Avenida Acueducto. Although it looks much older, the aqueduct was built between 1785 and 1788 to satisfy the city's growing water needs. With 253 arches stretching two km, it is an impressive sight, especially at night when spotlights illuminate the arches and the Tarascan fountain.

Bosque Cuauhtémoc & Museo de Arte Contemporaneo

The Bosque Cuauhtémoc, or Cuauhtémoc Forest, is a large park bordered on the north-east side by Avenida Acueducto. A couple of blocks from the Tarascan fountain, the Museum of Contemporary Art is at Avenida Acueducto 18, on one side of the park. It's open Tuesday to Sunday from 10 am to 2 pm and 4 to 8 pm, with changing exhibitions of modern art; admission is free.

Estatua Ecuestre al Patriota Morelos

This statue of Morelos on horseback trotting to battle is on Plaza Morelos, a plaza on the north-east side of Bosque Cuauhtémoc between Calzada Fray Antonio de San Miguel and Avenida Acueducto. Commissioned by the Porfirio Díaz government, the statue was built and erected by Italian sculptor Giuseppe Ingillieri between 1910 and 1913.

Museo de Historia Natural

Continuing around the borders of the Bosque Cuauhtémoc and turning south from Avenida Acueducto onto Calzada Ventura Puente, you come to the Natural History Museum, hugging another of the borders of the park. It is operated by the University of Michoacán, which has several more buildings on the same avenue labelled for the study of nursing, dentistry, etc. The museum is open every day except Tuesday, from 10 am to 6 pm; free admission.

Centro de Convenciones

Further south on Calzada Ventura Puente, the Centro de Convenciones complex, with extensive park-like grounds, holds a planetarium, an orchid house, and the Teatro Morelos.

The Planetario de Morelia, with a cupola 20 metres in diameter and a modern planetarium apparatus with 164 projectors, presents programmes on Friday and Saturday at 7 pm, Sunday at 6.30 pm; the programmes last about one hour and there's an admission charge of US$1.35. On Sunday at 5 pm there's a separate family programme, also for US$1.35; children must be five years old to attend it, or seven years old to attend the regular programme.

The Orquidario, or orchid house, is open every day from 7 am to 6 pm. There's no set admission fee but they sell entrance tickets costing US$0.20, US$0.35 and US$1.70; you can decide how much of a donation you want to make.

The Teatro Morelos is a large, modern theatre where cultural events are presented; you can find out the current schedule from the theatre itself, or from the cultural calendars given out free by the tourism office and the Casa de la Cultura.

The Centro de Convenciones is quite far to walk from the centre of town, but it's easily reached by local combi. From the centre, take the 'Ruta Amarilla' (Yellow Route) heading east on Calle Santiago Tapia-20 de Noviembre. This route stops running at 9 pm, so if you're out after that you'll have to take a taxi back to the centre.

Parque Zoológico Benito Juárez

The Benito Juárez Zoo is three km south of the zócalo on Calzada Juárez, which is an extension of Calles Galeana and

Nigromante. It's a pleasant zoo with many animals, a lake with rowboats for hire, a small train, picnic areas, and a children's playground. It's open every day except Tuesday from 10 am to 6 pm; admission is US$0.85 (US$0.20 for children under 10).

The maroon combi route ('Ruta Guión'), heading south on Nigromante from the stop on the east side of the Palacio Clavijero near the zócalo, will drop you off at the entrance to the zoo.

Markets
Three large mercados are within 10 blocks or so of the zócalo: the Mercado Nicolás Bravo on Nicolás Bravo between Corregidora and Guerrero; the Mercado Independencia at the corner of Vicente Santa María and Ana María Gallaga; and the Mercado Municipal Revolución at the corner of Revolución and Plan de Ayala.

Festivals
Feria de Morelia Morelia's major annual fair is celebrated from 29 April to 20 May with exhibits of handcrafts, agriculture and livestock from all over Michoacán, plus cultural events, regional dances, bullfights and fiestas.

Feria de Órgano The International Organ Festival is held during the first two weeks of May, in conjunction with the Feria de Morelia.

Founding of Morelia Morelia was founded on 18 May 1541. Its anniversary is celebrated every 18 May with cultural events, fireworks, and exhibitions of art and historical photos.

Festival Internacional de Música The International Music Festival takes place during the final week of July and the first week of August.

Día de Independencia Mexico's Independence Day is celebrated on 15 and 16 September with parades and other events.

Don José María Morelos y Pavón's Birthday This is celebrated on 30 September with a parade and events similar to those for the city's anniversary.

Día de la Virgen de Guadalupe The day of the Virgen de Guadalupe, Mexico's patron saint, is celebrated on 12 December at the Templo de San Diego. From 27 October to 12 December, typical Mexican foods are sold on the stone walking street Calzada Fray Antonio de San Miguel.

Feria Navideña The Christmas Fair is a moveable event taking place from approximately 1 December to 6 January, with traditional Christmas items, foods, handcrafts, and manufactured goods produced in Michoacán.

Places to Stay – bottom end
The cheapest place to stay in Morelia is the CREA youth hostel, *Villa Deportiva Juvenil* (☎ (451) 3-31-77), in the IMJUDE sports complex at the corner of Oaxaca and Chiapas, about a 15 or 20-minute walk south-west of the zócalo. The hostel is clean, with four beds (two bunks) and a locker in each room, and separate men's and women's areas. Travellers of any age are welcome; no hostel card is required, though there's a 10% discount if you have it. Cost is US$3.70 per bunk. In the sports complex are a swimming pool, a gym and several sports fields.

Otherwise, there are a number of good inexpensive hotels within a few blocks of the zócalo, including a couple near the bus station. The *Hotel del Matador* (☎ (451) 2-46-49), at Eduardo Ruíz 531 opposite the bus station door, is better than most hotels around bus stations. Its 57 clean rooms all have private bath and windows admitting light and air. Cost is US$12.70 for one or two people, US$3.35 extra if you want colour TV.

The *Hotel Concordia* (☎ (451) 2-30-52/54) at Valentín Gómez Farías 328, on the east side of the bus station, has singles/doubles at US$13.35/16.70. The rooms facing the street are the best, with little balconies and a whole wall of windows; the interior rooms are quieter but a bit dark.

A few blocks away, the *Hotel El Carmen* (☎ (451) 2-17-25) is at Eduardo Ruíz 63, between Juárez and Morelos, facing the small Plaza del Carmen. The rooms opening onto the plaza are quite pleasant, with small balconies; the interior rooms have no windows. Singles/doubles are US$6.70/10, or US$13.35 with two beds.

Around the corner, two blocks from the zócalo, the *Hotel Colonial* (☎ (451) 2-18-97) at 20 de Noviembre 15, on the corner of Avenida Morelos Norte, is a colonial-style hotel with 25 rooms at US$10/11.70. Street-facing rooms are good – large, with high beamed ceilings and small balconies – but this is a busy corner with much traffic noise; the interior rooms are quieter.

The *Posada Don Vasco* (☎ (451) 2-14-84) at Vasco de Quiroga 232 is a colonial-style hotel with rooms arranged around a courtyard with sitting areas and plants. It has a variety of rooms, some quite pleasant; all have carpet, phone, and hot-water private bath (6.30 am to 2 pm). Singles/doubles cost US$8.35/11.70. The hotel restaurant is popular and cheap.

Opposite the Don Vasco, the *Hotel Mintzicuri* (☎ (451) 2-06-64) at Vasco de Quiroga 227 has 37 small, clean rooms, all with carpet and phone, around a courtyard with parking spaces. Singles/doubles are US$11.50/14.35; they, too, have a restaurant.

Four blocks west of the zócalo, the *Hotel San Jorge* (☎ (451) 2-46-10) at Avenida Madero Poniente 719, on the corner of Guadalupe Victoria, has large, clean rooms with ample windows opening onto the interior walkway; cost is US$11/13.35.

Places to Stay – middle

Two blocks south-west of the zócalo, the *Hotel D'Atilanos* (☎ (451) 2-01-21) at Corregidora 465, on the corner of Ignacio Rayón, is a colonial-style hotel with 27 large rooms, all with colour TV and phone, arranged around a lovely covered interior courtyard. Singles/doubles are US$16.70/21.70.

A block further from the zócalo, the *Hotel Mansión del Quijote* (☎ (451) 2-67-93) at Quintana Roo 204, on the corner of Corregidora, is an attractive place with 12 large rooms, all with plenty of light and air and provisions for off-street parking. Singles/doubles are US$16.70/20.

The *Hotel Florida* (☎ (451) 2-18-19, 2-10-38) is half a block south of the zócalo at Avenida Morelos Sur 161. It's a clean, modern place where all rooms have colour TV, carpet, and phone; most rooms have good ventilation, and those facing the street catch the afternoon sun. Singles/doubles are US$15.70/22.

On the north side of the zócalo, the *Hotel Casino* (☎ (451) 3-10-03) at Portal Hidalgo 229 has 48 clean, comfortable rooms, all with carpet, phone and colour TV. Those facing the street have small balconies overlooking the zócalo; the interior rooms open onto a covered courtyard with a popular restaurant on the ground floor. Singles/doubles are US$22.60/28.25.

In the same block, the *Hotel Catedral* (☎ (451) 3-04-06, fax 3-04-67) at Zaragoza 37, opposite the cathedral, is another attractive colonial-style hotel with comfortable rooms around a covered courtyard, but at US$36.70/45.85 the rooms seem overpriced.

The *Hotel Real Victoria* (☎ (451) 3-23-00, 3-25-11) at Guadalupe Victoria 245 is a modern four-star hotel with 110 clean, pleasant rooms, all with colour TV and carpet, at US$28.35/34.45. There's enclosed parking and a restaurant on the ground floor of the covered interior courtyard.

Places to Stay – top end

On the north-west corner of the zócalo, the *Hotel Virrey de Mendoza* (☎ (451) 2-00-45) at Portal Matamoros 16 is the converted mansion of Antonio de Mendoza, the first viceroy of Mexico. The 52 rooms are elegantly furnished with antiques, crystal chandeliers and so on. Interior rooms cost US$47, those with balconies over the street are US$60, and suites are US$67.

Another good choice is the four-star *Hotel Posada de la Soledad* (☎ (451) 2-18-88) at Zaragoza 90, on the corner of Ocampo. Built around 1700, its long history includes periods as a carriage house, a convent, and a private mansion. It has 50 standard rooms at US$44/52, plus nine suites.

Back on the north-west corner of the zócalo, the four-star *Hotel Alameda* (☎ (451) 2-20-23, fax 3-87-27) at Avenida Madero Poniente 313 is a more modern, 116-room hotel. Rooms in the older section are US$43/54; in the new section they're US$59/74, suites US$67/84. It's an attractive hotel, with a popular restaurant and bar, but have a look at the Mendoza or the Soledad first.

Places to Eat

Morelia has a variety of good, economical restaurants to choose from. Opposite the front doors of the cathedral, at Portal Galeana 103 on the corner of Avenida Madero and Benito Juárez, the *Restaurant El Paraíso* is a good, basic restaurant with moderate prices for all meals. The comida corrida is US$3.35; they also serve a variety of breakfast combinations and a typical à la carte menu. It's open every day from 7.30 am to 11 pm.

In the next block west along Madero, opposite the zócalo, is a row of restaurants and sidewalk cafés, open every day from around 7.30 am to 10 pm. The *Café Catedral* is a popular spot, as is the *Restaurant Don Quijote*, the restaurant of the Hotel Casino, with tables both inside and out on the sidewalk. The sidewalk tables are popular all day and evening for coffee and people-watching.

Half a block off the zócalo, at Madero Poniente 327, the *Paletería La Michoacana* makes good fruit drinks and ice cream, good for taking to the zócalo and sitting on a bench under a tree. It's open every day from 8 am to 9 pm.

On the south side of the zócalo, Calle Hidalgo is a shopping street blocked off to traffic. The *Restaurant El Tragadero* at Hidalgo 63, half a block from the zócalo, is another good, basic restaurant for all meals;

it's open from 8 am to 11 pm Monday to Saturday, 8 am to 8 pm on Sunday.

The *Restaurante Woolworth* is a pleasant, clean cafeteria in a converted former church on Virrey de Mendoza, half a block south of Avenida Madero. In addition to the à la carte menu it has a selection of weekday combination meals for breakfast, lunch and dinner, all priced at US$1.65, an excellent deal. On weekends they have a breakfast buffet and a two-for-one comida corrida special where two can eat for US$5. It's open from 8 am to 9 pm Monday to Saturday, 9 am to 8 pm on Sunday.

For cheap eats, there are several restaurants near the bus station, open daily from around 7 am to midnight; a comida corrida might cost as little as US$1.35 here. Or there's a row of cheap eating stalls with tables under the covered arches running around three sides of the Plaza San Agustín, one block south of the zócalo; they're open every day from around 3 or 4 pm until around 1 am.

Vegetarian On the east side of the zócalo at Morelos Sur 39, in the building that used to house the Hotel Oseguera, the *Restaurant Hindu Vegetariano Govinda* is a quiet, attractive restaurant serving a selection of breakfasts, vegetarian burgers and comida corrida combos for US$2.35 to US$3.35; a vegie burger is US$1. It's open Monday to Friday from 9 am to 9 pm, Saturday from 9 am to 5 pm, closed Sunday.

On Hidalgo, the shopping street heading south from the zócalo, the *Restaurante Vegetariano Acuarius* at Hidalgo 75 is open from 1 to 5 pm every day, serving a good comida corrida for US$3.35. The restaurant is in a pleasant covered courtyard.

Queen of Morelia's vegetarian restaurants is the popular *Restaurante Vegetariano La Fuente*, five blocks east of the zócalo at Avenida Madero Oriente 493-B. It's open Monday to Saturday from 1 to 6 pm, serving a delicious and filling comida corrida for US$4.50, with selections changing daily. A guitarist entertains at lunch time; on Friday night there's food, music and other entertainment from 8 pm to midnight.

Entertainment

Being a university town as well as the capital of one of Mexico's most interesting states, Morelia has a lively cultural life. Stop by the tourist office and the Casa de la Cultura for their free monthly calendars listing films and cultural events around Morelia.

Morelia's two daily newspapers *El Sol de Morelia* and *La Voz de Michoacán* have cultural sections with events notices and theatre ads where you can see what's playing at the cinemas. There are several movie theatres around the centre.

International film series are presented by the Cine Club, with admission always free. The films are shown at the Museo Regional Michoacano on weekends (Saturday at noon and 5 pm, Sunday at noon) and at the Museo Casa Natal de Morelos during the week (Wednesday and Thursday at noon, 5 and 7 pm).

The Museo Casa Natal de Morelos also presents talks and various cultural events at its Viernes Culturales, on Friday at 7 pm. Cultural events including regional dances, music, stories, and exhibitions from the state of Michoacán are also presented every Wednesday at 7.30 pm at the Museo del Estado.

La Librería, a bookstore and coffee house at Calzada Fray Antonio de San Miguel 284, a couple of blocks east of the Tarascan fountain, is another enjoyable place to partake of culture, with a pleasant university atmosphere. Its Cine Club presents international films on Friday at 7 pm and Saturday at 7.30 pm; on Sunday at 7.30 pm they have live music. There's no charge for any of their events; just have a coffee, tea or a cake from the café.

The Restaurante Vegetariano La Fuente at Avenida Madero Oriente 493-B, five blocks east of the cathedral, hosts a Cena y Variedad on Friday evenings from 8 pm to midnight, a sort of Bohemian evening with music, singing, guitars, poetry and similar fare, in addition to the vegetarian foods, wines and *sangría*.

Then there are the weekend planetarium programmes; see the Centro de Convenciones for details on the planetarium.

For higher cultural entertainment, Morelia also has a number of discothéques, including the Disco Molino Rojo, the Baron Rojo, Aurum, Gyrovago's Laser Disco, the Club XO, Bambalina's, the Bol-Morelia, Las Moras, Inchátiro, and Los Quinqués.

Getting There & Away

Air The Francisco J Múgica airport (☎ 2-00-72, 2-02-00) is 27 km from Morelia, on the Morelia-Zinapécuaro highway.

Three airlines serve Morelia. Taesa (☎ 5-74-63, 5-74-65) has daily flights to Mexico City, Tijuana and Zacatecas. Aero Sudpacífico (☎ 5-24-13) has three flights daily to Uruapan and Lázaro Cárdenas, one flight daily to Mexico City and Guadalajara. Aeromar (☎ 3-05-55) has four flights daily to Mexico City.

Bus Morelia's Central Camionera is conveniently located in the centre of the city, just a few blocks from the zócalo, on Eduardo Ruíz between Valentín G Farías and Leon Guzman. In the bus station are a 24-hour office for local and long-distance telephone calls and fax, plus several cafeterias and places where you can store your luggage.

Bus routes departing from Morelia include:

Guadalajara – 367 km, five hours; 19 daily with Autobuses de Jalisco-La Linea (US$6.70); 14 daily with Servicios Coordinados (US$6.70); 11 daily with Autobuses de Occidente (US$6.20); 10 daily with Flecha Amarilla (US$6.20); six daily with Primera Plus (US$10); six daily with ETN (US$14.35).

Guanajuato – 176 km, four hours; eight daily with Flecha Amarilla (US$4.35).

Lázaro Cárdenas – 406 km, seven to eight hours; hourly, 24 hours, with Galeana (US$10.20 to US$14); eight daily with Ruta Paraíso (US$14); three daily with Tres Estrellas de Oro (US$10); one daily with Autobuses de Occidente (US$7.70).

León – 197 km, 3½ to four hours; every 30 minutes, 4.45 am to 10.30 pm, with Flecha Amarilla (US$4.60); six daily with Primera Plus (US$6); four daily with Servicios Coordinados (US$5).

Mexico City – 315 km, 4¼ to six hours, to both the Norte and Observatorio terminals; every 20 minutes, 24 hours, with Autobuses de Occidente (US$7.70); every 30 minutes, 4.15 am to 2.30 am, with Herradura de Plata (US$8.70 to US$11); hourly, 6.10 am to 4.30 pm, with Autobuses México-Toluca-Zinacantepec (US$7.70); 19 daily with Flecha Amarilla (US$7.70); 16 daily with ETN (US$16.70); eight daily with Primera Plus (US$11); five daily with Servicios Coordinados (US$8.50); three daily with Tres Estrellas de Oro (US$8.20); two daily with Transportes Norte de Sonora (US$7.35).

Pátzcuaro – 62 km, one hour; every 10 minutes, 6 am to 7.30 pm, with Galeana (US$1.75); nine daily with Flecha Amarilla (US$1.50).

Querétaro – 259 km, three to four hours; four daily with Flecha Amarilla (US$4.35); two daily with Transportes Frontera (US$5.70); one daily with Primera Plus (US$5.70).

San Luis Potosí – 397 km, six to seven hours; five daily with Primera Plus (US$12.70); four daily with Flecha Amarilla (US$9.20).

Uruapan – 124 km, two hours; every 15 minutes, 4 am to 9.50 pm, with Galeana (US$3.30 to US$4.20); every 30 minutes, 6 am to 9.30 pm, with Parhikuni (US$3.50); nine daily with Flecha Amarilla (US$2.95); six daily with Primera Plus (US$4.35).

Zitácuaro – 150 km, 2½ to three hours; hourly, 6.10 am to 4.30 pm, with Autobuses México-Toluca-Zinacantepec (US$3); 11 daily with Transportes Frontera (US$3.30); three daily with Autobuses de Jalisco-La Linea (US$3).

Train The Estación del Ferrocarril (☎ 6-16-97) is on Avenida Periodismo, on the south-west outskirts of the city. The ticket office is open from 5.30 to 6.30 am, 10 am to noon, 4 to 6 pm, and 10 to 11 pm. Trains departing from Morelia include:

Lázaro Cárdenas (via Pátzcuaro & Uruapan)
5.35 am – 1st-class cars US$13.05, 2nd-class cars US$3.60 (10 hours)
Mexico City (via Toluca)
10.30 am – 2nd class, US$3.10 (eight hours)
10.55 pm – 1st-class cars US$11.25, 2nd-class cars US$3.10 (eight hours)
Uruapan (via Pátzcuaro)
5.35 am – 1st-class cars US$4.25, 2nd-class cars US$1.20 (four hours)
5.30 pm – 2nd class, US$1.20 (four hours)

Getting Around

Local combis operate frequently from 6 am to 9 pm and cost US$0.25. The various combi routes are designated by colour, with the white Volkswagen vans marked by a broad coloured stripe and called the 'Ruta Roja', 'Ruta Amarilla' and so on. A few routes operate until 10 pm. Most places you'll want to visit in Morelia are within walking distance of the zócalo, but the combis are useful for getting to the zoo (the maroon route, 'Ruta Guinda') and the planetarium (yellow route, 'Ruta Amarilla').

Local buses marked 'Indeco' or 'Magisterio' run between the train station and the centre.

Taxis are plentiful in the centre; the average taxi ride costs around US$1.65. A taxi to the airport costs around US$13 to US$17, but you can also get there by bus.

MONARCH BUTTERFLY SANCTUARY

In the easternmost part of Michoacán, near the border of México state, is a Monarch butterfly sanctuary. Somewhere from 35 million to hundreds of millions of Monarch butterflies come here every year to mate and bear young, arriving around the end of October or beginning of November and departing again around the beginning or middle of April for their long migration back to the USA and southern Canada. When they are present, there are so many butterflies in the sanctuary that they cover the trees, turning them a flaming orange; it's a spectacular sight.

The sanctuary is open every day during the season the butterflies are present. The entrance fee of US$3.35 includes a guide who takes you through the sanctuary, explaining the butterflies' life cycle and so on. You can stay in the sanctuary as long as you like, but it only takes a couple of hours to tour it. It's a good idea to get there in the morning, when the butterflies are up in the trees. As the day warms up, they come down onto the ground where it's more humid, and there are so many that you can't avoid crushing some as you walk.

The sanctuary is quite 'off the beaten

track', but it is not difficult to reach. The first thing to do is to get to the city of **Zitácuaro** (population 67,000), a regional commercial centre on Highway 15, the highway from Mexico City through Toluca to Morelia. By bus, Zitácuaro is about three hours from Morelia (150 km), 2½ hours from Toluca (97 km) or 3½ hours from Mexico City (164 km); Autobuses de Occidente and Autobuses México-Toluca-Zinacántepec make the trip. At Zitácuaro you must change buses, taking a local bus for the 45-minute trip uphill to the village of Angangueo, about 25 km away. Zitácuaro's bus stations are separate, but they're on the same street.

Angangueo is a pretty mountain village, a former mining town with a population of about 3000 souls. While you're there you can enjoy strolling around, seeing the two churches and the Monument to the Miner, with a good view over the town. Angangueo has several places to stay, including the *Hotel Parakata* at Matamoros 7, with a sign on the main road; singles/doubles with private bath and hot water cost US$13.35/17.35. Behind the church are two similar hotels, the *Hotel Romero* and the *Hotel Ariaga*; the *Hotel Albergue Don Bruno* on Morelos, the main road, is more expensive. Beside the Hotel Albergue Don Bruno, the *Restaurant La Margarita* is a good place to eat, or there's a restaurant at the Hotel Parakata.

Camionetas, or vans, depart from the main road in Angangueo for the rugged nine km trip to the Monarch sanctuary, taking about an hour to get there; it's about another 15-minute walk from the parking place to the sanctuary. You have to hire the whole van, so the more people pitching in to share the cost, the better. Cost for the 10-person van is around US$25 to US$50 (depending on your bargaining power) for the round trip, including waiting while you visit the sanctuary. You'll have the best chance of finding other travellers to share the ride on weekends, but there are usually a few travellers around even during the week. To walk from Angangueo to the sanctuary is a steep uphill journey taking around three hours.

Another alternative is to visit the sanctuary from the town of Ocampo, 15 km from the sanctuary. Ocampo is not as attractive as Angangueo but it might be easier on your car if you're driving. There are places to stay in Ocampo, and organised tours going from there to the sanctuary.

PÁTZCUARO
Population: 42,500
Altitude: 2175 metres
Once the capital of a Purépechan Indian empire and then the seat of the bishopric of Michoacán, Pátzcuaro is a beautiful town with the atmosphere of an Indian village and the regal splendour of Spanish architecture. It stands about five km from the south-east shore of Lago Pátzcuaro along Highway 14, equidistant between Morelia and Uruapan (62 km to either place).

The Purépechans mysteriously appeared along Lago Pátzcuaro in the early 14th century. Anthropologists and archaeologists are still uncertain where they came from because they are not linked to any other peoples in the Americas. Their language does, however, resemble Zuni (spoken in the American Southwest), a Maya-Totonac dialect (once spoken in southern Mexico) and Quechua (spoken in Peru). The Spanish supposedly began calling the Purépeche Indians Tarascans because the Indians often used a word that sounded like *tarasca*.

In 1400, with the death of Purépechan King Tariácari, the kingdom was divided into three parts – Pátzcuaro, Tzintzuntzan and Ihuatzio – ruled together as a league. They remained a league until the Spanish arrived, first in 1522 and later in 1529 with soldiers and colonists who either killed the Indians or forced them into slavery for work in the mines. The Spanish soldiers, led by conquistador Nuño de Guzman, burned the Purépechan chief alive in their quest for gold.

Guzman's inhumanity to the Indians was so severe that the Catholic Church and the colonial government sent a bishop named Vasco de Quiroga to straighten out the mess. Quiroga arrived in 1536 to establish a bishopric and community of villages based on the humanistic ideals of Sir Thomas More's *Utopia*. To escape the cruelties of local Spanish mining lords and landowners, Quiroga successfully encouraged each village around Lago Pátzcuaro to establish its own craft specialities, a tradition that continues today. Not surprisingly, Quiroga is venerated for his work; streets, plazas, restaurants and hotels in Michoacán are named after him.

Quiroga made his base first at Tzintzuntzan, the Tarascan capital, 15 km north-east of Pátzcuaro. In 1540 he moved the seat to Pátzcuaro, whose Tarascan name means Seat of Ancient Temples; the Tarascans believed Pátzcuaro to be a place of access to the heavens. Quiroga later proclaimed Pátzcuaro as the capital of the province of Michoacán.

Orientation

Pátzcuaro is in a hilly region five km south of Lago Pátzcuaro. Most services and places of interest are in the centre of town, within easy walking distance. Docks for boats to Janitzio (the largest of five islands in Lago Pátzcuaro), the train station and a number of restaurants specialising in fish from the lake are on or near the lakefront.

Pátzcuaro has two principal plazas and several smaller ones. The main plaza is the Plaza Vasco de Quiroga, with a large statue of the venerated bishop gazing down benignly from the central fountain. The plaza is quaint and peaceful, bordered by a number of arched 17th-century mansions now used as hotels, restaurants and shops. The tourist office is on the north-west corner of the plaza.

One block north of this plaza, the smaller Plaza Gertrudis Bocanegra is named for a local heroine who was shot by firing squad in Plaza Vasco de Quiroga for her support of the independence movement. The town market opens onto the west side of this plaza; on the north side are a theatre, a library, and a small handcrafts market. Local buses and combis to the lake and to the train and bus stations depart from this plaza.

Driving in from Morelia, the highway par-allels the train tracks all the way to the lake and almost to the station. The road to downtown Pátzcuaro veers south from the highway just before the junction to the station, becoming Avenida Lázaro Cárdenas (also called Avenida or Calzada de las Américas) and then Calle Ahumada as it winds into town. When it reaches Calle Lloreda, Plaza Gertrudis Bocanegra is one block to your right. Watch the street names – some change with every block.

Information

Tourist Office The Delegación Regional de Turismo (☎ (454) 2-12-14) is on the northwest corner of Plaza Vasco de Quiroga, at Calle Ibarra 3, Interior 4, on the corner of Ibarra and Mendoza. Look for the large 'Sanatorio' sign over the doorway of the building. They give out free maps of Pátzcuaro, can help you find a hotel room or anything else you might need, and provide information on the state of Michoacán. Office hours are Monday to Friday from 9 am to 2 pm and 4 to 7 pm, Saturday and Sunday 9 am to 2 pm.

Post & Telecommunications The post office is at Obregón 13, half a block north of Plaza Gertrudis Bocanegra. It's open Monday to Friday from 8 am to 7.30 pm, Saturday 9 am to 1 pm.

The Telecomm office at Títere 15 offers telegram and fax services. It's open Monday to Friday from 9 am to 7 pm, Saturday from 9 am to noon.

There's a caseta de larga distancia in the lobby of the Teatro Emperador Caltzontzin, on the north side of Plaza Gertrudis Bocanegra. It's open every day from 7 am to 9.30 pm, offering local and long-distance telephone and fax services.

Another caseta, on the west side of Plaza Gertrudis Bocanegra in the upstairs lobby of the Hotel San Agustín, is open every day from 8.30 am to 10 pm.

The central bus station also has a caseta, open daily from 7.30 am to 9 pm.

Laundry The Lavandería Automática at

Terán 14, 1½ blocks west of Plaza Vasco de Quiroga, is open Monday to Friday from 9 am to 2 pm and 4 to 8 pm, Saturday from 9 am to 2 pm. Cost is US$3.35 for three kilos of laundry for wash, dry and fold.

Biblioteca Gertrudis Bocanegra

The Gertrudis Bocanegra Library occupies the former Church of San Agustín on the north side of the Plaza Bocanegra. A large, colourful Juan O'Gorman mural covering the rear wall depicts the history of Michoacán from pre-Hispanic times to the 1910 Revolution. A great selection of books in English at the back is testimony to the large number of gringos passing through; you may be able to borrow a book if you ask. The library is open Monday to Friday from 9 am to 7 pm, Saturday from 9 am to 1 pm.

Teatro Emperador Caltzontzin

Next door to the library, this theatre was a convent attached to the church until it was converted to a theatre in 1936. Movies and occasional cultural events are presented here. Murals in the main upstairs hall col-

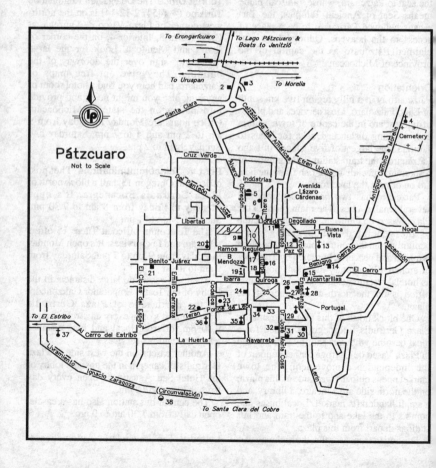

Pátzcuaro

Not to Scale

To Erongarícuaro
To Lago Pátzcuaro &
Boats to Janitzio
To Uruapan
To Morelia
To Erongarícuaro
Santa Clara
Calzada de las Américas
Efrén Uricho
Cemetery
Antiguo Camino a Morelia
Cruz Verde
Del Panteón
San José
Álvaro Obregón
Indústrias
Madero
Avenida Lázaro Cárdenas
Libertad
Lloreda
Degollado
Ahumada
Buena Vista
Nogal
Ramos Regules
Paz
Benigno Serrato
Ascensión
El Cerro
Benito Juárez
Emilio Carranza
B Mendoza
Ibarra
Quiroga
Alcantarillas
Esperanza
El Ciprés del Espejo
Cedros
Ponce de León
Portugal
To El Estribo
Al Cerro del Estribo
Terán
La Huerta
Navarrete
Dr José María Coss
León
Libramiento
Ignacio Zaragoza
(Circunvalación)
To Santa Clara del Cobre

ourfully remind movie-goers of various epochs in Michoacán's history, including the meeting of Tarascan King Tangahxuan II and the Spanish conquistador Cristóbal de Olid near Pátzcuaro in 1522, and the advance of technology in Michoacán during the years 1934 to 1940.

Mercado de Artesanías

The Mercado de Artesanías is along a passageway next to the Biblioteca Gertrudis Bocanegra, on the north side of the plaza by the same name. Some of the crafts sold here include thick, hand-woven wool sweaters, grotesque Tócuaro masks, intricately carved wooden forks and knives from Zirahuén, and pottery. Bargaining is the rule though prices are already low. Many other typical products of Michoacán are sold in the town market on the west side of the plaza.

On Friday mornings a ceramics market, with ceramics from different villages, is held

in Jardín Revolución, the small square one block west of Plaza Vasco de Quiroga.

Mercado

Pátzcuaro's busy mercado, or public market, opens onto the west side of Plaza Gertrudis Bocanegra. Here you can find everything from fruits, vegetables and fresh Lago Pátzcuaro fish to shoes and clothing, including the striped shawls, sarapes and *peruanas* (a kind of serape-shawl worn by women) distinctive of the region.

La Casa del Gigante

At Portal Matamoros 40 on the east side of Plaza Vasco de Quiroga, this mansion, built in 1663 for a count and countess, is a well-preserved example of colonial architecture, taking its name (House of the Giant) from a giant statue of a man holding up one of the columns in the interior courtyard. The last time we were in town it was being used as a private home and was not open to the public.

■	**PLACES TO STAY**	6	Telecomm
		7	Teatro Emperador Caltzontzin,
2	Hotel Posada de Don Vasco		Biblioteca Gertrudis Bocanegra &
3	Hotel Villa Pátzcuaro		Mercado de Artesanías
9	Hotel Posada de la Rosa & Hotel	8	Mercado
	de la Concordia	10	Plaza Gertrudis Bocanegra
11	Hotel Valmen	13	Basílica de Nuestral Señora de la
12	Hotel Posada de la Basílica		Salud
14	Hotel Posada de la Salud	15	Museo Regional de Artes Populares
18	Hotel Mansión Iturbe	16	Cine Michoacán
21	Hotel Posada La Terraza	19	Tourist Office
24	Hotel Los Escudos	20	Church of El Santuario
32	Hotel Mesón del Gallo	22	Lavandería Automática
34	Hotel Misión San Manuel & Hotel	23	Jardín Revolución
	Posada de San Rafael	25	Plaza Vasco de Quiroga
		26	Casa del Gigante
▼	**PLACES TO EAT**	27	Joaquinita Chocolate Supremo
		28	Church of La Compañia
17	Gran Hotel	29	Church of El Sagrario
33	Restaurant El Patio	30	Casa de los Once Patios
		31	Pila de San Miguel
	OTHER	35	Church of San Juan de Dios
		36	Church of San Francisco
1	Train Station	37	Church of El Calvario
4	Church of El Humilladero	38	Bus Station
5	Post Office		

Pila de San Miguel

Two blocks south of Plaza Vasco de Quiroga, on the corner of Dr José Maria Coss and Navarrete, the Pila de San Miguel is a centuries-old public fountain where the villagers of Pátzcuaro came to draw water. The painting of St Michael is faded, but still watches over the trough.

Casa de los Once Patios

The House of 11 Courtyards is just off Calle Enseñanza (also called Calle Lerin) and up a nameless cobblestoned street from Calle Dr José Maria Coss, one block south of Plaza Vasco de Quiroga. When Bishop Vasco de Quiroga had the house built, it was used as one of Mexico's first hospitals; later, Dominican nuns moved in and made it into a convent.

Today the house's well-preserved colonial-style buildings hold a plethora of tiny artesanía shops, each specialising in a particular craft of Michoacán. Copperware from Santa Clara del Cobre, straw goods from Tzintzuntzan, musical instruments and wooden creations from Paracho, hand-painted ceramics from a number of villages, as well as lacquerware, a variety of textiles, and more are represented. The shops are open every day from around 10 am to 7 pm.

Museo Regional de Artes Populares

The Regional Museum of Popular Arts is in a building founded by Vasco de Quiroga in 1540 as the Colegio de San Nicolás Obispo. Today it is a comprehensive museum of Michoacán arts and crafts. Exhibits include delicate white lace rebozos from Aranza, hand-painted ceramics from Santa Fe de la Laguna, copperware from Santa Clara del Cobre and clay pots from Tzintzuntzan. One room is set up as a typical Michoacán kitchen with a tremendous brick oven.

The museum is one block east of Plaza Vasco de Quiroga, on the corner of Calle Enseñanza and Calle Alcantarillas. It's open Tuesday to Saturday from 9 am to 7 pm, Sunday from 9 am to 3 pm (closed Monday). Admission is US$3.35, but free for children under 13 and seniors over 60; it's free for everyone on Sunday.

Casa de Cultura

Opposite the museum is the Iglesia de la Compañia, and attached to it is a large building which in the 17th century served as the Hospital of Santa María. Plans to restore the ex-hospital and make it into a cultural centre have been in the works for several years, with progress stalled for lack of funds.

Basílica de Nuestra Señora de la Salud

One block north of the museum, the basilica was originally intended as Vasco de Quiroga's grand contribution to the people of Pátzcuaro. He wanted a church that would be three times as large as Notre Dame of Paris, big enough for 30,000 worshippers, but this was ambitious. The present basilica, finished in the early 19th century, is only one nave of the original plan.

The basilica's most interesting sight is the figure of the Virgen de la Salud (Virgin of Health) made by local Tarascan Indians for Vasco de Quiroga in 1540, upon his request that they make an image of the Virgin. Soon the Indians began to receive miraculous healings, and Quiroga had the words 'Salus Infirmorum' (Healer of the Sick) inscribed at the figure's feet. The figure, which is made from a corn cob and honey paste called *tatzingue*, has miraculously survived more than four centuries of earthquakes, fires and other disasters.

Ever since Quiroga named it the Virgin of Health, pilgrims have come from all over Mexico on the eighth day of each month to ask the Virgin for a miracle. As at the Basílica de Guadalupe in Mexico City, the pilgrims crawl on their knees across the plaza to the basilica. You can walk up the stairs behind the altar to see the many small tin representations of body parts (hands, feet, legs, etc) that pilgrims have offered to the Virgin, now arranged into a sort of mosaic.

Other Churches

If you like old churches, Pátzcuaro has several others of interest, including the churches of La Compañia, El Sagrario, San Juan de Dios, San Francisco, El Santuario, El Calvario and El Humilladero. All are shown on the map.

El Estribo

El Estribo, a lookout point on a hill four km west of town, offers a magnificent view of the entire Lago Pátzcuaro area. It takes about 30 minutes to an hour, depending on your speed, to walk there from the centre of town; in a vehicle, it takes only a few minutes. Either way, you can reach it by taking Calle Ponce de León from the south-west corner of Plaza Vasco de Quiroga and following the signs. It makes a good destination for an early morning stroll.

Festivals

Las Pastorelas Processions in honour of the 'three wise men' take place on 6 January.

San Antonio del Abad Traditionally called The Blessing of the Animals, 17 January is the day people dress up their animals and bring them to the basilica.

Fiesta de la Candelaria In the village of Tócuaro, 10 km west of Pátzcuaro, this festival is celebrated on 2 February with a mass followed by music, traditional dances with devils in masks in which good and evil struggle together, a rodeo, and a village dance in the evening.

Procesión Tres Caídas On Good Friday the procession of Jesus bearing the cross to Calvary, and the crucifixion itself, is re-enacted in Pátzcuaro.

Procesión del Silencio The following day, on Sábado de Gloria (the day before Easter), Christ's death is mourned in a silent procession around Pátzcuaro, with candle-carrying mourners wearing hoods and long brown robes.

Día de los Muertos The Day of the Dead celebrations on the night of 1 November are held in veneration of the dead, from sunset until sunrise the following day, on the island of Janitzio in Lago Pátzcuaro. The candlelight procession, music and dances are world famous.

Similar candle-lit ceremonies take place in the graveyards of other local villages on that night, with villagers taking offerings of the dead ones' favourite foods to the graveyards of Tzintzuntzan, Ihuatzio, Jarácuaro and Erongarícuaro, but it's the ceremonies on Janitzio that have become famous and attract visitors.

Tiángüis Artesanal Artesanías from towns and villages all over Michoacán are brought to Pátzcuaro for this crafts fair held from 2 to 10 November in Plaza Vasco de Quiroga, with an abundant selection on display and for sale.

Nuestra Señora de la Salud Celebrations on 8 December honour the Virgin of Health with a colourful procession of Tarascan pilgrims and dancers. The traditional dances performed include Los Reboceros, Los Moros, Los Viejitos, Los Panaderos and Los Mojigangas.

Places to Stay – bottom end

Camping Pátzcuaro has two trailer parks on the road to the lake, and another nearby on the lakeshore itself.

The *Trailer Park El Pozo* (☎ (454) 2-09-37) is just off the Pátzcuaro-Morelia highway (No 120) across the train tracks on the lake. It has 20 sites with full hook-ups, hot showers and a dock. Watch carefully for the sign pointing across the tracks. Cost is US$10 for two in trailers or tents.

On the road to the lake, the *Hotel Villa Pátzcuaro* (read on) has a pleasant, well-maintained trailer park at the rear of the hotel. It's a small family park with eight trailer spaces with full hook-ups and a separate lawn area for tents. There's a small kitchen with a fireplace where campers congregate to cook and chat, and they can also use the hotel's tennis courts and swimming pool. Cost is US$5 for tents, US$6.70 to US$8.35 for vehicles, depending on their size.

Also on the road to the lake, the luxurious *Hotel Posada de Don Vasco* (read on) has a trailer park with 25 spaces with full hook-ups, plus spaces for tents. Guests here can use all the hotel's facilities (swimming pool, tennis, etc); cost is US$10 per space.

Hotels The *Hotel Valmen* (☎ (454) 2-11-61) at Lloreda 34, on the corner of Lloreda and Ahumada one block east of Plaza Gertrudis Bocanegra, is one of the best deals in Pátzcuaro despite having a rather fussy owner who posts signs saying (in Spanish) 'We beg you not to wash clothes' and 'Your silence helps the rest'. He locks the outside door at 10 pm and won't let you in after that (but there's not much to do in Pátzcuaro after 10 pm anyway). If this doesn't put you off, you'll probably enjoy the place; the 16 large, spotless rooms, all with private bath, steaming hot water, and large windows facing outside, are arranged around a lovely covered interior patio. The upstairs rooms have small balconies over the street. Singles/doubles are US$6.70/10.

On the west side of Plaza Gertrudis Bocanegra, the upstairs *Hotel Posada de la Rosa* (☎ (454) 2-08-11) at Portal Juárez 29 is another good choice. All the rooms open onto a central courtyard and have two beds; cost is US$5.35 per room with shared bath, US$6.70 with private bath. The communal baths are kept clean, there's a lavadero where you can wash clothes, and the management is friendly and accommodating.

Next door at Portal Juárez 31, the *Hotel de la Concordia* (☎ (454) 2-00-03) is not quite as good, but it too is cheap and has a variety of rooms.

The *Hotel Posada de la Salud* (☎ (454) 2-00-58) at Benigno Serrato 9, half a block behind the basilica, has 15 clean rooms with windows facing onto a grassy courtyard. Singles/doubles are US$10/12.85; two rooms have fireplaces but you have to buy your own wood.

Three long blocks west of the plazas, the *Hotel Posada La Terraza* (☎ (454) 2-10-27) at Benito Juárez 46 is a small family hotel with just eight rooms. They have an outdoor

area, an upstairs enclosed terrace with a bit of a view, and they offer breakfast if you like. Singles/doubles are US$10/12.70, and they also have a couple of larger rooms sleeping up to seven people for US$5.70 per person.

Places to Stay – middle
Several of the 17th-century mansions around Plaza Vasco de Quiroga have been refurbished into elegant colonial-style hotels, all with restaurants. Probably the most attractive is the *Hotel Los Escudos* (☎ (454) 2-01-38, 2-12-90) at Portal Hidalgo 73, on the west side of the plaza. All 30 rooms have colonial murals on the walls, carpeting, private bath and colour TV with parabolic antenna; some also have fireplaces. They're set around two lovely patios full of plants, and cost US$20/26.70 for singles/doubles. The hotel restaurant is highly recommended.

On the south side of Plaza Vasco de Quiroga, the *Hotel Misión San Manuel* (☎ (454) 2-13-13, 2-10-50) at Portal Aldama 12 is a former monastery which also has attractive rooms, all with fireplace, carpet, phone, painted tile bathrooms and beamed ceilings; singles/doubles are US$18.70/23.35. Nearby at Portal Aldama 18, the *Hotel Posada de San Rafael* (☎ (454) 2-07-70/79) has 104 more basic rooms, with carpeting but no fireplaces, at US$17.70/22.20.

On the north side of Plaza Vasco de Quiroga, the *Hotel Mansión Iturbe* (☎ (454) 2-03-68) at Portal Morelos 59 is a former mansion still retaining its colonial elegance; singles/doubles are US$25.35/28.50.

One block south of Plaza Vasco de Quiroga, the *Hotel Mesón del Gallo* (☎ (454) 2-14-74, 2-15-11), at Dr José Maria Coss 20, is a bit more modern and not quite as charming as the hotels on the plaza, but makes up for this by having a swimming pool, a pleasant lawn and garden area, plus two bars and a restaurant. The 20 singles/doubles are US$17.35/21.70; the five suites cost extra.

Away from the plaza, the *Posada de la Basílica* (☎ (454) 2-11-08), opposite the basilica at Arciga 6, is another elegant colonial mansion with plenty of character. Its 11 rooms are arranged around an open courtyard with plants, there are views over the red-tiled roofs of town; singles/doubles are US$18.35/23.35. The restaurant here has one of the best views in town.

The pleasant *Hotel Villa Pátzcuaro* (☎ (454) 2-07-57) at Calzada de las Américas 506 is set back from the road to the lake, about three km from the centre of town. The 12 cosy rooms all have fireplaces and parking spaces in front, like an US-style motel; singles/doubles are US$16.70/20. Tennis courts, a swimming pool, a trailer park and a large lawn area are in the rear. It's most convenient if you have a vehicle, but local buses marked 'Lago' pass by every five minutes or so for rides to the lake or to town.

Places to Stay – top end

The four-star *Hotel Posada de Don Vasco* (☎ (454) 2-02-27), about three km from the centre of town at Calzada de las Américas 450, is considered the best place in town; it's certainly the most expensive, with singles/doubles at US$53/62. It's part of the Best Western chain and has 102 luxurious rooms, plus tennis courts, swimming pool, games room, restaurant, bar, and so on.

Places to Eat

While you're in Pátzcuaro, try a couple of the town's typical foods. Most famous is the pescado blanco (whitefish), a small, tender fish caught on Lago Pátzcuaro by fishermen in canoes with large 'butterfly' nets *(las mariposas)*. Another specialty is the hearty Tarascan soup (sopa Tarasca).

All the colonial mansion hotels on Plaza Vasco de Quiroga have restaurant/bars. One of the most pleasant is the small restaurant at the *Hotel Los Escudos* on the west side of the plaza, with an attractive decor, plenty of hanging plants, and delicious food at moderate prices. It's open every day from 8 am to 9.30 pm. Also on Plaza Vasco de Quiroga, on the south side, the *Restaurant El Patio* at Portal Aldama 9 is another pleasant restaurant with moderate prices, open the same hours.

On the south side of Plaza Gertrudis Bocanegra, the restaurant at the *Gran Hotel* serves good food. The breakfasts are hearty,

and there's a filling comida corrida for US$5.35 served from 1.30 to 7.30 pm. It's open daily from 8 am to 8 pm.

For a marvellous view over town and the lake, try the restaurant at the *Posada de la Basílica*, opposite the basilica at Arciga 6. It's an attractive restaurant, with woven tablecloths and heavy ceramic plates typical of Michoacán.

One of the best places to try the fish fresh from the lake is beside the lakefront dock where the boats depart for Janitzio. A row of simple open-air restaurants all charge the same prices; you can choose your fish and they'll fry it up on the spot. Besides the famous pescado blanco there are also good-looking mojarra, trucha (trout) and charales (also called charalitos), a tiny fish, not quite as long as your finger, which is eaten whole.

On the way to the dock, between the railway station and the lake are several indoor restaurants serving the same selection of lake fish; look for the *Restaurant El Gordo, La Mansión del Lago* or the *Restaurant Las Redes*.

Near the museum in Pátzcuaro, at Calle Enseñanza 38, is a small shop called *Joaquinita Chocolate Supremo* run by an old woman who makes a very sweet homemade chocolate, good for making hot chocolate with milk. A big packet is US$3.35.

Entertainment

The area around Pátzcuaro has a number of traditional regional dances, complete with music, costumes and masks. To see most of them you have to be present at a festival when they're performed, but one of the most delightful dances, the Danza de los Viejitos (Dance of the Old Men), is presented twice weekly at the Hotel Posada de Don Vasco. The costumed dancers, wearing comical masks of grinning *viejitos* with long grey hair, hooked noses, rosy cheeks and no teeth, enter hobbling on skinny canes. Their dance gets more and more animated, with wooden sandals clacking on the tile floor, until finally they hobble off again, looking like they can barely make it to the door.

This dance is performed every Wednesday

and Saturday evening at 9 pm in the restaurant of the Hotel Posada de Don Vasco (☎ 2-02-27); you should reserve a table on the day of the performance, or one day before, if you plan to come for the dance. There's no charge for the performance, you only need have something to eat or drink. Music begins with a trio at 7 pm and the dance comes on at 9 pm, followed by a band of mariachis.

On the north side of Plaza Gertrudis Bocanegra, the Teatro Emperador Caltzontzin presents the usual fare of cinema in small-town Mexico, with grade F Kung Fu movies and the like; movies are screened from Saturday to Wednesday nights (none on Thursday and Friday). However, the theatre also hosts occasional cultural activities including performances of theatre, music and dance. Check for the current offerings. Another movie theatre, Cine Michoacán, is on Calle Iturbe between the two plazas.

Otherwise, there's not much to do around Pátzcuaro in the evening; the town seems to close up with a thud around 9.30 pm.

Getting There & Away
Bus Pátzcuaro's Central Camionera is on the outskirts of town, on the road called the Circunvalación, the Livramiento, or Avenida Ignacio Zaragoza. At the bus station are cafeterias, a guarda equipaje where you can store your luggage, a pharmacy, and a caseta de larga distancia.

Buses from Pátzcuaro include those to:

Erongarícuaro – 18 km, 30 minutes; every half-hour, 7 am to 8 pm, with Autobuses de Occidente (US$0.50).
Guadalajara – 347 km, six hours, US$6.35; two daily with Flecha Amarilla; one daily with Autobuses de Occidente; one daily with Tres Estrellas de Oro.
Lázaro Cárdenas – 342 km, seven hours; hourly, 6 am to 9 pm, with Galeana (US$6.85).
Mexico City – 377 km, seven hours (via Morelia and Toluca); hourly, 7.15 to 12.30 am, with Herradura de Plata (US$8.70); four daily with Flecha Amarilla (US$7.70 and US$8.70); two daily with Autobuses de Occidente (US$8.35).

Morelia – 62 km, one hour, US$1.35; buses every 15 minutes, 5.30 am to 9 pm, with Galeana; every half-hour, 7 am to 12.30 am, with Herradura de Plata; hourly, 4 am to 11.30 pm, with Flecha Amarilla; six daily with Autobuses de Occidente.
Quiroga – 22 km, 30 minutes; every 15 minutes, 5.50 am to 8.45 pm, with Galeana (US$0.70).
Santa Clara del Cobre – 18 km, 30 minutes; every half-hour, 5.45 am to 8.45 pm, with Galeana (US$0.70).
Tzintzuntzan – 15 km, 20 minutes; same bus as to Quiroga (US$0.50).
Uruapan – 62 km, one hour; buses every 15 minutes, 6 am to 9 pm, with Galeana (US$1.20).
Zirahuén – 20 km, 30 minutes; three buses daily, with Galeana (US$0.70).

Train The Estación del Ferrocarril (☎ 2-08-03) is near the lake, at the end of Avenida de las Américas. Trains departing from Pátzcuaro include:

Mexico City
    9 am – 2nd class, US$3.65 (12 hours)
    9 pm – 1st-class cars US$13.20, 2nd-class cars US$3.65 (10 hours)
Morelia
    same trains as to Mexico City; 1st-class cars US$1, 2nd class cars US$0.50 (1¼ hours)
Uruapan
    6.45 am – 1st-class cars US$1.30, 2nd-class cars US$0.65 (2¼ hours)
    6.45 pm – 2nd-class cars US$0.65 (two hours)
Lázaro Cárdenas
    6.45 am – 1st-class cars US$11.10, 2nd-class cars US$3 (eight hours)

Getting Around
Two useful local bus routes, served by buses and smaller Volkswagen combis, operate every day from around 6 am to 10 pm; cost is US$0.25. 'Lago' buses depart from the north-eastern corner of Plaza Gertrudis Bocanegra; they go along Avenida de las Américas to the lake, passing by the train station on their way to the docks where boats depart for Janitzio. 'Central' buses heading for the Central Camionera depart from the west side of Plaza Gertrudis Bocanegra, in front of the mercado. Both routes operate very frequently, with combis every five minutes or so.

Taxis charge around US$1.70 to go from

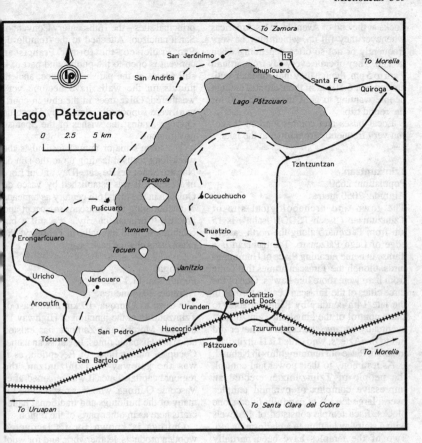

Lago Pátzcuaro

0   2.5   5 km

To Zamora

San Jerónimo

15

To Morelia

Chupícuaro

Santa Fe

San Andrés

Quiroga

Lago Pátzcuaro

Tzintzuntzan

Pacanda

Cucuchucho

Puácuaro

Ihuatzio

Yunuen

Erongarícuaro

Tecuen

Janitzio

Uricho

Jarácuaro

Janitzio
Boat Dock

Arocutín

Uranden

San Pedro

Huecorio

Tzurumutaro

Tócuaro

Pátzcuaro

To Morelia

San Bartolo

To Uruapan

To Santa Clara del Cobre

town to the bus or train stations. Once you're in town, everything is within walking distance.

AROUND PÁTZCUARO
Isla de Janitzio

Although many tourists visit the island of Janitzio, the largest in the lake, both the boat ride from Pátzcuaro's docks and a two-hour stroll around the island are worthwhile. The 20-minute boat trip offers views of the other towns along the shore and often boatside demonstrations of Tarascan fishermen's famous butterfly-shaped fishing nets. The

pescado blanco (whitefish) they catch is considered the regional speciality.

A popular tourist haunt, the island has an abundance of souvenir shops, fish restaurants, and a huge 40-metre statue of Morelos on the highest point. Inside the statue are a set of murals depicting Morelos' life; you can climb up inside the statue all the way to the giant's raised fist, from where there's a breezy lookout. It's worth making the climb to the top for the terrific view of the lake and all the towns around it. Admission to the statue is US$0.35.

Launches to Janitzio depart from the

docks at the end of Avenida de las Américas whenever they fill up, which may be very frequently or not so often depending when you go. They operate every day from around 7 am to 5 pm, though they may run later, until around 6 or 6.30 pm, if there are still enough people wanting to go. Cost is US$1.80 for the round trip.

Local buses and combis marked 'Lago' run very frequently from town to the lake.

Tzintzuntzan

Population: 2650
Altitude: 2050 metres

The town and archaeological site of Tzintzuntzan ('tseen-TSOON-tsahn') is 15 km from Pátzcuaro along the north-eastern edge of Lago Pátzcuaro. Tzintzuntzan is a Tarascan name meaning Place of Hummingbirds, though the Tarascan armies that came from here were more like hawks. One of the three cities of the Tarascan League formed in the late 14th century by King Tariácuri to share control of the kingdom, Tzintzuntzan eventually became the capital. It never did fall to the Aztecs, who called it Huitzitzilán, meaning Place of Hummingbirds in Nahuatl.

As testimony to their power and control, the people of Tzintzuntzan erected an impressive complex of pyramid temples over a large terrace of carefully fitted stone blocks. Each temple consisted of 12 levels with a stairway leading to a platform on top. Two of the temples have been partially restored; you can see them up on the hill, on the side of town away from the lake. The archaeological site, Las Yácatas, is open every day from 9 am to 6 pm; admission is US$2.70.

Vasco de Quiroga established his first base as the Bishop of Michoacán here in the Tarascan capital in 1538 at the Iglesia de Santa Ana, now in ruins. After he moved the seat to Pátzcuaro in 1540, Tzintzuntzan declined in importance.

Today in Tzintzuntzan, craftspeople display handpainted ceramics and straw figurines (the town's specialities) on Calle Principal, not far from another of the town's principal sites – the 16th-century Convent of San Francisco. Attached to the Templo de San Francisco, the former Franciscan convent is open to the public, and part of it still serves as the parish residence; ancient murals on the walls have become very weathered. Olive trees in the church courtyard were supposedly planted by Vasco de Quiroga against the wishes of the Spanish government.

The town's major annual festival is the week-long festival leading up to the Día de Nuestro Señor del Rescate (Day of Our Lord of Rescue). It was established by Vasco de Quiroga in the mid-16th century as a means of encouraging the Tarascans to accept and practise 'Christian charity'. It's still a big celebration, held annually in February; the exact dates change each year.

Quiroga

Population: 11,770
Altitude: 2074 metres

The town of Quiroga, 10 km north-east of Tzintzuntzan at the junction of Highway 15 between Morelia and Zamora, has existed since pre-Hispanic times. Its Tarascan name, Cocupao, meant Place of Reception, as it was the gateway to Tzintzuntzan, the regional capital. Later it was renamed after Vasco de Quiroga, who was responsible for many of the buildings and traditional handcrafts here as in other parts of the region.

Quiroga is known for its lacquered wooden products, leatherwork, and for wool sweaters and serapes. These and many other artesanías from around Michoacán are displayed and sold in the town.

On the first Sunday in July, the Fiesta de la Preciosa Sangre de Cristo (Festival of the Precious Blood of Christ) is celebrated with a long torchlight procession, led by a group carrying an image of Christ crafted from a paste of corn cobs and honey.

Erongarícuaro

Population: 2500

On the south-west edge of Lago Pátzcuaro, 16 km from Pátzcuaro, Erongarícuaro is one of the oldest settlements on the shores of the lake. It's not a big tourist destination; about all there is to see is the plaza, the church a block away, and the old seminary attached to the church. But it's a lovely, peaceful town where you can enjoy strolling through the streets still lined with old Spanish-style houses. Because the town's name is rather a mouthful, it's often called 'Eronga' for short.

On 6 January, the Fiesta de los Reyes Magos (Festival of the Three Kings) is celebrated with music, dances and much festivity.

Santa Clara del Cobre

Population: 9850

Santa Clara del Cobre, 18 km south of Pátzcuaro, was a copper-mining centre from about 1553 onwards. Though the mines no longer operate, the town still specialises in copper artisanship, with over 50 workshops where a variety of copper goods are made.

The Feria del Cobre (Copper Fair) is held for one week in August; the exact dates change each year.

Zirahuén

Population: 2200

Smaller than Lago Pátzcuaro, the blue lake beside the small colonial town of Zirahuén, 20 km from Pátzcuaro off the road to Uruapan, makes a peaceful spot for a day trip or for camping. Buses make the half-hour trip between Pátzcuaro and Zirahuén, but only a few times daily; alternatively, you could take a bus heading for Uruapan, get off at the Zirahuén turnoff and hitch the rest of the way.

Tingambato

Population: 5400

At Tingambato, a small village on the highway between Pátzcuaro and Uruapan, are the ruins of a pre-Hispanic pyramid. The only evidence you see from the road is a blue sign with a white pyramid and an arrow; follow the arrow and you come to the pyramid and ruins, about one km from the highway.

URUAPAN

Population: 187,650

Altitude: 1650 metres

When the Spanish monk Fray Juan de San Miguel arrived in 1533, he was so impressed with the Río Cupatitzio and lush vegetation surrounding it that he named the area Uruapan ('oo-roo-AH-pahn'), which translates roughly from Tarascan, the local Indian language, as Fruit and Flowers or Eternal Spring.

Juan de San Miguel laid the foundations of the town by having a large market square, hospital and chapel built and arranging the streets in an orderly chequerboard pattern. As the Spanish encomienda system, a feudal system of land grants to Spanish soldiers and serfdom for the Indians, spread in the surrounding countryside, Uruapan rapidly developed as a major agricultural centre.

Today, its continual water supply and temperate climate have maintained Uruapan's status as one of Mexico's most productive agricultural areas, renowned for its high-quality avocados and fruit. In addition, Uruapan's craftspeople are famed for their beautiful hand-painted cedar lacquerware, particularly trays and boxes.

Orientation

Uruapan is 320 km south-east of Guadalajara, 125 km south-west of Morelia, 62 km south-west of Pátzcuaro and 280 km north of Lázaro Cárdenas. It is situated in the highlands near the Volcano of Paricutín and at the junction of Highways 14 from Morelia and 37 from Lázaro Cárdenas.

The city lies on the east bank of the Río Cupatitzio, with most of the streets still arranged in the chequerboard pattern laid down by Fray Juan de San Miguel in the 1530s. Aside from the train and bus stations, everything of interest to travellers is within walking distance of the zócalo, which is actually three connected plazas making a long, narrow rectangle with the long way running east-west. Two colonial churches stand on the north side of the plaza at either end.

As with many cities in Mexico, watch

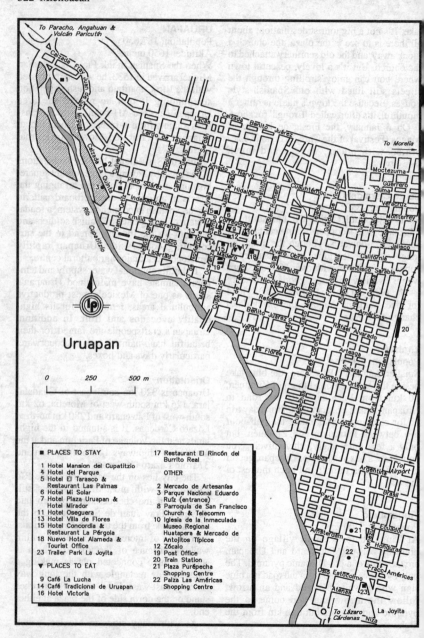

To Paracho, Angahuan &
Volcán Paricutín

To Morelia

Uruapan

0   250   500 m

PLACES TO STAY
1 Hotel Mansion del Cupatitzio
4 Hotel del Parque
5 Hotel El Tarasco &
  Restaurant Las Palmas
6 Hotel Mi Solar
7 Hotel Plaza Uruapan &
  Hotel Mirador
11 Hotel Oseguera
13 Hotel Villa de Flores
15 Hotel Concordia &
   Restaurant La Pérgola
18 Nuevo Hotel Alameda &
   Tourist Office
23 Trailer Park La Joyita

PLACES TO EAT
9 Café La Lucha
14 Café Tradicional de Uruapan
16 Hotel Victoria

17 Restaurant El Rincón del
   Burrito Real

OTHER
2 Mercado de Artesanías
3 Parque Nacional Eduardo
  Ruiz (entrance)
8 Parroquia de San Francisco
  Church & Telecomm
10 Iglesia de la Inmaculada
   Museo Regional
   Huatapera & Mercado de
   Antojitos Típicos
12 Zócalo
19 Post Office
20 Train Station
21 Plaza Purépecha
   Shopping Centre
22 Palza Las Américas
   Shopping Centre

To Lázaro
Cárdenas

To
Airport

La Joyita

street names because they often change every few blocks. In Uruapan, Álvaro Obregón is a dividing line with the names of intersecting streets different on each side of it. Obregón itself also changes to Emilio Carranza as it runs north-west and to Francisco Sarabia in the opposite direction. Unfortunately, no one is absolutely certain at which points the streets parallel to Obregón change names.

Paseo General Lázaro Cárdenas, one of the major streets in town, runs south-west towards the coast and north-east to intersect the highway to Morelia and the volcano of Paricutín.

Information

Tourist Office The Delegación de Turismo (☎ (542) 4-06-33) is at Calle 5 de Febrero 23, Interior 204, half a block south of the east end of the zócalo. The staff give out a good free map of Uruapan, brochures about Michoacán in English and Spanish, and are helpful with questions. It's open Monday to Saturday, 9 am to 2 pm and 4 to 7 pm.

Money There are a number of banks near the zócalo. Bánamex is one block south of the zócalo at the corner of Morelos and Cupatitzio. Banca Serfín is nearby at Cupatitzio 13; Banco Internacional is at Cupatitzio 23. Bancomer is at the corner of Emilio Carranza and 20 de Noviembre. Comermex Lázaro Cárdenas is at Juan Ayala and Independencia.

All of these banks are open Monday to Friday, 9 am to 2 pm, except Bánamex which is also open for an afternoon shift from 4 to 6 pm. If you need to change money outside these hours, try the Casa de Cambio Janitzio, on the south side of the plaza. It's open Monday to Friday from 9 am to 2 pm and 4 to 8 pm, Saturday 9 am to 2 pm; its rates are only slightly lower than the banks and it changes both travellers' cheques and cash.

Post The post office is at Calle Cupatitzio 36, 1½ blocks south of the zócalo. It's open Monday to Friday from 8 am to 7 pm, Saturday 9 am to 1 pm. Another post office branch is in the bus station.

Telecommunications The Telecomm office on Ocampo, half a block north of the west end of the zócalo, offers telegraph, telex, telegram and fax services. It's open Monday to Friday from 9 am to 8 pm, Saturday from 9 am to noon, closed Sunday.

Local and long-distance telephone calls may be made from the caseta de larga distancia at the Restaurant Las Palmas, one block north of the western end of the zócalo; it's open every day from 8 am to 10 pm. Another caseta is half a block south of the east end of the zócalo, at the Medicina Natural shop at Calle 5 de Febrero 4-B, opposite the Nuevo Hotel Alameda; it's open every day from 10 am to 2 pm and 4 to 8.30 pm.

The central bus station also has a caseta de larga distancia and a telegraph office.

Museo Regional Huatapera

For an interesting overview of Michoacán and Tarascan crafts, visit the Museo Regional Huatapera (also known as the Museo de la Huatapera), attached to the church on the north-east corner of the plaza. The building, erected by Fray Juan de San Miguel in 1533, was the first hospital in the Americas. The museum is open Tuesday to Sunday, 9.30 am to 1.30 pm and 3.30 to 6 pm (closed Monday); admission is free.

Parque Nacional Eduardo Ruíz

This national park contains the headwaters of the Río Cupatitzio, gushing forth out of the ground at a number of different springs. The river and springs keep the surrounding tropical vegetation lush, which makes for cool picnic grounds or a pleasant afternoon stroll on one of the several paths.

The park's main entrance is on Calzada Fray Juan de San Miguel (also called Calzada La Quinta) at the end of Calle Independencia; from the zócalo, walk seven blocks west on Independencia and you run right into it. The park is open every day from 8 am to 6 pm. Admission is US$0.35; for another US$0.20 you can get a map of the park showing all the springs, the pathways, and the well-known mural fountain (the Mural Mapeco).

Festivals

Domingo de Ramos Palm Sunday is celebrated with a procession through the city streets. Figures and crosses woven from palm fronds are sold after the procession. There's also a ceramics contest, with ceramics and other handcrafts (artesanías) typical of many of Michoacán's villages filling up the zócalo.

Semana Santa The exhibit of artesanías continues all through Holy Week, with the zócalo and two churchyards brimming with all manner of typical handcrafts for sale. Prices get lower as the week goes on.

San Juan Apóstol The Festival of Saint John the Apostle venerates the saint on 24 June with traditional dances and musical performances, fireworks and parades.

María Magdalena The Festival of Saint Mary Magdalene is celebrated on 22 July with a procession of decorated mule and oxen teams and traditional dances on the atrium of the church.

San Francisco Saint Francis, the patron saint of Uruapan, is honoured on 4 October with colourful festivities and the Canácuas dance by Tarascan women.

Día de la Raza Otherwise known as Columbus Day, 12 October is the day that Christopher Columbus 'discovered' the New World.

Festival de Coros y Danzas The Choir & Dance Festival is a contest of Tarascan dance and musical groups that lasts for three days around 24 October and offers a good opportunity to see and hear a variety of traditional Tarascan dances and music.

Feria del Aguacate The Avocado Fair, held

for two weeks in November, features expositions of agriculture, artesanías and industry. Exact dates vary; check with the tourist office.

Places to Stay – bottom end

Camping The *Trailer Park La Joyita* (☎ (542) 3-03-64) is at Estocolmo 22, 1½ blocks east of Paseo General Lázaro Cárdenas at the southern end of town. It's a small park with full hook-ups for 10 trailers, a lawn area for tents, a BBQ and 24-hour hot water in the showers. The owner keeps an eye on the place for security, locking the front gate at 10 pm (but he'll let you in if you stay out later). Cost for two people is US$8.35. Local buses marked 'FO-VISSSTE' operate frequently between here and the zócalo.

Another option for camping around Uruapan is the camping ground at Angahuan, the village beside the Volcán Paricutín (see Around Uruapan).

Hotels Of Uruapan's cheapies, the *Hotel del Parque* (☎ (542) 4-38-45) at Independencia 124, 6½ blocks west of the zócalo and half a block from the entrance to the national park, is not only one of the cheapest but also one of the most pleasant. Singles/doubles are US$5.70/7.35 in clean rooms with yellow or blue tile floors, private bath and 24-hour hot water. There's also an interior garden, a place where you can wash clothes, and enclosed parking.

Hotel Villa de Flores (☎ (542) 4-28-00) at Emilio Carranza 22, 1½ blocks west of the zócalo, is a well-kept colonial-style hotel with clean, comfortable rooms with private bath opening onto a pleasant interior courtyard with plants. Singles/doubles are US$10.70/13.35. The hotel's restaurant is open daily from 7 am to 10 pm.

Uruapan has several other cheap hotels which are old and rather worn, though they're kept clean enough. Try them if the first two places are full.

On the south-east corner of the zócalo, at the corner of Obregón and Degollado, the *Hotel Oseguera* (☎ (542) 3-98-56) has 29 rooms, all with private bath, 24-hour hot water, and windows facing outside. Singles/doubles are US$10/11.70.

The *Hotel Mirador* (☎ (542) 4-04-73) at Ocampo 9 is a large, 47-room hotel facing onto the west side of the zócalo; its rooms are dark but clean, all with private bath, some with tub, and many with windows opening onto the zócalo. Singles/doubles are US$6.35/8.35.

Under the same management, a block north of the zócalo, the *Hotel Mi Solar* (☎ (542) 4-09-12) at Juan Delgado 10 is a similar place, though smaller, with 20 rooms opening onto an interior courtyard. It's in slightly better shape than the Mirador and has the same prices.

Places to Stay – middle

Uruapan has many attractive and convenient places to stay in the middle range. Right on the zócalo, on the south side, the *Hotel Concordia* (☎ (542) 3-04-00, 3-05-00) at Portal Carrillo 8 is a modern and luxurious hotel with 63 large, spotless rooms, all with colour TV, phone, carpeting, and plenty of windows. It also has parking, a restaurant/bar, and a laundry. Cost is US$17.35/21.70 for singles/doubles.

Half a block south of the zócalo, the *Nuevo Hotel Alameda* (☎ (542) 3-41-00) at Calle 5 de Febrero 11 is another good middle-range hotel, similar to the Concordia; rates here are US$16.70/20.

The *Hotel El Tarasco* (☎ /fax (542) 4-15-00), half a block north of the zócalo at Independencia 2, is a step up in luxury, with 65 large, bright and attractive rooms with all the same features, plus a large swimming pool. Singles/doubles are US$26.35/32.70.

The four-star *Hotel Plaza Uruapan* (☎ (542) 3-35-99, 3-03-33, fax 3-39-80) at Ocampo 64 faces onto the west side of the zócalo. It's quite luxurious, with extra large, elegant rooms with floor-to-ceiling windows opening onto small balconies. Singles/doubles are US$28/35.

If you're driving a vehicle, you might like the *Motel Pie de la Sierra* (☎ /fax (542) 4-25-10), on Highway 37 four km north of

town, at Km 4, Carretera Uruapan-Carapan (the highway to Paracho). At the foot of the mountains, just as the name says, it has large, well-kept, landscaped grounds, a swimming pool, games room, a pleasant restaurant/bar, and 72 attractive rooms with fireplace, colour TV, private terraces and good mountain views. Rates are US$23.50/29.50 for singles/doubles. It's great if you have your own vehicle, but a bit inconvenient otherwise, as the local buses don't come this far out of town; a taxi to town costs about US$2.50.

Places to Stay – top end

The hacienda-style *Hotel Mansion del Cupatitzio* (☎ (542) 3-21-00, 3-20-60), at the north end of the Parque Nacional Eduardo Ruíz on Calzada Fray Juan de San Miguel, is considered one of the best hotels in Uruapan. Its restaurant has a fine view over the Rodilla del Diablo, where the Río Cupatitzio begins. There's a large swimming pool and grounds, laundry, etc; singles/doubles are US$45/56 in standard rooms, US$61/67 in junior suites.

Places to Eat

The *Mercado de Antojitos Típicos*, one short block north of the zócalo, is a good place to sample the regional dishes of Michoacán, with about 40 food stalls under a large awning serving up traditional dishes every day from around 6 am to midnight. Prices are cheap and the stalls are popular with local families.

On the south side of the zócalo, *El Rincón del Burrito Real* at Matamoros 7 has some of the best food in Uruapan. Try the Sopa Tarasca, a local Indian speciality, a hearty, spicy soup with crispy tortilla strips, cheese, sour cream and avocado pieces sticking out all over it; a large bowl for US$2.50 makes a filling meal. The comida corrida, served from 1 to 6 pm, is a good deal at US$4.85, and the salads here are safe to eat. It's open every day from 8 am to 11 pm.

Behind the church on the north-west side of the zócalo, *Restaurant Las Palmas* at Donato Guerra 2 is a good, basic, cheap restaurant; you can get a meal here for around US$3.35 and watch the world go by. It's open every day from 8 am to 10 pm.

Uruapan also has a couple of excellent cafés for enjoying good, strong coffee. One is *La Lucha*, half a block north of the zócalo on Calle García Ortíz, one of the small streets heading north out of the zócalo between the two churches. It's open every day from 9 am to 2 pm and 4 to 9 pm.

Another good café is the *Café Tradicional de Uruapan*, at Calle Emiliano Carranza 5-B, half a block west of the zócalo. It's a more expensive place, in the Spanish style with heavy carved Spanish furniture, but famous for its coffees, with a large selection to choose from. It's open daily from 8.30 am to 2 pm and 4 to 10 pm, Sunday from 9 am to 2 pm and 4.30 to 10 pm. They also serve breakfasts and desserts.

Also done up in the heavy Spanish style, the *Restaurant La Pérgola* at Portal Carrillo 4 on the south side of the zócalo is a popular and attractive restaurant. It's not cheap; the comida corrida costs around US$7.70, but it may include selections like filet mignon. It's open every day from 8 am to 11.30 pm.

If you're in Uruapan on a Sunday afternoon and can stand a splurge, try the Sunday buffets at either the *Hotel Plaza Uruapan* facing onto the west side of the zócalo or the *Hotel Victoria* half a block south of the zócalo at Cupatitzio 11. The Sunday buffets at both of these four-star hotels are something special, with an enormous spread of delectable foods accompanied by a pianist in the corner. The buffet at the Victoria is served from 2 to 5.30 pm and costs US$11.70; at the Plaza it's served from 1 to 6 pm and costs US$13.35 (children half price at both places).

Entertainment
Uruapan is not exactly New York City for nightlife, but besides lingering over coffee at a good café or going to church there are a couple of other things you can do in the evening.

Stop by the office of Promociones Culturales (☎ 3-17-00) in the Presidencia Municipal to ask about their free events. There's one entrance roughly opposite the La Lucha Café on Calle García Ortíz, a small street heading north from the zócalo between the two churches, and a separate theatre entrance on the tiny plaza behind the Church of San Francisco. On our last visit they were presenting international films on Wednesday and Friday evenings, classical guitar concerts on Thursday evenings and Latin American music concerts on Saturday evenings – all at no cost. The schedule varies so stop in during the day and check it out.

On the west side of the zócalo, the Hotel Plaza Uruapan has a bar, a disco, and live entertainment on weekends. Several of the other better-class hotels near the zócalo also have bars. Or there are a few cinemas in town.

Things to Buy
Various local specialities such as lacquered trays and boxes can be bought at the Mercado de Artesanías, on Calzada Fray Juan de San Miguel opposite the entrance to the Parque Nacional Eduardo Ruíz.

Getting There & Away
Air Uruapan's airport, about eight km south of the centre of town on the highway to Lázaro Cárdenas, is served by two local airlines. Aeromar (☎ 3-50-50) has one daily flight to Mexico City, for US$104. Aero Sudpacífico (☎ 4-53-55) has one daily flight to Guadalajara for US$66, and two daily flights to Lázaro Cárdenas for US$50.

Bus The Central Camionera is about three km from central Uruapan on the highway to Morelia. It has a post office, a telegraph office, a long-distance telephone office, cafeterias, a pharmacy and other shops.

Local buses between the bus station and the zócalo are marked 'Central Camionera' (or, more likely, 'Central' for short) and 'Centro'. You can catch them on the south side of the zócalo, and at the door of the bus station.

Buses from Uruapan include those to:

Angahuan (for Volcano Paricutín) – 33 km, one hour; hourly, 5.50 am to 6 pm, with Galeana (US$1). (Take bus heading for Los Reyes and get off at Angahuan.)

Guadalajara – 325 km, five hours; 11 daily with Autobuses de Occidente (US$6); nine daily with Servicios Coordinados (US$5.90); six daily with ETN (US$12.70); four daily with Flecha Amarilla (US$6); one daily with Galeana (US$6).

Lázaro Cárdenas – 280 km, six hours; hourly, 24 hours, with Galeana (US$6); three daily with Tres Estrellas de Oro (US$6.20); one daily with Autobuses de Occidente (US$6).

Mexico City – 440 km, six hours; nine buses daily with Autobuses de Occidente (US$10); six daily with ETN (US$21.70); five daily with Servicios Coordinados (US$14); four daily with Flecha Amarilla (US$14); four daily with Tres Estrellas de Oro (US$9.70).

Morelia – 125 km, two hours; direct buses every 15 minutes, 5.50 am to 9 pm, then every half-hour from 9 pm to midnight, with Galeana (US$2.50); 1st-class buses hourly, 6.40 am to 9 pm, also with Galeana (US$2.85); 12 daily, 5.30 am to 8.15 pm, with Parhikuni (US$2.85).

Paracho – 40 km, 40 minutes; every 40 minutes, 6.45 am to 10.30 pm, with Servicios Coordinados (US$0.70).

Pátzcuaro – 62 km, one hour; buses every 20 minutes, 6 am to 8 pm, with Galeana (US$1.20).

Zamora – 115 km, 2½ hours; every hal- hour, 5 am to 7.30 pm, with Autobuses de Occidente (US$2); nine daily with Servicios Coordinados (US$2.35).

Train The Estación del Ferrocarril (☎ 3-13-67, 3-18-19) is on Paseo Gral Lázaro Cárdenas at the east end of Calle Américas. Local buses marked 'Américas' go down Calle Américas between the train station and the zócalo. Heading from the centre of town to the train station you can catch this bus on Calle Cupatitzio, one block south of the zócalo, at the stop in front of the post office. Trains departing from Uruapan include:

Lázaro Cárdenas
10 am – 1st-class cars US$8.85, 2nd-class cars US$2.50 (six hours)

Mexico City
6.35 am – 2nd class, US$4.35 (14½ hours)
7.15 pm – *Purépecha* train – 1st-class cars US$15.50, 2nd-class cars US$4.35 (12¾ hours)

Morelia
6.35 am – 2nd class (four hours)
7.15 pm – *Purépecha* train – 1st & 2nd-class cars (3¾ hours)

Pátzcuaro
6.35 am – 2nd class (2¼ hours)
7.15 pm – *Purépecha* train – 1st & 2nd-class cars (2¼ hours)

Toluca
6.35 am – 2nd class (11½ hours)
7.15 pm – *Purépecha* train – 1st & 2nd-class cars (10¼ hours)

Getting Around

Most everything of interest to travellers is within walking distance of the zócalo, except the train and bus stations, which are served by local bus routes. The local buses run every day from around 6 am to 9 pm; cost is US$0.20.

Taxis are plentiful in Uruapan; from the bus station into town, or from town to the airport, costs around US$2.

AROUND URUAPAN
Tzaráracua Waterfalls

About 10 km south of Uruapan just off Highway 37, the Río Cupatitzio cascades over a 20-metre cliff into a couple of pools and, two km farther upstream, over a smaller cliff. These beautiful waterfalls are called Tzaráracua and Tzaráracuita and can be reached by foot or horse (US$2.75 round trip for both falls). 'Tzaráracua' buses depart frequently from the zócalo.

Paracho

Population: 14350

Paracho is 40 km north of Uruapan on Highway 37. This small town is world-renowned for its handmade guitars and is worth visiting to watch some of the world's best guitar-makers at work. They are also known for their high-quality violins, cellos, and many other woodcrafts, including furniture. If you're in the market to buy an instrument, this is the place to come; there are many shops to choose from.

Angahuan & Volcán Paricutín

Population: 3000

The story of Volcán Paricutín is the stuff that legends are made of – and it really happened, not so long ago.

On 20 February 1943, a farmer was ploughing his cornfield near the village of Paricutín, about 35 km from Uruapan, when at about 3 pm the ground in the field began moving and heating. Within hours it was spewing rocks, fire and smoke. The farmer tried at first to cover the moving earth, but when that proved impossible, it seemed best to keep a distance. Later on, a volcano started to rise from the spot. The Indians from the nearby villages of San Salvador Paricutín and San Juan Parangaricutiro moved away, as lava from the volcano engulfed and buried both villages.

The volcano continued to spew lava and fire for several years until one day, on 5 March 1954, it stopped as suddenly as it had begun. Since that day the volcano has never been heard from again, and its large, black cone stands mute on the landscape, surrounded by about 20 square km of hardened

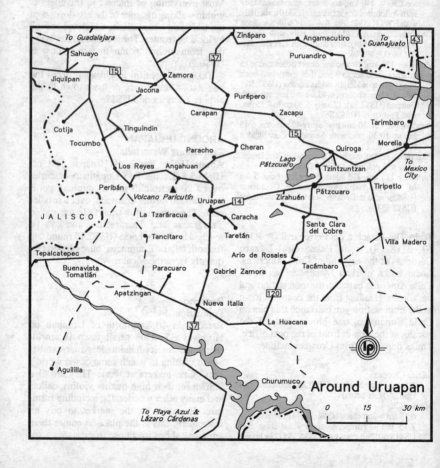

Around Uruapan

0   15   30 km

lava rock. The only trace of the villages buried beneath the lava flow is the top of San Juan's church; the highest point in the village, its spires protrude eerily above the lava.

An excursion to the volcano from Uruapan makes a memorable day trip. Get started early in the day, as you'll want plenty of time to explore the area around the volcano; stock up on snacks and water before leaving Uruapan.

From the Central Camionera in Uruapan, take a bus heading for Los Reyes and get off at the village of Angahuan, about an hour's ride from Uruapan.

There are a couple of options for visiting the volcano. If you want to go all the way to the crater, you'll probably want to go on horseback; three hours up and another three hours back down. Or you can make a shorter trip by going over the lava fields to the church spires of San Juan, looming up out of the lava. From Angahuan to the church takes about 1½ to two hours on horseback, or about three hours if you walk. Or you can walk up to El Mirador, a high spot about an hour's walk from Angahuan, with a good view of the volcano, the lava flow, and the church spires.

Arranging a guide in Angahuan for visiting the volcano is no problem because the villagers are accustomed to taking visitors to the volcano – for a price, of course. In fact you may be besieged by guides as soon as you alight from the bus. Going with a guide on horseback all the way to the crater costs around US$15 per person; going by horseback to the church costs around US$10 per person. Or there are guides who will take you hiking to the church over the lava, for around the same price of US$10.

Most visitors probably go by horseback but one traveller, Howard Scotland III, wrote us a glowing letter of a six-hour trek over the lava to the church and back:

... If one is in good physical shape, this has to be the way to see Paricutín. The horses are fine for an easy trip but you won't get the same experience of walking the distance through the twisted and broken lava flow.

Our guide's name was Francisco and he is easily recognisable by his having but one eye. His trek includes a stop in the village and all the history you care to ask about, a bit of Spanish going a very long way (the best slow conversational Spanish class I've ever attended). If Lonely Planet cites names, his is worth a mention as we couldn't have gotten a better tour or guide for the day.

When we went, we went on horseback and liked it just fine!

Other things to see in Angahuan include the Iglesia de Santiago Apostol, a small 16th-century church. Around to the right of the church, a couple of doors back from the plaza, there's an interesting wooden door carved with the history of Volcán Paricutín.

Festival days in Angahuan are the Fiesta de San Isidro Labrador on 15 May, with a weaving contest, and the Fiesta de Santiago Apostol on 25 July, with artesanías displays, music, contests and games.

Unless you plan to spend the night in Angahuan, be sure to find out what time the last bus passes through town for the return trip back to Uruapan; it's usually around 6 or 7 pm.

If you do want to stay in Angahuan, the *Centro Turístico de Angahuan* has cabañas (cabins) sleeping up to six people, each with a living room and fireplace, plus a trailer park with spaces for trailers and tents, and a restaurant with regional food. Or you can find the guide Francisco Lázaro, who our reader recommended, and stay at his house – his family rents rooms to visitors at US$5 for two, with meals costing extra if you want to eat with the family.

ZAMORA

Population: 109,750

Zamora, on Highway 15 about 150 km north-west of Morelia and 200 km south-east of Guadalajara, is the centre for a rich agricultural region. It's not much of a tourist destination, but you may pass through it if you're travelling between Michoacán and Jalisco. It's a pleasant town to stroll around in, with a curious unfinished Gothic cathedral. If you need to spend the night, Zamora has several hotels to choose from. The bus station is on the outskirts of town.

Zamora takes its name from the Spanish town of the same name. It was founded here in the Valle de Tziróndaro (whose name means Place of Marshes), on the banks of the Río Duero, in 1574.

LÁZARO CÁRDENAS

Population: 53,600

Lázaro Cárdenas is the largest city on the Michoacán coast. It's named after the reform-minded leader who served as governor of Michoacán from 1928 to 1932 and as president of Mexico from 1934 to 1940. In the late 1960s he encouraged then-President Díaz Ordaz to begin constructing a huge US$500 million Sicartsa iron and steel works and US$40 million port in the village of Melchor Ocampo. The project didn't get under way until after his death in 1970 and during the administration of President Luis Echeverría (1970-76).

Echeverría renamed the village Lázaro Cárdenas and erected what became a slum city around the project, which by this time was slated to cost over US$1 billion. The resulting plant produced steel wire, which Mexico really didn't need, and was run with coal imported from Colombia. The plant cost much more than it could ever earn and greatly contributed to the 450% increase in Mexico's foreign debt, which was more than US$19 billion by 1976.

Today the plant continues to run, supposedly with injections of British capital, but more emphasis seems to have been placed on the city's burgeoning port facilities. While not as much of an eyesore as it was in the past, the city has nothing of real interest to travellers. Reasons to stop here are to stock up on food and water, change buses, and head for Playa Azul, a beach resort 24 km to the west.

Getting There & Away

Bus While the town itself is not of much interest to travellers, Lázaro Cárdenas is a terminus for several bus routes, so you may

need to change buses here if you're travelling in this part of the country.

Lázaro has two bus terminals, two blocks from one another. The Galeana and Tres Estrellas de Oro bus lines (☎ 2-02-62), with services north to Manzanillo and inland to Uruapan and Morelia, share a terminal at Avenida Lázaro Cárdenas 1810, on the corner of Calle Constitución de 1814. Avenida Lázaro Cárdenas is the city's 'main drag' and there are many hotels, restaurants, shops, etc around the bus station.

The Flecha Roja, Estrella Blanca and Cuauhtémoc bus lines (☎ 2-11-71) have buses south to Zihuatanejo, Acapulco, and then inland from Acapulco to Mexico City. They share a separate terminal two blocks behind the Galeana terminal, at Calle Francisco Villa 164, half a block from Calle Constitución de 1814 (walk two blocks on Calle Constitución de 1814 to get from one terminal to the other).

Buses from Lázaro Cárdenas include:

Acapulco – 311 km, six hours; buses every half-hour, 2.30 am to midnight, from Flecha Roja terminal (US$7.35).

Manzanillo – 330 km, six hours; three daily, from Galeana terminal (US$6.55).

Mexico City – 711 km, 12 hours; three daily, via Zihuatanejo, Acapulco, Chilpancingo, Iguala and Cuernavaca, from Galeana terminal (US$18.70).

Morelia – 406 km, eight hours; hourly buses, 24 hours, from Galeana terminal (US$8.70).

Uruapan – 282 km, six hours; same bus as to Morelia (US$5.90).

Zihuatanejo – 72 km, two hours; same bus as to Acapulco (US$2.50).

Combis to Playa Azul, passing through La Mira, depart from a stop on Avenida Lázaro Cárdenas, opposite the Galeana bus terminal, every five or 10 minutes from 5 am to 9 pm. The 24-km trip takes about half an hour and costs US$0.85.

Train If you're heading inland towards the mountains of Michoacán, the train from Lázaro Cárdenas to Uruapan makes a pleasant alternative to the bus. It takes six hours to reach Uruapan, the same as the bus, but it does not have to negotiate as many curves as the highway, making for a smoother trip.

The train departs Lázaro Cárdenas every day at noon, arriving in Uruapan at around 6.15 pm. Seats in the 1st-class coaches cost US$8.85; in the 2nd-class coaches it's US$2.50.

PLAYA AZUL
Population: 3200
Playa Azul is a small beach resort town backed by lagoons formed by a tributary of the Río Balsas. Although it has mostly been a resort for Mexican families, foreign travellers are gradually being attracted by the beautiful beach and surfable waves. A strong undertow, however, makes swimming in the sea here extremely dangerous. Also beware of stingrays lying on the sand.

Orientation
Playa Azul is a small town of only a few blocks beside the sea. No one ever seems to use street names – everything is so close that there's little need for names, since everyone knows where everything is – but just in case you want to know, there are four street names in town, all running parallel to the beach. The beachside street, usually called the Malecón, is technically named Calle Emiliano Zapata. The next street inland is Calle Venustiano Carranza; the next one is Francisco I Madero; and the fourth is Independencia.

A Pemex petrol station (la gasolinera) at the corner of Independencia marks the beginning of town as you enter from the highway. This is a major landmark in the town, with buses and combis arriving and departing from here. The beach is three blocks straight ahead. A few blocks east (left as you face the sea) is a large plaza. Most everything you need in the town is found somewhere between the plaza and the gasolinera. A long row of enramadas, palapa-covered open-air seafood restaurants, stretches along the beach.

Information
The post office is on a rear corner of the plaza. It's open Monday to Friday from 8 am

to 1 pm and 3 to 6 pm, Saturday 8 am to 1 pm.

Activities
Swimming Since the beach is not safe for swimming, you may want to swim in one of the swimming pools. The Hotel Playa Azul has a swimming pool in its interior courtyard, with a poolside restaurant; if you come here to eat, you get free use of the pool. Behind the Hotel Playa Azul is another, larger pool with a toboggan water slide, open every day from 10 am to 6 pm. Admission is US$3.35 (children half price), but free for guests of the Hotel Playa Azul.

Horseriding Horses can be rented from the Hotel Delfín; cost is around US$3.50 per hour.

Places to Stay
Playa Azul has a number of pleasant, inexpensive places to stay. No matter where you stay, it's impossible to be more than three blocks from the beach in this town. All the places to stay have parking areas, convenient if you have a vehicle. They also all have private baths and hot water in the showers, a bit of a surprise in this warm climate.

Places to Stay – bottom end
Camping If you have a hammock, you can string it up at one of the enramadas along the beach; ask permission from the family running the restaurant, who probably won't mind, especially if you eat there a time or two. If you don't have your own hammock they may let you use one of theirs. There are public toilets and showers at a couple of the enramadas, and on the road running between the Pemex station and the beach.

The Hotel Playa Azul (read on) has a small trailer park in the rear, with full hook-ups for trailers, spaces for tents, and hot water in the showers. The cost of US$10 per night for one or two people includes use of the hotel's swimming pool.

Hotels & Bungalows The Bungalows de la Curva (☎ 6-00-58), one block towards the beach from the Pemex station at the entrance to town, is clean with a variety of rooms and a small swimming pool. Singles/doubles without kitchen are US$13.35/15. Rooms with kitchen for two or three people cost US$18.35, or there are also some larger rooms sleeping up to six people, also with kitchen, for US$25.

Next door, the *Hotel Delfín* (☎ 6-00-07) on Calle Venustiano Carranza is a pleasant place with clean, comfortable rooms arranged around a small swimming pool courtyard with a restaurant opening onto it. Singles/doubles are US$10/11.70.

Hotel Costa de Oro (☎ 6-00-86) on Calle Francisco I Madero, near the plaza, is a friendly place with 16 simple rooms. Singles/doubles are US$8.35/11.70; if you want TV it's US$10/13.35, or with both TV and air con it's US$13.35/15.

Hotel Maria Isabel (☎ 6-00-16/30), also on Calle Francisco I Madero but on the far side of the plaza, is a fine place to stay, with an attractive swimming pool and 30 extra large, clean rooms at US$12/15.

A more basic place is the *Hotel del Pacífico* (☎ 6-01-06), on the Malecón near the plaza, opposite the beachfront enramadas and just a few metres from the beach. With singles/doubles at US$6.70/10, it's actually only slightly cheaper than some of the more attractive places.

Places to Stay – top end

The large, 72-room *Hotel Playa Azul* (☎ 6-00-24/88) on Calle Venustiano Carranza is the big luxury hotel in this town. It has rooms at a variety of prices, starting at US$15.70/20.70 for singles/doubles with fan, rising to US$30.70/35.70 with air con. The restaurant/bar beside the swimming pool in the interior court is one of the town's more enjoyable places to eat. Hotel guests are also allowed free admission to the large swimming pool with toboggan water slide behind the hotel.

Places to Eat

The beachfront of Playa Azul is lined wall-to-wall with enramadas, palapa-covered open-air seafood restaurants. All charge the same prices and serve basically the same selection of seafood, fresh from the ocean.

Aside from these, there are a few other good places to eat in town. Two restaurants on the market street around the corner from the Hotel Playa Azul are often recommended by locals; both are cheap and serve good food. The *Restaurant Familiar Martita*, a pleasant little family restaurant with good, economical meals, is open every day from 7 am to 11 pm. Across Madero, the *Restaurant Galdy* is a much more basic place, with only a couple of tables inside and a few out on the sidewalk, but it too has good food, and is open the same hours.

The poolside restaurant/bar at the *Hotel Playa Azul* is a favourite with travellers. Open from 7 am to 11 pm, it serves hearty breakfasts and a wide selection of dishes; for example, there are 14 soups to choose from. If you come here to eat, you can swim in the pool for free.

The small poolside restaurant at the *Hotel Delfín* is also recommended by travellers.

Getting There & Away

Buses and Volkswagen combis run every five or 10 minutes from 5 am to 9 pm between Playa Azul and Lázaro Cárdenas, passing through La Mira. In Lázaro Cárdenas, catch either a bus or combi on the city's main street, Avenida Lázaro Cárdenas, opposite the Galeana bus terminal. The buses drop you off in front of Playa Azul's Pemex station, while the combis continue past the station and down Calle Carranza, dropping you off anywhere along Carranza. In Playa Azul, catch the combis on Carranza, or at the Pemex station. Fare for the half-hour trip to Lázaro Cárdenas is US$0.85.

Intercity buses do not pass through Playa Azul; instead they will drop you off 1½ km from town at the highway junction.

Guadalajara, Jalisco & Colima

The states of Jalisco and Colima are located in the central region of Mexico's Pacific coastline. Both are interesting for visitors, with warm Pacific resort towns – Puerto Vallarta is the largest and best known, but there are also several smaller ones – and cooler highland cities including Guadalajara, Mexico's second-largest city and the capital of Jalisco state, and Colima, capital of Colima state.

Jalisco

The Spanish arrived in this part of Mexico in 1530, led by the tyrannical Spanish conquistador Nuño Beltrán de Guzmán. Guzmán gave the name La Gran España (Greater Spain) to all of the area now occupied by the state of Jalisco, plus parts of the adjoining states of Colima, Michoacán, Guanajuato, Aguascalientes, Zacatecas and Nayarit. Two

years later, in 1532, he founded the first ill-fated settlement of Guadalajara in what is now the state of Zacatecas, but it was to move three more times before finally being established where it is today.

When the Spanish arrived they met several Indian groups living as simple agriculturalists and nomadic hunters. Guzmán hungered for wealth and used Indian slave labour to extract precious minerals for him. His mistreatment of the Indians caused the viceroy of Nueva España (New Spain) in Mexico City, Antonio de Mendoza, to boot him out. Mendoza installed Pérez de la Torre in Guzmán's place and the area was renamed Nueva Galicia (New Galicia) in honour of Spain's Galicia province.

It remained Nueva Galicia until 1821 – after independence from Spain – when most of the territory became the state of Jalisco. The name Jalisco is derived from Xalisco (The Sandy Place), one of four Chimalhuacán Indian kingdoms that con-

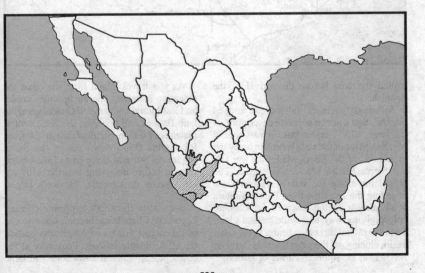

trolled the area before the arrival of the Spanish.

Although parts of Jalisco are indeed 'sandy', that's not an accurate description of this large, 80,137-sq-km state in west-central Mexico. Most of the state is broken up by the mountains of the Sierra Madre del Sur and the Sierra Madre Occidental ranges. The mountains along the state's south-western edge hug the coastline from Puerto Vallarta south almost to the town of La Cumbre before giving way to a wide coastal plain. Then the mountains creep nearer to the coast again, closing off the plain towards Barra de Navidad at the southern corner of Jalisco.

As you travel inland from the coast the elevation increases, the air becomes cooler and less humid and, around Guadalajara, the land flattens and becomes the great central plateau of Mexico. South of Guadalajara, the Río Lerma flows down out of the Sierra Madre del Sur and along part of the central plateau before emptying into the 1109-sq-km Laguna de Chapala, Mexico's largest lake.

Because of the area's temperate climate, Laguna de Chapala has become home to one of the largest groups of Americans outside the USA, mostly retirees. Proximity to the cosmopolitan cultural attractions and large airport of Guadalajara is another reason. The area is also popular with travellers.

On the coast, Puerto Vallarta is one of Mexico's most popular coastal resort cities, a touristy tropical paradise with hotels and restaurants for every budget, and a variety of easily accessible beaches. Farther south are the less visited but equally pleasant beach towns of Chamela, San Patricio-Melaque and Barra de Navidad.

GUADALAJARA

Population: 2,870,500
Altitude: 1563 metres

Second largest city in Mexico, Guadalajara has a reputation as the nation's most 'Mexican' city. Many 'typically' Mexican things and traditions were created here: the Jarabe Tapatío or Mexican Hat Dance, the broad-rimmed *sombrero* hat, charreadas (Mexican rodeos), mariachi music and tequila, which is often considered the national drink.

Guadalajara is full of attractions for travellers; the city centre has good places to stay

Sombrero hat

and eat in every budget range and there's plenty to do here every day of the week. Excursions to surrounding areas including Tlaquepaque, Tonalá and Laguna de Chapala, Mexico's largest lake, are also worthwhile. You'll never get bored in this town.

History

Guadalajara was founded where it is today only after three previous settlements on other sites had failed.

Shortly after the army led by Spanish conquistador Nuño Beltrán de Guzmán had brought the area's Indian tribes under submission in 1530, Spanish settlers arrived to colonise the region. Guzmán founded the first Guadalajara in 1532 with a group of 63 Spanish families and their dependents near Nochistlán in what is now the state of Zacatecas. He named it Guadalajara after his home city in Spain, close to Madrid; in Arabic the name means Valley Where Water Flows over the Rocks.

The first Guadalajara faced many difficulties; water was scarce, the land was not easy to farm, and the Indians there were hostile to the Spanish. In 1533 Captain Juan de Oñate ordered the settlement moved to the old Indian village of Tonalá, which today is a suburb of Guadalajara. However, Guzmán did not like Tonalá and a couple of years later, in 1535, he had the settlement moved again, this time to Tlacotán, near the confluence of the Río Santiago and Río Verde.

Around 1540 this settlement was attacked and destroyed by a confederation of local Indian tribes led by the great chief Tenamaxtli. The inhabitants, however, escaped and found refuge in the Indian village of Tetlán. Undecided where to go next, the colonists finally agreed on a site in the valley of Atemajac beside the San Juan de Dios creek, which ran where Calzada Independencia is today, in the centre of Guadalajara. On 14 February 1542, near where the Teatro Degollado now stands, the new settlement of Guadalajara was founded by Captain Juan de Oñate.

The settlement prospered and in 1560 it

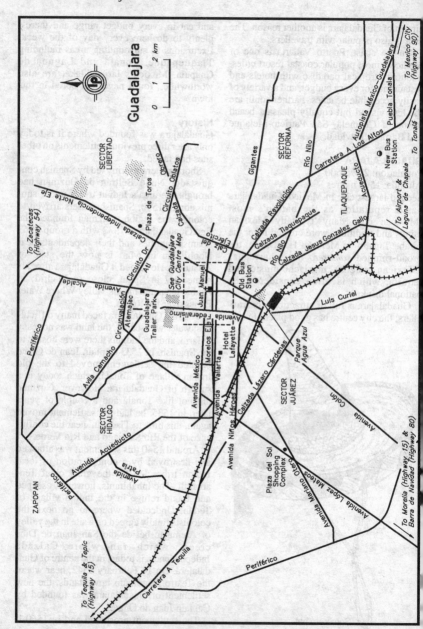

Guadalajara

was declared the capital of the Nueva Galicia province. It quickly grew into one of New Spain's largest and most important cities after Mexico City. After independence from Spain in 1821 the city continued to grow and prosper. Today it is Mexico's second-largest city and an important centre for commerce and industry, as well as the transport hub for the region.

In 1992, several large gas explosions blew up several streets in Guadalajara, causing several deaths and the destruction of many buildings. However, in spite of the impression television news reports gave, this all happened in one suburb of the city; as it is not a suburb that tourists normally visit, this terrible incident should not cause any inconvenience to travellers.

Orientation

Guadalajara's giant twin-towered cathedral is at the heart of the city. It is surrounded by four lovely plazas in the four cardinal directions. Behind the cathedral, the Plaza de la Liberación extends east for two blocks to the Teatro Degollado, another city landmark.

Behind the Teatro Degollado is the Plaza Tapatía, stretching half a km east to the Instituto Cultural Cabañas, yet another important historical edifice. Other historical buildings are grouped around the plazas near the cathedral. Just south of Plaza Tapatía is the Mercado Libertad, a huge three-storey market covering an area of four city blocks.

About 25 blocks west of the cathedral, the north-south Avenida Chapúltepec is Guadalajara's zona rosa (pink zone), a stylish area with a number of fine restaurants and shops. On the south-west side of the city, Plaza del Sol on Avenida López Mateos is a huge modern shopping mall with restaurants, entertainment, and a number of hotels and motels nearby.

Major arteries of the city include Avenida Chapúltepec, Avenida López Mateos and Calzada Independencia, beside the Mercado Libertad, which runs south to Parque Agua Azul and the train and old bus stations, and north to the zoo and planetarium, the Plaza de Toros and stadium, and the Barranca de Oblatos canyon. In the centre, the north-south streets change names on either side of Avenida Hidalgo, the avenue which runs along the north side of the cathedral, Plaza de la Liberación and Plaza Tapatía. The state tourist office in Plaza Tapatía provides an excellent free map of the greater central area.

Guadalajara is 535 km north-west of Mexico City and 345 km east of Puerto Vallarta. It is a major transit point, with Highways 15, 54, 70, 80 and 90 all converging here. All of these highways combine temporarily in Guadalajara to form a periférico, a transit highway making a ring around the city which allows bypass traffic to avoid the city centre. Guadalajara also has a busy train station, with routes to Mexico City, the west coast of Mexico (southbound and northbound), and to the borders of Arizona and California in the USA, plus a major bus station and international airport.

Information

Tourist Office The state tourist office (☎ (36) 658-22-22) is in Plaza Tapatía at Morelos 102, about 100 metres behind the Teatro Degollado, in an historic building called the Rincón del Diablo (Devil's Corner). It's open Monday to Friday from 9 am to 9 pm, Saturday and Sunday from 9 am to 1 pm. This is the place to come for free maps and information on Guadalajara and the state of Jalisco. English and Spanish are spoken in addition to a smattering of French.

This office offers a number of useful services including a listing of cultural and other events happening every day around the city, information on anything you could want to know from local bus routes to retirement in Mexico, and some useful publications. Ask for *Ver y Oír*, a monthly magazine listing cultural events in the city and environs, and *Let's Enjoy*, a bilingual monthly Spanish/ English general tourist magazine about the state of Jalisco. They also have a 'Teletur' programme, where you can telephone the office to ask about anything you might need to know.

The same office also operates a smaller information office in the Palacio del

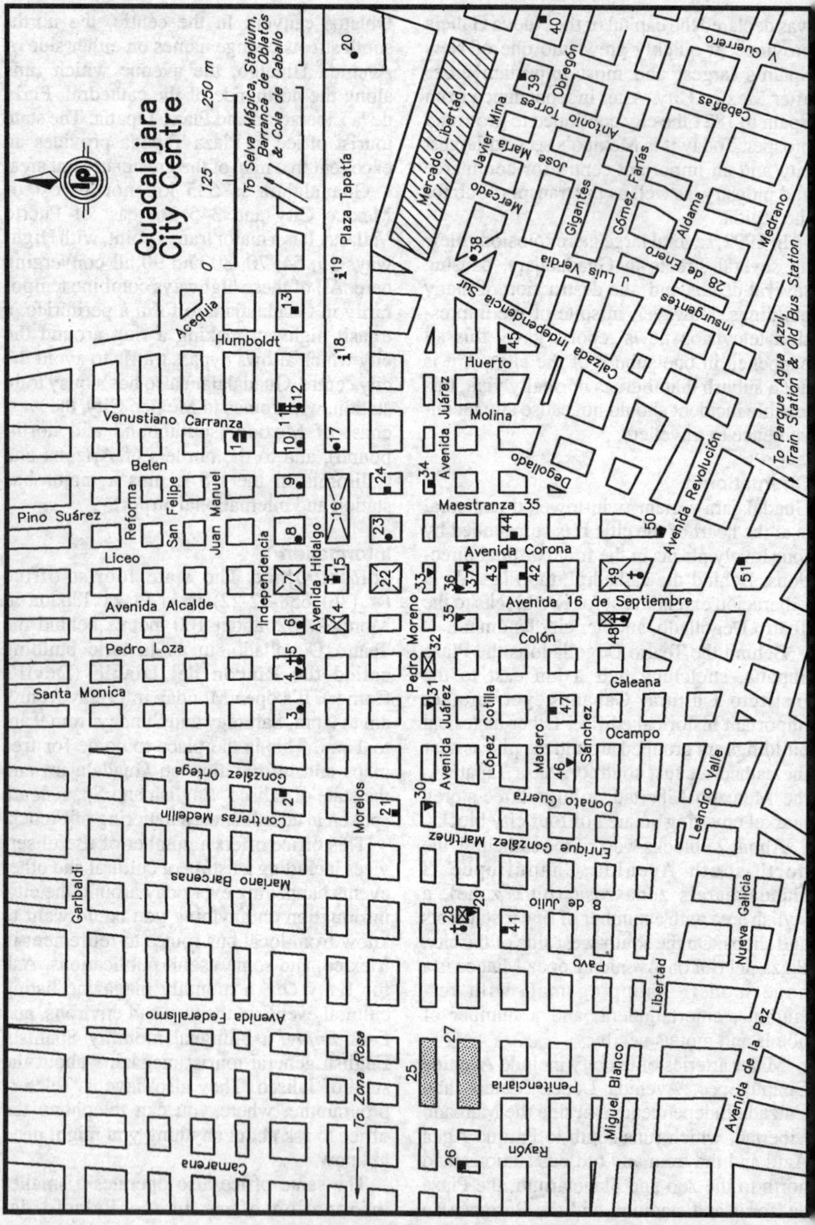

Guadalajara City Centre
0 125 250 m
To Selva Mágica, Stadium, Barranca de Oblatos & Cola de Caballo
Plaza Tapatía
Mercado Libertad
Acequia
Humboldt
Venustiano Carranza
Belen
Reforma
San Felipe
Juan Manuel
Pino Suárez
Liceo
Independencia
Avenida Hidalgo
Avenida Alcalde
Pedro Loza
Santa Monica
González Ortega
Contreras Medellín
Morelos
Mariano Barcenas
Garibaldi
Avenida Federalismo
Camarena
To Zona Rosa
Pedro Moreno
Avenida Juárez
Huerto
Molina
Maestranza
Avenida Corona
Avenida 16 de Septiembre
Colón
Galeana
López Cotilla
Madero
Sánchez
Ocampo
Donato Guerra
Enrique González Martínez
8 de Julio
Pavo
Penitenciaria
Rayón
Miguel Blanco
Libertad
Leandro Valle
Nueva Galicia
Avenida de la Paz
Avenida Revolución
To Parque Agua Azul, Train Station & Old Bus Station
Degollado
Calzada Independencia Sur
J Luis Verdia
Insurgentes
28 de Enero
Medrano
Aldama
Gómez Farías
Gigantes
Mercado
Javier Mina
José María
Antonio Torres
Obregón
Cabañas
Guerrero
1 2 3 4 5 6 7 8 9 10 11 12 13 14 15 16 17 18 19 20 21 22 23 24 25 26 27 28 29 30 31 32 33 34 35 36 37 38 39 40 41 42 43 44 45 46 47 48 49 50 51

Gobierno, facing the Plaza de Armas just south of the cathedral, where you can stop by for free maps and to ask information. It's open Monday to Friday from 9 am to 3 pm and 6 to 8 pm, Saturday 9 am to 1 pm.

SECTUR (☎ (36) 614-86-65), the federal tourist office, is in Plaza Tapatía at Paseo Degollado 50, a block from the state office. It's open Monday to Friday from 8 am to 3 pm; it has information on travel in other parts of Mexico outside Jalisco.

Money Banks are plentiful in Guadalajara, and are open for currency exchange and other services Monday to Friday from 9 am to 1.30 pm. In addition there are a number of casas de cambio on López Cotilla in the three blocks between Corona and Molina. These

are open longer hours; the Casa de Cambio Libertad at López Cotilla 171 is open Monday to Saturday from 9 am to 7 pm, Sunday 10 am to 2 pm, and there are plenty of others.

The American Express office and travel agency (☎ 630-02-00, 615-89-10) is at Vallarta 2440, opposite Plaza Vallarta. It's open Monday to Friday from 9 am to 6 pm, Saturday 9 am to 1 pm.

Post The main post office is on Carranza, between Juan Manuel and Calle Independencia. It's open Monday to Friday from 8 am to 7 pm, Saturday and Sunday 9 am to 1 pm.

Telecommunications The Telecomm office, with telegram, telex and fax services, is in

■ PLACES TO STAY		46	Restaurant Acuarius
2	Hotel González		OTHER
11	Hotel de Mendoza		
13	Hotel Las Américas	1	Main Post Office
21	Hotel Internacional	3	Mercado Corona
24	Hotel Francés	5	Templo de la Merced
26	Hotel del Parque	6	Presidencia Municipal
34	Hotel Calinda Roma	7	Rotonda de los Hombres Ilustres
39	Hotel Ana Isabel	8	Museo Regional de Guadalajara
40	Hotel México 70	9	Palacio Legislativo
41	Posada de la Plata	10	Palacio de Justicia
42	Posada San Pablo	12	Templo de Santa María de Gracia
43	Hotel Fenix Best Western	14	Plaza de los Laureles
44	Posada Regis	15	Cathedral
45	Hotel Maya	16	Plaza de la Liberación
47	Hotel Hamilton	17	Teatro Degollado
50	Hotel Aranzazú	18	State Tourist Office
51	Hotel Continental	19	Federal Tourist Office (SECTUR)
		20	Instituto Cultural de Cabañas
▼ PLACES TO EAT		22	Plaza de Armas
		23	Palacio del Gobierno
4	Restaurant La Terraza & Restaurant	25	Parque Revolución
	El Patio de la Merced	27	Parque Revolución
29	Restaurant Naturalissimo	28	Santuario de Nuestra Señora del
30	Café Madoka & Telmex		Carmen
31	Restaurant La Copa de Leche	32	Plaza de los Mártires
33	Café Madrid	38	Plaza de los Mariachis
35	Denny's	48	Templo de Aranzazú
36	Sanborns	49	Templo de San Francisco
37	Restaurant La Chata		

the Palacio Federal on Avenida Alcalde at Calle Hospital, opposite the Santuario church a few blocks north of the centre. It's open Monday to Friday from 9 am to 7 pm, Saturday 9 am to noon.

Telmex, the main caseta de larga distancia, is at Donato Guerra 84 near the corner of Juárez. It's open every day from 7 am to 8.30 pm.

Computel, with long-distance telephone and fax services, has several offices around the city. There's one in the Edificio Mulbar on Corona opposite the Hotel Fenix, between Madero and López Cotilla; it's open Monday to Saturday from 7 am to 8.30 pm. Another is at Avenida 16 de Septiembre 599. They also have offices at the train station and at both the old and new bus stations.

Foreign Consulates Over 30 countries have consular offices in Guadalajara. The state tourist office has a complete list, or you can contact the Consular Association (☎ 616-06-29) for information on consulates in the city. They include:

Canada
  Hotel Fiesta Americana, Local 30, Aurelio Aceves 225 (☎ 625-34-34)
France
  Avenida López Mateos 484 (☎ 616-55-16)
Germany
  Corona 202 (☎ 613-96-23)
Netherlands
  Calzada Lázaro Cárdenas 601, Zona Industrial (☎ 612-07-40)
UK
  Calzada González Gallo 1897 (☎ 635-89-27)
USA
  Calle Progreso 175 (☎ 625- 27-00)

Bookshops A fair selection of books and magazines in English is available at the gift shops of most major hotels. The Sandi Bookstore, Tepeyac 718, Colonia Chapalita also has a decent selection.

Useful Organisations & Publications The American-Canadian Club holds a free seminar on retirement in Mexico on Tuesday and Thursday at 10 am in the Hotel Plaza del Sol, on the corner of Avenida López Mateos

and Mariano Otero. It also offers a newsletter, information package and discount directory. You can contact them in their office in the lobby of the Hotel Plaza del Sol or phone them toll-free in the USA (☎ 1-800-882-8215) or Canada (☎ 1-800-368-0900).

MRTA (Mexico Retirement & Travel Assistance) publishes the book *Guadalajara – A Great Place to Visit or Retire* and an excellent newsletter, the *MRTA Guadalajara/Chapala Update*. You can pick up their newsletter free at the state tourist office. Their mailing address is PO Box 2190-23, Henderson, NV 89009-7009, USA.

Their book and another interesting English-language book, the 60-page *Guadalajara Walking Tours*, are available at the gift shops of most major hotels; in the centre, try the Hotel Fenix or the Hotel Calinda Roma.

Retirement in Guadalajara is another useful publication about retiring in the area, published by Fran & Judy Furton, who host a weekly open house and orientation seminar at their home in Guadalajara each Tuesday at 10.15 am. Contact them by phone (☎ 621-23-48, 647-99-24) or at their mailing address: Apdo Postal 5-409, Guadalajara, Jalisco.

Cathedral
Guadalajara's huge twin-towered cathedral is its most famous symbol and most conspicuous landmark. Begun in 1558 and consecrated in 1616, the cathedral is almost as old as the city. From a distance it is an impressive structure; up close you can see the hotchpotch of styles used in its design. Exterior decorations, some of which were completed long after the cathedral's consecration, include churrigueresque, baroque and Neoclassical styles. The towers were also added later, after an earthquake in 1848 destroyed the original towers; the present ones are much higher than the originals.

The interior includes 11 richly decorated altars given to Guadalajara by King Ferdinand VII of Spain (1784-1833), Gothic vaults and Tuscany-style pillars. In the sacristy, which you can ask an attendant to open or you, is *The Assumption of the Virgin*, painted by Bertolomé Murillo in 1650.

The cathedral is surrounded on four sides by attractive plazas: the Plaza de los Laureles, the Plaza de Armas, the Rotunda de los Hombres Ilustres, and the long Plaza de la Liberación.

Plaza de los Laureles & Presidencia Municipal

The Plaza de los Laureles is the plaza in front of the cathedral. As its name suggests, much of the plaza is planted with laurels. On its north side is the Presidencia Municipal (City Hall), which though it appears much older was actually constructed in this century, between 1949 and 1952. Above the interior stairway is a mural, depicting the founding of Guadalajara, by Jaliscan artist Gabriel Flores.

Plaza de Armas & Palacio del Gobierno

With the 16th to 17th-century cathedral on the north side and the 18th-century Palacio del Gobierno on the east, the Plaza de Armas is a pleasant place to sit and imagine how the city may have been in colonial times. Free concerts of typical Jaliscan music are held here on Thursday and Sunday, beginning at 6.30 pm. They've been doing this since 1898 and haven't missed a performance yet.

The Palacio del Gobierno (Government Palace) was finished in 1774 and, like the cathedral, was built in a combination of styles – in this case, a strange mix of simple, Neoclassical features and riotous Churrigueresque decorations. Its most interesting artistic feature is the huge 1937 portrait of Miguel Hidalgo painted by Mexican muralist José Clemente Orozco over the interior stairway, with an angry Hidalgo, father of Mexico's movement for independence from Spain, brandishing a torch with one fist raised high and the struggling masses at his feet.

In this mural Orozco also comments on the pressing issues of his time: communism, fascism and religion. Another Orozco mural in the upstairs Congreso (Congress Hall) depicts Hidalgo, Benito Juárez and other figures important in Mexican history. The murals can be viewed every day from 9 am to 9 pm.

Rotonda de los Hombres Ilustres & Museo Regional de Guadalajara

On the north side of the cathedral, the Rotonda de los Hombres Ilustres (Rotunda of Illustrious Men) is a monument to some of Jalisco's favourite characters. Around the outer edge of the plaza are statues honouring men important in the arts, including a poet, a composer, a writer, an architect, a historian, a university reformer and others. Their remains are buried beneath the large round pillared monument in the centre of the plaza.

Facing the east side of this plaza, at the corner of Avenida Hidalgo and Liceo, the Regional Museum of Guadalajara occupies the former seminary of San José, a late 17th-century baroque-style building with two storeys of arcades and an inner court.

The museum has an eclectic collection of exhibits covering the history and prehistory of western Mexico. Displays in the ground-floor archaeological section include the skeleton of a woolly mammoth, arrowheads, jewellery and ceramic figurines, some dating back to the Preclassic period (1500 BC to 300 AD). There's also a fibreglass replica of the 780-kilo Meteorite of Zacatecas, discovered in that state in 1792.

Upstairs, the exhibits include a gallery of paintings from the 17th century to the present. There is a separate gallery for European paintings, a history gallery covering life and events in Jalisco since the Spanish conquest, and an ethnography section with displays showing life among various Indian groups in Jalisco and the charro, or Mexican cowboy.

The museum is open Tuesday to Sunday from 9 am to 3.45 pm. Admission is US$4.35, but free for children under 13, seniors over 60, and for everyone on Sundays.

Plaza de la Liberación & Teatro Degollado

East of the cathedral on the former site of

several colonial buildings is the large Plaza de la Liberación stretching east for two blocks from the rear of the cathedral to the impressive Teatro Degollado. Begun in 1856 and inaugurated 30 years later, the Neo-classical-style theatre has been reconstructed at various times in its history. Over the columns in front of the theatre is a frieze depicting Apollo and the Nine Muses; inside, the five-tiered theatre filled with lush red velvet and gold decoration is crowned by a Gerardo Suárez mural based on the fourth canto of Dante's *Divine Comedy*.

Frequent performances are staged in the theatre (see the Entertainment section). The theatre can be visited for free Monday to Friday from 12.30 to 6 pm, Saturday 10 am to 6 pm.

Palacio de Justicia & Templo de Santa María de Gracia

Opposite the Teatro Degollado on Avenida Hidalgo, the Palacio de Justicia (State Courthouse) was constructed in 1588 as part of the Convento de Santa María, Guadalajara's first nunnery. A 1965 mural by Guillermo Chávez, depicting Benito Juárez and other figures in Mexico's legislative history, graces the interior stairway. Opposite this, on Avenida Hidalgo at the north side of the Plaza de la Liberación, is the Palacio Legislativo (State Congress), with massive stone columns in its interior courtyard.

Near the Teatro Degollado at the corner of Avenida Hidalgo and Carranza is the small Templo de Santa María de Gracia, which served as Guadalajara's first cathedral from 1549 to 1618.

Plaza Tapatía

Behind the Teatro Degollado, Plaza Tapatía is a modern plaza and pedestrian mall of shops, restaurants, street performers, fountains, statues, trees and the state and federal tourist offices. It stretches east for half a km from the Teatro Degollado to the Instituto Cultural de Cabañas.

Instituto Cultural de Cabañas

This huge Neoclassical gem on the east side of Plaza Tapatía was constructed between 1805 and 1810 by Spanish architect Manuel Tolsá. Called the Hospicio Cabañas after its founder Bishop Don Juan Cruz Ruíz de Cabañas, it served as an orphanage for over 150 years until 1980, sometimes housing up to 3000 children at a time. In addition, it occasionally served as an insane asylum, military barracks and jail. The orphanage acquired an important place in Mexican history when independence rebel leader Father Miguel Hidalgo signed a proclamation against slavery here in 1811.

More than a century later, between 1936 and 1939, Mexican muralist José Clemente Orozco painted a series of murals in the main chapel that are regarded by many critics as his finest work. Most notable is *The Man of Fire* in the dome; 53 other dramatic frescoes cover the walls and ceiling of the large chapel. Interpretations vary on what *The Man of Fire* means; a small book in both English and Spanish, *The Murals of Orozco in the Cabañas Cultural Institute*, on sale at the main entrance, gives background information on the artist, the murals here, how they were executed and the story behind each one.

Today the building is occupied by the Instituto Cultural Cabañas, a cultural institute containing a museum, a theatre and a school. All 23 courts and the chapel that Tolsá designed have remained intact. The museum features a permanent exhibition of over 100 Orozco drawings and paintings, plus temporary exhibits dedicated to painting, sculpture and engraving. The institute also hosts dance festivals, theatre performances, concerts and films.

The Instituto is open to the public Tuesday to Saturday from 10.15 am to 6 pm, Sunday 10.15 am to 3 pm. Admission is US$1.70 (children US$0.35) except on Sunday, when it's free.

Plaza de los Mariachis

The Plaza de los Mariachis, just south of the Mercado Libertad near the intersection of Javier Mina and Calzada Independencia Sur, is a small alley known throughout Mexico for the mariachi bands that play there at all hours of the day and night. Several restaurants have tables out on the plaza and the mariachi bands come around and offer a song to the customers – for a price, of course. They get strumming hardest late at night.

Colonial Churches

Besides the cathedral and the Templo de Santa María de Gracia there are 13 other churches in the centre of Guadalajara, some of them impressively beautiful. The baroque **Templo de La Merced**, near the cathedral at the corner of Avenida Hidalgo and Pedro Loza, was built in 1650; inside are several fine large religious paintings, crystal chandeliers, and lots of gold decoration.

The **Santuario de Nuestra Señora del Carmen**, facing the small plaza at the corner of Avenida Juárez and Calle 8 de Julio, is another lovely church, with lots of gold decoration, old religious paintings, and murals in the dome.

At the corner of Avenida 16 de Septiembre and Miguel Blanco, the Templo de Aranzazú, built from 1749 to 1752, has three splendidly ornate Churrigueresque golden altars. Beside it is the older and less ornate **Templo de San Francisco**, built two centuries earlier in 1550.

Parque Agua Azul

About 20 blocks south of the centre, near the south end of Calzada Independencia Sur, Parque Agua Azul is a large verdant park offering pleasant relief from the city hubbub, with an orchid house, a butterfly house, an aviary, and a childrens wading pool and playground. It's open Tuesday to Sunday from 10 am to 6 pm; admission is US$1 (children US$0.35).

Around the park are a number of interesting places to visit. The **Casa de las Artesanías de Jalisco** on the north side of the park can be entered through the park or through a separate entrance on Avenida González Gallo. It features handcrafts and arts from all over the state of Jalisco including ceramics, paintings, statues, textiles, wood and straw crafts, masks, furniture,

Huichol yarn art and more. Everything displayed is for sale; prices are high but the quality can't be beat. It's open Monday to Friday from 10 am to 7 pm, Saturday 10 am to 4 pm, Sunday 10 am to 2 pm; admission is free.

The **Museo de Arqueología del Occidente de México** is on Calzada Independencia Sur opposite the entrance to the park. Operated by the University of Guadalajara's Institute of Jaliscan Anthropology & History, it contains a small collection of pre-Hispanic figurines and artefacts from Jalisco and the neighbouring states of Nayarit and Colima.

On the east side of the park is the **Museo Infantil** (Children's Museum), reached through a separate entrance on Dr R Michel near the corner of González Gallo. It features exhibits on geography, space (with a small planetarium dome), prehistoric animals and more, with several hands-on exhibits. It's open Monday to Friday from 9 am to 1 pm and 3 to 7.30 pm; admission is free.

University of Guadalajara

On the west side of the centre, where Avenida Juárez meets Federalismo, is another shady park, **Parque Revolución**. Three blocks further west at Avenida Juárez 975 is one of the main buildings of the University of Guadalajara. Inside, the **Paraninfo** (theatre hall) contains large, powerful murals by José Clemente Orozco on the stage backdrop and dome.

Tequila Sauza Bottling Plant

The Tequila Sauza Bottling Plant is at Vallarta 3273, on the western outskirts of the city. Free tours of the plant – with free samples, of course – are offered Monday to Friday from 10 am to noon. Bus No 45 heading west on Madero will take you there.

Zoo, Selva Mágica & Planetarium

The zoo, the Selva Mágica amusement park and the planetarium are all near one another just off Calzada Independencia Norte on the northern outskirts of the city. Bus No 60 heading north on Calzada Independencia will drop you at the entrance monument, from where it's about a 10-minute walk to the actual entrances.

The Zoológico Guadalajara is a large zoo with over 500 animals on display. At one end is a view of the **Barranca de Huentitán**, similar to the view of the Barranca de Oblatos – it's all the same canyon. Other notable features are two pyramid-shaped aviaries, a herpetarium (snake house), a children's petting zoo, and a train that will take you around the zoo if you don't feel like walking. The zoo is open Tuesday to Sunday from 10 am to 5 pm; admission is US$1.35 (children US$0.70).

Beside the zoo is Selva Mágica, a children's amusement park with mechanical rides, a dolphin and seal show three times daily, and a trained bird show. It's open Tuesday to Sunday from 11 am until 7 or 8 pm; entrance is US$2.70 for adults or children. If you pay to visit the zoo, you can enter Selva Mágica for free, but you'll have to pay something to see the animal shows.

About a five-minute walk from the zoo is the planetarium, called the Centro de Ciencia y Tecnología (Centre of Science & Technology). It has exhibits on astronomy, space, aeroplanes, the history of telephones, the body, and other science topics. Planetarium shows are held at 11 am, noon, 1, 4, 5 and 6 pm. It's open Tuesday to Sunday from 10 am to 7.30 pm; admission is US$0.35 (free for children under 12), plus an extra US$0.85 to see the planetarium show.

Barranca de Oblatos & Cola de Caballo Falls

The Barranca de Oblatos is the same canyon you see from the zoo. Otherwise, you can take Bus No 60 north on Calzada Independencia to **Parque Mirador**, just a little further on past the entrance to the zoo, for a view of the canyon. The park is always open. This 670-metre-deep canyon rivals the Barranca del Cobre (Copper Canyon) in north-western Mexico for the title of 'Mexico's Grand Canyon', though the Barranca del Cobre is more spectacular.

Also in the canyon is the long Cola de Caballo (Horse Tail) waterfall. It flows all year but is most impressive in the rainy season. For a view of the falls take the Ixcatan bus from the Glorieta de la Normal on Avenida Alcalde about 10 blocks north of the cathedral, and get off at the Parque D Atl, from where there's a view of the falls.

Courses

The University of Guadalajara is the second largest university in Mexico, with an enrollment of 196,240 students. Its Foreign Student Study Center offers 12 levels of intensive five-week Spanish-language courses ranging from beginners to advanced. It also offers courses in history, culture, politics, economics, literature, art and other subjects, all taught in Spanish, which can be taken in addition to or independently of the Spanish-language courses. Workshops in folkloric dance, guitar and singing, Mexican cuisine, etc are also offered, as are special cultural events and excursions to other parts of Mexico.

The registration and tuition fees are US$395 for each five-week session. Lodging is arranged with local Mexican families at a cost of US$420 for the session. The workshops and excursions are an optional expense.

For more specific information and an application form, write to Universidad de Guadalajara, Centro de Estudios para Extranjeros (☎ (3) 653-60-24, 653-21-50 fax 653-00-40), Apartado Postal 1-4521 Guadalajara, Jalisco, CP 44100, México.

Many foreign universities in the USA Canada, Europe, Japan and Latin America have relations with the University of Guadalajara, making it easy for you to get credits in your country of origin for courses taken here. The Departamento de Intercambio Académico (☎ (3) 626-40-48) at Avenida Juárez 975 has a complete list of these universities.

In the USA, the University of Arizona (☎ (602) 621-4729) also offers a summer programme in Guadalajara. Write to Guadalajara Summer School, Robert Nugent

Building 205, University of Arizona, Tucson, Arizona 85721, USA.

Sports

There are plenty of opportunities for playing golf, tennis, squash and other sports around Guadalajara. For golf, try the 18-hole Club de Golf Santa Anita (☎ 686-03-86, 686-03-61), the 18-hole Club de Golf Atlas (☎ 689-00-85), the 18-hole Club de Golf San Isidro (☎ 633-23-91, 633-27-08) or the nine-hole Club de Golf Rancho Contento (☎ 621-68-89, 621-66-67). All are open to the public and have clubs for hire.

Tennis fans can visit the Tenis Patria tennis club (☎ 633-38-11) opposite the Plaza Patria in Zapopan. The Club Guadalajara 881 de Squash (☎ 625-88-81) is at Avenida Juárez 881, just a few blocks west of the centre.

The Hyatt Regency Hotel (☎ 622-59-32), near the Plaza del Sol at the corner of Avenida López Mateos Sur and Moctezuma, has an ice skating rink open every day. It costs US$4 for a 1¼ hour session, including skate rental.

Organised Tours

Panoramex (☎ 610-50-57, 610-50-05), at Calzada Federalismo Sur 944, operates a variety of all-day tours with English, French and Spanish-speaking guides.

Tour No 1 visits some of the main sights of Guadalajara (cathedral, Teatro Degollado, Palacio del Gobierno, fountains, monuments, etc) and Tlaquepaque; the cost is US$25 with lunch or US$13.35 without lunch.

Tour No 2, visiting the Laguna de Chapala towns of Chapala, Ajijic and Jocotepec, costs US$28.35 with lunch or US$16.70 without lunch.

Tour No 3 visits the the Barranca de Oblatos canyon, the Cola de Caballo waterfall, the Basilica of Zapopan with its Huichol Indian art museum, and ends at Amatitán with a tour of one of the area's oldest tequila distilleries. The cost is US$28.35 with lunch or US$15 without lunch.

On Sundays only, Tour No 4 goes to the village of Tapalpa; the cost is US$16.70 with lunch included.

Festivals

Several major festivals, in addition to a number of minor ones, are celebrated each year in Guadalajara and the towns nearby. They include:

Carnavales de Chapala Carnaval (Mardi Gras) is celebrated in Chapala during the week before Ash Wednesday, sometime between mid-February and early March (depending upon when Easter falls).

Feria de Tonalá The annual handcrafts fair in Tonalá, specialising in ceramics, is held during Semana Santa, the week before Easter.

Tlaquepaque Fiestas Tlaquepaque's annual fiesta and handcrafts fair is celebrated from mid-June to the first week of July.

Fiestas de Octubre Beginning with an inaugural parade on the first Sunday in October, the October Fiestas, lasting all month, are Guadalajara's principal annual fair. Every day from around noon to 10 pm there's continuous free entertainment in the fairgrounds at the Benito Juárez auditorium, plus livestock shows, art and other exhibits, and sporting and cultural events around the city.

Feria de Zapopan Zapopan's fair is held during the first two weeks of December.

Places to Stay – bottom end

Camping Guadalajara has three trailer parks, all a few km from the city centre. All offer full hook-ups and spaces for tents, trailers and motor homes, with discounted monthly rates.

Closest to the city centre is the *Guadalajara Trailer Park* (☎ (36) 660-67-54), at Prolongación Alcalde Norte 83, five km north of the centre. It has 200 spaces at US$12 per site for trailers or motor homes, a little cheaper for tents. Phone ahead to make sure they're still operating; the park was up for sale in 1992 and its future was uncertain. To reach it from the city centre, bus or drive north on Avenida 16 de Septiembre/Alcalde.

The *San José del Tacho Trailer Park* (☎ (36) 686-17-38) is 6½ km south of the city centre at Km 15 on Highway 15, the Carretera a Tepic. To get there from the centre, head south on Avenida López Mateos until you reach the park. Facilities include a swimming pool, tennis court, clubhouse, laundry, and 175 sites; cost is US$14 per site by the day, or US$300 by the month, a little cheaper for tents. They also have 15 apartments.

The *Hacienda Trailer Park* (☎ (36) 627-17-24, 627-18-43) is at Circunvalación Poniente 66, Ciudad Granja, near Highway 15 (the Carretera a Tepic) and the Periférico, about 12 km south of the centre. Features include a swimming pool, clubhouse, billiards, laundry, barbeque, plenty of trees, and 98 sites. Cost is US$11.35/13.35 for one/two people, with a day for free after you've stayed seven days.

Hostels The *CODE* youth hostel (☎ (36) 624-65-15) is at Alcalde 1360, in a sports complex about a 15-minute bus ride north of the centre. Any bus heading north on Avenida 16 de Septiembre, which changes its name to Avenida Alcalde north of Avenida Hidalgo, will take you there. It's a large hostel with 200 beds in separate-sex dorms; cost is US$5 a night. You must telephone ahead to make reservations. People of all ages are welcome and a youth hostel card is not required.

Hotels – Central District The *Posada San Pablo* (☎ (36) 613-33-12) at Madero 218 is a friendly, family-run guest house with just seven rooms around an upstairs covered patio filled with plants, tables and some cheerful parakeets. Many European and international travellers stay here; singles/doubles are US$9.35/11.70.

Around the corner, the *Posada Regis* (☎ (36) 614-86-33) at Avenida Corona 171 is an upstairs hotel in a converted 19th-century French-style mansion with high ceilings and ornate details. The 19 rooms with bath open onto a covered upstairs patio filled with plants, where economical meals are served; these rooms cost US$17.35/21.70 for singles/doubles. A few plainer but cheaper rooms at US$10/15 are up on the roof. Discounts are given for stays of a few days or more.

The *Posada de la Plata* (☎ (36) 614-91-46) at López Cotilla 619 is also popular, with 12 rooms with high ceilings and large bathrooms opening onto a covered central courtyard. Singles/doubles are US$9.35/12.70.

The *Hotel Las Américas* (☎ (36) 613-96-22, 614-16-04), at Avenida Hidalgo 76 opposite Plaza Tapatía, is one of the best deals for its price in Guadalajara – its only drawback is the traffic noise, but most of the rooms are set back from the street. The 49 rooms are clean and modern, with TV, telephone, carpeting, and large windows opening onto ample airshafts. The cost of US$13.35/15 seems remarkably cheap for what you get.

The *Hotel Hamilton* (☎ (36) 614-67-26) at Madero 381 is simple but clean, with singles/doubles at US$9.35/11.70. At the same price, the *Hotel González* (☎ (36) 614-56-81) at González Ortega 77 is a basic but friendly family-run hotel, with 24 rooms around an interior courtyard full of clotheslines which you are welcome to use.

Slightly more expensive, the *Hotel Continental* (☎ (36) 614-11-17) at Avenida Corona 450 is a bit more upmarket, with parking, a restaurant and 124 clean, comfortable, old-fashioned rooms, all with TV, carpeting and telephone, at US$15.40/19.80.

Hotels – near Mercado Libertad Several other popular budget hotels are found along Javier Mina, opposite Mercado Libertad and near the Plaza de los Mariachis. This part of town near the market is not quite as pleasant as the centre, it's not as safe for walking at night, and the hotels are large and can be noisy. Nevertheless this is another popular low-budget hotel zone.

The *Hotel Ana Isabel* (☎ (36) 617-79-20, 617-48-59), at Javier Mina 164, opposite the Mercado Libertad, is one of the best in this district. It has 50 small, clean rooms, with a private bath and ceiling fan, opening onto a narrow, covered interior courtyard-walkway. Cost is US$15 for one or two people.

The *Hotel México 70* (☎ (36) 617-99-78) at Javier Mina 230 has 80 simple but clean rooms with private bath at US$10/13.35 for singles/doubles.

The *Hotel Azteca* (☎ (36) 617-74-65, 617-74-66) at Javier Mina 311 has 70 rooms, a restaurant, parking, and a small 4th-floor terrace. All the rooms have a bath and ceiling fan. Cost is US$13.35/15 and for an extra US$3.35 you can get TV in your room.

The *Hotel Maya* (☎ (36) 614-54-54, 614-46-54), at López Cotilla 39 on the corner of Huerto, is in the same general area. It has a restaurant, garage, and 60 basic but clean rooms at US$11.35/13.35.

Places to Stay – middle

Central District One of the centre's most attractive middle-range hotels is the *Hotel del Parque* (☎ (36) 625-28-00, fax 626-66-48) at Avenida Juárez 845 near the Parque Revolución. It has a pleasant restaurant and lobby bar with sidewalk café tables, and 81 rooms in three price categories ranging from US$20.35/26.70 to US$30.35/36.70, with a variety of possible amenities including colour TV, bathtubs, servi-bar, and rooms with two separate bedrooms.

The *Hotel Internacional* (☎ (36) 613-03-30) at Moreno 570 has 112 carpeted rooms, some with colour TV and air conditioning, all at the same price of US$25.70/34.85.

More expensive but also more luxurious is the historic *Hotel Francés* (☎ (36) 613-11-90, fax 658-28-31) at Maestranza 35 near the Plaza de la Liberación. Founded in 1610 as an inn, with rooms upstairs and horses kept in the arched stone courtyard (which is now an elegant lobby bar with a fountain and music), it's one of the city's rather posh

hotels. It has 60 rooms at US$46/55 and nine suites at US$57/67, all with colour TV and ceiling fan, some with bathtub and shower. The exterior rooms have French doors opening onto small wrought-iron balconies; the quieter interior rooms open onto ample airshafts.

Near the Bus Station The *Hotel El Parador* (☎ (36) 659-01-42) at the new bus terminal is a large three-star hotel whose *raison d'etre* is that it's right beside the bus station. It's convenient for its proximity to the station, but inconvenient to the centre, which is about half an hour away. It has two swimming pools and 377 basic but clean rooms with colour TV at US$26.40.

Motels Avenida López Mateos, running north-south a couple of km west of the centre, is Guadalajara's 'motel row', with a number of motels to choose from. A good one is the *Hotel del Bosque* (☎ (36) 621-46-50, 621-47-00), at López Mateos Sur 265, just off the Glorieta Minerva. It has an interior garden, swimming pool, restaurant, bar, and its 64 rooms all have carpeting and satellite TV. Singles/doubles are US$44/47; suites with kitchen are US$47/54.

The *Motel de Las Américas* (☎ (36) 631-44-15), at López Mateos Sur 2400, opposite the Plaza del Sol shopping mall, is a four-star motel with swimming pool, air conditioning and other amenities; its 94 rooms cost US$52/65. There are plenty of other motels in this area near the Plaza del Sol.

Another popular motel, cheaper and closer to the centre, is the three-star *Motel Isabel* (☎ (36) 626-26-30), at J Guadalupe Montenegro 1572, one block from Avenida de la Paz and about eight blocks towards the centre from Avenida Chapúltepec. It has 50 rooms, a swimming pool, restaurant, bar and inside parking; cost is US$24.95/30.80 for singles/doubles.

Places to Stay – top end

The *Hotel de Mendoza* (☎ (36) 613-46-46,

614-26-21, fax 613-73-10), at Carranza 16 on the north side of the Teatro Degollado, was built as the convent to the church of Santa María de Gracia, which is still standing on one side of it. Today, the convent has been refurbished into a four-star hotel, with 104 modern rooms and all the amenities – colour TVs, air conditioning, restaurant, bar, swimming pool and parking. Rooms cost US$52/65 for singles/doubles, with suites more expensive.

Other fine four-star hotels in the centre include the *Hotel Calinda Roma* (☎ (36) 614-86-50, fax 613-05-57), Avenida Juárez 170, with 172 rooms at US$52/60; the *Hotel Fenix Best Western* (☎ (36) 614-57-14, fax 613-40-05), Avenida Corona 160, with 259 rooms at US$63/72; and the *Hotel Aranzazú* (☎ (36) 613-32-32, fax 614-50-45), Avenida Revolución 110, near the corner of Corona, with two towers and 500 rooms at US$59/66.

Then there's the lovely *Hotel Lafayette* (☎ (36) 615-025-2, fax 630-11-12), at Avenida de la Paz 2055, just west of Avenida Chapúltepec, in Guadalajara's plush zona rosa. It has 181 attractive rooms with carpeting, colour TV and air conditioning at US$58/72 for singles/doubles.

Several large hotel chains also have five-star and Grand Tourism category hotels in Guadalajara. They include the *Camino Real* (☎ (36) 647-80-00, 647-67-81) at Avenida Vallarta 5005; the *Holiday Inn Crowne Plaza Guadalajara* (☎ (36) 634-10-34, 634-06-50) at Avenida López Mateos Sur 2500; the *Hyatt Regency Guadalajara* (☎ (36) 622-66-88, 622-77-78) at Avenida López Mateos and Moctezuma; and the *Fiesta Americana Guadalajara* (☎ (36) 625-34-34, 625-48-48) at Aurelio Aceves 225.

Places to Eat

Central District For good traditional Mexican food, try the *Restaurant La Chata* at Avenida Corona 126. The speciality of the house (the most expensive thing on the menu) is the Platillo Jalisciense, with a quarter chicken, potatoes, a sope, an enchil-ada and a flauta, all for US$6; a little cheaper is the plate with chicken mole, chile relleno, rice and beans. Enchiladas or chiles rellenos are around US$3.50. It's not an elegant restaurant, but it's been there for over 50 years and when you taste the food you'll see why. It's open every day from 9 am to 10.30 pm.

Another favourite is the *Café Madrid* at Avenida Juárez 264, near the corner of Avenida Corona. It's a popular place open every day from 8 am to 10 pm, with good food, excellent coffee, and a comida corrida for US$6.

The larger *Café Madoka*, at González Martínez 78, just north of Avenida Juárez, is a clean, bustling restaurant popular for its good food at all meals, with a comida corrida for US$5.50. It's open every day from 8 am to 11.30 pm, to 10 pm on Sundays.

The *Restaurant La Terraza* on an upstairs terrace at Avenida Hidalgo 436, just off the Plaza de Armas, is another popular spot, especially in the evening when there's live music from 6 to 9 pm – we went on a Sunday evening and could barely squeeze in the door. It serves economical meals, with meat and chicken around US$4, cheeseburgers US$2, and a comida corrida for US$3.50. It's open every day from noon to 10 pm.

Downstairs, the *Restaurant El Patio de la Merced*, at Avenida Hidalgo 426, is entered through the *Nectar* frozen yoghurt and ice cream parlour. It serves up simple and inexpensive snacks like pizza, sandwiches, burgers, coffee and desserts in a clean, pleasant covered courtyard surrounded by stone arches every day from 8 am to 9 pm.

For a more elegant meal, try the *Restaurant/Bar La Copa de Leche*, at Avenida Juárez 414. It's a bit more expensive, with main dishes around US$10 and a comida corrida for US$7.20 (US$8.50 on Sundays), but the atmosphere is pleasant both in the downstairs dining room and on the upstairs terrace, with romantic candlelight in the evening. It's open every day from 7 am until around 10 or 11 pm.

All the fancy hotels also have classy restaurants. Check out the ones at the *Hotel Francés*, Maestranza 35, or the *Hotel de*

Mendoza, Carranza 16, both historic city landmarks near the Teatro Degollado.

The *Restaurant Las Jaulas*, in the Hotel Fenix at Corona 160 near the corner of López Cotilla, is open every day from 7 am to midnight. Monday to Friday they have a breakfast buffet from 8 am to noon (US$8.80) and an ample afternoon buffet from 1 to 4.30 pm (US$9.70).

Homesick gringos might like to know there's a *Denny's* at Avenida Juárez 305, on the corner of Avenida 16 de Septiembre. It has an English menu with all the familiar dishes, it's also air-conditioned, and is open 24 hours every day. On the opposite corner, the *Sanborns* department store has a similar air-conditioned restaurant, which is clean, popular, and open every day from 7.30 am to midnight.

The *Mercado Libertad* has hundreds of little restaurant stalls. They're probably the cheapest eats you'll find in the city, and they feed thousands of people a day. Sensitive stomachs, beware – the hygeine here is not always the best. If you eat in the market, be sure to choose a stall that looks clean. Customers tend to cluster around the best stalls, so you might want to pick one that's crowded.

Vegetarian The *Restaurant Acuarius* at Sánchez 416 is a popular vegetarian restaurant and health food store, especially at lunchtime when the comida corrida is served (US$5.50). They also serve soya-based meals, yoghurt with fruits, and similar vegetarian fare; it's open every day except Sunday, from 9.30 am to 8 pm.

Smaller and friendlier is the simple family-run *Restaurant Naturalissimo*, at Calle 8 de Julio 138. Their comida corrida for US$3.35 includes salad, soup, main dish, dessert, and all the cold fresh fruit juice you can drink. Other goodies include chop suey with brown rice (US$2.30), vegetarian pizzas (US$3.35 for the simplest small one to US$8.70 for the large one with everything on it), soyburgers (US$1.95) and yoghurt with fruit and honey (US$1.50). They're

open every day except Sunday, from 10 am to 6 pm.

Another tiny but popular vegetarian restaurant is the simple little *El Colmenar*, on Avenida Hidalgo opposite Plaza Tapatía, just east of the bridge. It has a simple menu based mostly on yoghurts, fruits and sandwiches. It was recommended by several readers; when we went to check it out one afternoon there was a queue of hungry customers extending out onto the sidewalk.

Near Avenida Chapúltepec Just a 10-minute bus ride from the city centre, Guadalajara's zona rosa is a much quieter district, with some fine restaurants worth the trip to reach them. Catch the 'Par Vial' bus heading west on Independencia, get off at Avenidas Chapúltepec and Vallarta, and they're all close by.

The *Restaurant Los Itacates*, at Chapúltepec Norte 110, is a pleasant restaurant/bar specialising in traditional Mexican foods *de la vieja cocina Mexicana* (from the old Mexican kitchen) at surprisingly inexpensive prices. Chicken mole with two cheese enchiladas, potatoes, rice and tortillas is US$4, chiles rellenos US$3.35, or there are tacos with 19 fillings to choose from at just US$0.50 each. The ample breakfast buffet for US$4, served every day from 8.30 am to noon, is a good deal. It's open every day from 8 am to 11 pm except on Sunday, when it closes at 7 pm.

Nearby, the *Restaurant/Bar Recco*, at Libertad 1981, just east of Chapúltepec, is a more elegant restaurant specialising in European and Italian foods, with main courses from around US$6 to US$11. It's open every day from 1 to 11.30 pm, except on Sunday when it closes at 10 pm.

Also nearby, the *Restaurant Vegetariano Las Margaritas* at López Cotilla 1477, just west of Chapúltepec, is a good vegetarian restaurant whose comida corrida at US$3.70 (US$4.70 on Sundays) runs out fast; you have to show up at around noon to get it. Their menu includes 13 safe-to-eat salads, 17 hot or cold sandwiches, and a variety of fruit and vegetable juices. It's open Monday to Saturday from 9 am to 9 pm, and Sunday 10 to 6 pm.

Near Avenida López Mateos About 20 blocks west of Avenida Chapúltepec, Avenida López Mateos is another large avenue with a number of better restaurants.

The *Restaurant La Trattoria* at Niños Héroes 3051, one block east of Avenida López Mateos, is one of the finest Italian restaurants in Guadalajara, but it's not expensive. A salad bar is included in the price of all meals, which range from US$4.50 for pastas to US$8.50 for meat and seafood meals. It's open every day from 1 pm to midnight; bus No 51-A or 51-B will bring you here from the centre. *El Italiano* at Avenida México 3130 is another excellent Italian restaurant.

The *Guadalajara Grill*, Avenida López Mateos 3711 Sur, at the corner of Conchita a few blocks south of the Plaza del Sol, is also popular. Part of the Carlos Anderson restaurant chain, it's a large, fun place with a lively atmosphere, good music, and dancing in the bar. It's a bit expensive, with steaks or shrimp at US$10, red snapper at US$8.35 and chicken at US$7, but it's a fun place for a special lunch or dinner out. It's open every day from 1.30 pm to midnight, and to 6 pm on Sundays. Bus No 258 will bring you here from the centre.

Another Carlos Anderson restaurant, *Nacho's & Charlie's*, is at Avenida Américas 1472, a bit closer to the centre.

Entertainment

Guadalajara has something going on to fit any taste, from rodeos to ice skating to classic films, philharmonic concerts and some of the best mariachi music in Mexico. The city is in love with music; concerts in many styles can be found any night of the week at a number of popular venues.

Phone or stop by the state tourist office (☎ 658-22-22) to check out their weekly schedule of events; the friendly bilingual staff will help you find something to suit your fancy. Also ask for their bimonthly magazine *Ver y Oír*, with listings for music and cultural events, film and video presentations, live theatre performances at a dozen different theatres, and art galleries – there are over 35 galleries throughout the city.

Ballet Folklórico Every Sunday from 10 am to noon the Ballet Folklórico of the University of Guadalajara stages a magnificent performance at the Teatro Degollado. Tickets range from US$3.35 (gallery) to US$16.70 (*luneta*); buy them any day of the week at the theatre ticket office, which is open every day from 10 am to 1 pm and 4 to 7 pm. This is Guadalajara's most renowned folkloric dance troupe.

If you're in town on a Wednesday night rather than a Sunday morning, check out the Ballet Folklórico of the Instituto Cultural Cabañas, performing there every Wednesday night starting at 8.30 pm. Tickets are US$5.

Philharmonic Orchestra The state philharmonic orchestra, called the Filarmónica de Jalisco, performs every Sunday at the Teatro Degollado from noon to 2 pm, right after the Ballet Folklórico, and on Friday nights at 8.30 pm. Tickets cost from US$3.35 (gallery) to US$10 (luneta) and are sold at the theatre any day of the week.

Plaza de los Mariachis To hear mariachi music in the place it was born, check out the Plaza de los Mariachis, one of Mexico's most famous alleys, near Calzada Independencia Sur just south of Mercado Libertad. Take a seat at one of the tables set out on the plaza, get a soda, a beer or a meal, and enjoy the magnificent music. The bands go from table to table offering to play (for a price, of course); they're out there at all hours, 24 hours a day, but they are best late at night.

Music & Cultural Events Cultural performances are held frequently at the Teatro Degollado (☎ 658-38-12) and the Instituto

Cultural Cabañas (☎ 617-43-22), both right in the centre.

Other popular venues include the Instituto Cultural Mexicano Norteamericano de Jalisco (☎ 625-58-38, 625-41-01) at Enrique Díaz de León 300; the Centro Cultural Centenario (☎ 626-95-42) at Cruz Verde 272 between Garibaldi and Reforma; the Peña Cuicacalli (☎ 625-46-90) at Niños Héroes 1988 near Avenida Chapúltepec; Las Tapas Tías (☎ 615-76-72) at Francisco de Quevedo 78-2, opposite Plaza Vallarta; Café y Arte Quetzal (☎ 616-02-01) at Avenida Unión 236; the Café Tlalocán (☎ 626-76-34) at Prisciliano Sánchez 772; and the Centro Cultural Las Calas (☎ 647-03-83, 647-02-79) at Avenida Tepeyac 1156 in Colonia Chapalita.

Some of these places have a regular schedule of different events happening throughout the week. For example, on our last visit to Guadalajara, Café y Arte Quetzal was featuring flamenco and classical guitar on Monday, South American music on Tuesday, ballads on Wednesday, blues on Thursday, flamenco on Friday, rock on Saturday, and nueva canción on Sundays. The Centro Cultural Centenario, the Peña Cuicacalli and Las Tapas Tías had similar schedules, with something different every night of the week.

Copenhagen 77 (☎ 625-28-03), facing the west side of Parque Revolución near the corner of López Cotilla, specialises in 'gourmet jazz', with live music Monday to Saturday from 3 pm to 12.30 am. In addition to other meals they serve a great Spanish paella.

Most of the large, fancy hotels offer music and entertainment. The attractive lobby piano bar of the Hotel Francés, at Maestranza 35 near the Plaza de la Liberación, is especially popular. The lobby bar of the Hotel Fenix at Corona 160 is also popular, and there are plenty of others.

Free concerts of *típico* Jaliscan music are held in the Plaza de Armas on Thursdays and Sundays beginning at 6.30 pm, always drawing a crowd.

Cinemas Guadalajara has a number of *cines* presenting both Mexican and international films. Check the tourist office and their magazine *Ver y Oír*, which has film listings for most of the city's finest theatres. The *Occidental* and *Informador* daily newspapers also have movie listings.

Some of the best places to catch international films are at the Cine Charles Chaplin (☎ 641-54-07) on López Mateos Sur; Cine Cinematógrafo (☎ 625-05-14) at the corner of Avenidas Vallarta and Argentina; the Sala Premier, at Eulogio Parra 2233 on the corner of Avenida Las Américas; the Cine-Teatro Cabañas (☎ 617-43-22) at the Instituto Cultural Cabañas on the east end of Plaza Tapatía; Bellas Artes (☎ 614-16-14) at Jesús García 720; the Alianza Francesa (☎ 625-55-95) at López Cotilla 1199; and the Centro de Investigación y Enseñanza Cinematográficas (☎ 653-03-02) at Avenida Vallarta 2181. The University of Guadalajara's Departamento de Video y TV (☎ 625-57-23), Avenida Hidalgo 1296, presents a wide variety of interesting international films and videos; it's open to the public.

Discos Guadalajara has a number of discos. Some of the most popular are Daddy'O at Avenida López Mateos 2185; Osiris, on Lázaro Cárdenas two blocks from the large Hotel Camino Real; and Genesis, in the Hotel Carlton at the corner of Niños Héroes and Avenida 16 de Septiembre. Coco & Coco, in the Hotel Fenix at Avenida Corona 160, has live music for dancing, as do several other of the major hotels.

Rodeos, Bullfights & Cockfights Rodeos (charreadas) are held every Sunday in the rodeo ring behind Parque Agua Azul. Charros come from all over Jalisco and other parts of Mexico to show off their skills.

The bullfighting season is from September to January, but bullfights are not held every Sunday as they used to be. There will be a couple for sure during the October Fiestas; the rest of the season they may be sporadic. Check with the tourist office for coming events. When bullfights are held, they're on Sundays at 4 pm in the Plaza de Toros on the northern end of Calzada Independencia; bus No 60 heading north on Calzada Independencia will take you there.

Tickets can be bought in advance at the bullfight office, Avenida de la Paz 1271, on the corner of Federalismo (☎ 625-19-74, 625-29-72) or at the Plaza de Toros on the day of the fight.

Cockfights are held regularly at the Palenque near Parque Agua Azul, and at the Palenques in Tlaquepaque and Zapopan.

Football Fútbol (soccer) is one of Guadalajara's favourite sports. The city has four teams (Los Leones, Los Tecos, Las Chivas and Las Atlas) playing at stadiums around the city during the season from September to May. The tourist office keeps abreast of the matches, or you can phone the Guadalajara Stadium (☎ 637-06-16, 637-06-64) to ask about the games. Take bus No 60 heading north on Calzada Independencia to reach the stadium.

Things to Buy

Handcrafts from Jalisco, Michoacán and other Mexican states are available in Guadalajara. In the centre, the Casa de las Artesanías, at González Gallo on the north side of Parque Agua Azul about 20 blocks south of the centre, has a good selection; prices are high but the quality is excellent. It's open Monday to Friday from 10 am to 6 pm, Saturday 10 am to 4 pm, Sunday 10 am to 2 pm. Bus No 60 heading south on Calzada Independencia will drop you at the entrance to Parque Agua Azul.

The Instituto de la Artesanía Jaliscense at Alcalde 1221, about 20 blocks north of the centre, has a similar selection. It's open Monday to Saturday from 9 am to 5 pm; any bus heading north on Avenida 16 de Septiembre/Alcalde will take you there. Or there's the Casa de la Artesanía La Tapatía, at Paseo Degollado and Pasaje Jugueteros in the Plaza Tapatía, open the same hours as the one at Parque Agua Azul.

Mercado Libertad, right in the centre, is a giant marketplace with three floors of shops and stalls covering an area equivalent to four city blocks. It's open every day. On Sundays you can check out the huge El Baratillo market stretching for blocks in every direction, beginning about 15 blocks east of Mercado Libertad.

In the suburbs south-east of the centre, Tlaquepaque and Tonalá are famous for ceramics. Jocotepec, near Lake Chapala, is known for its woollen sarapes.

Getting There & Away

Air Guadalajara's Aeropuerto Internacional Miguel Hidalgo (☎ 689-00-89) is 17 km south of the city centre, just off the highway to Chapala. It is a major international airport served by a number of airlines, with flights available to virtually anywhere in Mexico and the USA.

There are over 100 travel agencies in Guadalajara where you can make flight arrangements; look in the telephone directory yellow pages under 'Agencias de Viajes'. Airline offices are listed in the yellow pages under 'Aviación – Lineas de'. They include:

Aero California
 López Cotilla 1423 (☎ 626-19-62, 626-10-64)
Aeroméxico
 Avenida Corona 196, corner of Madero (☎ 615-65-65)
American Airlines
 Vallarta 2440 (☎ 616-40-90)
Continental
 Hyatt Hotel, Plaza del Sol (☎ 647-66-72, 647-66-75)
Delta
 López Cotilla 1701 (☎ 630-35-30)
Mexicana
 Mariano Otero 2353 (☎ 647-22-22)

Bus Guadalajara has two bus stations. The long-distance bus station, called the Nueva Central Camionera, is a huge terminal with seven separate buildings (*módulos*) in Tlaquepaque, about five km south-east of the centre; it opened just a few years ago.

Each of the módulos is the base for various

ous lines, with each módulo specialising in buses to particular destinations. Buses to Mexico City depart from all the módulos. You can get information on which módulo you need for other destinations from the tourist information kiosks staffed 24 hours a day in each módulo. Watch out for their information on hotels, however; they work for a chain of expensive hotels and will try to steer you to these. We checked them out by asking for a recommendation to a cheap hotel in the centre, and were told that hotel rates are very high in Guadalajara, but they could give us a good deal on a special hotel for US$50 a night!

Local bus Nos 275A or 275B running south on Avenida 16 de Septiembre will take you to the new bus station; cost is US$0.20 for the 25-minute trip. A taxi will cost around US$7.35. If you're arriving at the station, you can take any northbound local bus No 275 into the centre, but they only operate from 5.30 am to 10.30 pm. For a taxi into town, buy a taxi ticket from the booth at the exit doorway of each módulo; fares are regulated by zones (it's US$7.35 to the centre).

Distances and travel times from Guadalajara to other cities in the region include: Aguascalientes, 251 km, 3½ to four hours; Barra de Navidad, 291 km, six hours; Colima, 224 km, three hours; Guanajuato, 300 km, five to six hours; Mexico City, 535 km, eight hours; Morelia, 367 km, five hours; Puerto Vallarta, 397 km, six to seven hours; Querétaro, 348 km, five to six hours; San Luis Potosí, 354 km, five to six hours; Tepic, 228 km, four hours; Uruapan, 325 km, five hours; Zacatecas, 319 km, five hours.

Guadalajara's other bus station is called the Vieja Central Camionera, or old bus station; before the new bus station was built, this was Guadalajara's only bus terminal. It's on Calle Analco between Calle Los Angeles and Avenida 5 de Febrero, near the Parque Agua Azul about 20 blocks south of the centre. Local bus No 60 heading south on Calzada Independencia will take you there.

This old bus station now serves as the terminal for buses serving destinations nearer Guadalajara, including:

Ajijic – 47 km, 1¼ hours; hourly buses on the half-hour, same buses as to Chapala (US$2), or bus to Chapala and take a local bus from there.

Chapala – 40 km, one hour; buses every half-hour, 6 am to 9 pm (US$2).

Jocotepec – 69 km, two hours; 2nd-class buses every half hour, 6 am to 9 pm (US$1.70), or bus to Chapala or Ajijic and take a local bus from there.

Tequila – 50 km, 1¾ hours; buses every 20 minutes, 6.10 am to 9.10 pm (US$1.65).

Train The Estación del Ferrocarril (☎ 650-08-26, 650-04-44, ext 462) is at the southern end of Calzada Independencia Sur, about 20 blocks south of the centre.

Train tickets can be bought at the station, or in the centre at the Agencia de Viajes MaCull (☎ 614-70-14, 614-70-15), López Cotilla 163, near the corner of Degollado. It's open Monday to Friday from 9 am to 2 pm and 4 to 7 pm, Saturday 9 am to 2 pm. They sell tickets for the *El Pacífico* and *El Tapatío* trains, which can be bought in advance of your date of travel; tickets for Train No 92 to Colima and Manzanillo must be bought at the station an hour before the train departs, on the day of your journey.

The 1st-class *El Tapatío* train (Train No 6) to Mexico City departs Guadalajara daily at 9 pm, taking 11½ hours to reach Mexico City. Basic 1st-class seats cost US$21; a camarín (roomette) for one person costs an additional US$41, while an alcoba (roomette) for two people costs an additional US$82 over the 1st-class fare. Tickets for this train can be purchased at the train station any day from 8 am to 8.30 pm.

The 1st-class *El Pacífico* train (Train No 1) originates at Guadalajara, heads west to Tepic and then north up the Pacific coast to the USA border towns of Mexicali (near Calexico, California) and Nogales (near Nogales, Arizona). It's all one train until it reaches the switching station at Benjamin Hill, Sonora, where the cars bound for Mexicali and Nogales are separated and sent on their respective ways. This train departs Guadalajara every day at 9.30 am. Tickets for the *El Pacífico* train are sold at the train station Monday to Friday from 9 am to 1 pm.

Fares and arrival times at cities along its route include:

departs

Guadalajara	9.30 am	
arrives		
Tepic	1.55 pm	US$ 8.25
Mazatlán	6.50 pm	US$17.70
Culiacán	9.50 pm	US$24.30
Sufragio	12.35 am	US$30.60
Navojoa	2.00 am	US$34.80
Ciudad Obregón	3.30 am	US$36.90
Empalme	5.10 am	US$40.50
Hermosillo	7.10 am	US$44.70
Benjamin Hill	8.50 am	US$48.60
Nogales	11.05 am	US$52.80
Caborca	10.55 am	US$52.20
Puerto Peñasco	1.00 pm	US$57.00
Mexicali	4.30 pm	US$64.50

Coming in the other direction, departure and arrival times are:

departs

Mexicali	9.00 am
arrives	
Puerto Peñasco	12.30 pm
Caborca	2.30 pm
departs	
Nogales	2.20 pm
arrives	
Benjamin Hill	4.40 pm
Hermosillo	6.30 pm
Empalme	8.35 pm
Ciudad Obregón	10.15 pm
Navojoa	12.05 am
Sufragio	1.05 am
Culiacán	4.00 am
Mazatlán	7.00 am
Tepic	12.25 pm
Guadalajara	7.05 pm

A 2nd-class train heading up the same Pacific route as the *El Pacífico* departs Guadalajara daily at noon, but it's slower, more crowded, dirtier and much less pleasant than the *El Pacífico*. It's worth spending the extra money to travel on the *El Pacífico* train if you're travelling this route.

Another 2nd-class train departing from Guadalajara is Train No 92, heading south to Colima and on to Manzanillo. It departs

Guadalajara daily at 9 am, arriving in Colima around 3 pm (US$2.30) and in Manzanillo at around 5.15 pm (US$3.10).

Car Guadalajara has over 30 rental car agencies; they are listed in the telephone directory yellow pages under 'Automóviles – Renta de'. As always, it's best to shop around to compare prices. Several of the large US companies are represented in Guadalajara, but you may get a better deal from local companies. Many agencies will deliver the car to you at no extra cost.

Rental car agencies include:

Auto Rent de Guadalajara
    Federalismo Sur 542A (☎ 625-15-15, 626-20-14)
Avis
    Hotel Fiesta Americana, Aurelio Aceves 225 (☎ 615-48-25, 689-05-81)
Budget
    Niños Héroes 934 (☎ 613-00-27, 613-02-86).
Central de Rentas
    Federalismo Sur 542 (☎ 613-76-76, 613-76-96).
Dollar
    Circunvalación Agustín Yañez 2557 (☎ 630-01-17, 616-50-23)
    Airport (☎ 689-0522)
Hertz
    Niños Héroes 9 (☎ 614-61-62, 614-61-39)
    Hotel Camino Real, Vallarta 5005 (☎ 647-80-00, ext 1054)
    Airport (☎ 689-01-56).
National
    Niños Héroes & Manzano (☎ 614-71-75, 689-02-81).
Odin
    Avenida 16 de Septiembre 742 (☎ 614-71-20, 614-86-84)
    Airport (☎ 689-05-05).
Quick Rent A Car
    Niños Héroes 954 (☎ 614-22-47, 614-60-06)
    Airport (☎ 689-05-02).
Rente Un Auto
    Vallarta 3997 (☎ 622-13-54, 622-33-16).
Vega's
    Manzano 410 (☎ 613-19-20, 658-03-16)
    Hotel El Parador, new bus station (☎ 659-01-42).

Getting Around

To/From the Airport Combis run from the airport into the city, and are cheaper than the taxis. But from the city back to the airport the price is almost the same as the taxi fare

(US$13.35) if you have them come to pick you up. Auto Transportaciones Aeropuerto (☎ 612-93-37, 612-93-39) is the company that runs the combis. Alternatively, combi route No 625 runs down Avenida Juárez heading for the airport, but only once an hour. Taxis are probably the easiest option.

Bus Guadalajara has an excellent local bus system that will take you just about anywhere you could want to go in the city. Buses operate frequently, every five minutes or so on most major routes, every day from 5.30 am to 10.30 pm; they cost US$0.20.

The tourist office has a complete list of the 140 bus routes in Guadalajara, and can help you figure out how to get anywhere you want to go. Convenient routes from the centre include those to:

Parque Agua Azul, Train Station & Old Bus Station –
    Bus No 60 heading south on Calzada
    Independencia.
Zoo, Planetarium, Stadium, Plaza de Toros & Parque
    Mirador – Bus No 60 heading north on Calzada
    Independencia.
Avenida Chapúltepec & Zona Rosa – White 'Par Vial'
    bus heading west on Independencia.
Plaza del Sol – Bus No 258 heading west on Calle San
    Felipe, three blocks north of the cathedral.
Tlaquepaque & New Bus Station – Bus No 275A or
    275B, heading south on Avenida 16 de
    Septiembre.
Tonalá – Bus No 275 'Diagonal', heading south on
    Avenida 16 de Septiembre, goes through
    Tlaquepaque to Tonalá.
Zapopan – Bus No 275 'Diagonal' heading north on
    Avenida 16 de Septiembre.

Metro Two subway routes crisscross the city. Linea 1 runs north-south for 15 km below the Calzada del Federalismo, a few blocks west of the centre, going all the way from the Periférico Norte to the Periférico Sur. You can catch it at the stop at Parque Revolución, at the corner of Avenida Juárez. Linea 2 runs east-west for 10 km below Avenida Juárez. It stops at Mercado Libertad (called San Juan de Dios, another name for the market), the University of Guadalajara, Avenida Chapúltepec and Avenida López Mateos, among others. Both routes operate fre-

quently every day from 6 am to 11 pm; the fare is US$0.25 to any destination.

Taxi Taxis are plentiful in the centre. They are supposed to charge fixed rates, depending on the distance traversed. Typical fares from the centre are US$3.35 to the train station, old bus station or Parque Azul; US$5 to the Plaza del Sol; US$7.35 to Tlaquepaque, the new bus station, the zoo or Zapopan; US$10 to Tonalá; and US$13.35 to the airport. Always be sure to clarify the fare before you get into the cab.

AROUND GUADALAJARA
Zapopan
Situated on the north-western edge of Guadalajara, Zapopan was an Indian village before the Spanish arrived, an important maize-producing agricultural village during colonial times, and is now a suburb of Guadalajara. The large **Basílica de Zapopan**, built in 1730, houses the image of Nuestra Señora de Zapopan, a tiny statue visited by pilgrims from near and far. In the church courtyard a statue of Pope John Paul II with a small child commemorates his visit to the basilica on 30 January 1979.

To the right of the church entrance the small **Museo Huichol** is a museum of Huichol Indian art with many examples of colourful yarn art and other arts and crafts produced by the Huichols. Most of the items on display are for sale. The museum is open Monday to Friday from 10 am to 1.30 pm and 4 to 7 pm, Saturday and Sunday 10 am to 1 pm; admission is free.

Bus No 275 'Diagonal' heading north on Avenida 16 de Septiembre stops beside the Basílica de Zapopan, about 20 minutes north of the centre.

Also in Zapopan is the **Museo de Caza Benito Alvarrán** at Paseo de los Parques 3540, Colinas de San Javier, a museum of hunting with a collection of over 250 lifelike stuffed mammals and birds. To get there from the centre, take bus No 510 heading west on Madero; get off at the corner of Pablo Neruda and Circuito Madrigal and walk six blocks straight ahead on Madrigal, until you see the museum on your left. It's open Saturday and Sunday from 10.30 am to 2.30 pm; admission is free.

Tlaquepaque

About five km south-east of downtown Guadalajara, Tlaquepaque ('tlah-keh-PAH-keh') also used to be a separate town, but Guadalajara spread south-eastward and made it a suburb. The townspeople, who had long been artisans and craftspeople, decided to capitalise on their talents by cleaning and beefing up the central plaza, renaming many of the shops 'galleries' to attract tourist dollars. Fortunately, the throngs of crafts-hungry gringos who have descended on the place have not spoiled the refurbishment of central Tlaquepaque.

Many flowers, small benches and monuments now grace the plaza. The shops are full of ceramics, including bizarre anthropomorphic monsters, papier mâché animals and bronze figures. First, visit the **Museo Regional de la Cerámica y los Artes Populares de Jalisco** at Independencia 237 to get an idea of the best handcrafts available in Tlaquepaque. The museum is open Tuesday to Saturday from 10 to 4 pm, and Sunday 10 am to 1 pm; admission is free. Also visit the glass factory across the street from the museum. Many of the shops are closed on Sunday. The tourist office (☎ 635-05-96) is at Guillermo Prieto 80.

Tlaquepaque has a number of pleasant restaurant/bars where you can refresh yourself. Several have lively mariachi bands in the afternoon and evening. *El Patio* at Independencia 186 has live music and dining in a fine garden patio. The *Restaurant Abajeño* at Juárez 231 also has garden dining and a group of mariachis. The *No Name Restaurant* at Madero 80 is a favourite spot, with good food and live music in a lovely setting with parrots and peacocks. *Mariscos Progreso* at Progreso 80 specialises in seafood, which is served under the trees.

To get to Tlaquepaque, take local bus No 275A or 275B heading south on Avenida 16 de Septiembre. Cost is US$0.20 for the half-hour trip.

Tonalá

The Guadalajara suburb of Tonalá, near Tlaquepaque about eight km south-east of the centre, is the poorer, less touristy relative of Tlaquepaque. The shops here call themselves 'factories', not galleries – an accurate description considering that many of them manufacture the glassware and ceramics found in Tlaquepaque and other parts of Guadalajara. On Thursday and Sunday most of the town becomes a huge street market that takes hours to explore.

The **Museo Nacional de la Cerámica**, at Constitución 110 near the Presidencia Municipal, is open Tuesday to Saturday from 10 am to 4 pm, Sunday 10 am to 1 pm; admission is free. The tourist office (☎ 683-09-71) is at Morelos 180.

Bus No 275 'Diagonal' heading south on Avenida 16 de Septiembre will take you to Tonalá, passing through Tlaquepaque on the way. The fare is US$0.20 for the 40-minute trip.

Laguna de Chapala

Forty km south of Guadalajara, Mexico's largest lake is 85 km long and 28 km wide. A near-perfect climate in the northern lakeshore towns of Chapala, Ajijic ('ah-hee-HEEK') and Jocotepec ('ho-co-teh-PEC') have attracted a growing population of American and Canadian retirees. So many have settled in this area that it is now one of the largest communities of American expatriates in the world; estimates vary but 30,000 is frequently mentioned.

To ward off homesickness, almost every imaginable North American organisation has been established here, including the Masons, Shriners, Daughters of the American Revolution, Eastern Star, Rotary Club, Lions Club, Salvation Army, Humane Society, Knights of Columbus, Weight Watchers, Alcoholics Anonymous, US military veterans' posts and country clubs.

One of Chapala's country clubs, the Villa Montecarlo, was once the country estate of Mexican President Porfirio Díaz, who served from the late 1800s to the early 1900s. Later, British author D H Lawrence wrote

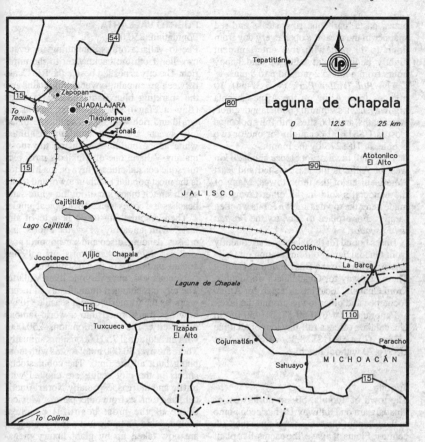

most of *The Plumed Serpent* while living at Calle Zaragoza 307 in Chapala. His former home has now been converted into the expensive *Quetzalcoatl Inn*.

Laguna de Chapala is beautiful at sunset, the only time you can really enjoy it. The lake is now polluted and clogged with a mass of vegetation that's quickly spreading from the shore.

Although all three towns along the north shore can easily be visited in a day trip, there are several hotels and a trailer park among them. In Chapala, the *Hotel Nido* (☎ 5-21-16) and its adjoining restaurant, at Madero 202 near the waterfront, are often recommended. Cost is US$13.35/16.70 for a single/double and US$7.70 for a huge comida corrida. *Beto's* restaurant beside it is also good.

In Ajijic there's the more expensive *La Nueva Posada* (☎ 5-33-95) at Donato Guerra 9 beside the lake. This small motor inn, run by an amiable Canadian couple, has 12 rooms with views of the lake or the swimming pool. Breakfast is included in the cost of US$47/54 for singles/doubles. *Restaurant Los Veleros*, on the highway in the heart of Ajijic, is reputed to have the best pizza, pasta, barbeque ribs, steaks and red snapper in the area; it's open every day from noon to 11 pm, with live entertainment nightly beginning at 8.30 pm and happy hours from noon to 2 pm and 6 to 8 pm.

The *Pal Trailer Park* (☎ 5-37-64), 10 minutes from Ajijic on the Ajijic-Chapala highway, has a swimming pool, laundry, hot-water baths, and 106 sites with full hook-ups. Cost is US$11.50 per night for one or two people, or US$275 by the month.

The small town of Jocotepec about 20 km west of Ajijic is the least visited and least Americanised of the three towns. Many of the handcrafts sold in the other towns are made here; the town is known for its woollen sarapes. For a place to stay, try the *Posada del Pescador*.

Buses bound for the lake depart frequently from Guadalajara's old bus station on Calle Los Angeles; see the Bus section in Getting There & Away for Guadalajara for details. From Chapala, local buses depart for Ajijic, Jocotepec and other towns around the lake.

Panoramex (☎ 610-50-57, 610-50-05) in Guadalajara offers a full-day tour of all three towns. Cost is US$28.35 with lunch or US$16.70 without lunch.

Tequila

The town of Tequila, 50 km north-west of Guadalajara on Highway 15, has been home to the liquor of the same name since the 17th century. Fields of agave, the cactus-like plant from which tequila is distilled, surround the town. You can almost get drunk just breathing the heavily scented air that drifts from the town's distilleries. The two largest distilleries – Sauza and Cuervo – offer public tours of their operations and, of course, free samples.

Since Tequila is on Highway 15, it's a main bus stop and easy to get to from either Guadalajara or cities and towns to the north. Local buses to Tequila depart every 20 minutes from Guadalajara's old bus station on Calle Los Angeles; see the Bus section in Getting There & Away for Guadalajara for details.

PUERTO VALLARTA

Population: 250,000

Puerto Vallarta offers something for every traveller, from the backpacker to the ultra-rich. The city is nestled beside the Río Cuale between green palm-covered mountains and the sparkling blue Bahía de las Banderas (Bay of Flags), seventh-largest bay in the world and rich with fish. The cobblestoned city streets are lined with old-fashioned white adobe buildings with red tile roofs, making Vallarta one of Mexico's most picturesque coastal cities. Playa de los Muertos is the most popular beach in town, and to the south stretch many km of idyllic white-sand beaches and coves backed by tropical jungle.

There's something to do here to fit any taste, with an array of water sports and cruises, dancing, disco and bar-hopping possibilities, Mexican handcrafts, art galleries and an abundance of fine restaurants.

Nonetheless, not everyone likes Vallarta. The city has changed dramatically in recent years, as the formerly quaint seaside village now has transformed into a world-famous resort city. The population tops 250,000, with an additional 750,000 visitors annually. There are over 30,000 hotel rooms with more being built all the time. The cobblestoned streets in the city centre are choked with traffic and tourists, especially North Americans and tourists from other parts of Mexico. Some of the most beautiful beaches, secluded and romantic just a few years ago, are now taken up by giant luxury mega-resorts with hundreds of rooms. English is almost as commonly spoken as Spanish; as tourism – Vallarta's only industry – has made this practically a bilingual city.

Even with all this, though, the natural beauty of Puerto Vallarta is still its dominant feature. We've seen it both ways, as it used to be and as it is today, and we have to admit we still like Vallarta.

History

Puerto Vallarta's history is not very long; the first recorded settlement here dates from 1851, when the Sánchez family came and made their home by the mouth of the Río

Cuale, which now divides the city. Farmers and fisherfolk followed several years later. By 1918 there were enough people living around the Río Cuale to give the settlement a name on the map. The name Vallarta was chosen in honour of Ignacio Luis Vallarta, a former governor of the state of Jalisco. It was called Puerto (port) because farmers had been shipping their harvests by boat from a small port area north of the Río Cuale.

Tourists first began to visit Vallarta in 1954 when Mexicana airlines started a promotional campaign and initiated the first flights here, landing on a dirt airstrip in Emiliano Zapata, an area which is now downtown Vallarta. But it was not until a decade later in 1964, when John Huston chose the nearby deserted cove of Mismaloya for the shooting of the film version of Tennessee Williams' *The Night of the Iguana*, that the town was put on the international tourist map.

The paparazzi of Hollywood descended to report on every development of the romance between Richard Burton and Elizabeth Taylor for hungry scandalmongers, while Burton's co-star Ava Gardner also raised more than a few eyebrows, and Puerto Vallarta suddenly became world-famous with an aura of steamy tropical romance. Tour groups began arriving not long after the film crew left and they've been coming ever since.

Orientation

Puerto Vallarta is about 400 km (6½ hours) west of Guadalajara and 210 km (3½ hours) north of Barra de Navidad.

The downtown area is centred around the Río Cuale, which bisects the city, with the small Isla Cuale island in the middle of the river and two bridges making easy passage between the two sides of town. To the north of the city is the airport (about 10 km away) and two recent developments: Marina Vallarta, with a large international-class yachting marina about a km south of the airport, and Nuevo Vallarta, further north around the bay about 25 km from the city centre. Also north of the city are a host of giant luxury hotels fanning out along the shore.

To the south of the city are more resorts and some of the most beautiful beaches in the area, including Punta Negra, Las Estacas, Mismaloya, Boca de Tomatlán (all of which can be reached by Highway 200, the coastal highway) and the more isolated beaches of Playa de las Ánimas and Quimixto, reachable only by boat. Further around the bay is Yelapa, once a tiny fishing village but now a favourite destination of day cruises. It has a population of over 2500 people, many of them North Americans.

The heart of the city centre is the Plaza Principal, also called Plaza de Armas, sitting by the sea between Morelos and Juárez, the

---

Bahía de las Banderas

The Bahía de las Banderas is a very large bay – seventh-largest in the world, with an area of about 34 km by 52 km, a 161-km shoreline and a depth of around 1800 metres, though depth-measuring instruments have never found the bottom. Supposedly the bay is formed by the sunken crater of a giant extinct volcano. This is difficult to see when you're on land, but they say that if you fly around the perimeters of the bay in a plane, it's quite easy to see from a bird's eye view.

The bay is teeming with life but it has the unusual distinction of being virtually a shark-free bay. This is because it's a dolphin bay, and dolphins are one of the few creatures that can overcome sharks. Numerous dolphins inhabit the bay, bearing their young here all year round, and to protect their colony they mount a patrol at the bay's entrance, not allowing sharks to enter.

Pilot and grey whales also bear their young in the bay but only at a certain time of year, from around February to April. If you're out on the bay in a boat you will probably see dolphins, and whales in season. Giant manta rays also inhabit the bay and they say that if you're here in April during their mating season you can see them from the Malecón, jumping up into the air. ■

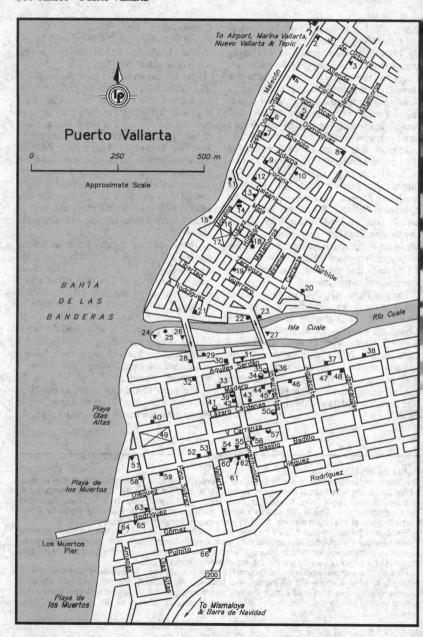

Puerto Vallarta

0   250   500 m

Approximate Scale

To Airport, Marina Vallarta,
Nuevo Vallarta & Tepic

BAHÍA
DE LAS
BANDERAS

Río Cuale

Isla Cuale

Playa
Olas
Altas

Playa de
los Muertos

Los Muertos
Pier

Playa de
los Muertos

To Mismaloya
& Barra de Navidad

city's two principal thoroughfares. The crown-topped cathedral, called the Templo de Guadalupe, towers behind the plaza on the mountain side; on the sea side of the plaza is an open-air amphitheatre with arches that have become a symbol of the town, and a wide seaside walkway known as the Malecón. The Malecón stretches north from the plaza from about 10 blocks to the Hotel Rosita, one of the city's first hotels.

The road running beside the Malecón,

Paseo Díaz Ordaz, is the major southbound route through the city, lined with bars, restaurants, nightclubs and boutiques. North of the Hotel Rosita it changes names, becoming Avenida México, and finally Highway 200 as it heads north out of town. On the other side of the plaza, Calle Juárez is the city's major northbound route.

The district south of the river is where the bus stations and many hotels and restaurants are found, in addition to the only two beaches in the city centre: Playa Olas Altas (poorly named because it doesn't really have 'big waves') and Playa de los Muertos, taking its strange name (Beach of the Dead) from a fierce fight there sometime in the distant past. Northbound traffic heads up Insurgentes and crosses the inland bridge over the river; southbound traffic comes over the seaside bridge, heads down Calle Vallarta and out of town on Highway 200.

Information

Tourist Office The tourist office (☎ (322) 2-02-42, 3-07-66, fax 2-02-43) is in the municipal building on the north-east corner of the Plaza Principal. They have abundant information on the city and bay region and the friendly staff can answer your questions in English, French or Spanish. They hand out free maps, mountains of tourist literature, and a free coupon book good for discounts around town. The office is open Monday to Saturday from 9 am to 9 pm.

Some of the more worthwhile publications to look for include *Places*, a useful little bimonthly magazine; *Vallarta Inside*, another useful magazine published annually; *Vallarta Today*, an interesting daily English-language newspaper for visitors and Vallarta's English-speaking community; and *Puerto Vallarta This Week*, a weekly tourist newspaper. All are distributed free at the tourist office.

Money Most businesses in Vallarta accept US dollars cash as readily as they accept pesos, though the rate of exchange they offer is usually less favourable than the banks, which offer the best rate. Many banks are found around the Plaza Principal; they are open Monday to Friday from 9 am to 1.30 pm but often have long queues.

There are also a great number of casas de cambio or currency exchange houses around Vallarta; their rates differ so it may pay to shop around. Though their rates are slightly less favourable than the banks, the difference often comes to only a few cents and the longer hours and faster service may make it worthwhile to change money here rather

than spending hours in the banks. They are usually open every day from around 9 am to 7.30 pm, sometimes with a lunch break from 2 to 4 pm.

On the north side of the Río Cuale there are a number of casas de cambio along the Malecón. Two others are on Calle Rodríguez opposite the Mercado Municipal, with another at Juárez 270 near the Plaza Principal.

On the south side of the river, there's a casa de cambio on Vallarta between Madero and Aquiles Serdán, beside the Hotel Posada Río Cuale; another at Vallarta 278 near the corner of Carranza; and another at Insurgentes 140, near the corner of Aquiles Serdán.

American Express (☎ 4-68-76, 4-68-77) has an office in the Villa Vallarta commercial centre, a few km north of the city. It's open Monday to Friday from 9 am to 6 pm, Saturday 9 am to 1 pm, and includes a travel agency in addition to cheque and card services.

Post The post office is on the Malecón at Morelos 444, on the corner of Mina. It's open Monday to Friday from 8 am to 7.30 pm, Saturday 9 am to 1 pm, and Sunday 9 am to noon.

Telecommunications The Telecomm office, with telegram, telex and fax services, is at Hidalgo 582 near the corner of Aldama. It's open Monday to Friday from 9 am to 5.30 pm, Saturday 9 am to noon.

Vallarta has many long-distance telephone offices, some with both telephone and fax. Most are on the south side of the Río Cuale. Offices with both telephone and fax include Computel, in the Tres Estrellas de Oro bus station at Carranza 322, open every day from 7 am to 1 am; Tierra, Mar y Sol at Constitución 129 opposite the GR supermarket, open Monday to Saturday from 8.30 am to 8.30 pm; and Larga Distancia on Lázaro Cárdenas facing Plaza Lázaro Cárdenas, beside the Hotel Eloisa, open every day from 8 am to 10 pm.

Offices with telephone only include Computel at Madero 296, open every day from 6.45 am to 1 am; and another in the Transportes del Pacífico bus station at Insurgentes 282, open daily from 9 am to 9 pm, except Sunday when it's open from 9 am to 3 pm.

Foreign Consulates There's a US Consulate (☎ 2-00-69) upstairs behind the La Fuente del Puente restaurant, just on the north side of the river opposite the Mercado Municipal; look up to the 2nd floor and you'll see the large American seal. It's open Monday to Friday from 9 am to 1 pm.

The Canadian Consulate (☎ 2-53-98) at Hidalgo 226 is open the same hours.

Laundry Several laundries are in the area south of the Río Cuale. The Lavandería Erendira II at Madero 428, and the Lavandería Blanquita at Madero 407-A, are open Monday to Saturday from 8 am to 9 pm and charge US$3 for three kg of laundry (wash, dry and fold).

Other laundries with about the same prices are the Lavandería Elsa at Olas Altas 385, the Lavandería Acuarius on the corner of Olas Altas and Púlpito, and the slightly more expensive Lavandería Adriana at Gómez 142. Another laundry is on Aquiles Serdán near the corner of Vallarta.

Museo del Cuale

This tiny museum on Isla Cuale barely qualifies as one because it has only a few ceramic statues recovered from archaeological sites in the area, with no commentary to tell you where they might come from or anything about them. More space is given to the changing art exhibits. The museum is open Monday to Saturday from 10 am to 4 pm; admission is free.

Art Galleries

More interesting than the museum are the numerous art galleries around Vallarta, showing everything from traditional Huichol Indian art to the latest in contemporary art and even 'art to wear' clothing designs. Some of the better known galleries include Arte Mágico Huichol at Corona 164, the Brooks de Gooyer gallery at Morelos 589, Galería Uno at Morelos 561, Galería Vallarta at Juárez 263 and the Galería Pacífico at Juárez 519.

Water Sports

Snorkelling, scuba diving, deep sea fishing, waterskiing, jet-skiing, windsurfing, sailing, parasailing, riding the 'banana' and of course just plain swimming are all popular water sports in Vallarta, as are serious work on tans and people-watching. Most water sports can be arranged on the beaches in front of any of the large hotels in and around the city. The tourist office can help to connect you with operators of just about any water sport you can imagine.

For snorkelling and diving, the most spectacular spots are the **National Underwater Park** at Los Arcos, an island rock formation just north of Mismaloya, and the **Islas Marietas** at the entrance to the bay, with impressive reefs, underwater caves, tunnels, walls, and a chance to see dolphins, whales and giant manta rays.

Vallarta has a number of diving and snorkelling operators to take you to these and other locations. Check out Chico's Dive Shop (☎ 2-18-95), on the Malecón at Paseo Díaz Ordaz 770-5, which offers several good diving and snorkelling trips as well as diving instruction. They do trips to Los Arcos (snorkelling US$25, diving US$47), to the Quimixto coves on the south side of the bay (snorkelling US$42, diving US$60), and to the Islas Marietas (snorkelling US$42, diving US$77).

Chico's dives can be arranged at their shop, or though any travel agency. Though Chico's is the oldest and most popular dive shop in Vallarta, several other diving operators also offer similar snorkelling and diving trips and instruction; ask at the tourist office for recommendations. See the Mismaloya section under the following Around Puerto Vallarta section for a cheaper way to get to Los Arcos.

Deep-sea fishing is popular all year, with a major international sailfish tournament taking place each November. Prime catches are sailfish, marlin, tuna, red snapper and sea bass. The tourist office can recommend fishing operators for the type of trip you have in mind.

Cruises

A host of cruises are available in Vallarta, including daytime cruises, sunset cruises and evening cruises, some including snorkelling stops at Los Arcos.

Yelapa, accessible only by water and formerly a tiny fishing village, is now probably the most popular cruise destination, and its cove is lined with tourists, restaurants, and parasailing operators. If you go to Yelapa, take a hike upriver to see the waterfalls.

Another popular destination is **Playa de las Ánimas** (Beach of the Spirits), a lovely beach with a smaller, less developed fishing village and some beachside palapa restaurants offering fresh seafood. This is another village that can only be reached by water and (so far) it is less commercialised than Yelapa.

Yet another lovely beach only accessible by water is **Quimixto**. It has a waterfall you can reach with a half-hour hike, or you can hire a pony on the beach to take you up.

The tourist office or any travel agency can tell you what cruises are operating, details of where they go, what they offer (many include meals, drinks, open bar, etc) and current prices.

If you just want to visit the beaches, forgoing the meals, drinks, etc, a cheaper way to get there is on the Water Taxi (see the Getting Around section).

Horseback Riding

There are several possibilities for horseback riding along the beach and into the jungle behind Puerto Vallarta. Horsemen along the beach charge around US$7 per hour for beach rides. The Rancho El Charro (☎ 2-49-94) comes highly recommended by those who love horses.

Golf & Tennis

Golf and tennis are both popular sports at Vallarta. The exclusive Marina Vallarta Golf Club (☎ 1-01-71) is an international-level course, but phone ahead to see if you can come to play there – it's a membership club with privileges for guests of certain hotels but not just anyone from the general public can show up and play. The less exotic 18-hole Los Flamingos Golf Club (☎ 8-02-80) is open to the public. Both golf courses are north of the city.

A favourite with tennis fans (or those who want to learn) is the John Newcombe Tennis Club (☎ 4-43-60), also north of the city. Most of the large luxury hotels also have courts; phone them to reserve a court time. The Sheraton Buganvilias (☎ 3-04-04) and the Hotel Krystal (☎ 4-02-02) both have courts available, and there are plenty of others.

Other

The Chess Club meets every Saturday at 10 am in the Plaza Hidalgo. Alcoholics Anonymous (☎ 2-60-60, ext 204, or 2-43-56) holds meetings in English as well as in Spanish.

Timeshares

As you will quickly discover while walking along any of Puerto Vallarta's main streets, it is easy to arrange a free or greatly discounted cruise, dinner, Jeep rental, horse ride or what-have-you by attending a timeshare presentation. On almost every block downtown there are at least two booths staffed by English-speaking hawkers with inviting smiles who try to coax you to their stands with sugary hellos and offers of Jeeps for US$5 per day or free tours.

Of course there's a catch to the offers. In exchange for listening to a 90-minute breakfast presentation about the benefits of investing in one of Puerto Vallarta's burgeoning timeshare condominium projects and then touring the project, you get one of the goodies mentioned. You must be over 25 years old, in possession of a major credit card, and employed; many timeshare projects require that you be married as well, and that both husband and wife attend the presentation. Breakfast is free and they will pay the taxi fare from your hotel to the project. You are under no obligation to buy or sign anything.

Travellers give mixed reports about the presentations. Some say it's a painless enough way to get a cheap Jeep, tour or cruise. Others are still angry days later when they've had to fend off the 'hard sell'. We won't recommend that you go or stay away – up to you. Just be wary of the seasoned professional salespeople who can sometimes come on very strong, and by all means, if you're thinking of buying, use your intelligence, keep your wits about you and be sure you understand the sneaky fine print in the contract.

Organised Tours
Also available through the tourist office and travel agents are a variety of tours on land, including city tours, jungle tours, tropical tours and horseback tours.

Festivals & Annual Events
Regatta Marina del Rey-Puerto Vallarta Held during February in odd-numbered years, this boat race begins at Marina del Rey, near San Diego, California, and ends with festivities here.

Semana Santa Holy Week, the week before Easter, is the busiest holiday in Puerto Vallarta, with hotels filling up and hundreds (or thousands) of excess visitors camping out on the beaches and partying. It's a wild time.

Fiestas de Mayo The entire month of May features the May Fiestas, a city-wide fair with cultural, sporting and other events, popular music concerts, carnival rides, art exhibits and more.

Torneo de Pesca A big International Sailfish Tournament is held each year in November, with dates variable according to the phase of the moon, which must be right for fishing. The tourist office can provide exact dates.

Día de Santa Cecilia The day of Santa Cecilia, patron saint of mariachis, is celebrated on 22 November with all the city's mariachis uniting as an orchestra for a musical procession to the Templo de Guadalupe cathedral in the early evening. They come playing and singing, enter the church where they sing homage to their saint, and then go out into the plaza and continue to play. During the entire day one or another group of mariachis stays in the church making music.

Fiestas Guadalupanas All of Mexico celebrates 12 December as the day of the country's patron saint, the Virgin of Guadalupe, but in Puerto Vallarta the celebrations are more drawn out, with pilgrimages and processions to the Templo de Guadalupe cathedral taking place day and night from 30 November on, leading up to the big bash on 12 December.

Places to Stay
Vallarta has a great number of places to stay – there are over 30,000 hotel rooms in and near the city, with good places in every price range.

Hotel prices are higher during Vallarta's high season, roughly from December to April. The rates we are giving here are those for the rest of the year, except where noted. If you're coming at the very busiest times – the week before Easter (Semana Santa) or between Christmas and New Year – rooms can still be hard to find, so at those times be sure to reserve in advance.

Places to Stay – bottom end
Camping *Tacho's Trailer Park* (☎ (322) 4-21-63) is several km north of the city centre, opposite the marina on the highway to Pitillal, about five blocks from the sea. It has a swimming pool and 99 trailer and tent spaces with full hook-ups; sites cost US$12 per space.

Hotels The cheapest places to stay are found south of the Río Cuale, with most concentrated along Madero. All are basic but clean, with fan and private bath.

Our favourite is the *Hotel Villa del Mar*

(☎ (322) 2-07-85) at Madero 440. Most of the 50 rooms open onto private brick balconies with chairs and flowering plants, and up on the roof are sitting areas with a bit of a view of the town. The quality you get for the price of US$8.70/11.35 per single/double makes this one of the best deals in Vallarta. They also have some studio apartments with fully equipped kitchens; the cost is US$16.70/20 a single/double by the day, or US$300/335 by the month.

The *Hotel Posada Castillo* (☎ (322) 2-02-36) at Madero 275 has 16 large, clean rooms with good ventilation. Regular rooms cost US$13.35, those with kitchen are US$16.70 to US$20; they provide pots but you must supply your own dishes. Nearby, the *Hotel Posada El Real* (☎ (322) 2-05-87) at Madero 285 is a clean family place with just eight rooms at US$10/13.35 for singles/doubles.

The *Hotel Hortencia* (☎ (322) 2-24-84) at Madero 336 has 18 rooms; those facing the street have sliding glass doors opening onto private balconies. Singles/doubles are US$11.70/13.35. Next door, the *Casa de Huéspedes García* at No 338 is basic but clean, with singles/doubles at US$10/11.70.

The *Hotel Analiz* (☎ (322) 2-17-57) at Madero 429 is more cheerful than some other places on Madero, with flowers on the walkway, ample windows for fresh air, and colourful decor. Its 22 singles/doubles are US$8.35/10. Another popular place on Madero is the larger 46-room *Hotel Azteca* (☎ (322) 2-27-50) at No 473, where clean singles/doubles are US$8/10.

Other basic hotels on Madero include the similarly priced *Hotel Lina* (☎ (322) 2-16-61) at No 377, the *Hotel Bernal* (☎ (322) 2-36-05) at No 423, and the *Hotel Cartagena de Indias* (☎ (322) 2-69-14) at No 428.

Several other economical choices are found off Madero. The *Motel Mayo* (☎ (322) 2-34-03) at Basilio Badillo 300 is an older hotel with a friendly and peaceful atmosphere, and it's one of the only cheapies with enclosed parking. Some of the 23 rooms have private terraces, and some have kitchens; regular singles/doubles are US$11.70/15, or US$15/18.35 with kitchen.

Nearer the beach, the pleasant *Hotel Yazmín* (☎ (322) 2-00-87) at Basilio Badillo 168, has singles/doubles at US$15/16.70. It is an excellent deal considering it's just half a block from Playa de los Muertos, the most popular beach in Vallarta.

Also near Playa de los Muertos, the *Apartamentos Posada Olas Altas*, Olas Altas 356 at the corner of Basilio Badillo, seems an anomaly in this district of fancier places. It has seven fully-equipped apartments with kitchen that are quite basic and perhaps only a true beach bum would like them. However, they have everything you need (fridge, stove, bed, ceiling fan, etc) and the price is right at US$13.35, with discounts by the month.

Places to Stay – middle

One of the most popular places to stay among foreign travellers, especially Americans and Canadians, is the *Hotel Posada de Roger* (☎ (322) 2-08-36, 2-06-39) at Basilio Badillo 237. It's famous for its friendly atmosphere, cleanliness and security, and has a pleasant courtyard swimming pool plus a convivial bar/restaurant, El Tucan, where good breakfasts are served. Singles/doubles are US$20/25 with ceiling fan, US$3.35 extra with air-conditioning.

The *Hotel Posada Río Cuale* (☎ (322) 2-04-50), at Aquiles Serdán 242 on the corner of Vallarta, is a pleasant hotel with a swimming pool, a gourmet poolside restaurant/bar, and 21 rooms with both air-conditioning and ceiling fan. Singles/doubles are US$20/25; the rooms by the pool, away from the busy Calle Vallarta, are quieter.

The *Hotel Encino* (☎ (322) 2-02-80, 2-00-51, fax 2-25-73) is at Juárez 122, just on the north side of the seaside bridge over the Río Cuale. There's a rooftop swimming pool and penthouse restaurant, the Lobster House, and here, as on the upper floors, there's a fine view of the sunset and the river meeting the sea. Singles/doubles are US$21.70/25, suites US$36.70 with one bedroom or US$50 with two; most rooms have air-conditioning.

Beside the beach on the north end of the centre, the *Hotel Rosita* (☎/fax (322) 2-10-

3, 2-21-71) at Paseo Díaz Ordaz 901 is a popular, older hotel with 112 rooms and a beachside swimming pool, restaurant and bar. Rates range from US$20/24 for singles/doubles on the street side to US$38 for beachfront suites.

Back on the south side of town, the *Hotel Eloisa* (☎ (322) 2-64-65) at Lázaro Cárdenas 179, opposite the Plaza Lázaro Cárdenas and half a block from Playa Olas Altas, has a rooftop terrace with a children's pool and 75 bright, clean rooms with air-conditioning at US$26.70/30 for singles/doubles.

A good deal for middle-range apartments is the *Estancia San Carlos* (☎ (322) 2-53-27) at Constitución 210. It has a courtyard swimming pool with a waterfall, covered parking, and 24 clean, modern apartments with fully-equipped kitchen, air-conditioning, cable TV, and private balcony. The daily cost is US$31.70/50 for one/two-bedroom apartments, with discounts by the week (US$175/315) or month (US$550/650). Prices are higher from November to April.

Places to Stay – top end

If you can afford it, Puerto Vallarta has many unbelievably beautiful places to stay at the upper end of the accommodation market. If you're here during the off-season, from April to mid-December, the discounts at these times bring even some of the loveliest places down to a more affordable level.

One of Vallarta's most beautiful, centrally located hotels is the four-star *Hotel Molino de Agua* (☎ (322) 2-19-07, 2-19-57, fax 2-60-56) at Vallarta 130, facing the beach just on the south side of the Río Cuale. Though it's in the city centre, it is remarkably quiet and peaceful, with 65 cabins, rooms and suites set among beautiful tropical gardens covering an area equivalent to two city blocks. Prices from 16 April to 20 December are US$44 for cabins, US$60 for double rooms with ocean views, and US$72 to US$80 for beachfront suites, including continental breakfast. From 21 December to 15 April the rates are 15% higher. It has every luxury including two swimming pools, an outdoor jacuzzi, and a garden restaurant/bar.

Also beautiful and central, one of Vallarta's best kept romantic secrets is the tiny *La Casa del Puente* (☎ (322) 2-07-49), tucked behind the Restaurant La Fuente del Puente beside the Río Cuale, just on the north side of the inland bridge. It's an elegant river-view place with just one regular room with bath, a one-bedroom apartment and a two-bedroom apartment. The apartments are huge and have well-equipped kitchens and bathrooms with a tub, and the whole place is remarkably clean and elegantly furnished. Molly Muir, the owner, is a wonderful hostess and impromptu tour guide for her guests. Rates are very reasonable at US$33 for either apartment and US$16.50 for the regular room during most of the year, rising to US$71.50 in the one-bedroom apartment, US$82.50 in the two-bedroom apartment, and US$27.50 in the regular room during the high season from 15 December to the week after Easter.

Another classy place to stay is the *Casa Kimberley* (☎ (322) 2-13-36) at Zaragoza 445. The former villa of Elizabeth Taylor and Richard Burton – he bought it for her as a birthday gift in 1964, before they were married – it's been converted to a B&B inn with eight rooms, a swimming pool and a large kitchen-terrace area where you can cook if you like. Since the house didn't have a swimming pool, Burton also bought the house across the street, put in a pool, and connected the two with a bridge arching over the street.

Photos of Liz and Richard decorate the villa, and the US owners can tell you much about the history of the famous couple who stayed here frequently from 1964 to 1974. Rates per room, breakfast included, are US$45 to US$75 from 16 August to 14 November, US$60 to US$100 from 16 May to 15 August, and US$80 to US$125 from 15 November to 15 May.

Top-end hotels line the beach at Playa de los Muertos, Vallarta's most popular beach. Typically they are high-rises with air-conditioning and beachfront swimming pools and restaurants. To take one example, the *Hotel Oro Verde* (☎ (322) 2-30-50, 2-15-55, fax 2-24-31) at Gómez 111 has 162 rooms priced at US$41 most of the year, higher in high season from December to April.

Many giant five-star and Grand Tourism-category hotels, often with hundreds of rooms, are found along the beaches both to the north and south of town. Those north of the city include the *Buenaventura, Omni, Fiesta Americana, Playa de Oro, Holiday Inn, Krystal, Marina Vallarta Resort, Marriott's, Melia Vallarta, Plaza Iguana, Sheraton Buganvilias* and the *Club Maeva*. South of the city are the *Camino Real, Costa Vida, Hyatt Coral* and *La Jolla de Mismaloya*. Travel agents can connect you with any of them; they do a big business in foreign package tours.

Places to Eat

The restaurant situation in Puerto Vallarta is similar to the hotel situation – there's something for every budget. Generally, the cheaper restaurants and food stalls are found near the cheaper hotels, particularly around Madero. Most of the expensive restaurants are attached to 1st-class and deluxe hotels.

South of the Río Cuale South of the river you'll find everything from the most economical restaurants to some of the best in town.

Several small, cheap, typical Mexican family-run restaurants are along Calle Madero. The *Restaurant El Corita* at Madero 340, open daily except Wednesday from 8 am to 10.30 pm, serves a comida corrida lunchtime meal (soup, rice, choice of main dish, coffee and dessert) for US$3.35, as does the *Restaurant Gilmar* at Madero 418, open daily except Sunday from 7 am to 11 pm. At *Antojitos Mexicanos Linita*, Madero 376, open daily except Tuesday from 7 am to 11 pm, the comida is US$4. All serve breakfasts for around US$2.50 and a typical selection of Mexican foods.

Half a block off Madero, the *Fonda La China Poblana* at Insurgentes 222 is a similar place with similar prices, a slightly more varied menu, and an upstairs dining terrace. It's open 24 hours every day.

Many other restaurants south of the rive are a step up in class; this being the city's main hotel district, most are heavily patron-ised by tourists, with the occasional loca thrown in.

Two restaurants a block apart on Basilio Badillo each claim to serve 'the best break-fast in Puerto Vallarta': *El Tucan*, connected to the Hotel Posada de Roger at the corner of Vallarta and Basilio Badillo, and *The Pancake House*, a block away at Basilio Badillo 289.

We tried them both and couldn't decide which was best, but they are both great places for breakfast, serving similar menus with about 25 varieties of pancakes and waffles (US$3 to US$4 at the Tucan US$3.35 to US$5 at the Pancake House) including some with exotic toppings like Black Forest, Kahlua & Chocolate, and a variety of fruits. Eggs with hash browns, toast, butter and coffee come to around US$3 at either place, and there are also a few treats like eggs Benedict, cheese blintzes and ome-lettes. Both are open from 8 am to 2 pm, the Pancake House every day, and the Tucan every day except Tuesday.

One of the best restaurants in Vallarta is *Pizza Joe* at Basilio Badillo 269, with tables set around a rear patio with a pool, waterfall and romantic candlelight in the evening. The spaghetti (US$5) and chocolate amaretto cheesecake (US$2.30) are some of the best we've ever tasted, and they also make good lasagna, pasta and pizza. It's open from 2 to 11 pm every day except Sunday.

Opposite this, *Puerto Nuevo* at Basilio Badillo 284 is a popular seafood restaurant where they bring out a platter with the fresh seafood of the day, from which you can make your selection. Main dishes range in price from fillet of fish (US$7) to giant prawns (US$13.35) but there are also a variety of snacks like manta-ray tacos (US$4.70). It's open every day from 1 to 11 pm.

More expensive but also popular for its good food is the *Adobe Café* at Basilio Badillo 300 on the corner of Constitución. Stylish and air-conditioned, it's open from 6 to 11 pm every day except Sunday.

Nearby, the *Karpathos Tavern* at Constitución 335 is a tiny Greek restaurant serving specialities including hummus (garbanzo bean dip), dolmadakia (stuffed grape leaves), saganaki (fried cheese), Greek salad, souvlaki, moussaka and baklava for dessert. Prices are a little high (dolmadakia US$4, souvlaki US$9.35 to US$11.35) but it's a good place, open from 5 to 11 pm every day except Monday.

One of Vallarta's best known restaurants is *Archie's Wok*, at Francisca Rodríguez 130, half a block from Playa de los Muertos. The former personal chef of film director John Huston, Archie now operates this small restaurant featuring wok specialities from many parts of Asia, with vegetarian or meat selections like Malaysian stir-fried vegetables (US$5.70), spicy Thai fried noodles with shrimp, chicken, bean sprouts and peanuts (US$7), or Thai coconut fish sautéed in coconut milk and Thai red curry sauce (US$8.70). Other sauces include Archie's own teriyaki sauce or sweet and sour. It's open from 1 to 10 pm every day except Sunday.

An old favourite in Vallarta, *Daiquiri Dick's* on Playa de los Muertos has been remodelled into a rather elegant beachside restaurant/bar with meat and seafood dishes from around US$7 to US$16. It's open every day from 9 am to 11 pm. In the same neighbourhood, *Las Tres Huastecas* at the corner of Olas Altas and Francisco Rodríguez is a cheerful little spot for simple meals; it's open every day from 7 am to 8.30 pm.

Up on the hill behind here, the *Restaurant Casa Vallarta* at Púlpito 220 is well worth the walk to get up there for the all-you-can-eat buffet served every evening from 5 to 10.30 pm. The cost is US$8.95 and the buffet changes nightly, with just a few nightly regulars including a 20-item salad bar, roast beef and barbeque spare ribs. The atmosphere is tropical and romantic, with a covered terrace, tropical plants, piano music and candlelight. Exotic tropical drinks are served from the bar.

Two hillside restaurants highly recommended for their fine views over the city and bay (especially at sunset) as well as for their excellent food are *El Palomar de los González*, Aguacate 425, and *Felipe's* at Prolongación Insurgentes 466. Both are open evenings only, from 6 to 11 pm (Felipe's every day, El Palomar every day except Sunday) and are reasonably priced.

Another elegant spot with a luxurious peaceful atmosphere is the garden restaurant of the *Hotel Molino de Agua* on Vallarta just south of the seaside bridge over the Río Cuale. It's open every day from 7 am to 11 pm.

North of the Río Cuale The Malecón is lined with boutiques and restaurant/bars. Many have upstairs terraces with fine views of the bay, but prices on the Malecón are considerably higher than in other parts of the city. If you don't mind the extra expense, stroll along here and see which place catches your fancy. Some of the more popular places include *Mr Tequila's Grill, Restaurante Zapata, Bar Océano, Casablanca, Las Palomas, Pizza Nova, Il Mangiare* and *Tsunami*.

Also along the Malecón are the *Hard Rock Café* and *Carlos O'Brian's*, both serving expensive food but nonetheless popular with visitors for their party-hard atmosphere, music and dancing in the evening. Various other places along the Malecón also offer music and dancing in the evening.

Just off the Malecón at Domínguez 181, *Rito's Baci* is a tiny Italian restaurant; the pizzas, pastas, lasagna, eggplant parmesan, and hot and cold sandwiches with selections like pastrami and Italian meatballs or sausage are all inexpensive and made with fresh ingredients daily. They offer free delivery within the city (☎ 2-64-48); it's open every day from 1 pm to midnight.

Another simple spot near the Malecón is the little *Tuti Fruti* on the corner of Morelos and Corona, with fresh juices, fruit shakes and simple snacks like hamburgers, sandwiches, burritos and breakfasts. It has just a few stools if you want to eat there, or you can take away. It's open every day from 8 am to 10 pm.

Up on the hill behind the Malecón is the *Restaurant El Panorama*, high up in the Hotel La Siesta at the corner of Domínguez and Miramar. Open for dinner every evening from 6 to 11 pm, it's known for its fine views and good food, but is quite expensive.

La Fuente del Puente on Insurgentes, at the north side of the inland bridge over the Río Cuale, is a pleasant open-air restaurant/bar with nightly mariachi music. It's open every day from 8 am to 11 pm, except Sunday when it's oopen for breakfast only.

Opposite this, the upstairs floor of the *Mercado Municipal* has a number of simple restaurant food stalls serving typical Mexican market foods every day from around 7 am to 8 pm.

A couple of American fast-food chains have made it to Vallarta, including *McDonald's*, on the corner of Paseo Díaz Ordaz and 31 de Octubre, and *KFC*, facing the Plaza Principal on the corner of Juárez and Zaragoza. Both are air-conditioned and open every day, but here they're not cheapies like in the USA – a Big Mac with large fries and a drink will set you back US$5.80, more than you'd pay to eat in a Mexican eatery.

If you're here in the heat of the summer you might like to know that the *Woolworth's Restaurant*, Juárez and 31 de Octubre, has the coolest air-conditioning in town. It also has 10 kinds of hamburgers served with French fries and salad (US$4.20) and an economical meal of the day, changing daily, with soup, main dish, rice and beans, bread and butter, a cold drink, dessert and coffee or tea, all for US$3.20; breakfasts are around US$2.20. It's open every day from 8 am to 9 pm.

The *Panadería Munguía* at Juárez 467 is an excellent bakery with cinnamon rolls, doughnuts, breads, cakes, cookies, tarts, pies and lots of sinfully rich chocolate goodies like brownies, German chocolate cake and other cakes. It's open from 7 am to 9 pm every day except Sunday. A smaller branch of the same bakery is at Aquiles Serdán 305 on the south side of the Río Cuale.

On Isla Cuale Several other restaurants are on the Isla Cuale in the middle of the river, including the *Franzi Café* and *Le Bistro*, both with jazz music on weekends, and *Chico Paradise II*, with a view of the sea. They're atmospheric but the food prices are higher than they need be.

Entertainment

Drinking and dancing are Puerto Vallarta's main forms of night-time entertainment. Stroll down the Malecón in the evening and take your choice – there's everything from romantic open-air bar/restaurants to riotous revelling. The Hard Rock Café along here has live rock music and dancing every night except Wednesday from around 10.30 pm until 1.30 am. The Zoo is another place with music and dancing. Or there's the ever-popular Carlos O'Brian's, a favourite drinking hole for fun-seeking, rabble-rousing gringos, with dancing into the wee hours.

Discos in Vallarta appear and disappear with some regularity. On our last visit the most popular were Cactus, on the south side of the river at the corner of Vallarta and Francisca Rodríguez, and Christine's, at the five-star Hotel Krystal about seven km north of the city. Elaine's, beside the Jack Tar Hotel in Nuevo Vallarta, about 25 km north of the city, is another popular disco with music and dancing going all night long, beginning every night around 10.30 pm.

Just off the Malecón, Brazz at the corner of Morelos and Galeana, 'the house of prime rib, Hereford steaks and seafood', has live mariachi music nightly from 9.30 pm. Mariachis also play nightly at the pleasant La Fuente del Puente restaurant on Insurgentes on the north side of the inland bridge over the Río Cuale. Out in Marina Vallarta, north of the city, there's a nightly flamenco show.

For jazz fans the Franzi Café and Le Bistro, both on the Isla Cuale, feature live jazz on weekends. The Isla Cuale makes a beautiful, quiet, romantic haven for strolling around at night, away from the city hustle.

La Iguana at Lázaro Cárdenas 311 is an old Vallarta favourite, presenting a 'Fiesta Mexicana' with traditional Mexican folk oric dances, mariachis, *ranchero* rope tricks, a piñata, bloodless cockfights, a huge Mexican foods buffet, an open bar, and a dance band for dancing under the stars. The fiesta is held every Thursday and Sunday evening from 7 to 11.15 pm. At US$28.35 per person it's not cheap, but it's a delightful event.

Other 'Fiesta Mexicana' nights, jazz nights, mariachi nights, etc are held at some of the giant luxury hotels around the area, including the Fiesta Americana, the Krystal, the Sheraton Buganvilias, the Camino Real and the Jack Tar Village. A weekly schedule is published in the English-language *Vallarta Today* newspaper, or ask at the tourist office for the current schedule.

Various sunset and evening cruises provide yet more evening entertainment. Ask about them at the tourist office or at travel agents.

There are several cinemas around town, including the Cine Bahía, on Insurgentes near Madero; the smaller Sala Elizabeth Taylor, just off Vallarta on the south side of the sea side bridge over the Río Cuale; the Cine Vallarta, on Calle Uruguay opposite the Conasupo supermarket on Avenida México a few blocks north of the centre; and the Cine Luz Maria, nearby at Avenida México 227. You can sometimes catch some good movies in Vallarta; often they're shown in English with Spanish subtitles. Stop by any theatre and check out the posters for what's on.

Bullfights are held every Wednesday all year round, starting at 5 pm in the bull ring across from the marina.

Things to Buy

Shops and boutiques in Puerto Vallarta sell just about every type of craft made in Mexico, but prices are higher here than elsewhere. Try the Mercado Municipal along the north bank of the Río Cuale between the bridges for haggling on everything from Taxco silver, sarapes and *huarache* sandals to hand-woven wool wall-hangings and blown glass. The market has over 150 shops and stalls and is open Monday to Saturday from 8 am to 8 pm, Sunday 9 am to 2 pm.

Supermarkets Conveniently placed in the centre of town, the Gutierrez Rizo ('GR') supermarket, at the corner of Constitución and Aquiles Serdán on the south side of the river, is a giant air-conditioned supermarket which will boggle your mind if you've been travelling a long time in Mexico. It has local merchandise and produce as well as thousands of items imported from the USA, plus magazines and paperbacks in English. It's open every day from 6.45 am to 10 pm.

Getting There & Away

Air Puerto Vallarta's international airport (☎ 1-12-98, 1-13-25) is about 10 km north of the city, off Highway 200. It is served by a number of national and international airlines with an array of flights, including:

Aero California (☎ 1-15-72) – daily flights to Guadalajara, Mazatlán, Phoenix and San Diego (California).

Aeroméxico (☎ 4-00-71, 1-10-30) – Juárez 255; daily flights to Guadalajara, Los Angeles, Mexico City, San Diego (California) and Tijuana; several flights weekly to Aguascalientes and León.

Alaska Airlines (☎ 3-03-50, 1-12-52) – daily flights to Los Angeles and San Francisco.

American Airlines (☎ 1-17-99, 2-30-19) – daily flights to Dallas.

Continental (☎ 1-10-25, 1-10-96) – daily flights to Houston.

Delta (☎ 1-19-19, 1-10-32) – daily flights to Los Angeles.

Mexicana (☎ 2-50-00, 1-11-38) – daily flights to Denver, Guadalajara, Los Angeles, Mazatlán and San Francisco; four flights weekly to Chicago, Dallas and San Antonio (Texas).

TAESA (☎ 1-10-41) – three flights weekly to Guadalajara and Laredo (Texas).

Bus Intercity bus lines operate from individual terminals on or near Madero and Insurgentes on the south side of the Río Cuale. They include: Estrella Blanca (☎ 2-06-13) at Insurgentes 180; Servicios Coordinados/Primera Plus (☎ 2-69-86) at Lázaro Cárdenas 267; Transportes Norte de Sonora (☎ 2-16-50) at Madero 343; Transportes del Pacífico (☎ 2-10-15) at Insurgentes 282; Transportes Cihuatlán (☎ 2-34-36) on the corner of Madero and

Constitución; and Tres Estrellas de Oro (☎ 2-66-66) at Carranza 322.

Long-distance buses departing from Puerto Vallarta include those to:

Barra de Navidad – 210 km, 3½ to 5 hours; same buses as to Manzanillo.

Guadalajara – 397 km, six to seven hours; 15 buses daily with Tres Estrellas de Oro (US$11.60 1st class, US$14.35 Plus); 10 daily with Transportes del Pacífico (US$11.35); five daily with Estrella Blanca (US$10.85); two daily with Servicios Coordinados/Primera Plus (US$11.70 1st class, US$13.35 Plus); two daily with Transportes Norte de Sonora (US$10.85).

Manzanillo – 302 km, five to six hours; hourly 2nd-class buses, 5 am to 6 pm, plus a bus at midnight, with Transportes Cihuatlán (US$6.70); three Primera Plus express buses daily with Transportes Cihuatlán (US$8.85); one daily with Tres Estrellas de Oro (US$7.35).

Mexico City – 932 km, 14 to 15 hours; two daily with Transportes del Pacífico (US$27.35); two daily with Tres Estrellas de Oro (US$28); two daily with Estrella Blanca (US$28.20 1st class, US$35.35 Plus); one daily with Transportes Norte de Sonora (US$24).

San Patricio-Melaque, 205 km, 3½ to 5 hours; same buses as to Manzanillo.

Tepic – 169 km, three to 3½ hours; buses every half-hour, 5 am to 8 pm, with Transportes del Pacífico (US$4.85); two daily with Transportes Norte de Sonora (US$4.35); two daily with Estrella Blanca (US$5).

Car Car rental agencies in Puerto Vallarta include Arrendadora de Alba (☎ 2-29-59), Avis (☎ 2-14-12, 1-11-12), Budget (☎ 2-67-66), Dollar (☎ 2-55-15), Hertz (☎ 2-00-24, 1-00-04), National (☎ 2-11-07), Odin (☎ 2-28-25), Popo's (☎ 2-23-56) and Quick (☎ 2-35-05).

Requirements for hiring a vehicle include that you be at least 25 years of age, have a valid driver's licence (a foreign one will do), and a major credit card. If you don't have a credit card you'll have to pay a large cash deposit.

Jeeps are the most popular vehicles. Discounts on Jeeps are frequently offered as an inducement to attend timeshare presentations – last time we were in Vallarta the streets were lined with signs saying 'Jeep – US$5 for 24 hours' with the catch that you had to attend the timeshare presentation to get the Jeep. This may be worthwhile if only to go to Eden de Mismaloya, four km inland from Mismaloya.

Getting Around

To/From the Airport Colectivo vans operate from the airport to town, but not from town to the airport. The cheapest way to get to the airport is on a local bus, costing just US$0.25; the 'Juntas' and 'Ixtapa' buses stop outside the airport entrance. Otherwise, a taxi from the city centre costs around US$7.35.

Bus Local buses operate from 6 am to 11 pm every five minutes on most routes and cost US$0.25. Plaza Lázaro Cárdenas at Playa Olas Altas is a major departure hub for buses heading both north and south.

Northbound buses marked 'Hoteles', 'Aeropuerto', 'Ixtapa', 'Pitillal' and others depart from this plaza and pass through the city heading north on Juárez, returning south along Avenida México, Paseo Díaz Ordaz (the Malecón), Morelos and Vallarta. The 'Hoteles', 'Pitillal' and 'Ixtapa' routes can take you to any of the large hotels stretched out around the bay north of the city.

Southbound 'Boca de Tomatlán' buses depart from this Plaza Lázaro Cárdenas and pass along the southern coastal highway past the fancy hotels and Mismaloya on their way to Boca de Tomatlán. These buses operate every 15 minutes from 6.40 am to 9 pm and cost US$0.25.

Taxi Taxi prices are regulated by zones; cost for a ride is determined by how many zones you cross. An average ride in town costs around US$1.70; a 10-km ride to the airport is US$7.35.

Boat In addition to taxis on land, Vallarta also has a water taxi (the 'Autobús Acuático') departing from Los Muertos Pier and heading south around the bay with stops at Mismaloya, Boca de Tomatlán, Playa de las Ánimas, Quimixto, and finally Yelapa taking 1½ hours to reach the end of the line. One-way cost to the first two destinations (which can also be reached by local bus) is US$3.35; to the last three (accessible only by water) it's US$6.70. The schedule is posted at the foot of the pier; the taxi departs daily at 9.30 am and 1 pm, leaving Yelapa for the return trip at 11 am and 4 pm.

Private yachts and boats *(lanchas)* can be hired from Playa de los Muertos just on the south side of the pier. They'll take you anywhere you want to go around the bay; most have gear aboard for snorkelling and fishing trips, and they can also take you to some lovely secluded beaches. The cost is around US$20 to US$25 per hour for the whole boat, holding seven to 10 people.

Another alternative for transport to Yelapa is the supply boat which operates every day except Sunday, departing Yelapa at 7 am and leaving for the return trip from the beach just south of the Hotel Rosita on the Malecón at around 11 or 11.30 am. It costs US$5 and takes an hour to reach Yelapa.

AROUND PUERTO VALLARTA
Mismaloya

About 10 km south of Puerto Vallarta is Mismaloya, the site where John Huston directed Richard Burton in *Night of the Iguana.* The cove stayed pretty much the same until 1990, when the giant 303-room La Jolla de Mismaloya Grand Tourism resort was built there, completely dominating the tiny cove. Nonetheless the buildings used in the film still stand deserted on the hill on the south side of the cove, and you can walk up to them.

Aside from the giant hotel, there's a row of palm-frond palapa restaurants lining the south side of the beach, specialising in seafood (of course). Most are open from around 9 am to 6 pm, with a couple staying open later, until around 10 pm.

Parasailing, diving and snorkelling trips can be arranged on the beach. This is the closest beach to **Los Arcos,** the offshore island rock formation now declared a National Underwater Park. Small-boat operators will take you from Mismaloya to Los Arcos for about US$14 using their snorkelling gear, half-price if you have your own

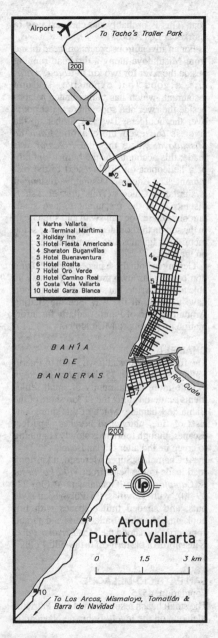

1 Marina Vallarta
   & Terminal Marítima
2 Holiday Inn
3 Hotel Fiesta Americana
4 Sheraton Buganvillas
5 Hotel Buenaventura
6 Hotel Rosita
7 Hotel Oro Verde
8 Hotel Camino Real
9 Costa Vida Vallarta
10 Hotel Garza Blanca

BAHÍA
DE
BANDERAS

**Around
Puerto Vallarta**

0   1.5   3 km

To Los Arcos, Mismaloya, Tomatlán &
Barra de Navidad

gear. This is probably the cheapest way to snorkel at Los Arcos.

For an adventurous excursion, head inland from Mismaloya along a dirt road running beside the river for two km to *Chico's Paradise*, a good (but expensive) seafood restaurant, which has tables under palapas beside the river at a spot where water pours over the boulders. Two km further up the river is the even more exotic *Eden de Mismaloya*, where the film *Predator* was made; this accounts for the burned-out hull of a helicopter on display next to the restaurant. The Eden de Mismaloya restaurant is similar to Chico's. Walk upriver a short distance past the restaurant to two small lagoons where you can swim and stretch out in the sun on the boulders. You may see some metre-long iguanas also sunning themselves on the rocks.

Getting to both these places is a hike if you don't have your own transport. You may be able to hitch a ride, but start early in case you have to walk all the way. See the Getting Around section of Puerto Vallarta for information on getting to Mismaloya.

CHAMELA

The first major coastal town south of Puerto Vallarta is Chamela, 152 km away. The town is little more a community of small settlements scattered along the 11-km shore of the Bahía de Chamela. Much of this shore consists of fine, untouched beaches – perfect escapes, though tourism is slowly beginning to creep in and alter the landscape.

At Chamela's Super Mercado, a km-long road leads to the beachfront *Villa Polinesia & Camping Club* (Guadalajara ☎ (36) 22-39-40), with 12 villas, 35 Polynesian-style huts, and shaded trailer spaces with full hook-ups. Another trailer park and motel, appropriately named the *Motel Trailer Park*, is just north of the turn-off to the Villa Polinesia.

SAN PATRICIO-MELAQUE
Population: 4525
The small beach resort town of San Patricio-Melaque on the lovely Bahía de Navidad is 60 km south-east of Chamela, just after Highway 80 from Guadalajara merges with Highway 200. Although it is a little larger than its twin resort town of Barra de Navidad two km along the beach to the south-east, it rarely appears on maps.

Another oddity is that it's officially known as San Patricio-Melaque, though locals usually call it simply Melaque. The reason for the double name is that two haciendas owned by foreigners (Irish, we presume?) used to stand side by side here, with the dividing line between the hacienda of San Patricio (on the east side) and Melaque (on the west) running where Calle López Mateos is today. Settlements gradually grew around the two haciendas, eventually merging into one town, which preserves the names of both.

In addition to being a popular beach resort for Mexican families when school is out, and a watering hole for yachties heading up and down the coast from November to May, the town is famous for its St Patrick's Day celebrations (Fiesta de San Patricio) in March, with the whole town putting on a raucous week-long party.

Orientation
Everything in Melaque is within walking distance. Most of the hotels, restaurants and public services are concentrated on or near Gómez Farías, running beside the beach, and López Mateos, the street coming in from the highway. Barra de Navidad is accessible via Highway 200 (five km) or the beach (two km).

Information
Tourist Office The tourist office in Barra de Navidad serves both Barra de Navidad and Melaque.

Money The Casa de Cambio Melaque at Local (shop) 11 in the Pasaje Comercial Melaque, on Gómez Farías opposite the main bus station, changes cash and travellers' cheques. It's open Monday to Saturday from 9 am to 2 pm and 4 to 7 pm, Sunday 9 am to 2 pm.

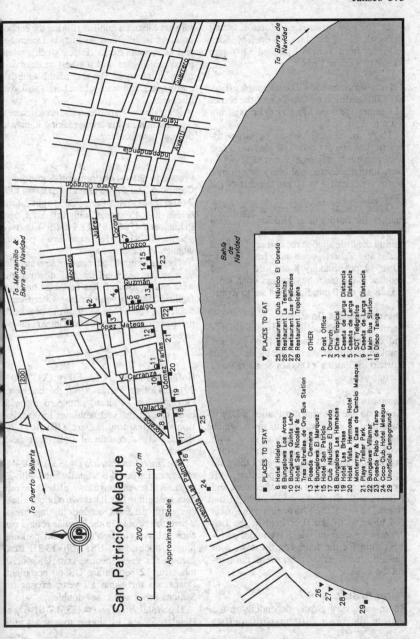

San Patricio-Melaque

0   200   400 m

Approximate Scale

To Puerto Vallarta

To Manzanillo & Barra de Navidad

To Barra de Navidad

Bahía de Navidad

PLACES TO STAY
6 Hotel Hidalgo
8 Bungalows Los Arcos
10 Bungalows Quinta Lety
12 Hotel San Nicolás &
   Tres Estrellas de Oro Bus Station
13 Posada Clemens
14 Bungalows El Marquez
15 Hotel San Patricio
17 Club Náutico El Dorado
18 Bungalows Las Hamacas
19 Hotel Las Brisas
20 Hotel Vista Hermosa, Hotel
   Monterrey & Casa de Cambio Melaque
21 Playa Trailer Park
22 Bungalows Villamar
23 Posada Pablo de Tarso
24 Coco Club Hotel Melaque
29 Unofficial Campground

▼ PLACES TO EAT
25 Restaurant Club Náutico El Dorado
26 Restaurant La Tesmiza
27 Restaurant Los Pelicanos
28 Restaurant Tropicana

OTHER
1 Post Office
2 Church
3 Cine Tropical
4 Caseta de Larga Distancia
5 Caseta de Larga Distancia
7 SCT Telegraph
9 Caseta de Larga Distancia
11 Main Bus Station
16 Disco Tanga

Post The post office is on Morelos, facing the north side of the plaza. It's open Monday to Friday from 9 am to 1 pm and 3 to 6 pm, Saturday 9 am to 1 pm.

Telecommunications The telegraph office, SCT Telégrafos, is on Orozco near the corner of Corona. It's open Monday to Friday from 9 am to 3 pm.

There are several casetas de larga distancia. The one at Corona 62 also has a fax; it's open every day from 8 am to 11 pm in busy tourist seasons, and every day from 8 am to 2 pm and 4 to 10 pm the rest of the time.

Other casetas include one at the Minimarket La Surtidora at Hidalgo 19, open every day from 7 am to 10 pm; another behind the little shop at the corner of Gómez Farías and Vallarta, open daily from 8 am to 10 or 11 pm, Sunday 8 am to 6 pm; and another at the main bus station, open daily from 8 am to 10 pm, Sunday 8 am to 2 pm.

Things to See & Do
Come to Melaque only if you want to relax and do nothing on the beach or join the drunken festivities during the Fiesta de San Patricio (St Patrick's Day) or Semana Santa (Easter week).

Festivals
Fiesta de San Patricio St Patrick's Day is celebrated in a big way in this town, which is named after Ireland's patron saint, with week-long festivities leading up to the saint's day on 17 March. During this week there are parties all day, domino competitions, bull races through the town every afternoon, and a fiesta with fireworks every night in the plaza. The day of the 17th begins with a mass and blessing of the fleet held in the Los Pelícanos restaurant, which is a major partying centre for the foreigners in town with pie-eating contests and other events throughout the week.

Places to Stay
Room rates vary greatly depending on the season; the town fills up with tourists (mostly Mexican families) during the school holidays in July and August, in December and at Semana Santa (Easter week), when prices are higher and it's best to reserve a room in advance. The rest of the time it's pretty quiet, and many of the hotels will give discounts.

Bungalows – apartments with kitchen – are common in this town, making it easy to do your own cooking.

Places to Stay – bottom-end & middle
Camping The *Playa Trailer Park* (☎ (333) 7-00-65) at Gómez Farías 205, right on the beach, has 45 spaces with full hook-ups. Prices are US$5.85/11.70 for one/two people, US$1.70 for each extra person, whether in trailers or tents.

There's an unofficial campground on a flat area by the beach all the way down at the west end of town. It has no water or other facilities, though you can buy water from a truck that comes by. Most of the beachside palapa restaurants nearby will let you have a free shower.

Hotels The *Posada Clemens* (☎ (333) 7-01-79), at Gómez Farías 70 on the corner of Guzmán, has 14 clean, simple rooms with bath, ceiling fan and windows for ventilation. Singles/doubles are US$10/11.70, rising only a couple of dollars at peak seasons.

The *Hotel San Patricio* (☎ (333) 7-02-44) at Gómez Farías 84 is a family hotel with 23 rooms and seven bungalows, all with private bath and ceiling fan. It has two outdoor kitchens, with pleasant outdoor dining areas, where the people in the regular rooms can cook, plus a children's pool and parking. Singles/doubles are US$10.70/13.35. Bungalows for eight people cost US$46.70; those for 12 people are US$60 per night. Prices are the same all year, except for Semana Santa when they double.

The *Hotel Hidalgo* (☎ (333) 7-01-61) at Hidalgo 56 has 14 simple rooms, all with ath and ceiling fan; singles/doubles are US$12/15.

The *Hotel San Nicolás* (☎ (333) 7-00-66) at Gómez Farías 54 has 10 upstairs rooms at US$13.35/16.70, rising about US$3 at holiday times. Rooms on the sea side have full-wall windows and a bit of a sea view.

The *Hotel Monterrey* (☎ (333) 7-00-04) at Gómez Farías 27, on the beach opposite the bus station, has a restaurant, parking, and 28 basic rooms with bath and ceiling fan, many opening onto a beachfront terrace. Singles/doubles are US$15/23.35, rising about US$2 during the busy tourist seasons.

The *Hotel Las Brisas* (☎ (333) 7-01-08) at Gómez Farías 9, also on the beach, has 28 rooms and six bungalows. All the rooms have a ceiling fan and a small fridge, with use of several small outdoor kitchens, but only the stoves and sinks are provided – unlike the other bungalows and kitchens in town, here you must bring your own pots, pans and dishes. Singles/doubles are US$19.10/23.85. The bungalows hold six people and cost US$52.45.

Bungalows *Bungalows Quinta Lety* (☎ (333) 7-00-64) at Gómez Farías 22 has four two-bedroom bungalows, each sleeping five people, with separate bedrooms opening onto outdoor kitchen/patios. The cost is US$33.35, except for a double bungalow for 10 people at US$66.70. Prices are the same all year except at Christmas and Semana Santa. It's a good place for families, with a children's pool, a table tennis table, and a handball and basketball court.

In the same block at Gómez Farías 2, *Bungalows Los Arcos* (☎ (333) 7-01-84) has eight bungalows; those for four people are US$37.35, and larger ones for eight people are US$66.

Beside the beach, *Bungalows Las Hamacas* (☎ (333) 7-01-13) at Gómez Farías 7 has 26 bungalows, parking, a small swimming pool and a beachfront restaurant. Bungalows for four people are US$37.35, for six people US$47.70, and for eight people US$65.35, with discounts when they're not busy. Some rooms have sea-view balconies.

Also on the beach, the *Hotel Vista Hermosa* (☎ (333) 7-00-02) at Gómez Farías 23, opposite the bus station, has a beachfront terrace, swimming pool, parking, and 26 bungalows at US$36.70 for one or two people, US$60 for five. Some open onto beachfront terraces. They also have 21 regular rooms at US$23.35/30 for singles/doubles.

Bungalows Villamar (☎/fax (333) 7-00-05) at Hidalgo 1 is a pleasant place with just five bungalows lined up beside a beachside garden with a small swimming pool. High-season rates of US$21.70 for two people and US$53.70 for eight are charged from November to February, in July and August, and at Semana Santa, with discounts the rest of the year.

Bungalows El Marquez (☎ (333) 7-02-13) at Gómez Farías 78 also has five bungalows, each for six people; they cost US$20.50/24.95 for singles/doubles, US$70.40 for six most of the year, and 20% higher during December and Semana Santa.

Places to Stay – top end
The *Posada Pablo de Tarso* (☎ (333) 7-01-17, 7-02-68) at Gómez Farías 408 is an attractive hotel with a large beachside pool and terrace. All the rooms have colour parabolic TV; suites also have air-conditioning. There are 12 bungalows for six people at US$99, 14 suites for four people at US$63, and just one regular room at US$14/31.20, with prices higher in July, August, December and during Semana Santa.

The four-star beachside *Club Náutico El Dorado* (☎ (333) 7-07-70/76, fax 7-02-39) at Gómez Farías 1-A, has a swimming pool, parking, a pleasant beachfront restaurant, and 56 well-appointed rooms with air conditioning, colour parabolic TV and other luxuries. Singles/doubles are US$50/63.

The most expensive place in town is the giant four-star *Coco Club Hotel Melaque* (☎ (333) 7-00-01, 7-03-64, fax 7-03-82). The price includes all meals, open bar, and a host of daily activities; singles/doubles are US$106/135 in regular rooms, US$120/150 in suites with kitchen, with one child free for each adult.

Places to Eat

A row of pleasant palm-thatched palapa restaurants stretches along the beach at the west end of town. Most popular with foreigners is the *Restaurant Los Pelícanos*, whose American-born owner/chef, the gregarious Philomena ('Phil') Garcia, provides a 'home away from home' for travellers and for the many yachties who anchor in the bay from November to May. She dishes up delicious food in large portions – try the barbeque shrimp for US$7.35, tender breaded octopus for US$8.35, or a big breakfast for US$2.35. It's open every day from 9 am to 9 pm.

Phil is also the author of several excellent cookbooks, which you can probably find at the restaurant, in addition to her book *Pelican's Pouch*, an informative little book about Mexico.

Other palapa restaurants along this stretch include the *Restaurant Tropicana*, open every day from 9 am to 6 pm with a dance every Sunday afternoon, and the *Restaurant La Tesmiza*.

A fancier beachside restaurant/bar is at the *Hotel Club Náutico*, with music in the evening and a great view of the bay. You could try a seafood combo or shrimp and steak shishkebab for US$9.35, fillet of fish with herbs and white wine sauce for US$8.35, or a chef salad for US$5.35. It's open every day from 8 am to 10.30 pm.

In the main bus station is a large, clean open-air restaurant open 24 hours a day, serving simple foods like hamburgers (US$2.70), fish (US$3.35), shrimp (US$5), sandwiches (US$2), enchiladas, tacos etc (US$0.35 each), quesadillas (US$0.50), or French toast with butter, maple syrup and coffee (US$1.70).

Entertainment

Disco Tanga on Gómez Farías, operated by the fancy Coco Club Hotel Melaque, is the only one in town. It's open every night from 10 pm until 3 am.

On Sunday afternoons, head down to the beach where the Restaurant Tropicana hosts a dance every Sunday from 2 to 6 pm.

Melaque has one movie house, the Cine Tropical, facing the south side of the plaza.

Getting There & Away

Air See the following Barra de Navidad Getting There & Away section for info on air services. Travel agents for flight arrangements are found in that town.

Bus Melaque has two bus stations. The main station, new in 1991, is on the corner of Gómez Farías and Carranza. It has a restaurant open 24 hours, a luggage storage room, and a long-distance telephone office.

Buses departing from this station include:

Barra de Navidad – five km, 10 minutes; buses every 15 minutes, 7 am to 8.30 pm (US$0.35). Southbound long-distance buses will also take you there.

Guadalajara – 294 km; six buses daily in primera clase (five hours, US$8); four buses daily with Primera Plus (five hours, US$10); 2nd-class buses hourly, 6.20 am to 11.20 pm, plus 2 and 4.20 am (seven hours, US$7.35).

Manzanillo – 97 km, 1½ hours; buses every half-hour, 5 am to midnight, plus 1 and 3 am (US$1.50 to US$2).

Puerto Vallarta – 205 km; three buses daily with Primera Plus (3½ hours, US$6.70); 2nd-class buses hourly, 6 am to 9.30 pm, plus 1 am (five hours, US$5).

The Tres Estrellas de Oro terminal is on Gómez Farías, 1½ blocks east of the main bus station. It has daily buses to Colima (three hours, US$5.35), Guadalajara (five hours, US$10) and Puerto Vallarta (four hours, US$6).

BARRA DE NAVIDAD

Population: 2185

The beach resort town of Barra de Navidad is around the bay from San Patricio-Melaque – a two km walk along the beach, or five km by road. The waves are bigger here than in Melaque – locals from Melaque often come over here for surfing, especially in January when the waves are best. Barra de Navidad has more restaurants than Melaque, and a number of places to stay, but the town itself is smaller, squeezed onto a sandbar between he Bahía de Navidad and the Laguna de Navidad.

Orientation

Legazpi, the main street, runs beside the beach. Veracruz, the town's other major street and the route to the highway, runs parallel to Legazpi before merging with it at the south end of town, which terminates in a finger-like sandbar.

Information

Tourist Office The tourist office (☎/fax 7-01-00) at Sonora 15 is open Monday to Friday from 9 am to 7 pm, Saturday 9 am to 1 pm. It has free maps and information on Barra de Navidad, Melaque and the state of Jalisco.

Money Banco Mexicano Somex, on the corner of Veracruz and Sinaloa, is open Monday to Friday from 9 am to 1.30 pm, but the hours for changing money (cash or travellers' cheques) are only from 10 to 11.30 am. They honour MasterCard, but for transactions with other credit cards you must go to Cihuatlán, 16 km south.

Post The post office is on Guanajuato near the corner of Mazatlán. It's open Monday to Friday from 9 am to 1 pm and 3 to 6 pm, closed on weekends.

Telecommunications The telegraph office, SCT Telégrafos, is at the corner of Veracruz and Guanajuato, on the south-east corner of the plaza. It's open Monday to Friday from 9 am to 3 pm.

There's a caseta de larga distancia on Calle Legazpi near the corner of Sonora; it's open Monday to Saturday from 9 am to 2 pm and 4 to 8.30 pm.

Travel Agencies Two travel agencies side by side on Veracruz, opposite the plaza, can make flight arrangements. The Agencia de Viajes Viacosta (☎ 7-02-58, 7-06-07) at Veracruz 206 is open Monday to Saturday

from 9 am to 2 pm and 4 to 7 pm. Next door, Isla Navidad Tours (☎ 7-06-65, 7-06-66, fax 7-06-67) is open the same hours.

Activities

Beach & Lagoons The beach, of course, is Barra de Navidad's prime attraction. Boating on the lagoon is also popular. The local boat operators' cooperative, the Sociedad Cooperativa de Servicios Turísticos Miguel López de Legazpi, on the lagoon at Veracruz 40, is open every day from 9 am to 6 pm, with a price list posted on the wall. Half-hour tours of the lagoon cost US$13.35 for a boat holding up to eight people; a bay tour is US$16.70. They also offer waterskiing (US$33.35 per hour) and deep-sea fishing (US$16.70 per hour).

The cooperative also does trips to the village of Colimilla across the lagoon; the round trip is US$10 for eight people. Or you can go halfway down the block and take boats to Colimilla for US$0.50 per person each way (US$1 return).

Tournaments National and international fishing tournaments are held four times a year for marlin, sailfish, tuna and dorado, with grand prizes including boats and cars. The most important annual tournament, the Torneo Internacional de Pesca de Marlin, Pez Vela y Dorado por Equipos, is held for three days around 15 to 20 January; dates vary slightly according to the phase of the moon.

The second most important tournament is the Torneo Internacional de Marlin Club de Pesca Barra de Navidad, held for three days during late May or early June. The same club sponsors another two-day tournament in early August. The final tournament of the year is held near the Mexican Independence Day on 15 and 16 September.

Places to Stay – bottom end

Camping You can camp for free by the beach on the north end of town, but there are no facilities provided.

Hotels The cheapest hotel in town is the

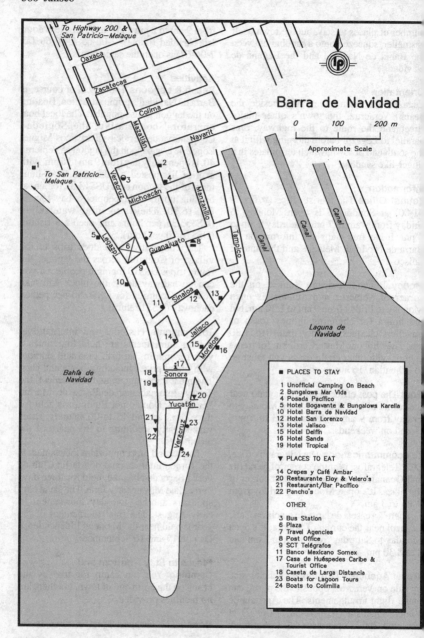

Barra de Navidad

0   100   200 m

Approximate Scale

Laguna de
Navidad

Bahía de
Navidad

■ PLACES TO STAY

1 Unofficial Camping On Beach
2 Bungalows Mar Vida
4 Posada Pacífico
5 Hotel Bogavante & Bungalows Karelia
10 Hotel Barra de Navidad
12 Hotel San Lorenzo
13 Hotel Jalisco
15 Hotel Delfín
16 Hotel Sands
19 Hotel Tropical

▼ PLACES TO EAT

14 Crepes y Café Ambar
20 Restaurante Eloy & Velero's
21 Restaurant/Bar Pacífico
22 Pancho's

OTHER

3 Bus Station
6 Plaza
7 Travel Agencies
8 Post Office
9 SCT Telégrafos
11 Banco Mexicano Somex
17 Casa de Huéspedes Caribe &
   Tourist Office
18 Caseta de Larga Distancia
23 Boats for Lagoon Tours
24 Boats to Colimilla

To Highway 200 &
San Patricio-Melaque

Oaxaca

Zacatecas

Colima

Nayarit

Mazatlán

To San Patricio-
Melaque

Veracruz

Michoacán

Manzanillo

Lepazpi

Guanajuato

Tampico

Canal

Canal

Canal

Sinaloa

Jalisco

Morelos

Sonora

Yucatán

Veracruz

simple little *Casa de Huéspedes Caribe* (☎ (333) 7-02-37) at Sonora 15. Its 10 rooms cost US$5 per person with general bath, or US$6.70 per person with private bath, rising to US$11.70/19.80 for singles/doubles at Christmas, Semana Santa and holidays.

The *Posada Pacífico* (☎ (333) 7-03-59) at Mazatlán 136, on the corner of Michoacán, is one of the best deals in town, with 25 large, clean rooms with bath and ceiling fan at US$10/12.70 for singles/doubles. The *Hotel San Lorenzo* (☎ (333) 7-01-39), at Sinaloa 7, on the corner of Mazatlán, has similar rooms at the same price, but the rooms aren't as bright.

The *Hotel Jalisco* (☎ (333) 7-04-47) at Jalisco 81 is an unremarkable place with 13 rooms, all with bath and ceiling fan, at US$11.70/14 for singles/doubles.

Places to Stay – middle

Barra de Navidad has a number of good middle-range places to stay. One of the best is the *Hotel Delfín* (☎ (333) 7-00-68, fax 7-10-20) at Morelos 23, opposite the lagoon. Its 26 rooms are large, clean and pleasant, looking out onto wide walkways with chairs outside each room where you can enjoy the view of the lagoon and the swimming pool below. They have an exercise and weights room and an outdoor restaurant with flowering plants and palapa-covered tables where a breakfast buffet for US$5 is served each morning. Singles/doubles are US$16.70/21.70 from June to October, rising to US$19.35/23.85 the rest of the year.

Over on Legazpi are several other good hotels right on the beach. Side by side are the *Hotel Bogavante* (☎/fax (333) 7-03-84), whose 22 rooms with bath and ceiling fan cost US$19/23.85 for singles/doubles; and the *Bungalows Karelia* (☎ (333) 7-01-87), with 10 one-bedroom apartments with kitchen at US$23.85 for one or two people. Both places have seafront terraces, but the rooms have no sea view.

Also on the beach is the *Hotel Tropical* (☎ (333) 7-00-20, fax 7-01-49) at Legazpi 96, a fancier place whose 42 rooms all have views – those on the beach side have

windows with a sea view, while those on the other side open onto private balconies with a view of the lagoon. At the hotel are a restaurant, bar, and children's pool; singles/doubles are US$23.50/29.35.

At the same price is the *Hotel Barra de Navidad* (☎ (333) 7-01-22, fax 7-03-03) at Legazpi 250, with a restaurant/bar and a beachside swimming pool. Of its 60 rooms, half open onto private beachfront terraces with fine views.

The *Hotel Sands* (☎ (333) 7-00-18), at Morelos 24 beside the lagoon, has 44 rooms, each with high, wood-beamed ceilings, a bath and a ceiling fan, opening onto a central courtyard with sitting areas. The lagoon-side outdoor restaurant and poolside bar are popular gathering spots at the afternoon happy hour. Singles/doubles are US$23.50/29.35 most of the year, dropping to US$18.80/23.50 in June, September, October and the first half of November.

It also has a couple of fine two-bedroom apartments with kitchen, sitting room and private balcony overlooking the lagoon. Each one can hold four people; they cost US$80 per night.

The *Bungalows Mar Vida* (☎ (333) 7-09-11, fax 7-03-49) at Mazatlán 168 is a fine little guest house with a swimming pool and just four studio apartments, all with colour satellite TV, at US$32/40 for singles/doubles.

Places to Eat

There are more good restaurants in Barra de Navidad than you would expect from the size of the town. Several are on terraces overlooking the beach, with a beautiful view of the sunset; several more are beside the lagoon; and still others are on Calle Veracruz, in the centre of town.

Beside the beach, the *Restaurant/Bar Pacífico* at Legazpi 206 has good food; its specialities are a large seafood platter for two people (US$18.35) and a Mexican antojitos platter (US$5). Other good dishes include fillet of fish (US$4.70) and filet mignon with shrimp (US$8.70). It's open every day from 8 am to 10 pm.

Almost next door, *Pancho's* at Legazpi 53 is a similar place, open every day from 8 am to 7 pm. Its food is also good but a little more expensive. Several other palapa-roofed restaurant/bars line the beach, and many of the beachside hotels also have restaurants.

Over beside the lagoon, the *Restaurante Eloy* at Yucatán 47 is a small, pleasant restaurant on a platform hanging out over the water. The specialities of the house are its filete de pescado a la casa for US$5, and the combination of shrimp, octopus and scallops cooked together in a special house sauce for US$6.70. Both are large, filling meals and there are plenty of other meals to choose from. It's open every day from 9 am to 9.30 pm.

Next door, *Velero's* is a somewhat fancier restaurant/bar with that same lagoon-side view. Specialities here include the shrimp and meat shishkebabs (US$10), and the shrimp dishes and steaks (US$8.35). It's open every day from noon to 10 pm.

One of the most pleasant restaurants in town, despite not being beside any water, is *Crepes y Café Ambar*, upstairs over the Ambar artesanías shop on the corner of Veracruz and Jalisco. It's a very clean '50% vegetarian' restaurant with fine atmosphere and good music, under a high palapa roof. It specialises in crepes, with 18 varieties, and salads that are safe to eat. Other treats include yoghurt with fruit, granola and honey, and Piña Ambar, half a pineapple filled with fruits and vanilla ice cream. Their coffee is probably the best in town. It's open every day from 8 am to noon and from 5 to 11 pm, except on Sunday when it's open on the evening shift only.

Entertainment

The one disco in town is Aladino's, aka El Galeón, at the Hotel Sands. It's naturally quite popular. The Hotel Sands' two-for-one happy hour, from 2 until 4 or 6 pm at the poolside bar, is also popular, especially since it includes the use of their lagoon-side pool.

Getting There & Away

Air Barra de Navidad and Melaque are served by the Playa de Oro international airport, 38 km south on Highway 200. To get there you must either take a taxi (half an hour, US$20), or a bus 16 km south to Cihuatlán and take a cheaper taxi from there. Aeroméxico has daily flights to Guadalajara, La Paz, Los Angeles and Mexico City; Mexicana has daily flights to Guadalajara, Los Angeles and Mexico City.

Bus The bus station is at Veracruz 228, near the corner of Nayarit. Local buses between Barra de Navidad and Melaque depart every 15 minutes from 6.30 am to 10 pm and cost US$0.35 for the 10-minute trip. Since the long-distance buses stop at both towns, any **northbound bus will also take you to Melaque.**

Long-distance buses departing from Barra de Navidad include those to:

Guadalajara – 291 km, six hours; seven buses daily (US$8 in primera clase, US$10 in primera Plus), plus a number of 2nd-class buses which take longer.

Manzanillo – 92 km, 1½ hours; buses every half-hour, 5 am to 10 pm (US$1.70).

Puerto Vallarta – 210 km; four buses daily with primera Plus (3½ hours, US$7); 2nd-class buses hourly, 7 am to 9 pm (five hours, US$5.35).

Colima State

With an area of only 5455 sq km, the state of Colima is Mexico's fourth-smallest after Tlaxcala, Morelos and Aguascalientes. Despite its relatively small area, the state is geographically diverse with everything from snowcapped volcanoes to tropical lagoons near the coast. More than three-quarters of Colima is covered with mountains and hills. The climate is equally diverse with higher temperatures and humidity along the coast and cool, sometimes freezing, temperatures in the highlands and mountains farther inland.

Colima borders the state of Jalisco to the north, east and west and the state of Michoacán to the south-east. To the north

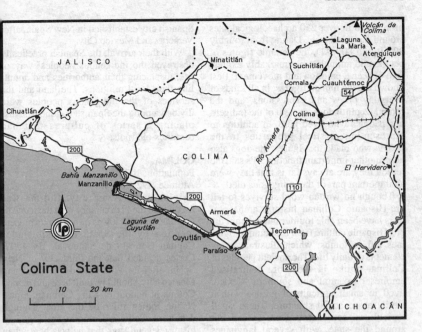

Colima State

0   10   20 km

and west, part of the border is delineated by the Río Cihuatlán. To the south-east and east, the Río Coahuayana, also known as the Río Tuxpan and the Río Naranjo, forms most of the border. The Río Armería, one of the state's largest rivers, flows down from the Sierra de Cacoma mountain range of Jalisco, crosses Colima from north to south and enters the Pacific Ocean through the Boca de Pascuales south-east of Manzanillo.

Colima's economy is based on agriculture, fishing, industry and tourism. The most important agricultural crops are coconuts, lemons, bananas and other fruits; fishing, highly important to the state, involves a number of species but the most significant are red snapper and shrimp. The largest part of the industrial sector is mining, with one of Mexico's richest iron deposits found in the Peña Colorada municipality of Minatitlán. The greatest tourist development is around Manzanillo.

There's something of interest for every

traveller in Colima. For beachlovers and fans of tropical paradise, there's plenty of both along the coast, particularly in and around Manzanillo and at the small beach resorts of Cuyutlán and Paraíso. Inland, Colima, the capital, is a quiet place where much of the original colonial-style architecture has been well preserved. Nearby, the white-washed town of Comala has also retained some of its colonial legacy, but today it is better known for its handcrafts, especially hand-carved furniture.

Overlooking both places are the steaming Volcán de Fuego de Colima (3960 metres) and the extinct snow-capped Volcán Nevado de Colima (4330 metres) of the Nevado de Colima National Park, both of which can be climbed by foot, horse or four-wheel drive, but only if you are feeling adventurous.

History

One of the things Colima is most known for is its pre-Hispanic ceramics, which have been found in over 250 archaeological sites around the small state. Dating from roughly 200 BC to 800 AD, the ceramic figures of people and animals are remarkably expressive of scene, emotion and movement. Best known are the human figures, in all kinds of everyday poses and expressions, and the rotund Izcuintli dogs, a totem of the indigenous peoples who lived here. In addition to representing mystical properties to the people who made the figures, the dogs also held another important function: it's said the reason they are always fat is that they were an important part of the indigenous diet!

Though no written word survives to tell pre-Hispanic Coliman history, archaeologists have been able to infer much about the pre-Hispanic culture from the ceramic figurines left in tombs, which illustrate many elements of daily life. The ancient peoples of Colima, unlike in the more centralised empires of central and southern Mexico, lived in small agricultural groups with a family-based social structure. These small agricultural settlements were spread out around the state, with several languages spoken, but they were not isolated. There is evidence of cultural contacts with many other parts of Mesoamerica, especially with the Altiplano cultures in Classic (Teotihuacán) and Postclassic (Mexica) times, along with evidence of materials, customs and traditions that came from greater distances.

To see an impressive collection of hundreds of these ancient ceramic figurines, visit the Museo de las Culturas de Occidente (Museum of Western Cultures) at the Casa de la Cultura in Colima city; it has one of the finest collections in Mexico.

After the fall of Tenochtitlán, the Spanish headed towards the Pacific coast. In the beginning of 1523, Capitán Rodríguez de Villafuerte penetrated Colima with Tarascan forces, but they were put down in the region of Tecomán. More successful was the advance of Capitán Gonzálo de Sandoval, who in the same year 'pacified' the region and founded the first villa of Colima in its present location in July 1523 – the third

Spanish city established in New Spain, after Veracruz and Mexico City.

With their arrival, the Spanish practically destroyed the indigenous peoples' way of life, displacing their authorities and annulling their local religions. The land and the services of the indigenous peoples were divided among the Spanish conquerors, displacing a series of cultures that had centuries-old roots.

COLIMA
Population: 107,000
Altitude: 492 metres

Originally an Aztec city, Colima was founded in the 11th century with the name of Cajitlán. In 1523 it was moved to its present location by the Spanish conquistador Capitán Gonzálo de Sandoval. By 1527, Cortés decided that the third city of New Spain, after La Villa Rica de Veracruz and Mexico City, should be built here and named Colima in honour of King Colimán, a past Nahua Indian ruler of the area. Though details of Colimán's empire are foggy in history, legend says that he was here when the Spanish first arrived and that he managed to chase them out four times before they finally succeeded in conquering the area.

Most of the buildings in Colima, however, were not built until after the Spanish left in the early 19th century. Although it was one of the first cities in Mexico, the area wasn't declared a state until 1857 and the city not a capital until a year later. Today, Colima is a pleasant tropical city, graced with palm trees, surrounded by farmland and not often visited by foreigners.

Orientation
Colima sits on a fertile plain surrounded by hills and mountains, the highest ones being the twin volcanic peaks of Nevado de Colima (4330 metres) and Fuego de Colima (3960 metres). Although it's only 45 km from the coast, the city is at a higher elevation and, consequently, cooler and less humid.

Central Colima spreads around three plazas, beginning with the Plaza Principal (also known as the Jardín Libertad), the Jardín Quintero behind the cathedral and, three blocks to the east, the Jardín Nuñez. As with most cities and towns in Mexico, street names change frequently, with the names of all streets in the centre changing on either side of the Plaza Principal.

Also like many towns in Mexico, Colima now has a shiny new bus terminal on the outskirts of the city, about two km east of the centre beside Highway 110, which heads 45 km south-west to the coast. Highway 110 also continues north-east from Colima, but if you're going to Guadalajara (224 km), Highway 54 is the faster route. The train station, about 10 blocks south of the Plaza Principal, is served by trains to/from Manzanillo and Guadalajara.

Information

Tourist Office The tourist office, called the Dirección de Turismo del Estado de Colima (☎ 2-43-60, ☎/fax 2-83-60), is moving to new offices at Portal Hidalgo 20, facing the Plaza Principal opposite the cathedral, and should be firmly esconced there by the time you read this book. They're open Monday to Friday from 8.30 am to 9 pm, Saturday 9 am to 1.30 pm. They have free maps, brochures and information on the city and state of Colima.

Money There are a number of banks around the centre where you can change money; they are open Monday to Friday from 9 am to 1.30 pm. Visa and MasterCard are honoured in Colima, but the American Express card is not.

The Majapara Casa de Cambio at the corner of Morelos and Juárez, on the southwest corner of Jardín Núñez, gives a rate similar to the banks and is open somewhat more convenient hours: Monday to Friday from 9 am to 2 pm and 4 to 6 pm, Saturday 9 am to 2 pm.

Post The post office is at Madero 247 on the corner of Revolución, at the north-east corner of Jardín Núñez. It's open Monday to Friday from 8 am to 7 pm, Saturday 8 am to noon.

Telecommunications The Telecomm office, with telegram, telex and fax services, is in the same building as the post office. It's open Monday to Friday from 9 am to 8 pm, Saturday 9 am to noon.

Colima has three Computel offices. Those in the centre have both long-distance telephone and fax; the one at the central bus station has telephone only. One Computel is at Morelos 234, facing Jardín Núñez; another is at Medellín 55 near the corner of Hidalgo. All three are open every day from 7 am to 10 pm.

Another caseta de larga distancia is at the Farmacia Colima at Madero 1, on the northeast corner of the Plaza Principal, opposite the cathedral; it's open Monday to Saturday from 8.30 am to 2 pm and 3.30 to 8.30 pm.

Laundry Lavandería Jando, on Juárez, facing the west side of Jardín Núñez, is open Monday to Saturday from 9 am to 2 pm and 4 to 8.30 pm, Sunday 9 am to 2 pm. The cost is US$0.85 per kilo for wash, dry and fold. Or there's the Lavandería Victoria, at Victoria 131, between Ocampo and De la Vega, with no sign out the front; the cost here is US$0.45 to wash three kilos of laundry if you do it yourself, US$1 if you drop it off to be washed only, or US$2 for three kilos for wash, dry and fold. It's open Monday to Friday from 7 am to 2 pm and 3 to 8 pm, Saturday 6 am to 8 pm.

Travel Agencies

The Avitesa travel agency (☎ 2-19-84, 2-69-70, fax 2-69-80) at the corner of Constitución and Zaragoza, a block north of the Plaza Principal, can make flight arrangements, and they speak English. They're open Monday to Friday from 8.30 am to 7 pm, Saturday 9 am to 2 pm.

Cathedral

On the east side of the Plaza Principal is Colima's Santa Iglesia cathedral, rebuilt several times since the Spanish first con-

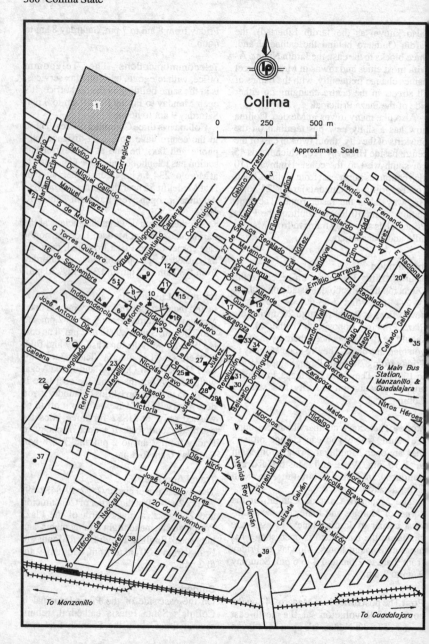

structed a cathedral here in 1527. The latest reconstruction dates from the 1940s just after the 1941 earthquake.

Palacio del Gobierno

Built between 1884 and 1904, the government palace is beside the cathedral on Plaza Principal where Colima's jailhouse once stood. Local artist Jorge Chávez Carrillo painted the murals, depicting Mexican history from the Spanish conquest to independence, on the walls of the stairway inside the palace in honour of independence hero Hidalgo's 200th birthday.

Museo de Historia de Colima

On Hidalgo facing the Plaza Principal is Colima's Museum of History. Its collection is not as extensive or well displayed as the one at the Museum of Western Cultures, but it's still worth stopping by to see its collection of ceramic vessels and figurines, mostly people and Izcuintli dogs, unearthed from

the 278 archaeological sites around the small state of Colima. Also here are displays of masks, textiles, clothing and costumes, basketry, shellwork from the coast of Colima, and temporary exhibits.

Outside the museum entrance is posted a monthly schedule of events at the museum, including films, theatre, conferences, workshops, book presentations, special exhibits and more. The museum is open Tuesday to Sunday from 10 am to 2 pm and 5 to 8 pm; admission is free.

Next door is the Sala de Exposiciones of the University of Colima, with changing art exhibitions; it's open the same hours as the museum and admission is free.

Teatro Hidalgo

The Hidalgo Theatre stands at the corner of Degollado and Independencia, one block from the Plaza Principal. It was built between 1871 and 1883 in a house donated by the famous independence hero Padre

---

■ PLACES TO STAY

6 Hotel San Cristóbal
9 Hotel Ceballos
25 Hotel América
27 Hotel Núñez & Lavandería Jando
29 Gran Hotel Flamingos
30 Casa de Huéspedes Miramar

▼ PLACES TO EAT

2 Ah Que Nanishe
11 Jugolandia
12 Giovanni's Pizza
15 Restaurant/Bar Los Naranjos
17 La Arábica
18 Restaurant Vegetariano Samadhi
34 Centro de Nutrición Lakshmi

OTHER

1 Jardín de la Corregidora
3 Instituto Universitario de Bellas Artes & Museo Universitario de Culturas Populares
4 Teatro Hidalgo

5 Tourist Office
7 Museo de Historia de Colima
8 Plaza Principal (Jardín Libertad)
10 Cathedral & Palacio del Gobierno
13 Computel
14 Jardín Quintero
16 La Taba
19 Sangre de Cristo Church
20 Casa de la Cultura & Museo de las Culturas de Occidente
21 Central de Boliche Bus Station
22 Buses to Comala
23 Mercado Constitución
24 Lavandería Victoria
26 Majapara Casa de Cambio
28 Computel
31 Antique Automobile Collection
32 Jardín Núñez
33 Post Office & Telecomm
35 Parque Piedra Lisa
36 Jardín Juárez
37 Parque Regional Metropolitano
38 Parque Hidalgo
39 Monument to Rey Colimán
40 Railway Station

Miguel Hidalgo, parish priest of the villa of Colima in 1792, long before his famous cry for the independence of Mexico in 1810. The theatre, named in his honour, was built in Neoclassic style during the later years of the Porfirio Díaz government, but destroyed in the earthquakes of 1932 and 1941, with reconstruction undertaken in 1942. Performances are held at the theatre; stop by to see what's on.

Casa de la Cultura & Museo de las Culturas de Occidente

The House of Culture, centre of cultural affairs for the state of Colima, is a government-run cultural complex at the intersection of Calzada Galván and Ejercito Nacional, a few blocks north-east of the centre.

In the main administrative building (☎ 2-31-55, 2-84-31), open every day from 9 am to 9 pm, is a permanent exhibit of the art of the renowned Coliman modernistic painter Alfonso Michel (1897-1957) and other temporary art exhibits. In another building, the **Edificio de Talleres**, are 20 workshops with classes in every kind of art, plus the Teatro Casa de la Cultura, an 800-seat theatre with frequent cultural performances. Downstairs is the Café Arte, with live music every night beginning around 8 or 9 pm.

In another building is the **Biblioteca Central del Estado**, the state library. Half a block away, the Cine Teatro USI presents cultural film series brought by the Casa de la Cultura (see the Entertainment section).

Most famous in the complex, though, is the **Museo de las Culturas de Occidente** – the Museum of Western Cultures. Here in a bright, modern and well-lit building are exhibited hundreds of specimens of pre-Hispanic ceramic vessels and figurines from archaeological sites around the state, with explanations about the figures and about the region in pre-Hispanic times. Most famous are the human figures and the fat Izcuintli dogs, but there are also a wide variety of other ceramic figures including simple vessels, musical instruments, mammals, reptiles, fish and birds, some of which still exist

in the area and others which have now disappeared.

The display is impressive, especially for the lifelike sense of movement and emotions in the ancient figures. The museum is open Tuesday to Sunday from 9 am to 7 pm; admission is free.

Museo Universitario de Culturas Populares

Housed at the Instituto Universitario de Bellas Artes (IUBA), on the corner of 27 de Septiembre and Manuel Gallardo, about eight blocks from the Plaza Principal, the University Museum of Popular Cultures used to be called the Museum of Masks & Dances. A small museum, it still has dance and mask displays from Colima and other Mexican states, but it has been expanded to include exhibits on many other popular art forms including textiles, clothing and costumes, ceramics, musical instruments, furniture and more. The museum is open Monday to Saturday from 9 am to 2 pm and 4 to 7 pm; admission is free.

Also at IUBA is the interesting **Taller de Reproducciones**, just inside the gate and off to your right, where you can see the process of reproducing the historical Coliman ceramic figurines. IUBA gives classes in all the arts, with performing arts presented here at a small theatre, the Foro Pablo Silva; also based here is the Ballet Folklórico de la Universidad de Colima. In the museum foyer is a shop where you can buy inexpensive handcrafts from Colima and other parts of Mexico, including the fat Izcuintli dogs and other figures made in the Taller de Reproducciones.

Colección de Automóviles Antiguos

One of Colima's most famous sights is the Collection of Antique Automobiles, housed in a shaky warehouse behind an auto parts store at Revolución 79, facing the east side of Jardín Núñez. Ask for Señor Francisco Zaragoza Vázquez, owner of the store and the collection, and he will lead you through a maze of shelves and old parts to the warehouse.

Since 1952 he has collected over 300 automobiles dating from 1912 to 1950; several horse-drawn carriages including an eerie old hearse date as far back as 1884. The collection here holds some fine, interesting specimens, but it is not the entire collection; more are housed at another site a few km from the centre.

Parks

There are a number of parks within walking distance of the centre of Colima. The **Parque Regional Metropolitano** on Degollado, a few blocks south-west of the centre, has a small zoo, a large pool with waves and toboggan water slides, an open-air theatre and a forest section with an artificial lake and rowboats.

Parque Piedra Lisa, east of the centre on Calzada Galván, is named for its famous Sliding Stone, which you'll see when you enter the park from the traffic circle at the intersection of Calzada Galván and Aldama. A legendary monolith, it has attracted generations of Colimans to slide on it, and just as drinking water from the Nile is said to ensure your return to Egypt, so traditional legend says that visitors who slide on this stone will return to Colima someday. The park contains a large children's playground and open green spaces.

The **Jardín de la Corregidora**, a few blocks north of the centre, is another popular park.

Festivals

Fiestas Charrotaurinas San Felipe de Jesús This festival, celebrated for 17 days in February beginning the first Saturday after 4 February, takes place in Villa de Alvarez, about five km north of the city centre. Each day of the festival except Tuesdays and Fridays, a large group on horseback departs from Colima's cathedral and rides to Villa de Alvarez preceded by giant *mojigangos*, figures of the village's mayor and wife, followed by musical groups. When they arrive at Villa de Alvarez the celebrations continue with food, music, dancing and bullfights.

Blessing of the Animals On the third Sunday in June at Lo de Villa, 3½ km from the centre of Colima on the northern outskirts of the city, Colimans bring their animals, seeds, grains and tractors to the Church of the Señor de la Expiración to receive a blessing.

Fiesta de San Rafael Arcangel The fiesta honouring this saint is celebrated from 10 to 24 October in Cuauhtémoc, 19 km north-east of Colima near the Colima airport. Celebrations include music and dancing in the town plaza, other concerts and dances, horseback processions, cockfights, bullfights, fireworks and more.

Feria de Todos los Santos Also called the Feria de Colima, the Colima state fair held from 27 October to 11 November includes exhibits of agriculture, livestock, commerce and industry, as well as handcrafts and popular arts, sporting and cultural events, open-air theatre, carnival rides, bullfights and more.

Día de la Virgen de Guadalupe Celebrations beginning around 1 December lead up to 12 December, the day of Mexico's patron saint. Pilgrims, many dressed in Indian costumes, come to pay homage at the Virgin's altar in the cathedral.

Places to Stay – bottom end

Colima doesn't have an abundance of places to stay, but you shouldn't have any problem finding a room.

A good place to stay if you're on a tight budget is the friendly little family-run *Casa de Huéspedes Miramar* (☎ 2-34-67) at Morelos 265, near the south-east corner of Jardín Núñez. The courtyard is full of flowers and plants, there's a lavadero where you can wash your clothes, and the atmosphere is peaceful and homely. It has 12 guest rooms; those with common bath cost US$8.35/10 for singles/doubles, those with private bath are US$8.35/13.35.

The Miramar is rarely full, but if it is you could try the *Hotel Núñez* (☎ 2-70-30) nearby at Juárez 88, facing the west side of Jardín Núñez. It's an older, very basic hotel; the 32 rooms facing an interior courtyard have no windows and so tend to be stuffy, but they're kept clean enough. Rooms with general bath cost US$6.70; those with private bath cost US$9.35 with one bed or US$12.70 with two beds.

Similar is the *Hotel San Cristóbal* (☎ 2-05-15) at Reforma 98, on the corner of Independencia, one block south-west of the Plaza Principal. The 21 rooms, with fans but no windows, cost US$6.70 with general bath, US$9.35 with private bath.

A great step up in quality is the *Gran Hotel Flamingos* (☎ 2-25-25, 2-25-26) at Avenida Rey Colimán 18, half a block from Jardín Núñez. Its 56 clean, modern rooms with bath and fan all have full-wall windows with sliding-glass doors opening onto private balconies, good for catching the breeze. The rooms on the upper floors offer a bit of a view over the town, with its many trees and the mountains surrounding it; those on the side away from the street and the bus stop out front are much quieter. Singles/doubles are US$14/15.70.

Places to Stay – top end

The *Hotel Ceballos* (☎ 2-44-44, fax 2-06-45) at Portal Medellín 12, facing the north side of the Plaza Principal, is the traditional fancy place to stay in the centre. The stately building, dating from 1880, has been the home of three of the state's governors. The 63 high-ceilinged, air-conditioned rooms are clean and pleasant, many with French doors opening onto small balconies; the cost for one or two people is US$33.35.

More modern is the four-star *Hotel América* (☎ 2-74-88, 2-95-96, fax 4-44-25) at Morelos 162, half a block west of Jardín Núñez. Its 75 rooms come with high wood-beamed ceilings, colour TV, phone, etc; facilities also include steam baths, swimming pool, restaurant, laundry and parking. Rooms are US$46.70 for one or two people.

Places to Eat

For a simple meal or snack there are many small restaurants, snack stands and sidewalk cafés around the Plaza Principal. Many offer cold drinks, ice cream and frozen paletas, welcome in this warm climate; the *Nevería La Flor de Michoacán* on one corner of the plaza has a good selection, and it's open every day from 8 am to 10 pm.

Just a few doors from the Plaza Principal, *Jugolandia*, at Madero 17 opposite the cathedral, is an inexpensive place for fresh juices, tortas, sandwiches, hamburgers, yoghurt, fruit salads and other snacks. It's open every day from 7 am to 11 pm.

The restaurant/bar *Los Naranjos* at Gabino Barreda 34, half a block north of Jardín Quintero, is a clean, pleasant restaurant with overhead fans; it's good for all meals. A pianist provides music from around 2.30 to 4.30 pm and from 9 to 11 pm; it's open from 8 am to 11.30 pm every day.

Pizza fans will probably like *Giovannís Pizza*, an Italian-style pizza parlour at Constitución 58 near the corner of Zaragoza. Prices range from US$5.70 for the simplest medium-size pizza up to US$19.35 for the giant size with everything on it, and it's pretty good pizza. If you like, you can phone them for free delivery (☎ 2-95-05, 2-95-30) and if it doesn't arrive in half an hour, it's free.

If you like vegetarian food, don't miss the *Restaurant Vegetariano Samadhi* at Filomeno Medina 125, opposite the Sangre de Cristo church, two blocks north of Jardín Núñez. Its graceful dining area occupies an arched courtyard with a large palm tree and other tropical plants.

The menu is large, varied and inexpensive, with selections including soyburgers with salad and French fries (US$2), spinach and cheese crepes (US$2), yoghurt with fruit and granola (US$1), mushroom and cheese omelettes (US$2.70), chicken Parmesan (US$3.35), a wide variety of vegetable and fruit juices, teas, and yoghurt or ice cream malts, and much more. The comida corrida, served from around 1 to 4 pm, including soup, salad, main course, dessert, and fresh juice, is a good deal at US$3.35. Samadhi is open from 8 am to 10 pm every day, except Thursday when it's open from 8 am to 5 pm.

The *Centro de Nutrición Lakshmi* is also near Jardín Núñez, at Madero 265. It includes a whole-grain bakery, a section with vitamins and health products, and a restaurant section serving soyburgers, flavoured yoghurts and fruit salads. It ; open Monday to Saturday from 8.30 am to 10 pm, Sunday 6 to 10 pm.

La Arábica, at Guerrero 162, near the corner of Obregón, is a small coffee house where people come to drink coffee and talk at the tables at the front or in the shady patio out the back. It's open Monday to Saturday from 9 am to 2 pm and 4.30 to 9 pm.

The *Café Colima,* in the middle of the Jardín de la Corregidora, is a favourite with locals, serving everything from tortas, nachos and burgers to meat and seafood meals. It's especially popular in the evening, when there's live music on the garden patio; it's open every day from 9.30 am to midnight.

Another favourite is *A Que Nanishe* at 5 de Mayo 257, five blocks north-west of the Plaza Principal, an attractive patio restaurant serving up traditional Oaxacan and Mexican dishes. House specialities include dishes of black huitlacoche mushrooms, flor de calabaza, Oaxacan tamales, huaraches (corn tortillas stuffed with a variety of fillings), meat dishes with three kinds of sauce (mole negro, mole verde and mole coloradita), and champurrado (a hot corn atole beverage with chocolate). Meat dishes are around US$5.35, huaraches US$1.70.

The restaurant's name means 'oh how delicious' in Zapoteco, the language of the owner's native Oaxaca. It's open every day from 1.30 pm until midnight, Wednesday from 7 pm until midnight.

Entertainment

Colima is basically a quiet city but there are a few things you can do in the evening.

There are several cafés featuring live music in the evening, known as *cafés cantante*. Most popular is the Café Colima, in the middle of the Jardín de la Corregidora, with music on the patio every night from around 9 pm to midnight. The Café Arte in the Casa de la Cultura complex also has live music nightly.

La Taba at Medellín 11, facing Jardín Quintero, is an Argentinian-style restaurant/bar with a dance floor and live music every night from around 9 pm until 2 or 3 am. Also on the Jardín Quintero is the upstairs Diego's Piano Bar, another restaurant/bar with live music nightly.

Colima has a few discos; best and most popular is Cheers at Zaragoza 528, several blocks east of the centre.

The Teatro Hidalgo, on the corner of Degollado and Independencia, one block from the Plaza Principal, the Teatro Casa de la Cultura, at the Casa de la Cultura complex on Calzada Galván, and the smaller Foro Pablo Silva theatre, at the Instituto Universitario de Bellas Artes at the corner of Manuel Gallardo and 27 de Septiembre, all host performing arts – dance, theatre, music, etc. You can stop by these places to see their posted schedules, or try phoning the Casa de la Cultura (☎ 2-31-55, 2-84-31), the organising body of cultural activities throughout the city and state, to ask what's on.

The Cine Teatro USI, half a block from the Casa de la Cultura on Calzada Galván, hosts film series presented by the Casa de la Cultura; the emphasis is on new Mexican films but international films are also shown. Drop by or phone the Casa de la Cultura to find out the current film schedule.

Other cinemas include the Cine Jorge Sthal at Avenida de los Maestros 110, the Cine Plaza del Rey at Avenida Rey Colimán 329, and the Cine Diana on Nigromante.

Cultural events including films, theatre, conferences, lectures and more are held at the Museo de la Historia de Colima on the Plaza Principal; their monthly events schedule is posted outside the entrance.

Things to Buy

Authentic-looking reproductions of the famous fat Izcuintli dogs and other artesanías are sold at the Museo Universitario de Culturas Populares. Casa Ceballos, at the corner of Medellín and Constitución on the north-east corner of the Plaza Principal, also has a collection of the dogs for sale, as does the Tienda de Artesanías DIF, a block away on the corner of Constitución and Zaragoza.

The big Mercado Constitución is on Calle Reforma, three blocks south of the Plaza Principal.

Getting There & Away

Air Colima's airport is in Buenavista, near Cuauhtémoc, about 20 minutes north-east of Colima off the highway to Guadalajara. It is served by only one airline, Aero California, which offers daily flights to Mexico City and Tijuana, with onward connections.

Bus Colima has three bus stations. The Central de Boliche, at Degollado 180, 2½ blocks south-west of the Plaza Principal, services only the Autobuses Colima-Manzanillo bus line, with buses to Manzanillo departing every 15 minutes from 4.30 am to 10 pm (US$2.35). One bus per hour goes direct to Manzanillo (1½ hours); the other three go via Tecomán (45 minutes, US$1) and Armería (one hour, US$1.20), taking two hours to reach Manzanillo.

A block further south-west on Degollado is an open lot from where local buses depart for towns near Colima. Buses to Comala depart from this lot every 15 minutes from 6 am to 10 pm.

Colima's main bus station, the Central Camionera, is about two km from the centre on the eastern outskirts of town, just off Avenida Niños Héroes where it meets Highway 110 coming from Manzanillo. At the station is a long-distance telephone office, a storage area for luggage, a pharmacy, and various restaurants and snack shops. Buses departing from this station include those to:

Armería – 45 km, 1¼ hours; 17 buses daily, 5.20 am to 10.30 pm via Tecomán, with Autotransportes del Sur de Jalisco (US$1.20).

Ciudad Guzmán – 50 km, one hour; 17 buses daily, 6.20 am to 8 pm, plus 3.40 am, with Autotransportes del Sur de Jalisco (US$2.85); five daily with Omnibus de México (US$3.20).

Guadalajara – 224 km, three hours; hourly buses, 6 am to 11.50 pm, plus 1.20 am and 4 am, with La Linea (US$7); hourly, 6.20 am to 8 pm, with Autotransportes del Sur de Jalisco (US$6.70); 11 daily with Primera Plus (US$8.35); 10 daily with Servicios Coordinados (US$7); nine daily with Omnibus de México (US$7); six daily with ETN (US$11.70); four daily with Tres Estrellas de Oro (US$6.70).

Lázaro Cárdenas – 267 km, six to seven hours; four daily with Autotransportes del Sur de Jalisco (US$8); two daily with La Linea (US$8.80); one daily with Tres Estrellas de Oro (US$8.35); or bus to Tecomán or Armería and change buses there.

Manzanillo – 101 km, 1¼ hours direct, 1¾ hours via Tecomán and Armería; hourly buses, 24 hours, with La Linea (US$2.65); 17 buses daily, 5.20 am to 10.30 pm via Tecomán and Armería, with Autotransportes del Sur de Jalisco (US$2.50); 11 daily with Servicios Coordinados (US$2.60); 10 daily with Primera Plus (US$3.35); eight daily with Tres Estrellas de Oro (US$2.70).

Mexico City – 742 km, 11 hours; three buses daily with Tres Estrellas de Oro (US$18.30); two daily with Servicios Coordinados (US$20.70); two daily with ETN (US$43.35); one daily with Primera Plus (US$24).

Tecomán – 42 km, one hour; 17 buses daily, 5.20 am to 10.30 pm, with Autotransportes del Sur de Jalisco (US$1.10).

Train The Estación del Ferrocarril (☎ 2-92-50) is about 10 blocks south of the Plaza Principal. Train No 91 departs Colima at 8.20 am and takes six hours to reach Guadalajara (US$2.30). Train No 92 departs at 3.15 pm, taking two hours to reach Manzanillo (US$0.85).

Tickets can only be bought half an hour before the arrival of the train, on the same day you're travelling. The trains are never early, but they are often late, and if so, the office won't open until half an hour before they are due to arrive. Schedules may vary; departure times are posted at the station.

Getting Around

To/From the Airport Arriving at the airport, there are combis ready to take you into the city, but none operate for the trip from the city back to the airport. A taxi to the airport costs US$11.70.

Bus & Taxi Local buses operate every day from 6 am to 9.30 pm; a ride costs US$0.20. Ones marked 'Central' will take you to the central bus station on the outskirts of town.

Taxis are plentiful and relatively cheap. The maximum fare around the city – from the bus station into town, for example – is US$1.70.

AROUND COLIMA
Comala
Population: 7570`

The small, picturesque town of Comala, nine km north of Colima, is known for its fine artesanías, especially its carved wood furniture but for other handcrafts as well. Special mercados de artesanías (handcrafts markets), called tianguis, are held twice a week: on Sundays in the Mercado La Trinidad, and on Mondays in the Mercado Municipal.

You can see the famous Comala furniture being made at the Sociedad Cooperativa Artesanías Pueblo Blanco, a handcrafts centre renowned for its colonial-style hand-carved furniture, wood paintings and ironwork. The centre is one km south of town, just off the road to Colima; it's open Monday to Friday from 9 am to 6 pm, Saturday 9 am to 2 pm.

There's a simple but beautiful church on the plaza, which has a fine white gazebo and trees blooming with brilliant yellow flowers. Under the arches along one side of the plaza are three attractive sidewalk cafés/patio restaurant/bars with a delightful tradition: when you order something to drink, they bring you all the *botanas* (snacks) you can eat, consisting of all kinds of typical regional foods. The *Restaurant Típico Los Portales* and beside it the *Restaurant/Bar Comala* are open daily from noon to 6 pm; the *Restaurant/Bar Fundador* is open from 10 am to 6 pm. Many people come to Comala just to enjoy these restaurants.

To get to Comala from Colima, take a bus from the open bus area on Calle Degollado, about four blocks south-west of the Plaza Principal. Buses to Comala depart every 15 minutes from 6 am to 10 pm; cost is US$0.40 for the 15-minute ride. In Comala, the buses back to Colima depart from the plaza.

NEVADO DE COLIMA NATIONAL PARK
Both volcanoes – Volcán de Fuego de Colima (3960 metres) and Volcán Nevado de Colima (4330 metres) – can supposedly be hiked in a day or two each, if you can start at the base trail/logging road of either one and not from Highway 54. That's the biggest problem because, aside from an occasional logging truck from the nearby paper-mill town of Atenquique and horseback riders from Fresnito, there are very few vehicles trudging up to either summit.

The trail/road from Fresnito is pleasant and begins climbing gradually, but expect to spend about two days hiking to the summit of Nevado de Colima. If you have the time, the hike is worthwhile just for the spectacular view, especially at sunrise, and for the experience of playing in the snow in Mexico. Nevado de Colima usually has snow on its summit year-round – they say it can reach a depth of eight metres in December and January. You can spend the night at a rustic cabin called La Joya a few km from the summit, but you must have your own water and all your own supplies.

To get to Fresnito, take a bus heading to Tonaya from Colima or Ciudad Guzmán and ask the driver to let you off at the Fresnito junction. Walk or hitch-hike to the village and ask locals for the trail to Nevado de Colima. It's easy to find because it begins at the main road through the village.

Another option is to bus to the town of Atenquique, 58 km from Colima on Highway 54 heading towards Guadalajara (be sure to take the old Carretera Libre highway, not the newer Carretera Cuota). At the entrance to the park is a sign saying 'Parque Nacional Nevado de Colima'. About seven trails start from here, heading to the summits of both volcanoes. The tourist office in Colima has a simple trail map and information on the volcanoes.

If you want to drive to either summit it's

best to do it in a four-wheel drive vehicle, although the fellow at the tourist office says you might also be able to make it in a normal car.

EL HERVIDERO & EL SALTO

Other attractions not far from Colima include **El Hervidero**, a natural thermal water resort 32 km south-east of Colima; and **El Salto**, a 30-metre waterfall forming a natural pool one km from the town of Minatitlán, 68 km west of Colima.

LAGUNA LA MARIA

Forty km north of Colima is the Laguna La Maria, popular for fishing, boating and hiking. It has restaurants serving fresh fish from the lake, and cabins where you can spend the night if you like. If you have a vehicle the lake is about a 40-minute drive from Colima – take the road to Comala and keep on heading north.

MANZANILLO

Population: 68,000
First and foremost, Manzanillo is a major port and industrial city. Before the Spanish arrived in the early 16th century, Manzanillo had been a port for more than 200 years for galleons shuttling to and from Asia. The urban (some might say squalid) sprawl has a centre that is a tangle of train tracks, shipping piers and traffic surrounded by stagnant marshy splotches locals call lagoons. Surprisingly, Manzanillo is also a beach resort with a few hotels, famous for its beaches and deep sea fishing.

Orientation

Manzanillo is 325 km south-west of Guadalajara and 101 km south-west of Colima. It extends for 16 km from north to south, the first five km of which are fingers of land squeezed between the Bahía de Manzanillo and the various lagoons of the Laguna de Cuyutlán. The resort hotels and finest beaches begin on Playa Azul across the Bahía de Manzanillo from Playa San Pedrito, the closest beach to downtown (about one km away).

Farther north-west is the Santiago peninsula, a rocky outcropping occupied by Las Hadas Resort and sheltering part of the Bahía de Santiago and the beaches of La Audiencia, Santiago, Olas Altas and Miramar. Just south of Miramar is the Santiago Lagoon.

Downtown Manzanillo is bound by the Bahía de Manzanillo to the north, the Pacific Ocean to the west, and the Laguna de Cuyutlán to the south-east and south. Avenida Morelos, the principal avenue, runs along the northern edge of the city beside the sea, west from Avenida Niños Héroes which leads to Highway 200. The city centre begins at the zócalo (also known as the Jardín Obregón) on Avenida Morelos, and continues southward with the major street, Avenida México, crossed from west to east by Allende, Cuauhtémoc, Guerrero and Nuñez. Many of these east-west streets change names on either side of Avenida México.

Information

Tourist Office The tourist office (☎ (333) 3-22-77) is around the bay in Salahua, near the Hotel Pacífico Azul. It's open Monday to Friday from 9 am to 3 pm.

Money Many banks are scattered around the centre of Manzanillo, including one on the north-west corner of the zócalo and several others on Avenida México. They are open Monday to Friday from 9 am to 1.30 pm.

Post The post office is one block east of the zócalo, on the corner of Juárez and 5 de Mayo. It's open Monday to Friday from 8 am to 7 pm, Saturday 9 am to 1 pm.

Telecommunications The Telecomm office, with telegram, telex and fax services, is in the government building on the south-east corner of the zócalo. It's open Monday to Friday from 9 am to 8 pm, Saturday 9 am to 1 pm.

Computel, with long-distance telephone and fax services, has two offices in the centre. One is at Madero 72, half a block south of the zócalo; the other is at Avenida

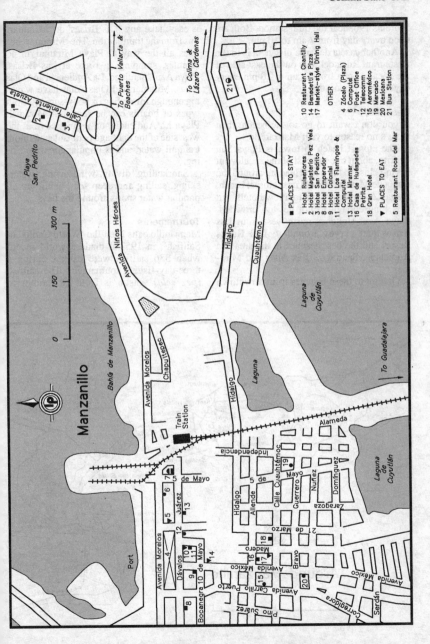

Manzanillo

PLACES TO STAY

1 Hotel Ruiseñores
2 Hotel Magisterio Pez Vela
3 Hotel San Pedrito
8 Hotel Emperador
9 Hotel Colonial
11 Hotel Los Flamingos & Computel
13 Hotel Miramar
16 Casa de Huéspedes Petrita
18 Gran Hotel

PLACES TO EAT

5 Restaurant Roca del Mar
10 Restaurant Chantilly
14 Benedetti's Pizza
17 Market-style Dining Hall

OTHER

4 Zócalo (Plaza)
6 Computel
7 Casa Post Office
12 Telecomm
15 Aeroméxico
19 Mercado
20 Mexicana
21 Bus Station

Morelos 196, near the train station. Both are open every day from 7 am to 10 pm.

Another caseta de larga distancia is in the Restaurant Roca del Mar on the east side of the zócalo, open from 7 am to 10 pm every day except Wednesday.

Beaches

If you don't want to go to the beach, then there's no reason to visit Manzanillo.

The closest beach to town is Playa San Pedrito, about one km east of the zócalo, but it's too close to the port. Heading around the Bahía de Manzanillo, the next closest beach, Playa Las Brisas, caters to a few hotels, but it is long enough to not get too crowded. Playa Azul stretches north-west from Las Brisas and curves around to Las Hadas Resort and the best beaches in the area: La Audiencia, Santiago, Olas Altas and Miramar.

Getting to these beaches from downtown

is easy: take any 'Las Brisas' or 'Miramar' bus from the train station. The 'Miramar' bus goes all the way to Playa Miramar in 40 minutes, stopping en route at Las Brisas, Playa Azul, Santiago, La Audiencia and Olas Altas. Miramar and Olas Altas have waves big enough for surfing or body-surfing. Both types of boards can be rented at Miramar. Playa La Audiencia, on a quiet cove at the west side of the Santiago peninsula, has more tranquil water, and is popular for waterskiing.

Snorkelling, diving, windsurfing, waterskiing, sailing and deep sea fishing are all popular water sports around the bay.

Tournaments

Manzanillo calls itself the 'World Capital of Sailfish'; in 1957 it made a world record when 336 sailfish were caught during a three-day fishing tournament. The sailfish *(pez vela)* season is from November to

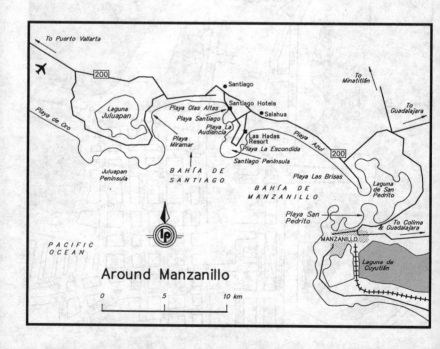

Around Manzanillo

March, with marlin, red snapper, sea bass, yellowtail and tuna also being important catches.

The biggest international sailfish tournament of the year takes place from around 18 to 20 November, with a smaller national tournament held again in February.

During the first part of February a sailing tournament coming from San Diego, California (every two years), or Puerto Vallarta (in the alternate two years) ends at the Las Hadas Resort, with parties, prizes and awards.

Places to Stay

The best places to stay in central Manzanillo are within a block or two of the zócalo. This area is safe and clean. A few blocks south, the centre of town also has a number of places to stay, but the centre is comparatively dirty and squalid.

Alternatively, you may prefer to stay at nearby Playa San Pedrito, which is not the best stretch of beach in the area but is convenient both to town and to buses to the better beaches. There are also places to stay at the better beaches all around the bay, though they tend to be more expensive; three relatively economical hotels are found out on a small bluff at Playa Santiago, a 10 or 15-minute walk (or five-minute ride) from Highway 200 and Santiago town.

Places to Stay – bottom end & middle
Camping Trailer parks at Miramar and La Audiencia beaches, and the *Trailer Park El Palmar* beside the highway in Salahua, have spaces for trailers and tents.

Near the Zócalo Just a few doors from the south-east corner of the zócalo, the *Hotel Miramar* (☎ (333) 2-10-08) at Juárez 122 has 37 clean rooms, all with bath and some with ceiling fan; many have windows facing onto an outdoor walkway good for catching the sea breezes. The cost is US$10/13.35 for singles/doubles.

Half a block from the south-west corner of the zócalo, the *Hotel Emperador* (☎ (333) 2-23-74) at Dávalos 69 is clean and friendly,

with 28 rooms with bath and ceiling fan. The construction of the building makes the rooms rather dark and cheerless, though they all open onto an interior airshaft/walkway. Singles/doubles here are US$8.35/11.70. The hotel restaurant downstairs has good food and is one of the most economical in town.

Half a block south of the zócalo, the *Hotel Los Flamingos* (☎ (333) 2-10-37) at Madero 72 is an unremarkable place with some of its 35 rooms opening onto the street, and others being interior rooms. All rooms have a bath; some have a ceiling fan. The cost is US$13.35 for one or two people.

The *Hotel Colonial* (☎ (333) 2-10-80, 2-12-30), at Bocanegra 100, on the corner of Avenida México a block south of the zócalo, is a fancy place to stay. A good hotel in a colonial style, with a restaurant and parking area, its 36 rooms were remodelled in 1992 and cost US$20.50 with ceiling fan, or US$22 with air-conditioning.

In the Centre The *Casa de Huéspedes Petrita* (☎ (333) 2-01-87) at Allende 20 is very basic but it's clean, friendly and economical. Rooms with one double bed and common bath cost US$10; those with two double beds and general bath are US$13.35; or with two double beds and private bath they're US$16.70.

The *Gran Hotel* (☎ (333) 2-03-88) at Cuauhtémoc 81 is unimpressive when you enter from the street, but the rooms aren't bad – they are clean, all have a bath and ceiling fan, and the large rooms on the street side have private balconies which, unfortunately, only overlook the dirty street below. The cost is US$10/16.70 for singles/doubles, with parking in the courtyard below.

Playa San Pedrito The *Hotel Magisterio Pez Vela* (☎ (333) 2-11-08) at Teniente Azueta 7 is one of the best deals in Manzanillo. It is operated by the Sindicato Nacional de Trabajadores de la Educación (national union of educational workers) and most of its guests are teachers and their families, though other people are also welcome to stay. Right on the beach, it has 36 clean rooms with private bath and ceiling fan arranged around a swimming pool courtyard; the cost is US$10/16.70 for singles/doubles.

A little further down Teniente Azueta, the *Hotel Ruiseñores* (☎ (333) 2-06-46) is a similar place, with a beachside swimming pool and 71 rooms which cost US$16.70/23.35 for singles/doubles. The *Hotel San Pedrito* (☎ (333) 2-05-35) at Teniente Azueta 3 is another similar hotel, also with a beachside pool; cost here is US$20/23.35.

Playa Santiago Out on the bluff at Playa Santiago, on a fine stretch of beach, are three reasonably priced hotels. Cheapest is the *Hotel Anita* (☎ (333) 3-01-61) with 91 rooms, all with private bath and ceiling fan, many opening onto a wide beachfront terrace. Cost is US$10/13.35 for singles/doubles.

Nearby, the *Hotel Marlyn* (☎ (333) 3-01-07) is a three-star hotel with a restaurant, swimming pool, and bungalows with kitchens as well as regular rooms. The bungalows cost US$83.35 per day and hold up to six people; regular rooms are US$16.70/23.35 for singles/doubles. All have private balconies overlooking the sea.

Next door is the more luxurious *Hotel Playa de Santiago* (☎ (333) 3-00-55, 3-02-70, fax 3-03-44), with a restaurant and bar, beachfront swimming pool, tennis courts and 105 rooms with private sea-view balconies. It has regular rooms at US$23.85, bungalows with kitchens at US$21.80, and suites at US$37.

Places to Stay – top end

Most of Manzanillo's middle and top-end hotels are on or near the beaches outside the city centre.

The best of the top-end hotels is *Las Hadas Resort* (☎ (333) 3-00-00, fax 3-04-30), a white Arabian-style resort on the Santiago peninsula conceived and financed by Bolivian tin magnate Antenor Patino. It is considered among the top 10 resorts in the world; the film *10* featuring Bo Derek was made here. Rooms start at US$130 per night.

Other top-end hotels around the bay include the newer *Hotel Sierra Manzanillo* (☎ (333) 3-20-00) near Las Hadas on Playa La Audiencia, and the *Hotel Maeva* (☎ 3-05-95) on the Bahía de Santiago.

More moderately priced and closer to town is the *Hotel La Posada* (☎ (333) 3-18-99), a friendly beachfront lodge at Lázaro Cárdenas 201 on Playa Azul, a stretch of beach good for snorkelling, windsurfing and swimming. It has a swimming pool and 23 rooms priced at US$46.70/51.70 from 1 May to 15 December, US$68 for one or two people the rest of the year, with breakfast included in the price.

Places to Eat

Around the zócalo are a number of good places to eat. The *Restaurant Roca del Mar* on the east side of the plaza is a pleasant restaurant/sidewalk café looking out onto the zócalo, with overhead fans whirring and a pleasant atmosphere. It is open from 7 am to 10 pm every day except Wednesday.

On the south side of the zócalo, the *Restaurant Chantilly*, a popular corner restaurant, is good for all meals. Antojitos (enchiladas, tacos, etc) are US$1.70 to US$3, meat and seafood meals around US$4.50 to US$6. Breakfasts for US$2.35 include waffles or eggs with bacon or ham. It's open from 7 am to 10 pm, every day except Saturday.

Restaurant Emperador, on the ground floor of the hotel of the same name at Dávalos 69, half a block west of the zócalo, is simple and small but it has good food at some of the most economical prices in Manzanillo. The comida corrida, with soup, rice, choice of main dish, dessert and coffee or tea is a good deal at US$3.35. Meat and seafood meals with selections like red snapper (huachinango), fillet of sole or filet a la Veracruzana also cost US$3.35, or you can get breakfast or enchiladas for just US$1.70. It's open every day from 8 am to 10.30 pm.

Also good, and just a little more expensive, is the pleasant colonial-style restaurant/bar at the *Hotel Colonial*, a block south of the zócalo on the corner of Avenida México and Bocanegra. Its comida corrida costs US$5; they're open from 8 am to 11 pm every day except Sunday.

Benedetti's Pizza, one block south of the zócalo at Avenida México 119, is a takeaway pizza chain with decent pizza. Prices range from US$5.70 for the simplest medium pizza up to US$19.35 for the extra large pizza with everything on it. They offer free delivery too (☎ 2-57-19, 2-58-19); if your pizza doesn't arrive in 30 minutes, it's free.

For the cheapest eats, check out the mercado-style dining hall on the corner of Madero and Cuauhtémoc, in the centre of town about six blocks from the zócalo. It's open every day from around 6.30 am until 9 or 10 pm, with a number of stalls to choose from.

Entertainment

If you happen to be in Manzanillo on a Sunday evening, stop by the zócalo where everyone from babies to teenagers and grandparents is out enjoying an ice cream, a visit with friends, and the balmy night air. A Sunday evening tradition which has disappeared in many parts of Mexico, the custom is still alive and well in Manzanillo. Sometimes a band plays in the gazebo to entertain the crowd.

Nightlife for the tourists in Manzanillo is mostly spread out around the bay. The Oui and Vog discos, both on the highway at Playa Azul, were the two latest raves on our last visit. Also on Playa Azul is the Carlos 'n' Charlie's Colima Bar Café, one of the Carlos Anderson bar/restaurant chain which puts on a good time for the tourists all over Mexico.

Getting There & Away

Air Manzanillo is served by the Playa de Oro international airport, 44 km north of the city on Highway 200. Aeroméxico and Mexicana are the two airlines with flights to and from this airport. Aeroméxico offers daily flights to Guadalajara, La Paz, Los Angeles and Mexico City; Mexicana has daily flights to Guadalajara, Los Angeles and Mexico City.

The Aeroméxico office (☎ 2-12-67, 2-17-11) is at Local 107, in the Centro Comercial on Avenida Carrillo Puerto between Allende and Cuauhtémoc; it's open Monday to Saturday from 9 am to 7 pm. The Mexicana office (☎ 2-17-01, 2-19-72) at Avenida México 382, is open Monday to Friday from 9 am to 7 pm, Saturday 9 am to 2 pm and 3 to 6 pm.

Bus The bus terminal is a few blocks east of central Manzanillo on the road to Colima. Services include a restaurant, a luggage-storage area, and a caseta de larga distancia.

Oddly enough, there are no local buses connecting the bus station with the centre; you have to either walk (about 15 minutes) or take a taxi (US$1.35). Local buses do run, however, from the bus station heading out around the bay to Playa Miramar and the beaches along the way, departing from the bus station every five minutes.

Buses departing from Manzanillo include those to:

Armería – 45 km, 45 minutes; buses every 15 minutes, 4.30 am to 9.30 pm, with Sociedad Cooperativa de Autotransportes Colima, Armería, Cuyutlán, Manzanillo (US$1.20).

Barra de Navidad – 92 km, 1½ hours; same buses as to Puerto Vallarta (US$1.70).

Colima – 101 km, 1½ to two hours; every 15 minutes, 4.30 am to 9.30 pm, via Armería and Tecomán, with Sociedad Cooperativa de Autotransportes Colima, Armería, Cuyutlán, Manzanillo (two hours, US$2.35); plus all the same buses as to Guadalajara (1½ hours, US$2.35 to US$3.35).

Guadalajara – 325 km, 4½ hours; 10 buses daily (every two hours) with La Linea (US$10); 10 daily with La Linea Plus (US$14.35); 10 daily with Servicios Coordinados (US$10); nine daily with Primera Plus (US$14.35); nine daily with Autocamiones del Pacífico (US$9.70); five daily with Autotransportes del Sur de Jalisco (US$9); three daily with Tres Estrellas de Oro (US$9.35).

Lázaro Cárdenas – 330 km, seven hours; three daily with Autotransportes del Sur de Jalisco (US$9); three daily with Galeana (US$8.35); one daily with Tres Estrellas de Oro (US$8.35).

Mexico City – 843 km, 12 hours; three daily with Tres Estrellas de Oro (US$21.70); two daily with Servicios Coordinados (US$23); one daily with Primera Plus (US$26.70).

Puerto Vallarta – 302 km, five hours; hourly, 4.30 am to 7.30 pm plus 11.30 pm, with Autocamiones del Pacífico (US$8.85); one daily with Tres Estrellas de Oro (US$7.20).

San Patricio-Melaque – 97 km, 1¾ hours; same buses as to Puerto Vallarta (US$1.70).

Train The train station is on Avenida Morelos, a couple of blocks east of the zócalo. The ticket office is open every day but only from 5 to 6 am, selling tickets for the one train of the day, Train 91, which departs at 6 am for Guadalajara (seven hours) via Colima (two hours). As with all trains, the schedule for this one is subject to change; the schedule is posted on the wall at the station.

Getting Around

To/From the Airport Transporte Colectivo Benito Juárez (☎ 3-21-80) operates a colectivo van to and from the airport, picking you up or dropping you off at your hotel. The cost is US$4.20 per person with three persons minimum, US$11.70 per person for less than three people, or US$31.70 for the whole van holding up to seven people. A taxi to the airport costs US$16.70.

Bus Local buses heading around the bay to San Pedrito, Salahua, Santiago, Miramar and all the beaches along the way depart from in front of the train station or from the main bus station every five minutes from 5 am to midnight. Buses cost is US$0.20 to San Pedrito and US$0.55 all the way to the end of the line at Playa Miramar. You can get on or off the bus anywhere along its route.

Taxi Taxis are plentiful but a bit expensive around Manzanillo. From the bus station into the centre is US$1.35; from town to Santiago is around US$7. Be sure you agree on the price for the ride before you get into the cab.

CUYUTLÁN & PARAÍSO

The small black-sand beach resort towns of Cuyutlán and Paraíso are on the coast southeast of Manzanillo off Highway 200. Cuyutlán, the more developed of the two, is near the south-eastern end of the Laguna de Cuyutlán, about 76 km south-east of Manzanillo and 62 km south-west of Colima – about an hour from either place. There's supposedly a road along the beach that connects Cuyutlán with Manzanillo and, six km to the south-east, Paraíso, but don't count on it.

Both towns have a few hotels and restaurants that are popular mostly with Mexican families and seldom visited by North Americans. Consequently, expect to pay much less here for beachfront accommodation than you would in places frequented by foreign tourists.

Information

Neither Cuyutlán or Paraíso have post offices or banks; for these services you'll have to go into Armería. Both do have long-distance telephone offices, however. Cuyutlán's caseta de larga distancia is on Calle Hidalgo in the little shop on the corner one block past the zócalo, heading away from the beach. In Paraíso it's in the little shop opposite the beach and the bus stop.

Getting There & Away

Cuyutlán and Paraíso are connected to the rest of the world through Armería, a dusty town on Highway 200 about 59 km southeast of Manzanillo and 45 km south-west of Colima. From Armería to Cuyutlán it's 17 km down a paved road passing through fruit orchards and coconut plantations to the coast; a similar road runs seven km from Armería to Paraíso.

To reach either place by bus involves going first to Armería and changing buses there. The local buses to Cuyutlán and Paraíso depart from the same stop in Armería, at the corner of Netzahualcóyotl (the main drag) and 5 de Mayo in front of the Restaurant Camino Real, a couple of blocks from the long-distance bus stop. There are no buses between the two beaches; to get from one to the other, you must return to Armería and change buses there.

Buses to Cuyutlán depart from Armería every 40 minutes from 6 am to 8 pm; they cost US$0.55 for the 20-minute trip. Buses to Paraíso depart every 45 minutes from 6 am to 7.30 pm; the cost is US$0.45 and the trip takes about 15 minutes.

If you miss the last bus, you can take a taxi from Armería to Cuyutlán for US$5; to Paraíso it's US$3.35.

Cuyutlán
Population: 1865

In Cuyutlán most of the hotels and places to eat are near one another on the beach or about half a block back from it. If you arrive in town by bus you'll be let off on Calle Hidalgo, on one side of the zócalo. Walk four blocks towards the sea on Hidalgo and you'll be right in the middle of the hotel and restaurant area beside the beach.

Aside from its long stretch of relatively isolated beach, Cuyutlán is also known for its 'green wave' in April and May, caused by little green phosphorescent critters.

Places to Stay At Christmas and Semana Santa (the week before Easter), all the hotels fill up with Mexican families on holiday. If you come at these times you should reserve in advance if you expect to find a room. Most of the hotels require that you take three meals a day included in the price at these times; the cost for the room and meals will be around US$27 per person.

To telephone the hotels from outside the town, you must dial the town caseta (☎ 91-332-41810); ask for the three-digit extension for the place you want and they will connect you.

Camping If you don't mind roughing it you can camp on the beach to the right of the hotels. A couple of simple thatch-roofed restaurants nearby have signs posted out front saying they rent showers and baths; some also have signs saying 'cuartos con baño', advertising simple rooms that may be only partitions in large halls behind the restaurants. At around US$8 for two people, these are the cheapest rooms in town.

Hotels As you come to the beach on Calle Hidalgo you'll reach the corner of Hidalgo and Calle Veracruz, the beachside road. On this corner are three good restaurants and two of Cuyutlán's most popular hotels. The other hotels are just a block or two to either side of this corner.

The *Hotel Morelos* (☎ 107), on this corner at Hidalgo 185, has clean, pleasant rooms with private bath; the cost is US$8.70 per person with fan and hot water, or US$6.70 per person with cold water and no fan. If you're coming in December, March or April you should reserve in advance and you'll probably have to take three meals a day with your room; the cost then is US$26.70 per person.

Opposite this, also on the corner of Veracruz and Hidalgo, the *Hotel Fénix* (☎ 147) is another good place; its 18 rooms with bath and ceiling fan are US$6.70 per person.

To your right are two similar hotels, both right on the beach, with beachfront terraces but no beach view from the rooms. The *Hotel Colima* (☎ 115) at Veracruz 22 has 43 simple but clean rooms with bath and good ventilation; cost is US$8.35 per person with fan, or US$6.70 per person with no fan. Next door, the *Hotel Tlaquepaque* (☎ 106) at Veracruz 30 has similar rooms, all with ceiling fan, at US$6.70 per person from May to November, US$10 the rest of the year.

A little more stylish is the *Hotel El Bucanero* (☎ 102), on the beachfront behind the Hotel Fénix. Its 50 rooms, all with bath and ceiling fan, cost US$8.35 per person for the interior rooms, or US$10 for those with a sea view.

Opposite this, also right on the beach, the large *Hotel Ceballos* (☎ 101) at Veracruz 10 is open only part of the year, from 1 December to 31 May. A three-storey concrete structure, all of its 73 rooms have private balconies and ceiling fans; the cost is US$18.33 per person for room only, or US$46.70 per person with three meals included.

To the left of this at Veracruz 46, the *Hotel Pensión San Rafael* (☎ 108) has a swimming pool; its 30 rooms all have a bath with hot water, and the beachfront rooms open onto a sea-view terrace. All are the same price at US$13.35/23.35 for singles/doubles.

Places to Eat Several of the hotels have good seafood restaurants. On the corner of Hidalgo and Veracruz are three of the town's best, all clean and pleasant: the *Restaurant Morelos* and *Restaurant Fénix* attached to the hotels of the same names, and the *Restaurant San Miguel*. The Morelos is open daily from 7 am to 10 pm; the Fénix from 8 am to 10 pm; and the San Miguel from 8 am to 7 pm. All offer similar meals at similar prices: the daily comida corrida is around US$5, breakfast and dinner each around US$4.

The *Hotel El Bucanero* and the *Hotel Pensión San Rafael* each have attractive beachfront restaurant/bars with a view of the sea, also with similar food at similar prices. Or you can grab a simple snack near the zócalo.

Paraíso

Population: 27

Paraíso is about six km south-east of Cuyutlán and seven km south-west of Armería. There's not much here, which is what makes it appealing; it has just two hotels side by side on the beach, a number of fishing boats, a black-sand beach and several

beachfront seafood restaurants which are simple thatched-roof structures called enramadas.

Places to Stay & Eat Of the two hotels, the fancy one is the three-star *Hotel Paraíso* (☎ in Colima 2-47-87, 2-10-32; in Tecomán 4-06-07). It has a swimming pool, ample terraces, a pleasant beachfront seafood restaurant with music, and 60 rooms which cost US$21.70 for up to two adults and two children. All the rooms have ceiling fan; many open onto beachfront terraces.

Next door, the *Hotel Villa del Mar* (☎ 4-29-10) has just seven simple rooms, all of them large and clean, with fan and private bath. Rooms cost US$11.70 for one or two people, US$16.70 for five.

Otherwise you could camp on the beach, or probably string up a hammock under one of the enramadas.

All the beachfront enramadas serve basically the same food at the same price: around US$6.35 for a meal of red snapper (huachinango), fillet of fish, shrimp (camarones), oysters (ostiones) or seafood soup. Fried fish or ceviche (cold seafood salad) are a bit cheaper, around US$4.70. Both hotels also have restaurants. Classiest for appearance is the poolside restaurant at the Hotel Paraíso; it and all the other restaurants are open every day from around 9 am to 6 pm.

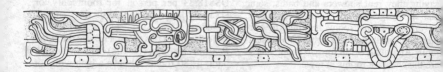

The Gulf Coast

The route from north-east to south-east Mexico lies along the hot coastal plain between the Gulf of Mexico and the country's central mountains. The two main cities, Tampico-Ciudad Madero and Veracruz, are both steamy tropical ports but Veracruz is much the more appealing, being also a holiday resort popular among Mexicans, with a famously festive atmosphere and the country's most riotous annual carnival. Veracruz lies, too, on the route from the centre of the country to the south-east.

This chapter covers the coast and hinterland from Tampico-Ciudad Madero to Coatzacoalcos in far south-east Veracruz state – just over 600 km as the crow flies but over 800 by Highway 180, following the curve of the coast. It's an area with an fascinating prehistory but only one major archaeological site – El Tajín, near Papantla, which shouldn't be missed as you travel through, and for ruins enthusiasts is even worth a trip from outside the region.

Southern Veracruz was probably the original homeland of the Olmecs but there's little to see there now. The best collections of Olmec artefacts – including several of the mighty 'Olmec heads' of sculpted basalt – are at Parque-Museo La Venta in Villahermosa (see the Tabasco chapter) and the Veracruz University anthropology museum in Xalapa (see the Mexico City to Veracruz chapter). The Xalapa museum has by far the best archaeological collection from the Gulf Coast as a whole.

HISTORY
Olmec
The first great centre of Central America's first civilisation, and Mexico's ancestral culture, the Olmec, flourished from about 1200 to 900 BC at San Lorenzo in the hot, wet far south of Veracruz state. After this centre fell, La Venta in neighbouring Tabasco was the main Olmec centre until it too was violently destroyed about 400 BC.

603

Olmec culture lingered, influenced gradually from elsewhere, for another 400 years or so at Tres Zapotes, west of San Lorenzo in Veracruz.

Classic Veracruz

In the Classic period (300-900 AD) the centres of civilisation on the Gulf Coast moved west and northwards. Cerro de las Mesas, near Ignacio de la Llave about 60 km south of Veracruz city, peaked around 400 to 600 AD and shows influences from several contemporary and earlier cultures.

In central and north Veracruz state a number of power centres arose which were politically independent but shared religion and culture. Together they're known as the Classic Veracruz civilisation. Their hallmark is a unique style of carving in which pairs of parallel lines are curved and interwoven to resemble nothing so much as Chinese Bronze and Iron Age work. The style often appears on three types of mysterious carved stone objects, probably connected with the ritual ball game which appears to have been very important. These are the U-shaped

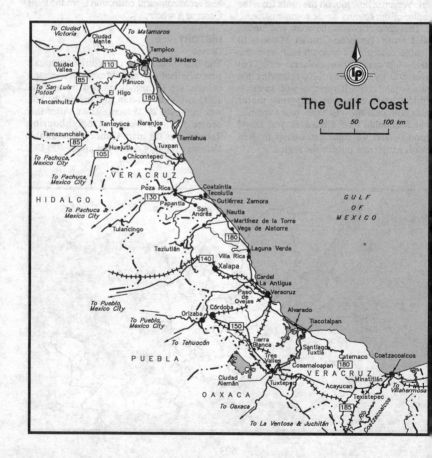

yugo, probably representing a wood or leather belt worn in the game, the long *palma*, and the *hacha*, a thin, axe-like head. The last two are thought to represent items attached to the front of the belt. Hachas may also have been court markers.

The most important Classic Veracruz centre, the multi-pyramided El Tajín near Papantla, was at its height about 600 to 900 AD and contains at least 11 ball courts. Other main centres were Las Higueras near Vega de Alatorre, close to the coast south of Nautla, and El Zapotal near Ignacio de la Llave.

Classic Veracruz exported cotton, rubber, cacao and vanilla to central Mexico and its influence is apparent in Teotihuacán, Cholula and elsewhere, while Veracruz sites in turn show Maya and Teotihuacán influence.

Totonac, Huastec, Toltec & Aztec

El Tajín was abandoned about 1200 AD, possibly destroyed by Chichimecs from the north. By this time the Totonacs, a people who may have occupied El Tajín in its later years, were establishing themselves from Tuxpan in the north to beyond Veracruz in the south. North of Tuxpan, the Huastec civilisation, another web of probably independent statelets, flourished from 800 to 1200. It was Mexico's chief cotton producer and the people built many ceremonial sites and developed great skill in stone carving. According to various accounts, emigrant Huastecs and/or early Totonacs helped build the great pyramids of Teotihuacán.

The warlike Toltecs, who dominated central Mexico in the early Postclassic age, also moved into the Gulf Coast area, occupying the Huastec centre Castillo de Teayo for some time between 900 and 1200. There's Toltec influence too at Zempoala, an important Totonac site near Veracruz city. In the mid-15th century the Aztecs subdued most of the Totonac and Huastec areas, exacting costly tribute of goods and sacrificial victims, and maintaining garrisons to control the frequent revolts.

Colonial Era

The situation was tailor-made for Hernán Cortés, who arrived on the Gulf Coast with his 11 ships and 550 men in 1519, aiming to conquer the Aztec empire and grab its fabulous riches. He turned the Totonacs of Zempoala, who wanted to throw off the Aztec yoke, into his first allies by telling them to imprison five Aztec tribute collectors and promising to protect them against reprisals.

Cortés set up a settlement, Villa Rica de la Vera Cruz (Rich Town of the True Cross), north of modern Veracruz city, then apparently scuttled his ships to remove any thought of retreat from his soldiers' minds. Leaving 150 men at Villa Rica he led the others to Tenochtitlán, the Aztec capital. When an expedition sent by Diego Velázquez, the governor of Cuba and original backer of Cortés' expedition, arrived to arrest him, Cortés returned with most of his men from Tenochtitlán and defeated the rival Spaniards at Zempoala in May 1520. Joined by many of the men he had defeated, Cortés then returned to Tenochtitlán and, after several near-fatal reverses, took it on 21 August 1521.

All the Gulf Coast was in Spanish hands by 1523. Control of Veracruz harbour became essential for anyone trying to govern Mexico and the fate of the country turned on events there many times – but for most inhabitants of the hot, damp coast, life was pretty miserable. The Indian population was slashed in the 16th century by a combination of diseases which had long plagued it and new ones like smallpox brought by the Spaniards. Large numbers of African slaves arrived and by 1600 there were about 140,000 people of African ancestry in Mexico.

19th & 20th Centuries

The population of Veracruz city actually shrank in the first half of the 19th century. But Mexico's first railway joined it to Mexico City in 1872, and some industries developed towards the end of the century under dictator Porfirio Díaz.

In 1901 oil was discovered in the Tampico area, which by the 1920s was producing a quarter of the world's oil. That proportion declined but by the 1980s, following the discovery of new fields in the south, the Gulf Coast had well over half Mexico's petroleum reserves and refining capacity.

GEOGRAPHY & CLIMATE

More than 40 rivers, running down from the inland mountains, cross the Gulf coastal plain. In the south-east they help create the low-lying, jungly, marshy area prone to flooding which saw the rise of the Olmec civilisation 3000 years ago.

The region receives warm, wet winds from the Atlantic in summer and autumn, and cooler winds from the north, usually dry but sometimes bringing drizzle, in winter and spring. Nevertheless it's warm and humid most of the time: hotter along the coast,

wetter in the foothills, hottest and wettest of all in the low-lying south-east. Two-thirds or more of the rain falls between June and September.

The city of Veracruz receives about 165 cm of rain a year, with temperatures well over 30°C from April to October and falling into the teens at night only from December to February. Tuxpan and Tampico, on the northern coast, are a bit drier, a little hotter in summer and a fraction cooler in winter. Coatzacoalcos in the south-east gets 300 cm of rain a year.

PEOPLE

The area covered by this chapter – mostly the state of Veracruz – has about seven million people. Veracruz, with over six million, is Mexico's third most populous state.

You may notice quite a few people with an African touch to their features on the Gulf Coast – these are the descendants of slaves brought by the Spaniards and of immigrants from Cuba. Of the region's nearly half a million Indians, the most numerous are the roughly 120,000 Totonacs (see El Tajín) and 100,000 Huastecs (see Tampico & The Huasteca).

Tampico & the Huasteca

The double city of Tampico-Ciudad Madero, about 500 km down the Gulf Coast from the US border, is one many travellers pass through but few linger in. Tampico, a few km upstream from the mouth of the Pánuco River, is the communications hub. Ciudad Madero, between Tampico and the coast, is the processing centre for the country's oldest oil fields.

Inland from Tampico is the fertile, often beautiful Huasteca ('wass-TEK-a') region, where the coast plain meets the fringes of the Sierra Madre Oriental. Spread over southern Tamaulipas, eastern San Luis Potosí and northern Veracruz, the region is named after the Huastec people who have lived here for about 3000 years. Highway 85, one of the main routes from the north-east to Mexico City, goes through the middle of it.

The Huastecs

The Huastec language is classified as one of the Mayance family. Other languages in this family in Mexico are spoken only in the south-east – including by the Yucatán Maya – and it has been theorised that they all stem from a language once spoken all down the Gulf Coast. One suggestion is that the Huastec language split from the rest of the family about 900 BC – which could be explained by the rise of the Olmec culture in the intervening area around that time.

Stories taken down by the Spaniards in the 16th century speak of 'inhabitants of Pánuco' – possibly emigrant Huastecs – who 'raised the hills in honour of the sun and moon' at Teotihuacán. The central-Mexican feathered serpent god Quetzalcóatl was probably of Huastec origin.

The Huastecs' greatest period was roughly 800 to 1200 AD. Under a number of independent rulers, they built many ceremonial centres, practised phallic fertility rites, and expanded as far west as north-east Querétaro and Hidalgo. They developed great skill in pottery and stone-and shell-carving. There are unfortunately no spectacular Huastec sites to visit; the two most interesting are Tamuín and Castillo de Teayo (see Tuxpan).

After the Spanish conquest, slavery and imported diseases cut the Huastec population from an estimated one million to probably under 100,000 during the 16th century. Rebellions went on into the 19th century.

Today, the roughly 100,000 Huastecs in the Huasteca live mostly between Ciudad Valles and Tamazunchale (see the San Luis Potosí section in the Bajío chapter), and east of Tantoyuca. Many of the women still wear quechquémitls, colourfully embroidered with traditional trees of life, animals, flowers and two-armed crosses. With they wear black skirts as well as coloured ribbons which are wound into the hair to keep it on top of the head. Huastecs still practise land fertility ceremonies, particularly dances.

TAMPICO-CIUDAD MADERO

Population: 600,000

Sweaty, smelly, seedy but jolly, Tampico detains few travellers. Somewhat faded since its 1920s heyday, it's still Mexico's busiest port, a tropical place where bars and cantinas stay open late. (But if tropical port atmosphere is what you're after, head on down to Veracruz city, which has it in spades.) Hotel prices are inflated by the oil business.

History

In 1523 Cortés defeated the native Huastec Indians and founded a colony called San Estéban, now Pánuco, 30 km upriver from Tampico. In the next few years he prevailed not only over the rebellious Huastecs – about 400 of whose leaders were apparently burnt to death by his sidekick Gonzalo de Sandoval – but also over Spanish rivals including Nuño de Guzmán who was appointed royal governor of the Pánuco area in 1527 but concentrated on pillage and slaughter in western Mexico. De Guzmán did however have time to organise a few slave raids north of the Pánuco. At the time 80 Indians could be sold for one horse. Eventually his misdeeds caught up with him and he was sent back to Spain.

Conversion of the Huastecs to Christianity began at a mission in Tampico in the 1530s. Tampico was destroyed by pirates in 1684 but was refounded in 1823 by families from Altamira, to the north. With the discovery of oil in the area from 1901, it suddenly became the world's biggest oil port: rough, tough and booming. Luckily it remained outside the main combat zones of the Mexican Revolution. The oil and its profits were under foreign control until a strike by Tampico oil workers in 1938 led to their nationalisation by President Lázaro Cárdenas.

Mexico's 1970s oil boom took place further down the coast, but the Tampico-Ciudad Madero area remains important.

Pipelines and barge fleets bring oil from fields north and south, onshore and offshore, to its refineries and harbour, and Ciudad Madero is the headquarters of the powerful oil workers' union, the STPRM.

Orientation

Tampico's bus station is in the north of the city, north of the Laguna del Carpintero, one of many lakes dotting this low-lying, marshy region near the mouth of the Pánuco River. If you walk out onto the road from the bus station, you'll see a line of large, decrepit cars that might be queuing to get into a wrecker's yard. These are in fact the colectivos which will take you to the city centre *(centro)* for US$0.20.

Downtown Tampico centres on two plazas. One is the zócalo or Plaza de Armas, with the 20th-century cathedral on its north side and the Hotel Inglaterra on its south side. One block south and one east is the Plaza de la Libertad. Hotels and restaurants of all grades are within a few blocks of these two plazas. Down a gentle hill south of either plaza you come to a smelly, sleazy area

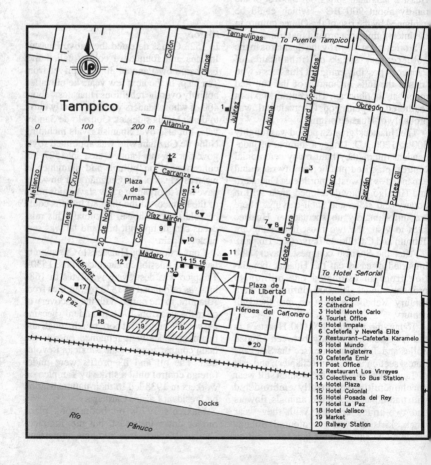

Tampico

0   100   200 m

1 Hotel Capri
2 Cathedral
3 Hotel Monte Carlo
4 Tourist Office
5 Hotel Impala
6 Cafetería y Nevería Elite
7 Restaurant—Cafetería Karamelo
8 Hotel Mundo
9 Hotel Inglaterra
10 Cafetería Emir
11 Post Office
12 Restaurant Los Virreyes
13 Colectivos to Bus Station
14 Hotel Plaza
15 Hotel Colonial
16 Hotel Posada del Rey
17 Hotel La Paz
18 Hotel Jalisco
19 Market
20 Railway Station

containing the market, railway station and riverside docks, which doesn't feel very safe at night.

Addresses on east-west streets usually have the suffix Ote (east) or Pte (west), while those on north-south streets are Nte (north) or Sur (south). The dividing point between east, west, north and south is the junction of Colón and Carranza at the north-west corner of the zócalo.

Information

Tourist Office Tampico tourist office (☎ (12) 12-00-07) is on the zócalo at Olmos Sur 101. Go up one flight of stairs beside Helados Chantal. The staff are willing but don't have very much of interest to tell you about. It's open Monday to Friday from 9 am to 7 pm and Saturday 9 am to 2 pm.

Post & Telephone The main post office is on Plaza de la Libertad at Madero 309. At the bus station, there's a post office in the 2nd-class hall, and Ladatel coin and card phones and a Lada caseta in the 1st-class hall.

Huastec Museum

The Museo de la Cultura Huasteca, in Ciudad Madero Technological Institute, has an extensive collection from the pre-Hispanic Huastec culture, and a good bookshop. From central Tampico take a 'Boulevard A López Mateos' bus north on Alfaro, and ask for 'Tecnológico Madero'. The museum is open Monday to Friday from 10 am to 5 pm and Saturday 10 am to 3 pm.

Beach

The 10-km-long Miramar Beach is about 15 km from downtown Tampico, beyond Ciudad Madero. Its waters are said to be surprisingly clean. Buses 'Boulevard A López Mateos' and 'Recreativo' north on Alfaro will take you to a part of the beach where there's a hotel with a swimming pool and, nearby, a miniature Chapultepec Park with a small zoo. There are several small seafood restaurants here.

Festivals

Semana Santa brings numerous Miramar Beach-based activities such as regattas, fishing and windsurfing competitions, sand-sculpture contests, music, dancing and bonfires. The anniversary of Tampico's 1823 refounding is celebrated with a procession on 12 April from Altamira, which passes through Tampico zócalo.

Places to Stay – bottom end

The only inviting bottom-end hotel we know is the *Hotel Capri* (☎ (12) 12-26-80) at Juárez 202 Nte, where small but clean rooms with ceiling fans, private baths and hot water cost US$8.50 for a single or double. The friendly owner, Guillermo Galván, has a beautiful pet ocelot and is an amateur archaeologist who often makes trips to Huastec sites.

Not surprisingly, the Capri is sometimes full. The poor second choice cheapie is the *Hotel Señorial* (☎ (12) 12-40-90) at Madero 1006 Ote, 400 metres east of the Plaza de la Libertad, with small singles/doubles for US$8.50/10. An upstairs exterior room, allowing the entry of some relatively fresh air, might be tolerable. Down among the foul smells, cheap cantinas, prostitution and air of nocturnal danger near the markets and docks are two possible desperation fall-backs, the *Hotel La Paz* (☎ (12) 14-11-19) at La Paz 307 Pte and the *Hotel Jalisco* (☎ (12) 12-27-92) at La Paz 120 Pte. Both are 40-room hotels charging US$17.75 a single or double for reasonably clean rooms with air-con. From the zócalo, go two blocks south along Colón, down a flight of steps, then one block more and turn right on La Paz.

Places to Stay – middle

The *Hotel Plaza* (☎ (12) 14-16-78) at Madero 204 on the corner of Olmos has clean, comfortable, sizeable rooms with air-con. It's good value for Tampico at US$21.75/26.75; for that reason you may find it full. The *Hotel Posada Del Rey* (☎ (12) 14-11-55) on the same block at Madero 218 Ote charges US$24/30 for air-con rooms which are large and carpeted but smell musty and, in our experience, lack hot water. Between the Posada Del Rey and the Plaza, and superior to both, is the *Hotel Colonial* (☎ (12) 12-76-76) at Madero 210 Ote, with clean, tasteful, air-conditioned, modern rooms for US$43.50/46.75. Prices are similar at the towering *Hotel Monte Carlo* (☎ (12) 14-10-93), also air-con, at López de Lara 107 Nte, and the *Hotel Impala* at Díaz Mirón 220 Pte, 1½ blocks west of the zócalo.

The *Hotel Mundo* (☎ (12) 12-03-60) at Díaz Mirón 413 Ote, rebuilt as new and reopened in 1991, has large, clean, no-frills but pleasant air-con rooms for US$30/35. It's a friendly place.

Places to Stay – top end

The top downtown place is the *Hotel Inglaterra* (☎ (12) 12-56-78) on the zócalo at Díaz Mirón Ote 116, with 120 comfortable air-con singles/doubles at US$66.75/73.50, its own good restaurant and a pool. If you arrive in Tampico by air this hotel will give you a free ride from the airport.

Out towards the airport at Avenida Hidalgo 2000, the *Hotel Camino Real* (☎ (12) 13-88-11) is Tampico's most luxurious hotel, with rooms and bungalows facing a tropical garden-courtyard, and a large pool. Prices are in the US$100/120 range.

Places to Eat

Carne asada Tampiqueña (grilled meat Tampico-style) is beefsteak marinated in garlic, oil and oregano and usually served with guacamole, strips of chile and totopos (maize chips).

Tampico restaurants are disappointing: even the most popular serve only so-so food. The best food downtown is probably to be found in the big hotels like the Inglaterra. The clean, air-conditioned *Restaurant Los Virreyes*, at the corner of Colón and Madero, a block from the zócalo, is open from 8 am to 10 pm and serves some of the better food downtown. Seafood (including crab) is mostly in the US$5 to US$6 bracket, meat dishes are US$4 to US$8 and breakfasts are US$2 to US$4.25. A seafood specialist is the busy *Cafetería y Nevería Elite* on Díaz Mirón half a block east of the zócalo, where you can get two stuffed crabs for US$4.25 or snapper for US$5.50 to US$7.

The *Cafetería Emir* at Olmos 107 Sur, half a block south of the zócalo, and the *Restaurant-Cafetería Karamelo* on Díaz Mirón between Aduana and López de Lara, are both adequate, offering quesadillas and enchiladas for around US$3.50 and meat dishes for US$4.50 to US$6.75. The Karamelo has salads too, and the Emir fish. There's another branch of the Emir on Calle Zapotal opposite the bus station.

Getting There & Away

Air Mexicana flies to/from Mexico City (one hour, US$60) three times daily. Aeromonterrey flies to/from Monterrey (1½ hours, US$103), once or twice daily; to/from Harlingen, Texas (four hours, US$155); and Veracruz and Matamoros five days a week. The office for both airlines (☎ (12) 13-96-00) is at Avenida Universidad 700-1. Aero Litoral (☎ (12) 2-90-20) also flies to/from Monterrey and Veracruz at least daily, as well as Poza Rica, Villahermosa and Aguascalientes. Aero Guadalajara flies to/from San Luis Potosí, Guadalajara (two hours, US$122), Zacatecas and Culiacán. Its office (☎ (12) 13-89-90) is at Avenida Hidalgo 4406.

Bus Buses go virtually anywhere sizeable that's north of Mexico City and down the Gulf Coast, and you needn't wait more than a few hours for main destinations. Tampico bus station is out on Calle Zapotal, about four km north of downtown. First-class is on the right side of the bus station as you enter, 2nd-class on the left. Departures include:

Ciudad Valles – 140 km, 2½ hours; seven 1st-class buses daily, mostly by Omnibus de Oriente, for US$2.75, and two or three 2nd-class buses an hour.

Matamoros – 500 km, eight hours; about 12 1st-class buses daily by various companies for US$11.50, and numerous 2nd-class buses.

Mexico City (Northern Terminal) – 515 km, 9½ hours; one luxury overnight bus by Uno for US$31.75, 11 1st-class buses daily by ADO and a few by other companies for US$12, and numerous 2nd-class buses.

Monterrey – 585 km, eight hours; six 1st-class buses daily by Transportes del Norte and a few by Omnibus de México for US$11, and several 2nd-class buses daily.

Nuevo Laredo – 820 km, 12 hours; four 1st-class buses daily by Transportes del Norte for US$15.50, seven 2nd-class buses daily by Transportes Frontera for US$14.

Pachuca – 380 km, nine hours; one or two 1st-class buses daily by ADO for US$9.75, and a few 2nd-class buses.

Poza Rica – 250 km, five hours; 11 1st-class buses daily by ADO for US$6, frequent 2nd-class buses.

Reynosa – 500 km, eight hours; several 1st-class buses daily by various companies for US$11, and numerous 2nd-class buses.

San Luis Potosí – 410 km, seven hours; seven 1st-class buses daily by Omnibus de Oriente and Tres Estrellas de Oro for US$7.50, plus some 2nd-class buses.

Tuxpan – 180 km, four hours; 11 1st-class buses daily by ADO for US$5, frequent 2nd-class buses.

Veracruz – 505 km, 10 hours; 12 1st-class buses daily by ADO for US$13.75.

Villahermosa – 980 km, 18 hours; seven 1st-class buses daily by ADO for US$22.75.

Xalapa – 540 km, 10½ hours; two 1st-class buses daily by ADO for US$11.50.

Car Highway 180 is in poor condition for much of the 95-km stretch between Aldama and Altamira, north of Tampico. Heading south out of Tampico, the highway soars over the Pánuco River on the Puente Tampico bridge, easily the most spectacular thing about the whole city. Car or motorbike toll on the bridge is US$4. Between here and Tuxpan there are more stretches of poor, bumpy road where you have to slow right down.

Getting Around

To/From the Airport Tampico airport is about 15 km north of the downtown area. Transporte Terrestre (☎ 28-45-88) runs colectivo combis from arriving flights to anywhere in Tampico-Ciudad Madero for US$3.50 per person, but only operates a taxi service (US$10) going *to* the airport.

'Aviación Boulevard' colectivos going to the left from the road outside the airport terminal will take you to López de Lara in central Tampico for US$0.30. 'Aviación' buses running north on Alfaro from downtown Tampico go to the airport.

To/From the Bus Station & Beach Decrepit colectivo taxis wait outside the bus station to take you downtown (US$0.20). From downtown to the bus station, take a 'Perimetral' or 'Perimetral-CC' colectivo from Olmos, a block south of the zócalo. 'Playa' buses or colectivos north on Alfaro will reach Playa Miramar.

TAMPICO TO PACHUCA

Highway 105 from Tampico to Pachuca (380 km) is part of an unusual scenic route to Mexico City. After crossing flat wetlands and a toll bridge at Pánuco, it climbs gradually into the beautiful Sierra Madre Oriental, a tortuous, sometimes foggy and in parts poorly-surfaced stretch. See under Tampico, in this chapter, and Pachuca, in the Near Mexico City chapter, for some info on buses on this route.

At **Huejutla** (165 km, population 40,000), you have entered Hidalgo state but are still in the semitropical lowlands. The big Sunday market in the square brings many Nahua Indians from outlying villages. The atrium of Huejutla's 16th-century fortress-monastery – one of many built in Hidalgo, which was frontier territory and subject to Indian attacks – forms part of the square. For accommodation try the *Hotel Posada Huejutla* (☎ 6-03-00) at Morelos 32 or the *Hotel Fayad* (☎ 6-00-40) on the corner of Hidalgo and Morelos.

Molango (240 km) and **Zacualtipán** (280 km) have more monasteries. In Molango try the *Hotel Plaza* (☎ 58) at Plaza de la República 27. The highway then leaves the forested Sierra Madre and drops several hundred metres to **Metzquititlán** (300 km) in the fertile Río Tulancingo Valley. The village of **Metztitlán**, 23 km north-west up the valley by paved road, has a reasonably well-preserved monastery. It was the centre of an

Otomí Indian state which the Aztecs couldn't conquer.

After an 800-metre climb up from the Tulancingo valley, there's another fortress-monastery at **Atotonilco el Grande** (345 km) where market day is Thursday.

Northern Veracruz

South of Tampico you enter the state of Veracruz, whose northern half is mostly rolling plains, lying between the coast and the southern end of the Sierra Madre Oriental. The major attraction is the ancient site of El Tajín, near Papantla.

TUXPAN
Population: 75,000
Tuxpan ('TOOKS-pahn') is a fishing town and minor oil port near the mouth of the Río Tuxpan, 310 km north of Veracruz city and 190 km south of Tampico. It's a cleaner, cooler and in every way more agreeable place to break a journey than Tampico, with something of a holiday atmosphere mainly thanks to its beach 12 km east. The town itself has a wide tropical river, pleasant little parks and decent-value hotels, and is within fairly easy reach of El Tajín, 75 km away.

Orientation
The town centre is on the north bank of the Río Tuxpan, spreading five or six blocks west (upstream) from the high toll bridge spanning the river. Reforma, the riverfront road, passes under the bridge and continues 12 km east to the beach. A block back from Reforma is Juárez, with many of the hotels. Parque Juárez at its west end functions as a zócalo and is crowded in the cool of the evening.

Information
There's a helpful tourist office (☎ (783) 4-01-77) on the west side of Parque Juárez, open daily. Outside is a bunch of Ladatel phones. There are banks on Juárez; the post office is at Morelos 12.

Museums
In the same building as the tourist office is a museum with Totonac and Huastec artefacts.

Fidel Castro spent 1956 in Tuxpan planning and preparing the Cuban revolution. The result is the Museo de la Amistad México-Cuba (Mexican-Cuban Friendship Museum) on Obregón south of the river, which tells of Spanish imperialism in the western hemisphere and the efforts of Castro, Che Guevara and others to change things. It's open daily and is free.

To reach it, take any of the lanchas (US$0.10) criss-crossing the river from landing points beside Reforma on the north bank. From the south bank, walk two or three blocks inland to Obregón, then turn right. The museum is at the end of Obregón, just before you reach the river again. On the bank beside the museum stands a replica of the wooden *Granma*, in which Castro sailed to Cuba at the end of the year.

Beach
A wide strip of sand stretches 20 km north from the mouth of the Río Tuxpan, 12 km east of the town. Its beauty has been diminished by a new power station two km north of the river mouth, but the water generally appears clean enough – and prices at the seafood palapas are low.

Some of the colectivos that line up at the east end of Juárez go to the beach for US$0.80. Or take a 'Playa' bus (US$0.50) from the Superbodega shop on Reforma, half a block east of Guerrero. The bus does a quick tour of the town centre before heading out to the beach.

The road passes docks with surprisingly big ships and, shortly before reaching the coast, crosses the mouth of the Tampamachoco Lagoon, stretching about 10 km north. The bus drops you just north of the river mouth.

Festivals
A big fishing tournament brings hundreds of visitors to Tuxpan in late June or early July, and festivities for the Assumption on 15 August continue for a week with folk-

dancing contests, bullfights and fireworks. The Totonac *voladores* (fliers) (see El Tajín) usually perform.

Places to Stay – bottom end

The *Hotel Posada El Campanario* (☎ (783) 4-08-55), at 5 de Febrero 9, isn't particularly welcoming to foreigners but its quite clean, sizeable singles/doubles with private bath and fan are decent value at US$5/6. The *Hotel Tuxpan* (☎ (783) 4-41-10) at the corner of Juárez and Mina has 30 rooms (fan only) at US$9.25/11.75. Some have big windows overlooking the street. Rooms in the *Hotel El Huasteco* (☎ (783) 4-18-59) at Morelos 41 are smaller and darker but they're air-conditioned, and the place is clean and friendly. Prices are US$10/11.75.

The upper front rooms of the 77-room *Hotel Florida* (☎ (783) 4-02-22) at Juárez 23 have superb river views. They're big and clean, though a few are beginning to get dilapidated and some beds have sagged. With fan only you pay US$11.75/16.75, which is good value. With air-con and TV they're US$20/25. There are wide balconies/sitting areas and a lift.

The *Hotel Plaza* (☎ (783) 4-07-38) at Juárez 39 has clean, air-conditioned but characterless rooms for US$15/18.50.

Places to Stay – middle

The most comfortable place in the town centre is the *Hotel Reforma* (☎ (783) 4-02-10) at Juárez 25, with TVs in air-conditioned rooms which are bigger than the Plaza's, and a pleasant covered courtyard with a fountain. Singles/doubles are US$22.50/26.85. There are more middle range places, aimed at motorists, on Adolfo López Mateos, the westward continuation of Moctezuma, as it loops round the north side of town towards the Tampico highway.

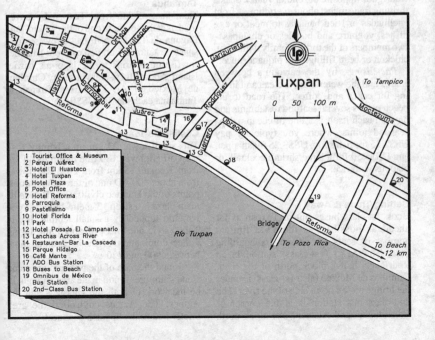

1 Tourist Office & Museum
2 Parque Juárez
3 Hotel El Huasteco
4 Hotel Tuxpan
5 Hotel Plaza
6 Post Office
7 Hotel Reforma
8 Parroquia
9 Pastelisimo
10 Hotel Florida
11 Park
12 Hotel Posada El Campanario
13 Lanchas Across River
14 Restaurant–Bar La Cascada
15 Parque Hidalgo
16 Café Mante
17 ADO Bus Station
18 Buses to Beach
19 Omnibus de México Bus Station
20 2nd–Class Bus Station

Tuxpan

0   50   100 m

To Tampico

Río Tuxpan

Bridge

To Pozo Rica

To Beach 12 km

Moctezuma

Reforma

Places to Eat

The restaurants of the hotels *Florida* and *Plaza*, and *Antonio's* in the Hotel Reforma, all on Juárez, serve some of the best fare, with a bias towards seafood. Of course you pay for the clean, orderly surroundings. The popular Hotel Florida restaurant is particularly quick and helpful, with comida corrida at US$5.50, while à la carte fish soup costs US$3.50 and shrimp salad US$6. Or opt for enchiladas or a sizeable hamburger (US$4). Sweet teeth can round things off with a Crepa Florida (pancake with ice cream, nuts and chocolate), also US$4. Antonio's is the dearest of these three restaurants and its helpings aren't always as big as you'd expect.

There are many more eateries on Juárez, and several bakeries towards the east end. The *Restaurant-Bar La Cascada*, also towards the east end, is a seafood place offering a range of breakfast bargains, too – eg juice, coffee, eggs and chilaquiles for US$1.75. The cheap *Cafe Mante* on Rodríguez opposite the end of Juárez does a thriving trade in just about everything – from enchiladas or fried bananas to meat or egg dishes, yoghurt, and bocoles or chalupas – two members of the tortilla family with meat, chicken or bean fillings and piquant sauce.

Pastelisimo, by the parroquia between Juárez and the waterfront, is clean and inviting for cakes and coffee. The road to the beach passes several seafood restaurants and on the beach itself is a line of cheap palapa seafood joints, where you typically pay US$2.25 for fish soup, US$3.25 for snapper, and US$5.50 for a large shrimp cocktail, or octopus with rice.

Getting There & Away

Book 1st-class buses out of Tuxpan as far ahead as possible, as there's a limited number of seats for passengers boarding here. The ADO (1st-class) station is on Rodríguez, half a block north of the river. Omnibus de México (also 1st-class) is under the bridge on the north side of the river. The 2nd-class bus station is at the corner of Constitución and Alemán, one block north

from the bridge then two east. Departures include:

Matamoros – 680 km, 12 hours; one or two 1st-class buses daily by ADO for US$16 plus one or two 2nd-class buses daily

Mexico City (Northern Terminal) – 355 km, six hours; 10 1st-class buses daily by ADO, and three by Omnibus de México, for US$7

Papantla – 90 km, 1¼ hours; five 1st-class buses daily by ADO for US$1.50

Poza Rica – 60 km, one hour; about 20 1st-class buses daily by ADO for US$1.25, 2nd-class buses every 10 minutes

Tampico – 180 km, four hours; about 20 1st-class buses daily by ADO for US$5, 2nd-class buses about half-hourly

Veracruz – 320 km, six hours; eight 1st-class buses daily by ADO for US$9

Villahermosa – 995 km, 14 hours; three 1st-class buses daily by ADO for US$18

Xalapa – 350 km, 6½ hours; five 1st-class buses daily by ADO for US$6.50

AROUND TUXPAN

Tamiahua

Tamiahua, 43 km from Tuxpan by paved road, is at the southern end of the 90-km-long Laguna de Tamiahua. It has a few seafood shack-restaurants and you can rent launches for fishing or trips to the lagoon's barrier island. About 10 1st-class buses by Omnibus de México or ADO go from Tuxpan to Tamiahua each day for US$0.80.

Castillo de Teayo

This small town, 23 km up a bumpy road west off Highway 180 (the turning's 44 km from Tuxpan, 15 km from Poza Rica), was from about 800 AD one of the southernmost points of the Huastec civilisation. Beside its main plaza is a steep 13-metre-high restored pyramid topped by a small temple. It's in Toltec style and was probably built during Toltec domination of the area some time between 900 and 1200.

Around the base of the pyramid are some stone sculptures found in the area, thought to be the work of both the Huastecs and the Aztecs. The Aztecs controlled the area briefly before the Spanish conquest.

EL TAJÍN

One of the least visited and understood of Mexico's ancient cities lies among hills covered in tropical vegetation a few km from Papantla. Its name ('el ta-HEEN') is Totonac for thunder, lightning or hurricane – all of which can happen here in summer. The ancient Totonacs may have occupied El Tajín in its later stages, but most of it was built before the Totonacs became important and little is known about these people. It is the highest achievement of Classic Veracruz civilisation.

El Tajín was first occupied about 100 AD but most of what's visible was built around 600 or 700. It was at its peak of activity and importance – seemingly a town as well as a ceremonial centre – from about 600 to 900, then abandoned about 1200, possibly after attacks by Chichimecs, and lay unknown to the Spaniards until about 1785, when an official came upon it while looking for illegal tobacco plantings.

Among El Tajín's special features are rows of square niches on the sides of buildings, a huge number (at least 11) of ball courts, and sculpture showing human sacrifice connected with the ball game.

The Mexican archaeologist who did much of the excavation here, José García Payón, believed that El Tajín's niches and stone mosaics symbolised day and night, light and dark, life and death in a universe composed of pairs of opposites. Other sources say the Tajín universe contained three parts – the sky above, the earth below and here in between. Despite intensive reconstruction of hitherto derelict pyramids and plazas in 1991, El Tajín retains an aura of mystery and a more 'lost in the jungle' feel than many of the more famous sites.

Information

The site is open daily from 9 am to 5 pm and is free on Sunday, US$3.50 other days. There are a few stalls selling drinks and handcrafts around the ticket kiosk. The whole site covers about 10 sq km. Two main parts have been cleared: the lower area where the Pyramid of the Niches stands, and, uphill, a group of buildings known as El Tajín Chico (Little El Tajín).

Totonac Voladores

Totonac Indians carry out the exciting voladores (fliers) rite most days from a 20-metre-high pole standing permanently next to the El Tajín car park. While it's in a way sad to see a sacred act turned into a show for tourists, the feat is dangerous and spectacular and the people who do it say they need the money because they have no land. They collect donations from the audience after the performance. (So feel free to postpone your own payment if you're approached individually beforehand, as seems to happen to some gringos.)

The fliers begin whenever there's enough of a crowd to make it worthwhile. They sometimes fly two or three times a day, but between 11 am and 1 pm is usually a reliable time. Five men in colourful costumes climb to the top of the pole. Four sit on a tiny wooden platform, each tying a rope to one ankle, while the fifth dances, bangs a drum and plays a whistle on an even tinier platform above them. Suddenly he stops and the others launch themselves into thin air. Upside down, arms outstretched, they slowly revolve round the pole and descend to the ground as their ropes unwind.

This pre-Hispanic ceremony is packed with symbolism. One interpretation is that it's a fertility rite and the fliers are macaw-men who make invocations to the four corners of the universe before falling to the ground, bringing with them the sun and rain. You may also be told that each flier circles the pole 13 times, giving a total of 52 revolutions, which is not only the number of weeks in the modern year but was an important number in pre-Hispanic Mexico which had two calendars – one corresponding to the 365-day solar year, the other to a ritual year of 260 days – with a day in one meeting a day in the other only every 52 solar years.

The voladores are representatives of the (approximately) 180,000 Totonacs in modern Mexico, who live between Tecolutla on the Veracruz coast and the southern Sierra

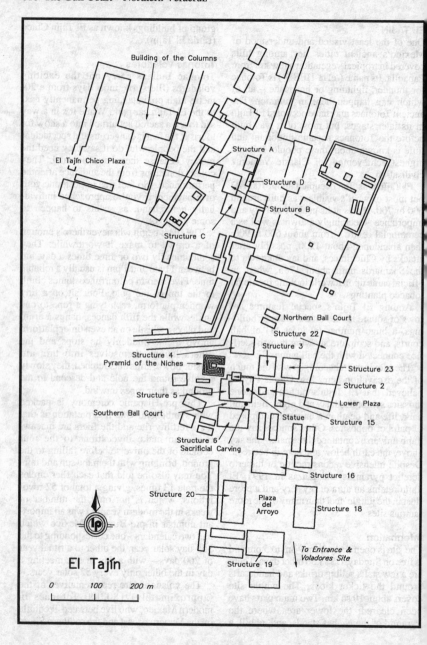

Building of the Columns

El Tajín Chico Plaza

Structure A

Structure D

Structure B

Structure C

Northern Ball Court

Structure 22

Structure 3

Structure 4
Pyramid of the Niches

Structure 23

Structure 2

Structure 5

Southern Ball Court

Structure 15

Lower Plaza

Statue

Structure 6
Sacrificial Carving

Structure 16

Structure 20

Plaza del Arroyo

Structure 18

To Entrance &
Voladores Site

El Tajín

Structure 19

0   100   200 m

Madre Oriental in northern Puebla. Roman Catholicism is superimposed on more ancient Totonac beliefs, with traditional customs stronger in the mountain areas. The chief Totonac deities are their ancestors, the sun (which is also the maize god) and St John (also the lord of water and thunder). Venus and the moon are identified with Qotiti, the devil, who rules the kingdom of the dead beneath the earth. Some Totonacs apparently believe that the world is flat, the sky is a dome, and the sun travels beneath the earth at night. The Feast of the Holy Cross (3 May) coincides with ceremonies for fertility of the earth and new seeds.

Lower Plaza

Inside the site, after the unremarkable Plaza del Arroyo, you reach the Lower Plaza, part of El Tajín's main ceremonial centre, with a low platform in the middle. A statue on the first level of Structure 5, a pyramid on the plaza's west side, represents either a thunder-and-rain god who was especially important at El Tajín, or Mictlantecuhtli, a death god. Structure 5's staircase bears traces of its original blue and red paint. Structure 3, a pyramid on the north side of the plaza, has traces of blue. All the structures around this plaza were probably topped by small temples.

Southern Ball Court

The 60-metre-long ball court between Structures 5 and 6 is one of Mexico's most famous because of six sculptures, from about 1150, on its walls.

North Corners The panel on the north-east corner (immediately on the right as you enter the court from the Lower Plaza) is the easiest to make out. Three ballplayers wearing knee-pads are in the centre. One has his arms held by the second while the third is about to plunge a knife into his chest in a ritual post-ball-game sacrifice. A skeletal death god on the left and a presiding figure on the right look on. Another death god hovers over the victim. The panel at the far (north-west) end of the same wall is thought to represent a

ceremony which preceded the ball game. Two players face each other, one with crossed arms, the other holding a dagger. Speech symbols emerge from their mouths. To their right is a figure with the mask of a coyote – the animal which conducted sacrificial victims to the next world. The death god is on the right.

South Corners The south-west panel seems to show the initiation of a young man into a band of warriors associated with the eagle. A central figure lies on a table; to the left another holds a bell. Above is an eagle-masked figure, possibly a priest. On the south-east panel one man offers a bunch of spears or arrows to another, possibly part of the same ceremony.

Central Panels These are devoted to the ceremonial drinking of the cactus-beer pulque. In the northern central panel, a figure holding a drinking vessel signals to another leaning on a pulque container. Quetzalcóatl sits cross-legged beside Tláloc, the fanged god of water and lightning. On the south panel Tláloc, squatting, passes a gourd to someone in a fish mask who appears to be in a pulque vat. On the left is the maguey plant, from which pulque is made.

The top sections of both these panels represent two dancing figures and, in the middle, a laughing drunken face with its tongue out. The two dancing figures may symbolise the sacred 'second' state induced by pulque. Maguey is not native to this part of Mexico, which points to influences from central Mexico (possibly Toltec) at this late stage of El Tajín.

Pyramid of the Niches

The Pyramid of the Niches, 35 metres square, is just off the Lower Plaza, by the north-west corner of Structure 5. The six lower levels, each surrounded by rows of small square niches, climb to a height of 18 metres. The wide staircase on the east side was a late addition, built over some of the niches.

There were originally 22 niches on each

side of the lowest level, 19 on the next level up, then 16, 13, 10 and seven. Some archaeologists reckon the temple on top, of which little remains, had five niches on three sides plus two on its east side – making a total of 365, the number of days in a year, and suggesting that the building may have been used as a kind of religious calendar. The insides of the niches were painted red, and their frames blue. The theory that they held statues of gods is now out of favour.

The only known similar building is a seven-level niched pyramid at Yohualichán near Cuetzalan, 50 km south-west of El Tajín. This was probably an earlier site than El Tajín and didn't reach the same artistic heights.

El Tajín Chico

The path north towards El Tajín Chico passes the Northern Ball Court, smaller and earlier than the southern one, but also with carvings on its sides.

Many of the buildings of El Tajín Chico, thought to have been the administrative centre of El Tajín, have geometric stone mosaic patterns known as Greco (Greek). They bear more resemblance to later decorations in Mitla, Oaxaca, than any others.

The main buildings, probably 9th-century, are on the east and north sides of El Tajín Chico Plaza. Structure C, on the east side, with three levels and a staircase facing the plaza, was originally painted blue. Next to it, Structure B was probably living quarters for priests or officials. Structure D, behind Structure B and off the plaza, has a large lozenge-design mosaic. A passage runs under it from east to west.

On the north side of the plaza, Structure A has a façade like a Maya roofcomb, with a stairway leading up through an arch in the middle. The construction of the arch, with the two sides jutting closer and closer to each other until they are joined at the top by a single slab, is known as 'corbelled' and is typical of Maya architecture – yet another piece in the confusing jigsaw of interaction between pre-Hispanic cultures. From the top

of the stairway a corridor leads all the way round the building.

Uphill to the north-west of El Tajín Chico Plaza is the as yet unreconstructed Building of the Columns, with large staircases that were probably only decorative. It originally had an open patio inside and, with adjoining structures stretching over the hillside for nearly 200 by 100 metres, was one of the most important buildings.

Getting There & Away

El Tajín is 15 km south-east of the dirty, noisy oil city of Poza Rica and 10 km west of the country town of Papantla, which is the nearest accommodation centre. Papantla and Poza Rica are both on Highway 180, 25 km apart. The entrance to El Tajín is on the Poza Rica-San Andrés road, marked by a big 'Zona Arqueológica El Tajín' sign, from which it's a 10-minute walk to the ticket office.

There are frequent local buses to El Tajín from both Papantla and Poza Rica. They're rather more frequent from Papantla, but getting to Poza Rica in the first place is easier because it's bigger and has more long-distance bus links – including 10 to 20 1st-class ADO buses daily from each of Tampico (250 km, five hours, US$6), Tuxpan (60 km, one hour, US$1.25), Veracruz (250 km, five hours, US$7.75) and Xalapa (285 km, 5½ hours, US$5.75), and over 30 from Mexico City Northern Terminal (260 km, five hours, US$5.75). You can also fly to Poza Rica from Tampico several days a week with Litoral. Long-distance transport to/from Papantla is covered in the Papantla section.

From Papantla White microbuses go on the hour to El Tajín for US$0.60 from 16 de Septiembre, the street on the south (uphill) side of Papantla's Juárez market. They take about 20 minutes. Alternatively you can do the trip in two stages by getting a bus from the same stop to the road junction village of El Chote, then any of the frequent buses going west (to the right) from El Chote, to the El Tajín turning. Other buses from

Papanta to El Chote leave from the Transportes Papantla terminal.

From Poza Rica Transportes Papantla's hourly buses to Coyutla from the 2nd-class side of Poza Rica bus station will drop you at the El Tajín entrance road. The fare is US$0.50 and the trip should take about 30 minutes but may be lengthened by stops to wait for more passengers on the way out of Poza Rica. Other buses destined for El Chote, Agua Dulce or San Andrés, by Autotransportes Coatzintla and other 2nd-class companies, should also get you to El Tajín. Ask for *'Desviación El Tajín'* (El Tajín turning).

PAPANTLA

Population: 97,000

Altitude: 290 metres

Set on a hillside among the outliers of the southern Sierra Madre Oriental, Papantla is an interesting base for visiting El Tajín. Some Totonacs still wear traditional costume here: the men sport baggy white shirts and trousers, the women embroidered blouses and quechquémitls. Voladores perform here most Sunday evenings and during the Corpus Christi festival in late May and early June.

Orientation

Papantla lies on Highway 180, which is running south-eastward on this stretch from Poza Rica. The centre of town is uphill (south) from the main road. To get from the ADO bus station to the centre, walk up to the main road, cross it and go straight on up Juárez. At the top of Juárez turn right on Enríquez to the zócalo, officially called Parque Téllez. Papantla's two markets, the Juárez and the Hidalgo, stand at the south-west and north-west corners of the zócalo respectively. Calle 20 de Noviembre runs down the right side of the Hidalgo market back to Highway 180, passing the Transportes Papantla bus terminal; Azueta goes down its left side.

Zócalo

The south wall of the zócalo, supporting the cathedral, is decorated with a 50-metre-long concrete mural by local artist Teodoro Cano depicting Totonac and Veracruz history. A serpent stretches along most of the mural. In the middle can be seen the Pyramid of the Niches. You can also pick out voladores, a pre-Hispanic stone carver and the modern oil industry. The roof of the kiosk in the middle of the plaza has a painting on a similar theme. Inside the Palacio Municipal are copies of carvings from the southern ball court at El Tajín.

The zócalo really comes alive on Sunday, when voladores usually perform in the cathedral yard.

Volador Monument

At the top of the hill above the zócalo, towers a 1988 statue of a volador musician playing his pipe as preparation for the four fliers to launch themselves into space. A red light adorns one of his fingers to warn off passing aircraft. Take the street heading uphill from the corner of the cathedral yard to reach the statue. Inscriptions around its base give an explanation of the voladores' ritual.

Festivals

Corpus Christi For the last week or so of May and the first couple of days of June, Papantla is thronged for the parades, dances and other celebrations of the Corpus Christi fiesta. Voladores perform specially, maybe two or three times a day. The main procession is on the first Sunday. Other dances you might catch are Los Negritos, Los Huehues (The Old Men) and Los Quetzalines.

Places to Stay

The *Hotel Tajín* (☎ (784) 2-06-44) at Nuñez 104 – a few metres uphill from the left end of the zócalo mural – has singles/doubles with fan for US$15.50/20.50 or with air-con for US$21/26. The rooms vary a lot in outlook, those at the front being blessed with balconies looking over the town, but all are clean, sizeable and in good shape.

The cheaper *Hotel Pulido* (☎ (784) 2-00-

36) at Enríquez 205, a short distance east of the north side of the zócalo, has smaller and dirtier rooms around a central parking area. It's quite friendly, though. Singles cost US$10; doubles are US$11.75 for one bed, US$13.50 for two beds.

The recently rebuilt *Hotel Premier* (☎ (784) 2-00-80) on the north side of the zócalo at Enríquez 3 has large, clean, comfortable, modern rooms, all with air-con, for US$34.75 a single or double.

Places to Eat

Papantla food is strictly Mexican, with an emphasis on meat in this cattle-raising area. The restaurant of the *Hotel Tajín* is adequate, if nothing special, with a long, not too expensive menu, though portions aren't huge. Various beefsteak filetes (US$3.50) are served: the Tampiqueño is strips of beef with fried bananas, small tortillas, guacamole, frijoles, salad and cheese; al carbón is charcoal-grilled with chips, frijoles and salad. Eggs dishes cost US$1 to US$2.50, most antojitos about US$2.

The *Restaurant Sorrento* at Enríquez 105, on the north-east corner of the zócalo, is very ordinary and not overwhelmingly clean but still more enticing than the market comedors. Antojitos, chicken and meat dishes are all US$2.50 to US$3.50.

On the same (north) side of the zócalo, the *Restaurante Enríquez* in the Hotel Premier is the air-conditioned Smart Place in Town. The menu is appetising with lots of fish and seafood in the US$6 to US$7 bracket, and meats around US$5.50 to US$6.75, but the service is very puzzling: when we wanted dinner about 8 pm we were told the place had closed at 6 pm despite the fact that six people were still dining merrily away in there. A pretty average breakfast next morning was accompanied by deafening pop tapes.

Things to Buy

The Hidalgo market has Totonac costumes (some quite pretty), good baskets and vanilla. Papantla is Mexico's leading vanilla-growing centre and you can buy it in extract form, in the original pods or in *figuras* – pods woven into the shape of flowers, insects, etc. The Juárez market sells mainly food.

Getting There & Away

Few long-distance buses stop here and there's no service at all to/from Tampico (change at Tuxpan or Poza Rica). Try to book your bus out of Papantla as soon as you arrive. If desperate consider going to Poza Rica and getting one of the much more frequent buses from there. ADO at Juárez 207 is the only 1st-class line serving Papantla. The unappealing 2nd-class alternative is Transportes Papantla on 20 de Noviembre, with slow, old vehicles. See Orientation for directions to/from the terminals. Departures from Papantla include:

Mexico City (Terminal Norte) – 290 km, 5½ hours; four 1st-class buses daily by ADO for US$6.

Poza Rica – 25 km, 30 minutes; eight 1st-class buses daily by ADO, 2nd-class buses about every 15 minutes by Transportes Papantla for US$0.50.

Tuxpan – 90 km, 1¼ hours; two 1st-class buses daily by ADO for US$1.50.

Veracruz – 230 km, five hours; five 1st-class buses daily by ADO for US$7.50 and five 2nd-class buses by Transportes Papantla.

Xalapa – 260 km, 5¼ hours; five 1st-class buses daily by ADO for US$5.25 and two 2nd-class buses by Transportes Papantla.

NORTHERN VERACRUZ TO PACHUCA

The 200 km Poza Rica-Pachuca road, Highway 130, is the direct approach to Mexico City from the northern part of Veracruz state. It climbs across the semitropical north of Puebla state into Hidalgo, crossing the scenic, sometimes misty southern extremities of the Sierra Madre Oriental. The area's population has a high proportion of Nahua and Totonac Indians. See under Pachuca in the Near Mexico City chapter for some info on buses along this route.

Huauchinango, roughly halfway between Poza Rica and Pachuca, is the centre of a flower-growing area. You'll also find embroidered textiles in the busy Saturday market. A week-long flower festival, including traditional dances, focuses on the third Friday in Lent. **Acaxochitlán**, about 25 km beyond Huauchinango, past the large El

Tejocotal Reservoir, is in Hidalgo state. Its market is on Sunday; specialities include fruit wine and preserved fruit. The Nahua women here often wear richly embroidered blouses.

The traditional Nahua village of **Pahuatlán**, source of many of the cloths woven with multicoloured animals and plants that you see in central Mexico markets, is reached from a turning north off Highway 130 about 10 km past Acaxochitlán. A spectacular 27-km dirt road winds several hundred metres down to the village, which holds a sizeable Sunday market. There's at least one hotel, with a restaurant, here. About half an hour's drive beyond Pahuatlán is **San Pablito**, a traditional Otomí village, where colourfully embroidered blouses abound. At least until recently, San Pablito was still producing amate (bark paper) by the pre-Hispanic method of boiling bark until it's soft, laying it in strips as a mesh, then beating it with a stone hammer.

Tulancingo (population 70,000, altitude 2222 metres), the second-biggest town in Hidalgo, is just 46 km short of the state capital, the Toltec capital briefly before Tula and there's a Toltec pyramid at the foot of a cliff at Huapalcalco, three km north. Market day is Thursday.

The remote Otomí village of **Tenango de Doria**, 40 rugged km north of Tulancingo by sometimes impassable dirt roads, is the source of more of the embroidered cotton cloths already mentioned under Pahuatlán. In **Huehuetla**, 50 km north of Tulancingo, one of the few communities of the tiny Tepehua Indian group embroiders colourful floral and geometric patterns on its quechquémitls and enredos.

PAPANTLA TO VERACRUZ

Highway 180 runs close to the coast for most of the 230 km from Papantla to Veracruz city. Swimmers should watch out for undertow on this coast.

Tecolutla & the Costa Esmeralda

Eleven km north-east from Highway 180 at Gutiérrez Zamora, 30 km east of Papantla, Tecolutla, at the mouth of the Río Tecolutla, is a minor seaside resort with a palm-fringed beach and a few hotels. There are ADO and Transportes Papantla buses to/from Papantla.

The Costa Esmeralda is the name given to the 40 km of coast between Gutiérrez Zamora and Nautla. Numerous hotels, rental bungalows, restaurants and at least three trailer parks dot the strip between highway and beach, with a concentration towards the Nautla end. Nautla, a small fishing town, has a handful of cheap but respectable hotels and a long beach where you can eat seafood.

Laguna Verde & Villa Rica

Mexico's first, controversial, nuclear power station is at Laguna Verde, about 80 km north of Veracruz city, on the coastal side of Highway 180. The fishing village of Villa Rica, 69 km before Veracruz, is where Cortés probably founded the first Spanish settlement in Mexico. There are traces of a fort and a church on the Cerro de la Cantera.

Zempoala

The ruins of the pre-Hispanic Totonac town of Zempoala (or Cempoala), which holds a key place in the story of the Spanish conquest of Mexico, stand in a modern town of the same name 42 km north of Veracruz city, three km west of Highway 180. The turnoff is by a Pemex station, eight km north of Cardel. Voladores perform at the ruins most Saturdays and Sundays around noon to 2 pm.

The site is attractive, with lines of palms, and mountains in the background. Most of the buildings are faced with smooth, rounded riverbed stones and are constructed as a series of narrow platforms. Their typical feature is battlement-like 'teeth' called *almenas*.

History Zempoala became an important Totonac centre after about 1200 and may have been the leader of a 'federation' of southern Totonacs. It fell subject to the Aztecs in the mid-15th century and many of the buildings are in Aztec style. The town had a system of defensive walls, underground water and drainage pipes and, when the Spanish came in May 1519, about 30,000 people. As Cortés approached the town one of his scouts reported back that its buildings were made of silver – but it was only white plaster or paint shining in the sun.

Zempoala's portly chief Chicomacatl, known to history as 'the fat *cacique*' from a description by Bernal Díaz del Castillo, struck an alliance with Cortés for protection against the Aztecs. But his hospitality didn't stop the Spanish from smashing his gods' statues and lecturing the Zempoalans on the virtues of Christianity. Zempoalan carriers went with the Spaniards when they set off for Tenochtitlán in August 1519. The following year, it was at Zempoala that Cortés defeated the expedition of Pánfilo de Narváez, sent by the governor of Cuba to arrest him.

By the 17th century Zempoala had virtually ceased to exist. Its population, devastated by new diseases, was down to eight families and soon afterwards it was abandoned. The present town dates from 1832.

Orientation The main ruins are at the end of a short track to the right as you enter Zempoala, where a sign says 'Bienvenidos a Cempoala'. They're open daily from 8 am to 6 pm. Entrance is US$1.75 except on Sunday, when it's free.

Templo Mayor The Main Temple is an 11-metre-high, 13-platform pyramid on a base 65 by 40 metres. Originally it was plastered and painted. A wide staircase ascends to the remains of a three-room shrine on top. This was probably Pánfilo de Narváez' headquarters in 1520, which Cortés' men captured by setting fire to the thatched roof of the shrine.

Las Chimeneas (The Chimneys) This is where Cortés and his men were lodged on their first visit to Zempoala. Its name comes from the hollow columns at the front, which were once filled with wood. A temple probably topped its seven platforms.

Western Structures The two main structures on the west side are known as the Gran Pirámide (Great Pyramid) and the Temple of the Wind God. Two stairways climb the Great Pyramid's three platforms in typically

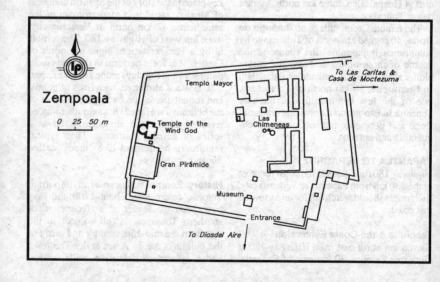

Toltec and Aztec style. It faces east and was probably devoted to the sun god. The round Temple of the Wind God, with a rectangular platform and ramps in front, is similar to Aztec temples to Ehecatl, a wind god.

Others Beyond the irrigation channel behind Las Chimeneas, you'll see a building called Las Caritas (The Little Heads) on your right. It once held large numbers of small pottery heads in niches. A large wind god temple, known as Dios del Aire, is reached by going back down the site entrance road, straight on over the main road, and round the corner to the right.

Getting There & Away Zempoala is most easily approached from Cardel, which is a stop for most buses on Highway 180. From Veracruz bus station the very frequent buses to Cardel cost US$1 by 1st-class ADO, US$0.80 by 2nd-class AU. From the bus stop at Cardel frequent green-and-white colectivo taxis (US$0.60) and some buses (US$0.30) run to Zempoala. Total journey time from Veracruz to Zempoala is about one hour.

La Antigua

This riverside village 23 km north of Veracruz, a km east of the highway, is where Cortés is thought to have scuttled his ships. It was one of the sites of Villa Rica, the Spanish settlement that preceded Veracruz, and boasts a house that was supposedly occupied by Cortés, and the very early Ermita del Rosario Church, probably dating from 1523. Small seafood restaurants here are popular with daytrippers from Veracruz.

Veracruz

Population: 450,000

As a coastal resort alone, the sweaty port city of Veracruz is hardly worth the stop, its beaches and waters being surpassed by many places on the Pacific or Yucatán coasts (though its relative cheapness makes it a favourite among Mexicans). But it's one of the most festive Mexican cities, with a hedonistic tropical port atmosphere, a zócalo that becomes a party every evening, and the biggest annual carnival between Rio de Janeiro and New Orleans. Its people, known as Jarochos, are good-humoured and relaxed.

Veracruz is a historic place too, having been Mexico's main gateway to the outside world from the day Cortés landed here in 1519 until the coming of the aeroplane. Invaders and pirates, incoming and exiled rulers, settlers, silver, slaves – all came and went to make the city a linchpin in Mexico's history, second to none except the capital.

People from Mexico City flood down here at weekends and holiday times. At Christmas, Carnival (the week before Ash Wednesday), and Semana Santa (the week before Easter), the city and nearby beaches are jam-packed with visitors. You need to book accommodation and transport in advance for these times.

If you fancy a trip outside the city, try the pre-Hispanic ruins at Zempoala (see the earlier Papantla to Veracruz section).

History

The Spanish Anchoring off the island of San Juan de Ulúa on Good Friday, 21 April 1519, Cortés made his first contact with Moctezuma's envoys, and baptised the place Villa Rica de la Vera Cruz. The harbour here immediately became the Spaniards' most important anchorage but Cortés' first settlement appears to have been another Villa Rica, 69 km north. It seems to have later moved to La Antigua, between Veracruz and Zempoala, before being established on the present site of Veracruz in 1598.

Until 1760 Veracruz was the only port allowed to handle trade with Spain. Tent cities blossomed for trade fairs when the annual fleet from Spain arrived, but because of frequent seaborne raids and an unhealthy coastal climate, with malaria and yellow fever rampant, Veracruz never became one of Mexico's biggest cities.

In 1567 nine English ships under John Hawkins, which sailed into Veracruz harbour

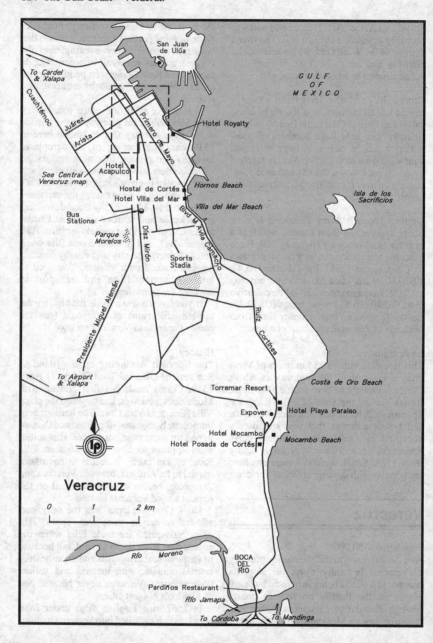

GULF
OF
MEXICO

San Juan
de Ulúa

To Cardel
& Xalapa

Cuauhtémoc

Juárez

Arista

Primero de Mayo

Hotel Royalty

Hotel
Acapulco

See Central
Veracruz map

Hostal de Cortés
Hotel Villa del Mar

Hornos Beach

Villa del Mar Beach

Isla de los
Sacrificios

Bus
Stations

Parque
Morelos

Díaz Mirón

Blvd M Avila Camacho

Sports
Stadia

Presidente Miguel Alemán

Ruiz Cortines

To Airport
& Xalapa

Costa de Oro Beach

Torremar Resort

Expover

Hotel Playa Paraíso

Hotel Mocambo
Hotel Posada de Cortés

Mocambo Beach

Veracruz

0   1   2 km

Río Moreno

BOCA
DEL
RÍO

Pardiños Restaurant

Río Jamapa

To Córdoba   To Mandinga

with the intention of selling some black slaves, were trapped by a Spanish fleet and only two escaped. One of them, however, carried Francis Drake, who went on to harry the Spanish endlessly in a long career as a sort of licensed pirate. The most vicious attack came in 1683 when the Frenchman Lorencillo with 600 men held the 5000 inhabitants in the church with little food or water, killed any who tried to escape, piled the Plaza de Armas with loot, got drunk, raped many of the women, threatened to explode the church unless the people revealed their secret stashes, and left a few days later 600,000 pesos richer.

19th Century In 1838 General Antonio López de Santa Anna, fresh from his rout by the Americans after the Alamo two years earlier, fled Veracruz in his underwear under bombardment from a French fleet in the Pastry War. But he replied heroically, driving the invaders out and losing his left leg in the process.

When the 10,000-strong army of Winfield Scott attacked Veracruz in 1847 in the Mexican-American War, over 1000 Mexicans including many civilians were killed in a week-long bombardment after which the city surrendered.

In 1859, during Mexico's internal Reform War, Benito Juárez' Veracruz-based liberal government promulgated the reform laws that nationalised church property and put education into secular hands. In 1861 when Juárez, having won the war, said Mexico couldn't pay its foreign debts, a joint French-Spanish-British force occupied Veracruz. The British and Spanish planned only to take over the customs house and recover what Mexico owed them, but Napoleon III of France intended to conquer Mexico. Realising this, the British and Spanish went home while the French marched inland to begin their five-year intervention.

Mexico's first railway was built between Veracruz and Mexico City in 1872, and under the dictatorship of Porfirio Díaz, investment poured into the city.

20th Century In the civil war that followed Díaz's departure in the 1910-11 Revolution, US troops occupied Veracruz in 1914 to stop a delivery of German arms to the conservative dictator Victoriano Huerta. The Mexican casualties caused by the intervention alienated even Huerta's opponents. Later in the civil war Veracruz was for a while the capital of the reformist Constitutionalist faction led by Venustiano Carranza.

Veracruz is now officially titled 'four times heroic' in reference to the final expulsion of the Spanish in 1825, the triumph over the French in the Pastry War and the resistance to the Americans in 1847 and 1914.

Orientation

The two centres of the city's action are the Plaza de Armas or zócalo – site of the cathedral, the Palacio Municipal (City Hall), and numerous cafés and restaurants – and the harbour, half a km east, with San Juan de Ulúa fort on its far side. Beaches are dotted down the coast south of the harbour. About 700 metres south of the zócalo along Independencia is Parque Zamora, a multiple road junction with a wide green area in the middle. Near here is the main market. The 1st and 2nd-class bus stations are two km south of Parque Zamora along Díaz Mirón.

Information

Tourist Office The city and state tourist office (☎ (29) 32-99-42) is on the ground floor of the Palacio Municipal, on the zócalo, open 9 am to 9 pm daily. Staff are well informed (even about city buses) and sometimes English-speaking.

Money Banamex and Bancomer are both on Independencia one block north of the zócalo. But you can save time on money exchange by going to the Casa de Cambio La Amistad, half a block east of the same corner at Juárez 112, where the rate for cash dollars is almost as good as at banks. It's open Monday to Friday 9 am to 2 pm and 4 to 7 pm, Saturday 9 am to 1 pm. MasterCard holders can get

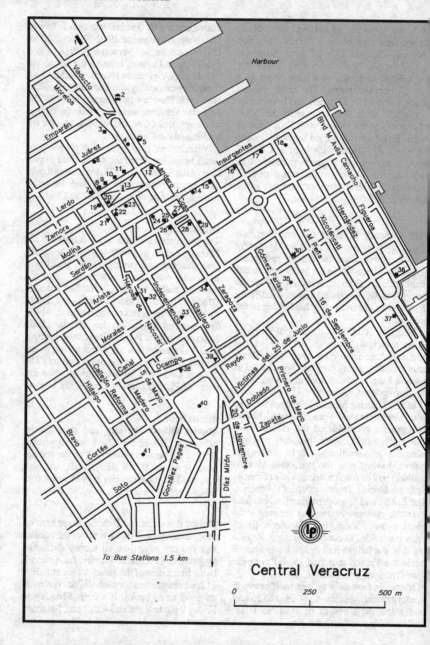

Central Veracruz

0   250   500 m

ash from a machine at Banamex. The American Express representative Viajes Olymar (☎ (29) 31-31-69) at Blvd M Avila Camacho 221, next to the Hostal de Cortés hotel, will exchange cash and travellers' cheques from 9 am to 1 pm and 4 to 6 pm Monday to Friday, 9 am to noon Saturday.

Post & Telecommunications The main post office at Plaza de la República 213, a five-minute walk north of the zócalo, is normally open 8 am to 8 pm Monday to Friday and 8 am to 1 pm Saturday. At the time of writing rebuilding had forced all business except stamp sales to move temporarily a few blocks west to the Transbordos Postales Marítimos Internacionales building, on Montesinos between Madero and Hidalgo.

The telégrafos office next door to the main post office has public fax, telegram and telex services, open 8 am to 8 pm Monday to Friday and 9 am to 7 pm Saturday. There are Ladatel phones, including one for credit cards, on the zócalo, but they work erratically.

Foreign Consulates The US Consulate (☎ (29) 31-01-42) is at Victimas del 25 de Junio 388, east of Parque Zamora. The tourist office has details on at least 14 other consulates in the city including several European countries.

Zócalo
The Veracruz zócalo, also called the Plaza de Armas, Plaza Lerdo and Plaza de la Constitución, is the hub of the city for Jarochos and visitors alike. It's a fine-looking place with palm trees, a fountain, a 17th-century Palacio Municipal on one side and an 18th-century cathedral, also known as the *parroquia* (parish church), on another.

But what makes it unique is its people. Each evening as the sweat cools off Veracruz bodies, the zócalo becomes a swirling, multifaceted party. From one of the cafés under the portales along the north side you might witness, in two blinks, a Mexico City couple celebrating their anniversary with wild, energetic dancing, prostitutes meeting Korean sailors, a holidaying middle-class family trying to control its children, a politician making a campaign speech, a vendor hawking leaping foam-rubber lizards with flashing eyes – all to the accompaniment of half a dozen groups of wandering mariachis, marimba-players, trumpeters and guitarists vying to be heard above each other and find some café customers who'll pay for personal serenades. The anarchy increases as the evening progresses and more and more alcohol is consumed, reaching a crescendo somewhere between midnight and 2 am. Some evenings there's formal entertainment too, in the shape of visiting musicians or dancers on a temporary stage.

Harbour

Veracruz harbour, about 250 metres east of the city centre, is still busy, though these days overshadowed by oil ports like Tampico and Coatzacoalcos. Stroll along Insurgentes (also called Paseo del Malecón) and view the ships and cranes across the water. In front of the Carranza Lighthouse (see Museums) the Mexican Navy goes through an elaborate parade early each morning. At the corner of Insurgentes and Blvd M Avila Camacho are monuments to the city's defenders against the Americans in 1914, and to all sailors who gave their lives to the sea. Boats from near this corner give one-hour harbour tours for around US$3.50 per person.

San Juan de Ulúa

This fortress protecting Veracruz harbour was once an island but is now linked to the mainland by a causeway across the north side of the harbour. In 1518 the Spaniard Juan de Grijalva landed here during an exploratory voyage from Cuba and found four priests at a shrine to Tezcatlipoca, the Aztec smoking mirror god. The next year Cortés also landed here and it became the main entry point for Spanish newcomers to Mexico. The Franciscan chapel is thought to have been built in 1524 and the first fortifi-

cations in the 1530s, but what we see now mostly dates from 1552-1779. The Spanish garrison here refused to surrender until 1825 four years after the last viceroy had recognised Mexican independence.

The fortress has acted not only as a garrison and defence but also a prison – most notoriously under Porfirio Díaz who reserved three stinking cells called El Purgatorio, La Gloria and El Infierno (Purgatory, Heaven and Hell), in the central part of the fortress, Fuerte San José (San José Fort), for political prisoners. They were so damp that stalactites formed (they're still there). Many inmates died of yellow fever or tuberculosis. Díaz himself left for exile from San Juan de Ulúa, but didn't savour one of his own dungeons.

Today San Juan de Ulúa is an empty ruin of passageways, battlements, bridges and stairways, which you can wander round between 9 am and 4.30 pm Tuesday to Sunday (entry US$3.50, except Sunday and holidays when it's free). Guided tours are available in Spanish for US$3.50 'per family'.

To get there, take a 'San Juan de Ulúa' bus (US$0.20) from the east side of Plaza de la República. The last bus back to town leaves at 6 pm.

Museums

Carranza Lighthouse On Insurgentes between Xicoténcatl and Hernández stands the Carranza Lighthouse, with a statue of the revolutionary hero Venustiano Carranza in front. Inside is the small Carranza Museum, devoted to the man whose government was based in Veracruz for a time. One room is preserved as it was when Carranza and others formulated the Mexican constitution here in 1914-15. The museum is open from 9 am to 1 pm and 4 to 6 pm Tuesday to Saturday. Entry is free.

Baluarte de Santiago Of the nine forts which once surmounted Veracruz' defensive wall, the Baluarte (Bastion) de Santiago at the corner of Canal and 16 de Septiembre is the only survivor. It was built in 1526. It now houses small exhibitions – open daily from 9 am to 5 pm, admission free.

Veracruz City Museum The Museo de la Ciudad de Veracruz, at the corner of Zaragoza and Morales, covers the city's history well but tails off a bit when it comes to customs, costumes and Carnival. Hours are 10 am to 5 pm Tuesday to Saturday and 9 am to 2.30 pm Sunday. Entry is US$0.70.

Beaches & Lagoons

Few people venture into the grubby water at Playa de Hornos or Playa Villa del Mar, both south of the city centre. Cleaner public beaches are found in the south of the city at Costa de Oro and, easier to reach by public transport, Mocambo which is 10 km south of the centre. At Mocambo people do go in the water (though few put their heads under). There's a friendly, relaxed atmosphere: you can rent a palapa sunshade for US$1 and even have drinks served – at a price. At the back of the beach is a tree-shaded Olympic pool with restaurant and bar (entry US$3.50).

To reach Mocambo take a 'Boca del Río–Mocambo' bus (see Getting Around) to the Expover exhibition hall on Calzada Mocambo, and walk down the street to the left of the Hotel Mocambo.

Beyond Mocambo the road crosses the Río Jamapa at Boca del Río. Over the bridge, the left fork continues along the coast to Isla del Amor and Mandinga (21 km from Veracruz), both of which have a few seafood restaurants and boats for hire to explore the lagoons behind them.

Carnival

Veracruz breaks into a nine-day party before Ash Wednesday (February or March) each year. Starting the previous Tuesday, brilliantly colourful parades wind through the city every day, beginning with one devoted to the 'burning of bad humour' and ending with the 'funeral of Juan Carnaval'. Other organised events include fireworks, dances, music (plenty of salsa and samba), children's parades and handcrafts, food and folklore

shows. Informally, everyone's hellbent on having as good a time as possible and a festive atmosphere takes over the whole city. It's easy to pick up a programme of events when you're there.

Places to Stay

Hotel prices in Veracruz are reasonable. Outside the peak seasons of mid-November to mid-January, Carnival, Semana Santa and mid-June to early September, some places give lower rates than we have mentioned here. The best value is generally around the zócalo, though there are some good deals on the seafront too. There are also a few decent cheap hotels near the bus stations. Several of the more expensive hotels are in the beach suburb of Mocambo, 10 km south of the centre.

Places to Stay – bottom end

In the cheapest city hotels you might not get hot water.

Zócalo Area Right on the zócalo at Lerdo 153, the *Hotel Imperial* (☎ (29) 31-16-41) is an ancient place with coats of arms on the walls and an antique caged lift rising from a cavernous lobby. It hasn't been decorated for years but somehow that adds atmosphere. Rooms are slightly musty but bearably clean and have fans and private baths. Singles/ doubles are US$11.75/15. Some have balconies over the zócalo for which you sometimes have to pay US$2 more.

Also on the zócalo, the *Hotel Concha Dorada* (☎ (29) 31-31-21) at Lerdo 77 has clean, small, hot rooms with fan and private bath for US$11.75/15, or air-con ones with a balcony over the zócalo for US$17/21.75. The *Hotel Rex* (☎ (29) 32-54-36), round the corner at Morelos 226, is a decaying ex-convent with lots of cats, friendly, eccentric staff, lovely tiles and two church domes rising behind an untidy courtyard. The rooms at US$5.75/8.50 are big, with bathrooms, fans, peeling paint and shabby furniture, and front a noisy road.

Other cheap hotels are grouped a couple of blocks south-east of the zócalo. The *Hotel*

Santo Domingo (☎ (29) 32-82-85) at Serdán 451 has small but clean rooms with private bath for US$11.75/15 with fan, US$16.75/20 with air-con. The older *Hotel Amparo* (☎ (29) 32-27-38) across the street at Serdán 482 is a basic but clean place with spartan tiled floors, uniformly lime-green walls and blue-and-white striped bedspreads. The small rooms with fan and private bath are US$10.75/13.50. The slightly bigger, though worn, rooms in the nearby *Hotel Santillana* (☎ (29) 32-31-16) at Landero y Coss 209 have the same colour scheme and cost US$11.75 single, US$15 double with one bed, US$20 double with two beds.

City Seafront Area Actually four blocks from the sea but on a quiet street looking across to the Baluarte de Santiago, the *Hotel Baluarte* (☎ (29) 36-08-46) at Canal 265 is excellent value for its clean, modern, well kept rooms – with TV and air-con – at US$19/21.50. It's on the corner of 16 de Septiembre, 800 metres south-east of the zócalo.

The budget seafront hotels face a not very fragrant harbour area about a km south-east of the zócalo – but their rooms are mostly OK and they *are* directly across the street from salt water! The *Hotel Villa Rica* (☎ (29) 32-48-54) at Blvd M Avila Camacho 7 isn't bad with small, tidy, fan-cooled rooms at US$11/14. A fraction further north at the corner of Blvd M Avila Camacho and Figueroa, the larger, busy *Hotel Mar y Tierra* (☎ (29) 32-02-60) has both an older front section with rooms at US$13.50/18.50 and a rear extension at US$20/27.50. All rooms are air-con but the rear rooms have newer air-con, plus TVs and carpets. Look before you choose.

The *Hotel Royalty* (☎ (29) 36-10-41) at the corner of Blvd M Avila Camacho and Abasolo has frill-less but clean balconied rooms for US$16.75 single or double with fan, US$21.75 with air-con. There are particularly good views, both out to sea and inland, from its upper floors.

Bus Station Area The best deal is just over a km from the bus stations but worth the effort. It's the *Hotel Acapulco* (☎ (29) 32-92-87) at Uribe 1327, just west of Díaz Mirón nine blocks north of the bus stations. Very clean, fairly bright, fan-cooled rooms of a reasonable size go for US$12/15, and the staff are friendly.

The *Hotel Central* (☎ (29) 37-22-22), half a block north of the 1st-class bus station at Díaz Mirón 1612, fronting a very noisy road, is cleanish and very busy, with fan-cooled rooms at US$11/14.50 and air-con doubles at US$18.50 with one bed, US$25 with two beds.

The *Hotel Rosa Mar* (☎ (29) 37-07-47) at Lafragua 1100, opposite the 2nd-class bus station, is clean enough. Sizeable fan-cooled rooms with private bath cost US$8.75 single, US$11.75 double with one bed, US$15 double with two beds. *Hotel Cheto* (☎ (29) 37-42-41) at 22 de Marzo 218 on the corner of Orizaba, a block east from the 2nd-class bus station, is a yellow bungalow with a small pink courtyard and a friendly owner. Rooms have one bed, fans, and private baths which could be cleaner, for US$8.75/10.75.

Places to Stay – middle
Zócalo Area Right on the zócalo there's a choice of three middle-range hotels, of which the best all-round value is the 180-room *Hotel Colonial* (☎ (29) 32-01-93) at Lerdo 117 which has an indoor pool and tiled terraces overlooking the square on the 5th and 6th floors. Interior rooms are dark but quite comfortable and half a dozen of them are fan-cooled for US$11.75/16.75. Other interior rooms, and exterior ones at the rear, have air-con and TV and cost US$21.75/27.50. Rooms at the front with balconies over the zócalo (but also with more noise) are US$25/30.75. Make sure the air-con is really working before checking into a room.

The *Hotel Prendes* (☎ (29) 31-02-41) at the corner of Lerdo and Independencia has comfortable rooms with air-con, phone, TV and, if you're lucky, a window and balcony, for US$23.50/26.75. The *Hotel Diligencias* (☎ (29) 31-22-41), on the west side of the zócalo at Independencia 1115, has 134 clean, modern, air-con rooms, most decorated with attractive sketches of Indian costumes. Bright exterior rooms are US$35/43, windowless interior ones US$25.50/30.75.

Just off the zócalo at Lerdo 20 on the corner of Landero y Coss, the *Hotel Oriente* (☎ (29) 31-24-90) has clean but not very big air-con rooms at US$21.50/28.75. Outside rooms have balconies, more light and more noise.

City Seafront The *Hotel Villa Del Mar* (☎ (29) 31-33-66) at Blvd M Avila Camacho 2707 opposite Villa del Mar beach, 2½ km south of the zócalo, is good value if you can get a room away from the noisy road. There's a good open-air pool, and the rooms, all air-con, are in both a central block and garden bungalows. Few have a sea view owing to buildings on the other side of the road, but at least it's a breezy location. Rooms are US$28/30.75. There are also suites at US$44 double.

Mocambo The *Hotel Mocambo* (☎ (29) 21-39-90, toll-free 800-2-90-01), on Carretera Veracruz-Mocambo in Mocambo, 10 km south of the city centre, offers a taste of luxury at reasonable prices. It's a long-established place – once top of the line in Veracruz and only ever-so-slightly faded – with over 100 rooms in low wings at the top of fine terraced gardens with three sizeable pools (two indoors). The rooms, all air-con with TVs, have varying outlooks but are all a good size. Doubles are US$46.75 with one bed, US$74.75 with two. Mocambo beach is a minute's walk from the foot of the gardens.

If you can't afford the Hotel Mocambo, try the little *Hotel Posada de Cortés* (☎ (29) 37-96-88). 'Junior suites' – in fact clean, pleasant, moderately-sized, air-con rooms with one double bed – go for US$28.50. 'Bungalows' – larger rooms – which can hold four people are US$38.50. A garden and small pool are at the centre of things. The hotel faces the inland side of Carretera Veracruz-Boca del Río, a couple of hundred metres south of the roundabout by the Hotel Mocambo, but its address is Suárez 1314 and

the entrance is from the first street on the right south of the roundabout.

Places to Stay – top end
Zócalo & Harbour The most central top-end place is the fully modernised *Hotel Veracruz* (☎ (29) 31-22-33, toll-free 800-2-92-33) at the corner of Independencia and Lerdo overlooking the zócalo, where carpeted, well-decorated, air-con rooms, some with balconies, cost US$67.50/76.75. There's a rooftop pool. The *Hotel Emporio* (☎ (29) 32-75-20, toll-free 800-2-90-19) towers over the harbour at the corner of Insurgentes and Xicoténcatl. An outside lift soars above three swimming pools to a roof garden. The 200 rooms and suites range upward from 'standard' air-con singles/doubles (which are comfortable but could be bigger) at US$66/71. The 50 suites all have jacuzzis which enables the hotel to claim that it has more jacuzzis than any other in the world. Make sure you get a room with a view!

City Seafront The *Hostal de Cortés* (☎ (29) 32-00-65, toll-free 800-2-98-00) at the corner of Blvd M Avila Camacho and Las Casas, facing Hornos Beach, is the first top-end hotel on the way south down the coast. It's a modern-style place with about 100 air-con rooms, some with sea-view balconies, and a pool. Rooms are US$70/77.

Mocambo The *Hotel Playa Paraíso* (☎ (29) 35-50-33, toll-free 800-2-90-10), at Ruíz Cortínes 3500 in Mocambo, has 34 air-con rooms and suites in bungalows in tree-filled grounds that front its private beach for US$66/71.50. The eight-storey *Torremar Resort* (☎ (29) 21-34-75, toll-free 800-2-99-00), next door at Ruíz Cortínes 4300, has 180 rooms, all with sea view, at US$66/82.50. Again there's a garden fronting a private beach. Both places have their own pools, too.

Places to Eat
Veracruzana sauce, found on fish all over Mexico, is made from onions, garlic, tomatoes, olives, green peppers and spices.

Zócalo Area The cafés under the zócalo portales are more for beer, tequila and atmosphere than for food. Stroll along the line and see which one grabs you. You can buy shrimps from passing vendors to nibble while you sit. For a meal here the air-conditioned *Restaurant Colonial*, beside the entrance to the Hotel Colonial, isn't bad value. Jamón a la plancha (a thick slice of ham with chips for US$3.50) and ensalada mixta de verduras (a plate of vegetables, US$2.50) or ensalada de frutas (US$2) makes a big meal. Fish and most meat dishes are US$5 to US$7.

The best value food on the zócalo itself is out of the limelight on the south side, at *La Paella*, where a filling plate of tender fish filete and salad costs just US$4.50. Chicken and seafood paella is the tasty speciality at US$5.50, or there are shrimps at US$7, antojitos at US$1.50 to US$2 and comida corrida at US$4.

Veracruz's essential eating experience is a few metres off the zócalo at Independencia 105, on the corner of Zamora. It's the big, convivial, noisy *Café de la Parroquia*, the city's favourite meeting place, echoing with the clinking of spoons on glasses by customers in need of a refill of the good café con leche (US$0.70). The food is straightforward and good, the waiters quick and the menu long: fish and meat are US$6 or US$7 (the ración de pavo is five large slabs of turkey breast in gravy with a bowl of jalapeño peppers), enchiladas and egg dishes US$2 to US$2.75. Huevos en tortilla con esparragos (asparagus omelette) is a breakfast treat for US$2.50. The Parroquia is open from 6 am to 1 am and packed most of the time.

A different Veracruz tradition can be found at *Cayetano*, at Molina 88 a block from the zócalo, famous for its deliciously cool juices, licuados and nieves concocted from a wide range of tropical fruits. Creations like mondongo de frutas, a large fruit salad topped with nieve for US$2, are almost meals in themselves. Licuados con leche cost US$1.50.

For possibly the best-value comida corrida in the zócalo area, head to *El Jarocho* at the corner of Emparán and Madero, open 8 am to 9 pm and always crowded for its US$2 lunch. There's à la carte fare, too – meat dishes around US$3.50, eggs US$1.50, juices US$1. *El Profeta* on the nearby corner of Juárez and Madero is a vegetarian restaurant doing lunch only, for US$2.50 Monday to Saturday, and US$3.50 on Sunday, when it's a buffet.

Harbour Area The *Gran Café de la Parroquia*, even larger than the original Café de la Parroquia on Independencia, sits at Insurgentes 340 facing the harbour. The menu's the same and the atmosphere almost as jovial. Navy brass hats breakfast here.

Navy other ranks are to be found on the top floor of the municipal fish market on Landero y Coss, which is packed with comedors doing bargain fish filete or shrimps al mojo de ajo for US$3. These close in the early evening. There are a few fish restaurants along Insurgentes, one of the busiest being *El Parador* where most main courses cost US$7 or US$8.

For a good steak in North American steakhouse-type surroundings, go to *Tilingo Charlie's* beside the Hotel Emporio entrance on Insurgentes. The going rate for your hunk of meat is US$9.50, or there's chicken for US$6 or US$7 and seafood cocktails at US$4.50.

Parque Zamora Area *La Merced* at Rayón 81 on the corner of Clavijero is Parque Zamora's jolly answer to the Café de la Parroquia, complete with clinking coffee spoons. A good, filling comida corrida of chicken soup, ham and chips, bread and a drink is US$5, while on the regular menu, fish and meat courses are mostly US$5 to US$7 and antojitos around US$2 to US$3. The nearby *Café Catedral*, at Ocampo 202 in Pasaje Castillo, half a block west of Independencia, is a similar but slightly more subdued place with the same sort of prices.

At Independencia 1520 between Parque Zamora and the zócalo, the *Cafetería Emir* is clean and cool with good antojitos (US$3) and licuados (US$1.50).

Cocina Económica Elia and *El Coyol*,

both on Héroes de Nacozari, a pedestrian street half a block west of Independencia between Morales and Arista, do comidas corridas of soup, rice, chicken or meat and maybe a dessert for US$2.

Down the Coast The non-hotel restaurants we have tried at Mocambo beach are either overpriced or disappointing. The best bets are the coffee shops in the Mocambo or Torremar hotels. A good breakfast in the Mocambo's is US$4 or so.

A seafood meal in the rivermouth village of **Boca del Río**, 13 km south of Veracruz centre, is an indispensable part of a visit to Veracruz for many Mexicans – and a long Sunday lunch is the favourite way to do it. *Pardiño's* at Zamora 40 in the centre of the village is the biggest and best-known restaurant, but there are several more by the riverside, where typical prices are US$3.50 for two stuffed crabs, US$5 for octopus or filete Veracruzana relleno de camarones (fish in Veracruzana sauce, stuffed with shrimp). Minstrels wander among the tables as you feed.

Mandinga, about eight km further along the coast from Boca del Río, is also known for its seafood (especially prawns) and has a clutch of small restaurants.

Entertainment

A café seat under the zócalo portales is a ringside ticket to the best entertainment in town but if you hanker for something more formal, the tourist office has info on exhibitions, concerts and other cultural events. La Capilla and Morucho's in the Prendes and Emporio hotels are two of the better discos.

Things to Buy

The Plaza de las Artesanías at the corner of Insurgentes and Landero y Coss, and the line of stalls across the street, are devoted more to seaside knick-knacks than genuine artisanry. But if you need a sailor cap or a '*Veracruz – Ciudad Del Amor*' T-shirt, drop by.

Ordinary Jarochos shop for their daily needs at the Mercado Hidalgo, a block southwest of Parque Zamora between Cortés and Soto. Shops are on Independencia and the streets to its west.

Getting There & Away

Air Mexicana flies four times daily to/from Mexico City (45 minutes, US$55). Its Veracruz office (☎ (29) 32-22-42) is at 5 de Mayo 1266, on the corner of Serdán, downtown. Taesa (☎ (5) 758-55-86) flies to/from Mexico City twice a week for around US$40 – Viajes Ahinco (☎ (29) 31-43-48) in the Hotel Veracruz sells its tickets, along with those of the Veracruz-based airline Litoral and other lines.

Litoral flies to/from Villahermosa (one hour), Poza Rica (30 minutes) and Tampico (one hour) usually twice daily. Its own ticket office (☎ (29) 31-52-32) is in the Hostal de Cortés hotel on Blvd M Avila Camacho facing Hornos beach. Aeromonterrey flies to/from Tampico five days a week.

Aerocaribe flies daily to/from Mérida (2½ to 3½ hours) via Minatitlán and/or Villahermosa. Its office (☎ (29) 35-05-68) is at Blvd M Avila Camacho 2983 between Bolívar and Valencia, about 3½ km south of the zócalo. Aeromar flies to/from Uruapan, Morelia and other central Mexico cities.

Bus Veracruz is a major hub, with good services up and down the coast and inland along the Puebla-Mexico City corridor. The 1st and 2nd-class bus stations (Centrales de Autobuses) are back-to-back between Díaz Mirón and Lafragua, two km south of Parque Zamora and 2¾ km south of the zócalo. The 1st-class side (almost exclusive to ADO) fronts Díaz Mirón at the corner of Xalapa. The 2nd-class side is at the rear, entered from Lafragua.

Note that tickets for AU's ordinario buses are sold not in the main 2nd-class ticket hall but from a separate taquilla by the 2nd-class platforms. Try to avoid the slow, uncomfortable buses of Autotransportes Los Tuxtlas for all but short hops. Departures (all 1st-class are by ADO) include:

Acayucan – 250 km, five hours; 16 1st-class buses daily for US$5.

Campeche – 925 km, 15 hours; two 1st-class evening departures for US$17.75.

Cancún – 1390 km, 22 hours; one 1st-class evening departure for US$27.

Catemaco – 165 km, three hours; four 1st-class buses daily for US$3.25, a few 2nd-class directo buses daily by AU and Autotransportes Los Tuxtlas, 2nd-class ordinario buses every 10 minutes by Autotransportes Los Tuxtlas.

Córdoba – 125 km, two hours; 13 1st-class buses daily for US$2.50, 22 directo 2nd-class buses daily by AU.

Chetumal – 1050 km, 17 hours; three 1st-class buses daily for US$20.

Matamoros – 1000 km, 18 hours; two 1st-class buses daily for US$24.75.

Mérida – 1175 km, 18 hours; two evening 1st-class departures for US$21.50.

Mexico City (TAPO) – 430 km, 6½ hours; four luxury buses daily by Uno for US$27.50, about 35 1st-class buses daily for US$9.

Oaxaca – 460 km, 8½ hours via Teotitlán del Camino; 540 km, 10½ hours via Huajuapan de León; one 1st-class bus daily by each route for US$10.25, one 2nd-class directo bus via Teotitlán del Camino by AU, two 2nd-class buses daily via Tuxtepec by Cuenca (tickets sold in the 1st-class station).

Orizaba – 150 km, 2¼ hours; 18 1st-class buses daily for US$3, 21 2nd-class directo buses by AU.

Papantla – 230 km, five hours; two 1st-class buses daily for US$7.50.

Poza Rica – 250 km, five hours; 14 1st-class buses daily for US$7.75.

Puebla – 300 km, five hours; one luxury bus daily by Uno for US$18, 10 1st-class buses daily for US$6.25, 19 2nd-class directo buses daily by AU.

Salina Cruz – 485 km, nine hours; two 1st-class buses daily for US$11.75.

San Andrés Tuxtla – 155 km, 2¾ hours; about 30 1st-class buses daily for US$3.

Santiago Tuxtla – 140 km, 2½ hours; eight 1st-class buses daily for US$2.75, 2nd-class buses every 10 minutes by Autotransportes Los Tuxtlas.

Tampico – 500 km, 10 hours; 13 1st-class buses daily for US$13.75.

Tapachula – 800 km, 14 hours; one evening 1st-class departure for US$17.75.

Tuxpan – 320 km, six hours; 14 1st-class buses daily for US$9.

Tuxtla Gutiérrez – 750 km, 14 hours; one 1st-class bus daily for US$15.50.

Villahermosa – 475 km, eight hours; 19 1st-class buses daily for US$9.25.

Xalapa – 100 km, two hours; 1st-class buses every 15 or 30 minutes 3 am to 10 pm, for US$2.25; 2nd-class buses every 15 minutes by AU.

Train The overnight sleeper *El Jarocho* between Veracruz and Mexico City is slower and dearer than a bus but you get more chance of sleep. It leaves Mexico City at 9.15 pm, Veracruz at 9.30 pm, and passes through Córdoba, Fortín de las Flores and Orizaba. The full trip is supposed to take 10 hours but allow for a couple of hours' delays. A camarín for one person to/from Mexico City costs US$16.50, an alcoba for two US$33, a primera especial seat US$10. Book as far ahead as you can. There are two other daily trains on the same route without sleeper accommodation, on which a primera seat is US$3.50, segunda US$2.

Incurable railway buffs could take a train to Tapachula, 885 km away on the Chiapas-Guatemala border. The daily service takes an alleged 23 hours 40 minutes for US$7 (primera) or US$4 (segunda). Down the line in Chiapas, station staff say these trains can turn up any time of day or night.

Veracruz station is at the north end of Plaza de la República, a five-minute walk from the zócalo.

Car At Veracruz the Tampico-Cancún Highway 180 meets Highway 140 from Mexico City, Puebla and Xalapa, and Highway 150 from Mexico City, Puebla and Córdoba. See the Mexico City to Veracruz chapter (especially under Puebla) for info on the routes to/from Mexico City, and elsewhere in this chapter for the roads south and north along the Gulf.

Car rental agencies in Veracruz include Auto Rentas Fast (☎ (29) 36-14-16) at Lerdo 245; Autos Laurencio (☎ (29) 32-70-60) at Serdán 3 in the Hotel Emporio building; Avis (☎ (29) 32-25-16) in the Hotel Veracruz; Budget (☎ (29) 31-21-39) at Díaz Mirón 1123 (corner of Alacio Pérez); Dollar (☎ (29) 32-00-65) in the Hostal de Cortés hotel; Hertz (☎ (29) 32-40-21) at Autover, Serdán 14; and National (☎ (29) 31-17-56) at Díaz Mirón 1036.

Getting Around
To/From the Airport Veracruz airport is a km south of Highway 140 to Paso de Ovejas

and Xalapa, about 11 km from central Veracruz. Transportación Aeropuerto (☎ 32-35-20) at Hidalgo 826 runs an airport colectivo (US$2) and taxi (US$9) service. It will pick you up from your hotel.

To/From the Bus Stations For the city centre, take bus 'Díaz Mirón' (US$0.20) from in front of the Hotel Central, on Díaz Mirón half a block north of the 1st-class bus station. The bus goes to Parque Zamora then up Madero. For the zócalo, get off at the corner of Madero and Lerdo. Returning to the bus stations, pick up the same bus going south on 5 de Mayo. A taxi is US$1.75.

To/From Mocambo, Boca del Río & Mandinga Bus 'Mocambo – Boca del Río' (US$0.20), every few minutes from the corner of Zaragoza and Serdán near the zócalo, goes to Parque Zamora then down the seafront Blvd M Avila Camacho to Mocambo (15 minutes) and Boca del Río (25 minutes). A taxi from the centre to Mocambo is usually US$3.

AU ordinario 'Antón Lizardo' buses from the 2nd-class bus station, every 20 minutes from 6 am to 8.45 pm, stop at Boca del Río, Isla del Amor and Mandinga. The last one back leaves Antón Lizardo (eight km beyond Mandinga, 29 km from central Veracruz) at 8 pm. The less frequent directo buses to Antón Lizardo stop at Boca del Río only.

Southern Veracruz

South-east of Veracruz city is a flat, hot, wet region crossed by many rivers but broken by hills only in the Los Tuxtlas area about 150 km from Veracruz, where the volcanic Sierra de los Tuxtlas rises above 1800 metres then sweeps down to the sea.

If you're not in a hurry, consider stopping in Los Tuxtlas – the green, fertile area around the towns of Santiago Tuxtla, San Andrés Tuxtla and Catemaco, described by the 19th-century traveller Alexander von Humboldt as the 'Switzerland of Veracruz'. His comparison was far-fetched but the area does have several lakes and waterfalls, and a quiet coastline, and is one of the most agreeable and climatically comfortable parts of Veracruz. Mexican vacationers come to Catemaco, a small lakeside resort, but few foreign tourists do.

Los Tuxtlas is also the western fringe of the ancient Olmec heartland, with interesting Olmec museums at Santiago Tuxtla and nearby Tres Zapotes. The basalt for the huge Olmec heads of San Lorenzo, 60 km south of Los Tuxtlas, was quarried from Cerro Cintepec in the east of the Sierra de los Tuxtlas, then transported probably by roller and raft.

ALVARADO
Population: 60,000

The busy fishing town of Alvarado, 67 km down Highway 180 from Veracruz city, stands on a spit of land separating the Gulf from the Laguna de Alvarado, which is the meeting point of several rivers including the Papaloapan. East of the town a long toll bridge (US$1.75 per car) crosses the channel from the lagoon to the sea.

Alvarado has a few hotels, and a restaurant in the Port Authority building with a name for excellent seafood at good prices. Carnival celebrations here are timed to start immediately after the Veracruz carnival finishes. You can hire boats for trips on the lagoon or up the river to Tlacotalpan (about two hours).

TLACOTALPAN
Population: 15,000

A quiet, old town beside the wide Río Papaloapan, 10 km south of Highway 180 from a turning 16 km east of Alvarado, Tlacotalpan has some very pretty streets, churches and plazas. The Museo Salvador Ferrando, open daily except Monday, is mainly devoted to the late 19th century, including furniture and women's costumes of that time. You can rent boats for river trips. Tlacotalpan's lively Candelaria festival, in late January and early February, features bull-running in the streets and several river-based events. In one of these an image of the Virgin is followed along the river by a flotilla of small boats.

There are two small hotels – the *Posada Doña Lala* and the *Hotel Reforma* – on Carranza, the main street.

Highway 175 (narrow in parts) goes from Tlacotalpan up the Papaloapan Valley to Tuxtepec then twists and turns over the mountains to Oaxaca (320 km from Tlacotalpan).

SANTIAGO TUXTLA

Population: 11,000
Altitude: 285 metres

Here, 140 km from Veracruz city, you are in the rolling green foothills of the volcanic Sierra de los Tuxtlas, where lots of maize and cattle are raised. Santiago, founded in 1525, is a pretty valley town with a river running through it, worth visiting for the Olmec remains and museums in the town and at Tres Zapotes, 23 km away. After a day among these relics, don't be surprised if the modern-day locals take on Olmec facial features too!

Orientation & Information

Buses arriving in Santiago drop you where Calle Morelos runs off the highway at a small 'Museo Arquelógico' sign. Calle Ayuntamiento runs off Morelos at right angles to the zócalo. The post office is on the zócalo, the telégrafos office on Morelos. There's a Multibanco Comermex on the zócalo too, but the nearest place to change travellers' cheques is San Andrés Tuxtla.

Things to See

The Olmec head in the zócalo is known as the Cobata head, after the estate where it was found on the Cerro (hill) de Vigía, west of Santiago. It's thought to be a very late or even post-Olmec production, but is the biggest Olmec head found so far, and unique in that its eyes are closed.

Along one side of the zócalo stands the Santiago museum. Among the Olmec exhibits (all carved in stone) are a colossal head from Nestepec west of Santiago, a rabbit head from Cerro de Vigía and a copy of Monument F or 'El Negro' from Tres

Zapotes which is an altar or throne with a human form carved into it. The museum is open 9 am to 6 pm Tuesday to Saturday (US$2.75), and 9 am to 3 pm Sunday (free).

Festivals

Santiago celebrates the festivals of San Juan (24 June) and Santiago Apóstol (St James 25 July) with processions and dances including the Liseres, in which the participants wear jaguar costumes.

Places to Stay & Eat

Hotel Morelos (☎ 7-04-04) has Morelos 12 as its address but its entrance is actually on Obregón, which runs off Morelos almost opposite the Autotransportes Los Tuxtlas bus station. Rooms cost US$8.50/11.75 and have fans and private bath with hot water but aren't very big. Some are brighter than others.

The tall *Hotel Castellanos* (☎ 7-02-00) on the zócalo at the corner of 5 de Mayo and Comonfort, is amazingly good for a small town, with a clean swimming pool and 48 bright, clean, panoramic, air-conditioned rooms of varying sizes. Singles/doubles are US$20/26.75. It also has a pleasant restaurant where egg dishes cost US$3, meat or chicken US$5 to US$7 and seafood a bit more. Cheaper eateries line up on the far side of the zócalo.

Getting There & Away

Santiago is served by fewer 1st-class ADO buses than San Andrés Tuxtla: if there are no convenient services use San Andrés as your transport hub and travel to/from Santiago by the frequent but cramped and suspension-free 2nd-class buses of Autotransportes Los Tuxtlas, or by taxi (US$5). The ADO station is at the junction of Morelos and the highway. Autotransportes Los Tuxtlas is a short way along Morelos from there.

Leaving Santiago, ADO has a few de paso buses each day to Acayucan (US$2, two hours), Veracruz (US$2.75, 2½ hours), Xalapa (US$5, 3½ hours), Puebla (US$9.50, seven hours) and Mexico City (US$12.50, 8½ hours).

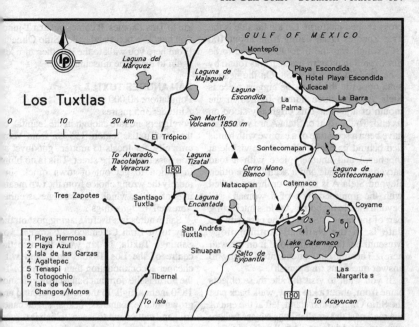

Los Tuxtlas

0   10   20 km

1 Playa Hermosa
2 Playa Azul
3 Isla de las Garzas
4 Agaltepec
5 Tenaspi
6 Totogochio
7 Isla de los Changos/Monos

Autotransportes Los Tuxtlas departs every few minutes for San Andrés Tuxtla (US$0.30), Catemaco (US$0.60) and Veracruz (US$2.50), and about hourly to Acayucan (US$2).

TRES ZAPOTES

The important late Olmec centre of Tres Zapotes is now just a series of mounds in maize fields, but many interesting finds are displayed at the museum in the village, 23 km across the plains west of Santiago Tuxtla.

History

Tres Zapotes was probably first occupied while the great Olmec centre of La Venta in Tabasco still flourished. It carried on after the destruction of La Venta in about 400 BC, in what archaeologists regard as an 'epi-Olmec' phase when the spark had gone out of Olmec culture, and other civilisations – notably Izapa – were also leaving their mark

here. Most of the finds are from this later period.

At Tres Zapotes in 1939 Matthew Stirling, the first great Olmec excavator, unearthed part of a chunk of basalt with an epi-Olmec were-jaguar carving on one side and, on the other, a series of bars and dots apparently giving part of a date in the Maya Long Count dating system. Stirling decoded the date as 3 September, 32 BC – which would mean that the Olmecs had preceded the Maya, who until then were believed to have been Mexico's earliest civilisation. Much controversy followed but other finds over the next decades supported Stirling's discovery. In 1969 a local farmer came across the rest of the stone, now called Stele C, which bore the missing part of Stirling's date.

Museum

Tres Zapotes museum is open daily 9 am to 4 pm. Entry is US$1.75 (free on Sunday and holidays). The objects are arranged on a cross-shaped platform. On the far side is the Tres Zapotes head, dating from about 100 BC, which was the first Olmec head to be discovered in modern times; it was found by a hacienda worker in 1858. On the nearest side, opposite the head, the biggest piece is Stela A, with three human figures in the mouth of a jaguar. This originally stood on its end. To the right of Stela A are what may have been a sculpture of a captive with hands tied behind its back ('fingers' are visible at the base) and another piece with a toad carved on one side and a skull on the other. Beyond Stela A is an altar or throne carved with the upturned face of a woman, and beyond that, in the corner, the less interesting part of the famous Stela C (the part with the date is in the National Anthropology Museum but there's a photo of it on the wall here). The museum attendant is happy to answer questions (in Spanish).

If you want to visit the site these objects came from, about a km away, walk back past the Sitio Olmeca taxi stand, left at the end of the road past the small village square (where you can get drinks at a small café), on over the bridge and along the road.

Getting There & Away
Autotransportes Los Tuxtlas runs buses to Tres Zapotes from San Andrés Tuxtla (US$1.25) via Santiago Tuxtla (US$1), supposedly every 1½ hours from 5.30 am to 2.30 pm, taking about an hour from San Andrés, but the schedule is unreliable. The last buses back supposedly leave Tres Zapotes at 1.30 and 3.30 pm.

The alternative is to get to Santiago Tuxtla first then take a green-and-white taxi to Tres Zapotes, for US$1 if it's going colectivo or US$6 if you have it all to yourself. They leave from the Sitio Puente Real, on the far side of the pedestrian bridge at the foot of Zaragoza, the street going downhill beside the Santiago Tuxtla museum.

A 'Zona Arqueológica' sign points the way to Tres Zapotes as you enter Santiago Tuxtla on Highway 180 from San Andrés Tuxtla. Eight km down this road, you fork right onto a decent dirt track for the last 15

km to Tres Zapotes. It comes out at a T-junction next to a taxi stand called Sitio Olmeca. From here you walk to the left, then turn left again to reach the museum.

SAN ANDRÉS TUXTLA
Population: 80,000
Altitude: 365 metres
Foreigners are rare enough in the 'capital' of the Los Tuxtlas region, 155 km from Veracruz city, for locals to mutter 'goodbye' as you pass them on the street. This is no blunt invitation to get out of town quick, but merely the wrong choice from the two meanings of *adiós*, which can translate as either 'farewell' or 'greetings'.

San Andrés is a useful staging post on the way to or from Catemaco, 12 km east, or Santiago Tuxtla, 14 km west. It's also the centre of the Los Tuxtlas area, and with cheaper accommodation than Catemaco. To the north is the dormant San Martín volcano, 1850 metres high. In the country around are grown maize, bananas, beans, sugar cane, fruit and cattle; and tobacco, which is turned into cigars *(puros)* in the town.

Orientation & Information
San Andrés' bus stations (except Autotransportes Los Tuxtlas) are on Juárez, which runs downhill to the town centre from Highway 180 on the west side of town. The church takes up a large part of the zócalo. The building immediately on your right as you enter the zócalo is the Palacio Municipal. Most to stay and eat are on or near Juárez or the plaza.

Banks on the zócalo and Juárez will change cash and travellers' cheques. The post office is on Lafragua: head down 20 de Noviembre directly across the zócalo from the Palacio Municipal and follow it round to the left. The market is three blocks down Rascón (the street between the Hotel Del Parque and the Canada shoe shop) from the zócalo.

Things to See
One or two spots in the country around San Andrés are worth considering if you have

me to spare in Los Tuxtlas. The **Laguna Encantada** ('Enchanted Lagoon'), a lake with the odd habit of rising in dry weather and falling when it rains, occupies a small volcanic crater three km north-east of San Andrés. A dirt road goes there but no buses.

A 242-step staircase leads down to the 40-metre-high, 40-metre-wide **Salto de Eyipantla** waterfall, 12 km from San Andrés. Autotransportes Los Tuxtlas buses (US$0.50) run about half-hourly to Eyipantla, taking 40 minutes. The route follows Highway 180 east for four km to Sihuapan, then turns right down a dirt road.

At Cerro del Gallo near **Matacapan**, just east of Sihuapan, is an early Classic (300-600 AD) pyramid in Teotihuacán style. It may have been on the route to Kaminaljuyú in Guatemala, the farthest-flung Teotihuacán outpost.

Places to Stay

For the cheapest hotels turn left when you hit the zócalo from Juárez, then take the second right, Pino Suárez. The *Hotel Catedral* (☎ (294) 2-02-37) at the corner of Pino Suárez and Bocanegra has large, quite clean rooms with fan, private bath and 24-hour hot water for US$5/6.75. A bit further up the street, the *Hotel Figueroa* (☎ (294) 2-02-57) also has clean rooms with fan, private bath (not always so clean) and hot water, for US$5/8.25. Some are a lot better than others.

Hotel San Andrés (☎ (294) 2-06-04) at Madero 6 (turn right when you hit the zócalo from Juárez) is fair value and therefore sometimes full. Its 31 clean rooms with TV and private bath cost US$11.75/16.75 with fan, US$13.50/18.50 with air-con. Some have balconies. The staff are friendly.

The two top places in town are the 48-room *Hotel Del Parque* (☎ (294) 2-01-98) at Madero 5 on the zócalo and the *Hotel De Los Pérez* (☎ (294) 2-07-77) at Rascón 2, down the street beside the Del Parque. The newer De Los Pérez is our preference for its clean, sizeable, modern, air-con rooms with TV at US$14.50/20 uncarpeted or US$16.25/21.75 carpeted. The Del Parque's rooms,

also air-con and with TV, are lighter but a little faded, for US$16/21.50.

Places to Eat

San Andrés has a fine corner seafood restaurant that you'd hardly notice if you didn't know it was there. It's *Mariscos Chazaro* at Madero 12, just along from the Hotel San Andrés. Surroundings (apart from a cartoon of the owner as the 'alchemist of the sea') are nothing special, even flyblown, but each order is prepared before your eyes with multiple ingredients and much care, and the results are delicious. Sopa de mariscos (US$4.50) is a tasty meal in itself.

The *Hotel Del Parque* restaurant is the social centre of town and its service is professional but the food is nothing inspired (egg dishes US$1.75 to US$2.75, meat or chicken US$5 to US$8, seafood around US$8). For vaguely Westernised fare visit the *Cafetería California* at Rascón 2, beneath the Hotel De Los Pérez. You'll get a respectable burger for US$2.50, tuna salad for US$2.50, carrot or other juices for US$1.50.

Things to Buy

The Santa Lucia factory at Blvd 5 de Febrero 10 (Highway 180), about 200 metres from the top of Juárez, has short, long, fat and thin cigars at factory prices. Even if you don't want to buy, the sights and smells of cigar-making are interesting.

Getting There & Away

Bus San Andrés is the transport centre for Los Tuxtlas, with fairly good bus services in every direction – though many are de paso, with limited seats, so try to book ahead. First-class buses are by ADO, whose station is at the top of Juárez, on the corner of Highway 180. AU (2nd-class) is a couple of blocks down Juárez towards the town centre. The 2nd-class buses of Autotransportes Los Tuxtlas – old, dirty and slow but often the quickest way of getting to local destinations – leave from the corner of Independencia and Rafael Solana Norte. From the zócalo head down Rascón (beside the Hotel Del Parque) for three blocks to the market; then turn right and take the first left. Departures from San Andrés include:

Acayucan – 95 km, 1½ hours; a few 1st-class buses daily for US$1.75, seven 2nd-class buses daily by AU, 2nd-class buses by Autotransportes Los Tuxtlas about every half-hour.

Campeche – 770 km, 12½ hours; two 1st-class buses daily for US$14.75.

Catemaco – 12 km, 20 minutes; 2nd-class buses by Autotransportes Los Tuxtlas every few minutes.

Mérida – 1020 km, 15 hours; two 1st-class buses daily for US$18.50.

Mexico City (TAPO) – 550 km, nine hours; eight 1st-class buses daily for US$12.50.

Puebla – 420 km, seven hours; five 1st-class buses daily for US$8.75.

Salina Cruz – 330 km, 6½ hours; one overnight 1st-class bus for US$8.75.

Santiago Tuxtla – 14 km, 20 minutes; 2nd-class buses by Autotransportes Los Tuxtlas every few minutes for US$0.30.

Veracruz – 155 km, 2¾ hours; 28 1st-class buses daily for US$3, 2nd-class buses by Autotransportes Los Tuxtlas every few minutes.

Villahermosa – 320 km, six hours; nine 1st-class buses daily for US$6.

Xalapa – 250 km, 4½ hours; nine 1st-class buses daily for US$5.

Taxi A taxi to or from Catemaco or Santiago Tuxtla costs about US$5.

CATEMACO
Population: 25,000
Altitude: 370 metres

This small, scruffy town on the western shore of a beautiful lake, 12 km east of San Andrés Tuxtla, makes most of its living from fishing and from Mexican tourists who flood into it in July, August, and particularly around Christmas, New Year and Semana Santa. The rest of the year it's a quiet, economical place to visit. An annual convention of *brujos* (witch doctors) is held on Cerro Mono Blanco (White Monkey Hill) north of Catemaco on the first Friday in March.

Orientation & Information
Catemaco is small and easily walkable, sloping gently down to the lake shore. You can change cash and travellers' cheques at Multibanco Comermex on the zócalo. The post office is on Aldama, two blocks down

from the zócalo. The market is on Madero 1½ blocks from the zócalo.

Laguna Catemaco
The lake, surrounded by volcanic hills, is roughly oval, 16 km long and averages about six km wide. It has several islands; on the largest, Tenaspi, Olmec sculpture has been found. Streams flowing into the lake are the source of Catemaco and Coyame mineral water.

Boat Trips There are always plenty of boats ready to take people out from the moorings just down from the zócalo. Prices for different destinations are posted, but you can try bargaining, especially out of season. Sometimes they go on a colectivo basis, with each of up to six passengers paying about a quarter of the fare that would be demanded for the whole boat.

One of the most popular trips is to Tanaxpillo Island, better known as Isla de los Monos or Isla de los Changos (Monkey Island). Around 60 red-cheeked *Macaca Arctoides* monkeys, originally from Thailand, live here. They belong to the University of Veracruz which uses them for research purposes. Despite pleas from the university for the animals to be left alone, boat operators bring food for them so that tourists can get close-up pictures. The posted price for up to six people for the half-hour trip to Monkey Island and back is US$13.50 but you should be able to cut it to about US$10.

Lake Walk
The lakefront road turns into a path at the eastern edge of the town for a pleasant hour's waterside stroll as far as the big Hotel Playa Azul. On the way, at El Tegal, is a grotto topped with a blue cross where the Virgin is believed to have appeared in the 19th century. Further on is Playa Hermosa, less a beach than a narrow strip of grey sand. The water's a bit murky but not too cold.

East of the Lake
To explore the villages and country east of the lake, where the mountain Santa Mart

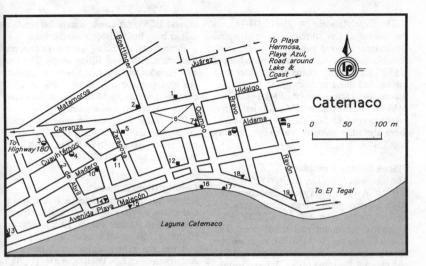

Catemaco

1   Hotel Catemaco
2   Hotel Acuario
3   AU Bus Station
4   Autotransportes Los Tuxtlas Bus Station
5   Hotel Gallardo
6   Zócalo
7   Church
8   ADO Bus Station
9   Post Office
10 Hotel Los Arcos
11 Market
12 Hotel Julita
13 Hotel Del Lago
14 La Luna Restaurant
15 La Ola Restaurant
16 Boats
17 Fisherman Monument
18 Bar El Pescador
19 Los Sauces Restaurant

stands out, take a local bus going to Las Margaritas. They leave every hour or two from the corner of Juárez and Rayón, by the Tienda La Surtidora del Sur.

Festivals
The pretty domed and towered church of the Virgen del Carmen in Catemaco's zócalo is a pilgrimage centre for a couple of days leading up to 16 July.

Places to Stay
Catemaco has accommodation across the price range, but add 30% to 50% at the peak periods.

Places to Stay – bottom end
Camping *Restaurant Solotepec* at Playa Hermosa, 1½ km east of town along the road round the lake, has a small camping area/trailer park close to the water. The road out of town starts where the rutted town streets end; start by going down Hidalgo from the zócalo. The *Hotel Canarias*, outside town on Highway 180 to Acayucan, has a trailer park.

Hotels The *Hotel Julita* at Avenida Playa 10, near the waterfront just down from the zócalo, has a few basic but sizeable and clean rooms with fan and private bath for US$7/8.50. The *Hotel Gallardo* on Zaragoza has fan-cooled rooms with private bath for US$7.50/9.25. Most are tiny but adequately clean: upstairs is airier. You only get hot water here if you ask for it to be turned on.

The *Hotel Acuario* (☎ (294) 3-04-18), on the zócalo at the corner of Carranza and Boettinger, is good value with large, comfortable singles/doubles with private bath at US$9/11.25. Some rooms are brighter than others, and those upstairs are in better condition. *Hotel Los Arcos* (☎ (294) 3-00-03) at Madero 7 on the corner of Mantilla has clean, bright rooms with fans and private baths, and there are wide balcony walkways. Rooms cost US$9.25/11.50.

Places to Stay – middle

The lakefront *Hotel Del Lago* (☎ (294) 3-01-60) on Avenida Playa at the corner of Abasolo, has good, clean, if not very big air-con rooms with TV for US$20/23.50. There's a restaurant and small pool. The *Hotel Catemaco* (☎ 3-00-45), right on the zócalo, also has rooms with air-con and TV, and charges the same prices. It has a restaurant, video bar and pool.

The *Hotel Playa Azul* (☎ (294) 3-00-01), 2½ km east of town by the lake, has 80 bright, clean, modern rooms, half of them air-con, in single-storey blocks around a garden. Singles/doubles are US$30/35 and there is also a restaurant, volleyball court, boat rental and disco (in season). The lakeside *Hotel La Finca* (☎ (294) 3-03-22), two km out of town on the Acayucan road, has 36 rooms with air-con, balconies and lake views at US$25/30. A taxi to either place from town costs around US$1.50.

Places to Eat

The lake provides the specialities here, among them the tegogolo, a lake snail reputed to be an aphrodisiac and best eaten in a sauce of chile, tomato, onion and lime; chipalchole, a soup with shrimp or crab claws; mojarra, a type of perch; and anguilas (eels). Tachogobi is a hot sauce sometimes served on mojarra; eels may come with raisins and hot chile.

The waterfront is dotted with restaurants where you can dine from lake, sea or land. *La Ola* is popular for its lovely setting though its cooking's only average: a main course of mojarra or tegogolo here costs around US$5. *La Luna*, across the road, is just as busy but without quite the view.

Further east the *Hotel Julita* has a cheaper restaurant with good, filling soups. The *Bar El Pescador* and the *Los Sauces* restaurant are also popular and about 20% to 25% cheaper than La Ola. Most of these places are closed by 7 pm out of season.

The *Hotel Catemaco* restaurant serves quite good food – spaghetti US$4, chicken and meat dishes US$4.50 to US$7.50, mojarra en tachogobi US$4.

Getting There & Away

Relatively few long-distance buses reach Catemaco, so you may find it easier to travel to/from San Andrés Tuxtla, 12 km west on Highway 180, or Acayucan, 80 km south, and use the grimy, noisy local buses of Autotransportes Los Tuxtlas, or a taxi (US$5 from San Andrés), to get to/from Catemaco. ADO, at the corner of Aldama and Bravo, is the only 1st-class bus company here. AU, 2nd-class, is on 2 de Abril just off Carranza. Autotransportes Los Tuxtlas is on Cuauhtémoc near the corner of 2 de Abril. Departures from Catemaco include:

Acayucan – 80 km, 1¼ hours; two 1st-class buses daily for US$1.75, seven 2nd-class buses daily by AU, 2nd-class buses by Autotransportes Los Tuxtlas about every half-hour.
Mexico City (TAPO) – 565 km, nine hours; one 1st-class bus daily for US$12.75 and four 2nd-class buses by AU.
San Andrés Tuxtla – 12 km, 20 minutes; four 1st-class buses daily for US$0.25, eight 2nd-class buses daily by AU, 2nd-class buses by Autotransportes Los Tuxtlas every few minutes.
Santiago Tuxtla – 25 km, 40 minutes; four 1st-class buses daily for US$0.60, 2nd-class buses by Autotransportes Los Tuxtlas every few minutes.
Veracruz – 165 km, three hours; about five 1st-class buses daily for US$3.25, 2nd-class buses by Autotransportes Los Tuxtlas every few minutes.
Villahermosa – 310 km, 5½ hours; one 1st-class bus daily for US$6 and one 2nd-class bus by AU.
Xalapa – 265 km, five hours; one 1st-class bus daily for US$5.75, three 2nd-class buses by AU.

THE COAST NEAR CATEMACO

About four km east of Catemaco, a rutted dirt

road heads north off the Coyame road to a little-visited part of the Gulf Coast. This is mainly ranchland, horses are a common form of transport, and green hills roll right down to the shore.

Sontecomapan, 18 km from Catemaco at the head of a lagoon, has a couple of restaurants and you can hire boats on the lagoon. To La Barra (a small fishing settlement at the mouth of the lagoon) and back costs about US$10.

From Sontecomapan the track climbs over a hill, with a superb view of the lagoon below. After about nine km is a small junction where a half-hidden sign points to 'Playa Escondida, El Eden de Dios 2 km'. The walk down this sidetrack takes you past the long grey-sand beach of **Jicacal**, with a small, poor fishing village, then up to a forested headland where the *Hotel Playa Escondida* stands. This unassuming establishment has basic rooms (shower but no hot water) for US$12/15 and a small restaurant. There are great views down to Playa Jicacal and the smaller Playa Escondida on the other side. It's that rare thing in Mexico – a rural retreat. A steep path leads down from the hotel to Playa Escondida.

Back on the 'road' you pass a biological research station next to one of the few tracts of unspoiled rainforest left on the Gulf Coast. Station staff may be able to point you to paths through the forest. The end of the road is at Montepío, about seven km from Playa Escondida.

Getting There & Away

Autotransportes Los Tuxtlas buses from Catemaco bump, grind and lurch as far as Montepío five or six times daily between 6 am and 3 or 4 pm, traumatising the numerous piglets by the roadside. To Playa Escondida takes 1½ hours for US$1. Alternatively the Hotel Los Arcos and one or two other places in Catemaco run eight-hour tours out here for US$20 including a meal. A round trip by taxi costs about US$20 to Sontecomapan, US$35 to Playa Escondida. Hitching a lift is possible but not wholly reliable.

ACAYUCAN

Acayucan is a road-junction town where Highway 185 heads off south across the Isthmus of Tehuantepec from Highway 180, leading to the Pacific coasts of Oaxaca and Chiapas. It sometimes makes sense to change buses here, while for drivers it may be a convenient overnight stop. Archaeology fans might want to seek out the Olmec site of San Lorenzo, 35 km away.

Orientation & Information

To reach the central Plaza de Armas from the bus stations on the east side of town, go back to Hidalgo, the road your bus has just turned off, turn left, and walk six blocks. The Plaza de Armas has a dovecot in the middle, a modern church on one side and the town hall on the other. Bancomer on Hidalgo, just down the hill from the Plaza de Armas, changes travellers' cheques.

Places to Stay

The *Hotel Ritz* (☎ 5-00-24), between the bus stations and the central plaza at Hidalgo 7, has quite big, reasonably clean singles/doubles with fan and private bath for US$7.50/9. On the plaza, the *Hotel Joalicia* (☎ 5-08-77) at Zaragoza 4 on the corner of Victoria, is good value for its clean, sizeable rooms with private bath, balcony, reading light and telephone (for all those long-lost friends you want to call in Acayucan) at US$9/14 with fan, or US$14.50 single or double with air-con. The top place is the *Hotel Kinaku* (☎ 5-04-10) at Ocampo Sur 7, a block from the plaza, behind the church. Spacious, comfortable air-con rooms, with TV, cost US$30/40.

Places to Eat

The restaurant in the *Hotel Joalicia* is a good place to eat, with antojitos around US$2, and meats at US$3.50 to US$6. There are also a few restaurants on Hidalgo in the Plaza de Armas – *La Parrilla* looks the best. The restaurant in the *Hotel Kinaku*, open 7 am to 11 pm, is the smartest place in town.

Getting There & Away

If you're driving south across the isthmus from Acayucan, be warned that around La Ventosa shortly before Juchitán, very strong winds sometimes blow high vehicles off the road.

The bus station is by the market, off Hidalgo six blocks east of the Plaza de Armas. Departures include:

Catemaco – 80 km, 1¼ hours; two 1st-class buses daily by ADO for US$1.75, seven 2nd-class buses daily by AU, half-hourly 2nd-class buses by Autotransportes Los Tuxtlas.

Juchitán – 195 km, three hours; several buses daily by Cristóbal Colón (1st-class, US$3.75) and Sur (2nd-class).

Mexico City (TAPO) – 750 km, 11 hours; several 1st-class buses daily by ADO and Cristóbal Colón for US$14.25, and 2nd-class buses by AU.

Salina Cruz – 210 km, four hours; several buses daily by Cristóbal Colón (1st-class, US$4.50) and Sur (2nd-class).

San Andrés Tuxtla – 95 km, 1½ hours; a few 1st-class buses daily by ADO for US$1.75, several 2nd-class buses daily by AU, 2nd-class buses by Autotransportes Los Tuxtlas about half-hourly.

Santiago Tuxtla – 110 km, two hours; a few 1st-class buses daily by ADO for US$2, 2nd-class buses by Autotransportes Los Tuxtlas about hourly.

Tapachula – 550 km, nine hours; a few buses daily by Cristóbal Colón (1st-class, US$10.75) and Sur (2nd-class).

Tuxtla Gutiérrez – 500 km, eight hours; one 1st-class bus each daily by Cristóbal Colón and ADO for US$8.50.

Veracruz – 250 km, five hours; about 15 1st-class buses daily by ADO for US$5.

Villahermosa – 225 km, 3½ hours; several 1st-class buses by ADO and Cristóbal Colón daily for US$4.75, and 2nd-class buses by AU.

SAN LORENZO

The first of the two great Olmec ceremonial centres, which flourished from about 1200 to 900 BC, is about 35 km south-east of Acayucan, near the Río Chiquito, a tributary of the Coatzacoalcos. Most of the main finds are in museums elsewhere.

The extraordinary main structure is a platform about 50 metres high, 1¼ km long and 700 metres wide, thought to have been built by human hands. Ridges jutting from its sides may have been meant to produce a bird or animal-shaped ground plan.

Eight Olmec heads have been found here, and other large stone objects have been detected underground. Some very heavy stone thrones, with figures of rulers carved in the side, were also found, as well as butchered and burnt human bones which indicate cannibalism, and tools of the black volcanic glass, obsidian, imported from Guatemala or the highlands of Mexico. Such wide contacts, and the labour involved in building the site and transporting the basalt for the heads and thrones from the Sierra de los Tuxtlas, show how powerful the rulers of San Lorenzo were. San Lorenzo also had an elaborate stone-pipe drainage system. During its dramatic destruction, which occurred around 900 BC, most of the big carvings were mutilated, dragged on to the ridges and covered with earth.

Getting There & Away

From Acayucan take a bus to Texistepec (south of the Coatzacoalcos road), then another to San Lorenzo, a total journey of 1½ to two hours. San Lorenzo proper is three km south-west of the village of Tenochtitlán. Finds have also been made at Tenochtitlán and at Potrero Nuevo, three km south-east of San Lorenzo.

MINATITLÁN & COATZACOALCOS

These two towns 50 and 70 km respectively east of Acayucan, now bypassed, mushroomed into transport and refining centres of nearly half a million people each in the oil boom of the late 1970s. The area is an industrial wilderness though Coatzacoalcos, until a couple of decades ago an easygoing fishing port, retains its pleasant central plaza and has an impressive new bridge over the river which it's named after. There are plenty of hotels here for the oil people but nothing to make anyone else want to stay.

Oaxaca State

The rugged southern state of Oaxaca (wa-HA-ka) reaches to within just 250 km of Mexico City but, divided from central Mexico by ranks of hard-to-penetrate mountains, remains a world away in atmosphere. It enjoys a slower, sunnier existence which requires a little adjustment if you come upon it suddenly – by a Mexico City-Oaxaca flight, for instance. Its special, somehow magical, quality has something to do with the rugged dry landscape, the remoteness, the bright southern light, the sparse population, and the high number of Indians, who are the driving force behind the state's specially fine handcrafts.

Oaxaca city has become a big travel destination, but remains beautiful, lively, artistic and colonial. Nearby in the Central Valleys of Oaxaca are thriving village markets and spectacular ruins of pre-Hispanic Indian towns like Monte Albán and Yagul. On the Oaxaca coast, Mexico's newest mega-resort is being born on the lovely Bahías de Huatulco (Bays of Huatulco). Puerto Escondido and Puerto Ángel are older beach spots which will probably always remain small-scale and laid-back.

In the aforementioned places, mestizo influence is at its strongest. There's also enough Indian-inhabited back country, as far from Oaxaca city in culture and travelling time as Oaxaca is from Mexico City, to offer a lifetime's exploring – though initially you may get a cautious reception since the people have been driven to these retreats by centuries of conflict.

HISTORY
Zapotecs & Mixtecs
Pre-Hispanic Oaxaca traded with other parts of Mexico, and the influence of the Olmecs, Teotihuacán and the Maya was felt here, but until the Aztecs arrived in the 15th century, Oaxaca's several cultures were left more or less undisturbed to reach heights rivalling those of central Mexico.

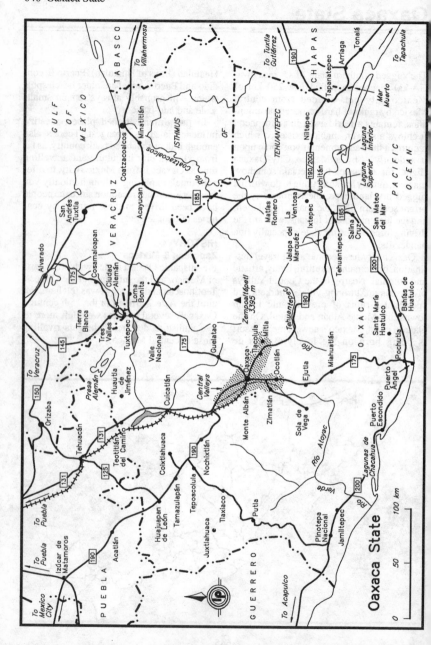

Oaxaca State

The Central Valleys have always been the hub of life in Oaxaca and building began at the magnificent hilltop site of Monte Albán about 500 BC. This became the centre of the Zapotec culture, which extended its control over the Central Valleys and other parts of Oaxaca by conquest. Zapotec civilisation peaked between 250 and 750 AD, by which time there were at least 200 other settlements or ceremonial sites in the Central Valleys, plus extensive irrigation. Monte Albán grew into a town of perhaps 25,000 people. But it declined suddenly, and by about 750 AD, along with many other Zapotec sites in the Central Valleys, was deserted.

From about 1200 those that remained came under the growing dominance of the Mixtecs, renowned potters and metalsmiths from what are now the north-west uplands of the state. Mixtec and Zapotec cultures became entangled in the Central Valleys before, with the north-west, they fell to the Aztecs in the mid-15th and early 16th centuries, and became tribute-payers.

Colonial Era

The Spaniards received a very hostile reception in Oaxaca, sending at least four expeditions before the city of Oaxaca was founded in 1529. Cortés donated large parts of the Central Valleys to himself and was officially named Marqués del Valle de Oaxaca. The Indian population slumped disastrously. The Central Valleys, which had about 150,000 Indians in 1568, had only 40,000 to 50,000 just 70 years later. Rebellions continued into the 20th century but the different peoples rarely united to form a serious threat.

Juárez & Díaz

Benito Juárez, the great reforming leader of the liberal side in mid-19th-century Mexico, was a Zapotec from northern Oaxaca. He served two terms as state governor, opening new village schools and cutting the bureaucracy, between 1848 and his election as national president in 1861.

Juárez appointed Porfirio Díaz, son of a Oaxaca horse trainer, state governor in 1862.

Díaz rebelled against Juárez' presidency in 1871 and went on to control Mexico with an iron fist from 1877 to 1910. While his rule kept the peace and brought the country into the industrial age, it fostered corruption, repression, foreign ownership of resources and, eventually, the Revolution. In Valle Nacional in northern Oaxaca, for instance, tobacco planters set up virtual slave plantations, most of whose 15,000 workers, according to the American writer J K Turner who visited them, had to be replaced annually because of deaths from disease, starvation or beating.

20th Century

The revolutionary decade, 1910 to 1920, saw Oaxaca dissolve into a chaos of shifting allegiances. In 1913 a group of *jefes serranos* (strongmen from the hills) won control and decided to dissociate Oaxaca from the national factions, declaring self-government. Though Oaxaca city was taken by the liberal Constitutionalists in 1916, the jefes serranos carried on fighting and in 1920 they allied with Álvaro Obregón to depose the national Constitutionalist government. They again controlled Oaxaca briefly but were replaced as Obregón and Plutarco Calles consolidated their hold on the country.

About 300 ejidos were set up in the 1930s, but land ownership is still a source of friction today. With little industry, Oaxaca is one of Mexico's poorest states. Many peasants are forced to seek work in the big cities or the USA – a situation worsened in some areas by deforestation, overuse of land and erosion. Tourism is increasingly important to the economy of Oaxaca city and some places on the coast.

GEOGRAPHY & CLIMATE

At 94,000 sq km, Oaxaca is Mexico's fifth biggest state. Its western two-thirds are rugged and mountainous; towards the east it occupies the southern half of the hot, low-lying Isthmus of Tehuantepec, Mexico's narrow 'waist'. Oaxaca also includes a thin plain along the Pacific coast, and a low-lying north-central region bordering Veracruz.

The western mountains are basically two ranges. The Sierra Madre del Sur (average height 2000 metres) enters Oaxaca from the west and stretches along the coast to the Isthmus of Tehuantepec. The Sierra Madre de Oaxaca (average height 2500 metres) runs down the west-central part of the state from Mexico's central volcanic belt. The two ranges meet roughly in the centre of the state. Between them lie the Central Valleys, containing the city of Oaxaca. The highest peak is Zempoaltépetl (3395 metres) near Zacatepec.

The Central Valleys are warm and dry. Centigrade temperatures range from the low teens on winter nights to the low 30s during the day in summer. Most of the annual 60 cm of rain falls from June to September. On the coast and in the low-lying areas it's hotter and a bit wetter.

PEOPLE

Oaxaca's 3.2 million population includes about a million Indians of at least 17 different peoples, a fifth of all Indians in Mexico. Each people has its own language and only perhaps three-quarters of Oaxaca Indians speak Spanish (as a foreign language). Some Indian ways are buckling under the pressure of change – colourful costumes for instance are seen less and less in Oaxaca city and the coastal resorts – but there's a strong Indian presence everywhere, noticeable in handcrafts, markets and festivals as well as dress.

Indian land is often the poorest in the state. Typically, Indians live in small, often single-room, houses, own land communally and share work. Relations between Indian groups', and with the mestizos who dominate property, business and politics, are often strained. When Indian organisations fight for land rights, the reaction of the powers-that-be is sometimes literally murderous.

Virtually all visitors come into contact with Oaxaca's most numerous Indian people, the Zapotecs – though often without realising it since there are few obvious signs to identify them. Some 350,000 Zapotecs live mainly in and around the Central Valleys

and on the Isthmus of Tehuantepec. Most are farmers, though they're also involved in trading their produce, which includes handcrafts and mezcal. Many, however, have to emigrate temporarily for work.

The Mixtecs are second-biggest Indian people, and some 300,000 of them are spread around the mountainous borders of Oaxaca, Guerrero and Puebla, with over two-thirds in western Oaxaca. The two other most numerous are the 100,000-plus Mazatecs in the far north, who retain much of their traditional dress and belief in a magical and ritual world; and the 80,000 Mixes, spread over the isolated highlands north-east of the Central Valleys.

Another group you may well see in Oaxaca city, since the women, wearing bright red huipils, populate some craft markets there, are the Triquis from western Oaxaca. They are perhaps only 12,000 strong.

DRUGS

Oaxaca is one of Mexico's main marijuana-growing areas, and magic mushrooms, used by some Indians for ceremonial or medical purposes, are common too. If you want either, take care who you buy them from.

Oaxaca

OAXACA
Population: 220,000
Altitude: 1550 metres

The state's capital and only sizeable city is a Spanish-built place of narrow, straight streets liberally sprinkled with lovely colonial buildings. It stands at the meeting point of the three Central Valleys of Oaxaca.

What's special about Oaxaca is its atmosphere – at once relaxed and energetic, remote and cosmopolitan. The sun, the dry mountain air, the city's manageable scale, its old buildings, plazas and cafés help slow the pace of life. At the same time the Indian peoples' millennia of residence in the area, an artistic liveliness and their Indian and

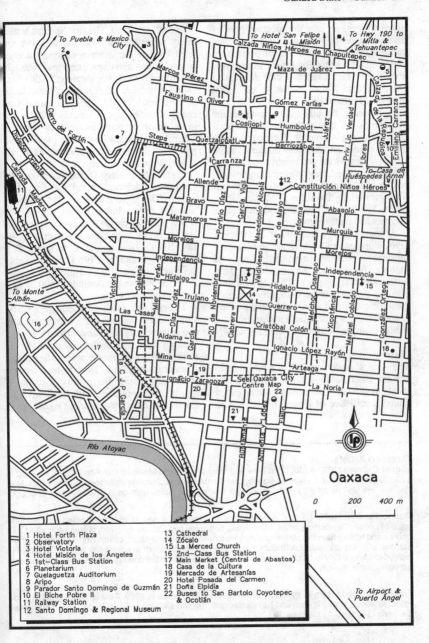

To Puebla & Mexico City

To Hotel San Felipe Misión

To Hwy 190 to Mitla & Tehuantepec

Calzada Niños Héroes de Chapultepec

Maza de Juárez

Marcos Pérez

Faustino G Oliver

Gómez Farfás

Cosijopi

Humboldt

Quetzalcóatl

Berriozábal

Carranza

Allende

Constitución Niños Héroes

To Casa de Huéspedes Arnel

Bravo

Abasolo

Matamoros

Murguía

Morelos

Morelos

Independencia

Independencia

Hidalgo

Hidalgo

Trujano

Guerrero

Las Casas

Cristóbal Colón

Aldama

Mina

Ignacio López Rayón

Arteaga

Ignacio Zaragoza

See Oaxaca City Centre Map

La Noria

Río Atoyac

To Monte Albán

Cerro del Fortín

División Oriente

Calzada Madero

Calzada de la República

Emiliano Carranza

Victoria

Galeana

Mier Y Terán

Díaz Ordaz

P García

A C J P García

20 de Noviembre

Cabrera

Porfirio Díaz

García Vigil

Macedonio Alcalá

5 de Mayo

Reforma

Melchor Ocampo

Xicoténcatl

Manuel Doblado

González Ortega

Priv Lic Verdad

Libres

Juárez

Valdivieso

Fiallo

Bustamante

Armenta y López

Oaxaca

0   200   400 m

To Airport & Puerto Ángel

1 Hotel Fortín Plaza
2 Observatory
3 Hotel Victoria
4 Hotel Misión de los Ángeles
5 1st–Class Bus Station
6 Planetarium
7 Guelaguetza Auditorium
8 Aripo
9 Parador Santo Domingo de Guzmán
10 El Biche Pobre II
11 Railway Station
12 Santo Domingo & Regional Museum

13 Cathedral
14 Zócalo
15 La Merced Church
16 2nd–Class Bus Station
17 Main Market (Central de Abastos)
18 Casa de la Cultura
19 Mercado de Artesanías
20 Hotel Posada del Carmen
21 Doña Elpidia
22 Buses to San Bartolo Coyotepec & Ocotlán

Spanish heritage, and the meeting here of diverse Oaxacan, Mexican and international cultures, all create a current of excitement which makes some foreigners return year after year. There's rarely a dull moment in Oaxaca. Head for the zócalo to get a first taste of the atmosphere.

Not least of the city's attractions are the abundant local handcrafts on sale. Experiencing Oaxaca is a matter of giving yourself time to ramble and see what markets, crafts, cafés and festivities you might come across. There are also many fascinating places within day-trip distance in the Central Valleys, notably the ruins at Monte Albán, Mitla, Yagul and Cuilapan, and the village markets and craft centres.

Accommodation in Oaxaca is inexpensive. Foreign and Mexican tourists are numerous, and an important source of income, but Oaxaca accommodates them with minimal impact. The unwelcome changes that have come to the city – notably the traffic din and fumes that make many central streets a pedestrian's nightmare – are part of changes in Mexican life in general.

History

The Aztecs' settlement here – established to enforce their hold over the tribute-paying locals in the late 15th century – was called Huaxyacac (Place of Gourds), from which

'Oaxaca' is derived. The first Spanish settlement, Segura de la Frontera, was 1½ km north-east of the modern centre, but after several Indian uprisings, a new town was laid out around the existing zócalo in 1529. It was called Antequera (after a part of Andalucía, Spain) until 1532, when its name was changed to Oaxaca. It quickly became the most important town in southern Mexico. The religious orders based here played a big part in pacifying the region's Indians by relatively humane conduct.

Eighteenth-century Oaxaca grew rich on exports of cochineal, a red dye from tiny insects. The boom ended in 1783 when the Spanish crown banned debt slavery, by which many of the 30,000 peasants producing cochineal were bound to traders in the city. But Oaxaca continued to thrive as a textile centre and by 1796 it was probably the third-biggest city in New Spain, with about 20,000 people (including 600 clergy) and 800 cotton looms.

The city elite were opposed to the early-19th-century independence movement and two envoys from the insurgent leader Miguel Hidalgo were shot in the city in 1810 (the street Armenta y López is named after them). A major earthquake in 1854 destroyed much of the city. Under the mainly peaceful, if repressive, presidency of Porfirio Díaz towards the end of the century Oaxaca began

Oaxacan Artists

Miguel Cabrera (1695-1768) Born here and went on to found Mexico's first Academy of Painting in 1753. Most of his best canvases, on religious themes, are in churches including Oaxaca's San Juan de Díos. He also painted a famous portrait of the nun Sor Juana Inés de la Cruz, the love poet.

Rufino Tamayo (1899-1991) A Zapotec born in Oaxaca, Tamayo is widely regarded as the fourth great Mexican 20th-century artist, with Rivera, Siqueiros and Orozco. His work is less concerned with politics and history than the others' and may be more abstract or stylised, or intent on everyday scenes. Tamayo also experimented with colour combinations which seem to reflect the light of Oaxaca. He moved to Mexico City in 1911 and lived much of his life outside the country, but gave his pre-Hispanic art collection to the city.

Francisco Toledo Born in 1940 in Juchitán; moved to Oaxaca in 1969. As well as his paintings, his woodcarvings are well known and he has designed blankets woven in Teotitlán del Valle. He founded the city's Graphic Arts Institute. ■

to grow again; in the 1890s its population passed 30,000.

During the Revolution, the Establishment was again conservative. The decade of turmoil cut the population from over 35,000 to under 28,000. An earthquake in 1931 left 70% of the city uninhabitable. Its major expansion has come in the past two decades with tourism and other new industries encouraging migration from the countryside.

Orientation

The centre of Oaxaca is the big, traffic-free zócalo. Adjoining it to the north-west is another traffic-free plaza, the Alameda, with the cathedral on its east side. Streets in the central area are on a grid plan and usually change their names when they pass the north-east corner of the cathedral. Macedonio Alcalá, running north from this corner to Santo Domingo church, a famous Oaxaca landmark, is mostly pedestrians-only.

Many hotels, restaurants and other services are within a few blocks of the zócalo. In general the few blocks north of the zócalo are smarter, cleaner and less traffic-infested than those to the south, especially the south-west, where cheap hotels and some markets congregate.

Highway 190 winds round the slopes of the Cerro del Fortín on its way in from the north, then runs eastward across the city as Calzada Niños Héroes de Chapultepec, 1¼ km north of the zócalo. The 1st-class bus station is beside this road, a 20-minute walk north-east of the zócalo. The 2nd-class bus station is almost a km west of the centre, near the main market.

Information

Tourist Offices Oaxaca has two tourist offices. Standards depend on who's on duty but on our last visit we found the info from the Palacio Municipal office (☎ (951) 6-38-10), at the corner of García Vigil and Independencia facing the Alameda, to be more reliable than that from the state tourist office (☎ (951) 6-48-28) at the corner of 5 de Mayo and Morelos. The latter has lower standards of English too – but better maps.

The Palacio Municipal office should be able to give initial help in emergencies. Both places are open 9 am to 8 pm daily.

Money Oaxaca bank queues are long and slow. The 1½ cents per dollar levied by the casas de cambio is a bargain for the time and aggravation they save – but beware of attempts to short-change you. Two near the zócalo, giving more or less identical rates when we checked, are Interdisa, a few steps up Valdivieso from the north-east corner of the zócalo, open 8 am to 8 pm Monday to Saturday and 9 am to 5 pm Sunday, and La Estrella at Alcalá 201, open 9 am to 1.30 pm and 4 to 7 pm, Monday to Saturday only.

If you have to use a bank, Bancomer at García Vigil 204 and Banamex at Hidalgo 821 are both about a block from the zócalo. (Bancomer's other building at García Vigil 202 doesn't do foreign exchange.) Most banks open from 9 am to 1 pm Monday to Friday, with foreign exchange closing at 11.30 am, but Banamex also does exchange from 4 to 5 pm.

Visa and MasterCard holders can get cash from the caja permanente machine in the Banamex lobby. MasterCard holders can also use the machine in Multibanco Comermex at Independencia 801.

The American Express representative is Viajes Micsa (☎ 6-27-00) at Valdivieso 2.

Post & Telecommunications The main post office, open Monday to Friday 9 am to 8 pm and Saturday 9 am to 1 pm, is on the Alameda, beside Independencia. Viajes Micsa, the American Express representative at Valdivieso 2, runs a client mail service. You can send or receive telegrams or faxes at the Telégrafos office on Independencia, next door to the post office and open the same hours. There are Ladatel phones at the north-west and south-west corners of the zócalo; one of those at the north-west takes credit cards. There's a long-distance phone caseta on Trujano between J P García and 20 de Noviembre.

Foreign Consulates The US consular agent

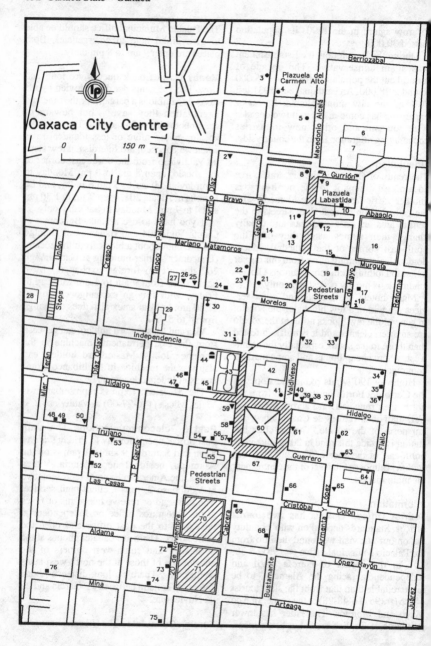

Oaxaca City Centre

0   150 m

(☎ 4-30-54) is at Alcalá 201. The Canadian and British representative (☎ 6-56-00) is at Hidalgo 817/5.

Laundry Superlavandería Hidalgo at the corner of Hidalgo and J P García, and Lavandería Automatica at 20 de Noviembre 605, both charge US$3.50 for a same-day service wash of up to 3.5 kg.

Media, Bookshops & Libraries The *Oaxaca Times*, a free monthly paper for tourists in English, contains much useful information. You can pick it up at Plaza Alcalá on the corner of Alcalá and Bravo, home of the Instituto de Comunicación y Cultura which publishes it.

The Biblioteca Circulante de Oaxaca (Oaxaca lending library) at Alcalá 305 has

---

■ PLACES TO STAY

1	Hotel Las Golondrinas
10	Posada Margarita
14	Hotel Calesa Real
16	Hotel Stouffer Presidente
17	Hotel Principal
19	Hotel Parador Plaza
24	Hotel Pombo
35	Posada San Pablo
38	Hotel Real de Antequera
45	Hotel Monte Albán
46	Hotel Central
48	Hotel Del Pacifico
49	Hotel San José
51	Hotel San Fernando
52	Hotel Vallarta
56	Hotel Las Rosas
58	Hotel Señorial
66	Hotel Gala
68	Hotel Aurora
69	Hotel Trebol
72	Hotel Rivera
73	Hotel Chayo
74	Hotel Pasaje
75	Hotel Típico
76	Hotel Mesón del Angel & Buses to Monte Albán

▼ PLACES TO EAT

2	Candela
9	Pizzería Alfredo da Roma
12	El Topil
23	Cafetería Bamby
25	Restaurant Flor de Loto
26	Plaza Gourmet
32	Quicklys
33	Restaurant Santa Fé
36	Los Chalotes
39	El Mesón
50	Cafetería Alex
53	Restaurant Flami

54	Cafetería Chip's
57	Café-Bar Del Jardín & El Asador Vasco
59	Mi Casita
61	El Zaguán
63	Restaurant Del Vitral
65	Restaurant La Flor de Oaxaca

OTHER

3	Museo Casa de Juárez
4	Carmen Alto Convent
5	Graphic Arts Institute
6	Museo Regional
7	Santo Domingo Church
8	Palacio Santo Domingo
11	Plaza Alcalá
13	Biblioteca Circulante
15	El Sol y La Luna
18	State Tourist Office
20	Casa de Cambio & US Consulate
21	Bancomer
22	Casa de Cambio
27	Museo Rufino Tamayo
28	La Soledad Church
29	San Felipe Neri Church
30	El Carmen Bajo Church
31	Palacio Municipal Tourist Office
34	Mexicana
37	Banamex
40	Viajes Micsa
41	Casa de Cambio
42	Cathedral
43	Alameda
44	Post Office
47	Aeroméxico
55	La Compañía Church
60	Zócalo
62	Aerovías Oaxaqueñas
64	San Agustín Church
67	Palacio de Gobierno
70	Juárez Market
71	20 de Noviembre Market

quite a big collection of books and magazines in English and Spanish, many of them on Oaxaca and Mexico. It's open 10 am to 1 pm Monday to Saturday plus 4 to 7 pm Monday to Friday. For a joining fee of US$8.50 you can borrow books. The library has a copy of *Lawrence in Oaxaca* by Ross Parmenter, an account of D H Lawrence's time in the state, where he wrote and set part of his novel *The Plumed Serpent*. The city's public library is also on Alcalá, at the corner of Morelos. The Graphic Arts Institute at Alcalá 507 has an excellent art library which visitors can consult.

The best Spanish bookshop is Proveedora Escolar at the corner of Reforma and Independencia. Its local history, archaeology and anthropology section, upstairs, is excellent. But you'll find more English books in Librería Universitaria, at Guerrero 108 just off the zócalo, or the bookshop upstairs in Palacio Santo Domingo at the corner of Alcalá and Allende. The regional and Rufino Tamayo museums also sell books. Good maps of outlying parts of the state are available from INEGI at Calzada Porfirio Díaz 241.

Zócalo & Alameda

The zócalo is the geographical and social heart of Oaxaca. Shady, traffic-free and lined with cafés and restaurants, it's the perfect place to relax and watch the city go by. The adjacent Alameda, without the cafés, is also a popular local gathering place.

The south side of the zócalo is lined by the **Palacio de Gobierno**, where the stairway has a mural depicting Oaxacan history. Its centre panel is devoted mainly to the 19th-century reformers, notably Juárez (shown with his wife Margarita) and Morelos. Porfirio Díaz appears below in blue. At bottom right, Guerrero's death at Cuilapan is shown. The left wall shows ancient Mitla while the right wall is dominated by women, notably Juana Inés de la Cruz, the 17th-century nun and love poet.

Oaxaca's **cathedral**, begun in 1553 and finished (after several bouts with earthquakes) in the 18th century, stands on the north side of the zócalo, partly behind the Hotel Marqués del Valle. Its main (west) façade on the Alameda has some fine baroque carving.

Buildings Near the Zócalo

Colonial churches with fine carved façades in the old market area are **La Compañía** (by the south-west corner of the zócalo) and the popular **San Juan de Díos**, dating from 1526 and the oldest church in Oaxaca, at the corner of Aldama and 20 de Noviembre. Carvings on **San Agustín**, on Guerrero 1½ blocks east of the zócalo, show scenes from the saint's life. The 1903 **Teatro Macedonio Alcalá** at the corner of 5 de Mayo and Independencia is in the French style fashionable under Porfirio Díaz. Its entrance hall is Louis XV, with a marble stairway. The five-tier auditorium holds 1300 people.

Alcalá

Calle Alcalá has been closed to traffic, and its fine stone buildings cleaned up and restored, to make a walking route to Santo Domingo church from one block north of the cathedral. Tourist-oriented shops and restaurants are scattered along the street but are in keeping with its colonial appearance.

Santo Domingo

Santo Domingo, four blocks north of the cathedral, is the most famous and splendid of Oaxaca's churches. Built mainly between 1570 and the early 17th century, it was the church of the city's Dominican monastery. The finest artisans were reputedly brought from Puebla and elsewhere to help create it and, like other large buildings in this earthquake-prone region, it has immensely thick stone walls. During the 19th-century wars and anti-clerical movements it was used as a stable.

Among the fine carving on the baroque façade, the figure holding a church is Santo Domingo de Guzmán, the 13th-century Spanish monk who founded the Dominican order, with its emphasis on study and teaching of the holy writ and strict vows of poverty, chastity and obedience. In Mexico the Dominicans gave the Indians some protection from the worst excesses of other colonists.

The church is usually locked from 1 to 4 pm. The interior, with lavish ornamentation in gilded and polychromed stucco, has a magically warm glow during candlelit evening services. Just inside the main door, on the ceiling, is an elaborate family tree of Santo Domingo de Guzmán. The 18th-century Capilla de la Virgen del Rosario (Rosary Chapel) on the south side is a profusion of yet more gilt.

Regional Museum

The highlight of the Museo Regional de Oaxaca, housed in the beautiful green stone cloister attached to Santo Domingo, is the Mixtec treasure from Tomb Seven at Monte Albán. This and other archaeological sections make most sense if you visit them after seeing some sites in the Central Valleys. All explanatory matter is in Spanish and there are no on-the-spot guides. The museum is open 10 am to 6 pm daily except Monday and entry is US$3.50 (free on Sunday and holidays).

The Mixtec trove – on the museum's upper floor – dates from the mid-14th century when the Mixtecs reused an old Zapotec tomb at Monte Albán to bury one of their kings and his sacrificed servants. With the bodies they placed a hoard of beautifully worked silver, turquoise, coral, jade, amber, jet, pearls, finely carved jaguar and eagle bone, and above all, gold. It was discovered in 1932 by Alfonso Caso. One superb gold pectoral on show is copied as earrings in numerous shops around the town. Other sections of the museum cover the history of Oaxaca state since the Spanish conquest, the state's Indian peoples, its archaeology, and the history of the Dominican order.

Graphic Arts Institute

The Instituto de Artes Gráficas de Oaxaca at Alcalá 507, almost opposite Santo Domingo, houses changing exhibitions of graphic art in a beautiful colonial house given by the artist Francisco Toledo, and has an excellent library. Opening hours are 10 am to 2 pm and 4 to 7 pm Wednesday to Saturday and Monday, 11 am to 5 pm Sunday. Donations are requested when you enter.

Museo Casa de Juárez

The Juárez house museum, at García Vigil 609 opposite Carmen Alto convent, is where Benito Juárez found work as a boy. A Zapotec with only a few words of Spanish, he came to Oaxaca in 1818 from the village of Guelatao, 60 km to the north. His employer Antonio Salanueva, a lay preacher and bookbinder, spotted the boy's potential

---

Benito Juárez

Juárez trained for the priesthood but abandoned it for law. He worked as a lawyer for poor villagers and became a member of the city council, then of the state government. Then, from 1848 to 1852, he became a liberal state governor, opening schools and cutting the bureaucracy. Exiled by the conservative government in 1853, Juárez returned in the 1855 Revolution of Ayutla with General Santa Anna and became justice minister in a liberal national government. His Ley (Law) Juárez, transferring the trials of soldiers and priests charged with civil crimes to ordinary civil courts, was the first of the Reform Laws which sought to break the power of the Church. They provoked the Reform War of 1858 to 1861 in which the liberals, after setbacks, defeated the conservatives.

Juárez was elected national president in 1861 but had only been in office a few months when the French, supported by many conservatives and clergy, invaded Mexico and forced him into exile again. In 1866, with US military support, he returned to oust the French and their puppet emperor Maximilian. He made primary education theoretically free and compulsory. He died in 1872, a year after being elected to his fourth presidential term. Countless statues and streets, schools and plazas named after him preserve his memory, and his maxim *El respeto al derecho ajeno es la paz* (Respect for the rights of others is peace) is widely quoted. ■

and helped pay for an education he otherwise might not have received.

The house, round a central courtyard, shows how the early-19th-century Oaxaca middle class lived. The binding workshop is preserved, along with pictures and a death mask of Juárez, some of his correspondence and other documents. It's open daily except Monday from 10 am to 7 pm. Entrance is US$1.75 (free on Sunday and holidays).

Museo Rufino Tamayo

This museum in a fine old house at Morelos 503, donated to Oaxaca by the artist Rufino Tamayo, focuses on the aesthetic qualities of pre-Hispanic artefacts and is so arranged as to trace artistic developments in the pre-conquest era. It's strong on the Preclassic era and lesser known civilisations like Veracruz. Hours are 10 am to 2 pm and 4 to 7 pm Monday and Wednesday to Saturday, 10 am to 3 pm Sunday. Admission is US$2.75.

La Soledad & San Felipe Neri Churches

The 17th-century La Soledad church, five blocks west of the Alameda along Independencia, is much revered because it contains the image of Oaxaca's patron saint, the Virgen de la Soledad (the Virgin of Solitude). The church, with a rich baroque facade, stands where the image is said to have miraculously appeared in a donkey-pack. Today the image is adorned with a two-kg gold crown, 600 diamonds and a huge pearl. The adjoining convent buildings contain a religious museum, open 10 am to 2 pm Monday to Saturday and noon to 2 pm on Sunday (entry US$0.50).

San Felipe Neri church, also 17th-century, three blocks back towards the centre from La Soledad, has a baroque mixture of styles on its southern façade, facing the street. Here Benito Juárez and Margarita Maza, daughter of the family for whom his sister had been a servant, were married in 1843.

Cerro del Fortín

This wooded hill overlooking the city from the north-west is a great place to escape the city noise and smells, with fine views and pleasant (if uphill) walking. From the large open-air Guelaguetza auditorium just above the highway that winds round the middle slopes, a quiet road leads up to the Cerro del Fortín observatory. Between the auditorium and the observatory a track branches to the Nundehui planetarium. On foot you can reach the auditorium by the Escalera del Fortín, a long stairway climbing up from Crespo. It's about two km, uphill all the way, from the zócalo to the observatory. Beyond the observatory, a foot trail leads to the top of the hill, marked by a cross, 20 to 30 minutes' walk further up.

Language Courses

Language students we have met from the Instituto Cultural Oaxaca (☎ 5-34-04), at Juárez 909 on the corner of Calzada Niños Héroes de Chapultepec, seem to have a good time and make friends as well as improve their Spanish. The school also runs Mexican literature and Zapotec, Mixtec and Mixe language courses. Twelve four-week sessions, with six hours' tuition (including craft workshops) five days a week, are run each year but it's usually possible to start any Monday. The fee for four weeks is US$350.

The Instituto de Comunicación y Cultura (☎ 6-34-43), upstairs in the Plaza Alcalá at Alcalá 307 on the corner of Bravo, offers three hours' small class tuition, Monday to Friday, for US$75 a week or US$300 a month. Classes can start any Monday. Other schools spring up during the North American summer holidays. Other places to ask about classes are the University of Oaxaca on the corner of Alcalá and Independencia, and the Casa de la Cultura at the corner of López Rayón and González Ortega, 800 metres south-east of the zócalo. Private tutors are fairly easy to find.

Schools can usually arrange family or hotel accommodation for students. Staying with a family costs around US$10 to US$15 a night, depending on how many meals are provided.

Organised Tours

Oaxaca's a compact city, and half the fun of

trips around the Central Valleys is making your own way there, but if you're short of time several companies offer day tours in and around the city. Two with a wide choice of itineraries are Viajes Turísticos Mitla (☎ 6-61-75), in the Hotel Mesón del Angel at Mina 518, and Viajes Xochitlán (☎ 4-36-64), in Plaza San Cristóbal at Bravo 210.

Festivals

Guelaguetza The Guelaguetza, a brilliant feast of folk dance bringing all Oaxaca state together, takes place – usually on the first two Mondays after 16 July – in a big amphitheatre on Cerro del Fortín. The festival is also known as Lunes del Cerro (Mondays on the Hill). Thousands of people flock into the city and a festive atmosphere builds for days beforehand. Hotel rooms quickly fill. On the appointed days the whole hill comes alive with hawkers, food stalls, and picnickers.

From about 10 am to 1 pm troupes of magnificently costumed dancers from the seven regions of Oaxaca perform a succession of dignified, lively and even comical traditional dances to live music, each tossing generous offerings of local produce to the crowd as they finish. Excitement climaxes with the incredibly colourful pineapple dance by women of the Papaloapan region and the final stately, prancing Zapotec feather dance (Danza de las Plumas), by men wearing glorious feather headdresses, which symbolically re-enacts the Spanish conquest of Mexico.

Seating in the auditorium, which holds perhaps 10,000, is divided into four areas *(palcos)*. For the two nearest the stage you must buy a ticket (US$33 or US$23) from the 5 de Mayo tourist office or other outlets in town. The two rear areas are free but, though much bigger than the first two, they fill up early. You need to be in by 8.30 am to ensure a seat. By 10 am you'll be lucky to get even standing room. Tickets for the front areas guarantee a seat but you should still arrive by 9 am if you want one of the better ones. For all areas take a hat and something to drink as you'll be sitting under the naked sun for hours.

Virgen del Carmen The streets around Carmen Alto Church on García Vigil become a vast fairground for a week or more before the day of the Virgen del Carmen on 16 July. The nights are lit by processions and fireworks.

Blessing of Animals Pets are dressed up and taken to La Merced church about 5 pm on 31 August.

Virgen de la Soledad The city's patron saint's day, 18 December, and the two previous nights, see processions and traditional dances focused on La Soledad church.

Noche de los Rábanos (Night of the Radishes) Amazing figures carved from radishes are displayed in the zócalo on 23 December. You're supposed to eat *buñuelos* (a type of crisp pancake) and throw your bowl in the air afterwards.

Christmas Eve A week of festivities

Origins of the Guelaguetza

The pre-Hispanic Zapotecs, Mixtecs and Aztecs of the Central Valleys held a festival in the same place at the same time of year in honour of their maize gods. Christian priests replaced this with masquerades associated with the feast of the Virgen del Carmen (16 July), before such semi-pagan goings-on were abolished altogether in 1882. But people continued to make pilgrimages and have picnics on the hill on the two Mondays following 16 July. Celebrations in something like their present form began in the 1930s and the purpose-built amphitheatre was opened in 1974.

The only time Guelaguetza is not held on the first two Mondays after 16 July is when 18 July (the anniversary of Benito Juárez' death) falls on a Monday, in which case Guelaguetza is celebrated on 25 July and 1 August. ■

climaxes with an image of the baby Jesus and other floats being paraded round the zócalo and churches.

Places to Stay – bottom end

Most places are in the noisy, crowded streets within five blocks south or west of the zócalo, but several of the better deals are to be found on the other sides of town. Streetside rooms everywhere are likely to be noisy.

Camping The large, fairly shady *Trailer Park Oaxaca* (☎ (951) 5-27-96) is 3½ km north-east of the centre at the corner of Violetas and Heroica Escuela Naval Militar. The rate for a vehicle with all hook-ups is US$10. To get there turn north up Calzada Manuel Ruíz off Calzada Niños Héroes de Chapultepec, five blocks east of the ADO 1st-class bus station, and go seven blocks. Ruíz becomes Violetas.

South & West of the Zócalo One of the better bets among the real cheapies is the *Hotel Aurora* (☎ (951) 6-41-45), at Bustamante 212, with singles/doubles at US$5/6.75. Bathrooms are shared, and hot water irregular, but the rooms, round a wide single-storey courtyard, are large, cool and tidy and the management is friendly.

Elsewhere, similar prices usually mean tiny, dark, sporadically cleaned rooms. Some have private bathrooms but hot water is often limited to a couple of hours in the morning. The *Hotel La Cabaña* (☎ (951) 6-59-18) at Mina 203 on the corner of Cabrera has moderately clean rooms but gloomy, smelly, noisy corridors. Rooms are US$5/7 with shared bath, US$8.50/10 with private bath. The *Hotel San José*, at Trujano 412, a dank, passage-like place with no private baths, has seemingly no hot water at all. The asking price for rooms is US$5/7. The *Hotel Del Pacífico* (☎ (951) 6-57-53), just along from the San José at Trujano 420, is cleaner and its rooms, all with private bath, are a bit bigger and brighter – but for US$9/11.50, there are better deals elsewhere.

The *Hotel San Fernando* (☎ (951) 6-00-75), at Díaz Ordaz 307, one of a clutch of

hostelries just south of Trujano on Díaz Ordaz, has tolerably clean if small rooms with private bath for US$6.75/8.50, and a few hours' hot water each morning. The *Hotel Vallarta* (☎ (951) 6-49-67) next door at Díaz Ordaz 309 is a small step up – well kept, clean and bright, with rooms for US$6.75/13.50, which isn't bad for a single – but read on for better value doubles...

The friendly *Hotel Pasaje* (☎ (951) 6-42-13), at Mina 302, half a block west of the 20 de Noviembre market, is a travellers' favourite as much for its parrot Lorenzo – who not only talks but whistles at women and renders the Mexican national anthem each morning – as for its rooms, which are very clean but small. Singles/doubles with private bathroom are US$10/11.75.

Calle 20 de Noviembre has several hotels of similar design, typically two three-storey rows of box-like but presentable rooms facing each other across a long, narrow courtyard. The *Hotel Chayo* (☎ (951) 6-41-12) at No 508 opposite the 20 de Noviembre market and the *Hotel Típico* (☎ (951) 6-41-11), a block beyond at No 612, both charge US$9/11.50 for clean, basic, smallish rooms with private bathrooms.

Better is the *Hotel Posada del Carmen*, a block further out at No 712, which has spruced-up paintwork and furnishings, and friendly staff. Rooms are US$11.75/13.50. The larger *Hotel Rivera* (☎ (951) 6-38-04) at 20 de Noviembre 502 on the corner of Aldama has big, clean rooms but also higher prices (US$13.50/16.75), offhand staff and echoing, institutional corridors. It's a reliable fallback if everywhere else you've tried is full.

North & East of the Zócalo The eccentric *Hotel Pombo* (☎ (951) 6-26-73), at Morelos 601, a block north of the Alameda, is a rambling place with 50 rooms and nearly always some vacancies. It's spartan, and clean if you don't look too closely. Try to see more than one room before deciding, as they're very varied. The best are quite spacious and bright. In some you are given woodshavings wrapped in newspaper to make a fire to warm the water. Singles/doubles with private bath cost from US$6/8.50 to US$8/10.75. With shared bath they're mostly older, damp and enclosed, and only a little cheaper.

Not bad value for its very central position is the *Hotel Central* (☎ (951) 6-59-71), at 20 de Noviembre 104, with adequately clean, smallish rooms, mostly round an untidy little roofed courtyard for US$8.50 single, US$10 double with one bed, US$11.75 double with two beds.

A 20-minute walk from the centre but within 10 minutes of the 1st-class bus station in a quiet cobbled neighbourhood, the family-run *Casa de Huéspedes Arnel* (☎ (951) 5-28-56) is geared up for backpackers and deservedly popular, with an international crowd usually in residence. The small but very clean rooms are on two storeys around a big, jungly, parrot-inhabited courtyard. With private bath they're US$10/13.50, with shared bath US$7/10. There's 24-hour hot water and clothes-washing facilities. Breakfast is served and you can book here for buses to the coast. Casa Arnel is at Aldama 404 on the corner of Hidalgo in Colonia Jalatlaco, 1½ km north-east of the zócalo.

On Plazuela Labastida, four blocks north of the zócalo, the friendly *Posada Margarita* is another good family-run place with a surprising view of the towers of Santo Domingo from its courtyard. The clean if rather dark rooms have private baths and vary in size, costing between US$11.75 and US$13.50 a double.

Places to Stay – middle
The lower middle range has some exceptional-value hotels with prices kept low by competition – some within a block of the zócalo. One is the *Hotel Las Rosas* (☎ (951) 4-22-17) at Trujano 112. The entrance is up a flight of stairs and the well-kept rooms, with private baths, are on two levels round a pleasant courtyard. The price is US$14/17.25 and there's a TV lounge, a place to wash clothes on the roof, and tea and coffee available in the lobby.

Prices are the same at the *Hotel Real de Antequera* (☎ (951) 6-46-35) at Hidalgo 807 half a block east of the zócalo. An apricot facelift has made the Antequera brighter and more inviting than it used to be and with its central position it's good value. There's a wide stone staircase up from the courtyard café to the rooms, which are clean, medium-sized and have TVs. Everything is roofed over, which retains the heat.

The *Hotel Trebol* (☎ (951) 6-12-56), almost hidden opposite the Juárez market at the corner of Las Casas and Cabrera, is a minor revelation when you get inside. Sizeable, bright, clean, well-furnished rooms round a modern courtyard go for US$13.75/17, with private bath.

A great recent arrival on the Oaxaca hotel scene is the *Hotel Las Golondrinas* (☎ (951) 4-21-26) at Tinoco y Palacios 411, 4½ blocks north and two west of the zócalo. An oasis of calm, lovingly tended by friendly owners and staff, Las Golondrinas (The Swallows) has about 18 rooms opening on to a trio of lovely plant-strewn little courtyards. Rooms vary considerably: none are vast but each is individually and tastefully planned and decorated, and immaculately clean. There's a TV room and good breakfasts are served from 8 to 10 am. Singles/doubles with private bath are US$13.75/17.25 which, for the doubles in particular, is some bargain. There are a few rooms with shared bathrooms (again immaculate) for US$2 less.

A long-established travellers' favourite still providing good rooms at a reasonable price is the *Hotel Principal* (☎ (951) 6-25-35), 3½ blocks north-east of the zócalo at 5 de Mayo 208. It's very well kept, with large old rooms opening on a sunny, peaceful courtyard. Doubles are US$20.75. Only a couple of the 16 or so rooms are offered as singles (US$17) but several will function as triples. The Principal is sometimes full but if not, be sure to look at the room you're offered since a few – notably in the less attractive rear courtyard – are smaller than the others.

The *Hotel Monte Albán* (☎ (951) 6-27-77), facing the cathedral at Alameda de León

1, is one of the best of a gaggle of hotels charging just under US$30 a double. It's about 400 years old with a beautiful pillared courtyard-restaurant (unfortunately covered), where folk dance shows take place nightly. Rooms are on two floors around this and cost US$23/28.75. Those at the front are bigger but the whole place is comfortable and has a colonial atmosphere.

The *Hotel Gala* (☎ (951) 4-22-51) at Bustamante 103, half a block south of the zócalo, is a modernised 1930s building with sizeable, comfortable, well-decorated rooms and good tiled bathrooms. Prices here, too, are US$23/28.75.

The *Hotel Calesa Real* (☎ (951) 6-55-44) at García Vigil 306, 1½ blocks north of the Alameda, is prettily tiled and very clean but the rooms, with fan and TV, are mostly windowless, and small for US$23/28.75. A block and a half east, the *Hotel Parador Plaza* at Murguía 104 has been attractively modernised and brightened up, but many rooms still lack natural light and one or two already show traces of damp. The best are around the courtyard. Singles/doubles are US$23.50/28.50.

The *Hotel Señorial* (☎ (951) 6-39-33), on the zócalo at Portal de Flores 6, has over 100 rooms ranging from small, dark, interior ones which are poor value at US$20/23.50, to bigger, airier ones with lots of daylight for US$30/33.50. The best are generally on the top floor. All are clean and have TV. There's a good restaurant.

The three top middle-range hotels are all in the north of the city. The modern *Hotel Fortín Plaza* (☎ (951) 5-77-77) is at Venus 118, immediately above Highway 190 as it winds down from Cerro del Fortín, about 1¼ km from the centre. Though its six storeys make it a skyscraper in Oaxaca, its ambience is low-key and pleasant, with tile and marble decor. The rooms are bright and fairly spacious, with balconies. Those at the front have views over the city. The hotel is used by both tour groups and individual travellers. Singles/doubles are US$40/50.

The 164-room *Hotel Misión de los Ángeles* (☎ (951) 5-15-00), also just north of Highway 190 at Calzada Porfirio Díaz 102 (about 700 metres east of the Fortín Plaza), has over 100 large, comfortable rooms among tropical gardens, plus tennis and a pool. Singles/doubles are US$50/60.

Calzada Porfirio Díaz also leads to the similarly priced *Hotel San Felipe Misión* (☎ (951) 5-01-00), further north at Jalisco 15 in Fraccionamiento San Felipe del Agua, which has 154 balconied rooms, more gardens, and a pool. There's a golf course close by. A shuttle bus runs between this hotel and the city centre; a taxi is about US$3.

Apartments The *Posada San Pablo* (☎ (951) 6-49-14), two blocks east of the zócalo at Fiallo 102, is worth checking if you plan an extended stay. Once part of a convent, its 20 or so clean, stone-walled rooms face a colonial courtyard. They're well kept – though short of natural light – and are billed as furnished apartments since each has a cooker, fridge and private bathroom. The management prefers to rent by the month at US$233.50/266.75 single/double, which is such good value that the place is often full. If you're lucky enough to get a room by the day it'll cost US$13.50 single or double.

The spacious, clean, well-furnished, modern apartments of the *Parador Santo Domingo de Guzmán* (☎ (951) 4-10-19) at Alcalá 804, 8½ blocks north of the zócalo, are some of the best of all middle-range accommodation. Each has a bedroom with two double beds, a sitting room, a bathroom and a well-equipped kitchen. There's hotel-style room service with clean sheets daily, and a café adjacent. You can rent by the day at US$26.75 a single, US$30.50 a double, US$34 a triple, or by the week at US$160/183.50/200.

If you want to rent your own apartment or house, check the ads in the *Oaxaca Times* and the notice boards in the Instituto Cultural Oaxaca language school or Cafetería Chip's.

Places to Stay – top end
The *Hotel Stouffer Presidente* (☎ (951) 6-

06-11), at 5 de Mayo 300, four blocks north-east of the zócalo, is Oaxaca's most expensive hostelry, and its ultimate in colon-ial atmosphere. The entire 16th-century convent of Santa Catalina was converted to create it in the 1970s: the old chapel is a banquet hall, one of the courtyards contains a swimming pool, and the bar is lined with books on otherworldly devotion. Thick stone walls – some still bearing original frescoes – keep the place cool. There are 91 varied, well-decorated rooms costing US$120 single or double. If you can, choose one upstairs and away from the street and the kitchens. The noises and smells of the kitch-ens pervade one or two parts of the hotel. Some think the service here should be better, but the setting's hard to beat!

The *Hotel Victoria* (☎ (951) 5-26-33) stands above Highway 190 on the lower slopes of the Cerro del Fortín, about 1½ km north-west of the zócalo. Many of the 150 large rooms and suites look over the city and the hotel has an Olympic pool set in big gardens. Its restaurant gets good reports, too. Standard doubles cost US$77. This is a good place for those with cars – but the walk to the city centre is only 20 to 30 minutes in any case. The hotel also runs a shuttle bus to the city in the mornings, returning in the evening.

Places to Eat
Specialities Good Oaxaqueño cooking is spicily delicious, though it offers limited choice for vegetarians. (Oaxaca's other res-taurants, however, offer vegetarians more choice than is usual in Mexico.) Some Oaxaca specialities include:

Amarillo con Pollo – Chicken in a yellow cumin and chile sauce.
Chapulines – Grasshoppers fried, often with onion and garlic; high in protein and good with a squeeze of lime.
Coloradito – Pork or chicken in a red chile and tomato sauce.
Mole Oaxaqueño or *Mole Negro* – A dark sauce made from chiles, bananas, chocolate, pepper and cin-namon, usually served with chicken.

Picadillo – Spicy shredded pork, often used for the stuffing in chiles rellenos.
Tamale Oaxaqueño – Tamale with a mole Oaxaqueño and (usually) chicken filling.
Quesillo – Oaxacan stringy cheese.
Verde con Espinazo – Pork back in a green sauce made from beans, chiles, parsley and epazote (goose-foot or wild spinach).

Probably the two best places specialising in Oaxaqueño food, at opposite ends of the price spectrum, are El Biche Pobre II and Mi Casita – both open only for lunch, which can begin as late as 5 pm.

El Biche Pobre II is at Calzada de la República 600, 1½ km north-east of the zócalo, near the Casa de Huéspedes Arnel. It's open from 1 to 6.30 pm daily – an infor-mal, friendly place with about a dozen tables, some long enough to stage lunch for a whole extended Mexican family. For an introduc-tion to Oaxacan food you can't do better than order a US$4 botana surtida (assortment of snacks). This brings you a dozen tasty little items which add up to a meal. Alternatively you can order a full serving of some of the botana items or of other main dishes, several of which are al horno (baked in the oven), mostly for around US$3.50.

Mi Casita (☎ 6-92-56) is a lot more expen-sive, its cuisine more delicate, and its location much more central, upstairs at Hidalgo 616, which is the north-west corner of the zócalo. It's open 1 to 6 pm daily except Friday. The equivalent of a botana surtida here is the platillo Oaxaqueño, with nine items for US$18.50. An order of quesadillas or empanizadas are US$5 or US$6, and meat or chicken dishes mostly about US$10. The chiles rellenos de picadillo, delicious at US$9.50, are about half a meal.

Cheap Oaxaqueño meals can be found in the 20 de Noviembre market a couple of blocks south of the zócalo. Many of the small comedors that congregate here serve up local specialities, with a main dish typically costing US$1.50 or US$2. The busiest will usually be the best. Many of the comedors stay open till early evening but their fare is freshest earlier in the day.

Other restaurants where you can find

some Oaxacan specialities include Doña Elpidia, the Santa Fé and El Topil (see below).

Zócalo All the cafés and restaurants beneath the zócalo arches are great places to watch the life of Oaxaca but the fare and service vary widely. We like the *Café Bar Del Jardín* at the south-west corner and the cheaper *El Zaguán* on the east side. The Del Jardín, always bustling, is a favourite with locals. When you get a table, you can linger over a coffee or beer – or eat a snack or meal from the long menu of Oaxacan and international food. The omelettes at US$2.50 are big and excellent.

El Zaguán is a friendly place with just a few tables doing good-value breakfasts – eg juice, eggs, frijoles, bolillo and coffee for US$2.50 – or a three-course lunch for US$3. The unnamed juice bar next door will do you a big carrot or orange juice for US$1.50 and licuados con leche for US$1. On the other side of El Zaguán, the *Café y Restoran Guelatao* retains the Oaxaca Zócalo Slow Service Award which it won in the previous edition of this book. The staff apparently think they're of some species superior to the poor homo sapiens gasping at their tables. On our most recent visit we witnessed a mother with a crying baby being made to wait no less than 45 minutes for change, herself being reduced to tears in the process.

El Asador Vasco (☎ 6-97-19), above the Del Jardín at the zócalo's south-west corner, has an attitude problem too, which is a pity because it serves good, if not cheap, Basque, Mexican and international food. Here they look down their noses if you order one dish between two people, and when they bring the bill they like to point out that service is not included. Evening diners are serenaded by musicians who deposit a tambourine inscribed 'Thankyou for your tip' beside your elbow. Main dishes are mostly in the US$7 to US$9 bracket and portions of some are on the mean side. Steaks and brochetas (kebabs) are among the best choices. For a table overlooking the zócalo, book earlier in the day.

The *Restaurant Señorial* inside the hotel of the same name on the west side of the zócalo efficiently serves up good-value fare in a large, pleasant dining room. A breakfast of juice, eggs, bacon, coffee and assorted bread rolls is US$3.

You can eat as well at *El Mesón*, at Hidalgo 805 just off the north-east corner of the zócalo, as anywhere on the square itself. A wide selection of tasty, mainly charcoal-grilled Mexican food is prepared at ranges in the centre of the restaurant, and at lunchtime there's a good US$4 all-you-can-eat buffet of meat and bean dishes, rice, fruit, salad and maize. If you're not having the buffet, you tick off your order on a printed list – and if you don't understand what the items are, the waiters will patiently try to explain. Tacos and quesadillas are specialities but they don't come cheap at between US$1 and US$1.75 each. Alambres (meat kebabs on tacos) and tacos razas con crema (bean tacos with cream) are both delicious.

A few metres from the opposite corner of the zócalo, on Trujano, *Cafetería Chip's* looks on its last legs but serves up probably the best café con leche in Oaxaca for US$0.50, big orange juices for just US$1, and a variety of excellent-value snacks from torta vegetariana, a big avocado, cheese, tomato and lettuce roll for US$1.25, to ensalada supersonica, a mound of fruit salad, honey, yoghurt and granola for US$1.50. *Tartamiel*, just along the street, is a French bakery dealing good croissants and cakes.

South & West of the Zócalo The clean, lively, little *Cafetería Alex*, with just 11 tables at Díaz Ordaz 218 near the corner of Trujano, is well worth finding for great-value breakfasts, served from 7 am to noon daily, or an inexpensive lunch or dinner up to 9 pm any day except Sunday. Breakfast possibilities range from yoghurt-and-granola to chilaquiles or huevos rancheros. For example, US$2 buys you juice, scrambled eggs with potato and bacon or cheese, frijoles, bread or tortillas, and coffee. And portions are generous. Later in the day choose from soups (US$1), chicken and chips (US$2.25), an order of enchiladas or tacos for US$2.50, or egg dishes at US$2. There's always a mixed Mexican and gringo crowd and service is friendly and quick.

A few steps from the Alex at Trujano 322, the even smaller *Comedor Familiar Piscis* does an adequate vegetarian comida corrida from 1 to 7 pm for US$2.50. On the same block, *Restaurant Flami* at Trujano 301, an extensive, busy place with mainly Mexican customers, does a decent four-course carnivore's comida – soup, rice, choice of three lean meat courses, and flan for the same price. On the á la carte menu, egg dishes are around US$1.50, chicken US$1.75.

Doña Elpidia at Cabrera 413, 5½ blocks south of the zócalo, has been serving up one of Oaxaca's most substantial and carefully prepared comidas for decades. Open lunchtime only, it's in a shabby part of town with only an appropriately shabby 'Restaurant' sign outside, but inside you enter a large, greenery and birdsong-filled courtyard: the dining area is on the far side. The six-course meal, for US$5.50, usually starts with a botana and proceeds to dessert by way of soup, rice and a couple of skilfully seasoned meat dishes.

North of the Zócalo *Quicklys*, at Alcalá 101, 1½ blocks from the zócalo, is a good standby for a reliable and inexpensive, if bland, feed. The fare, like the ambience, is a gringo-Mexican mix. Parrilladas – big grilled veg and rice platters topped with melted cheese and served with tortillas and guacamole – are guaranteed to fill you for US$3 to US$5. Some varieties have meat too. You can also choose from a variety of burgers (including vegetarian ones) with chips, or an order of six tacos, for around US$2.50.

Just off Alcalá 2½ blocks further up, in Plazuela Labastida, *El Topil* serves individualistic Oaxacan and Mexican dishes which have the touch of home cooking. Tasajó (a slab of pounded beef) with guacamole and vegetables is one speciality for US$4.75, and there's a range of soups – of which garbanzo (chick pea, US$2.75) is delicious – plus

some good antojitos. Vegetarians could choose nube especial, a large queso fundido and raw vegetable salad with guacamole for US$5.

Standards at *Pizzeria Alfredo da Roma*, at Alcalá 400 just below Santo Domingo church, have slipped but you can get a passable Italian feed. Pastas are mainly in the US$4 range, while pizzas – which when we were last there looked dry, over-cheesy and under-Italian – come in over 20 combinations and four sizes. Lei-lui, for two people, are mostly US$5 to US$7. There are salads too, and you can rinse it all down with sangría (US$1.50 a glass) or wine (from US$2 a glass to US$18 a bottle).

For a breakfast splurge, the all-you-can-eat buffet in the *Hotel Stouffer Presidente* at 5 de Mayo 300 costs US$12. At night the food in *El Sol y La Luna* at Murguía 105 is good – but this is primarily a music place: see Entertainment.

If you're near Santo Domingo between 1 and 6 pm, you could do little better than eat at *Candela*, 1½ blocks west of the church at Allende 211. The building looks like a private house but inside there's a large dining room with a short menu of tasty, inexpensive Mexican dishes, which you can eat in or take away. Most of them will be prepared as you wait. We have tried spaghetti marinara, verduras al vapor (steamed vegetables), chiles rellenos (all US$2 or less) and filete pescado a la crema (US$2.75), all of which were delicious. In the evenings, when Candela becomes a live music venue (see Entertainment), food quality sinks *and* you have to pay a cover charge.

The bright, sparkling clean *Cafetería Bamby* at García Vigil 205, 2½ blocks north of the zócalo, is open 8 am to 10 pm daily except Sunday and serves up sizeable portions of plain but good Mexican and gringo food – salads US$2 to US$2.75, spaghetti dishes US$2.75 to US$4, chicken and meats US$4 to US$6, burgers US$2.75. There's also a comida corrida – eg mushroom soup, creamed spaghetti, roast chicken, dessert and coffee – for US$4. The Bamby bakery, just down the street on the corner of Morelos, is a convenient stop for bolillos, rock cakes and pan integral.

Three blocks north-west of the zócalo at Morelos 509 on the noisy corner of Porfirio Díaz, the vegetarian *Restaurant Flor de Loto* is good for soups and juices (including carrot and beetroot) at US$1 or less. The main dishes we have tried were small and ordinary, but the bread's good and the four-course daily menu especial is reasonable value for US$2.75. There are also breakfast deals. The *Plaza Gourmet* at Morelos 509, just along from the Flor de Loto, is generally better value – it's a fairly successful stab at pleasing a range of gringo palates. For vegetarians, the crepas de verduras (veg pancakes) and verduras al gratin (veg with melted cheese) are both good at US$2.50. For carnivores there are good chicken and meat dishes around US$4, pasta or burgers for US$2 to US$3. The US$3.75 comida corrida, which includes veggie options, is a real meal.

East of the Zócalo The *Restaurant Santa Fé* at 5 de Mayo 103, one block east and 1½ north from the zócalo, is clean, reliable and popular with tourists, but hardly inspired. It's larger than it looks from the street since there are three floors. The menu combines Oaxacan tamales, mole or enchiladas (all US$4 to US$5) with other Mexican and some gringo dishes (steaks mostly US$7 to US$8). Three blocks south at Armenta y López 311, the clean *Restaurant La Flor de Oaxaca*, open daily 7.30 am to 10 pm, has meat and non-meat Mexican food – again reliable, with main dishes around US$4 or US$5. The comida corrida (US$3.50) is popular.

Between the Santa Fé and the Flor de Oaxaca, just off Armenta y López at Guerrero 201, the *Restaurant Del Vitral* (☎ 6-31-24) is Oaxaca's most elegant and probably most expensive eatery. Upstairs in an imposing town mansion, its ambience is that of pre-revolutionary privilege, with smooth, efficient staff. The cuisine is 'Oaxaca Meets Europe'. You might try the lemony grasshoppers for starters and order

flambé steak in mustard sauce to ensure a taste treat to follow. Without wine or any other drink, you're looking at US$25 or more for dinner. The Del Vitral is open from lunchtime to 11.30 pm.

In the same area, and less pricey, is *Los Chalotes* at Fiallo 116. The cuisine is French, and it's run by a Frenchman. Boeuf Bourguignon and navarin d'agneau (rack of lamb) are good main courses at US$7 and US$8 respectively. Starters – eg shrimp mousse and salsa verde – are US$2 to US$3.50. Opening hours are 2 to 10.30 pm, daily except Monday.

Pastelería Quemen at the corner of Morelos and Reforma is Oaxaca's most tempting cake and pastry shop – stop for a coffee and drool over the choices – while *Panificadora La Luna* at Independencia 1105, half a block east of Juárez, must be the city's most varied bakery, with good croissants and several types of pan integral on offer.

Entertainment

Oaxaca has a lively entertainment scene thanks mainly to its student and tourist population. To start with there's live music – usually marimbas or a brass band – Sunday lunchtimes and most nights in the zócalo.

If you've ever dreamed about tropical rhythms, Latin American folk or jazz on a balmy Mexican night, don't miss El Sol y La Luna at Murguía 105, five minutes' walk north of the zócalo. The deep courtyard of an old house – now with a roof, which stops rain spoiling things but takes away the fun of being under the stars – is packed with tables where you can sit and hear good live bands from 7 or 8 pm until late every night except Sunday. Cover is US$2 and these days they more or less insist that you have a meal too, unless you can sneak in late when no one's looking too closely. The food's good – pasta or hamburger US$4, steaks US$10, and, we reckon, the best pizzas in town at US$5.50 one-person size.

Also good is Candela, at Allende 211, 1½ blocks west of Santo Domingo church. The music is mainly salsa and rumba, sometimes with a rock band as support. You sit at tables, restaurant-style, but though Candela *is* also a restaurant (see Places to Eat) you can stick to drinks only. The music goes from about 8.30 pm to about 1 am and cover is US$2. Candela is open every night and is popular with students, especially on Friday and Saturday.

The Hotel Monte Albán stages *danzas folkloricas* at 8.30 pm nightly in its court-yard. The 1½-hour show is the same every night – worthwhile if you don't get any other chance to see Oaxacan dance. Tickets are US$3.50 and it's advisable to book a day ahead.

Oaxaca's best discos are attached to the expensive hotels in the north of town. On our last visit the Yonkee video disco at the Hotel San Felipe Misión (you'll need a taxi to get there) and the Victoria at the Hotel Victoria were more in favour than Kaftan's at the Hotel Misión de los Angeles. The Victoria has great views from its bar. Opening times and charges vary but expect all three to be open at least Tuesday to Saturday from about 10 pm to 2 am. On Saturday you pay about US$6 entry at any of them, but often less on other nights.

The Casa de la Cultura Oaxaqueña, in an ex-monastery east of the zócalo at González Ortega 403 between Colón and Rayón, runs an almost daily programme of exhibitions, concerts, dance, theatre, classes, etc. Craft, art and photo exhibitions, open-air or street theatre, dance, music and talks are likely to pop up anywhere in Oaxaca any time.

Things to Buy

The state of Oaxaca has one of Mexico's richest, most inventive folk art scenes and the city is the chief clearing house for its products. In general, the better work is found in the tourist shops along Alcalá, García Vigil and nearby streets north of the zócalo, with the very best in just a handful of places. But prices are lower in the markets. Oaxaca crafts are generally cheaper in Oaxaca than outside the state, and not necessarily dearer in the city than in the villages where they are made.

Some completely new folk art forms have been born in recent decades as traditional artefacts adapt to the international market that now buys them. The brightly painted copal wood animals which became the rage in the late '80s and early '90s developed from toys that Oaxacans had been carving for their children for centuries. The three villages where most of them are carved, San Martín Tilcajete, Arrazola, and La Unión Tejalapan, have suddenly become relatively rich, with one in three families involved in carving and many able to build new houses and buy new land and cars. Craft techniques, however, are still often very traditional – the backstrap loom is used alongside the pedal loom, and pottery is turned by hand.

Local crafts to look out for include the distinctive black pottery from the village of San Bartolo Coyotepec; dark green-glazed pottery and intricate light brown 'em-broidered' clay figures from Atzompa; blankets and rugs from Teotitlán del Valle; huipils and other Indian clothing from any-where (those from Yalalag and the Triquis are among the prettiest); and stamped and coloured tin from Oaxaca itself, which has been a boom business ever since someone thought of making Christmas decorations from the stuff.

In jewellery, Oaxaca's speciality is gold earring replicas of some of the Mixtec trea-sure from Monte Albán – the best pairs cost around US$500. Silver and precious-stone jewellery are also sold here – the best shops are on Alcalá – but you're likely to find prices a bit higher than in Mexico City or Taxco. In the markets you'll also find lots of leather, bags, hats, textiles, shoes and clothes – not necessarily local.

Markets The vast main market, the Central de Abastos (Supplies Centre), is in the west of town next to the 2nd-class bus station. Saturday is the big day, but the place is a hive of activity any day. Zapotec women are among the traders here and you can find almost anything if you look for it long enough. Each type of goods has a section to itself – so you'll find 20 or so woven-basket sellers grouped here, a couple of dozen pottery stalls there, and so on. The care that goes into the displays of food, particularly vegetables, would put any Western shop-window to shame. Every bunch of chiles becomes a work of art. In addition to the everyday items that Oaxacans buy and sell here, there are some handcrafts. You may also find medicinal herbs and numerous things whose identity you can only discover by asking.

Nearer the city centre are various more specialised markets. The indoor Juárez market, a block south of the zócalo, concentrates on food (more expensive than the Central de Abastos) but there are also flowers and, at the zócalo end and down the 20 de Noviembre side, a fair range of handcrafts. The 20 de Noviembre market, in the next block south, is mainly taken over by comedors but there are a few craft stalls on its west and south sides.

The official Mercado de Artesanías (Crafts Market), at the corner of Zaragoza and J P García, a block south-west of the 20 de Noviembre market, gets few customers because, though only a few minutes' walk from the zócalo, it's off the beaten track. It's strong on rugs and other textiles. Vendors seize on anyone who looks interested and you may pick up some bargains.

Two smaller street craft markets function every day in plazas off Alcalá. In Plazuela Labastida you'll find jewellery, carved animals and belts, while Plazuela del Carmen Alto is the place for weavings, embroideries, rugs and other textiles. Triqui women weave at backstrap looms here.

Shops The highest quality crafts are found in about half a dozen shops. Yalalag at Alcalá 104, near the corner of Independencia, is one, dealing in fine goods from Oaxaca and further afield and specialising in pottery and textiles. Further from the centre, but worth finding, is Aripo at García Vigil 809, which is run by the state government. Different rooms are devoted to different crafts – table cloths, clothing, pottery, tin, woodwork, etc; much of it is among the best you'll find in Oaxaca. Weavers work at treadle looms in a back room and the shop is open Sunday morning as well as 9 am to 1.30 pm and 4 to 7.30 pm every other day.

Other good shops include Fonart at the corner of García Vigil and Bravo, Artesanías Chimalli at García Vigil 513 (good for stamped tin) and El Cactus at Alcalá 401 (for blankets and rugs). Casa Brena at Pino Suárez 58 out towards the 1st-class bus station focuses on ceramics and costumes: you can walk round its own workshops in the back. Nearly all these shops will mail things home for you if you want.

The Oaxaca area is one of Mexico's chief mezcal brewing zones and several shops south-west of the zócalo sell nothing but the stuff, in a variety of strange vessels. Try Mezcal Perla del Valle and El Rey de Mezcales, both on Aldama between J P García and Díaz Ordaz.

Getting There & Away

Air Mexicana, Aeroméxico and Aviacsa between them fly to/from Mexico City (one hour, US$55) five to seven times daily. One of the Mexicana flights starts/finishes in Veracruz, and one of Aeroméxico's in Guadalajara.

Aviacsa and the Mexicana feeder airline Aerocaribe both do daily jet hops to/from Cancún (about five hours, US$215) with stops at Tuxtla Gutiérrez (US$85), Villahermosa (US$100) and Mérida (US$160). Aerocaribe also flies four days a week to/from Acapulco (US$67, one hour).

There are daily direct flights by at least two airlines to/from both Puerto Escondido and Huatulco – see those towns for more details.

Airline offices in Oaxaca include: Aerocaribe, Aerocozumel (both (☎ 5-63-73) at the Hotel Misión de los Angeles; Aeroméxico (☎ 6-37-65) at Hidalgo 513; Aerovega (☎ 6-27-77) at Alameda de León 1; Aerovías Oaxaqueñas (☎ 6-38-24) at Armenta y

López 209; Aviacsa (☎ 3-18-09) at the Hotel Misión de los Angeles; and Mexicana (☎ 6-84-14) at Fiallo 102. For Aeromorelos, go to the travel agency Viajes Micsa (☎ 6-30-10), at Valdivieso 2 just off the zócalo. Other useful travel agents for air tickets are Centroamericana de Viajes (☎ 6-29-76) on the west side of the zócalo and Viajes Turísticos Mitla (☎ 6-61-75) in the Hotel Mesón del Angel at Mina 518.

Bus Reaching Oaxaca from any direction involves several hours travel through the mountains. From Puebla and Mexico City there are two routes, each taken by some buses – one, rougher but quicker, through the La Cañada area via Teotitlán del Camino and known as the Vía Corta; the other, smoother but slower, via Huajuapan de León.

The 1st-class bus station, used by ADO and Cristóbal Colón, is where you arrive or depart for most intercity trips and some shorter ones within Oaxaca state. It's at Calzada Niños Héroes de Chapultepec 1036, 1¾ km north-east of the zócalo. The large 2nd-class bus station, swarming with hundreds of people and dozens of bus companies, is about 900 metres west of the zócalo, between Trujano and the main market. It's the departure point for almost everywhere in the Central Valleys and many buses elsewhere within the state, and for some slower, less comfortable buses to more distant places. For info on buses to the Oaxaca coast – Puerto Escondido, Puerto Ángel, Pochutla and Huatulco – see the Oaxaca Coast section.

On the less frequent 1st-class services out of Oaxaca, such as to San Cristóbal de las Casas, it's always advisable to book in advance. This you can do at least a week ahead with Cristóbal Colón, a month ahead with ADO.

The following information covers 1st-class and some 2nd-class buses from Oaxaca to most main long-distance destinations. Services to Oaxaca are almost always of similar frequency.

Mexico City – 500 km, nine hours via Teotitlán del Camino; 580 km, 11 hours via Huajuapan de León; two overnight luxury Cristóbal Colón Plus buses for US$17.50; 22 1st-class buses (nine directo) daily by ADO, 11 by Cristóbal Colón, for US$11. Most services are overnight and use the eastern terminal, TAPO, in Mexico City. A couple use the southern Tasqueña terminal. The main 2nd-class lines from Mexico City to Oaxaca are AU and Sur.

Puebla – 370 km, seven hours via Teotitlán del Camino; 450 km, nine hours via Huajuapan de León; four 1st-class buses daily by ADO and two by Cristóbal Colón for US$8; numerous 2nd-class buses daily by Fletes y Pasajes for US$7.

San Andrés Tuxtla – 340 km, eight hours; one 2nd-class bus daily by the Cuenca del Papaloapan line from the 1st-class bus station for US$8.

San Cristóbal de las Casas – 630 km, 12 hours; one 1st-class bus daily by Cristóbal Colón for US$12.50.

Tapachula – 675 km, 12 hours; two overnight 1st-class buses daily by Cristóbal Colón for US$13.50; a few 2nd-class buses by Servicios Unidos del Istmo for US$11.50.

Tehuantepec – 250 km, 4½ hours; six 1st-class buses daily by Cristóbal Colón for US$4.75; several 2nd-class buses daily by Fletes y Pasajes and Servicios Unidos del Istmo for US$4.25.

Tuxtla Gutiérrez – 550 km, 10 hours; one overnight luxury Cristóbal Colón Plus bus for US$18; three 1st-class buses daily by Cristóbal Colón for US$11; four 2nd-class buses daily by Fletes y Pasajes for US$9.25.

Veracruz – 460 km, 8½ hours via Teotitlán del Camino; 540 km, 10½ hours via Huajuapan de León; two 1st-class buses daily by ADO for US$10.25; two 2nd-class buses daily by Cuenca del Papaloapan from the 1st-class bus station for US$7.25.

Villahermosa – 700 km, 12 hours; two 1st-class buses daily by Cristóbal Colón for US$14.

Train The *El Oaxaqueño* sleeper is a reasonable way of travelling between Mexico City and Oaxaca. Though much slower than the buses; it takes a more scenic route. The train leaves both Mexico City and Oaxaca at 7 pm nightly, arriving supposedly at 9.30 am next morning but in practice usually around midday. Stops include Puebla. Southbound, you spend the morning daylight hours winding through the spectacular Sierra Madre de Oaxaca; northbound you spend them passing by a series of volcanoes on the approach to the capital. Oaxaca-Mexico City fares, including two meals, are: alcoba for two US$62.50, camarín for one US$31.25; primera especial US$12.75; primera regular US$5. Take your own drinks.

Oaxaca station is on Calzada Madero (the westward continuation of Independencia) about two km west of the zócalo. You can buy *El Oaxaqueño* tickets for no extra charge at the Centroamericana de Viajes travel agency at Portal de Flores 8 on the west side of the zócalo.

Car In addition to the two routes taken by buses from Mexico City (see Bus), a third option for motorists is the 525-km route through Cuautla, Izúcar de Matamoros and Acatlán de Osorio. All three routes traverse long, isolated, twisting mountain stretches as they enter Oaxaca state.

East of Oaxaca city, Highway 190, the Pan-American, descends to Tehuantepec (250 km) then crosses the Isthmus of Tehuantepec before climbing again into Chiapas.

Car Rental Budget (☎ 6-06-11) in the Hotel Stouffer Presidente, Dollar (☎ 6-63-29) at Matamoros 100, and Hertz (☎ 6-54-78) at Plazuela Labastida 115 all have uniquely confusing ways of quoting car rental prices. Insurance, tax and kilometrage are the extras that have to be added to the basic figure. Once you've clawed your way through their intricacies you may find that one particular deal is better suited to your plans, but in general you pay around a total US$75 plus petrol for a day and 200 km in a VW sedan. Bigger cars go up to about twice that.

Getting Around

Most points of importance in the city are within walking distance of each other. You can walk from the bus stations too, and even the railway station if you like, but there are transport alternatives.

To/From the Airport Oaxaca airport is about six km south of the city off the road to Ocotlán and Pochutla. Tickets for the yellow combi colectivos which meet incoming flights are sold at the airport's Transporte Terrestre desk. These will take you anywhere in the city centre for US$2.75. If you have a lot of baggage they may charge you for an extra person. A taxi costs about US$10 – or you could walk the half-km to the main road and pick up one of the frequent buses that pass.

You can book Transporte Terrestre from the city to the airport by visiting or phoning the office (☎ 4-43-50) at Alameda de León 1-6. Its hours are 9 am to 2 pm and 5 to 8 pm, Monday to Saturday. Buses going to San Bartolo Coyotepec or Ocotlán (see Central Valleys South) will stop at the airport approach road.

To/From the Bus & Train Stations For a bus from the 1st-class bus station to the centre, walk 300 metres left (west) along Calzada Niños Héroes de Chapultepec to a crossroads with traffic lights and take any bus going left (south) from there down Juárez. All go within a few blocks of the zócalo – watch your map to decide where to get off. An 'Etapa Blanco Juárez Colón' bus going north up Reforma will take you back to the same traffic lights. All city buses are US$0.15. From the railway station to the centre, take a 'Centro' bus.

A taxi to the zócalo should cost US$2 from the 1st-class bus station or the railway station, US$1.50 from the 2nd-class bus station.

MONTE ALBÁN

The ancient Zapotec capital (MON-teh al-BAN – White Mountain) stands on a long, artificially-flattened hilltop 400 metres above the valley floor, nine km west of Oaxaca. Its distinctive outline can be clearly seen from the airport and from some places in the city if you know what you're looking for. Monte Albán's hilltop position, with views over the often dry, moonscape-like hills and valleys for many km around, makes it spectacular even if you're bored by old stones.

History

The site was first occupied some time between 800 and 400 BC, probably by Zapotec-speakers from the outset. One theory about its origins is that when the peoples of the Central Valleys first became a political unit they agreed – or were forced – to create one central governing and religious settlement. Some of its founders probably had cultural connections with the Olmec to the north-east. Archaeologists divide its history – and that of the Central Valleys as a whole – into five phases:

Monte Albán I The years up to about 200 BC saw the levelling of the hilltop, the building of temples and probably palaces, and the growth of a town of 10,000 or more on the hillsides.

Monte Albán II Between 200 BC and about 300 AD the city came to dominate more and more of Oaxaca. The arrow-shaped Building J (the observatory) was erected and lined with engraved slabs recording military victories. Some early Maya influence is apparent in pottery. Buildings were typically made of huge stone blocks with steep walls.

Monte Albán III The city was at its peak from about 300 to 700 AD. The slopes of the main and surrounding hills were terraced for dwellings and the population reached about 25,000 – a size not exceeded by Oaxaca until the late 19th century. There was extensive irrigation and at least 200 other settlements and ceremonial centres were established in the Central Valleys. Monte Albán was the centre of a highly organised, priest-dominated society. Its people ate tortillas, corn dough, beans, squash, chile, avocado and other plants plus, sometimes, deer, rabbit and dog. In the dry season water was probably carried up to them from the valley.

Most of what we see today dates from this time. Many of the buildings were plastered with stucco and painted red. The use of talud-tablero architecture probably indicates influence from Teotihuacán, with which Monte Albán seems to have co-existed peacefully. Nearly 170 underground tombs from Phase III have been found – many of them elaborate and decorated with frescoes.

Monte Albán IV The period between about 700 and 950 AD was the one of Monte Albán's decline. During its first century the city was largely abandoned – perhaps because supplying its growth was now beyond the Central Valleys' resources. Monte Albán gradually fell into ruin and Zapotec life centred instead around other places in the Central Valleys.

Monte Albán V The final period, from about 950 to 1521 (the Spanish conquest), saw minimal life at Monte Albán, except that when the Mixtecs arrived in the Central Valleys some time between 1100 and 1350 they re-used old tombs at Monte Albán to bury their own dignitaries. In Tomb 7 they left one of the greatest treasure hoards in the Americas, which is now in Oaxaca's Regional Museum.

Information

Try to take a torch so that you can look in the tombs and tunnels but ask at the ticket desk which tombs are open, since many main ones often aren't and some are a bit of a walk from the rest of the site. Official guides offer their services outside the ticket office. There's a cafeteria and a couple of shops here too. Entry to the site is US$3.50 (free on Sunday) and it's open from 8 am to 5 pm daily.

Gran Plaza

The track up from the museum comes out at the north-east corner of the Gran Plaza, which was the centre of Monte Albán. It's about 300 metres long, 200 metres wide, and aligned roughly north-south. The visible structures are nearly all from Monte Albán III. Some were temples, others residential.

Ball Court As you go along the east side of the plaza, this deep, I-shaped court is the first structure. The stone terraces were probably part of the playing area, not stands for spectators. The round stone in the middle may

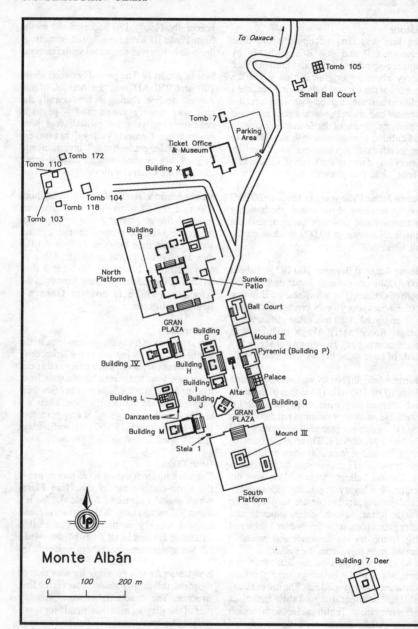

To Oaxaca

Tomb 105

Small Ball Court

Tomb 7

Parking Area

Ticket Office & Museum

Tomb 172
Tomb 110
Building X
Tomb 104
Tomb 103
Tomb 118

Building B

North Platform

Sunken Patio

Ball Court

GRAN PLAZA

Building G

Mound II

Pyramid (Building P)

Building IV
Building H

Building I
Palace

Building L
Building J
Altar
Building Q

Danzantes
GRAN PLAZA

Building M

Stela 1
Mound III

South Platform

Monte Albán

0   100   200 m

Building 7 Deer

have been used for bouncing the ball at the start of the game.

Building P A small pillared temple stood on top of Building P, a pyramid half way down the east side of the plaza. From the altar in front of the pyramid came a well-known jade bat-god mask, probably from Monte Albán II and now in the National Anthropology Museum.

Palace This structure, towards the south end of the east side, has a broad stairway. Under the inner patio on top was found a cross-shaped tomb, probably from Monte Albán IV, constructed after the site had been largely abandoned.

South Platform The south end of the plaza is dominated by this big mound with a wide staircase, good for a panorama of the plaza. Two or three hundred metres south-east is a big structure called Building Seven Deer, from an inscription on its entrance lintel.

Building J This arrowhead-shaped Monte Albán II building, riddled with tunnels and inner staircases, stands at an angle of 45° to the other Gran Plaza structures and is widely believed to have been an observatory. It has significant alignments with the bright star Capella. Figures and hieroglyphs carved on its walls probably record military conquests.

Building M The remains of four columns of a temple stand on top of this southernmost building on the west side of the plaza. There's also a cross-shaped tomb on top, but Building M was not primarily funerary. Only its front part is Monte Albán III, having been added, like the front of Building IV on the same side of the plaza, to an earlier structure in an apparent attempt to conceal the plaza's lack of symmetry. (The great rock mounds on which the south and north platforms are built are not directly opposite each other.)

Danzantes Building L, north of Building M, is an amalgam of a Monte Albán I structure which contained the famous Danzante (Dancer) carvings, and a Monte Albán III structure built over it. The Danzantes – some of which are seen around the lower part – represent slain enemies. They generally have open mouths (sometimes down-turned in Olmec style) and closed eyes, and in some cases blood flows where their genitals have been cut off. Hieroglyphic dates and possibly names accompanying them are the earliest known true writing in Mexico. Some of the Danzantes were later moved and used again elsewhere in the site.

Building IV A tunnel from Building IV's north side enables you to see the big stone block construction typical of Monte Albán II. Stela 18 (originally five metres high) close to the tunnel entrance is also Monte Albán II.

Buildings G, H & I These are one complex, lined up from north to south on top of a rocky eminence in the middle of the plaza. They were probably topped with altars.

North Platform

This huge structure, built, like the South Platform, over a rock outcrop, is almost as big as the Gran Plaza. Chambers on either side of the main staircase contained tombs, and columns at its top once supported the roof of a hall. Behind is the sunken patio, with an altar in the middle and, on its west side, Building B which was probably a late Mixtec addition.

Tombs

Most of the tombs are open very irregularly, but it is usually possible to see into a couple.

No 104 A marked path branching north from the track to the Gran Plaza leads to the 5th-century underground Tomb 104. It's the only major tomb that's open regularly – usually from 9 am to 1 pm and 2 to 4 pm (if you're out of luck, there's a full-size replica in the National Anthropology Museum!). Above its elaborate underground entrance stands an urn in the form of Pitao Cozobi, the Zapotec maize god, wearing a mask of Cocijo, the rain god whose forked tongue represents lightning. The heavy stone slab covered with hieroglyphs in the antechamber originally blocked the doorway of the tomb proper.

The tomb walls are covered with frescoes in Teotihuacán-like style. The figure on the left wall is probably Xipe Tótec, the Zapotec flayed god and god of spring; on the right wall wearing a big snake and feather headdress is Pitao Cozobi again. The tomb contained a male skeleton and several urns.

It's possible to descend or look into a few more tombs in the large mound behind Tomb 104.

No 7 This partly restored tomb, just off the car park, dates from Monte Albán III but in the 14th or 15th century it was re-used by Mixtecs to bury a dignitary along with two other bodies – probably sacrificed servants – and the great treasure hoard now in the Oaxaca Regional Museum.

No 105 On the hill called Cerro del Plumaje, east of the Monte Albán access road, is another tomb reproduced in the National Anthropology Museum. Its somewhat decayed Teotihuacán-influenced murals show four figures walking along each side. These and other figures may represent nine gods of death or night and their female consorts. A band of decoration round the top seems to show eyes (or stars) falling from divine jaws.

Getting There & Away

The only buses to the site are run by Autobuses Turísticos (☎ 6-53-27) from the Hotel Mesón del Ángel at Mina 518 in Oaxaca, a 10 to 15-minute walk south-west of the zócalo. Call or consult tourist offices for current schedules. Most of the year there are four buses spaced through the day, departing for the 20-minute trip at fixed times. At peak tourism periods there are up to seven services a day. The US$1.75 fare includes a return trip 2½ hours after you leave Oaxaca. If you want to stay longer than this schedule allows, you must hope there'll be a spare place on a later return bus – and pay a further US$1 if there is.

A taxi from Oaxaca to Monte Albán costs US$5 to US$7 but coming down you may have to pay up to US$10. Other possibilities are hitching (don't leave it too late to come down) or a city bus from Trujano, outside Oaxaca's 2nd-class bus station, to the suburb of Colonia Monte Albán, about two km below the site on the road up from Oaxaca.

Central Valleys

Three valleys radiate from the city of Oaxaca: the valley of Tlacolula to the east, the valley of Zimatlán to the south, and the valley of Etla to the north. Their population is mostly Zapotec. The east and south valleys provide a variety of goals for day trips from Oaxaca, ranging from pre-Hispanic ruins to craft villages and lively country markets, one or more of which is held daily except Saturday.

To the east, ancient Mitla, with its mosaic-like stonework, is almost as well known as Monte Albán, while the ruins of Yagul are arguably the region's most dramatic and the Tlacolula market one of its busiest. The weavers of Teotitlán del Valle are among Mexico's most famous artisans. To the south are the beautiful old monastery at Cuilapan, the renowned potters of San Bartolo Coyotepec and more busy markets at Zaachila and Ocotlán.

Market Days

Tlacolula market (east of Oaxaca) is on Sunday, Miahuatlán (south) Monday, Soledad Etla (north) Tuesday, Zimatlán (south) and San Pedro y San Pablo Etla (north) Wednesday, Zaachila and Ejutla (both south) Thursday, and Ocotlán (south) Friday. They're at their busiest in the morning and start to wind down in early afternoon.

CENTRAL VALLEYS – EAST

Most of the places mentioned here are on or within walking distance of the Oaxaca-Mitla

Top: The Palace, Palenque, Chiapas (JL)
Bottom: Temple of the Inscriptions, Palenque, Chiapas (TW)

Top: Crafts market, Plazuela de Carmen Alto, Oaxaca (JN)
Left: Chac-mool wall carving, tomb at Monte Albán, Oaxaca state (RMcK)
Right: Interior, Iglesia Santo Domingo, Oaxaca (RMcK)

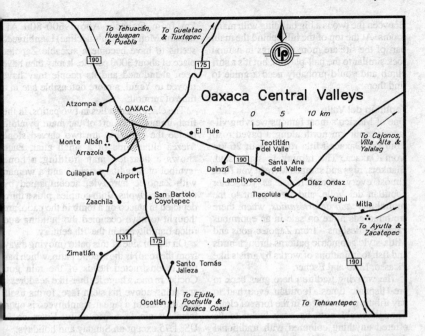

Oaxaca Central Valleys

0   5   10 km

To Tehuacán, Huajuapan & Puebla

To Guelatao & Tuxtepec

Atzompa
OAXACA
El Tule
Teotitlán del Valle
Santa Ana del Valle
Monte Albán
Arrazola
Dainzú
Lambityeco
Díaz Ordaz
Cuilapan
Airport
Tlacolula
Yagul
Mitla
San Bartolo Coyotepec
Zaachila
To Cajonos, Villa Alta & Yalalag
To Ayutla & Zacatepec
Zimatlán
Santo Tomás Jalieza
Ocotlán
To Ejutla, Pochutla & Oaxaca Coast
To Tehuantepec

road, and Transportes Oaxaca-Istmo's buses to Mitla, every 15 minutes from Gate 9 of the 2nd-class bus station in Oaxaca, will drop you wherever you want on this road.

El Tule

A vast *ahuehuete* tree (a type of cypress) in the churchyard here, 10 km along the Mitla road, is claimed to have the biggest girth of any tree in the world. It's 42 metres round, 2000 or more years old, and protected by a fence so you can't get too close. It stands right by the road, so you might get a glimpse from the bus if you don't want to get off. The annual Feria del Árbol (Fair of the Tree) is on the second Monday in October.

Dainzú

Twenty-one km from Oaxaca along the Mitla road, a track leads a km south across a hillside to the small but interesting ruins of Dainzú ('dine-ZOO'), open daily from 10 am to 6 pm. Entry is US$1.75 except Sunday

and holidays. Dainzú has remains from several periods between 300 BC (or earlier) and 1000 AD.

To the left as you approach is the pyramid-like Building A, 50 metres long and eight metres high, built about 300 BC. Along its bottom wall (mostly to the right of the stairs) are a number of engravings from the same date or earlier, similar to the Monte Albán Danzantes. The Dainzú carvings nearly all show ball players – with masks or protective headgear, protective handgear and a ball in the right hand. Some experts say these figures, like the Danzantes, have 'Olmecoid' features. Behind the ball-players' wall, steps descend to a tomb, converted from a stairway about the 7th century AD – when the stairway up the middle of the building was added. Among the ruins on the hillside below Building A are, to the right as you look down, a sunken tomb with its entrance carved in the form of a crouching jaguar and, to the left, a half-restored ball court from about 1000 AD.

Between the two is a big building with many rooms. At the top of the hill behind the main part of the site are more carvings in natural rock similar to the ball-players, but it's a stiff climb and you'd probably need a guide to find them.

Teotitlán del Valle

One of Mexico's most famous weaving villages is four km north along a paved road from the Oaxaca-Mitla road, about 26 km from Oaxaca. The turning is signposted. Blankets, rugs and sarapes wave at you from almost every second house as you enter Teotitlán del Valle, and signs point to the central *mercado de artesanías*, where there are hundreds more on sale in an enormous variety of designs – from Zapotec gods and Mitla-style geometric patterns through birds and fish to imitations of works by artists like Picasso, Miró and Escher.

The weaving tradition here goes back to pre-Hispanic times. Teotitlán even had to pay tribute to the Aztecs in the form of cloth. Though you'd now be very lucky to be offered anything coloured with traditional dyes made from cochineal, sea snails, wood, moss or leaves, the quality is still very high in many cases. You can see people at work on treadle looms and sometimes spinning their own wool. Prices in Teotitlán are not necessarily lower than for their products in Oaxaca, but there's probably a bigger choice here. The very best work may well be hidden away in weavers' houses; if you show interest you will probably be asked in to see someone's techniques and merchandise.

Teotitlán celebrates the fiesta of the Virgen de la Natividad on 3 April with the Feather Dance.

Buses of Autotransportes Valle del Norte run every hour or two all the way to Teotitlán from Oaxaca's 2nd-class bus station, and the last one returns from the village about 6 pm. It's not too hard to get a lift to/from the main road.

Lambityeco

The small archaeological site of Lambityeco lies on the south side of the Mitla road, 29 km from Oaxaca. About 600-800 AD (around Monte Albán's decline) Lambityeco seems to have become a sizeable Zapotec place of about 3000 people. It may then have been abandoned and its people may have moved to Yagul, a more defensible site in a time of turmoil.

The chief interest lies in two patios. In the first, immediately left of the main pyramid beside the car park, are two carved stone friezes either side of a small altar. Each shows a bearded man holding a bone (symbol of hereditary rights) and a woman with Zapotec hairstyle, accompanied by their name glyphs. Both couples, plus a third depicted in stucco on a tomb in the patio, are thought to have occupied the building and ruled Lambityeco in the 7th century.

On the far side of this patio (moving away from the road) is the second patio, which has two reconstructed heads of the rain god Cocijo. In one, a huge feather-like headdress, spreading above his stern face, forms itself into the face of a jaguar. Lambityeco is open from 10 am to 6 pm daily. Entrance is US$1.75 except on Sunday and holidays.

Tlacolula

Four km beyond Lambityeco and 33 km from Oaxaca, this town of about 20,000 people holds one of the Central Valleys' major markets every Sunday. The area around and behind the church becomes a packed throng. Teotitlán blankets are among the goods sold. Like Ocotlán's, this market has even more of an Indian feel than Oaxaca's. An extra-big market is held on the second Sunday in October. Buses from Oaxaca cost US$0.60.

Church Tlacolula's church was one of several founded in Oaxaca by Dominican monks. Inside, the domed chapel of Santo Cristo is a riot of golden, Indian-influenced decoration comparable with the Rosary Chapel in Santo Domingo, Oaxaca. Martyrs can be seen carrying their heads under their arms. There's a lot of silver too. The chapel gate and the pulpit are fine colonial wrought-iron work.

Santa Ana del Valle

A turn north off the main road at Tlacolula, towards Díaz Ordaz, brings you after about a km to a junction. Here, if you go left, you enter Santa Ana del Valle, a village with a textile tradition going back to before the Spaniards. Today it produces mainly blankets, sarapes and bags made of wool on treadle looms. Natural dyes have not entirely disappeared and traditional designs – flowers, birds, geometric – are still in use. Prices in the co-operatively-run textile market are considerably lower than in Teotitlán del Valle or the Oaxaca shops. Santa Ana also has a small museum covering archaeology, history and traditional textile methods, including the preparation of cactus and cochineal dyes. There's also a richly decorated 18th-century church. Minibuses run frequently from Tlacolula to the village.

The Zapotec Sierra

The road through Díaz Ordaz leads to a remote mountain Zapotec region served only by dirt roads, of which San Ildefonso Villa Alta, about 60 km north of Santa Ana, is the heart. Yalalag, source of some of Oaxaca's loveliest huipils, is in this region, a few km east of Cajonos which is about two-thirds of the way to Villa Alta. Flecha de Zempoaltépetl buses go infrequently to Yalalag (US$4, about five hours) and Villa Alta from gate 36 of Oaxaca's 2nd-class bus station.

Yagul

The ruins of Yagul are among the most spectacular in Oaxaca. They stand on a cactus-covered hill, with good views around sunset, 1½ km by paved road north from the Oaxaca-Mitla road. The signposted turning is 35 km (US$0.70 by bus) from Oaxaca. The site is open from 9 am to 5.30 pm daily and entry is US$1.75 (free on Sunday and holidays). The attendants nearly always have some excuse not to open the interesting tombs. You may be luckiest if you visit at a quiet time, and not too late in the day.

History Yagul became a leading Central Valleys settlement some time after the decline of Monte Albán. Most of what's visible is from after 900 AD. Yagul was probably Zapotec for most of its history, with some Mixtec influence in the later period from which the main structures date. But no one's sure when or for how long Mixtecs occupied Yagul. It may even have remained inhabited by Zapotecs under Mixtec political and cultural influence.

Patio of the Triple Tomb Entering the site from the car park you see, down to the left, this plaza which was surrounded by four temples. On the east side is a stone-carved animal, probably a jaguar. Next to the central platform is the entrance to one of several underground triple tombs at Yagul. Steps go down to a tiny court, with one tomb on each side and one in front. Carvings in the court are in the Mitla 'stepped fret' design. The largest tomb, to the left, has stone heads either side of its entrance.

Ball Court The beautifully restored court is the largest known in the Central Valleys. To its west, on the edge of the hill, is Patio 1, with the narrow council hall along its north side. Behind the council hall is a pathway with Mitla-style stone mosaics.

Palace of the Six Patios This maze of a building was probably the leader's residence. Mitla-style structures were built over earlier Zapotec ones. The walls were made of clay and stone, then faced with cut stone, plastered and painted red.

Fortress It's well worth ascending this huge rock which towers above the ruins. The path passes Tomb 28, made of cut stone. A few steps lead down to it and you can look in. From the top of the fortress the views are great. On the north side there's a sheer drop of 100 metres or more. There are overgrown ruins of several structures up here.

Caballito Blanco Returning to the main road, you may be able to make out white drawings on a cliff to the left. These are probably ancient human figures. Nearby is the little that's left of a 250 BC building similar to the mysterious Building J at Monte Albán.

Mitla

The pre-Hispanic stone 'mosaics' on the 'palaces' of Mitla are unrivalled in Mexico. The modern Zapotec town in which they stand is nothing special.

History Though often referred to as a Mixtec capital, Mitla was a Zapotec settlement from as early as 100 AD and has probably

remained so for most of its history. After the decline of Monte Albán, about 750 AD, it became one of the most important Zapotec centres. What we see now dates almost entirely from the last two or three centuries before the Spanish conquest in 1521, and seems to point to a short period of Mixtec domination followed by a Zapotec reassertion before the Aztecs conquered the town in 1494. Nearly all the 14th-century pottery found at Mitla is Mixtec, but when the Spaniards arrived they found the place peopled only by Zapotecs. The style of

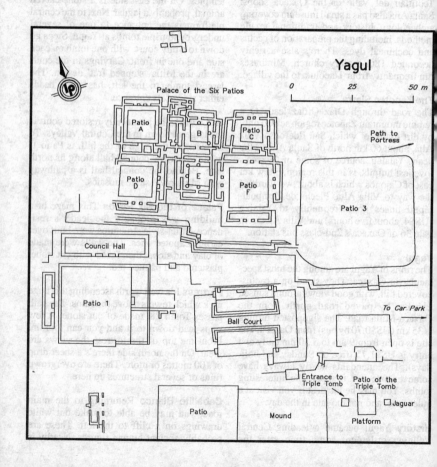

Palace of the Six Patios

Patio A

Patio B

Patio C

Patio D

Patio E

Patio F

Patio 3

Path to Portress

Council Hall

Patio 1

Ball Court

To Car Park

Entrance to Triple Tomb

Patio of the Triple Tomb

☐ Jaguar

Patio

Mound

Platform

Yagul

0   25   50 m

stonework for which Mitla is famous does not appear in the Mixtec heartland in north-west Oaxaca, but something like it had appeared on early Zapotec pottery at Monte Albán, and at Lambityeco, another Zapotec site.

According to the 17th-century monk Francisco de Burgoa, Mitla had been the main Zapotec religious centre, dominated by high priests who performed literally heart-wrenching human sacrifices. Somewhere beneath the town may be a great undiscovered tomb of Zapotec kings and heroes; Burgoa wrote that Spanish priests found it but sealed it up.

It's thought that each of the groups of buildings we see at Mitla today was reserved for specific occupants – one for the high priest, one for lesser priests, one for the king, one for his officials, etc.

Orientation If you tell the bus conductor from Oaxaca that you're heading for *las ruinas*, you'll be dropped at a junction at the entry to the town, where you go left up to the central square. Here there's a restaurant-museum. For the ruins, continue straight on through the square towards the three-domed San Pablo church. The site's open 8 am to 5 pm daily. Admission is US$2.75 (free on Sunday and holidays).

Group of the Columns This group of buildings, to the right as you approach the church, has two main patios each surrounded on three sides by long rooms. The northern patio is nearer to the site entrance. At the top of the steps on its north side is the Hall of the Columns, 38 metres long and seven metres wide, with six thick columns. At one end of the Hall of the Columns, a passage leads to the additional Patio of the Mosaics with a room along each side, one of which has a roof reconstructed to its original design. Some of the best stonework at Mitla lines this small patio and its rooms. Each little piece of stone was cut to fit the design and then set in mortar on the walls, and painted. There are 14 different geometrical designs at Mitla,

thought to symbolise the sky, earth, and feathered serpent, among other things.

The southern patio of the Group of the Columns holds two underground tombs. The one on the north side contains the Column of Life – if you put your arms round it, the number of hand widths between your finger tips is supposed to measure how many years' life you have left.

Other Groups The most substantial is the Church Group, in similar style to the Group of the Columns but less well preserved. Its northern patio has some remains of a painted frieze, showing figures with their names in hieroglyphs. Similar paintings once adorned many Mitla buildings. The church was built on top of one patio in 1590.

The Arroyo Group is the most substantial of the other, unexcavated, groups. The Adobe Group is topped by a hideous brick chapel. The remains of forts, tombs and other structures are scattered over the country for many km around.

Museum The Frissell museum (open 9 am to 5 pm daily, free) in the Posada La Sorpresa building has a sizeable collection of small archaeological pieces.

Places to Stay & Eat *Posada La Sorpresa* (☎ 4) at Independencia 40 off the town square no longer has rooms, but still serves very good breakfasts (US$4) and lunches (US$7 or US$8) at tables round a beautiful, peaceful courtyard. The modernish but fading *Hotel La Zapoteca* at 5 de Febrero 8 (☎ 26), between the town square and the ruins, has rooms with private bath for US$16 around an untidy courtyard, while the basic *Hotel Mitla* (☎ 12) at Independencia 12, across the road from La Sorpresa, charges US$6/7 for singles/doubles, also with bath.

Things to Buy Mitla's streets are spattered with shops selling mezcal and textiles – embroidered dresses, rebozos, table cloths, rugs, even hammocks. There's a craft market strategically placed next to the ruins, with the same sort of stuff, much of it made here in

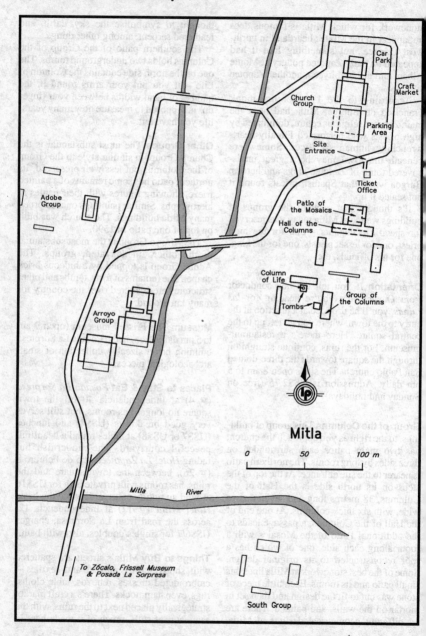

Car Park

Church Group

Craft Market

Parking Area

Site Entrance

Ticket Office

Patio of the Mosaics

Hall of the Columns

Column of Life

Group of the Columns

Tombs

Adobe Group

Arroyo Group

Mitla River

To Zócalo, Frissell Museum & Posada La Sorpresa

South Group

Mitla

0   50   100 m

Mitla. Some striped rebozos are an original Mitla design.

Getting There & Away Mitla is 42 km from Oaxaca, the last four km being up a side road east off Highway 190. Bus fare is US$0.75.

The Mixe Region

Beyond Mitla is the isolated country of the Mixe Indians, about 80,000 of whom are spread through the mountains towards the Isthmus of Tehuantepec. The Mixe are among the least modernised, most shy and self-contained of Oaxaca's Indians, but are courteous and friendly. Some Spanish is essential if you come here. The Mixes in low-lying areas produce some cash crops, but those from the poorer highlands often have to emigrate temporarily for work. Mixe illnesses may be diagnosed and treated by witch-doctors, sometimes with the help of magic mushrooms.

Ayutla & Zacatepec Two of the main settlements are Ayutla (population 4000), about 30 km east of Mitla, and Zacatepec (population 3000), a further 40 km north-east. Zacatepec has a municipal hotel opposite its telegraph office. Travellers can stay for US$2.25 per person – rooms are big and clean, if musty; water is by bucket from a barrel. The *Restaurant Chely* below the primary school, off the main square, does a decent basic meal plus a beer for around US$2.50. Ayutla has a hotel too.

Villages within walking distance of Zacatepec include San Pedrito (officially San Pedro Ayacaxtepec, about three hours) and San Juan Cotzocón (four hours from San Pedrito). It should be possible to lodge with families on overnight trips from the towns.

Both towns are served by one 2nd-class Fletes y Pasajes bus daily to/from Oaxaca. Oaxaca-Zacatepec takes eight hours for US$4.50. Only parts of the road from Mitla are paved. Market day in Zacatepec is Wednesday. In Ayutla (which has a bigger market) it's Sunday. There's local transport between the two places on market days at least.

CENTRAL VALLEYS – SOUTH

Three roads head south from Oaxaca. Highway 175 to Pochutla and the Pacific coast goes through San Bartolo Coyotepec, Ocotlán, Ejutla and Miahuatlán. Estrella del Valle/Oaxaca Pacífico buses go down here at least as far as Ejutla, every 15 or 30 minutes from a small terminal half a km south of the Oaxaca zócalo, on Armenta y López just north of Burgoa. Highway 131, which veers south-west off Highway 175 about 14 km from Oaxaca, a couple of km beyond San Bartolo Coyotepec, is a cross-country route to Puerto Escondido, paved for the first 75 km to Sola de Vega, then dirt for another 170 km to Puerto Escondido. The third road goes to Cuilapan and Zaachila, to which Autobuses de Oaxaca runs from gate 28 of Oaxaca's 2nd-class bus station every 20 minutes.

Cuilapan

Shortly before the Spanish conquest Cuilapan (kwi-LAP-an), 12 km from Oaxaca, was a Mixtec town of over 10,000 people. Today it's one of the few Mixtec enclaves in the predominantly Zapotec Central Valleys. The attraction for visitors is the ruins of its big, beautiful, historic Dominican monastery (open daily 10 am to 6 pm, entry US$1.75). Probably begun in 1555, its pale stone seems almost to grow out of the land. Part of the monastery church still functions, but is closed when not in use. Autobuses de Oaxaca stop right by the monastery. The fare from Oaxaca is US$0.20.

In 1831 the Mexican independence hero Vicente Guerrero was executed at the monastery by soldiers supporting the rebel conservative Anastasio Bustamante, who had just thrown the liberal Guerrero out of the presidency. The fleeing Guerrero booked passage on a ship out of Acapulco but its captain handed him over to the authorities for 50,000 pieces of gold. Guerrero was transported to Cuilapan to die.

From the entrance you first reach the long, low, elegant, roofless capilla abierta. Beyond is part of the original monastery church. Round its right-hand end you reach the two-storey cloister, a rare example of pure Renaissance architecture in Mexico. The rear rooms on its ground floor have some 16th and 17th-century murals. A painting of Guerrero hangs in the room where he was held. Outside, a monument stands on the spot where he was shot.

The closed part of the church is said to contain the Christian tombs of Juana Donají (daughter of Cocijo-eza, the last Zapotec king of Zaachila) and her Mixtec husband.

Zaachila

The part-Mixtec, part-Zapotec village of Zaachila (za-CHEE-la), six km beyond Cuilapan, has a busy Thursday market. At Carnival it's the scene of a masked mock-battle in which *curas* (priests) defend themselves with crosses and buckets of water from whip-wielding *diablos* (devils). Zaachila was a Zapotec capital from about 1400 to the Spanish conquest but was controlled for some of that period by the Mixtecs. Its last Zapotec king, Cocijo-eza, became a Christian with the name Juan Cortés and died in 1523.

Bus fare from Oaxaca is US$0.25. From Zaachila bus station, walk up the main street to the zócalo (where six pre-Hispanic monoliths stand and the market is held) and church. When you return to Oaxaca you can take a colectivo taxi (US$0.60) from the zócalo.

Tombs Up the road behind the church, then up a path to the right marked 'Zona Arqueológica', are mounds containing at least two tombs used by the ancient Mixtecs. In one of them, Tomb 2, was found a Mixtec treasure hoard comparable with that from Tomb 7 at Monte Albán. It's now in the National Anthropology Museum. So strong was local opposition to disturbance of these relics that the famous Mexican archaeologists Alfonso Caso and Ignacio Bernal were forced to flee when they tried to dig in the 1940s and 1950s respectively. Roberto Gallegos excavated the tombs under armed guard in 1962.

There doesn't appear to be any greater enthusiasm in the village for outsiders to see the tombs today: they're nominally open from 10 am to 6 pm daily (admission US$1.75, free on Sundays and holidays) but there's rarely anyone around to open them up. Market day is probably the best day to try. Ask in the Palacio Municipal on the zócalo if you can't find anyone to help you.

The tombs are beneath the sparse remains of a Mixtec patio in front of the site kiosk. Much typical Mixtec polychrome pottery was found in both tombs.

San Bartolo Coyotepec

All the polished, black, amazingly light pottery you see in Oaxaca comes from San Bartolo Coyotepec (san barr-TOL-o co-yo-te-PEC), a small village about 12 km south of the city on Highway 175. Look out for the roadside sign to the *alfarería* (pottery) of Doña Rosa, up one of the village's few streets, east of the road. Several village families make and sell the blackware but it was Rosa Valente Nieto Real who, a few decades ago, invented the method of burnishing it with quartz stones for the distinctive shine. She died in 1979, but her family carries on and gives skilful demonstrations on Fridays from about 9 am to 2 pm. The pieces are hand-moulded by an age-old technique in which two saucers play the part of a potter's wheel, then fired in pit kilns. They go black because of the iron oxide in the local clay and because smoke is trapped in the kiln.

The village saint's day, 24 August, is celebrated with dances, including the Feather Dance. Bus fare from Oaxaca to San Bartolo is US$0.30.

Santo Tomás Jalieza

This little Zapotec village just east of Highway 175, about 25 km south of Oaxaca, holds a Friday textiles market to coincide with market day in Ocotlán. Its cotton waist-sashes have pretty animal or plant designs.

Ocotlán

The big, bustling Friday market at Ocotlán, 35 km from Oaxaca, goes back to pre-Hispanic days. Local specialities include reed baskets, and there's other merchandise from far and wide – Mitla embroidery, palm hats from Huajuapan de León, Teotitlán del Valle rugs, San Bartolo blackware, and green Atzompa pottery. Buses from Oaxaca take about 45 minutes; fare is US$0.70.

Ejutla

Some 60 km from Oaxaca down Highway 175, Ejutla (e-HOOT-la) has a Thursday market and is known for its engraved knives, machetes and swords – and for its mezcal, reputedly the finest in Oaxaca. Bus fare from Oaxaca is US$1.30.

The Mixteca

Oaxaca's Mixteca (land of the Mixtecs) comprises three adjoining western areas. The north-west borderlands around Huajuapan de León are part of the Mixteca Baja (Low Mixteca) which stretches across into Puebla at 1000 to 1700 metres. The Mixteca Alta (High Mixteca) is the rugged area between the Mixteca Baja and the Oaxaca Central Valleys, mostly above 2000 metres, where settlements tend to be small and scattered. The Mixteca de la Costa (Coast) is a remote south-western zone stretching back up into the hills from the coast.

Three 16th-century Dominican monasteries in the Mixteca Alta, at Yanhuitlán, Coixtlahuaca and Teposcolula, are among colonial Mexico's finest works of art, their restrained stonework fusing Medieval, Plateresque, Renaissance and Indian styles.

History

The Mixteca has been the heartland of the Mixtec people for at least 1200 years. It was an 11th-century king of the Mixtecs of Tilantongo, south-west of Nochixtlán, called Eight Deer, who began to spread Mixtec dominion to the Central Valleys and the Tehuantepec area. Coixtlahuaca was probably the most pre-eminent of a collection of small 15th-century Mixtec states that exerted a measure of control over the Zapotecs of the Central Valleys. The Mixteca Alta was sub-

jugated by the Aztecs in the 15th century. Famed as workers of gold and precious stones, the Mixtecs also developed a fine painted pottery known as Mixteca-Puebla which, it is said, was the only type the Aztec emperor Moctezuma would eat from.

After the Spanish conquest the Mixtecs suffered servitude, epidemics and loss of lands. During the Revolution many supported Zapata's radical land-reform goals. Today much of the Mixteca is eroded by over-farming and deforestation, and politics and business are dominated by mestizos. Many Mixtecs have to emigrate for work. The *juego de pelota Mixteca*, probably descended from the pre-Hispanic ball game, is sometimes still played.

Places to Stay

You can visit the Mixteca Alta and Baja in a long day trip from Oaxaca, but there are also basic hotels in Nochixtlán, Yanhuitlán and Coixtlahuaca, and slightly better ones in Tlaxiaco and Huajuapan de León.

Getting There & Away

Huajuapan, Yanhuitlán and Nochixtlán are all on Highway 190 from Oaxaca to Mexico City or Puebla, served by several 1st-class and numerous 2nd-class buses daily. Huajuapan is about four hours from Oaxaca for US$3.75 1st class; Yanhuitlán is 2½ hours and US$2.50.

For Teposcolula, Tlaxiaco and other places on Highway 125, you can either take one of the frequent minibuses down Highway 125 from Highway 190 for about US$3, or one of the less frequent direct buses from Oaxaca to Teposcolula and Tlaxiaco by Cristóbal Colón (1st class) or Fletes y Pasajes (2nd class). Fletes y Pasajes also goes from Tlaxiaco to Putla and Pinotepa Nacional. There are buses from Mexico City (TAPO) to Teposcolula, Tlaxiaco and Putla.

YANHUITLÁN

The most easily reached of the Mixteca monasteries, Yanhuitlán (yan-wit-LAN) towers beside Highway 190, 120 km from Oaxaca. It was designed not only to impress, but also

The Mixteca

0   12.5   25 km

COIXTLAHUACA

The monastery in this small town (pronounced coyss-tla-WAC-a), 22 km north-east of Highway 190 by a paved road, is if anything more beautiful than Yanhuitlán. The turnoff, 142 km from Oaxaca, is at Tejupan ('te-HOO-pan'), which has its own giant 16th-century Dominican church. Colectivo taxis (US$2.25) wait at Tejupan to take people to Coixtlahuaca. There are some remains of pre-Hispanic Coixtlahuaca in the town, but the local people don't want them excavated. The town holds a big procession, rodeo and firework show on 27 December for the feast of San Juan Evangelista.

Beside the monastery church stands its graceful, ruined capilla abierta. The church itself is usually locked because of its art treasures. Enlist the caretaker of the cloister museum to help open it. The interior has a lovely rib-vaulted roof with carved keystones.

The *Hotel Marina Sol* has big, spartan rooms for US$6 per person with private bath.

TEPOSCOLULA

The small town of San Pedro y San Pablo Teposcolula lies on Highway 125, 13 km south of Highway 190. The monastery is beside the zócalo, which borders the road through the town. Its chief glory is a stately capilla abierta of three elegant open bays, in pure Renaissance style, immediately north of the west end of the monastery church. The church itself is a replacement for the 16th-century original, which was probably destroyed by an earthquake. Some carved saints from the original stand on the west façade. The cloister is a museum (open 10 am to 6 pm daily, admission US$1.75).

TLAXIACO

Before the Revolution, Tlaxiaco (tla-hi-ACo), 43 km south of Teposcolula on Highway 125, was known as 'Paris Chiquita' (Little Paris), because of the quantities of French luxuries like clothes and wine imported for its few rich land and mill-owning families. Today the only signs of that elegance are

to withstand earthquakes and serve as a defensive refuge. Abandoned – possibly after an epidemic – in the 17th century, the monastery was used by royalist in 1812, French and other troops in various wars, so it's surprising that so much remains.

The cloister has an interesting little museum of items from the monastery (open daily 10 am to 6 pm, admission US$1.75). The church contains valuable works of art and is usually locked. Ask the museum caretaker to open it. Its nave has a Gothic rib vault, and the fine timber roof supporting the choir is in Mudéjar style.

some surprisingly grand portales round the zócalo and a few large houses with courtyards. Foreigners are a rarity.

There's a 16th-century monastery two blocks south of the zócalo but most of it now seems to be a court and prison. Its church, still in use, has gold-painted ribs on its Gothic vault and a Plateresque façade. The market area is off the south-east corner of the zócalo – Saturday is the main day.

Places to Stay & Eat

The *Hotel Del Portal* (☎ 2-01-54) on the zócalo has big clean rooms with private bath round a pleasant courtyard and charges US$11.75/18.50 for singles/doubles. *Casa Habitación San Michell* on Independencia is the other of the town's better places, charging a couple of dollars less. Cheaper still is the *Hotel Colón*, one block east of the zócalo at the corner of Colón and Hidalgo, where rooms are US$6 with private bath, US$4 with shared bath.

The best food is at the *Cafe Uni-Nuu* next to the Hotel Del Portal with comida corrida at about US$3.50 plus a wide ranging menu on which shrimps are about US$6.50 and most other main courses US$3.50, and great coffee. The *Restaurant Superior* on Hidalgo also serves decent meals, but make sure you establish the price in advance.

TLAXIACO TO PINOTEPA NACIONAL

South of Tlaxiaco, Highway 125 winds through the Sierra Madre del Sur to Pinotepa Nacional on the coastal Highway 200 between Acapulco and Puerto Escondido. The only sizeable place on the way is Putla, 95 km from Tlaxiaco. Check the state of this road before setting out on it.

Before Putla is San Andrés Chicahuaxtla in the small territory of the Triqui Indians. There may be a chance to pick up Triqui crafts here. The Spaniards found the Triqui rebellious and nearly impossible to Christianise. Even today Triqui witch doctors reputedly carry out cures in churches after services, and a history of conflict between Triquis and mestizos or Mixtecs continues over land rights. Some Triquis have to rent

their land to mestizo cattle-raisers and then work on it as labourers.

Santa María Zacatepec, 49 km south of Putla, has a population of Tacuate Indians whose men are instantly recognisable by their white cotton shirts and trousers embroidered with hundreds of tiny, colourful animals, birds and insects. The Amuzgo Indians of San Pedro Amuzgos, 73 km south of Putla, are known for their fine huipils.

Northern Oaxaca

TUXTEPEC & GUELATAO

Tuxtepec, on the Papaloapan River, 128 km from Alvarado on the Veracruz coast, is the 'capital' of a low-lying area of northern Oaxaca which in culture and geography is equally akin to Veracruz. Highway 175 winds 210 km through the mountains from Oaxaca, so Tuxtepec is on a possible coast-to-coast route. It has several moderately priced hotels and is served by ADO and Cristóbal Colón (1st class) and AU (2nd class) buses from most places in Oaxaca and Veracruz.

On the way to Tuxtepec, 74 km from Oaxaca, is Guelatao, birthplace of Benito Juárez. There's a mausoleum with his remains, at least two statues of him, a museum devoted to him (open Tuesday to Saturday, 10 am to 2 pm and 4 to 6 pm, admission US$1.75), and more memorabilia in the Palacio Municipal. In Ixtlán, a km north of Guelatao on Highway 175, is the 16th-century church where baby Benito was baptised. Buses of the Benito Juárez line go at least three times daily to Guelatao (US$1.25, 2½ hours) from Oaxaca's 2nd-class bus station.

HUAUTLA DE JIMÉNEZ

The hallucinogenic mushrooms *(hongos)* used for spiritual renewal by the Mazatec Indians of Huautla de Jiménez (WOWT-la de him-EYN-ez) once acted as a magnet to young Mexicans and travellers. Now the flow of outsiders is a trickle, and mainly in rainy June, July and August, when los hongos appear. (Out of season they can still be obtained, preserved in honey.) Locals disapprove of mushroom-taking just for thrills, but it's OK if aimed at 'cleaning the mind' under the direction of a 'guide' or *curandero*. Huautla's most famous curandera, María Sabina, regarded by many Oaxacans as a *diosa*, died in 1986.

Places to Stay & Eat

Casa de Huéspedes Primero de Mayo (☎ 41) at Juárez 30, just east of the market, has rooms for US$4/5.50 with shared bath, US$5.50/7 with private bath. It's also possible to rent rooms or cabins from families for US$2 or so. *Restaurant Karina* a few doors from the Primero de Mayo does good basic food and its friendly owner will talk about mushroom traditions.

Getting There & Away

Huautla is 67 km east into the hills from Teotitlán del Camino on Highway 131 between Oaxaca and Tehuacán. There's at least one 2nd-class bus daily from Oaxaca to Huautla for US$3.25, taking six hours.

Oaxaca Coast

For some travellers, Oaxaca city is only a stopover on the way to a laid-back stint on the Oaxaca coast. Though newly paved roads have brought this isolated area closer to the rest of Mexico in the last 15 years, the two fishing villages-cum-travellers' rests of Puerto Escondido and Puerto Ángel are still smaller and more relaxed than most Pacific resorts. In contrast, to their east, Mexico's 'new Cancún' is being built on the once empty Bahías (Bays) de Huatulco.

Getting There & Away

Air There are daily flights to Puerto Escondido and Huatulco from both Oaxaca and Mexico City. Flights to/from Acapulco are an on-off affair – check with Aerolibertad and possibly Aeromorelos.

Bus & Car The Acapulco-Salina Cruz coastal Highway 200 leads into the area from west and east. It passes through Puerto Escondido, and close to Puerto Ángel and the Bahías de Huatulco. From Oaxaca, Highway 175 (all paved) winds 260 km down through the spectacular Sierra Madre del Sur to meet Highway 200 at Pochutla, just north of Puerto Ángel. Highway 131, which goes more directly from Oaxaca to Puerto Escondido, is unpaved for its last 170 km from Sola de Vega.

For Puerto Ángel or Huatulco it's often easiest to take a bus to Pochutla then transfer to local transport. The best Puerto Escondido service is the twice daily 'directo de turismo' bus by Estrella del Valle/Oaxaca Pacífico to/from Oaxaca. This is up to normal 1st-class standards and costs US$7.50 for the six to seven-hour trip. You can get off at Pochutla but for no saving in cost. Departures are at 8 am and 10.45 pm in both directions, leaving from the Hotel Mesón del Angel at Mina 518 in Oaxaca, and from the Estrella del Valle/Oaxaca Pacifico terminal on Hidalgo in Puerto Escondido. In Oaxaca, book at the travel agency Centroamericana de Viajes (☎ 6-37-25) on the west side of the zócalo, or at Autobuses Turísticos (☎ 6-53-27) in the Hotel Mesón del Angel.

Apart from the few Cristóbal Colón buses, most other buses serving this coast are 2nd-class, including Estrella del Valle/Oaxaca Pacifico's so-called '1st-class' services. Frequent buses link Puerto Escondido and Pochutla with Acapulco – but travel to/from Chiapas is less simple, as only one daily service (by Cristóbal Colón between Pochutla and San Cristóbal de las Casas) goes right through. The confusing, slow alternative is to change buses at Salina Cruz or Juchitán (often both) on the Isthmus of Tehuantepec. More detail is given under each town.

PUERTO ESCONDIDO

Population: 35,000

A haunt of surfers since long before paved roads reached this part of Oaxaca, Puerto Escondido (PWERR-toh ess-con-DEED-oh, which means Hidden Port) is more resort than fishing village now, but remains small and cheap. Scattered across a hillside above the ocean, it has few paved streets and hasn't made it on to the package holiday map.

There are several beaches in and near the town, a range of reasonable accommodation, cafés and restaurants, and a spot of nightlife. It's a convivial place for travellers to get together, and Puerto Ángel, even more laid-back, is only 1½ hours east.

Puerto Escondido is hotter and much more humid than the highlands of Oaxaca. Any breath of breeze can be at a premium and you're more likely to get one up the hill a bit, rather than down at sea level. The rainy season is May to October, with May, June, early July and September the wettest times. At these times tourism slumps and Puerto Escondido puts on its worst face in other ways too – you may feel a resentment towards tourists, and crime against tourists, never to be dismissed here, seems to increase.

Orientation

The town is on a hillside rising from a small, south-facing bay (the Bahía Principal). Highway 200 runs across the hill half way up, dividing the upper town where the locals live and work – and buses arrive – from the lower, tourism-dominated part. Avenida Pérez Gasga, the partly pedestrianised main street of the lower town, is the heart of Puerto Escondido's 'resort area', with cafés, restaurants, shops and some hotels. The west end of Pérez Gasga winds up the slope to meet the highway at a crossroads known simply as El Crucero.

The Bahía Principal curves round, at its east end, to the long Zicatela Beach – good for surfing but dangerous for swimming – which is backed by several newer, mostly bottom-end, places to stay. Other beaches line a series of bays to the west.

Information

Money Happily a casa de cambio, named Money Changer, now exists on Avenida Pérez Gasga to save you an hour or so's queueing at the aggravating Bancomer along the street. Both give lower rates than their equivalents in Oaxaca and the difference between them is only a few pesos per dollar. Money Changer observes its posted hours – 9 am to 2 pm and 5 to 8 pm – erratically. The bank is open 9.30 am to 1 pm, Monday to Friday.

Post & Telecommunications The post and telegraph office is in the upper part of town, a 20 or 30-minute uphill walk from the seafront. It's on 7a Norte at the back of a blue building fronting on Oaxaca, open Monday to Friday 8 am to 7 pm, Saturday 9 am to noon. There are Ladatel phones in front of the Farmacia Cortés on Pérez Gasga. One of them works on credit cards or phone cards sold by the farmacia, which also sells postage stamps.

Dangers & Annoyances Crime against tourists can be a problem here. At the time of writing, stories of knifepoint robberies, coshings with bags of stones, even stabbings, have become too numerous not to be taken seriously by everybody. The beaches – notably Zicatela – after dark are notoriously dangerous, but one reader also wrote to tell us of her knife-point mugging on a sparsely populated Bacocho Beach at 1 pm.

Beaches

Bahía Principal The main town beach is long enough to accommodate a few restaurants at its west end, a small fishing fleet in the middle, sun-worshippers at the east end (known as Playa Marinero), and occasional flights of pelicans winging in inches above the waves. A few hawkers wander up and down offering textiles and necklaces. The smelly water entering the bay from the inaptly named Laguna Agua Dulce will put you off dipping anywhere other than Playa Marinero, so don't get too close to the rocks.

Zicatela The waters of Zicatela, beyond the rocky outcrop at the east end of Playa Marinero, have a literally lethal undertow

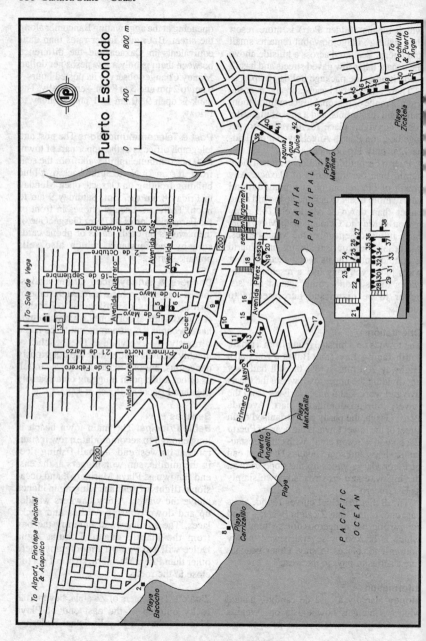

and are for strong-swimming surfers only – though landlubbers can still enjoy the sand and the acrobatics of the board-riders on the 'Mexican Pipeline'. After dark, Zicatela is a renowned haunt of muggers.

Puerto Angelito The bay of Puerto Angelito, about a km west of the Bahía Principal as the crow flies, has two small beaches separated by a few rocks which you can walk across. The sea floor here slopes a bit more steeply than in the Bahía Principal but the bay is sheltered. Snorkelling's good and you can rent equipment at the small restaurant. At weekends and holiday times Puerto Angelito can get as busy as the Bahía Principal.

Lanchas (motor launches) from the Bahía Principal beach will take you to Puerto

Angelito for about US$10 round-trip. The boat returns at an agreed pick-up time. If there's no boat waiting somewhere in front of the Palmas de Cortés, stand there looking expectant. By land, go west along Highway 200 for a few hundred metres from El Crucero. A sign points left down to Puerto Angelito. On the way down, fork left at the Pepsi sign – altogether a 30 to 40-minute walk from Avenida Pérez Gasga. A taxi from town costs about US$2.

Carrizalillo The small cove of Carrizalillo, just west of Puerto Angelito, is rockier but OK for swimming, with a little beach. Lanchas from the Bahía Principal will bring you here too. By land, a path down from the Trailer Park Carrizalillo reaches the cove. From the town, follow the directions for

---

■ PLACES TO STAY

2 Posada Real
3 Hotel Luz del Angel
4 Hotel Posada del Puerto
8 Trailer Park Carrizalillo
9 Hotel San Juan
10 Hotel Paraíso Escondido
11 Casa de Huéspedes Naxhiely
12 Casa de Huéspedes Las Dos Costas
14 Hotel Virginia
15 Hotel Nayar
16 Hotel Loren
25 Hotel Casablanca & Turismo Rodimar
31 Hotel Las Palmas
32 Hotel Rincón del Pacifico
37 Palmas de Cortés
38 Neptuno
40 Hotel Flor de María
41 Aldea Marinero
43 Hotel Santa Fé
44 Casas de Playa Acali
47 Casa de Huéspedes Pako-Lolo
48 Hotel Arco Iris
49 Bungalows Acuario
50 Beach Hotel Inés
51 Rockaway

▼ PLACES TO EAT

19 Restaurant Junto al Mar

20 Restaurant La Posada D'Loren
26 Restaurant San Angel
28 Restaurant Los Crotos
30 Restaurant Alicia
34 Ostería del Viandante da Ugo
35 Cafetería Cappuccino
36 Cafetería Bananas
42 Restaurant Liza's
46 Cipriano's Pizza

OTHER

1 Post Office
5 Transportes Oaxaca-Istmo Bus Station
6 Transportes Gacela/Lineas Unidas del Sur Bus Station
7 Estrella del Valle/Oaxaca Pacifico Bus Station
13 Transportes Aeropuerto y Turístico
17 Lighthouse
18 Hertz
21 Coco
22 Farmacia Cortés
23 El Son y La Rumba
24 Bancomer
27 Tío Mac
29 Moneychanger
33 Aerovías Oaxaqueñas
39 La Patisserie
45 Las Olas

Puerto Angelito but fork right at the Pepsi sign to get to the trailer park. Ascending from Puerto Angelito, cut left through the trees and across to the trailer park.

Bacocho This long, straight beach, on the open ocean just west of the Posada Real hotel, has dangerous undertow and a reputation for muggings of tourists who leave the safety of numbers.

Organised Tours

One or two tour companies on Pérez Gasga run trips to places along the coast to the west – see the West of Puerto Escondido section.

Places to Stay

In the peak tourist season – Christmas to April – the most popular places may be full. Your best chance in such places then, if you haven't booked ahead, is to ask at about 9 or 10 am. High season prices, especially in the bottom and middle-ranges, may be up to 60% higher than the levels described here. Out of season, bargaining will get you a discount at some places.

The surfers, the space and the most laid-back scene are on Playa Zicatela, where there's both bottom and middle range accommodation. Calle del Morro, the track that leads along the rear of Zicatela to these places, is said to be safe from the criminals who haunt the beach itself at night – but if in doubt, use taxis.

Places to Stay – bottom end

Playa Zicatela *Casas de Playa Acali* (☎ (958) 2-02-78) and *Bungalows Acuario* both provide wooden cabañas for up to three or four people with mosquito nets, fans, fridge, private shower and toilet, and filtered water. You pay about US$13 a cabaña, adding or subtracting a dollar or two for more or less than two people. *Rockaway*, further along, has good cabañas around a pool for similar prices. *Las Olas* has just a couple of

cabañas, of fair standard but with communal bathroom, for about US$10 single or double.

Casa de Huéspedes Pako-Lolo, another surfers' favourite, with a friendly English-speaking owner, is at the top of the little hill behind Zicatela and catches some breeze. Steps lead up from the gate beside Cipriano's Pizza. A room with mosquito nets, fan and private bath is about US$11.50/15 single/double, and there are fridges and gas cookers.

Bahía Principal The cabañas on Playa Marinero are mostly smaller, shabbier, dirtier and crowded together in what's a pretty crowded area anyway. The best are at *Aldea Marinero* in a small lane going back from the beach. They have mosquito nets and shared bathrooms for US$7.50 single or double. You can rent a fan for US$1.75 extra.

Neptuno in the centre of the Bahía Principal has some small, basic cabañas (no mosquito nets, a few mosquitoes) for US$8.50, but the communal showers are grubby. There's a grassy area for camping (US$4.50 per person), with electrical hook-ups available, and a big central fireplace.

The *Palmas de Cortés* campground/trailer park next door to Neptuno has more shade but less space, charging US$4.50 per person and US$2.25 per vehicle, with showers and electrical hook-up available, and fireplaces.

Pérez Gasga The *Casa de Huéspedes Las Dos Costas* (☎ (958) 2-01-59) at Pérez Gasga 302, on the left going up the hill, has bare, shabby, only moderately clean singles/doubles with fan and private bath for US$8.50/10. *Casa de Huéspedes Naxhiely* over the road at No 301 has adequate but small and breezeless rooms for US$9.50/11.50.

The *Hotel Virginia* on Alfaro, a track leading off Pérez Gasga lower down, has a few rooms with fan and private bath for US$12.50/15. They're getting dilapidated, especially the bathrooms, but are tolerable. You'll catch more breeze upstairs.

Dearer and more of a walk, but better value, is the *Hotel San Juan* (☎ (958) 2-03-36) just east of Pérez Gasga immediately below El Crucero. Rooms are little more than functional – if quite well kept – but there's a great rooftop sitting area for catching the sun, the view or the breeze. Singles/doubles with private bathroom are US$13.50/16.75.

Above the Highway There's little reason to stay up here unless perhaps your bus has arrived late and you can't be bothered walking down the hill, or you have an urge to be among locals rather than tourists. The *Hotel Posada del Puerto* (☎ (958) 2-02-64) at Avenida Hidalgo 104 has about 15 basic two-bed rooms with fan and private bath round a courtyard for US$11.75 double.

Better is the *Hotel Luz del Angel* (☎ (958) 2-01-22) at Avenida Díaz 102 where the 16 clean rooms with fan and private bath cost US$13.50/17. The front rooms at the top have good views.

West About 1½ km west of the town, the *Trailer Park Carrizalillo* is big and bare, with a fine clifftop position. Water and electrical hook-ups are included at US$10 for two people. Follow the 'Puerto Angelito' sign to the left off Highway 200 going out of town, then fork right at the Pepsi sign.

Places to Stay – middle
Playa Marinero & Playa Zicatela The *Hotel Arco Iris* (☎ (958) 2-04-32) on Playa Zicatela has 20 big, clean, fan-cooled rooms with balconies looking straight on to the surf, plus a large pool and a good upstairs bar-restaurant open to the breeze. A mixed crowd of surfers and others uses this friendly, relaxed hotel where singles/doubles are US$16.25/20.

A little further along Zicatela, the *Beach Hotel Inés* has a lovely pool area with a café serving excellent food, and spotlessly clean, fan-cooled rooms with private bath for US$17 double. Unfortunately our stay was spoiled by the attitude of the Germans running the place, who were so cool as to be icy.

If the *Hotel Flor de María* (☎ (958) 2-05-36) stood somewhere more prepossessing than a little dirt lane leading back from Playa Marinero to the highway, it could be the best deal in town. This relatively new hotel, run by a friendly, English-speaking, Mexican-Italian couple, has 24 ample, clean rooms with fan, two double beds and private bath, round a central court. The pretty decorations demonstrate the personal care of the owners. There's a rooftop sitting area with a small pool, a TV room and a restaurant. Singles/doubles range from US$14/16.75 in low season to US$23/27 in high season.

Beside the rocky outcrop that divides Playa Marinero from Playa Zicatela, the *Hotel Santa Fé* (☎ (958) 2-01-70) is one of the best designed hotels in southern Mexico, with 40 individual rooms set around small terraces and a palm-fringed pool. The stairways are tiled and there's a lovely airy restaurant/bar overlooking Playa Zicatela. Rooms vary in size and outlook, but good design – with tiles again cleverly used – makes most of them agreeable. Many have air-conditioning as well as a fan. Singles/doubles are US$40/50. The hotel's postal address is Apartado Postal 96, Puerto Escondido.

Pérez Gasga The *Hotel Las Palmas* (☎ (958) 2-00-56) and the *Hotel Rincón del Pacífico* (☎ (958) 2-00-56), side by side on the pedestrianised part of Avenida Pérez Gasga, are outwardly similar, with 20-odd big-windowed, fan-cooled rooms round palmy courtyards that open towards the beach. Both are slightly dilapidated and have their own café/restaurants right on the beach.

But while some Las Palmas staff were in our experience sullen to the point of rudeness, the Rincón del Pacifico's remained cheery and helpful – and their rooms, though a touch smaller, were better kept. With prices of US$13.75/17.50 against the Las Palmas' US$16.75/20, the Rincón del Pacifico wins. It's also that much further from the drain smell that often pervades the western end of the Pérez Gasga mall. Streetside rooms in both places are assailed by loud late-night music from outside.

In some ways a better bet than either is the *Hotel Casablanca* (☎ (958) 2-01-68) across the street at Avenida Pérez Gasga 905. It faces the street, not the beach – but since there's no traffic that's no hardship. It has just a dozen or so good, large, modern rooms, with big bathrooms and, on the street side, balconies. Rooms are US$16.75/20 with fan, US$21.75/25 with air-con.

A minute uphill from the Pérez Gasga mall are the *Hotel Loren* (☎ (958) 2-00-57) and the *Hotel Nayar* (☎ (958) 2-03-19), both charging US$14/18 for bare, no-frills, but adequate rooms. The Nayar, being the higher, gets more breeze in its wide sitting areas/walkways. Its 36 rooms have fans and small balconies; some have sea views. But the Loren has slightly bigger rooms and a friendlier air.

Top place in this part of town is the *Hotel Paraíso Escondido* (☎ (958) 2-04-44) on little Calle Unión, which shortcuts the bend in Avenida Pérez Gasga. It's a rambling, old-fashioned whitewash-and-blue-paint place on several levels with lots of tile, pottery and stone sculpture decoration. There's an attractive restaurant/bar/pool area. The 24 clean though moderately sized rooms are air-conditioned. Some have stained-glass panes. Views are better upstairs. Rooms are US$31/41.

Places to stay – top end

The Best Western-owned *Posada Real* (☎ (958) 2-01-33) is about three km west of town on Boulevard Benito Juárez in the still-to-be-developed Fraccionamiento Bacocho, off Highway 200. It has 100 air-conditioned rooms with balconies in three four-storey buildings among big palm-shaded gardens, on a headland overlooking Bacocho beach. There's a pool, three bars (one on the beach) and a restaurant. Rooms are between US$60 and US$80 depending on the season. You can book in Mexico City (☎ 575-50-58 or 525-90-81).

Places to Eat

Puerto Escondido's restaurants and cafés are mostly simple, half open-air places, and most of the better ones are near the better places to stay – on Avenida Pérez Gasga and Playa Zicatela.

There's a clutch of reasonably priced restaurants serving what we have always found to be fresh seafood around the west end of the Pérez Gasga mall. Several open on to the beach so you can observe their current popularity from the sands in front. This end of Pérez Gasga is sometimes afflicted by drain smells, so check wind direction, too, before picking your restaurant! On our last visit we tried the unpretentious *Restaurant Junto Al Mar* and the *Restaurant La Posada D'Loren*, which has minor airs. Both served up a good meal. Most seafood cocktails or fish dishes – such as a whole juicy snapper (huachinango) with rice or chips and a little salad – go for US$4 to US$5 in either place. A good, big avocado or mixed salad for accompaniment is around US$2.75. For shrimps or prawns you'll generally pay US$7 to US$9. The Junto Al Mar's flavoursome fish soup is almost a meal in itself, with whole large chunks of tender fish, for US$2.75.

Towards the east end of the Pérez Gasga mall, the *Restaurant San Ángel* always seems crowded, but its location – opening on to a busy part of the street – rather than the food, which seems ordinary, must be the reason for this. Prices are similar to the Junto Al Mar or Posada D'Loren's and there are more chicken and meat choices as well as seafood. Cheaper and better value is the little *Restaurant Alicia*, neighbouring the Hotel Las Palmas, with cocktails and fish dishes around US$3.50. It also has some cheap breakfast deals.

The *Osteria del Viandante da Ugo* on Avenida Pérez Gasga is an Italian-run Italian restaurant, and a good one at that – though standards seem to slip a little when *il signor* isn't present in person. There's a range of pasta dishes and one-person pizzas for US$2.50 to US$4.75, some good salads around US$2.50 to US$3.75 (including avocado and octopus), plus fish and meat (steaks around US$8). *Cafetería Cappuccino*, almost next door, serves probably the best coffee in town, plus good bowls of yoghurt, fruit salad and granola, and decent crepas (pancakes). Its owners must be the politest of Puerto Escondido caterers, which makes a difference.

The *Hotel Santa Fé* restaurant is one of the few eateries with a touch of flair in both its design – spacious and open to the breezes on a raised platform looking down Playa Zicatela – and its cuisine, which includes some tasty seafood and vegetarian fare (but be ready for your choice to be unavailable). The extra thought that goes into the food takes it out of the budget range: fish and seafood dishes are mostly US$7 to US$10, antojitos, pasta, and tofu and soyburger offerings mostly US$3 to US$5.

Further along Zicatela, *Cipriano's Pizza* does the best pizza we've found in town, with a thin crisp base and lots of good cheese, baked in a brick oven by the friendly family whose front garden the restaurant occupies. There's a range of pizza toppings and the only size available, costing US$3.50 to US$5, is enough for two.

Beyond Cipriano's, the restaurant of the *Hotel Arco Iris*, with a good upper-storey position, serves a straightforward but tastily prepared mix of Mexican and international fare designed to satisfy the surfers down this part of town. Pasta and antojitos go for around US$3, fish and meat courses for US$4 to US$7 (though you'll probably need, say, a vegetable salad to really fill up), giant shrimps for US$8.50.

Good wholegrain and banana breads, and croissants, are made and sold at a tiny bakery, *La Patisserie*, just up from the Hotel Flor de María on the little lane leading back from Playa Marinero to the highway.

Entertainment

Many Puerto Escondido evenings start at the happy hours – usually lasting from about 6 to 9 pm – in Pérez Gasga café-bars like Coco, Bananas or Tío Mac, or the Hotel Las Palmas, or Restaurant Liza's on Playa Marinero. Then there's usually at least a couple of places with live music into the early hours – on our last visit El Son y La Rumba just up from the Pérez Gasga mall had an excellent Mexican salsa/samba band, while Coco thumped along to a gringo blues/reggae/rock trio.

Getting There & Away

Air Deregulation has brought a rush of airlines to join the ageing 28-seat DC-3s of Aerovías Oaxaqueñas on the Oaxaca-Puerto Escondido route. At present, for the spectacular half-hour hop over the Sierra Madre del Sur, you have the choice of four different daily services in both directions, all with one-way fares in the US$50 to US$55 bracket. The newcomers are Aeromorelos, the Mexicana feeder airline Aerocaribe, and Aerovega whose Cessna 'commuter flights' go twice daily each way. The airlines' Oaxaca ticket offices are listed under Oaxaca.

In Puerto Escondido, Aerovías Oaxaqueñas (☎ 2-01-32) and Aerovega (☎ 2-01-51) are both on Avenida Pérez Gasga, while Aeromorelos tickets are sold by Turismo Rodimar (☎ 2-07-34), also on Pérez Gasga, and Aerocaribe is handled by Mexicana (☎ 2-03-00) at the airport. Aerovías Oaxaqueñas also has an office (☎ 510-01-62) at Balderas 32, Mexico City.

Mexicana flies daily to/from Mexico City (one hour) for US$65.

Bus The Estrella del Valle/Oaxaca Pacifico and Transportes Gacela/Lineas Unidas Del Sur bus stations are both on Avenida Hidalgo, two blocks uphill from El Crucero.

To/From Oaxaca See the Oaxaca Coast introductory Getting There & Away section for info on the twice-daily Estrella del Valle/Oaxaca Pacifico 'directo de turismo' bus, which is the best Oaxaca-Puerto Escondido service. The same companies' other half-dozen daily services on the route are called '1st-class ordinario' but are more like 2nd-class, and leave from Oaxaca's 2nd-class bus station. They take longer because they make stops, and cost US$5.75. La Solteca's two low-seatback 2nd-class buses daily take the mostly unpaved crosscountry route via Sola de Vega, for US$5.50.

Along The Coast From 5.30 am to 7.30 pm Estrella del Valle/Oaxaca Pacifico run hourly buses to/from Pochutla (72 km, 1½ hours, US$1.50). Transportes Oaxaca-Istmo runs five daily 2nd-class buses to/from Huatulco (110 km, 2½ hours, US$2.50) and Salina Cruz (250 km, five hours, US$4.50). Tickets are sold at the café on the corner of 5 de Mayo and Avenida Hidalgo, opposite the station of Transportes Gacela/Lineas Unidas Del Sur, which itself runs 20 2nd-class buses daily to/from Pochutla and Huatulco, and frequent 2nd-class services to/from Acapulco (390 km, seven hours, US$7.75). Four of the Acapulco runs (two overnight, two morning departures) are directo, costing US$8.50.

Car Hertz (☎ 2-00-35), beside the Hotel Rocamar on Pérez Gasga, has vehicles for hire at normal Hertz rates, which means that a day trip in a VW sedan to Puerto Ángel and Huatulco, covering about 280 km, costs nearly US$90 plus petrol. The office is supposedly open 8 am to 7 pm Monday to Saturday and 8 am to noon on Sunday, but siestas are long.

Getting Around

To/From the Airport The airport is about four km west of the town centre on the north side of Highway 200. For more than one person, a taxi is the cheapest way into town if you can find one and agree on a reasonable price (US$2 to US$3).

Otherwise, colectivo combis (US$2 per person) meet incoming flights and will drop you anywhere in town. You can book them to take you back to the airport at Transportes Aeropuerto y Turístico (☎ 2-01-23) at the corner of Avenida Pérez Gasga and Calle Unión. Turismo Rodimar on Pérez Gasga runs a similar service, picking you up from your hotel, for US$1.75. There should be no problem finding a taxi to go out to the airport for a reasonable fare.

Taxi & Lanchas Lanchas (motor launches) and taxis are the only transport to or from the central Pérez Gasga/Bahía Principal area if you don't want – or think it's unsafe – to walk. Taxis wait by the barriers at the ends of Pérez Gasga's pedestrian strip. Their standard fare to Playa Zicatela is US$1.75, Puerto Angelito US$2.

WEST OF PUERTO ESCONDIDO

Highway 200, heading towards Acapulco, passes through a coastal region whose people are of notably mixed ancestry. In addition to the indigenous Mixtecs and the Spanish input, there are descendants of African slaves who escaped here from the Spaniards, of itinerant Asians, and of Chileans shipwrecked on their way to the California goldrushes. The latter inspired a local folk music known as la Chilena.

Getting There & Away

Frequent Transportes Gacela/Lineas Unidas Del Sur buses from Pochutla and Puerto Escondido will drop you anywhere along this route – the 145 km from Puerto Escondido to Pinotepa Nacional take 2½ hours for US$2.75. A couple of Puerto Escondido tour companies run trips to places like Manialtepec and Chacahua and the markets in Jamiltepec or Pinotepa Nacional. Look out for their signs on Pérez Gasga.

Manialtepec

The jungle and the 12 km-long mangrove-surrounded lagoon here, 13 km from Puerto Escondido, are the haunt of raccoon (*mapache*), badger (*tejón*), heron (*garza*), pelican and diver. You can get here by road; then find a local boat operator to take you out on the lagoon. A five-hour bird-spotting tour from Puerto Escondido with an English-speaking guide costs about US$30.

Tututepec

Tututepec, nine km north of the village of Santa Rosa about 70 km along the highway from Puerto Escondido, was the capital of a southern Mixtec kingdom which fought off the Aztecs in the 15th century. Remains include stone carvings of a jaguar and a telamon.

Chacahua

The area around the three coastal lagoons of Chacahua, La Pastoría and Tianguisto forms the Parque Nacional Lagunas de Chacahua. Highway 200 at this point – about 75 km from Puerto Escondido – is nearly 20 km from the coast but a road leads south into the park. Mangrove-fringed islands in Chacahua lagoon harbour ibis, roseate spoonbills and other birds, plus black orchids, mahogany trees, deer, alligators and turtles. Tours usually board lanchas at Zapotalito and stop for a swim at Morro Hermoso or Chacahua fishing village. If you got here under your own steam you should be able to rent a local lancha.

Jamiltepec

The mainly Mixtec town of Jamiltepec, 105 km from Puerto Escondido, has a Sunday market. It figures in D H Lawrence's *The Plumed Serpent*.

Pinotepa Nacional

The biggest town between Puerto Escondido and Acapulco has a high Mixtec population, a Sunday market, an unfriendly reputation and several places to stay, of which probably the best is the *Hotel Carmona* (☎ 3-22-22) at Porfirio Díaz 510. There's also the *Hotel Rodríguez* at Juárez 402. Some Fletes y Pasajes buses take Highway 125 north to Tlaxiaco, 212 km away (see The Mixteca).

In one Semana Santa ceremony here, white-painted youths called Judíos (Jews) recite old Mixtec formulae and fire arrows into the air. Pinotepa de Don Luis, one of the most traditional Mixtec villages, is about 15 km north-east of Pinotepa Nacional. Its main fiesta is for the Assumption (15 August, dances and horse races).

POCHUTLA

Pochutla is the crossroads town where Highway 175 from Oaxaca, 238 km north, meets the coastal Highway 200 running from Acapulco and Puerto Escondido to Huatulco and Salina Cruz. Puerto Ángel is 12 km south. There's not usually any need to stay overnight in Pochutla, but you may have to change buses here. Pochutla also has the nearest bank to Puerto Ángel.

Orientation

Highway 175 passes through Pochutla as Cárdenas, the narrow, busy, north-south main street. Its junction with Highway 200 is about a km south of the main built-up area. The bus stations of Cristóbal Colón and Oaxaca Pacífico/Estrella del Valle are nearly opposite each other on Cárdenas towards the south end of the built-up area. The bus station of Transportes Gacela, Lineas Unidas Del Sur and Flecha Roja is 300 to 400 metres north and a block east, on Hidalgo, which runs off Cárdenas between Cárdenas 77 and the blue health centre. Madero, east off Cárdenas two blocks north of Hidalgo, leads to the Plaza de la Constitución, or zócalo, where the church stands.

Information

Bancomer at the corner of Cárdenas and Allende (a block south of Hidalgo) changes travellers' cheques and foreign cash from 9 or 10 to 11 am, Monday to Friday. Sometimes a cash shortage imposes a maximum transaction of US$25 or, occasionally, zero. The nearest other banks are at Huatulco and Puerto Escondido.

Places to Stay & Eat

The most comfortable option is the *Hotel Costa Del Sol* on Cárdenas just north of Madero, where clean, modern rooms cost US$13.75/16.75 for singles/doubles with fan or US$ 17/20 with air-con. The *Hotel Pochutla* (☎ 4-00-33) at Madero 102 has 33 humid but reasonably clean and large rooms with private *baño* for US$8.50/10. *Los Arcos* on Cárdenas opposite Madero is one of the busiest restaurants. There are others on Cárdenas and the zócalo.

Getting There & Away

To/From Oaxaca Oaxaca Pacífico/Estrella del Valle '1st-class ordinario' buses go to/from Oaxaca's 2nd-class bus station eight times daily for US$4.50, taking about 6½ hours. Quicker but dearer is the same companies' 'directo de turismo' service (see Oaxaca Coast introductory Getting There & Away).

Along The Coast Cristóbal Colón runs five 1st-class buses daily to/from Santa Cruz Huatulco (35 km, one hour, US$1) and Salina Cruz (180 km, four hours, US$3.50).

Oaxaca Pacífico/Estrella del Valle runs buses to Puerto Escondido and Santa Cruz Huatulco hourly from 5.30 am to 7.30 pm, and to Puerto Ángel half-hourly from 6 am to 8 pm.

Flecha Roja/Lineas Unidas del Sur/Transportes Gacela 2nd-class buses leave about 20 times daily for Puerto Escondido and Acapulco, and about 15 times daily for Santa Cruz Huatulco between 6 am and 5 pm.

To/From Chiapas Cristóbal Colón's daily 1st-class service to/from San Cristóbal de las Casas (555 km) takes about 12 hours for US$11. Intermediate stops include Juchitán (five hours, US$4.50) and Tuxtla Gutiérrez (10 hours, US$9.50).

PUERTO ÁNGEL

Puerto Ángel (PWERR-toh ANN-hell) is still little more than a fishing village and small-time port straggling round a little bay guarded by two rocky headlands. There's a tiny beach on one side of the bay, but what makes Puerto Ángel a travellers' haven is the beaches a few km either side of the village – in particular the long, empty stretch of pale sand called Zipolite, fabled as southern Mexico's ultimate place to lie back in a hammock and do as little as you like, in as little as you like, for almost as little as you like. Puerto Ángel itself also has a number of good, cheap places to stay and eat.

Fifteen years ago access to Puerto Ángel was only by unpaved road over the Sierra Madre del Sur from Oaxaca. Now you can fly to Puerto Escondido, a couple of hours away by bus, and paved roads lead from Oaxaca, Salina Cruz and Acapulco. But Puerto Ángel is still a sleepy place where a small naval base makes as little difference to the tenor of local life as its slow growth in

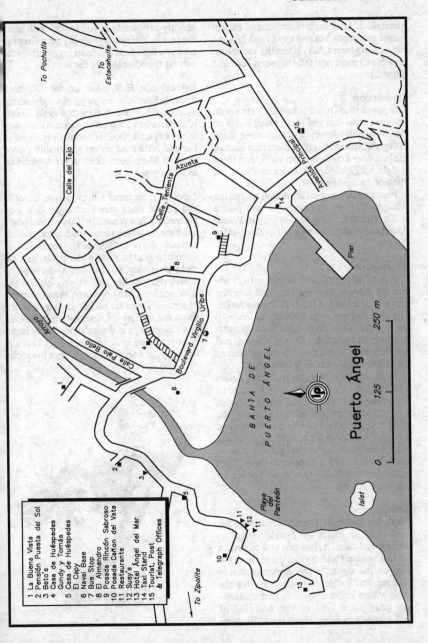

To Pochutla

To Estacahuite

Calle del Tajo

Azueta

Calle Teniente

Avenida Principal

15

Pier

Boulevard Virgilio Uribe

Calle Palo Bello

Arroyo

9

8

14

7

1

6

4

2

3

5

250 m

125

0

BAHÍA DE PUERTO ÁNGEL

Puerto Ángel

Playa del Panteón

11
12
11

10

13

To Zipolite

Islet

1   La Buena Vista
2   Pensión Puesta del Sol
3   Beto's
4   Casa de Huéspedes
    Gundy y Tomás
5   Casa de Huéspedes
    El Capy
6   Naval Base
7   Bus Stop
8   El Almendro
9   Posada Rincón Sabroso
10 Posada Cañon del Vata
11 Restaurants
12 Susy's
13 Hotel Ángel del Mar
14 Taxi Stand
15 Tourist, Post
    & Telegraph Offices

tourism. Like Puerto Escondido, Puerto Ángel gets pretty hot and any breath of wind can be a big bonus. May is usually the hottest month and most rain falls between June and September.

Orientation

The paved road from Pochutla, 13 km north, emerges at the east end of the small Bahía de Puerto Ángel, where you can see most of the village. The road winds on round the back of the bay, over a creek bed, up a hill, then forks – right to Zipolite, left down to Playa del Panteón in the bay itself.

Places to stay and eat are dotted around the village, and there are numerous basic places at Zipolite too. Some people stay in Puerto Ángel and make their way out to Zipolite for the day.

Information

The post, telegraph and tourist offices are side by side on Avenida Principal near the pier at the east end of Bahía de Puerto Ángel. The first two are open Monday to Friday 9 am to 3 pm. The nearest bank is in Pochutla but Casa de Huéspedes Gundy y Tomás and possibly other hostelries will change cash or travellers' cheques at their own rates.

Theft can be a problem in Puerto Ángel and Zipolite – one traveller even wrote to us about being robbed in a taxi going between the two! Another told us that going to the Puerto Ángel police *can* help. Thieves had broken a window in his vehicle one night and helped themselves, but he got his possessions back within a couple of days. Take equal care with drugs – you never know who might set you up.

Beaches

Playa del Panteón
The little beach on the west side of Bahía de Puerto Ángel is shallow and calm. At low tide you can swim out to a sandspit which joins the shore to the islet on the right. In the evenings diving pelicans and locals in boats may fish the same waters inshore. You can rent snorkelling gear from one of the handful of café-restaurants here, whose touts disagree-

ably try to buttonhole you as you walk on to the beach. You could probably get a fisher to take you for a boat trip from here or from the pier on the other side of the bay.

Estacahuite
Half a km up the hill back towards Pochutla, a sign points right, along a path to this beach '500 metres' away. In fact it's 700 metres but worth it to reach three tiny sandy bays, all good for snorkelling. A small bar and restaurant serves reasonably priced seafood. More Eden-like beaches stretch east as far as you can see.

Zipolite
Time takes a back seat in Zipolite and people often stay far longer than they planned *(if* they planned). This remote place has a magic which stems from some combination of the pounding sea and sun, open-air sleeping, strange rocket-like palm huts on rocky pinnacles, and (no doubt) the dope.

But the Zipolite surf is *deadly*, fraught with riptides, changing currents and a strong undertow. There are no life-saving facilities and some visitors drown most years. Locals don't swim here and won't even bring boats inshore. Going in deeper than your knees is risking your life. Keep away from the rocks

at both ends of the beach. If you do get swept out, your best hope is to swim calmly parallel to the shore to get clear of the current pulling you outward.

The wide, palm-fringed beach is a couple of km long. You reach it by a track from Puerto Ángel, which can be walked in about 45 minutes – or a taxi will cover it in 10 minutes for about US$2.25 to the near end, US$3 to the far end. Some taxis operate as colectivos for about US$0.40 per person. A taxi from Pochutla to Zipolite is about US$6.

Lining the end of Zipolite nearest Puerto Ángel is a collection of palm shelters which serve as fisherfolk's homes, restaurants, and bargain accommodation. At the far end rise those rocks with the rocket-shaped huts. Some are part of the Shambhala Posada, called the Casa Gloria after its North American owner. A track, passable for vehicles, leads along behind the beach to Casa Gloria.

Nudity is usually no problem on the beach – just occasionally, men in uniforms wander along asking people to cover up.

Beyond Zipolite A path behind Casa Gloria leads to two more long, sandy beaches. At the first, about a km away, pelicans fishing from a rock may be the only living creatures. The second is the site of a turtle slaughterhouse, where dogs sniff round giant turtles flapping on their backs in the sand, waiting to die and be shipped out in trucks as meat. If you want a reason to become vegetarian, pay a visit.

Places to Stay
Puerto Ángel Some of Puerto Ángel's best accommodation is run by Mexican-North American or Mexican-European couples who have settled here. Places with an elevated position are more likely to catch any breeze there might be. Some have a water shortage; there's usually enough to wash yourself but not always your clothes. What follows is in east-to-west order, as you'll come to them when you arrive.

The little *Posada Rincón Sabroso*, up a flight of steps to the right as you start to wind your way round the bay, is one of the best,

with friendly young owners. Its handful of clean, fan-cooled rooms sits on a greenery-shaded terrace, with a hammock outside each. They have private bathrooms but there's water for only a few hours a day. Singles/doubles are US$11.75/13.50. *El Almendro*, up a little lane a few metres past the Rincón Sabroso steps, is also OK. It has the same prices and is similarly clean, with a shady garden, but the rooms are mostly a bit smaller and darker.

The friendly *Casa de Huéspedes Gundy y Tomás*, breezily placed up a path opposite the naval base, has a variety of rooms ranging from US$7.75/8.50 with a clean shared bathroom to a double with fan and private bath for US$13.50. All have either mosquito nets or mosquito screens on the windows. The cheaper ones are mostly higher up and feel airier. You can also hang or rent an open-air hammock for US$2.50. There's enough water for washing clothes. Food is available and there are pleasant sitting areas.

To reach one of our top choices, *La Buena Vista*, turn right along the creek, then go a short way up the first track on the left. There are about a dozen big clean rooms here ranging from US$10/11.75 to US$12.75/15, all with private bathrooms and opening on to breezy balconies overlooking the bay. They have fans and mosquito screens – though that doesn't always stop the mozzies squeezing between the top of the walls and the roof. A recent addition is an airy terrace restaurant.

The German-owned *Pensión Puesta del Sol* is up to the right beyond the creek. Rooms are sizeable and clean and have fans – but no mosquito screens or nets – for US$6.75/8.25. The shared showers and toilets are clean, and food is available.

Casa de Huéspedes El Capy, on the right as the road descends to Playa del Panteón, has a few clean, cool, though not huge rooms with fan, private bath and mostly good views for US$10/11.75. A good restaurant is part of the same friendly establishment.

The *Posada Cañon del Vata* has just a few comfortable rooms (with fans and private bathrooms) artistically scattered among the foliage on a quiet hillside. This is a good place to stay if you're seeking a quiet retreat, and there's snorkel gear available. Dinner is served at long tables in a lovely palm-roofed, open-sided dining room. Singles/doubles cost US$11.75/15 or US$13.50/16.75 and there's also a bungalow with two double beds for US$20. To get there, follow the road down to Playa del Panteón, then go on round to the right. The entrance is up a flight of steps on the right.

Almost opposite is the start of the road up to the hilltop *Hotel Ángel del Mar*, Puerto Angel's miserable, decaying attempt at an upper-bracket hotel. 'Creepy', 'bug infested' and 'really dirty' are among the descriptions bestowed by readers who had the misfortune to pay its US$24.50/28.25 prices.

Zipolite Several of the palm abodes or comedors at the near end of the beach will rent you a hammock or small room, or let you sling your own hammock. Pick one whose owner will look after, and preferably lock up, your things for you. A hammock space usually costs US$1 to US$1.50, a rented hammock about US$1.75. Places with rooms – mostly US$6 double with shared bathroom but rarely running water – include the *Lola* and *Genesis* restaurants.

The *Shambhala Posada* or *Casa Gloria*, on the hill at the far end of the beach – with great views back along it – offers spaces in a communal hammock area for US$1 with your own hammock or US$1.75 with a rented one, or cabañas with room for one hammock at US$1.75, for two hammocks at US$3.50.

Nowhere at Zipolite has free drinking water so you must add the cost of drinks to your budget there.

Places to Eat
Puerto Ángel Some of the best food is served at two small restaurants round the bay a bit. One is *Beto's*, on the way up the hill past the creek, where a tasty fish filete – which could be Veracruzana, al mojo de ajo, or natural – goes for just US$2.50, a whole snapper for US$4.50, and shrimp dishes for US$5.50. There are seafood cocktails, salads

and meat options too. Beto's is open evenings only. Dearer but usually a treat is the terrace restaurant – deliciously cool in the evenings – of *Casa de Huéspedes El Capy*. Shrimps and snapper (Veracruzana or in garlic sauce) are both US$6.75, a serving of guacamole US$1.50, of papas fritas US$1.75. There are decent breakfasts too for around US$2.

The trio of beach restaurants on Playa del Panteón serves up some fair seafood, but be careful about its freshness in the low tourist season. *Susy's* for instance does big seafood cocktails for US$3.50 to US$5.50, fish dishes around US$3, and shrimp dishes for US$5.50.

Non-residents can eat in the excellent restaurant at the *Posada Cañon del Vata*, where a good dinner (often vegetarian) of soup, main course and salad is served for US$5. Book earlier in the day. From about 7.30 am to 4 pm you can get things like yoghurt with granola and bananas, sandwiches of cheese, avocado, tomato and onion, or enchiladas for around US$2.

Zipolite A fresh fish costs around US$2.50 or US$3 at most of the simple comedors. *Genesis* and *Lola* both have good food – and Lola's does a fine Veracruzana sauce. *Casa Gloria* serves vegetarian food (most items US$2 or less).

Getting There & Away
To/from Oaxaca there's one overnight Estrella del Valle/Oaxaca Pacífico '1st-class' bus – more like what the rest of Mexico understands by '2nd-class', costing US$4.75 and taking about 7½ hours. Southbound, it leaves Oaxaca's 2nd-class bus station at 10.30 pm. Otherwise reaching Puerto Ángel is a matter of reaching Pochutla, 13 km north, then taking local transport. Estrella del Valle buses run between Pochutla and Puerto Ángel every half hour from 6 am to 8 pm for US$0.35. The bus stop in Puerto Ángel is in front of El Árbol restaurant, between the pier and naval base. Colectivos (US$0.60) and taxis (about US$3) also cruise around to take people between the two places.

HUATULCO

Mexico's new mega-resort for the 21st century began taking shape in the late 1980s on a series of picturesque sandy bays, now called the Bahías de Huatulco ('wah-TOOL-koh'), some 35 km east of Pochutla. 'The new Cancún' is a common and apt label for what's being created: along a coastline where formerly only one small fishing village stood, Huatulco is planned to have 9000 hotel rooms and a population of 100,000 – nearly half Cancún's present size – by the turn of the century, and to carry on growing thereafter. In contrast to Cancún, six storeys is the maximum building height.

For the moment the only accommodation actually on the coast is in top-end resorts. You can pick your way between building sites to less expensive places to stay and eat inland, though there's nothing bottom end and nowhere in the laid-back mould of Puerto Ángel or Puerto Escondido. Why come? Well, the jungle-backed bays and beaches are indeed beautiful, and most are still tranquil, while there's an unusual excitement in the brand-new towns popping up where before was only tangled forest. It's also oddly fascinating to witness jungle becoming instant modern city before your eyes.

The seed of the project is said to have been sown one day in 1982 when President José López Portillo took a boat trip along the coast with his Minister of Tourism Rosa Luz Alegría. Until then, this barely peopled coast was known to only a few outsiders as a great place for a quiet swim in translucent waters, and good fresh seafood. During the early years of development some locals complained of official pressure and trickery over compensation for their lands.

Orientation

From west to east, the eight bays are San Agustín, Chachacual, Cacaluta, Maguey y Organo, Santa Cruz, Chahue, Tangolunda and Conejos. It's about 20 km as the crow flies from San Agustín to Conejos. The village of Santa Cruz Huatulco on Santa Cruz Bay is one initial centre of tourist devel-

opment; the other is Tangolunda Bay, where the first top-end resorts have gone up.

Both are linked to each other and to the Acapulco-Pochutla-Salina Cruz Highway 200 by new roads: Santa Cruz Huatulco is four km from the highway, Tangolunda seven km. Between Santa Cruz Huatulco and the highway is La Crucecita, the brand new service town for the area.

Huatulco airport is on the north side of Highway 200, 12 km west of the turning to the resorts. Santa María Huatulco, north of the highway between the airport and the turning, is being turned into the area's administrative and commercial centre.

Information

Banamex has a branch on Juárez in Santa Cruz Huatulco and there's a casa de cambio across the street from the Sheraton at Tangolunda Bay. There are travel agents in the big hotels and on the zócalo at La Crucecita.

Things to See & Do

Santa Cruz Huatulco, where most of the tourist-oriented shops are destined to be, so far consists of little more than one boulevard – Juárez – a km or so long. But it has a pretty little harbour, with a silver and handcrafts market on one side. This is the starting point for lanchas to the other bays. Fixed prices are posted for a round trip for up to 10 people, which can include a stay of several hours up to no later than 5 pm: for example Tangolunda or Maguey y Organo Bay US$16.75, Chachagual Bay US$46.75. Some beaches are also accessible by road.

La India beach on Chachagual Bay is so far undeveloped and one of the most beautiful. Maguey and Organo beaches, separated only by a thin strip of vegetation, have clear calm waters good for snorkelling. La Entrega (The Handover) beach on Santa Cruz Bay is where in 1831 the Mexican independence hero Vicente Guerrero was delivered to his enemies by an Italian sea captain who had betrayed him for 50,000 pieces of gold. Guerrero was taken to Cuilapan, near Oaxaca, and shot.

There's a golf course at Tangolunda and

the top-end resorts all lay on varied sporting and other activities. Some also lay on day tours by plane to Oaxaca, Monte Albán, Mitla and so on for US$200 or so.

Places to Stay

Prices in Huatulco vary wildly with the seasons. The low season is May to July. Prices start to rise in August and in the peak months of December to April may even double.

La Crucecita The service town for the resort area, beside the road leading from Highway 200 to Santa Cruz Huatulco and Tangolunda, has the cheapest options. Most are grouped around the wide Plaza Principal, or zócalo. The *Hotel Posada Del Parque* on the south side of the zócalo has adequately comfortable but moderate-sized fan-cooled rooms with private bath for US$27 single or double in low season. Prices and rooms are similar at the *Hotel Grifer*, a block east of the zócalo at the corner of Guamúchil and Carrizal. You get a small balcony with some rooms at the Grifer.

Suites Bugambilias (☎ (958) 7-00-18) on Bugambilia just off the south-east corner of the zócalo has slightly more comfortable fan-cooled rooms, opening on to upstairs walkways, for US$27/33 singles/doubles in low season. Top place is the pink *Hotel Flamboyant* (☎ (958) 7-01-13) on the north-west corner of the zócalo, with a pleasant interior courtyard, air-conditioned rooms at US$46 single or double (low season), and its own restaurant and pool.

Santa Cruz Huatulco The *Posada Binniguenda* (☎ (958) 4-00-77) at Boulevard Juárez 5 (towards the far western end) is Huatulco's oldest hotel, dating from 1987. It's a pleasant place with colonial decor, its own restaurant and coffee shop, and 75 air-con rooms ranging between about US$70 and US$123 single or double.

The only other hotel near completion on our visit was the *Hotel Castillo de Huatulco* (☎ 7-00-51) by the roundabout at the start of Boulevard Juárez, which may be in a slightly cheaper bracket than the Binniguenda.

Tangolunda Bay The biggest *Club Med* (☎ (958) 1-00-33, toll-free in the USA 800-258-2633) in the western hemisphere stands alone on the west side of Tangolunda Bay, reached by its own half-km approach from the Santa Cruz-Tangolunda road. It's in 20-hectare grounds with three pools, four beaches, and 500 bungalow-style air-con and fan-cooled rooms with hammock-slung balconies.

Most guests come on packages which include air fare, three meals a day, and a vast array of activities from tennis and volleyball through windsurfing and snorkelling to shows and discos. If you exclude the airfare you'll usually be paying between US$200 and US$300 double per night.

On the east side of Tangolunda Bay, 1½ km from the Club Med, a town is growing up. Its seafront is taken up by the pink *Sheraton Huatulco Resort* (☎ (958) 1-00-55, toll-free in the USA 800-325-3535) and the adjacent *Royal Maeva* resort (☎ (958) 1-00-00, toll-free in the USA 800-431-2138), both with 300-plus ocean-view rooms, fine beaches, gardens, pools, sports facilities and entertainment.

At the less hectic Sheraton rates start from about US$200 double, room only, while at the Club Med-like Royal Maeva a similar price includes meals and activities. You can also visit the Royal Maeva just for a day (US$67 per person, low season) or an evening (US$33.50).

Places to Eat

In La Crucecita there's a wide range of eateries on the zócalo – walk round and make your choice. Prices are a bit higher than in Puerto Escondido or Puerto Ángel. There are a few cheaper places, plus a pizzeria, along Gardenia, which runs north from the zócalo's north-west corner.

Santa Cruz Huatulco has a number of comedors near the harbour but is, so far, short on classier restaurants, though that will doubtless change. Tangolunda Bay has a pizzeria and one or two other restaurants across the street from its hotels. There are palapa seafood joints on some of the beaches including El Maguey.

Getting There & Away

Air The airport is called both Huatulco and Bahías de Huatulco, so look for both names in timetables. Aerocaribe and Aeromorelos both fly daily to/from Oaxaca (40 minutes, US$55). Aeroméxico and Mexicana both fly twice daily to/from Mexico City (one hour, US$70). Aerolibertad flies between Huatulco and Acapulco (US$85) each Friday at the time of writing. Aerocaribe and Méxicana share an office (☎ 7-02-23) in the Hotel Castillo de Huatulco on Boulevard Juárez in Santa Cruz Huatulco. Aeroméxico (☎ 4-03-28) is currently at the airport only.

Bus Make sure your bus is heading to Santa Cruz Huatulco or La Crucecita, not Santa María Huatulco, which is a long, long way from the coast. If it's marked 'Bahías de Huatulco', it'll be OK. In La Crucecita, most bus terminals are on Gardenia, leading north off the zócalo.

Along The Coast Santa Cruz Huatulco is on the routes of several services on the coastal Highway 200. Second-class fares and journey times include: Pochutla (35 km) one hour, US$1; Puerto Escondido (105 km) two hours, US$2.50; Salina Cruz (150 km) three hours, US$2.50. Services include:

Lineas Unidas Del Sur/Transportes Gacela/Flecha Roja – 2nd-class buses to/from Pochutla and Puerto Escondido at least hourly, about 6 am to 5 pm.
Oaxaca Pacífico/Estrella del Valle – 2nd-class buses to/from Pochutla hourly until 8 pm.
Cristóbal Colón – 1st-class buses to/from Pochutla and Salina Cruz five times daily.
Transportes Oaxaca-Istmo – 2nd-class buses to/from Salina Cruz, Pochutla and Puerto Escondido five or six times daily.

Others Between Oaxaca and Santa Cruz Huatulco there's one overnight 1st-class service each way by Cristóbal Colón via Salina Cruz (eight hours, US$8), plus two daily Estrella del Valle/Oaxaca Pacífico services, '1st-class' in name only, using the 2nd-class bus station in Oaxaca, taking seven hours for US$5.50.

Cristóbal Colón runs a daily bus each way to/from San Cristóbal de las Casas (US$10.50) via Tuxtla Gutiérrez.

Car Budget (☎ 7-00-34) has offices in La Crucecita and the Royal Maeva and Posada Binniguenda hotels. Dollar (☎ 1-00-38) is in the Sheraton.

Getting Around

To/From the Airport Transporte Terrestre provides colectivo combis to Santa Cruz Huatulco for US$6.75 per person and Tangolunda Bay for US$7.75, or taxis for US$19.75 and US$22.75 respectively. Get tickets at their airport kiosk.

Taxi A taxi between any two of La Crucecita, Santa Cruz Huatulco and Tangolunda Bay costs about US$3.

Isthmus of Tehuantepec

Eastern Oaxaca occupies the southern half of the 200 km-wide Isthmus of Tehuantepec (teh-wan-teh-PECK), Mexico's narrowest point and only coast-to-coast stretch of lowland. This is sweaty, unpretty country. Of its three towns, Tehuantepec is the most appealing but Salina Cruz and Juchitán – each with a sizeable share of Oaxaca's limited industry – are more likely places to change buses.

If you want a bus along the Oaxaca coast to Huatulco, Pochutla or Puerto Escondido, get to Salina Cruz where most of them start. For buses into Chiapas or north across the isthmus, go to Juchitán. Frequent local buses link all three isthmus towns. If you do spend a night or two here – perhaps waiting for a bus connection – you'll probably be agreeably surprised by the people's liveliness and friendliness.

Fifteen km east of Juchitán, around La Ventosa where Highway 185 to Acayucan, Tabasco and Veracruz diverges from Highway 190 to Chiapas, strong winds sweep down from the north and sometimes blow high vehicles off the road.

History & People

In 1496 the isthmus Zapotecs repulsed the Aztecs from the fortress of Guiengola near Tehuantepec, and the isthmus never became part of the Aztec Empire. Later some of the strongest resistance against the Spaniards took place here, notably from 1524 to 1527 (by an alliance of Zapotecs, Mixes, Zoques and Chontals), and in the 1660 Tehuantepec rebellion.

Isthmus women are much more open and confident than women in most of Mexico. They're physically well-built and take a leading role in business and politics. They're also famous for their costumes. Many older women still wear embroidered huipils and voluminous printed skirts. For fiestas, Tehuantepec and Juchitán women turn out in velvet or sateen huipils and skirts embroidered with fantastically colourful silk flowers. They also deck themselves in gold and silver jewellery, a sign of wealth. Many isthmus fiestas feature the curious Tirada de Frutas in which women climb on roofs and throw fruit on the men below.

Miguel Covarrubias, the Mexican artist who wrote one of the best books on the culture of Bali, did the same for the Isthmus of Tehuantepec with *Mexico South*, published in 1946. It's a fascinating read but sadly a lot of what he describes has now disappeared.

TEHUANTEPEC

Population: 47,000

Tehuantepec is a jolly, friendly town where there's often a fiesta going on in one of the barrios. A curious form of local transport is the *motocarro* – a kind of three-wheel buggy in which the driver sits on a front seat while the passenger stands behind on a platform.

Orientation & Information

The Oaxaca-Tuxtla Gutiérrez Highway 190 meets Highway 185, from Salina Cruz, just west of Tehuantepec then skirts the north edge of the town. Tehuantepec's bus stations, collectively known as 'Terminal', are just off Highway 190 on the north-eastern side of town, about 1½ km from the centre. Some buses, including most local ones to/from Salina Cruz, also stop where the highway passes the end of 5 de Mayo, opposite the Posada Colonial, only a minute's walk from the zócalo. The street along the west side of the zócalo, which 5 de Mayo meets beside the dark, smelly market, is Romero. Parallel to Romero on the far, eastern side of the zócalo is Juárez. Across the north side is 22 de Marzo, with the post and telegraph offices.

Guiengola

The hilltop Zapotec stronghold of Guiengola, where the Aztecs were defeated in 1496, is seven km north of the Oaxaca road from a turning about 11 km out of Tehuantepec. A sign points to 'Ruínas Guiengola 7' just past the 240-km marker. The site is open daily from 10 am to 6 pm and you can see the remains of a big pyramid, a few smaller buildings, and a thick, high defensive wall.

Festivals

Each Tehuantepec barrio has its own main fiesta, which continues for several days around the allotted saint's day and includes tiradas de frutas and lots of marimba music. Barrios and fiestas are:

Lieza – San Sebastián, 22 January.
Guichiveri & Atotonilco – San Juan, 24 June.
Vishana – San Pedro, 30 June.
Santa María, San Jacinto & Santa Cruz – Assumption, 15 August.
Laborio – Birth of the Virgin Mary, 10 September.
San Jerónimo & Cerrito – San Miguel, 1 October.

Places to Stay

Hotel Donají (☎ 5-00-64) at Juárez 10, two blocks south of the zócalo, has clean rooms with private bath (intermittent hot water) on two upper floors, most of them round a central court with wide, open-air walkways. Singles/doubles with fan are US$8.50/12, with air-con US$16.75/21.75. The rooms in the middle are quietest. *Hotel Oasis* (☎ 5-00-08) at Ocampo 8 on the corner of Romero, one block south of the zócalo, has slightly smaller, fan-cooled rooms and similar standards, for US$8.50/12.50.

Casa de Huéspedes Istmo at Hidalgo 31 – Hidalgo is the street heading north beside the post office on the zócalo – has a nice courtyard and small, only tolerably clean rooms for US$6.75/10 with shared bath, or US$13.50 double with private bath.

On Highway 200 about two km east of town, *Hotel Calli* (☎ 5-00-85) has air-conditioned rooms in the US$25 to US$45 range.

Places to Eat

Mariscos Rafa on the north side of the zócalo is an unpretentious little seafood restaurant doing excellent fish dishes for around US$5.50, seafood cocktails for US$2.50 to US$4.75 and shrimps several ways at around US$7. The aguacate relleno de camarones (avocado stuffed with shrimps) turns out to be a whole, generous plateful of the two items and a meal in itself at US$4.50. On the same side of the zócalo, *Restaurant La Carreta* does good fish Veracruzana for US$4.75 and antojitos for around US$3.50. In the evenings tables are set up in the zócalo for cheap open-air eating.

Getting There & Away

See Orientation and Getting Around for where to find the buses. The 250-km trip from Oaxaca takes 4½ hours in a 1st-class bus. You're winding downhill for the middle 160 km – spot the dead vehicles on the slopes below.

Cristóbal Colón runs five daily 1st-class buses to Oaxaca (US$4.75), plus one or two daily to Mexico City (US$18.50, 14 hours), Tuxtla Gutiérrez (US$5.50, five hours), Tapachula (US$8, 6½ hours), Huatulco (US$3, three hours), Pochutla (US$4, four hours) and Veracruz (US$11.50, eight hours). Most departures are late at night or very early in the morning. The 2nd-class line

Sur has a few buses to Oaxaca, Tapachula and Tuxtla Gutiérrez.

From the local bus station, across the street from the long-distance terminal, buses run to Juchitán (25 km, US$0.45) and Salina Cruz (15 km, US$0.35) at least every half-hour, taking half an hour to either place.

Getting Around

Taxis (about US$0.75), colectivos (US$0.20) and 'Centro-Terminal' buses all run between the zócalo and the bus stations. On foot, take Romero north out of the zócalo, turn right on to Guerrero after two or three blocks, then left up Avenida Héroes after another block or two.

SALINA CRUZ

When a railway was built across the isthmus at the turn of the century, Salina Cruz became an important port. But a lack of major oil finds and the cutting of the Panama Canal further south soon ended its prosperity. In recent years the area has received some spin-offs from the oil boom in Tabasco, Veracruz and Chiapas, and Salina Cruz has developed again as a pipeline terminal, with a big refinery. It has a bit of a Wild West feel today.

Orientation

Highway 200 from Puerto Escondido and Pochutla meets the Salina Cruz-Tehuantepec road, Highway 185, on the northern edge of Salina Cruz, about three km from the town centre. Salina Cruz's many bus stations lie on or just off the road between here and the town centre: the tiny orange-and-white terminal of Transportes Oaxaca-Istmo (2nd class) is just across the railway tracks from the junction of the two highways; Sur (2nd class) is on Obrero, a few paces off the main road nearly half way to the centre; Cristóbal Colón (1st class) is on Primero de Mayo, just off the main road two blocks past Obrero; local buses from Tehuantepec and Juchitán and a collection of other small bus lines congregate in an open area beside the railway, opposite Primero de Mayo.

If your bus connections work out right, you may not need to venture into the centre with its wide, windy zócalo, at all. The road from Tehuantepec becomes Avenida Tampico as it nears the centre, passing a block west of the zócalo, which is to the left. The market is on the far left corner as you enter the zócalo from Avenida Tampico.

Places to Stay

You needn't stray off 5 de Mayo, the street along the east side of the zócalo, if you need to stay in Salina Cruz. Side by side on 5 de Mayo, 1½ blocks south of the zócalo between Coatzacoalcos and Libertad, are the *Hotel Altagracia*, with clean air-con rooms for US$24/28.50, a good little restaurant and friendly management, and the less welcoming but reasonably clean *Posada Bonampak* with sizeable fan-cooled rooms at US$8.50/11.75.

Half a block north of the zócalo at 5 de Mayo 43, the *Hotel Magda* (☎ 4-01-07) has ordinary but again reasonably clean rooms with fans for US$10.75/13.50. External, upstairs rooms are airier. The *Hotel Bugambilias* a couple of blocks further north on 5 de Mayo, at the corner of Manzanillo, looks like the top place in town.

Places to Eat

The *Restaurant El Lugar* on 5 de Mayo at the south-eastern corner of the zócalo has clean, modern surroundings and a mixed menu of decently-prepared food from egg dishes or hamburguesas at US$2 to US$3 to carne asada at US$4, fish or steaks at US$5 to US$6. At the north-eastern corner of the zócalo the *Restaurant La Jaiba Loca* is a big, echoing, concrete-floored place busy with locals downing a beer with their fish filete (US$4.50), seafood cocktail (US$2.50 or US$4.50) or shrimps (US$6).

Getting There & Away

See Orientation for the location of bus stations.

Along The Oaxaca Coast Cristóbal Colón on Primero de Mayo runs five daily 1st-class buses to/from Santa Cruz Huatulco (150 km, US$2.50, three hours) and Pochutla (180 km, US$3.50, four hours). From 4 am to 8 pm there are hourly 2nd-class departures to the same places plus Puerto Escondido (250 km, US$4.50, five hours) from the rabbit hutch-like office of Transportes Del Istmo and other minor lines, in the yard by the railway opposite Primero de Mayo. Transportes Oaxaca-Istmo runs six daily 2nd-class buses to the same places.

To the East There are more eastbound buses from Juchitán, but Cristóbal Colón (1st class) still goes to Tuxtla Gutiérrez (US$6, 5½ hours, twice daily), San Cristóbal de las Casas (US$7.50, 7½ hours, once daily), Tapachula (US$8.50, seven hours, once daily) and Villahermosa (US$9, eight hours, twice daily). Sur runs two 2nd-class buses daily to Tapachula, one to Tuxtla Gutiérrez, and 11 to Acayucan (US$4.25, four hours). From 4.15 am to 11.15 pm there are hourly buses to Acayucan and Coatzacoalcos by Transportes Del Istmo, etc, from the station opposite Primero de Mayo.

To Tehuantepec & Juchitán Buses leave at least half-hourly from the railway-side yard opposite Primero de Mayo. Tehuantepec is 15 km and half an hour away for US$0.35; Juchitán is 40 km and an hour for US$0.80.

To Oaxaca & Mexico City Cristóbal Colón runs four daily buses to Oaxaca and six to Mexico City; Sur runs two and Transportes Oaxaca-Istmo five to Oaxaca.

Getting Around

Blue city buses (US$0.20) run along the road between the bus terminals and the city centre every few minutes. Their departure point on the zócalo is the south-eastern corner, where 5 de Mayo meets Acapulco. Tell the conductor which bus station you want.

JUCHITÁN

Population: 55,000
This town mainly serves as a bus junction for nearby towns.

Top: Tziscao village, Lagos de Montebello, Chiapas (JN)
Left: Lagos de Montebello, Chiapas (JN)
Right: Sumidero Canyon, Chiapa de Corzo, Chiapas (JN)

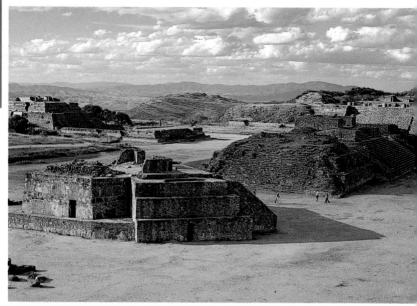

Top: Observatory, Monte Albán, Oaxaca state (JN)
Left: Iglesia Santo Domingo, Oaxaca (TW)
Right: Church of Coixtlahuaca, Oaxaca (JN)

Orientation

Local buses from Salina Cruz and Tehuantepec turn right from Highway 190 into Prolongación 16 de Septiembre, at a crossroads as they hit the edge of Juchitán. The main long-distance bus terminal is on the right after about 100 metres. The 2nd-class buses of Fletes y Pasajes and Autotransportes Tuxtla Gutiérrez use the separate FYPSA terminal, separated from the main one by the Pemex station at the crossroads.

Places to Stay & Eat

Hotel Malla, upstairs in the bus station, has cool, tolerably clean rooms with private bathrooms for US$8/10 singles/doubles. The more comfortable *Hotel La Mansión* (☎ 2-10-55) at Prolongación 16 de Septiembre No 11, two blocks into town from the bus station, has air-con rooms for US$18.75/20.50, and its own restaurant. *Restaurant La Oaxaqueña* at the crossroads does good carne asada for US$3.50. There are five or six other meat and fish dishes available. *Café Colón*, oddly located at the rear of the petrol station across the road, is the rather plush alternative with bow-tied waiters, wine, and higher prices.

Getting There & Away

The majority of buses are de paso and at busy times you may have to wait some hours before getting a place.

To Chiapas If you're going to Tuxtla Gutiérrez and things get desperate, consider taking a bus to Arriaga (135 km, two hours) then another to Tuxtla from there. Cristóbal Colón has six 1st-class buses daily to Tuxtla Gutiérrez (250 km, US$5, five hours), two to San Cristóbal de las Casas (335 km, US$6.50, seven hours), two to Tapachula (390 km, US$7.50, six hours), and one just to Tonalá (160 km, US$3.25, 2½ hours). Sur (2nd class) runs seven daily buses to Tapachula and four to Tuxtla Gutiérrez. Fletes y Pasajes and Autotransportes Tuxtla Gutiérrez run four daily buses to Tuxtla Gutiérrez and 18 to Arriaga. The last to Arriaga is at 7 pm.

To Veracruz & Tabasco Cristóbal Colón 1st-class buses go to Villahermosa (420 km, US$8.25, seven hours) four times daily and Veracruz (445 km, US$10.75, eight hours) twice daily. Sur (2nd class) has seven daily locales to Acayucan (195 km, US$3.50, three hours). AU (2nd class) has one or two daily to Veracruz and Xalapa.

To Oaxaca & Mexico City Cristóbal Colón 1st-class buses go to Oaxaca (270 km, US$6, five hours) eight times daily – mostly in the small hours of the morning – and to Mexico City (US$17.75, 14 hours) three times. Sur runs five and Fletes y Pasajes/Autotransportes Tuxtla Gutiérrez 18 daily 2nd-class buses to Oaxaca. AU runs five 2nd-class buses to Mexico City daily.

To the Oaxaca Coast Cristóbal Colón runs two daily 1st-class buses to Huatulco and Pochutla but there are many more departures from Salina Cruz.

To Tehuantepec & Salina Cruz Local buses go every half-hour or less from the the long-distance terminal to Tehuantepec (15 km, 30 minutes, US$0.45) and Salina Cruz (40 km, one hour, US$0.80).

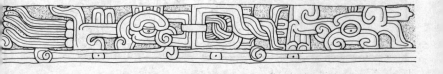

Chiapas

Mexico's southernmost state has enormous variety and is one of our favourites. At the centre of Chiapas is San Cristóbal de las Casas, a cool, tranquil hill-country colonial town surrounded by mysterious, very traditional Indian villages. Two hours west – and nearly 1600 metres lower – the surprisingly modern state capital, Tuxtla Gutiérrez, has probably Mexico's country's best zoo, devoted entirely to Chiapas' very varied fauna. Only a few km from Tuxtla is the 1000-metre-deep Sumidero Canyon, through which you can take an awesome boat ride.

Three hours south-east of San Cristóbal, near the border with Guatemala, with which Chiapas has always had much in common, is the lovely Montebello Lakes region. Chiapas also has a steamy Pacific coast, where Puerto Arista near Tonalá is a very laid-back beach spot.

About four hours north of San Cristóbal are the Agua Azul waterfalls, among

Mexico's most spectacular. A little further on are the ruins of Palenque, one of the most beautiful of all ancient Maya sites. Further east are the other fine Chiapas Maya sites Yaxchilán and Bonampak, both deep in the Lacandón jungle, one of Mexico's largest areas of tropical rainforest. You can even go from Palenque to Flores and Tikal in Guatemala's El Petén.

If you're heading for Guatemala, Chiapas is the main gateway. If you're not, try to fit Chiapas into your plans anyway. Most travellers who have stumbled upon it by chance have stayed longer than they planned.

HISTORY
Pre-Hispanic civilisations straddled the Chiapas-Guatemala border, and for most of the colonial era Chiapas was governed from Guatemala.

Pre-Hispanic
Central and coastal Chiapas came under the

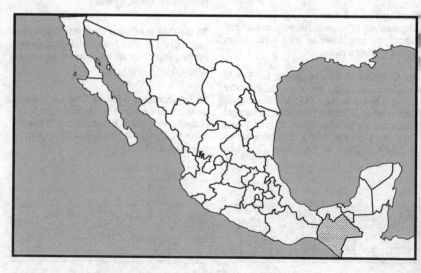

influence – conquest, trade or missionary – of the Olmecs, who flourished on the Gulf Coast from about 1300 to 400 BC. Izapa, in the southern corner of Chiapas near Tapachula, was the centre of a culture which peaked around 200 BC to 200 AD and is thought to be a link between the Olmec and the Maya.

During the Classic era (approximately 300-900 AD) coastal and central Chiapas were relative backwaters, but low-lying, jungly eastern Chiapas gave rise to two important Maya city-states, Palenque and Yaxchilán, which both flourished in the 7th and 8th centuries. Toniná and Chinkultic

Polychrome Maya statue

were lesser Maya centres. The Chiapas Maya sites were more closely related to those of Petén in northern Guatemala than to those of Yucatán, whose art style was less realistic.

After the Classic Maya collapse, highland Chiapas and Guatemala came to be divided among a number of often warring mini-empires, many with cultures descended from the Maya but some also with rulers claiming central Mexican Toltec ancestry. Coastal Chiapas, a rich source of cacao from which chocolate is made, was conquered by the Aztecs at the end of the 15th century and became their most distant province, under the name Xoconochco (from which its present name, Soconusco, is derived).

Spanish Era

Soconusco was subdued by the Spanish in 1524, lying as it did on Pedro de Alvarado's route to conquer Guatemala. Central Chiapas didn't come under effective Spanish control until the 1528 expedition of Diego de Mazariegos, who defeated the dominant, warlike Chiapa Indians, many of whom jumped to death in Sumidero Canyon rather than be captured. Outlying areas of Chiapas were subdued in the 1530s and 1540s, though the Spanish never gained control of the Lacandón forest which remained a Maya refuge.

Soconusco and inland Chiapas were administered separately, both from Guatemala, for most of the Spanish era, which meant that they lacked supervision for long periods and there was little check on colonists' excesses against the Indians. Aside from being sold into slavery, forced to work on encomiendas and paying severe taxes, the Indians were moved out of their villages into small settlements where they could be more easily controlled. New diseases were brought by the Spanish and one epidemic in 1544 killed about half the Indians of Chiapas. Numerous rebellions were brutally put down.

The only light in the Indians' darkness was the work of some Spanish church figures, among them the Dominican monks. Pre-eminent was Bartolomé de las Casas

(1474-1566), appointed the first bishop of Chiapas in 1545. Las Casas had come to the Caribbean as an ordinary colonist, but in 1510 he entered the Dominican order and spent the rest of his life fighting for Indian rights in the new colonies. His achievements, including partly observed laws reducing compulsory labour (1543) and banning Indian (but not black) slavery (1550), earned him the hostility of the colonists but the affection of the Indians. He spent only six months in his diocese, being occupied with campaigns on a wider scale.

19th & 20th Centuries

In 1821, with the end of Spanish rule over Mexico and Central America, Chiapas' leaders declared their wish to join Mexico, were accepted, and sent deputies to the national congress. The Central American states (including Guatemala) were annexed by Mexico in 1822. When the Mexican congress was dissolved in 1823, a Chiapas junta, with representatives from each of its districts, was set up to govern temporarily. The Central American states declared themselves independent as the United Provinces of Central America.

Chiapas rejoined Mexico in 1824 after a referendum in which 96,829 Chiapanecos voted to rejoin Mexico against 60,400 in favour of joining Central America. Support for the Central American option had been stronger in Soconusco and only in 1882 did Guatemala (by then a separate country) officially recognise Mexican rule over Soconusco.

Lands continued to be taken from the Indians and the most symbolic event of the 19th century was the 1869 to 1870 Chamula rebellion. It was sparked by the arrest of a young Tzotzil girl who was at the centre of a religious cult, which spread through central Chiapas and narrowly failed to take San Cristóbal de las Casas.

San Cristóbal was capital of the state until 1892, when the title went to Tuxtla Gutiérrez – apparently because of hostility in San Cristóbal toward the Mexican dictator Porfirio Díaz, who encouraged the takeover

of peasant land by big landowners. In the same era the Soconusco coffee plantations were notorious for the near-slavery of their Indian workers.

The question of which city was to be the state capital was not taken lightly. In 1911 there was a mini-war between the two rivals with Tuxtla victorious and many Tzotzil Indians massacred.

Today, just 1% of Chiapas' landowners – now including descendants of Nazi-era German immigrants in the Soconusco as well as the older Spanish-descended families – hold nearly half the state and there are still clashes over land rights. Samuel Ruíz García, the bishop of San Cristóbal, who follows in the las Casas tradition of support for Indian causes, is nicknamed *El Obispo Rojo* (The Red Bishop) by the establishment press. The powers-that-be clamp down, often violently, against movements like OCEZ, the Organización Campesina Emiliano Zapata, which campaigns for the return of land awarded to the peasants by the courts but not handed over. In 1991 OCEZ members staged a hunger strike beside the Tuxtla Gutiérrez zócalo in protest against the deliberate burning down of some villages and the imprisonment of villagers.

Refugees

Between 1981 and 1983 Guatemalan Indians streamed into Chiapas to escape the savage Guatemalan army. The first arrivals were sent back at gunpoint but others replaced them and by the next year there were tens of thousands of Guatemalan refugees in Chiapas in makeshift camps.

In the mid-1980s Mexico, perhaps afraid that the arrivals would upset its relations with Guatemala and stir discontent in Chiapas, moved nearly half the 46,000 recognised refugees to new camps in Campeche and Quintana Roo. Most of the remainder stayed on in 100 or more poorer camps in Chiapas, mainly near the border in the Comalapa, Lagos de Montebello and other areas, where conditions slowly improved over the years.

Other Guatemalans not recognised as refugees, and fugitives from the civil war in El

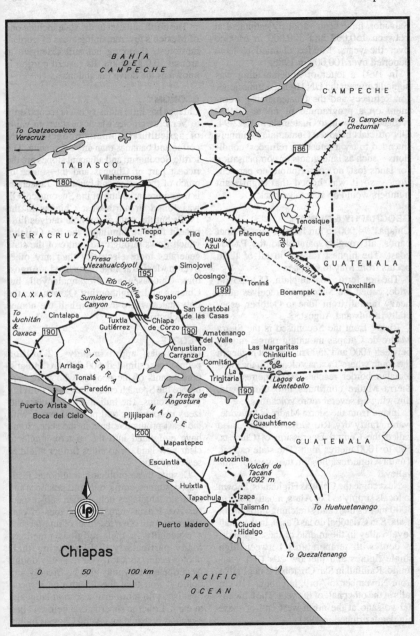

Chiapas

0   50   100 km

Salvador, have been variously estimated at between 150,000 and 300,000 in Mexico over the years. Mexico claimed to have deported over 100,000 in 1986.

In 1991 a letter of understanding was signed between the UN High Commissioner for Refugees and the Guatemalan government on a programme of up to 30,000 refugees returning to Guatemala in 1992-94. UN officials believed Guatemala genuinely intended to try to meet the refugees' conditions – such as land grants or compensation for lands lost, no conscription, no persecution – so it was hoped that significant numbers would be able to go back.

GEOGRAPHY & CLIMATE
Chiapas' 74,000 sq km fall into five distinct bands, all roughly parallel to the Pacific coast. The highest rainfall in all of them occurs from May to October.

The hot, fertile coastal plain, 15 to 35 km wide, called the Soconusco, receives quite heavy rainfall from June to October, especially in July and August.

Rising from the Soconusco is the Sierra Madre de Chiapas mountain range, mostly between 1000 and 2500 metres but higher in the south where Tacaná volcano on the Guatemalan border reaches 4092 metres. The Sierra Madre continues into Guatemala, throwing up several more volcanoes.

Inland from the Sierra Madre is the wide, warm, fairly dry Río Grijalva valley, also called the Central Depression of Chiapas, 500 to 1000 metres high. The state capital, Tuxtla Gutiérrez, lies in the west of this valley.

Next come the Chiapas Highlands, known to locals simply as Los Altos, mostly 2000 to 3000 metres high and stretching into Guatemala. San Cristóbal de las Casas, in the small Jovel valley in the middle of these uplands, is cool with temperatures between high single figures and the low 20s (°C) year-round. Rainfall in San Cristóbal is negligible from November to April, but about 110 cm falls in the other half of the year. The Chichonal volcano at the north-west end of these highlands erupted in 1981.

The north and east of the state include one of Mexico's few remaining areas of tropical rainforest, shrinking but still extensive at around 10,000 sq km. Its eastern portion is known as the Selva Lacandona.

ECONOMY
Chiapas has little industry but is second only to Veracruz among Mexican states in value of agricultural output, producing more coffee and bananas than any other state. The fertile Soconusco and adjacent slopes are the richest part of Chiapas and the source of much of the coffee and bananas. Tapachula is the commercial hub of the Soconusco. Oil was found in north-west Chiapas in the 1970s but the state as a whole derives little benefit from it. Similarly, the Río Grijalva which flows through the centre of the state generates more electricity than any other river in Mexico at huge dams like La Angostura, Chicoasén and Nezahualcóyotl, but Chiapas and neighbouring Oaxaca are the only states where less than half the homes have electricity.

PEOPLE
Of Chiapas' approximately 3.2 million people, an estimated 600,000 are Indians, descendants of the peoples who were here before the Spanish came, including outlying Maya groups. The Indians are 2nd-class citizens in economic and political terms, with the least productive land in the state. Some have emigrated into the eastern jungle to clear new land, or to cities further afield in search of jobs.

Despite these problems, traditional festivals, costumes, crafts, religious practices and separate languages help Indian self-respect survive. Indians remain suspicious of outsiders, and are often resentful of interference – especially in their religious practices. Many particularly dislike having their photos taken, so ask if you're in any doubt. Nevertheless they may also be friendly and polite if you treat them with due respect. Spanish is no more than a second language to them. Belief in supernatural beings called *naguales* is shared by several Chiapas Indian peoples. A person who has a nagual can usually take on other human or animal forms and commit either harmful or protective deeds. Disease is widely believed to result either from the actions of naguales or from failure to pay homage to a particular deity. Curanderos cure illness by ritual and herbal methods.

Indian Peoples

The Indian people that travellers are most likely to come into contact with are the 150,000 or so **Tzotzils** around San Cristóbal de las Casas. Tzotzil textiles are among the most varied, colourful and elaborately worked in Mexico. You may also encounter the **Tzeltals**, another strongly traditional people, about 220,000 strong, who inhabit the region just east of San Cristóbal.

Other Chiapas Indians include about 80,000 **Chols** on the north side of the Chiapas highlands and the low-lying areas beyond, east and west of Palenque; an estimated 20,000 Mexican **Mames** near the Guatemalan border between Tapachula and Ciudad Cuauhtémoc, including some on the slopes of Tacaná (many more Mames – around 300,000 – are Guatemalans); and the **Zoques**, some 25,000 of whom used to inhabit western Chiapas, but were dispersed by the 1981 Chichonal eruption. Some have moved back to the area and there are hopes that the damage is not irreversible.

There are still a few hundred **Lacandóns**, the last true inheritors of ancient Maya traditions, in the eastern Chiapas rainforest, with a language related to Yucatán Maya which they themselves call 'Maya'. The past four decades have wrought more changes in Lacandón life than the previous four centuries: 100,000 land-hungry settlers have arrived in the forest, and North American missionaries have succeeded in converting some Lacandón to Christianity.

TUXTLA GUTIÉRREZ

Population: 300,000
Altitude: 532 metres

Many travellers simply change buses in Chiapas' state capital as they head straight through to San Cristóbal de las Casas. But if you're not in a hurry this clean, surprisingly lively and prosperous modern city has several things worth stopping for – among them probably Mexico's best zoo (devoted solely to the fauna of Chiapas), and easy access to exhilarating motor-boat trips through the 1000-metre-deep Sumidero Canyon – though both these trips could also be made in a long day from San Cristóbal de las Casas. There's plenty of decent middle-range accommodation in Tuxtla but the bottom end is mostly poor value.

Tuxtla Gutiérrez is towards the west end of Chiapas' hot, very humid central valley. Its name comes from the Nahuatl *tuchtlan*, 'where rabbits abound', and from Joaquín Miguel Gutiérrez, a leading light in Chiapas' early 19th-century campaign not to be part of Guatemala. It was unimportant until it became the state capital in 1892.

Orientation

The centre of Tuxtla Gutiérrez is the large Plaza Cívica or zócalo, with the cathedral on its south side. The main east-west artery, here called Avenida Central, runs across the zócalo in front of the cathedral. As it enters the city from the west the same road is Blvd Dr Belisario Domínguez, to the east it becomes Blvd Ángel Albino Corzo.

The Cristóbal Colón bus station is two blocks west of the zócalo's north-west corner. The main 2nd-class bus station, Autotransportes Tuxtla Gutiérrez, is on 3 Sur Ote just west of 7 Ote Sur – from the southeast corner of the cathedral that's four blocks east, one south, one more east, and one south. The last block is pedestrians only, through a small market.

Most hotels, places to eat and services are within a few blocks of the zócalo, but the tourist office and some middle and top-end hotels are in the west of the city on Blvd Dr Belisario Domínguez.

The central point for Tuxtla's street-naming system is the corner of Avenida Central and Calle Central beside the cathedral. East-west streets are called Avenidas – 1 Sur, 2 Sur, etc as you move south from

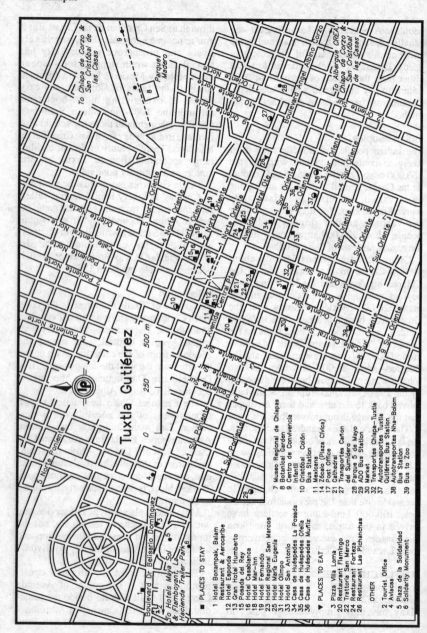

Tuxtla Gutiérrez

0   250   500 m

PLACES TO STAY

1   Hotel Bonampak, Balam
    Restaurant & Aerocaribe
12 Hotel Esponda
13 Gran Hotel Humberto
15 Posada del Rey
16 Hotel Casablanca
18 Hotel Mar-Inn
19 Hotel Fernando
23 Hotel Regional San Marcos
25 Hotel María Eugenia
31 Hotel Olimpo
33 Hotel San Antonio
34 Casa de Huéspedes La Posada
35 Casa de Huéspedes Ofelia
36 Casa de Huéspedes Muñiz

PLACES TO EAT

3   Pizza Villa Lorna
20 Restaurant Flamingo
22 Trattoria San Marco
24 Restaurant Forteza
26 Restaurant Las Pichanchas

OTHER

2   Tourist Office
4   Aviacsa
5   Plaza de la Solidaridad
6   Solidarity Monument
7   Museo Regional de Chiapas
8   Botanical Garden
9   Centro de Convivencia
    Infantil
10 Cristóbal   Colón
    Bus Station
11 Mexicana
14 Zócalo (Plaza Cívica)
17 Post Office
21 Cathedral
27 Transportes Cañon
    del Sumidero
28 Parque 5 de Mayo
29 ADO Bus Station
30 Market
32 Transportes Chiapas–Tuxtla
37 Autotransportes Tuxtla
    Gutiérrez Bus Station
38 Autotransportes Nha–Bolom
    Bus Station
39 Bus to Zoo

Avenida Central, and 1 Norte, 2 Norte, etc moving north. North-south streets are Calles – 1 Pte, 2 Pte and so on to the west of Calle Central; 1 Ote, 2 Ote, etc to the east. It all gets a bit complicated with the addition (sometimes) of secondary names: each Avenida is divided into a Pte part (west of Calle Central) and an Ote part (east of Calle Central) – thus 1 Sur Ote is the eastern half of Avenida 1 Sur. Likewise Calles have Norte and Sur parts: 1 Pte Norte is the northern half of Calle 1 Pte.

Information

Tourist Office The Chiapas tourist information office (☎ (961) 3-51-86) is 1¾ km west of the zócalo, on the ground floor of the Edificio Plaza de las Instituciones, the building beside Bancomer oppposite the Hotel Bonampak. The staff are helpful, but don't speak much English, and the office is open 9 am to 8 pm every day.

Money Banamex, at the corner of 1 Pte and 1 Sur, and Bancomer, at the corner of Avenida Central Pte and 2 Pte, do foreign exchange Monday to Friday 10 am to noon.

Post & Telecommunications The main offices are on a pedestrians-only block of 1 Norte Ote, just off the east side of the zócalo. The post office is open 8 am to 6 or 7 pm Monday to Saturday for all services, and 9 am to 1 pm Sunday for stamps only. Telegram, telex and fax services are available from 9 am to 8 pm Monday to Friday and 9 am to 5 pm Saturday. The American Express representative, Viajes Marabasco (☎ 2-69-98) at Plaza Bonampak, Local 14, on Blvd Belisario Domínguez across the road from the tourist office, has a client mail service.

There are Ladatel phones on the west side of the zócalo, in the Cristóbal Colón bus station, and by the Choco Centro shop behind the east end of the cathedral. One of those outside Choco Centro takes credit cards.

Laundry Laundromats include Gaily II at 1

Sur Pte 575, open 8 am to 2 pm and 4 to 8 pm, Monday to Saturday.

Maps You can get good Chiapas maps at the Instituto Nacional de Estadística, Geografía e Información on 1 Norte Ote just east of the zócalo. Many hotels hang large state maps in their lobbies.

Plazas

Tuxtla's lively zócalo, the Plaza Cívica, occupies two blocks, with the modern San Marcos cathedral facing it across Avenida Central at the south end. A plaque by the cathedral's north door recalls a 1990 visit by Pope John Paul II. On the hour the cathedral clock tower plays a tune to accompany a parade of saintly images revolving out of one of its upper levels. There's live music in the zócalo on Sunday nights.

The Plaza de la Solidaridad, overlooking Blvd Belisario Domínguez 1¾ km west of the zócalo, commemorates the 1824 union of Chiapas and Mexico. You can ascend its tall monument – worth a look if you're staying at the nearby Hotel Bonampak.

Zoo

Chiapas, with its huge range of environments, claims the highest concentration of animal species in North America – among them several varieties of big cat, 1200 types of butterfly and 641 bird species. You can see a good number of them in Tuxtla's excellent Zoológico Miguel Alvárez del Toro (ZOOMAT), where they're kept in relatively spacious enclosures in a hillside woodland area just south of the city. Most species are accompanied by charts showing their range of habitat and chances of avoiding extinction. (This conservation message has clearly not sunk in with all Chiapas citizens: shortly after visiting the zoo John was invited to join a jaguar shoot by a hotel manager.)

Among the creatures you'll see are ocelot, jaguar, puma, tapir, red macaw, boa constrictor, the monkey-eating harpy eagle (aguila arpia) and some mean-looking scorpions and spiders. And there's a special display of 'the most dangerous species, destroyer of nature and probably of itself'.

The zoo is open 8.30 am to 5.30 pm daily except Monday, and entry is free. It has a bookshop. To get there take a 'Cerro Hueco' bus (US$0.15) from the corner of 1 Ote Sur and 7 Sur Ote. They leave about every 20 minutes and take 20 minutes. A taxi – easy to pick up in either direction – costs US$1.50.

Parque Madero Complex

This is a museum-theatre-park area about 1¼ km north-east of the city centre. If you don't want to walk, take a colectivo along Avenida Central to Parque 5 de Mayo at the corner of 11 Ote, then another north along 11 Ote.

The **Museo Regional de Chiapas** has fine archaeological and colonial history exhibits and costume and craft collections, all from Chiapas, plus often interesting temporary exhibitions. It's open 9 am to 4 pm daily, except Monday. Next door is the 1200-seat **Teatro de la Ciudad**. Nearby there's a shady **botanical garden**, with many species labelled – it's open 9 am to 6 pm daily except Monday; entry is free.

Also in Parque Madero is an open-air children's park, the **Centro de Convivencia Infantil**, which 'adults' may enjoy too; it's open daily except Monday. It has models and exhibits on history and prehistory, a mini-railway, pony and boat rides and mini-golf.

Sumidero Canyon Lookouts

The best way to see Sumidero Canyon is by boat along the Río Grijalva from Chiapa de Corzo, a few km east of Tuxtla, which you can easily do in a day from Tuxtla (see the Sumidero Canyon and Chiapa de Corzo sections). But if you want to see Sumidero from the top, Transportes Cañon del Sumidero (☎ 2-06-49), at 1 Norte Ote 1121, eight blocks east of the zócalo, will take up to six people in a minibus for a two-hour tour of miradores (lookout points) on the canyon edge for US$10.

Places to Stay – bottom end

Tap water in the cheapies is 'al tiempo' (not heated) but, since this is a hot town, not cold either. Keep your eye open for big bottles of agua purificada in lobbies, etc – these can save you dollars on drinks.

The cleanest real cheapie is the *Albergue CREA Youth Hostel* (☎ (961) 3-34-05) at Blvd Ángel Albino Corzo 1800, about two km east of the centre. For a bed in one of the small, separate-sex dormitories you pay US$2.75 and place a deposit of US$1.75 for sheets. You don't need a youth hostel card. Water supplies are reportedly erratic. From the city centre take a colectivo east along Avenida Central. The hostel is on the right beside a yellow footbridge, just before the black statue of Ángel Albino Corzo on a white base in the middle of the road.

If you're desperate for somewhere cheap to lay your head near the Autotransportes Tuxtla Gutiérrez bus station, there are three small guest houses within a couple of blocks. Mosquitoes can be vicious in all of them. When full at night, they lock up tight and are impossible to find.

Closest to the bus station and least often full is the *Casa de Huéspedes Muñiz* at 2 Sur Ote 733, across the street from the north end of the bus yard, with a variety of muggy, grubby rooms, a few fans and obliging management. You pay US$8.50 a single or double with one bed, US$11.75 for a double with two beds. Bathrooms are shared.

The *Casa de Huéspedes Ofelia*, on the same block at 2 Sur Ote 643 just east of 5 Ote, has no sign but '643' is visible above its doorway if you look very hard. Rooms are fanless but clean – and often full. Singles are just US$3.50, doubles US$6.75; bathrooms are shared. The *Casa de Huéspedes La Posada* (☎ (961) 2-29-32) at 1 Sur Ote 555 has a sign but it's very minimal. Reasonably clean singles/doubles with fans are US$8.50/11.75 with private bath inside the room, US$6.75/10 with private bath outside. The family is friendly.

If you can manage a few dollars more, the friendly *Hotel San Antonio* (☎ (961) 2-27-13), at 2 Sur Ote 540, is much better. Very clean rooms with fan and private bath, in a young building with a small interior courtyard, are US$11.75/15. The upper floors are breezier.

If all else fails, the rambling *Hotel Olimpo* (☎ (961) 2-02-95) at 3 Sur Ote 215 will always have a room. It'll be small and muggy but with fan and private bath, and kept just about clean despite holes in the ceiling, flaking plaster, etc. Singles are US$6.75, doubles US$10 with one bed, and US$13.50 with two. Again the upper floors are breezier.

Another good street for cheap hotels is 2 Norte Ote. The relatively new *Hotel Casablanca*, half a block off the zócalo is very bare and basic, with small rooms, but exceptionally clean for the price – US$10 a single or double with fan and private bath, US$8.50 a single or double with shared bathroom and no fan.

Further along at 2 Norte Ote 341 the *Hotel Mar-Inn* (☎ (961) 2-19-00) has 60 sizeable, quite well-kept rooms, with wide, plant-lined walkways, but also a roof over everything that keeps humidity in. Singles/doubles are US$11.75/15. The *Hotel Fernando* at 2 Norte Ote 515 is also not bad for its US$6.75/8.50 price, with quite big, clean-ish rooms that include fan and private bath. Exterior rooms are bright, with big windows, and desk staff are helpful.

Stepping up a rung, the *Hotel Regional San Marcos* (☎ (961) 3-18-87), a modern building a block east of the cathedral at 2 Ote Sur 269, on the corner of 1 Sur Ote, is reasonable value at US$13.75/17.50. The rooms are smallish, and not all the lights work, but they're clean and tidy, and the attached bathrooms are prettified with tiles. Some have air-con, some a fan.

At the *Hotel Esponda* (☎ (961) 3-67-84) at 1 Pte Norte 142, a block west of the zócalo, you pay US$15/18.75 for tolerably clean two-bed fan-cooled rooms with big bathrooms.

La Hacienda Trailer Park (☎ (961) 2-79-86), at Blvd Belisario Domínguez 1197 on the west edge of town beside a roundabout, has a pool, cafeteria and all hook-ups for US$10 a double.

Places to Stay – middle

There are options in the city centre and at the west end of town on Blvd Belisario Domínguez.

The *Gran Hotel Humberto* (☎ (961) 2-20-80) at Avenida Central Pte 180, a block west of the zócalo, has big, clean rooms with air-con, TV and vast showers. Singles/doubles are US$24/29 – good value for this downtown location if you get one of the exterior rooms, some of which have fine views. Inner rooms look on to interior wells. Try to avoid 8th-floor rooms on Friday and Saturday nights because of noise from the 9th-floor nightspot.

The *Posada del Rey* (☎ (961) 2-28-71), on the north-east corner of the zócalo at 1 Ote Norte 310, is a dollar cheaper but poorer in quality. Rooms are air-conditioned, light and clean, and some overlook the zócalo, but they could be bigger and some need new paint or plaster. Singles/doubles are US$23/28. The building seems to lean, like the Tower of Pisa.

The best downtown hotel is the *Hotel María Eugenia* (☎ (961) 1-01-85) at Avenida Central Ote 507, three blocks east of the zócalo. The ample, clean, comfortable, air-con rooms are pleasingly fitted out and cost US$33/41. The hotel has a decent restaurant.

The *Hotel Bonampak* (☎ (961) 3-20-50) at Blvd Belisario Domínguez 180, 1¾ km west of the zócalo, is among the oldest of Tuxtla's better hotels, but is well renovated and comfortable with air-con rooms at US$33.50/41 and fan-cooled rooms at US$21.50/27.75. Some rooms are in the main block, others are in bungalows in the grounds. A big, clean pool, jai-alai and tennis courts, and good restaurants make the Bonampak good value. There's a copy of Chiapas' famous Bonampak prisoner mural in the lobby (which is much more vivid than the original!).

About 1¼ km further west is the *Hotel Maya Sol* (☎ (961) 2-34-13) at Blvd Belisario Domínguez 1380. Here clean, decent-sized air-con rooms with TV and phone, in a greenery-draped block away from the road, cost US$32.75/40.75. There's a coffee shop, restaurant and pool. A 'Fuente' colectivo west along Avenida Central or Blvd Belisario Domínguez will take you to the roundabout with a fountain just short of the hotel.

Places to Stay – top end

Tuxtla's most luxurious hostelry is the 119-room *Hotel Flamboyant* (☎ (961) 1-05-05) at Blvd Belisario Domínguez Km 1081, four km west of the zócalo. It lives up to its name with the ultimate in modern Arabic architecture draped in hanging foliage, and the rooms set round a large swimming pool, with tennis courts, restaurants and bars nearby. The Disco 'Sheik' (get it?) out front looks like a mosque. Singles/doubles are US$61/76. You'd pay several times as much for the same in Cancún.

Places to Eat

The cafés and restaurants lined up behind the east end of the cathedral aren't the cheapest but they're a good place to sample the city's atmosphere.

Even Italians enjoy the pizza – US$4.50 one-person size, US$6 two-person – at the *Trattoria San Marco*, the place with tables under a red-and-white awning. Another treat here if you're feeling generous to yourself is papa rellena, a baked potato with cheese, ham or tuna filling for US$3.25. There are sweet and savoury crepas too. At busy times service can be slow. *Choco Centro*, a small shop beside the cinema entrance here, sells tubs of tasty mango yoghurt for US$1.

For Chiapaneco fare it's well worth making the short trek to the *Restaurant Las Pichanchas*, 6½ blocks east of the zócalo at Avenida Central Ote 857 (look for the sign with a black pot on a pink background and the words Sientase Chiapaneco). This is an open-air restaurant in a plant-filled courtyard with a long menu of local specialities which friendly, efficient waiters will explain for you. Try chipilín, a maize-based cheese-and-cream soup for US$2; and for dessert chimbos, made from egg yolks and cinnamon (US$1.75). In between you could go for any of six types of tamales at US$2.50 a pair,

or meat courses like carne asada Chamula around US$6.50. Vegetarians can enjoy ensalada betabel con zanahorías (beetroot and carrot salad) for US$2. Every evening except Monday there's live marimba music and Chiapas folk dances.

The *Restaurant Flamingo*, a few metres down a passage at 1 Pte 17, 1½ blocks from the zócalo, is a quiet, air-conditioned, slightly superior place with good food and service. An order of three tacos or enchiladas is US$4.50, salads are US$3.50 to US$5, meat and fish dishes US$7.50 to US$11. There's a good comida corrida for US$4.75. The restaurant of the *Hotel María Eugenia*, on Avenida Central Ote three blocks east of the zócalo, also does a good comida corrida, for US$5. For a cheaper meal the *Restaurant Forteza* at Avenida Central Ote 453, half a block west of the María Eugenia, is reasonable. Many varieties of taco are US$0.40 each, egg dishes around US$1.50, queso fundido US$2, carne asada US$3.

Out west, the good cafeteria at the *Hotel Bonampak* does spaghettis and tamales for US$3 or so, plus grills, sandwiches and antojitos. A breakfast of eggs, fruit, toast, jam and coffee is US$4.75. The hotel's roadside outdoor *Balam Restaurant* serves some of Tuxtla's best meat dishes at reasonable prices – around US$7 a main course. *Pizza Villa Loma*, two blocks east of the Hotel Bonampak on the south side of Blvd Belisario Domínguez, does good pizzas at around US$6 two-person size. It's open from 8 am to midnight.

Tuxtla juice bars offer some original lines like licuados made from milk, granola and fruit, for US$1 at places like *Jugos California* and *La Michoacana* on Avenida Central in the first couple of blocks west of the zócalo.

Entertainment

Tuxtla's best disco at the time of writing is reportedly Colors in the Hotel Arecas at Blvd Belisario Domínguez Km 1080, a couple of hundred metres west of the Hotel Flamboyant. Entry is US$5 to US$7 depending on the day – Friday is busiest – and drinks are

US$1.75 and up. The Hotel Bonampak's Singles Bar is a disco too and provides the main competition to Colors.

Things to Buy

The Casa de las Artesanías de Chiapas, next to the tourist information desk in the Edificio Plaza de las Instituciones, beside Bancomer opposite the Hotel Bonampak, has a good selling display of Chiapas crafts – open Monday to Saturday 9 am to 2 pm and 5 to 8 pm.

Tuxtla's main market spreads round Calle Central Sur, two to three blocks south of the cathedral.

Getting There & Away

Air Mexicana and Aviacsa both fly to/from Mexico City (US$85, 1¼ hours) once or twice daily. Aviacsa and Aerocaribe both fly to/from Oaxaca (US$85, one hour) and Cancún (US$155) via Villahermosa (US$50) and Mérida (US$105) daily – Aviacsa is a bit quicker, taking three hours to Cancún against Aerocaribe's four. Aviacsa also flies daily to/from Tapachula (US$55, 30 minutes).

Tuxtla has two airports. Aeropuerto San Juan, 35 km west on Highway 190, handles bigger jets, at present used only by Mexicana. Aviacsa and Aerocaribe use Aeropuerto Terán, two km south of Highway 190 from a signposted turning about five km west of the zócalo.

Mexicana (☎ 2-00-20) is at Avenida Central Pte 206, a block west of the zócalo. Aerocaribe (☎ 2-20-32) is at Bungalow 414 in the Hotel Bonampak at Blvd Belisario Domínguez 180, but you can also book through Mexicana. Aviacsa (☎ 2-68-80) is at Avenida Central Pte 1144, 1¼ km west of the zócalo.

Bus Cristóbal Colón, at the corner of 2 Norte Pte and 2 Pte Norte, two blocks north-west of the zócalo, is the major 1st-class bus line serving Tuxtla Gutiérrez. ADO, at the corner of 5 Sur Pte and 9 Pte Sur, about 1¼ km west of the zócalo then five blocks south, has a limited number of services. The ageing 2nd-class buses of Autotransportes Tuxtla

Gutiérrez (ATG) congregate in a yard on 3 Sur Ote, half a block west of 7 Ote Sur, nearly a km south-east of the zócalo. Much newer 2nd-class buses are used on the San Cristóbal run by Autotransportes Nha-Bolom from 8 Ote Sur 330, two blocks east then half a block north of Autotransportes Tuxtla Gutiérrez. Departures from Tuxtla include:

Arriaga – 155 km, three hours; hourly 1st-class buses from 7 am to 10.30 pm by Cristóbal Colón for US$3, hourly 2nd-class buses until 8 pm by ATG.

Chiapa de Corzo – 12 km, 20 minutes; Transportes Chiapa-Tuxtla microbuses leave 3 Sur Ote, near the corner of 3 Sur Ote, every few minutes from 5 am to 7 pm, for US$0.25.

Ciudad Cuauhtémoc (Guatemalan border) – 255 km, four hours; two morning 1st-class buses by Cristóbal Colón for US$5, an early morning directo 2nd-class bus by ATG.

Comitán – 170 km, 3½ hours; hourly 1st-class buses from 5.30 am to 6.30 pm by Cristóbal Colón for US$3.25, 15 2nd-class buses daily by ATG.

Juchitán – 250 km, five hours; three 1st-class buses daily by Cristóbal Colón for US$5.

Mérida – 995 km, 16 hours; one luxury Cristóbal Colón Plus bus daily for US$30, a lunch time 2nd-class bus by ATG.

Mexico City – 1000 km, 19 hours; two luxury Cristóbal Colón Plus buses daily for US$33.50, eight 1st-class buses daily by Cristóbal Colón and five by ADO for US$22.75.

Oaxaca – 550 km, 10 hours; one morning 1st-class bus by Cristóbal Colón for US$11, an evening 1st-class bus by ADO for US$10.50, three 2nd-class buses daily by ATG.

Palenque – 295 km, eight hours; about six buses daily by ATG.

Pochutla – 470 km, 10 hours; one morning 1st-class bus by Cristóbal Colón US$9.50.

Salina Cruz – 300 km, six hours; two 1st-class buses daily by Cristóbal Colón for US$6.

San Cristóbal de las Casas – 85 km, two hours; one luxury Cristóbal Colón Plus bus daily for US$3.50, hourly 1st-class buses from 4.30 am to 9 pm by Cristóbal Colón for US$1.75, 2nd-class buses by ATG every half-hour until 6 pm, about a dozen 2nd-class buses daily by Autotransportes Nha-Bolom.

Tapachula – 405 km, seven hours; 18 1st-class buses daily by Cristóbal Colón for US$7.50.

Tonalá – 180 km, 3½ hours; hourly 1st-class buses from 7 am to 10.30 pm by Cristóbal Colón for US$3.50, 11 2nd-class buses daily by ATG.

Veracruz – 750 km, 14 hours; evening 1st-class buses daily by Cristóbal Colón for US$15.50, four days a week by ADO for US$13.50.

Villahermosa – 295 km, six hours; one luxury Cristóbal Colón Plus bus daily for US$10.75, six 1st-class buses daily by Cristóbal Colón for US$5.50.

Colectivos The quickest way to/from San Cristóbal de las Casas is a colectivo taxi which does the trip in 1¼ hours for US$3.50 per person. In Tuxtla Gutiérrez drivers wait outside the Autotransportes Tuxtla Gutiérrez bus station and leave when they have six passengers.

Car Rental companies include Budget (☎ 2-55-59) at Blvd Belisario Domínguez 2510; Dollar (☎ 2-89-32) at 5 Norte Pte 2260; Gabriel Rent-a-Car (☎ 2-07-57) at Belisario Domínguez 780, half a km west of the Hotel Bonampak, and Hertz in the Hotel Bonampak.

Getting Around

To/From the Airport Transporte Terrestre combis (☎ 2-15-54) run to/from Aeropuerto San Juan for the Mexicana flights to/from Mexico City. The fare is US$3.25 per person. They'll drop you anywhere in the city. Going out to the airport you can board at the Gran Hotel Humberto two hours before take-off, or they'll collect you anywhere else in the city if you telephone at least two hours before you need to be picked up. For Aeropuerto Terán you need a taxi – US$3 to/from the city centre.

Local Transport All colectivo combis (US$0.10) on Blvd Belisario Domínguez-Avenida Central-Blvd Albino Corzo run at least as far as the tourist office and Hotel Bonampak in the west, and 11 Ote in the east. Their official stops are marked by blue 'Ascenso'/'Descenso' signs but they'll sometimes stop for you elsewhere. Taxis are abundant.

TUXTLA GUTIÉRREZ TO VILLAHERMOSA

After travelling 50 km from Tuxtla Gutiérrez on Highway 190 (beyond Chiapa de Corzo; see below), you come to the junction with

Highway 195. Go straight on to San Cristóbal de las Casas (34 km), or turn left (north) to Villahermosa on Highway 195 (264 km).

The village of **Bochil** (population 13,000), 94 km from Tuxtla Gutiérrez at an altitude of 1272 metres, is inhabited by Tzotzil Maya. It has two hotels: the tidy *Hotel Juárez* on the main road, and the more modest *Hotel María Isabel* set back a bit from the road. There's also a Pemex fuel station, the only one for many km.

Five km before the Teapa turnoff, on the right-hand (east) side, is the **Balneario El Azufre** (Sulphur Baths), as you can tell by the odour when you descend into the valley to cross a stream and the stink of sulphur rises to meet you. The highway bypasses Teapa to the west, 60 km from Villahermosa. The railway to Mérida passes through Teapa.

CHIAPA DE CORZO

Population: 32,000
Altitude: 500 metres
Chiapa de Corzo is a little colonial town on the Río Grijalva. It is the starting point for trips to Sumidero Canyon.

History

Chiapa de Corzo has been occupied almost continuously since about 1500 BC. Its sequence of cultures – in a crossroads area where Olmec, Monte Albán, Maya and Teotihuacán influences were all felt – makes it invaluable to archaeologists trying to trace pre-Hispanic cultural developments.

In the couple of centuries before the Spanish arrived, the warlike Chiapa, the dominant people in western Chiapas at the time, had their capital, Nandalumí, a couple of km downstream from Chiapa de Corzo, on the opposite bank of the river near the canyon mouth. When the Spanish under Diego de Mazariegos arrived in 1528 to occupy the area, the Chiapa, realising defeat was inevitable, apparently hurled themselves by the hundreds – men, women and children – to death in the canyon rather than surrender.

Mazariegos then founded Chiapa de Corzo – at first called Chiapa de los Indios –

but a month later shifted his base to a second new settlement, Villa Real de Chiapa (now San Cristóbal de las Casas), where the climate and the Indians were less hostile.

In 1863 Chiapa de Corzo was the scene of the decisive battle for Chiapas between liberals supporting national president Benito Juárez and pro-Church conservatives supporting the French invasion of Mexico. The conservatives, led by Juan Ortega, had taken San Cristóbal de las Casas but were defeated by forces from Chiapa de Corzo and Tuxtla Gutiérrez, organised by the liberal state governor Ángel Albino Corzo and led by Salvador Urbina. The name of Corzo, who was born and died here, was given to the town in 1888.

Orientation & Information

Chiapa de Corzo's large, slightly sloping zócalo is called Plaza General Ángel Albino Corzo. Buses stop on 21 de Octubre, the street running east from the top end of the zócalo. For boats into the canyon, walk down the west side of the zócalo (5 de Febrero) and go straight on for a couple of blocks to the *embarcadero* on the river front.

There's a post office on the way down, opposite the large church. Bancomer on La Mexicanidad (the east side of the zócalo) will change foreign cash and travellers' cheques. The market is on La Mexicanidad opposite the east end of the church. There are a few artesanías shops around the zócalo.

Things to See

The fine eight-sided **Spanish Fountain**, called La Pila, towards the bottom of the zócalo was built in 1562 and is said to be inspired by the Spanish crown. A block beyond the bottom of the zócalo, the large **Santo Domingo Church** is mid-16th century. One of its towers has an enormous gold, silver and copper bell of famed sonority, made in 1576 (one of the earliest in Latin America).

On the west side of the zócalo is an interesting little **Museo de Laca** (Lacquer Museum) dedicated to the craft of lacquered wooden objects or gourds (*jícaras*), of which

Chiapa de Corzo is a centre. The practical and symbolic importance of gourds is explained here (the Maya *Popol Vuh* epic says the sky is a big, blue, upside-down gourd), and lacquerware from other centres like Uruapan, Pátzcuaro and Olinalá shows the variety of styles. The museum also has masks of the type used in Chiapa's January festivities. Hours are Tuesday to Sunday 9 am to 7 pm, Monday 9 am to 1 pm and 4 to 7 pm; admission is free.

The staircase of the **Palacio Municipal** (Town Hall) on La Mexicanidad has a mural of local history and a map of the 1863 battle. The mural shows three churches crowning small hills around the top of the town, all liberal defence points in 1863 and now good viewpoints.

The **Pre-Hispanic Ruins** will interest only the most enthusiastic. One small restored pyramid which contained a tomb, Montículo 32, stands about a km east of the zócalo along 21 de Octubre, at the junction of the bypass. There are more stone-faced pyramids and stairways, mostly from 100 BC to 200 AD, through some backstreets south-east of here.

Festivals

Some of Mexico's most colourful and curious fiestas, together known as the **Fiesta de Enero**, happen in Chiapa de Corzo every January.

From 9 January, young men dressed as women and known as Las Chuntá dance through the streets nightly – a custom said to derive from a distribution of food to the poor by the maids of a rich woman of colonial times, Doña María de Angulo.

Processions and dances of the bizarre Parachicos – men with wooden masks and ixtle 'hair', representing Spanish conquistadors – take place in daylight hours on 15, 17 and 20 January. They shake tin maracas and are accompanied by little girls. They too are said, in part, to go back to the same Doña María de Angulo. A curandero who cured her crippled son allegedly advised her to provide entertainment for the boy (*para el chico*) in his convalescence, so she instructed some of her servants to shake maracas for him.

There's a musical parade of just about everyone on 19 January, then on the night of 21 January there's the Combate Naval – an hour-long mock battle on the river, enacted by people in canoes, with spectacular fireworks. This probably goes back to waterborne encounters between Spanish conquistadors and local Indians – the Irish traveller Thomas Gage recorded something similar in 1626 – but the modern version was inspired by a film of the battle of Port Arthur in the Russo-Japanese War, seen locally in 1905!

The celebrations usually close with another parade and general merrymaking on 22 or 23 January. Women wear colourful, exquisitely worked dresses.

Places to Stay
The *Hotel Los Angeles* (☎ 6-00-48), on La Mexicanidad at the bottom corner of the zócalo, is nothing special but it's fairly clean and the rooms quite sizeable. Hot water is intermittent and mosquito nets would be a distinct improvement. Singles/doubles are US$10/13.50.

Places to Eat
There are several restaurants by the embarcadero but more appealing is the friendly *Restaurant Jardines de Chiapa*, in a garden off the La Mexicanidad side of the zócalo. The menu is long and explains everything in English as well as Spanish. Sopa Fiesta (US$2), with macaroni, egg, avocado and chicken, and pollo entomatada (chicken in tomato sauce, US$5.50) are both good.

Getting There & Away
It's possible to visit Sumidero Canyon and Chiapa de Corzo in a day trip from San Cristóbal de las Casas on public transport, though starting out from Tuxtla Gutiérrez or even Chiapa de Corzo itself is more leisurely. There are also Sumidero Canyon tours from San Cristóbal, but be sure what you're paying for with these – many don't include the cost of the boat trip itself.

To/From Tuxtla Gutiérrez Transportes Chiapa-Tuxtla microbuses run every few minutes up to about 7 pm between 3 Ote Sur, near the corner of 3 Sur Ote in Tuxtla, and a yard on 21 de Octubre, half a block east of the Chiapa de Corzo zócalo. Fare for the 12 km, 20 minute trip is US$0.25.

To/From San Cristóbal de las Casas Cristóbal Colón runs three morning and two afternoon 1st-class buses from San Cristóbal to Chiapa de Corzo – US$1.50 for the 1½-hour trip. Autotransportes Tuxtla Gutiérrez (ATG) runs about 15 2nd-class buses daily for a little less. Both stop at their offices on 21 de Octubre in Chiapa. Cristóbal Colón's is a white building a block from the zócalo, and ATG is at No 284, three-quarters of a block further up on the opposite side. Conductors don't always announce that you've reached Chiapa de Corzo, so keep alert.

From Chiapa de Corzo to San Cristóbal, all three daily Cristóbal Colón buses are usually fully booked in advance. ATG has far more frequent services, and you can usually leave your baggage with its friendly office while you visit the canyon. Another alternative is to backtrack to Tuxtla Gutiérrez and get a bus or colectivo from there.

Other ATG runs 2nd-class buses to Palenque (US$5.25, three times daily), Villahermosa (US$5), Comitán (US$3), Ciudad Cuauhtémoc (US$4.50) and Tapachula (US$7).

SUMIDERO CANYON
The Cañon del Sumidero is a daunting fissure in the countryside a few km east of Tuxtla Gutiérrez, with the Río Grijalva or Río Grande de Chiapas flowing north through it. When the Chicoasén dam was completed at its north end in 1981, the canyon became a long, thin reservoir. Fast passenger launches speed along its 35-km length between near-sheer walls 900 to 1200 metres high. This two to three-hour trip can cost as little as US$5 – a bargain for a crocodile's-eye view of some of Mexico's most awesome scenery.

Highway 190, heading east from Tuxtla

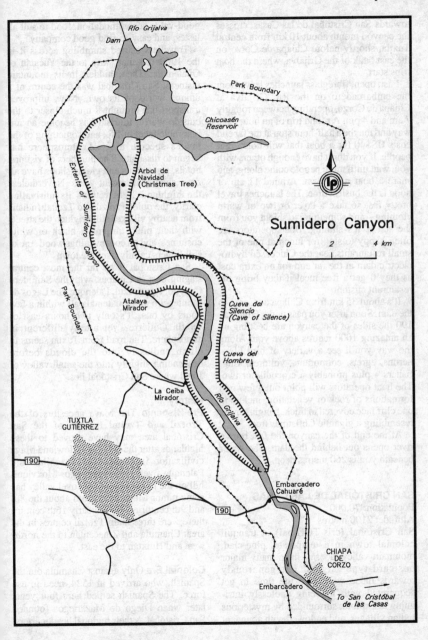

Río Grijalva

Dam

Park Boundary

Chicoasén
Reservoir

Arbol de
Navidad
(Christmas Tree)

Extents of Sumidero Canyon

Sumidero Canyon

0   2   4 km

Atalaya
Mirador

Cueva del
Silencio
(Cave of Silence)

Park Boundary

Cueva del
Hombre

Río Grijalva

La Ceiba
Mirador

TUXTLA
GUTIÉRREZ

190

190

Embarcadero
Cahuaré

CHIAPA DE
CORZO

Embarcadero

To San Cristóbal
de las Casas

towards San Cristóbal de las Casas, crosses the canyon mouth about 10 km from central Tuxtla, shortly before Chiapa de Corzo on the east bank of the Grijalva, where the boat trips start.

Fast, open, fibreglass launches leave from the embarcadero on the Río Grijalva at Chiapa de Corzo, operating between roughly 7 am and 4 pm. A round trip of an hour each way and maybe a half-hour stop at the far end costs US$40 for a boat that will hold eight people. If you don't have enough others with you, wait until more people come along, and share a boat with them. Around 11 am or noon is the busiest time. The launches travel pretty fast so take a layer or two of warm clothing – and something to shield you from the sun if it's shining. Boat operators are often happy to stop for lunch at one of the small restaurants near the Chicoasén hydro-electric dam at the far end for no extra cost as they'll get a free meal if they bring the restaurant custom.

It's about 35 km from Chiapa de Corzo to the dam. Soon after you pass under Highway 190 the sides of the canyon are beetling up an amazing 1000 metres above you. Along the way you'll see a variety of bird life – herons, egrets, cormorants, vultures, kingfishers – plus probably a crocodile or two. The boat operators will point out a few odd formations of rock or vegetation, including one cliff face covered in thick, hanging moss resembling a gigantic Christmas tree.

At the end of the canyon the fast brown river opens out behind the dam. The water beneath you is 260 metres deep.

SAN CRISTÓBAL DE LAS CASAS
Population: 70,000
Altitude: 2100 metres
San Cristóbal (cris-TOH-bal), a tranquil colonial town in a temperate, pine-clad, mountain valley, doesn't have many major postcard-type 'sights' but generously rewards those who have the time to get acquainted with it, being endlessly intriguing to explore, surrounded by mysterious Indian villages, and endowed with abundant good-value accommodation, food to suit all tastes, and easy-to-find good company.

Travellers started stumbling across it in the 1960s on their way to the Yucatán or Guatemala. Then, hidden in its mountain fastness, San Cristóbal was the centre of a unique world of its own. Now, improved transport has brought it much closer to the outside world, tourism has become an un-ignorable facet of life, and something of the town's special, magical, atmosphere has begun to dissipate. The numbers of visitors, hotels, restaurants and glossy shops have all risen sharply in recent years. Nevertheless the highland light retains its unrivalled clarity, the quiet Tzotzil and Tzeltal Indians from nearby villages still brighten the streets with their pink, turquoise, black or white costumes, and on cool evenings wood smoke still lingers calmly over the town.

San Cristóbal is by far the most central staging-post in Chiapas, with the Sumidero Canyon, Agua Azul, Palenque, the Lagos de Montebello and Guatemala all within a few hours by bus. It's only two hours east of Tuxtla Gutiérrez yet utterly different in atmosphere. The road from Tuxtla seems to climb endlessly into the clouds before descending slightly into the small valley of Jovel where San Cristóbal lies.

History
Pre-Hispanic The Maya ancestors of the Tzotzil and Tzeltal Indians of the San Cristóbal area may have moved to these highlands after the collapse of lowland Maya civilisation in places like Yaxchilán and Palenque over 1000 years ago. Moxviquil hill on the north side of the Jovel valley has some minor Maya ruins from about the 8th and 9th centuries. By the early 16th century there were three main Tzotzil centres in the area: Chamula and Zinacantán to the northwest and Huixtán to the east.

Colonial Era Only against Chamula did the Spanish, who arrived in 1524, need to use force. The Spanish settled here four years later when Diego de Mazariegos founded San Cristóbal as their regional headquarters.

In the early days the Spanish, perhaps 200 in number, occupied the area around the zócalo, known as El Recinto. Outside this were areas for Indian allies who had arrived with the Spanish; Aztecs, Tlaxcalans and Oaxacans settled in the Mexicanos, Tlaxcala and San Antonio barrios, Guatemalans in San Diego and Cuxtitali. A sixth barrio, El Cerrillo, was founded by freed Tzotzil slaves in 1549. The outlying villages were taken as encomiendas and, later, haciendas by the Spanish.

For most of the colonial era San Cristóbal's Spanish citizens made their fortunes – usually from wheat – at the cost of the Indians, who lost their lands, and suffered diseases, taxes and forced labour. Early on, the church gave the Indians some protection against colonist excesses. Dominican monks arrived in Chiapas in 1545 and made San Cristóbal their main base. Bartolomé de las Casas (after whom the town is now named), appointed bishop of Chiapas that year, and Juan de Zapata y Sandoval, bishop from 1613 to 1621, are both fondly remembered.

19th & 20th Centuries San Cristóbal was state capital from 1824, when Chiapas joined independent Mexico, to 1892, when Tuxtla Gutiérrez took over.

One day in 1867, at a place called Tzajalhemel, a Chamula girl named Agustina Gómez Checheb found three pieces of obsidian which seemed to talk. She entrusted them to a local Indian official, Pedro Díaz Cuzcat, who said they woke him at night with their noise inside a wooden box. Tzajalhemel became an Indian pilgrimage centre where Agustina and Díaz would interpret the 'oracles' of the stones. Díaz baptised 12 Indians as saints of the cult, which soon won more followers than the Catholic Church in many Indian villages north of San Cristóbal. This alarmed the church and civil authorities and in December 1868 the pair were imprisoned in San Cristóbal.

Now enter the revolutionary Ignacio Fernández Galindo. Identifying himself with San Salvador or the Tzotzil god Cul Salik, he came from San Cristóbal to rouse the Chamulas to win back their lands and stop burdensome taxes. In June 1869 the schoolmaster and Catholic priest in Chamula were murdered and the rebels went through the countryside killing more mestizos. At San Cristóbal, they successfully demanded the release of Agustina and Díaz but were persuaded to leave Galindo and his wife as hostages.

When the hostages were not released, Díaz, joined by many Tzotzils, attacked San Cristóbal, but the authorities had time to gather reinforcements and the rebels were beaten. Galindo was sentenced to death, other rebels were shot or deported to remote parts of Mexico. Díaz survived to lead a short-lived uprising of hacienda servants in 1870.

The road from Tuxtla Gutiérrez wasn't paved until the 1940s, and only in the 1970s was a tunnel built to provide adequate drainage for the Jovel valley and stop the floods which had periodically struck the town since its founding.

Since the mid-1970s San Cristóbal's mostly mestizo population has been swelled by many of a reported 13,000 Tzotzils expelled from Chamula and other villages. The exiles live in makeshift colonies on the edges of town and most of the street hawkers are drawn from their numbers. Two explanations are commonly given for their expulsion from their native villages: one is that they turned Protestant as a result of the missionary efforts of the Summer School of Linguistics from the USA; the other is that they oppose the PRI.

Names San Cristóbal de las Casas is the town's eighth official name. The others were: Villa Real de Chiapa (1528-29); Villaviciosa de Chiapa (after the birthplace of its first Spanish judge; 1529-31); San Cristóbal de los Llanos de Chiapa (1531-36); Ciudad Real de Chiapa (1536-1829); San Cristóbal (1829-48); San Cristóbal las Casas (1848-1934); Ciudad las Casas (1934-43). It has also had two popular names: Jovel (which is still current) and Chiapa de los Españoles.

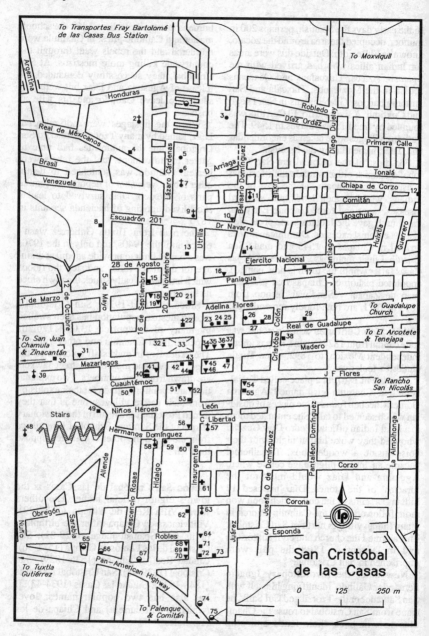

To Transportes Fray Bartolomé
de las Casas Bus Station

To Moxviquil

Argentina

Honduras

Robledo

Díaz Ordaz

Diego Dujelay

Real de Méxicanos

Primera Calle

Brasil

Tonalá

Venezuela

Lázaro Cárdenas

D Arriaga

Belisario Domínguez

Utrilla

Chiapa de Corzo

Comitán

Tapachula

Huixtla

Guerrero

Escuadrón 201

Dr Navarro

13

14

28 de Agosto

Ejercito Nacional

5 de Mayo

16 de Septiembre

Paniagua

J M Santiago

12° de Marzo

12 de Octubre

1° de Marzo

20 de Noviembre

Adelina Flores

To Guadalupe
Church

To San Juan
Chamula
& Zinacantán

Cristóbal Colón

Real de Guadalupe

To El Arcotete
& Tenejapa

Mazariegos

Madero

J F Flores

To Rancho
San Nicolás

Cuauhtémoc

Niños Héroes

León

C Libertad

Stairs

Hermanos Domínguez

Allende

Insurgentes

Corzo

La Almolhonga

Crescencio Rosas

Hidalgo

Josefa O de Domínguez

Pantaleón Domínguez

Corona

Obregón

Sarabia

Núño

Robles

Juárez

S Esponda

San Cristóbal
de las Casas

Pan-American Highway

0   125   250 m

To Tuxtla
Gutiérrez

To Palenque
& Comitán

Members of San Cristóbal's few-hundred-strong Spanish-descended ruling caste are known as Coletos.

Orientation

San Cristóbal is easy to walk around, with straight streets rambling up and down several gentle hills. The Pan-American Highway passes across the south side of town, with the main bus stations just off its north side. From these terminals, you walk north (slightly uphill) to the zócalo (Plaza 31 de Marzo), which has the cathedral on its north side. From the Cristóbal Colón terminal it's six blocks up Insurgentes to the zócalo; from Autotransportes Tuxtla

■ PLACES TO STAY

4	Posada El Candil
8	Hotel Parador Mexicanos
13	Posada Santo Domingo
14	Posada El Cerrillo
15	Hotel Español
17	Posada Jovel
21	Hotel Posada Diego de Mazariegos
24	Hotel Real del Valle
25	Hotel San Martín
27	Posada Santiago
28	Casa Margarita
29	Posada Tepeyac
30	Hotel Mansión del Valle
38	Posada Virginia
42	Hotel Ciudad Real
43	Hotel Santa Clara
44	Posada San Cristóbal
47	Hotel Los Angeles
49	Posada Los Morales
53	Hotel Fray Bartolomé de las Casas
55	Casa de Huéspedes Lupita
60	Hotel D'Monica & Restaurant Unicornio
62	Posada Lucella
69	Posada Insurgentes
71	Posada Lupita
72	Hotel Capri
73	Posada Vallarta

▼ PLACES TO EAT

10	La Parrilla
16	El Bazar
18	Café-Restaurant Del Teatro
19	Café Olulu
20	La Salsa Verde
31	El Taquito
34	Restaurant La Faisán
35	Restaurant Los Arcos
36	Fulano's Restaurant
37	Restaurant Flamingo
41	La Galería

45	Restaurant Tia Maty
46	Restaurant La Misión del Fraile
51	Cafetería San Cristóbal
52	Restaurante Tuluc
54	Comedor Familiar Normita II
56	Madre Tierra Restaurant & Panadería
64	Cafetería y Lonchería Palenque
68	Restaurant Chamula
70	Restaurant Tikal

OTHER

1	Combis to San Juan Chamula, Zinacantán & Tenejapa
2	Church
3	Market
5	City Museum
6	Sna Jolobil Gallery
7	Santo Domingo Church
9	La Caridad Church
11	Church
12	Na Bolom
22	Cathedral
23	Casa de Cambio Lacantún
26	Casa de las Imagenes
32	Tourist Office
33	Zócalo (Plaza 31 de Marzo)
39	La Merced Church
40	Post Office
48	Cerro (Hill) & Church of San Cristóbal
50	Centro de Investigaciones Ecológicas del Sureste
57	San Francisco Church
58	El Carmen Church
59	Bellas Artes Auditorium
61	Hospital
63	Santa Lucía Church
65	Autotransportes Tuxtla Gutiérrez Bus Station
66	Colectivos to Tuxtla Gutiérrez
67	Transportes Lacandonia Bus Station
74	Cristóbal Colón Bus Station
75	Autotransportes Nha-Bolom Bus Station

Gutiérrez it's five blocks up Allende, then two to the right along Mazariegos.

Places to stay and eat are scattered all around town, but there are concentrations on Insurgentes, and on Real de Guadalupe and Madero which lead east from the zócalo.

Information

Tourist Office This is at the north end of the Palacio Municipal on the west side of the zócalo. It's open 8 am to 8 pm Monday to Saturday, and 9 am to 2 pm Sunday (☎ (967) 8-04-14). Staff are helpful and most speak English.

Money The banks on and near the zócalo only do foreign exchange from 9 to 11 am and queues can be slow. It's much easier and quicker to change your money or travellers' cheques at Casa de Cambio Lacantún at Real de Guadalupe 12A, half a block from the zócalo, where rates are only about 50 pesos per dollar worse than at the banks. The minimum transaction is US$50 and hours are 8.30 am to 2 pm and 4 to 8 pm Monday to Saturday, 9 am to 1 pm Sunday.

Post & Telecommunications The post office is on the corner of Cuauhtémoc and Crescencio Rosas, one block west and one south of the zócalo. It's open 8 am to 7 pm Monday to Friday, 9 am to 1 pm Saturday, Sunday and holidays. For telegrams and telex go to the Telégrafos office at Diego de Mazariegos 29, 2½ blocks west of the zócalo.

There are Ladatel phones on the west side of the zócalo and in the Cristóbal Colón bus station, and lada casetas in the Dulcería Santo Domingo at the corner of Adelina Flores and Utrilla, Zapatería Jalc's at Insurgentes 67, and the Autotransportes Tuxtla Gutiérrez bus station.

Foreign Consulates There is no Guatemalan Consulate in San Christóbal; the nearest is in Comitán.

Laundry Lavasec, at Crescencio Rosas 12 just north of Hermanos Domínguez, open Monday to Saturday 8 am to 6 pm, will wash and dry three kg for US$3.25, or just wash it for US$1.75, and have it ready the same day if you take it in by about 10 am. There's also Lavarama, at Guadalupe Victoria 20A, just west of 5 de Mayo.

Books, Bookshops & Libraries Graham Greene came to San Cristóbal in 1938 and devoted most of a chapter of *The Lawless Roads* to it, calling it Las Casas. Also worth seeking out are the historical novels of Rosario Castellanos (1925-74). *Balún Canán* (1957, translated into English as *The New Watchmen*) tells of a Chiapas landowner reluctant to give up his property under the Cárdenas reforms of the 1930s. *Ciudad Real* (1960) is set in San Cristóbal this century.

Librería Soluna, at Real de Guadalupe 13B, less than a block from the zócalo, is probably the best bookshop in town, with many books in English and a good selection of novels, and books of local interest and anthropology.

Interested outsiders can use the library at Na Bolom from 9 am to 1 pm, Tuesday to Saturday. Its 14,000 books include one of the world's biggest collections on the Maya, and many more on other aspects of Chiapas and Central America.

The Centro de Investigaciones Ecológicas del Sureste, at the corner of Cuauhtémoc and Crescencio Rosas, has a library and a good collection of large-scale maps of Chiapas. It's open 3 to 7 pm Tuesday to Friday, 10 am to 1 pm Saturday.

Zócalo

Officially called Plaza 31 de Marzo, this is the old Spanish centre of town, used for markets until early this century. Today it's a fine place to sit and watch the life of the town happen around you. The cathedral, on the north side, was begun in 1528 but completely rebuilt in 1693. Its gold-leaf interior has a baroque pulpit and altarpiece. The Hotel Santa Clara on the south-east corner was the house of Diego de Mazariegos, the Spanish conqueror of Chiapas. It's one of the few non-ecclesiastical examples of the Plateresque style in Mexico.

Santo Domingo

North-west of the centre, opposite the corner of Lázaro Cárdenas and Real de Mexicanos, Santo Domingo is the most beautiful of San Cristóbal's many churches – especially with its pink façade is floodlit at night. Together with the adjoining monastery – which now houses the outstanding Sna Jolobil textile gallery and saleroom, and the city museum – it was built from 1547 to 1560. The church's baroque façade (on which can be seen the double-headed Hapsburg eagle, symbol of the Spanish monarchy) was added in the 17th century. There's plenty of gold inside. Chamulan women conduct a daily crafts market around Santo Domingo and La Caridad church (1712) immediately to its south. Taxes levied on Indians for the building of La Caridad sparked the 1712 Tzeltal rebellion of Cancuc, the most famous Chiapas Indian uprising of colonial times.

Sna Jolobil San Cristóbal's outstanding display of Indian textiles is exhibited – and offered for sale – in the Santo Domingo monastery buildings by Sna Jolobil, an organisation of 650 women backstrap-loom weavers from 20 Tzotzil and Tzeltal villages. It was founded in the late 1970s to foster this important folk art both as an income-earner and to preserve Indian identity and tradition. The aims of Sna Jolobil – Weavers' House in Tzotzil – include the revival of forgotten techniques and designs, and development of natural dyes.

Each Chiapas highland village has its own distinctive dress. Most of the seemingly abstract designs on these costumes are in fact stylised snakes, frogs, butterflies, birds, saints and so on. Some motifs can still perform a religious-magical function: scorpions, for example, can be a symbolic request for rain, since scorpions are believed to attract lightning. The sacredness of traditional costume is shown by the dressing of saints' images in old and revered garments at festival times.

Some designs have pre-Hispanic origins: for instance, the rhombus shape on some huipils from San Andrés Larráinzar is also found on the garments shown on Lintel 24 at Yaxchilán. The shape represents the old Maya universe, in which the earth was cube-shaped and the sky had four corners. Other costumes are of more recent origin: the typical men's ensemble from Chamula – long-sleeved shirt, wool tunic, belt and long trousers – stems from the Spanish, who objected to the relative nudity of the loin-cloth and cloak that Chamulan men used to wear.

Sna Jolobil is open from 9 am to 2 pm and 4 to 6 pm daily except Sunday. There are shawls, sashes, ponchos, hats and more. Prices range from a few dollars for some small items up to US$400 or US$500 for the

Weaver with backstrap loom

best huipils from Magdalenas and San Andrés Larráinzar. Across the road at Lázaro Cárdenas 42 is the Sna Jolobil Galería Textil, a small non-selling exhibition of the very finest garments.

City Museum The Museo Arqueología, Etnografía, Historia y Arte deals mainly with the history of San Cristóbal itself. All explanatory material is in Spanish. Hours are Tuesday to Sunday, 9 am to 2 pm, and entry is US$2.75.

Market

The flavour of outlying Indian villages can be tasted at San Cristóbal's busy market, between Utrilla and Belisario Domínguez eight blocks north of the zócalo. Many of the traders are Indian villagers – for whom buying and selling is the main reason to come into town – and fresh food is the stock-in-trade. Some may be offering just a few bunches of carrots or other small produce from their plots. One local speciality is cream cheese.

The Indians generally keep their distance from the mestizo population, the result of centuries of exploitation. But they can be friendly and humorous – and hard bargainers. Their quiet dignity contributes much to the town's atmosphere.

The market has covered and open-air sections. Both stay open till late afternoon daily, except Sundays – when markets are held in the outlying villages (see Around San Cristóbal).

Na Bolom

A visit to Na Bolom, a house at Guerrero 33 on the corner of Chiapa de Corzo six blocks north of Real de Guadalupe, is one of San Cristóbal's most fascinating experiences. For several decades it has been the home of Swiss anthropologist and photographer Gertrude (Trudy) Duby-Blom, now over 90, and (until his death in 1963) of her husband, Danish archaeologist Frans Blom.

The pair shared a passion for Chiapas and particularly its Indians. While Frans explored and dug at ancient Maya sites, Trudy devoted much of her life to studying and campaigning for the tiny Lacandón Indian population of eastern Chiapas. One building at Na Bolom is reserved for Lacandóns to use. Her energy continued into old age, with emphasis on campaigning to save the endangered Lacandón rainforest and starting a tree nursery for Indian villagers. She also attracted criticism for allegedly shielding the Lacandón too zealously from change.

The house, whose name is Tzotzil for Jaguar House as well as a play on the owner's name, is full of photographs, archaeological and anthropological relics and books – a treasure-trove for anyone with an interest in Chiapas. Visits are only by guided tour (US$1.75) daily except Monday at 4.30 pm. The tours are given in English and Spanish by volunteers from several countries, who are happy to chat with visitors. These are some of the least formal guided tours you'll find anywhere. At the end you can pay an extra US$0.70 for a film on the Lacandón and Trudy Blom's work. The house's large library is open separately (see the San Cristóbal Information section).

If you like the feel of Na Bolom, you can stay here (see Places to Stay – middle) – or dine with the assembled company for US$5 at lunch or dinner (give three hours' notice). Some say lunch is more relaxed since the 28-seat table is not so full then.

El Carmen & Bellas Artes

El Carmen church stands at the corner of Hidalgo and Hermanos Domínguez. Formerly part of a nunnery built in 1597, it has a distinctive 1680 tower resting on an arch, erected to replace one destroyed by floods 28 years earlier. Next door is the Casa de Cultura, containing an art gallery, library and the Bellas Artes auditorium.

Centro de Investigaciones Ecológicas del Sureste

The headquarters of this organisation is a large building on the Pan-American Highway at the south-eastern edge of San Cristóbal, but its museum and library on the corner of Cuauhtémoc and Crescencio Rosas

...as displays on Chiapas' vegetation, geology and ecology. Opening hours are Tuesday to Friday 3 to 7 pm, Saturday 10 am to 1 pm.

Hills & Walks

San Cristóbal & Guadalupe The most prominent of the several small hills over which San Cristóbal undulates are the Cerro de San Cristóbal in the south-west quarter of town, reached by steps up from Allende, and the Cerro de Guadalupe, seven blocks east of the zócalo along Real de Guadalupe. Both are crowned by churches and afford good views. There's an amazing Crucifixion sculpture made entirely of vehicle number plates behind the San Cristóbal church – but there have been reports of attempted rapes here too.

Moxviquil Cerro de Moxviquil, about 1½ km north of the town, has some Maya ruins which were excavated by Frans Blom but are now overgrown. The walk, involving a climb of about 200 metres, is pleasant. Head north out of town on Santiago, from Real de Guadalupe, to the settlement of Ojo de Agua just north of the unpaved Periférico Norte (northern ring-road).

From Ojo de Agua head for two timber shacks which are the highest buildings you can see. The trail is steep and rough but eventually you enter a valley and the gradient reduces. When a long narrow maize field appears on the left, backtrack 50 metres and take the path branching uphill round the left side of the field. The wooded hill now up to your left is Moxviquil and the path is strewn with rough pottery shards. To climb the hill, continue 300 metres and find a faint path on the left. The ruins are little more than big heaps of rough stone.

Ecatepec, Huitepec & Tzontehuitz A trail leads up to Cerro Ecatepec, south of the town, from Los Sumideros, the caves that drain the Jovel valley's small rivers, on the Periférico Sur. A tunnel made in the 1970s to increase Los Sumideros' drainage capacity and prevent flooding also starts near Los Sumideros. You can ascend Cerro Huitepec (2750 metres), west of the town, either from the church in the south-western barrio of San Felipe or by striking up from the Periférico Oeste, between the Pan-American Highway and the road to Chamula.

Cerro Tzontehuitz, 10 km north-east of the town, is the highest peak in the Chiapas highlands at 2900 metres.

El Arcotete

This natural limestone arch over the Río Quinta, in pleasant country seven km east of the town, is a popular local outing. Follow Madero east from the town centre and continue along the Tenejapa road. About 4½ km from the town centre a sign points to El Arcotete down a dirt track to the right. Start down the track and keep asking as you go, as there are one or two not-too-obvious turns.

Grutas de San Cristóbal

The grutas (caves) are in fact a single long cavern nine km south-east of San Cristóbal, among lovely pine woods a five-minute walk south of the Pan-American Highway. The first 350 metres or so of the cave have a wooden walkway and are lit. You can enter for US$0.40 from 9 am to 5 pm daily, and though the cave itself doesn't take long to visit, there are some good walks in the lovely country around, which is tranquil except on Sundays. Often there are ponies available for hire too.

To get there take an Autotransportes Tuxtla Gutiérrez 'Comitán' bus, or any bus heading down the highway from opposite the Cristóbal Colón terminal, and ask for 'Las Grutas' (US$0.40). A fee of US$0.70 is charged for any car entering the caves area, which is named the Parque Recreativo San Cristóbal. Camping is allowed (see Places to Stay).

Huitepec Ecological Reserve & Pro-Natura

The Reserva Ecológica Huitepec is a two-km interpretative nature trail on the slopes of Cerro Huitepec, rising through various vegetation types to rare cloud forest. The ascent is about 45 minutes.

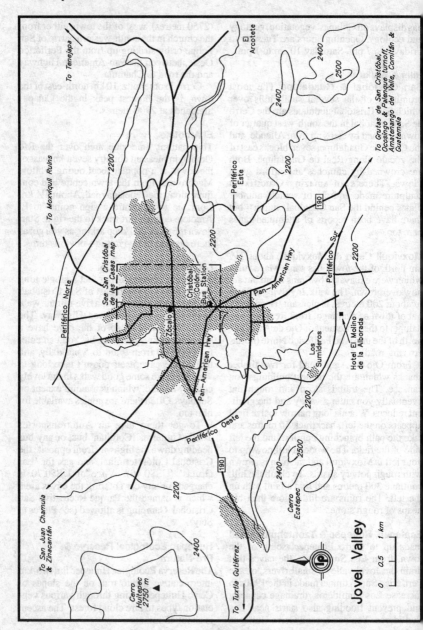

Jovel Valley

0 0.5 1 km

It's 3½ km out of San Cristóbal on the Chamula road, open from 9 am to 4 pm daily except Monday. No entry fee is charged but donations are requested. The reserve is run by Pro-Natura, an independent organisation staffed by volunteers and funded by private donations, which also conducts bird-watching trips and occasional other ecological tours. Its office is at Primero de Marzo 21 in San Cristóbal.

Activities

The Centro Bilingue language school (☎ 8-41-57) at Insurgentes 57 has received some good reports for its one-to-one tuition.

Notice boards outside the tourist office and in the Casa Margarita, the Casa de las Imagenes, and elsewhere advertise live music, horses riding, weaving courses, lifts, tours, and more.

Horse Riding

You can arrange a ride at several places around town. The Casa Margarita for instance charges about US$17 for a five or six-hour guided ride to Chamula or Las Grutas. You can often rent ponies on the spot at Las Grutas. Zinacantán and El Arcotete are other possible goals. Try to find out, before you commit yourself, what the animals are like – whether they're real horses or just ponies, fiery or docile, fast or slow – and whether you'll have a guide. José Hernández (☎ 8-10-65), at Elías Calles 10 near Na Bolom, and the Rancho San Nicolás campground also provide mounts. Carlos (☎ 8-18-73) was advertising 'true horses' on our last visit.

Organised Tours

A few travel agencies in San Cristóbal offer tours to nearby Indian villages. They rarely go anywhere you couldn't reach under your own steam, though they may be able to offer information or combinations of destinations that you couldn't manage easily. Some of the most interesting tours are the small groups (about eight people) led daily by Mercedes Hernández Gómez, a fluent English speaker who grew up in San Juan Chamula. You can find Mercedes at 9 am near the kiosk in the zócalo. The cost is about US$13.50 for five or six hours, travelling by public transport and foot, and the itinerary varies from day to day.

There are also organised day trips further afield for those who are badly short of time. The minibus tours run from the Casa Margarita are some of the cheapest. Usually requiring a minimum of four people, these include Palenque and Agua Azul, the Sumidero Canyon, the Lagos de Montebello, and Toniná ruins. The 12-hour Palenque and Agua Azul trip, for instance, gives you just two hours at each place for about US$27 per person; the eight-hour Montebello trip includes three hours among the lakes for US$18.50. The Hotel Real del Valle, at Real de Guadalupe 14, runs similar trips.

With any Sumidero Canyon trip, establish whether or not the price includes the canyon boat trip itself. On many trips, amazingly, this is extra.

Viajes Pakal (☎ 8-28-19) at the corner of Hidalgo and Cuauhtémoc, and Servicios Turísticos Yaxchilán (☎ 8-12-19), in the Plaza de la Calle Real on Real de Guadalupe half a block from the zócalo, both run road and plane day trips of about 10 hours to Yaxchilán (where you stay two hours) and Bonampak (one hour) for about US$140 per person in a group of four, or US$280 each if just two go. The flights are from Ocosingo, 100 km north of San Cristóbal. Taxis Aereos Ocosingo (☎ 8-25-74 in San Cristóbal) does air trips to Palenque, Yaxchilán, Bonampak and even Tikal in Guatemala from the airstrip at Ocosingo.

Festivals

San Cristóbal's calendar has a liberal sprinkling of festivals. Ask at the tourist office what's on while you're there. In spring Semana Santa, with processions on Good Friday and the burning of 'Judas' figures on Holy Saturday, is followed by the Feria de la Primavera y de la Paz (Spring & Peace Fair) the next week, with more parades, bullfights, and so on. Sometimes the celebrations for the anniversary of the town's founding (31 March) fall in the midst of all this too!

Also look out for events marking the feast of San Cristóbal (17-25 July), the anniversary of Chiapas joining Mexico in 1824 (14 September), National Independence Day (15 and 16 September), the Day of the Dead (2 November), the feast of the Virgin of Guadalupe (10-12 December) and preparations for Christmas (16-24 December).

Festivals are a big feature of life in the Indian villages too – see the Around San Cristóbal section.

Places to Stay – bottom end

Camping The *Rancho San Nicolás* camping and trailer park (☎ (967) 8-00-57) is two km east of the zócalo: continue along León for a km after it becomes a dirt track. The atmosphere's friendly – though the showers and toilets may be mucky – and the cost per person is US$1 in a tent or US$2.50 in a cabin. It's US$4 for a caravan or camper with full hook-ups.

Camping is also permitted in the fine pinewoods around the Grutas de San Cristóbal, nine km south-east of town (see the earlier Grutas section), for US$1.75 per vehicle.

Hotels & Casa de Huéspedes Several cheap hostelries are dotted along Insurgentes, the street leading from the Cristóbal Colón bus station to the zócalo. But with a few exceptions they're dingy and uncared for, and many better deals can be found along Real de Guadalupe, which heads east off the zócalo, and elsewhere.

Insurgentes The *Posada Vallarta* (☎ (967) 8-04-65), actually off Insurgentes at Hermanos Piñeda 10 (the first street on the right as you go up Insurgentes), is clean and modernish. Singles/doubles with private bath are US$10/13.50. Upstairs rooms open on to a balcony. The *Posada Lucella* (☎ (967) 8-09-56) at Insurgentes 55 on the corner of Obregón, is clean and quiet, with a courtyard that more could be made of. Singles/doubles using clean shared baths are US$8.50/12. Doubles with private bath are US$16.75 – a bit overpriced.

Posada Lupita at Insurgentes 46, charging US$8/10, and the *Posada Insurgente* (☎ (967) 8-24-35) nearly opposite at No 73 charging US$5/6.75, both have small, dark rooms and just tolerable common bath rooms. The Lupita is pervaded by the smell of the chicken pen out the back.

The best bottom-end place on Insurgentes is the *Posada San Cristóbal* at No 3, less than a block from the zócalo, which has just a dozen or so airy, sizeable, clean, quite colourfully decorated rooms with recently added showers, set round a courtyard with a fountain and plants. At US$12.50/15.50 it's good value. Hot water is limited to a few hours a day.

Real de Guadalupe The *Hotel Real del Valle* (☎ (967) 8-06-80) at Real de Guadalupe 14, within half a block of the zócalo, has good, clean, largeish rooms with private bath for US$12.50/15.50. Some rooms – the older ones – are round a front courtyard, other newer ones are in a rear extension. What makes this place extra good value is the friendly atmosphere generated by its very helpful, English-speaking owner. The *Hotel San Martín* (☎ (967) 8-05-33), next door at No 16, has a narrow courtyard with tiers of bright, clean and basic rooms rising above. Prices are identical to the Real del Valle's.

The *Posada Santiago* (☎ (967) 8-00-24) at Real de Guadalupe 32, 1½ blocks from the zócalo, is a friendly place where decent, carpeted, medium-sized rooms with private bath go for US$13.50 a double.

The *Casa Margarita* (☎ (967) 8-09-57), at Real de Guadalupe 34, just beyond the Posada Santiago, has long been a very popular budget travellers' halt. It remains so despite a more businesslike, slightly less laid-back atmosphere now that a younger generation of the owning family has taken charge, and the in-house restaurant has spread into the courtyard where guests' washing used to hang. The house is a fine single-storey building with some rooms round the wide courtyard, others along a variety of corridors. The rooms are totally bare, but clean, and the beds are comfortable. If you're alone ask for a *dormitorio* bed, or find other travellers to share a double, triple or quadruple room with you. A dormitorio bed is US$4.50, a double US$9.75, a triple US$13. Bathrooms are communal but very clean. The Margarita is a good travellers' meeting place and will hold mail for you.

A block further up Real de Guadalupe, the *Posada Tepeyac* (☎ (967) 8-01-18) at No 40 is basic but clean, a rambling place where the rooms at the back are lighter. Prices are US$6.75/8.50 with shared bath, US$10/11.75 with private bath.

The *Posada Virginia* (☎ (967) 8-00-24), at Christóbal Colón 1 just south of Real de Guadalupe, has nice, clean rooms, with a bit of thought put into the furnishings, and nice, clean tiled bathrooms. Some rooms have nice little balconies and altogether the place has that bit more comfort and...nice-ness than most others in the bottom range. More rooms are being added to the existing handful, so check the stage building has reached – and likely noise levels – before booking in. Doubles are US$16.75, rooms with one double and two single beds US$20.

Elsewhere Some of the best value is found further from the town centre (which is little hardship because nowhere is really far from the zócalo).

Two blocks north of Real de Guadalupe, at Paniagua 28 between Colón and Santiago, the small, family-run *Posada Jovel* (☎ (967) 8-17-34) attracts real budget travellers with its friendly atmosphere and prices of US$6.75/10 with shared bathroom, US$8.50/11.75 with private bath. Rooms are small but, like the shared bathrooms, fairly clean. Breakfast is available and from the rooftop there are good views over this little-touristed part of town.

Posada El Candil (☎ (967) 8-27-55), at Real de Mexicanos 7, 1½ blocks west of Santo Domingo church, has quite bright rooms which are a good size for what's charged – US$5 for a room with a double bed and shared bath, US$6.75 for two single beds, US$10 for a double with private bath. The whole place is kept pretty clean.

Other posadas with small, rather tired rooms, but worth considering if nowhere comparable is readily available, are the *Posada Santo Domingo*, three blocks north of the zócalo on 28 de Agosto between 20 de Noviembre and Utrilla, the *Posada El Cerrillo*, at Belisario Domínguez 27 just north of Ejercito Nacional, four blocks from the zócalo, and the *Casa de Huéspedes Lupita* at Juárez 12, one block east and 1½ south of the zócalo.

The family-run Santo Domingo is probably the cleanest, charging US$5/6.75; El Cerrillo has a small courtyard and costs US$6.75 with one double bed, US$8 with two singles, US$10 with two doubles; the Lupita charges US$5 per person (singles available) for rather dowdy rooms. The shared bathrooms in all these places are average.

Posada Los Morales (☎ (967) 8-14-72) at Allende 17 has a dozen bare little white-washed two-person 'bungalows' for US$13.50 a night, looking out from a hillside garden on the lower slopes of the Cerro de San Cristóbal. The setting is great but the bungalows are variable, some being dark and rather dank, others being cleaner, brighter and more comfortable. Each has a bathroom with shower, fireplace, gas stove and inter-mittent hot water. Some have one double bed, others two singles. Bedding is provided.

Places to Stay – middle

Insurgentes A block and a half up from the Cristóbal Colón bus station, the *Hotel Capri* (☎ (967) 8-00-15) at Insurgentes 54 has modern, clean rooms round a narrow, flowery, covered courtyard for US$16/20. It's nothing special. Don't confuse it with the vile Posada Capri a block down on the other side of the street.

Further up, at Insurgentes 33, the *Hotel D'Mónica* (☎ (967) 8-29-40) is good value, if low on atmosphere since European tour groups flood through it regularly. Three floors of spacious, tasteful, clean, comfort-able rooms with TV and fireplaces look down on a pretty little garden. Singles/doubles are US$16/20. The in-house Restau-rant Unicornio will send a good pizza, salad and beer up to your room – far better than the endless wait for service at one of its tables.

The *Hotel Fray Bartolomé de las Casas* (☎ (967) 8-09-32), at the corner of Insurgentes and Niños Héroes, is just two blocks from the zócalo. There's a variety of rooms – the larger seem also to be the darker – on and off a lovely pillared courtyard (used for parking). All are clean, with private bathrooms, though some visitors have complained of excessively lumpy pillows and lukewarm water. Try to avoid the noisy Insurgentes side. Rooms are again US$16/20.

Zócalo & Around Back in the 16th century, the *Hotel Santa Clara* (☎ (967) 8-08-71) at Insurgentes 1, the south-east corner of the zócalo, was the home of Diego de Mazariegos, the Spanish conqueror of Chiapas. Rooms are clean and mostly sizeable and comfortable, and there's a pleasant courtyard brightened by some caged red macaws, plus a restaurant, bar/lounge and even a heated pool. Singles/doubles are US$24.50/28.75.

A couple of doors along at Plaza 31 de Marzo 10, with the same prices, the *Hotel Ciudad Real* (☎ (967) 8-18-86) is another Spanish mansion but slightly less spacious. The central courtyard is covered and functions as the dining room. Rooms are clean, neat and well decorated but on the small side; try to get one higher up to lessen noise from the courtyard.

The *Hotel Los Angeles*, half a block east of the zócalo on Madero, is an old but well-converted building with wood-beamed ceilings, and a pleasant courtyard roofed in wood and glass, not the usual plastic. Rooms are clean and fairly spacious if a bit dark, and again cost US$24.50/28.75.

West of the Zócalo The *Hotel Español* (☎ (967) 8-04-12) at Primero (1°) de Marzo 15 on the corner of 16 de Septiembre, is a quiet, old place with a lovely garden beautified by Talavera tiles and a fountain. Graham Greene stayed here in the 1930s. Rooms are comfortable but a little dark and moderately sized. Those opening on the garden are

pleasant, those at the back less thrilling. Wood is provided for the fireplaces in the rooms. The management can be offhand and prices are a little high at US$20 a single, US$24.50 for one double bed, US$28.75 for two beds.

Three blocks further north-west, the *Hotel Parador Mexicanos* (☎ (967) 8-00-55), at 5 de Mayo 38 just south of Escuadrón 201, has two floors of clean, comfortable, sizeable rooms flanking its garden-cum-drive, at the end of which is a tennis court. There are pleasant verandahs, a restaurant and a lobby lounge. The rooms are fair value at US$16/20.

The *Hotel Mansión del Valle* (☎ (967) 8-25-82) at Diego de Mazariegos 39, 3½ blocks west of the zócalo, is modern, clean, comfortable and lacking in atmosphere. The rooms have a TV but could be bigger for US$21/26.75.

Elsewhere The *Hotel El Molino de la Alborada* (☎ (967) 8-09-35) is a rural retreat at the foot of the hills on the south side of the Jovel valley, about four km from the town centre. The dozen or so cottage-style rooms set in large grounds, costing US$16/20, are spacious and clean, with fireplaces and wood. But check for water marks – some of the roofs leak when it rains seriously. There's a good restaurant and a lounge with a marvellous collection of *National Geographic* magazines.

From the town, follow Insurgentes southward, straight on over the Pan-American Highway and past the old airfield on the right, until its second leftward bend, just before the Tortillería María Auxiliadora. Here fork right up a straight track which meets the unpaved Periférico Sur after about 300 metres. Turn right and the hotel appears on the left after about half a km. If you have no vehicle, the management can sometimes run you in and out of town: otherwise a taxi is US$1.75 from town to hotel, US$3.50 vice-versa. 'María Auxiliadora' microbuses from the market or post office go as far as the tortillería.

If you like the atmosphere of *Na Bolom* at

Guerrero 33 (see the earlier Na Bolom section) you can stay in one of its 11 well-decorated guest rooms for US$30/35.

Places to Stay – top end

The elegant, colonial *Hotel Posada Diego de Mazariegos* (☎ (967) 8-05-13) occupies two fine buildings around lovely courtyards either side of Utrilla, one block north of the zócalo. The main reception is in the western building, at 5 de Febrero 1. Rooms are tastefully furnished and most have a TV and a fireplace. But their sizes vary and not all are in quite the pristine condition you would expect for US$32/41. The hotel has a restaurant, bar and crafts shop.

Places to Eat

San Cristóbal has a range of small, clean restaurants and cafés to suit all kinds of palate. The categories into which we divide them are not hard and fast: some 'International' restaurants for instance serve vegetarian food, though without specialising in it, while others dole out Mexican staples as well. The main concentrations of eateries are along Insurgentes and a couple of blocks in all directions from the zócalo, particularly along Madero.

Wholefood/Vegetarian The *Madre Tierra Restaurant*, at Insurgentes 19 on the corner of Hermanos Domínguez, is a vegetarian's oasis in the land of carnes and aves. The emphasis is on fresh, wholefood ingredients, and the range of filling soups, main dishes (mostly US$2.50 to US$3.50), salads (US$1.75 or so), sandwiches and drinks is eclectic and appetising. Brown rice (arroz integral), alfalfa sprouts, that old standby granola, yoghurt and fruit (US$2.50), and even lassi all make their appearance. There are breakfasts too. Excellent whole-wheat bread (pan integral) is served with meals. The only gripe is that some main dishes are a bit stodgy. There are tables both in a small courtyard and in three rooms off it, and live music upstairs some evenings.

The *Panadería Madre Tierra* next door to the Madre Tierra is a wholefood bakery

selling a variety of tasty breads, cakes and snacks like 'pizza' – good for a bite if you don't need a sit-down feed.

El Bazar at Paniagua 2, in the building marked 'Plaza San Cristóbal', is another combined courtyard-and-indoor eatery with a wholefood emphasis, though there are also more standard offerings like hot cakes, spaghetti and meat dishes. The fare is a bit cheaper than the Madre Tierra's and less well prepared. Breakfasts are US$1.75 to US$2.50. El Bazar is open till 11 pm.

International The *Casa Margarita* restaurant at Real de Guadalupe 34 does a very reliable mixture of Western and Mexican food including vegetarian options – it's not fancy, but is good, satisfying and served with efficiency and a smile, though not particularly cheap. For a main course you could choose from several quiches or eight types of spaghetti all for around US$3, enchiladas or queso fundido around US$3.50, chicken done various ways at around US$5, or meat filetes for about US$6.50. There are tables both indoors and outside in the courtyard – the latter are pleasant for the Margarita's good, filling breakfasts, such as fruit salad, eggs, toast, jam, butter and coffee for US$3.50.

Another wide and reliable range of fare is to be found at *La Galería*, at Hidalgo 3 a few doors from the zócalo, which was inhabited at various times past by Diego de Mazariegos, Francisco de Montejo and various bishops of Chiapas. Today the waiters are bow-tied and the typical customer not poverty-stricken. Downstairs is a video and piano bar, upstairs a restaurant and cafeteria. There are good soups and salads (eg Ensalada La Galería – lettuce, tomato, beetroot, cucumber, carrot and dressing), mostly for US$2.50 or so. Main course choices include chicken dishes at US$4 or the good beef filete in mushroom sauce (salsa de champiñon) at US$5.75. Plenty of good whole-wheat bread is served too. La Galería is also open for breakfast.

A third popular central eatery is the *Restaurante Tuluc* at Insurgentes 5, a block and a bit from the zócalo. It can be hard to get a table here at dinner time: again the food is reliable, though served in smaller quantities than at the last two mentioned eateries. Two good choices, both around US$4, are the tasty filete Tuluc, a beef filete rolled round cheese and spinach, with bacon and beans on the outside, and served with chips; and pescado Veracruzana which is good fish with an excellent rich Veracruz sauce. The sopa de verduras is good and chunky. Some people are annoyed by the note 'Service is not included – Thankyou' which arrives with the bill, but the Tuluc scores with its 6.15 am opening time, allowing for a decent breakfast – eg eggs, toast, jam, butter, small juice and coffee at US$2 – before you catch an early bus.

Further down Insurgentes is the *Restaurant Unicornio* in the Hotel D'Monica at No 33, which combines some of the slowest service in town with some of the best pizza (about US$8 for two with a good vegetable salad). Further south on Insurgentes are a trio of small, cheap, friendly and good places: the *Cafetería y Lonchería Palenque*, at No 40 opposite the corner of Robles, the *Restaurant Chamula*, at No 69, and the *Tikal Restaurant* just a block before the Pan-American Highway.

The Palenque serves a mixture of travellers' favourites and orthodox Mexican fare – guacamole or yoghurt, granola and honey for US$1.25, chicken or carne asada with chips and salad for US$2.75. In the Chamula, chicken, meat or enchiladas are all around US$3, and there's a good US$3.50 comida corrida of lentil, vegetable or another soup, spaghetti or rice, meaty main course, and fruit dessert. The Tikal – with a Guatemalan theme to its decor – serves generous spaghettis (such as Genovesa, with cheese, nutmeg and spinach) and salads, and good guacamole with totopos, all at US$2.50, and also hamburguesas at US$2 and meat filetes at about US$5.

On Madero, *Restaurant La Faisán* at No 2, just off the zócalo, used to be a cheap hangout where you could make a lemon tea last for several games of chess. Now it's glassed in, tarted up and has some pretensions. Most main dishes, like chicken or filete with beans, chips and green salad are US$6 or US$7; humble quesadillas are US$3.50. Tax of 15% is added to the menu prices. A few doors up, *Fulano's Restaurant* and the *Restaurant Flamingo*, with similar sorts of fare, both present respectable, reasonably priced food that's nothing special. Spaghettis and salads are US$2.50 and up, pizzas US$4 or US$5, meat dishes around US$5.50. The Flamingo does a fair US$4 comida which might be carrot soup, rice, a main course of chicken, chile relleno or meat, dessert and coffee.

The *Café-Restaurant Del Teatro* upstairs at Primero de Marzo 8 near the corner of 16 de Septiembre, is one of San Cristóbal's top restaurants. The well-prepared food is French and Italian-based, with wood-fire oven-baked pizzas, crepes, and good filetes and desserts. The US$6 daily set meal – for example soup, vegetable salad with vinaigrette dressing, spaghetti Bolognese or lasagne or chicken tacos, and a dessert – is available up to 10 pm.

Mexican A block from the zócalo at Insurgentes 10, the corner of J F Flores, the *Restaurant La Misión del Fraile* is a long, high-beamed, tile-roofed room with colonial hill-town ambience. Tasty anafres, which are sizzling cheese or meat platters for US$5 to US$10 for two, are the main speciality but there are also Mole Jovel and enchiladas de Coletas – of chicken, with a brown sauce and rice – at US$3.75 each, plus salads and a variety of more common Mexican dishes.

Several more workaday Mexican eateries are strung down Insurgentes, among them the *Restaurant Tia Maty* half a block up from the Misión del Fraile, with many meat dishes under US$3 or an order of chicken tacos for US$1.75.

Just off the zócalo on Madero, the *Restaurant Los Arcos* is bigger and much cheaper than its smarter neighbour, La Faisán, and its four-course comida at US$4 is well worth the money. Pollo frito or carne asada is US$3.50, quesadillas just US$2.

Possibly the best, and certainly the most

expensive, tacos in San Cristóbal are served up at *La Salsa Verde* on 20 de Noviembre 1½ blocks north of the zócalo. Over a dozen varieties can be prepared on the open range while you watch – nearly all meaty, though nopal (a type of cactus) makes an interesting change. But the smart service and surroundings contribute to the very hefty price of US$0.70 a taco, US$0.85 with cheese. Quesos fundidos and full meat dishes are also available at around US$5.

At the humbler *El Taquito*, on the corner of Diego de Mazariegos and 12 de Octubre, tacos are half the price and still good. You can also enjoy filete al queso a la parrill (grilled meat filete with a cheese topping) for US$4, or fruit cocktail with granola and honey for US$1.75.

La Parrilla at the corner of Belisario Domínguez and Dr Navarro – open from 6.30 pm to midnight, Sunday to Friday – serves excellent carnes and quesos al carbón (char-grilled meats and cheeses). A main course, dessert and drink will cost you about US$10.

The *Comedor Familiar Normita II*, on the corner of J F Flores and Juárez, has been around a long while. Now it's spruced up with a bright paint job (hence the 'II') but the cooking remains local and good. Pozole, a soup of maize, pork, cabbage, radishes and onions (US$2 or US$2.75), and Plato Típico Coleto, a kind of San Cristóbal mixed grill with two types of pork sausage plus chops, frijoles and guacamole for US$5, are specialities but there's plainer fare too like carne asada with chips for US$3 or pollo al gusto for US$2.50.

Cafés Probably the best coffee in town, and some good cakes, are served in the little *Cafetería San Cristóbal*, on Cuauhtémoc just off Insurgentes. The clientele is mainly Mexican men who bring along chess sets and newspapers and relax.

Sweet-tooths looking for a treat should head for the *Café Olulu* in the courtyard of the Plaza Xama at 20 de Noviembre 4, 1½ blocks north of the zócalo, where the Crepa Olulu wraps yoghurt, honey, fruit and granola all into one pancake for US$3.50.

Entertainment

San Cristóbal's a fairly early-to-bed town, and conversation in cafés, restaurants or rooms will occupy many of your evenings. A handful of eateries – the Madre Tierra, Casa Margarita, and La Galería on our most recent visit – has live music, often Latin folk, most nights.

The Casa de las Imagenes at Belisario Domínguez 11, just north of Real de Guadalupe, is an art gallery cum bookshop cum café with a small cinema showing some interesting films – drop by and look at their programme. There are fairly regular musical and theatrical performances in the Bellas Artes auditorium at the corner of Hidalgo and Hermanos Domínguez.

Local youth consume burgers and music videos at the Café Rock, on Madero next to the Restaurant Flamingo. There are two discos – the Crystal and the Princess – on opposite sides of the Pan-American Highway, about half a km in the Comitán direction from the bottom of Insurgentes. Friday and Saturday are the lively nights – the music goes on till almost dawn.

Things to Buy

Chiapas' Indian crafts are among Mexico's most colourful and inventive, and hosts of shops in San Cristóbal sell them. Guatemalan crafts are sold here too. The heaviest concentrations of shops are along Real de Guadalupe and towards the market end of Utrilla. But most things sold in shops can also be found – sometimes cheaper – at the large, informal, daily crafts market around Santo Domingo church. The items you won't find there are the upmarket, expensive jewellery, boots, fashions and so on sold in places like the Plaza de la Calle Real, on the first block of Real de Guadalupe.

Indian textiles – shawls, scarves, rebozos, blouses, blankets, huipils, belts, sashes, bags – are the outstanding items, and Tzotzil weavers are among the most skilled in Mexico. To see the best in different village styles and get an idea of prices, go to the Sna Jolobil weaving cooperative salesroom beside Santo Domingo (see the earlier Sna

Jolobil section). Sna Jolobil shows and sells woven, embroidered and brocaded cloth mostly in the forms used by the Indians themselves, while the market outside and the shops in the town deal also in goods that adapt Indian styles to tourist tastes, such as shoulder bags or purses with colourfully embroidered panels.

Around town you'll also find plenty of the appealing, cheap Amatenango del Valle pottery including *animalitos* (little animals), and some good leather belts.

You can find many things in more than one place but buying a few things from the same seller is one way of achieving a worthwhile overall discount. Indians are no softer than anyone else when it comes to haggling. Some shops have fixed prices.

San Cristóbal's busy market, open daily except Sunday between Utrilla and Belisario Domínguez, eight blocks north of the zócalo, is where locals go for food and their other day-to-day needs – it's as much a place to observe local life as to shop for anything other than basic necessities. (See the earlier Market section.)

Getting There & Away

San Cristóbal is on the Pan-American Highway, No 190, between Tuxtla Gutiérrez, 85 km west, and Comitán 85 km south-east. The Guatemalan border at Ciudad Cuauhtémoc (165 km) is 80 km beyond Comitán. The road to Ocosingo (100 km), Agua Azul (155 km) and Palenque (210 km) turns north off the Pan-American 12 km south-east of San Cristóbal. For Villahermosa (300 km), you turn north off the Pan-American between Tuxtla Gutiérrez and San Cristóbal, onto Highway 195.

Air Scheduled flights come no nearer than Tuxtla Gutiérrez. There's an Aviacsa office at Pasaje Mazariegos 16, just off the first block of Real de Guadalupe. Travel agents can make bookings on other airlines.

Bus San Cristóbal has a reasonable 1st-class bus service by Cristóbal Colón, but you need to book ahead where possible. For some trips you may have to fall back on a variety of 2nd-class lines.

A new Central de Autobuses is planned in the south of the town but for the moment each company has its own terminal. Cristóbal Colón is at the junction of the Pan-American Highway and Insurgentes. The main 2nd-class lines are Autotransportes Tuxtla Gutiérrez (ATG), on Allende half a block north of the Pan-American Highway; Transportes Lacandonia on the Pan-American Highway between Hidalgo and Crescencio Rosas (1½ blocks west of Cristóbal Colón); Autotransportes Nha Bolom on the Pan-American Highway half a block east of Cristóbal Colón; and Transportes Fray Bartolomé de las Casas on Avenida Salomon González Blanco, the continuation of Utrilla, 300 metres north of the market.

ATG is, overall, the best equipped 2nd-class company, but it's still nothing to write home about. Transportes Lacandonia calls some of its services '1st-class' – they aren't, though they're better than normal 2nd-class.

For transport to highland villages near San Cristóbal see the Around San Cristóbal section. Other bus departures from San Cristóbal include:

Chetumal – 700 km, 13 hours; one evening Transportes Lacandonia '1st-class' bus for US$12.50.

Chiapa de Corzo – 70 km, 1½ hours; five 1st-class buses daily for US$1.50, several 2nd-class buses by ATG.

Ciudad Cuauhtémoc (Guatemalan border) – 165 km, three hours; two morning and one afternoon 1st-class buses for US$3.25 (take the first, early morning, bus if you plan to get any distance into Guatemala the same day).

Comitán – 85 km, 1½ hours; 13 de paso 1st-class buses daily for US$1.75 (tickets sold from two hours before departure), about 15 2nd-class ATG buses (mostly de paso) daily.

Huatulco – 520 km, 11 hours; one morning 1st-class bus for US$10.50.

Mérida – 770 km, 15 hours; one evening Transportes Lacandonia '1st-class' bus for US$13.75.

Mexico City – 1085 km, 21 hours; one Cristóbal Colón Plus luxury bus daily for US$36.75, two evening 1st-class buses for US$23.75.

Oaxaca – 630 km, 12 hours; one evening 1st-class bus for US$12.50.

Ocosingo – 100 km, three hours; about eight 2nd-class buses daily by ATG for US$1.75, 12 by Transportes Lacandonia and several by Transportes Fray Bartolomé de las Casas for US$1.50.

Palenque – 210 km, six hours; five 2nd-class buses daily by ATG for US$4 (advance tickets, up to two days ahead, sold for the 6 am and 12.30 pm buses only), seven by Transportes Lacandonia for US$4, two by Transportes Fray Bartolomé de las Casas for US$3.75.

Pochutla – 555 km, 12 hours; one morning 1st-class bus for US$11.

Tapachula – 485 km, nine hours via Arriaga; one morning 1st-class bus via Arriaga for US$9.25, about 12 de paso 2nd-class buses via Arriaga daily by ATG, one daily 2nd-class bus via Motozintla (350 km, eight hours) by ATG for US$7.25.

Tonalá – 265 km, 5½ hours; one morning 1st-class bus daily for US$5.

Tuxtla Gutiérrez – 85 km, two hours; 17 1st-class buses daily including four morning locales for US$1.75 (advance booking possible on some services only), about 18 2nd-class buses (mostly de paso) daily by ATG and 13 by Autotransportes Nha-Bolom.

Villahermosa – 300 km, seven hours; one morning 1st-class bus by Cristóbal Colón for US$6, one morning Transportes Lacandonia '1st-class' bus.

Colectivo The quickest way to/from Tuxtla Gutiérrez is a colectivo taxi, which costs US$3.50 per person and takes 1¼ hours. In San Cristóbal they wait at the corner of Allende and the Pan-American Highway, and leave when full (six passengers).

Car The only car rental agency is Budget (☎ 8-18-71) at Auto Rentas Yaxchilán at Diego de Mazariegos 36, 2½ blocks from the zócalo. Opening hours are Monday to Saturday 8 am to 2 pm and 3 to 8 pm, Sunday 8 am to noon and 5 to 7 pm. At busy periods you may need to book your car a few days in advance. The cheapest, a VW Sedan, is around US$40 a day plus US$0.20 a km, insurance and taxes included.

AROUND SAN CRISTÓBAL DE LAS CASAS
Tzotzil & Tzeltal Indians

The Tzotzils and Tzeltals of highland Chiapas – descendants of the ancient Maya – are among Mexico's most traditional Indians, with some distinctly pre-Hispanic elements in their nominally Catholic religious life, and Spanish very much a second language. Their costume, too, marks them as the inheritors of ancient Maya traditions.

Very roughly, the 150,000 or so Tzotzils occupy an area about 50 km from east to west and 100 km from north to south, with San Cristóbal at its centre. Tzeltal territory is a similar size and shape, immediately east of the Tzotzil area. Most of the people live in the hills outside the villages, which are primarily market and ceremonial centres. Both peoples are strongly differentiated from place to place. You'll notice this most obviously in the strikingly different costumes: for instance the Tzotzil men from Zinacantán wear pink while those of Chamula go for woolly black or white tunics. (For more on costume see the individual village sections and Sna Jolobil in the San Cristóbal section.)

Most of these Indians are poor. Many men from San Juan Chamula and Mitontic, for instance, have to spend half the year away from home working on Soconusco coffee plantations. Some Tzotzil have moved to the Lacandón forest in search of land. Despite long repression, the Tzotzils' and Tzeltals' relatively large numbers have enabled them to maintain their group pride. These Indians guard their traditions fiercely; approach them with respect.

Social Organisation Women are generally restricted to domestic work, including weaving. Men hold the community leadership positions. *Cargos* – temporary posts, usually held for a year – bring prestige but cost a lot, making it very difficult for individuals to accumulate wealth. Senior *cargo* holders among the Tzotzil, called *mayordomos*, are responsible for the care of saints' images in the churches. These saints are often identified with pre-Hispanic deities, and their saint's days are marked by important ceremonies. The *cargo* of an *alférez* involves organising and paying for these fiestas. The *capitanes'* job is to dance and ride horses at fiestas. *Principales* are men who have carried out important *cargos* and entered the ranks of 'village elders'.

Photography In some villages, particularly those nearest San Cristóbal, you may be greeted with wariness, the result of centuries of oppression and the desire to preserve traditions from interference. Cameras are at best tolerated – and sometimes not even that. The San Cristóbal tourist office displays a sign stating that photography is banned in the church and during festivals at Chamula, and banned completely at Zinacantán. A tale has circulated for years that two tourists were killed for taking photos in the Chamula church. Whether or not it's true, it's certainly evidence of the hostility that can be aroused by insensitive behaviour. If in any doubt at all, ask before taking a picture.

Markets & Festivals The villages' weekly markets are nearly always on Sunday. Proceedings start very early and wind down by lunch time.

Festivals often give the most interesting insight into Indian life, and there are plenty

Chiapas Highlands

f them. Apart from fiestas for a village's patron and other saints, occasions like Carnival (for which Chamula is famous), Semana Santa, the Day of the Dead (2 November) and the day of the Virgin of Guadalupe (12 December) are celebrated almost everywhere.

San Juan Chamula

The Chamulans put up strong resistance to the Spanish in 1524 and launched a famous rebellion in 1869. Today they are one of the most numerous Tzotzil groups – 40,000-strong – and their village 10 km north-west of San Cristóbal is the centre for some unique religious practices. A big sign at the entrance to the village says it is strictly forbidden to take photos in the church or anywhere rituals are being performed.

The centre of the village is at the bottom of a hill leading down from the paved road from San Cristóbal. The church stands on the far side of a large plaza. A sign on its door tells visitors to ask at the 'tourist office', also on the plaza, for tickets (US$0.70) to enter. If the sense of intruding doesn't overwhelm you, the atmosphere inside is extraordinary. The rows of burning candles, the thick clouds of incense, the chanting worshippers kneeling with their faces to the pine-needle-carpeted floor, are all as reminiscent of an Asian temple as of anywhere else. Saints' images are surrounded with mirrors and dressed in holy garments. Among the candles stand Pepsi and Coke bottles – perhaps offerings to appease the deities of the outside world that has broken so quickly over Chamula in recent decades.

From dawn on Sundays, people stream into town from the hills for the weekly market. In addition to the regular basic commodities, there's now a craft section to take advantage of the increasing number of tourists who visit the market, some even in coaches from San Cristóbal. Otherwise there's little to do except imbibe the atmosphere.

Chamulans believe Christ rose from the cross to become the sun. Christian festivals are interwoven with older ones: the pre-Lent Carnival celebrations, which are among the most important and last several days in February or March, also mark the five 'lost' days of the ancient Maya Long Count calendar, which divided time into 20-day periods (18 of these make 360 days, which leaves five more to complete a full year). Other festivals include ceremonies for San Sebastián (mid-late January); Semana Santa; San Juan, the village's patron saint (22-25 June); and the annual change of *cargos* (30 December-1 January).

On such occasions a strong alcoholic brew called *posh* is drunk and you may see groups of ceremonially attired men, carrying flags and moving slowly round in tight, chanting circles. At Carnival, troops of strolling minstrels called *mash* wander the roads strumming guitars and wearing sunglasses (even when it's raining) and tall pointed hats.

Cargo holders wear black tunics instead of the usual white ones.

Zinacantán

This Tzotzil village, centre for the roughly 15,000 Zinacantecos, is 11 km north-west of San Cristóbal. The road to it forks left off the Chamula road, then down into a valley. Zinacantán has two churches. Photos are banned altogether here.

The men wear very distinctive red-and-white striped tunics (which appear pink), and flat, round, ribboned palm hats. Unmarried men's hats have longer, wider ribbons. A market is usually held only at fiesta times. The most important celebrations are for the patron saint, San Lorenzo, between 8 and 11 August, and San Sebastián (January).

Zinacantecos venerate the geranium which, along with pine branches, is offered in rituals to bring a wide range of benefits. The crosses dotting the Zinacantán countryside mostly mark entrances to the abodes of the important ancestor gods or the Señor de la Tierra (Earth Lord), all of whom have to be kept happy with offerings at the appropriate times.

Tenejapa

Tenejapa is a Tzeltal village 28 km north-east

of San Cristóbal, in a pretty valley with a river running through it. There are about 20,000 Tenejapanecos in the surrounding area. A quite busy market fills the main street (round behind the church) early on Sunday mornings. *Cargo* holders wear wide, colourfully beribboned hats, and chains of silver coins round their necks. Women wear brightly brocaded or embroidered huipils.

Tenejapa has a few comedors in the main street and one basic posada, the *Hotel Molina*, but it's not always open. The main festival is for the patron saint, San Ildefonso, on 23 January.

Amatenango del Valle

The women of this Tzeltal village, by the Pan-American Highway 37 km south-east of San Cristóbal, are renowned potters. Amatenango pottery is still fired by the pre-Hispanic method of burning a wood fire around the pieces, rather than putting them in a kiln. In addition to the pots, bowls, urns, jugs and plates that the village has turned out for generations, young girls in the last 15 years or so have made animalitos (little animals) which find a ready market with tourists. These are small, appealing and cheap, if fragile. If you visit the village, expect to be surrounded within minutes by girls selling them.

The women wear white huipils embroidered with red and yellow, wide red belts and blue skirts. Amatenango's patron saint, San Francisco, is fêted on 4 October.

Andrés Larráinzar

This is a hilltop Tzotzil and mestizo village 28 km north-west of San Cristóbal. Sometimes, confusingly, it's called San Andrés Chamula. It's 18 km beyond San Juan Chamula (where the road ceases to be paved and becomes pretty rough in parts). A turnoff uphill to the left, 10 km after San Juan Chamula, leads through spectacular mountain scenery to San Andrés.

A weekly Sunday market is held and the people seem less reserved towards outsiders than those of San Juan Chamula and Zinacantán. Men wear a red, black and white combination of tunic, long-sleeved shirt and cotton trousers with colourfully ribboned palm hats. Women have white blouses with red and black brocaded patterns, red belt and dark blue wool skirts.

People from Magdalenas, another Tzotzil village a few km north, attend the San Andrés market. Magdalenas' superb ceremonial huipils are among the finest of all Chiapas Indian garments.

It's not possible, as far as we could discover, to get to San Andrés and back by bus from San Cristóbal in one day. The patron saint's day is 30 November. Carnival celebrations are lively, with plenty of posh going down the men's throats.

Mitontic & San Pedro Chenalhó

The plaza at Mitontic, a small Tzotzil village a few hundred metres left of the Chenalhó road, 23 km beyond San Juan Chamula, has both a picturesque, ruined 16th-century church and a more modern working one. *Cargo* holders here wear white hats with multicoloured ribbons. The patron saint, San Miguel, is honoured from 5 to 8 May.

San Pedro Chenalhó is a Tzotzil village in a valley with a stream running through it, 1500 metres high, 27 km beyond and quite a descent from San Juan Chamula. It's the centre for about 14,000 people in the surrounding area. There's a weekly Sunday market and Chenalhó has accommodation possibilities. One is a pink house with green pillars, opposite a green house with pink trimmings, along the street which forks right at the three crosses as you enter the village. The same house also serves basic meals. A second is Señora Consuelo Aguilar Gordillo's house, on the corner of the third street on the left along Avenida Central (the grandly named main street – don't fork right at the three crosses). Señora Gordillo charges about US$2 for a bed.

If neither of these places can take you, look up the friendly priest, Padre Miguel Chanteau, a Frenchman who has been here since 1965. His house is immediately to the right of the church in the main square, and it

..as a dormitory where he told us travellers could stay.

Chenalhó men traditionally wear black unics, leather belts, white trousers and .ometimes ribboned hats. The main fiestas .re for San Pedro (27-30 June), San Sebasián (16-22 January) and Carnival.

Getting There & Away
There are paved roads to San Juan Chamula, Zinacantán, Amatenango del Valle, and most of the way to Tenejapa. Reaching the other villages mentioned involves long stretches of pretty rough dirt track, but buses make it along them and so can a VW sedan (slowly).

Bus and colectivo schedules are geared to getting villagers into town early and back home not too late.

Combis to the villages nearest San Cristóbal leave from the north-western corner of San Cristóbal market, between Utrilla and Cárdenas. They depart for San Juan Chamula and Zinacantán every 20 minutes or so up to about 5 pm; the fare is US$0.50. For Tenejapa they leave about half-hourly, take an hour and cost US$0.90. Return services from Tenejapa start getting scarce after noon.

To Amatenango del Valle, take a Comitán bus (see San Cristóbal, Getting There & Away). The fare is US$0.90.

Transportes Fray Bartolomé de las Casas (see San Cristóbal, Getting There & Away) runs buses to Chenalhó (US$1, 2½ hours) four times daily, and to San Andrés Larráinzar (US$0.90, 2½ hours) at 2 pm. The return bus from San Andrés leaves at 7 am.

SAN CRISTÓBAL TO PALENQUE
This roughly 210-km journey – 12 km south-east down the Pan-American Highway from San Cristóbal, then north on Highway 199 – takes you from cool, misty highlands to steaming lowland jungle, and is dotted with interesting stopovers. Ocosingo, 100 km from San Cristóbal, is the jumping-off point for the little-known Maya ruins at Toniná. The turnoff for the superb cascades of Agua Azul is about 50 km beyond Ocosingo. Another beautiful waterfall, Misol-Ha, with

a good swimming hole, is two km off the road 40 km after the Agua Azul turning.

The San Cristóbal-Palenque road is now all paved, though a few bits are in poor repair.

HUIXTÁN & OXCHUC
Huixtán, 32 km from San Cristóbal and the centre for the roughly 12,000 Tzotzils, was one of the main pre-Hispanic Tzotzil centres and has a 16th-century church. Its women wear attractive white shawls with delicate floral patterns. Oxchuc, 20 km beyond Huixtán, is a small Tzeltal and mestizo town dominated by the large colonial church of Santo Tomás. Costume leans heavily towards pink and red. Women generally wear very long white huipiles adorned with coloured rectangles and stripes. The men's costume, when they wear it, is a knee-length cotton tunic, with a coloured square on the chest, and striped arms.

OCOSINGO
Population: 20,000
Ocosingo is a small, easygoing, mestizo and Tzeltal valley town on the San Cristóbal-Palenque road.

Orientation & Information
The town spreads downhill to the east of the main road. Avenida Central runs straight down from the main road to the zócalo. Most of the bus stations are on Avenida 1 Norte, parallel to Avenida Central a block north. Everything else is within five minutes' walk of the zócalo. To orient yourself on the zócalo, remember that the church is on the east side and the Hotel Central on the north side. The large market is three blocks east along Avenida 1 Sur Ote from the church.

None of the banks in town will change dollars or travellers' cheques, though this may change as Ocosingo edges on to the tourist map.

Places to Stay
The *Hotel Central* (☎ 3-00-24) on the north side of the zócalo has good clean rooms with fans, and private baths with hot water, for US$10 a single, US$13.50 a double. The

Posada Agua Azul, at 1 Ote Sur 127, two blocks south of the church, has medium-sized, not very clean rooms round a courtyard which harbours a few tightly caged anteaters, hawks and macaws. Singles are US$6.75, doubles US$8.50 with one bed, US$10 with two.

At the really cheap end there's the *Hospedaje La Palma*, on the corner of Calle 2 Pte and Avenida 1 Norte, just down the hill from the Autotransportes Tuxtla Gutiérrez bus station. It's an extremely basic, just about clean, family-run place, with a flowery courtyard. Singles/doubles are US$3.50/5.50 and bathrooms are communal. The *Hospedaje San José* (☎ 3-00-39) at Calle 1 Ote 6, half a block north of the north-east corner of the zócalo, has dark, small but clean enough rooms. A one-bed double with fan and private bath is US$8.50. There are also cheaper rooms without fan and with shared bath.

Places to Eat

Ocosingo is famous for its queso amarillo (yellow cheese), which comes in three-layered one-kg balls. The two outside layers are like chewy Gruyére, the middle is creamy.

Restaurant La Montura has a prime location on the north side of the zócalo, with tables on the Hotel Central's verandah as well as indoors. It has a sizeable menu and is good for breakfast (fruit cocktail, eggs, coffee, bread, butter and honey for US$3). *Restaurant & Pizzería Troje* on the opposite side of the zócalo has only a few pizzas but serves queso amarillo in its quesadillas (US$2) and its plato especial de queso fundido con chorizo (melted cheese with spicy suasage, US$3).

La Calesa just west of the zócalo on Avenida Central specialises in char-grilled (al carbón) meats and cheeses, but also offers eggs and antojitos. It's open till 11 pm. A little further along the same street, the *Restaurant San Cristóbal* offers a US$3.50 comida corrida. A sample is beefsteak with chips, sopa de arroz, tortillas, frijoles, salad and refresco.

Getting There & Away

Air Taxis Aereos Ocosingo (☎ 3-01-88) run air tours to Palenque, Yaxchilán, Bonampak and even Tikal in Guatemala. Yaxchilán and Bonampak in one day cost around US$350 for up to four people. The office is at the airstrip, just east of the market.

Bus All buses are 2nd class. Those of Autotransportes Tuxtla Gutiérrez, with about half a dozen buses to/from both Palenque and San Cristóbal daily, are the least uncomfortable. Their terminal is on Avenida 1 Norte – from the zócalo, one block west then one north, then half a block uphill. Buses start here for Palenque (US$2.25, three hours), San Cristóbal (US$1.75, three hours) and Tuxtla Gutiérrez (US$3.25, five hours) at 6 am, and there are six de paso buses to Palenque and seven in the other direction daily.

Transportes Lacandonia, on the same street a little higher up, runs older, slower buses to/from both Palenque (US$2.25) and San Cristóbal (US$1.50). They leave Ocosingo both ways hourly from 8 am to 5 pm. Transportes Fray Bartolomé de las Casas, on the far side of the main road at the top of Avenida 1 Norte, has a mixture of modern microbuses and decrepit old blue buses. It has six or seven daily buses to/from San Cristóbal for US$1.50, and at least two a day to/from Palenque for US$2.

TONINÁ

The Maya ruins at Toniná, 14 km east of Ocosingo, are relatively hard to reach and don't compare with Palenque for beauty or importance, but form a sizeable, interesting site with some big structures on terraces cut from a hillside. Some reconstruction hasn't reduced Toniná's 'lost in the jungle' feel. The ruins are open from 9 am to 4 pm daily, for US$2.75. The house opposite the ticket office sells refrescos.

Toniná was probably a city-state independent of both Palenque and Yaxchilán, though it declined at the same time as they did, around 800 AD. Dates found at the site range rom 500 to 800 and like Palenque and Yaxchilán it peaked in the last 100 years or o of that period.

The caretaker may be willing to go round he site with you, which can be helpful as here are few signs. If you have already visited Palenque or Yaxchilán, imagine a similar splendour here. Many of the stone facings and interior walls were covered in coloured paint or frescoes.

The track goes past the small museum which holds quite a number of good stone carvings – statues, bas-reliefs, altars, calendar stones – then over a stream and up to a flat area from which rises the terraced hill supporting the main structures. As you face his hillside, behind you in a field are an overgrown outlying pyramid and the main ball court. The flat area contains a small ball court and fragments of limestone carvings. Some appear to show prisoners holding out offerings, with glyphs on the reverse sides.

The most interesting area of the terraced hillside is the right-hand end of its third and fourth levels. The stone facing of the wall rising from the third to fourth levels here has a zig-zag x-shape, which may represent Quetzalcóatl and is also flights of steps. To the right of the base of this are the remains of a tomb, with steps leading up to an altar. Behind and above the tomb and altar is a rambling complex of chambers, passageways and stairways, believed to have been Toniná's administrative hub.

Over towards the centre of the hillside are remains of the central stairway, which went much of the way up the hillside. One level higher than the top of the zig-zag wall is a grave covered in tin sheeting, which you can lift to see a stone coffin beneath. Here were found the bodies of a ruler and two others. To the left on the same level is a shrine to Chac, the rain god. To the right at the foot of a crumbling temple is a carving of the *monstruo de la tierra*. Higher again and to the left are two more mounds. The left-hand one, the pyramid of life and death, may have supported the ruler's dwelling. At the very top of the hill rise two more tall pyramid-temple mounds.

Getting There & Away

The track from Ocosingo is dirt and in parts rough, but crosses pleasant, flat ranchland with lots of colourful birds.

In your own vehicle, follow Calle 1 Ote south from Ocosingo church. Before long it curves left and you pass a cemetery on the right. At the fork a couple of km further on, go left. At the next fork, the site is signposted to the right. Finally a sign marks the entry track to Toniná at Rancho Guadalupe on the left. From here it's another km to the site itself.

Otherwise you have the options of a taxi (about US$20 round trip with an hour at the ruins), hitching (maybe six vehicles an hour pass Toniná), or a passenger truck from Ocosingo market (several a day, most frequent from late morning, about US$1) or a bus of Carga Mixta Ocosingo from their yard near the market. There appear to be two or three buses to Guadalupe (near the ruins) and back each day. The ride costs US$1 and takes about 45 minutes. The Rancho Guadalupe sometimes puts people up for the night or allows them to camp.

For minibus day trips to Toniná with English-speaking guides, ask at the Casa Margarita in San Cristóbal de las Casas. A 10 or 12-hour trip costs about US$20 per person.

AGUA AZUL

Just over 60 km from Palenque and 4½ km off the highway, scores of dazzling white waterfalls thunder into turquoise pools surrounded by jungle. The Agua Azul cascades are among the wonders of Mexico.

The temptation to swim is great but take extreme care – the current is deceptively fast and there are many invisible submerged hazards like rocks and dead trees. Use your judgement to identify slower, safer areas. Drownings are all too common, as memorials to foreign travellers and others who have died here show. During the height of the rainy season, the waters can turn brackish with brown silt.

A vehicle track leads down from Highway 199 to a section of the falls with a car park, a collection of reasonable comedors and, nearby, a small village. A fee of US$1.75 is charged for each car (including its passengers) entering the *parque natural* centred on Agua Azul, or US$0.70 for each individual. At holiday times there'll be crowds of Mexican and foreign tourists here; at other times you'll have few companions.

The falls stretch some distance up and downstream. Upstream, a trail takes you over some swaying, less-than-stable foot bridges and up through jungle. An experienced female traveller walking alone above the falls here reported that she was attacked, escaping only through a strategically aimed kick to the groin. Several travellers have also reported thefts at Agua Azul even at gunpoint, so take care.

Places to Stay

The Agua Azul *Camping* charges US$1 per person for camping or hammock-slinging, US$2.75 to rent you a hammock or a bed. Ask at the small kiosk with a 'Camping' sign about 100 to 150 metres upstream from the car park. The site is a minute's walk to the left from there.

Getting There & Away

The Agua Azul junction, or *crucero*, on Highway 199 is about 50 km north of Ocosingo and 60 km south of Palenque. The 4½ km to the falls is downhill all the way – OK to walk down, but very hard work in the heat and humidity going back up. Hitching is possible but you can't rely on it.

An easy way of visiting Agua Azul is a day trip from Palenque with transport laid on. Several travel agents in Palenque offer such trips, lasting about seven hours with typically three hours at Agua Azul and half an hour at Misol-Ha, for about US$6.50 per person including entrance fees. The colectivo combis of Autotransportes Chambalu in Palenque, departing from Allende near the corner of Hidalgo at 8 and 10 am and 12 noon, charge only US$5.50 and get back to Palenque 6½ hours later. Be there half an hour early to ensure a seat.

Alternatively you can travel by 2nd-class bus to the crucero and trust your legs an luck from there. Any bus between Palenqu and San Cristóbal or Ocosingo will drop yo there. The trip is about four hours (US$3 from San Cristóbal, one hour (US$1) from Ocosingo and 1¼ hours (US$1) from Pale nque. Try to book ahead on these buse unless you want to stand. Catching a bu from the crucero when you leave almos certainly means standing, to start with a least. Some travellers have hitched from th crucero, but don't count on this.

Another possibility is to find car traveller with whom to share an Agua Azul trip, an its cost. Try asking around at the Hotel L Cañada Restaurant, or the Maya Restauran near the zócalo, in Palenque.

MISOL-HA

About 20 km from Palenque, a waterfal drops nearly 35 metres into a beautiful wid pool safe for swimming. The Misol-Ha (o Misol-Ja) cascade and its jungle surround ings, though less visited than Agua Azul, ar spectacular enough to be the setting for a Arnold Schwarzenegger epic.

The waterfall is 1½ km west by dirt roa off Highway 199 and the turning i signposted. Near the waterfall, though out o sight from it, are a café, and some self-cater ing cabins under construction. A fee o US$1.75 per visitor car, or US$0.40 pe visitor without a vehicle, is charged Camping is allowed in a small area near th waterfall.

See Agua Azul for info on getting to an from Misol-Ha. Buses stop at the Misol-H junction (crucero) just as they do at the Agu Azul crucero.

PALENQUE

Surrounded by emerald jungle, Palenque' setting is superb and its Maya architectur and decoration are exquisite. It's a site yo shouldn't miss.

From Palenque you can trek into th Lacandón jungle, one of Mexico's larges areas of tropical forest, to visit the May ruins at Yaxchilán and Bonampak. Usin Palenque as a base you can take a quick tri to Nututun for swimming, a longer excursion to the beautiful waterfall and chilly jungle pool at Misol-Ha, or an even longer one to the cascades at Agua Azul. For details on these sites, see the earlier section San Cristóbal to Palenque.

History

The name Palenque means Palisade in Spanish and has no relation to the ancient city, the real name of which is still uncertain or unknown. It could be Nachan, (City of Snakes), Chocan, (Sculptured Snake), Culhuacán, Huehuetlapalla, Xhembobel Moyos, Ototium...No one knows for sure.

Evidence from pottery fragments indicates that Palenque was first occupied more than 1500 years ago. It flourished from 600 to 800 AD, and what a glorious two centuries they were! The city first rose to prominence under Pakal, a club-footed king who reigned from 615 to 683 AD. Archaeologists have determined that Pakal is represented by hieroglyphics of sun and shield. He lived to a ripe old age, possibly 80 to 100 years.

During Pakal's reign, many plazas and buildings, including the superlative Temple of Inscriptions, were constructed within the 20 sq km of the city. The structures were characterised by mansard roofs and very fine stucco bas-reliefs. Hieroglyphic texts at Palenque state that Pakal's reign was predicted thousands of years prior to his ascension and would be celebrated far into the future.

Pakal was succeeded by his son Chan-Balum, symbolised in hieroglyphics by the jaguar and the serpent. Chan-Balum continued Palenque's political and economic expansion as well as the development of its art and architecture. He completed his father's crypt in the Temple of the Inscriptions and presided over the construction of the Plaza of the Sun temples, placing sizeable narrative stone stelae within each. One can see the influence of Palenque's architecture in the ruins of the Maya city of Tikal in Guatemala's Petén region and in the pyramids of Comalcalco near Villahermosa.

Not long after Chan-Balum's death, Palenque started on a precipitous decline. Whether this was due to ecological catastrophe, civil strife or invasion has been disputed, but after the 10th century Palenque was largely abandoned. Situated in an area receiving the heaviest rainfall in Mexico, the ruins were overgrown with vegetation and lay undiscovered until the latter half of the 18th century.

Orientation

There are two Palenques: the town (population 70,000; altitude 80 metres) and the archaeological zone, 6.5 km apart. Coming south from Highway 186, you'll go about 20 km before passing through the settlement of Pakal-Na at the Palenque railway station; the town is several km farther on. If you arrive by train, try hitching into town, or take a taxi for US$3.

Several more km bring you past the airstrip on the left (east), and then to a fork in the road. You'll know the fork by the huge, bombastic statue of a Maya chieftain's head. Bear left at the statue for Palenque town (one km) or bear right for the ruins (5½ km) within the national park. The road to the right toward the ruins also leads to the turn (left) for Nututun, Misol-Ha, Agua Azul and San Cristóbal de las Casas.

Though most hotels and restaurants are in the town centre, the camping areas and several middle and top-end hotels and restaurants are located along the road to the ruins. There are also a few good hotels and restaurants just to the left of the Maya statue as you come in from the highway.

Though relatively small, the town is spread out. From the Maya statue at its western limit to the Hotel Misión Palenque at the eastern end is about two km. But most of the bus offices are clustered a few hundred metres east of the Maya statue past the Pemex fuel station on the way into town, and the walk to most hotels is 800 metres or less.

The main road from the Maya statue into town is Avenida Juárez, which ends at the town's main square, known as simply el parque (the park). Juárez is also the centre of the commercial district.

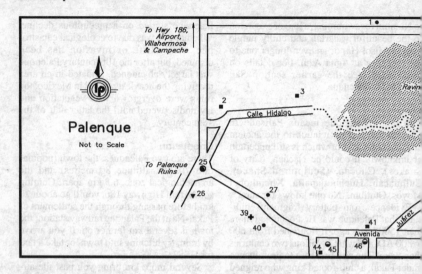

To Hwy 186,
Airport,
Villahermosa
& Campeche

Palenque

Not to Scale

To Palenque
Ruins

Calle Hidalgo

Ravin

Juárez

Avenida

■ PLACES TO STAY		35	Taquerías
		36	'Restaurant Row'
2	Hotel Maya Tulipanes	47	Restaurant Las Tinajas
3	Hotel La Cañada	49	Tienda Naturista Esconpion
4	Casa de Huéspedes León		
8	Hotel La Croix		OTHER
21	Hotel Misol-Ha		
23	Hotel Casa de Pakal & Restaurant	1	Market
	Castellano	5	Post Office & Telegraph Office
24	Hotel & Restaurant Chan-Kah	6	Palacio Municipal & Tourist Office
30	Hotel Kashlan	9	Farmacia Santa Fe (24 hours)
31	Hotel Regional	10	Clinica Santa Fe
37	Hotel Vaca Vieja & Restauarnt Yunuén	11	Colectivos Chambalu
38	Hotel Misión Palenque	12	Anfitriones Turísticos de Chiapas
41	Hotel La Avenida	16	Banamex
43	Hotel Palenque	17	Bancomer
44	Hotel Santa Elena	19	Mercado de Artesanías
48	Posada Charito	22	Farmacia Centro
		25	Maya Head Statue
▼ PLACES TO EAT		27	Pemex Fuel Station
		28	ADO (1st-Class) Bus Station
7	Restaurant Arsemio's	29	Lavandería Automática
13	Piccolino's Pizza	32	Farmacia Principal
14	Restaurant Paisanos	39	Hospital General
15	Restaurant El Herradero	40	Centro de Salud (Clinic)
18	Restaurant Maya	42	Casa de la Cultura
20	Restaurant La Kan-Ha	45	Transportes Dag-Dug Bus Station
26	Restaurant-Bar Hardy's (La Selva)	46	Autotransportes Tuxtla Gutiérrez Bus
33	Expendio de Pan Virginia		Station
34	Cookshops	50	Church

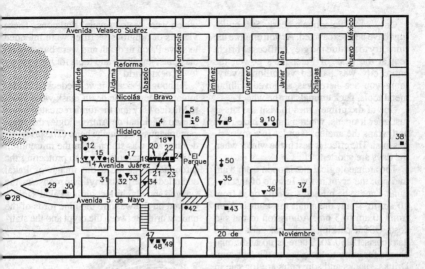

It's always sweltering in Palenque, and there's rarely any breeze.

Information

Tourist Office Located just off the park in part of the Palacio Municipal, the tourist office has English-speaking staff but no adequate map of either the ruins or the town. The office is open Monday to Saturday 8 am to 2 pm and 5 to 8 pm, Sunday 9 am to noon.

Money Bancomer, 1½ blocks west of the park on Avenida Juárez, changes money between 10 and 11.30 am Monday to Friday. Banamex, 2½ blocks west of the park, changes money from 10.30 am to noon Monday to Friday. Hotels and better restaurants will also change money, though at less favourable rates.

Post & Telecommunications The post office is just off the park on the left side of the Palacio Municipal. It's open Monday to Friday 8 am to 1.30 pm and 4 to 6 pm, Saturday 8 am to noon. The postal code is 29960.

You can place long-distance telephone calls from the ADO bus station. Uncom-

pleted person-to-person or collect (reverse-charge) calls are subject to a fee. The telegraph office is on Independencia near the corner with Nicolás Bravo, a block north of the park.

Laundry There is a laundromat, the Lavandería Automática a few steps uphill from the ADO bus station on the opposite side of the street.

Medical Services Palenque has a Hospital General across from the Pemex station near the Maya statue, a Centro de Salud Urbano (Urban Health Centre) next door, and various pharmacies. The Farmacia & Clinica Santa Fe, on Hidalgo at Javier Mina two blocks east of the park, is open 24 hours a day. Don't expect to see the lights on day and night, but feel free to wake them in an emergency.

Palenque Ruins

The archaeological zone of Palenque is situated in a much larger reserve, the Parque Nacional Palenque. You pass through a thatched gateway into the national park a km or so before coming to the ruins.

Only 34 of Palenque's nearly 500 buildings have been excavated. As you explore the ruins, try to picture the grey edifices as bright red; at the peak of Palenque's power, the entire city was painted vermilion. Everything you see here was achieved without metal tools, pack animals or the wheel.

One of the prime times to visit the site is just after it opens, when a humid haze rises and wraps the ancient temples in a mysterious mist. The effect is best in the winter when the days are shorter.

The archaeological site is open from 8 am to 5 pm; the crypt in the Temple of Inscriptions – not to be missed – is only open from 10 am to 4 pm; the small museum is open from 10 am to 5 pm. Admission to the site costs US$5; parking in the car park by the gate costs US$0.20. There is no additional charge for entry to the crypt or the museum. Drinks, snacks and souvenirs are for sale in stands facing the car park.

Temple of Inscriptions After you enter the enclosure and walk along the path, look for a small stone structure on the left-hand side. This is the tomb of Alberto Ruz Lhuillier, the tireless archaeologist who revealed many of Palenque's mysteries between 1945 and 1952.

The magnificent pyramid on the right is the tallest and most prominent of Palenque's buildings. Constructed on eight levels, it has a central staircase rising some 23 metres to a temple which crowns the structure; it once had a tall roofcomb as well. Between the doorways are stucco panels with reliefs of noble figures. On the temple's rear wall are three panels with a long inscription in Maya hieroglyphs which gives the temple its name. The inscription, dedicated in 692 AD, recounts the history of Palenque and of the temple.

Ascend the 69 steep steps to the top, both for a magnificent vista of Palenque and surrounding jungle and for access to stairs down to the tomb of Pakal (open 10 am to 4 pm). This crypt lay undiscovered until 1952 when Lhuillier, who had been excavating the staircase, found a sealed stone passageway in

which were seated several skeletons. These victims of religious sacrifice were intended to serve Pakal in death and were buried with clay pots, jewellery and tools for his journey to the next world.

Although Pakal's jewel-bedecked skeleton and jade mosaic death mask were taken to Mexico City and the tomb recreated in the Museo Nacional de Antropología, the stone sarcophagus lid remains here. (The priceless death mask was stolen from the museum in 1985.) The carved stone slab protecting the sarcophagus includes the image of Pakal encircled by serpents, mythical monsters, the sun god and glyphs recounting Pakal's reign. Carved on the wall are the nine lords of the underworld. Between the crypt and the stair-

Stucco head found in the Temple of Inscriptions tomb

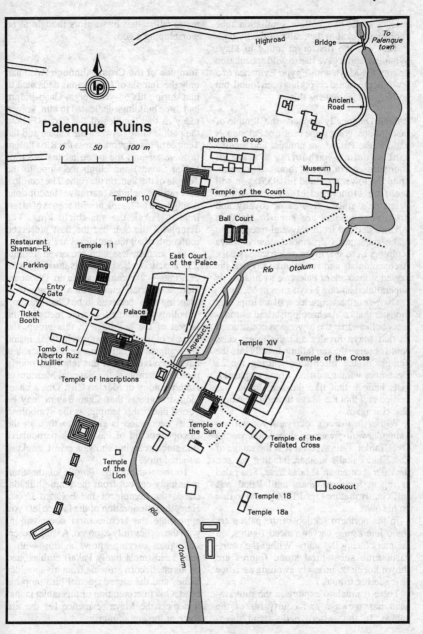

Palenque Ruins

0   50   100 m

To Palenque town

Highroad

Bridge

Ancient Road

Northern Group

Museum

Temple of the Count

Temple 10

Ball Court

Restaurant Shaman–Ek

Temple 11

East Court of the Palace

Río Otolum

Parking

Entry Gate

Palace

Ticket Booth

Temple XIV

Temple of the Cross

Tomb of Alberto Ruz Lhuillier

Temple of Inscriptions

Aqueduct

Temple of the Sun

Temple of the Foliated Cross

Temple of the Lion

Lookout

Temple 18

Temple 18a

Río Otolum

case, a snake-like hollow ventilation tube connected Pakal to the realm of the living.

This was the first crypt found in Maya pyramids, and it gave rise to wild speculation linking the Maya with Egypt. Evidence of a few other pyramid crypts has been found, but nothing as elaborate as this.

Palace Diagonally opposite the Temple of Inscriptions, lying in the centre of Palenque's park, is the Palace, an unusual and significant structure harbouring a maze of courtyards, corridors and rooms. If you walk up to the tower (restored in 1955), you will see fine stucco reliefs on the walls. Palenque's stucco figures of royalty and prominent priests are superb. Using a mixture derived from clay and tree bark to make the stucco dry more slowly, Maya sculptors were able to create intricate details. Archaeologists and artists alike say that the carved stonework of Palenque's ruins stands unparalleled among Maya sites in Mexico.

On the northern interior wall are imposing monster masks. Archaeologists and astronomers believe that the tower was constructed so that Maya royalty and the priest class could observe the sun falling directly into the Temple of the Inscriptions during the 22 December winter solstice. Some archaeologists believe that like the sun, Pakal was deified and that the Maya thought he would also rise again.

Within the tower's courtyard, you will see a singular well-preserved stone known as the Oval Tablet. Engraved on it is the image of Zac-Kuk, Pakal's mother, handing her son the ruler's ceremonial headdress. She ruled as regent for three years until Pakal was sufficiently mature (aged 12½ years) to rule on his own.

In the northern section of the palace are some interesting carved stucco figures, on the piers facing the stairs. Within the courtyard, nine substantial stone figures are shown kneeling, possibly awaiting sacrifice or rendering tribute.

There is much to explore in the subterranean passageways and courtyards of the palace. In the eastern patio stand three-metre-tall statues of warriors thought to be worshipping a god.

Temples of the Cross Although Pakal had only the Temple of Inscriptions dedicated to him during his 68-year reign, Chan-Balum had three buildings dedicated to him, known today as the Temples of the Cross. Follow the path leading between the Palace and the Temple of Inscriptions, cross the Río Otolum (a mere stream; the name means Place of Fallen Stones) and climb the slope to the Temple of the Sun, on the right. The temple's decoration includes narrative inscriptions dating from 642, replete with scenes of offerings to Pakal, the sun-shield king. The Temple of the Sun has the best preserved roofcomb of all the buildings at Palenque.

The smaller, less well-preserved Temple XIV next door also has tablets showing ritual offerings – a common scene in Palenque. Here a woman makes an offering to a 'dancing man' believed to be Chan-Balum.

Follow the path a few more metres to the largest of the buildings in this group, the Temple of the Cross, restored in 1990. Inside are sculpted narrative stones; some tablets have been taken from this relatively poorly preserved temple to the National Museum of Anthropology in Mexico City. One archaeologist suggests that Chan-Balum may be buried under this temple, as the symbolism of its decoration is similar to that on the sarcophagus lid of Pakal. One particularly fine stucco carving shows a priest smoking a sacred pipe.

To the right of the Temple of the Sun, seemingly cut out from the jungle hillside, stands the Temple of the Foliated Cross. Here, the deterioration of the façade lets you appreciate the architectural composition, with the arches fully exposed. A well-preserved tablet carving shows a king with a sun-shield (most likely Pakal) emblazoned on his chest, corn growing from his shoulder blades and the sacred quetzal bird atop his head. One interpretation of this tablet is that it depicts the Maya reverence for the life force of the god of maize.

Other Ruins & Museum Cross the park, heading away (north) from the Temple of Inscriptions, and follow the road around to the north side of the Palace. On your left is the Northern Group of buildings, unrestored; on your right, just north of the Palace, the ruins of a ball court. Crazy Count de Waldeck lived in one of the temples of the Northern Group – hence its name, Temple of the Count. Constructed in 647 AD under Pakal, it is one of Palenque's oldest mansard-roofed buildings.

Continue on the road keeping the Palace on your right, then through a clearing and you'll reach the museum, on the left by the river. Among the small museum's most interesting exhibits are stone tablets covered with finely wrought calendar glyphs, votive figurines, statues and a chart of Maya history. The musuem is open from 10 am to 5 pm.

Organised Tours

Several companies in Palenque town operate transport and tour services to Palenque ruins, Agua Azul and Misol-Ha, Bonampak and Yaxchilán, and La Palma (for the boat to Flores in Guatemala), usually offering similar features at similar prices. Often there is a minimum number of passengers required for the minibus to go. Here are the agencies:

Amfitriones Turísticos de Chiapas, on Allende between Avenida Juárez and Hidalgo (☎ (934) 5-02-10; fax 5-03-56)
Colectivos Chambalu, at the corner of Hidalgo and Allende
La Posada, Fraccionamiento La Cañada, behind the Hotel Maya Tulipanes (☎ (934) 5-04-37)
Transportes Palenque, on Allende between 20 de Noviembre and Corregidora
Viajes Toniná, Juárez 105, near Allende (☎ (934) 5-03-84)
Viajes Shivalva, at the Hotel La Cañada on Hidalgo (Merle Green) near the Maya statue (☎ (934) 5-04-11; fax 5-03-92)

To Agua Azul & Misol-Ha

Taking a tour, though more expensive than the bus, eliminates standing for hours on crowded buses and walking (perhaps with all your luggage) the 1½ km in from the highway to (and back out from) Misol-Ha, and the 4½-km walk

downhill from the highway to Agua Azul proper – and then back uphill when it comes time to leave.

Most tours depart around 10 am, returning by 3.30 pm, costing US\$6 per person.

Places to Stay

The quality of Palenque's hospitality services reflects its popularity. Hotels are not very well maintained and service is lackadaisacal, but the magnificent ruins nevertheless draw crowds of tourists.

Places to Stay – bottom end

Camping Campers can string a hammock or pitch a tent at the *Camping Mayabell*, on the southern side of the road to the ruins, within the national park boundaries. The Mayabell charges US\$2 per person and the same for a car. It offers toilets and showers, some shade, full hook-ups, snacks and drinks for sale, and is only two km from the ruins, though the walk is all uphill.

Camping María del Mar, three km from the ruins on the opposite side of the road, is similar but with less shade, at the same price.

You can also camp on the grounds of the *Hotel Nututum Viva*, 3½ km along the road from Palenque to San Cristóbal de las Casas, on the banks of the Río Usumacinta. You use the hotel's facilities. The fee is US\$2 per person, and US\$2.75 per vehicle.

Hotels Hotels in town are cheaper than those on the road to the ruins, with the notable exception of the camping grounds.

Posada Charito (☎ (934) 5-01-21), 20 de Noviembre 15, two blocks south-west of the park, has numerous advantages. It's quiet here, the rooms are kept in fairly good shape by its religious family owners and prices are low: US\$8/10/13 a single/double/triple for a room with private shower, clean sheets, ceiling fan, and Gideon Bible (in Spanish) on your pillow. The Templo Evangélico Emmanuel is right next door.

Hotel Santa Elena, behind the Transportes Dag-Dug bus station, has small, breezy, pleasant, mahogany-panelled rooms with fan and shower for US$15, which is good value for money. You're a few minutes' walk from the centre here, but very near the bus stations.

Posada Santo Domingo (☎ (934) 5-01-36), 20 de Noviembre 119, fairly near the bus stations yet reasonably quiet, charges only US$10 for acceptable double rooms with fan and private shower.

Hotel La Avenida (☎ (934) 5-01-16), Avenida Juárez 183 opposite the Auto-transportes Tuxta Gutiérrez bus station, lets you hear every thunderous, unmuffled bus. Though you may lack sleep, you won't lack camaraderie which (along with the broken bathroom fixtures) is infectious here. A single/double with cold-water shower costs US$10/12.

For other rock-bottom accommodation, try the *Casa de Huéspedes León*, on Hidalgo between Abasolo and Independencia.

La Posada (☎ (934) 5-04-37), Fraccionamiento La Cañada, is located behind the Hotel Maya Tulipanes, in a quiet countrified setting with a nice garden. It caters to backpackers, with decent rooms at decent prices (US$14 a double with floor fan), a good bulletin board, and table tennis. They'll change cash and travellers' cheques for you, and book your tour or transport to Agua Azul and Misol-Ha, Bonampak and Yaxchilán, or to La Palma for the boat trip into Guatemala. La Posada is operated by the same folks who run the Restaurant Las Tinajas.

Hotel Chablis, Fraccionamiento (barrio) La Cañada near the hotels Maya Tulipanes and La Cañada, has a restaurant, video bar, and simple, quiet rooms with shower and fan for US$14 a double.

Hotel La Croix (☎ (934) 5-00-14), Hidalgo 10, is conveniently situated on the north side of the park opposite the church, with ground-floor rooms facing the park. It can be a bit noisy but with its pretty interior courtyard, potted tropical plants and adequate rooms with fan and bath, La Croix, which used to be the cheapest place in town, is still popular. It now charges US$18 a double; there's no hot water.

The *Hotel Regional* (☎ (934) 5-01-83), Avenida Juárez at Aldama, has white stucco walls and black steel windows around a small plant-filled courtyard. The rooms, which are adequate but nothing to write home about, are on two levels; each has a private shower and fan. The price is good, at US$13/17/20 a single/double/triple.

Places to Stay – middle
The top moderate choice is just out of town near the Maya statue, a 10 to 15-minute walk from the park. *Hotel La Cañada* (☎ (934) 5-01-02), at the end of Calle Hidalgo (also called Merle Green or Cañada), is a group of cinder-block cottages in a quiet spot surrounded by jungle. Most of the cottages are air-conditioned and all come with baths; many have huge ceramic tubs. This was a favourite with archaeologists working at the ruins, and still maintains its legendary attraction for many visitors. Cottages cost US$21/26 for a single/double with fan.

La Cañada has a good thatch-roofed restaurant and the attractive Restaurant La Selva is close by. The hotel is worth the walk, and is actually as close to the bus and colectivo stations as are the hotels in the centre.

Sharing some of La Cañada's advantages is the nearby *Hotel Maya Tulipanes* (☎ (934) 5-02-01), Calle Cañada 6, only 100 metres from the Maya statue and the highway. Rooms are on two levels; the upstairs ones tend to catch more of the breeze and thus are a bit cooler. With ceiling fans, rooms go for US$24/29 a single/double; add US$2 per person for air-con. If business is slack, expect reductions.

In the centre of town near the ADO bus station, your best bet is the *Hotel Kashlan* (☎ (934) 5-02-97; fax 5-03-09), Avenida 5 de Mayo 105 at Allende. Clean, bright and modern, the Kashlan offers its rooms with ceiling fan and shower for decent prices of US$18/21 a single/double.

Hotel Vaca Vieja (☎ (934) 5-03-88), Avenida 5 de Mayo 42 at Chiapas, three blocks east of the park, is well maintained and has pleasant rooms with fan and tiled bathrooms priced at US$14/22 for a single/

double. The proprietor used the proceeds from the sale of his cattle herd to fund the construction of the hotel, hence its name (Old Cow) and the sign. The Restaurant Yunuén is off the lobby.

On Avenida Juárez half a block west of the park is the basic but clean *Hotel Misol-Ha* (☎ (934) 5-00-92), with serviceable if bare rooms going for US$17/21/25 a single/double/triple, private shower and fan included. Try haggling if business is slack as these prices are a bit high.

Hotel Palenque (☎ (934) 5-01-88; fax 5-00-39), Avenida 5 de Mayo No 15 between Jiménez and Guerrero, was once the most comfortable place to stay, but is now only moderately so due to ageing. Look at your room before you sign in. Bonuses here are the convenient location, very pretty gardens in the interior court, a small and often presentably clean swimming pool, and rooms with either ceiling fan (US$16 a double) or air-con (US$22 a double); it's good value.

The *Hotel Casa de Pakal*, on Avenida Juárez near Independencia and the park, has 14 small rooms with air-conditioning, TV and private bath, and prices are not unreasonable if you must have coolness: US$23/30 a single/double.

Hotel Chan-Kah (☎ (934) 5-03-18; fax 5-04-89), above the restaurant of the same name at the corner of Avenida Juárez and Independencia overlooking the park, has 16 very nice rooms, with private shower and fan, for US$25/30 a single/double. Lots of extras here: a lift, insect screens, two double beds in each room, little balconies, some with a view of the town.

Readers with their own cars might want to consider staying at the new *Hotel El Paraíso* (☎ (934) 5-00-33/45), Carretera a las Ruinas Km 2.5, which, as the address indicates, is 2½ km along the road to the ruins, on the right-hand side. Large, airy, clean rooms here with two double beds, gleaming tiled bathrooms and individual air-conditioning units cost US$34 a double. Most rooms are at the back of the Restaurant El Paraíso and thus farther from the road, although there is little noise but that of the jungle out there.

Places to Stay – top end

Palenque's top accommodation in terms of comfort is at the *Hotel Misión Palenque* (☎ (934) 5-02-41, 5-01-10; in Villahermosa (931) 4-05-08; toll-free in Mexico (800) 9-00-38), Rancho San Martín de Porres, Palenque, Chiapas 29960, at the far eastern end of town along Avenida Hidalgo. The Misión Palenque is large (160 rooms) and attractive with well-kept gardens and a decor of wood, stone and stucco; it also has air-conditioned rooms, a swimming pool, restaurant and bar. The rate is US$75 a double. The hotel's minibus shuttles guests to the ruins and back every two hours (four trips per day).

The most attractive and interesting lodgings at Palenque are at *Chan-Kah* (☎ (934) 5-03-18; fax 5-04-89), three km from town on the road to the ruins. Individual cottages here are done in a style similar to that of the Chan-Kah's sister hotel in Palenque town. The vast palapa-topped restaurant and enormous stone-bound swimming pool, the lush jungle gardens and other accoutrements are lavish, but sparsely populated. The reason may be the high price (US$62 a double), the remoteness from town, and the fact that the cottages have only ceiling fans, not air-conditioning.

South of town 3½ km on the road to San Cristóbal is the *Hotel Nututum Viva* (☎ (934) 5-01-00/61), overlooking the Río Usumacinta just to the left of the road. The modern motel-style buildings are nicely arranged in spacious jungle gardens shaded by palm trees. Large air-conditioned rooms with bath cost US$45 to US$50 a double. You can also pitch your tent or park your camper here for US$2 per person or US$2.75 per vehicle. A swim in the hotel's river balneario costs US$1.

Places to Eat – bottom end

Cheapest fare in Palenque is at the open-air cookshops on Abasolo (a pedestrian stepstreet) between Juárez and 5 de Mayo. Next cheapest comes from the taquerías on Jiménez at 5 de Mayo, along the western (park) side of the block where the church is.

Try *Los Farolitos* or *Refresquería Deportista* for a plate of tacos at US$2 to US$2.75.

Restaurant Arsemio's is a family-run place at the corner of Jiménez and Hidalgo. Everything here seems to cost about US$2.75 to US$3.50, whether it be filete, chicken, or traditional Mexican antojitos. This is a simple, tidy place where Mamá does the cooking and her daughter waits on tables: honest work, honest food, honest prices.

Restaurant Las Tinajas, 20 de Noviembre at Abasolo, a few steps from the Posada Charito, is run by the family which operates La Posada. *Las Tinajas* means Earthen Jars, and the building is quaintly woody, with a few tables set out on the small terrace in front to allow you to watch the street action as you eat. Breakfasts cost US$3 to US$3.75, chimichangas, tacos and quesadillas go for slightly less. For a splurge, have the filete a la Tampiqueña for US$6.

Sooner or later you'll probably drop in for a meal at the popular *Restaurant Maya* (☎ 5-00-42), at the corner of Independencia and Hidalgo at the north-west corner of the park. The food is típico, the service Palenque-ish, the hours long (7 am to 11 pm). Breakfast can be eggs, juice and coffee for US$3, or the cheaper granola with milk. Lunch and dinner favourites are enchiladas con mole (with spicy, bitter chocolate sauce), steak and french fries, and tamalitos chiapanecos (little tamales Chiapas-style). Prices range from US$3.50 to US$10 for a full meal.

Right next door to the Maya at the corner of Independencia and Juárez, also facing the park, is the *Restaurant Chan-Kah*. Stone pillars, wrought-iron grillwork, ceiling fans for a breeze and a bit of jungle ambience make this the more atmospheric place to dine, and prices are only slightly higher than at the Maya. A popular choice here is the Mexican variety plate with an assortment of antojitos for US$5, but you can also get tacos, tostadas or enchiladas for US$3. The simple daily comida corrida costs US$6.

'Restaurant Row' is the name we give to Avenida 5 de Mayo at Mina, where you will find six food places lined up. Besides the cheap restaurants *Cenaduria, Capricornio*

and *Shisho's*, there is a fruiterer and two ice cream shops, *Holanda* and *El Oasis*. For natural foods, however, seek out the *Tienda Naturista Escorpion*, on 20 de Noviembre near Independencia, close to the Posada Charito. They sell natural food products, vitamins and the like.

The Hotel Vaca Vieja's little *Restaurant Yunuén*, corner of 5 de Mayo and Chiapas, has good breakfasts for US$3 to US$3.75, and reasonably priced típico meals for US$4 to US$7.

Several good, cheap small eateries are to be found along Avenida Juárez west of the park. *Restaurant La Kan-Ha*, Avenida Juárez 20 near Abasolo, serves breakfast for US$1.50 to US$3, meat and chicken plates for US$3.75 to US$6. It's neat, nice and only slightly overpriced.

Restaurante Paisanos, on Avenida Juárez between Aldama and Allende, is a tidy, cheaper workers' place where everything seems to cost US$2.25 (chicken dishes, daily special plates), with a few meat dishes going for US$3. The nearby *Restaurant El Herradero* is similar, but distinguishes itself by its fried-egg placemats.

At *Piccolino's Pizza* (☎ 5-03-32), on Avenida Juárez at Allende, good pizzas range in price from the small cheese (US$4) to the big combination (US$12).

Expendio de Pan Virginia, or Virginia's Bakery, across the street from Bancomer on Avenida Juárez between Abasolo and Aldama, sells good breads and rolls for picnics.

Places to Eat – middle

The Hotel Casa de Pakal's *Restaurant Castellano*, on Avenida Juárez near Independencia and the park, has the advantage of air-conditioning, a rare service among Palenque restaurants. The food is OK and the prices not bad (US$8 to US$13 for a full meal) considering the cool air.

The town's two best restaurants are near the Maya statue, 10 to 15 minutes' walk from the park. Bear left at the statue and walk 100 metres along the road toward the ruins to reach the *Restaurant-Bar Hardy's*, named after owner Zacarias Hardy González, but more commonly known as La Selva (☎ 5-03-63).

The food here is a cut above that available in the rest of Palenque. It offers filete tampiqueña, fajitas norteñas and a number of fairly expensive house specialities. Chiapan musicians sometimes play during dinner. Expect to spend US$8 to US$14 for a full lunch or dinner, though you could spend US$20 for a speciality with wine. Breakfasts are quite expensive. La Selva is open every day from 7 am to 11 pm.

Hotel La Cañada has its own thatched restaurant which is less pretentious than La Selva, but you still get careful service and moderate prices. Tacos go for US$3, most meat dishes for US$4 to US$8. The restaurant maintains its tradition of attracting travellers with a serious interest in archaeology, who stay after dinner and long into the evening discussing the ruins over cold beer or other drinks from the bar.

Getting There & Away

Air Palenque has a small airstrip north of town, used mostly for air-taxi and charter flights. Occasionally there are short-hop services to and from Tuxtla Gutiérrez, capital of Chiapas. Check with the tourist office or a travel agency in Palenque.

Bus There is less thievery on the bus than on the train, but some bus passengers have reported goods stolen. Don't leave anything of value in the overhead rack, and stay alert. Your gear is probably safest in the luggage compartment under the bus, but watch as it is stowed. Robberies of the night bus from Palenque to Mérida have been reported, but in one case the robbers didn't bother to open the luggage compartments, being content to fleece the passengers sitting above.

The bus stations are all fairly close to one another, between the Maya statue and the centre of the town. 1st-class ADO is at the confluence of Avenida Juárez and 5 de Mayo. To spot the 1st and 2nd-class Autotransportes Tuxtla Gutiérrez and Transportes Fray Bartolomé de las Casas bus station,

look for the easily identifiable Restaurant Pam-Pam. Both stations have left-luggage (baggage check) rooms (US$0.75 per piece per day). The 2nd-class Transportes Dag-Dug is a block west of the Autotransportes Tuxtla station. Transportes Lacandonia drop passengers near the mercado on Avenida Velasco Suárez.

It's a very good idea to buy your onward ticket from Palenque a day in advance if possible. Though many buses are de paso, originating somewhere else, some originate here, allowing you to reserve your seat in advance.

Here are some distances, times and prices:

Agua Azul Crucero – 60 km, 1½ hours; five 1st-class buses (US$1.15) by Autotransportes Tuxtla. Except for the 8 am bus which goes only to the crucero, these buses go on to Ocosingo, San Cristóbal and Tuxtla Gutiérrez; seats are sold to those passengers first. Tickets to Agua Azul go on sale 30 minutes before departure, and if all seats are sold, you must stand all the way to the Agua Azul turn. You may also take a combi (see the Getting Around section).

Campeche – 362 km, 5½ hours; one direct 1st-class bus (US$6) by ADO, and one 2nd-class bus at 5 pm (US$7.25) by Transportes Dag-Dug; you can also catch a bus (six daily) or combi, or hitchhike the 27 km north to Catazajá, on the main Villahermosa-Escárcega highway, and catch one of the buses which pass every hour or two.

Catazajá – 27 km, half an hour; five 1st-class buses daily by ADO (US$0.70) at 7 and 8 am, noon, 3 and 5 pm; one 2nd-class bus daily at 8 am by Transportes Dag-Dug (US$0.60).

Chetumal – 487 km, seven hours; one 1st-class bus daily at 10 pm by ADO (US$10).

Escárcega – 212 km, three hours; one 1st-class morning bus (US$5) by ADO, three 2nd-class buses (US$4) by A del Sur.

Mérida – 556 km, 10 or 11 hours; one 1st-class bus (US$12) by A del Sureste directly to Mérida; one 1st-class ADO night bus at 9 pm. Many more 1st-class daylight buses pass by the main highway junction at Catazajá, 27 km to the north of the town.

Misol-Ha – 47 km, one hour; five 1st-class buses (US$0.75) by Autotransportes Tuxtla. Tickets go on sale 30 minutes before departure, and you may have to stand during the trip.

Mexico City – 1020 km, 16 hours; one 1st-class bus at 6 pm (US$23) by ADO.

Ocosingo – 85 km, two hours; five 1st-class buses (US$2.25) by Autotransportes Tuxtla.

San Cristóbal de las Casas – 190 km, 5½ hours; five 1st-class buses (US$3.75) by Autotransportes Tuxtla.

Tuxtla Gutiérrez – 275 km, 7½ hours; five 1st-class buses (US$6) by Autotransportes Tuxtla; two 2nd-class buses (8 am and 1 pm, US$8) by Transportes Dag-Dug which go the long way (eight hours) via Villahermosa.

Villahermosa – 150 km, 2½ hours; six 1st-class buses (US$3) by ADO at 7 and 8 am, noon, 3, 5 and 7 pm; two 2nd-class buses (8 am and 1 pm, US$2.85) by Transportes Dag-Dug.

Yajalon – 133 km, three hours; one bus daily (US$3) by Autotransportes Tuxtla.

Train It's not a good idea to take the train to or from Palenque. There are no dormitorios to lock on board and robberies are common between Palenque and Mérida. So take the bus – it's quicker and you are not as likely to lose your gear.

Getting Around

All of the hotels listed in town are within two to 10 minutes' walk of both bus stations. The railway station is six km north of town at Pakal-Na. Taxis are available at the park and the bus stations.

To Palenque Ruins Colectivos Chambalu, at the corner of Hidalgo and Allende, operates combis (VW minibuses) frequently between Palenque town and the ruins. Service is every 10 minutes (so they say) from 6 am to 6 pm daily. Transportes Palenque, Allende between 20 de Noviembre and Corregidora, runs a similar service. The minibus will stop to pick you up anywhere along the town-to-ruins road, which makes it especially handy for campers. Fare is US$0.30. ADO runs one huge bus daily from Palenque town to Palenque ruins at 10.30 am for the same fare.

BONAMPAK & YAXCHILÁN RUINS

The ruins of Bonampak – famous for frescoes – and the great ancient city of Yaxchilán are accessible on camping excursions from Palenque, or by chartering an aircraft from Palenque, San Cristóbal or Tenosique.

The frescoes at Bonampak have deteriorated greatly since they were discovered and do not provide the expected thrill. Go instead to look at the site, and then examine copies of the murals in books or in the Museo Nacional de Antropología in Mexico City. The site at Yaxchilán is more rewarding, and the trek through the jungle and across the Usumacinta is a thrill in itself.

Bonampak and Yaxchilán have neither food nor water, so make certain you are well supplied if you come on your own. It's bug-infested in these parts – bring insect repellent. Don't leave your gear unattended, as thefts have been reported on previous trips. Finally, carry a torch to see dark parts of the ruins better and for any camping emergencies.

The Mexican government was, until recently, planning to build a dam on the Usumacinta which would have resulted in the inundation of Bonampak and Yaxchilán. The dam proposal has been abandoned, however, and the ruins are preserved for visitors at least for the forseeable future.

Bonampak

Lying about 155 km south-east of Palenque near the Guatemalan frontier, Bonampak was hidden from the outside world by dense jungle until 1946. A young WW II conscientious objector named Charles Frey fled the draft and somehow wound up here in the Lacandonian rainforest. There he was virtually adopted by local Indians and shown what the Indians told him was a sacred site of their ancestors. Impressed by what he saw, Frey enthusiastically revealed his findings to Mexican officials and archaeological expeditions were mounted. Frey died in 1949 trying to save an expedition member from drowning in the turbulent Usumacinta.

The ruins of Bonampak lie around a rectangular plaza. Only the southern edifices of the plaza are preserved; the rest is little more than heaps of stone. It was the frescoes of a temple in the Southern Group, today designated Building 1, that excited Frey and the archaeologists who followed. They saw three rooms covered with paintings depicting ancient Maya ways. Painted in profile are warriors decked with quetzal feathers, kings and royal families, priests, shamans, dancers, musicians and war captives. The details of costumes themselves reveal much about Maya life and the murals are complete with glyphs.

The murals' original colours were brown, green and vermilion, with the figures outlined in black. Unfortunately, 12 centuries of weather deterioration were accelerated when the first expedition attempted to clean the murals with kerosene. On the positive side, some restoration has been undertaken and reproductions installed for comparison. Generally the murals are so difficult to decipher that you may wonder what all the fuss was about. If you look closely (or view the reproductions) though, you may think you are looking at artwork from ancient Egypt.

Some of the murals depict the victory of the Maya over the Olmecs. One panel shows dancing at a celebration, another prisoners waiting to be sacrificed, and a third the giving of thanks to the gods for victory.

To best see what these faded frescoes originally looked like, inspect the Bonampak mural reproductions in the Museo Nacional de Antropología in Mexico City, or the ones at the Museo Regional de Antropología Carlos Pellicer Cámara in Villahermosa. Tuxtla Gutiérrez's Hotel Bonampak has a full reproduction of the central room's mural in its lobby.

Other than some narrative stelae at the foot of the hill leading to Building 1, the Temple of the Frescoes, the eight other buildings of the Southern Group are badly ruined.

Yaxchilán

Set above the jungled banks of the Usumacinta, Yaxchilán was first inhabited about 200 AD, though the earliest hieroglyphs found have been dated from 514 to 807 AD. Although not as well restored as Palenque, the ruins here cover a greater extent, and further excavation may yield even more significant finds.

Yaxchilán rose to the peak of its prominence in the 8th century under a king whose name in hieroglyphs was translated into Spanish as Escudo Jaguar, or Shield Jaguar. His shield-and-jaguar symbol appears on many of the site's buildings and stelae. The city's power expanded under Escudo Jaguar's son, Pájaro Jaguar, or Bird Jaguar (752-70). His hieroglyph consists of a small jungle cat with feathers on the back and a bird superimposed on the head.

Building 33 on the south-western side of the plaza has some fine religious carvings over the northern doorways, and a roofcomb which retains most of its original beauty. At the front base of the temple are narrative carvings of a ball game.

The central plaza holds statues of crocodiles and jaguars. A lintel in Building 20 shows a dead man's spirit emerging from the mouth of a man speaking about him, and stelae of Maya making offerings to the gods. In front of Building 20 are exceptional stelae featuring Maya royalty.

Be certain to walk to Yaxchilán's highest temples, which are still covered with trees and are not visible from the plaza. Building 41 is the tallest of these, and the view from its top is one of the highlights of a visit to Yaxchilán. Some tour guides do not want to

Bonampak Ruins

Building 3

Stone 1

Stela 2   Stela 3   Stone 2

Stela 1   Building 1 (Temple of the Frescoes)

Main Plaza

0   50   100 m

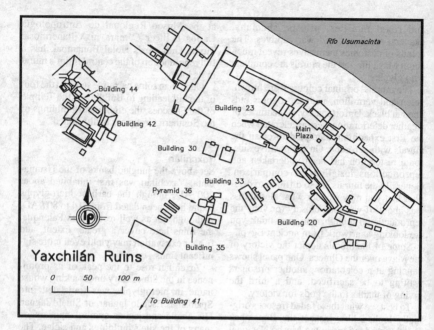

Yaxchilán Ruins

Building 44

Building 23

Building 42

Main Plaza

Building 30

Building 33

Pyramid 36

Building 20

Building 35

Río Usumacinta

0   50   100 m

To Building 41

make the effort to show you Building 41 – insist on it!

Organised Tours

Combi & Boat Tours Various travel agencies in Palenque run two-day road and river tours to Bonampak and Yaxchilán; see Organised Tours in the Palenque section.

The rate for a two-day tour by land to Yaxchilán and Bonampak is US$90, including transportation and all meals. A minivan takes you within 10 km of Bonampak and you walk the rest of the way. Tents are provided for overnight. The next morning, you are driven to the Río Usumacinta, where an outboard motor boat takes you for an hour through the jungle to Yaxchilán.

There are also one-day tours to Bonampak for US$30 to US$45, or to Yaxchilán and back for US$45 to US$60.

Viajes Pakal in Palenque offers the following two-day trip for US$85 per person (if five or six people sign up), US$115 per person (if three or four), or US$213 per person (if two): drive from Palenque to the Lacandón settlement of Caribal Lacanjá by car, take a two-hour walk to Bonampak (stay 1½ to two hours), walk back to Caribal Lacanjá and camp or sleep in a Lacandón house. Next morning, travel by car to Frontera Echeverría, then boat along the Río Usumacinta to Yaxchilán, stay three hours, and then return to Palenque by boat and car.

Getting There & Away

Air Those with more money than time can charter a small plane to Bonampak and Yaxchilán from Palenque, San Cristóbal, Comitán or Tenosique. For current information on the travel agencies operating these flights, ask at the tourist office in each town.

In Palenque, Amfitriones Turísticos de Chiapas (☎ (934) 5-02-10), on Allende between Avenida Juárez and Hidalgo, can give you details on air tours, as can Viajes Shivalva (☎ (934) 5-04-11; fax 5-03-92),

Fraccionamiento La Cañada, Avenida Hidalgo (Merle Green). Cost is about US$130 per person.

In San Cristóbal de Las Casas, flights and tours to Yaxchilán and Bonampak can be arranged through Viajes Pakal (☎ (967) 8-28-18/19), at the corner of Hidalgo and Cuauhtémoc, or Amfitriones Turísticos in the Hotel Posada Diego de Mazariegos. The flight option, with a scheduled total of 3½ hours at the two sites, costs about US$130 per person. The flights go from Comitán or Las Margaritas (near Comitán) if San Cristóbal airport is out of action; transport to and from the airstrip is included.

Car Despite what you may hear, it is possible to drive to Bonampak and the trip doesn't even require 4WD – although the local car-rental company might not be too pleased if they knew where you intended to take their Volkswagen Beetle. A full tank of fuel might just get you from Palenque to Bonampak, Yaxchilán and back but you'd be better off buying a plastic container and carrying some additional fuel. The round trip is a bit over 300 km.

The Bonampak turnoff is about 10 km south of Palenque on the Ocosingo and San Cristóbal road. It's marked 'Chancalá', not 'Bonampak', and it's wise to ask directions. It takes about three hours from the main road turnoff to the Bonampak turnoff and the road is passable, although it tends to be dusty and you must beware of rocks and potholes. Eventually you reach the Bonampak turnoff to the right and the road deteriorates to a rougher one-lane track. After about 10 km a sign indicates Bonampak to the left. Despite what the sign may say, the distance is about 15 km.

There's a campsite close to this junction and from here it's wise to walk, particularly if it has been raining, although a Volkswagen can make it in good weather. There are several streambeds and shaky bridges to be crossed, so be careful if you try to drive all the way to the site.

To continue to Yaxchilán you have to drive on to Frontera Echeverría, a border town to Guatemala which is on the Río Usumacinta upstream from Yaxchilán. From the Bonampak turnoff continue another 20 km to where a sign indicates the direction to the border, from there you travel along another 30 km of rough track. Boats to the ruins can be hired from this sprawling village; you might be asked around US$40 for a complete boat but should be able to knock that down. Yaxchilán is about 20 km downstream, and while you get there quite fast, the return trip against the swift current can take over two hours. Come prepared for the fierce sun.

The comedor above the river in Echeverría is good for dinner or breakfast. Buses occasionally come down the road from Palenque as far as the Bonampak turnoff and sometimes all the way to Echeverría.

COMITÁN

Population: 84,000
Altitude: 1630 metres

Comitán, a pleasant enough town, is the jumping-off point for the Lagos de Montebello and the last place of any size before the Guatemalan border at Ciudad Cuauhtémoc.

The first Spanish settlement in the area, San Cristóbal de los Llanos, was set up in 1527. Today the town is officially called Comitán de Domínguez, after Belisario Domínguez, a local doctor who was also a national senator during the presidency of Victoriano Huerta. Domínguez had the cheek to speak out in the senate in 1913 against Huerta's record of political murders and was himself murdered for his pains.

Orientation

The wide, attractive zócalo is bound by Avenida Central on its west side and Calle 1 Sur on the south. The 1st-class Cristóbal Colón bus station is out on the Pan-American Highway, which passes through the western edge of the town, about 20 minutes' walk from the centre. To reach the zócalo, turn left out of the bus station along the highway, take the first right (downhill along 4 Sur Pte but it's not marked), go six blocks (up and down hills – and the first two blocks are long), then turn left on to Avenida Central Sur and go three blocks.

Information

Tourist Office There's a tourist information office in the Palacio Municipal on the north side of the zócalo, open 8.30 am to 8 pm.

Money Bancomer is on the south-east corner of the zócalo. Banamex is a block south at the corner of 2 Sur Ote and 1 Ote Sur.

Post & Telephone The post office (open Monday to Friday 8 am to 7 pm, Saturday 8 am to 1 pm) is on Avenida Central Sur between 2 and 3 Sur, 1½ blocks south of the zócalo. There's a Ladatel phone at the south-west corner of the zócalo, and a lada caseta on 2 Sur Pte, half a block west of Avenida Central Sur.

Foreign Consulates The Guatemalan Con-sulate (☎ 2-26-69) is at 2 Pte Norte 28, open 8 am to 1 pm and 2.30 to 4.30 pm, Monday to Friday. Visas normally take about half an hour, for a US$10 fee.

Things to See

Located on the east side of the zócalo, **Santo Domingo church** dates from the 16th century. The adjacent **Casa de la Cultura** on the south-east corner of the zócalo was being renovated on our last visit to include an exhibition gallery, book and craft shop, library, auditorium, cafeteria, and a museum with sections on archaeology, ethnography and the local writer Rosario Castellanos.

The family home of martyr-hero Belisario Domínguez at Avenida Central Sur 29, half a block south of the zócalo, has been turned into a **museum** that provides interesting insight into medical practices and the life of the professional classes in turn-of-the-century Comitán. It's open 10 am to 6.45 pm

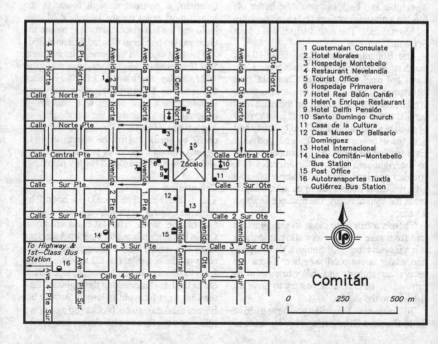

1 Guatemalan Consulate
2 Hotel Morales
3 Hospedaje Montebello
4 Restaurant Nevelandia
5 Tourist Office
6 Hospedaje Primavera
7 Hotel Real Balún Canán
8 Helen's Enrique Restaurant
9 Hotel Delfín Pensión
10 Santo Domingo Church
11 Casa de la Cultura
12 Casa Museo Dr Belisario Domínguez
13 Hotel Internacional
14 Linea Comitán—Montebello Bus Station
15 Post Office
16 Autotransportes Tuxtla Gutiérrez Bus Station

Comitán

0   250   500 m

Tuesday to Saturday, and 9 am to 12.45 pm Sunday, for US$0.40.

Places to Stay – bottom end

Comitán has quite a few hotels since a lot of people pass through en route to or from Guatemala. The *Hotel Delfín Pensión* (☎ 2-00-13), at Avenida Central 19A on the west side of the zócalo, is one of the better value bottom-end places. Its fairly spacious rooms have private baths (hot water intermittent) and those at the back are modernish and overlook a leafy courtyard. Singles/doubles are US$9.50/13.50.

The *Hotel Morales* (☎ 2-04-36) at Avenida Central Norte 8, 1½ blocks north of the zócalo, resembles an aircraft hangar with rooms perched round an upstairs walkway. Small rooms with private bath are US$9.50/11.75.

Comitán also has several cheap posadas, some OK for a night. Among the better ones is the *Hospedaje Primavera*, around two small courtyards at Central Pte 4, a few steps west of the zócalo. Small, dark rooms with one double bed cost US$5 a single or double; bigger ones with two beds go for US$6.75. The whole place, including the shared bathrooms, is clean. Another is the *Hospedaje Montebello* (☎ 2-17-70), a block further north at 1 Norte Pte 10, with rooms of varied shapes and sizes round a wide courtyard. All those we have seen have private bathrooms. A room with a double bed is US$8.50 for one or two persons.

Places to Stay – middle

The *Hotel Internacional* (☎ 2-01-10), a block south of the zócalo at Avenida Central Sur 16, on the corner of Calle 2 Sur, has clean, bright but no-frills rooms for US$16.50/20.

The modern *Hotel Real Balún Canán* (☎ 2-10-94), a block west of the zócalo at Avenida 1 Pte Sur No 7, is the top place. Prints of Frederick Catherwood's 1844 drawings of Maya ruins decorate the stairs of the front section. Rooms cost US$27/33.50 and are comfortable enough, with TV and phone, but aren't big. At this price try to ensure you get one looking on to the outside world, not the sometimes noisy interior of the hotel.

Places to Eat

Several reasonable cafés line the west side of the zócalo. *Helen's Enrique Restaurante*, beside the Hotel Delfín Pensión, is the most imposing and its food is respectable, but portions are moderate and service tardy. Chicken and meat dishes are between US$4 to US$7; antojitos, spaghetti, or a breakfast of eggs, juice, coffee and toast are US$2 to US$3. *Restaurant Acuario* and *Restaurant Yuly* in the same row are more basic and cheaper.

Probably better value than any of them is the popular *Restaurant Nevelandia* on the north-west corner of the zócalo, where hamburgers, spaghetti and antojitos all go for around US$2.50 (though a plate of Chiapas cheeses is US$6.75), and meat dishes typically for US$5. There's a comida corrida of four courses plus coffee for US$5.

At the Hotel Real Balún Canán's *El Escocés Restaurant*, open until 11 pm, the food is perfectly palatable and in fairly generous servings but nothing special. Meat courses are mostly around US$5.50, spaghetti and antojitos US$2.75.

Getting There & Away

Buses on the Pan-American Highway 190 are regularly stopped for document checks by immigration officials, both north and south of Comitán – so don't forget your passport.

Cristóbal Colón provides the 1st-class bus service, Autotransportes Tuxtla Gutiérrez (ATG) the main 2nd-class one. The Cristóbal Colón station is on the Pan-American Highway (see the Orientation section). ATG is at 4 Sur Pte 55 between Avenida 3 and 4 Pte Sur, three blocks south from the zócalo then 3½ west. Buses for the Lagos de Montebello go from the Linea Comitán-Montebello terminal at Avenida 2 Pte Sur 17B, between 2 and 3 Sur Pte, two blocks west and 1½ south of the zócalo (see the

Lagos de Montebello section for more info on services). Buses from Comitán include:

Ciudad Cuauhtémoc – 80 km, 1½ hours; three de paso 1st-class buses daily (two morning, one afternoon) for US$1.50 and 10 2nd-class buses daily, mostly de paso, by ATG.

Mexico City – 1170 km, 22 hours; one luxury Cristóbal Colón Plus afternoon bus for US$40 and two 1st-class buses daily for US$26.

Palenque – 275 km, seven hours; two morning buses by Línea Comitán-Montebello.

San Cristóbal de las Casas – 85 km, 1½ hours; 11 1st-class locales daily (the last at 7 pm) for US$1.75; 14 2nd-class buses, mostly de paso, by ATG.

Tapachula – 260 km, seven hours (via Motozintla); one afternoon 2nd-class bus by ATG for US$4.50, several 2nd-class buses daily by Autotransportes San Francisco Motozintla for US$4.25.

Tuxtla Gutiérrez – 170 km, 3½ hours; 11 1st-class locales daily for US$3.25 and 14 2nd-class buses daily, mostly de paso, by ATG.

LAGOS DE MONTEBELLO

The temperate forest along the Guatemalan border south-east of Comitán is dotted with about 60 small lakes – the Lagos or Lagunas de Montebello. The area is beautiful, refreshing, not hard to reach, and quiet. The many little-used vehicle tracks through the forest provide some excellent walks. Some Mexican weekenders come down here in their cars, but the rest of the time you'll probably see only resident villagers and a small handful of visitors. There are two very basic hostelries and a campground. At one edge of the lake district are the rarely visited Maya ruins of Chinkultic. A number of Guatemalan refugee camps are in and around the lakes area.

Orientation

The paved road to Montebello turns east off the Pan-American Highway 16 km south of Comitán, just before the town of La Trinitaria. Running first through flat ranchland, it passes Chinkultic after 30 km, entering the forest and the Parque Nacional de Montebello five km further on. At the park entrance (no fee) the road splits. The paved section continues three km ahead (north) to the Lagunas de Colores, where it dead-ends at two small houses 50 metres from Laguna Bosque Azul. To the right (east) from the park entrance a dirt road leads to turnings for several more lakes and to the village and lake of Tziscao (nine km).

Chinkultic

These dramatically sited ruins lie two km along a track north off the La Trinitaria to Montebello road, 30 km from the Pan-American Highway. A sign 'Chinkultic 3' marks the turning. Doña María at La Orquidea restaurant, a km further along the road, has a map and book on Chinkultic.

Chinkultic was on the far western edge of the ancient Maya area. Dates carved here extend from 591 to 897 AD – the last of which is nearly a century after the latest dates at Palenque, Yaxchilán and Toniná. These years no doubt span Chinkultic's peak period, but occupation is thought to have started around 200 AD and continued until after 900. Of the 200 mounds scattered over a wide area, only a few parts have been cleared, but these are worth the effort.

The track brings you first to a gate with a hut on the left. Here take the path to the left, which curves round to the right. On the overgrown hill to the right of this path stands one of Chinkultic's major structures, E23. The path reaches a long ball court where several stelae – some carved with human figures – lie on their sides, some under thatch shelters.

Follow the track back to the hut and turn left, passing what could be a parking area, soon after which you can spot a few stone mounds in the undergrowth to the right. On the hillside that soon comes into full view ahead is the partly restored temple called El Mirador. The path goes over a stream and steeply up to El Mirador, from which there are good views over the surrounding lakes and down into a big 50-metre-deep cenote.

The Lakes

Lagunas de Colores The paved road straight on from the park entrance leads through the Lagunas de Colores, so called because their colours range from turquoise

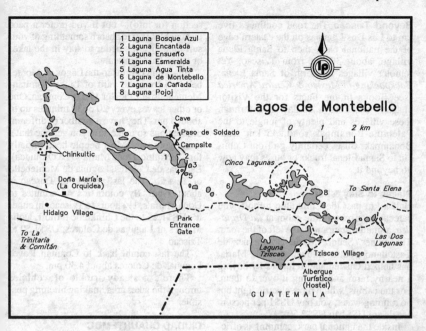

1 Laguna Bosque Azul
2 Laguna Encantada
3 Laguna Ensueño
4 Laguna Esmeralda
5 Laguna Agua Tinta
6 Laguna de Montebello
7 Laguna La Cañada
8 Laguna Pojoj

Lagos de Montebello

0   1   2 km

Cave
Paso de Soldado
Campsite
Chinkultic
Cinco Lagunas
Doña María's
(La Orquídea)
To Santa Elena
Hidalgo Village
Park
Entrance
Gate
Las Dos
Lagunas
To La
Trinitaria
& Comitán
Laguna
Tziscao   Tziscao Village
Albergue
Turístico
(Hostel)
GUATEMALA

to deep green. The first of these, on the right after about two km, is Laguna Agua Tinta. Then on the left come Laguna Esmeralda followed by Laguna Encantada, with Laguna Ensueño on the right opposite Encantada. The fifth and biggest is Laguna Bosque Azul, on the left where the road ends.

Two paths lead on from the end of the road. Straight on, 800 metres brings you to the *gruta* – a cave shrine where locals make offerings (take a torch with you). To the left, you reach Paso de Soldado, a picnic site beside a small river after 300 metres. The track goes on; an old man sitting beside it once told us it reaches a place called Ojo de Agua after '1½ leagues'.

Laguna de Montebello About three km along the dirt road towards Tziscao from the park entrance, a track leads 200 metres left to the Laguna de Montebello, one of the bigger lakes, with a flat, open area along its shore where the track ends. About 150

metres to the left is a stony area which is better for swimming than the muddy fringes elsewhere.

Cinco Lagunas A further three km along the Tziscao road another track leads left to these 'five lakes'. Only four of them are visible from the road, but the second, La Cañada, on the right after about 1½ km, is probably the most beautiful of all the Montebello lakes – it's nearly cut in half by two rocky outcrops. The track eventually reaches the village of San Antonio and, amazingly, is a bus route.

A km further along the Tziscao road from the Cinco Lagunas turning, a track leads to Laguna Pojoj, a km north.

Laguna Tziscao This comes into view on the right another km along the road. The junction for Tziscao village is a little further, on the right. The village has pleasant grassy streets and friendly people.

Beyond Tziscao The road continues five km to Las Dos Lagunas on the eastern edge of the national park, then to Santa Elena village, about 30 km from Tziscao. Yet remoter villages lie north of Santa Elena; *Backpacking in Mexico & Central America* (see Books in the Facts for the Visitor chapter) describes a 10-day hike through these villages and plenty of jungle to the Palenque-Bonampak road, 45 km from Bonampak. Buses certainly go from Comitán to Santa Elena; trucks or buses may now go beyond it.

Places to Stay & Eat

Half a km past the Chinkultic turnoff, you can camp or rent a little cabin at *La Orquidea*, a small restaurant on the left of the road. The owner, Señora María Domínguez de Castellanos, better known as Doña María, has helped Guatemalan refugees by buying a nearby farm and turning it over to them. For the cabins, which have electric light but no running water, you pay US$1 per person. Meals are US$1 to US$2.50.

Inside the national park, camping is officially allowed only at Laguna Bosque Azul. There are toilets and water and one of the small houses here sells drinks and food.

Tziscao village has a hostel – the *Albergue Turístico* – where you pay US$2 per person for a dormitory bunk or a wooden cabana. The hostel lies on the shore of one of the most beautiful lakes – you can rent a rowing boat – and Guatemala is just a few hundred metres away. Entering the village, turn right beside a corner store soon after you come level with the small church on the hill, and follow the track down towards the lake, then round to the left. The señora will cook fish & chips, or eggs, frijoles and tortillas, for around US$1.50, and there's a fridge full of refrescos. The toilets seem to be in permanent desperate need of a good clean.

Getting There & Away

It's possible to make a whirlwind tour of Chinkultic and the lakes in a day from San Cristóbal – either by public transport or tour (see the San Cristóbal Organised Tours section for info) – but if you prefer a pace that enables you to absorb something of your surroundings, it's better to stay in the lakes or at least at Comitán.

Buses and combis to the Lagos de Montebello go from the yard of Linea Comitán-Montebello at 2 Pte Sur 17B in Comitán. One or other leaves every 20 or 30 minutes up to about 5 pm. They have a number of different destinations so make sure you get one that's going your way. Most people head initially for Chinkultic, Doña María's (La Orquidea), Lagunas de Colores, Laguna de Montebello or Tziscao. The last vehicle to Tziscao is about 2 pm. By combi it's 45 minutes to Doña María's, 1¼ hours to Tziscao. In either it's US$1.25 to the Chinkultic turnoff, Doña María's or Lagunas de Colores, US$1.50 to Tziscao.

The last combi back to Comitán leaves Lagunas de Colores about 4.30 pm.

There's a steady trickle of vehicles through the lakes area, making hitching possible.

CIUDAD CUAUHTÉMOC (Guatemalan Border)

This 'city' is just a few houses and a comedor or two, but it's the last/first place in Mexico on the Pan-American Highway. Comitán is 80 km north, San Cristóbal 165 km. Ciudad Cuauhtémoc is the Mexican border post; the Guatemalan one is three km south at La Mesilla. There are taxis (US$1.50), combis and trucks (US$0.50) across the no-man's-land.

Travellers have reported that those who need Guatemalan visas can get them at La Mesilla, but check the latest situation and if in doubt, get your paperwork sorted out in advance at the Guatemalan Consulate in Comitán or the embassy in Mexico City.

There's no bank at this border. Individual moneychangers operate but give fewer quetzals than a bank would. Try to get some in Mexico before you head for the border.

Getting There & Away

Cristóbal Colón runs three 1st-class buses daily each way between Ciudad Cuauhtémoc and Comitán (US$1.75, 1½ hours), San Cristóbal de las Casas (US$3.25, three hours) and Tuxtla Gutiérrez (US$5, five hours). At the time of writing departures from the border are at 6 am, 12.30 pm and 3.30 pm. But it's often easier to use one of the 20 or so daily 2nd-class buses of Autotransportes Tuxtla Gutiérrez or Autotransportes San Francisco Motozintla, between Ciudad Cuauhtémoc and Comitán, and another bus on from (or to) Comitán.

Guatemalan buses depart La Mesilla for main points inside Guatemala like Huehuetenango, Quezaltenango (Xela) and Guatemala City. Lake Atitlán and Chichicastenango both lie off the Huehuetenango-Guatemala City road and if you want to reach them in one day you should be through the border by about 11 am. Before boarding a bus, try to find out when it's leaving and when it reaches your destination. This could save you several hours.

MOTOZINTLA

The small town of Motozintla lies in a deep valley in the Sierra Madre 70 km south-west of Ciudad Cuauhtémoc. A good road leads to it from the Pan-American Highway a few km north of Ciudad Cuauhtémoc, then continues down to Huixtla on the Chiapas coast near Tapachula – a spectacular, unusual trip. Be sure to carry your passport as there are immigration checks along the way. About half a dozen buses of Autotransportes San Francisco Motozintla cover the route daily on their seven-hour Tapachula-Comitán (and vice-versa) run, calling at Ciudad Cuauhtémoc.

ARRIAGA

Population: 40,000
Altitude: 40 metres

Arriaga, on the hot Chiapas coastal plain, is where the Juchitán-Tapachula coastal Highway 200 meets the road snaking down through the mountains from Tuxtla Gutiérrez. A number of buses start or finish their journeys here so it's a place where you might find yourself changing buses on the

way along the coast or to/from Tuxtla Gutiérrez.

Orientation

The modern Central de Autobuses is at the corner of 5 Ote and 7 Sur, about 15 minutes walk south-east of the town centre. To reach the centre, turn left out of the bus station and go three blocks along 5 Ote, then turn right along 1 Sur, which crosses the railway after three blocks and becomes 1 Norte. Hotels are on 1 Norte, 4 Ote (the third street to the right off 1 Norte after the railway), and 3 Norte (the second right off 4 Ote).

Places to Stay & Eat

The *Hotel Albores II*, on 3 Norte between 4 Ote and 2 Ote, has small, dark cubicles with minuscule private baths for US$8.50/10.50. The *Hotel Colón* (☎ 2-01-20), a block south at 3 Norte 8 half a block from the railway, is clean and marginally brighter, charging US$9/11 for similar-sized rooms.

The *Hotel Panamericana* (☎ 2-03-57), at the corner of 4 Ote and Callejón Independencia, a block east of 1 Norte, is fairly friendly and reasonably clean though dingy. Singles/doubles with private bath are US$12/18. The best town-centre place is the *Hotel Ik Lamaal* (☎ 2-17-18) at 1 Norte 7, just over a block north of the railway. It occupies the upper floors of a modern building, with a shopping mall below. Big, clean, well-kitted-out, air-con rooms with TV go for US$23/29.

A few small restaurants dot 2 Ote east of the Pemex station on the corner of 3 Norte. There's a restaurant attached to the *Hotel Ik Lamaal* too.

Getting There & Away

Bus Arriaga has quite good bus services. Departures include:

Juchitán – 135 km, two hours; a few 1st-class buses daily by Cristóbal Colón for US$2.75, many 2nd-class buses daily by Sur and Fletes y Pasajes/ Transportes Oaxaca-Istmo.

Mexico City (TAPO) – 900 km, 16 hours; a few 1st-class buses daily by Cristóbal Colón for US$19.75, 2nd-class buses by Fletes y Pasajes/ Transportes Oaxaca-Istmo.

Oaxaca – 400 km, seven hours; a daily evening bus by Cristóbal Colón for US$8.75, a few 2nd-class buses by Sur and Fletes y Pasajes/Transportes Oaxaca-Istmo.

Salina Cruz – 175 km, three hours; a few buses daily by Cristóbal Colón (1st-class) for US$3.25 and Sur (2nd-class).

San Cristóbal de las Casas – 240 km, five hours; one 1st-class bus daily by Cristóbal Colón for US$4.50, several 2nd-class buses by Auto-transportes Tuxtla Gutiérrez.

Tapachula – 245 km, 3½ hours; numerous buses daily by Cristóbal Colón (1st-class) for US$4.75, and by Sur and Autotransportes Tuxtla Gutiérrez (2nd-class).

Tonalá – 23 km, 30 minutes; Transportes Arriaga-Tonalá microbuses every few minutes for US$0.50.

Tuxtla Gutiérrez – 155 km, three hours; numerous buses daily by Cristóbal Colón (1st-class) for US$3, and by Sur and Autotransportes Tuxtla Gutiérrez (2nd-class).

TONALÁ

Population: 25,000
Altitude: 40 metres

Twenty-three km south-east of Arriaga on Highway 200, Tonalá has little more intrinsic appeal but is the jumping-off point for the laid-back beach spot of Puerto Arista. A tall pre-Hispanic stele in the Tonalá zócalo appears to depict Tláloc, the central Mexican rain god. There's a small regional museum at Hidalgo 77, with some archaeological pieces found in the region.

Orientation & Information

Highway 200 runs north-south through the middle of Tonalá under the name Avenida Hidalgo, forming the west side of the zócalo. Bus stations are several blocks from the centre, at each end of the town on this road.

The tourist office (☎ 3-01-01), on the ground floor of the Palacio Municipal on the Hidalgo side of the zócalo, is knowledgeable and helpful, and can even tell you the pros and cons of the various nearby beaches. It's open 9 am to 3 pm and 6 to 8 pm Monday to Friday, and 9 am to 2 pm Saturday.

Bancomer and Banamex both have branches on Hidalgo a few doors from the zócalo. The post office is a block north of the zócalo at Hidalgo 148.

Places to Stay

Tonalá has no great accommodation deals. If you're heading for Puerto Arista, go straight there if you can. The *Hotel Galilea* (☎ 3-02-39), on the south side of the zócalo, has clean, air-conditioned rooms with private bath, but is a bit overpriced at US$16/19 for singles/doubles. More expensive but fairer value is the *Hotel Grajandra* (☎ 3-01-44) at Hidalgo 204 next to the Cristóbal Colón bus station. Clean, sizeable, air-con rooms with TV cost US$23/28.75.

The *Hotel Tonalá* (☎ 3-04-80) at Hidalgo 89, roughly halfway from Cristóbal Colón to the zócalo, has decent doubles for US$15 with fan, US$18 with air-con, but the singles (US$12) are either grotty or hideously close to the heavy trucks which roar through Tonalá all night.

Places to Eat

On the north side of the zócalo, behind a red and yellow awning at the corner of Hidalgo, *Café Sambor's* serves good seafood. Filete de pescado empanizado (fish fillet fried in breadcrumbs) with salad, or a large shrimp and avocado salad, costs US$5. But nothing can drown out the traffic noise here even when they turn the TV to full volume.

The *Hotel Galilea* and the *Hotel Grajandra* also have respectable restaurants. More cafés and small restaurants dot Hidalgo between the zócalo and the Cristóbal Colón bus station.

Getting There & Away

Bus Services out of Arriaga are often better so if things look bad in Tonalá, make your way there. Tonalá's Cristóbal Colón 1st-class bus station is six blocks north of the zócalo on Hidalgo. Autotransportes Tuxtla Gutiérrez (2nd-class) is a similar distance south of the zocálo on Hidalgo. You can pick up other 2nd-class buses on the road outside these terminals. If you're going south, you have more chance of a seat if you wait at the

Top: San Christóbal de las Casas, Chiapas (RMcK)
Bottom: Chamula kids in marketplace, San Christobal de las Casas, Chiapas (RMcK)

Top: Temple of the Warriors, Chichén Itzá,Yucatán state (TW)
Left: Washing radishes, Mérida market, Yucatán state (GE)
Right: Puerto Juárez pier, Cancún, Quintana Roo (GE)

north end of town (outside Cristóbal Colón), and vice-versa. Departures include:

Arriaga – 23 km, 30 minutes; Transportes Arriaga-Tonalá microbuses every few minutes for US$0.50 from the corner of Rayón and Independencia, two blocks off the south-east corner of the zócalo.

Juchitán – 160 km, 2½ hours; a few buses daily by Cristóbal Colón (1st-class) for US$3.25 and Sur (2nd-class).

Mexico City (TAPO) – 925 km, 17 hours; one luxury evening bus by Cristóbal Colón Plus for US$30, two 1st-class buses daily by Cristóbal Colón for US$20.50.

Oaxaca – 425 km, 7½ hours; one or two buses daily by Cristóbal Colón (1st-class, US$9.25) and Sur (2nd-class).

Salina Cruz – 200 km, 3½ hours; one or two buses daily by Cristóbal Colón (1st-class, US$3.75) and Sur (2nd-class).

San Cristóbal de las Casas – 265 km, 5½ hours; one 1st-class bus daily by Cristóbal Colón for US$5.

Tapachula – 220 km, three hours; numerous buses daily by Cristóbal Colón (1st-class) for US$4.25, and by Sur and Autotransportes Tuxtla Gutiérrez (2nd-class).

Tuxtla Gutiérrez – 180 km, 3½ hours; numerous buses daily by Cristóbal Colón (1st-class) for US$3.50, and by Sur and Autotransportes Tuxtla Gutiérrez (2nd-class).

PUERTO ARISTA

Puerto Arista, 18 km south-west of Tonalá, is a km-long collection of palm shacks and a few more substantial buildings in the middle of a 30-km grey sand beach, where the food's mostly fish, you get through a lot of refrescos, and nothing else happens except the crashing of the Pacific waves...until the weekend, when a few hundred Chiapanecos cruise in from the towns, or during Semana Santa or Christmas, when they come in their thousands and the residents make their money for the year.

Usually, the most action you'll see is when an occasional fishing boat puts out to sea, or a piglet breaks into a trot if a dog gathers the energy to bark at it. The temperature's mostly sweltering if you stray more than a few yards from the shore, and it's humid in summer.

The sea is clean but don't go in more than knee-deep: there's an undertow, and rip tides

known as *canales* can sweep you a long way out in a short time.

The paved road to Puerto Arista forks right off Highway 200 three km south-east of Tonalá, then crosses flat ranchland. Puerto Arista's landmark is a lighthouse, where the Tonalá road meets the only street, Blvd Zapotal, which runs parallel to the shore.

Places to Stay

Turn left at the lighthouse, then take the first right and you come to the *Restaurante Playa Escondida*. Bare little rooms, just about clean, with mosquito nets cost US$5 (shower and toilet separate) or US$6.75 (with private toilet). This and similar places will also rent you a hammock to sleep in or let you sling your own for US$1.75.

Two blocks in the opposite direction from the lighthouse, then left towards the sea, the seafront *La Puesta del Sol* has big, clean rooms with two double beds, fan and private bath for US$23.50 at the front, US$20 behind. Other places on the same 'street' have dirtier rooms at around US$8 single, US$13 double. Off-season you can bargain them down a bit. Also up this end of town is *La Casa Diana*, with a choice of bed, hammock or tent accommodation, which claims to be clean with good food, plenty of fresh water, and rock 'n roll music.

The top place is the *Hotel Arista Bugambilias* (☎ Tonalá 3-07-67), towards the north end of Blvd Zapotal, where clean, air-con rooms with TV cost US$32 per single or double. They're nothing fancy but a step up from everywhere else. The hotel has a pool and a garden reaching to the beach.

Places to Eat

Every second beachfront palapa will serve fried fish, eggs or soup any time of year but for slightly more choice and similar prices try *La Puesta del Sol* on the seafront two blocks north of the lighthouse. A good mojarra grande (a big perch-type fish) with salad and tortillas here is US$4; huevos a la Mexicana are US$2.

Getting There & Away

Colectivo taxis go to Puerto Arista from the corner of Matamoros and 5 de Mayo in Tonalá for US$1 per person. They leave when full (six passengers). From Tonalá zócalo, walk two blocks south along the main street, Hidalgo, then turn right down 5 de Mayo for one block to Matamoros.

Transportes Rodulfo Figueroa buses also go from Tonalá to Puerto Arista, about half-hourly from 7 am to 5 pm, for US$0.40. Continue along 5 de Mayo for one block past the colectivo stop, then turn left on to Juárez. The stop is on the right almost immediately. Rodulfo Figueroa also runs a few buses to Boca del Cielo (US$0.80, 1¼ hours) each day. From Puerto Arista to Boca del Cielo you could wait for one of these buses at the junction three km inland, or take a taxi for about US$7.

A taxi from Tonalá is around US$5 to Puerto Arista, US$10 to Boca del Cielo.

AROUND PUERTO ARISTA
Boca del Cielo

About three km from Puerto Arista on the Tonalá road, a turning to the right (south-east) leads to this little fishing settlement at the mouth of an *estero* (estuary) 17 km away. There are some very relaxed palapa seafood restaurants and you can take a launch along the mangrove-fringed estuary or to a beach.

TAPACHULA

Population: 220,000

Most travellers come to Mexico's southern-most city only because it's a gateway to Guatemala, though for ruins buffs Izapa, 11 km east, is worth a visit. The proximity of Guatemala is quickly apparent from the abundance of quetzals (banknotes, not birds) and strange vehicle number plates. Guate-malans hop over the border for three main purposes: business (which may involve smuggling), shopping, and refuge from the fighting in their own country.

Tapachula is the 'capital' of the Soco-nusco, Chiapas' coffee and banana-growing coastal plain, and a busy commercial centre. You may notice some blonde Mexicans and

Chinese names in Tapachula; these are mostly the descendants of German immigrants from the Nazi era and Kuomin-tang supporters who fled China in the 1940s. All this, plus the heat, give the place a livelier atmosphere than most Chiapas towns; even women go around in shorts, a rarity in Mexico outside beach resorts.

Tapachula is overlooked by the 4092-metre Tacaná volcano to its north-east, the first of a chain of volcanoes stretching down into Guatemala. The village of Unión Juárez, 40 km from Tapachula, reportedly provides good views of the volcano, and the surround-ing country has hiking possibilities.

Orientation

The axes of Tapachula's street grid are Avenida Central, running nearly north-south, and Calle Central (east-west), but the large zócalo, Parque Hidalgo, is between Avenidas 6 and 8 Norte, three blocks west of Avenida Central, with Calle 5 Pte on its north side. Accommodation is mostly near the zócalo. Bus stations are scattered north, east and west. Avenidas are even-numbered west of Avenida Central, odd-numbered east of it, and suffixed Norte or Sur depending on whether you're north or south of Calle Central. Calles are even-numbered south of Calle Central, odd-numbered north of it, with the suffix Ote or Pte (East or West).

Information

Money If you're going to Guatemala try to get some quetzals in Tapachula; rates at the borders are less advantageous. Several banks around the city centre will change dollars and quetzals but for a little extra commis-sion, the Casa de Cambio Tapachula at the corner of Calle 3 Pte and Avenida 4 Norte is quicker and open longer – 7.30 am to 7.30 pm Monday to Saturday, 7 am to 1 pm Sunday.

Post & Telephone The post office is several blocks from the centre at the corner of Calle 1 Ote and Avenida 7 Norte – open 8 am to 6 pm Monday to Friday, 8 am to noon Satur-day. There are lada casetas on Calle 17 Ote,

1½ blocks west of the Cristóbal Colón bus station, and in Farmacia Monaco next to the Hotel Don Miguel on Calle 1 Pte.

Foreign Consulates The Guatemalan Consulate is at Calle 2 Ote 33, between Avenidas 7 and 9 Sur. It's open 8 am to 4 pm Monday to Friday. Visas are usually issued quickly and, according to reports, without any photos required.

Soconusco Regional Museum
The Museo Regional del Soconusco on the west side of the zócalo has archaeological and folklore exhibits, including some finds from Izapa. Entry is US$2.75.

Places to Stay – bottom end
The friendly *Hospedaje Las Américas* (☎ 6-27-57), at Avenida 10 Norte 47 north of the zócalo, is good value: small but clean rooms with private bath round a planted courtyard

are just US$5/6.75. The *Hospedaje Colón*, on Avenida Central Norte, a couple of doors north of Calle 9 Ote, has small, noisy, mosquito-inhabited rooms with fans for US$8.75/11.75. Bathrooms are shared.

The *Hospedaje Colonial* (☎ 6-20-52), at Avenida 4 Norte 31 half a block north of Calle 3 Pte, has quiet, clean, bright rooms with private baths along a balcony above an amazingly sweet-smelling garden and courtyard. Singles are US$8.50, doubles/twins are US$14.75/US$17. Ring the bell to enter.

Places to Stay – middle
The *Hotel Santa Julia* (☎ 6-31-40) at Calle 17 Ote 5, next door to the Cristóbal Colón bus station, has clean air-con rooms with TV and private bath for US$16/20.

The *Hotel Fénix* (☎ 5-07-55), at Avenida 4 Norte 19 near the corner of Calle 1 Pte, has an encouraging lobby but a very mixed bag of medium-sized rooms within. Some fan-

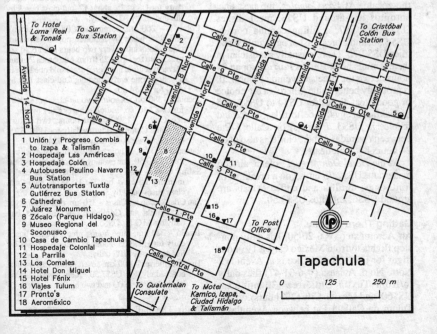

1 Unión y Progreso Combis
   to Izapa & Talismán
2 Hospedaje Las Américas
3 Hospedaje Colón
4 Autobuses Paulino Navarro
   Bus Station
5 Autotransportes Tuxtla
   Gutiérrez Bus Station
6 Cathedral
7 Juárez Monument
8 Zócalo (Parque Hidalgo)
9 Museo Regional del
   Soconusco
10 Casa de Cambio Tapachula
11 Hospedaje Colonial
12 La Parrilla
13 Los Comales
14 Hotel Don Miguel
15 Hotel Fénix
16 Viajes Tulum
17 Pronto's
18 Aeroméxico

Tapachula

0   125   250 m

cooled rooms at US$15.50/20 are far less dilapidated than some air-con ones at US$19/23.50.

The modern *Hotel Don Miguel* (☎ 6-11-43) at Calle 1 Pte 18, is the best city centre hotel, with good, clean, light, air-con rooms with TV for US$23/27.50. There's a good little restaurant here.

Places to Stay – top end

The two top hotels, both with air-conditioned rooms and swimming pools, are the *Motel Kamico* (☎ 6-26-40), on Highway 200 east of the city (singles/doubles US$33/44), and the *Hotel Loma Real* (☎ 6-14-40), just off Highway 200 on the west side of town, charging US$32/42.

Places to Eat

Machacado – chopped fruit with ice, water and sugar – is a popular, refreshing drink in steamy Tapachula. Another cooler is frozen yoghurt (helado de yoghurt).

Several restaurants line the south side of the zócalo. At *Los Comales*, the best one, antojitos are around US$3, meat dishes US$4 to US$7, a filling comida corrida US$4.50, and a breakfast of eggs, coffee and juice US$2.75. There's usually a musician in the evenings here. But *La Parrilla*, open 24 hours across the street at Avenida 8 Norte 20, is probably better value. There's a big choice of good meat dishes for US$4 to US$5, and a breakfast of eggs, juice, tortillas, coffee and frijoles is US$3. *Pronto's*, on Calle 1 Pte between Avenidas 4 and 2 Norte, is also open 24 hours but a bit dearer.

At the *Hotel Don Miguel's* clean, air-con restaurant, US$2.75 buys you a breakfast of fruit, eggs, tortillas and coffee. Meats are around US$6, antojitos US$3.50.

Getting There & Away

Air Aeroméxico (☎ 6-20-50) has daily non-stop flights to/from Mexico City, a 1½-hour flight for US$135. Its office is at Avenida 2 Norte No 6. Aviacsa (☎ 6-31-47) flies daily to/from Tuxtla Gutiérrez (30 minutes, US$60) and Mexico City (2¼ hours). Viajes Tulum on Calle 1 Pte between Avenidas 2

and 4 Norte, and Diverti Viajes at the corner of Calle 1 Pte and Avenida Central Norte, sell Aviacsa, Aeroméxico and Mexicana tickets.

Bus Cristóbal Colón is the only 1st-class bus line serving Tapachula. Its terminus is at the corner of Calle 17 Ote and Avenida 3 Norte, five blocks east and six north of the zócalo. To reach the zócalo go west (left) along 17 Ote for two blocks, then six blocks south (left) down Avenida Central Norte and three west (right) along Calle 5 Pte.

The main 2nd-class bus stations are Sur at Calle 9 Pte 63, a block west of Avenida 12 Norte; Autotransportes Tuxtla Gutiérrez (ATG), at the corner of Calle 9 Ote and Avenida 3 Norte; and Autobuses Paulino Navarro, at Calle 7 Pte 5, half a block west of Avenida Central Norte.

Buses to/from the Guatemalan border are covered in the Talismán & Ciudad Hidalgo section. Other departures include:

Arriaga – 245 km, 3½ hours; nine 1st-class buses daily for US$4.75, about 12 2nd-class buses by Sur and six by ATG daily.

Comitán – 260 km, seven hours (via Motozintla); 2nd-class buses by Autotransportes San Francisco Motozintla every two hours from 6.30 am to 2.30 pm for US$4.25 (from Autobuses Paulino Navarro station, numbered seats sold one hour in advance), one early morning 2nd-class bus by ATG for US$4.50.

Juchitán – 380 km, six hours; two 1st-class buses daily for US$7.50, six 2nd-class buses daily by Sur.

Mexico City – 1150 km, 20 hours; two luxury Cristóbal Colón Plus buses daily for US$36.75, eight 1st-class buses daily for US$24.75.

Oaxaca – 650 km, 11 hours; one evening 1st-class bus for US$13.50, one evening 2nd-class bus by Sur.

Salina Cruz – 420 km, seven hours; one early-morning 1st-class bus for US$8.50, two 2nd-class buses daily by Sur.

San Cristóbal de las Casas – 350 km, eight hours (via Motozintla and Comitán); one 2nd-class bus daily by ATG for US$5.75.

Tonalá – 220 km, three hours; nine 1st-class buses daily for US$3.25, about 12 2nd-class buses by Sur and six by ATG daily.

Tuxtla Gutiérrez – 400 km, seven hours; 15 1st-class buses daily for US$7.50, about six 2nd-class buses daily by ATG and two by Sur.

Train The daily trains between Tapachula

and Veracruz via Ixtepec, Medias Aguas and Tierra Blanca are for Patagonian Express freaks only. They leave Tapachula at 3 pm and Veracruz at 9 am and are supposed to arrive just under 24 hours later. There are no sleeping accommodation or reserved seats. Fares to/from Veracruz are US$7 in primera, US$4 in segunda. Tapachula station is just south of the intersection of Avenida Central Sur and Calle 14.

Getting Around

To/From the Airport Tapachula airport is 18 km south of the city off the Puerto Madero road. Transporte Terrestre (☎ 5-12-87) at Avenida 2 Sur 40A runs colectivo combis between the airport and any hotel in Tapachula for US$2.75 per person. A taxi is US$7.50.

IZAPA

If this site was in a more visited part of Mexico it would have a constant stream of visitors, for it's not only important to archaeologists as a link between the Olmec and the Maya but interesting to walk around. It flourished from approximately 200 BC to 200 AD. The Izapa carving style – typically seen on stelae with altars placed in front – is derived from the Olmec style and most of the gods shown are descendants of Olmec deities, with their upper lips grotesquely lengthened. Early Maya monuments from lowland north Guatemala are similar.

Northern Area

Most of this part of the site has been cleared and some restoration has been done. There are a number of platforms, a ball court, and several carved stelae and altars. The platforms and ball court were probably built some time after Izapa was at its peak.

Southern Area

This is less visited than the northern area. Go back about ¾ km along the road towards Tapachula and take a dirt road to the left. Where the vehicle track ends, a path leads to the right. The three areas of interest are separated by less-than-obvious foot trails and

you may have to ask the caretaker to find and explain them. One is a plaza with several stelae under thatched roofs. The second is a smaller plaza with more stelae and three big pillars topped with curious stone balls. The third is a single carving of jaguar jaws holding a seemingly human figure.

Getting There & Away

Izapa is 11 km east of Tapachula on the road to Talismán. You can reach it by the combis of Unión y Progreso from Calle 5 Pte, half a block west of Avenida 12 Norte in Tapachula. The main (northern) part of the site is marked on the left of the road.

TALISMÁN & CIUDAD HIDALGO (Guatemalan Border)

The road from Tapachula to Guatemala heads 20 km east past Izapa ruins to the border at Talismán bridge, opposite El Carmen, Guatemala. A branch south off this road leads to another border crossing at Ciudad Hidalgo (38 km from Tapachula), opposite Ciudad Tecún Umán. Both crossings are open 24 hours.

At the time of writing it was possible to obtain Guatemalan visas as well as tourist cards at the border, but check this in advance. There's a Guatemalan Consulate at Central Ote 10 in Ciudad Hidalgo, as well as the one in Tapachula. The Guatemalan border posts may make various small charges as you go through, and insist on being paid in either dollars or quetzals – so get some before you leave Tapachula.

Getting There & Away

The combis of Unión y Progreso shuttle between Calle 5 Pte in Tapachula, half a block west of Avenida 12 Norte, and Talismán every few minutes. The fare is US$0.50. A taxi from Tapachula to Talismán takes 20 minutes and costs US$5.

Autobuses Paulino Navarro makes the 45-minute journey between Tapachula and Ciudad Hidalgo for US$1, every 15 minutes.

There are two daily Cristóbal Colón 1st-class services between Talismán and Mexico City for US$25.50.

Many of the longer distance buses leaving the Guatemalan side of the border head for Guatemala City (about five hours away) by the coastal slope route through Retalhuleu and Escuintla. If you're heading for Lake Atitlán or Chichicastenango, you need to get to Quezaltenango (Xela) first, for which you may have to change buses at Retalhuleu or at Malacatán on the Talismán-San Marcos-Quezaltenango road.

Tabasco

Tabasco is a low-lying coastal area to the north of Chiapas, kept fertile by huge rivers which slice through the state on their way to the Gulf of Mexico. It was in this unlikely country that the Olmecs developed Meso-america's first great civilisation. Besides its cultural wealth, Tabasco is noted for its mineral riches, particularly petroleum, which in recent years have brought great prosperity.

The state capital Villahermosa is a convenient jumping-off point for an exploration of the Yucatán Peninsula, and to visit the splendid Maya sites of Palenque, Bonampak and Yaxchilán in Chiapas. For more details, see the Yucatán and Chiapas chapters.

History

What is now called the state of Tabasco was once the home of the Olmecs, the first great Mesoamerican civilisation (1200-400 BC), whose religion, art, astronomy and architec-

ture would deeply influence the civilisations that followed in its wake. The Olmec capital, La Venta, was situated in the western part of the state. Major artefacts, including some of the famous gigantic heads, were moved from that site to Villahermosa's Parque-Museo La Venta to save them from damage during oil exploration. The Chontal Maya who followed the Olmecs built a great ceremonial city called Comalcalco outside present-day Villahermosa. By the time the Spaniards landed, Comalcalco had long been abandoned and lost in the jungle.

Cortés, who disembarked on the Gulf coast near present-day Villahermosa in 1519, initially defeated the Maya and founded a settlement called Santa María de la Victoria. The Maya regrouped and offered stern resistance until they were defeated by Francisco de Montejo, who pacified the region by 1540. Nonetheless, this tranquillity was short-lived. The depredations of pirates forced the original settlement to be moved

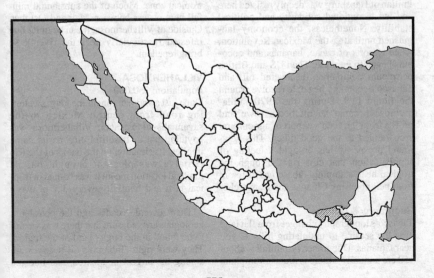

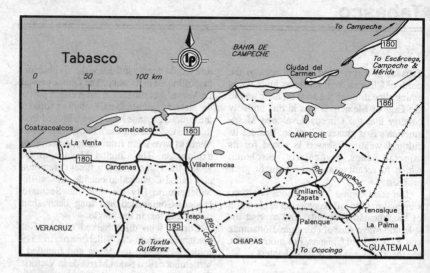

inland from the coast and renamed Villa-hermosa de San Juan Bautista.

After independence was won from Spain, various local land barons tried to assert their power over the area, causing considerable strife. The 1863 French intrusion under Maximilian of Hapsburg was deeply resisted here and led to regional solidarity and political stability. Nonetheless, the economy languished until after the Mexican Revolution, when exports of cacao, bananas and coconuts began to increase. Then US and British petroleum companies discovered oil, and Tabasco's economy began to revolve around the liquid fuel. During the 1970s Villahermosa became an oil boom town and profits from the state's export of agricultural crops added to the good times. This newfound prosperity has brought a feeling of sophistication that cuts right through the tropical heat, stamping Tabasco as different from neighbouring Chiapas and Campeche.

Geography & Climate

Tabasco's topography changes from flat land near the seaside to undulating hills as you near Chiapas. Due to heavy rainfall – about 150 cm annually – there is much swampland and lush tropical foliage. Outside Villahermosa, the state is rather sparsely populated for Mexico, with a little more than a million people inhabiting about 25,000 square km.

Be prepared for sticky humidity in this tropical zone. Much of the substantial rainfall here occurs between May and October. Outside of Villahermosa, it can be quite bug infested (particularly near the rivers), so bring repellent.

VILLAHERMOSA

Population: 250,000

Once just a way-station on the long, sweltering road from central Mexico to the savannahs of Yucatán, Villahermosa was anything but a 'beautiful city' as its name implies. Its situation on the banks of the Río Grijalva was pleasant enough, but its lowland location meant it was bathed in tropical heat and humidity every day of every year.

Then several decades ago the petroleum geologists arrived, sure that there was wealth to be found in the boggy land of the region. They were right. Tabasco's oil reserves are among the largest in Mexico, and boosted

Mexico's position on the short list of countries with proven oil reserves.

With the boom came money – lots of it – and the people of Villahermosa spent much of it to beautify their city. Today Villahermosa is indeed a beautiful city with wide, tree-shaded boulevards, sprawling parks, fancy hotels (for the oilies) and excellent cultural institutions.

If you want to see everything here, you will have to stay at least one night. The open-air Olmec archaeological museum, called the Parque-Museo La Venta, is one of

Mexico's great archaeological exhibits, and will take you most of a morning. The excellent Museo Regional de Antropología (Regional Archaeological Museum) deserves at least an hour or two. And just a short bus ride from the city are the ruins of ancient Comalcalco, complete with a formidable pyramid and temples constructed with mortar made from oyster shells.

Orientation

Villahermosa is a sprawling city, and you will find yourself walking some consider-

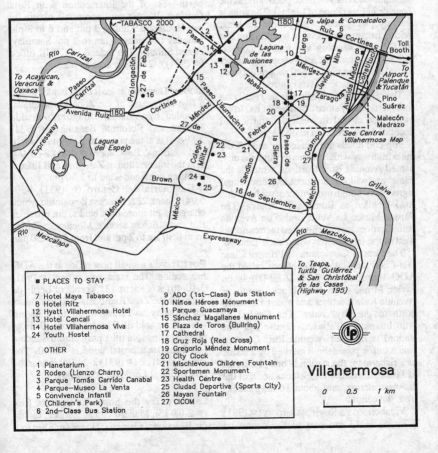

PLACES TO STAY

7 Hotel Maya Tabasco
8 Hotel Ritz
12 Hyatt Villahermosa Hotel
13 Hotel Cencali
14 Hotel Villahermosa Viva
24 Youth Hostel

OTHER

1 Planetarium
2 Rodeo (Lienzo Charro)
3 Parque Tomás Garrido Canabal
4 Parque–Museo La Venta
5 Convivencia Infantil
  (Children's Park)
6 2nd–Class Bus Station

9 ADO (1st–Class) Bus Station
10 Niños Héroes Monument
11 Parque Guacamaya
15 Sánchez Magallanes Monument
16 Plaza de Toros (Bullring)
17 Cathedral
18 Cruz Roja (Red Cross)
19 Gregorlo Méndez Monument
20 City Clock
21 Mischievous Children Fountain
22 Sportsmen Monument
23 Health Centre
24 Ciudad Deportiva (Sports City)
26 Mayan Fountain
27 CICOM

Villahermosa

0   0.5   1 km

able distances – in the sticky heat – and occasionally hopping on a minibus (combi) or taking a taxi, unless you have your own wheels.

Bottom-end and middle-range hotel and restaurant choices are mostly in the older commercial centre of the city between the Plaza de Armas, between Independencia and Guerrero, and Parque Juárez, the small main plaza about five blocks to the north bound by streets named Zaragoza, Avenida Madero and Juárez. This section has been renovated in recent years and is known, because of those renovations, as the Zona Remodelada (Remodeled Zone) or, more poetically, as the Zona de la Luz (Zone of Lights). The zona is a lively place, busy with people strolling, licking frozen yogurt cones, snacking on fast food, bench-warming and making conversation, and – most of all – shopping. Every Saturday evening is a virtual shopping fiesta, and Avenida Madero is its centre.

The city centre can be navigated easily on foot, particularly since a number of its streets have been closed to vehicular traffic and decorated as pedestrian malls.

Top-end hotels are located on and off the main highway which passes through the city, named Avenida Ruiz Cortines, which is the name you will see on street and directional signs, even though most older maps have this road labelled as Boulevard Grijalva. The Parque-Museo La Venta is also on Avenida Ruiz Cortines, several hundred metres north-west of the intersection with Paseo Tabasco.

The Central Camionera de Primera Clase (1st-Class bus station, sometimes called the ADO terminal, (☎ (931) 2-89-00) is on Javier Mina, three long blocks south of Avenida Ruiz Cortines and about 12 blocks north of the city centre. The Central de Autobuses de Tabasco (2nd-class bus station) is right on Avenida Ruiz Cortines near a traffic roundabout marked by a statue of a fisherman; the station is one block east of Javier Mina, four long blocks north of the 1st-class station, and about 16 long blocks from the centre.

Villahermosa's Rovirosa airport (☎ (931) 2-75-55) is 13 km east of the centre on Highway 180, on the other side of the bridge across the Río Grijalva.

Information

Tourist Offices There's a tourist information booth at the ADO bus station run by the Tabasco Hotel & Motel Association, but its hours are erratic, as are the capabilities of its staff. Similar booths are at Parque-Museo La Venta and Rovirosa airport.

The large, glitzy main Tabasco state tourist office (☎ (931) 5-06-94) is in the government complex known as Tabasco 2000, at Paseo Tabasco 1504, half a km north-west of the intersection with Ruiz Cortines. It's not very accessible except by car. Hours are 9 am to 3 pm and 6 to 8 pm Monday to Friday, 9 am to 1 pm Saturday, closed Sunday. The federal SECTUR office (☎ (931) 6-28-91) is here as well.

Money There are at least eight banks within a five-block area of the Zona Remodelada, bounded by Aldama, Zaragoza, Avenida Madero and Reforma. Banamex (☎ (931) 2-89-94) is at the corner of Avenida Madero and Reforma; Bancomer (☎ (931) 2-37-00) is at the intersection of Zaragoza and Juárez. Banking hours are 9 am to 1.30 pm.

Cambiaria del Centro (☎ (931) 4-30-53/4), Saenz 222, is a casa de cambio which charges a bit more than banks, but provides fast and efficient service Monday to Friday from 8.30 am to 2 pm and from 4 to 6.30 pm.

Post There's a small post office at the ADO bus station. The main post office (☎ (931) 2-10-40) is at Saenz 131, corner of Lerdo de Tejada in the Zona Remodelada. Postal hours are Monday to Friday 8 am to 5.30 pm (stamps are sold till 7 pm), Saturday 9 am to noon (stamps sold till 1 pm), closed Sunday. Villahermosa's postal code is 86000. The telegraph office (☎ (931) 2-24-94) is near the post office at Lerdo de Tejada 601.

Laundry Try the Super Lavandería Rex (☎ 2-08-15), Madero 705 at Méndez, facing the Restaurant Geminis. Hours are 8 am to 8 pm, Monday to Saturday. A three-kg load costs US$3 for overnight service.

Parque-Museo La Venta

History Parque-Museo La Venta exists thanks to unusual circumstances. Off the Gulf Coast some 129 km west of Villahermosa, near Tabasco's border with Veracruz, a great religious site of the Olmec civilisation was first excavated by the archaeologist Frans Blom in 1925. The Olmec city of La Venta, built on an island where the Río Tonalá runs into the Gulf, was originally constructed in about 1500 BC, and flourished from 800 BC to 200 AD. After the original work by Blom, Tulane and California universities continued the excavations, and many archaeologists took part. M W Sterling is credited with having discovered, in the early 1940s, five massive heads sculpted from basalt.

When, about this time, petroleum engineers drained a nearby marsh, more of the city was revealed. The additional discoveries came to the attention of Villahermosa's 'Renaissance man', Carlos Pellicer Cámara. Pellicer, a poet, historian and archaeologist, was appalled when he heard that oil drilling jeopardised the La Venta ruins.

Exerting political pressure and influence on the state's politicians, Pellicer arranged to have the significant finds from La Venta, including several of the gigantic heads, moved to a park on what was then the outskirts of Villahermosa. Today, Parque-Museo La Venta is a monument to Pellicer's efforts; a magnificent museum without walls in a lush green setting that enables your imagination to picture these sculptures in their original Olmec city.

Three colossal Olmec heads, intriguingly African in their facial composition, were moved to the park. The largest weighs over 24 tonnes and stands more than two metres

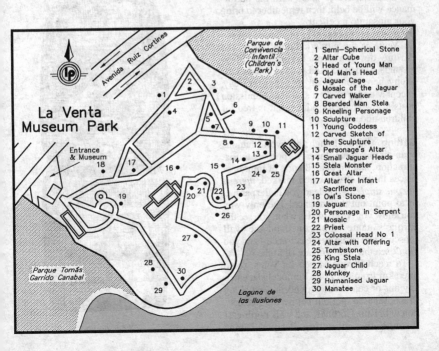

La Venta Museum Park

1 Semi—Spherical Stone
2 Altar Cube
3 Head of Young Man
4 Old Man's Head
5 Jaguar Cage
6 Mosaic of the Jaguar
7 Carved Walker
8 Bearded Man Stela
9 Kneeling Personage
10 Sculpture
11 Young Goddess
12 Carved Sketch of the Sculpture
13 Personage's Altar
14 Small Jaguar Heads
15 Stela Monster
16 Great Altar
17 Altar for Infant Sacrifices
18 Owl's Stone
19 Jaguar
20 Personage in Serpent
21 Mosaic
22 Priest
23 Colossal Head No 1
24 Altar with Offering
25 Tombstone
26 King Stela
27 Jaguar Child
28 Monkey
29 Humanised Jaguar
30 Manatee

tall. It is a mystery how, originally, the Olmecs managed to move the basalt heads as well as religious statues some 100 km without the use of the wheel.

The park is a maze of paths with numbered artefacts set amidst jungle foliage. As well as the heads, you will see intricately carved stelae and sculptures of manatees, monkeys and, of course, the jaguar.

Admission Parque-Museo La Venta (☎ (931) 5-22-28) is open every day from 8 am to 4.30 pm. Entry costs US$1. Officially the guides' services are free, but tips are expected. In the past, self-guidance brochures were available at the entrance for a small charge, or from the tourist office for free.

If your Spanish is up to snuff, come for the evening sound-and-light show (US$1.25) on Tuesday, Thursday, Friday or Saturday, weather permitting, at 7 or 8 pm. Check with the tourist office to make sure the performance will be held, then remember to bring your mosquito repellent.

On the north-east side of Parque-Museo La Venta is the city's children's park, the Parque de Convivencia Infantil. Playgrounds, a small zoo and aviary keep the kids happy here from 9 am to 5 pm any day, except Monday when it's closed. Admission costs a few cents for adults, but is free for children under 12.

Getting There Though this world-famous open-air museum is the city's primary tourist attraction, and though all sorts of important places in this city are well marked, *there is not one single sign* to lead you to the parque, or to point out the entrance! The only way you know you've arrived is when you see the parque's name emblazoned on the wall (obscured by trees) by the entrance – and you won't see this until you are right there.

To reach Parque-Museo La Venta, some three km from the Zona Remodelada, catch any bus or combi heading north-west along Paseo Tabasco, get out before the intersection with Ruiz Cortines, and walk north-east through the sprawling Parque Tomás

Garrido Canabal, a larger park which actually surrounds Parque-Museo La Venta.

CICOM & Regional Museum of Anthropology

The Center for Investigation of the Cultures of the Olmecs & Maya (CICOM) is a complex of buildings on the bank of the Río Grijalva one km south of the Zona Remodelada. The centrepiece of the complex is the Museo Regional de Antropología Carlos Pellicer Cámara, dedicated to the scholar and poet responsible for the preservation of the Olmec artefacts in the Parque-Museo La Venta. Besides the museum, the complex holds a theatre, research centre, an arts centre and other buildings.

The Anthropology Museum (☎ (931) 2-32-02) is open 8 am to 7 pm every day; admission costs US$0.50.

Olmec figure

Just inside the front door is a massive Olmec head, one of those wonders from La Venta. The best way to proceed with your tour of the museum is to turn left, take the lift to the 2nd (top) floor (3rd floor American-style) and work your way down. Although the museum's explanations are all in Spanish, they are often accompanied by photos, maps and diagrams.

On the top floor, exhibits outline Meso-america's many civilisations, from the oldest stone-age inhabitants to the more familiar cultures of our millennium.

After you've brushed up on the broad picture, descend one flight to the 1st (middle) floor where the exhibits concentrate on the Olmec and Maya cultures. Especially intriguing are the displays concerning Comalcalco, the ruined Maya city not far from Villahermosa.

Finally, the ground floor of the museum holds various changing and travelling exhibits.

Getting There CICOM is one km south of the city centre, or 600 metres south of the intersection of Malecón Madrazo and Paseo Tabasco. You can catch any bus or colectivo ('CICOM' or 'No 1') travelling south along Madrazo; just say 'a CICOM?' before you get in, and pay the few cents' fare.

Tabasco 2000 & Parque La Choca

The Tabasco 2000 complex is a testimonial to the prosperity the oil boom brought to Villahermosa, with its modern Palacio Municipal, chic boutiques in a gleaming mall, a convention centre and pretty fountains. There's also a planetarium, where Spanish-language Omnimax cinema shows are presented Tuesday to Friday at 4, 5.30, 7 and 8.30 pm. Admission is US$1.50, half-price for students. If you are coming from the city centre, take a 'Tabasco 2000' bus along Paseo Tabasco.

Parque La Choca, just beyond the Tabasco 2000 complex, is the site of a state fair, complete with livestock exhibitions and a crafts festival in late April. It is also a pleasant place to picnic, has a swimming pool and

is open Monday to Saturday from 7 am to 9 pm.

Places to Stay – bottom end

Camping It might be possible to set up a tent or caravan/trailer at the *Ciudad Deportiva* in the southern part of the city. Ask at the fieldhouse adjacent to the Olympic Stadium during the day. The Tamolte bus runs out here. There's trailer parking also at Parque La Choca on Paseo Tabasco north-west of Tabasco 2000, but no tents are allowed.

Hotels Most of Villahermosa's inexpensive hotels are conveniently located in the Zona Remodelada, but there is at least one cheap choice near the 1st-class bus station.

Excellently located on Lerdo de Tejada between Juárez and Madero are three small, plain, cheap hotels all in a row. The family-run *Hotel San Miguel* (☎ (931) 2-12-85), Lerdo 315, in the mall off Avenida Madero at Lerdo 315, is the best of the lot, renting its plain rooms for US$9 a double, US$13 a twin, or US$15 a double with air-conditioning.

Hotel Tabasco (☎ (931) 2-00-77), Lerdo 317, is a step down from the neighbouring San Miguel, but will do if price is important. Rooms with ceiling fans and sorry beds go for US$9 a double. *Hotel Oviedo* (☎ (931) 2-14-55), Lerdo 303, is the worst of the lot, with less comfortable, hardly charming rooms going for US$8/9/12 a single/double/triple.

Hotel Providencia (☎ (931) 2-82-62), Constitución 210, just north of Reforma, has tiny rooms and even tinier baths that are usually acceptably clean. It's certainly well priced at US$8 per room, single or double, with fan. Among the problems here is noise, as the hotel faces busy Constitución, with its back on the even busier Malecón. To find the hotel, look for the odd sign saying 'Hotel P', with an eye peering from a triangle.

Hotel Buenos Aires (☎ (931) 2-15-55), Constitución 216, a few doors north of the Hotel Providencia, offers dispiriting rooms, usually at prices a bit higher than the preferable Hotel P. Singles and doubles here are

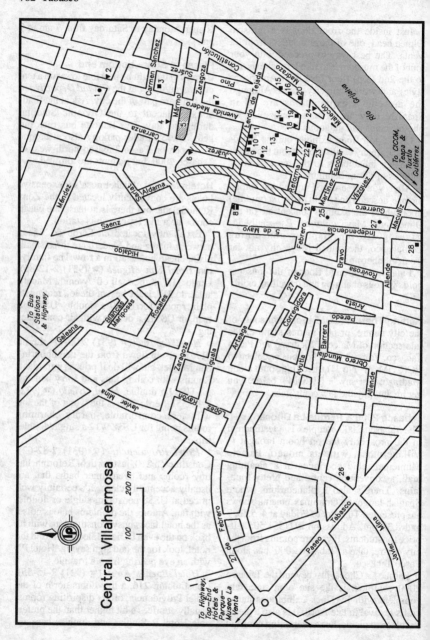

Central Villahermosa

0   100   200 m

To Bus Stations & Highway

To Highway; Top-End Hotels & Parque La Venta; Museo La Venta

To CICOM, Teapa, Tuxtla Gutiérrez

■ PLACES TO STAY

3	Hotel San Francisco
7	Hotel Palma de Mallorca
9	Hotel Tabasco
10	Hotel San Miguel
11	Hotel Oviedo
13	Hotel Oriente
14	Hotel Don Carlos
15	Hotel Buenos Aires
16	Hotel 'P' (Providencia)
17	Hotel Miraflores
19	Hotel Madan
20	Casa de Huéspedes Terecita
22	Hotel Madero
28	Hotel Plaza Independencia

▼ PLACES TO EAT

2	Restaurant Mexicanito
4	Panificadora y Pastelerá
6	Panificadora Los Dos Naciones
18	Restaurant Madan
23	El Torito Valenzuela
24	Restaurant Shally-mar

OTHER

1	Super Lavandería Rex
5	Parque Juárez
8	Post & Telegraph Office
12	Telephone Office
21	Patria es Primo Fountain
25	Palacio de Gobierno
26	Inter Ticket Office
27	Plaza de Armas

for the price: US$13 for a double with one bed and fan, or US$16 for a double with two beds and air-con.

Hotel Oriente (☎ (931) 2-01-21, 2-11-01), Avenida Madero 425 near Lerdo, is very simple and cleanish, with its own good, cheap little restaurant on the ground floor. Singles with private shower and ceiling fan go for US$10, doubles for US$12.

Hotel Madero (☎ (931) 2-05-16), Avenida Madero 301 between Reforma and 27 de Febrero, is in an old building with some character, run by an engaging man who seems to have guests' interests at heart. The clean, pleasant, small rooms are among the best at this price in the city: US$13/15 a single/double with ceiling fan and private shower, and US$18 a double with air-con. Keep street noise in mind when you choose your room.

Hotel Palma de Mallorca (☎ (931) 2-01-44/5), Avenida Madero 516 between Lerdo de Tejada and Zaragoza, is slightly more comfortable, but does not offer particularly good value for money. Rooms with ceiling fan rent for US$16/18 a single/double, or US$21 a double with air-conditioning.

Hotel Palomino (☎ (931) 2-84-31), is at Javier Mina 222 at the corner of Pedro Fuentes, right across from the main entrance to the ADO (1st-class) bus station. A modern place with well-used facilities, it rents serviceable but sometimes noisy rooms for US$14 a double with ceiling fan and private shower, or US$18 with air-con. This may be your first choice if you arrive in Villahermosa late at night by bus in a near-liquid state.

Places to Stay – middle

Middle-range hotels are also in the Zona Remodelada. The well-located *Hotel Miraflores* (☎ (931) 2-00-22/54), Reforma 304 just west of Avenida Madero, was extensively renovated in 1991, and now offers the best mid-range value in both rooms and restaurant. The nicely appointed air-con rooms with bath cost US$30/32/36 a single/double/triple. Here you have the benefits of a relatively quiet pedestrian-street location, and the services of a travel agency and rental car

generally quoted at US$8. *Casa de Huéspedes Terecita* (☎ (931) 2-34-53), Constitución 224, on the east side of the street across from the Hotel Madan, has slightly better rooms up one flight from the street. Price is US$8, single or double.

Another hotel to try for budget rooms with air-conditioning is the 28-room *Hotel San Francisco* (☎ (931) 2-31-98), Avenida Madero 604 between Mármol and Carmen Sánchez. The hotel is a mixed bag: a lift does away with the sweaty hike upstairs; tidy, pleasant hallways lead to the rooms; the bathrooms are neat and tiled, but may not have a seat on the toilet; and the curtains may be heading earthward. Still, it's pretty good desk. Prices may rise to pay for the renovations, though.

Hotel Plaza Independencia (☎ (931) 2-12-99), Independencia 123 at the southern end of the Zona Remodelada near the Plaza de Armas, is a pleasant three-star hotel with 90 air-conditioned rooms with TVs, clean private baths, and even balconies to enjoy the view (try for a room on an upper floor). A pleasant restaurant, bar and small swimming pool, plus a car park, add to the hotel's appeal. Prices are excellent: US$30 a single, US$33 a double, US$36 a triple. The hotel adds a ridiculous telephone charge of US$0.50 per day to your room bill.

Hotel Madan (☎ (931) 2-16-50, 4-05-24), Pino Suárez 105 just north of Reforma, has 20 modernish air-conditioned rooms with bath in a modern, conveniently located building. The hotel entrance is at the eastern end of the building on Pino Suárez; the western end on Madero houses the restaurant (see Places to Eat). Room rates here are US$26 a single, US$30 a double.

Hotel Don Carlos (☎ (931) 2-24-92/99; fax 2-46-22), Avenida Madero 418 between Reforma and Lerdo, facing the Hotel Oriente, has 116 air-conditioned rooms with private baths, TVs and telephones. The lobby is lavish in its mirrors and marble, but the rooms are musty and the furniture creaky. The hotel has seen better days, but is still priced as though it were in its prime at US$30 a single, US$33 a double, and US$36 a triple.

For a moderately priced hotel near the bus stations, try the *Hotel Ritz* (☎ (931) 2-16-11), Madero 1013, a modernised three-storey building one block south of Ruiz Cortines (Highway 180), about five blocks east of both the 1st and 2nd-class bus stations. The 62 rooms here all have individual air-conditioners, private baths, and reasonable prices of US$26 a single, and US$30 a double. The Ritz is a popular place, so pin down a room early if you can.

If you want a cool, safe haven, the place for you is the *Hotel Maya Tabasco* (☎ (931) 2-11-11; fax 2-10-97), four blocks north of the 1st-class ADO bus station, a block west of the 2nd-class bus station, right near the

intersection of Javier Mina and Ruiz Cortines. Its 160 air-conditioned rooms offer TVs with satellite hook-ups; the hotel has a swimming pool, lobby bar, two restaurants (Mexican and international), a disco, hairdresser and newsstand. Rates for this refuge are US$45, single or double.

Places to Stay – top end

As an oil boom town, Villahermosa has no shortage of luxury lodgings. Three of the best hotels are located near the intersection of Paseo Tabasco and Avenida Ruiz Cortines (Highway 180), a pleasant 10-minute walk from Parque-Museo La Venta.

Poshest of the posh is the *Hyatt Villahermosa* (☎ (931) 3-44-44; toll-free in Mexico (800) 5-07-77; fax 5-12-35), Juárez 106, Colonia Lindavista 85050, south-west off Paseo Tabasco on the Laguna de las Ilusiones, south-east of Avenida Ruiz Cortines. The Hyatt is the best in town, with all the expected luxury services at US$110 a double, tax included.

Consider the pretty *Villahermosa Viva* (☎ (931) 2-55-55), right at the the intersection of Paseo Tabasco and Avenida Ruiz Cortines (Highway 180). The comfortable air-conditioned rooms are in two-storey motel-style white stucco buildings placed around a large swimming pool; the restaurant, bar and disco club (sometimes with live entertainment) keep you entertained in the evenings. Singles are US$50 to US$60, doubles US$60 to US$75, tax included.

The price leader in this high-rent area is undoubtedly the *Hotel Cencali* (☎ (931) 5-19-96/97/99; fax 2-18-62), Calle Juárez off Paseo Tabasco, more or less between the Hyatt and the Viva (a different Calle Juárez from the one in the city centre!). The Cencali has a nice layout amidst tropical foliage, lawns, with a good restaurant, clean swimming pool, and pleasant, modern, air-conditioned rooms with TVs. Prices are a reasonable US$54/56 a single/double, tax included.

Holiday Inn Villahermosa (☎ (931) 3-44-00/80; toll-free in Mexico (800) 0-09-99; fax 3-55-69), Paseo Tabasco 1407 in the Tabasco

2000 complex (86036), is Villahermosa's newest luxury lodging, a modern slab-like building with very comfortable rooms, a pool, restaurants and bars. Prices are US$95/115 a single/double.

Places to Eat – bottom end

There are a number of good, cheap little eateries clustered around the 1st-class bus station on Javier Mina, several right across the street from the main entrance. But the main stem for cheap eateries is undoubtedly Avenida Madero; the pedestrian streets of the Zona Remodelada (Lerdo, Juárez, Reforma, Aldama) also have lots of snack and fast-food shops.

El Torito Valenzuela, 27 de Febrero 202 at the corner with Avenida Madero, open 8 am to midnight, is perhaps Villahermosa's most popular and convenient cheap taquería. Tacos made with various ingredients are priced at US$0.60 to US$1.80 apiece and similarly varied tortas (sandwiches) go for exactly twice as much. With its corner location, you can watch the busy street life as you munch.

Restaurant Mexicanito, Madero 704 north of Méndez, is a bit of a walk from the Zona Remodelada, but makes up for it with a variety of dishes at reasonable prices. This plain little lonchería serves chilaquiles (red or green) with chicken for US$3, meat dishes for about US$4, and a variety of breakfasts for US$2 to US$3.25.

Panificadora y Pastelería on Mármol facing Parque Juárez, is the place to go for sweet rolls, bread and pastries for snacks, make-your-own breakfasts, or picnic supplies. Another useful bakery is the *Panificadora Los Dos Naciones*, at the corner of Juárez and Zaragoza.

Places to Eat – middle

Avenida Madero and Constitución have a number of suitable middle-range dining places. The restaurant at the *Hotel Miraflores* (☎ 2-00-22/54), Reforma 304 just west of Madero, has a pleasant decor, decent food, and full meals for US$10 to US$15. *Restaurant Madan*, on Avenida Madero just north of Reforma, is bright and modern, with booths, pseudo-colonial tables and chairs, air-con, and a pleasant informal ambience. A genuine espresso machine hisses in one corner, promising an excellent post-prandial cup of coffee. A full meal of fruit cocktail, filete tampiqueña (beef in savoury tomato sauce), dessert, drink, and espresso, costs about US$12 to US$14, though you can have a hamburger and a beer instead for US$5. Hours are 8 am to 11 pm every day.

Restaurant Shally-mar, on Constitución just south of Reforma, specializes in seafood, which is not particularly cheap, but which can be good if it's fresh. Expect to spend US$15 to US$18 for a meal.

Los Faroles, on Malecón Madrazo north of Reforma, is a nice patio place with brick arches and a river view. The menu bears all the Mexican favourites, at prices which might bring your bill to US$10 or US$14.

Besides the dining rooms of the luxury hotels, there are several garden restaurants along Paseo Tabasco between the river and Avenida Ruiz Cortines. If you get hungry while visiting the Museo Regional de Antropología, try the *Restaurant Los Tulipanes* (☎ 2-92-09, -17) in the CICOM complex, open from noon to 1 am every day. A full lunch might cost US$15, dinner a few dollars more (perhaps to pay for the live music). On Sunday, there's a buffet.

For a splurge you can cruise the Río Grijalva while eating so-so cuisine on the *Capitán Beúlo* (☎ 2-92-09/17), a restaurant boat docked next to the Restaurant Los Tulipanes. The meal-and-cruise is most interesting during the day (departures daily except Monday at 1.30 and 3.30 pm) when you can observe life on the river. Evenings, (at 9.30 pm) you see little, but those who enjoy dinner cruises may find it romantic. Prices are higher than in shore restaurants, of course, but not all that bad: steaks for US$11, shrimp dishes for US$13, full meals for US$20 or US$25.

Entertainment

Teatro Esperanza Iris at the CICOM complex offers folkloric dance, theatre or comedy

Wednesday to Saturday at 7 and 9.30 pm. Ask at the tourist office or your hotel for details.

The planetarium at Tabasco 2000 has Omnimax cinema shows and Parque La Venta has sound-and-light shows Tuesday, Thursday, Friday and Saturday; see those sections for details.

Discos can be found in the Villahermosa Viva, Hyatt, Cencali and Maya Tabasco luxury hotels, open every evening except Sunday and Monday from about 10 pm on. Cover charge is about US$8. For other cultural goings-on, call the Instituto de la Cultura (☎ 2-79-47) or check their bulletin of events distributed to the museums and bigger hotels.

Getting There & Away

Air Villahermosa's Rovirosa airport (symbol: VSA; ☎ (931) 2-75-55) is 13 km east of the centre on Highway 180, on the other side of the bridge across the Río Grijalva.

Inter (formerly Aerocaribe) (☎ (931) 4-32-02/03; fax 4-30-17), Javier Mina 901-A (or 1202), Edificio Alejandra, between Paseo Tabasco and Pedrazo, flies between Villahermosa and Mérida daily, with extra flights on Friday and Sunday. They also currently have a flight to Flores in Guatemala (near Tikal) on Monday, Wednesday and Saturday, but check to see if it's still operating when you arrive.

Flights to and from Mérida, Cancún and Mexico City are operated by Aeromexico (☎ (931) 2-69-91, 2-95-54, 2-09-04), Avenida Carlos Pellicer Cámara 511, Plaza CICOM No 2 (next to the Regional Museum, and Mexicana (☎ (931) 3-50-44), Avenida de los Ríos 105, Tabasco 2000.

Aviacsa (☎ (931) 3-67-51, 3-69-10, 4-57-70/80; fax 4-57-90) flies daily between Villahermosa and Mérida (one hour, US$65 to US$71), Cancún (two hours, US$125), Oaxaca and Tuxtla Gutiérrez; and from Tuxtla Gutiérrez to Tapachula. They also have routes connecting Mexico City with Oaxaca, Ixtepec, Chetumal and Tuxtla Gutiérrez.

Litoral (☎ (938) 2-43-64; fax 2-43-63), a small airline based in Ciudad del Carmen, Campeche state, flies daily on the route Ciudad del Carmen-Villahermosa-Veracruz-Tampico-Monterrey and return. Inquire at the airport or at a travel agency for more information.

Smaller local airlines fly to Tuxtla Gutiérrez and Oaxaca. For information, contact Turismo Grijalva (☎ (931) 2-25-96, 2-43-94), Zaragoza 911 in the Zona Remodelada.

Bus The 1st-class (ADO) bus station, Javier Mina 297, has a small post office, a tourist information booth, and a selection of little eating places. If you're looking for a hotel near the bus station, refer to Places to Stay and the Hotel Palomino (bottom end), Hotel Ritz and Hotel Maya Tabasco (middle). While there is no *guardería* for your luggage, you might be able to tip a baggage handler to watch your gear for a few hours.

The two main 1st-class companies serving Villahermosa are ADO and Omnibus Cristóbal Colón; UNO, the luxury line, has several buses to central Mexico. Villahermosa is an important transportation point, but many buses serving it are de paso, so buy your onward ticket in advance.

All of the buses and fares listed below are 1st-class:

Acayucan – 225 km, 3½ hours; several buses by ADO for US$5.50.

Campeche – 450 km, seven hours; 18 1st-class ADO buses daily for a fare of US$9; 14 of these buses will drop you at Catazajá (Palenque junction, US$2.50).

Cancún – 915 km, 14 hours; nine buses daily by ADO for US$22.

Chetumal – 575 km, nine hours; 10 ADO buses daily for US$12.

Comalcalco – 53 km, 1½ hours; three buses daily for US$2.

La Venta – 140 km, two hours; nine buses daily by ADO for US$2.50.

Mérida – 700 km, 10 hours; 18 by ADO for US$13.

Mexico City – 820 km, 14 hours; two 1st-class buses (US$19) and one deluxe (US$30) daily by Cristóbal Colón, 32 1st-class by ADO, for US$19.

Oaxaca – 700 km, 13 hours; two buses daily (7.30 and 9.30 pm) by Cristóbal Colón for US$15.

Palenque – 150 km, 2½ hours; seven buses daily (4.30, 6, 6.20 and 8 am; 1.30, 4.30 and 6 pm) by ADO for US$2.85; if you want to go directly to the ruins, be sure to buy a ticket for a 'zona arqueológica' bus (US$3).

Paraíso – 75 km, two hours; three buses daily for US$1.80.

Playa del Carmen – 848 km, 14 hours; eight ADO buses daily for US$18.

San Andrés Tuxtla – 320 km, six hours; 23 buses daily by ADO for US$6.

San Cristóbal de las Casas – 308 km, eight hours; one bus daily by Cristóbal Colón for US$6.

Tapachula – 735 km, 13 hours; one bus daily (6 pm) by Cristóbal Colón for US$16.

Teapa – 60 km, one hour; five buses daily by Cristóbal Colón for US$1.25.

Tenosique – 290 km, four hours; nine buses daily by ADO for US$4.

Tuxtla Gutiérrez – 294 km, six hours; seven buses daily by Cristóbal Colón for US$6.

Veracruz – 475 km, eight hours; 24 buses daily by ADO for US$10.

The 2nd-class Central de Autobuses de Tabasco bus station is on the north side of Avenida Ruiz Cortines (Highway 180) across the highway from the Euzkadi Radial building, just east of the intersection with Javier Mina. It's about five blocks from the 1st-class bus station as the crow flies; use one of the pedestrian overpasses to cross the busy highway.

A number of smaller companies serve local destinations within the state of Tabasco, but there are also 2nd-class buses run by Autobuses Unidos to Acayucan (four a day for US$4.25), Veracruz (one daily for US$12) stopping along the way at Catemaco (US$5.50), and to Mexico City (three a day for US$18). Buses to La Venta depart four times daily at a fare of US$2.25.

For Comalcalco, hop on a bus run by Servicio Somellera. They run every 15 minutes throughout the day for US$1.25.

Train The nearest railhead to Villahermosa is 58 km away at the town of Teapa and it's just as well, as the slow trains through Tabasco are less comfortable and safe than the bus.

Getting Around
To/From the Airport The colectivo Trans-porte Terrestre minibuses charge US$3 per person for the trip into town; a taxi costs US$12. Buy your tickets from a counter in the terminal. The 13-km trip takes about 20 minutes to the centre and 25 to 30 minutes to top-end hotels.

To/From the Bus Terminals From the 1st-class ADO bus station, it's generally about 15 to 20 minutes walk to the recommended hotels (those closer are noted). Ordinarily we'd suggest that you do the journey on foot, but Villahermosa's heat and high humidity may make taking a taxi a better option (figure around US$2 to US$2.75 in the cheaper Volkswagen Beetle taxis for almost any ride in the city). Local bus fares are only a few pesos.

As you exit the front of the ADO station, go left for two blocks to the corner of Javier Mina and Zozaya, where buses stop en route to the Zona Remodelada and Avenida Madero, the main thoroughfare. If you are walking, go out the ADO station's front door, cross Javier Mina and follow Lino Merino five blocks to the principal plaza, Parque de la Paz on Avenida Madero, and turn right.

Bus & Minibus A dozen municipal (SAETA) bus routes link the centro with outlying areas of the city; but the green-and-white minibuses and combis are more useful than the larger city buses. The minibuses travel tortuous, twisting routes, but it is easy enough to get where you want as they bear the names of major landmarks scrawled in their windscreens. Catch a 'Palacio Mpal' minibus along Paseo Tabasco to get to Tabasco 2000 and the tourist offices; 'Chedraui' for the big department stores on Javier Mina, 1½ blocks from the ADO bus station; and 'Centro' to get to the Zona Remodelada.

Although the major sights listed are far from the centre, there is local bus service to them. See each particular listing for the appropriate bus destination.

COMALCALCO RUINS
If you have the time and are interested in

archaeology, a day trip from Villahermosa to the ruins of Comalcalco is worth your while. Admission is US$3 and Comalcalco is open daily from 8 am to 5 pm.

Comalcalco was constructed during the Maya Late Classic period between 500 and 900 AD, when the region's agricultural productivity prompted population expansion. The principal crop which brought Indian peasants from Palenque to this region was the cacao bean, still the chief cash crop (the Comalcalcoans traded it with other Maya settlements).

Although Comalcalco in many ways resembles Palenque in architecture and sculpture, it is unique in its composition. Because stone was in short supply, the Maya made bricks from clay, sand and – ingeniously – oyster shells. Mortar was provided with lime obtained from the oyster shells. This unique mortar was also used in the sculpting of elaborate stucco façades with multicoloured reliefs, grotesque masks, and human and animal representations. Comalcalco is thought by archaeologists to be among the first cities built of brick.

You will have to look carefully to see some of the stucco sculpture. The government has simplified the task of finding the best carvings by erecting thatch roofs to

shelter them. Look on the right-hand side of the pyramid and you will see some remains of the stucco sculptures which once covered the pyramid. Then walk through the plaza to the main Acropolis area where, particularly on the northern section, you will find the remains of fine stucco carvings.

Although the west side of the Acropolis once held a crypt comparable to Palenque's Pakal, the tomb was vandalised before the area was known to the outside world; the sarcophagus was stolen. Continue up the hill to the ruin called the Palace, and from this elevation enjoy the breeze while you gaze down on unexcavated mounds.

Since all the structures are built of stucco and brick, you don't want to assist the erosion process by climbing on them. The 'No Subir' signs are also for your safety; a tourist broke a leg here not long before I visited the site.

Getting There & Away

The 55-km journey takes about an hour. A virtual shuttle service operates between Comalcalco and the 2nd-class bus station in Villahermosa, with buses departing every 15 minutes throughout the day; fare is US$1.25. When you get to the town of Comalcalco, get out at the intersection of Highways 187 and 195, catch a VW minibus (combi) headed south, and mention that you want to get out at 'las ruinas'. The driver will charge you US$0.50 and drop you at the access road to the ruins, from where it is a walk of one km. A taxi from Comalcalco town costs about US$2.50 each way.

RÍO USUMACINTA

The mighty Río Usumacinta snakes its way north-westwards along the border between Mexico and Guatemala. A journey along the Río Usumacinta today reveals dense rainforest, thrilling bird and animal life, and ruined cities such as Bonampak and Yaxchilán (see the Chiapas chapter). You can visit these ruins by air if time is short and money plentiful, but a journey by car and boat is cheaper and much more exciting. You can also use a tributary of the Usumacinta as your water-road into El Petén, Guatemala's vast jungle province, with its stupendous ruins at Tikal.

To Flores & Tikal (Guatemala)

For those in a real hurry, Inter (formerly called Aerocaribe) flies between Villahermosa and Flores three days a week; see Getting There & Away in the Villahermosa section for details.

You can also go from Tenosique to Flores, in Guatemala's Petén province near Tikal, by bus and boat in two days of fairly hard travel, or in one day if you're willing to pay a bit more.

For the one-day trip from Palenque, contact La Posada (see Organised Tours in the Palenque section of the Chiapas chapter) for a reservation on their special minibus, which departs at 4.30 am to Tenosique (US$12) and La Palma (US$18), arriving at 7 am. The boat on the Río San Pedro departs La Palma at 8.30 am, arriving in El Naranjo at noon. After passing through Guatemalan customs, you catch a bus departing El Naranjo at 1 pm for Flores, arriving at 7 pm. Viajes Shivalva also runs a tour travelling from Palenque to Flores in one day, and other agencies may do so as well.

To do it on your own, which takes two days but is slightly cheaper, take an early morning bus from Palenque to the town of Emiliano Zapata, about 40 km north-east of Palenque on the banks of the Usumacinta. From Zapata, take another bus to Tenosique and, after lunch, change for yet another bus (1½ hours, US$1) due east to La Palma.

For a bit more money, join the special minibus run by Amfitriones Turísticos de Chiapas (☎ (934) 5-02-10), on Allende between Avenida Juárez and Hidalgo in Palenque, which departs Palenque at 10 am (US$15). Doing it this way, you must spend the night – or at least part of it – in El Naranjo in primitive shelters rented for the purpose. It's best to have your own camping equipment and warm gear as it can actually get cold here at night. You then catch the 3 am bus for Flores, arriving at 9 am.

Tenosique

Tenosique, due east of Palenque on the opposite bank of the Usumacinta, is the last town of any size on the lower part of the river; the next town is Sayaxché, Guatemala, on the Río de la Pasión, some 150 km to the south-east.

Second-class buses run regularly from Villahermosa, and trains stop here en route to Mexico City and Mérida. The bus station is one km from the centre; the railway station is one km from the plaza.

Places to Stay & Eat The best budget hotel in Tenosique is the *Hotel Azuleta*, on Pino Suárez, where singles with fan and bath are US$7, doubles US$10. There are cheap restaurants around the plaza.

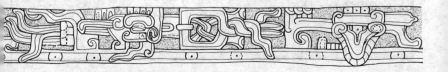

The Yucatán Peninsula

When you cross the Río Usumacinta into Yucatán, you are crossing into the realm of the Maya. The appearance of the countryside changes, as do the houses and the people in

them. Heirs to a glorious and often violent history, the Maya live today where their ancestors lived a millenium ago. The Maya are proud to be Mexicans, but even prouder to be Maya, and it is the Mayab (the lands of the Maya) that they consider their true country.

Though it's flat and hot, Yucatán has surprising diversity. There are archaeological sites galore, several handsome colonial cities, Mexico's most popular seaside resort, and quiet coastlines populated mostly by exotic tropical birds.

Yucatán's rainy season is from mid-August to mid-October. During this time it's normal for an afternoon shower to come down most days.

HISTORY
The Maya
At the height of Maya culture during the Late Classic Period (600 to 900 AD), the Maya lands were ruled not as an empire but as a

collection of independent but also interdependent city-states. Each city-state had its noble house, headed by a king who was the social, political and religious centre of the city's life.

By the end of the Late Classic Period, the focus of Maya civilisation had shifted from Guatemala and Belize to northern Yucatán, where a new civilisation developed at Chichén Itzá, Uxmal and Labná.

During the Early Postclassic Period (900 to 1200), classic Maya civilisation collapsed. Weakened, the Maya were prey to wave of invaders from central Mexico. The Toltecs of Tula (near present-day Mexico City) conquered Teotihuacán, then marched and sailed eastwards to Yucatán. They were led by a fair-haired, bearded king named Quetzalcóatl (Plumed Serpent), who established himself in Yucatán at Uucil-abnal (Chichén Itzá). He left behind in Mexico, and then in Yucatán, a legend that he would one day return from the direction of the rising sun. The culture at Uucil-abnal flourished after the late 800s, when all of the great buildings were constructed, but by 1200 the city was abandoned.

The Spaniards

Cortés' expedition of 1519, departing from Cuba, first made landfall at Cozumel off the Yucatán peninsula. After their conquest of central Mexico, the Spaniards turned their attention to Yucatán. The Spanish monarch commissioned Francisco de Montejo (El Adelantado, the Pioneer) with the task of conquest, and he set out from Spain in 1527 accompanied by his son, also named Francisco de Montejo. Landing first at Cozumel on the Caribbean coast, then at Xel-ha on the mainland, the Montejos discovered that the local people wanted nothing to do with them.

The Montejos then sailed around the peninsula, conquered Tabasco (1530), and established their base near Campeche, which could be easily supplied with necessities, arms and new troops from New Spain (central Mexico). They pushed inland, but after four long, difficult years were forced to retreat and to return to Mexico City in defeat.

The younger Montejo (El Mozo, The Lad) took up the cause again, with his father's support, and in 1540 he returned to Campeche with his cousin named (guess what?) – Francisco de Montejo. These two Francisco de Montejos pressed inland with speed and success, allying themselves with the Xiú Maya against the Cocom Maya, defeating the Cocoms and gaining the Xiús as converts to Christianity.

The Montejos founded Mérida in 1542, and within four years had almost all of Yucatán subjugated to Spanish rule. The once proud and independent Maya became peons, working for Spanish masters without hope of deliverance except in heaven.

Independence Period

The harshness of Spanish rule resulted in frequent revolts. When Mexico finally won its independence from Spain in 1821, the new Mexican government urged the peoples of Yucatán, Chiapas and Central America to join it in the formation of one large new state. At first Yucatán and Chiapas refused and Guatemala accepted, but all later changed their minds. Yucatán and Chiapas joined the Mexican union, and Guatemala lead the formation of the United Provinces of Central America.

Though independence brought new prosperity to the creoles (Mexicans of Spanish descent), it worsened the lot of the Maya. The end of Spanish rule meant that the Crown's few liberal safeguards, which had afforded the Indians minimal protection from the most extreme forms of exploitation, were abandoned. Maya claims to ancestral lands were largely ignored and huge plantations were created for the cultivation of tobacco, sugar cane and henéquen (agave). The Maya, though legally free, were enslaved by debt peonage to the great landowners.

Not long after independence, the Yucatecan ruling classes again dreamed of independence, this time from Mexico, and perhaps of union with the USA. With these goals in mind, the *hacendados* made the mistake of arming and training their Maya peons as local militias in anticipation of an invasion from central Mexico. Trained to use modern weaponry, the Maya envisioned a release from their own misery and boldly rebelled against their Yucatecan masters.

War of the Castes

The War of the Castes began in 1847 in Valladolid, a city known for its oppressive laws against the Maya. The Maya rebels quickly gained control of the city in an orgy of vengeful killing and looting. Supplied with arms and ammunition by the British through Belize, they spread relentlessly across Yucatán.

In little more than a year the Maya revolutionaries had driven their oppressors from every part of Yucatán except Mérida and the walled city of Campeche. Seeing the Whites' cause as hopeless, Yucatán's governor was about to abandon the city when the rebels saw the annual appearance of the winged ant. In Maya mythology, corn (the staff of life) must be planted at the first sighting of the winged ant. The sowing is not to be delayed, or Chac, the rain god, will be affronted and respond with a drought. The rebels abandoned the attack on Mérida and returned quickly to their farms to plant the corn.

This gave the Whites and mestizos time to regroup and to receive aid from their erstwhile enemy, the government in Mexico City. The counter-revolution against the Maya was vicious in the extreme. Between 1848 and 1855, the Indian population of Yucatán was halved. Some Maya combatants sought refuge in the jungles of southern Quintana Roo and continued to fight until 1866.

Yucatán Today

Although the post-WW II development of synthetic fibres led to the decline of the henéquen (rope) industry, it still employs about a third of the peninsula's workforce. The slack has been more than picked up by the oil boom in Tabasco, the fishing and canning industries of the peninsula, and the rapid growth of tourism in the past decade. Though the power elite is still largely of Spanish or mestizo parentage, Yucatán's Maya are better off today than they have been for centuries.

A good number of Maya till the soil as their ancestors have done for centuries, growing staples like corn and beans. Subsistence agriculture is little different from the way it was in the Classic period, with minimal mechanisation.

GEOGRAPHY

The Yucatán Peninsula is one vast flat limestone shelf rising only a few metres above sea level. The shelf extends outward from the shoreline for several km under water. If you approach Yucatán by air, you should have no trouble seeing the barrier reef which marks the limit of the peninsular limestone shelf. On the landward side of the reef the water is shallow, usually no more than five or 10 metres deep; on the seaward side is deep water. The underwater shelf makes Yucatán's coastline wonderful for aquatic sports, keeping the waters warm and the marine life (fish, crabs, lobsters, tourists) abundant, but it makes life difficult for traders. The only anomaly on the flat shelf of Yucatán is the low range of the Puuc Hills near Uxmal, which attains heights of several hundred metres.

Because of their geology, northern and central Yucatán have no rivers or lakes. The people on the land have traditionally drawn their fresh water from cenotes, limestone caverns with collapsed roofs, which serve as natural cisterns. Rainwater which falls between May and October collects in the cenotes for use during the dry season from October to May. South of the Puuc Hills there are few cenotes, and the inhabitants traditionally have resorted to drawing water from limestone pools deep within the earth.

Yucatán is covered in a blanket of dry thorny forest, which the Maya have traditionally slashed and burned to make space for planting crops or pasturing cattle. The soil is red and good for crops in some areas, poor in others, and cultivating it is hot, hard work.

Campeche State

Campeche is the least visited state on the Yucatán Peninsula. This is a blessing for the traveller who wants to get away from the Caribbean tourist mobs and explore a richly historical region. The impressive walled city of Campeche with its ancient fortresses or *baluartes* propels the visitor back to the days of the buccaneers. Those who explore the region's ancient Maya Chenes-style ruins of Edzná, Dzibilnocac and Hochob may find they have the sites all to themselves.

CAMPECHE

Population: 185,000

Tranquil, cheap and filled with historic buildings, Campeche is a worthwhile stop-over between Villahermosa and Mérida. Worthwhile, yes, for its picturesque buildings, streets and baluartes, but not for its beaches. They are few, small and generally not of any interest.

History

Once a Maya trading village called Ah Kim Pech (Lord Sun Sheep-Tick), Campeche was invaded by the conquistadors in 1517. The Maya resisted and for nearly a quarter of a century the Spaniards were unable to fully conquer the region. Campeche was founded in 1531, but later abandoned due to Maya hostility. Finally, by 1540 the conquistadors had gained sufficient control, under the leadership of Francisco de Montejo the Younger, to found a settlement here which survived. They named it the Villa de San Francisco de Campeche. The settlement soon flourished as the major port of Yucatán.

For two centuries the depredations of pirates terrorised Campeche. In their most gruesome of assaults, in early 1663, the various pirate hordes set aside their jealousies to converge upon the city as a single flotilla, massacring many of Campeche's citizens in the process.

It took this tragedy to make the Spanish monarchy take preventive action. Starting in 1668, 3.5-metre-thick ramparts were built. After 18 years of construction, a 2.5-km hexagon incorporating eight strategically placed baluartes surrounded the city. A segment of the ramparts extended out to sea so that ships literally had to sail into a fortress to gain access to the city.

Originally part of the state of Yucatán, Campeche became an autonomous state of Mexico in 1863.

Orientation

Though the baluartes (bulwarks) still stand, the city walls themselves have been razed and replaced by streets which ring the city centre just as the walls once did. This is the Avenida Circuito Baluartes, or Circular Avenue of the Bulwarks.

The centre of the old city is Plaza Moch-Cuouh, on the western side near the waterfront. Along the waterfront on the western edge of the city is Avenida Ruiz Cortines. The top hotels are located between Plaza Moch-Cuouh and this avenida; cheaper hotels and restaurants overlook the plaza from its eastern side, or are located a block or two off the plaza in the grid of streets to the east.

According to the compass, Campeche is oriented with its waterfront to the north-west, but tradition and convenience hold that the water is to the west, inland is east. The street grid is numbered so that streets running north-south have even numbers, while east-west streets have odd numbers; street numbers ascend towards the south and the west.

Information

Tourist Office The State Tourism Office (☎ (981) 6-60-68, 6-67-67) is in a fortress-like, partly subterranean structure located near the southern end of the Plaza Moch-Cuouh, on Calle 61 between Avenidas 16 de Septiembre and Ruiz Cortines. The entrance, facing the sea, is not visible until you're at it. The staff are friendly and available Monday to Saturday from 8 am to 2.30 pm and 4 to 8.30 pm, closed Sunday.

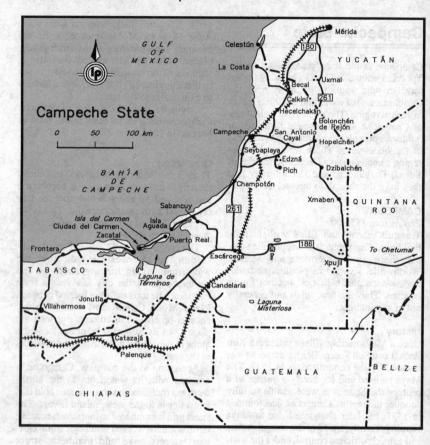

Money There are several banks, all open Monday to Friday from 9 am to 1 pm. Bancomer is across from Baluarte de la Soledad at Calle 59 No 2A and at Avenida 16 de Septiembre. Banco del Atlantico is at Calle 50 No 406, and Banamex at Calle 10 No 15.

Post The central post office (☎ (981) 6-21-34), at the corner of Avenida 16 de Septiembre and Calle 53, is in the Edificio Federal near the Baluarte de Santiago at the north-western corner of the old town. Hours are Monday to Friday 8 am to 7 pm, Saturday 8 am to 1 pm and Sunday 8 am to 2 pm.

Walking Tour

Campeche, the first city in the New World completely encircled by walls, began to modernise by tearing down some of its impressive baluartes. Fortunately, in homage to its heritage (and also to lure tourists), seven bulwarks still stand; four of them are of great interest. You can see them all by following the Avenida Circuito Baluartes around the city on a two-km walk.

Close to the modern Palacio de Gobierno, at Avenidas Circuito Baluartes and Justo Sierra, near the intersection of Calles 8 and 65 and a ziggurat fountain, is the **Baluarte**

de San Carlos. The interior of the bulwark is now arranged as the **Sala de las Fortificaciones**, or Chamber of Fortifications, with some interesting scale models of the city's fortifications in the 18th century. You can also visit the dungeon, and look out over the sea from the roof. Baluarte de San Carlos is open from 9 am to 1 pm and 5 to 7.30 pm daily; there is no charge for admission.

From the Baluarte de San Carlos, head north along Calle 8. At the intersection with Calle 59, notice the **Puerta del Mar**, or Sea Gate, which provided access to the city from the sea before the area to the north-west was filled in. The gate was demolished in 1893 but rebuilt in 1957 when its historical value was realised.

The **Baluarte de la Soledad**, on the north side of the Plaza Moch-Cuouh close to the intersection of Calles 8 and 57, is the setting for the **Museo de Estelas Maya**. Many of the Maya artefacts here are badly weathered, but the precise line drawing next to each stone shows you what the designs once looked like. The bulwark also has an interesting exhibition of colonial Campeche. Among the antiquities are 17th and 18th-

century seafaring equipment and armaments used to battle pirate invaders. The museum is open 9 am to 2 pm and 3 to 8 pm Tuesday to Saturday, 9 am to 1 pm on Sunday, closed Monday. Admission is free.

Just across the street from the baluarte is **Parque Principal**. Whereas the sterile, modernistic, shadeless Plaza Moch-Cuouh was built to glorify its government builders, Parque Principal (Plaza de la Independencia) is a pleasant place where locals relax. Construction was begun on the **Catedral de la Concepción**, situated on the north side of the plaza, shortly after the conquistadors established the town, but it wasn't finished for centuries. One of the church's towers is called the **Spanish Tower** because it was completed during Spanish rule. The other, the **Tower of Campeche**, was completed after independence. The cathedral is usually open in the morning and evening. The attractive, arcaded former **Palacio de Gobierno** (or Palacio Municipal) dates only from the 19th century.

Continue north along Calle 8 several blocks to the **Baluarte de Santiago**, at the intersection of Calles 8 and 51. It houses a

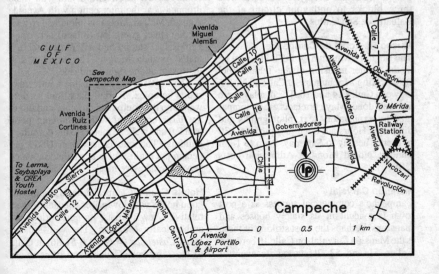

minuscule yet lovely tropical garden, the **Jardín Botánico Xmuch Haltun**, within its walls. There are 250 species of tropical plants set around a lovely courtyard of fountains. Tours of the garden are given in Spanish every hour or so in the morning and evening, and in English at noon and 4 pm. The garden is open Tuesday to Saturday from 9 am to 8 pm and Sunday 9 am to 1 pm. Admission is free.

From the **Baluarte de Santiago**, walk south-east (inland) along Calle 51 to Calle 18, to the Baluarte de San Pedro, sited in the middle of a complex traffic intersection. Within the bulwark is the **Exposición Permanente de Artesanías**, a regional exhibition of crafts, open Monday to Friday from 9 am to 1 pm and 5 to 8 pm. Admission is free.

Continue south along Avenida Circuito Baluartes to the **Baluarte de San Francisco** at Calle 57 and, a block farther along at Calle 59, the **Puerta de Tierra**, or Land Gate. The **Baluarte de San Juan**, at Calles 18 and 65, marks the south-westernmost point of the old city walls. From there, bear right (southwest) along Calle 67 (Avenida Circuito Baluartes) to the intersection of Calles 14 and 67 and the **Baluarte de Santa Rosa**, now a municipal library. Walk north-west three blocks to end your circuit at the Baluarte de San Carlos.

Museo Regional de Campeche

The Regional Museum (☎ 6-91-11) is set up in the former mansion of the Teniente del Rey, or King's Lieutenant, at Calle 59 No 36, between Calles 14 and 16. The displays here are well done: Maya artefacts are accompanied by explanatory text, photographs and diagrams. Hours are 8 am to 2 pm and 2.30 to 8 pm Tuesday to Saturday, 9 am to 1 pm Sunday, closed Monday. Admission costs US$1.

Mansión Carvajal

Campeche's commercial success as a port town is evident in its stately houses and mansions. Perhaps the most striking of these is the Mansión Carvajal, on Calle 10 between Calles 51 and 53. It started its eventful history as the city residence of Don Fernando Carvajal Estrada and his wife Sra María Iavalle de Carvajal. Don Fernando was among Campeche's richest hacendados, or hacienda-owners.

The mansion is open every day except Sunday from early morning until late in the evening, when the craft shops close; you can walk around and have a look for free.

Edzná Ruins Tours

Should you want to visit the ruins at Edzná from Campeche, you can go on a tour organised by one of the larger hotels about US$22. See the section on Edzná for more information.

Places to Stay – bottom end

Hostels Campeche's *CREA Youth Hostel* (☎ (981) 6-18-02), on Avenida Agustín Melgar, is 3½ km south-west of the Plaza Moch-Cuouh off the shore road; the shore road is Avenida Ruiz Cortines in town, but changes its name to Avenida Justo Sierra, then to Avenida Resurgimiento as it heads out of town toward Villahermosa. Buses marked 'Lerma' or 'Playa Bonita' will take you there. Ask the driver to let you off at the Albergue de la Juventud and you'll be dropped near the intersection with Avenida Agustín Melgar. Melgar is unmarked so look for the street going left (inland) between a Pemex fuel station and a VW dealership – that's Avenida Melgar. The hostel is 150 metres up on the right-hand side.

The hostel is actually inside a university sports complex. To find the hostel section, walk into the compound entrance and out to the large courtyard with swimming pool, turn left and walk 25 metres to the dormitory building. The rate is less than US$3 per person per night. There is a cafeteria which serves inexpensive meals.

Hotels Central Campeche has a number of good hotels with low prices. Because it gets relatively few tourists, its hotel prices are authentically Mexican. The well-located *Hotel Castelmar* (☎ (981) 6-51-86) at Calle 61 No 2, between Calles 8 and 10, is an old house surrounding an interior courtyard set with a few plants. The rooms are fairly clean, have fans and hammock hooks and the rooms at the front of the building are large and airy. A room with hot shower and (in some rooms) a balcony is only US$8/10 a single/double. The hotel's name is in huge letters on the façade, visible from the Plaza Moch-Cuouh.

The *Hotel Roma* (☎ (981) 6-38-97) is at Calle 10 No 254, between Calles 59 and 61. Undeniably cheap, its rooms with fan and shower go for US$6.50/8.75 a single/double.

Hotel Reforma (☎ (981) 6-44-64), Calle 8 No 257, between Calles 57 and 59, facing the Baluarte de la Soledad, has a prominent location, low price (US$7.50 a double) and very grungy rooms and showers. If all else fails, or if you're desperate to save a dollar, take a look here.

The *Hotel Colonial* (☎ (981) 6-22-22), Calle 14 No 122, between Calles 55 and 57, offers more comfort for a bit more money. The hotel was once the mansion of Doña Gretrudis Eulalia Torostieta y Zagasti, the former Spanish governor of Tabasco and Yucatán. The well-furnished rooms have good showers with hot water. Price is US$10 a single, US$12 a double, a few dollars more for a room with air-conditioning.

Places to Stay – middle

Hotel América (☎ (981) 6-45-88/76), Calle 10 No 252 (Apdo Postal 94), is a fine colonial house with large, nicely furnished rooms, equipped with good bathrooms, overlooking the interior courtyard. Rooms go for US$15 a single/double with fan; an extra person in a room costs US$4.25 more.

Similarly good value is the *Posada del Angel* (☎ (981) 6-77-18), Calle 10 No 309, between Calles 55 and 53, just off Parque Principal on the east side of the church. The rooms remind one of a cell block, but they're modern and clean, with air-conditioning, for US$18/20 a single/double.

Hotel López (☎ 6-33-44), Calle 12 No 189, between Calles 61 and 63, offers similarly clean rooms with showers at US$15 a

double with a fan, and US$19.50 a double with air-conditioning. It's tidy and quiet.

Places to Stay – top end

The 119-room *Ramada Inn Campeche* (☎ (981) 6-22-33) is at Avenida Ruiz Cortines No 51, just west of Plaza Moch-Cuouh. It has all the standard comforts: air-conditioned rooms with balconies, a swimming pool, restaurant, bar, nightclub, coffee shop and a fenced parking area. Prices are reasonable: US$46/60/70 for a single/double/triple; suites cost US$80 to US$92.

Just south of the Ramada is its competition, the older but still comfortable *Hotel Baluartes* (☎ (981) 6-39-11), Avenida Ruiz Cortines s/n. The Baluartes' well-used rooms are still air-conditioned and comfortable, and cheaper at US$40/50 for a single/double. The hotel has a pool, a nice dining room, an air-conditioned garden café, a nightclub and a vast open car park.

Places to Eat

Campeche has some good, reasonably priced seafood – particularly its shrimp *(camarones)*, as this is a major shrimping port.

Places to Eat – bottom end

The cheapest eats are at the Mercado Pedro Saiz de Baranda, at the eastern end of Calle 53 across Avenida Circuito Baluartes Este.

Among the cheapest eateries is the *Restaurant Marganzo* (☎ 6-23-28), Calle 8 No 265, between Calles 57 and 59. Seafood plates cost US$7 or so, traditional Mexican plates for much less.

Also quite cheap is the *Cafetería y Nevería Continental* (☎ 6-22-66), Calle 61 No 2, at the corner of Calle 8. They have ice cream, cakes, desserts and drinks, and also a few cheap lunch items. Filete de pescado goes for US$3.25. The hearty soup *caldo xochitl* is only half that much.

For sweet rolls, biscuits, bread or cakes, head for the *Panificadora Nueva España*, Calle 10 at the corner of Calle 61, which has a large assortment of fresh baked goods at very low prices.

The *Café y Restaurant Campeche* (☎ 6-

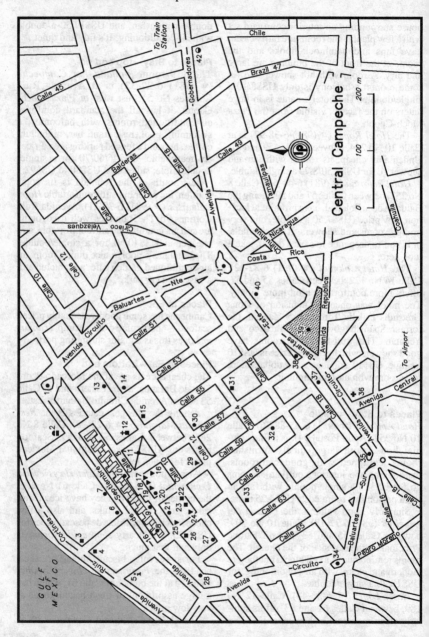

Central Campeche

■ PLACES TO STAY

3 Ramada Inn Campeche
4 Hotel Baluartes
15 Posada del Angel
18 Hotel Reforma
22 Hotel América
23 Hotel Roma
26 Hotel Castelmar
31 Hotel Colonial
33 Hotel López

▼ PLACES TO EAT

16 Café & Restaurant Campeche
17 Restaurant del Parque
18 Restaurant Marganzo
19 Restaurant-Bar Familiar La Parroquía
24 Panificadora Nueva España
25 Restaurant Miramar
26 Cafetería y Nevería Continental
29 Restaurant Vegetariana Natura 2000

OTHER

1 Baluarte de Santiago & Jardín
   Botánico

2 Post Office (Edificio Federal)
5 Tourist Office
6 Bank
7 Bank
8 Plaza Moch-Cuouh
9 Puerta del Mar
10 Baluarte de la Soledad
11 Parque Principal
12 Catedral de la Concepción
13 Mansión Carvajal
14 Bank
20 Bank
21 Bank
27 Bank
28 Baluarte de San Carlos
30 Cine Selem
32 Museo Regional de Campeche
34 Baluarte de Santa Rosa
35 Baluarte de San Juan
36 IMSS Hospital
37 Puerta de Tierra
38 Baluarte de San Francsico
39 Alameda
40 Market
41 Baluarte de San Pedro
42 ADO (1st-Class) Bus Terminal

21-28), Calle 57 No 2, at Calle 55, is beneath the very beat-up Hotel Campeche facing Parque Principal. The restaurant is very simple, loud and bright. Prices are refreshingly low: the *platillo del día* (daily special) usually costs only US$3. Fish and meat dishes cost up to US$5. The Campeche is open early for breakfast.

Near the Campeche is the *Restaurant del Parque* (☎ 6-02-40), Calle 57 No 8, a cheerful little place serving fish dishes for about US$5, meat and shrimp for up to US$7 or US$8. Fruit drinks, alcoholic beverages and desserts are served and the restaurant opens early for breakfast.

Near the Restaurant Campeche is the aptly named *Café Literario El Murmullo* (The Murmur), where the mostly male clientele sip and murmur.

Restaurant Vegetariano Natura 2000, corner of Calles 12 and 59, is plain and simple. Fruit, granola, tofu, yoghurt and similar good, healthy stuff is combined in imaginative ways and served at reasonable prices, usually not exceeding US$2.75 per item. It's open every day from breakfast until tea, but closes at 4.30 pm. You can also get good health food at the *Natura 2000* health food shop on Calle 12 between 55 and 57.

Places to Eat – middle

Campeche's most famous traditional seafood place is the *Restaurant Miramar* (☎ 6-28-83), corner of Calles 8 and 61 a block south of the Puerta del Mar. Oyster cocktails are US$4, and chicken, shrimp and beef dishes cost US$7 to US$9. If you're on a strict budget, have the rice with seafood platter for US$5. Miramar is open 8 am to midnight Monday to Friday, till 1 am Saturday, and 11 am to 7 pm Sunday.

Perhaps the best known restaurant in town is the *Restaurant-Bar Familiar La Parroquía* (☎ 6-18-29), now in a new location at Calle 8 No 267, between 57 and 59, facing the Puerta del Mar. La Parroquía serves breakfasts for US$1.75 to US$3.50 from 7 to 10 am Monday to Friday, and substantial lunches and dinners like chuleta de cerdo (pork chop), filete a la tampiqueña, shrimp cocktail, shrimp salad and even fresh pampano, for US$4 to US$9. You can have a full meal here for US$6 to US$16.

The air-conditioned restaurants in the two top hotels also offer good food at decent prices. The *Restaurante La Almena* in the Hotel Baluartes has a *long* menu with everything from enchiladas and tacos to fish and shrimp to chicken; there are 20 meat dishes. Expect to spend US$10 to US$22 per person here.

Entertainment

On Friday evenings at 8 pm from September to May (weather permitting), the state tourism authorities sponsor Estampas Turísticas, performances of folk music and dancing, in Plaza Moch-Cuouh. Other performances, sponsored by the city government, take place in Parque Principal on Thursday, Friday and Saturday evenings at about 7 pm. Be sure to confirm these times and places with the tourist office.

Campeche's most popular discos are at the Ramada Inn and Hotel Baluartes. Local cinemas sometimes have English-language films with Spanish subtitles.

Getting There & Away

Air The airport is west of the railway station at the end of Avenida López Portillo (Avenida Central), or 3½ km from Plaza Moch-Cuouh. You must take a taxi (US$4) to the city centre.

Bus Campeche's ADO bus terminal is on Avenida Gobernadores, 1½ km from the centre. City buses marked 'Gobernadores' or 'Centro' run past the bus station on Avenida Gobernadores. As you leave the bus station, turn left and you'll be looking down Avenida Gobernadores in the direction of the centre of town. The taxi fare is about US$2 to any hotel, more to the youth hostel.

Daily buses go to the following places from Campeche. Prices and times are for 1st class; 2nd class is slightly cheaper and may be slower.

Acayucan – 690 km, 10 hours (US$13.75), three evening buses.

Cancún – 512 km, nine hours; change at Mérida.

Chetumal – 422 km, seven hours (US$7), two buses.

Edzná – 66 km, 1½ hours; or take a faster bus to San Antonio Cayal (45 km) and hitch south from there.

Escárcega – 150 km, 2½ hours (US$6), eleven 1st-class buses.

Mérida – 195 km (short route via Becal), three hours; 250 km (long route via Uxmal), four hours; 33 1st-class buses (US$7), by ADO round the clock; 13 2nd-class buses, US$6.50, by Autobuses del Sur.

Mexico City – 1360 km, 21 hours (US$26), eight buses.

Palenque – 362 km, 5½ hours (US$7.25), one direct bus at 6.30 pm; many other buses drop you at Catazajá (Palenque turnoff), 27 km north of Palenque village.

San Andrés Tuxtla – 770 km, 12½ hours; two 1st-class buses daily for US$14.75.

San Cristóbal de las Casas – 820 km, 14 hours; change at Villahermosa.

Tuxtla Gutiérrez – 736 km, 12 hours; change at Villahermosa.

Uxmal – 171 km, 2½ hours; see Mérida (long route) schedule.

Veracruz – 925 km, 15 hours; two 1st-class evening buses for US$17.75.

Villahermosa – 450 km, seven hours; 15 1st-class (US$9) buses; they'll drop you at Catazajá (Palenque junction).

For village buses to Cayal, Pich and Hool (for Edzná), go to the market at the eastern end of Calle 53 across Avenida Circuito Baluartes Este.

Train The railway station is three km east of the centre, south of Avenida Gobernadores on Avenida Héroes de Nacozari in the district called Colonia Cuatro Caminos. Buses departing from a stop to the right (west) as you leave the station will take you to the centre.

Getting Around

To/From the Airport The airport is east of the railway station at the northern end of Avenida López Portillo. To reach the air terminal you must go east to Avenida López

Top: Lagoon at Xel-Ha, a coastal inlet near Tulum, Quintana Roo (RB)
Bottom: View of Nun's Quadrangle at Uxmal, showing corbel arch entrance, Yucatán state (RB)

Top: House of the Halach Uinik at coastal ruins of Tulum, Quintana Roo (RB)
Left: Governor's Palace, Uxmal, Yucatán state (JL)
Right: Platform of Venus, Chichén Itzá, Yucatan state (TW)

Portillo, then north to the terminal, 3½ km from Plaza Moch-Cuouh.

Bus The ADO bus terminal is 1½ km north-east of Plaza Moch-Cuouh along Avenida Gobernadores (Highway 180).

Train The railway station is three km north-east of the centre, south of Avenida Gobernadores on Avenida Héroes de Nacozari in the district called Colonia Cuatro Caminos.

AROUND CAMPECHE
Forts
Four km south of the Plaza Moch-Cuouh along the coast road stands the Fuerte de San Luis, an 18th-century fortress of which only a few battlements remain. Near the fort, a road off to the left (south-east) climbs the hill one km to the Fuerte de San Miguel, a restored fortress once housing the archaeological museum but now closed to the public. The view of the city and the sea is beautiful, but the walk uphill is a killer.

Getting There & Away To reach the Fuerte de San Luis, take a 'Lerma' or 'Playa Bonita' bus south-west along the coastal highway (toward Villahermosa).

Beaches
The Balneario Popular, four km south of Campeche along the coastal road just past the Fuerte de San Luis, should be avoided. A few km farther along is Playa Bonita, which has some facilities (restaurant, lockers, toilets) but water of questionable cleanliness and, at the weekends, wall-to-wall local flesh.

If you're really hard up for a swim, head south-west to the town of Seybaplaya, 33 km from Campeche. The highway skirts narrow, pure-white beaches dotted with fishing smacks, the water is much cleaner, but there are no facilities. The best beach here is called Payucan.

ESCÁRCEGA
Population: 18,000
Most buses passing through Escárcega stop here to give passengers a refreshment break, and some travellers change buses. There is no other reason to stop in this town, located at the junction of highways 186 and 261, 150 km south of Campeche and 301 km from Villahermosa.

The town is spread out along two km of Highway 186 toward Chetumal. If you plan to spend the night or change bus companies here, you may find yourself walking a km or two.

It's 1½ km between the ADO and Autobuses del Sur bus stations. Most hotels are nearer to the Autobuses del Sur bus station than to the ADO; most of the better restaurants are near the ADO bus station.

ESCÁRCEGA TO CHETUMAL
Highway 186 heads due east from Escárcega through the scrubby jungle to Chetumal. Right on the border between the states of Campeche and Quintana Roo near the village of Xpujil, 153 km east of Escárcega and 120 km west of Chetumal, are several important Maya archaeological sites: Xpujil, Becan, Chicanna and Río Bec. These pristine unrestored sites, largely free of tourists, will fascinate true ruins buffs, but be forewarned that those expecting park-like sites such as Uxmal and Chichén Itzá will be disappointed. Most of what you see here is jungle and rubble. Exploring these sites remains a pleasure reserved for the very adventurous with camping gear and lots of insect repellent, or those with their own cars, as Xpujil has no services.

CAMPECHE TO MÉRIDA – SHORT ROUTE (HIGHWAY 180)
This is the fastest way to go and if you simply buy a bus ticket from Campeche to Mérida your bus will follow this route. If you'd prefer to go the long way via Edzná, Kabah and Uxmal, you must ask for a seat on one of the less frequent long route buses. If you'd like to stop at one of the towns along the short route, catch a 2nd-class bus.

Hecelchakan, Calkini & Becal
Hecelchakan, 77 km north-east of Campe-

che, is the home of the Museo Arqueologíco del Camino Real, where you will find some burial artefacts from the island of Jaina, as well as ceramics and jewellery from other sites. The museum is open from Monday to Saturday from 9 am to 6 pm, closed Sunday. The Church of San Francisco is the centre of festivities on the saint's day, 4 October. From 9 to 18 August a popular festival called the Novenario is held, with bullfights, dancing and refreshments.

After Hecelchakan, it's 24 km to **Calkini**, site of the 17th-century Church of San Luis de Tolosa, with a Plateresque portal and lots of baroque decoration. Each year the Festival of San Luis is celebrated on 19 August.

Becal is eight km from Calkini just before you enter the state of Yucatán. It is a centre of Yucatán's Panama hat trade. The soft, pliable hats, called jipijapa by the locals, have been woven by townfolk from the fibres of the huano palm tree in humid limestone caves since the mid-19th century. The caves provide just the right atmosphere for shaping the fibres, keeping them pliable and minimising breakage.

From Becal it's 85 km to Mérida.

EDZNÁ

Most travellers take the long route (Highway 261) from Campeche to Mérida, in order to visit the various ruin sites. The closest ruins to Campeche are at Edzná, south of Highway 261.

Edzná, meaning House of Grimaces or House of Echoes, may well have been host to both, as there has been a settlement here since about 800 BC. Most of the carvings are of a much later date: 550 to 810 AD. Though a long way from such Puuc Hill sites as Uxmal and Kabah, some of the architecture here is similar to Puuc style.

The site is open from 8 am to 5 pm daily, for US$4 admission.

Although the archaeological zone covers two sq km, the best part is the main plaza, 160 metres long and 100 metres wide, surrounded by temples. Every Maya site has huge masses of stone, but at Edzná there are

cascades of it, terrace upon terrace of bleached limestone.

The major temple here, the 30-metre-high Temple of Five Levels, is to the left as you enter the plaza from the ticket kiosk. Built on a vast platform, it rises five levels from base to roofcomb, with rooms and some weathered decoration of masks, serpents and jaguars' heads on each level. A great central staircase of 65 steps goes right to the top. On the opposite (right) side of the plaza as you enter is a monumental staircase 100 metres wide, which once led up to the Temple of the Moon. At the far end of the plaza is a ruined temple that may have been the priests' quarters.

Getting There & Away

The ruins of Edzná are 20 km south of the village of San Antonio Cayal, which is 44 km east of Campeche on Highway 261.

From Campeche's market, at the eastern end of Calle 53 across Avenida Circuito Baluartes Este, catch a 2nd-class village bus early in the morning headed for Edzná. This will probably mean taking a bus going to the village of Pich, some 15 km south-east of Edzná, or to Hool, about 25 km south-west. Either bus will drop you at the access road to the site. A sign just north of the junction says 'Edzná 2 km', but don't let it fool you. The ruins are just 500 metres beyond the sign, only about 400 metres off the highway. Coming from the north and east, get off at San Antonio Cayal and hitch or catch a bus 20 km south to Edzná.

If you're coming from the south (Palenque) in your own car and you don't plan to visit Campeche, you can bypass that city and head directly for Edzná via the village of Hool. This road bypasses Campeche completely, turning east and north from the coast near Champotón. When you leave you'll have to depend on hitching or buses to get you to San Antonio Cayal, from where you can hitch or catch a bus west back to Campeche, or to the north-east towards Uxmal.

Alternatively, guided tours (US$22 per person) are set up by the larger hotels in Campeche if they have enough people.

BOLONCHÉN DE REJÓN & XTACUMBILXUNAAN

Heading east from San Antonio Cayal, 40 km brings you to Hopelchén, where Highway 261 turns north. The next town to appear out of the flat, dry jungle is Bolonchén de Rejón, after 34 km. The local festival of the Santa Cruz is held each year on May 3rd.

Bolonchén is near the Grutas de Xtacumbilxunaan, located about three km south of town.

You can visit the cavern by taking a 30 to 45-minute tour with the guide/caretaker for the price of a tip. The cave is 'open' whenever the caretaker is around, which is most of the time during daylight hours.

Highway 261 continues into Yucatán state to Uxmal, with a side road leading to the ruin sites of the Puuc Route. See these sections for more information.

Yucatán State

MÉRIDA

Population: 600,000

The capital of the state of Yucatán is a proud charming city of narrow streets, colonial buildings and shady parks. It has been the centre of Maya culture in Yucatán since before the conquistadors arrived; today it is the peninsula's centre of commerce as well. There are lots of hotels and restaurants of every class and price range and good transportation services to any part of the peninsula and the country.

Mérida seems busiest with tourists in high summer (July and August), which is the worst time to visit because of the humidity. In winter there are fewer visitors and there's plenty of room for everybody.

History

Francisco de Montejo the Younger founded a Spanish colony at Campeche in 1540. From this base he was able to take advantage of political dissension among the Maya, conquering Tihó (now Mérida) in 1542. By the end of the decade, Yucatán was mostly under Spanish colonial rule.

When Montejo's conquistadors entered defeated Tihó, they found a major Maya settlement of lime-mortared stone which reminded them of Roman architectural legacies in Mérida, Spain. They promptly renamed the city after its Spanish likeness and proceeded to build it into the colonial capital. Mérida took its colonial orders directly from Spain, not from Mexico City, and Yucatán has had a distinct cultural and political identity ever since.

During the War of the Castes (1847-55) only Mérida and Campeche were able to hold out against the rebel forces; the rest of Yucatán came under Indian control. On the brink of surrender, the ruling class in Mérida was saved by reinforcements sent from central Mexico in exchange for Mérida agreeing to take orders from Mexico City. Though Yucatán is certainly part of Mexico, there is still a strong feeling of local pride in Mérida, a feeling that the Mayab (Maya lands) are a special realm set apart from the rest of the country.

Orientation

Mérida's street grid makes it relatively easy to find your way around. Odd-numbered streets run east to west, with higher numbered streets to the south; even-numbered streets run north to south, with higher numbered streets to the west. The main plaza, or Plaza Mayor, is bound by Calles 60, 62, 61 and 63. Be advised that house numbers may progress very slowly; you cannot know whether Calle 57 No 481 and Calle 57 No 544 are one block or ten blocks apart. Perhaps for this reason, addresses are usually given in this form: Calle 57 No 481 X 56 y 58 (between Calles 56 and 58). Most of the hotels and restaurants recommended here are within a five-block walk of the main plaza.

Though the centre of Mérida is around the Plaza Mayor, many important buildings and services are along the grand Paseo de Montejo, a wide boulevard which begins nine blocks north of the plaza and extends northwards to the outskirts of the city.

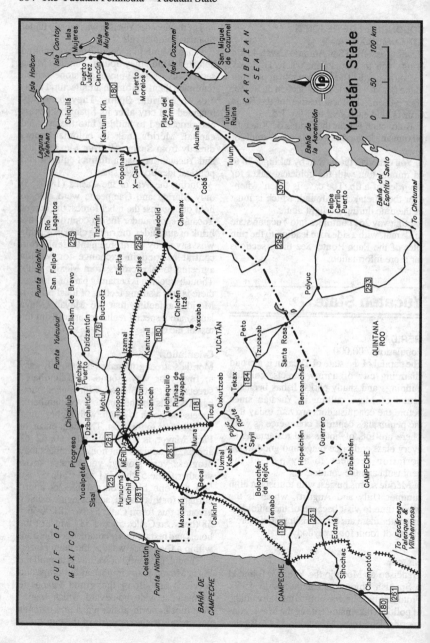

Information

Tourist Office There are information booths of minimal usefulness at the airport and the 1st-class bus station. Preferable is the Tourist Information Centre (☎ (99) 24-92-90, 24-93-89), at the corner of Calles 60 and 57, in the south-west corner of the huge Teatro Peón Contreras, less than two blocks north of Plaza Mayor.

Money Banamex operates a casa de cambio in the Casa de Montejo on the main plaza. It's open from 9 am to 1.30 pm Monday to Friday. In addition, there are lots of banks along Calle 65 between Calles 60 and 62 Banking hours are generally 9.30 am to 1.30 pm, Monday to Friday. Casa de Cambio del Sureste (☎ 28-21-52), Calle 56 No 491 X 57 y 59, is open Monday to Friday 9 am to 5 pm, Saturday and Sunday 9 am to 1 pm. Note that there are no currency exchange facilities at Mérida's airport.

Post & Telecommunications The main post office (Correos) (☎ (99) 21-25-61) is in the market area on Calle 65 between Calles

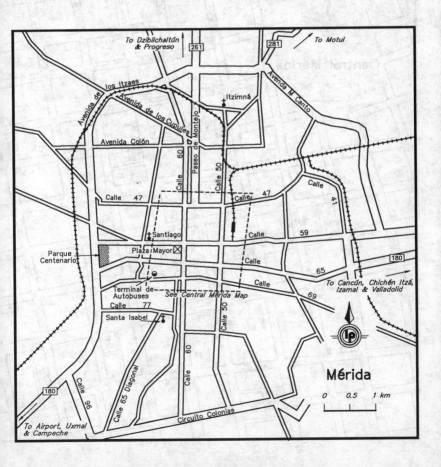

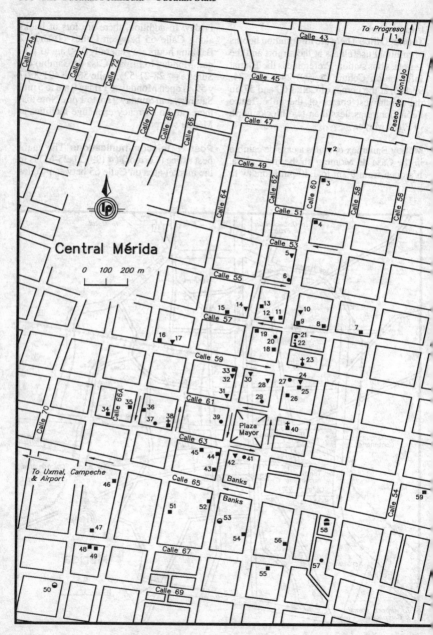

Central Mérida

0   100   200 m

To Progreso

Calle 43
Calle 45
Calle 47
Calle 49
Calle 51
Calle 53
Calle 55
Calle 57
Calle 59
Calle 61
Calle 63
Calle 65
Calle 67
Calle 69

Calle 74a
Calle 74
Calle 72
Calle 70
Calle 68
Calle 66
Calle 64
Calle 62
Calle 60
Calle 58
Calle 56
Calle 54

Calle 66A
Calle 70

Paseo de Montejo

Plaza Mayor

Banks
Banks

To Uxmal, Campeche
& Airport

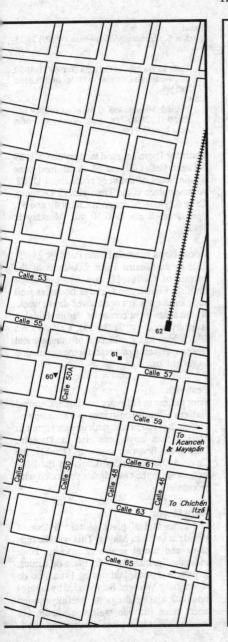

■ PLACES TO STAY

3   Hotel Los Aluxes
4   Hotel Trinidad Galería
7   Hotel Mucuy
8   Posada Toledo
9   Hotel Casa del Balam
11 Hotel Mérida Misión Park Inn
13 Hotel Trinidad
15 Hotel El Castellano
16 Hotel del Gobernador
18 Hotel del Parque
19 Hotel Colonial
25 Hotel Caribe
26 Gran Hotel
33 Hotel Reforma
34 Hotel Las Monjas
35 Hotel Latino
36 Hotel Margarita
43 Hotel Sevilla
44 Casa de Huéspedes Peniche
45 Hotel Lord
46 Casa Bowen
47 Posada del Angel
48 Hotel New Victoria
49 Hotel Casa Becil
51 Hotel María Teresa
52 Hotel Oviedo
54 Hotel México
55 Hotel América
56 Hotel Peninsular
59 Hotel Dolores Alba
61 Hotel Janeiro

▼ PLACES TO EAT

2   Restaurant La Casona
5   Patio de las Fajitas
10 Restaurant El Tucho
12 Pop Cafetería & Restaurante Portico
    del Peregrino
14 Las Mil Tortas
17 Restaurant Cedro del Libano
24 Restaurant Tiano's
28 Café-Restaurant Express
30 Pizzería de Vito Corleone
31 El Louvre
32 Jugos El Trapiche
42 Panificadora Montejo
60 Los Almendros

    OTHER

1   Anthropology Museum (Palacio
    Cantón)

*   KEY CONTINUED NEXT PAGE

6	Parque Santa Lucia
20	Universidad de Yucatán
21	Teatro Peón Contreras
22	Tourist Information Centre
23	Iglesia de Jesús
27	Parque Hildalgo
29	Palacio de Gobierno
37	Casa de los Artesanías
38	Ex-Convento de las Monjas
39	Palacio Municipal
40	Cathedral
41	Casa de Montejo (Banamex)
50	Terminal de Autobuses
53	Progreso Bus Station
57	Mercado Municipal
58	Main Post Office
62	Railway Station

56 and 56A, open Monday to Friday from 8 am to 7 pm and Saturday from 9 am to 1 pm. There are postal service booths at the airport and the 1st-class bus station, open on weekdays. There is an American Express office which holds mail for clients at the Hotel Los Aluxes, Calle 60 No 444, at the corner of Calle 49.

To make long-distance telephone calls, go to the casetas at the airport, at the corner of Calles 59 and 62 or Calles 64 and 57, or on Calle 60 between Calles 53 and 55. The main bus station has a caseta, Ladatel phones, and a public fax machine.

Foreign Consulates A number of countries have consulates in Mérida. If yours is not listed here, call your embassy in Mexico City.

Belgium
    Calle 25 No 159, between Calles 28 & 30 (☎ (99) 25-29-39)
Belize
    You can get information about travel in Belize at the British Vice-Consulate (see below), weekday mornings from 9.30 am to noon.
Denmark
    Calle 32 No 198 at Calle 17, Colonia Garcia Ginerés
France
    Avenida Itzaes 242 (☎ (99) 25-46-06)

Spain
    Km 6, Carretera Mérida-Uman (☎ (99) 29-15-20)
UK
    Calle 53 No 489, at Calle 58 (☎ (99) 21-67-99, 28-39-62), open Monday to Friday from 8.30 am to 5 pm.
USA
    Paseo de Montejo 453, at Avenida Colón (☎ (99) 25-50-11, 25-86-77), open Monday to Friday from 8 am to 4 pm.

Laundry There's a good laundry on Calle 59 between Calles 72 and 74. A full load done within hours of delivery costs about US$2. Another place is the Tintorería El Danubio, Calle 62 No 426, between Calles 49 and 51, open from 8 am to 6.30 pm, Monday to Friday.

Bookshops Librería Dante Peón (☎ 24-95-22), in the Teatro Peón Contreras at the corner of Calles 60 and 57, has some English, French and German books as well as Spanish ones. It's open seven days a week. At the south-west corner of Parque Hidalgo is Hollywood (☎ 21-36-19), Calle 60 No 496, which has a selection of international newspapers, magazines and some novels and travel guides.

Festivals
Prior to Lent in February or March, Carnival features colourful costumes and nonstop festivities. It is celebrated with greater vigour in Mérida than anywhere else in Yucatán. During the first two weeks in October, the Cristo de las Ampollas (Christ of the Blisters) statue in the cathedral is venerated with processions.

Plaza Mayor
The most logical place to start a tour of Mérida is in Plaza Mayor. This was the religious and social centre of ancient Tihó; under the Spanish it was the Plaza de Armas, or parade ground, laid out by Francisco de Montejo the Younger. Surrounded by harmonious colonial buildings, its carefully pruned laurel trees provide welcome shade. On Sunday, the main plaza's adjoining road-

ways are off limits to traffic. Plaza Mayor is bound on all sides by some of the city's most impressive buildings.

Cathedral On the east side of the plaza, on the site of a Maya temple, is Mérida's huge, hulking, severe cathedral, begun in 1561 and completed in 1598. Some of the stone from the Maya temple was used in the cathedral's construction.

Walk through one of the three doors in the baroque façade and into the sanctuary. To your right is a painting of Tutul Xiú, *cacique* (local ruler) of the town of Maní, paying his respects to his ally Francisco de Montejo at Tihó. Xiú's descendants still live in Mérida.

Look in the small chapel to the left of the principal altar for Mérida's most famous religious artefact, a statue called Cristo de las Ampollas, or the Christ of the Blisters. Local legend has it that this statue was carved from a tree in the town of Ichmul. The tree, hit by lightning, supposedly burned for an entire night yet showed no sign of fire. The statue carved from the tree was placed in the local church where it alone is said to have survived the fiery destruction of the church, though it was blackened and blistered from the heat. It was moved to the Mérida cathedral in 1645. The faithful still make pilgrimages here.

The rest of the church's interior is very plain, its rich decoration having been stripped by angry peasants at the height of anticlerical feeling during the Mexican Revolution.

Palacio de Gobierno On the north side of the plaza, the Palacio de Gobierno houses the state of Yucatán's executive government offices. It was built in 1892 on the site of the palace of the colonial governors. The palace is open every day from 8 am to 8 pm.

See also the historical murals painted by local artist Fernando Castro Pacheco. After 25 years of work, the murals were completed in 1978.

In vivid colours, the murals portray a symbolic history of the Maya and their interaction with the Spaniards. Over the stairwell is a painting of Maya sacred corn,

the 'ray of sun from the gods'. On Sunday at 11 am, there's usually a concert (jazz, classical pops, traditional Yucatecan) in the Salón de la Historia of the Palacio de Gobierno.

Palacio Municipal Facing the cathedral across the square, the Palacio Municipal (Town Hall) is topped by a clock tower. Originally built in 1542, it has twice been refurbished, in the 1730s and the 1850s.

Today the building also serves as the venue for performances of Yucatecan dances (especially the *jarana*) and music at the weekly Vaquería Regional, a regional festival held to celebrate the branding of the cattle on haciendas. Performances are on Monday evenings at 9 pm.

Every Sunday at 1 pm, the city sponsors a re-enactment of a colourful mestizo wedding at the Palacio Municipal. The performance is by the city's ballet folklorico and the police orchestra.

Casa de Montejo From its construction in 1549 until the 1970s, the mansion on the south side of the plaza was occupied by the Montejo family. Sometimes called the Palacio de Montejo, it was built at the command of the conqueror of Mérida, Francisco de Montejo the Younger. These days the great house shelters a branch of Banamex and you can look around inside whenever the bank is open (usually from 9 am to 1.30 pm, Monday to Friday).

If the bank is closed, content yourself with a close look at the Plateresque façade, where triumphant conquistadors with halberds hold their feet on the necks of generic barbarians (who are not Maya, but the association is inescapable). Also gazing across the plaza from the façade are busts of Montejo the Elder, his wife and his daughter. The armorial shields are those of the Montejo family.

Walking Tour
A block north of the Plaza Mayor is the shady refuge of **Parque Hidalgo**. The park's benches always hold a variety of conversationalists, lovers, taxi drivers, hammock pedlars and tourists.

At the far end of the park, several restaurants, including Café El Mesón and Tiano's, offer alfresco dining. Tiano's often has a marimba band in the evening. The city sponsors free marimba concerts here on Sunday mornings at 11.30 am as well.

Just to the north of the parque rises the 17th-century **Iglesia de Jesús**, also called the Iglesia El Tercer Orden. Built by the Jesuits in 1618, it is the surviving edifice in a complex of Jesuit buildings which once filled the entire city block. Always interested in education, the Jesuits founded schools which later gave birth to the Universidad de Yucatán nearby. The 19th century General Cepeda Peraza collected a library of 15,000 volumes, which is housed in a building behind the church.

Directly in front of the church is the little **Parque de la Madre**, sometimes called Parque Morelos. The modern madonna and child statue, which is a common fixture of town squares in this nation of high birth rates, is a copy of a statue by Lenoir which stands in the Jardin du Luxembourg in Paris.

Just north of Parque de la Madre you confront the enormous bulk of the great **Teatro Peón Contreras**, built from 1900 to 1908 during Mérida's henéquen heyday. Designed by Italian architect Enrico Deserti, it boasts a main staircase of Carrara marble, a dome with frescos by Italian artists imported for the purpose and, in its southwest corner, the Tourist Information Centre.

The main entrance to the theatre is at the corner of Calles 60 and 57. A gallery inside the entrance often holds exhibits by local painters and photographers; hours are usually 9 am to 2 pm and 5 to 9 pm Monday to Friday, 9 am to 2 pm Saturday and Sunday. To see the grand theatre itself, you'll have to attend a performance. Perhaps the most interesting performance is Yucatán y sus Raices (Yucatán & its Roots). See the Entertainment section for more details.

Across Calle 60 from the theatre is the entrance to the main building of the **Universidad de Yucatán**. Though the Jesuits provided education to Yucatán's youth for centuries, the modern university was only established in the 19th century by Governor Felipe Carrillo Puerto and General Manuel Cepeda Peraza. The story of the university's founding is rendered graphically in a mural done in 1961 by Manuel Lizama. Ask for directions to the mural.

The central courtyard of the university building is the scene of concerts and folk performances every Tuesday or Friday evening at 9 pm (check with the Tourist Information Centre for performance dates and times).

A block north of the university, at the intersection of Calles 60 and 55, is the pretty little **Parque Santa Lucia**, with arcades on the north and west sides. When Mérida was a lot smaller, this was where travellers would get into or out of the stagecoaches which bumped over the rough roads of the peninsula, linking towns and villages with the provincial capital.

Today the park is the venue for orchestral performances of Yucatecan music on Thursday at 9 pm and Sunday at 11 am. Also here on Sunday at 11 am is the Bazar de Artesanías, the local handicrafts market.

Paseo de Montejo

The Paseo de Montejo was an attempt by Mérida's 19th-century city planners to create a wide European-style grand boulevard, similar to Mexico City's Paseo de la Reforma or Paris's Champs Elysées. Since this is Mérida, not Paris, the boulevard is more modest. But it is still a beautiful swath of green and open space in an urban conglomeration of stone and concrete.

As Yucatán has always looked upon itself as distinct from the rest of Mexico, the peninsula's powerful hacendados and commercial barons maintained good business and social contacts with Europe. Europe's architectural and social influence can be seen along the paseo in the surviving fine mansions built by wealthy families around the turn of the century. Many other mansions have been torn down to make way for the banks, hotels and other establishments. Most of the remaining mansions are north of Calle

37, which is three blocks north of the Anthropology Museum.

Anthropology Museum The great white palace at the corner of Paseo de Montejo and Calle 43 is the Museo Regional de Antropología de Yucatán, housed in the Palacio Cantón. The great mansion was designed by Enrico Deserti, also responsible for the Teatro Peón Contreras. Construction took place from 1909 to 1911. The mansion's owner, General Francisco Cantón Rosado (1833-1917) lived here for only six years before his death. No building in Mérida exceeds it in splendour or pretension. It's a fitting symbol of the grand aspirations of Mérida's elite during the last years of the Porfiriato.

Admission to the museum costs US$0.75; it's open Tuesday to Saturday from 8 am to 8 pm, Sunday from 8 am to 2 pm, closed Monday. The museum shop is open from 8 am to 3 pm (2 pm on Sunday). Labels on the museum's exhibits are in Spanish only.

The museum covers the peninsula's history from the very beginning, when mastodons roamed here. Exhibits on Maya culture include explanations of the forehead-flattening which was done to beautify babies and other practices such as sharpening teeth and implanting them with tiny jewels. If you plan to visit archaeological sites near Mérida, you can study the many exhibits here – lavishly illustrated with plans and photographs – which cover the great Maya cities of Mayapán, Uxmal and Chichén Itzá, as well as lesser sites.

Monumento a la Patria At the intersection with Avenida Colón is the Parque de las Américas, which boasts trees and shrubs collected from many countries of the western hemisphere. Walking north two blocks from Avenida Colón brings you to the Monument to the Fatherland, an elaborate sculpture in neo-Maya style executed in 1956 by Rómulo Rozo. The fatherland, here, takes on a distinctly Maya appearance.

Parque Centenario
On the western edge of the city, 12 blocks from the Plaza Mayor, lies the large, verdant Parque Centenario, bordered by Avenida de los Itzaes, the highway to the airport and Campeche. There's a zoo in the park which specialises in exhibiting the fauna of Yucatán. To get there, take a bus westwards along Calle 61 or 65.

Places to Stay
Mérida has an excellent array of lodgings in all price ranges, from the basic but very cheap to international luxury class. Most of the cheap and middle-range hotels are within about six blocks of the plaza; the largest concentration of luxury hotels is along the Paseo de Montejo, 12 to 16 long blocks from the plaza.

Places to Stay – bottom end
Prices for basic but suitable double rooms in Mérida range from about US$12 to US$22. This price can get you a small but clean room with fan and private shower, only a short walk from the plaza. All hotels should provide purified drinking water at no extra charge (ask for *agua purificada*). The list below is in order of price, from the cheapest up.

Hotel Las Monjas (☎ (99) 21-98-62), Calle 66A No 509 at the corner of Calle 63, is one of the best deals in town. All 26 rooms in this little place have ceiling fans and running water (sinks or private baths with hot and cold water). Rooms are tiny and most are dark, but they are clean. The price is US$12 to US$14 a double.

Hotel Margarita (☎ (99) 23-72-36), Calle 66 No 506, between Calles 61 and 63, is a favourite with foreigners because of its low price, convenient location and clean (if very small) rooms with fan and running water for US$10.75 a single, US$12 a double, US$14 a twin, US$17 a triple and US$19 a quad. Air-conditioning is available in some rooms for a few dollars more.

Casa de Huéspedes Peniche (☎ (99) 21-31-35), Calle 62 No 507, between 63 and 65, has some nice period touches but is woefully rundown. All rooms have a fan (showers are shared) and the Peniche is close to the plaza. Rates are different for each room, but generally about US$7/10 a single/double. Make sure your room door locks before you rent.

Hotel Latino (☎ (99) 21-48-31), Calle 66 No 505 between Calles 61 and 63, takes the overflow from the Hotel Margarita. The Latino lacks something of the Margarita's convivial spirit and prices are a bit higher, but it's still pretty good value.

Hotel Mucuy (☎ (99) 21-10-37), Calle 57 No 481, between Calles 56 and 58, is a pleasant family-run place with 26 tidy rooms on two floors facing a courtyard. Sra Ofelia Comin and her daughter Ofelia speak English and Sr Alfredo Comin understands it. Rooms with ceiling fan and private shower cost US$13.50/17/20 a single/double/triple.

Hotel María Teresa (☎ (99) 21-10-39), Calle 64 No 529 between Calles 65 and 67, could be a bit tidier but most of the bare rooms are acceptable. With fan and private bath, doubles cost US$14 to 17; with air-con US$20.

Hotel El Caminante (☎ (99) 23-67-30), Calle 64 No 539, between 65 and 67, is a half-block south of the María Teresa. The cell-like rooms are neat and well kept by the friendly Pérez Hernández family. Doubles cost US$17 with fans. The court serves as a car park.

Casa Bowen (☎ (99) 21-65-77), Calle 66 No 521B between Calles 65 and 67, is a longtime favourite with budget travellers. It's a large old Mérida house which has been converted to a hotel; the building next door has been joined to it and renovated. Rooms are very simple, even bare, and some are quite dark, but all have the necessary fans and showers. Rates are US$12.50 a single, US$14.50 a double with fan and US$20 a double with air-con.

There are a few suitable hostelries near Mérida's central bus station. The ones facing the station are unbearably noisy and hot, but others on nearby streets are better, if slightly overpriced. The *Hotel Casa Becil* (☎ (99) 21-29-57), Calle 67 No 550C between Calles

66 and 68, is a converted town house with small guest rooms at the back. With a private shower and fan, the price is US$16 to US$20 a double.

Hotel New Victoria (☎ (99) 24-09-72), Calle 67 No 552C between 66 and 68, a few steps west of the Casa Becil, is clean and bright, with small rooms along a narrow court. All is kept ship-shape by Sra María Elena Selem, who charges US$20 a double with fan, US$27.50 with air-con. There's a lunch counter in the lobby.

Hotel Sevilla (☎ (99) 23-83-60, 28-24-81), is at Calle 62 No 511, on the corner of Calle 65. It's conveniently located and has a certain faded elegance, but most rooms are musty and dark. It costs US$13.50/15/17 for a single/double/triple.

Another of Mérida's faded glory hostelries is the *Hotel Oviedo* (☎ (99) 21-36-09), Calle 62 No 515 between Calles 65 and 67, a 33-room former town house with a nice courtyard. The rooms are small, with ceiling fans and private showers, but marginally better than those of the nearby Hotel Sevilla.

Hotel América (☎ (99) 21-51-33), Calle 67 No 500 between Calles 58 and 60, is modern, but the rooms at the front are noisy. All 43 rooms have ceiling fans and showers, and cost US$12/14 a single/double.

Hotel México (☎ (99) 24-70-22), Calle 60 No 525, between Calles 65 and 67, has 30 modern rooms with ceiling fans and showers. It's not too bad at US$14/15/17 a single/double/triple.

Hotel Trinidad (☎ (99) 21-30-29, 23-20-33), Calle 62 No 464 between Calles 55 and 57, has been a budget favourite for several years. Owner and artist Manolo Riviera, who speaks some English, has decorated the hotel with modern Mexican paintings. The guest rooms are all different, as are their facilities; they range in price from US$14.50 for a small double with sink to US$32 a double for a large room with private bath and air-conditioning. Discounts are granted if you pay cash.

The Trinidad's sister hotel, the *Hotel Trinidad Galería* (☎ (99) 23-24-63), Calle 60 No 456 at the corner of Calle 51, was once a gracious residence, then an appliance show-room and is now an unlikely hotel. It has a small swimming pool, a bar, an art gallery and antique shop, as well as presentable rooms with fans and private showers for US$13/17/21 a single/double/triple.

Hotel Lord (☎ (99) 23-93-71, 23-96-77), is at Calle 63 No 516, between Calles 62 and 64. It's clean, bright and barracks-like and reasonably well run. An adjoining café can provide breakfast and light meals. Rooms are fairly expensive at US$20 a double with a fan or US$23 a double with air-con.

Hotel Peninsular (☎ (99) 23-69-96), Calle 58 No 519 between Calles 65 and 67, is in the midst of Mérida's market district. The rooms are behind the restaurant. It's well kept and costs US$16/20/22 a single/double/triple with private bath and fan; add a few dollars for air-conditioning.

Hotel del Parque (☎ (99) 24-78-44), Calle 60 No 497 at Calle 59, is only a few steps from Parque Hidalgo and Parque de la Madre. The rooms are small but clean and bright, with ceiling fans and private showers. Those at the front are very noisy. Singles/doubles/triples cost US$22/26/29.

Posada del Angel (☎ (99) 23-27-54), Calle 67 No 535 between Calles 66 and 68, is two blocks north-east of the bus station and is quieter than most other hotels in this neighbourhood. It's tidy and convenient, with its own little restaurant and car park. Clean rooms with fan and bath cost US$22 a double, or US$25 a double with air-con.

Places to Stay – middle

Mérida's middle-range places provide surprising levels of comfort for what you pay. Most charge US$25 to US$60 for a double room with air-conditioning, ceiling fan and private shower; most of these hotels have restaurants, bars and little swimming pools.

Hotel Dolores Alba (☎ (99) 21-37-45), Calle 63 No 464 between Calles 52 and 54, is one of the top choices in Mérida. It's run by Sr Angel Sánchez, and has a pleasant courtyard, a beautiful swimming pool and clean, comfortable rooms priced at US$24 a double (slightly more for air-conditioning).

The Sánchez family also owns the Hotel Dolores Alba at Chichén Itzá, so you can make reservations for it here.

Another hotel owned by the Sánchez family is the *Hotel Janeiro* (☎ (99) 23-36-02), Calle 57 No 435, between Calles 48 and 50. Rooms and facilities are similar to those at the Dolores Alba and the price for a room is identical.

Hotel Caribe (☎ (99) 24-90-22), Calle 59 No 500 at the corner of Calle 60, is actually at the back corner of Parque Hidalgo. It's centrally located and has a swimming pool, a central courtyard and two restaurants. Most rooms have air-conditioning and cost US$28 to US$34 a single, US$32 to US$38 a double, and US$35 to US$42 a triple. There are also a number of rooms with just ceiling fans, which are not quite as well kept but still serviceable, for US$3.50 per room less. Air-conditioned suites cost US$52 to US$70. All rooms have private showers. The Caribe is often booked solid, so reserve in advance, or arrive early in the day to claim a room.

Also on Parque Hidalgo is the *Gran Hotel* (☎ (99) 24-76-22, 24-77-30), Calle 60 No 496, between Calles 59 and 61, on the southern side of the park. True to its name, this was Mérida's grand hotel about a century ago. It's well kept, and rooms with a private shower and a ceiling fan cost US$27/33/38 for a single/double/triple; a suite is US$70. Perhaps even more evocative of 19th-century Mérida is the *Posada Toledo* (☎ (99) 23-22-56, 23-16-90), at Calle 58 No 487, on the corner of Calle 57. It has a dining room straight out of the 19th century and small, modernised rooms with a private shower and either a fan or air-con for US$23/27/33 a single/double/triple. The staff are very friendly and helpful. A breakfast buffet is served in the dining room each morning (US$4.50).

Hotel Reforma (☎ (99) 24-79-22), Calle 59 No 508, corner of Calle 62, is an old hotel that preserves a little of its 19th-century elegance. The old-fashioned rooms have high ceilings, fans, bathrooms and are priced at US$27 a double (US$32 with air-con). A TV set is about US$1 more per day. The hotel has a small swimming pool. *Hotel Colonial* (☎ (99) 24-21-20, 23-64-44; fax 28-39-61), Calle 62 No 476 on the corner of Calle 57, is anything but colonial. It's a recently renovated modern structure with 73 modern air-conditioned rooms, each with TV and telephone, priced at US$66 for a single/double. There's a small swimming pool, restaurant and bar. *Hotel del Gobernador* (☎ (99) 23-71-33), Calle 59 No 535 at the corner of Calle 66, is an attractive, modern hotel with efficient service, air-conditioning and pleasant, comfortable rooms. Off the lobby is a cheerful, bright restaurant. The price is US$50/60 a single/double.

At the *Hotel Paseo de Montejo* (☎ (99) 23-90-33), at Paseo de Montejo 482, the rooms are simpler and older than those of its top-end cousin the Hotel Montejo Palace across the road; but it's comfortable and well priced at US$42 a double. Between the two establishments you have your choice of six restaurants and bars. The swimming pool at the Montejo Palace is open to guests staying at the Paseo de Montejo as well.

Places to Stay – top end

Top-end hotels charge between US$60 and US$125 for a double room. All rooms in this class are air-conditioned and each hotel has a restaurant, bar, swimming pool and probably other services like a travel agency, newsstand, hairdresser and nightclub.

Holiday Inn Mérida (☎ (99) 25-68-77; in the USA (800) 465-4329), Avenida Colón 498 at the corner of Calle 60, is Mérida's most luxurious establishment, complete with US satellite TV, a swimming pool and tennis courts. Its 213 air-con rooms all have minibars and purified water and cost US$125, tax included. The Holiday Inn is often full, so reserve a room in advance.

The *Hotel Los Aluxes* (☎ (99) 24-21-99, fax 23-38-58; in the USA call (800) 782-8359), is at Calle 60 No 444, at the corner of Calle 49. This relatively new 109-room hotel is an easy walk from the city centre and Paseo de Montejo, is comfortable and convenient though a bit expensive, and has all of the top-end services. It's intriguing name

aluxes ('ah-LOO-shess') refers to the Maya equivalent of leprechauns or wee folk, benevolent but usually invisible fairies. Rates are US$100 for a single/double, US$115 for a triple, and US$140 for a suite.

Hotel Mérida Misión Park Inn (☎ (99) 23-95-00, toll-free (800) 9-00-38; in the USA (800) 648-7818), is centrally located at Calle 60 No 491, on the corner of Calle 57. Renovated in 1991, it's very comfortable and convenient. Rates for the 150 air-con rooms, all with colour satellite TV and phone, are US$65 for a single or double. It has a swimming pool, a dining room, and contains a branch of the Wini Cafetería chain.

Hotel Casa del Balam (☎ (99) 24-88-44; fax 24-50-11), Calle 60 No 488 at Calle 57, has a swimming pool, restaurant, bar and travel agency. It's popular with groups, which may account for the brusque and hurried service. Air-conditioned rooms with TV and mini-bar are priced fairly high at US$85 a double, but the location is excellent.

Hotel El Castellano (☎ (99) 23-01-00; fax 23-01-10), is at Calle 57 No 513, between Calles 62 and 64. Its well-maintained 12-storey building holds 170 air-conditioned rooms, a swimming pool, solarium, restaurant, bar and coffee shop. Rates are US$65 for a single or double and US$76 for a triple/suite.

Hotel El Conquistador (☎ (99) 26-21-55; fax 26-88-29), Paseo de Montejo No 458 at Calle 35, has 90 air-conditioned rooms and suites in a modern nine-storey structure; the rooms have two double beds, colour TV and all the other expected comforts. There is a restaurant, coffee shop and lobby bar, and a small enclosed pool on the second floor. Rates are US$64 for a single/double, US$72 a triple and US$80 for a junior suite.

Hotel Montejo Palace (☎ (99) 24-76-44), Paseo de Montejo 483-C, faces the Hotel Paseo de Montejo across the Paseo at Calle 41. Both hotels are under the same management. The Montejo Palace, on the west side of the Paseo, is slightly fancier with 90 rooms at US$60 a single/double; the rooms have two double beds, a colour TV and a mini-bar.

Places to Eat

Mérida's restaurants offer Yucatecan, Mexican, American, Italian, French and even Lebanese cuisine. The best restaurants are moderately priced and the market eateries are cheap and good.

Places to Eat – bottom end

The cheapest full meals are, as usual, in and around the market. From the western side of the market at Calle 67, go up the flight of steps past the touristy Mercado de Artesanías. At the top of the ramp, turn left and you'll see a row of two dozen market eateries with names like *El Chimecito, La Temaxeña, Saby, Mimi, Saby y El Palon, La Socorrito, Reina Beatriz* and so forth.

Comidas corridas here are priced from US$2.25 to US$3, big main-course platters of beef, fish or chicken with vegetables and rice or potatoes go for US$2 to US$3.25, and specialities such as frijol con puerco (Yucatán-style pork and beans) for US$2. Bistec (beefsteak) and chuletas (chops, veal or pork) cost only a bit more. Though no place in Mérida can be called cool, it's at least shady and breezy here. The market eateries are open from early morning until late afternoon every day.

Along Calle 62, between Calles 54 and 61, there are also lots of cheap eating places. *El Louvre* (☎ 21-32-71), Calle 62 No 499 on the corner of Calle 61, is a bright, bare, well-used place with efficient waiters and low prices. Sandwiches go for US$1.25 to US$2.50, full breakfasts for US$3 and the daily comida corrida for about US$4.50. Try the other places along Calle 62, including *Cafetería Erik's* next door.

For cheap sandwiches, try the tiny *Las Mil Tortas*, Calle 62 between Calles 57 and 55. Though it doesn't really offer a thousand different sandwiches, they are cheap, ranging from US$1 to US$2.25. Breakfast is served here for US$2 to US$3.25.

Another place for takeaway food is the *Pizzería de Vito Corleone* (☎ 23-68-46), Calle 59 No 508 at the corner of Calle 62. Small one-person pizzas go for US$3 to US$4.50 depending upon ingredients; larger

pizzas cost US$7.50 to US$10. If you decide to eat there, head for the upstairs dining room to lessen street noise.

Around the corner from Vito Corleone, *Jugos El Trapiche*, Calle 62 No 491, has cheap pizzas and good sandwiches for US$2.50 and up, as well as freshly squeezed fruit juices.

For fairly cheap food in clean, modern surroundings and air-conditioned comfort, try the soups, sandwiches, tortas, salads and desserts at the *Wini Cafetería*, Calle 60 No 491, in the Hotel Mérida Misión Park Inn. Another branch is at Paseo de Montejo 466. Though a huge club sandwich costs US$6.50, those with ham, cheese, pork or chicken go for US$3.50 to US$4; tortas are about the same. They serve several good Mexican dishes such as burritas, enfrijoladas and enchiladas as well. Desserts are a speciality, from pies and cakes to banana splits and sweet crepes.

The best cheap breakfasts can be had by picking up a selection of pan dulces (sweet rolls and breads) from one of Mérida's several *panificadoras* (bakeries). A convenient one is the *Panificadora Montejo* at the corner of Calles 62 and 63. Pick up a metal tray and tongs, select the pastries you want and hand the tray to a clerk who will bag them and quote a price, usually US$2 or so for a full bag.

Places to Eat – middle

Around Parque Hidalgo are several pleasant restaurants. The least expensive is the *Cafetería El Mesón* (☎ 21-92-32) in the Hotel Caribe. Meat, fish and chicken dishes are priced from US$4.25 to US$9, but sandwiches and burgers are only US$2.75 to US$4.50. They often have Montejo beer here, which is not easily found elsewhere. El Mesón is open for breakfast, lunch and dinner daily.

Next door is *Tiano's* (☎ 23-71-18), Calle 59 No 498 at the corner of Calle 60, a fancier version of El Mesón. In the evening the restaurant often hires a marimba group to entertain its patrons. A full meal like sopa de lima, puntas de filete, dessert and a drink is around US$17. A main course of red snapper or chicken costs US$8 and a sandwich less than half that. The menu is long and varied, with steaks, seafood and a few Yucatecan dishes. Tiano's is supposedly open 24 hours a day, but it's usually locked up from midnight to 7 am.

In the Gran Hotel is *El Patio Español* which serves good Mexican and Yucatecan food at moderate prices. Filling spaghetti dishes go for US$2.75 to US$3.25 and main meat courses are about US$5.50. You can get breakfast here, as the restaurant is open from 7 am to 11 pm every day.

Across Calle 60 is an old Mérida standard, the *Café-Restaurant Express* (☎ 21-37-38), at Calle 60 No 502. Express is a bustling meeting place, but the food is acceptable. Most main-course plates cost US$4.50 to US$6. Breakfast is good as well. Hours are 7 am to midnight daily.

Pop Cafetería (☎ 21-68-44), is at Calle 57 between Calles 60 and 62, on the north side of the street. It's air-conditioned and open from breakfast to dinner. The menu is limited but adequate, with hamburgers for US$2, big plates of spaghetti for US$3.50 and main-course platters such as chicken in mole sauce for US$4 to US$5. Breakfasts cost from US$2.25 for pan dulce and coffee to US$3.50 for bacon, eggs and the works. The restaurant is named after the first month of the Maya calendar. For food or snacks on Plaza Mayor try the *Restaurant Nicte-Ha* (☎ 23-07-84), Calle 61 No 500, on the north side of the square beneath the arcade of the Palacio de Gobierno. The selection is varied, from tacos and enchiladas to sandwiches and full-course lunches and dinners. Prices are low and you can fill up for US$3 to US$6.

Also on the north side of Plaza Mayor is the *Dulcería y Sorbetería Colón*, a good place for a pastry (US$0.65), ice cream (US$1.40) or a soft drink (45c). Next door is *Jugos California*, which has higher prices.

Restaurant Cedro del Líbano (☎ 23-7531), Calle 59 No 529 between Calles 64 and 66, is a simple and clean Lebanese restaurant. Lebanese traders made up a significant minority in the population during the 19th century and their descendents remain loyal citizens of Mérida to this day. Berenjena con tijini (eggplant with tahini), labne (yogurt), tabule, kibi and alambre de kafta (ground meat mixed with spices and grilled on skewers) are a few of the choices you'll have. For a full meal, expect to pay US$7 to US$11. Hours are 11.30 am to 11.30 pm every day.

Places to Eat – top end

Mérida's better restaurants are surprisingly good and inexpensive when compared to eateries of similar rank in Europe or North America. You can have an excellent three-course repast, either continental or Yucatecan, for US$10 to US$15 per person, wine, tax and tip included.

Among the city's most dependable dining places is the *Restaurante Portico del Peregrino* (☎ 21-68-44), Calle 57 No 501 between Calles 60 and 62, right next to Pop. Yucatecan dishes are its forte, but you'll find many continental dishes as well. Lunch (noon to 3 pm) and dinner (6 to 11 pm) are served every day and a full meal is about US$14 to US$20 per person.

La Casona (☎ 23-83-48), Calle 60 No 434 between Calles 47 and 49, is a fine old city house now serving as a nice restaurant. Italian dishes crowd the menu, with a few Yucatecan plates to top it off. Besides the inevitable pollo pibil, there are lots of steak, fish and pasta platters. Plan to spend anywhere from US$11 to US$20 per person, everything included; the highest prices are reserved for those shrimp and lobster dishes. La Casona is open every evening for dinner; on weekends, you might want to make reservations.

Los Almendros (☎ 21-28-51), Calle 50A No 493 between Calles 57 and 59, is Mérida's branch of this Yucatecan culinary chain. Its speciality is authentic Yucatecan country cuisine such as pavo relleno negro (grilled turkey with hot peppered pork stuffing), papadzul (tacos filled with egg smothered in a fiery sauce), sopa de lima (chicken broth with lime and tortillas) or Los Almendros' most famous dish, the zingy onion-and-tomato pork dish poc-chuc. All meals are served with hot handmade tortillas. For those who don't read Spanish, there is a photo-menu of each dish. It's hearty and tasty food; sopa de lima, poc-chuc, dessert and a bottle of beer costs US$12 to US$15.

Restaurant El Tucho (☎ 24-23-23), Calle 60 No 482 between Calles 57 and 55, features a menu of Yucatecan specialities including cochinita pibil, pavo en escabeche, poc-chuc and pan de cazón. The dining room looks like an enormous na, with thatched roof and bamboo walls. It's not fancy, but rather a place where the locals come for eating, drinking and singing, from 6 pm to midnight, seven days a week. Most main courses cost US$6 or US$7 and a full meal is US$12 to US$15. Beware of the high prices for drinks; a beer costs US$2.50 and a mere soft drink almost US$2.

Mérida's most famous French restaurant is the *Yannig Restaurante* (☎ 27-03-39), some distance from the centre at Avenida Pérez-Ponce No 105, near the Iglesia de Itzamná. Chef Yannig Oliviero is from France and his menu has classic French dishes as well as those which might be termed *nouvelle Yucatán*. Dinner is served Monday to Saturday from 5 to 11.30 pm; on Sunday there's lunch and dinner from 1 to 10.30 pm. A full meal costs US$15 to US$20 per person, with wine.

Patio de las Fajitas (☎ 28-37-82), Calle 60 No 467 at the corner of Calle 53, is a fine old colonial mansion. Fajitas (beef, chicken, pork, etc) are the speciality and are priced from US$8.50 to US$10. It's open from 1 to 11 pm daily (closed Monday).

Entertainment

Concerts & Folklore Proud of its cultural legacy and attuned to the benefits of tourism, the city of Mérida offers nightly folkloric events by local performers of considerable skill. Admission is free to city-sponsored events.

Yucatán y sus Raíces (Yucatán & its Roots), a ballet folklorico show sponsored by the university, is held at 9 pm every night in the Teatro Peón Contreras, at the corner of Calles 60 and 57. Admission costs US$4.50.

Monday – A regional Vaquería features the city's ballet folklorico accompanied by the local Jarana Orchestra; it is staged behind the Municipal Palace in the Garden of the Composers at 9 pm.

Tuesday – A city band plays music from the past and present. Performances are in Santiago Park, at the intersection of Calles 59 and 72.
Some Tuesdays there are concerts in the university courtyard; check with the tourist office.

Wednesday – Mérida's string ensemble plays light classical and popular music in Santa Ana Park at the corner of Calles 60 and 47.

Thursday – Traditional Yucatecan folkloric dancers and troubadours entertain in the Parque Santa Lucia at Calles 60 and 55 at 9 pm.

Friday – Local theatre is presented in the Garden of the Composers at the back of the Palacio Municipal. Also, in the university's patio in a building at the intersection of Calle 60 and 57, entertaining folkloric dances and music are performed.

Saturday – Musical performances (jazz, classical pops and traditional Yucatecan) at 11 am in the Salón de la Historia of the Palacio de Gobierno on the Plaza Mayor.
City sponsored marimba concerts take place in Parque Hidalgo, Calles 60 and 59, at 11.30 am.
At 1 pm, the city sponsors a re-enactment of a colourful mestiza wedding by the city's ballet folklorico and police orchestra at the Palacio Municipal.
The weekly Bazar de Artesanías is held from 11 am to 3 pm in Parque San Lucia. As the bazaar begins, there's a performance of traditional folk dancing and music.
A number of travel agencies promote the Maya Spectacular presented at Tulipanes Restaurant at Calle 42 No 462A. In my estimation, the show is melodramatic and the food doesn't make up for what the show lacks. Admission is US$6, not including dinner. For a more contemporary Maya experience, go for dinner to the Restaurant El Tucho, described above.

Cinemas Many English films, some of fairly recent release, are screened in Mérida with Spanish subtitles. Buy your tickets (usually about US$1 or US$2) before showtime and well in advance on weekends. The popular Cine Cantarell, Calle 60 No 488, next door to the Restaurant Express, and Cine Fantasio, facing Parque Hidalgo between the Gran Hotel and Hotel Caribe, are convenient. There's also the Cine Olimpia

Vistarama, Calle 60 between Calles 57 and 55, next to the Hotel Mérida Misión, the Cine Premier, at the corner of Calles 57 and 62, and the Cinema 59, Calle 59 between Calles 68 and 70.

Things to Buy

From standard shirts and blouses to Maya exotica, Mérida is *the* place on the peninsula to shop. Purchases you might want to consider include traditional Maya clothing such as the colourful women's embroidered blouse called a huipil, a Panama hat woven from palm fibres, local craft items and of course the wonderfully comfortable Yucatecan hammock which holds you gently in a comfortable cotton web.

Mérida's main market, the Mercado Municipal Lucas do Gálvez, is bounded by Calles 56 and 56A at Calle 67, four blocks south-east of the Plaza Mayor. The market building is more or less next door to the city's main post office (Correos) and telegraph office, at the corner of Calles 65 and 56. The surrounding streets are all part of the large market district, lined with shops selling everything one might need.

The Bazar de Artesanías, Calle 67 at the corner of Calle 56A, is set up to attract tourists. You should have a look at the stuff here, then compare the goods and prices with independent shops outside the Bazar.

Handicrafts The place to go for high-quality craft and art items is the Casa de los Artesanías, Estado de Yucatán on Calle 63 between 64 and 66; look for the doorway marked 'Dirección de Desarrollo Artesanal DIF Yucatán'. It's open Monday to Friday from 8 am to 8 pm, Saturday from 8 am to 6 pm, closed Sunday. This is a government-supported marketing effort for local artisans. The selection of crafts is very good, quality usually high and prices reasonable.

You can also check out locally made crafts at the Museo Regional de Artesanías on Calle 59 between Calles 50 and 48. The work on display is superlative, but the items for sale are not as good. Admission is free and it's open from Tuesday to Saturday from 8 am to 8 pm and Sunday 9 am to 2 pm, closed Monday.

Guayaberas Kary's on Calle 64 between Calles 65 and 67 sells a good selection of traditional Yucatecan guayaberas (fancy dress shirts) at reasonable prices. Check the cut, fit and stitching carefully before you buy any guayabera.

Panama Hats Panama hats are woven from *jipijapa* palm leaves in caves and workshops in which the temperature and humidity are carefully controlled, as humid conditions keep the fibres pliable when the hat is being made. Once blocked and exposed to the relatively drier air outside, the hat is surprisingly resilient and resistant to crushing. The Campeche town of Becal is the centre of the hat-weaving trade, but you can buy good examples of the hatmaker's art in Mérida.

The best quality hats have a very fine, close weave of slender fibres. The coarser the weave, the lower the price should be. Prices range from a few dollars for a hat of basic quality to US$25 or more for top quality.

A store famous for its Panama hats is appropriately named Becal and is located at Calle 56 No 522. Another is El Becaleño, Calle 65 No 483, at the corner of Calle 56A. A third is La Casa de los Jipis, Calle 56 No 526 near Calle 65.

Hammocks The fine strings of Yucatecan hammocks make them supremely comfortable. In the sticky heat of a Yucatán summer, most locals prefer sleeping in a hammock, where the air can circulate around them, rather than in a bed. Many inexpensive hotels used to have hammock hooks in the walls of all guest rooms, though the hooks are not so much in evidence today.

Yucatecan hammocks are normally woven from strong nylon or cotton string and dyed in various colours; there are also natural, undyed versions. In the old days, the finest, strongest, most expensive hammocks were woven from silk.

Hammocks come in several widths. From

smallest to largest, the names generally used:
are *sencillo* (about 50 pairs of end strings,
US$12), *doble* (100 pairs, US$14 to US$18),
matrimonial (150 pairs, US$18 to US$25)
and *matrimonial especial* or *quatro cajas*
(175 pairs or more, US$20 and up). You must
check to be sure that you're really getting the
width that you are paying for. Because hammocks fold up small and the larger
hammocks are more comfortable (though
more expensive), consider the bigger sizes.

During your first few hours in Mérida you
will be approached on the street by hammock
pedlars. They may quote very low prices, but
a price is only as good as the quality is high
and street-sold hammocks are mediocre at
best. Check the hammock very carefully.

You can save yourself a lot of trouble by
shopping at a hammock store with a good
reputation. La Poblana (☎ 21-65-03), at
Calle 65 No 492 between Calles 58 and 60,
is fairly good. In theory, prices are set, but
some travellers report a small measure of
success with bargaining. La Poblana will
safely mail your purchase home for you,
saving you the typical post office hassle.
Some travellers report slightly cheaper
prices for good quality at El Aguacate, Calle
58 No 604 at the corner of Calle 73. El
Campesino, at Calle 58 No 548 between
Calles 69 and 71, is cheaper but provides less
guidance – so you should really know what
you are looking for and check quality.

You may be able to save a little money on
your hammock purchase if you bus out to the
nearby village of Tixcocob to watch them
being woven. The bus runs regularly from
the Progreso bus station south of the main
plaza at Calle 62 No 524 between Calles 65
and 67.

Getting There & Away

Air Most international flights to Mérida are
connections through Mexico City or Cancún; the only nonstop international services
are Aeroméxico's two daily flights from
Miami and Aviateca's flights to Guatemala
City. Domestic flights are operated mostly
by smaller regional airlines, with a few
flights by Aeroméxico and Mexicana.

Aerolíneas Bonanza (☎ (99) 28-04-96, 24-62-28),
Calle 56A No 579, between Calles 67 and 69,
flies round-trips twice daily from Mérida to
Chetumal and once daily to Ciudad del Carmen.

Aeroméxico (☎ (99) 27-95-66, 27-92-77), Paseo de
Montejo 460, has a few flights as well.

Aviacsa (☎ (99) 26-32-53, 26-39-54; fax 26-90-87),
at the airport, flies nonstop to Cancún and
Villahermosa, and direct to Tuxtla Gutiérrez, the
airline's home base. They also have routes
linking Tuxtla with Chetumal, Mexico City,
Oaxaca and Tapachula.

Aviateca (☎ (99) 24-43-54), at the airport, flies to
Tikal and Guatemala City several times per
week.

Inter (☎ (99) 24-95-00, 23-00-02), Paseo de Montejo
476A, flies between Mérida and Cancún
(morning and evening flights, US$75 one way,
US$110 round-trip excursion), Chetumal,
Mexico City, Oaxaca, Tuxtla Gutiérrez (for San
Cristóbal de las Casas), Veracruz and Villahermosa.

Litoral (☎ toll-free (91-800) 2-90-20), based in Veracruz, flies to Ciudad del Carmen, Veracruz and
Monterrey.

Mexicana (☎ (99) 24-66-33), Calle 58 No 500, has
nonstop flights to and from Havana, Cancún and
Mexico City.

Bus The Terminal de Autobuses (☎ 24-37-
43), operated by the Unión de Camioneros
de Yucatán, is on Calle 69 between Calles 68
and 70, about six blocks south-west of the
main plaza. This is the main bus station in
the city. (If you're arriving from points east,
such as Cancún, Valladolid or Chichén Itzá,
your Autobuses de Oriente Mérida-Puerto
Juárez bus might make a stop, or even terminate the journey, at its garage on Calle 50
between Calles 65 and 67.) At the Terminal
de Autobuses, you'll find a bank, telegraph
office, travel agency, Yucatán state tourism
booth, an instant B&W photo booth and a
bank of Ladatel coin-operated long-distance
telephones, as well as a public fax machine.

Half a dozen different companies use the
Terminal de Autobuses. Each company
specialises in services to a certain part of the
region or the country, but some companies'
territories overlap. Shop around a bit before
you buy your ticket, as fares, travel times and
comfort can vary from one company to the
next. Here's a quick rundown on the compa-

nies (their abbreviated name appears after the company name):

Autobuses de Oriente (ADO) – long-haul 1st-class routes to Campeche, Mexico City, Palenque, Veracruz and Villahermosa.

Autotransportes Peninsulares (A Peninsulares) – frequent 1st-class buses to Chetumal, some 2nd-class buses to Chetumal, Felipe Carrillo Puerto and Ticul.

Autotransportes de Oriente Mérida-Puerto Juárez (A de O M-PJ) – frequent buses between Mérida and Cancún stopping at Chichén Itzá, Valladolid and Puerto Juárez (for Isla Mujeres boats); they also run buses to Tizimín, to Playa del Carmen (for Cozumel boats), to Tulum and to Akumal.

Autotransportes del Sur (A del Sur) – frequent buses to Uxmal, Kabah and Campeche and one bus a day to Villahermosa.

Autotransportes del Caribe (A del Caribe) – nine buses daily to Ticul; also 1st and 2nd-class buses to Akumal, Bacalar, Cancún, Chetumal, Felipe Carrillo Puerto, Oxcutzkab, Playa del Carmen and Tulum.

Autotransportes del Sureste en Yucatán (A del Sureste) – dozens of 2nd-class buses daily to Campeche, some stopping at Becal; one bus daily to Palenque (many more to the Palenque turnoff at Catazajá), one to Tuxtla Gutiérrez and San Cristóbal de las Casas via Tenosique and Ocosingo.

Here's information on trips to and from Mérida; all buses are daily and all times are by 1st-class bus (2nd class may be slower):

Akumal – 350 km, six or seven hours; three 2nd-class buses daily by A de O M-PJ and three by A del Caribe.

Bacalar – 420 km, 8½ hours; four 1st-class buses (US$8.75), four 2nd-class buses (US$7.50) by A del Caribe.

Campeche – 195 km (short route via Becal), three hours; 250 km (long route via Uxmal), four hours; 44 1st-class buses (US$7) by ADO, one bus at least every hour from 6 am to 11.30 pm; 21 2nd-class buses (US$6.75) daily by A del Sureste; 11 2nd-class buses (US$6.50) by A del Sur.

Cancún – 320 km, 5½ to six hours; almost every 30 minutes 1st class (US$7.50) by A de O M-PJ; 2nd-class buses (US$7) on the hour from 5 am to midnight (except no buses at 4, 7, 8, 9 and 10 pm) by A de O M-PJ; several 1st-class by A del Caribe (US$11) as well.

Chetumal – 456 km, eight to nine hours; seven 1st-class buses (US$11) by A Peninsulares and four 1st-class buses (US$10) by A del Caribe; nine 2nd-class buses (US$9) by A del Caribe and three (US$10) by A Peninsulares.

Chichén Itzá – 116 km, 2½ to three hours; four 1st-class (US$3), and 15 2nd-class buses (US$2.75) by A de O M-PJ, heading for Valladolid, Cancún and Playa del Carmen, pass nearby. A special round-trip (US$5.50) excursion bus by A de O M-PJ departs from Mérida at 8.45 am and returns from Chichén Itzá at 3 pm.

Felipe Carrillo Puerto – 310 km, 5½ to six hours; two 1st-class buses (US$5) by A del Caribe and two (US$7) by A Peninsulares; others of this line may stop there as well. One 2nd-class bus (US$6.50) by A de O M-PJ.

Kabah – 101 km, two hours; six 1st-class buses (US$2) by A del Sur.

Mexico City – 1505 km, 26 hours; eight 1st-class buses (US$31) by ADO.

Palenque – 556 km, 10 or 11 hours; two 1st-class buses (US$12) by A del Sureste and one (US$13) night bus by ADO directly to Palenque. Many more, including nine 2nd-class (US$11) buses by A del Sureste, will drop you at Catazajá, the main highway junction 27 km to the north of the town, from which you can hitchhike or catch another bus to the town.

Playa del Carmen – 378 km, eight hours; six 1st-class buses (US$8.50) and six 2nd-class buses (US$7) by A de O M-PJ; several 1st-class buses by A del Caribe (US$10) go via Ticul and Felipe Carrillo Puerto.

Progreso – (leaves from another terminal – see below).

Ticul – 85 km, 1½ hours; nine 2nd-class buses (US$1.25) by A del Caribe, and two (US$1.75) by A Peninsulares.

Tizimín – 210 km, four hours; two 1st-class buses (US$4.25) by A de O M-PJ; one 2nd-class (US$3.75) by A de O M-PJ; or take a bus to Valladolid and change there for Tizimín.

Tulum – 320 km, six hours; three 2nd-class buses (US$8.75) via Cobá by A del Caribe; three 1st-class buses (US$9) via Cancún by A de O M-PJ take two hours longer.

Tuxtla Gutiérrez – 1296 km, 20 hours; one 1st-class bus (US$18) by A del Sureste (which also goes to San Cristóbal), or take a bus to Villahermosa and change there for Tuxtla.

Uxmal – 80 km, 1½ hours; six 2nd-class buses (US$2) by A del Sur, or take a bus bound for Campeche or beyond by the inland (longer) route and get off at Uxmal.

Valladolid – 160 km, three hours; 24 1st-class (US$3.75) by A de O M-PJ, 15 2nd-class (US$3) by A de O M-PJ.

Veracruz – 1175 km, 18 hours; two 1st-class buses (5.30 and 9 pm, US$21.50) by ADO.

Villahermosa – 700 km, 10 hours; 17 1st-class buses (US$14) by ADO; one 2nd-class bus (US$11.50) by A del Sur.

If you take an all-night bus, don't put anything valuable in the overhead racks, as there have been several reports of gear being stolen at night.

For Progreso and the ruins at Dzibilchaltún, go to the Progreso bus station at Calle 62 No 524 between Calles 65 and 67. Nonstop buses depart every 15 minutes for Progreso (33 km, 45 minutes, US$1.25), and stopping buses every 40 minutes. The latter stop at the Dzililchaltún access road (15 km, 30 minutes, US$1).

There are several departures a day to the Celestún flamingo region from the Autotransportes del Sur station, at Calle 50 No 531 on the corner of Calle 67.

For Río Lagartos or San Felipe, Autotransportes del Noroeste buses depart three times daily, from Calle 52 between Calles 63 and 65.

Train In the Yucatán Peninsula, buses are preferable to trains in that they are considerably faster and infinitely safer. Rail robberies in some areas (between Mérida, Campeche and Palenque in particular) have reached epidemic proportions.

There is a night train for Campeche, Palenque and ultimately Mexico City (two days' journey). The railway station is at Calle 55 between Calles 46 and 48. Tickets should be bought several hours in advance.

Car Rental cars are expensive in Mexico, but cheaper in Mérida than in Cancún. Assume you will pay about US$65 per day for the cheapest car offered, usually a bottom-of-the-line Volkswagen or Nissan. If you can find others to share the cost, car rental is the best way to see the Puuc Route sites. The longer the rental, the less you'll spend per day for the car.

A small, local car rental company, Mexico Rent a Car (☎ (99) 27-49-16, 23-36-37), at Calle 62 No 483E between Calles 59 and 57, has a good reputation. It's owned and operated by Alvaro and Teresa Alonzo and their daughter Teresa. Numerous friends of ours have used them for years with no complaints. They offer VW Beetles and larger Nissans for all-inclusive rates that are considerably lower than the big-name competition. If the office on Calle 62 is closed, look for them at their parking lot beside the Hotel del Parque on Calle 60 at Calle 59 (open 8 am to 12.30 pm and 6 to 8 pm).

The big international car rental companies all have agencies in Mérida, the most active of which is Budget Rent-a-Car (☎ (99) 27-87-55), Paseo de Montejo Prolongación 497. There are also car rental desks for Avis, Budget, Dollar, Hertz, Max, National and VW Rent at the airport.

Getting Around
Most parts of Mérida that you'll want to visit are within five or six blocks of the Plaza Mayor and are thus accessible on foot. Given the slow speed of city traffic, particularly in the market areas, travel on foot is also the fastest way to get around.

To walk from the Terminal de Autobuses to Plaza Mayor, exit the terminal to the street in front (Calle 69), turn right and walk three blocks to Calle 62. Turn left and walk the remaining three blocks north to the plaza.

To/From the Airport Mérida's modern airport is 12 km south-west of the centre off Highway 180 (Avenida de los Itzaes). Bus 79 ('Aviación') travels infrequently between the airport and city centre for US$0.35.

Most arriving travellers use the Transporte Terrestre minibus colectivos (US$2.75). Prices are displayed prominently at the ticket-seller's desk in front of the airport by the bus stops. Be sure to ask for a *colectivo* ticket; the ticket-seller may automatically assume that you want an *exclusivo* (private minibus) ticket for US$6. To return to the airport you must take a taxi for an outrageous US$8.

Bus The city's bus system is confusing at

best, with routes meandering through the city, finally terminating in distant suburban neighbourhoods. For exact route information, ask at the tourist office.

The bus system is supplemented by minibus jitneys, which are easier to use as they run shorter and more comprehensible routes. The minibus (colectivo) you're liable to find most useful is the Ruta 10 (US$0.30), which departs the corner of Calles 58 and 59, half a block east of Parque Hidalgo, and travels along the Paseo de Montejo to Itzamná.

Taxi The official taxi rate from the Terminal de Autobuses to the Plaza Mayor or thereabouts is about US$2.50 to US$3.50; to the Holiday Inn on Paseo de Montejo about US$4. If you walk a block or two away from the bus terminal and catch a taxi, you can probably get a lower rate.

DZIBILCHALTÚN

This was the longest continuously utilised Maya administrative and ceremonial city, serving the Maya from 1500 BC or earlier until the European conquest in the 1540s. At the height of its greatness, Dzibilchaltún covered 80 sq km. Today there is little for the casual visitor to see except a few ruined pyramids, a sacbé (ceremonial road) or two, the interesting little Temple of the Seven Dolls and a cool, clear cenote swimming pool.

Dzibilchaltún (Place of Inscribed Flat Stones) is a large site, open from 8 am to 5 pm every day; admission costs US$3.

Getting There & Away

Bus Buses depart every 15 minutes from Mérida to the Dzibilchaltún access road (15 km, 30 minutes, US$1) on the right (east) side of the highway. It's five km from the highway to the entrance of the ruins along a sleepy country road and through a little village; the best time to hitch a ride is in the morning. From the site entrance, it's another 700 metres to the building housing the museum, ticket window and soft drinks stand.

PROGRESO

Population: 30,000

This is a seafarers' town, the port for Mérida and north-western Yucatán. The Yucatecan limestone shelf declines so gradually into the sea that a marvellously 6.5 km-long muelle (pier) had to be built to reach the deep water. This same gradual slope of land into water is what makes Progreso's long beach so inviting.

Progreso is normally a sleepy little town, but on weekends, especially in summer, it seems as if all of Mérida is here. If it's crowded, walk six km east along the palm-fringed beach to the tiny village of Chicxulub, a pleasant escape from the crowds. Alternatively, five km west of Progreso is Yucalpetén, whose new harbour is stealing some of the thunder from Progreso's business. For true solitude, walk a few km west of Yucalpetén to the tranquil sands of Chelem and Chuburná.

Orientation

Progreso is long and narrow, stretched out along the seashore. Though it has an apparently logical street grid, it illogically is subject to two numbering systems fifty numbers apart. One system has the city centre's streets numbered in the 60s, 70s and 80s, another has them in the 10s, 20s and 30s. Thus you might see a street sign on Calle 30 calling it Calle 80 or on a map Calle 10 might also be referred to as Calle 60. We've included both systems on our map.

What anyone coming to Progreso wants to find first are the beach and the muelle. The highway into town becomes Calle 78 (one-way northbound) which leads past the main square directly to the muelle. To the right (east) of the muelle is the Malecón, or seaside promenade and beach, stretching for one km eastward. The Malecón, extending from Calle 60 (also called Calle 10) in the east to Calle 78 (28) and the muelle in the west, is one way westbound for cars.

The bus stations are near the main square. It's six short blocks from the main square to the Malecón and the muelle.

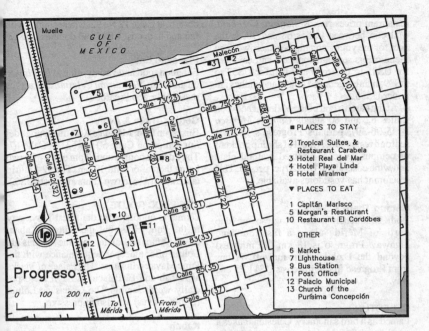

Progreso

PLACES TO STAY
2 Tropical Suites &
  Restaurant Carabela
3 Hotel Real del Mar
4 Hotel Playa Linda
8 Hotel Miralmar

PLACES TO EAT
1 Capitán Marisco
5 Morgan's Restaurant
10 Restaurant El Cordóbes

OTHER
6 Market
7 Lighthouse
9 Bus Station
11 Post Office
12 Palacio Municipal
13 Church of the
   Purísima Concepción

Places to Stay

Progreso is a resort, and thus a bit expensive. On Sunday in July and August, even the cheapest hotels fill up.

The best of Progreso's budget inns is the *Hotel Miralmar* (☎ (993) 5-05-52), Calle 27 No 124 at the corner of Calle 76, which offers rooms with private shower, fan and one double bed for US$14, with two beds for US$16.50. Several good lodging places are located right on the Malecón. *Hotel Playa Linda* (☎ (993) 5-11-57), Malecón at Calle 76, is a simple little two-storey place. Double (two bed) rooms with a private shower and a fan rent for US$16.50. It has a small shop selling souvenirs, snacks and cold drinks, and a moped rental agency.

At the corner of Malecón and Calle 70 are two more hotels. *Tropical Suites* (☎ (993) 5-12-63) is the nicest, with tidy rooms with showers and fans going for US$19 a double.

Hotel Real del Mar (☎ (993) 5-05-23), behind the Restaurant Pelicanos, is an older

hostelry, but still a good deal. Rooms with a shower and fan cost US$16.50 a single/double for one bed, US$21 a double/triple for two beds, or US$24 for a suite.

Places to Eat

Seafood is the strong point on the menus of Progreso's restaurants. Note that if you come on a day trip to Progreso, you can change clothes at the *vestidores* (changing cubicles) attached to most beachfront restaurants.

An inexpensive eatery is *Restaurant El Cordóbes*, at the corner of Calles 81 and 80 on the north side of the main square. It's open from early morning until late at night. Standard fare – tacos, enchiladas, sandwiches and chicken – costs from US$2.25 to US$5; fish, at US$5 to US$7.50, is the strong suit.

Morgan's, on the Malecón between Calles 80 and 78, is a Mexican beach restaurant where you can get a full fish dinner for about US$10, everything included.

As you move eastward along the Malecón,

restaurant prices rise. *Restaurant Carabela*, Malecón between Calles 68 and 70, is the spot for the young and hip beach crowd. The menu offers seafood cocktails and ceviches for US$5 to US$6.50 and fish for US$7 to US$9; hamburgers and other sandwiches are under US$5.

At the eastern end of the Malecón between Calles 62 and 60 stands *Capitán Marisco* (☎ 5-06-39), perhaps Progreso's fanciest seafood restaurant. A meal of shrimp cocktail or octopus ceviche, a mixed seafood plate and wine costs about US$20 per person. This restaurant has vestidores available.

Getting There & Away
Both Dzibilchaltún and Progreso are due north of Mérida along a fast four-lane highway. Progreso is 18 km (20 minutes) beyond the Dzibilchaltún turn-off. A bus from Progreso to Mérida costs US$1.25 one way.

CELESTÚN
Famed as a bird sanctuary, Celestún makes a good beach-and-bird day trip from Mérida. Although this region abounds in anhingas and egrets, most birdwatchers come here to see the flamingos.

The town is located at the southern tip of a spit of land between the Río Esperanza and the Gulf of Mexico. The beach here is not the peninsula's most appealing and on some days fierce afternoon winds swirl clouds of choking dust through the town. The dust makes the sea silty and therefore unpleasant for swimming in the afternoon.

Given the winds, the best time to see birds is in the morning. Hire a boat from the bridge where launches are docked about one km from the town. The rental should run to about US$14 for a 1½ hour tour of the flamingo-inhabited areas.

Places to Stay
The *Hotel Gutiérrez*, Calle 12 No 22, is the top budget choice, with well-kept rooms with fan and bath costing US$13. Cheaper and not as nice is the *Hotel San Julio* (☎ 1-

85-89), at Calle 12 No 92, where singles with fan and bath cost US$7 and doubles US$12.

Places to Eat
For good food and variety, dine at *La Playita* on the shore. *Restaurant Celestún* also serves reasonably good seafood.

Getting There & Away
Buses run from Mérida's Autotransportes del Sur station on Calle 50 No 531 at Calle 67. They depart hourly until 2 pm and every two hours thereafter until 10 pm. The 92-km trip takes about 1½ to two hours and costs US$2.

THE PUUC ROUTE
Uxmal is undoubtedly the finest Maya city in the Puuc Hills, but the ruins at Kabah, Sayil, Xlapak, Labná and the Grutas de Loltún offer a deeper acquaintance with the Puuc Maya civilisation. The Palace of Masks at Kabah and El Palacio at Sayil are especially worth seeing. The Grutas de Loltún (Loltún Caves) are also impressive.

Kabah
The Zona Arqueológica Puuc and the ruins of Kabah, just over 18 km south-east of Uxmal, are right astride Highway 261. The site is open from 8 am to 5 pm; admission costs US$4.

The guard shack and souvenir shop are on the east side of the highway as you approach. Cold drinks and junky snacks are sold.

Undoubtedly the most impressive building here is the **Palace of Masks**, or Codz Poop, set on its own high terrace on the right-hand (east) side of the highway. It's an amazing sight, with its façade covered in nearly 300 masks of Chac, the rain god or sky serpent.

To the north of the Palace of Masks is a small **pyramid**. Behind and to the left of the Palace of Masks is **El Palacio**, with a broad façade having several doorways; in the centre of each doorway is a column, a characteristic of the Puuc architectural style. Walk around the left side of El Palacio and follow a path into the jungle for several hundred metres to the **Temple of Columns**,

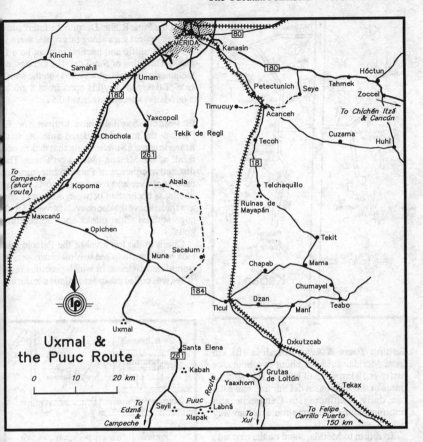

Uxmal & the Puuc Route

0   10   20 km

called the Tercera Casa, famous for the rows of semi-columns on the upper part of its façade. Cross the highway to the west side, walk up the slope and on your right you'll pass a high mound of stones that was once the Gran Teocalli, or **Great Temple**. Continue straight on to the sacbé, or cobbled elevated ceremonial road, and look right to see a monumental arch with the Maya corbelled vault (two straight stone surfaces leaned against one another, meeting at the top). This arch is ruined, however. It is said that the sacbé here runs past the arch and through the jungle all the way to Uxmal,

terminating at a smaller arch; in the other direction it went to Labná. Once all of Yucatán was connected by these marvellous 'white roads' of rough limestone.

Beyond the sacbé, about 600 metres farther from the road, are several other complexes of buildings, none as impressive as what you've already seen. The **Western Quadrangle** (Cuadrángulo del Oeste) has some decoration of columns and masks. North of the quadrangle are the Temple of the Key Patterns and the Temple of Lintels; the latter once had intricately carved lintels of tough sapodilla wood.

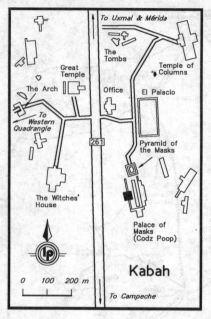

Kabah

this is the Puuc Route. Despite the interesting archaeological sites along this route, there is not much traffic and hitchhiking can be difficult. The ruins of Sayil are 4½ km east of the junction with Highway 261, on the south side of the road. Sayil is open from 8 am to 5 pm daily; admission costs US$1.

El Palacio Sayil is best known for El Palacio, the huge three-tiered building with a façade some 85 metres long that makes one think of the Minoan palaces on Crete. The distinctive columns of Puuc architecture are used here over and over, as supports for the lintels, as decoration between doorways and as a frieze above the doorways, alternating with huge stylised Chac masks and 'descending gods'.

Climb to the top level of the Palacio and look to the north to see several *chultunes*, or stone-lined cisterns, in which precious rainwater was collected and stored for use during

Getting There & Away Kabah is 101 km from Mérida, a ride of about two hours, or just over 18 km south of Uxmal. Six 1st-class buses of the Autobuses del Sur line make the run daily, continuing to Campeche and returning along the same route; a one-way ticket costs US$1.70.

To return to Mérida, stand on the east side of the road at the entrance to the ruins and flag down a bus. Try hitchhiking as well, because the buses are often full and thus won't stop. You may have the same problem of full buses if you stand on the west side of the highway and flag down a bus to take you to the Puuc Route turn-off, five km south of Kabah, or to other sites along Highway 261 farther south.

Many visitors come to Kabah by private car and may be willing to give you a lift southwards on the Puuc Route.

Sayil
Five km south of Kabah a road turns east:

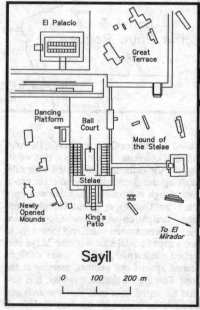

Sayil

the dry season. Some of these chultunes can
hold more than 30,000 litres.

El Mirador If you take the path southwards
from the palace for about 400 metres you
come to the temple named El Mirador, with
its interesting rooster-like roofcomb once
painted bright red. About 100 metres beyond
El Mirador by the path to the left is a stela
beneath a protective palapa which bears a
relief of a phallic god, now badly weathered.

Xlapak
From the entrance gate at Sayil, it's six km
east to the entrance gate at Xlapak ('shla-
PAK'). The name means Old Walls in Maya
and was a general term among local people
for ancient ruins, about which they knew
little. The site is open from 8 am to 5 pm;
admission is US$1.

The ornate palace at Xlapak is smaller
than those at Kabah and Sayil, measuring
only about 20 metres in length. It's decorated
with the inevitable Chac masks, columns and
colonnettes and fretted geometric latticework of the Puuc style. To the right is the
rubble of what were once two smaller buildings.

Labná
From the entrance gate at Xlapak, it's 3½ km
east to the gate at Labná. The site here is open
from 8 am to 5 pm; admission costs US$1.

The Arch Labná is best known for its magnificent arch, once part of a building which
separated two quadrangular courtyards. It
now appears to be a gate joining two small
plazas. The corbelled structure, three metres
wide and six metres high, is well preserved
and stands close to the entrance of Labná.
The mosaic reliefs decorating the upper
façade are exuberantly Puuc in style.

If you look at the ornate work on the
north-eastern side of the arch, you will make
out mosaics of Maya huts. At the base of
either side of the arch are rooms of the
adjoining building, now ruined, including
upper lattice patterns constructed atop a ser-
pentine design.

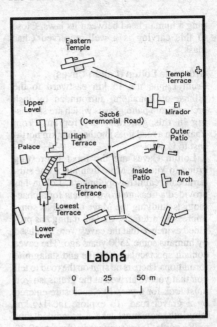

Labná

0   25   50 m

El Mirador Standing on the opposite side of
the arch and separated from it by the lime-
stone-paved sacbé is a pyramid with a temple
atop it called El Mirador. The pyramid itself
is poorly preserved, being largely stone
rubble. The temple, with its five-metre-high
roofcomb, true to its name, looks like a
watchtower.

Palace Archaeologists believe that at one
point in the 9th century, some 3000 Maya
lived at Labná. To support such numbers in
these arid hills, water was collected in
chultunes, or cisterns. At Labná's peak there
were some 60 chultunes in and around the
city; several are still visible.

The palace, the first edifice you come to
at Labná, is connected by a sacbé to El
Mirador and the arch. One of the longest
buildings in the Puuc Hills, its design is not
as impressive as its counterpart at Sayil.
There's a ghoulish sculpture on the eastern
corner on the upper level of a serpent grip-

ping a human head between its jaws. Close to this carving is a well-preserved Chac mask.

Grutas de Loltún (Loltún Caves)

From Labná it's 15 km eastward to the village of Yaaxhom, surrounded by lush orchards and palm groves which are surprising in this generally dry region. From Yaaxhom a road goes another four km northeast to Loltún.

Loltún Caves are the most interesting grutas in Yucatán. More than just a fine subterranean realm for spelunkers, Loltún has provided a treasure trove of data for archaeologists studying the Maya as well as some impressive artefacts. Carbon dating has provided evidence that the caves were first used by humans some 2500 years ago. The caves contain spectacular stalactite and stalagmite formations There is no sign on the road to tell you that you've arrived at the grutas, so you must look for a park-like enclosure entered by a gravel road. To explore the 1½-km labyrinth, you must take a scheduled tour. with a guide. Tours supposedly depart at 9.30 and 11 am and at 12.30, 2 and 3.30 pm, but may depart early if enough people are waiting. The guides may be willing to take you through at other hours if you offer a substantial tip (a few dollars). Occasionally there is a guide on the premises who speaks English – check to see if the tour will be in a language you understand.

Admission to the caves costs US$3.50, children under 12 free. The guides, who are not paid by the government, expect a tip at the end of the hour-long tour.

For refreshments there's the *Restaurant El Guerrero* near the exit of the caves, a walk of eight to 10 minutes (600 metres) along a marked path from the far side of the parking lot near the cave entrance. Comida corrida costs about US$9. They serve icy-cold drinks, but a simple soft drink costs more than US$1.

Getting There & Away Loltún is on a country road leading to Oxkutzcab (8 km) and there is usually some transport along the

road. Try hitching, or catch a ride for US$0.30 in one of the colectivos which ply this route. A taxi from Oxkutzcab may charge US$6 or so one way.

Buses run frequently every day between Mérida and Oxkutzcab via Ticul.

If you're driving from Loltún to the Puuc Route site of Labná, drive out of the Loltún car park, turn right and take the next road on the right, which passes the access road to the restaurant. Do not take the road marked 'Xul'. After four km you'll come to the village of Yaaxhom, where you turn right to join the Puuc Route westwards.

UXMAL

Set in the Puuc Hills, which lent their name to the architectural patterns in this region, Uxmal was an important city during the Late Classic period (600-900 AD) of a region which encompassed the satellite towns of Sayil, Kabah, Xlapak and Labná. Although Uxmal means Thrice Built in Maya, it was actually reconstructed five times.

That a sizeable population flourished at all in this area is a mystery, as there is precious little water in the region. The Maya cisterns (chultunes) must have been adequate.

History

First occupied in about 600 AD, the town is influenced by highland Mexico in its architecture, most likely through contact fostered by trade. The well-proportioned Puuc architecture is unique to this region.

Given the scarcity of water in the Puuc Hills, Chac the rain god was of great significance. His image is ubiquitous here in stucco monster-like masks protruding from façades and cornices.

There is much speculation as to why Uxmal was abandoned in about 900 AD. Drought conditions may have reached such proportions that the inhabitants had to relocate. One widely held theory suggests that the rise to greatness of Chichén Itzá drew people away from the Puuc Hills.

The first written account of Uxmal by a European came from the priest López de Cogullado in the 16th century. The next

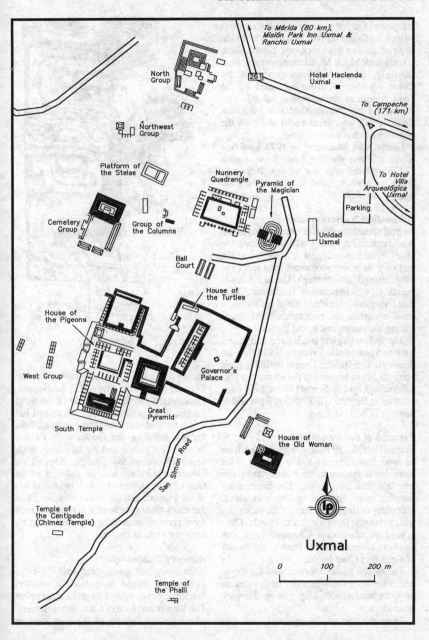

To Mérida (80 km),
Misión Park Inn Uxmal &
Rancho Uxmal

261

Hotel Hacienda
Uxmal

To Campeche
(171 km)

North Group

Northwest
Group

Platform of
the Stelae

Nunnery
Quadrangle

Pyramid of
the Magician

To Hotel
Villa
Arqueológica
Uxmal

Parking

Cemetery
Group

Group of
the Columns

Unidad
Uxmal

Ball
Court

House of
the Turtles

House of
the Pigeons

West Group

Governor's
Palace

Great
Pyramid

San Simon Road

South Temple

House of
the Old Woman

Temple of
the Centipede
(Chimez Temple)

Uxmal

0   100   200 m

Temple of
the Phalli

influential European account of the site was written by Count de Waldeck in 1836. In the hope of selling his work, the Count made Uxmal look like a Mediterranean ruin. Fortunately, misconceptions generated by Count de Waldeck were corrected by the great American archaeologist John L Stephens and his British illustrator Frederick Catherwood, who wrote about and drew the site with accuracy.

Uxmal was excavated in 1929 by Frans Blom. His was the first modern excavation and paved the way for others. Although much has been restored, there is still a good deal to discover.

Orientation & Information

As you come into the site from the highway, you'll enter a car park (US$0.85 per car); the Hotel Villa Arqueológica is to the left at the end of a short entrance road. You enter the site through the modern Unidad Uxmal building, which contains Restaurant Yax-Beh. Also in the Unidad Uxmal are toilets, a small museum, an auditorium, and shops selling souvenirs, crafts and books.

The archaeological site is open daily from 8 am to 5 pm; admission costs US$6 (free on Sunday). The Unidad Uxmal building stays open till 10 pm because of the 45-minute Luz y Sonido (Light & Sound) show, held each evening in English (US$2.50) at 9 pm and in Spanish (US$1) at 7 pm.

Pyramid of the Magician

This tall temple, 39 metres high, was built on an oval base. The smoothly sloping sides have been restored; they date from the temple's fifth incarnation. The four earlier temples were covered in the rebuilding, except for the high doorway on the west side, which remains from the fourth temple. Decorated in elaborate Chenes style, the doorway proper takes the form of the mouth of a gigantic Chac mask.

The ascent to the doorway and the top is best done from the west side. Heavy chains serve as handrails to help you up the very steep steps.

From the top of the pyramid, you can

Chac mask

survey the rest of the archaeological site. Directly west of the pyramid is the Nunnery Quadrangle. On the south side of the quadrangle, down a short slope, is a ruined ball court. Further south stands the great artificial terrace holding the Governor's Palace; between the palace and the ball court is the small House of the Turtles. Beyond the Governor's Palace are the remains of the Great Pyramid, and next to it are the House of the Pigeons and the South Temple. There are many other structures at Uxmal, but most have been recaptured by the jungle and are now just verdant mounds.

Nunnery Quadrangle

Archaeologists guess that this 74-room quadrangle might have been a military academy, royal school or palace complex. The long-nosed face of Chac appears everywhere on the façades of the four separate temples which form the quadrangle. The northern temple, grandest of the four, was built first, followed by the south, east and west.

Several decorative elements on the façades show signs of Mexican, perhaps Totonac, influence. The feathered serpent (Quetzalcóatl) motif along the top of the west temple's façade is one of these. Note also the stylised depictions of the *na*, or Maya thatched hut, over some of the doorways in the northern and southern buildings.

Ball Court

Pass through the corbelled arch in the middle of the south building of the quadrangle and continue down the slope to the ball court, which is much less impressive than the great ball court at Chichén Itzá.

House of the Turtles

Climb the steep slope up to the artificial terrace on which stands the Governor's Palace. At the top on the right is the House of the Turtles, which takes its name from the turtles carved on the cornice. The frieze of short columns or 'rolled mats' which runs around the top of the temple is characteristic of the Puuc style. Turtles were associated by the Maya with the rain god Chac. According to Maya myth, when the people suffered from drought so did the turtles and both prayed to Chac to send rain.

Governor's Palace

The magnificent façade of the palace, nearly 100 metres long, has been called 'the finest structure at Uxmal and the culmination of the Puuc style' by Mayanist Michael D Coe. Buildings in Puuc style have walls filled with rubble, faced with cement and then covered in a thin veneer of limestone squares; the lower part of the façade is plain, the upper part festooned with stylised Chac faces and geometric designs, often lattice-like or fretted. Other elements of Puuc style are decorated cornices, rows of half-columns and round columns in doorways. The stones forming the corbelled vaults in Puuc style are shaped like boots.

Great Pyramid

Adjacent to the Governor's Palace, this 32-metre mound has been restored only on the northern side. There is a quadrangle at the top which archaeologists theorise was largely destroyed in order to construct another pyramid above it. This work, for reasons unknown, was never completed. At the top are some stucco carvings of Chac, birds and flowers.

House of the Pigeons

West of the great pyramid sits a structure whose roofcomb is latticed with a pigeon-hole pattern – hence the building's name. The nine honeycombed triangular belfries sit on top of a building which was once part of a quadrangle. The base is so eroded that it is difficult for archaeologists to guess its function.

House of the Old Woman & Temple of the Phalli

Both sites are located between the main highway and the San Simon road, south-west of the Governor's Palace. The House of the Old Woman, which is now largely rubble, was according to Maya mythology the home of a dwarf magician's mother, a sorcerer. Just to the south sits the Temple of the Phalli, which is festooned with phallic sculptures. Some of these served as spouts to drain water from the roof. Some archaeologists think the temple was constructed by later invaders, as the Maya are not believed to have had any phallic cult.

Cemetery Group

Lying on the path west of the ball court, these stone altars have skull-and-crossbone sculptures, but there is no real evidence that this was a cemetery.

Places to Stay & Eat – bottom end

As there is no town at Uxmal, only the archaeological site and several top-end hotels, you cannot depend upon finding cheap food or lodging. Campers can pitch their tents five km north of the ruins on Highway 261, the road to Mérida, at *Rancho*

Uxmal. The rate is US$3 per person. Several serviceable guestrooms with shower and fan go for US$19 a double, a bit expensive for what you get, but cheap for Uxmal. You can have a filling lunch or dinner platter in the thatch-roofed restaurant for about US$5 or US$7. It may take you 45 to 55 minutes to walk there from the ruins; there's some possibility of hitching a ride.

Other than the Rancho Uxmal, there's no cheap lodging in the area. If you don't want to return to Mérida for the night, make your way to Ticul.

For food, the best thing to do is to bring your own with you from Mérida. Otherwise try the *Restaurant Yax-Beh* in the Unidad Uxmal. Breakfasts here cost US$4.50 to US$8, sandwiches US$5 or US$6, and main courses at lunch or dinner about US$8 or US$10. Even a cold soft drink and a snack will set you back more than US$2. It's not cheap, but it is air-conditioned.

Or try the *Posada Uxmal Restaurant Nicté-Ha*, just across the highway from the road to the ruins, on the grounds of the Hotel Hacienda Uxmal. This simple eatery is open from 12.30 to 7 pm daily and offers sandwiches, fruit salads and similar fare at prices slightly lower than those at the Yax-Beh. Often they'll allow you to use the hotel's swimming pool after you've bought a meal.

Places to Stay & Eat – top end

The *Hotel Hacienda Uxmal* (☎ 4-71-42), originally housed the archaeologists who explored and restored Uxmal. It's an exceptionally pleasant and comfortable place to stay and has a beautiful swimming pool.

Meals in the dining room are a bit pricey at US$9 for breakfast and US$20 for lunch or dinner. Rooms cost US$60 to US$75 a single or double, but with breakfast and dinner included the price rises to more than US$120 a double. You can supposedly make reservations in Mérida at the Mérida Travel Service in the Hotel Casa del Balam (☎ (99) 24-88-44), at the corner of Calles 60 and 57, but they seem not to know the correct room prices and have always told me the hotel is full, even if it isn't.

Hotel Villa Arqueológica Uxmal (In Mérida, contact through Apdo Postal 449, (☎ (99) 24-70-53) is the closest lodging to the ruins. Run by Club Med, this attractive modern hotel offers a swimming pool, tennis courts, a good French-inspired restaurant and air-conditioned guestrooms for US$50 /58 a single/double. Spacious two-bedroom family rooms cost US$65. In the restaurant, you can have a very good dinner for US$20 to US$34 per person. A cold beer by the pool costs US$2.50.

The *Misión Park Inn Uxmal* (in Mérida (☎ (99) 24-73-08) is the newest of the hotels, set on a hilltop 2 km north of the turn-off to the ruins. Many rooms have balcony views of Uxmal and all are air-conditioned. Facilities include a swimming pool, restaurant and bar. Rooms are priced at US$46/50 a single/double.

Getting There & Away

Air An airstrip is under construction near Uxmal. When it is finished, air routes from Cancún will be developed, making it possible to visit Uxmal on a day excursion.

Bus It's 80 km (1½ hours) from Uxmal to Mérida and services are frequent. Eight 2nd-class (US$1.70) buses of the Autobuses del Sur line make the trip daily and there are other buses as well. For the trip to Mérida, wait by the Hotel Hacienda Uxmal and flag down a bus as it approaches. In late afternoon there may be standing room only.

If you're going to Ticul, hop on a bus heading north, get off at Muna and get another bus eastwards to Ticul.

For buses to Kabah, the Puuc Route turnoff and points on the road to Campeche, flag down a southbound bus at the turnoff to the ruins.

Car If you rent a car in Mérida, plan on at least two days and preferably three, exploring the area. You can spend the first day driving from Mérida to Uxmal, with a stop along the way at the Hacienda of Yaxcopoil. Spend the night at Uxmal and continue to Kabah and the Puuc Route sites the next day.

You can return to Mérida for the night, or to Uxmal, or go to Ticul. Returning via Yucatán state Highway 18, you can stop for a visit to the ruins of Mayapán and a look at the pyramid in Acanceh.

TICUL

Ticul, 30 km east of Uxmal, is the largest town south of Mérida in this ruin-rich region. It has several serviceable hotels and restaurants, and good transport. It's also a centre for fine *huipil* weaving – the embroidery on these dresses is extraordinary. For both quality and price, Ticul is a good place to buy this traditional Maya garment. Ticul's main street is Calle 23, sometimes called the Calle Principal, going from the highway north-east past the market and the town's best restaurants to the main plaza.

Places to Stay – bottom end

Hotel Sierra Sosa (☎ (997) 2-00-08/53),

Calle 26 No 199A, half a block north-west of the plaza, has very basic rooms for US$6/8.50 a single/double. A few rooms at the back have windows, but most are dark and dungeon-like; all are fairly beat-up. Before you move in, check to be sure the ceiling fan works. If no one seems to be around at the hotel, check next door in the electronics shop.

Similarly basic but more expensive is the *Hotel San Miguel* (☎ (997) 2-03-82), Calle 28 No 195, near Calle 23 and the market. Singles cost US$7.50 with fan and bath, doubles US$9 to US$12, triples US$12 to US$16 and rooms for four cost US$16 to US$19.

Places to Stay – middle

Ticul's better hotels don't really offer too much more in the way of comfort and both are on the highway on the outskirts of town,

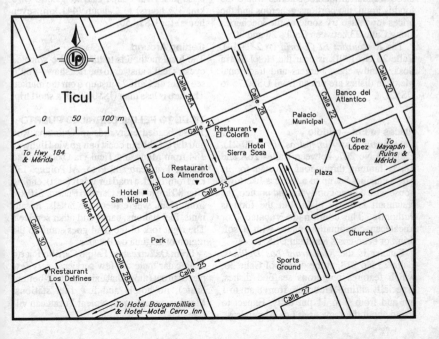

Ticul

0   50   100 m

To Hwy 184 & Mérida

Calle 26A
Calle 21
Restaurant El Colorín
Hotel Sierra Sosa
Calle 26
Calle 28
Restaurant Los Almendros
Hotel San Miguel
Market
Calle 30
Calle 23
Park
Calle 28A
Restaurant Los Delfines
Calle 25

Banco del Atlantico
Palacio Municipal
Calle 22
Calle 20
Cine López
To Mayapán Ruins & Mérida
Plaza
Church
Sports Ground
Calle 27

To Hotel Bougambillias & Hotel-Motel Cerro Inn

an inconvenient two-km walk from the centre, but fine if you have a car.

Best in town is the new *Hotel Bougambillias* (☎ (997) 2-01-39), near the junction of the western end of Calle 25 and the highway to Muna and Mérida. The darkish rooms are simple but newer and cleaner than the competition's. Prices are US$14 a double and US$26 for a twin, but you can often haggle the price down.

A hundred metres north-west of the Bougambillias on the opposite side of the highway is the older *Hotel-Motel Cerro Inn* (no phone). Set in spacious, shady grounds, it has nine well-used rooms with private shower and ceiling fan for US$12 to US$16 a double. A palapa restaurant provides drinks and snacks.

Places to Eat – bottom end

Ticul's lively market provides all the ingredients for picnics and snacks. It also has lots of those wonderful market eateries where the food is good, the portions generous and the prices low. Also try some of the loncherías along Calle 23 between Calles 26 and 30.

The *Restaurant El Colorín* (☎ 2-03-14), Calle 26 No 199B, is near the Hotel Sierra Sosa. Sandwiches, burgers and traditional Mexican dishes are priced from US$0.75 to US$2.

Places to Eat – middle

Restaurant Los Almendros (☎ 2-00-21), Calle 23 No 207, between Calles 26A and 28, is famous throughout Yucatán for its Maya cuisine. Set up in a fortress-like town house with a large courtyard and portico, the restaurant is fairly plain, but the food is authentic. The combinado yucateco, or Yucatecan combination plate, with a soft drink or beer, costs less than US$10.

Fancier is the *Restaurant Los Delfines*, Calle 23 No 218, at the corner of Calle 30, which features numerous seafood dishes, especially shrimp. Hours are from 8 am to 1 pm and from 5 to 11 pm daily. Expect to spend about the same as at Los Almendros.

Getting There & Away

It's 85 km between Ticul and Mérida, a 1½-hour journey. Nine 2nd-class buses of the Autobuses del Caribe line run daily, charging US$1.25 one way.

You can catch a minibus (combi), from the intersection of Calles 23 and 28, to Oxkutzcab ('osh-kootz-KAHB') 16 km to the south-east. From Oxkutzcab a minibus or pickup truck (colectivo) goes to Loltún (eight km); ask for the camión to Xul ('SHOOL'), but get off at Las Grutas de Loltún.

Minibuses to Santa Elena (15 km), the village between Uxmal and Kabah, also depart from the intersection of Calles 23 and 28, taking a back road and then leaving you to catch another bus north-west to Uxmal (15 km) or south to Kabah (3½ km). You may find it more convenient to take a minibus or bus to Muna (22 km) on Highway 261 and another south to Uxmal (16 km).

Autobuses del Caribe runs occasional 1st-class buses via Felipe Carrillo Puerto (215 km, 3½ hours) to Cancún (441 km, seven hours) for US$8.50.

Getting Around

The local method is to hire a three-wheeled cycle, Ticul's answer to the rickshaw – you'll see them on Calle 23 just up from the market. The fare is less than US$0.50 for a short trip.

TICUL TO FELIPE CARRILLO PUERTO

Those headed eastwards to Quintana Roo and the Caribbean coast can go via Highway 184 from Muna and Ticul via Oxkutzcab to Tekax, Tzucacab and Peto. At Polguc, 130 km from Ticul, a road turns left (east), ending after 80 km in Felipe Carrillo Puerto, 210 km from Ticul, where there are hotels, restaurants, fuel stations, banks and other services. The right fork of the road goes south to the region of Laguna de Bacalar.

From Oxkutzcab to Felipe Carrillo Puerto or Bacalar there are few services: very few places to eat (those that exist are rock-bottom basic), no hotels and few fuel stations. Mostly you see small, typical Yucatecan villages.

TICUL TO MÉRIDA
Via Muna & Yaxcopoil
From Ticul to Mérida you have a choice of routes. The western route to Muna, then north on Highway 261, is fastest, with the best bus services.

Muna, an old town 22km north-west of Ticul, has several interesting colonial churches, including the former Convento de la Asunción and the churches of Santa María, San Mateo and San Andrés.

The **Hacienda of Yaxcopoil**, 29 km north of Muna on the west side of Highway 261, has numerous French Renaissance-style buildings which have been restored and turned into a museum of the 17th century. This vast estate specialised in the growing and processing of henéquen. From Yaxcopoil it's 16 km north to Uman, and then another 17 km to the centre of Mérida.

Via Ruinas de Mayapán
The eastern route north follows Yucatán state Highway 18 from Ticul via the ruins of Mayapán to Tecoh, Acanceh and Mérida. Transport on this route is difficult without your own car. It might take the better part of a day to get from Ticul via the ruins of Mayapán to Mérida by bus.

Those taking this route should be careful to distinguish between Ruinas de Mayapán, the ruins of the ancient city, and Mayapán, a Maya village some 40 km south-east of the ruins past the town of Teabo. Buses and colectivos run fitfully along this route, so you should plan the better part of a day, with stops in Ruinas de Mayapán and Acanceh, to travel the route by public transport.

If you're driving, follow the signs from Ticul north-east via Chapab to Mama (25 km), which has a peculiarly fortress-like church, then farther north-east to Tekit (seven km). At Tekit, turn left (north-west) on Yucatán state Highway 18 toward Tecoh, Acanceh and Kanasin; the Ruinas de Mayapán are eight km north-west of Tekit, on the left (west) side of the road.

RUINAS DE MAYAPÁN
The city of Mayapán, once a major Maya capital, was huge, with a population estimated at around 12,000. Its ruins cover several sq km, all surrounded by a great defensive wall. Over 3500 buildings, 20 cenotes and traces of the city wall were mapped by archaeologists working in the 1950s and in 1962. The workmanship was inferior to the great age of Maya art; though the Cocom rulers of Mayapán tried to revive the past glories of Maya civilisation, they succeeded only in part.

History
Mayapán was supposedly founded by Kukulcán (Quetzalcóatl) in 1007, shortly after the former ruler of Tula arrived in Yucatán. His dynasty, the Cocom, organised a confederation of city-states which included Uxmal, Chichén Itzá and many other notable cities. Despite their alliance, animosity between the Cocoms and the Itzaes led to the storming of Chichén Itzá by the Cocoms during the late 1100s, which forced the Itzá rulers into exile. The Cocom dynasty under Hunac Ceel Canuch emerged supreme in all of northern Yucatán and obliged the other rulers to pay tribute.

Cocom supremacy lasted for almost 2½ centuries, until the ruler of Uxmal, Ah Xupán Xiú, led a rebellion of the oppressed city-states and overthrew Cocom hegemony. The great capital of Mayapán was utterly destroyed and was uninhabited ever after.

But there was no peace in Yucatán after the Xiú victory. The Cocom dynasty recovered and frequent struggles for power erupted until 1542, when Francisco de Montejo the Younger founded Mérida. The ruler of the Xiú people, Ah Kukum Xiú, submitted his forces to Montejo's control in exchange for a military alliance against the Cocoms. The Cocoms were defeated and – too late – the Xiú rulers realised that they had willingly signed the death warrant of Maya independence.

Information
At the caretaker's hut 100 metres in from the road, pay the admission fee of US$3.50 and enter the site any day between 8 am and 5

pm. If you have camping equipment, the caretaker may grant you permission to camp near his hut. Facilities consist of a latrine and a well with a bucket.

Ruins

Jungle has returned to cover many of the buildings, though you can visit several cenotes (including Itzmal Chen, a main Maya religious sanctuary) and make out the large piles of stones which were once the Temple of Kukulcán and the circular Caracol. Though the ruins today are far less impressive than those at other sites, Mayapán has a stillness and a loneliness (usually undisturbed by other tourists) that seems to fit its melancholy later history.

MAYAPÁN TO MÉRIDA

About two km north of the Ruinas de Mayapán is **Telchaquillo**. Beneath the village plaza is a vast cenote, or limestone cavern, filled with rainwater. It's still used as a water source during the dry months.

From Telchaquillo it's 11 km north to **Tecoh**, with its church and well-kept Palacio Municipal separated by a green football pitch. From Tecoh it's only 35 km to Mérida, but you should plan a short stop in Acanceh.

The road enters **Acanceh** and goes to the main plaza, which is flanked by a shady park and the church. To the left of the church is a partially restored pyramid, and to the right are market loncherías if you're in need of a snack. In the park, note the statue of the smiling deer; the name Acanceh means Pond of the Deer. Another local sight of interest is the cantina Aqui Me Queda (I'm Staying Here), a ready-made answer for wives who come to the cantina to urge their husbands homeward.

Continuing north-west you pass through Petectunich, Tepich, San Antonio and Kanasin before coming to Mérida's periférico (ring road).

IZAMAL

Population: 40,000

In ancient times, Izamal was a centre for the worship of the supreme Maya god Itzamná and the sun god Kinich Kakmó. A dozen temple pyramids in the town were devoted to these or other gods. Perhaps this Maya religiosity is why the Spanish colonists chose Izamal as the site for an enormous and very impressive Franciscan monastery.

Today Izamal is a small, quiet provincial town with the atmosphere of life in another century. Its two principal squares are surrounded by impressive arcades and dominated by the gargantuan bulk of the Convento de San Antonio de Padua. There are a few small, cheap hotels and eateries.

Convento de San Antonio de Padua

When the Spanish conquered Izamal, they destroyed the major Maya temple, the Popul-Chac pyramid and in 1533 began to build from its stones one of the first monasteries in the hemisphere. The work was finished in 1561.

The monastery's principal church is the Santuario de la Virgen de Izamal, approached by a ramp from the main square. Walk up the ramp and through an arcaded gallery to the Atrium, a spacious arcaded courtyard in which the fiesta of the Virgin of Izamal takes place each 15 August.

Entry to the church is free. The best time

to visit is in the morning, as it may be closed during the afternoon siesta.

If you wander around town, you may come across remnants of the other 11 Maya pyramids. The largest is the temple of Kinich Kakmó; all are unrestored piles of rubble.

Getting There & Away

There are direct buses several times daily from Mérida (72 km, 1½ hours, US$1.75). Four 2nd-class buses (US$2.75) serve Izamal from Valladolid; if you don't catch one of these, you must change buses at Hóctun. If you're driving eastward, turn north at Hóctun; if westward, at Kantunil.

CHICHÉN ITZÁ

The most famous and best restored of Yucatán's Maya sites, Chichén Itzá will awe the most jaded of ruins visitors. Many mysteries of the Maya astronomical calendar are made clear when one understands the design of the 'time temples' here. But one astronomical mystery remains: why do most people come here from Mérida and Cancún on day trips, arriving at 11 am, when the blazing sun is getting to its hottest point and departing around 3 pm when the heat finally begins to abate? You'd do better to stay the night nearby and do your exploration of the site either early in the morning or late in the afternoon.

Should you have the good fortune to visit Chichén Itzá on the vernal equinox (20 to 21 March) or autumnal equinox (21 to 22 September), you can witness the light-and-shadow illusion of the serpent ascending or descending the side of the staircase of El Castillo. The illusion is almost as good in the week preceding and the week following the equinox.

History

Chichén Itzá (The Mouth of the Well of the Itzaes) had two periods of greatness and was abandoned between those epochs.

Most archaeologists agree that Chichén Itzá's first major settlement, during the Late Classic period between 550 and 900 AD, was pure Maya. In about the 10th century, the city was largely abandoned for unknown reasons.

The city was resettled about 1100 AD. Shortly thereafter, Chichén seems to have been invaded by the Toltecs, who had moved down from their central highlands capital of Tula, north of Mexico City. The Toltecs fused their culture with that of the Maya, incorporating the cult of Quetzalcóatl (Kukulcán in Maya). You will see images of both Chac, the Maya rain god, and Quetzalcóatl, the plumed serpent, throughout the city.

The substantial fusion of highland central Mexican and Puuc architectural styles make Chichén unique among Yucatán's ruins. The fabulous El Castillo, the Temple of Panels and the Platform of Venus are all outstanding architectural works built during the height of Toltec cultural input.

After a Maya leader moved his political capital to Mayapán while keeping Chichén as his religious capital, Chichén Itzá fell into decline. Why it was subsequently abandoned in the 14th century is a mystery, but the once-great city remained the site of Maya pilgrimages for many years.

Orientation

Most of Chichén's lodgings, restaurants and services are ranged along one km of highway in the village of Piste ('PEESS-teh'), to the west (Mérida) side of the ruins. It's 1½ km from the western entrance of the ruins to the first hotel (Pyramide Inn) in Piste, or 2.5 km from the ruins to Piste village square (actually a triangle), which is shaded by a huge tree. Buses generally stop at the square; you can make the hot walk to or from the ruins in 20 to 30 minutes.

On the eastern (Cancún) side, it's 1½ km from the highway along the access road to the eastern entrance to the ruins. On the way you pass the Villa Arqueológica, Hacienda Chichén and Mayaland luxury hotels. The moderately priced Hotel Dolores Alba is 3 km east of the eastern entrance to the ruins, on the highway to Cancún.

Chichén's little airstrip is north of the

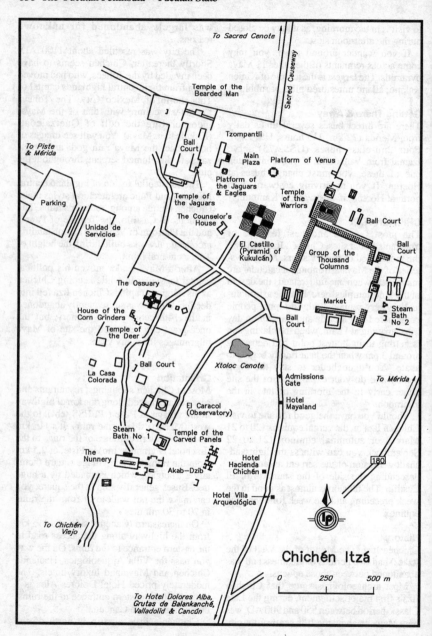

To Sacred Cenote

Sacred Causeway

Temple of the Bearded Man

Tzompantli

Main Plaza

Platform of Venus

Ball Court

Platform of the Jaguars & Eagles

Temple of the Warriors

To Piste & Mérida

Parking

Temple of the Jaguars

The Counselor's House

Ball Court

Ball Court

Unidad de Servicios

El Castillo (Pyramid of Kukulcán)

Group of the Thousand Columns

The Ossuary

House of the Corn Grinders

Temple of the Deer

Market

Ball Court

Steam Bath No 2

La Casa Colorada

Ball Court

Xtoloc Cenote

Admissions Gate

To Mérida

El Caracol (Observatory)

Hotel Mayaland

Steam Bath No 1

Temple of the Carved Panels

Hotel Hacienda Chichén

The Nunnery

Akab–Dzib

180

Hotel Villa Arqueológica

To Chichén Viejo

Chichén Itzá

0   250   500 m

To Hotel Dolores Alba, Grutas de Balankanché, Valladolid & Cancún ruins, on the north side of the highway, three km from Piste's main square.

Information

Money Changing money can be a problem in Piste, and you may have to depend upon your hotel or the Unidad de Servicios at the western entrance to the ruins, as the Banamex branches seem to have closed down.

Telephone For long-distance telephone calls you must go to the Teléfonos de México caseta de larga distancia in Piste. Look for the Restaurant Xaybe, across the highway from the Hotel Misión Chichén Park Inn; the caseta is in the same group of buildings, open from 8 am to 9 pm.

Archaeological Zone

Chichén Itzá is open every day from 8 am to 5 pm; the interior passageway in El Castillo is open only from 11 am to 1 pm and from 4 to 5 pm. Admission to the site costs US$6.25 (free on Sunday), US$11 extra for a video camera and US$8 extra if you use a tripod with your camera. Admission is free to children under 12.

The main entrance is the western one, which has a large car park (US$0.85) and a big, modern entrance building called the Unidad de Servicios, open 8 am to 10 pm. The Unidad has a small but worthwhile museum (open 8 am to 5 pm) with sculptures, reliefs, artefacts and explanations of these in Spanish, English and French. The Chilam Balam Auditorio next to the museum has audio-visual shows about Chichén in English at noon and 4 pm. In the central space of the Unidad stands a scale model of the archaeological site, and off towards the toilets is an exhibit on Thompson's excavations of the sacred cenote in 1923. There are two bookshops with a good assortment of guides and maps; a currency exchange desk (open 9 am to 1 pm); and a *guardarropa* at the main ticket desk where you can leave your belongings (free) while you explore the site.

Sound-and-light shows (35 minutes) are held each evening in Spanish from 7 to 7.35 pm for US$1.25, and in English from 9 to 9.35 pm for US$2.25.

El Castillo As you pass through the turnstiles from the Unidad de Servicios into the archaeological zone, El Castillo rises before you in all its grandeur. Standing nearly 25 metres tall, El Castillo (The Castle) was originally built before 800 AD, prior to the Toltec invasion. Nonetheless, the plumed serpent was sculpted along the stairways and Toltec warriors are represented in the doorway carvings at the top of the temple.

Climb to the top for a view of the entire site. This is best done early in the morning or late in the afternoon, both to beat the heat and to see Chichén before the crowds arrive.

The pyramid is actually the Maya calendar formed in stone. Each of El Castillo's nine levels is divided in two by a staircase, making 18 separate terraces which commemorate the 18 20-day months of the Vague Year. The four stairways have 91 steps each; add the top platform and the total is 365, the number of days in the year. On each façade of the pyramid are 52 flat panels, reminders of the 52 years in the Calendar Round.

Most amazing of all, during the spring and autumn equinoxes (around 21 March and 21 September), light and shadow form a series of triangles on the side of the north staircase which mimic the creep of a serpent. The illusion lasts three hours and 22 minutes.

This pyramid holds more surprises: there's another pyramid *inside* El Castillo. When archaeologists opened it, they found a brilliant red jaguar throne with inlaid eyes and spots of shimmering jade. The inner sanctum also holds a Toltec chac-mool figure.

The inner pyramid is only open from 11 am to 1 pm and 4 to 5 pm. Entry is not a good idea for claustrophobes or those who hate close, fetid air.

Principal Ball Court The principal ball field, the largest and most impressive in Mexico, is only one of the city's eight courts, indicative of the importance the games held here. The field is flanked by temples at either end and bound by towering parallel walls with stone rings cemented up high.

There is evidence that the ball game may have changed over the years. Some carvings show players with padding on their elbows and knees and it is thought that they played a soccer-like game with a hard rubber ball, forbidding the use of hands. Other carvings show players wielding bats; it appears that if a player hit the ball through one of the stone hoops, his team was declared the winner. It may be that during the Toltec period the losing captain, and perhaps his team-mates as well, were sacrificed.

Along the walls of the ball court are some fine stone reliefs, including scenes of decapitations of players. Acoustically the court is amazing – a conversation at one end can be heard 135 metres away at the other end, and if you clap, you hear a resounding echo.

Temple of the Bearded Man & Temple of the Jaguars The structure at the northern end of the ball court, known as the Temple ' of the Bearded Man and named for a carving inside it, has some finely sculpted pillars and reliefs of flowers, birds and trees. See also the temple at the end of the court facing out on El Castillo. This Temple of the Jaguars (the south-eastern corner of the ball court) has some rattlesnake-carved columns and jaguar-etched tablets. Inside are faded mural fragments depicting a battle, possibly between the Toltecs and the Maya.

Tzompantli The Tzompantli, a Toltec term for Temple of Skulls, is between the Temple of the Jaguars and El Castillo. You can't mistake it because the T-shaped platform is festooned with carved skulls and eagles tearing open the chests of men to eat their hearts. In ancient days this platform held the heads of sacrificial victims.

Platform of the Jaguars & Eagles Adjacent to the Temple of Skulls, this platform's carvings depict jaguars and eagles gruesomely grabbing human hearts in their claws. It is thought that this platform was part of a temple dedicated to the military legions responsible for capturing sacrificial victims.

Platform of Venus Near the path to the Sacred Cenote, looking north from El Castillo and east from Tzompantli, is the Platform of Venus. Rather than a beautiful woman, the Toltec symbol for the planet Venus is a feathered serpent bearing a human head between its jaws. The platform is decked with feathered snake figures. Some maps refer to this as the Tomb of Chac-Mool because a figure of the reclining god was found within the structure.

Sacred Cenote Near the Platform of Venus, you will see a 300-metre dirt path running north to the huge sunken well that gave this city its name. The Sacred Cenote is an awesome natural well, some 60 metres in diameter and 35 metres deep. The walls between the summit and the water's surface are ensnared in tangled vines and other vegetation.

Although some of the guides enjoy telling visitors that female virgins were sacrificed by being thrown into the cenote to drown, divers in 1923 brought up the remains of men, women and children.

Skeletons were not all that was found in the Sacred Cenote. Artefacts and valuable gold and jade jewellery from all parts of Mexico were recovered.

The artefacts' origins show the far-flung contacts the Maya had (there are some items from as far away as Colombia). It is believed that offerings of all kinds, human and otherwise, were thrown into the Sacred Cenote to please the gods.

Group of the Thousand Columns Comprising the Temple of the Warriors, Temple of Chac-Mool and Sweat House or Steam Bath, this group takes its collective name from the copious number of pillars in front. The platformed temple greets you with a statue of the reclining god, Chac, as well as stucco and stone-carved animal deities. The temple's roof caved in long ago; columns entwined with serpents once served as roof supports. If you have been to Tula, you will see some similarities between its Toltec temple and this one.

A 1926 restoration revealed an edifice inside the Temple of the Warriors, constructed prior to it – the Temple of Chac-Mool. You can enter via a stairway on the north side. The temple walls have murals (which have largely deteriorated) of what is thought to be the Toltecs' defeat of the Maya defenders here.

Just east of the Temple of the Warriors sits the rubble of a Maya sweat house, with an underground oven and drains for the water. The sweat houses were regularly used for ritual purification.

Market If you walk south from the Temple of the Warriors, you will come to some colonnaded chambers once thought to house Chichén's elite. Nearby is a remnant of what may have been an area of walled market stalls. None of these structures are in good condition.

Ossuary The Ossuary, otherwise known as the Bonehouse or High Priest's Grave, is a deteriorated pyramid, the first building you come to as you take the dirt path south from El Castillo. As with most of the buildings in this southern section, the architecture is more Puuc than Toltec, adding to the belief that when the Toltecs took control they moved the focus of the city north. During excavation of the Ossuary, the remains of a man believed to be a high priest were found in a natural grotto over which the pyramid was built. This structure may be restored soon.

La Casa Colorada La Casa Colorada or The Red House, on the right fork leading from the Ossuary, was named by the Spanish, who saw the red paint of the deteriorating mural on its doorway. This building has little Toltec influence and its design largely shows a pure Puuc-Maya style. Referring to the stone latticework at the roof façade, the Maya named this building Chichán-Chob, or House of Small Holes. What was thought to be a Toltec

ball court to its rear has now been carbon dated to three centuries prior to the Toltec invasion, adding to the debate over who originally conquered whom.

Temple of the Deer Until it deteriorated in the 1920s, the mural of a deer gave this classical little Maya structure its name. The only reason to see this edifice is to go to the back of the building and climb to the top for a nice view of the surrounding ruins.

El Caracol Take the path to the left from the Ossuary to reach Chichén's observatory. Called El Caracol (The Giant Conch Snail) by the Spaniards due to its interior spiral staircase, the observatory is one of the most fascinating and important of all of Chichén Itzá's buildings. Its circular design resembles some central highlands structures, though, surprisingly, not those of Toltec Tula. In a fusion of architectural styles and religious imagery, there are Maya Chac rain god masks over four external doors facing the cardinal directions.

The windows in the observatory's dome are aligned with the appearance of certain stars at specific dates. From the dome the priests decreed the appropriate times for rituals, celebrations, corn-planting and harvests. The observatory was built over several centuries and is a product of Toltec times, though its base was undertaken earlier.

Nunnery & Annexe Thought by archaeologists to have been a palace for Maya royalty, the Nunnery, with its myriad rooms, resembled a European convent to the conquistadors, hence their name for the building. The Nunnery's dimensions are imposing: its base is 60 metres long, 30 metres wide and 20 metres high. The construction is Maya rather than Toltec, though a Toltec sacrificial stone stands in front. A small building added onto the west side is known as the Annexe. These buildings are in the Puuc-Chenes style, particularly evident in the lower jaw of the Chac mask at the opening of the Annexe. There are several other Chac statues on the façade of the Nunnery.

The Church Near the Annexe sits a relatively small building, notable only for upper façade masks alternating Chac with animal gods called *bacabs* – crab, turtle, snail and armadillo – who Maya mythology claims hold up the sky.

Akab-Dzib On the rough path east of the Nunnery, the Akab-Dzib is thought by some archaeologists to be the most ancient structure excavated here. The central chambers date back to the 2nd century. Akab-Dzib means Obscure Writing in Maya, referring to the south-side Annexe door whose lintel depicts a priest with a vase etched with hieroglyphics. The writing has never been translated, hence the name. Note the red fingerprints on the ceiling, thought to symbolise the deity Itzamná, a sun god from whom the Maya sought wisdom.

Chichén Viejo Chichén Viejo, or Old Chichén, comprises largely unrestored, basically Maya ruins (some have Toltec additions). Visiting Old Chichén is best done with a guide. The path to it runs south-west from the Nunnery.

Grutas de Balankanché

In 1959 an archaeological guide was exploring a cave on his day off. Pushing against one of the cavern's walls, he is said to have broken through into a larger subterranean opening. Archaeological exploration revealed a path that runs some 300 metres past carved stalactites and stalagmites, terminating at an underground pool.

The Grutas de Balankanché (Balankanché Caves) are six km east of the ruins of Chichén Itzá, two km east of the Hotel Dolores Alba on the highway to Cancún. Second-class buses heading east from Piste toward Valladolid and Cancún will drop you at the Balankanché road; the entrance to the caves is 350 metres north of the highway.

As you approach the caves, you enter a pretty botanical garden displaying many of Yucatán's native flora, including many species of cacti. In the entrance building is a little museum, a shop selling cold drinks and souvenirs and a ticket booth. Plan your visit for an hour when the compulsory tour and Light & Colour Show will be given in a language you understand. The 40-minute show (minimum six persons, maximum 30) is given in the cave at 11 am, 1 and 3 pm in English; at 9 am, noon, 2 and 4 pm in Spanish; and at 10 am in French. Tickets are sold from 9 am to 4 pm daily. Admission costs US$3.50

Discovered in the caves and now on exhibition are offerings to Tláloc, the Toltec central Mexican rain god (similar to the Maya Chac). Among the offerings were incense burners carved with the image of Tlaloc and some miniature metates used for grinding corn. These are found principally in two places: in a large domed cavern called The Throne where you'll find a fused pillar of stalactites and stalagmites (Balankanché means Hidden Throne in Maya), and the subterranean pool area.

Places to Stay

Most of the lodgings close to Chichén are in the middle and top-end price brackets. Haggle in the off season (May to October) to get a reduction. In Piste, to telephone any of the hotels you must dial (985) 6-25-13, which gets you the long-distance telephone exchange, and leave a message.

Places to Stay – bottom end

Camping There's camping at the *Pirámide Inn & Trailer Park* on the eastern edge of Piste (closest to the ruins). For under US$5 per person, you can pitch a tent, enjoy the Pirámide Inn's pool and watch satellite TV in the lobby. There are hot showers and clean, shared toilet facilities. Those in vehicles pay US$11 for two for full hook-ups.

Hotels Unfortunately, there's not much. Your best bet is the *Posada Chac-Mool* in Piste, just east of the Hotel Misión Park Inn on the opposite (south) side of the highway.

It has ceiling fans and insect screens. Rates are US$16/18 a single/double.

The similar *Posada El Paso* is a few dozen metres west of the Stardust Inn. An L-shaped motel-style building, it has insect screens on the windows, ceiling fans and private showers. Rooms are overpriced but often full, so try to arrive by lunchtime to book.

Posada Poxil, in the western part of town on the highway, is behind the restaurant of the same name. Rooms are about the same and cost the same as at the Chac-Mool.

Places to Stay – middle

Hotel Dolores Alba (☎ in Mérida (99) 21-37-45), Carretera Km 122, is just over three km east of the eastern entrance to the ruins and two km west of the road to Balankanché, on the highway to Cancún. There are more than a dozen rooms here surrounding a small, clean swimming pool. The dining room is good and prices moderate, which is important since you're pretty much at their mercy, with no other eating facility nearby. The Sánchez family, who own the hotel, will transport you to the ruins, but you must take a taxi or a bus or walk back.

Single/double rooms with fan and shower cost US$22/24. There are a few air-conditioned rooms for about US$5 extra. If you're coming here by bus, remind the driver to drop you off shortly after the eastern access road to the ruins.

The newest hotel in Piste is the *Stardust Inn* (☎ in Mérida (99) 24-41-94, 24-05-42), next to the Pirámide Inn and less than two km from the ruins. It's an attractive place with 57 rooms surrounding a little swimming pool. Each room has air-conditioning, TV and private bath and costs US$70 for singles/doubles in high season. There's a good little restaurant, too. Their reservations office in Mérida is at Calle 81A No 550D, Colonia Obrera.

The *Pirámide Inn*, next door to the Stardust Inn and the bus station, has been here for years. It has very pretty grounds and a swimming pool. The rooms are all air-conditioned and priced (in high season) at US$55/60/65/75 a single/double/triple/quad. It's as close as you can get to the archaeological zone's western entrance.

Places to Stay – top end

Hotel Mayaland is 200 metres from the eastern entrance to the archaeological zone. It's the oldest and most gracious of the hotels at Chichén, having been built in 1923. Extensive renovations in 1989 added air-con, telephones and satellite TV to the rooms; the hotel has a gymnasium, beauty parlour, tennis courts and riding stables. Rooms are US$120 a double. For reservations, call the Mérida office of Mayaland Tours (☎ (99) 25-23-42, 25-22-46; fax (99) 25-70-22).

Its sister hotel is the *Hotel Hacienda Chichén*, just a few hundred metres farther from the ruins on the same eastern access road. This was the hacienda where the archaeologists lived when excavating Chichén. It has a swimming pool, and rooms in the garden bungalows have ceiling fans and private baths, but no TVs or phones; they rent for US$110 a double. The Hacienda Chichén closes from May to October. For reservations, call Mayaland Tours in Mérida.

The *Hotel Villa Arqueológica* (☎ (985) 6-28-30), Apdo Postal 495, Mérida, is a few hundred metres east of the Mayaland and Hacienda Chichén. Run by Club Med, it has a good restaurant, plus tennis courts and a swimming pool. Rooms are fairly small but comfortable and air-conditioned and priced at US$75/85 a single/double.

In Piste, the *Misión Park Inn Chichén* (☎ in Mexico City (5) 533-05-35 to -39; fax 533-13-89) is two km west of the ruins entrance on the north side of the highway. The rooms are around a nice swimming pool and it has a huge restaurant and bar. Air-conditioned singles/doubles cost US$70/80.

Places to Eat

The cafeteria in the *Unidad de Servicios* at the western entrance to the archaeological zone serves mediocre food at high prices (ham and cheese sandwich and chips for US$5) in pleasant surroundings. It's not air-conditioned.

The highway through Piste is lined with

little restaurants, most of them fairly well tarted up in a Maya villager's conception of what foreign tourists expect to see. Prices are fairly high for what you get and most of these places serve only table d'hôte meals at lunch.

Of the Piste restaurants, the *Restaurant Sayil*, facing the Misión Park Inn, is probably the cheapest, a plain little *restaurante económico* serving cochinita or pollo pibil for US$3, rice with garnish for US$1.25 and egg dishes for US$2.

Another simple little eatery is the *Restaurant Parador Maya*, where meat and chicken platters cost less than US$5, egg dishes even less, and tacos less than US$2.50.

Prices are only slightly higher at the attractive, family-run *Restaurant Carrousel*, where you can order a platter of pollo pibil or cochinita pibil for under US$5, eggs and a few antojito choices for even less. The big palapa-covered dining room is pleasant and open from 10.30 am to 6.30 pm.

Restaurant Poxil, at the western edge of town, is a bit far from the ruins and therefore a bit cheaper. Eggs and tortillas cost US$2, pollo pibil only US$6.

The *Restaurant Xaybé* opposite the Misión Park Inn, has excellent cuisine, usually served buffet style in an air-conditioned dining room. Figure on US$10 for lunch, and just slightly more for dinner, for all you can eat. Customers of the restaurant get to use its swimming pool for free, but even if you don't eat here you can still swim for about US$1.

The fantastical *Restaurant Fiesta* has bombastic murals of busty Maya maidens and muscular warriors – worth a look if not a meal. The luncheon table d'hôte goes for US$9.50, but you can order from the menu in the evening, when substantial portions of meat cost US$6.50 and tacos US$3.50 to US$5.50.

Restaurant Nicte-Há is a good place for light fare, with sandwiches for US$1 or less (club sandwich for US$1.60), or steak with mushrooms for US$6.50.

The luxury hotels all have restaurants, with the *Villa Arqueológica* serving particularly distinguished cuisine. Count on around US$35 to US$50 for dinner for two at the Villa, including a bottle of wine and the tip. Light meals like hamburgers are around US$6. At the Misión Park Inn in Piste, the five-course comida corrida at lunch costs US$11.

Getting There & Away
Air Inter runs excursions by air from Cancún to Chichén Itzá in little planes, charging US$90 for the flight. If you want to get to Chichén, see a lot and return to Cancún the same day, this is your best bet.

Bus At least two dozen of the buses (both 1st and 2nd-class) which travel daily between Mérida, Valladolid and Cancún pass by Chichén Itzá, and many stop in the neighbouring village of Piste. Ask about stopping in Piste or Chichén when buying your ticket and also when boarding your bus. Some bus routes from Piste:

Cancún – 205 km, three to 3½ hours, US$2.75 to US$3.
Izamal – 95 km, two hours, US$2.75, change buses at Hóctun.
Mérida – 116 km, 2½ to three hours, US$2.75 to US$3.
Valladolid – 42 km, 30 to 45 minutes, US$1.

Getting Around
Be prepared for walking in the hot sun at Chichén Itzá. For the Grutas de Balankanché, you can set out to walk early in the morning when it's cooler (it's eight km from Piste) and then hope to hitch a ride or catch a bus for the return.

A few taxis are available in Piste and sometimes at the Unidad de Servicios car park at Chichén Itzá, but you cannot depend upon finding one unless you've made arrangements in advance.

VALLADOLID
Population: 80,000
Valladolid is only 40 km (half an hour) east of Chichén Itzá and 160 km (about two hours) west of Cancún but as it has no sights of stop-the-car immediacy, few tourists do

stop here; most prefer to hurtle on through to the next major site. It's just as well, for this preserves Valladolid for the rest of us who want to enjoy it.

History

The Maya ceremonial centre of Zací was here long before the Spaniards arrived. The initial attempt at conquest in 1543 by Francisco de Montejo, nephew of Montejo the Elder, was thwarted by fierce Maya resistance, but the Elder's son Montejo the

Younger ultimately conquered the Maya and took the town. The Spanish laid out a new city on the classic colonial plan.

During much of the colonial era, Valladolid's distance from Mérida, its humidity and surrounding forests kept it isolated from royal rule and thus relatively autonomous. Banned from even entering this town of pure-blooded Spaniards, the Maya rebelled, and in the War of the Castes of 1847 they made Valladolid their first point of attack. Besieged for two months, Valladolid's defenders were finally overcome; many of

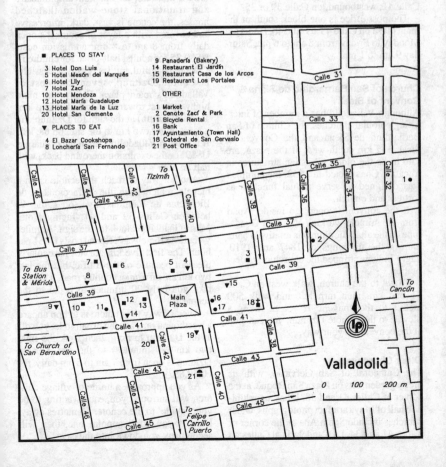

PLACES TO STAY

- 3 Hotel Don Luis
- 5 Hotel Mesón del Marqués
- 6 Hotel Lily
- 7 Hotel Zací
- 10 Hotel Mendoza
- 12 Hotel María Guadalupe
- 13 Hotel María de la Luz
- 20 Hotel San Clemente

PLACES TO EAT

- 4 El Bazar Cookshops
- 8 Lonchería San Fernando

- 9 Panadería (Bakery)
- 14 Restaurant El Jardín
- 15 Restaurant Casa de los Arcos
- 19 Restaurant Los Portales

OTHER

- 1 Market
- 2 Cenote Zací & Park
- 11 Bicycle Rental
- 16 Bank
- 17 Ayuntamiento (Town Hall)
- 18 Catedral de San Gervasio
- 21 Post Office

Valladolid

0   100   200 m

the citizens fled to the safety of Mérida and the rest were slaughtered by the Maya forces.

Orientation & Information

Streets are on a numbered grid. Odd-numbered streets run east-west, even-numbered streets north-south. Recommended hotels are on the main plaza, called the Parque Francisco Cantón Rosado, or just a block or two away from it. The plaza is bound by Calles 39 and 41, and 40 and 42.

The main highway goes right through the centre of town. Eastbound, you travel on Calle 41; westbound, on Calle 39 or 35.

The post office is one block south of the main plaza on Calle 43 at Calle 40. Hours are Monday to Friday from 8 am to 6 pm, Saturday 9 am to 1 pm.

Church of San Bernardino de Siena & Convent of Sisal

Although Valladolid has a number of interesting colonial churches, the Church of San Bernardino de Siena and the Convent of Sisal, 1½ km south-west of the plaza, are said to be the oldest Christian structures in Yucatán. Constructed in 1552, the complex was designed to serve a dual function as fortress and church.

If the convent is open, go inside. Apart from the miracle-working Virgin of Guadalupe on the altar, the church is relatively bare. During the uprisings of 1847 and 1910, angry Indians stripped the church of its decoration.

To get to the church, walk west on Calle 41 one km, then turn left and walk 500 metres to the convent. If you're riding a bicycle to the Cenote Dzitnup, you can stop at the convent on your way.

Other Churches

The Cathedral of San Gervasio, with its pretty garden, sits on Plaza San Roque, at the corner of Calles 41 and 38. It has an exhibition hall of Maya artefact photographs. Other churches include Santa Ana at the corner of Calles 41 and 34, La Candelaria at Calles 44 and 35, San Juan Iglesia at the corner of Calles 49 and 40, and Santa Lucía at the corner of Calles 40 and 27.

Cenotes

Cenotes, those vast underground limestone sinkholes, were the Maya's most dependable source of water. The Spaniards used them also. The Cenote Zací, Calle 36 between Calles 39 and 37 is Valladolid's most famous.

Set in a pretty park which also holds the town's museum, an open-air amphitheatre and traditional stone-walled thatched houses, the cenote is vast, dark, impressive and covered with a layer of scum. It's open daily from 8 am to 8 pm; admission costs US$0.85 for adults, half-price for children.

More beautiful, but less easily accessible, is Cenote Dzitnup, seven km west of Valladolid's main plaza. Follow the main highway west towards Mérida for five km. Turn left (south) at the sign for Dzitnup and go just under two km to the site, on the left. A taxi from Valladolid's main plaza charges US$9 for the excursion there and back, with half an hour's wait.

Another way to reach the cenote is on a bicycle rented from the Refaccionaría de Bicicletas de Paulino Silva, on Calle 44 between Calles 39 and 41, facing Hotel María Guadalupe; look for the sign 'Alquiler y Venta de Bicicletas'. Rental costs US$1 per hour. The first five km are not particularly pleasant because of the traffic, but the last two km are on a quiet country road. It should take you only 20 minutes to pedal to the cenote.

Another way to get there is to hop aboard a westbound bus, ask the driver to let you off at the Dzitnup turning, then walk the final two km (20 minutes) to the site. Cenote Dzitnup is open from 7 am to 6 pm daily, for US$0.85.

As you approach, a horde of village children will surround you, each wanting to be your 'guide' to the cenote, 10 metres away. Even if you don't appoint one, they will accompany you down into the cave.

Places to Stay – bottom end

The best budget choice in town is the *Hotel María Guadalupe* (☎ (985) 6-20-68), Calle 44 No 188 between Calles 39 and 41. Kept clean and in fresh paint, the simple rooms here go for US$12/15/18 a single/double/triple with private shower and fan. Arrive early in the day to get a room.

Hotel Zací (☎ (985) 6-21-67) is at Calle 44 No 191, between Calles 37 and 39. The Zací's rooms are built around a quiet, pleasant garden courtyard complete with swimming pool. Choose from rooms with fan for US$15/18/22 a single/double/triple or with air-conditioning for about US$2 or US$3 more.

Across the street and down a few doors is the *Hotel Lily* (☎ (985) 6-21-63), Calle 44 No 190, between Calles 37 and 39. Rooms are cheaper here, as they should be for what you get: US$9 a double with shared bath and US$11/13 a single/double with private bath and fan. The housekeeping could be better.

Places to Stay – middle

All the following hotels have secure parking facilities.

The best in town is *Hotel Mesón del Marqués* (☎ (985) 6-20-73), Calle 39 No 203, on the north side of the main plaza. The modernised guestrooms look onto two beautiful colonial courtyards here, one of which has a clean swimming pool. The hotel has a dining room as well. All rooms have air-con, some have fans as well. There are three categories of rooms, priced from US$30 to US$44 for a single, US$32 to US$50 for a double.

Next best is the *Hotel San Clemente* (☎ (985) 6-22-08), Calle 42 No 206 at the corner of Calle 41. The 64 rooms have private baths and either air-con or fans. The hotel has a swimming pool and a decent little restaurant named Los Cupules. Large families or small groups should ask about renting adjoining rooms; some rooms sleep up to five people. With ceiling fan/air-con, rooms cost US$16/20 a single, US$18/24 a double, US$23/27 a triple.

The *Hotel Don Luis* (☎ (985) 6-20-08),

Calle 39 No 191 at the corner of Calle 38, is a modern motel-style structure with a palm-shaded patio and swimming pool, and acceptable rooms. Singles with fan and bath cost US$9, doubles US$21. If you want air-conditioning, the price goes up US$1 or US$2.

The cheapest air-conditioned rooms on the plaza are in the *Hotel María de la Luz* (☎ (985) 6-20-70) on Calle 42 near Calle 39. The rooms surround a tiny court with trees and a much-used swimming pool. Rooms are US$20/24 a single/double with private bath and air-con, a dollar or two cheaper with fan.

Places to Eat – bottom end

The bus station has its own cafeteria, but the restaurants just outside and across the street are cheaper and often better.

El Bazar is a collection of little open-air market-style cookshops at the corner of Calles 39 and 40, north-east corner of the plaza. This is a great place for breakfast: a huge glass of freshly squeezed orange juice costs only US$1, eggs with ham, beans and bread only US$2.50. At lunch and dinner-time, a comida corrida of soup, main course and a drink costs just over US$3.25. There are a dozen eateries here open from 6.30 am to 2 pm and from 6 pm to about 9 or 10 pm.

For a bit more you can dine at the breezy tables in the *Hotel María de la Luz,* overlooking the plaza. Substantial sandwiches sell for US$2 to US$3.50, main course platters of meat or chicken for about twice as much.

Places to Eat – middle

Restaurant Casa de los Arcos (☎ (985) 6-24-67), on Calle 39 between Calles 38 and 40, serves Yucatecan cuisine. The menu is in English and Spanish. You might start with sopa de lima, continue with pork loin Valladolid-style (in a tomato sauce) or grilled pork steak with *achiote* sauce, and finish up with guava paste and cheese. With drink, tax and tip, the bill will be US$12 to US$15 per person. If you're confused by Yucatecan cooking, order the combination plate (US$5). The restaurant is open every day from 7 or 8 am to 10 pm.

The *Hotel El Mesón del Marqués*, Calle 39 No 203, also has a good middle-range restaurant.

Getting There & Away

Bus Autotransportes de Oriente Mérida-Puerto Juárez handles most of the buses between Cancún and Mérida via Valladolid, from their terminal on Calle 37 between Calles 54 and 56. Most buses are de paso, meaning that they've originated their journeys somewhere else; there may or may not be seats free. Often, you won't know until half an hour or less before departure time.

Cancún/Puerto Juárez – 161 km, two to 2½ hours; the two early-morning 1st-class (US$3.75) and two 2nd-class (US$3) *local* buses may be jam-packed with commuters; there are de paso buses (both 1st-class and 2nd-class) more or less on the hour from 6 am to 9 pm.

Chetumal – 305 km, five hours; two 2nd-class (US$6).

Chichén Itzá – 42 km, 30 to 45 minutes (US$1); most buses going to Mérida will stop here if you remind the driver.

Chiquilá – 141 km, three hours; two 2nd-class (US$3) *local* buses, at 2 and 11.30 am.

Cobá – 115 km, two hours; two 2nd-class (US$2.75) *local* buses at 4.30 am and 1.15 pm.

Izamal – 115 km, two hours; four 2nd-class (US$2.75) buses daily; Autobuses del Centro del Estado de Yucatán runs five buses daily to Mérida via Izamal.

Mérida – 160 km, three hours; 24 1st-class (US$3.75) buses daily, with *locals* at 6 and 7 am, 4.30 pm and 12.30 am; 20 2nd class (3½ hours, US$3) more or less on the hour from 6 am to 9 pm. Autobuses del Noroeste en Yucatán and Autobuses del Centro del Estado de Yucatán run buses to Mérida via routes (and towns) to the north of the main highway.

Playa del Carmen – 213 km, four hours (via Cancún); 1st-class (US$5) *local* at 6 am, and seven de paso; five local 2nd-class (US$4.50) via Cancún, and two ruta corta (short route) buses via Cobá and Tulum.

Tizimín – 51 km, one hour; one 1st-class (US$1) daily at 8.15 pm; five 2nd-class (US$0.80) buses; Autobuses del Noroeste en Yucatán also has 2nd-class buses at 10 am and 1.30 pm.

Tulum – 360 km, six hours (US$7); there are buses at 1.30, 5 and 8 am and 2 pm.

Taxi A quicker, more comfortable but more expensive way to Cancún is by taking one of the shared taxis parked outside the bus station, which leave as soon as all seats are filled. The trip costs about twice the bus fare.

TIZIMÍN

Many travellers bound for Río Lagartos change buses in Tizimín (Place of Many Horses), the second-largest city in the state of Yucatán. There is little to warrant an overnight stay, but the main plaza is pleasant.

Two great colonial structures, the Convento de los Tres Reyes Magos (Monastery of the Three Wise Kings) and the Convento de San Francisco de Assis (Monastery of Saint Francis of Assisi) are worth a look. Five lengthy blocks from the plaza, northwest on Calle 51, is a modest zoo, the Parque Zoológico de la Reina.

The Banco del Atlantico, next to the Hotel San Jorge on the south-west side of the plaza, changes money between 10 am and noon from Monday to Friday.

Places to Stay

Several decent hotels such as the *Hotel San Jorge* (☎ (986) 3-20-37), Calle 53 No 411, near Calle 52, the *Hotel San Carlos* (☎ (986) 3-20-94), Calle 54 No 407, and the *Hotel Tizimín* (☎ (986) 3-21-52), Calle 50 at the corner of Calle 53, can put you up for US$12 to US$16 a double.

Getting There & Away

Bus Autotransportes de Oriente Mérida-Puerto Juárez runs between Tizimín and Valladolid (51 km, one hour) five times daily (2nd-class, US$1); Autobuses del Noreste en Yucatán operates daily buses from Valladolid to Tizimín (US$1) at 10.30 am and 1.30 pm. From Cancún and Puerto Juárez, there are direct buses to Tizimín at 7.30 am, and 1.30 and 6.30 pm (215 km, four hours, US$4.75). There are several daily 1st and 2nd-class buses between Tizimín and Mérida via Valladolid. For Río Lagartos there are three 1st-class departures and five daily 2nd-class buses which continue to San Felipe.

RÍO LAGARTOS

It is worth going out of your way to this little fishing village, 103 km north of Valladolid and 52 km north of Tizimín, to see the most spectacular flamingo colony in Mexico. The estuaries are also home to snowy egrets, red egrets, great white herons and snowy white ibis. Although Río Lagartos (Alligator River) was named after the once substantial alligator population, don't expect to see any as hunting has virtually wiped them out.

The town of Río Lagartos itself, with its narrow streets and multihued houses, has little charm, though the panorama of the boats and the bay is pleasant. Were it not for the flamingos, you would have little reason to come here. Although the state government has been making noises about developing the area for tourism, this has not happened yet.

At the centre of town is a small triangular plaza, the Presidencia Municipal (Town Hall) and the Conasupo store.

Flamingos

If you walk some of the 14 km along the beach from the lagoon out to Punta Holohit on the sea, you will most likely see colourful bird life. Among the species common here are egrets, herons, flamingos, ibis, cormorants, stilts, pelicans and plovers.

As for boats, a short trip (two to three hours) to see a few nearby local flamingos and to have a swim at the beach costs US$18 to US$22 for a five-seat boat. The much longer voyage (four to six hours) to the flamingos' favourite haunts costs US$60 or so for the boat, or about US$12 per person for a full load. If you can't put together a suitable itinerary by yourself, you might inquire at the *Hotel Nefertiti* (☎ 14-15), Calle 14 No 123, the only hostelry in town. It charges US$19 a double with bath and fan. For transport information, see the Getting There & Away sections for Valladolid and Tizimín.

SAN FELIPE

Population: 400

This tiny fishing village of painted wooden houses on narrow streets, 12 km west of Río Lagartos, makes a nice day trip from Río Lagartos. While the waters are not Caribbean turquoise and there's little shade, in spring and summer scores of visitors come here to camp. Other than lying on the beach, birdwatching is the main attraction, as just across the estuary at Punta Holohit there is abundant bird life.

There are no hotels in San Felipe, but the proprietor of La Herradura grocery store near the pier will tell you about inexpensive house rentals. Spartan rooms are sometimes available for rent above the Cinema Marrufo. Campers are ferried across the estuary to islands where they pitch tents or set up hammocks.

The town's sole eatery, *Restaurant El Payaso*, is cheap and quite good for seafood.

Some buses from Tizimín to Río Lagartos continue to San Felipe and return. The 12-km ride takes about 20 minutes.

Quintana Roo

CANCÚN

Population: 250,000

In the 1970s Mexico's ambitious tourism planners decided to build a brand new world-class resort on a deserted sandspit offshore from the little fishing village of Puerto Juárez. The island sandspit was shaped like a lucky '7'. The name of the place was Cancún.

Yucatán's major international airport is here, as are doctors, modern hospitals, consular representatives, rental car agencies and many other services.

Dozens of mammoth hotels march along the island's shore as it extends from the mainland nine km eastward, then 14 km southward, into the turquoise waters of the Caribbean. At the north the island is joined to the mainland by a bridge which leads to Ciudad Cancún; at the south a bridge joins a road leading inland to the international airport.

The Mexican government built Cancún as an investment in the tourism business.

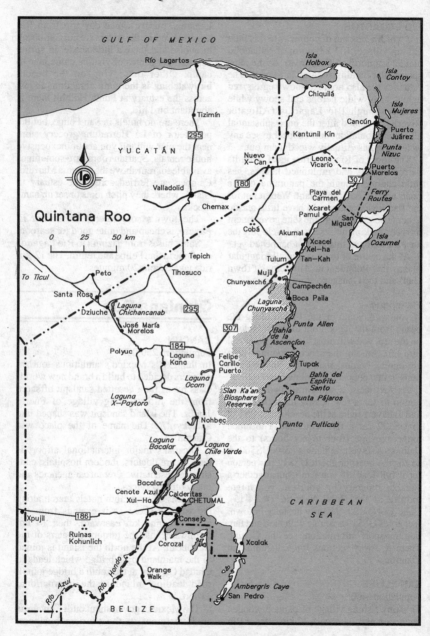

Cancún's reason-for-being is to shelter planeloads of tourists who fly in (usually on the weekend) to spend one or two weeks in a resort hotel before flying home again (usually on a weekend). They have a good time. This is the business of tourism.

Orientation

Ciudad Cancún is a planned community on the mainland. On the 23-km-long sandy island is the Zona Hoteles, or Zona Turística, with its towering hotels, theme restaurants, convention centre, shopping malls, golf course and so on.

If you want to stay right on the beach, you must stay in the Zona Hoteles, out on the island. With the exception of the youth hostel, there are no budget hotels here. You can choose from among the few older, smaller, moderately priced hotels, or the many new, luxurious, pricey hotels.

Restaurants in the city centre range from ultra-Mexican taco joints to fairly smooth and expensive places where the Zona Hoteles people come to 'find someplace different for dinner'.

Several landmarks will help you find your way around this vast resort. In Ciudad Cancún, the main north-south thoroughfare is called Avenida Tulum; it's a one-km-long tree-shaded boulevard lined with banks, shopping centres, small hotels, restaurants and touts selling time-share condominiums.

The central portion of Avenida Tulum is bound north and south by large traffic roundabouts. The northern roundabout has a soaring steeple-like concrete sculpture at its centre, the Monument to the History of Mexico; the southern one has an open iron-work construction, the Monument to the North-South Dialogue (!).

Between the roundabouts, prominent on the east side of the boulevard, is the city hall, marked 'Ayuntamiento Benito Juárez' and set back from the roadway across a wide plaza. The bus station is half a block north-west of the northern roundabout. The road out to the Zona Hoteles begins at the southern roundabout.

Travellers should note that addresses in Cuidad Cancún often include the words *supermanzana* (super city block), *manzana* (city block) or *retorno* (a U-shaped loop street). Thus addresses are sometimes given as 'Hotel X, S.M. 22, Retorno 3'. For a town planner, this makes the place easy to find; but on the street, the manzanas are not marked at all and the retornos are given street names. So if your hotel card has no better address than the type listed above, seek further instructions.

Isla Cancún is shaped like a '7'. Coming from Ciudad Cancún, the main road is Blvd Kukulcán (sometimes called Avenida or Paseo Kukulcán), a four-lane divided high-way which goes east along the top of the '7'. The youth hostel and the few moderately priced hotels are located in the first few kms of Blvd Kukulcán. After nine km, the road reaches the convention centre near Punta Cancún, and turns south for another 14 km to Punta Nizuc and then rejoins the main-land.

Cancún International Airport is about eight km south of Avenida Tulum. Puerto Juárez, the port for passenger ferries to Isla Mujeres, is about three km north of Avenida Tulum. Punta Sam, the dock for the slower car ferries to Isla Mujeres, is about five km north of Avenida Tulum.

Information

Tourist Offices There are tourist kiosks open daily at several points along Avenida Tulum.

The Quintana Roo State Tourism Office (Delegación Estatal de Turismo) (☎ (988) 4-80-73) is at 26 Avenida Tulum, next to the Multibanco Comermex. Hours are 9 am to 9 pm, seven days a week.

The Federal Tourism Office (Delegación Federal de Turismo de Quintana Roo) (☎ (988) 4-32-38, 4-34-38) is in a stone-faced building at the corner of Avenidas Cobá and Carlos J Nader. It is open Monday to Friday from 8 am to 3.30 pm, closed weekends.

Money Banks on Avenida Tulum are open from 9 am to 1.30 pm, but many limit foreign

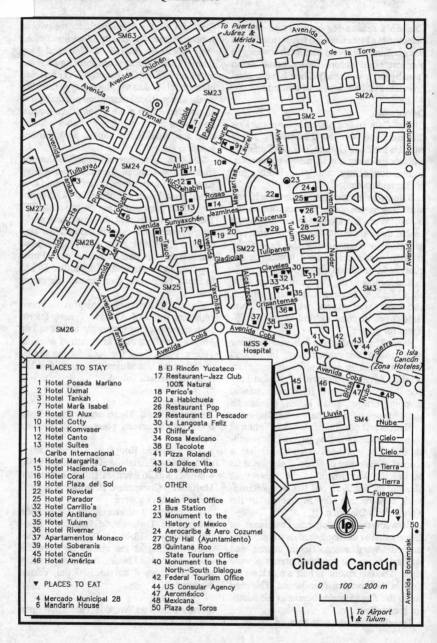

■ PLACES TO STAY

1 Hotel Posada Mariano
2 Hotel Uxmal
3 Hotel Tankah
7 Hotel María Isabel
9 Hotel El Alux
10 Hotel Cotty
11 Hotel Komvaser
12 Hotel Canto
13 Hotel Suites
   Caribe Internacional
14 Hotel Margarita
15 Hotel Hacienda Cancún
16 Hotel Coral
19 Hotel Plaza del Sol
22 Hotel Novotel
25 Hotel Parador
32 Hotel Carrillo's
33 Hotel Antillano
35 Hotel Tulum
36 Hotel Rivemar
37 Apartamentos Monaco
39 Hotel Soberanis
45 Hotel Cancún
46 Hotel América

▼ PLACES TO EAT

4 Mercado Municipal 28
6 Mandarin House

8 El Rincón Yucateco
17 Restaurant—Jazz Club
   100% Natural
18 Perico's
20 La Habichuela
26 Restaurant Pop
29 Restaurant El Pescador
30 La Langosta Feliz
31 Chiffer's
34 Rosa Mexicana
38 El Tacolote
41 Pizza Rolandi
43 La Dolce Vita
49 Los Almendros

OTHER

5 Main Post Office
21 Bus Station
23 Monument to the
   History of Mexico
24 Aerocaribe & Aero Cozumel
27 City Hall (Ayuntamiento)
28 Quintana Roo
   State Tourism Office
40 Monument to the
   North—South Dialogue
42 Federal Tourism Office
44 US Consular Agency
47 Aeroméxico
48 Mexicana
50 Plaza de Toros

Ciudad Cancún

0   100   200 m

To Airport
& Tulum

exchange transactions to between 10 am and noon. Casas de cambio usually are open from 8 or 9 am to 1 pm and again from 4 or 5 pm till 7 or 8 pm; some casas are open seven days a week. There's a handy one next to the Dollar Rent-a-Car office near the Denny's restaurant at the north traffic roundabout on Avenida Tulum; it's half a block from the bus station.

Other casas are along Avenida Tulum. Travel agencies, hotels and the youth hostel will change money, but at rates less advantageous than the banks.

Some restaurants along Avenida Tulum (usually the more expensive ones) will accept US dollars in payment at rates equal to or better than the banks.

Post The main post office (Oficina de Correos, Cancún, Quintana Roo 77500) is at the western end of Avenida Sunyaxchén, which runs west from Avenida Yaxchilán; the post office is four or five short blocks from Avenida Yaxchilán. Hours for buying stamps and picking up Lista de Correos (poste restante) mail are from 8 am to 7 pm Monday to Friday, 9 am to 1 pm Saturday and holidays, closed Sunday. For international money orders and registered mail, hours are 8 am to 6 pm Monday to Friday, 9 am to noon Saturday and holidays, closed Sunday.

The Cancún office of American Express (☎ (988) 4-19-99), c/o Hotel América, Suite A, Avenida Tulum, Cancún, Quintana Roo 77500), is in the Hotel América, just south of Avenida Cobá and the southern traffic roundabout on Avenida Tulum. Hours are 9 am to 1 pm and 4 to 5 pm, Monday to Friday, 9 am to 1 pm Saturday, closed Sunday.

Telephone You'll find Ladatel phones in both the arrival and departure terminals of Cancún's airport, in the bus station off Avenida Tulum and in front of the post office at the western end of Avenida Sunyaxchén. There are also special Ladatel phones which accept credit cards in the Plaza Caracol Shopping Centre on Isla Cancún, near the McDonald's restaurant and in the hall near the Gucci shop.

Foreign Consulates The US Consular Agent (☎ (988) 4-24-11) is located at the offices of Intercaribe Real Estate, 86 Avenida Cobá, one block east off Avenida Tulum as you go towards the Zona Hoteles. Though the office is open from 9 am to 2 pm and 3 to 6 pm daily, except Sunday, the consular agent is only on duty from 10 am to 2 pm Tuesday to Saturday. If the agent is not available, call the US Consulate General in Mérida (open 7.30 am to 3.30 pm weekdays) at (99) 25-50-11; in an emergency after hours or on holidays, call (99) 25-54-09. There is always a duty officer available to help in an emergency.

Other countries have consular agents reachable by telephone. If yours is not listed here, call your consulate in Mérida, or your embassy in Mexico City (see the Foreign Embassies & Consulates section in the Mexico City chapter).

Canada
  ☎ (988) 4-37-16
Costa Rica
  in the Omni Cancún Hotel (☎ (988) 5-02-26, 5-07-14); hours are 9 am to 1 pm, Monday to Friday
Germany
  in the Club Lagoon (☎ (988) 3-09-58, 3-28-58)
Italy
  ☎ (988) 3-21-13
Spain
  ☎ (988) 4-18-95
Sweden
  In the office of Rentautos Kankun in Ciudad Cancún (☎ (988) 4-72-71, 4-11-75)

Bookshops The best selection of English-language material (including *The Mexico City News*, *Wall Street Journal*, *USA Today*, etc) is at Librería Don Quijote at Avenida Uxmal 18, on the corner of Margaritas, across Uxmal from the bus station. They have some Spanish, French and German publications and cassette tapes, snacks and medicines as well. Hours are 8 am to 10 pm, seven days a week.

Another store with periodicals and books

in several languages is Fama, 105 Avenida Tulum, near the corner with Tulipanes.

Laundry & Dry Cleaning There are several shops offering these services. The Lavandería Maria de Lourdes, near the hotel of the same name, is on Calle Orquideas off Avenida Yaxchilán. Or try the Lavandería y Tintorería Cox-Boh, Avenida Tankah 26, Supermanzana 24. Walk toward the post office along Avenida Sunyaxchén; in front of the post office, bear right onto Avenida Tankah and Cox-Boh is on the right-hand side of the street.

Laundry costs US$2 per kg for bulk service. To have a pair of trousers washed and ironed costs US$2.30, or $5 for dry cleaning. Washing and ironing a shirt costs US$1.70. Cox-Boh is open every day except Sunday.

Maya Ruins

Zona Arqueológica El Rey, on Isla Cancún, is fairly unimpressive – a small temple and several ceremonial platforms. Heading south along Blvd Kukulcán from Punta Cancún, watch for the marker for Km 17.8. Just past the marker there's an unpaved road on the right which leads to the ruins, open from 8 am to 5 pm every day; admission costs US$2.

For just a quick glimpse, continue on Blvd Kukulcán 700 metres past the Km 17 marker and up the hill. At the top of the hill, just past the restaurant La Prosperidad de Cancún, you can survey the ruins without hiking in or paying the admission charge.

The tiny Maya structure and chac-mool statue set in the beautifully kept grounds of the Sheraton Hotel are actually authentic ruins found on the spot.

Archaeological Museum

The Museo de Antropología y Historia, next to the Convention Centre in the Zona Hoteles, has a limited collection of Maya artefacts. Although most of the items, including jewellery, masks and skull deformers, are from the Postclassic period (1200-1500 AD), there is a Classic period hieroglyphic staircase inscribed with dates from the 6th century as well as the stucco head which gave the local archaeological zone its name of El Rey (The King).

The Cancún Convention Centre is being expanded considerably and it's possible that the museum will be moved to another site.

Beaches

The dazzling white sand of Cancún's beaches is light in weight and cool underfoot even in the blazing sun. That's because it is composed not of silica but rather of microscopic plankton fossils called disco-aster (a tiny star-shaped creature). The coolness of the sand has not been lost on Cancún's ingenious promoters, who have dubbed it 'air-conditioned'. Combined with the crystalline azure waters of the Caribbean, it makes for beaches that are pure delight.

All of these delightful beaches are open to you because all Mexican beaches are public property. Several of Cancún's beaches are set aside for easy public access, but you should know that you have the right to walk and swim on any beach at all. In practice it may be difficult to approach certain stretches of beach without going through a hotel's property, but few hotels will notice you walking through to the beach in any case.

Starting at Ciudad Cancún and heading out to Isla Cancún all the beaches are on the left-hand side of the road as you go; the lagoon is on your right. They are: Playa Las Perlas, Playa Linda, Playa Langosta, Playa Tortugas, Playa Caracol, and then Punta Cancún, the point of the '7'. South from Punta Cancún are the long stretches of Playa Chac-Mool and Playa del Rey, reaching all the way to Punta Nizuc at the base of the '7'. The beach at the Club Méditerranée, near Punta Nizuc, is noted for its nude bathing.

Beach Safety As any experienced swimmer knows, a beach fronting on open sea can be deadly dangerous and Cancún's eastern beaches are no exception. Though the surf is usually gentle, undertow is a possibility and sudden storms (called *nortes*) can blacken the sky and sweep in at any time without warning. The local authorities have devised a system of coloured pennants to warn beachgoers of potential dangers. Look for the coloured pennants on the beaches where you swim:

Blue: Normal, safe conditions.
Yellow: Use caution, changeable conditions.
Red: Unsafe conditions: use a swimming pool instead.

Getting There & Away To reach the beaches, catch any bus marked 'Hoteles', or 'Zona Hoteles' going south along Avenida Tulum or east along Avenida Cobá. The cost of a taxi depends upon how far you travel. For details, see Getting Around at the end of the Cancún section.

Places to Stay – bottom end
Though there are more than 20,000 hotel rooms in Cancún, this resort offers the low-budget traveller the worst selection of cheap accommodation at the highest prices of any place in Mexico. But if you are about to catch a plane, or if you simply must try out Cancún's air-conditioned beaches, a night in Cancún need not bankrupt you.

The following hotel recommendations are arranged as walking itineraries starting from the bus station. All you need do is get off the bus and follow the itinerary until you come to a hotel which has a vacant room that suits your budget. If you arrive by air and take a minibus into town (see below under Getting Around), your minibus driver will drop you at your chosen hotel at no extra charge.

In general, bottom-end rooms range from US\$20 to US\$45 a double, tax included, in the busy winter season. Prices drop 15% to 20% in the less busy summer months. In most of the rest of Mexico, including Mexico City, a room costing US\$45 would be moderate or even deluxe. In expensive Cancún it's at the high end of the budget price range. For this amount of money you'll get a room with private bathroom, fan and probably air-conditioning and the hotel might even have a small swimming pool.

Youth Hostel The IYHF youth hostel is the only low-budget lodging on Isla Cancún, in the Zona Hoteles four km from the bus station. Officially called the *Villa Deportiva Juvenil* (☎ (988) 3-13-37), it's at Blvd Kukulcán Km 3.2, on the left-hand (north) side of the road. Look for the sign which reads 'Deportiva Juvenil'.

Single-sex dorm beds (there are over 600 of them) go for US\$8.50, with a US\$10 deposit. Camping costs US\$5 on the hostel's grounds; for that price you get a locker and the right to use the hostel's facilities as there are none for the camping area itself. Meals are available in the hostel's cafeteria; breakfast is US\$3, lunch or dinner costs US\$4. Coming from the airport by minibus, the driver will drop you here at no extra charge. From the bus station, walk out to Avenida Tulum and catch a local bus (Ruta 1, 'Hoteles') heading south.

Avenida Uxmal Except for the youth hostel, all of Cancún's cheap hotels are in Ciudad Cancún and many are within a few blocks of the bus station. Turn left as you leave the bus station waiting rooms and walk to Avenida Uxmal. Turn right on Avenida Uxmal and you'll come to the following cheap lodgings:

Hotel El Alux (☎ (988) 4-06-62, 4-05-56, 4-66-13), Avenida Uxmal 21, is a tidy little place on the right-hand side of the road. Air-conditioned doubles with shower go for US\$40. They'll rent you a moped here, as well.

Across Avenida Uxmal on the south side is the *Hotel Cotty* (☎ (988) 4-13-19, 4-05-50), Avenida Uxmal 44, a motel-style place with 48 reasonably quiet rooms. Doubles with shower and air-con cost US\$30, slightly more if you want a room with two double beds and a TV. If you're driving, they offer off-street parking.

A few steps farther along the north side of Avenida Uxmal is Calle Palmera, one of Cancún's loop streets. The *Hotel María Isabel* (☎ (988) 4-90-15), Calle Palmera, SM 23, is a tiny place with window screens, and a quiet location. Doubles with private shower and air-con cost US\$30.

One long block farther, on the left-hand side just before the corner of Avenida

Chichén Itzá, stands the *Hotel Uxmal* (☎ (988) 4-22-66, 4-23-55), Avenida Uxmal 111, a clean, family-run hostelry where US$30 will buy you a double room with fan or air-con, TV and off-street parking.

Rock-bottom lodgings are available just a bit farther along at the *Hotel Posada Mariano* (☎ (988) 4-39-73), Avenida Chichén Itzá near Avenida Uxmal, SM 62. The lobby door has iron bars and basic double rooms go for US$17 with fan, private shower and hot water.

Avenida Yaxchilán On Avenida Yaxchilán is one of the richest concentrations of cheap and moderately priced hotels in Cancún.

The *Hotel Komvaser* (☎ (988) 4-16-50) at Avenida Yaxchilán 15 offers a swimming pool and well-kept air-conditioned rooms, with hot plates to heat stuff up and fridges to keep stuff cold. Singles/doubles/triples with bath cost US$30/34/38. The hotel has no sign, so look for the largeish building on the west side which has lots of rooms with glass doors and beach towels hanging out on the balconies.

A short distance along Avenida Yaxchilán, past the Komvaser near Avenida Sunyaxchén, is the *Hotel Canto* (☎ (988) 4-12-67) on Calle Tanchactalpen (Manzana 22, Retorno 5), behind Pizza Bambino's. Being on a side street it's fairly quiet. Rooms with private shower and air-con cost US$30. There's a caseta de larga distancia adjoining the lobby.

Avenidas Sunyaxchén & Tankah Just off Avenida Yaxchilán stands the *Hotel Hacienda Cancún* (☎ (988) 4-12-08, 4-36-72), Avenida Sunyaxchén No 39-40, on the right-hand (north) side. This place is hardly budget, but it offers exceptional value. For US$40 (single or double) you get an air-conditioned room with colour TV and private bath, use of the hotel's pretty swimming pool and patio and a good location.

Farther along Sunyaxchén on the opposite (left) side of the street is the *Hotel Coral* (☎ (988) 4-05-86), Avenida Sunyaxchén 30 (Supermanzana 25, Manzana 3), at Calle

Grosella. There's a tiny swimming pool, but the attraction is the air-conditioned rooms with shower going for US$22/26/32/40 a single/double/triple/quad. This is good value, as Cancún goes.

Continue along Avenida Sunyaxchén to the post office and bear right onto Avenida Tankah. On the right-hand side is the *Hotel Tankah* (☎ (988) 4-44-46, 4-48-44), Avenida Tankah 69, an undiscovered place charging only US$20 for a double with fan, a few dollars more for a similar room with air-con.

Avenida Cobá From the intersection of Avenidas Yaxchilán and Sunyaxchén, continue south and bear left onto Avenida Cobá. Soon, on the left-hand (north) side, you'll come to *Apartamentos Monaco* (☎ (988) 4-52-19), Avenida Cobá 31 (Supermanzana 22), next to the Clinica Cobá. Here you can rent a complete little apartment with two beds, a fridge, cooker and air-con for US$46 per day or US$300 per week.

Avenida Tulum Hotels along the main street tend to be noisy and not particularly well kept, but the location is certainly central.

Heading north on Avenida Tulum is the *Hotel Rivemar* (☎ (988) 4-11-99, 4-13-72, 4-17-08), near Calle Crisantemas, on the left-hand side. The air-conditioned rooms with bath, favoured mostly by men rather than couples, cost US$30 for one or two people, US$44 for three.

A bit farther on the same side, the *Hotel Tulum* (☎ (988) 4-13-55), charges US$36/42/48/60 for a single/double/triple/quad for somewhat nicer rooms, right in the middle of town.

Places to Stay – middle
Middle-range hotel rooms cost from US$50 to US$120 in the busy winter season, somewhat less during the summer. During the very slow times (late May to early June, October to mid-December), prices may be only half of those quoted here, particularly if you haggle a bit. These hotels offer air-conditioned rooms with private bath, a swimming pool, restaurant and perhaps

some other amenities such as a bar, lifts (elevators) and shuttle vans from the hotel to the beach. Much of the clientele of these places is small tour groups.

A walk around the loop formed by Avenidas Tulum, Cobá, Yaxchilán and Uxmal takes you past virtually all of Ciudad Cancún's moderately priced hotels. Starting from the northern traffic roundabout near the bus station, walk south along Avenida Tulum.

Avenida Tulum Just south of the roundabout on the left-hand (east) side of the road is the *Hotel Parador* (☎ (988) 4-13-10, 4-10-43, 4-19-22), Avenida Tulum 26, a modern building with 66 air-conditioned rooms, all with two double beds, TV and tiled private shower. The small restaurant off the lobby was closed during my last visit, but other eating places are nearby. The hotel has its own small parking lot and charges US$70 a single/double.

Directly across Avenida Tulum from the Parador, on the west side, is the *Hotel Novotel* (☎ (988) 4-29-99), Avenida Tulum 75 (Apdo Postal 70); despite its name, it is not a member of the French hotel chain. The 40 rooms here all have private baths, air-conditioning and colour TV and some have tiny balconies. Rooms with fan go for US$55 a single/double, US$62 a triple, slightly more with air-con.

Walk south along Avenida Tulum and look for Calle Claveles, the fifth little street. The *Hotel Carrillo's* (☎ (988) 4-12-27), Calle Claveles (Supermanzana 22, Retorno 3), is behind the restaurant of the same name. Rooms here are usable, though nothing special, but quieter than those right on the avenue. Prices are US$52 a single/double, US$63 a triple.

Perhaps my favourite city hotel from the standpoint of friendliness, value for money, comfort and quiet is the *Hotel Antillano* (☎ (988) 4-15-32, 4-11-32), on Calle Claveles, a block farther along from Carrillo's. The Antillano's 48 guestrooms are all air-conditioned, with private shower and colour cable TV; there's a small pool, a disco

and a bar. Rates are a reasonable US$56 a single, US$62 a double, US$68 a triple.

Avenida Yaxchilán At the intersection with Avenida Sunyaxchén are three good middle-range lodgings. The large *Hotel Plaza del Sol* (☎ (988) 4-38-88), Avenida Yaxchilán 31, corner of Jazmines, has 87 air-conditioned rooms with bath, two double beds and colour TV, priced at US$100/125 a single/double. It has a pretty swimming pool with swim-up bar, a restaurant and coffee shop, and a private car park.

A block farther along Avenida Yaxchilán, at the other end of the loop formed by Calle Jazmines, stands the *Hotel Margarita* (☎ (988) 4-93-33; fax 4-92-09), with services similar to the Plaza del Sol. The price for a room is US$85 a single/double. You can call toll-free for reservations in the US and Canada (☎ (800) 223-9815; in New York (212) 545-8469).

Directly across Avenida Yaxchilán from the Margarita is the huge *Hotel Suites Caribe Internacional* (☎ (988) 4-30-87; fax 4-19-93), Avenidas Yaxchilán con Sunyaxchén 36). The 80 rooms include double rooms with two beds, cable colour TV and private bath; and junior suites with two beds, colour cable TV, private bath, and a kitchenette with cooker and refrigerator. Prices (tax included) are US$120 a single/double, US$130 a triple, and US$150 a double for a junior suite, US$18 for an extra person.

Zona Hoteles A few of the older, smaller or simpler hotels on Isla Cancún charge rates of US$100 for a double room during the high winter season. In summer, many more bargains are to be had. Driving out along Blvd Kulkulcán from Ciudad Cancún, you will come to these moderately priced hotels in the following order; all are on the left-hand (north or east) side of the road.

The *Playa Blanca Hotel & Marina* (☎ (988) 3-03-44; in the USA (800) 221-4726), Apdo Postal 107, is at Km 3.5; it's a 161-room hotel with lush gardens, comfortable air-conditioned rooms, several bars and three restaurants. Rooms cost US$90 to

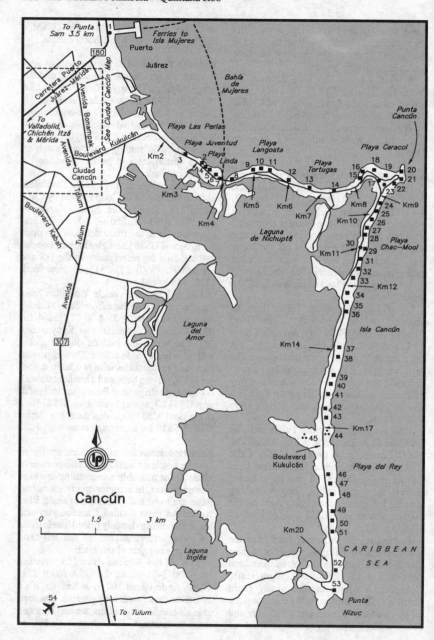

Cancún

0   1.5   3 km

■ PLACES TO STAY

2	Villa Deportiva Juvenil (Youth Hostel)
3	Club Verano Beat
4	Playa Blanca Hotel & Marina
5	Hotel Carrousel
6	Aquamarina Beach Hotel
8	Calinda Cancún Beach
9	Hotel Casa Maya Cancún
10	Hilton International Cancún
11	Villas Tacul
12	Hotel Maya Caribe
13	Hotel Dos Playas
14	Stouffer Presidente
15	Hotel Viva
16	Fiesta Americana Cancún
18	Hotel Camino Real Caribe
19	Fiesta Americana Coral Beach Cancún
20	Camino Real Cancún
21	Hyatt Regency Cancún
22	Krystal Cancún
24	Hotel Aristos Cancún
25	Miramar Misión
26	Hotel Inter-Continental
27	Hyatt Cancún Caribe
28	Fiesta Americana Plaza Cancún
29	Hotel Aston Flamingo
31	Hotel Brisas del Caribe
32	Hotel Baccara

33	Hotel Beach Club Cancún
34	Meliá Turquesa Hotel
35	Sheraton Cancún Resort & Towers
36	Paraíso Radisson Cancún
37	Hotel Tropical Oasis
38	Cancún Palace
39	Marriott's Cancún Resort
40	Meliá Cancún Hotel
41	Fiesta Americana Condesa
42	Hotel Oasis Cancún
43	Omni Cancún Hotel
46	Holiday Inn Crowne Plaza Cancún
47	Cancún Playa Hotel
48	Hotel Solymar
49	Ramada Renaissance Hotel Cancún
50	Aston Solaris Cancún
51	Hotel Casa Maya Caribe
52	Hotel Conrad Cancún
53	Club Méditerranée

OTHER

1	Ferry Service Office
7	Playa Linda Marine Terminal
17	Plaza Caracol Shopping Centre
23	Convention Centre
30	Flamingo Plaza
44	San Miguelito Archaeological Site
45	Zona Arqueológica El Rey
54	International Airport

US$130 in winter, depending upon the month.

The newer *Aquamarina Beach Hotel* (☎ (988) 3-14-25, 3-13-44, 3-19-37; fax 3-17-51; in the USA (800) 446-8976), is at Blvd Kulkulcán Km 3.9 (Apdo Postal 751). The rooms are comfortable, with the requisite colour cable TV, private bath and air-conditioning. Some have kitchenette and refrigerator, but cost no more – ask for one of these when you reserve your room. The price is US$125 a double in winter.

The *Hotel Maya Caribe* (☎ (988) 3-20-00), Blvd Kukulcán Km 6 (Apdo Postal 447), has 64 rooms, each with two double beds, minibar, balcony, a hammock and a view of either the ocean or the lagoon. Three swimming pools, two restaurants, a bar and water sports equipment round out the services. Rooms go for US$120 in winter.

Just before coming to Punta Cancún, at about Km 8.3, you'll see the great white block of the *Hotel Viva* (☎ (988) 3-01-08 or 3-08-00). Though the Viva is cheek-by-jowl with several far more luxurious hotels, its rooms and services are in the middle range, as are its prices. In winter a nice room with a sea view, two double beds, a refrigerator and other comforts costs US$145, perhaps a bit less if you haggle.

Following Blvd Kukulcán around past Punta Cancún and southward brings you to the *Hotel Aristos Cancún* (☎ (988) 3-00-11), Blvd Kukulcán Km 9.3 (Apdo Postal 450), with 250 comfortable air-conditioned rooms, restaurant, bar and pool. Prices in winter are US$140 or US$90, depending upon how full the hotel is – they're sensitive to supply and demand and adjust prices accordingly.

Places to Stay – top end

Cancún's top places range from comfortable but boring to luxurious full-service hostelries of an international standard. Prices range from US$160 to US$250 and more for a double room in winter, but few people pay these 'rack rates'. Most people sign up for package tours which include airfare and hotel, which cuts the cost of staying in these places considerably. Off-season rates (June to November) are considerably lower – perhaps 30% to 40%.

All the top places are located on the beach, many have vast grounds with rolling lawns, tropical gardens, swimming pools (virtually all with swim-up bars – a Cancún necessity) and facilities for sports such as tennis, handball, waterskiing and sailboarding. Guest rooms are air-conditioned, equipped with minibar and TV linked to satellite receivers for US programmes.

As with middle-range hotels, I'll describe the hotels as you'll see them coming from the city centre, travelling east and south. All are on the eastern (left) side of Blvd Kukulcán Addresses along Blvd Kukulcán are usually given in km from the centre.

Km 4 to Km 6 *Calinda Cancún Beach* (☎ (988) 3-16-00; in the the USA (800) 221-2222) faces the Playa Linda Marine Terminal across the channel connecting Bahía de Mujeres with Laguna de Nichupte. Though it has most of the luxury services, prices for the 280 rooms are at the lower end of the luxury range.

Hotel Casa Maya Cancún (☎ (988) 3-05-55; fax 3-11-88), Blvd Kukulcán, is an enormous building with some ancient Maya architectural features. Each of the 250 rooms has a balcony with ocean view and all the conveniences.

Hilton International Cancún was under construction at the time of writing. For current information on the hotel call Hilton Reservation Service (in the USA ☎ (800) 445-8667).

Km 8 *Stouffer Presidente* (☎ (988) 3-02-00; fax 3-25-15; in the USA (800) 468-3571), Blvd Kukulcán Km 7.5, has recently been renovated. All 294 rooms face the Caribbean, some are specially equipped for the handicapped, others are set aside for nonsmokers. The beach is among the best and safest and one of the swimming pools is equipped with five whirlpool baths.

Fiesta Americana Cancún (☎ (988) 3-14-00; in the USA (800) 343-7821) is an oddity among Cancún hotels. While all its neighbours boast sleek, space-age architecture, the Fiesta Americana resembles an old-city streetscape, an appealing jumble of windows, balconies, roofs and other features.

Punta Cancún (Km 9) *Fiesta Americana Coral Beach Cancún* (☎ (988) 3-29-00, fax 3-25-02; in the USA (800) 343-7821), Blvd Kukulcán, is one of the most luxurious hotels. Many of the 602 rooms are actually large junior suites with all the luxuries; master suites even have their own private whirlpool baths.

Camino Real Cancún (☎ (988) 3-01-00, 3-12-00; fax 3-17-30; in the USA (800) 228-3000) was one of Cancún's first luxury hotels and thus had the best pick of locations. Situated at the very tip of Punta Cancún, the Camino Real enjoys panoramic sea views, and has lots of restaurants and bars.

Hyatt Regency Cancún (☎ (988) 3-09-66; fax 3-13-49; in the USA (800) 228-9000), Apdo Postal 1201, shares Punta Cancún with the Camino Real and several other hotels. The Hyatt is actually a gigantic cylinder, with a lofty open court at its core and the 300 guestrooms arranged round it.

Krystal Cancún (☎ (988) 3-11-33; fax 3-17-90; in the USA (800) 231-9860), Punta Cancún, is also in an excellent location near the Convention Centre. It has 330 guestrooms, and a striking swimming pool complex.

Km 10 *Miramar Misión* (☎ (988) 3-17-55; in the USA (800) 648-7818), Blvd Kukulcán, has lanai terraces, one on each of the 225 rooms, all with views of both the Caribbean and the Nichupté lagoon.

Hyatt Cancún Caribe (☎ (988) 3-00-44; fax 3-15-14; in the USA (800) 228-9000), Blvd Kukulcán, has recently been fully modernised; its 180 rooms are more comfortable than ever.

Km 11 *Fiesta Americana Plaza Cancún* (☎ (988) 3-10-22; fax 3-22-70, 5-14-03; in the USA (800) 343-7821), Blvd Kukulcán Km 11, is a gigantic hotel designed as an interconnected mass of Spanish-style villas.

Km 12 & 13 *Hotel Beach Club Cancún* (☎ (988) 4-16-43; in the USA (800) 346-8225), Blvd Kukulcán, is smaller than its neighbouring megahotels and has more of a club's atmosphere. Of the 160 rooms, 117 are suites.

Meliá Turquesa Hotel (☎ (988) 3-25-44; fax 5-12-41; in the USA (800) 336-3542), Blvd Kukulcán Km 12, prides itself on its European-style service. The Turquesa has 408 guestrooms.

Sheraton Cancún Resort & Towers (☎ (988) 3-19-88; fax 5-00-83, 3-14-50; in the USA (800) 325-3535), Blvd Kukulcán (Apdo Postal 834), has 748 guestrooms with the usual Cancún luxuries, in a complex of three large Maya step-pyramid buildings and a V-shaped Towers section. Suites in the Towers building have sea views.

Paraíso Radisson Cancún (☎ (988) 5-01-12, 5-02-33, fax 5-09-99; in the USA (800) 333-3333), Blvd Kukulcán, is a moderately sized hotel right on the beach, offering 300 very comfortable rooms at prices surprisingly lower than its neighbours.

Km 14 to Km 16 *Cancún Palace* (☎ (988) 5-05-33; fax 5-15-93; in the USA (800) 346-8225), Blvd Kukulcán (Apdo Postal 1730), is not part of a big international chain, so it works extra hard to offer good value. The 421 rooms and suites have all the amenities and services you'd expect, including balconies with water views.

Marriott's Cancún Resort (☎ (988) 5-20-00; fax 5-17-31; in the USA (800) 228-9290), Blvd Kukulcán, is a six-storey hotel with 450 rooms, all with private balconies, in-room safe deposit boxes, hair dryers, plus all the usual luxuries.

Meliá Cancún Hotel (☎ (988) 5-11-60; fax 5-10-85; in the USA (800) 336-3542), Blvd Kukulcán Km 15, will startle you with its dramatic geometry. The 447 rooms and suites have all the comforts.

Fiesta Americana Condesa (☎ (988) 5-10-00, 5-12-66; fax 5-18-00; in the USA (800) 343-7821), Blvd Kukulcán (Apdo Postal 5478), has 500 luxury rooms in three buildings around a large swimming pool.

Ruinas El Rey (Km 17.8) *Hotel Oasis Cancún* (☎ (988) 5-08-67; fax 5-01-31; in the USA (800) 446-2747) lives up to its name as a huge (960-room) self-contained resort boasting a pyramidal central building and four accommodation buildings arranged around a marvellous system of interconnected swimming pools almost half a km long.

Omni Cancún Hotel (☎ (988) 5-01-74; fax 5-00-59; in the USA (800) 843-6664), Blvd Kukulcán (Apdo Postal 127), has 320 guestrooms with private balconies.

Holiday Inn Crowne Plaza Cancún (☎ (988) 5-10-50, 5-10-22; fax 5-17-07 ext 6100; in the USA (800) 465-4329), Blvd Kukulcán Km 18.5 (Apdo Postal 5-477), is a dramatic glass-fronted building with 366 guestrooms, and all of the expected luxury services.

Cancún Playa Hotel (☎ (988) 5-11-11/15; fax 5-11-51, 5-10-76; in the USA (800) 683-4482), Blvd Kukulcán (Apdo Postal 203), looks like a cross between a modern luxury hotel and several Maya step-pyramids. There are 388 luxury rooms.

Km 18 *Ramada Renaissance Hotel Cancún* (☎ (988) 5-01-00; fax 5-03-54; in the USA (800) 228-9898), Blvd Kukulcán Km 19, is smaller (226 rooms) and more congenial than many Cancún mega-hotels.

Aston Solaris Cancún (☎ (988) 5-06-00; fax 5-09-75; in the USA (800) 922-7866), Blvd Kukulcán Km 20, bills itself as 'Mexico's Mediterranean village on the Caribbean'. Less lavish than many of its neighbours to the north, the Solaris has 'character' and decent prices.

Punta Nizuc *Hotel Conrad Cancún* (☎ (988) 5-00-86, 5-05-37; fax 5-00-74; in the USA (800) 445-8667), Blvd Kukulcán Km 20 (Apdo Postal 1808), is a new, 391-room hotel very near Punta Nizuc, with all the luxuries and most up-to-date features.

Club Méditerranée (☎ (988) 4-29-00; fax 4-24-09; in the USA (800) 258-22633), Punta Nizuc, has a central building with the usual facilities, and accommodation in two and three-storey beachfront buildings.

Places to Eat
Places to Eat – bottom end
As with hotels, so with eating places: Cancún is much more expensive than the rest of Mexico. But the local people, who live on Mexican workers' incomes, have to eat and they eat good meals at low prices. Bottom-end meals cost between US$3.50 and US$8 or so.

Ciudad Cancún As usual, market eateries provide the biggest portions at the lowest prices. Ciudad Cancún's market, near the post office, is more modern than most. To find it, walk from the post office (Correos) and bear left down Avenida Xel-ha. A hundred metres along on the right is a building set back from the street and emblazoned with the name 'Mercado Municipal Artículo 115 Constitucional'.

Called simply 'Mercado 28' (that's 'mercado veinte y ocho') by the locals because it is in Supermanzana 28, this large, spacious, modern maze of buildings extends well back from the street in a series of courtyards. Shops selling fresh food, prepared meals and a thousand other things surround the courtyards.

In the second courtyard in from the street are the eateries: these are pleasant, simple places with tables beneath awnings and industrious señoras cooking away behind the counter. Most are open for breakfast, lunch and dinner and all offer full meals (comidas corridas) for as little as US$3.50, and individual sandwiches and platters for even less.

El Rincón Yucateco, Avenida Uxmal 24, across from the Hotel Cotty, serves good Yucatecan *típico* food at decent prices from 7 am to 10 pm every day. The Maya classics such as cochinita pibil, poc-chuc and papadzules are offered, as are fish dishes. Main courses cost US$3 to US$5.

El Tacolote on Avenida Cobá, across from the big red IMSS hospital, has ceiling fans, is brightly lit and attractive, and has lots of Mexican families in attendance. Tacos are the draw, with a dozen types priced from US$1.10 to US$3.75 per portion. El Tacolote (the name is a pun on taco and *tecolote*, owl) is open from 7 to 11.30 am for breakfast, then till 10 pm for tacos.

Between the Hotel Parador and the Ayuntamiento is the *Restaurant Pop* (☎ 4-19-91), Avenida Tulum 26, a bright, simple, modern place with an air-conditioned dining room and shaded patio tables. The food is not exciting, but you can have yoghurt, fresh fruit salads, hamburgers, sandwiches, soups spaghetti, cakes and desserts. Expect to spend about US$5 or $8 for a good, filling meal. Pop (the name of the first month of the Maya calendar) is open from 8 am to 10.30 pm (closed Sunday).

Chiffer's, is in the big San Francisco de Assis department store on the east side of Avenida Tulum. It has air-conditioning. A huge club sandwich plate goes for US$6, hamburgers, chicken tacos, or enchiladas suizas for even less. You can spend as much as US$12 for a full, heavy meal with dessert and drink, but most people keep their bill below US$8, the price of the four-course set-price meal. Chiffer's is open from 7 am to 11 pm daily.

Isla Cancún There is little in the way of cheap eateries in the Zona Hoteles. Bring your own sandwiches for a day at the beach.

Mr Papa's specialises in big baked potatoes topped with mushrooms, cheese, bacon, creamed spinach or broccoli and more, for US$3.50 to US$8. Burritos and burgers are in the same range. Look for their modern upbeat decor in the Terramar Plaza shopping centre (☎ 3-14-11), and in the Flamingo Plaza (☎ 3-31-06). Mr Papa's is also downtown on Avenida Tulum (☎ 4-06-91). They're open for lunch and dinner every day.

Otherwise, there's *Otto's*, Blvd Kukulcán Km 9, on the lagoon side of the road just west of the Convention Centre and just past the big Mauna Loa restaurant complex. Pizzas, burgers, sandwiches and drinks fill the menu, mostly costing US$7 or US$9 (pizzas go as high as US$12). An all-you-can-eat breakfast costs less than US$6. Otto's is open from 7 am to midnight every day.

Places to Eat – middle
If you're willing to spend between US$12 and US$25 for dinner you can eat fairly well in Cancún. Most of these restaurants concentrate more on their food than do the elaborately decorated expensive places.

Ciudad Cancún Most of the moderately priced restaurants are located in the city centre. The *Restaurant El Pescador* (☎ 4-26-73) is at Tulipanes 28. The streetside dining terrace is small, but is the best place to sit. Cooling is by ceiling fans. The menu lists lime soup and fish ceviche for starters, charcoal-grilled fish, red snapper in garlic sauce and beef shishkebab for main courses, among many others. Full meals cost US$14 to US$25 per person. El Pescador is open for lunch and dinner (closed Monday). Most nights it's full by 7 pm; by 7.30 pm there's a long waiting line.

Pizza Rolandi (☎ 4-40-47), Avenida Cobá 12, just off the southern roundabout, is an attractive Italian eatery open every day. It serves elaborate, tasty one-person pizzas (US$5 to US$8), spaghetti plates and more substantial dishes of veal and chicken. Ceiling fans circulate the air. Watch out for drink prices, which can swell your bill surprisingly. Hours are 1 pm to midnight (Sunday, 4 pm to midnight).

Many visitors to Cancún make the pilgrimage to *Los Almendros* (☎ 4-08-07), Avenida Bonampak at Calle Sayil, the local incarnation of Yucatán's most famous restaurant chain. Started in Ticul in 1962, Los Almendros set out to serve *platillos campesinos para los dzules* (country food for the bourgeoisie, or townfolk). The chefs at Los Almendros (The Almond Trees) claim to have created poc-chuc, a dish of succulent pork cooked with onion and served in a tangy sauce of sour orange or lime.

Waiters scurry about bearing papadzules (tortillas wrapped around chopped egg and marrow seeds, topped with tomato sauce), rice soup with fried bananas, tangy lime soup with rafts of floating tortillas, cochinita pibil (suckling pig flavoured with achiote sauce, wrapped in banana leaves and baked in a pit oven, or pib) and other Yucatecan specialities such as turkey in a dark sauce. If you don't know what to order, try the combinado yucateco. A full meal here costs about US$15 per person, all included. Come any day for lunch or dinner. The restaurant is at the southern end of Avenida Bonampak directly across from the bullring, more than a km from the centre of town.

Restaurant-Jazz Club 100% Natural (☎ 4-36-17), Avenida Sunyaxchén at Avenida Yaxchilán, is a pleasant, airy café. Though the menu lists several natural food items such as fruit salads and juices, green salads and milkshakes with granola or yoghurt or vegetables, they also serve hamburgers, fish fillets, enchiladas and burritos, not to mention wine and beer. A glass of orange juice, a plate of burritos and a serving of apple pie is about US$10.

Perico's (☎ 4-31-52), Avenida Yaxchilán 71 at Calle Marañón, is quintessential Cancún, a huge thatched structure stuffed with stereotypical Mexican icons. Waiters in exaggerated Mexican costumes don't serve so much as 'dramatise your dining experience'. But Perico's is not a bad place to have dinner. The food is decent, the menu heavy with the macho fare most popular with group tourists: filet mignon, jumbo shrimp, lobster, barbecued spareribs. 'Pancho Villa's Plate' will get you an assortment. A meal costs US$25 to US$35 per person. It's supposedly open from noon to 2 am, but may in fact serve only dinner.

You can get Chinese food at *Mandarin House* (☎ 4-71-83), Avenida Sunyaxchén at Avenida Tankah, across from the post office. The Cantonese classics are on the menu for lunch and dinner every day (except Wednesday when it's closed); a full meal costs only US$12, or less.

Isla Cancún You can dine well without blowing your moderate budget at *Casa Rolandi* (☎ 3-18-17) in the posh Plaza Caracol shopping centre at Km 8 near Punta Cancún. Northern Italian, Mexican and international dishes fill the menu, things like carpaccio of salmon and cabrito al horno de leña (wood-roasted kid). The catch of the day comes as a fillet or as a whole fish. A full dinner goes for US$20 to US$35 per person; lunch costs less. It's open from 1.30 to 11.30 pm daily and from 6 to 11.30 pm on Sunday.

Los Rancheros (☎ 3-27-13) in the Flamingo Plaza (Blvd Kukulcán Km 11) specialises in Mexican favourites interpreted for visiting gringos and gringas: nachos, caldo tlalpeño (spicy chicken soup), beef tenderloin filete tampiqueña (in savoury tomato sauce) and red snapper fillet. There's even a 'make-a-taco' plate of beef, chicken, pork, guacamole and beans – you roll your own. Full dinners cost US$20 to US$35 per person. Hours are 8 am to 11 pm every day.

Places to Eat – top end

Traditionally, Mexican restaurants have followed the European scheme of simple decor and elaborate food. Cancún, however, caters mostly to the sort of sun-baked North Americans who seem to prefer simple food served in elaborate surroundings. Half the menus in town are composed of such grill-me items as steak, jumbo shrimp, fish fillet and lobster tail.

Thus Cancún's expensive restaurants are elaborate, with rhapsodic menu prose, lots of tropical gardens, mirrors, waterfalls, paraphernalia, even fishtanks and aviaries of exotic birds. The food can be good, forgettable or execrable. If it's the last, at least you'll have pleasant music and something to look at as you gnaw and gag.

Here are the exceptional places:

Ciudad Cancún A long-standing favourite is *Rosa Mexicano* (☎ 4-63-13), Calle Claveles 4, the place to go for unusual Mexican dishes. Rosa used to offer many traditional recipes but recently, however, more concessions to Cancún have appeared, such as good tortilla soup and puntas de filete. For dessert, have the dulce de camote, a Puebla delicacy of yams baked in brown sugar and cinnamon, served with mild yellow cheese. Dinner, served daily from 5 to 11 pm, goes for about US$30.

Another dependable favourite is *La Habichuela* (☎ 4-31-58) Margaritas 25 just off Parque Las Palapas. The menu tends towards dishes easily comprehended and easily perceived as elegant: shishkebab flambé, lobster in champagne sauce, jumbo shrimp and beef tampiqueña. But the food is good, the service experienced and the prices not bad: US$34 to US$42 per person for dinner. Hours are 1 pm to about 11 pm, every day of the year. La Habichuela ('LAH-b'CHWEH-lah') means The Stringbean.

La Dolce Vita (☎ 4-13-84), Avenida Cobá 87 just east of Avenida Nader, is a nice little place that's been serving good food for years. Though the menu includes Italian favourites (lots of veal and pasta), there's also sea conch and calamari sautéed in garlic, herbs and soy sauce and tournedos of beef. Full dinners, served from 5 pm to midnight daily, cost US$25 to US$45 per person.

Isla Cancún Visiting gringos flock to *Carlos 'n' Charlie's* (☎ 3-13-04), Blvd Kukulcán Km 5, opposite the Casa Maya, because they enjoy the who-cares atmosphere, jokey waiters, purple menu prose and decent food, and they don't mind paying US$28 to US$45 for dinner. Trendy Mexican dishes (guacamole, fajitas, ceviche) join the requisite steaks, shrimp and lobster on the menu. You pay US$3 for a beer, US$4 for anything stronger. There's dancing by the water after dinner.

Entertainment

There are discos at most of the luxury hotels in the Zona Hoteles, but the action depends very much upon the clientele in residence. A convention of Golden Agers will leave the disco sleepy, but busloads of body types will make it thunder.

Most of the nightlife is loud and bibulous as befits a supercharged beach resort. If the theme restaurants don't do it for you, take a dinner cruise on a mock pirate ship.

The local Ballet Folklorico performs some evenings at various halls for about US$30 per person, which includes dinner. The dancers come on at 8.30 pm. Don't expect the finesse and precision of the one in Mexico City.

Bullfights (four bulls) are held each Wednesday afternoon at 3.30 pm in the Plaza de Toros at the southern end of Avenida Bonampak, about one km from the centre of town. Tickets cost about US$20 and can be purchased from any travel agency.

Things to Buy

There are gift shops and touts everywhere in Cancún, with crafts from all over Mexico at sometimes exorbitant prices. Save your shopping for other Mexican destinations. If you hanker for a hammock, buy it in Mérida. Still, window-shopping in Cancún is good fun. The Plaza Caracol near Punta Cancún is very posh, with arctic air-conditioning. Also, have a wander around the Plaza Nautilus with its art galleries and boutiques.

Getting There & Away

Air Cancún's international airport is very busy with scheduled flights and also lots of charter traffic. Be sure to ask your travel agent about charter and group flights, which can be quite cheap, especially in summer.

For information on transport to and from the airport, see Getting Around, below.

Of the scheduled flights from North America, most are by Aeroméxico, American, Mexicana, Continental, Delta, Northwest and United. Most flights in the USA come from Baltimore, Chicago, Dallas/Fort Worth, Denver, Detroit, Houston, Los

Angeles, Miami, New Orleans, New York, Philadelphia, San Francisco, Tampa/St Petersburg and Washington, DC.

Domestic flights are mostly handled by smaller regional airlines such as Aerocaribe and Aviacsa. Mexicana have recently merged Aero Cozumel, Aerocaribe and Aero Monterrey into a new airline called Mexicana Inter. But as the merger process is still in a transitionary phase, airline offices and tickets may still bear the old name.

Here are sample fares (one-way): Chetumal US$80, Ciudad del Carmen US$140, Cozumel US$45, Mérida US$80, Mexico City US$190, Oaxaca US$230, Veracruz US$199 and Villahermosa US$160. A special excursion fare from Cancún to Mérida and return is US$120. You can also book a flight to Chichén Itzá and return for US$89.

Aeroméxico (☎ (988) 4-35-71, 4-10-97, 4-11-86), is on the south side of the road at Avenida Cobá 80, SM 3, between Avenida Tulum and Avenida Bonampak. It's open 8 am to 6.30 pm every day. It has daily nonstop flights to Mérida, Mexico City, Houston, Miami, New York and New Orleans, and a Saturday nonstop service to Paris.

American (☎ (988) 4-29-47, 4-26-51) is at the airport.

Aviacsa (☎ (988) 4-23-11, 7-66-95; fax 7-67-95) is at the airport. Based in Tuxtla Gutiérrez, Chiapas, it flies Cancún-Mérida-Villahermosa-Tuxtla Gutiérrez, and Mexico City-Oaxaca-Tuxtla Gutiérrez-Chetumal.

Continental (☎ (988) 4-25-40, 4-27-06) is at the airport.

Inter (☎ (988) 4-81-03, 4-13-64), the important regional carrier with flights to Chichén Itzá, Mérida, Uxmal, Cozumel and other points in Yucatán and beyond, is in a complex at the intersection of Avenidas Tulum and Uxmal. It also presently runs flights to Belize City, and to Flores (for Tikal) in Guatemala.

Inter (☎ (988) 4-36-83) at the airport has short-hop flights in light aircraft to Chichén Itzá, Cozumel, and other regional tourist centres.

Lacsa (☎ (988) 4-12-76), the Costa Rican airline, at Avenida Yaxchilán 5, has flights to San José (Costa Rica), and from there to other Central American points, as well as to New York.

Mexicana (☎ (988) 7-44-44), Avenida Cobá 13, not far from the Aeroméxico office, flies nonstop to and from Cozumel, Mérida, Guadalajara, Dallas/Fort Worth, Los Angeles, Miami and Tampa/St Petersburg.

Northwest (☎ (988) 4-09-46, 4-50-44) is at the airport.

United (☎ (988) 4-28-58, 4-25-28) is at the airport.

Bus Several companies share the traffic to and from Cancún. The bus station on Avenida Uxmal just west of Avenida Tulum and the northern traffic roundabout, serves them all. The station has a cafeteria, snack shops and a newsstand, but no left-luggage lockers.

Autotransportes de Oriente Mérida-Puerto Juárez (A de O M-PJ), in the right-hand portion of the bus station, handles most of the traffic to and from Mérida.

Autotransportes del Caribe (A del Caribe), in the left-hand portion of the bus station, runs buses south along the coast to Puerto Morelos, Playa del Carmen, Akumal, Xelha, Tulum, Felipe Carrillo Puerto, Limones, Bacalar and Chetumal, as well as west to Ticul and Muna.

Autobuses de Oriente (ADO) does the long routes to Mexico City via Villahermosa and Veracruz.

Bacalar – 350 km, five hours; five 2nd-class (US$7.50) buses daily by A del Caribe.

Chetumal – 382 km, seven hours; five 2nd-class (US$8.75) buses daily by A del Caribe.

Chichén Itzá – 205 km, three to 3½ hours; two 1st-class (US$4) departures (7.15 and 11.45 am) by A de O M-PJ; many Mérida-bound buses (including 2nd-class ones for US$3.75) will also drop you at Chichén Itzá.

Felipe Carrillo Puerto – 226 km, 3½ hours; nine 1st-class (US$6), and several 2nd-class (US$5.25) by A del Caribe.

Mérida – 320 km, 5½ to six hours; 32 1st-class (US$7.50) and 12 2nd-class (US$6.25) by A de O M-PJ.

Mexico City – 1772 km, 27 hours; ADO runs six 1st-class buses (US$36.50) daily.

Playa del Carmen – 65 km, one hour; six 1st-class (US$2.25) and seven 2nd-class (US$1.90) by A de O M-PJ, all de paso; A del Caribe also has eight buses daily.

Puerto Morelos – 36 km, half an hour; see Playa del Carmen.

Ticul – 441 km, seven hours (via Felipe Carrillo Puerto); one 1st-class bus (US$8.50) daily by A del Caribe.

Tizimín – 212 km, four hours; A de O M-PJ runs one 1st-class (US$4.50) at 5.45 pm, and four 2nd-class buses (US$4) daily; otherwise, change at Valladolid.

Tulum – 131 km, two hours; four 1st-class (US$3.75) daily by A de O M-PJ.

Valladolid – 161 km, two hours; 32 1st-class (US$3.75) and nine 2nd-class (US$3) by A de O M-PJ.

Veracruz – 1390 km, 22 hours; one 1st-class bus (US$27) daily by ADO.

Villahermosa – 915 km, 14 hours; nine 1st-class buses (US$22) daily by ADO.

Car A Volkswagen Beetle or similarly sized Nissan without air-conditioning, radio, or other comforts can cost over US$70 per day with unlimited kilometrage. If you don't rent with unlimited kilometrage, keep in mind that distances in Yucatán are great and that the kilometrage will end up being your biggest cost, far more than the daily rental charge. When estimating costs, be sure to take into consideration the high collision damage waiver costs and the 15% IVA (value-added tax) as well.

The rental agency desks at the airport are as good a place as any to haggle over rates (and haggling does help), but don't expect to get a cheap car, no matter how much you haggle.

Here are the major companies:

Budget – Avenida Tulum (☎ (988) 4-07-30, 4-02-04)
Dollar – Avenida Tulum (☎ (988) 4-20-39)
Econo-Rent – Calle Tulipanes 16 (☎ (988) 4-18-26, 4-14-35)
Hertz – Calle Reno 35 (☎ (988) 4-46-92)
National (Europcar, Tilden) – Avenida Chichén Itzá Lote A 2-2 Altos, SM 63 (☎ (988) 4-99-08)
Thrifty – Avenida Yaxchilán 160 (☎ (988) 4-26-99, 4-28-99; fax 7-50-12)

Boat There are frequent passenger ferries to Isla Mujeres from Puerto Juárez, about three km north of Avenida Tulum. Car ferries, which also carry passengers, depart from Punta Sam, about five km north of Avenida Tulum. There are also three daily ferries to Isla Mujeres from the Playa Linda Marine Terminal, Blvd Kukulcán Km 4 on Isla Cancún, just west of the bridge between the Aquamarina Beach and Calinda Cancún hotels.

Getting Around

To/From the Airport You must take an airport van or a taxi; there are no buses. The airport vans ('Transporte Terrestre') cost US$6.50.

The route from the airport is invariably via Punta Nizuc and north up Isla Cancún along Blvd Kukulcán, passing all of the luxury beach-front hotels before reaching the youth hostel and Ciudad Cancún. If your hotel is in Ciudad Cancún, the ride to your hotel may take as long as 45 minutes.

The alternative to the van is to take a taxi, or hire a van for a private trip, straight to your hotel. This costs US$22. If you walk out of the airport and follow the access road, you may be able to flag down a taxi which will take you for less because the driver is no longer subject to the expensive regulated airport fares.

To return to the airport you must take a taxi; you cannot call or wave down one of the airport vans. The fare to the airport is US$11 from anywhere in Ciudad Cancún or Isla Cancún.

Bus Local buses are operated by various companies and charge between US$0.35 and US$1.25 per ride; the fare is often written in the windscreen.

Although you can walk everywhere in Ciudad Cancún, to get to the Zona Hoteles, catch a 'Ruta 1, Zona Hoteles' local bus heading southward along Avenida Tulum. They proceed down Avenida Tulum to Avenida Cobá, turn left and continue along Blvd Kukulcán almost to Punta Nizuc. There are never enough buses and they are always packed.

To reach Puerto Juárez or Punta Sam for the ferries bound for Isla Mujeres, take a Ruta 8 bus ('Pto Juárez' or 'Punta Sam'). Returning from Isla Mujeres to Punta Sam, note that the bus drivers seem to have been pressured by the *taxistas* to depart *just before the ferry arrives*, thereby forcing passengers to take taxis back to Ciudad Cancún. If you're willing to wait, another Ruta 8 bus will come. The bus waits on the road outside the gate to the ferry area.

Taxi Cancún's taxis do not have meters so you must haggle over fares. Some of the large hotels have fares to various points posted on signs near their front entrances. Generally, the fare between Ciudad Cancún and Punta Cancún (Hyatt, Camino Real and Krystal hotels and the Convention Centre) is US$2 or US$2.50, the same or slightly less to shuttle between two of the big hotels on Isla Cancún.

To go from Ciudad Cancún all the way down to the Club Med at Punta Nizuc might cost US$6 or US$8. To the airport costs US$11, a flat rate from any point in the city or on the island. To Puerto Juárez you'll pay about US$3.75, to Punta Sam about US$4.50 or US$5.

Because there are never enough buses, at peak travel times (late morning, before dinner in the evening) there are also never enough taxis. You will find transport difficult at these times, no matter how you wish to travel or what you're willing to spend.

ISLA MUJERES
Population: 13,500
Isla Mujeres (Island of Women), has a reputation as a 'backpackers' Cancún', a place where one can escape the high-energy, high-priced mega-resort for the laid-back life of a tropical isle – at bargain prices. Though this was true for many years, it is less true today. Cancún has been so successful that its version of the good life has spilled over onto its neighbouring island.

The chief attribute of Isla Mujeres is its relaxed social life in a tropical setting with surrounding waters that are turquoise blue and bathtub warm. If you have been doing some hard travelling through Mexico, you will find many travellers you met along the way taking it easy here. Others make it the site of a one to two-week holiday.

History
Although it is said by some that the Island of

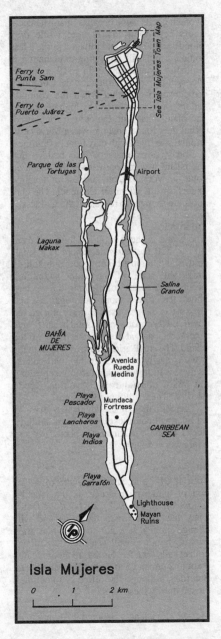

Isla Mujeres

Women got its name because Spanish buccaneers kept their lovers here while they plundered galleons and pillaged ports, a less romantic but still intriguing explanation is probably more accurate. In 1519, a chronicler sailing with Hernández de Córdoba's expedition wrote that when the conquistadors' ships were forced by high winds into the island's harbour, the crew reconnoitred. What they found onshore was a Maya ceremonial site filled with clay female figurines.

Today, some archaeologists believe that the island was a stopover for the Maya en route to worship their goddess of fertility, Ixchel, on the island of Cozumel. The clay idols are thought to represent the goddess.

Orientation

The island is about eight km long and from 300 to 800 metres wide. There is a small mid-island airstrip. The good snorkelling areas and some of the better swimming beaches are to the south along the western shore; the eastern shore faces open sea and the surf is dangerous. The ferry docks, the town and the most popular sand beach (Playa Cocoteros) are at the northern tip of the island. The small grid of narrow streets in the town is easily comprehensible, particularly as there is little vehicular traffic except along the main coastal road, Avenida Rueda Medina. There are few street signs.

There is a main plaza which also serves as a basketball court just inland from the ferry docks, a municipal market, a post office and a largeish cemetery.

Information

Tourist Office Located on Guerrero, at the end of a narrow passage, is the island's tourist office (☎ (988) 2-01-73, 2-01-88). They have crude map handouts and will change money at a not-so-great rate after banking hours, as well as make international collect calls for a fee. Hours are theoretically 9 am to 2 pm and 5 to 7 pm from Monday to Saturday, although the office is sometimes closed during these hours.

Money The island's Banco del Atlantico, at

Juárez 5, and Banco Serfin, at Juárez 3, are so packed during the two hours a day (10 am to noon, Monday to Friday) when foreign currency may be exchanged that many travellers change money at a lower rate at a grocery store, their hotel or at the tourist office.

Laundry The family that runs the Posada San Jorge has opened a laundromat (lavandería) (☎ 2-01-55) at Avenida Juárez 29, just in front of the posada. Come any day between 6 am and 8 pm, drop off three kg of laundry and your choice of detergent and you'll pay US$3.25 to have it washed, US$1.50 to have it dried, or US$4.50 for wash and dry.

Playa Cocoteros

Walk north along Calle Hidalgo or Guerrero to reach Playa Cocoteros, sometimes called Playa Los Cocos, the town's principal beach. The slope of the beach is very gradual and the transparent and calm waters are only chest-high far from the shore. However, the beach is relatively small for the number of sunseekers and while there are some palapathatched huts for shelter from direct rays, the

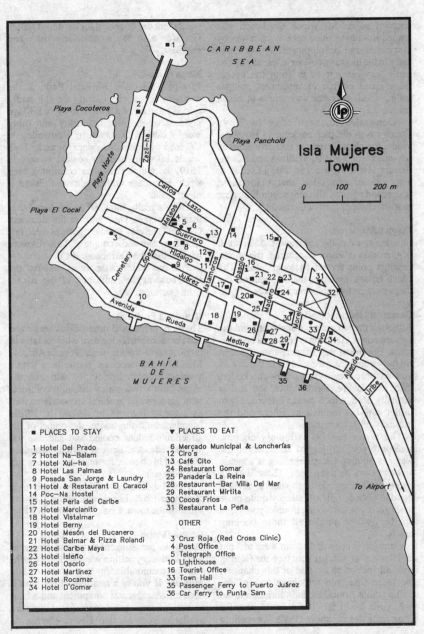

CARIBBEAN
SEA

Playa Cocoteros

Playa Panchold

Playa Norte

Playa El Cocal

Isla Mujeres Town

0   100   200 m

BAHÍA
DE
MUJERES

To Airport

■ PLACES TO STAY

1 Hotel Del Prado
2 Hotel Na–Balam
7 Hotel Xul–ha
8 Hotel Las Palmas
9 Posada San Jorge & Laundry
11 Hotel & Restaurant El Caracol
14 Poc–Na Hostel
15 Hotel Perla del Caribe
17 Hotel Marcianito
18 Hotel Vistalmar
19 Hotel Berny
20 Hotel Mesón del Bucanero
21 Hotel Belmar & Pizza Rolandi
22 Hotel Caribe Maya
23 Hotel Isleño
26 Hotel Osorio
27 Hotel Martinez
32 Hotel Rocamar
34 Hotel D'Gomar

▼ PLACES TO EAT

6 Mercado Municipal & Loncherías
12 Ciro's
13 Café Cito
24 Restaurant Gomar
25 Panadería La Reina
28 Restaurant–Bar Villa Del Mar
29 Restaurant Mirtita
30 Cocos Fríos
31 Restaurant La Peña

OTHER

3 Cruz Roja (Red Cross Clinic)
4 Post Office
5 Telegraph Office
10 Lighthouse
16 Tourist Office
33 Town Hall
35 Passenger Ferry to Puerto Juárez
36 Car Ferry to Punta Sam

coconut palms for which the beach was named have long since been swept away by hurricanes and development. Try to come early in the morning or later in the day. If you can't tear yourself away from the beach, there are a couple of restaurant palapas selling food, beer and soft drinks at beach prices.

Along the northern edge of Playa Cocoteros at the pier adjacent to Hotel del Prado, the clear water and colourful aquatic life make for good snorkelling and it's infinitely less crowded than Playa Garrafón. There is no admission charge for these waters and you can also rent snorkelling gear in town cheaper than at Garrafón.

Playa Lancheros
Four km south of the town and 1½ km north of Garrafón is Playa Lancheros, the southernmost point served by local buses. The beach is less attractive than Cocoteros, but there are free festivities on Sundays.

Garrafón National Park
Although the waters are translucent and the fish abundant, Garrafón is perhaps a bit overrated. Hordes of day trippers from Cancún fill the water during the middle of the day, so you are more often ogling fellow snorkellers than aquatic life. Furthermore, the reef is virtually dead, which makes it less likely to inflict cuts but reduces its colour and the intricacy of its formations.

The water can be extremely choppy, sweeping you into jagged areas. When the water is running fast snorkelling is a hassle and can even be dangerous. Those without strong swimming skills should be advised that the bottom falls off steeply quite close to shore; if you are having trouble, you might not be noticed amidst all those bobbing heads.

Garrafón is open daily from 8 am to 5 pm and the earlier you get here (see the Getting Around section at the end of this chapter), the more time you will have free of the milling mobs from Cancún. Admission to the park costs US$1.50. There are lockers for your valuables for about US$2. Snorkelling

equipment can be rented for the day at US$5. Garrafón also has a small aquarium and museum.

Maya Ruins
Just past Garrafón National Park, at the southern tip of the island, are the badly ruined remains of a temple to Ixchel, Maya goddess of the moon, fertility and other worthy causes. Observed by Hernández de Córdoba when his ships were forced by high winds into the island's coastal waters in 1519, the temple has been crumbling ever since. Hurricane Gilbert almost finished it off in 1988.

There's really little left to see here other than a fine sea view and, in the distance, Cancún. The clay female figurines were pilfered long ago and a couple of the walls were washed into the Caribbean.

You can walk to the ruins, beyond the lighthouse at the south end of the island, from Garrafón.

Mundaca Fortress
The story behind the ruins of this house and fort are more intriguing than what remains of them. A slave-trading pirate, Fermin Antonio Mundaca de Marechaja, fell in love with a visiting Spanish beauty. To win her, the rogue built a two-storey mansion complete with gardens and graceful archways as well as a small fortress to defend it. While Mundaca built the house, the object of his affection's ardour cooled and she married another islander. Brokenhearted, Mundaca died and his house, fortress and garden fell into disrepair.

The Mundaca fortress is east of the main road near Playa Lancheros, about four km south of the town. Look for signs.

Scuba Diving
Diving to see sunken ships and beautiful reefs in the crystalline waters of the Caribbean is a memorable way to pass time on Isla Mujeres. If you're a qualified diver, you'll need a licence, rental equipment and a boat to take you to the good spots. All of these are available from Mexico Divers (Buzos de

México, ☎ (988) 2-01-31), Avenida Rueda Medina at Madero. Costs range from US$50 to US$85 depending upon how many tanks you use up.

Places to Stay

During the busy seasons (late December to March and midsummer), many island hotels are booked solid by midday; at these times prices are also highest. From May to mid-December prices are lower and you may even be able to haggle them still lower if business is slack. Double rooms will usually be rented as singles at a slightly lower price if demand for rooms is not high.

Places to Stay – bottom end

Poc-Na (☎ (988) 2-00-90), on Matamoros at Carlos Lazo, is a privately run youth hostel and an international travellers' hangout. The fan-cooled dormitories, which take both men and women together, are clean as are the communal toilets. Poc-Na is close to both the beach and the town, yet the location is fairly quiet. The cafeteria serves decent food at inexpensive prices; the patio dining room is a great meeting place for travellers. The charge for bunk and bedding is US$5; you must put down a deposit of US$8.50 on the bedding.

Hotel El Caracol (☎ (988) 2-01-50), Matamoros 5 between Hidalgo and Guerrero, is run by a smiling and efficient señora and her family who keep everything clean and neat. The tidy restaurant off the lobby serves meals at decent prices. Rooms have insect screens, ceiling fans, clean tiled bathrooms and many have two double beds. You pay US$22 a double if you stay only one night, US$18 per night for two or more.

The *Hotel Martínez* (☎ (988) 2-01-54) Madero 14 is an older family hotel that's been fairly well maintained. Some rooms have sea views, all have ceiling fans and private baths. Doubles go for US$17. It's dependable for cheap, clean accommodation.

Almost across the street is the *Hotel Osorio* (☎ (988) 2-00-18), Madero at Juárez. The older part of the hotel, on the opposite side of the street from the Martinez (the building with the odd façade of rounded stones), has huge, clean rooms with fan and bath; the newer building facing it across Madero has more up-to-date rooms. The rate for a double is US$16 to US$20, depending upon the room, the season and your bargaining abilities.

Cheaper still is *Posada San Jorge* (☎ (988) 2-01-55), Juárez 29A, behind the laundromat of the same name. Its bare, basic rooms are acceptably clean and quite inexpensive. Singles with fan and bath cost US$12, doubles US$15. *Hotel Las Palmas* (☎ (988) 2-04-16), Guerrero 20, across from the Mercado Municipal, offers nice, clean, new rooms with fan and bath for US$14/18 a single/double. It's near the market's cheap eateries and closer to the beach than most hotels in town.

Hotel Caribe Maya (☎ (988) 2-01-90), Madero 9 between Guerrero and Hidalgo, charges $US16 a double, and offers good value for money. Rooms are simple but clean, with a fan and private shower.

Hotel Marcianito (☎ (988) 2-01-11), Abasolo 10 between Juárez and Hidalgo, is a place to try if everything else is full. Rooms here are serviceable, but more closed-in and older than those in nearby hotels; and the price here is a bit higher, at US$19 a double with fan and shower.

Hotel Isleño (☎ (988) 0-03-02), Madero 8 at the corner of Guerrero, has rooms with ceiling fans and good cross-ventilation, but without running water, for US$14 a double. There's a shared bathroom for every three guest rooms, so the facilities aren't really overcrowded. Upper-floor rooms are quieter.

Hotel Vistalmar (☎ (988) 2-00-96), Avenida Rueda Medina between Abasolo and Matamoros, is a final place to look if all else is full. True to its name, the Vistalmar has nice sea views from its front porch, but its rooms are as simple and functional as any in town yet cost a bit more than most: US$19 a double.

Places to Stay – middle

Moderately priced hotel rooms cost anywhere from US$26 to US$75 a double. For this you usually (but not always) get air-conditioning, more in the way of decor, perhaps a balcony and/or a nice sea view and sometimes other services such as a restaurant, bar and swimming pool. All rooms have private bathrooms.

Hotel Perla del Caribe (☎ (988) 2-04-44, 2-03-02), Madero east of Guerrero, right on the eastern beach, has 63 rooms on three floors, most with balconies, many with wonderful sea views and good cross-ventilation. There's a cafeteria, snack bar and a swimming pool. Rooms are in four categories (all doubles): for US$42, you can have a room, with fan or air-con, facing the town; for US$58, your room has a sea view, but is on a lower floor; for US$64 you get a similar room on an upper floor; and for US$76 one of the newest, most luxurious rooms.

Hotel Belmar (☎ (988) 2-04-29/30; fax 2-04-29), Hidalgo between Abasolo and Madero, is right above the Pizza Rolandi restaurant and run by the same family. Though it doesn't look like much from its entrance, the hotel's rooms are very nicely decorated and well kept, with fan, air-con and TV. The price, US$35 a double, is good for what you get. The new *Hotel D'Gomar* (☎ (988) 2-01-42), Hidalgo 5, is easily visible from the ferryboats as you dock. The guestrooms, arranged on four floors above a boutique, rent for a reasonable US$35 a double. Each has a fan and two double beds.

The *Hotel Rocamar* (☎ (988) 2-01-01) is on the opposite side of the town from the ferry above the main square where Guerrero meets Bravo. This was the first real hotel to be built here and though it now shows its age a bit, maintenance is good. It still has the advantages of an excellent hilltop site, wonderful sea views and very good cross-ventilation. The hotel's restaurant, El Limbo, shares the fine sea view. Singles/doubles/triples with fan and bath cost US$40/46/50.

The 40 rooms at the *Hotel Berny* (☎ (988) 2-00-25/26), on Abasolo at the corner of Juárez, are built around a central court with a small swimming pool. The rooms are comfortable and modernish though not fancy;

with ceiling fan and private bath, they cost US$34 a double.

The brand-new *Hotel Xul-ha*, on Hidalgo not far from López Mateos, is a stucco structure with up-to-date rooms, all with balconies and air-con, renting for US$42 a double.

Hotel Mesón del Bucanero (☎ (988) 2-02-36), Hidalgo 11 between Abasolo and Madero, is above the restaurant of the same name. Rooms at the Bucanero are nice enough and they come with ceiling fans, but the prices are upscale at US$45 to US$58 a double.

Places to Stay – top end
The island's poshest place is the *Hotel Del Prado* (☎ (988) 2-00-29/43, 2-01-22), Islote del Yunque. The dramatic inclined façade faces north across the water from its perch on a tiny islet at Isla Mujeres' northernmost point, just 100 metres north of Playa Cocoteros. The 100 rooms here have all the conveniences and most of the luxuries; there's a restaurant and bar, a pool and a tiny beach, though most of the islet is jagged rock. Singles/doubles cost US$92/110, tax included. Call toll-free for reservations in Mexico (☎ (800) 9-04-44; in the USA (800) 782-9639).

Hotel Na-Balam (☎/fax (988) 2-04-46), Calle Zazil-Ha 118, faces Playa Cocoteros at the northern tip of the island. The two-storey structure holds 12 spacious junior suites, most with a fabulous sea view, ceiling fan, refrigerator, two double beds and private bath. Prices for suites with balcony are US$70 a double in season, US$50 off season; without a balcony, prices are US$5 lower. More hotels similar to the Na-Balam (the name means House of the Jaguar) are being built facing the beach here.

Places to Eat – bottom end
On Guerrero, near the intersection with López Mateos, is the Mercado Municipal opposite the Hotel Las Palmas. Beside the market are several *cocinas económicas* (economical kitchens) serving simple but tasty and filling meals at the best prices on the

island. Sit in the shade and have a big plate with fried chicken, chips and salad for US$3.50, or various Mexican antojitos for US$2.50. Tacos are even cheaper. Prices are not marked, so ask before you order. These market eateries are nicer than those in most Mexican towns and only a bit more expensive. Hours are usually (and approximately) 7 am to 6 pm.

Fresh baked goods are available at *Panadería La Reina*, on Madero between Juárez and Hidalgo, a good place to stop for breakfast or picnic supplies.

Café Cito, a tiny place on Guerrero near the corner with Matamoros, has a New Age menu which includes 10 varieties of crepes, ingenious sandwiches, huge salad plates and tempting daily special platters. The menu is in English and German. Expect to spend US$3.50 to US$7 for a meal here. Hours are 9 am to noon and 6 to 10 pm, closed Monday.

Self-Catering To buy your own supplies, there's the municipal market, the Supermercado Mirtita at Juárez 14, on the corner of Nicolas Bravo one block inland from the ferry docks, or the Super Betino on the main plaza.

Places to Eat – middle

Most of the island's restaurants fall into the middle category. Depending upon what you order, breakfast goes for US$3.25 to US$6 and lunch or dinner for US$7 to US$18 per person, unless you order lobster.

El Bucanero (☎ 2-02-36), Avenida Hidalgo 11, between Abasolo and Madero in the Hotel Mesón del Bucanero, has a long and interesting menu: breakfast omelettes of ham and cheese (US$3.25), fried chicken or fish (US$5) and Mexican traditional foods (enchiladas, tacos, etc) for about the same. Besides the usual, they serve offbeat things like asparagus au gratin with wholemeal bread. It's open every day for all three meals.

Pizza Rolandi (☎ 2-04-30), directly across Hidalgo from El Bucanero, serves pizzas and calzones, cooked in a wood-fired oven, and pastas with various sauces for US$5 to US$9 per person. The menu includes fresh salads, fish and lobster as well as some Italian specialities. Hours are 1 pm to midnight daily, 6 pm to midnight on Sunday.

Restaurant El Peregrino (☎ 2-01-90) at Madero 8 adjoining the Hotel Caribe Maya, has a small streetside dining area and several pleasantly decorated interior rooms. Though the menu is similar to those at the aforementioned places, the prices here are lower and the food is as good.

Restaurant La Peña (no phone), Guerrero 5, behind the bandstand on the main square, serves platters designed for the tourist trade: fish or beef brochettes with salad, chips and a glass of beer or wine for US$7.50. Colour photographs by the entrance show you what you're supposed to get. Prices are fairly reasonable, but sometimes portions on the real-world platters don't quite live up to the photographs. The restaurant has many complicated and expensive drinks. La Peña is open daily from 8 am to midnight.

Another place favoured mostly for ambience is *Cocos Frios* at Hidalgo 4. Specials here are not chilled coconuts so much as fried chicken, chicken tacos, fried fish and beef served in various ways. Breakfast here is a favourite – again, more for the mood than the food.

Somewhat more expensive is *Restaurant Gomar* (☎ 2-01-42), on Hidalgo at the corner with Madero, which serves excellent seafood and chicken dishes. The huge VCR shows movies while you dine. There are tables outside on the verandah as well. Expect to spend about US$9 to US$12 for a decent seafood dinner here. Hours are supposedly from 8 am to 11 pm.

Ciro's, on Matamoros at Guerrero, serves a varied menu of sandwiches, soups, chicken, meats, fish and lobster at moderate prices, but the real draw here is the air-con dining room. It's open from 2 to 10 pm daily. A large club sandwich with chips costs US$3.50 and most meat, chicken and fish plates are about US$5.

Restaurant Mirtita (☎ 2-01-57) faces the ferry dock on Avenida Rueda Medina. The menu is in English. Portions are a bit on the small side and prices on the big, but it's convenient to the ferry. Another choice is the nearby *Restaurant Tropicana*, also on Avenida Rueda Medina at the corner of Nicolas Bravo, which is more favoured by *isleños*.

Also facing the ferry docks is the *Restaurant-Bar Villa Del Mar* (☎ 2-00-31), Avenida Rueda Medina 1 Sur, which is fancier in decor and ambience but not all that much higher in price.

Places to Eat – top end
Big spenders from Cancún and well-heeled visitors to Isla Mujeres often head for *María's Kan-Kin Restaurant Française* (☎ 3-14-20, 2-00-15), several km down the coast near Garrafón and open daily from 8 am to 9 pm. The lobsters are live, the prices for the continental-inspired cuisine are high, but the food is said to be good.

Entertainment
The first place to go is the main plaza, where there's always something to watch (a football match, a basketball or volleyball game, an impromptu concert or serenade) and lots of somebodies watching it.

The island's only cinema, the Cine Blanquita on Morelos is on the north-west side of the square. It sometimes has foreign films in English with subtitles in Spanish, but ask – don't assume.

As for discos, there's Buho's (☎ 2-00-86), which is also a restaurant and bar, in the Hotel Cabañas María del Mar, Avenida Carlos Lazo 1 at Playa Cocoteros. Nearby is the Bad Bones Café, next to the north lighthouse. Tequila Video Bar (☎ 2-00-19), at the corner of Matamoros and Hidalgo, is a favourite with locals, but draws a respectable number of foreigners as well. Hours are 9 pm to 3 am every day except Monday.

Getting There & Away
Bus Most people travelling to Isla Mujeres from Cancún take a Ruta 8 bus heading north on Avenida Tulum (US$0.60) or a taxi (US$3.75) to Puerto Juárez, about three km north of Ciudad Cancún's Avenida Tulum; a

Cancún airport minibus will take you to Puerto Juárez on a private trip for about US$22, but it'd be cheaper to ride the minibus with others into Ciudad Cancún (US$6.50 per person) and then take a taxi from there. There are also direct buses to Puerto Juárez from Mérida, Chichén Itzá and Valladolid.

To get to Punta Sam, take the Ruta 8 bus (US$0.90, 25 minutes) heading north from Avenida Tulum, or a taxi (US$4.50 or US$5, 15 minutes).

Boat There are three points of embarkation from the mainland by ferry to Isla Mujeres, 11 km off the coast. Two are north of Ciudad Cancún, the other is on Isla Cancún.

To/From Puerto Juárez The official schedule says that passenger ferries depart every hour on the half-hour from 8.30 am to 8.30 pm, with extra boats at 6 and 10 am. In practice, the schedule depends upon demand and if few people show up for a particular voyage, it'll be cancelled. One-way fare is US$2.75, or US$4 if you take the fancier and more comfortable *Caribbean Queen*. The voyage takes about 30 minutes. Return schedules from Isla Mujeres are equally frequent; most hotels on the island have schedules posted.

To/From Punta Sam The dock at Punta Sam, about five km north of Avenida Tulum and 3½ km north of Puerto Juárez, is the departure point for car ferries to Isla Mujeres. These offer greater stability (and less chance of seasickness) than the Puerto Juárez passenger ferries, but the car ferries are slower, taking 45 minutes to an hour to reach the island.

Ferries leave Punta Sam at 7.15 and 9.45 am, at noon and at 2.30, 5.15, 7.45 and 10 pm. Departures from Isla Mujeres are at 6, 8.30 and 11 am and at 1.15, 4, 6.30 and 9 pm. Passengers pay US$2; a car costs US$8.50. If you're taking a car, be sure to get to the dock an hour or so before departure time. Put your car in line and buy your ticket early or you may have to wait for the next voyage.

To/From Playa Linda Marine Terminal
Three times daily, *The Shuttle* (☎ (988) 4-63-33, 4-66-56) departs from Playa Linda on Isla Cancún for Isla Mujeres. Voyages are at 8 and 11 am and 2 pm from Playa Linda; return voyages depart Isla Mujeres at 9.30 am and 12.30 and 5 pm. The round-trip fare is US$16, but this includes free beer and soft drinks on board.

Show up at the Playa Linda Marine Terminal, Blvd Kukulcán Km 4 on Isla Cancún, just west of the bridge between the Aquamarina Beach and Calinda Cancún hotels, at least 30 minutes before departure so you'll have time to buy your ticket and get a good seat on the boat.

Getting Around
The town of Isla Mujeres is small and everything's within walking distance. If you arrive with heavy luggage, little boys will wheel it on push-bikes to your hotel. If you walk to Garrafón, bring some water – it's a hot, two-hour, six-km walk.

Bus By local bus from the market or dock, you can get within 1½ km of Garrafón; the terminus is Playa Lancheros. The personnel at Poc-Na youth hostel can give you an idea of the bus's erratic schedule. (Locals in league with taxi drivers may tell you the bus doesn't exist.)

Taxi It costs about US$3.50 to Garrafón and just under US$2 to Playa Lancheros. Rates are set by the municipal government and are posted at the ferry dock, though the sign is frequently defaced by the taxi drivers.

Bicycle & Moped Bicycles can be rented from a number of shops on the island including Sport Bike, on the corner of Juárez and Morelos, a block from the ferry docks. Before you rent, compare prices and the condition of the bikes in a few shops, then arrive early in the day to get one of the better bikes. Costs are US$3 to US$7 for four hours, only a bit more for a full day; you'll be asked to plunk down a deposit of US$12 or so.

Many people rent motorbikes or mopeds. Shop around, compare prices and check these items: new or newer machines in good condition, full gas tanks and reasonable deposits. Cost per hour is usually US$4 to US$6 with a two-hour minimum, US$25 all day, or even cheaper by the week. Shops away from the busiest streets tend to have better prices, but not necessarily better equipment.

When driving, remember that far more people are seriously injured on motorbikes than in cars. Your enemies are inexperience, speed, sand, wet or oily roads and other people on motorbikes. Don't forget to slather yourself with sunblock before you take off. Be sure to do your hands, feet, face and neck thoroughly, as these will get the most sun.

AROUND ISLA MUJERES
Isla Contoy Bird Sanctuary
You can take an excursion by boat to tiny Isla Contoy, a national bird sanctuary, about 25 km north of Isla Mujeres. It's a treasure trove for birdwatchers, with an abundance of brown pelicans, olive cormorants and red-pouched frigates, as well as frequent visits by flamingos and herons. There is good snorkelling both en route and just off Contoy.

Getting There & Away For a private trip, contact Ricardo Gaitan and he will take you to Contoy in his 10-metre sailboat, *Providencia*. Gaitan will supply food and snorkelling equipment for the two-day venture at roughly US$30 per person. You will need suntan lotion, insect repellent and a sleeping bag.

If you just want a one-day excursion, for about US$20, ask at the Sociedad Cooperativa Transporte Turística 'Isla Mujeres' (☎ (988) 2-02-74), on Avenida Rueda Medina to the north of the ferry docks.

ISLA HOLBOX
If you're looking to be close to nature, Isla Holbox (pronounced 'HOHL-bosh') might appeal to you, but note that the most basic facilities are in short supply and the beaches are not Cancún-perfect strips of clean, air-

conditioned sand. To enjoy Isla Holbox, you must be willing to rough it.

The 25-km by three-km island has sands that run on and on, as well as tranquil waters where you can wade out quite a distance before the sea reaches shoulder level. Moreover, Isla Holbox is magic for shell collectors, with a galaxy of shapes and colours. The fishing families of the island are friendly – unjaded by encounters with exotic tourists or the frenetic pace of the urban mainland.

However, the seas are not the translucent turquoise of the Quintana Roo beach sites, because here the Caribbean waters mingle with those of the darker Gulf. Seaweed can create silty waters near shore at some parts of the beach. While there are big plans to develop Isla Holbox one day, at the time of writing there is only one modest hotel, the aptly named *Hotel Flamingo* (with doubles for US$6) and a few snack shops. Most travellers camp or stay in spartan rooms rented from locals.

Getting There & Away
To reach Isla Holbox, take the ferry from the unappealing port village of Chiquilá. Buses make the 2½-hour trip three times a day from Valladolid to Chiquilá and in theory the ferry is supposed to wait for them. However, it may not wait for a delayed bus or may even leave early (!) should the captain feel so inclined. If you're coming from Cancún, you'll probably need to change buses at the highway junction to Chiquilá.

It is therefore recommended that you reach Chiquilá as early as possible. The ferry is supposed to depart for the island at 8 am and 3 pm, and takes an hour. Ferries return to Chiquila at 2 and 5 pm. The cost is US$1.50.

Try not to get stuck in Chiquilá, as it is a tiny hole of a port with no hotels, no decent camping and very disappointing food.

PUERTO MORELOS
Puerto Morelos, 32 km south of Cancún, is a sleepy fishing village known principally for its car ferry to Cozumel. There is a good budget hotel here and travellers who have reason to spend the night here find it refreshingly free of tourists. A handful of scuba divers come to explore the splendid reef 600 metres offshore, reachable by boat.

Places to Stay & Eat
For good basic budget lodging, stay at the *Posada Amor* (no phone). Family-run, the Posada is a wood and white stucco place with lots of plants and a happy atmosphere. Rooms with fan and a clean shared bathroom cost US$26, a single or double. Good breakfasts in the cosy dining room go for US$4 to US$6, lunches and dinners for US$8 to US$10.

On the main square (parque) in the centre of the village is the *Hotel Plaza Morelos* (no phone), with uninspired but serviceable rooms with private bath for US$34 a double.

The *Hotel Playa Ojo de Agua*, a block north of the main square, has a swimming pool, restaurant and bar. Divers receive a special rate if they make use of the hotel's dive-shop excursions and equipment rental. Rooms and three meals cost US$135. For reservations and information write to Nery Vada, Apdo Postal 299, Cancún, Quintana Roo 77500.

La Ceiba Beach Hotel, on the beach north of Puerto Morelos, has a restaurant, small swimming pool and dive shop which runs scuba excursions. Rooms come with refrigerators and have balconies overlooking the beach. Singles or doubles cost about US$120, with a discount for divers. For reservations, write to the hotel, Apdo Postal 1252, Cancún, Quintana Roo 77500.

Getting There & Away
All 2nd-class and many 1st-class buses stop at Puerto Morelos coming from or en route to Cancún, 34 km (45 minutes) away. Buses generally come by every few hours during the day.

The car ferry (transbordador; ☎ in Cozumel (987) 2-08-27, 2-09-50) to Cozumel leaves Puerto Morelos daily early in the morning, returning at midday. Departure times vary from season to season. Unless you plan to stay for awhile on Cozumel, it's hardly worth shipping your vehicle. You must get in line two or three hours before departure time and hope there's enough space on the ferry for you. Fares for the 2½ to four-hour voyage are US$4.50 per person, US$30 per car. Note that rough seas often prevent the ferry from sailing. At times, it has remained in port for up to a week until the weather cleared.

PLAYA DEL CARMEN

For decades Playa (as it's called) was just a simple fishing village on the coast opposite Cozumel. With the construction of Cancún, however, the number of travellers roaming this part of Yucatán increased by an order of magnitude. Playa, as the jumping-off point for Cozumel, got plenty of new traffic.

Playa is still something of a 'raw' beach town, with unpaved sand streets and an 'instant' infrastructure of cheaply constructed buildings, few telephones, and even fewer services. Most of the hotels are owned and run by foreigners for foreigners, at prices higher than Mexican-run establishments. Sometimes it seems as though the locals and tourists could be living on different planets. The beach resort parts of Playa are like a poor person's Cozumel pasted onto a subsistence Yucatecan fishing town. Even so, Playa is pleasant, with good beaches, snorkelling and scuba diving and a more authentically Yucatecan ambience than either Cancún or Cozumel.

Orientation

It's just over one km from Highway 307 along Avenida Principal, the town's only wide, divided street, to Playa's main square and the docks for the ferries to Cozumel. Avenida Quinta, the street a block inland from the beach, is the main commercial thoroughfare. Town blocks are about 100 metres square. In half an hour's strolling you can see the entire settlement.

The Beach

The beach runs on and on, with palms shading the sands and bathtub-warm waters.

You can walk out quite a distance in the quiet seas before the water reaches to your shoulders.

Playa has one of the few nude beaches in Mexico. Go north from the Blue Parrot Inn around the point and you will see the beach. It's long enough to let you stake out some isolated sands.

If you want to snorkel, walk to the northern end of the nude beach where there's a small reef. Or take a day trip to Cozumel for snorkelling and scuba. Since Playa has beaches superior to Cozumel's and is cheaper, many travellers prefer to stay in Playa and make occasional day trips to Cozumel.

Places to Stay – bottom end

Many of Playa's budget lodging places, busy all the time in winter, are fairly empty in summer. Several even close down for the summer months.

Places to Stay – bottom end

Camping As Playa develops rapidly, locations which were once campgrounds turn into hotels and bungalows. Look for the camping areas north-east of the main square along the beach. Theft of belongings is a problem for campers in Playa. Before you camp anywhere, stop and ask other campers whether they've heard of – or had – any such problems.

Hostels *Villa Deportiva Juvenil* (youth hostel; no phone), 1½ km from the ferry docks, is a modern establishment offering the cheapest clean lodging in town, but it's quite a walk to the beach and you sleep in single-sex dorm bunks. On the positive side, the hostel is cheap at US$4.50 per bunk (US$3 deposit). The hostel rents several modern cabañas with fan and private shower for US$16 (US$5 deposit), and also has an inexpensive café serving breakfast for about US$2.50 and lunch and dinner for US$3.50.

Hotels Alternatives to the hostel include the *Posada Lily* on Avenida Principal, just a block inland from the main square. It offers

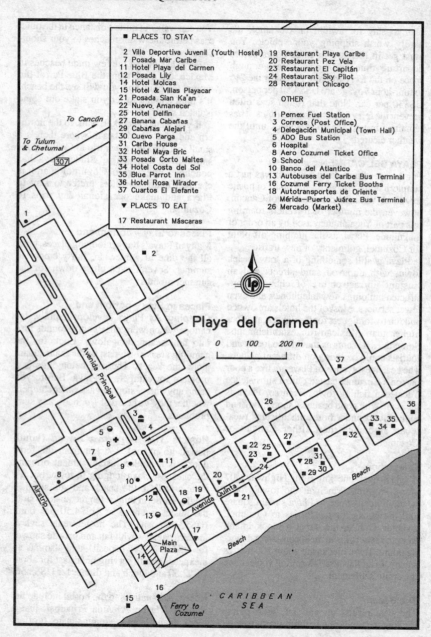

■ PLACES TO STAY

2 Villa Deportiva Juvenil (Youth Hostel)
7 Posada Mar Caribe
11 Hotel Playa del Carmen
12 Posada Lily
14 Hotel Molcas
15 Hotel & Villas Playacar
21 Posada Sian Ka'an
22 Nuevo. Amanecer
25 Hotel Delfin
27 Banana Cabañas
29 Cabañas Alejari
30 Cuevo Parga
31 Caribe House
32 Hotel Maya Bric
33 Posada Corto Maltes
34 Hotel Costa del Sol
35 Blue Parrot Inn
36 Hotel Rosa Mirador
37 Cuartos El Elefante

▼ PLACES TO EAT

17 Restaurant Máscaras

19 Restaurant Playa Caribe
20 Restaurant Pez Vela
23 Restaurant El Capitán
24 Restaurant Sky Pilot
28 Restaurant Chicago

OTHER

1 Pemex Fuel Station
3 Correos (Post Office)
4 Delegación Municipal (Town Hall)
5 ADO Bus Station
6 Hospital
8 Aero Cozumel Ticket Office
9 School
10 Banco del Atlantico
13 Autobuses del Caribe Bus Terminal
16 Cozumel Ferry Ticket Booths
18 Autotransportes de Oriente
    Mérida–Puerto Juárez Bus Terminal
26 Mercado (Market)

To Cancún

To Tulum & Chetumal

307

Playa del Carmen

0   100   200 m

Avenida Principal

Airstrip

Avenida Quinta

Main Plaza

Beach

Beach

CARIBBEAN SEA

Ferry to Cozumel

clean rooms with private shower and fan for US$17 a double. Watch out for street noise here; try to get a room at the back.

Another favourite is the quaint little *Posada Sian Ka'an* (☎ in Mérida (99) 29-74-22), Apdo Postal 135, Playa del Carmen, Quintana Roo 77710, with clean, simple rooms in semirustic buildings not far from the beach. Though it's charming it's a bit expensive: US$23 for a double without running water, US$36 for a double with private shower and fan.

Places to Stay – middle

My favourite place in Playa is the *Hotel Maya Bric*, a smallish establishment with rooms clustered around a small swimming pool. Rooms are fairly large and airy, with two double beds, ceiling fan, and a private shower. A small dive shop and snack stand is attached. Rates vary with the seasons, but range from US$24 in summer to US$55 or more in winter. The manager likes to fill his rooms, however, so haggling may get you a reduction if the hotel is not full.

Hotel Delfin, Apdo Postal 38, Playa del Carmen, Quintana Roo 77710, is a newish concrete block building offering standard rooms, with ceiling fan and tiled bathroom, for US$27 to US$42 a double. You can make reservations in the USA by calling (718) 297-6851.

In the grounds of *Nuevo Amanecer* Californian proprietor Arlene King has installed a hot tub, and each of the cabañas is equipped with a hammock. Comfortable rooms with fan and bath cost US$50 for the smaller cabañas and US$58 for the larger. For reservations write to Arlene King, Apdo Postal 1056, Cancún, Quintana Roo 77500.

Cueva Pargo is run by a helpful couple, Huacho and JoAnne Corrales, and has a variety of thatch-roofed cabañas at a variety of prices, which include good breakfasts served in the cabañas' Sailorman Pub next door on the beach. A cabaña with clean shared bath costs US$35/44 a single/double; a cabaña for two with private bath costs US$48. A beach house costs US$90 and there is a large cabaña for four costing

US$105. The Cueva Pargo also has a sailboat for day or month-long snorkelling/scuba excursions. To make reservations, write to Cueva Pargo, Apdo Postal 838, Cancún, Quintana Roo 77500.

The cabañas at the *Blue Parrot Inn* provide a touch of paradise. The thatch-roofed cabañas, set on a pretty stretch of sands, are well maintained by former Florida resident Rick Jones. The Blue Parrot also has a terraced restaurant serving some of the best food in Playa. If you make reservations or are extremely lucky, there is one small cabaña with shared bathroom for US$45 for one or two people. Other beachfront cabañas cost US$50 to US$75, depending upon facilities. For reservations, write to the Blue Parrot Inn, PO Box 652737, Miami, Florida 33265, USA.

Next to a tropical garden is the popular *Banana Cabañas*. Run by the friendly Sam and Martha Beard, the cabañas are reasonably priced at US$25 for one or two people. Larger cabañas sleeping up to four cost from US$35 to US$45. A cabaña with a kitchenette costs US$42.

Places to Stay – top end

Those seeking luxury lodging in town will find the *Hotel & Villas Playacar* to their liking. The cabañas have kitchens, and the hotel offers tennis, waterskiing and scuba trips. During the high season, prices range from US$150 to US$290; during the low season (summer) they range from US$90 to US$200.

Built above the ferry dock, with pretty seaside views, the *Hotel Molcas* charges US$80 to US$120 (depending upon the season) for its comfortable air-conditioned double rooms. For reservations, write to Apdo Postal 79, Playa del Carmen, Quintana Roo 77710 (☎ Mérida (99) 25-69-90, Cancún (988) 4-64-33, Cozumel (987) 2-04-77, Miami (305) 534-3716; fax (305) 534-0541).

Places to Eat

Eating establishments can be divided into two categories: those run by Mexicans for

Mexicans, and those run by foreigners for foreigners. The former are cheap and basic, the latter are more atmospheric and expensive, with fancier food that may not taste much better. Many of the 'foreign' restaurants operate only during the winter season.

A favourite for any meal, especially an early breakfast, is the simple *Restaurant Playa Caribe*, which seems to be a bit cheaper than the other local places. Hotcakes go for US$2.75, full breakfasts for less than US$4.50.

The *Restaurant Máscaras*, on the main plaza, is the most famous and long-lived of the more expensive places. It has American music from the 1950s and '60s, and you can dine on fish for US$8, and pizza or pasta for US$6 to US$14. Drinks are fairly expensive.

A better choice for food is the *Restaurant Limones*, next to Banana Cabañas, where the atmosphere is more sedate, and the food is a bit more expensive but well worth it.

Friends of ours recommend the *Restaurant La Terraya*, around the corner from the Hotel Maya Bric and down on the beach, which is filled each evening with divers, fishing buffs and nautical wannabes. Fish is served many ways: a la plancha (roasted on a board), al mojo de ajo (in garlic sauce), a la mantequilla (in butter), and a la Veracruzana (in a tomato sauce), just to name a few. Prices for fish range from US$5 to US$8.

Entertainment

Playa's restaurants are the main venues for evening entertainment, which consists of eating, drinking, conversation, seeing and being seen. The Restaurant Sky Pilot on Avenida Quinta had the hippest music and people on our last visit.

Getting There & Away

Air Aero Cozumel (in Cozumel ☎ (987) 2-05-03, 2-09-28), with an office next to Playa's airstrip, runs little aircraft across the water from Cozumel to Playa and return every two hours from 8 am to 6 pm during the winter season. In summer there are usually four flights per day in each direction,

departing from Cozumel at 9 and 11 am, and 3 and 5 pm, returning from Playa del Carmen 20 minutes later. The flight costs US$14 one way.

Bus Three companies serve Playa del Carmen, and each has its own terminal. By far the most useful line is Autotransportes de Oriente Mérida-Puerto Juárez, with 1st and 2nd-class buses to major destinations throughout Yucatán. Autotransportes del Caribe is the line to take if you're going south to Felipe Carrillo Puerto or Chetumal, or west to Oxkutzcab, Ticul or Uxmal. ADO (Autobuses de Oriente) has only a few long-distance buses passing through Playa.

Cancún – 65 km, one hour; six 1st-class (US$2.25), seven 2nd-class (US$1.90) by Autotransportes de Oriente M-PJ; Autotransportes del Caribe also has eight buses daily.

Chetumal – 315 km, 5½ hours; five 1st-class (US$7), and five 2nd-class (US$6) by Autotransportes del Caribe, stopping at Felipe Carrillo Puerto and Bacalar.

Cobá – 113 km, two hours; Autotransportes de Oriente has three 1st-class (US$1.25) and two 2nd-class buses (US$1) daily on the route Tulum-Cobá-Valladolid.

Mérida – 378 km, eight hours; six 1st-class (US$8.50), six 2nd-class (US$7) by Autotransportes de Oriente M-PJ; these buses stop at Valladolid and Chichén Itzá. Several A del Caribe 1st-class buses to Mérida go via Oxkutzcab, Ticul and Muna.

Tulum – 63 km, one hour; Autotransportes de Oriente's Cobá buses stop at Tulum (US$1), but Autotransportes del Caribe has the most traffic, with 10 buses daily heading south via Tulum to Chetumal.

Valladolid – 213 km, four hours; the many Autotransportes de Oriente buses to Mérida stop at Valladolid (US$5 1st-class, US$4.50 2nd-class), but it's faster to go on the ruta corta (short route) via Tulum and Cobá.

Boat A variety of watercraft ply the seas between Playa del Carmen and Cozumel, taking between 30 and 75 minutes and charging US$3.50 to US$5.50 one way. Schedules, particularly in summer, are highly mutable, and I advise that you buy one-way tickets only. That way, if your chosen boat doesn't materialise for a scheduled return trip, you can buy a ticket on another line.

Fastest boats are the waterjets *México*, *México 2*, and *Cozumeleño*, charging the top price, but whisking you across the water in the shortest time. The catamaran hull gives a smooth ride and these boats have air-con. Soft drinks, beer and snacks are sold on board. The waterjets are scheduled to run about every two hours from dawn to dusk, but voyages may be cancelled at the last moment if the boat breaks down or if there aren't enough passengers. Note also that 'fast boat' emblazoned on ticket offices and billboards may not mean 'waterjet', and the 'fast boat' may actually be slower than the waterjet.

The next best boat is the *Playa del Carmen*, offering only slightly less in the way of comfort, speed and price.

The slowest, oldest, least comfortable but cheapest boat is the *Xel-Ha*, which is best avoided by those prone to seasickness.

COZUMEL

Population: 175,000

Cozumel floats in the midst of the Caribbean's crystalline waters 71 km south of Cancún. Its legendary Palancar Reef was made famous by Jacques Cousteau and is a lure for divers from all over the world. Scuba diving is not an inexpensive sport and visitors to Cozumel tend to be better heeled than those staying at Isla Mujeres or Playa del Carmen. Prices are not cheap by Mexican standards, but you can stay and eat at Cozumel on a moderate budget. If you're looking for a low-budget room, plan to take an early boat or plane from Playa del Carmen and pin down your chosen room by mid-morning.

Though it has that beautiful offshore reef, Cozumel does not have many good swimming beaches. The western shore is mostly sharp, weathered limestone and coral, and the eastern beaches are often pounded by dangerous surf. If you're looking for diving, Cozumel is the place; if you prefer good beaches, spend your time in Cancún, Isla Mujeres or Playa del Carmen.

History

Measuring 53 km long and 14 km wide, Cozumel is the largest of Mexico's islands. Maya settlement here dates from 300 AD. During the Postclassic period, Cozumel flourished both as a commercial centre and as a major ceremonial site. The Maya sailed here on pilgrimages to shrines dedicated to Ixchel, the goddess of fertility and the moon.

Although the first Spanish contact with Cozumel in 1518 by Juan de Grijalva was peaceful, it was followed by the Cortés expedition in 1519. Cortés, en route to his conquest of the mainland, laid waste to Cozumel's Maya shrines. The Maya offered staunch military resistance until they were conquered in 1545. The coming of the Spanish brought smallpox to this otherwise surprisingly disease-free place. Within a generation after the conquest, the island's population had dwindled to only 300 souls, Maya and Spanish.

While the island remained virtually deserted into the late 17th century, its coves provided sanctuary and headquarters for several notorious pirates including Jean Lafitte and Henry Morgan. Pirate brutality led the remaining populace to move to the mainland and it wasn't until 1848 that Cozumel began to be resettled by Indians fleeing the War of the Castes.

At the turn of the century, the island's population – which was now largely mestizo – grew thanks to the craze for chewing gum. Cozumel was a port of call on the chicle export route and locals harvested chicle on the island. Although chicle was later replaced by synthetic gum, Cozumel's economic base expanded with the building of a US air force base here during WW II.

When the US military departed, the island fell into an economic slump and many of its people left. Those who stayed fished for a livelihood until 1961, when underwater scientist Jacques Cousteau arrived, explored the reef, and told the world about Cozumel's beauties. A resort destination was born.

Orientation

It's easy to make your way on foot around

the island's only town, San Miguel de Cozumel, where most of the budget lodgings are. Some of the middle-range places are here as well. For top-end hotels, you'll probably have to take a taxi up or down the coast. The airport, two km north of town, is accessible only by taxi or on foot.

The waterfront boulevard is Avenida Rafael Melgar; on the west side of Melgar south of the ferry docks is a narrow but usable sand beach. Just opposite the ferry docks (officially called the Muelle Fiscal) on Melgar in the centre of town is the main plaza. Running inland (eastward) from the main plaza is Avenida Benito Juárez, the main east-west thoroughfare. Avenida Juárez divides the town into norte (north) and sur (south). North-south streets (parallel to Avenida Melgar) are called avenidas, east-west streets (parallel to Avenida Juárez) are calles. Calles north of Juárez have even numbers, those south of Juárez have odd numbers.

Information

Tourist Office The local tourist office (☎ (987) 2-09-72) is in a building facing the main square to the left of the Bancomer, on

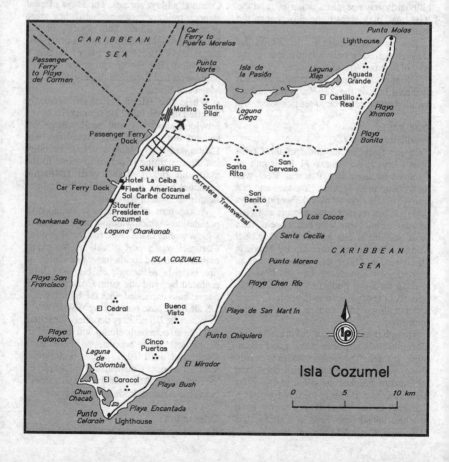

Isla Cozumel

the 2nd floor; hours are Monday to Friday from 9 am to 3 pm and 6 to 8 pm. There's also a little booth in the main plaza, open (in theory) from 8 am to 1.30 pm and 5.30 to 8 pm, but the hours are really at the caprice of the clerk.

For the federal (SECTUR) tourism headquarters, head south on Avenida Melgar past the post office and look for SECTUR on the right. This is not an information office, but they might help with special problems.

Money For currency exchange, Bancomer and Banco del Atlantico off the main plaza change money from 10 am to 12.30 pm only, Monday to Friday. Banpaís, facing the ferry docks, will change your travellers' cheques from 9 am to 1.30 pm Monday to Friday for a 1% commission. Most of the major hotels, restaurants and stores will change money at a less advantageous rate when the banks are closed.

Post The post and telegraph office (☎ (987) 2-01-06) is south of Calle 7 Sur on the waterfront just off Avenida Melgar. Hours are Monday to Friday from 9 am to 1 pm and 3 to 6 pm, and Saturday from 9 am to noon. Cozumel's postal code is 77600.

Laundry The clean and tidy Margarita Laundromat, Avenida 20 Sur 285 between Calle Salas and Calle 3 Sur, is open Monday to Saturday from 7 am to 9 pm, Sunday from 10 am to 6 pm. It charges US$2 to wash a load (US$0.40 extra if you don't bring your own detergent), US$1.20 for 10 minutes in the dryer, or US$2 for 20 minutes. Ironing and folding services are available at an extra charge. Look for the sign reading 'Lavandería de Autoservicio'.

Bookshops The Zodiac Bookstore, on the south-east side of the plaza, 40 metres from the clock tower next to Bancomer, is open seven days a week selling English, French, German and Spanish books, and English and Spanish magazines and newspapers.

Activities
Scuba Diving For equipment rental, instruction and boat reservations, there are numerous dive shops on Avenida Melgar along San Miguel's waterfront. Generally, a two-tank, full-day scuba trip will cost US$55 to US$75 and an introductory scuba course about US$90.

The most prominent scuba destinations are: the five-km-long Palancar Reef, where stunning coral formations and a 'horseshoe' of coral heads in 70-metre visibility offer some of the world's finest diving; Maracaibo Reef, for experienced divers only, which offers a challenge due to its current and aquatic life; Paraiso Reef, famous for its coral formations, especially brain and star coral; and Yocab Reef, shallow yet vibrantly alive and great for beginners.

Snorkelling You can go out on a boat tour for US$20 to US$30 or, far cheaper, rent gear for about US$8 and snorkel at the following places: Chankanab Bay, Playa San Francisco, La Playa Ceiba near the car ferry dock (where a plane was purposely sunk for the film *Survive*), Presidente Hotel and Palancar.

Glass-Bottom Boat You can enjoy the coral formations and aquatic life by taking a tour by glass-bottom boat. The boats are supposed to leave the car ferry dock area every day at 10 am, noon and 2 pm, but generally wait until they are filled. They cost US$10 to US$15, but outside the tourist high season, bargain for a lower price.

Places to Stay – bottom end
You will have to pay more for a room on Cozumel than on the mainland. Indeed, you had better think less of cost and more about availability, as the cheapest lodgings fill up early.

Camping To camp anywhere on the island you'll need a permit from the island's naval authorities, obtainable 24 hours a day, for free, from the naval headquarters south of the post office on Avenida Rafael Melgar. Best

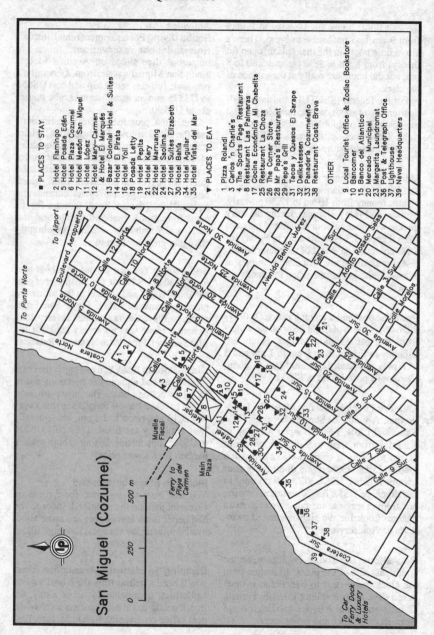

San Miguel (Cozumel)

■ PLACES TO STAY

2 Hotel Flamingo
5 Hotel Posada Edén
6 Hotel Plaza Cozumel
7 Hotel Mesón San Miguel
11 Hotel López
12 Hotel Mary-Carmen
13 Bazar Colonial Hotel & Suites
14 Hotel El Marqués
16 Hotel El Pirata
18 Hotel Yoli
19 Posada Letty
21 Hotel Pepita
22 Hotel Kary
24 Hotel Marruang
27 Hotel Saolima
30 Hotel Suites Elizabeth
34 Hotel Bahía
35 Hotel Aguilar
       Hotel Vista del Mar

▼ PLACES TO EAT

1 Pizza Rolandi
3 Carlos 'n Charlie's
4 The Sports Page Restaurant
8 Restaurant Las Palmeras
17 Cocina Económica Mi Chabelita
25 Restaurant La Choza
26 The Corner Store
28 Mr Papa's Restaurant
29 Pepe's Grill
31 Tacos y Quesos El Sarape
32 Delikatessen
33 Panadería Cozumeleño
38 Restaurant Costa Brava

OTHER

9 Local Tourist Office & Zodiac Bookstore
10 Bancomer
15 Banco del Atlántico
20 Mercado Municipal
23 Margarita Laundromat
36 Post & Telegraph Office
37 Lighthouse
39 Naval Headquarters

camping places are along the relatively unpopulated eastern shore of the island.

Hotels *Hotel Flamingo* (☎ (987) 2-12-64), Calle 6 Norte 81 between Avenida Melgar and Avenida 5 Norte, is not the cheapest place in town, but it's undoubtedly the best value for money. The 21 rooms in this fairly new but simple place go for US$25 to US$35 a double, depending upon the season.

Hotel Marruang (☎ (987) 2-16-78, 2-02-08), Calle Adolfo Rosado Salas 440 facing the municipal market, is new and its rooms have ceiling fans. A clean room, with one double and one single bed, costs US$22 to US$28, depending upon the season. The entrance to the hotel is down a passageway opposite the market. If there's no one in evidence, ask at the juice bar (fuente de sodas) on the right at the beginning of the passageway.

Hotel Posada Edén (☎ (987) 2-11-66, 2-15-82), Calle 2 Norte 12 between Avenidas 5 and 10 Norte, also called the Edem, is a simple, uninspiring but fairly cheap and quiet place charging US$13/22 a single/double for a room with private shower and ceiling fan.

Posada Letty (☎ (987) 2-02-57), Calle 1 Sur at Avenida 15 Sur, is among the cheapest lodgings in town, a small, plain place marked only by a minuscule sign. Ask for rooms at the small shop to the left on the corner. Well-used rooms with ceiling fan, decent cross-ventilation and private tiled shower go for US$17 in summer, US$22 in winter.

Hotel Yoli (☎ (987) 2-00-24), Calle 1 Sur 164 between Avenidas 5 and 10 Sur, is family-run and though the rooms are a bit dingy, they are fairly clean. Because of its convenient location the Yoli (or Yoly) fills up fast. The very plain rooms with fan and bath cost US$15 a single or double.

Hotel Saolima (☎ (987) 2-08-86), Calle Adolfo Salas 268 between Avenidas 10 and 15 Sur, is among the best deals in town. The Saolima has clean, pleasant rooms in a quiet locale, with ceiling fans and private showers, for US$16/18 a single/double.

Hotel López (☎ (987) 2-01-08), Calle 1 Sur (Apdo Postal 44), on the south side of the plaza, used to be a divers' hangout but now caters to budget travellers. The simple rooms with good private baths go for US$22 a single (with fan), US$34 a double (with air-con) in summer, somewhat higher in winter. If the hotel is not full, haggle with the owner, Sr Miguel López Vivas, for a discount.

Places to Stay – middle
Middle-range hostelries, though still simple, offer welcome amenities such as air-conditioning and swimming pools. Prices are not too much higher than at bottom-end places. All of the rooms in these hotels have private bathrooms.

Hôtel Vista del Mar (☎ (987) 2-05-45; fax 2-04-45), Avenida Rafael Melgar 45 at Calle 5 Sur, has it all including a restaurant, liquor store and a rental car and travel agency. Some rooms have balconies with sea views. The price in summer is US$50 a double, rising to US$70 in winter.

Clean, comfortable lodgings are yours at the *Hotel Mary-Carmen* (☎ (987) 2-05-81), Avenida 5 Sur 4. Enter the courtyard to find a small reception desk and shop, behind which is a large mamey tree and 27 tidy air-con rooms with private baths, and prices of US$40 a double in summer.

Equally pleasant is the accommodation at *Hotel Suites Elizabeth* (☎ (987) 2-03-30), Calle Adolfo Salas 44 (Apdo Postal 70), half a block east of Avenida Rafael Melgar. These clean and well-kept suites offer air-con bedrooms with kitchenettes (cooker, refrigerator and utensils) for US$30 to US$40 a double in summer, US$50 to US$58 in winter.

Yet another good value place is the *Hotel Pepita* (☎ (987) 2-00-98), Avenida 15 Sur 2 on the corner of Calle 1 Sur. Well-maintained air-con rooms in a tranquil part of town go for US$30 to US$40 in summer, US$45 to US$50 in winter. Most rooms have two double beds, insect screens, fans and little refrigerators. The hotel runs scuba diving tours as well.

Bazar Colonial Hotel & Suites (☎ (987) 2-05-06; fax 3-03-09, 2-13-87), Avenida 5

Sur 9, has the distinction of being one of the few hotels in town with a lift. The modern, attractive rooms are studio or one-bedroom suites (some of which can sleep up to four people) with kitchenette (cooker, refrigerator, utensils) and air-con. Rates are a reasonable US$42 to US$50 a double in summer, US$50 to US$60 in winter.

Hotel Bahía (☎ (987) 2-02-09), Avenida Rafael Melgar at Calle 3 Sur, operated by the same people as the Bazar Colonial, has pleasant modern suites with air-con, satellite TV, telephones and kitchenettes for US$55 to US$60 a double in summer, US$60 to US$75 in winter. It's good value for small groups or families.

Hotel El Pirata (☎ (987) 2-00-51, 2-15-28), Avenida 5 Sur 3-A, offers decent air-con rooms for US$34 a double in summer, US$50 in winter.

Hotel Aguilar (☎ (987) 2-03-07), Avenida 5 Sur at Calle 3 Sur, has bungalows grouped around a small swimming pool. All rooms are air-conditioned, and go for US$30 a single and US$40 a double in summer, US$48 to US$55 a double in winter. The management often seems more interested in the moped rental business, but it's a serviceable place. The hotel has touts working the docks. Don't believe their rates; they get a commission if they bring you here and you pay extra for it. Simply find the Aguilar on your own and the rates will be cheaper.

Hotel Costa Brava (☎ (987) 2-14-53), Avenida Rafael Melgar 601, south of the post office and inland from the naval base, is set well back from the street behind the Restaurant Costa Brava, and is therefore fairly quiet. The modern rooms are comfy if simple, with good cross-ventilation and ceiling fans (air-con in some). Rates are US$30 a double in summer, US$45 in winter.

Hotel Kary (☎ (987) 2-20-11), Calle Adolfo Rosado Salas at Avenida 25 Sur, is just east of the municipal market. The location is a bit out of the way, but the hotel offers nice double rooms grouped around a swimming pool for US$22 to US$32 a double with fan, US$29 to US$38 with air-con; higher prices apply during the busy winter season.

Hotel Plaza Cozumel (☎/fax (987) 2-00-66), Calle 2 Norte 3 just off Avenida Melgar, is a new, modern, comfortable hotel. It has a lift, and each room is air-conditioned and equipped with two large beds, satellite TV, and an up-to-date bathroom. The price? A moderate US$57 in summer, US$88 in winter.

Hotel Mesón San Miguel (☎ (987) 2-02-33, 2-03-23), Avenida Juárez 2-B on the north side of the plaza, has a convenient location, a swimming pool, restaurant, and 97 air-con rooms with balconies. There's also a separate club with water sports facilities seven blocks from the hotel on the water. Rates in summer are US$45 a double, and US$68 a double in winter.

Hotel El Marqués (☎ (987) 2-05-37, 2-06-77), Avenida 5 Sur 12, has lackadaisical and inept management. It also has a good location and fairly cheap, presentable air-con rooms for US$34 a double in summer, US$50 in winter.

Places to Stay – top end

Several km south of town are the big luxury resort hotels of an international standard. North of town along the western shore of the island are numerous smaller, more modest resort hotels, usually cheaper than the big places, but catering mostly to package tour groups.

South of town, the *Stouffer Presidente Cozumel* (☎ (987) 2-03-22; fax 2-13-60), Carretera a Chankanab Km 6.5, is hard to miss with its 259 rooms, many with sea views, set amidst tropical gardens. The water sports facilities are particularly good, and there are numerous restaurants and bars. It has many other recreational facilities. The price for double rooms in the high winter season range from US$198 to US$290 a double, tax included. You can expect substantial discounts in summertime.

Fiesta Americana Sol Caribe Cozumel (☎ (987) 2-70-00; fax 2-13-01), Playa Paraíso Km 3.5 (Apdo Postal 259), Cozumel, Quintana Roo 77600, has 321 luxurious rooms and a lavish layout with plenty of facilities. There are six restaurants and bars. Winter season prices are US$185 to US$210 a double, with hefty reductions available in summer. Fiesta Americana has a slightly cheaper hotel, the *Fiesta Inn*, not far away from the Sol Caribe. For reservations at either hotel, call (800) 343-7821 in the USA.

Meliá Mayan Cozumel (☎ (987) 2-02-72; fax 2-15-99), Playa Santa Pilar, is a 200-room resort with numerous seafood restaurants, bars and the usual facilities. Another Meliá hotel, the *Sol Cabañas del Caribe* (☎ (987) 2-01-61, 2-00-17; fax 2-15-99) caters mostly to divers. For reservations, call (800) 336-3542 in the USA.

Places to Eat – bottom end

Cheapest of all eating places, with fairly tasty food to boot, are the market loncherías, seven in all, located next to the Mercado Municipal on Calle Adolfo Rosado Salas between Avenidas 20 and 25 Sur. All of these little señora-run eateries offer soup and a main course plate for about US$3, with a large selection of dishes available. Latin music issuing from multiple boom boxes is provided for your dining pleasure. Hours are 6.30 am to 6.30 pm daily.

Restaurant Costa Brava (no phone), on Avenida Rafael Melgar just south of the post office, is among the more interesting – read funky – places to dine on the island. Besides good ambience, the Costa Brava provides cheap breakfasts (US$2 to US$3.50), and such filling dishes as chicken tacos, grilled steak and fried fish or chicken for US$3.50 to US$8. Hours are 6.30 am to 11.30 pm daily.

The Corner Store, at the corner of Calle Adolfo Rosado Salas and Avenida 5 Sur, is an excellent place to have a healthy breakfast, light lunch or vitamin-filled snack. Fresh fruit juices are priced at US$1.25 to US$2.25, sandwiches from US$2 to US$3; the house speciality, a fruit salad with granola and yoghurt goes for US$2.75 to US$3.50.

Restaurant La Choza, Calle Adolfo Rosado Salas 198 at the corner of Avenida 10 Sur, specialises in *cocina típica Mexic-ana*, authentic Mexican traditional cuisine, which is not all tacos and enchiladas. An open-air place shaded by a palapa, it provides eggs served in a multitude of ways, brochettes of beef or chicken, and numerous other dishes. Among my favourites is the pozole, a spicy meat-and-hominy stew. With a soft drink, you pay US$8 for a huge bowl.

Tacos y Quesos El Sarape, Avenida 5 Sur between Calles 1 and 3 Sur, is a tiny and tidy glass-fronted place selling simple meals for low prices. It's closed Sunday.

Cocina Económica Mi Chabelita, Avenida 10 Sur between Calle 1 Sur and Calle Adolfo Rosado Salas, is a tiny, fairly cheap eatery run by a señora who serves up decent portions of decent food at decent prices. It's not the cheapest in town, but good for the money. You can fill up for US$5.50 or less here. It opens for breakfast at 7 am; don't linger over dinner as it closes at 7 pm.

Places to Eat – middle

Restaurant Las Palmeras (☎ 2-05-32) is at the edge of the main plaza by the ferry docks. The food can be fairly mediocre, but the location is so good for people watching, and so convenient to everything, that it's usually full. A bowl of sopa de lima is a good bet at US$3.75, as is a big fruit plate for US$7.50. Most Mexican traditional dishes go for US$6 to US$8, fish and squid for US$9 to US$14.

Pizza Rolandi, Avenida Rafael Melgar between Calles 6 and 8 Norte, serves one-person (20-cm diameter) pizzas: the Margherita with tomato, cheese, basil and olive oil costs US$7.50; the Four Seasons with ham, asparagus, mushrooms and olives is US$10. Wine is sold by the quarter and half-litre; beer and other drinks are served as well. Come to Rolandi from 11.30 am to 11.30 pm; it's closed Sunday.

Among the restaurant chains spawned by Cancún's development, *Mr. Papa's* is among the better ones. The name is a pun on *papas* (potatoes), and indeed potatoes, filling, healthy and delicious, are the main course. They come topped with sauces laden with meats, vegetables and spices, and cost between US$6 and US$8.

Cozumel is so Americanised that it has its own sports buffs' watering hole: *The Sports Page* (☎ 2-11-99) at the corner of Calle 2 Norte and Avenida 5 Norte. For a full meal, of guacamole or stuffed potato skins, a bacon cheeseburger, and a drink, you'd pay US$12, which is also the price for a plate of fajitas. Steak, lobster and shrimp cost US$15 to US$25; fruit plates and omelettes are only a few dollars.

For picnic supplies, head for the *Delikatessen*, Avenida 10 Sur 264 between Calle Adolfo Rosado Salas and Calle 3 Sur. Open from 9 am to 9 pm (closed Sunday), the Deli sells delicacies: smoked salmon, provolone, camembert, brie, imported biscuits and meats, etc. It's not cheap, but if your picnic demands brie, this is the place to find it.

Places to Eat – top end
Cozumel's traditional place to dine well is *Pepe's Grill* (☎ 2-02-13), on Avenida Rafael Melgar at Calle Adolfo Rosado Salas. Flaming shrimps, grilled lobster, caesar salad and other top-end items can take your bill to US$40 or US$50 per person, but the food is good. Call for reservations in season.

Entertainment
Cinemas Far cheaper than live entertainment are the town's two cinemas which sometimes screen English-language films with Spanish subtitles. Cine Borgues is on Avenida Juárez at Avenida 35, Cine Cozumel is on Avenida Rafael Melgar at Calle 4 Norte, two blocks north of the plaza.

Discos Nightlife in Cozumel is pricey, but if you want to dance, the most popular disco is Disco Neptuno, five blocks south of the post office on Avenida Rafael Melgar. Cover charge is US$5, with drinks (even Mexican beer) for US$3 and up. Another hot spot, similarly priced, is Disco Scaramouche at the intersection of Avenida Melgar and Calle Adolfo Rosado Salas. For Latin *salsa* music, try Los Quetzales, Avenida 10 Sur at Calle 1 Sur, a block from the plaza. It's open every evening from 6 pm.

A block and a half north of the plaza on Avenida Rafael Melgar is the local incarnation of the Carlos 'n Charlie's chain. Unlike the other restaurants, which combine hip menus, sassy waiters and decent food with moderately high prices, this one is more like a rowdy bar.

The luxury hotels (Stouffer Presidente, Fiesta Americana Sol Caribe and La Ceiba) have discos with similarly lofty cover charges and drink prices.

Things to Buy
Near the plaza and along Avenida Rafael Melgar are numerous boutiques selling the favourite local souvenir, jewellery made with black coral. Legitimate shops will probably not try to cheat you on quality, but beware the cut-price merchants who substitute black plastic for the real thing. True black coral is 'weathered', with gold-coloured streaks in it. It is very light – lighter than the plastic fakes – and true coral will not burn, as does plastic.

Getting There & Away
Air Cozumel has a surprisingly busy international airport, with numerous direct flights from other parts of Mexico and the USA. Flights from Europe are usually routed via the USA or Mexico City. There are nonstop flights on Continental (☎ (987) 2-02-51) and American (☎ (987) 2-08-99) from their hubs at Dallas, Houston, and Raleigh-Durham, with many direct flights from other US cities via these hubs. Mexicana (☎ (987) 2-02-63) has nonstops from Miami and direct flights from Mérida and Mexico City.

Aero Cozumel (☎ (987) 2-09-28, 2-05-03), with offices at Cozumel airport, operates flights between Cancún and Cozumel about every two hours throughout the day for US$40 one way. Reserve your seat in advance, as many of these little planes are filled by groups of divers coming for a day's plunge. Aero Cozumel also runs convenient and inexpensive flights to and from Playa del Carmen. In summer there are usually four flights per day in each direction, departing from Cozumel at 9 and 11 am and 3 and 5 pm, and returning from Playa del Carmen 20 minutes later. The flight costs US$14 one way.

Boat For details on taking the fast waterjet passenger ferries from Playa del Carmen, see that section. If you must bring your car to Cozumel, you'll have to take a car ferry from Puerto Morelos. Details are in that section.

Getting Around
To/From the Airport The airport is about two km north of town. You can take a minibus from the airport into town for less than US$2, slightly more to the hotels south of town, but you'll have to take a taxi (US$4 or US$5) to return to the airport.

Bus & Taxi Cozumel's taxi drivers have a lock on the local transport market, defeating any proposal for a convenient bus service. A single bus leaves daily from the tourist booth on the plaza in town (near the ferry) at 11 am, heading south toward Chankanab bay, returning at 5 pm. Fare is US$1.50. The walk from the Stouffer Presidente Hotel south to Chankanab is about one km.

For other points on the island you will have to take a taxi. Fares average US$4 or US$5 for every 15 minutes of travel, or roughly US$20 per hour.

Car & Moped Rates for rental cars are upwards of US$60 to $70 per day, all inclusive. You could probably haggle with a taxi driver to take you on a tour of the island, drop you at a beach, come back and pick you up, and still save money; keep this shocking fact in mind when you consider renting a car.

Rented mopeds are popular with those who want to tour the island on their own. It seems that every citizen and business in San Miguel – hotels, restaurants, gift shops, morticians – rents mopeds, generally for US$30 to US$38 per day (24 hours), though some rent from 8 am to 5 pm for US$22. Insurance and tax are included in these prices. It's amusing that a 24-hour rental of two mopeds (for two people) almost equals the cost of renting a car (for up to four people) for the same period of time.

You must have a valid driving licence, and you must use a credit card, or put down a hefty deposit (around US$60).

The best time to rent is first thing in the morning, when all the machines are there. Pick a good one, with a working horn, brakes, lights, starter, rear-view mirrors, and a full tank of fuel; remember that the price asked will be the same whether you rent the newest, pristine machine or the oldest, most beat-up rattletrap. (If you want to trust yourself with a second-rate moped, at least haggle the price down significantly.) You should get a helmet and a lock and chain with the moped.

When riding, keep in mind that you will be as exposed to sunshine on a moped as if you were roasting on a beach. Slather yourself with sunblock (especially the backs of your hands, feet and neck, and your face), or cover up, or suffer the consequences. Also, be aware of the dangers involved. Of all motor vehicle operators, the inexperienced moped driver on unfamiliar roads in a foreign country has the highest statistical chance of having an accident, especially when faced by lots of other inexperienced moped drivers. Drive carefully.

AROUND ISLA COZUMEL
In order to see most of the island (except for Chankanab Bay) you will have to rent a moped or bicycle, or take a taxi (see Getting Around for San Miguel). The following route will take you south from the town of San Miguel, then anticlockwise around the island.

Chankanab Bay Beach
This bay of clear water and fabulously coloured fish is the most popular on the island. It is nine km south of the town.

You used to be able to swim in the adjoining lagoon, but so many tourists were fouling the water and damaging the coral that Chankanab lagoon was made a national park and put off limits to swimmers. Don't despair – you can still snorkel in the sea here and the lagoon has been saved from destruction.

Snorkelling equipment can be rented for US$8 per day. Divers will be interested in a reef offshore; there is a dive shop at the beach, and scuba instruction is offered.

There is also a restaurant and snack shop. The beach has dressing rooms, lockers and showers, which are included in the US$2.50 admission price to the National Park, open 9 am to 5 pm daily. The park also has a botanical garden with 400 species of tropical plants.

Getting There & Away There's one daily local beach bus which leaves San Miguel at 11 am, returns at 5 pm and costs US$1.50. The taxi fare from San Miguel to Chankanab Bay is about US$7.

San Francisco & Palancar Beaches

Playa San Francisco, 14 km from San Miguel, and Playa Palancar, a few km to the south, are the nicest of the island's beaches. San Francisco's white sands run for more than three km, and rather expensive food is served at its restaurant. If you want to scuba or snorkel at Palancar Reef you will have to sign on for a day cruise or charter a boat.

El Cedral

To see these small Maya ruins, the oldest on the island, go 3½ km down a paved road a short distance south of Playa San Francisco. Although El Cedral was thought to be an important ceremonial site, its minor remnants are not well preserved.

Punta Celarain

The southern tip of the island has a picturesque lighthouse, accessible via a dirt track, four km from the highway. To enjoy truly isolated beaches en route, climb over the sand dunes. There's a fine view of the island from the top of the lighthouse.

East Coast Drive

The eastern shoreline is the wildest part of the island and highly recommended for beautiful seascapes of rocky coast. Unfortunately, except for Punta Chiquiero, Chen Río and Punta Morena, swimming is dangerous

on Cozumel's east coast due to potentially lethal riptides and undertow. Be careful! Swim only in coves protected from the open surf by headlands or breakwaters. There are small eateries at both Punta Morena and Punta Chiquiero and a hotel at Punta Morena. Some travellers camp at Chen Río.

El Castillo Real & San Gervasio Ruins

Beyond where the east coast highway meets the Carretera Transversal (cross-island road) that runs to San Miguel, intrepid travellers may take the sand track about 17 km from the junction to the Maya ruins known as El Castillo Real. They are not very well preserved and you need luck or a 4WD vehicle to navigate the sandy road.

If you are a real ruins buff, there is an equally unimpressive ruin called San Gervasio on a bad road from the airport. 4WD vehicles can reach San Gervasio from a track originating on the east coast, but most rental car insurance policies do not cover unpaved roads such as this. The jungle en route is more interesting than the ruins.

Punta Molas Lighthouse

There are some fairly good beaches and minor Maya ruins in the vicinity of the northeast point, accessible only by 4WD vehicle or foot.

BEACHES ALONG THE COAST

Some of the world's most beautiful beaches lie between Cancún and Tulum. If you want a beach of your own, away from the tourist throngs of Cancún and Isla Mujeres, this stretch of Caribbean coast may make your dreams come true.

Privacy does come at a cost. Several of the beaches are difficult to reach, others have no lodging or only expensive hotels. If you have a tent, hammock and mosquito netting, you will be rewarded for roughing it.

Although buses run between Cancún and Tulum during the day (see Getting There & Away in the Cancún section for details), 1st class is often full and may not stop to pick you up. Even if 2nd class is not full, all of the seats may be; you'll be lucky to get standing room, and will have to stand with your baggage because time is rarely taken to put it underneath in the luggage compartment. During the day, Caribbean coastal buses tend to run at roughly two-hour intervals.

While you are waiting for the bus to get you between beaches, try hitchhiking. Every day, scores of tourists who have rented cars in Cancún go day-tripping down the coast. Beachcombers find it relatively easy to catch a ride if they start out early enough. The bus fare between beaches is generally less than US$1.50 so don't bother hitching just to save money. The highway itself is straight and dull; dense vegetation spills back from the road on both sides and there's little sign of habitation. Access roads to the beaches are not always well marked; you may only see a narrow unpaved road heading eastwards one or two km to the beach. But the less well marked it is, the emptier it may be.

Xcaret (Km 290)

Look for the *Restaurant Xcaret* on the east side of the highway; this marks the access road to this beautiful spot. The road cuts through the Rancho Xcaret turkey farm, to which you must pay an admission fee of US$2, before reaching several small tumbledown Maya ruins, and then a beautiful inlet, or *caleta,* filled with tropical marine life. Bring your snorkelling gear. A small restaurant provides refreshments at resort prices. Inland a few metres from the coast is Xcaret cenote, a limpid pool in a limestone cave, which is also an excellent place for a swim.

Pamul (Km 274)

Although Pamul's small rocky beach does not have long stretches of white sand like some of its Caribbean cousins, the palm-fringed surroundings are inviting. If you walk only about two km north of Pamul's little hotel, you will find an alabaster sand beach to call your own. If you're collecting coral, try the shores just south of Pamul. The least rocky section is the southern end, but watch out for spiked sea urchins in the shallows offshore.

Giant sea turtles come ashore here at night

in July and August to lay their eggs. Why they return to the same beach every year is a mystery not understood by zoologists. If you run across a turtle during your evening stroll along the beach, keep a good distance from it and don't use a light, as this will scare it. Do your part to contribute to the survival of the turtles, which are endangered: let them lay their eggs in peace.

Places to Stay & Eat *Hotel Pamul* offers basic but acceptable rooms with fan and bath for US$15 a single and US$25 a double. There is electricity in the evenings until 10 pm. The friendly family that runs this somewhat scruffy hotel and campsite also serve breakfasts and seafood at their little restaurant for reasonable prices.

The fee for camping is US$7 for two people per site. There are showers and toilets.

Puerto Aventuras (Km 269.5)

The Cancún lifestyle spreads inexorably southward, dotting this recently pristine coast with yet more sybaritic resort hideaways. One such is the *Puerto Aventuras Resort* (☎ (987) 2-22-11), PO Box 186, Playa del Carmen, Quintana Roo, a modern luxury complex of hotel rooms, swimming pools, beach facilities and other costly comforts.

Yal-Ku Lagoon (Km 256.5)

One of the secrets of snorkelling aficionados, Yal-Ku Lagoon is not even signposted. Its dirt road turn-off is across from a stone-walled house with a windmill. The tiny lagoon is a good place to snorkel, filled with a delightful array of aquatic life. Best of all, you may have the lagoon to yourself.

Yal-Ku is basically for day trips, as there is little shade and not much in the way of decent places to pitch a tent. Bring your own refreshments and snorkelling gear.

Akumal (Km 255)

Famed for its beautiful beach shaded by graceful palm trees (often photographed for travel brochures), Akumal suffered some damage from Hurricane Gilbert in 1988. Many of its palms were swept away by the storm, but enough remain to keep this a beautiful place. Akumal (Place of the Turtles in Maya), does indeed see giant turtles come ashore to lay their eggs during the summer.

Beach Activities There are two dive shops here where you can rent snorkelling gear. The best snorkelling is at the north end of the bay; or try Yal-Ku Lagoon, 1.5 km north of Akumal.

World-class divers come here to explore the Spanish galleon *Mantancero* which sank in 1741. You can see artefacts from the galleon at the museum at nearby Xel-ha. The dive shops will arrange all your scuba excursion needs. Beginners' scuba instruction can be provided for less than US$120; if you want certification, the dive shops offer three-day courses. They will also arrange deep-sea fishing excursions.

Places to Stay Accommodation here is in the top end category, and favours vacationers spending a week or more. The least expensive of this resort's three hotels is the *Hotel-Club Akumal Caribe Villas Maya*, where basic two-person air-conditioned cabañas with bath cost US$90 to US$125 a double. Make reservations through Akutrame, (☎ (915) 584-3552, or toll-free outside Texas (800) 351-1622), PO Box 13326, El Paso, Texas 79913, USA.

The *Hotel Ina Yana Kin Akumal Caribe* on the south end of the beach is an attractive two-storey modern lodge with swimming pool and boat rental. Spacious air-conditioned rooms equipped with refrigerators cost US$110. These can sleep six people.

On the north side of the beach you will find the cabañas of *Las Casitas Akumal* (☎ (987) 2-25-54) consisting of a living room, kitchen, two bedrooms and two bathrooms. Bungalows cost US$160 in the busy winter season and US$110 in summer. For reservations write to Las Casitas (☎ (201) 489-6614; fax (201) 489-5070), 270 River St, Box 522, Hackensack, NJ 07602, USA.

Places to Eat Even the shade-huts near the beach are expensive for light lunches and snacks. Just outside the walled entrance of Akumal is a grocery store patronised largely by the resort workers; if you are day-tripping here, this is your sole inexpensive source of food. The store also sells tacos and other típico food.

For those willing to splurge, both the *Zasil Restaurant*, next to Las Casitas, and the *Lol Ha* next to the dive shop have a reputation for fine cuisine. Somewhat cheaper is the restaurant owned by the *Hotel Ina Yana Kin*.

Las Aventuras (Km 250)

Developers got the first chance at Las Aventuras, which now has a planned community of condominiums, villas, and the beautiful *Aventuras Akumal Hotel*, which has double rooms for about US$115. All rooms face the sea and each has a balcony looking out on the fine stretch of beach. There's some coral just offshore and the resort also has a pool and bar. The resort's *Los Tucanas* restaurant is pleasant, and dinner for two with beer, dessert and coffee will cost about US$35.

Chemuyil (Km 248)

This is a beautiful alabaster sand beach shaded by coconut palms. There is good snorkelling in the calm waters, which have exceptional visibility, and fishing from the shore is said to be good.

Chemuyil is being developed, with some condos already built. During winter's high season there are a fair number of campers here.

The cheap accommodation is spartan screened shade huts with hammock hooks. Enquire about availability at the bar; they cost US$15, and showers and toilets are communal.

Local fare is prepared at the bar, including some seafood.

Xcacel (Km 247)

Xcacel ('shkah-CELL') has no lodging other than camping (US$2.75 per person), no electricity and only a small restaurant stall. This is actually fortunate, because if Xcacel was more developed, this magnificent Caribbean beach would be overrun. As it stands, you can enjoy this patch of paradise in relative privacy for a day-use charge of only US$1.50.

For fine fishing and snorkelling, try the waters north of the campground. The rocky point leads to seas suitable for snorkelling, and the sandy outcropping is said to be a good place to fish from. The waters directly in front of the campground are not the best to swim in as there is no reef to break the waves. Swimming, like snorkelling, is best from the rocky point to the north end of the beach.

Xcacel offers good pickings for shell collectors, including examples of that aquatic collector, the hermit crab. There are also some colourful and intricate coral pieces to be found. When beachcombing here, wear footgear.

Take the old dirt track which runs two km north to Chemuyil and three km south to Xel-ha, and you may spy parrots, finches or the well-named clockbird (mot-mot) with its long tail.

Xel-ha Lagoon (Km 245)

Once a pristine natural lagoon brimming with iridescent tropical fish, Xel-ha ('SHELL-hah') is now a Mexican national park with landscaped grounds, changing rooms, restaurant and bar. However, the fish are regularly driven off by the dozens of busloads of day-trippers who come to enjoy the beautiful site and to swim in the pretty lagoon.

It's best to come off-season (in summer), or in winter, either very early or very late in the day to avoid the tour buses. Bring your own lunch as the little restaurant here is overpriced. Entry to the lagoon area costs US$4; it's open from 8 am to 6 pm daily.

If you're lucky enough to swim at Xel-ha when there are few other swimmers around, you'll enjoy a feast for the eyes. Brightly coloured, improbably shaped parrot, angel and butterfly fish are among the nearly 50 species here. You can rent snorkelling equip-

ment; the price is a high US$8, and you may get a mask that's been worn to the point of no longer being watertight. If a rented mask is not suitable for you, ask for another no matter how much the vendor tells you that the mask is fine and you are to blame for not snorkelling correctly.

Museum & Ruins The small maritime museum contains artefacts from the wreckage of the Spanish galleon *Mantancero*. The galleon sank in 1741 just north of Akumal and in 1958 Mexican divers started their salvage operation. On display are guns, cannons, coins and other items. There are also items from some more recent wrecks as well as Maya artefacts. Admission costs US$0.85.

There is a small archaeological site on the west side of the highway, 500 metres south of the lagoon entry road, open from 8 am to 5 pm for US$2. The ruins, which are not all that impressive, date from Classic and Postclassic periods, and include El Palacio and the Templo de los Pajaros.

TULUM

The ruins of Tulum, though well preserved, would hardly merit rave notices if it weren't for their setting. Here the grey-black buildings of the past sit on a palm-fringed beach, lapped by the turquoise waters of the Caribbean.

While Tulum literally means City of the Dawn in Maya, a looser translation is City of Renewal. For those travellers who are 'ruined out', the dramatic environs of Tulum will renew their desire to explore antiquities.

Like Chichén Itzá, Tulum's proximity to the tourist centres of Cancún and Isla Mujeres make it a prime target of tour buses. To best enjoy the ruins, visit them either early in the morning or late in the day. The ruins are open from 8 am to 5 pm and there is a US$6 admission charge. Around midday, when Tulum's fortress city is besieged by busloads of tourists, it is best to make use of either the ruin's beaches or the sands south of here. After a siesta, you'll be refreshed

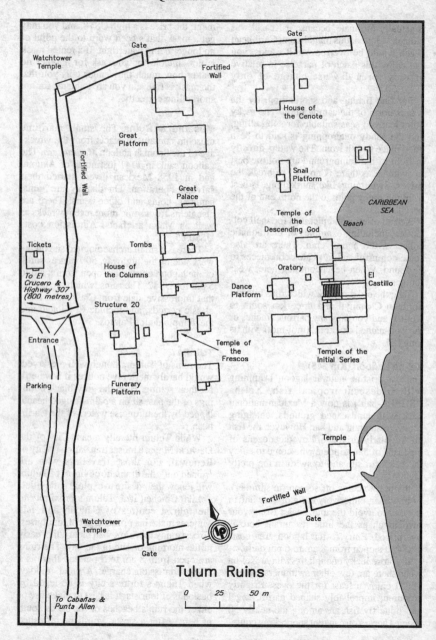

Tulum Ruins

0   25   50 m

enough to return to the more lightly populated ruins in the late afternoon.

History

Although a stele has been found at Tulum dating from 546 AD, most archaeologists believe the stone was moved much later to the site and that Tulum was actually settled during the decline of Maya civilisation in the Early Postclassic period (900-1200). The city-fortress may have been built as late as 1200. In fact, Tulum was probably still occupied after first contact with the Spanish, as a mural found here depicts Chac, the rain god, riding a four-legged animal. Since horses were unknown until the conquistadors brought them to the New World, some archaeologists therefore conclude that Tulum was still settled at the time of initial European intrusion.

The ramparts that surround three sides of Tulum (the fourth side being the sea) leave little question as to its strategic function as a fortress. Averaging nearly seven metres in thickness and standing three to five metres high, the walls have an interior walkway from which Tulum's defenders could throw spears or rocks at invaders. There is evidence of considerable strife between Maya city-states during the Late Classic period. Another theory holds that the wall separated the priest class and nobility living within the city from the peasant huts built outside.

When Juan de Grijalva's expedition sailed past Tulum in 1518, he was amazed by the sight of this walled city with its buildings painted a gleaming red, blue and white and a ceremonial fire flaming atop its seaside watchtower. The city was abandoned about three-quarters of a century after the conquest. Maya pilgrims continued to visit over the years and Indian refugees from the War of the Castes took shelter here from time to time.

In 1842, explorer and archaeologist John L Stephens and illustrator Frederick Catherwood visited Tulum by boat. They made substantial drawings and notes which, published in 1848, aroused the curiosity of the outside world. Subsequent expeditions were mounted, the most important being the 1916 to 1922 investigations by the Carnegie Institution. If you look north along the coast, you will see beyond the walls the huts of archaeologists working here today.

Don't come to Tulum expecting majestic pyramids or anything comparable to the architecture of Chichén Itzá or Uxmal. The buildings here, decidedly Toltec in influence, were the product of Maya civilisation in decline. Nonetheless, the dramatic setting and well-preserved structures give a striking sense of the past.

Orientation & Information

There are two Tulums, Tulum Ruinas and Tulum Pueblo. The ruins are 800 metres south-east off Highway 307 along an access road. The village *(pueblo)* of Tulum straddles Highway 307 about three km south of the Tulum Ruinas access road, or two km south of the Cobá road.

South of Tulum Ruinas, a road passes several collections of beachfront bungalows before entering the huge Sian Ka'an Biosphere Reserve. The road, unpaved, continues for some 50 km past Boca Paila to Punta Allen.

Tulum Pueblo has one lodging-place; no doubt more will open in the near future. The junction of Highway 307 and the Tulum Ruinas access road, called El Crucero, has several little hotels and restaurants. At the ruins themselves there are soft drink stands and one or two small eateries. The bungalows south of Tulum can provide shelter and food as well.

Structure 20 & the Funerary Platform

As you enter the Tulum city gate, look to the first building on your right, Structure 20. The roof caved in about 1929, making it a bit difficult to envision what once was a royal palace. Fragments of paintings remain on the walls. Just to Structure 20's right is a Funerary Platform with a cross-shaped grave in its centre. Here archaeologists found skeletons and animal offerings, the latter to provide sustenance for the deceased on the journey to the next world.

Temple of the Frescoes

If you walk straight toward the sea from Structure 20, you will come to the relatively well-preserved Temple of the Frescoes. Thought to have been built initially in about 1450, the temple has been added to on several occasions. Here you will see a carved figure very much in evidence at Tulum, the diving god. Equipped with wings and a bird's tail, this fascinating deity has been linked by some archaeologists with the Venus morning-star symbol of Quetzalcóatl. On the western façade are stucco masks thought to symbolise Quetzalcóatl in another form.

Inside the temple the best preserved of the greenish-blue-on-black murals may be seen through protective bars. The mural is painted in three levels demarcating the three realms of the Maya universe: the dark underworld of the deceased, the middle order of the living and the heavenly home of the creator and rain gods. Look closely at the middle level and you will see a god astride a four-legged beast – an image probably indicating knowledge of the conquistadors' horses.

The Great Palace

To the left of the Temple of the Frescoes, as you face the sea, is the Great Palace. Smaller than El Castillo, this largely deteriorated site contains a fine stucco carving of a diving god.

El Castillo

Look straight toward the sea from the Temple of the Frescoes and you can't miss Tulum's tallest building, a watchtower fortress overlooking the Caribbean, appropriately named El Castillo by the Spanish. Over the years, El Castillo was built as a series of additions. It started as a palace-like base, upon which a staircase and a crowning temple were constructed.

Note the serpent columns of the temple's entrance, with rattlers' tails supporting the roof and their heads adjoining the floor. Chichén Itzá's Temple of the Warriors has a similar columnar design influenced by the Toltec plumed serpent. On top of the entrance columns of El Castillo's temple is a fine carving of the diving god.

Take the pyramid-like staircase to the summit's temple for the view. On one side you'll see the luminous Caribbean shimmering in the tropical sun and on the other the antiquities of Tulum. This watchtower guarded the city against sea invasion. Imagine how surprised the Maya of Tulum must have been to spy the sails of the first Spanish ships along this coast.

Look down to the north from El Castillo and you will see a good small beach, great for sunning and a refreshing dip. There's a bit of an undertow here, so swim with caution.

Temple of the Descending God

Facing north (left as you face the sea) from the front of El Castillo, you will see the Temple of the Descending God. True to its name, there is a good stucco carving of a diving god on top of the door. If you ascend the inner staircase, you will see paint fragments of a religious mural.

Temple of the Initial Series

At the south flank of El Castillo stands a restored temple named for a stele now in the British Museum, which was inscribed with the Maya date corresponding to 564 AD. At first this confused archaeologists, who had evidence that Tulum was not settled until some time later. Today, scholars believe that the stele was moved here from a city founded much earlier. This temple has a handsome arch and windows on three sides.

Places to Stay

There are no very cheap lodgings near Tulum, but if you're willing to spend a bit more you can find places at El Crucero, Tulum Pueblo, and along the road south to Punta Allen.

El Crucero Right at the junction of Highway 307 and the Tulum access road are several hotels and restaurants, including the *Motel El Crucero* (no phone). Older rooms with fan and private shower rent for US$20 a double.

There's a restaurant and a shop selling ice, pastries, snacks and souvenirs.

Facing the Motel El Crucero across the access road is the *Hotel El Faisan y El Venado* (no phone), which is slightly fancier with better rooms, but also a bit more expensive at US$22 a double for a room with fan, private bath and TV with a satellite hook-up. There's a small swimming pool out the back and a decent restaurant as well.

Tulum Pueblo The *Hotel Maya Tulum* is on the west side of Highway 307 as it passes through the village, right near the village bus stop. Opened in 1990, this simple hotel charges US$18 for a double room with ceiling fan and private bathroom. The problem is that here you're four km (almost an hour's walk) from the ruins. For reservations, call the caseta (village telephone office; ☎ (987) 2-16-33) and leave a message for Irma Cruz, manager of the hotel.

Boca Paila/Punta Allen Road South of the archaeological zone is a paradise of palm-shaded white beach dotted with collections of cabañas, little thatched huts of greater or lesser comfort, and simple wooden or concrete bungalows. Most of these places have little eateries at which you can take your meals, and some have electric generators which provide electric light for several hours each evening. There are no phones.

The cheapest way to sleep here is to have your own hammock, preferably with one of those tube-like mosquito nets to cover it; if you don't carry your own, several of the cheaper places will rent you what you need. If you have candles or a torch, it'll come in handy here. In the cheapest places you'll have to supply your own towel and soap.

Unfortunately, these lodgings are located some distance south of the ruins and there is no public transport along the road. Though you may occasionally be able to hitch a ride, you can depend only upon your own two feet to get you from your bungalow to the ruins, which may be up to seven km away.

I'll start by describing the places closest to Tulum ruins, then head south.

Closest to the ruins are *Cabañas El Mirador* and *Cabañas Santa Fe*, on the beach about 600 metres south of the Tulum ruins parking lot. Of the two, the Santa Fe is preferable, though a bit more expensive, charging US$2.75 per person for a campsite, US$6.75 to hang your hammocks in a cabin, single or double.

One km south of the parking lot is *Cabañas Don Armando*, another step up the price and quality scale. For US$11 (single or double) you get one of 17 cabins built on concrete slabs, with lockable doors, hammocks or beds (you pay a deposit for sheets and pillows), mosquito netting, good showers, and a good, cheap restaurant. Lighting is by candles. This place is fun, right on the beach, and still only a 10-minute walk to the ruins.

Next to the south is the *Hotel El Paraíso*, 1½ km south of the ruins, which approaches a conventional hotel in its services. Some of the rooms are in older bungalow units, others in newer motel-style structures up on the hill; all benefit from the constant cooling onshore breezes. The newer rooms, with two double beds and private bath, cost US$30. There's a nice little restaurant with a good sea view.

South of El Paraíso it's over three km to the next lodgings, *Cabañas Familia Canché*, 4½ km south of the ruins. Just south of the Canché is *La Perla Restaurant*, and after that the paved road ends, giving way to a good sand track.

Cabañas Chac-Mool are just north of the Sian Ka'an Biosphere Reserve entrance, about 6 km south of the ruins. You can camp here or rent one of the comparatively expensive cabañas, and dine in the cosy vegetarian restaurant.

As you go south the cabañas get a bit more expensive, comfortable and scuba-diver-oriented, charging between US$26 and US$38 for a double room. *Los Arrecifes*, seven km south of the ruins, has large, fairly luxurious (for Tulum) bungalows on the beach for US$60, or much cheaper, simpler ones back from the beach (no view) for US$27. Despite the lofty prices, there's no electricity.

Restaurant y Cabañas de Anna y José is

next door to the south, with simple lodgings but a decent if plain restaurant.

The last set of cabañas in this group is *Cabañas Tulum*, over seven km south of the ruins, where little concrete bungalows look out through the palm shade to the sea and the beach. Each has two double beds, light bulb, window screens, cold-water private shower, a table, and a porch perfect for hammock-hanging; the rate is US$26 per night, single or double. The electric generator runs (if it's working) from dusk to 10 pm each evening.

Places to Eat

El Crucero The *Motel El Crucero* has a popular, very simple but somewhat expensive restaurant. Go the American route with a cheeseburger plate for US$4.50, or have Yucatecan cochinita pibil for the same price. Tacos and enchiladas go for US$4, and it's a good idea to stick to these simple items rather than to hazard money on the fancier dishes costing several times as much. The seafood, for instance, would be of questionable freshness.

At the *Restaurant El Faisan y El Venado* across the street the surroundings are a bit more attractive, the food similar and the prices just a bit higher.

Tulum Ruinas The car park at the ruins is surrounded by little stalls selling souvenirs. Most of these used to be tiny eateries, but the profits are in cheap souvenirs so the eateries got driven out. A few survive, however, including the *Restaurant México*, on the left as you come into the car park from the highway. It serves decent sandwiches of cheese, ham or chicken for US$3.75, and fried chicken for US$5. Sometimes they have spaghetti or fish, and they always have cold beer and soft drinks.

The little restaurant right next door to the left of the Restaurant México is similar but not quite so nice. At the far end of the parking lot near the road to Punta Allen is the *Restaurant Garibaldi.*

Getting There & Away

Getting to Tulum from Cancún, Playa del Carmen, Chetumal or Felipe Carrillo Puerto is no problem: you simply buy a ticket for a seat on the bus and get off at El Crucero near Tulum Ruinas. But getting away from Tulum may be difficult as you must depend upon passing buses to pick you up, and these are often full. Sometimes a sympathetic tourist in a rented car will give you a lift if you hitchhike. In any case, plan to wait a while for a bus, and don't expect to find a seat on the first one that stops. During the day, northbound and southbound buses stop at El Crucero about every two hours.

TULUM TO BOCA PAILA & PUNTA ALLEN

If you think you might find a tourist-free paradise by taking the unpaved road to land's-end some 50 km south of Tulum past Boca Paila, forget it. The scenery en route is the typically monotonous flat Yucatecan terrain. Furthermore, the beaches are far from spectacular, though there's no doubt you will find plenty of privacy.

You ultimately meet land's-end at the lobster-fishing village of Punta Allen. While not without some charm, its beaches are less attractive than, say, the sands around Cabañas Los Arrecifes just a short drive from Tulum.

It's important to have plenty of fuel before heading south from Tulum as there is no fuel available on the Tulum-Punta Allen road.

Places to Stay

One of the two hotels on the road to Punta Allen is *La Villa de Boca Paila*, where luxury cabañas complete with kitchens cost about US$90 per double, including two meals. The clientele is predominantly affluent American sport fishers. For reservations write to Apdo Postal 159, Mérida, Yucatán, Mexico. Boca Paila is 25 km south of the ruins.

Ten km south of Boca Paila you cross a rickety wooden bridge. Beyond it is *El Retiro Cabañas* where you can hang hammocks or camp for a few dollars.

Punta Allen does have some rustic lodgings. The *Curzan Guest House* has cabañas with hammocks for about US$25 a double.

The couple who run it prepare breakfast and lunch at a cost of US$6.50 per person and charge US$14 for dinner. They can arrange snorkelling and fishing expeditions, or visits to the offshore island of Cayo Colibri, known for its bird life. To write for reservations, the address is Curzan Guest House, c/o Sonia Lillvik, Apdo Postal 703, Cancún, Quintana Roo 77500.

If you wish to camp on Punta Allen's beach, simply ask the Maya in front of whose house you would be sleeping for permission.

COBÁ

Fifty km north-west of Tulum lies a more impressive, yet less frequently visited, ruined Maya site. Perhaps the largest of all Maya cities, Cobá – whose ruins extend at least 50 sq km – offers the chance to explore mostly unrestored antiquities set deep in tropical jungles. Prepare to do some walking on jungle paths and dress for humidity, wear decent footgear and cover yourself with repellent because the forest here can be thick with mosquitoes. It's also a good idea to bring a canteen of water because it's hot and the refreshment stands are outside the main gate. Avoid the midday heat.

Don't let all this put you off; no other site in the Yucatán peninsula offers such an opportunity to play at being an archaeologist. The estimated 5% of Cobá that has been unearthed will reward you by letting you walk the streets of one of the Maya's greatest cities.

Cobá is worth visiting for other reasons. On jungle walks, you are likely to see tropical birds, butterflies, reptiles and insects.

History

Cobá was settled earlier than Chichén or Tulum, its heyday dating from 600 AD until the site was abandoned about 900 AD. Cobá's architecture is a mystery; its towering pyramids and stelae resemble the architecture of Tikal, several hundred km away, rather than that of Chichén Itzá and other sites of northern Yucatán.

While there is not yet a definitive explanation, some archaeologists theorise that an alliance with Tikal was made through marriage to facilitate trade between the Guatemalan and Yucatecan Maya. Stelae appear to depict female rulers from Tikal holding ceremonial bars and flaunting their power by standing on captives. These Tikal royal females, when married to Cobá's royalty, may have brought architects and artisans from Guatemala with them.

Archaeologists are also baffled by the network of extensive stone-paved avenues or *sacbeob* in this region, with Cobá as the hub. The longest runs nearly 100 km from the base of Cobá's great pyramid Nohoch Mul to the Maya settlement of Yaxuna. In all, some 40 sacbeob passed through Cobá. Why did the Maya build such an extensive road network if they had no pack animals to traverse the wide (some measuring 10 metres across) straight roads? The best guess is that the sacbés' function was mostly ceremonial, perhaps allowing Maya astronomers to get an early fix on a rising celestial body. In effect, the sacbeob may have been part of the huge astronomical 'time machine' that was evident in every Maya city.

Archaeologists believe that this vast city once held 40,000 Maya. They don't know why it was abandoned. The small populace presently inhabiting the region raises the question of what happened to all the people.

The first excavation was by the Austrian archaeologist Teobert Maler. Hearing rumours of a fabled lost city, he came to Cobá alone in 1891. There was little subsequent investigation until 1926 when the Carnegie Institute financed the first of two expeditions led by J Eric S Thompson and Harry Pollock. After their 1930 expedition not much happened until 1973, when the Mexican government slowly began to finance excavation. Archaeologists now estimate that Cobá contains some 6500 structures of which just a small percentage have been excavated and restored.

Orientation & Information

About 650 metres after you bear left at a fork in the road to approach Cobá village, notice a sign marked 'Mirador'. At my last visit there was nothing to see from this 'viewpoint' except jungle, but several years ago the jungle had been cut back to reveal part of the sacbé which went from Cobá to Yaxuna. Perhaps when you visit the jungle will have been attacked again (but ultimately it always wins).

The small village of Cobá, 1½ km past the Mirador, is what you see first as you approach the archaeological site. Just past the village is the lake; turn left for the ruins, right for the Villa Arqueológica Cobá hotel.

The village has several small, simple and cheap lodging and eating places. There are also four small cookshops by the entrance to the archaeological site. The site is open from 8 am to 5 pm; admission costs US$5.

Cobá Group

Soon after you enter the site, you will see a right fork designated 'Cobá Group'. Take this path past unexcavated mounds and the rubble of ruins until you come to the enormous pyramid called the Temple of the Churches. Climb to the top of this steep edifice for a view of the Nohoch Mul pyramid to the north and shimmering lakes to the east and south-west. If you continue along this path you will ultimately come to Lake Cobá.

Las Pinturas Group

From the Temple of the Churches, come back to the main path and follow it until you see the sign for the Conjunto de las Pinturas, or the Temple of Paintings, located on a trail branching off from the main path. En route to the temple, you can take a one-km circular subtrail past some stelae dubbed Grupo Ma Can Xoc. Some of the stelae on this trail are very fine, others badly deteriorated. It is from one of these that archaeologists theorised that the carved woman with the ceremonial bar as well as the woman standing arrogantly on a captive were royal females from Tikal.

Returning to the trail to the Temple of the

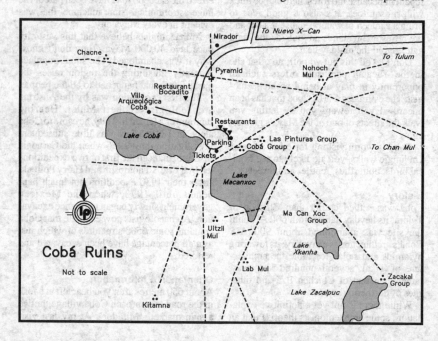

Cobá Ruins
Not to scale

Paintings, you will find disappointingly bare walls upon reaching the temple. Today there remain mere fragments of the murals which once gave this edifice its name. Take the trail from the temple entrance to a break in the bush and you will see a huge stele. Here, a regal-looking man stands over two figures, one of them kneeling with his hands bound behind him. Sacrificial captives lie beneath the feet of a ruler at the base of the deteriorating stela.

Nohoch Mul – The Great Pyramid

Return to the main trail and follow the signs to Nohoch Mul. It's a 1½-km walk through lush, humid jungle and though you may be hot and tired at this point, the trek is well worth the effort. At a splendid 42 metres high, the Great Pyramid is the tallest of all Maya structures in the Yucatán Peninsula. Climb the 120 steps for a panoramic view of the surrounding jungle, observing the Maya carved shell-like forms where you put your feet.

There are some diving gods carved over the doorway of the Nohoch Mul temple at the top, similar to the sculptures at Tulum. Apparently this temple at the summit was added long after the pyramid was constructed.

From the Great Pyramid's face, look to the right in the plaza and you will see Temple 10. The building itself is not particularly noteworthy, but in front of it is the exquisitely carved Stele 20, with a ruler standing over two kneeling captive slaves.

There are unexcavated ruins as far from the entrance as Ixtil, 19 km distant. For those seeking the unusual, there is a three-storeyed pyramid near Kucilan (eight km south of Cobá's centre) which unlike other Maya structures of its kind has lower storeys, which were never filled in, to support the added level.

Places to Stay & Eat

In the village of Cobá is the *Restaurant Isabel*, which also offers rooms for rent. In fact on my last visit lodging was the only business being done as the restaurant bore a sign reading 'No Functione'. The spartan but basically acceptable rooms with fans and shared bath here cost US$8 a single and US$10 a double.

Fifty metres from Hotel Isabel, *Restaurant Bocadito* has clean doubles with bath for US$10 a single, US$14 a double. The manager is very helpful and will do his best to make you comfortable. As for the restaurant, it's your best bet for a cheap meal in these parts. More pleasant and cheaper than the eateries facing the parking lot at the archaeological site entrance, Bocadito (Little Mouthful) offers ham and cheese sandwiches for US$3, guacamole for just a bit more, and main course platters such as beef, pork or chicken for US$5.

Next door to the Bocadito is *Cabañas Económicas*, which was not open at my last visit, but these places have a way of opening and closing without warning, so have a look in any case.

As for camping, there's no organised spot, though you can try finding a place along the shore of the lake.

For upscale lodging and dining the choice is easy: there's only the *Villa Arqueológica Cobá* (Cancún ☎ (988) 4-25-74). This pleasant hotel is a gathering spot for archaeologists and those interested in antiquities. There is a library here with the focus on Maya culture and history, and a study of Mexican, Guatemalan and Honduran archaeological sites. The very pleasant hotel has a swimming pool and good restaurant. Air-conditioned rooms cost US$70 a single, US$80 a double and US$90 a triple. Lunch or dinner in the good restaurant might cost US$20 to US$30.

For reservations in the USA, phone (800) 528-3100; or in Mexico City call 203-38-86. You can supposedly make bookings through the travel agent at the Hotel Antillano lobby in Cancún. He's a helpful guy but there's no guarantee that you'll actually find a room reserved for you when you arrive in Cobá! If there's no room available in Cobá they may let you sleep in the library or fix you up with a room in the employees' quarters.

Getting There & Away

Buses veer onto the Cobá road from Highway 307, north of Tulum Pueblo, at 6 and 11 am on their way to Valladolid via Nuevo X-Can. The 50-km trip to Cobá takes about an hour and costs US$2.75. From Valladolid, buses leave for Cobá at 4 am and noon, arriving about two hours later. Be sure to mention to the driver that you want to get out at Cobá, because the road does not pass directly through the village of Cobá and thus you might miss it. If the driver drops you at the junction with the dead-end road to the village and the ruins, you'll have a 2-km walk to the village and a 2½-km walk to the ruins.

A more comfortable, dependable but expensive way to reach Cobá is by taxi from the parking lot at the Tulum ruins. Find some other travellers interested in the trip and split the cost, about US$20 or US$30 round-trip, including two hours at the site.

If you start out early enough from Tulum and are willing to be patient, you may have some luck hitching a ride with tourists in rented cars.

Coming from Chichén Itzá or Valladolid, simply catch one of the two daily buses which depart from Valladolid at 4 am or noon. From Cancún you must take a bus to Nuevo X-Can and wait at the junction with the Cobá road for the bus from Valladolid.

By the way, many maps show a road from Cobá to Chemax, but this road is not practicable and should not really be shown. The only passable road north from Cobá is the one to Nuevo X-Can.

FELIPE CARRILLO PUERTO

Population: 17,000

The dusty town of Felipe Carrillo Puerto, 155 km from Chetumal, was once called Chan Santa Cruz. During and after the War of the Castes, Chan Santa Cruz was a centre of rebel activities. After the suppression of the Maya rebels, the town was renamed in honour of a progressive governor.

History

In 1849 the War of the Castes went against the Maya of northern Yucatán, who made their way to this town seeking refuge. Regrouping their forces, they were ready to sally forth again in 1850, just when a 'miracle' occurred. A wooden cross erected at a cenote on the western edge of the town began to 'talk', telling the Maya they were the chosen people, exhorting them to continue the struggle against the Whites, and promising the Maya forces victory. The talking was done by a ventriloquist who used sound chambers, but the people nonetheless looked upon it as the authentic voice of their aspirations.

The oracular cross guided the Maya in battle for eight years, until their great victory in conquering the fortress at Bacalar. For the latter part of the 1800s, the Maya in and around Chan Santa Cruz were virtually independent of governments in Mexico City and Mérida. In the 1920s a boom in the chicle market brought prosperity to the region and the Maya decided to come to terms with Mexico City, which they did in 1929. Some of the Maya, unwilling to give up the cult of the talking cross, left Chan Santa Cruz to take up residence at small villages deep in the jungle, where they still revere the talking cross to this day. You may see some of them visiting the site where the cross spoke in its little park, especially on 3 May, the day of the Holy Cross.

You can visit the **Sanctuario del Cruz Parlante** five blocks west of the Pemex fuel station on the main street (Highway 307) in the commercial centre of town. Besides the cenote and a stone shelter, there's little to see in the park, though the place reverberates with history.

Places to Stay & Eat

El Faisan y El Venado (☎ (983) 4-00-43), across from the Pemex station 100 metres south of the traffic roundabout, has 13 clean rooms with private showers and either ceiling fans or air-con. Prices are US$8.50 to US$15 a single, US$11 to US$17 a double and US$13 to US$19 a triple, the higher prices being for those with air-con, of course. They have a decent restaurant, too. Just a few dozen metres to the south near the Pemex station is the *Restaurant 24 Horas*, also family-run, equally pleasant, but a bit cheaper.

Just off the main plaza is the *Hotel Chan Santa Cruz* (☎ (983) 4-01-70), with acceptable if plain rooms around a courtyard priced similarly to those at El Faisan y El Venado.

Getting There & Away

Buses running between Cancún (224 km) and Chetumal (155 km) stop here, as do buses travelling from Chetumal to Valladolid (150 km). There are also a few buses between Felipe Carrillo Puerto and Mérida via Ticul (change there or at Muna for Uxmal).

Note that there are few services on the route from Felipe Carrillo to Ticul.

LAGUNA BACALAR

Nature has set a turquoise jewel in the midst of the scrubby Yucatecan jungle – Laguna Bacalar. A large, clear fresh-water lake with a bottom of gleaming white sand, Bacalar comes as a surprise in this country of tortured limestone. Bacalar, for all its beauty, has hardly been developed at all. While this preserves its beauty, it also makes it difficult to put up here for the night.

The small, sleepy town of Bacalar, just east of the highway some 125 km south of Felipe Carrillo Puerto, is the only settlement of any size on the lake. It's noted mostly for its old fortress and its swimming facilities.

The fortress was built over the lagoon to protect citizens from raids by pirates and Indians. It served as an important outpost for the Whites in the War of the Castes. In 1859, it was seized by Maya rebels who held the fort until Quintana Roo was finally conquered by Mexican troops in 1901. Today, with formidable cannons still on its ramparts, the fortress remains an imposing sight. It houses a museum exhibiting colonial armaments and uniforms from the 17th and 18th centuries. The museum is open daily from 8 am to 1 pm and has a small admission charge of US$0.50.

A divided avenue runs between the fortress and the lakeshore northward a few hundred metres to the balneario, or bathing facilities. Small restaurants line the avenue and surround the balneario, which is very busy on weekends.

Costera Bacalar & Cenote Azul

The road which winds southward along the lakeshore from Bacalar town to Highway 307 at Cenote Azul is called the Costera Bacalar. It passes a few lodging and camping places along the way.

About 2½ km south of the town is the *Meson Nueva Salamanca*, Costera 51, with tidy little motel-type rooms for US$25 a double. There's no restaurant, but a little shop sells cold drinks and snacks.

Hotel Laguna (☎ (983) 2-35-17 in Chetumal, (99) 27-13-04 in Mérida), 3½ km south of Bacalar town along the Costera, is only 150 metres east of Highway 307, so you can ask a bus driver to stop here for you. The Laguna is a hidden paradise: clean, cool and hospitable, with a wonderful view of the lake, a nice swimming pool, breezy terrace and restaurant, and bar. Rooms at the Laguna cost US$40 a single or double with fan, and private bath. In the restaurant, sandwiches go for US$3, and fried chicken, fish or beef for US$5 to US$7.50.

Only 700 metres past the Hotel Laguna along the Costera is a nameless little camping area on the shore run by a family who live in a shack on the premises. You can camp in the dense shade of the palm trees for US$5.75 per couple. Bring your own food and drinking water, as the nearest supplier is the restaurant at the Hotel Laguna.

The **Cenote Azul** is a 90-metre-deep natural pool on the south-western shore of Laguna Bacalar, 200 metres east of Highway 307. Being a cenote there's no beach, just a few steps leading down to the water from the vast palapa which shelters the restaurant. A small sign purveys the traditional wisdom: 'Don't go in the cenote if you can't swim'.

The restaurant has its own little aviary with colourful peacocks and macaws; main course dishes of fish or meat are US$5 to US$11; you might pay US$9 to US$15 for the average meal here.

Getting There & Away

Coming from the north, have the bus drop you in Bacalar town, at the Hotel Laguna, or at Cenote Azul, as you wish (check before you buy your ticket to see if the driver will stop).

From Chetumal, catch a minibus from Combi Corner. Departures are about every 20 minutes from 5 am to 7 pm for the 39-km (40 minutes, US$2.75) run to the town of Bacalar; some northbound buses (US$1.75) departing from the bus station will also drop you near the town of Bacalar. Along the way they pass Laguna Milagros (14 km), Xul-ha (22 km) and the Cenote Azul (33 km), and all four of these places afford chances to swim in fresh water. The lakes are gorgeous, framed by palm trees, with crystal clear water and soft white limestone-sand bottoms.

Heading west out of Chetumal, you turn north onto Highway 307; 15½ km north of this highway junction is a turn on the right marked for the Cenote Azul and Costera Bacalar.

CHETUMAL

Population: 130,000

Laid out on a grand plan with many wide, divided boulevards, Chetumal has yet to grow into its obvious destiny as the important capital city of the state of Quintana Roo. In times BC (Before Cancún), the sparsely populated territory of Quintana Roo received special tax relief from the Mexican federal government to encourage immigration from other parts of the country. Quintana Roo was upgraded from a territory to a state in 1974, but Chetumal still enjoys lower taxes than other parts of the country (6% tax on imports, instead of the 15% elsewhere). You'll see many shops selling fancy imported goods at the low-tax prices in this town.

Before the conquest, Chetumal was a Maya port for shipping gold, feathers, cacao and copper from this region and Guatemala to northern Yucatán. After the conquest, the town was not actually settled until 1898 when it was founded to put a stop to the

■ PLACES TO STAY

1	Posada Pantoja
3	Hotel & Restaurant Ucum
6	Hotel Continental Caribe
10	Hotel Del Prado
14	Hotel & Restaurant Jacaranda
17	Hotel María Dolores & Restaurant Sosilmar
19	Hotel Baroudi
21	Hotel El Dorado
22	Albergue CREA (Youth Hostel)

▼ PLACES TO EAT

4	Restaurant Pantoja
13	Restaurant Típico El Taquito
15	Restaurant Pollo Brujo
16	Restaurant Señorial
18	Panadería La Muralla & Restaurant Campeche
20	Sergio's Pizzas

OTHER

2	Combi Corner (Minibus Stops)
5	Mercado (Market)
7	Tourist Information Kiosk
8	Hospital Morelos
9	Centro de Salud (Clinic)
11	Teléfonos de México
12	Correos (Post Office)
23	Palacio de Gobierno & Tourist Office

illegal trade in arms and lumber carried on by the descendants of the War of the Castes rebels. Dubbed Payo Obispo, the town's name was changed to Chetumal in 1936. Chetumal was virtually obliterated by Hurricane Janet in 1955, which is why the centre of the city is modern.

Besides its special tax status, Chetumal is the gateway to and from Belize, and you may encounter groups of Belizeans coming to the 'big city' to shop.

Orientation

Despite its sprawling street grid layout, the centre of this small city is easily manageable on foot. Once you find the all-important intersection of Avenida de los Héroes and Avenida Alvaro Obregón, you're within 50

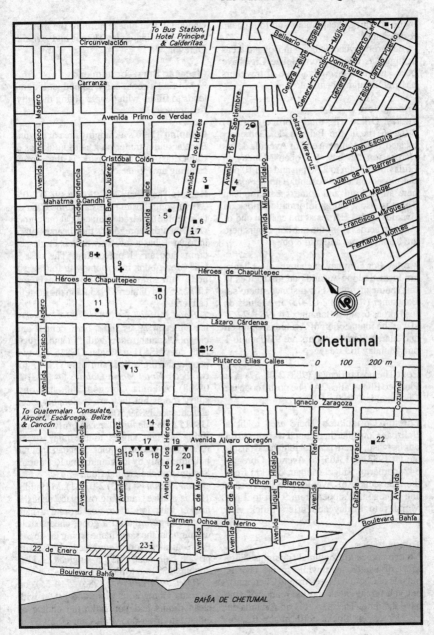

Chetumal

0   100   200 m

metres of three cheap hotels and four cheap restaurants.

Be careful when walking in isolated areas at night, as thieves from Belize City have been known to take advantage of travellers passing through Chetumal.

Information

Tourist Office The tourist office (☎ (983) 2-02-66) is in the Palacio de Gobierno, located at the southern end of Avenida de los Héroes, on the bay. It's open Monday to Friday from 8 am to 2.30 pm and 6 to 10 pm, but closed on the weekend. The personnel here are helpful and some speak English. There is also a tourist information kiosk on Avenida de los Héroes at the eastern end of Aguilar, across from the market. Hours here are 8 am to 1 pm and 5 to 8 pm.

Money For currency exchange, most banks are located along Avenida de los Héroes in the centre of town. For instance, there's a Bancomer (☎ (983) 2-02-05) at Avenida de los Héroes 6, and a Banamex (☎ (983) 2-27-10) at the intersection of Avenidas Obregón and Juárez. Banking hours are 9.30 am to 1 pm, Monday to Friday.

Post The post office (☎ (983) 2-00-57) is at Plutarco Elías Calles 2A. The postal code for Chetumal is 77000.

Foreign Consulates There used to be a Belizean Consulate here, but it was closed on our last visit. There is a Guatemalan Consulate (☎ (983) 2-13-65) at Avenida Obregón 342, corner of Rafael Melgar, one km from the intersection of Avenidas de los Héroes and Obregón. It's open from 9 am to 2 pm Monday to Friday and offers quick visa service.

Things to See

No one comes to Chetumal for sightseeing. Most of what's worthwhile in the area is outside of Chetumal (see Around Chetumal), but you might check out the market if you have the time. The market is on Avenida de los Héroes ten blocks north of the Bay of

Chetumal, five blocks north of the intersection of Avenida de los Héroes and Avenida Obregón.

Places to Stay – bottom end

Try to find a room early, as budget lodging tends to fill up with people plying the duty-free trade.

Camping There's a camping area at Laguna Bacalar and a trailer park with hook-ups at Calderitas; the trailer park is the closest camping area to the city.

Hostels The *Albergue CREA* (☎ (983) 2-05-25), or youth hostel (also called the Casa de la Juventud), Calzada Veracruz at the corner with Avenida Obregón, is the cheapest place in town. It has a few drawbacks: single-sex dorms and an 11 pm curfew. The cost is US$4 for a bunk in a room with four or six beds and shared bath. Breakfasts are US$2.25 and dinners US$3.25 in the hostel's cafeteria.

Hotel Baroudi (☎ (983) 2-09-92), Avenida Obregón 39, is stark, bare, central and cheap. Cleanish rooms with fan and private bath cost US$11 a single, US$15 for two people sharing a bed, and only US$17 for two beds. *Hotel María Dolores* (☎ (983) 2-05-08), Avenida Obregón 206, has tiny, stuffy rooms but they are reasonably clean and cheap at US$9.50 a single and US$12 to US$15 a double with fans and private bath. Being at right angles to the busy street, rooms here are fairly quiet. You can spot the building easily by looking for the Restaurant Sosilmar on the ground floor.

Hotel Ucum (☎ (983) 2-07-11), M Gandhi 167, is a large, rambling old place near the market with lots of rooms around a bare central courtyard, and a good, cheap, little restaurant of the same name facing the street. Plain but cheap rooms equipped with fan and private bath cost US$8 a single, US$11 a double, US$14 a triple.

Hotel Jacaranda (☎ (983) 2-14-55), on Avenida Obregón, is plain and bright with clean rooms and you have the choice of either fan or air-con. Rates are US$9.50 to

US$11 a single, US$13 to US$16 a double, US$16 to US$20 a triple; the higher prices get you the air-con. Note that this hotel has many noisy rooms. The Restaurant Jacaranda is next to the hotel lobby.

Want a very clean, quiet room with good cross-ventilation, fan, TV and private bath for only US$15 a single, US$17 a double? Then find your way to the *Posada Pantoja* (☎ (983) 2-39-57), Lucio Blanco 95, one km north-east of the market in a peaceful residential area. This tidy, modern establishment is run by the same family responsible for the popular Restaurant Pantoja (see Places to Eat). To find it, walk five blocks north from the market along Avenida de los Héroes to Camelias, turn right, walk two blocks to Calzada Veracruz, cross over this main street and walk a short distance north-east on it to Lucio Blanco, on the right. The Posada is 4½ short blocks along Lucio Blanco, between Heriberto Jara and Felipe Carrillo Puerto.

At Avenida Obregón 193 is the *Hotel Quintana Roo*. Pleasant double rooms with fan and bath at this well-managed hotel cost US$12.

Places to Stay – middle

Hotel El Dorado (☎ 2-03-15), Avenida 5 de Mayo 42 (Apdo Postal 30), a block east of Avenida de los Héroes between Avenidas Obregón and O Blanco, is perhaps the best of the mid-range places. Here you will find large, tidy rooms with fan or air-conditioning for US$20 to US$33 a single, US$30 to US$40 a double, US$35 to US$40 a triple, US$38 to US$55 a quadruple, the higher prices being for rooms with air-conditioning.

Places to Stay – top end

Hotel Del Prado (☎ (983) 2-05-42), Avenida Héroes at Chapultepec, is generally regarded as the best hostelry in town, with a nice swimming pool and a decent restaurant. Air-conditioned rooms with TV cost US$88 a single or double.

Two blocks further north along Avenida de los Héroes, on the right-hand side near the tourist information kiosk, is the *Hotel Continental Caribe* (☎ (983) 2-10-50, 2-13-71), Avenida de los Héroes 171 (Apdo Postal 1); its comfortable rooms overlook several swimming pools, a restaurant and bar. Air-conditioned rooms cost US$48 a single, US$58 a double; junior suites are US$70 a single, US$85 a double.

Hotel Príncipe (☎ (983) 2-51-67, 2-47-99), Prolongación Avenida de los Héroes 326, is on the northern extension of Avenida de los Héroes, about 1½ km from the centre and also 1½ km from the bus station. This new, modern building set back from the street holds five floors of rooms with all the comforts: TV, air-con, private bath. Rates are unbeatable value: US$35 a single or double, US$44 for a suite.

Places to Eat

As with inexpensive hotels, so with restaurants: the first place to look is near the intersection of Avenidas Obregón and de los Héroes. On the south side of Avenida Obregón just west of Avenida de los Héroes are no fewer than five eateries all in a row, with another one on the northern side of the street.

Nearest to Avenida de los Héroes is the quaint old *Restaurant Campeche*, in a Caribbean-style wooden building which may give way to the bulldozers and rampant modernisation at any moment. Until it does, you can enjoy cheap food in an old Chetumal atmosphere.

Next door is the *Panadería La Muralla*, providing fresh baked goods for bus trips, picnics, and make-your-own breakfasts.

Restaurant Sosilmar, next along Avenida Obregón, is perhaps the cleanest, tidiest and brightest of the eateries in this area. Filling platters of fish or meat go for US$4 to US$5.

Next along is the *Restaurant Señorial*, and next to that is *Pollo Brujo*, a roast chicken place where you can roll your own burritos. The roast chicken goes for US$4.75 for half a chicken, US$8.50 for a whole one; wheat tortillas (tortillas de harina) are US$0.65, and soft drinks US$0.40.

On the north side of Avenida Obregón is a serviceable hotel eatery, the *Restaurant*

Jacaranda (in the Hotel Jacaranda), where you can get a plate of four tostadas, panuchos or salbutes for US$3.50, or six chicken tacos for US$3.50.

The family-owned and operated *Restaurant Pantoja*, on the corner at M Gandhi 164 and Avenida 16 de Septiembre 181, is a neighbourhood favourite serving decent, inexpensive Mexican fare. A bright, newish place, it opens early for breakfast, and later provides a comida corrida for US$3.50, enchiladas for US$2.40, and meat plates such as bistec or liver and onions (higado encebollado) for US$4.75. The nearby *Restaurant Ucum*, in the Hotel Ucum, also provides good cheap meals.

To sample the typical traditional food of Quintana Roo, head for the *Restaurant Típico El Taquito*, Avenida P E Calles 220 at Avenida Juárez. It has an airy, simple dining room where good, cheap food is served: beef tacos for US$0.70 each, hamburgers for US$2.25, and frijoles refritos, the speciality of the house, for US$1.10. It's straightforward, good value, and always busy.

Sergio's Pizzas (☎ 2-23-55), Avenida Obregón 182 a block east of Avenida de los Héroes, is actually a full-service restaurant. Enter the delightfully air-conditioned dining room, order a cold beer in a frosted mug or one of the many wines offered, and select a pizza priced from US$4.75 (small, plain) to US$20 (large, fancy). A small ham and pineapple pizza (US$5) is plenty for one person, enough for two with heat-shrunk appetites at lunch. Sergio's is open from 1 pm to midnight every day.

Chetumal doesn't have many places for an upscale meal. The hotel restaurants are serviceable without being inspiring. The *Restaurant El Grill* at the Hotel Del Prado serves a comida corrida for US$11.50 plus drink and tip, and at dinner such dishes as a cheeseburger for US$6.75, puntas de filete a la Mexicana for US$12, or shrimp in garlic sauce for US$16.50. The restaurant at the Continental Caribe is similar, if a bit cheaper.

Getting There & Away

Air Chetumal's small airport is less than two km north-west of the city centre along Avenida Obregón and Avenida Revolución. You can walk the distance from the intersection of Avenidas de los Héroes and Obregón in less than half an hour; otherwise take a taxi.

Inter (☎ (983) 2-66-75 at the airport) operates flights to Mérida, Cozumel and Cancún.

Aviacsa (☎ (983) 2-76-89, 2-76-76; at the airport 2-77-87) flies nonstop to Mexico City, and also to Tuxtla Gutiérrez. From Tuxtla you can fly to Mérida, Oaxaca, Tapachula or Villahermosa.

For flights to Belize City (and on to Tikal) or to Belize's cayes, cross the border into Belize and fly from Corozal.

Bus Chetumal's large new bus station, two km north of the city centre at the intersection of Avenida de los Insurgentes and Avenida Belice, handles buses running west to Escárcega, then on to Campeche or Palenque, Villahermosa and beyond; north to Mérida, to Valladolid, and along the coast to Cancún; and south to Corozal and Belize City.

The dominant company to points in Mexico is Autobuses del Caribe, with 1st and 2nd-class services, some run in conjunction with Autobuses de Oriente (ADO). All buses listed below run daily by Autobuses del Caribe unless otherwise specified. For Belize there are two lines, Venus Bus Line and Batty's Bus Service, with ticket offices right in the Chetumal bus station and very frequent services.

Akumal – 275 km, five hours; seven 2nd-class (US$5.50) by A del Caribe, and five 1st-class (US$4.75) by A del Caribe.

Bacalar – 39 km, 45 minutes; nine 2nd-class (US$1.75).

Belize City – 160 km, four hours (express 3¼ hours); Venus has buses every hour on the hour from 4 am to 10 am for US$5; Batty's has buses every two hours on the hour from 4 am to 6 pm for the same price. The one express bus departs Chetumal at 2 pm.

Campeche – 422 km, seven hours; 1st-class buses (US$7) at 12.30 and 7 pm.

Cancún – 382 km, seven hours; five 2nd-class (US$9.50) and seven 2nd-class (US$8.75).

Corozal (Belize) – 30 km, one hour with border formalities; see the Belize City schedule, or catch a minibus for the 12-km ride to the border at Subteniente López (see Minibus).

Escárcega – 275 km, four hours; 10 1st-class buses (US$6).

Felipe Carrillo Puerto – 155 km, three hours; five 1st-class (US$4) and nine 2nd-class (US$3.25).

Kohunlich – 67 km, 1¼ hours; take a bus heading west to Xpujil or Escárcega and get off just before village of Francisco Villa and walk nine km (1¾ hours) to site.

Mérida – 456 km, eight to nine hours; seven 1st-class (US$11) by A Peninsulares, and eight 1st-class (US$10) by A del Caribe; nine 2nd-class (US$9) by A del Caribe.

Muna – 375 km, seven hours; nine 2nd-class (US $7.50).

Playa del Carmen – 315 km, 5½ hours; five 1st-class (US$7), and seven 2nd-class (US$6).

Puerto Morelos – 350 km, 6¼ hours; seven 2nd-class (US$7).

San Cristóbal de las Casas – 700 km, 13 hours; one evening 2nd-class bus for US$12.50 by Autotransportes del Caribe (who use the Transportes Lacandonia bus station in San Cristóbal).

Ticul – 352 km, 6½ hours; nine 2nd-class (US$7.50).

Tizimín – 352 km, 6½ hours; two 2nd-class (US$8) at 8.30 am and 4.50 pm.

Tulum – 251 km, four hours; five 1st-class (US$6) and seven 2nd-class (US$5).

Tuxtla Gutiérrez – 762 km, 16 hours; one 2nd-class (US$12.50) at 1.15 pm.

Valladolid – 305 km, five hours; two 2nd-class (US$6) at 8 am and 4 pm.

Villahermosa – 575 km, nine hours; two 1st-class (US$12) and one 2nd-class (US$9) at 1.15 pm.

Xpujil – 120 km, two hours; three 2nd-class (US$3) at 6.30 am, noon and 7.30 pm.

Minibus Not far from the market are several minibus departure and arrival points. Volkswagen combi minibuses run from here to points in the vicinity of Chetumal such as Laguna Bacalar and the Belizean border at Subteniente López. Combi Corner, as we call it, is the intersection of Avenidas Primo de Verdad and Hidalgo, two blocks east of Avenida de los Héroes.

AROUND CHETUMAL
Calderitas
If you want to go out to a beach, catch a Calderitas bus on Avenida Belice between Colón and Gandhi, just by the market, for a 15 to 20-minute, six-km ride to Calderitas

Bay and its rocky beach. Palapas (thatched roofs) here shelter you from the sun; refreshment stands provide snacks and drinks. If you wish to pitch a tent, there's a campsite. Note that on Sundays the beach is packed with locals and their families on their day off.

KOHUNLICH RUINS
West of Chetumal along Highway 186 is the archaeological site of Kohunlich. It is only partly excavated, with many of its nearly 200 mounds still covered with vegetation. The surrounding rainforest is thick, but the archaeological site itself has been cleared selectively and is now a delightful forest park. Kohunlich's caretaker, Señor Ignacio Ek, may offer you a tour, after which a tip is in order. Otherwise, admission to the site costs US$2, and is open from 8 am to 5 pm daily. Drinks are sold at the site, but nothing else.

These ruins, dating from the late Preclassic (100-200 AD) and Early Classic

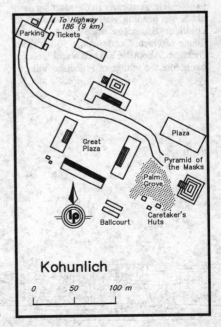

Kohunlich

(250-600 AD) periods, are famous for the impressive Pyramid of the Masks: a central stairway is flanked by huge, three-metre-high stucco masks of the sun god. The thick lips and prominent features are reminiscent of Olmec sculpture. Though there were once eight masks, only two remain after the ravages of archaeology looters. The masks themselves are impressive, but the large thatch coverings which have been erected to protect them from further weathering also obscure the view; you can see the masks only from close up. Try to imagine what the pyramid and its masks must have looked like in the old days as the Maya approached it across the sunken courtyard at the front.

The hydraulic engineering used at the site was a great achievement; nine of the site's 21 hectares were cut to channel rainwater into Kohunlich's once enormous reservoir.

Getting There & Away

There is no public transport running directly to Kohunlich. To visit the ruins without your own vehicle, start early in the morning, and take a bus heading west from Chetumal to Xpujil or Escárcega, then watch for the village of Nachi-Cocom some 50 km from Chetumal. About 9½ km past Nachi-Cocom, just before the village of Francisco Villa, is a road on the left (south) which covers the nine km to the archaeological site. Have the bus driver stop and let you off here, plan to walk and hope to hitch a ride from tourists in a car. To return to Chetumal or head westward to Xpujil or Escárcega you must hope to flag down a bus on the highway.

INTO BELIZE

Corozal, 18 km south of the Mexican/Belizean border, is a pleasant, sleepy, laid-back farming and fishing town, and an appropriate introduction to Belize. There are several decent hotels covering a full range of prices, and restaurants to match. For complete details on travel through, within and beyond Belize, get hold of Lonely Planet's *La Ruta Maya – a travel survival kit* and/or *Central America on a shoestring*.

Buses run directly from Chetumal's bus station to Belize City via Corozal and Orange Walk. From Belize City you can catch westward buses to Belmopan, San Ignacio, and the Guatemalan border at Benque Viejo, then onward to Flores, Tikal, and other points in Guatemala.

A special 1st-class bus service goes directly between Chetumal's bus terminal and Flores (near Tikal in Guatemala) once daily (350 km, nine hours, US$35).

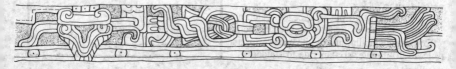

Glossary

Note: For names of food and drinks, see Food and Drinks in Facts for the Visitor; for bus and train terms, see Getting Around.

AC – *antes de Cristo* (before Christ); equivalent to BC

adobe – sun-dried mud brick; often used for building dwellings

agave – maguey

aguardiente – literally 'ardent water'; strong liquor usually made from sugarcane

albergue de la juventud – youth hostel; in Mexico these are often dormitories in a Villa Deportiva Juvenil (Youth Sport City) complex

alfíz – rectangular frame about a round arch; an Arabic influence on Spanish and Mexican buildings

Altiplano Central – dry plateau stretching across north central Mexico between the two Sierra Madre ranges

amate – paper made from tree bark

Apdo – abbreviation for *Apartado* (Box) in addresses; hence *Apartado Postal* means Post Office Box.

arroyo – brook, stream

artesanías – handicrafts, folk arts

atlas (s), atlantes (pl) – sculpted male figure(s) used instead of a pillar to support a roof or frieze, another name for *telamon*

atrium – churchyard, usually a big one

autopista – expressway, dual carriageway

azulejo – painted ceramic tile

balneario – bathing-place, often a natural hot spring

baroque – ornate architectural style dominant in the 17th and first half of the 18th centuries

barrio – neighbourhood of a town or city, often a poor neighbourhood

billete – bank note

boleto – ticket

brujo – witch-doctor, shaman

caballeros – literally 'horsemen', but corresponds to 'gentlemen' in English; look for it on toilet doors

cabaña – cabin, simple shelter with roof and walls

cacique – Aztec chief, also used to describe provincial warlord or strongman of newly independent Mexico

calle – street

callejón – alley; small, narrow or very short street

calzada – grand boulevard or avenue

capilla abierta – open chapel; used in early Mexican monasteries for preaching to large crowds of Indians

casa de cambio – exchange house; place where currency is exchanged, usually at a rate only marginally lower than at a bank, but much faster to use

caseta de larga distancia – long-distance telephone station, often in a shop; now being replaced by special coin and card phones; see Lada, Ladatel

cazuela – clay cooking-pot; usually sold in a nested set

cenote – in Yucatán, a limestone sinkhole filled with rainwater; used as a reservoir and sometimes for ceremonial purposes

central camionera – bus terminal

Chac – Maya god of rain

chac-mool – pre-Hispanic stone sculpture of a hunched, belly-up figure; the stomach was used as a sacrificial altar

charro – Mexican cowboy

chilango – citizen of Mexico City

chinampas – floating gardens of the Aztecs at the time of the Spanish invasion; versions still exist at Xochimilco near Mexico City

chingar – literally 'to fuck'; it has a wide range of colloquial usages in Mexican Spanish equivalent to those in English

chultún – cement-lined brick cistern found in the *chenes* (wells) region of Yucatán in the Puuc hills south of Mérida

Churrigueresque – Spanish late baroque style; found on many Mexican churches

cigarro – cigarette

Coatlicue – Aztec goddess of death

colectivo – minibus, microbus or car which picks up and drops off passengers along a predetermined route

colonia – neighbourhood of a city, often a wealthy residential area

comedor – literally 'dining room', an eating stall or small cheap restaurant

completo – full up; a sign you may see at hotel desks

conasupo – government-owned store that sells many everyday basics at subsidised prices

conquistador – early Spanish explorer-conqueror

criollo – Mexican-born person of Spanish parentage; in colonial times considered inferior by peninsular Spaniards (see *gachupines, peninsulares*)

Cristeros – Roman Catholic rebels of the late 1920s

DC – *después de Cristo* (after Christ); equivalent to AD (anno Domini)

damas – ladies; the sign on the toilet doors

de lujo – deluxe; often used with some licence

delegación – in Mexico City, a large urban governmental subdivision comprising numerous colonias; equivalent to a *municipio*

descompuesto – broken, out of order

DF – Distrito Federal (Federal District); where Mexico City is located

ejido – communally owned Indian land organised under a programme inspired by President Lázaro Cárdenas

encomienda – a grant of land and Indians made to a *conquistador*; the conquistador was supposed to protect and convert the Indians, but usually treated them as serfs

enramada – thatch-covered, open-air restaurant

enredo – wrap-around skirt

esq – abbreviation of *esquina* (corner) in addresses

estación ferrocarril – railway station

estípite – long, narrow, upside-down pyramid-shaped pilaster; the hallmark of Churrigueresque architecture

ex-convento – former convent or monastery; now usually devoted to a different use

excusado – toilet

faja – waist sash used in traditional Indian costume

feria – fair

ferrocarril – railway

fonda – eating stall in market, small restaurant

fraccionamiento – subdivision; similar to a *colonia*, often modern

frontera – border between political entities; more often the border between the USA and Mexico

gachupines – derogatory term for the colonial *peninsulares*

Green Angels – government-funded mechanics who patrol Mexico's major highways in green vehicles; they help motorists with fuel, spare parts and service

guarda equipaje – room for storing luggage, eg in a bus station

gringo – European or North American visitor to Latin America; female is *gringa*

Grito – literally 'shout'; the 'cry' for independence by parish priest Miguel Hidalgo y Costilla in 1810 which sparked the struggle for independence from Spain

güero – white man; *una güera* is a blonde woman

guarache – also *huarache*, woven leather sandal, often with car-tyre tread as the sole

guayabera – also *guayabarra*, thin fabric man's shirt with pockets and appliquéd designs up the front, over the shoulders and down the back; worn in place of a jacket and tie in hot regions

hacienda – estate; Hacienda (capitalised) is the Treasury

hay – there is, there are; you're equally likely to hear *no hay* (there isn't, there aren't)

henequén – agave fibre used to make sisal rope; grown particularly around Mérida in Yucatán

hombres – men; sign on toilet doors

huevos – eggs; also slang for testicles

huipil – Indian woman's sleeveless tunic, usually highly embroidered. Can be thigh-length or reach the ankles

INAH – Instituto Nacional de Antropología e Historia; the body in charge of most ancient sites and some museums

indígena – indigenous, pertaining to the Indians, the original inhabitants of Latin America; can also refer to the people themselves

INI – Instituto Nacional Indigenista; set up in 1948 to improve the lot of Indians and integrate them better into society, sometimes accused of paternalism and trying to stifle protest

IVA – *impuesto al valor agregado*, or 'ee-bah'; a sales tax which can range as high as 15% and is added to the price of many items

ixtle – maguey fibre

jaguar – panther native to Central America; principal symbol of the Olmec civilization

Jarocho – citizen of Veracruz

jefe – boss or leader, especially political

jorongo – small poncho for men

Kukulcán – Maya name for the plumed serpent god Quetzalcóatl

Lada – short for *larga distancia*

Ladatel – automatic coin or card-operated long-distance telephone

ladino – more or less the same as *mestizo*

larga distancia – long-distance; usually refers to the telephone network

latifundio – large landholding; these sprang up after Mexico's independence from Spain

latifundista – powerful landowner who usurped communally owned land to form a *latifundio*

libramiento – a free road running parallel to a toll highway

licenciado – university graduate, abbreviated as Lic and used as an honorific before a person's name; a status claimed by many who don't actually possess a degree

lista de correos – literally 'mail list', a list displayed at a post office of people for whom letters are waiting; similar to General Delivery or Poste Restante, but names are not posted up in Mexico's Poste Restante service

lleno – full, as with a car's fuel tank

machismo – maleness, masculine virility; an important concept in Mexico

madre – literally 'mother', but the term can be used colloquially with an astonishing array of meanings

maguey – cactus with thick pointed leaves growing straight out of the ground, also called agave; tequila and mezcal are made from its sap

malecón – waterfront street, boulevard or promenade

mañana – literally 'tomorrow' or 'morning'; in some contexts it may mean 'sometime in the future'

maquiladora – assembly-plant operation in a Mexican border town or city; usually owned, at least in part, by foreigners and allowed to import raw materials duty-free on the condition that the products manufactured are re-exported to the USA

mariachi – small ensemble of street musicians playing guitars and trumpets; from the French *mariage* (wedding), at which such groups played during the French intervention in Mexico (1864-67)

marimba – wooden xylophone-type instrument, popular in Veracruz

mercado – market; usually a building near the centre of a town, with shops and open-air stalls in the surrounding streets

mestizaje – mixedness, Mexico's mixed-blood heritage; officially an object of pride

mestizo – person of mixed (usually Indian and Spanish) ancestry, ie most Mexicans

metate – shallow stone bowl with legs, for grinding maize and other foods

mezcal – strong alcoholic drink produced from maguey cactus

minibus – small bus, bigger than a Volkswagen microbus (Combi)

milpa – peasant's small cornfield, often cultivated by the slash-and-burn method

Montezuma's revenge – Mexican version of Delhi-belly or travellers' diarrhoea

mordida – literally 'little bite', a small bribe

to keep the wheels of bureaucracy turning; giving a *mordida* to a traffic policeman may ensure that you won't have to pay a bigger fine later

Mudéjar – Moorish architectural style, imported to Mexico via Spain

mujeres – women; seen on toilet doors

municipio – small local-government area; Mexico is divided into 2394 of them

Noche Triste – the 'Sad Night', when Cortés was besieged by the Aztecs and retreated from Tenochtitlán with massive losses

Nte – abbreviation for *norte* (north), used in street names

Ote – abbreviation for *oriente* (east), used in street names

palacio de gobierno – state capitol, state government headquarters

palacio municipal – town or city hall, headquarters of the municipal corporation

palapa – thatched roof, thatched-roof shelter, usually on a beach

pan integral – whole-grain bread

paquetería – room for storing luggage, usually in a bus station

parada – bus stop, usually for city buses

parado – standing up, as you often are on 2nd-class buses

parroquia – the parish church; often a large church in a city which does not have a bishop and hence a cathedral

paseo – boulevard, walkway or pedestrian way; also the tradition of strolling in a circle around the plaza in the evening, men and women moving in opposite directions

Pemex – government-owned petroleum mining, refining and retailing monopoly

peninsulares – those born in Spain and sent by the Spanish government to rule the colony in Mexico (see *criollo, gachupines*)

petate – mat, usually of palm or reed

peyote – hallucinogenic mezcal cactus

piñata – clay pot decorated with papier mâché, tissue paper, ribbons to resemble an animal, pineapple, star etc; filled with sweets and gifts and smashed open at festivals, particularly Christmas

plazuela – small plaza

Poblano – person from Puebla, or something in the style of Puebla

Porfiriato – Porfirio Díaz's reign as president-dictator of Mexico for 30 years until the 1910 Revolution

portales – arcades

presidio – fort or fort's garrison

PRI – Partido Revolucionario Institucional (Institutional Revolutionary Party); the political party which has ruled Mexico since the 1930s

propina – tip; different from a *mordida*, which is closer to a bribe

Pte – abbreviation for *poniente* (west), used in street names

pulque – thick, milky drink of fermented maguey cactus juice; a traditional intoxicating drink which is also nutritious

quechquémitl – Indian woman's shoulder cape with an opening for the head; usually colourfully embroidered, often diamond shaped

Quetzalcóatl – plumed serpent god of pre-Hispanic Mexico

rebozo – long wool or linen scarf covering the head or shoulders

Regiomontano – person from Monterrey

rejas – wrought-iron window guards

retablo – small altarpiece or painting on wood, tin, cardboard, glass, etc; placed in a church to give thanks for miracles, answered prayers, etc

s/n – *sin número* (without number); used in street addresses

sacbe – ceremonial avenue between great Maya cities

sanatorio – hospital, particularly a small private one

sanitario(s) – toilet(s), literally 'sanitary'

sarape – traditional woollen blanket

Semana Santa – holy week, the week before Easter; Mexico's major holiday period, when accommodation and transport get very busy

sitio – taxi stand

stele – standing stone monument, usually carved (pl *stelae*)

supermercado – supermarket; anything from a small corner store to a large, North American-style supermarket

Sur – south; often seen in street names

taller – shop or workshop; a *taller mecánico* is a mechanic's shop, usually for cars; a *taller de llantas* is a tyre-repair shop

talud-tablero – building style typical of Teotihuacán, in which the rising sections of a stepped building consist of both vertical *(tablero)* and sloping *(talud)* sections

Tapatío, Tapatía – citizen of Guadalajara

taquilla – ticket window

telamon – statue of a male figure, used instead of a pillar to hold up the roof of a temple; see also atlas

telar de cintura – backstrap loom; the warp (lengthways) threads are stretched between two horizontal bars, one of which is attached to a post or tree, the other to a strap round the weaver's lower back, and the weft (cross) threads are then woven in

templo – church; anything from a wayside chapel to a cathedral

tequila – vodka-like liquor; like pulque and mezcal, it is produced from maguey cactus

Tex-Mex – an Americanised version of Mexican food

Tezcatlipoca – Aztec god; as a smoking mirror he could see into your heart, as the sun god he needed the blood of sacrificed warriors to ensure he would rise again, as

Quetzalcóatl he was the lord of life and enemy of death

típico, típica – typical or characteristic of a region; particularly used to describe food

tianguis – Indian market

topes – anti-speed bumps; found on the outskirts of many towns and villages, they are sometimes marked by signs

viajero – traveller

voladores – literally 'flyers', the Totonac Indian ritual in which men whirl around a tall pole, suspended by their ankles, known as The Dance of Those Who Fly

War of the Castes – bloody Maya uprising in the Yucatán peninsula (1847-66)

yácata – stone ceremonial structure with an eternally burning flame, constructed by the Tarascan civilization

zaguán – vestibule or foyer, sometimes a porch

zócalo – a town's main plaza or square; a term used in some, but by no means all, Mexican towns; from the Zócalo in Mexico City

Zona Rosa – literally Pink Zone, an area of expensive shops, hotels and restaurants in Mexico City, frequented by the wealthy and tourists; by extension, a similar area in another city

Index

TEXT

Thanks

Thanks to the many travellers who wrote in with comments about our last edition, and with tips and comments about Mexico:

Marcello Accinni (D), Dana Adler (USA), Miriam Akhtar (UK), Geoff Alexander (USA), Scott Anderson (USA), Ernest Atencio (USA), Carl Babcock (USA), Roger Barlow (UK), Dr R Barnes (UK), Jana Bashor (USA), William Beaty (USA), Mara Beinarovics (C), Vincenzo Beiser (USA), Peter Bienstock (USA), Fiona Black (Aus), Richard Blumburg (USA), Joyce Bogner (USA), Andy Bolton (Aus), Mike Boon (Can), A H & S J Boon (Nl), Barbara Borowitz (USA), John Bouffard (USA), Geoffrey Bowyer, Greg & Kathleen Brewer (USA), Paul Bridge (Aus), Iain Brodie, Tony Brooks (UK), Mark Brundage (USA), Veronica M Burns (Mex), Anna Stewart Burt (C), Alan Callow (UK), Virginia Campbell, I Carlssin, DI Carlsson (Sw), Ingemar Carlsson (Sw), Brian Carter (C), Gillian Chetty (C), Lance Chilton (UK), Dale E Chrestenson (USA), Rustin Chrisco (USA), Sandy & Ed Clarke (Mex), Berne Clausen (Dk), Diana Clement (UK), Bruce Clifford (Aus), the legendary Lee Clinch (USA), Jackie Cohen (USA), Brigitte Compton, Amy Conger (USA), Dennis Conway (USA), Harriet Corbett (USA), Kevin Craig (USA), Alice Craje (Nl), Mark Crapelle, John Cross (USA), Erich Dahlmanns (D), Alex Darquea (USA), Tobb Dell'Oro (USA), Jasmine Dellal (UK), John Dickinson (Aus), Ken Dickson (Aus), AM Diffley (USA), David & Donna Dobkin (USA), Tamar Dothan (Isr), Andrew Downing (UK), E Duggan (Ire), D Joy Dyke (Aus), Tara Ehrcke (C), Lois S Ehrlich (USA), Bijan Elmdust (D), Alex Encel (Aus), Ms M Engel (Nl), Douglas Engelman (USA), Emmanuel Ermidis (USA), Benjamin Evans (USA), Clare Ferguson (B), Marco Antonio Fimbres (Mex), Hugh Finsten (C), Gavin Fredric (NZ), Steven Freilich (USA), Nellie Friedman (Mex), Elizabeth Galbraith (UK), Dirk George (D), John Gibbs, Diana Gibson (USA), Michele Goodwin (USA), Nikki Grant (UK), Chris Green (UK), Rachel & Laurie Greenberg (USA), Paul Greenway (Aus), Stephen Greig (Aus), Cathryn Gruyler (UK), Claire Guarniere (Mex), Dan Gubbels (USA), Gote Gustafsson (SW), A R Haigh (UK), Adrienne Hale (UK), Joseph Halpin (USA), Eric Hamovitch (C), Helle & Svend Harders (Dk), Ole-Johan Harm (N), Eric Harnett (USA), Vivian B Harvey (USA), Mark Harvey (UK), Peter Hatch (USA), Sarah Hayward (UK), Elaine Heaver (UK), Klaus & Sylvia Heyer (C), Roger Hicks (USA), Mrs W W Holladay (UK), Y Holmes (NZ), Stephen Hopkins, A A Hysette (USA), Stephen Hyskin (USA), Kerrin Isaacs (UK), Iain Jackson (UK), Eric Jacobsen (USA), Mrs A D Johnston (Aus), Linda Johnston (UK), Judith Jones (USA), Tracy Jordan (USA), Carlos Juillen (USA), Kryss Katsiavriades (UK), Nicholas Kenrick (C), Jill Key (UK), Bill Koulopoulos (C), Jessica Krakow (USA), Ulf Kristofferson (Sw), Jenny Landen (USA), Peter Larrett (USA), Douglas Lattey (UK), Stephen & Barb Lee (C), Christine Lem (C), Daniel Lieberfield (USA), Charles & Linda Link (USA), Jorg Linow (D), N Lofstrom (USA), Rick Logan (CH), Susan Long (USA), Kathy & Ruth Lotscher, Kathy Luke (USA), Lilla Lunnabol, Jim Lux (USA), Margaret MacDonald (USA), Emelda Mangune (C), Samuel Manickam, Alexander Matthaei (UK), John D McComish (USA), Bill McDonald (Aus), Frederic Medici (It), Liesbeth Meijer (Nl), Eric Menning (USA), Francis Middel (USA), Wolfgang Minas, Linda Mitchell (USA), M Monarty (USA), Dawn Montgomery, Bill Morton (USA), Leslie Moy, Sven Schaumburg Muller (Dk), Anne M Murray (US), Christophe Nauchien (F), John Nehring (USA), Chris & Kay Nellins (UK), Andrea Nguyen (USA), A Nicolas (UK), Ryszard Niedzielski (P), Tetsuya Noguchi (Jap), Jim O'Daniel (Mex), Sharon O'Day (USA), Robert Obrzut (A), Yannig Oliviero (Mex), David W Olson (US), Liesbeth van Ommeren (Nl), Anton Opperman (Nl), Lilly Otto (USA), Martha Palomares (Mex), Gabriella Paradisi (It), Simon H Parson (UK), Helen Payne (UK), Jo Pearce (Aus), Janique Perrin (CH), Rosemary Perry, Peter Phelan (Aus), Phil & Dale (Aus), Peter Pilbrow (UK), Ann Pinzl (USA), Marion Pluim (Nl), Melissa Pollok (Aus), Markus Pomper (US), Annette & Edgar Portillo (Mex), Janet Powell (UK), Russ Prather (USA), Freddy Rabenau (D), Boyden Ralph (USA), Micheal Ramsey (USA), John Ratcliffe (UK), Holly Reiter (USA), Oliver Renzler (It), Shirley Richardson (USA), Conrad Richter (Can), Anita Riermersma (Nl), Gary Roberto (USA), Richard Robinson (UK), Claudia Roeckle (D), Mrs Barbara Rogers (UK), Marie-Ange Rombauts (UK), Cristina & Luca Rosso (D), Lori Rubens (USA), Carlos Ruiz (Mex), Dr Louis Ruprecht (USA), Federico G Russek, Katie Russell (UK), Urs Rutishauser (CH), Catarina Sandgren (Sw), Beatrice Scherrer (CH), Jutta Schmitt (D), Deborah Schorsch (USA), Paul Schwink (USA), Howard Scotland (USA), Caroline Searby (USA), Guilietta Sestini (Aus), Robert Shepard (USA), Robert Shepard (USA), Silver Dan (USA), Sarah Slater (UK), Anne Small (NZ), David Smith (USA), Tony Smyth, Jimmie Soulecki (USA), Martin Spencer (Aus), Sally Spencer (USA), Tony & Lynne Stark (UK), John Steedman (UK), Linda Steele (UK), Dorothy Strickland (USA), Storma Swanson (USA), Bob Synder (Can), Ron Szili (Aus), Kitty Tacklebox (USA), Owen Teeters (Mex), Steve & Gaby Telander (Mex), Ronny Temmerman (B), Mac Thomson (USA), Nick Tolan (UK), Lucero Topete (Mex), Carol Towson (USA), Henk Tukker (Nl), Eric Turkewitz (USA), Tim Uden (Aus), Sergio Valdes (Mex), Juan Carlos Vega (Mex), Graziella Verazzo (UK), Ineke Visser (Nl), John Wagner (USA), Anita M Walter

(USA), Caroline Walton, Kathleen Wasser (USA), Daniel Watson (UK), John Wedlick (Aus), Mrs J M Welbank (UK), Claudia Wenzel (Mex), Eric A Wessman (USA), Marian & Peter Whelan (Aus), Albert M White (Aus), George Whiting (C), Louise Whiting (Aus), Ian M Wilkinson (Aus), Steven Williams (USA), Diarmuid Wilson (UK), Kerry Wilson (C), Jill Yesko (USA), Claire Zenner (B), Robert A Zimmerman (USA), Werner Zwick (D)

A – Austria, Aus – Australia, B – Belgium, C – Canada, CH – Switzerland, D – Germany, Dk – Denmark, F – France, Jap – Japan, Ire – Ireland, Isr – Israel, It – Italy, Mex – Mexico, N – Norway, Nl – Netherlands, NZ – New Zealand, Sw – Sweden, UK – United Kingdom, USA – United States of America

Keep in touch!

We love hearing from you and think you'd like to hear from us.

The Lonely Planet Newsletter covers the when, where, how and what of travel. (AND it's free!)

When...*is the right time to see reindeer in Finland?*
Where...*can you hear the best palm-wine music in Ghana?*
How...*do you get from Asunción to Areguá by steam train?*
What...*should you leave behind to avoid hassles with customs in Iran?*

To join our mailing list just contact us at any of our offices. (details below)

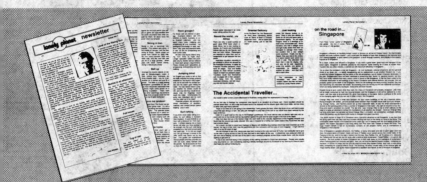

Every issue includes:

- *a letter from Lonely Planet founders Tony and Maureen Wheeler*
- *travel diary from a Lonely Planet author - find out what it's really like out on the road*
- *feature article on an important and topical travel issue*
- *a selection of recent letters from our readers*
- *the latest travel news from all over the world*
- *details on Lonely Planet's new and forthcoming releases*

Also available Lonely Planet T-shirts. 100% heavy weight cotton (S, M, L, XL)

LONELY PLANET PUBLICATIONS
Australia: PO Box 617, Hawthorn, 3122, Victoria (tel: 03-819 1877)
USA: Embarcadero West, 155 Filbert Street, Suite 251, Oakland, CA 94607 (tel: 510-893 8555)
UK: Devonshire House, 12 Barley Mow Passage, Chiswick, London W4 4PH (tel: 081-742 3161)

Lonely Planet Guidebooks

Lonely Planet guidebooks cover every accessible part of Asia as well as Australia, the Pacific, South America, Africa, the Middle East, Europe and parts of North America. There are five series: *travel survival kits*, covering a country for a range of budgets; *shoestring guides* with compact information for low-budget travel in a major region; *walking guides*; *city guides* and *phrasebooks*.

Australia & the Pacific
Australia
Bushwalking in Australia
Islands of Australia's Great Barrier Reef
Fiji
Melbourne city guide
Micronesia
New Caledonia
New Zealand
Tramping in New Zealand
Papua New Guinea
Bushwalking in Papua New Guinea
Papua New Guinea phrasebook
Rarotonga & the Cook Islands
Samoa
Solomon Islands
Sydney city guide
Tahiti & French Polynesia
Tonga
Vanuatu
Victoria

South-East Asia
Bali & Lombok
Bangkok city guide
Cambodia
Indonesia
Indonesia phrasebook
Laos
Malaysia, Singapore & Brunei
Myanmar (Burma)
Burmese phrasebook
Philippines
Pilipino phrasebook
Singapore city guide
South-East Asia on a shoestring
Thailand
Thai phrasebook
Vietnam
Vietnamese phrasebook

North-East Asia
China
Beijing city guide
Mandarin Chinese phrasebook
Hong Kong, Macau & Canton
Japan
Japanese phrasebook
Korea
Korean phrasebook
Mongolia
North-East Asia on a shoestring
Seoul city guide
Taiwan
Tibet
Tibet phrasebook
Tokyo city guide

West Asia
Trekking in Turkey
Turkey
Turkish phrasebook
West Asia on a shoestring

Middle East
Arab Gulf States
Egypt & the Sudan
Arabic (Egyptian) phrasebook
Iran
Israel
Jordan & Syria
Yemen

Indian Ocean
Madagascar & Comoros
Maldives & Islands of the East Indian Ocean
Mauritius, Réunion & Seychelles

Mail Order

Lonely Planet guidebooks are distributed worldwide. They are also available by mail order from Lonely Planet, so if you have difficulty finding a title please write to us. US and Canadian residents should write to Embarcadero West, 155 Filbert St, Suite 251, Oakland CA 94607, USA; European residents should write to Devonshire House, 12 Barley Mow Passage, Chiswick, London W4 4PH; and residents of other countries to PO Box 617, Hawthorn, Victoria 3122, Australia.

Indian Subcontinent
Bangladesh
India
Hindi/Urdu phrasebook
Trekking in the Indian Himalaya
Karakoram Highway
Kashmir, Ladakh & Zanskar
Nepal
Trekking in the Nepal Himalaya
Nepali phrasebook
Pakistan
Sri Lanka
Sri Lanka phrasebook

Africa
Africa on a shoestring
Central Africa
East Africa
Trekking in East Africa
Kenya
Swahili phrasebook
Morocco, Algeria & Tunisia
Arabic (Moroccan) phrasebook
South Africa, Lesotho & Swaziland
Zimbabwe, Botswana & Namibia
West Africa

Central America
Baja California
Central America on a shoestring
Costa Rica
La Ruta Maya
Mexico

North America
Alaska
Canada
Hawaii

Europe
Baltic States & Kaliningrad
Dublin city guide
Eastern Europe on a shoestring
Eastern Europe phrasebook
Finland
Greece
Hungary
Iceland, Greenland & the Faroe Islands
Ireland
Italy
Mediterranean Europe on a shoestring
Mediterranean Europe phrasebook
Poland
Scandinavian & Baltic Europe on a shoestring
Scandinavian Europe phrasebook
Switzerland
Trekking in Spain
Trekking in Greece
USSR
Russian phrasebook
Western Europe on a shoestring
Western Europe phrasebook

South America
Argentina, Uruguay & Paraguay
Bolivia
Brazil
Brazilian phrasebook
Chile & Easter Island
Colombia
Ecuador & the Galápagos Islands
Latin American Spanish phrasebook
Peru
Quechua phrasebook
South America on a shoestring
Trekking in the Patagonian Andes

The Lonely Planet Story

Lonely Planet published its first book in 1973 in response to the numerous 'How did you do it?' questions Maureen and Tony Wheeler were asked after driving, bussing, hitching, sailing and railing their way from England to Australia.

Written at a kitchen table and hand collated, trimmed and stapled, *Across Asia on the Cheap* became an instant local bestseller, inspiring thoughts of another book.

Eighteen months in South-East Asia resulted in their second guide, *South-East Asia on a shoestring*, which they put together in a backstreet Chinese hotel in Singapore in 1975. The 'yellow bible' as it quickly became known to backpackers around the world, soon became *the* guide to the region. It has sold well over half a million copies and is now in its 7th edition, still retaining its familiar yellow cover.

Today there are over 120 Lonely Planet titles in print – books that have that same adventurous approach to travel as those early guides; books that 'assume you know how to get your luggage off the carousel' as one reviewer put it.

Although Lonely Planet initially specialised in guides to Asia, they now cover most regions of the world, including the Pacific, South America, Africa, the Middle East and Europe. The list of *walking guides* and *phrasebooks* (for 'unusual' languages such as Quechua, Swahili, Nepalese and Egyptian Arabic) is also growing rapidly.

The emphasis continues to be on travel for independent travellers. Tony and Maureen still travel for several months of each year and play an active part in the writing, updating and quality control of Lonely Planet's guides.

They have been joined by over 50 authors, 54 staff – mainly editors, cartographers, & designers – at our office in Melbourne, Australia, 10 at our US office in Oakland, California and another three at our office in London to handle sales for Britain, Europe and Africa. In 1992 Lonely Planet opened an editorial office in Paris. Travellers themselves also make a valuable contribution to the guides through the feedback we receive in thousands of letters each year.

The people at Lonely Planet strongly believe that travellers can make a positive contribution to the countries they visit, both through their appreciation of the countries' culture, wildlife and natural features, and through the money they spend. In addition, the company makes a direct contribution to the countries and regions it covers. Since 1986 a percentage of the income from each book has been donated to ventures such as famine relief in Africa; aid projects in India; agricultural projects in Central America; Greenpeace's efforts to halt French nuclear testing in the Pacific and Amnesty International. In 1993 $100,000 was donated to such causes.

Lonely Planet's basic travel philosophy is summed up in Tony Wheeler's comment, 'Don't worry about whether your trip will work out. Just go!'